MELTING THE DARKNESS

MELTING THE DARKNESS

THE DYAD AND PRINCIPLES OF CLINICAL PRACTICE

Warren S. Poland, M.D.

JASON ARONSON INC.
Northvale, New Jersey
London

Production Editor: M'lou Pinkham

This book was set in 11 pt. New Aster by Alpha Graphics of Pittsfield, New Hampshire, and printed and bound by Book-mart Press of North Bergen, New Jersey.

Library of Congress Cataloging-in-Publication Data
Poland, Warren S.
    Melting the darkness : the dyad and principles of clinical
practice / Warren S. Poland.
        p.   cm.
    Includes bibliographical references and index.
    ISBN 1-56821-816-8 (hc : alk. paper)
    1. Psychoanalysis.   2. Psychodynamic psychotherapy.
3. Psychotherapist and patient.   I. Title.
    [DNLM: 1. Psychoanalytic Therapy.   2. Professional-Patient
Relations.   3. Psychoanalytic Interpretation.   WM 460.6 P762m 1996]
RC509.P65   1996
616.89'17—dc20
DNLM/DLC
for Library of Congress   96-4643

Manufactured in the United States of America. Jason Aronson Inc. offers books and cassettes. For information and catalog write to Jason Aronson Inc., 230 Livingston Street, Northvale, New Jersey 07647.

For
Janice,
Hylla, Marc and Carol
Piper, Ariel and Danielle

The charm dissolves apace;
And as the morning steals upon the night,
Melting the darkness, so their rising senses
Begin to chase the ignorant fumes that mantle
Their clearer reason.

—SHAKESPEARE
The Tempest V:i

Contents

Acknowledgments

Stars shooting through the darkness, guild the Night
With sweeping Glories, and long trails of Light.
—DRYDEN

Passionate as a teacher dedicated to psychoanalysis as a form of inquiry and to full respect for the separate authenticity of other persons, Jacob Finesinger was the first to train me to see and attend to the powers at play in the hidden darkness of a human soul. It was he who first exposed for me the potent forces active in patients outside their own awareness, and then, in the relevance of that human immediacy, led me to the incendiary brilliance of Freud's work. The effulgence of Freud's genius, despite errors inevitable in work ever in process, has sparked the secondary flames that have lighted our glimpses into a mind's secret side.

I have worked during the subsequent years with a wide range of patients and have come to sense and to see psychoanalysis as the basic science of the clinical treatment of troubled minds. When a psychiatrist in training, I was responsible for the care of individuals who were severely disturbed; only later did I have the opportunity to listen at length to those whose inner disturbances account for much of what is called normal life. (Across the years the only definition of normality that for me has stood the test of time is that a normal person is one you don't know well yet.)

Paths of training as customarily arranged seem designed backwards, like much else in the world. Just as I had learned underlying basic physiology before I could grasp the dynamics of disease, I believe it would have been better to have learned basic psychoanalysis before turning to conduct psychotherapy. Psychotherapy, properly conducted with appreciation of the hidden powers at work in the interchange between patient and therapist, seems to me much more difficult and demanding than classical psychoanalysis. Having given all of my clinical time in the first half of my posttraining career to psychoanalysis, it is only in the second half that I have taken on the challenge of less intensive psychotherapy.

Every time in this volume that for succinctness I use the term *psychoanalysis*, I intend to imply both psychoanalysis and dynamic psychotherapy. All of my observations are applicable both to formal analysis and to insight therapy—work that is less intensive than classical psychoanalysis but that also takes as its goal mastery of difficulties through insight into underlying internal conflicts. Thus, the word *analysis* in this volume should always be taken to imply both psychoanalysis and dynamic psychotherapy.

Recognition of the implications of much that one learns as a child comes into emotional fullness only after many years of personal life experience. The same is also true in one's professional life. In the beginning I read many works in which clinical writers expressed appreciation to their patients. In candor, I thought at first this might be an authorial form of vanity, a way of showing one's superiority by adopting a posture of modesty. Through years of work I have come to realize how wrong I was!

I often feel amazed and awed by the wealth of private life to which others have allowed me entrée. Each patient is another person, fully real, fully alive, each leading me by the hand into private areas of that one's soul. At times I feel stunned by the privilege; at times frightened by the responsibility. There can be no doubt about the depth of my indebtedness to my patients. At times they have lost patience with me; at times I with them. Yet in their own wish to be clearly understood, they have borne with me while I struggled to get it right, necessarily never getting it exactly right.

I would credit my teachers and my friends but find myself unable to draw a line between these two groups. Whenever one taught me something I could use, my gratitude always was accompanied by affection. Whenever a friend would be there for me, candid and open, critical or reassuring, I would learn and find my affection doubled and redoubled. Drs. Kenneth Grigg and Stanley Needell have been steady presences, valuable and cherished, throughout my career, their ideas contributing to my thinking in such regular ways as to become at times indistinguishable from my own thoughts. Drs. William Granatir, Milton Meltzer, and Stanley Olinick have enriched my life first as teachers and then also as friends.

My vision of the world has broadened, become deeper and more subtly complex, thanks to Dr. Theodore Jacobs and *grace à* Dr. René Major. Each has taught me to look at the world afresh, from new and different angles, and each has been wondrously generous of himself, of his friendship. Drs. Robert Gardner and James McLaughlin were first teachers at a distance, then friends, friends from whom I have never ceased to learn. Dr. Stanley Shapiro has been a friend and colleague whose quiet, profound wisdom is consistently presented with subtle, dry humor. To live with such friends is to live among poets. From all of them I have learned about patients, I have learned about friendship, I have learned about myself, and, thrillingly, I have learned something of how to use language.

Two others have been of especial value to me despite their distance across time and across geography. When I read and reread *The Rambler*, I am constantly awed by the wonder and genius of Samuel Johnson, a linguistic architect with insights into human vanity that remain unmatched in modern times, and, like Freud, an ever-original, delightful wit. Anyone who has met Johnson only through Boswell has yet to discover the delight of knowing Johnson directly.

As Johnson has enriched me across time, so has Dr. Jacob

Arlow across distance. It is only in recent years that I have had the privilege of knowing him personally, yet whatever path I have taken as I have proceeded with this work, I have seen Dr. Arlow's footsteps ahead, footsteps that have always assured me I was on the right track.

Drs. Ruth Lax, Stanley Leavy, David Raphling, Gail Reed, and Owen Renik have assisted and enriched me, my thinking, and my work. Each has reviewed sections of this work and each has given to me in ways far beyond those valuable contributions.

Isaac Bashevis Singer once remarked that every writer has to have an address. I have been fortunate to have two. In regular and immensely enjoyable discussions over more than a quarter century, my colleagues in Group VIII at The Center for Advanced Psychoanalytic Studies have nourished me with their own ideas, helping me shape mine. And for many years I have also taken the editorial board of *The Psychoanalytic Quarterly* as my home. No exercise has so sharpened my thinking as has that of trying to grasp and critique outstanding psychoanalytic writing and reading the anonymous reports of others on the editorial board. I have been surrounded by scholars who respect originality, who do not confuse cant with basic concepts.

To credit Janice, my wife, is in many ways to credit myself, since so often I cannot tell what is part of me, what is part of her. She is and has been an endlessly dependable source of help. She has read and she has criticized, offered new ideas and corrected some of my wrongful ways of thinking. She has frequently saved me from the humiliation of presenting ideas still but half-baked. I could not imagine this book without her.

Dr. Michael Moskowitz has also been essential to this work. For years I had resisted the seductions of personal vanity and the encouragement of others, turning down invitations to prepare this volume. It was not only Dr. Moskowitz's encouragement but, importantly, his vision in helping me discern threads in my own thinking that made this volume possible. Any honest writer knows the reality of his editor's contributions. It has been a blessing to have an editor who is so knowledgeable a psychoanalyst.

Similarly, I have benefited from M'lou Pinkham's uncommon combination of aesthetic sensitivity, technical expertise, and personal good humor. She has turned the production of this volume into a pleasure.

I am in the profound debt of all of these people and the numberless others from whom I have taken every step of my way. My cup, truly, doth run over. Were I to list each person who has contributed to the field in general and to my own understanding in particular, my bibliographies would be longer than my texts and would still be incomplete. My conclusions are my own responsibility, but I do not claim credit for the awesome contributions of those who have gone before and those who have gone along with me. My decision to follow the flow of ideas without continuously citing scholarly references should be taken to imply recognition and respect for the contributions of many others whose work I follow with my own efforts of integration.

And, dear reader, do not think for a moment that I leave you off the list of those to whom I am indebted. As I hope to make clear throughout, we are all in this work together and no one has the last word. With the courage of my temporary convictions I shall spell out how I have come to understand the psychotherapeutic process. In your reading, you will—as you must—modify what I intend. Let us hope that together we continue to expand the area of light into the edge of darkness.

Parts of this volume have already been published in earlier, less developed form. For permission to publish modified versions of that work I thank the following:

The Psychoanalytic Quarterly:
    "Transference: An 'Original' Creation," 1992, 61:185–205
    "An Analyst's Slip of the Tongue," 1992, 61:85–87
    "The Gift of Laughter," 1990, 59:197–225
    "Insight and the Analytic Dyad," 1988, 57:341–369
    "The Analyst's Words," 1986, 55:244–272
    "On Surmise," 1983, 52:599–600

The Journal of the American Psychoanalytic Association, International Universities Press, publisher:
    "From Analytic Surface to Analytic Space," 1992, 40: 389–412

"On the Analyst's Neutrality," 1984, 32:283–300
"Pilgrimage: Action and Tradition in Self Analysis," 1977, 25:399–416

The International Journal of Psycho-Analysis:
"Tact as a Psychoanalytic Function," 1975, 56:155–162

Psychoanalytic Psychology
"On Long Analyses," in press

The Analytic Press:
"Self and Other in Self-Analysis," in *Self-Analysis: Critical Inquiries, Personal Visions* (1993), edited by J. W. Barron, pp. 219–235
"At Work," in *Analysts at Work: Practice, Principles, and Techniques of Contemporary Psychoanalysis* (1985), edited by J. Reppen, pp. 145–164
"On Empathy In and Beyond Analysis," in *Empathy I*, edited by J. Lichtenberg, M. Bornstein, and D. Silver (1984), pp. 331–349

International Universities Press:
"Foreward," in *The Use of the Self: Countertransference and Communication in the Analytic Situation*, by T. Jacobs (1991), pp. xi–xv

Philadelphia Association for Psychoanalysis
"On Empathy in Analytic Practice," 1974, *Journal of the Philadelphia Association for Psychoanalysis*, pp. 284–297

* * *

I

ORIENTING PRINCIPLES

*It is easier to know man in general
than to understand one man in particular.*
—LA ROCHEFOUCAULD

To start, in conclusion . . .

In an analysis, one always starts in the present, in the immediacy of the moment, only with difficulty teasing out and tracing to their sources the threads that brought that moment to realization. History flows forward but our view of the past looks in the opposite direction, backward. We start with the present as the conclusion to a puzzle and then search in reverse for the developmental steps that led to the end from which we begin. Such is the nature of clinical work. Hoping to broaden possibilities for later, we start from now and trace back to before.

So it is, also, for us. What follows in this volume are efforts to puzzle out questions that have perplexed me through the years as I have listened and tried to be of help to others in their struggle toward insight. Now, an introduction for you is a retrospective for me. To orient you, I begin with current conclusions, with some of the concepts I have come to find most enduring in my continuing wonderings.

Indeed, when I began to practice psychoanalysis and psychoanalytic therapy, I did not guess that the issues that came to preoccupy me would later be questioned. Working with people suffering from symptoms and inhibitions, my assumption was that my greatest challenge would come from trying to learn the subtleties of psychopathology, trying to understand the intricacies and theories underlying neuroses, psychoses, character disorders, and perversions.

From the start I was already aware of the need to attend to disease processes rather than symptoms, and I knew that I would deal with *people* who had these disorders, not with "cases." But I had no serious inkling that it would be the people themselves—the questions of how they came to be who they were and how that could be discovered by exploring what they and I were doing together—that would become the center of our work. Beyond disease and disorder lies the profound riddle of what it is like to be someone else. The task of the analyst and analytic therapist is to help another know that other's self and come to peace with that other's unique actuality and singular personal potential.

Technique matters in this task. The issues of technique that first concerned me were those taught under familiar rubrics, such as the interpretation of resistance. However, just as it is that life is what happens while plans are being made, I eventually came to realize that psychoanalysis is what happens while resistance is being interpreted. Technique matters immensely. The analyst's discipline is essential. Yet while technical discipline is the necessary means to understanding, it is not understanding itself. There is a danger in turning the mastery of technique from a means into its own goal. Neutrality and abstinence are less problematic when they are respected within the context of being means toward the end of facilitating the patient's self-exploration. Whatever the motivations that bring the analyst to the work, that work is done in the service of the patient's self-inquiry.

Across the decades I have been privileged to take part in clinical discussions with colleagues of seriousness and dedication from the wide range of analytic orientations unfolding around the world. Whether these others were the great minds who have founded schools of thought or more modest and junior co-workers in the analytic vineyards, all tried intensely to grasp the pathodynamics behind the sufferings of the patients under consideration.

To my surprise, even in these group discussions I repeatedly had the impression that behind honest debates and polemical disputes lay the more fundamental questions of just what it was the therapist and the patient were trying to do. What true but hidden forces had brought them together? What was going on in each clinical partner's mind as the collaborative couple went through the routines of meeting and engaging? Whether seeing it in my own practice or inferring it as the profound issue underlying clinical discussions among colleagues, I found deeply embedded in all my exposure to analysis and therapy the fundamental questions of just what *is* psychoanalysis and what *is* insight therapy. What is the analyst's job, what are the analyst's responsibilities, what is the analyst trying to do?

Once, many years ago, I worked with a severely obsessional man who had been sent for analysis by his wife who decided she could not stand living with him any longer unless he changed. I quickly learned what the wife must have had in mind: this man was consumed by his need to refine, ever more minutely, the details of any thought he expressed, thoughts he never seemed able to perfect well enough to bring to conclusion. Indeed, his descent from idea to endless trivial modifications was so pervasive that he often could not finish sentences. He had been driving his wife mad and now I felt he was driving me mad.

About six months after we started, his wife asked him how his analysis was going. "Quite well," he proudly assured her, adding, "Why shouldn't it? It isn't anything personal."

Too often, clinical presentations sound as if the analyst too found them not anything personal rather than the essence of personal. In analysis—and as stated earlier I shall include all analytic therapy within that word—the patient is known through associations and emotional engagements as communicated within the experience of personal actualizations in the analytic field. To come to know the patient the analyst must be able to hear both words and music. Without the latter, the analyst sounds like a professional imitation of my obsessional patient.

The analytic situation is a creation of both patient and analyst. It is a new venture, brought to life in the engagement of the two partners. Even though the roles of each partner are constrained by vast differences and are thus asymmetric, and even though there are necessary and appropriate restrictions on the analyst's contribution to enactments with the patient, it is only in the shared engagement that a clinical analysis can come to life.

Speaking of the analyst's part in the experience, I have more in mind than only what has come to be called *countertransference in the broad sense.* The analyst, in a properly disciplined and aim-inhibited manner, is open to emotional engagement with the patient. However, that engagement not only informs the analyst but, together with the patient's more apparent contributions, constructs the analytic situation.

Who is this person, the patient, and what are the patient and analyst trying to do? Questions about the analytic process combine the basic questions of what it means to be a person and how it is that a person is changed by what goes on in interactions. When two people share an experience, they go through the moment together, yet what each savors is individual, not truly a shared taste of the other's experience. Just as no man is an island, so also is every man an island.

HISTORICAL CONTEXT

The problem of balancing awareness of self with professional dedication to the place of the other is as old as our field, having been structured into our thinking in part as an inevitable result of our history. Psychoanalysis, with all the bright benefits that have flowed from it, was originally conceived and delivered in the lonely agony of one genius's pained but relentless self-scrutiny. However far we have been carried by subsequent learning, the courage and brilliance of Freud's self-analysis continues to cast its awesome and humbling spell.

Freud's revolutionary breakthrough has both led and mis-led us. So astonishing were his discoveries that we have spent most of this century extending his search into the individual unconscious. But for too long we struggled with our patients, forgetting that our model was derived from a *self*-analysis.

As a result of starting from a self-analysis, Freud was delayed in recognizing the significance of transference and countertrans-ference in clinical work, the effects of two different persons on each other. And, following Freud, for too long we continued to view the mind of the patient as if it stood alone, with ourselves as detached outsiders.

There is no blame to be set for such an oversight. So amaz-ing and compelling were their wondrous findings in the first half of this century of depth psychology that the first generations of investigators were slow in noticing the influences they had brought with them in their explorations.

Although it was slow, at last attention moved on to the vital interchange between the two participants in the clinical venture. There is resistance in the progress of a science just as there is in the progress of an analysis, and the resistance in part grows from good and sufficient reasons in each instance. The resistance to new attention to "the interpersonal" arose not only from unyield-ing conservatism but also from a valid perception that "interper-sonal" was often used as a sophisticated defense against crediting the power of active unconscious forces. Many of the "interper-sonalists" in the middle of the century, like many in new schools now, saw themselves as their generation's revolutionaries. And then, like now, new concepts that might have enriched analytic understanding often served to screen out unconscious forces.

Allegiances led to antagonisms and controversies flared; such is the dialectic nature of progress. Yet for all of those who established and defended fixed positions, there were others who strove to integrate. Because of the considerable advances made in the last half of the twentieth century, the analytic field is no longer described as the mind of the patient inspected from the remote detachment of the analyst like a test tube viewed at arm's length by a white-coated scientist.

Recognition of the importance of the engagement of the analytic partners has grown greatly—so greatly that some of those attending to dyadic enactments have raised warnings against the analyst's listening *for* the transference rather than *to* the transference.

Emphasis on the importance of interaction and the analytic space as the matrix of the clinical work—once viewed as subversive thought—is now accepted almost as received truth. With this gain of current attention to dyadic interaction comes the risk of a loss—the focus on the centrality of the exploration of the patient as a unique other, which is the primary task of all analysis and insight therapy. The mistaken absenting of the analyst from consideration ought not be corrected by the analyst's pushing the patient from center stage into the wings. *The dyadic clinical field offers the medium for analysis, but the primary purpose of the analysis remains the exploration and understanding of the functioning of the patient for the sake of the increased freedom that comes from genuine insight and consequent mastery.*

INTRODUCTORY CONCLUSIONS

Where does this bring us? What is an analysis? What is the relationship of the individual patient to the specific analyst and to the work at hand? How can attention to the uniqueness of an individual patient be balanced with the inevitable pressures of the clinical partnership? And, put in the other direction, how can respect for the inevitable imperatives of the dyadic field be balanced with the primacy of the exploration of the patient's mind? How can the interactive context of clinical work be credited without compromising the centrality of the search for meanings derived from unconscious forces within the patient as a singular individual?

I begin this volume with some of the conclusions I have come to out of the journey reflected in the text. Like answers given in the back of an algebra text, these statements may seem at times arbitrary, at times merely restating the obvious. Nonetheless, it is only by repeated working through of these questions that I now more fully realize some of what may at first seem obvious.

1. The analyst works in the service of the patient and specifically in the service of the patient's analysis. That is, while the analyst may engage in many activities believed to facilitate the patient's growth, the basic clinical orientation is for the analyst's mind to be put in the service of the exploration of the patient's mind. Indeed, *the fundamental principle from which all other principles of analytic technique derive is regard for otherness, the analyst's profound and genuine respect for the authenticity of the patient's self as a unique other, an other's self as valid as the analyst's own.*

2. Patient and analyst come together, each bringing multiple underlying motivations, each looking for both merger and differentiation. Whatever the analyst's own personal urges and fantasies, the analyst works to tame them in the service of the fundamental task of giving priority to the exploration of the workings of the patient's mind.

3. Each of the partners in the asymmetric collaborative task is driven to change the other in multiple ways, destructive as well as beneficial. Each is interested in self-gratification, and each is pulled toward that one's own self-analysis.

4. The patient takes precedence. The clinical work is the patient's show, that is, the analyst must struggle to defer any private agenda for the sake of the task at hand. There is both propriety and benefit captured by the thought "Analysts do it with aim inhibition."

5. Despite the seductive appeal of the belief that an analyst can have mystical entry into a patient's mind or unconscious, one person can never truly know what it is like to be another person, how another person feels or thinks.

6. An analyst must struggle to learn whatever can be learned of the patient's psychic reality, but the analyst cannot function validly as if there were no psychic reality of the

analyst's own. The analyst's task first requires recognition of the presence and power of the patient's and the analyst's psychic reality and then demands special attention to the importance of the discrepancy between the two. It is in navigating the area at the edge of darkness within the analytic space between and within the differing psychic realities of the analytic pair that valid analytic exploration can lead to genuine insight.

7. In this analytic negotiation, analyst and patient are pre-occupied by trying to size each other up, each driven to know (in fantasy to capture and master) how the other feels, how the other thinks. While the analyst is trying to understand the patient, the patient—with brilliance, empathy, and important distortions and errors—continuously monitors everything about the analyst, doing so with greater intensity than that of the analyst, since it is the patient's life that is more directly at stake. While anonymity cannot and should not be total, the analyst ought not intrude more than is inevitable or minimally necessary in the work. I suspect that what may be genuinely mutative for the patient derives in part from the patient's reading of the metacommunications buried within and behind the analyst's behavior and interventions, including interpretations. Nonetheless, the patient's potential is maximized when the analyst's intrusions are minimized.

The patient and the analyst are separate people engaged in a shared task that elicits parallel mutual regressions, with the analyst's self-scanning (on the whole more often than the patient's) serving to awaken both from threateningly excessive regression and helping to expand the areas of feelings and inner experience in which the patient can have the words to say it by.

Collaboration depends on equality of respect and value of the partners, with recognition that the purposeful asymmetry of the two partners' positions is a temporary necessity for the clinical task, not a difference in essential superiority and inferiority.

The separateness of the two people is crucial. Each partner regresses in efforts toward fusion, the analyst's trial identification arising in the face of felt separation as the patient begins to regress. The analyst's discipline of work together with the analyst's own defensive pressure to protect personal integrity and identity lead to interpretative responses that implicitly contain within them the message, "No, I am not you nor am I your ghosts, but together as separate people we can put words to name your desires, your terrors, and your ghosts." Thus, merger is replaced by contact and the essential otherness of each is respected. While providing a great personal gain, this shift simultaneously feels like a loss. As the prophet said, "Who increases knowledge increases sorrow."

WHAT IS TO FOLLOW

The chapters to follow are not prescriptions for technique; rather, they are attempts to think through the principles by which to evaluate matters of technique. The section "The Dyadic Analytic Context" is an effort to sketch broadly an integrated wholeness in the clinical situation. Whatever we study abstracted from the unity of the clinical engagement is seriously distorted unless it is placed back into the wholeness of its phenomenological context. Indeed, such contextualization has come to seem so important to me that I now consider it one of the basic truths that must regularly be applied to whatever subject is under consideration. To be examined seriously, any field must be narrowed so that scrutiny can be applied to fine details. However, unless that narrow focus is eventually broadened, the study of a microscopic slide will be taken inappropriately to be an equivalent of the study of life.

With this principle in mind, in the next section, "The Analyst at Work," I move from an overview of the unique partnership of the clinical situation to more specific aspects of the clinical engagement. Starting with a consideration of neutrality, the examination of the supraordinate attitude the analyst adopts toward the patient and the patient's analytic work, I turn next to the actual words the analyst speaks, followed by questions of empathy and tact, principles involved in the analyst's understanding of and activity toward the patient.

In the section "Manifest Clinical Issues," I turn from a narrowly technical orientation to see how some of the questions raised play out from more varied angles. Here I examine such issues as the place of a sense of humor in clinical work, the problems of long or interrupted analyses, even the place of action outside clinical work in furthering insight. Finally, in the section entitled "Self-Analysis," I examine the place of the other in an area that seems solitary, self-analysis.

Having begun with the conclusions I have come to through the work reflected in this volume, I think it appropriate to end with the questions that now open before me. Some of these are spelled out in "Continuing Questions."

I have added an appendix of personal self-introduction, "At Work." For a book of comparative analytic styles, I was once asked to describe the nature of my practice, myself at work, some of the ways I approach common problems in practice, the sources that have influenced me. I am aware, as anyone concerned with fantasies and unconscious activities must be, of the differences that are bound to exist between what one says and thinks one does and what one actually does. The current appendix comes as near as possible to conveying how I *think* I work in my office. I include it for those who may wonder more about who it is who has written the rest.

Now, let us proceed.

II

THE DYADIC ANALYTIC CONTEXT

1

From Analytic Surface to Analytic Space

"Meeting a friend in a corridor, Wittgenstein said: 'Tell me, why do people always say it was natural for men to assume that the sun went round the earth rather than that the earth was rotating?' His friend said, 'Well, obviously, because it just looks as if the sun is going round the earth.' To which the philosopher replied, 'Well, what would it have looked like if it had looked as if the earth was rotating?'"
—Stoppard (1972)

Our earliest views of the world are always shaped by a vantage point that has ourselves as its center. With experience and learning we come to understandings more complex, subtle, and modest regarding our own centrality. But the new elegant edifice of sophistication is shaped by the naive self-centeredness around which it grew. It is so in our individual lives, and it is so in our science. In our effort to help others confront themselves, we traditionally thought that what we saw first was the surface of the patient's mind. Such a view seems self-evident from our earliest sense of the patient as someone in the world out there, and it continues to engage our primitive tendency to see the universe as a series of spheres surrounding our own observing center.

Our original clinical sense of the patient as a person who brought symptoms for our knowing examination was informed by Freud's early (1901) introduction of the notion of the surface as that which the patient's "unconscious happens to be presenting" (p. 12). This image has kept its appeal despite generations of changes in the way we conceptualize mental models and the analytic process.

It is tempting to think that the idea of the surface keeps its favor because of its ready clinical heuristic value, but close reconsideration suggests that the idea of a surface may often be misleading. The analyst listens to associations, notices affective movements, and comments on what is seen. The surface has been the name for what the analyst believes is coming from the patient. Yet what we focus our conscious analytic attention on inevitably includes vital areas that lie outside our conscious realizations.

Recent efforts have been made to explore more precisely the place of the analytic surface in a theory of technique. Paniagua (1985) emphasized the surface as "the level of observables" (p. 323), later (1989) proposing the term "clinical surface" for the data that can be observed without conjecture. Levy and Inderbitzen (1990) have attempted to move the concept from that of simple clinical observation readily shared by patient and analyst to another level of abstraction, a more theoretical structure, that of a yardstick by which different clinical approaches could be compared and evaluated. They distinguished the surface as a level of consciousness (what can be seen on top) from the surface as the aspect of the patient's productions "to which the analyst specifically and selectively attends in order to gain access to what is hidden" (p. 372). By moving from manifest surface, the direct observation of the patient's mind, to what might be termed an implied surface, that is, to the level at which clinicians appear to intervene—a level that implies what those clinicians deal with as the functional surface—they attempted to utilize the concept of surface as a way of comparing different clinicians' approaches to patients.

This attempt was brought into question by Boesky (1990) who, doubting that surface concepts could be divided away from ideas of consciousness, asked how surface as a way of organizing data differed from the concept "focus of attention." Boesky's questions have triggered much discussion of whether the clinical implication of thinking in terms of the surface implied narrowing of interventions to resistance interpretations. One implication of the place of the surface to which I shall return concerns the way the structural model is used and how that might be modified by new appreciation of the significance of compromise formations.

The idea of the surface of the patient's mind as something noticed and described from outside by a detached observer developed historically at an early time before the significance of both transference and countertransference were realized. Now, almost a century later, we are aware that exploration of the patient's mind unfolds within a unique clinical dyad. The clinical practice of analysis is no mere spectator activity where action on the field is viewed and commented on from the detached security of the sidelines.

When Freud first spoke of the surface he was struggling with discoveries about the depths; his orientation, necessarily, did not yet include awareness of the import of his own role in the clinical work. Now that we are sensitive to the complexities of the analyzing instrument—knowing that even when working at best the analyst too has an unconscious and a presence—our effort is to reexamine the place of the surface when two people with complex mental structures collaborate to explore the depths of one of them. Our primary clinical task remains unchanged: the exploration of the workings of one person's, the patient's, mind. Attuned to the impact that the unique two-person analytic field has on the unfolding of that task, we are led to reevaluate the concept of the surface of the patient's mind.

After briefly considering implications of the word "surface" itself, I shall move to a clinical vignette to demonstrate some of the complexities at hand. My view is, first, that surface in analysis implies engagement in the immediacy of the analytic moment; second, that surface is consequently determined by both partners; third, that the clinical goal of all of this is to extend the patient's self-knowledge as far as possible beyond the surface; and fourth, that the analytic engagement involves affective communicative resonances and searching out by each partner of the other, unconsciously as well as consciously, with each hearing the other beyond the apparent surface. Indeed, I believe the analytic surface can only be appreciated within its context in the analytic space.

THE ANALYTIC SURFACE

The idea of the surface of the patient's mind implicitly maintains the flavor of its roots in the early topographical theory, referring as it does to what is shown on the top, to the outside, what the analyst can look upon and see as the uppermost appearance of what is presented by the patient's mind. The word "surface" itself is defined as "the outermost boundary . . . of any material body, immediately adjacent to the air or empty space, or to another body." Secondarily, the *Oxford English Dictionary* goes on to add that the word is "usually denoting that part or aspect of anything which presents itself to a slight or casual mental view." The very word "surface" implies separation without engagement.

A boundary implies a division between two objects, in an analysis the separation between the patient's mind and that of the analyst. Indeed, the two minds *are* separate, but they also are *not* simply separate as they engage and exist in the interactive analytic context. Each mind is shaped by concerns over what the other thinks, means, and intends. The analytic situation is, therefore, structured to open maximally the patient's hidden intentions and, simultaneously, to allow the analyst's psychology to be put in the service of the task at hand, the analysis of the patient's mind. Thus, the two minds are separate and yet they are not simply separate. What comes to be thought of as being on the surface of the other's mind is the outcome of internal forces within each mind as it processes experiences of the other.

When Freud (1911, p. 92) said that the analyst "should always be aware of the surface of the patient's mind at any given moment," when Fenichel (1941, p. 44) spoke of "beginning at the surface," when current students are taught the clinical adage that they ought always interpret what is on the surface—in each of these there is an implication of detached separateness of the analyst from the field the analyst observes.

For the idea of the analytic surface to be maintained, it must be understood within its context. Indeed, in the analytic situation the surface refers to the variegated, diverse and multicolored, alive and shifting, multiple-meaninged and multiple-leveled boundaries of the uniquely analytic dyadic engagement. I use the plural because in the affective space of the analytic process, in the transferences buried in the manifest words of both associations and interpretations, there are communicative connections on *all* levels, including unconscious ones. The analyst, too, in the course of analytic work comes to know things about the patient before the analyst knows they are known. Unlike the surface of a painted landscape circumscribed by a frame and viewed by an onlooker whose watchful presence in the gallery does not change the picture, the analytic surface is interpenetrating. Also, what is perceived as surface here is both unitary and wildly fragmented, with closeness and distance existing side by side, objects both seen and hidden, seen and not known to be seen, and seen illogically from front and back at the same time, all present in each overwhelmingly condensed moment. The organizing forces that shape what and how the patient relates are the patient's unconscious fantasies. But who we are, how we experience, how much we are open to the forces in the depths of the patient and ourselves are our—the analysts'—contributions to defining what gets called the surface. I say "what gets called the surface" because I consider the surface a technically defined aspect that is artificially abstracted from the engagement, which is a complex but unitary living phenomenon.

CLINICAL ILLUSTRATION

To aid in consideration of the concept of the analytic surface, I offer a clinical vignette chosen on the basis of two criteria: that it be current, alive at the time I write, and that it be an ordinary, garden-variety, analytic moment. My wish is to illustrate dynamic forces at work on all levels in both the patient and the analyst, with messages going back and forth and processed by each on all levels. This vignette, like any, can only demonstrate, not prove.

This young man came for analysis because of difficulty leaving an empty marriage. He had chosen his Tibetan wife mainly for her exotic qualities. In fact, he said, his "entire love life" had been limited to involvement with women culturally or racially exotic. So little background, and already we realize that my words may speak on the surface but that many other worlds are inevitably implied. His "entire love life" manifestly referred to the world of his adult outer actualities. Yet we already know enough to be skeptical. Our minds wander and we wonder not only about childhood development (can a mother be exotic? can she not be exotic?), but also about masturbation fantasies. Who are the selves and who are the others in such an "entire love life"? *Manifest words on the surface—the very words themselves—imply questions about the presence of their complements, that which the words seemingly exclude, that which exists below the surface.*

So that you may know what I knew as this unfolded, I add that this man's father died when this man was only 9, and that this man has a continuing conviction that he has been fatherless and raising himself throughout life. Also, his mother, now dead six years, was always seen by him as "weird," an embarrassment to him throughout his life.

During the hour at hand, the young man, who is white, bemoaned his rejection by a beautiful young black woman from Angola. He spoke of the wonderful impression he usually made, of how seductively promising he could seem. He considered the various ways he adjusts his appearance to play to his sense of his immediate audience. Could I hear such a statement without wondering how he now was playing to me? *Manifest words that on the surface appear to be about a third party relationship imply below the surface questions about their import for the immediate two-party relationship.*

I tend to consider all that a patient says to me for its possible implications regarding how he is experiencing our engagement at the moment because I believe this immediacy offers a primary point of access to the unconscious forces come alive.

Though premature interpretation interferes with further open-ing of this line of meaning, it would be difficult to exaggerate the importance of considering transferential meanings of anything that seems on the surface.

A man who would not generally allow himself uncomfort-able feelings, he nonetheless spoke of his fear of losing power. He had tried many ways of winning, of adjusting his facade. In the course of his continuing distress, one statement of his espe-cially caught my ears. As he described his attempt to be charm-ing he spoke of it as being like "trying out a new piece of equip-ment" that didn't work. He went on to say that when he would feel upset by rejection he would try to persuade himself that it was only a piece of his facade, not himself, which had been rejected.

I wondered to myself what this man experienced as his true self, how it could be that parts of himself felt detached, "trying out a new piece of equipment." *The factors by which we choose what we will call the surface always include our own selections and translations.* That is so for all of us. No analyst who has ever shared clinical discussions, especially with colleagues from dif-ferent schools, could ever believe there is an analytic unanimity when deciding what to call the surface. Indeed, any analyst who does not conceptualize some aspects of dynamics differently from the way they would have been seen in earlier years must worry whether "basic concepts" have been allowed to become private rigidities.

But back to the moment in the session. What we hear from our patients is understood in many ways, touching all aspects of our own prior experiences, including experiences with other patients. When my patient spoke of reassuring himself, I fleet-ingly remembered a patient I thought I had forgotten from many years ago. That was a man who suffered from insistent vanity, one who did much analytic work before he could allow himself to feel the envy hidden behind his vanity. When that man for the first time could allow himself to notice a competitor who could outdo him in verbal pyrotechnics, he comforted himself after a very brief moment by thinking, "I don't have to be jealous of him.

I could talk as well as he does, if I were he." My hearing of my present patient, my understanding that envy might lie behind his vanity, was informed by my prior patient. *What the analyst views and how that view is conceptualized is shaped by the analyst's prior experience, both clinical and personal.*

Also, while the successful analyst for the most part may have mastered internal conflicts, still the analyst's words, language, and understandings are colored by private history and personal psychology. Our minds are put in the service of the analysis of the other, but they still are our minds. The way I heard and responded was inevitably colored by the weaknesses and strengths, the shames and the prides, I had come to know growing up in childhood, in adolescence, and even in my professional childhood and adolescence. The analyst's mastery, like that of any person, is always a matter of degree. Neither by magical empathy nor by absolute detached observation can any one person know the true or full flavor of another person's inner experience. Every hearing and every consideration of something as surface involves personal processing, which includes personal translations. *The analyst's objectivity does not come from being apart from the analytic field, but it comes from the relentless candor of the analyst's self-analysis and from the ruthlessness with which the analyst acts to stay in the service of the patient's continuing investigation.*

Let us return to the clinical moment. I said to the patient that the division between his public and private views of himself were linked by his concern over "trying out new equipment." Now, as I reflect and write, I wonder whether in part I too was trying out new equipment with a new, partial interpretation. Consciously, I had at that moment remembered something the patient had pushed away—his having spoken earlier about his secretly masturbating at 13 and 14. He had felt himself an outsider, something of a freak in junior high school and high school, but he made a "radical change" when he went to college. Then he replaced thick glasses with contact lenses, dressed well, and began his involvement with "exotic" girls. To me it seemed that what was primary in what I at that moment considered the surface was his pain with rejection, and that the main deep implication likely had to do with a painfully fragmented sense of self rooted in a body image, and especially a sexual body image, that was also fragmented.

What we are able to recognize, what we can readily see and thus call the surface, is also informed by what we have learned through the patient's actions apart from his words. My office is in a suite shared with colleagues. We have a bathroom opening onto the waiting room, which the patients use, and another opening onto the inner hall to the individual offices, which the doctors use. Through the years I have learned that a patient's using or not using the inner bathroom has importance. One day my patient, uncomfortable from waiting for the outer bathroom, asked my permission to use the inner one. This was a man who spoke of himself as never really having had a father and never having to submit to a male authority, one whose tone to me was often cockily disdainful. Although I did not think it was the time to question his request, I attributed great significance to his asking. And I experienced and considered what he was telling me implicitly about feeling strong or weak, big or little, during the hour at hand within the context of how he had been both acting and speaking in enacting his own strong-big and weak-little feelings in relation to me. There seem to me two main inferences to be drawn here. First, *what gets called the surface is vitally influenced by the unspoken evocative power of current personal interactions, those which derive from actions apart from words as well as those structured within words.* And second, *what gets called the surface can never be removed from the context of the experiences over time in the shared engagement of the two persons involved.*

The moments of engagement in which we search for what to call the surface include the analyst, no matter how silent he may seem, as well as the patient. My own mind responded to the complexities of my patient—his multiple current and past messages and my multiple readings—by thinking that the struggles over his sense of self and body, and especially phallic roots, were what was central on the surface.

Aiming in the direction of underlying, organizing unconscious fantasies, I addressed the patient using his own metaphor, one I felt could appeal on multiple levels. He immediately heard the phallic implication of my choice of the words "trying out a new piece of equipment," and he contemptuously wondered whether I was building a case on a meaningless turn of phrase. (Of course, in doing so, the whole issue of which one of us was more powerful was also at the same time being reenacted.) I replied, "You try to tuck what you're saying away."

In retrospect I am struck by other possible reactions I might have offered. Focusing on transference demands, I might have chosen to speak to the competitive concern over domination and submission. Focusing on resistance, I might have chosen to speak to the shift of the patient's position to his repudiation of what he had just said, questioning what went through his mind at the moment of that shift. However, with this patient I had already learned that exclusive attention to resistance, even resistance within the transference, was subtly used by him to avoid matters of shame in the development of his sense of body and sexual weakness. At that moment in the hour I had the impression that the patient felt a repressed or suppressed piece of himself was caught out in the open, and it seemed to me then that most was to be gained by holding on to it and not being easily shaken loose.

Interpretation of resistance is a vital part of the analytic work, and I believe the transference is the primary medium of this work. But neither resistance nor transference interpretation is the ultimate goal. Both are vehicles to that goal, and both can also be used to avoid the goal—the patient's maximum access to all parts of his mind at work. It was because I felt in that clinical moment that the emerging level of conflict was sufficiently clear to me and that the patient was sufficiently ready to acknowledge that level that I chose to address the conflicted self-image behind the immediate resistance. *Both the analyst's theoretical mind-set in general and personal mind-set at the moment influence how the analyst contributes to structuring the surface.*

Even though I had never used the phrase "tucking away" with my patient, how could I have unwittingly chosen such a word without recognizing that both of us would think of phallic defense, tucking one's tail between one's legs? While consciously attending to what appears on the surface, *both* the analyst and the patient process their experiences of each other in and out of awareness.

The patient next spoke about the distinction between two worlds—that of his public suave image and that of his uncertain secret private fantasies where excitement was naked, not under sophisticated, cool control. With great discomfort (and, I think, also great relief) he went on to talk of the difference between his private feelings of smallness, impotence, old shame over bed-wetting, and the fragility of his man-of-the-world facade.

I have selected a pedestrian moment rather than a full-blown interpretation to show how the surface is the point from which the analyst aims ever more deeply to define the patient's organizing unconscious fantasies, eventually to reconstruct in the living here and now of the transference their genetic roots. In my own hearing and processing of the patient's verbal, emotional, and interactive messages, I recognized meanings deeper than those he consciously thought were on the surface. By not limiting myself to defense interpretations but speaking instead to the deeper meanings I felt were accessible behind the defense, I helped the patient go beyond his conscious surface, aiming deeper. Neutrality in clinical work does not imply an analyst's indifference to selecting between the superficial and the deeper.

THE ANALYTIC SURFACE AND
THE ANALYTIC SPACE

If we consider the relationship of the analytic surface to the deep, we discover difficult intrinsic problems. Where is the surface and where is the deep? If we say that the surface is the only way we can come to know the deep, and that the deep can be known by examining the surface, then the word *surface* may become so all-inclusive as to be useless. It suggests that whatever of the deep is active, even if unconsciously, is therefore on the surface. If surface is not merely another way of speaking of conscious access, if it includes even the activity and representations of repressed forces, then surface includes the deep and loses its usefulness.

Another way of conceiving of the relationship of surface and deep is the tempting metaphor of levels. The onion skin, peeled layer by layer, is an appealing image, but it is, I believe, misleading in analytic experience. The surface is not simply the *edge* of the unconscious, it is the current apparent manifestation of very complex compromises, which themselves reflect and contain underlying powerful forces.

We have a dilemma. We cannot simply say that surface includes everything, nor can we say that it is a layer that excludes the deep. Both are true and both are untrue. Despite our preference for conventional dualistic logic, deep structures are at one and the same time both implicit in the apparent surface and buried beyond it.

In the interaction within the analytic situation each partner shapes and is shaped by forces arising both in the self and in the other. The analyst's clinical task is to maximize mastery of personal inner forces, to utilize them as much and as best as can be done in the service of the other's self-exposure and self-inquiry. But mastery is neither self-absence nor self-omnipotence. Like any conscious thought, what the analyst conceives as the surface of the patient is a compromise representing all levels of forces.

We now recognize that even when an analyst speaks as a person, separate from the patient, who tries to focus the patient's attention on shifts in the patient's own associations, still the analyst affects and colors what unfolds. What analysts choose to say and not to say all inform the patient. Even when the analyst's words are the most dispassionately objective, they carry buried metacommunications. Even manifest attention to what is thought on the surface always carries with it significant messages and interactions beyond the surface.

Recognition of the dyadic vitality of the analytic process may also clarify a common question about deep interpretations. Often, when it is said that an analyst must not interpret too deeply, deep analysis is being confused with wild analysis. We tend to underestimate the strength of the patient's ego, of what the patient can take. A crucial question in evaluating an interpretation is whether it rises from the actuality of the analytic moment or whether it comes from some theoretical concept carried in the analyst's mind (at times a rationalized unconscious fantasy of the analyst's own). It may be that a patient can tolerate almost any interpretation that arises deeply, provided it comes from a genuine experience in the actuality of the analytic process. What undermines analysis is interpretation that arises untruthfully, that is, not out of the immediacy of the experience of the analysis but from the analyst's detached theories. Then the analyst is speaking within an analytic setting but from outside the analytic process, and what results is wild analysis, not deep analysis. Rather than being clinically valid, wild analysis—reading the patient as a text rather than from the words and music of the affective moment—is a form of applied analysis—or, more precisely, of misapplied analysis.

From our early detached view of the surface of the other's mind we now move to a different view, one in which we examine phenomena not as observers apart but as ones who know our very act of observing takes place within and affects the analytic universe. We move from the analytic surface to a recognition of the complexities of the analytic space, to use Viderman's (1974) felicitous phrase.

THE ANALYTIC SPACE

There is no surface apart from context. The artists of the earliest prehistoric drawings in the caves of the Dordogne used the natural shapes of the cave walls to create a bas relief, giving semi-sculptural qualities to their figures. As Modell has pointed out (1968), "the created environment and the 'real' environment . . . were interpenetrated" (p. 16). Such a model for all relationships also applies to the analytic relationship, modifying the early paradigm of perfectionistic or absolute analytic neutrality by recognizing that the contours of the analyst, like the contours of the wall, influence the transference images painted upon it.

Acknowledging that the wall has shape is insufficient. In fact, the analyst has never been an inanimate wall. (This is so despite the frequency with which those who would rather avoid the discipline and technical value of the abstinence principle suggest otherwise.) Even when functioning with appropriate abstinent restraint, the analyst is always a living person and thus is involved in active unconscious engagement as well as in the conscious reading of apparent surfaces.

Ten years after he spoke about the surface, Freud (1915a) said, "It is a very remarkable thing that the *Ucs.* of one human being can react upon that of another, without passing through the *Cs.* This deserves closer investigation . . . but, descriptively speaking, the fact is incontestable" (p. 194). The analytic literature reporting this investigation is by now substantial in detailing the subtleties of the analytic process which unfold behind manifest associations and interpretations (see especially Jacobs 1991). These considerations have addressed how analysts' inner forces influence their perception of and interaction with patients, including how analysts' very choices of words are shaped by their own psychologies and carry buried messages structured within those words to patients. Certainly, in my clinical work with the young man described above, he and I were constantly feeling each other out in trying to understand the impact and influence each was having on the other.

What we have been calling the analytic surface exists within the analytic space. The shift of vantage point from analytic surface to analytic space turns out to be considerably more true to our daily clinical experiences. Now we have room to notice that both surface and depth are within the field of the affective engagement of patient and analyst as each experiences the unfolding transferences within the analytic situation. *The analytic space lies in the affective engagement of the two partners in the uniquely structured analytic situation.*

Not only does attention to the analytic space not alter traditional discipline, it depends on that discipline. "The fundamental rule, that of free association, cannot be conceived of, and would probably be inoperative, without the other coordinates which constitute the specific analytic field: i.e. without the diametrically opposed positions of the two organizers of the situation" (Viderman 1974, p. 470). Within the context of the different positions of the patient and the analyst in the analytic setting, it is thanks to the mastered psychology of the analyst "that a deep and incomparable understanding can be established between two unconscious minds bound in an affective experience" (Viderman 1974, p. 472).

Transferential forces and countertransferential forces (in the broadest sense) are present and can be in the service of or against the service of the analytic task. Indeed, these forces in each analytic partner serve both analytic progress and analytic resistance at one and the same time. As a result, appropriate mistrust of countertransference demands the analyst's steady self-analysis in relation to each continuing clinical analysis. Such disciplined restraint is essential in order to realize rather than to dissipate analytic potential. Whether the analyst works as if on automatic pilot—with self-analysis functioning preconsciously and unconsciously—or whether the analyst maintains conscious self-monitoring, the clinical exposure of the patient's mind takes place within a matrix, an affective space, that includes the analyst's personal emotional receptivity, self-inquiry, and necessary silent turning of those forces to the service of the manifest exploration of the patient's mind.

As a consequence of the vitality of the analytic space, communications can be seen to occur between the analytic partners both in and out of conscious awareness. The therapeutic goal is to bring the unconscious aspects to conscious view, to put them into words. As has been stated, unconscious communication is not only the nonverbal. Even the words spoken carry buried messages that can be and are read unconsciously by both patient and analyst. Each hears messages buried deep in the structure of the other's words, and each may hear those messages before being able consciously to acknowledge them.

THE ANALYTIC SPACE AND COMPROMISE FORMATION

The shift from analytic surface to analytic space is a clinical-level consideration that parallels the theoretical shift from early structural theory to current understandings. Tripartite structuralism has made possible vast progress in analytic understanding. But just as conscious-preconscious-unconscious systems proved inadequate models for psychic functioning, id-ego-superego systems have similarly proved to be valuable but insufficient.

"It is compromise formation one observes when one studies psychic functioning" (Brenner 1982, p. 109). Any mental activity expresses forces from each part of the tripartite model. One clinical evidence of this is in the observation that any transferential position carries both expressive and resistant aspects. Indeed, at times that which is expressive on one level is simultaneously resistant on another, as in the use of partial insights to defend against further emerging forces. Thus, there is an artificiality to the position that one can restrict oneself to interpretations of ego defenses. We can address id, ego, or superego aspects, or expressive or defensive aspects of a patient's functioning within the analysis, but the supraordinate principle of compromise formation reminds us that each piece of behavior reflects all vital forces in condensation.

We are left with other technical conflicts of our own. To hear the unconscious messages within the affective and verbal associations the analyst must listen with evenly hovering attention. Yet to address the significance of any specific conflict, the analyst must focus attention and interpretively call the patient to temporarily focused attention. It is in the realm of focused attention that the concept of the surface of the patient's mind has its transient heuristic value. As the partial view abstracted from the experiential whole is reintegrated—by returning to the overview of the patient's free associations and the analyst's free-float-ing attention—the artifice of surface is internalized by the pa-tient in the experience of the analytic space. Free associations without interpretive structuring would result in chaos, not ana-lytic change, and focused interpretation without free associations and evenly hovering attention would result in indoctrination, not analytic change.

Gray (1986) has provided a most thorough study of the circumscribed sequential examination of those aspects of the patient's mind that are ego defensive. By focusing on resistance analysis he has explored and mapped what can be observed by both analyst and—with the analyst's help—the patient of func-tions evident on the apparent surface of the patient's mind. To succeed in this task, Gray has necessarily moved from the posture of evenly hovering attention to one of closely focused attention. "Even-hovering attention and skillful, id-resonating interpreta-tions in a transferentially enhanced authoritative atmosphere are, by themselves, relatively ineffective in bringing into the patient's awareness the unconscious ego activities that carry out repeti-tive forms of defense as resistance. To observe the simple or in-tricate defenses at work against specific id impulse derivatives, the analysand requires a form of observation distinguishable from the 'experiential observation' . . . that serves free associa-tion" (p. 245).

The analyst's mind is in a constant state of multiple tensions, including a tension between aim-inhibited regression that per-mits evenly hovering attention and the more alert state of con-scious focusing of attention necessary to pinpoint observations. Each function must be allowed its appropriate sway, and cau-tion is ever necessary lest any favored analytic stance serve to defend against others.

Attention must be directed in order to focus on any part, but such partial abstraction must always be placed in its overall con-text or else distortion takes the place of accuracy. Recognizing the value of appropriate closely focused attention, consideration must also be extended to a danger presented by such attention. As with any technical maneuver, looking at something requires looking away from something else. The fact that the analyst is describing and demonstrating an immediate bit of the patient's mental functioning does not remove that very act from participating in its own engagement, which opens new transferential meanings. To discuss the course of the patient's associations as if these could then be examined and spoken of in isolation runs the risk of implying that parts of analysis can take place outside and apart from contextual transferential and dyadic implications.

Pure resistance analysis implies a reification of the structural theory, which undermines its value by segmenting functions into *either* id *or* ego *or* superego. The benefits of considering psychic processes from the structural point of view could hardly be exaggerated, but to separate "this part" as id from "that part" as ego is like dividing an arc into its concave and convex parts. Brenner's recognition that all psychic activity involves compromise formations that integrate forces from all parts of the psychic apparatus including considerations of reality has provided a major conceptual step forward in our understanding and use of the structural model. It extends understanding by integrating conceptual fragments into a unitary whole.

Resistance interpretation presumably addresses ego defenses as the latter are manifest on the surface. The shift from surface of the patient's mind to recognition of the analytic space is parallel to the shift from pure ego defense to recognition of compromise formation. It carries with it a vital technical implication that can result in a sea change in the clinical atmosphere. Consistently to address resistance as primary, the manifestation of defense, risks implying that the organizing question in the back of the analyst's mind is "What is it that the patient is not or can not tell us now, and why not?" To address clinical resistance as a compromise formation, expressive as well as defensive, implies a significantly different organizing question in the back of the analyst's mind, namely, "What is it that the patient is telling us and struggling to tell us now?" Clinical resistance is expression of psychic conflict, a struggle that reveals itself. It is the analytic work unfolding.

Interpretation calls for the analyst to speak to a particular surface, but also always to be aware of the distortions incurred by such abstraction from the psychic whole, to be prepared to step back to an even consideration of the psychic space in order to learn how the interpretation is taken in, modified, and used by the patient. Recognition of the overall affective analytic space within which attention to seeming surface manifestations can take place protects against the risks of single-minded resistance interpretation. Surface understood in the context of the analytic space includes all the accessible messages, meta-messages, transferential evocations, and provocations that fill the analytic air. With all included, surface in the analytic space comes alive in the immediacy of the analytic moment.

THE ANALYTIC SPACE AND INTERPERSONALISM

Attention to the dyadic nature of the analytic space is not a rubric for legitimizing countertransferential enactments. Avoidance of pseudo-objectivity and reductionism in formulations based on the surface does not relieve us of the need to make clinical choices, the need to stay alert to implications of technique. The shift from a simple view of the surface of the patient's mind to one open to the hidden forces active at work even while the analyst appears to be objectively viewing that surface does not diminish the analyst's need for discipline. Attention to the analytic space does not imply that since everything has multiple meanings the analyst can do or say anything at all, as if all is somehow bound to end up in the service of the clinical work (a theory we might call a "loose canon"). Instead, such attention demands even greater self-scrutiny and discipline on the analyst's part. Recognition of the multiple levels of interchange in the analytic space demands more, not less, mastery by the analyst.

This concern with the analytic space is not merely an old interpersonal view brought out in new dress. The present attention to the power of the affective communicative matrix within which an analysis unfolds is different from customary interpersonal psychology. This new vantage point does not minimize the centrality of unconscious forces. To the exact contrary, consideration of the analytic space extends respect for unconscious forces in both analytic participants. At times old interpersonal dynamics seemed to absent the power of the patient's unconscious, attending instead to those interchanges between patient and analyst that were close to the surface. A current incarnation of that old tendency may be present in the shift from considering the totality of the patient's psychic state to considering the patient's so-called mental state, moving from a total picture including unconscious forces to a segmental attention to an "experience-near" conscious sense of self.

Earliest analytic understanding viewed the analytic partners as a pair within which it was the patient who brought unconscious forces to the engagement. Defensive interpersonalism (whether in old or new dress) attends to the analyst as an active participant in the analytic engagement but often dilutes the import of the patient's active unconscious forces. Attention to the analytic space as an affective area of engagement within a disciplined analytic situation is more like a model of three-dimensional chess. While keeping to the traditional goals and basic technical concepts of analysis, this orientation opens analytic consideration to the full range of unconscious forces alive within the analytic field.

CLOSING QUESTIONS

My intent has been to define some of the limits of the concept of "the surface of the patient's mind," aiming to extend our view to a fuller realization of the analytic space, which contains a perceived surface. However, as we achieve new clarities, other questions are brought into the open. Now that we are alert to the affective field created by the partners in the unique psychoanalytic situation we are left with further paradoxes, ones intrinsic to every personal interaction. The dyadic analytic interaction is the best laboratory yet conceived for examining the nature of how one person relates to another.

How can it be that no man is an island and that at the same time every man is an island? As an analysis progresses, both patient and analyst share in the actual experience of the unfolding analysis. But what does it mean to say that they share? True, each goes through the moment along with the other, but what each tastes is individual, never a truly shared taste of the other's experience of the moment. How often does it happen that we think or say, "I know what you mean" and the other's answer is, "Almost, but that's not exactly how I meant it"? Indeed, must we not be suspicious of those moments when someone feels understood? Is it not likely that the sense of relief derives from the contact, from the feeling that the other has come very close, rather than from the feeling of being known for what one's inner life fully is? As Shapiro (1990) put it, "Language makes such understanding communicative rather than simply communal" (p. 43).

Shared experiences are privately known in separate firsthand ways that nonparticipants can only know about, never directly know. It is misleading to speak glibly of one-person psychology versus two-person psychology. No single person exists outside a human, object-connected field; the analytic space colors how such a single person comes to understanding by the other and to insight. At the same time, the mind of any individual can be engaged by another yet is always crucially apart, a private universe of inner experience. Empathy at its best is trial identification, at its worst, distorting projection. Empathy is not symbiosis.

There is an affective interaction between patient and analyst. Each constantly monitors the other and each constantly struggles with and against the emotional impact of the other. To survive and keep any clinical utility the concept of the analytic surface must move from simple topography—the analyst's conscious observation of what appears on the top of the patient's mind. Its extension into consideration of the analytic space necessitates the analyst's modesty when sizing up what appears to be on top of the patient's mind. It necessitates the analyst's constant self-analytic monitoring in an effort to be alert to affective pressures not yet accessible to words, pressures originating both in the patient and in the analyst. Those forces within the analyst include the inevitable consequences of trying to follow the patient, intrinsic forces beyond neurotic countertransference distortions that self-evidently also demand mastery.

Recognition of the analytic space implies ever greater consideration for the subtleties of unconscious pulls.

ENVOY

I would like to close by referring to the story told by linguist Allen Walker Read (as cited by M. Stacey in *The New Yorker* [1989]). He told of three baseball umpires describing their decisions. Regarding the balls and strikes, one said that he called them as they were. The second said that he called them as he saw them. Then the last stated, "They ain't nothin' till I calls 'em." Read noted that the umpire who called them as they were had an absolutist and rigid attitude. The second, he noted, had a different world view, recognizing that his own reactions were involved in his decision, while the third, more extreme, was aware that he himself imposed a pattern on a changing world.

The student of psychoanalysis, just like the student of semantics, struggles with consideration of his own place in the world he structures as well as describes. Appreciation of the affective communicative aspects of the analytic space opens the analyst's mind to the greatest breadth of understanding of what is alive, whether apparent yet or not, in the analytic process.

2

Transference:
"An Original Creation"

Reflecting on the now does not imply relinquishing the future or forgetting the past: the present is the meeting place for the three directions of time.
PAZ (1991)

Just as the seeming surface of interaction between patient and analyst is abstracted from a broader emotional space, so, too, is exposure of the past abstracted from a broader context of engaged immediacy in the present. Transference, though its roots are in the past, comes into existence as it is actualized within the world of the present. As Laplanche and Pontalis (1973) put it, in psychoanalysis transference is "a process of actualization of unconscious wishes. Transference uses specific objects and operates in the framework of a specific relationship established with these objects. . . . In the transference, infantile prototypes reemerge and are experienced with a strong sense of immediacy" (p. 455). Transference exists in the now.

Dazzled by the past, in analysis we have at times lost our bearings in the present, as if we could reach for the past without putting our full weight on the present. Only the past that is alive in the present, even if buried within it, can ever be grasped in our hands. This is the past that is alive as it is recalled into present feelings by present sensations, or as it is revived in analytic en-

actments. The untouchable past is that which we can only reconstruct, inferring its shape by its imprint on the unconscious fantasies we come to know through present experience.

In an attempt to place the present within the analytic process I shall try to make these points: (1) that life exists in the
present moment; (2) that like a crystalline drop of water mirroring the universe, the worlds of past and present, self and others,
are made visible by exploring the reflections in the tiny and fragile
drop of the immediacy of the moment; (3) that what we see when
we look closely at those reflections are the lights of the present—
the past does not merely repeat itself in the present, but the
present creates our pictures of the past; and, (4) lastly, that it is
the emotional sensations experienced in the moment that shine
the light that makes possible our seeing and knowing the inner
universe of buried dynamics and of the past.

To approach these ideas, I shall start with a brief statement
of the basic principle behind the psychoanalytic process and
move on to a definition of transference. Then, after describing a
clinical incident, I shall address current concerns with process
and interaction in the context of the centrality of the present
moment in analysis. Finally, I shall address the place of sensations in the present in the exploration of memories about the past.

TRANSFERENCE AND BASIC
ANALYTIC CONCEPTS

There could hardly be an analytic concept more basic than
that of the centrality of unconscious forces acting powerfully
behind mental functioning. Indeed, the fundamental principle
that makes clinical analysis possible is that every person behaves
in the world as that person does because it is the best way of
getting along in the world as that person sees it. Whether we call
this the centrality of an active unconscious or the repetition compulsion or the supraordinacy of the adaptive principle does not
matter. What matters is that people repeat patterns based on
hidden inner forces. Regardless of how unreasonable manifest

behavior might seem to others, our basic principles tell us that it could all be understandable, it would all make good sense, if only one knew the hidden meanings alive behind the manifest appearance, that is, how one came to see the world in the way that one does. Thus, the clinical task is to set up a situation where patterns of mental functioning can be brought most clearly to life and where their exploration can reveal the hidden forces that combine to create them.

Recognizing this, it did not take long for Freud to realize that adult patterns were shaped by developmental patterns and experiences in infancy and childhood. However, it would be too simple, an error, to say that because the infantile neurosis lies behind the adult neurosis it is alone the cause of the adult neurosis.

Behind the present lies the past. But in analysis the border between the past and the present is not something temporal, not something that resides in the linear actuality of time. When we speak of the psychoanalytic past, it is, rather, something that is present now, something within the deep structure of the mind that is nevertheless an enduring piece of the mind alive. We refer to reverberations of the past as they are alive in the present framework of the patient's mind whether or not they are accessible in the conscious tales of memory.

Our clinical interest in the past arises because our goal is mastery through insight. However, our interest in the past is not an academic historicity but a concern for bringing to the patient's free access all the parts we can of the innermost recesses of the patient's mind as it is alive and active even when hidden from itself. We aim not only to identify patterns but also to try to define the secret complex of feelings and ideas that have organized and shaped those mental patterns. If we were to use our theories to translate presenting stories and fantasies directly to ideas of childhood roots, we would be practicing wild analysis. We would be functioning in the manner of revisionist history in which a story is presented that most comfortably fits the historian's preferences, or like the lawyer who starts a summation to the jury by saying, "And these, ladies and gentlemen, are the conclusions on which I base my facts."

Where, then, do we find the past? Like good historians, we seek primary sources. The primary source in analysis is not something external, like childhood diaries and letters. We even acknowledge that stories recalled as memories are themselves not primary sources by speaking of those tales as screen memories. Primary sources in psychoanalysis are the current expressions of those internal forces that, even when not directly visible and even though themselves shaped by the past, are now alive and give shape to the present. It is *not* essential that psychic forces be obvious on the surface for us to consider them valid; it *is* essential that they be implicit and thus potentially discoverable within present experience, even when they are beyond a person's awareness. We call this cluster of functions that shape unfolding adult life, this set of implicit organizing principles, the unconscious fantasies.

The present is now. Unconscious fantasies—those hidden principles that give such consistency to a personality that we can say that something does or does not ring true about someone—are the bridges between the past and the present. The set of unconscious fantasies developed out of past drives and experiences then shape present drives, urges, daydreams, and ways of relating in the world. *The past is not directly alive in the present as the past incarnate. The past is alive as it has shaped unconscious fantasies, and it is this set of unconscious fantasies that is alive in the present.*

This is of clinical, not merely academic, importance. To tie together infantile neurosis and adult neurosis without including the unconscious fantasies is to convert a living human experience into an academic intellectualization. *Recognition of the meaningfulness of organizing fantasies alive in the present is the doorway to the relevance of the past.*

TRANSFERENCE AS AN ORIGINAL CREATION

Transference, as defined at the beginning, involves the patient's inner forces coming to life within the clinical situation. A valuable light is cast on the transferential process by a statement about three-quarters of a century old drawn from one whom we often overlook. On the short list of those extraordinary students of the mind who have lighted thought throughout the twentieth century were two early contemporaries whose writings give no indication that either was aware of the other, Sigmund Freud and Marcel Proust.

It is curious now to reflect on how it was that it was Proust who emphasized the more modern definition of transference. Interiority, sexuality, dreams, and the unconscious were in the air in western culture, perhaps even more so at the last fin de siècle than at this one. Freud was a doctor, and so he came to his work with the eye of the physician, looking on at his patient as a separate person under clinical scrutiny. Consequently, he saw the disease and he saw the patient, but only later did he come to recognize the importance of his own relationship with the patient.

Proust, on the other hand, was a novelist. Like Freud, he was concerned with the hidden forces in people's lives, but his ultimate aim was to offer descriptions of truth cloaked in the robes of fiction. As a result, Proust from the start was preoccupied by relationships. Proust saw, as Freud later came to understand, that transference is not merely the detached sound of the past echoing by us but apart from us. It is the past alive in present relationships.

As I quote Proust's definition, the clarity of its brief wording will be apparent. The concerns about time and experience that seem most special are in its closing phrases, on which I shall focus.

In *The Captive*, a volume in *Remembrance of Things Past*, Proust (1913–1927, vol. 3) wrote: "When we have passed a certain age, the soul of the child that we were and the souls of the dead from whom we sprang come and shower upon us their riches and their spells, asking to be allowed to contribute to the new emotions which we feel and in which, erasing their former image, we recast them in an original creation" (p. 73).

That the souls of our childhood selves and others contribute to our new emotions is well known. The past clearly and undoubtedly influences the present, but, Proust adds, the present shapes our views of the past. It is in regard to our early ghosts that Proust says, *"erasing their former image, we recast them in an original creation."*

The present shapes our view of the past at the very moment that the past shapes the present. That is how it occurs within the clinical transference. What is latent comes alive not simply on a blank screen but rather as actualized in the immediacy of the affective moment within the unique and encouraging two-person analytic relationship. This is also, I believe, what Leavy (1980) meant when he wrote that "the past begins now and is always becoming" (p. 94).

CLINICAL ILLUSTRATION

Let us turn to an unusual moment in an analysis as a way of approaching and highlighting what goes on in more usual analytic moments.

Although I do not routinely answer the telephone during a patient's hour, I did answer it one time when Ms. R was late and I thought it might be her call, explaining her absence. To my surprise, however, I heard a voice on a far-sounding call speaking Italian, a language I do not know. I assumed it was a wrong connection, but in rapid and urgent tones the speaker repeatedly used my name.

The speaker spoke no English and my feeble French was of no avail. I found myself feeling not as if I were at home in my own office but as if *I* were the one with a language problem, as if I were lost and alone in a country where I could not speak the language.

It was just then that Ms. R walked in and found me looking confused and in need of rescue. And, just then, I remembered that Ms. R had lived for a year in Italy. I must have looked pathetic and perhaps even urgent as I held out the receiver for help. At that instant, feeling lost, I was not thinking of good technique. I did what I did: I turned the phone over to my patient.

Ms. R took the phone, spoke briefly, hung up, and told me that the voice at the other end was someone who wanted to invite me to Milan and who would write with details. The entire incident, which occurred during the middle of Ms. R's third year of analysis, took only a minute or two, but it opened a world between Ms. R and me.

Ms. R was the first child in her immediate family, itself a unit within an East European extended family that, though not royal, was of such prestige and power as to be referred to in dynastic terms. Raised primarily by governesses, Ms. R was thought to be quite privileged. Unfortunately, as we already knew, those material privileges rarely extended to warmth and affection. By age 6 she knew the customs of high etiquette; she could debone a fish flawlessly. She did not, however, know how to play.

Her analysis had, until the incident I just described, unfolded as might be expected. Ms. R tried very hard to be a proper analysand but felt desperately inadequate at trying to do what "good patients who could really analyze" should do. She had been in something of a bind as she tried to describe her childhood in a way that never implied criticism of her parents. Along with this, she had seemed wary of me, on guard against any spontaneous exposure of feelings concerning our interaction. At times I wondered whether something she said had in it extremely subtle implications of criticisms or, at other times, some extremely subtle implicit humor. But efforts to push the boundary to expose such possible implications had never succeeded.

Taking the couch after having taken the phone, Ms. R was briefly silent and then turned to current events in her familiar proper but detached style. Some time passed before I recognized that what I had thought was her routine style was running out of steam. Ms. R seemed subtly distracted.

I noticed the slight change and asked about the incident around the telephone. I already knew that Ms. R kept her private mind severely separate from her public life, and that, despite genuine efforts to associate freely, she rarely gave me entry to her private thoughts. I had even shared with her my image of her as someone who survived by existing secretly in the underground while appearing to live normally in an occupied country.

With great hesitation, Ms. R let me know some of what she had really felt when I had handed her the receiver. A whole world had flashed through her mind within an instant: rage, outrage, the impulse to walk out but the quick sense that to be free she would have to finish her analysis and that if she were to walk out she would have to walk back in. So she stayed and took the phone, all in an instant.

Taking the phone brought powerful feelings, a world of experiences she thought she had forgotten. They were, certainly, experiences that had never been recalled with full feelings. Her mother was always late, always expecting the world to be ready and waiting whenever she would arrive. Ms. R was 7 when the mother, knowing she was late, sent her young daughter to the train station to tell the conductor to hold the train until the mother would show up. Trains and planes, to my own naive surprise, would, in fact, wait at the mother's imperious demand, but they would not change their schedules at the request of a frightened 7-year-old. Mother never understood this as a difficulty for the daughter but, rather, she took it to be a sign of the daughter's hostile subversion. Accordingly, the mother punished the daughter severely.

Ms. R's reaction to the stimulus I had provided was indignant rage and a sense of impotence. Her decision to stay in the analysis, however, was not merely another submission. Instead, it reflected a sense that staying was in part in her own interest. Of course, Ms. R might have stayed and refused to accept the telephone receiver, but at that time she was very far from such a sense of power and freedom.

The sensation of seeing me with phone in outstretched hand brought to life similar sensations from memories until then only latent. That is, the new sensation experienced in the interaction with me brought forth similar sensations from the distant past, forgotten, and perhaps even repressed, but still powerful in Ms. R's unconscious reservoir.

Ms. R's *unconscious fantasy* was of herself in a world in which her own needs were without power even to the point of her invisibility, and in which she was vulnerable to the capricious needs of others who were seen as powerful and sadistically dangerous. This buried view of herself organized the way she related to and experienced her relationships in the world. Though I was in the instance at hand manifestly weak and needy, she could see me no other way than imperious. That was her transferential tide. Those latent forces, always seeking a moment in current experience to carry them into actualization, required the immediacy of experience to be fulfilled. That was how the specifics of her transference came alive as an original creation of our shared moment.

We were able to develop the *genetic reconstructions* of Ms. R's probable emotional history secondary to our shared clarification of the organizing unconscious fantasies as they came alive in the present. Personal myths of history as originally offered by Ms. R could thus be modified by exploration of Ms. R's associations to her increasingly recognized patterns. Sensations and feelings now alive in this present context added to the recall of lost memories, offering a growing ring of truth to the approximations of reconstructions.

In retrospect, it seems somewhat surprising to me that in all of Ms. R's long associations to this incident she always seemed to identify me with the imperious side of her mother, rather than seeing me directly as manifesting a helplessness akin to her own. But, I believe, that is in part what makes this particular vignette clarifying.

An analytic clinical observation of long-standing value is that children identify with the *unconscious* conflicts of their parents.

Thus, in a sense, it often seems that a full analysis extends to a speculative analysis of the parents. Analysis of what arose within Ms. R when I peremptorily gave her the phone led to interpretation of previously repressed rage at her mother, interpretation of those current unconscious fantasies that shaped her seemingly accommodating personality. However, we were able to hypothesize reconstructions plausible behind those interpretations. Later consideration of the possibility of the mother's own sense of helplessness and Ms. R's identification with that side of the mother's personal conflicts led to a great broadening of Ms. R's awareness of both her own helplessness and her own secret imperiousness. The outcome was ultimately greater acceptance of those qualities in herself and less anger and even some new sympathy for the presence of these conflicting forces in the mother.

Part of what was newly remembered had earlier been spoken of in broad intellectual terms. Had reconstructions of a probable past been offered without drawing them from interpretations themselves based on the emotionally experienced present, we would have had possibly brilliant but nonetheless useless formulations. It was only when the present exposed the patterns of relating that structured how Ms. R's mind worked that she and I could come to know the shape of her unconscious fantasies, that we could come to sketch the probable roots of those unconscious fantasies.

The incident I have described has the disadvantage of being eccentric—it arose after an unusual intrusive action on my part, not from a seemingly ordinary analytic moment. My action, of course, had served as the trigger, but the subsequent chain reaction could not have unfolded unless the ground had already been prepared in an increasingly trusting analytic engagement.

The advantage of such an incident is that, like pathology in relationship to normal behavior, it exposes through magnification what otherwise might be hidden from view. *The context of the partnership within the analytic situation provides the medium in which the patient's transference can be actualized.* In an analysis, as in life, one thing leads to another, and meaningfulness within analysis derives from those "things" coming to life as unfolded and actualized within the analytic relationship. I am reminded of one time during Ms. R's analysis when, sitting during a long and labored silence, I cleared my throat. Ms. R burst out, "Since you bring the subject up," and went on to a painful area of which we had never heard. *The forces within the patient push toward expression, but they require the present analytic context in order to be actualized.*

The vignette around the telephone was a tiny sliver in the vastly complex mosaic that was Ms. R's ultimate analysis. The work with her was for me among the longest and most difficult in my experience. I think it was also among the most valuable. Ms. R was a woman who ultimately turned out to fit Shengold's (1989) description of "soul murder." It took many years of work before she was able substantially to overcome her fears and expose to our shared scrutiny her sense of her world as she had known it. After about eight years she decided to settle for the work then done and to stop. That decision was like an important, and I now suspect necessary, enactment of her impulse to walk out during the interchange over the telephone. She returned a year later, relieved that I had accepted her stopping with respect. It was then that for the first time she was able more fully to lay claim to our work together as hers rather than mine, that she was able with courage to explore more deeply her world of inner dread and pain.

My knowledge of analytic theory helped me in understanding what unfolded as we worked together. But my understanding and Ms. R's insights derived from what we discovered together, not simply from what I brought in the way of theoretical knowledge. The clinical relationship between Ms. R and me was shaped by our mutual presence—I turned my mind to her service and her unconscious fantasies exerted the primary influence on the way our present relationship was actualized. It was from our collaborative study of her experienced immediacy that unconscious fantasies were interpreted and, then, from recognition of unconscious fantasies, historical past was reconstructed. I can add that as part of that work my own self-analysis reluctantly but valuably also progressed, though to a much lesser degree.

DISCUSSION

I have tried to illustrate that we live within the present and that we explore the past from within experience of that present. Where does this fit into analytic thinking? Our questions are of process and of interaction. Is there an intrinsic analytic process, one which unfolds singly within the patient who is engaged in introspective work? And what is the relationship of that singular inner unfolding to the field of the two-person interaction in which it comes to life?

Psychoanalytic Process as Internal Dialectic

First, process. The classical sense of the analytic process has been the examination of the mind of a single person, the patient. That classical viewpoint has been succinctly stated by Calef (1987) who distinguished what has been learned through years of clinical work from the analytic process itself. Analysis is not to be defined in terms of accumulated analytic wisdom but by its process, and, as Calef added, "the process of psychoanalysis is a dialectic" (p. 11). "The suggestion," he wrote, "may come as a surprise to some—even as a shock—that dynamic formulations, the discovery of meaning, significance, and symbolism, the unveiling of unconscious contents and genetic reconstructions associated with the recall of childhood memories, collectively or individually, do not define analysis. . . . Though some or all of these achievements may be products of analysis, they do not reflect the psychoanalytic observations per se, or the methodology by which deductions are reached" (pp. 12–13).

Calef defined clinical analysis as the inner dialectic process of the unfolding of intrapsychic forces. He allowed no ambiguity, writing that "shifts in the resistances are the observational facts of psychoanalysis and the evidence of the process, rather than the unveiling of the unconscious, the reconstruction of development, and the realities of an individual's personal history" (p. 17).

Although uncommonly succinct, Calef reflected a major trend in analytic thinking. Indeed, some theorists consider the interpretation of resistance and the inquiry into the motivations of those obstacles' to comprise the whole of the psychoanalytic process. Calef did not take so limited a view, but he did define that part of the work as central to the psychoanalytic tool. The analytic process is the internal dialectic unfolding of the patient's mind.

Psychoanalytic Interaction as Dialogue

But if the analytic process is the shifting of forces of resistance and expression within one person's mind, then where does the analyst fit in? If the analytic process is an inner dialectic, what is the place of the analyst and of the analytic interaction as a dialogue?

At its very beginning, analysis was Freud's self-analysis. Freud and his early analytic colleagues then examined the patient's mind as if it existed in itself in toto, uninfluenced by the field of the analytic partnership. Thus, the significance of dyadic clinical interactions was either unnoticed or minimized, as if clinical work were essentially the same as the private inner analytic work Freud had carried out and described. In fact, transference, when finally noticed, was first seen as an interference to the work at hand, as, for much longer, countertransference was similarly viewed.

Freud very early made a statement fateful for subsequent theoretical thought. While sorting out instinctual forces in *Three Essays on Sexuality*, Freud explored sexual drives and distinguished their sources from their aims and their objects. He then said, "The sexual instinct and the sexual object are merely soldered together" (1905a, p. 148). With the objects seemingly readily interchangeable, attention was focused on the sources and vicissitudes of drives. For a long period, during which much of depth psychology was valuably charted, the place of the object, including the place of the analyst as the patient's current other person, was set aside.

Psychoanalysis is a tool. Any tool, like analysis, like the microscope, or like the telescope, has a specific use. In analysis, the tool is intended for the use of looking at the inner workings of the patient's mind. Following this comparison, the analyst seems an outside observer, one who describes what he sees in an interpretation, like the scientist's describing what is present on the slide under the microscope.

But the tool determines the phenomenon examined. What is seen to be on a microscopic slide is determined not only by the contents of the slide but also by the focus of the viewer. The microscope "allows only for a choice among several enlargements . . . but does not give us the 'true' structure" of what exists on the slide (Viderman 1974, p. 474). What is seen depends on where the looker focuses. What you look for is what you see is what you get.

The analytic instrument is the patient's and analyst's *shared* examination of their unfolding analytic relationship. Thus, the context of investigation is at the same time an essential part of the object of investigation. What Calef referred to as the inner dialectic unfolding of the patient's mind can now be recognized as taking place within the context of a current clinical interaction, the clinical dialogue.

"Dialectic" is a word that derives from the Greek, *dialektikos*, meaning conversation. In fact, the word "dialogue" derives along its own parallel line from the same original source. However, "dialectic" and "dialogue" are not the same. "Dialectic," as Calef used it, speaks to the back and forth flow of forces within a single structural context, here within a single person. "Dialogue" implies separate people, separate subjects in a conversation, an interpersonal dialectic. It is the relation of the individual dialectic to the dyadic dialogue that now provides us our greatest challenge in understanding the psychoanalytic process. The two, while not synonymous, are linked in the present affectively charged living moment.

The split between drive and object-relationships is seductive in its seeming clarity, but it betrays the essentially unitary nature of human phenomena. No drive is realized outside the fabric of human connectedness, even when that fabric has been internalized, and no object relationship is alive without the motive force of unconscious drives within each partner.

We are all part of our times, even analysts, and analytic concerns inevitably parallel ones alive in the air in general. Literary studies offer a similar current dilemma. Is there simply an intrinsic meaning in a text or is each text to be understood only by the meanings that each reader brings to a reading? My emphasis is that the answer does not lie in a choice between the two but rather must include both views. The patient has a core personality shaped by the power of currently alive unconscious fantasies. It is in the analysis of those present-tense unconscious fantasies that the past unfolds as it comes into view. And the dialogue of interactive experiences, the human field of the analysis, provides the context in which the dialectic processes of those individual forces are actualized and can be explored.

The immediacy of experience and its attendant psychic state are not to be confused with what is often called "experience-near." "Experience-near" generally implies a degree of conscious awareness of one's affective state. "Self-sense" and "self-state" have similarly carried the implication of conscious awareness of one's self and mood. In contrast, emotional immediacy, as I use the phrase, refers to the entire psychic state including sources of feelings for which the person lacks conscious awareness. What matters is not that forces be close to the patient's conscious awareness but that they be inferred from present mental actuality as recognized in the unfolding of the patient's mind within the immediacy of the clinical moment.

To explore present experience in search of hidden sources one must avoid the temptation of selective allegiance to the vantage points of either the one-person dialectic of process or the two-person dialogue of interaction. Taking the immediacy of the emotional experience of the clinical moment as our recurrent starting point offers our greatest protection as we proceed.

The division between process and interaction, between dialectic and dialogue, is artificial. The analytic inner unfolding is latent, only a potential until it is actualized in the unique clinical relationship. Our minds take the order that seems logical: drives exist first and actualization comes after. However, that seemingly correct view is not true to our phenomenological experience. We, patient and analyst, *experience* the drive derivatives now, in their immediate actualization, and only *infer* the structurally more deep, the historically more early. It is the "now" to which we must regularly return if what we infer is to be authentic.

An interpretation, from this point of view, refers to a statement that extends to a new level the understanding of dynamics or genetics as based on an affective experience within the analytic moment. The analyst's understanding can, thus, contribute to the patient's insight by helping the patient see how current experience, feeling, and behavior are organized by a unique inner framework of unconscious fantasies.

A reconstruction, in contrast, hypothesizes a historical past that could explain, with plausibility and probability, the formation and shape of the patient's unconscious fantasies. Such reconstructions offer a cognitive aid to the patient in working through prior constrictions and exploring the possibilities of new beginnings. Their validity is tested by their effectiveness in broadening a patient's range of thought, feeling, and action.

In short, interpretations link immediate experience with unconscious fantasies, while reconstructions offer links between unconscious fantasies and possible or probable historical pasts. Interpretations necessarily entail the analyst's translating, after personal inner processing, those associations that the patient previously had had to translate into words from deeper nonverbal levels. As a result, all interpretations are translations of translations, and, inevitably, all interpretations are trial interpretations. Nonetheless, interpretations can come very close to approximating psychic truth. In contrast, reconstructions, useful as they are, are unavoidably more speculative.

In work that rings true to common clinical experience, Viederman (1991) addressed the actualities of the analyst, beyond formal technical procedures, for their contribution to the development of the patient's transferences. Emphasizing exploration of the realities of the analytic process rather than suggesting altered technique, Viederman offers both clinical examples and a thoughtful consideration of the implications of the analyst's presence on traditional principles such as neutrality, abstinence, and anonymity. In so doing he demonstrates the clear benefits of starting from clinical experience and inferring transference only secondarily to that.

MEMORIES AND SENSATIONS

"Ou sont les neiges d'antan?"—where are the snows of yesteryear? Where are memories, in the past or the present? As we listen to free associations, to the patient's descriptions of the past as consciously remembered, we find ourselves having to locate the power of the past within the present. What is the place of memory in relation to time?

A widow whose children had grown and left home was mourning the imminent sale of the large family home in which she now lived alone. With tears she said that it would be hard to give up her home. "There are so many memories there."

Another patient, a man, spoke of looking through an album filled with snapshots of the lifetime of vacations he and his wife had taken together. With great feeling he commented on the album. His words were the same, "There are so many memories there."

Where is "there"? Memories, of course, lie within the minds of that widow and of that man, not in the objects of the house or the pictures of the album. Yet there must be truth in what each said, a truth that resonates with our own experiences.

Memories are alive as present emotional experience. Their actuality is in the present even as their subject is the past. For the connections to the past to come alive in the present, for them to be active memories rather than academic historical tales, there must be a link to emotional sensation. The old home and the old snapshots are said to contain memories because they offer the sensations that call to life the emotions around the past. The interaction between the patient and the analyst in the analytic situation offers the clinical equivalent of the widow's home or the album photographs. It is the analytic dyadic context that permits the sensations that allow latent memories to be recalled to life with emotional immediacy.

Once again, Proust has much to offer us. Like Freud, Proust discovered that the simple stories of memory are insufficient to expose personal truth. In each of many moments of profound insight he discovered and rediscovered that it was the experience of sensation that brought back earlier sensations in which lost time and prior experience remained alive. It is in association to those sensations that other sensations and memories long-buried can be reclaimed. Indeed, that was the main thesis of Proust's *magnum opus*.

The past is alive and can be known only in its continuity to the emotions and sensations experienced in the present. One is not free to choose memories and build upon them but must take them as they come. As Proust (1913–1927) said,

> It was precisely the fortuitous and inevitable fashion in which . . . sensations had been encountered that proved the trueness of the past which they brought to life, of the images which they released. . . . Here too was the proof of the whole picture formed out of those contemporaneous impressions which the first sensation brings back in its train, with those unerring proportions of light and shade, emphasis and omission, memory and forgetfulness to which conscious recollection and conscious observation will never know how to attain. [p. 913]

Psychoanalysis is chiefly the analysis of transferences. It is as we explore the depths of our present sensations that we come to know the hidden worlds alive within our minds. Sensations in the relationship with the analyst provide the vehicle for actualization of the ready-to-emerge unconscious stimuli: current sensations evoke remembered sensations and emerging sensations attach to current sensations. Thus does transference come as an original creation.

The interaction of patient and analyst creates an original universe of experience that permits the latent forces in the patient to be realized. The analyst's aim inhibitions, the analyst's own mind being put into the service of the patient's introspective goals, allow the patient's patterns and stories to take center stage. As a result, both the stories in conscious memories and forgotten experiences and relationships can emerge to be seen. Memories, cogent as they are alive in the immediacy of the analytic moment, can then be explored and found to be, themselves, condensations of other fantasies, experiences, and memories. The past, then, is reconstructed only secondarily, from derivatives of the unconscious fantasies that frame the immediacy of the present.

Proust's work repeatedly demonstrated the multiple levels of engagements that are built into current experience. Both the voices of oneself as a former child and the echoes of voices of those who mattered—voices that carry in themselves the echoes of others across generations—all combine into the actualization of the moment. Proust described the multiple layers built into the present moment in the paragraph from which I took the first quotation. He was in the midst of reflecting on how Marcel's present love for Albertine and his behavior toward her captured multiple reflections from his past and from the pasts of those who were with him in his past.

> As if it were not enough that I should bear an exaggerated resemblance to my father . . . as if it were not enough that I should allow myself to be ordered by my aunt Léonie to stay at home and watch the weather . . . here I was talking now to Albertine, at one moment as the child that I had been at Combray used to talk to my mother, at another as my grandmother used to talk to me. When we have passed a certain age, the soul of the child that we were and the souls of the dead from whom we sprang come and shower upon us their riches and their spells, asking to be allowed to contribute to the new emotions which we feel and in which, erasing their former image, we recast them in an original creation.

Thus my whole past from my earliest years, and, beyond these, the past of my parents and relations, blended with my impure love for Albertine the tender charm of an affection at once filial and maternal. We have to give hospitality, at a certain stage in our lives, to all our relatives who have journeyed so far and gathered round us. [pp. 73–74]

All of this happens in analysis as Proust describes. The past matters as it is alive, its forces coming together, combining, and condensing all now, all within the immediacy of the present analytic moment, all within the emotional universe created by the two clinical partners together.

3

Insight and the Analytic Dyad

Wisdom, where shall it be found?
And where is the place of understanding?
—Job 28:12

The universe of an analysis is broad. In space it is at once superficial and deep. In time it condenses farthest personal history and longest future expectations all into the immediacy of a present moment. Yet with all its complexities, the analytic universe is unitary in nature. What brings us into this universe is the aim to help another person, a patient seeking some desired improvement, some greater personal comfort and freedom. Looking beyond the relief of symptoms, we work toward insight.

Insight, important as it always has been to analytic thinking, has never found an easy place in analytic conceptualizations. However the goal of analysis is described, at its center are self-exploration and self-knowledge, introspection and insight. Transference, resistance, associations, and dreams are basic units of the work, but they are the tools not the purpose of clinical inquiry. Looking within, reflecting, and knowing what is seen—inquiry for the sake of mastery and freedom through insight—is the heart of clinical analysis. Symptomatic relief without insight may be at times an appropriate therapeutic end, but the further

goal of insight is the hallmark of psychoanalysis and psychoanalytic therapy.

Central as it is, insight has never fit neatly into models of
theory. It is too large. A mind is more than its structural components, and insight combines aspects of all areas of mental functioning. We study by categorizing, but the parts we examine are
ever more distorted as they are removed from context. By narrowing attention to focus on detail, by abstracting, we modify
what we are examining. Of the many advantages to current concern with mental activity as compromise formations, one may
be most important, that is, the implication of wholeness, the
recognition that intrapsychic experience is unitary, not divided
into the pieces we focus on in our discussions. Similarly, in clinical practice the process of working through represents, along with
continuing exploration, the need for repeated reconnection of the
pieces abstracted in our effort to understand.

In its original general use insight referred both to the process of looking within and to what is seen. The earliest notion
was of insight as the eyes of the mind. Only later did the word
come to refer also, and now mainly, to what is seen by the act of
looking within. In analysis we tend to make a division between
the process, which we call introspection, and the knowledge
learned—the content, which we then call insight. But there are
problems in too neat a division: analytically we know that structure is a relatively stable constellation of functions, that what one
knows and the act of knowing are not fully separable. Moreover,
when we say someone values insight, we mean one values the
knowing of oneself, not simply some specific piece of knowledge.
I shall use the word insight, therefore, in its broad sense of referring both to looking within and to what is learned by that search.

While clinical analysis is structured for the very purpose of
aiding the growth of insight, self-knowledge grows in many ways.
It can grow in privacy, at times flourishing in the reflections of
solitary reverie. It can grow in an interchange with the inanimate,
such as in an aesthetic experience. And it can grow in personal
relationships. In clinical analysis the forces of private reflection

are actualized in the analytic dialogue. Here, the search for insight, while referring to an inner mental process, is manifest in the interpersonal context of the analytic situation.

Insight is internal, an individual's inner viewing. Yet, as there is no portrait without an underlying canvas, there can be no intrapsychic process without a fabric of human connectedness. Drives imply objects, and imagoes of objects are significant in a person's thinking even when that person appears to be alone. My aim now is to consider the analyst's place in the clinical development of the patient's insight. My intention is, first, to observe an internal aspect of insight: that self-knowledge becomes insight by connection and integration into the whole cloth of one's psychic reality; and, then, to move toward the two-person clinical context in which analytic insight grows.

The goal of psychoanalysis is the exploration of the mind of the patient. Attention to the dyadic aspects of the development of insight does not imply alteration of that goal or of customary technique. Rather, my purpose is to consider what takes place behind the manifest level while the psychoanalysis proceeds.

ILLUSTRATION

First, an instance of daily work, chosen not for its drama but for its familiar nature in adding to a patient's insight.

Most of the preceding work with Mr. N, a bright foreign service officer, dealt with his avoidance of success, his fear of competitiveness, his terror of surpassing his father. He had been born in Eastern Europe about the time the Nazis took over, and a non-Jewish family kept him as their own while his Jewish parents hid. He had no memory for it but was only told that after the war the couple who had kept him wanted a great deal of money to give him up, so the "true" parents had had to kidnap him to get him back. Once with his returned parents, the first three and a half years and the lost parents who had raised him were never spoken of, never to be mentioned.

Approaching the third summer vacation in the analysis he was unusually curious whether I would be in town or going away. He was not so concerned with not seeing me but was preoccupied by *where* I would be. Thoughts turned to the awesome upheaval in his life when he was 3½ and to areas spoken of before, particularly the possibility I had mentioned that the warmth of his personality suggested that in his first years he had known love, not simply meanness, and the possibility that the family that had kept him had wanted to continue keeping him as their own. Now I said that his concern over where I would be sounded like what he must have felt as a small child taken to strangers and told he must never look back, undergoing his own sudden personal holocaust—the destruction of the whole world he had known all his life, without ever being able to mourn or even speak of what was lost.

His thoughts turned to gaps, with instances of the terror that gaps inspired in him. Again, the question of where I would be. Not knowing brought back the terror. Knowing would put it into words; I would still exist. I asked him to consider not only the overwhelming change he must have known as a 3-year-old, but the fact that it was for him literally unspeakable. There were no words to name his prior life, not even names for his former parents.

Much of this we had known as it had arisen from his ambivalent struggles with his father. Father, successful and prestigious before the war, was hidden and hunted during the war, then severely disadvantaged after it. The father's own conflicts as reconstructed from their shadows in the son were of impotence and power, helplessness and vindication. The possibility that the son had known any love in his first three years had had to be denied to protect the father. Understandable though it was, there were tragic consequences for him of his parents' need to rewrite their own personal history in a way that not only betrayed the truth of his reality but could not even tolerate having questions about these realities put into words.

How could he mourn what was not ever even to have existed? Gaps were filled with terror. Relief would be great if only he could have words, an image and a speakability that the missing ones did exist. He went on. He and his girlfriend had been at the library. He went to the bathroom and returned, but when he came back she was on the other side of a post. For the moment he didn't see her he was panicked. Had he imagined the whole thing? Was he alone? In that instant of terror, remembering her name reassured him. Again, would I be in town or would I be away? Last summer, he recalled, he had gotten a psychologic self-help book during the vacation. He didn't read it, but it served as a reminder I really had been present. Over and over, examples of glossing over the gap.

Not only was success, surpassing his father, a threat. He was confronted by the question of whether he would have to deny reality or else threaten and betray his father. To speak of a gap was forbidden. He was required to pretend his life had started at age 3. No acknowledgement was made of the existence of a loss. No names were given to what was missing, to the people gone.

Where was I while all of this was going on? When I first sat to write this, the hour had seemed like an ordinary and easy one: I had not been anxious or bored, brilliant or dull, just in a commonplace pre-vacation session. But reflection revealed personal areas on the edge of my conscious thinking. As only one example among very many, there was the fleeting sense of panic and hatred I had felt as a 5-year-old when my father momentarily hid in a crowded store, as I later came to realize, so that he could watch my frightened reaction and share my relief when he then popped out. I could understand a son's ambivalence, fearing and longing for a father seen both as weak and as strong. And I could understand a father's similar ambivalence to his son, his conflicts that could color and complicate how he treated his son. I could understand these because I had tasted experiences close enough, yet different enough, to allow me both to see and to distinguish their parallels in the intimacy of the analytic field. From that I could flash in an instant on the results of years of self-analytic work.

The instance from my own childhood and my own father was but one of numberless instances of my edge-of-awareness self-analysis that allowed me to attend consciously to my patient and to engage in the struggle for genuine understanding. There was, of course, more. With the inevitable mixed feelings of any good father, my own father not only accepted but also encouraged my surpassing him, walking the fine line of trying to make life easy but not too easy for me. Matching of similarities permits partial trial identification. Differences, however, are as vital as similarities to recognition, mastery, and understanding.

None of this did I say to my patient. Indeed, I had seemed to say very little of this consciously to myself. What I said to aid my patient's insight into the workings of his mind appeared to be detached offerings of links entirely between elements of which *he* had spoken. But even when I thought I was working in a routine and automatic way, my own personal meanings provided the bond of significance that made understanding possible.

Let us return to Mr. N, a man who was struggling against inhibitions, the results of conflicts he knew only from their after-effects. He suffered not only from early traumas but also from having identified with unconscious conflicts in his parents. Those conflicts had deprived him of the words and even of the right to words to deal with such matters in himself. Talking with an analyst, he found his underlying conflicts coming to life in the new relationship. Through his analysis he developed greater ease with himself, increased mastery of his conflicts, and a freer sense of legitimacy. What made the difference? How much was it the putting into words and how much was it the reliving of the underlying pattern in a new situation? Where is insight to be placed in the analytic situation? To work toward an understanding, let us briefly consider the background of insight and then examine insight and the analytic dyad.

BACKGROUND OF CONCEPT
OF INSIGHT IN ANALYSIS

Insight is defined by Webster as "seeing into a situation . . . the act *or* result of apprehending the inner nature of things" (emphasis added). Early clinical use of "insight" was more descriptive than analytic: recognizing behavior as abnormal was called insight. The doctor was apart and above. Michels (1986) only half joked when he said that insight at first referred to whether the patient agreed with the psychiatrist's view of the patient and judgment first referred to whether the patient agreed with the psychiatrist's view of everyone else.

In early dynamic work the cure was seen as deriving from the patient's becoming aware of traumatic memories previously denied consciousness. Insight thus became more internal, the recognition of blocked memories. Though there was greater depth, insight was still seen as purely conscious and existing in a one-person psychology. A second person's role was limited to that of an outsider who could assist in returning buried trauma to awareness.

The development of the structural point of view emphasized both unconscious ego functions and intrasystemic conflicts. It was now clear that not only drives but also regulatory functions work in the dark, beyond conscious awareness; the ego as well as the id included unconscious functions. Insight was reflected in mastery beyond conscious attention as well as that within. Indeed, purely conscious knowledge of the self fell from prior prominence to devaluation as intellectual insight. This shift necessarily opened the question of unconscious insight, deep knowledge beyond the reach of words.

In clinical practice unconscious connections were noted to precede conscious ones, with continuity from one insight to the next maintained only late in analyses (Kris 1956). As a result, insight has come to be seen as involving a continuum of ever expanding stages, not a final point of perfect knowledge. When a defense is interpreted and a patient remembers something previously repressed, we speak of insight. When current dynamic implications of that memory are recognized by the patient, again we speak of insight. When the implications of that recall are expanded to reconstruct or recall other genetics, again we speak of insight. When, without consciously thinking of it, new situations are faced in new and more open ways, yet again we speak of insight. Each is insight, yet each is different. There are levels or degrees of insight. Perhaps the deepest level is that in which understanding is most thoroughly integrated, so integrated that one's character and mental functioning utilize the understanding without having to resort to conscious thought.

Because of the varied subtleties of multiple determination, because of the depth of the unconscious and the limits of conscious capacity to see, insight can be more or less, but it can never be complete. Also, because of the multiple levels of functioning, insight can be valid and simultaneously be used defensively. A partial insight is at times emphasized to protect against the pain threatened by recognition of some deeper insight. The defensive aspect of insight is most clearly suspect whenever it does not lead to further psychic opening or does not translate into new ways of action in the world.

Hatcher (1973) clarified the distinction between self-observation and insight. Observation of the self necessarily precedes insight but it is not necessarily followed by insight. Insight requires more than self-observation. Recognizing the importance of one's reflecting on associations, ego psychology emphasized mastery rather than depth. Attention to regulatory functions raised the question of the relationship of insight to cure. Does insight cause cure or result from cure? Ego integration, seen by Bibring (1937) as the foundation of cure, is clearly necessary to permit insight development. Yet insight clearly promotes ego growth.

As with any developing concept, there were excesses. Ego integration was defined as evidence of mature mental functioning and then, circularly, proclaimed as the cause of the attainment of that state, the cure. The extreme of substituting naming for understanding came in an ever expanding list of ego functions: organizing, integrating, synthesizing, and many others.

(Just as Stoppard's philosopher had suggested there was no problem that could not be solved if only one had a big enough plastic bag, so for a while it seemed there was no question that could not be answered if only one had enough names.)

Realization that psychic growth required more than intellectual self-observation led Strachey (1934) to address insight in relation to technique. In his classic paper he pointed out that for interpretations to have effect they must deal with impulses alive in the moment of the transference. Strachey was seminal in linking ego growth to experience and analysis of transference.

Reid and Finesinger (1952) offered the broadest ego psychological view of insight, emphasizing the importance of connections rather than content. Noting that insight can grow outside conscious attention, they observed that insight generalizes, with the good analytic situation serving as "a spreading factor." This is especially important because it suggests insight is not limited to knowledge gained directly from interpretation but grows internally, perhaps around understanding gained in the seeding crystal of interpretation. Analysis of central currents yields changes in areas not themselves directly examined.

They went on to question whether it is the truth of an insight that determines efficacy, saying that unless truth is defined very crudely, "It is misleading . . . to talk as if the aim of a therapist in making interpretations is to state hypotheses that are true" (p. 733). They felt the most useful insights the analyst offers are those that stimulate new insights, not that give facts.

The place of the clinical dyad was approached by Richfield (1954), who agreed the analytic goal was not knowledge but was the mobilization of mental forces. Distinguishing *knowledge of* by firsthand acquaintance from *knowledge about* by secondhand description, he emphasized that insight requires both the experiential and the descriptive, writing that "when our insights are knowledge by description, we have truths about the repressed enemy, not the enemy itself" (p. 403). Though emphasizing the need for the patient to experience conflicts as actual, he stopped short of addressing the transference neurosis and its dyadic context.

We jump a quarter of a century to the next wave of attention to insight. At an international forum on insight in analysis, Anna Freud (1981) suggested that insight, attention to the inner world, be distinguished from orientation to the outside world, which may simply be termed understanding. She pointed out that the barrier against experiencing inner unpleasure is very high, in contrast to the less strong resistance to noticing external unpleasure. People more readily recognize adverse matters on the outside than in the inside. The difference between how one can know oneself and how one can know someone else is vast and crucial. Now put more precisely, how does an analyst's understanding aid the patient's capacity for insight?

INSIGHT AND THE DYAD

In the course of work with the man who was terrified of gaps, I offered many interpretations. In order to analyze my patient, I privately had to analyze myself. Transference is ubiquitous, and the analyst cannot be defined as the one in the clinical pair who is without an unconscious. Ideally the analyst is the one more open to unconscious derivatives and less impelled to their enactment. But just as my own private psychology had to be distinguished from that of the patient, the *way* I could know myself differed from the *way* I could know my patient.

This point is a continuation of Anna Freud's. Appreciation of another person's mind differs vastly from knowing oneself. We aid clarity by accepting the usage of "insight" as limited to oneself, by speaking of an analyst's *insight* into the analyst's own self and the analyst's *understanding* of a patient. This distinction is especially important given the current context of preoccupation with empathy, with some at times sounding as if they believe the analyst could know the patient's mind as well as or in the same way as the patient could. *Knowing* and *knowing about* are not the same.

Confusion of insight with understanding is reflected in the multiple ways we use the word "analyze." In our self-analyses we analyze ourselves; in clinical work we analyze patients. The use of the same word at times obscures important differences. When two people go through experiences together we say they share the experience. But what each of the participants experiences is crucially unique, different from the other's experience. One can never know another in the way one knows oneself, truly from the inside. Stein (1983) put it most provocatively when he said, "The only person in an analysis an analyst can analyze is himself." The two uses of the word analyze, personal inner searching and working in the service of another's analysis, are easily confused. The difference between analyzing ourselves and analyzing others is implied in Anna Freud's distinction that limits "insight" to self-knowledge and "understanding" to knowledge of others.

Similarly, an analyst cannot "give" an insight. Interpretations can offer new knowledge, interactions can give new emotional experience, but the patient must translate and digest the knowledge or experience to turn those into insight.

Insight and Meaningfulness

The analytic task involves a specialized form of searching for meanings. Both quantitative and qualitative aspects are essential to the development of insight. A meaning can be cognitively interpreted without resulting in insight if the matter considered has not been brought into the immediacy of emotional meaningfulness.

Let us return again to Mr. N. When Mr. N first consulted me he told me both of his fear of unexpected changes and of the unexplained replacement of the world he knew by a new, strange world. He already knew of both, but he could not make use of that knowing. He spoke *about*, not from *within*, the experience. Engagement in the actuality of the two-person analytic field allowed thoughts and potentials to be experienced, to come to life. The analytic situation made possible the immediate meaningfulness of latent meanings.

Analysis not only exposes, it intensifies. Just as routines are patterned into rites to create traditions, analysis is structured into patterns to intensify the transference experience, to bring latent meanings into the fuller experience of the examined present. This is so even when what is truly meaningful is disguised by a patient's seeming indifference.

Transference, which actualizes the carryover from the past, is universal. The analyst contributes to the formation of the transference neurosis by recognizing the presence of the past in the immediacy of all the patient says and does. Thus, as well as referring to the presence of the past, the transference neurosis is also defined by the intensity of the patient's emotional investment in the analysis, sharpened by the analytic situation and facilitated and partially defined by the analyst.

Addressing the immediacy of the psychic moment gives an interpretation its impact, even when it is the historic past that is under discussion. A person's mind is a unified whole. Examination of any part—past or present, content or process—is alive in the experience of the immediate moment if it rings true as an authentic part of discovery and working through.

Meaningfulness is not the same for analyst and patient. A patient brings a mental life suffused with hidden meanings. In the course of analytic work the analyst's own meanings come to life as they are informed by and can themselves inform the patient's meanings. It is then that an analyst can understand. Thus, by the analyst's scrutiny of resonances and disharmonies, by listening to both the music and the words, by sorting out what the patient says plus what the patient evokes, the truths in the patient's hidden meanings can be brought to life.

Insight and Truth

How valid are the meanings the analyst interprets? Reid and Finesinger (1952) doubted that simple truth is exposed in any analytic interpretation. A vital fact for my patient Mr. N was his sudden change of worlds at age 3. Mr. N had known that fact from the start. But for that fact to become part of his truths, it had to assume its connections to his personal context. The transference offered the opportunity to link facts to personal truths.

Truth implies a breadth beyond the range of immediate conscious attention, a resonance with deeper levels, distant echoes ringing true. Truth, here, refers to meaningfulness that bears validity for the rest of one's psychic reality. It is not the "Truth with a capital T" of religions or other fervent world views.

Immediacy in the analytic process implies the unconscious come alive. Attention to the actuality, the singularity of the analysand's mind currently at work, evokes the feeling of truth that comes from the act of discovering for oneself, even when discovering with someone else. Analytic truth develops more from discovery than from revelation.

Facts are not the same as truth. Documentary data from extra-analytic sources can be invaluable in writing biographies, but the work of an analysis is that of psychic exploration and integration. Genetic aspects of insight are authentic when they derive from unfolding in the transference. They then stand in strong contrast to the pseudo-interpretations offered out of an analyst's defensive misuse of theory, which amounts to indoctrinating rather than exploring. As we reconstruct from developments within the shared analytic field, we would never say, "The *facts* shall set you free." Indeed, facts can be used selectively to obscure truth.

Obviously, we never wish to aim toward the false. Our allegiance to the truth moves to the center of our attention those data that we can know firsthand, the data revealed in the transference. A major criticism of reconstruction is that it may be a way the analyst builds a tendentious version of a story to make both analyst and patient more comfortable, that is, a story that seems liberating in a more sophisticated way than paranoid or religious stories but that is nevertheless limiting by virtue of being contrived. Protection, as Freud pointed out in distinguishing scientific from religious views, comes from readiness to revise rather than to defend explanations. Attention to shifts in the patterns of transference are as valuable as are the manifest associations in determining the effect of reconstructions.

Psychic truth is partial but cumulative. As a result, reconstructions may hold true and be of use in opening new possibilities of understanding beyond the question of their external historical accuracy. How the patient came to see the world is more cogent than how others saw events, though history gotten from others can be valuable to the patient in opening new questions. However, the fidelity of statements to psychic reality, both of the moment and of the background of the moment, matters more than does the picture of past events as seen by others.

Just as focus on reconstruction of history without attention to the shared process of the moment can undermine the truth value of interpretations, inappropriate concern with narration can similarly be misleading. Some have suggested that the essence of an analysis is the telling and amendment of a life story. The literary quality of analysis as life narrative is compelling but limited. As the experience of the transference–countertransference in process gives meaning to memories and spoken fantasies, so, too, attention to the analytic dialogue corrects distortions that would develop from special concern with the construction of an autobiography.

Location of the Analyst

Where is the analyst's place in this work of developing insight in the patient, someone who emotionally starts out resisting insight (Joseph 1986)? The task of the analyst has been compared to that of the fool with Lear (Rose 1969), or of Teiresias with Oedipus (Abrams 1981, Michels 1986). However, those models emphasize the role of the analyst as the one who knows either the secrets of the patient's mind (as does Teiresias) or the truths of reality (as does Lear's fool).

The analyst does know many things important to the patient, such as the experience of analysis and the principles of technique for using the analytic tool to assist someone else with that experience. In a very rough way, the analyst also knows a bit about how the mind works as well as how analysis works, knowledge that helps minimize the impact of potential blind spots. To the extent the analyst has the belief of knowing the patient's mind better than the patient does or necessarily knowing reality better than the patient does, to that extent the analyst is likely to fall into countertransference enactments of power. (Historical implications of this have been studied incisively by Roustang 1983.)

Our basic analytic ideal is of quiet observation followed by neutral interpretation. But to observe is to intervene, to structure an analysis is to suggest delay of discharge, to speak or to be silent is to be active. Despite the implications of this one model, that of an analyst's absolute detached neutrality, the analyst's very presence is an act of intervention. On the other hand, despite the recommendation by another currently popular model for the analyst to be warmly understanding, analytic inquiry implies that the patient is understandable, not already understood or even easily understandable. The struggle toward insight is a shared task, actualized in the patient–analyst engagement.

Where is the analyst during the work? One view, stated in the extreme, would have the analyst a separate body, *in* but not *of* the patient's field. Here, the analyst observes from outside the patient, from time to time sending interpretations as cognitive messages to help the patient. This image is reminiscent of those old films in which an untrained person replaces a disabled pilot, informs an expert on the ground of cockpit readings, and is guided to landing by helpful directions returned by radio. Another view, again in the extreme, considers the two who are engaged in analytic work a symbiotic union. Here, two become one, each part of the other as each works to cure both self and other.

These differences carry over to views of how an analyst contributes to a patient's insight. Do the two send verbal messages back and forth from separate psychologic universes or do they share the same mind? Efforts to avoid on the one hand the extreme of seeing the patient as a mind in a test tube removed from actual emotional interactions with the analyst or on the other hand that of seeing patient and analyst as symbiotic have

led to the view of the analytic process as a communicative relationship (Southwood 1974). In this view, open examination of
one takes place in a matrix of a more deeply buried pair of reciprocal self-inquiries (Gardner 1989). Here, the analyst's mental
processes parallel and diverge from those of the patient but do
not truly merge.

Clearly, the analyst's mind must be emotionally engaged. As
observed by Stein, even at the first moments of psychoanalysis,
when he introduced the Irma dream, Freud (1900) spoke of transference as the way an observer learns the mind of the other. Freud
said, "And now I must ask the reader to make my interests his
own for quite a while, and to plunge, along with me, into the
minutest details of my life; for a transference of this kind is peremptorily demanded by our interest in the hidden meaning of
dreams" (pp. 105–106).

To understand the other is to plunge along with the other.
Thus, the analyst necessarily makes a "transference," a purposeful regression for the service of understanding, not the regression of countertransference distortion. Structuring the analytic
field and becoming a vital part of that field, the analyst experiences a partial regression separately but under influence of the
patient and simultaneously consciously and unconsciously has
impact on the patient. The analyst does not, however, become a
part of the patient's mind.

The view of reciprocating self-inquiries lying behind the
manifest inquiry into the patient's mind gives room for the patient to learn both from the analyst's manifest words and from
the hidden processes structured in and behind those words. How
meanings flow between the intrapsychic and the interpersonal,
between inside and outside, remains the question. Although both
analyst and patient experience much of the work in the uncertainty of transitional phenomena, there is a crucial difference
from other transitional experiences. Describing the intermediate area between inside and outside, Winnicott (1953) emphasized that the question of location of the transitional object
between mother and child was not to be asked, not even to be
formulated. Yet in an analysis the position of not asking in whose

mind a feeling or thought occurred is always taken temporarily in the course of further exploration. The question of distinguishing the minds of analysand and analyst is always an essential part of the total analytic inquiry.

Knowing that sharing takes place and knowing that shared experiences are never the same for the partners sharing, how can we resolve the paradox of "sharing" with the uniqueness of individual inner worlds? A concept of reciprocating self-inquiries underlying the manifest inquiry into the patient keeps open for further study both the interplay of mental processes in the dyad and the question of how external experience becomes internalized. While problems remain, this view for now allows us to proceed in examining the collaborative analytic work.

The Location of Insightful Ideas

Describing the analysand's development of insight, Meyerson (1965) says, "An attempt at mastery through the use of fantasy and imagination is a prerequisite for meaningful observations of the conflictual impulses which are expressed in the fantasy" (p. 780). What happens in the analyst? The regression of the analyst at work has also been described (Olinick et al. 1973), but to what extent does the analyst's imagination also take part in the development of understanding?

Let me briefly detour to an observation I began having during my early morning commute to the office. Over time I noticed that out of the group of morning roadside runners one was so regular as to become for me a landmark. After I noticed that I had noticed him, I became curious. Why did he run so much, so hard? How did he come to be a runner? Did he have a wife and children, and where did his running fit into their lives? I wished I could speak with him, interview him. I was full of questions. I had moved from notice and mental attachment to curiosity.

At that time I had a patient who was a novelist. During his analysis he spoke of strangers who caught his eye, but, I realized, with reactions quite different from mine. At first he made mental notes, a study of mannerisms to use for characters in future works. Then he would imagine, creating stories and detailed lives for the strangers. He moved from notice and mental attachment to imagination.

Though each of us had noticed strangers, we reacted to the unknown differently. I filled the empty mental space with questions; he, with imagined answers. Might our different styles reflect different, complementary, and even partially mutually exclusive functions characteristic of our different careers?

In a parallel partial regression, an analyst's own fantasies are evoked by experience of the patient's transference. But the analyst does not give full freedom to those awakened urges, instead partially reining them in so as to use them for information rather than untamed gratification. Instead of the satisfactions of reveries, personal fantasies are put to the scrutiny of professional curiosity. Thus, the analyst at work uses private associations not to impose personal imaginings but to refine curiosity to be a route ever closer to the patient's meanings.

Analysands learn this skill of submitting imagining to curious reflection without having to learn the content of the analyst's imaginings. Though distorted by transference, the analysand is able to read *how* the analyst's mind works more than we generally credit. The analyst's aim inhibition of imagination, that is, the analyst's using imagination for information rather than gratification, may be a critical model for the patient's coming to take self-inquiry and insight as valued goals. This process of learning emotionally the value of attending to *how* one thinks may be as crucial to the analytic work as learning the analyst's interpretations of *what* one thinks. As insight develops in the course of a successful analysis, the patient develops an increasing capacity for self-analysis. Insight can become part of a patient's ego ideal, replacing the transferential image of the analyst as the object of longed-for infantile gratifications.

The problem of locating the partners in this enterprise raises also the question of the source of insights. Interpretation is our model. When a new connection is recognized, the analyst tells the analysand. Does interpretation only expose meaning that already exists or does it create new meaning? Where in the dyad does an insight arise? For convenience, let us consider the extremes.

Viderman (1974) wonders where latent ideas come from when first an analyst interprets them. He sees unconscious fantasy as a bare outline of instinct, which the analyst gives a name by interpretation. "It is less a discovery of the instinct that he makes, than a creation" (p. 473). "*To create* is to give a name to and to unify by interpretation that which is only vague desire, nameless, obscure, barely outlined" (p. 474). Were latent thoughts truly in the patient's mind or do they take existence from the analyst's hypothesizing what could be missing? When an analyst says the reference to six roses in the patient's dream represents feelings about the *cirrhose* (cirrhosis—*six roses* and *cirrhose*, homophones in the original French) that killed the patient's father, Viderman (1979) asks which of the two actually had the idea in mind, adding it "was more in the mind of the analyst than in that of the patient" (p. 265).

Friedman (1985), in contrast, says that "Freudian theory describes latency and potentiality, not just inevitability and actuality. Potentiality is the roundhouse from which various end points can be reached by an individual. . . . It is a peculiarity of experience that 'actuality' contains various levels of potentiality, such that someone can say, 'That is exactly how I feel, and it wasn't apparent to me until you said it'" (pp. 396–397). The concept of potentiality appears to suggest that whatever an analyst might interpret was already in the patient's mind.

Viderman, suggesting that the latent became manifest and thus arose in the analyst's rather than the patient's mind, seems to void the centrality of the patient's unconscious fantasies. And Friedman seems to minimize the analyst's initiating new knowledge, the patient's learning of an inner matter through being told about it by the analyst. Interpetations are neither omnipotent nor impotent. It would be wrong to follow the extreme path that the unconscious of one person is created by the unconscious of the other and also wrong to adopt the view that the analyst offers nothing new, that all is already present within the patient's mind. The patient on some level knew what it was that needed to be repressed, or there would have been no repression. But the patient did not know why that repression was needed. The labor of analytic work, of exposing and resolving resistance, belies the view that the analyst does no more than put into words what the patient already knew and was almost ready to acknowledge.

This does not imply that all insight derives from the analyst's understanding. When the analysis has gone far enough for the patient to value insight, the patient will often arrive at a new connection or realization the analyst has not yet recognized. The analyst contributes valuably by acceptance of uncertainty and mental exploration even when unable to impart new interpretations. Indeed, one of the most underappreciated yet essential and valuable of the functions an analyst serves is that of standing as a witness to the patient's unfolding work.

My silence in the face of Mr. N's anxious questions about my absence plus my remarks about his fear of gaps explicitly contributed knowledge to him about his conflicts and implicitly evidenced my tolerance of gaps, the way I tame my own forces by reflection and mastery. What accounted for Mr. N's gradual insight and freeing up? Would he have benefited if told about his history earlier? Did the reconstruction take effect not because of what it offered but because of what it followed—prior work by both analyst and patient together?

We seem to arrive at a paradox in the evolving definition of insight. The patient's and analyst's minds reflect, resonate, differ, and interact, but they do not merge. The regressive pull to fuse self and object representations yields to a move to a higher level of ego functioning, that of contact, union through psychological touching while acknowledging essential separateness. The clinical engagement is shared, but as in the early definition of insight the analyst is still an outsider, an other who assists in bringing insight. The analyst's emotional participation is intrinsic to the analytic task, but the analyst does not "give insight" by becoming a part of the patient's mind.

Insight, Interpretations, and Time

Collaborative exploration of associations in the transferential context makes possible linking past and present in a truthful way. In this process, interpretations, like all human functions, are multiply determined and, consequently, carry multiple levels of messages. Words carry implicit temporal connections even when only one temporal aspect is in the manifest message.

How do insight, language, and time interrelate? Humans have been defined as time-binding, able to form symbols, able to remember. As a result, thought can serve as trial action and a special communicative relationship can become a talking cure. At a mature level, such time-binding brings integration of identity, a sense of continuity of self across time. Psychic structure implies time.

Memories are more than the content of stories. Past experiences shape the *way* the mind works, and memories exist in the manners of thinking, the tones of relating, the accents of thought. The stories of memory are moments of experience in time, organized at the moment and reorganized at later moments. Analytic elucidation of a person's private stories is not, therefore, the improvement of an autobiography, but is a study in current experience of *how* a person's mind works. Clinical analysis is a unique fragment of life in action; it is not merely applied analysis, applied to the history of a person.

In addition to historic time, time flows in the analysis itself. (It is the unconscious that is timeless, not the analysis or the participants.) To the extent that a patient's associations become increasingly free, new and even surprising connections are revealed. As the analyst listens, what the patient says evokes memories of matters the patient had spoken of earlier, even many years earlier in the analysis. Old memories, often of something not in the front of the analyst's mind, come back. In order to come back, those memories had had to be allowed to fade from immediate view.

The analyst's memory has been called an indispensable condition for the analytic process, providing the containing matrix for the patient's associations (Rizzuto 1985). This is so, but it is only part of the story. To work toward insight the analyst at times *partially* forgets in order to come to remember, sets aside in order to discover, to participate with the patient in the work of discovery. The analyst is paradoxically both pulled to set aside "memory and desire" so as to follow the patient and at the same time pushed to recall memory in order to permit new integrations and understandings.

An analyst's defensively forgetting, repressing what has been heard, is neurotic, but it happens there are times when an analyst finds some of what has been heard has moved to a greater distance from attention, moved in memory to a place where it is not immediately known even though still reclaimable. This partial setting aside is necessary for the analyst to be along with the patient at work. Facts fixed as immutable in the analyst's mind would interfere with analytic inquiry as much as would the analyst's being wedded to a favored formulation. Cold data, even that from an initial history, is not the same as insight gained through hard exploration. The facts I had known about Mr. N from early on had faded from my attention. I both knew them and did not know them as they returned in a new and useful way when they came alive in the transference.

Were the patient's story not remembered, the analyst could not make new connections. However, if the analyst were to keep with total ease immediate access to everything the patient said, it is unlikely the analyst would be together with the patient working toward discovery. Indeed, it is the analytic search more than the conclusion that leads to self-analytic abilities.

In contrast, an analyst can appear impressive, making brilliant-sounding interpretations using theoretical knowledge as power. Despite their academic accuracy, such explanations obscure important parts of the truth of the dyadic moment. This seems what Bird (1957) must have meant when he spoke of the "curse of insight," the result, in fact, of insufficient insight. It is attention to immediacy of psychic experience, especially in the transference, that distinguishes analysis from wild analysis, from those academic interpretations Freud (1910a) called "distribution of menu-cards in a time of famine" (p. 225).

Insight, Interpretations, and Words

What is the place of words and the growth of insight in the talking cure? Mr. N's early terrors were unspeakable. Because they could not be named they were amorphous, overwhelming, and disintegrating. To put names on feeling and experience implies that they not only can be known but can be contained, put in mental bounds. A colleague once told me that the main thing he learned in his own analysis was that even life and death were not "life and death" issues. Matters to be feared need not be disorganizing if they can be put into words. Interpretations offer inner reconnections, understanding communicated by cognitive explanation implies the possibility of mastery.

Words are the analyst's main tools, the way understanding is conveyed to the patient. But words are not crystallized concepts. They are reflections of ideas, carrying their own distortions and limitations. Indeed, the subtle differences between what the analyst tries to capture of the patient's mental experience and what the analyst actually says may be of major importance in the patient's ability to recognize that the analyst is only a different person, a helpful and skilled other person but not the realization of an idealized infantile imago.

The structure of words assures they will fall short when expressing mental experiences suffused with feelings. Flaubert expressed it well when he wrote, "No one can ever give the exact measure of his needs, his thoughts or his sorrows; and human speech is like a cracked drum on which we beat a tune that sets bears to dance when we would move the stars to pity."

Experience is whole, but words are fragments, categorical. A mind in process is fluid, with time and urges, wishes and memories at one in mental experience. At any single moment thoughts work both for the satisfaction of the moment and for that of earlier forces alive in the moment. Multiple determination is our theoretical way of moving from dualistic thinking into a maximal number of smaller categories. But psychic reality is not divided.

While our minds work with fluidity, moving experience, affect, and symbols in free-flowing ways, manifest words work by categories and comparisons, by contrasts and distinctions. Words identify by abstracting, dividing, and subdividing. Language is categorical; human experience is undivided. Language is substantially fixed and linear; human experience is fluid, circular, indirect, overlapping with self and time and other experience.

General semanticists have summarized this in comparing the word and phenomena represented to the map and territory. They describe the following principles:

1. The map is not the territory, the word is not the thing.
2. The map does not represent *all* of the territory, the word does not represent *all* of the thing.
3. The word, like the map, is self-reflective, that is, it reflects itself and its maker.

We are led to yet another paradox. The partial nature of words plus the integrity of the human mind allow interpretations both to miss the point, to fall short, and yet simultaneously to have impact in broad areas of the patient's mind. If the word is not the thing, then our language returns us to our earlier problem of how interpretation works, how a verbal message converts to insight. Clearly, what the analyst says can only be a part truth, stated with limited precision. Insight is not submission; a concept simply swallowed remains a foreign body. Yet a person can digest an understanding, altering it to render it assimilable. Meaning comes to life only as the specific textual meaning of interpretive words is placed by the patient into the context of inner mental life, both in the past and within the psychoanalytic relationship.

The manifest message of words and their deeper communicative impact are not the same. Both are essential in analysis. However, the manifest content of words has limits that speech transcends. The self-reflective nature of words may provide an important means by which interpretive words can succeed in aiding insight despite the innate limits of words. It seems likely that the words that carry partial answers to the questions under overt examination by the patient also carry buried information valuable for the patient's introspection.

When a statement is heard, it is heard with the listener's own connotations. The speaker's buried messages, self-reflective aspects of an analyst's words, can be heard by the patient, at times outside of conscious awareness. But what is heard is then digested for the patient's own meanings. The word taken in is not the same as the word spoken. As a result, although they cannot give insight, interpretations can facilitate insight.

Words, as products of mental functioning, have a place in time. Despite our preference for fixity and precision, words themselves change, though with less fluidity than do our minds. This disparity, too, may add to the ways words help tame inner forces. Just as words change in their general use over time, their meanings are ever in flux in the analytic work. The changing import of words in an analysis reflects the history of dyadic analytic progress.

Words, thus, have performative as well as informative effects. They carry manifest messages but also act through their implicit messages. Even the kinesthetic experience of speech may carry information to deepest levels, reverberating with early preverbal communication between mother and child.

Words do more than just offer the patient the words to say it by. They are, in addition, new acts, new life events that add fresh experience to the patient's life beyond that of increased cognitive ways of dealing with old unconscious processes (Leavy 1980). Words do both less and more than they are intended to do. They do less because of built-in inadequacies of expressing and identifying. And they do more by adding modifications of experience and understanding beyond those consciously intended. Words diminish by abstracting, removing from context. They add the new collaborative experience of analytic inquiry.

CONCLUSION

To stay true to the larger nature of insight, let us step back to the clinical overview. All insight is partial. Self-exploration, the search for insight, threatens one by exposing both dangerous impulses and vulnerability. It takes courage to be a patient. Beyond trust in the analyst, trust must grow for the analytic process. Great trust in the reality principle is necessary to engage in continuing introspection, and, as with any development of the reality principle, such trust is possible only as a refinement of the preference for pleasure.

In everyday speech, being understanding implies being sympathetic. To feel understood is to feel comforted. Although the analyst's attitude to the patient differs from and cannot satisfy those desires longed for in early childhood, the analyst's tolerance of free association is rooted in authentic acceptance of the patient. Might not insight, self-understanding, evidence a parallel? Being at-one-with in authentic understanding—while two are engaged together in ruthlessly honest searching—can be internalized as a model for valuing introspection and insight as important parts of the ego ideal.

As greater comfort is gained from new insights, the patient becomes more willing to risk danger in the search for ever greater freedom. Insight can increase immediate pain, yet ultimately insight strengthens. The firsthand experience of growing insight leads to faith in the value of further insight, and that faith allows the risk of further pain in exploration. It is from the experience of beginning insights that the sense develops that maximum knowledge of oneself is worth both the danger and the labor.

Insight relieves anxiety in part by extending perspective, placing immediate inner conflicts in the context of a broader view of one's dynamic and genetic self. As a result, insight enlarges, giving comfort not by closing but by opening. But also as a result, insight raises ever more questions, ever greater possiblities of self-understanding and the tolerance for broader uncertainties.

The psychoanalytic building of insight comes in collaborative work. The analyst is the patient's professional assistant participating in the patient's search for insight even though that may not have been the patient's original wish, even though the journey is at times rough and painful, and even though most of the analyst's work is done silently, mentally, behind the scenes.

In summary, insight reflects the unitary nature of psychic activity in contrast to the fragmentation created in abstracting categories for the purpose of study and discussion. The unique analytic clinical dyad offers a structure in which intrapsychic fragments can be actualized and integrated. As a result, the analyst's contribution is more crucially one of exploration than of revelation.

Whatever the area of examination, past or present, the link to analytic immediacy offers the opportunity to make meanings meaningful, to convert known facts to psychic truths. The analyst's clinical task requires private self-analysis as part of the collaborative exploration of how the patient's mind works. Higher-level ego functioning, including acutely active remembering, is at times transiently loosened in order for the analyst to share in the clinical work of discovery.

The words the analyst uses to communicate an understanding convey only approximate manifest meanings, although they structurally reveal deeper messages of importance to the patient. These verbal approximations help stimulate self-reflection in the analysand as a step in the process of gaining insight.

III

THE ANALYST AT WORK

1

The Analyst's Neutrality

Power must always feel the check of power.
—Brandeis

We have opened with an overview of the analytic situation, its multiplicity of levels of consciousness all condensed and its sense of time past and time future also all combined in the immediacy of the affective moment. From that, we moved on to the place of insight as a goal that colors the entire analytic context, looking particularly at the power of the collaboration of both partners in the clinical task.

Now, before moving to the specific technical issues that confront the analyst at work, it is proper to consider the attitude the analyst takes in approaching both the patient and their shared enterprise. In contrast to the early discoveries of depth psychology, the matter of the analyst's neutrality at work did not command consideration historically until relatively late.

It was not until 1915, a year after psychoanalysis had grown to such an extent that he had already published a paper on the history of the psychoanalytic movement (Freud 1914) and five years after he first spoke of countertransference (Freud 1910b), that Freud for the very first time used the word "neutrality" in the psychoanalytic sense in his writings. "In my opinion . . . we ought not to give up the neutrality towards the patient, which we have acquired through keeping the countertransference in check" (Freud 1915b, p. 164).

So long a delay in the appearance of so important a clinical concept is not hard to understand. Clinical psychoanalysis had been born as a product of Freud's own revolutionary insights into his personal unconscious conflicts. Thus, it was a self-analysis that served as both germ and organizing principle for the developing life of our field.

As already pointed out, great consequences have resulted from this seminal role of a self-analysis—the lateness in recognition of the significance of the transference and the countertransference, the effect of two different persons on each other.

The unfolding theory of clinical technique has been made more difficult by the need to shift from the original model of a one-person to a two-person process. How could one conceive of the question of neutrality in a self-analysis? The closest we come is in the familiar saying that the major problem of self-analysis is countertransference, though in deference to Freud and in candor to ourselves, I suggest that the primary problem in self-analysis is that of case selection.

In contrast, in clinical analysis a new world of two-party relations is introduced, a world that raises the issue of the responsibilities implicit in one person's impact on another, one person's power over another. The analyst's neutrality is the basic technical concept addressing that problem. The application of the principle of neutrality brings clinical work full-circle back to its origins, taking as the dyadic clinical goal the development in the analysand of a functioning capacity for self-analysis.

In everyday usage neutrality is defined as having two clusters of meanings, those related to appearance and those related to power. With respect to appearance, neutrality implies absence of color: something may appear neutral, that is, indifferent, achromatic. With respect to power, neutrality implies a form of action: something may act neutral, that is, remain nonaligned with any power grouping.

This general definition also applies to neutrality in its technical analytic usage. Respect for the distinction between these two categories—appearance as a noun, action as a verb—has a clinical import to which I shall return.

In an analysis the patient's intrapsychic life is exposed through its actualization in the transference neurosis, the analyst's own inner forces being employed in an aim-inhibited manner in the service of understanding. No longer dominant is the myth of the analyst's total, somehow nonhuman detachment, with understanding and interpreting throught of as arising exclusively from outside the patient's mental state. Therefore, it is necessary to add a third aspect to appearance and power in the definition of clinical neutrality, taming and mastery of the analyst's own inner processes.

To maintain this self-mastery for the sake of the analysis, the analyst monitors what unfolds internally. The regressive pull of an analysis calls to life in the experience of both partners the hidden forces in the inner world of the patient. It is in this context that the significance of the classical mirror metaphor can best be understood. The analytic mirror must be substantially opaque in what it reflects back of itself in order to offer the best possible reflection of the patient, but it is only as a living mirror—one whose own inner sources can bring to light the hidden aspects of the patient—that the analyst can recognize the patient's active unconscious by noting, examining, and mastering parallels and distinctions in the analyst's own self.

Analysis of dreams, analysis of the content of free associations, and so on, are absolutely essential, but are academic and clinically sterile outside the context of the transference process of the analytic situation. This provides the basic rule for the analyst, equal in import and coinciding with that for the patient—*all* the analyst's own internal experiences must be considered and examined in relation to the analysis for their informational value, with the analyst accepting as data for evaluation all inner observations, never ignoring or dismissing anything out of hand. This is, of course, a rule demanding the analyst's examination, not rationalizing unmastered action or development of a two-party group therapy. But neutrality is not a cover story for analytic blind spots. As Anna Freud (1954) pointed out, analytic technique was not designed for the defense of the analyst.

Neutrality is, therefore, a principle used to circumscribe the interpersonal aspect of the transference process from eccentric intrusions by the analyst's intrapsychic forces. It is a major contribution the analyst utilizes to sustain and nurture the patient's observing ego in the presence of the transference. It is thus that the analyst works for the patient.

Neutrality, then, involves the analyst's nonself-serving availability for observing who and where the patient is. True neutrality originates in genuine respect for the patient's individuality. This fundamental regard for the essential otherness of the patient, for the uniqueness of the patient's self in its own right, is so basic a condition of psychoanalysis as to be taken for granted. Although in lists of basic analytic concepts it usually goes without saying, the analyst's respect for the authenticity of the patient's self as a genuine other, equal in validity to the analyst's self, may be the most profound of all clinical psychoanalytic principles.

A crucial consequence of respectful neutrality is that the analyst follows rather than tries to lead, letting the unfolding transference, not a theoretic bias, direct the course of the work. This principle adds the caution (Nacht 1965) against the analyst's inappropriately viewing a change of subject by the patient as defensive rather than as the patient's readiness to move on.

Difficulty derives from the very presence of two individuals rather than one as well as from the question of why the two have come together. At times one hears the suggestion that the research aspect of an analysis is not in the service of a therapeutic goal but replaces it, as if there should be no therapeutic attitude at all, even as if the analyst ought be neutral to the progress and very survival of the analysis itself. On the contrary, however, neutrality does not imply the absence of any goals.

The substantial long-term analytic goal of insight and structural change demands inhibition of short-term helpfulness. Wallerstein (1965) pointed out the distinction between goallessness as a procedural stance required by analytic technique and the long view goal of structural change as the major aim toward which the analysis works.

Clinical psychoanalysis is not a spectator sport. The dedication of psychoanalytic principles and techniques is not done in the service of furthering a movement, but in the primary service of each analysand. Appropriate analytic technique frustrates transferential demands not to force the patient into a preconceived mold but to lead to the freedom consequent to insight and mastery. Neutrality is required for the sake of the patient's analytic work; it is not an unconcerned indifference.

Thus the analyst at work in the service of the patient inhibits short-term helpfulness exactly because of a basic realization of the implications of the principles of psychic determinism. This includes the knowledge that work based on a ruthless dedication to honesty, the importance of psychic reality and the unconscious, and the possibility of freedom and growth through the mastery to be gained from insight are the most the analyst can offer to patients. No matter the dedication to scientific research, if the analyst's work has no impact on the analysand, the analyst is meaningless. The diatrophic presence (Spitz 1956), the role of the healer (McLaughlin 1961), the support given to the patient (Gitelson 1962)—all provide the background context of clinical psychoanalysis. They are the raison d'être of clinical practice, providing the occasion for analytic neutrality. To repeat, the analyst's neutrality is never indifference to the course and success of the analysis itself.

Neutrality as a position, therefore, is to be distinguished from the technical principle of abstinence. Both are active processes. Neutrality is a global concept implying the analyst's openness to all experiences and processes in the analysis, in the patient, and in the analyst's self. By contrast, abstinence implies the more narrow limitation, perhaps titration, of transference gratification in order to promote further psychological work, the not giving on one level in order to facilitate regression to a deeper level of hidden meanings. Analytic abstinence is, therefore, a way of guarding the patient from undue intrusion by the analyst, a technical position for the purpose of promoting analytic work, not for the analyst's comfort or gratification.

Clearly, abstinence is not lack of emotional engagement by the analyst. In direct contrast to that, it is a way the analyst holds back from offering an immediate satisfaction so that roots of transference longings can be exposed. Rather than giving the quick gratification that might leave both analysand and analyst briefly feeling good, the analyst withholds enough satisfaction so as to open the question of what feelings the patient would experience were manifest urges not to be discharged. The narrow principle of abstinence, like the more basic principle of neutrality, is a derivative of the analyst's working in the service of the patient by trying to help the patient be open to the widest range of inner feelings possible.

The analyst's too-ready attitude of supposed understanding can block the true understanding that results from exposure of those deeper roots. Appreciation of psychic determinism allows the analyst to know that meanings are *potentially* understandable, not that they are *easily* understood. Uncompromising efforts toward insight are the most an analyst can give to a patient, a gift unique and more valuable than any transference gratification.

At times the concept of abstinence is opposed and characterized as a form of adversarial attitude, when in fact the application of the abstinence principle is directly in the service of mutual collaboration toward analytic goals. Abstinence is required to sustain the progress of the analysis, not to satisfy the analyst's perfectionistic superego. Detachment in the service of the analyst's superego or of a fantasy that defines analytic technique according to an imagined model of remote perfection is actually antianalytic. Such a posture is radically different from appropriate activity in the service of the work.

Appropriate technique frustrates transference demands not for the purpose of forcing a reaffirmation of a theory but in order to lead to accurate understanding. While basic analytic concepts are inviolable, allegiance to an analytic school—no matter which—compromises the analyst's neutrality to the patient. In each instance, analysis must be practiced for the sake of the specific analysand.

It is here that a recent clinical controversy has arisen. New understanding of the significance of developmental aspects of psychology has led some to embrace what seems an excess of therapeutic activity, positing for analysis a clinical role that includes the task of providing a new active influence in order to attain developmental levels previously unreached. Statements by Freud regarding the analyst's educative influence often are used to buttress a shift in perspective without considering the extent to which such a shift may undermine and even betray the basic psychoanalytic orientation to mastery through understanding. Freud (1919) both acknowledged this problem and took a position on the clinical posture required:

> We refused most emphatically to turn a patient who puts himself into our hands in search of help into our private property, to decide his fate for him, to force our own ideals upon him, and with the pride of a creator to form him in our own image and see that it is good. I still adhere to this refusal. . . . We cannot avoid taking some patients for treatment who are so helpless and incapable of ordinary life that for them one has to combine analytic with educative influence; and even with the majority, occasions now and then arise in which the physician is bound to take up the position of teacher and mentor. But it must always be done with great caution, and *the patient should be educated to liberate and fulfill his own nature, not to resemble ourselves*. [pp. 164–165; emphasis added]

Having addressed the question of the analyst's tactical goallessness for the sake of strategic therapeutic goals, I now would like to address neutrality as it relates to empathy and tact. Empathy has a special link to neutrality, both having roots in the conflicting pressures toward merger and differentiation. Empathic perception arises in the context of felt separateness, an effort to open into the feelings of the other. Neutrality is the technical manifestation of respect for the essential otherness of the patient.

The phrase "empathic response" has gained currency to denote the combination of both sensitive attention and appropriate response. In fairness to those who use the phrase, I emphasize the word "appropriate," which differs from "warm and appreciative." Nonetheless, as Einstein said, it is good to make things as simple as possible—but not *more* simple; I suggest that this tempting phrase, "empathic response," at times obscures more than it clarifies.

A contrasting model takes note of the distinctions among the analyst's sensory imaging, inner mastery, and then active intervention. All of these component functions of the analyst at work require active internal processing. "Evenly hovering attention" is a form of activity. Neutrality is an attitude, an approach, not simple passivity.

First, on the sensory level, is empathy, which I shall discuss in greater detail in a later chapter. The concept of empathy as a mode or perception rather than reaction has a long history within the analytic community, traditionally referring to that temporary, partial trial identification by which, as Freud (1923a) said, the analyst tries "to catch the drift of the patient's unconscious with his own unconscious" (p. 239). Recent focus on the developmental impact of faulty empathic responses has led to a shift in the use of the word "empathy" from a form of perception to a global constellation blending perception and response. This shift has not been universally accepted and has caused some misunderstandings. While it is true that appropriate response depends on accurate empathic perception, "empathic response" is often used to imply a too readily positive reaction that can interfere with full understanding.

The distinctive meaning of other concepts essential to neutrality is also clouded by this view of empathic responsiveness. The various developmental levels of the transference require differing attention depending on how cohesive or distorted are the early self- and object representations.

Whatever the theoretic framework for conceptualizing it, the underlying object relation between analyst and analysand provides the object relation canvas on which the tableau of the transference neurosis is painted. During the course of a customary analysis, the analyst tends to the understanding of the painted world the analysand portrays and elicits. When there is a tear in the canvas, in the fundamental capacity for interpersonal ties—a situation more common with the now-widened scope of analysis—the analyst's direct attention is required for the underlying object-connections. Thus the analyst has technical responsibilities toward all levels of transference, including both the transference neurosis and the primary transference.

To obscure this particular distinction is to interfere with the analyst's neutral availability to all of the patient's issues. The most common manifestation of such interference is the analyst's resistance to acknowledging and accepting hate in the patient, defending against aggression in the transference by insistently seeing it as only a result of narcissistic hurts. Then, rather than explore unfolding transference hate, the analyst hurries to repair the presumed basic rent, acting as if only underlying wounds could explain the rage. The assumption that a negative current in the transference neurosis must be a defect in the primary transference often results from the analyst's underlying fear of the analyst's own sadistic impulse. As a result, too often such an ostensibly humane response is an analyst's reaction formation, a failure of empathic accuracy. An atmosphere of acceptance implies full openness, not a selective filter for the comfort of the analyst.

It is not, of course, a flaw of requisite neutrality for the analyst to reveal an interest in the analytic work, an interest manifest even while proceeding to analyze the meanings the patient attaches to that interest. But true empathic ambiance stays open to hate as well as to love, to the murderous impulse as well as to the wounded feeling.

Human experience is unitary. Affect and cognition are not totally separate phenomena but are different facets of intrinsically integrated events. Therefore, a genuinely neutral reading of the patient requires a combination of both empathic and cognitive modes of perception. Empathic perception alone too quickly fades into the projection present in the empathic imagination. Cognitive reading alone too quickly fades into wild analysis. For true neutrality, music and words must be combined. Either alone is misleading.

After the level of the analyst's perception comes that of response. Neutrality is an attitude in the presence of conflicts, of competing forces. It is as an impartial referee working for the patient's growing introspective skills that the analyst remains equidistant from all parts of the psychic apparatus. In fact, it is through freedom to speak of the multiple pulls of the patient's conflicts that the analyst becomes more neutral, which is another way of stating that interpretation nurtures the analytic alliance. Defensive diffidence is a form of taking sides in the patient's conflicts. To be neutral is not the same as to be neutered.

Neutrality also implies the analyst's avoidance of imposing self or personal values, demanding an inhibition of the urge to dominate, to have power over the other person. This applies even to the power of interpretation. Interpretations inevitably fall short of perfect truth to the patient's meanings by virtue of having passed through the analyst's mental processing. The analyst, while actively interpreting resistance and the unconscious, has also to guard against overweening self-certainty. While clinical instances are usually more subtle, for clarity's sake an egregious model of such an imposition disguised as interpretation can be seen in the well-known words of Goethe's biographer who wrote: "Of all the women he had ever known, Goethe said he loved Fredereka the most. Here Goethe was wrong."

We must remain aware of the multiple impacts of any intervention. Good analytic form can provide a vehicle for suggestion, whether intentionally or unintentionally. Indeed, questioning an inhibition or the urgency of an action can direct by selection of attention more effectively than any command.

Analytic tact, which I shall also discuss further in a later chapter, is an aspect of the analyst's mode of action toward the patient and, like empathy, it is subordinate to the requirement for neutrality. But tact is separate from empathy. It is a mode of intervention that extends the limits of what the patient can tolerate without violating either honesty or neutrality.

Empathy, trial identification, gives us a taste of what goes on inside the patient. Tact derived from the sense of touch, especially the touch of the mothering one during the earliest phases of separation-individuation. It refers to the manner of handling, of responding, whether in explicit interpretation or in silence. Thus tact follows empathy. By examination of associations and by empathic tasting of process—by combining both the words and the music—the analyst comes to understand what to interpret or about what to remain silent. Tact has to do with the *how* of the analyst's activity.

Tact is a clinical derivative of the neutral respect for the patient's autonomy. The empathic process arises in the face of separation as a pull to reestablish connection between self and object. Tact shifts to the level of attempting contact, that is, union through touching while acknowledging essential separateness. There is in the use of tact the respectful recognition of the distinction between other and self.

Indeed, this is why both aggression and narcissistic wounds can be dealt with directly through interpretation. Like the mother's touch, tact permits the candor of harsh reality. Without unrealistic and obscuring warmth, tactful interpretation integrates, allowing the assimilation of information, permitting further exposure. Its ability to expose aggression by implicit binding is the integrative function of tact that is mutative, permitting a person to become honestly intact.

Our main concern is with maintaining neutrality. Analytic tact is not cowardice or self-serving ingratiation. It is not prudence in the service of avoiding anxiety, or behavior demonstrating the analyst to be the loving and accepting, pure, superior, or more secure contrast to the bad parent. It is not softness of voice or kindness that documents goodness. Analytic tact always takes as its goal the ruthless exposure of psychic reality and it is this dedication to a collaborative goal that enables shame, guilt, and disintegrating narcissistic damage to yield to shared work.

Having considered the need for neutrality, for the analyst to be of a relatively consistent and even, moderate, but human color in structuring the analytic situation, let us turn to the related matter of the analyst's self-scrutiny—turning inner motivations to a tamed or sublimated neutral level in the service of the analytic work—a task that demands unceasing self-analysis.

The analyst's own unconscious and infantile sources of work motivation cover the full range of psychic development. Well known among these are rescue fantasies, urges to master both objects and drives, the urge to symbiotic regression, scopophilic and exhibitionistic urges, and aggressive forces. Each genetic level contributes to the stream ending in the ego functions of the adult at work, but each requires mastery, aim-inhibition.

Violations of the analyst's neutralization of underlying motivations result in countertransferential distortions, a subject of great breadth. There is, however, one particular form of such countertransference that merits special notice here in that it presents itself manifestly as a false neutrality, a countertransference posture in the guise of analytic technique.

Collaborative ignorance provides an exemplary instance of false neutrality. We are familiar with the problems of collusion, such as the possible hidden collusion between sadist and masochist. And we are alert to the dangers of such hidden collusion within the analytic situation. By collaborative ignorance I refer to the covert sustenance and support of such a sadomasochistic dyad by those in the surrounding object world, those who participate by acting as if they see nothing. The parent who is blind to child abuse by the marital partner, the presumably ordinary citizen who acts as if ignorant while living next door to a death camp—these are examples of collaborative ignorance as distinguished from collusion within the dyad. Such collaboration is necessary to maintain the collusive pair. Collusion refers to the two-person mutual enactment of forbidden covert wishes; collaborative ignorance refers to the third-person support, generally obscured and unnoticed, which provides the background structure permitting and supporting the two-person collusion.

The analyst's maintenance of the relatedness of the primary transference, as has been described, is essential to the development and analysis of the transference neurosis. But silence can communicate assent, and pseudo-neutrality, the avoidance of questioning as if in the name of protecting the analysis, can functionally support sadistic exploitation. Though imitating good analytic technique, this serves an eccentric need of the analyst.

Analytic dedication to neutrality is not based on a sense of "anything goes," which means, in practice, "anything goes unnoticed," but for the respect that *all* analytic activity, including that of seeming inactivity, carries complicated meanings that must be examined.

Alert to the vicissitudes of the dyadic relationship, the analyst must also be alert to the use to which the patient may try to put both analyst and analysis regarding the patient's actions outside the analytic chamber. Most often this can be best handled by waiting in attentive silence, but at times a transference interpretation is essential. There is the danger of pseudo-neutrality serving as a disguise for collaborative ignorance on the analyst's part.

I offer an extreme instance. A young analyst presenting a fragment of a case to colleagues revealed in passing that the troubled young woman who was his patient could not afford a baby-sitter. Therefore, she daily locked her 5-year-old son in a small room so he could be left unattended for the almost two hours needed for her analytic sessions. When the colleagues responded with horror, alert to the statements of the child's increasing problems, the analyst explained that his task was not to feel guilty but rather to analyze the material as it arose. In fact, he had never questioned or commented to the patient on the peculiar arrangements. In the guise of neutrality, he had become a silent partner.

Such dramatic pseudo-neutrality is, one hopes, rare. But what of the less dramatic posture of purported neutrality, of supposed nonjudgmental attitude that is adopted in the service of obscuring an aspect of the analyst's views? The analyst who could not interpret the defensive nature of a perverse patient's life style rationalized his position in terms of analytic neutrality, not wishing to place a value judgment on the perversion. Of course, judging is precisely what the analyst was doing. The resultant analytic stalemate arose not from good technique, but from a functional encouragement of sadism "out there" to avoid the mixed dangers of seduction and aggression "in here," in the analysis.

These are specific instances of countertransference distortion. On such occasions the analyst's lack of comprehension arises not from simple ignorance but from personal neurotic conflicts. In the broad spectrum of countertransference, false neutrality based on collaborative ignorance is evidenced specifically in such interchanges as these where the analyst fails to interpret acting out.

In addition, countertransferential defensive silence can be present even when masked by a purposeful partial interpretation or premature interpretation. In each of these instances the analyst, for private countertransference needs, imitates appropriate neutral technique in order to inhibit regression in an area that seems threatening. Indeed, this likely explains the well-known difficulties with premature interpretations, which are said to give rise to stubborn resistances. That very statement itself may indicate the analyst's role, serving as it does to shift attention, responsibility, and often blame to the analysand.

Gitelson (1952) stated succinctly: "It is of primary importance for the analyst to conduct himself so that the analytic process proceeds on the basis of what the patient brings to it" (p. 7). Countertransference distortions can intrude in any of the areas of the analyst's functioning. We know that the analyst's objectivity resides in an attitude toward the analyst's own subjectivity. Thus, modesty is an essential aspect of the recognition that absolute neutral objectivity can never be totally achieved.

Moreover, beyond the human limits relating to countertransferential distortions, there is within the analytic process itself an intrinsic limiting feature. Here we note a paradox that has been present throughout the entire consideration of neutrality. Can the principle of neutrality be reconciled with the presence of an analytic goal, even that of structural change consequent to self-knowledge, self-mastery, and a functioning capacity for self-analysis? Much of this apparent paradox has been set aside by the distinction of differing levels—short-term abstinence for the sake of ultimate self-realization—with neutrality derived from the respect for the uniqueness of the patient's own present and ultimate self.

This distinction, however, loses its tidiness when the bridge between those two levels is brought into view. In order to employ customary analytic technical tactics, the analyst must believe in their usefulness for the ultimate goal. Despite all the work done on evaluating analyzability, the analyst at the outset and throughout the work functions not simply on the basis of who the observed patient *is*, but also on the sense of what the patient *might become*—someone with a capacity for realizing further ego growth. Between the short-term and the long-term aims lies the bridge of the analyst's expectations based on a sense of the rudiments of the emerging core of the patient's self (Loewald 1960).

Efforts to sidestep this problem, such as ones offered by those who would presumably do away with judgments by dismissing them with the pejorative label of "health morality," quickly disintegrate when case presentations are examined closely. Can an analyst truly interpret and not trivialize without selecting some issues as more related to anxiety, to defense, to inhibition, than others? Can an analyst in practice truly deal with symptoms of constriction as if they were not the result of a conflicted compromise formation?

These very dilemmas demand the analyst's constant caution of protecting the analysis by respecting the analytic neutrality. It is in the very desire to help develop the self-analytic function that the analyst becomes fully committed to efforts at maintaining neutrality. It is in the context of the collaborative analytic work that the analyst abstains from unnecessary transference gratifications, not to be cold and unresponsive, but in order to protect and further the patient's analysis.

The analyst is a technically skilled assistant at work in the patient's service, welcomed into this other person's life to serve a very special function. All the technical implications of the principle of neutrality are reasonable, logical, and inevitable consequences of remembering *who* the analyst is and *why* the analyst is there.

2

The Analyst's Words

*Language is the armoury of the human mind;
and at once contains the trophies of its past
and the weapons of its future conquests.*
—COLERIDGE

Having considered the overall attitude with which the analyst approaches the patient and the work, let us again start from what we see and trace backwards. Let us begin with the words the analyst actually speaks to the patient. Words are at the heart of the "talking cure," and although powerful forces beyond speech are active in the analytic situation, spoken words serve as the major pathway in our work toward insight.

In the analytic situation the patient relates the inner world to the analyst, relating in words and relating in the transference process. "To relate" means both—"to connect with" and "to tell." For the analysand it is in relating through words that an analysis comes to life, becoming a talking cure. And for the analyst words are the primary avenue of technical interventions. In light of the severe limitations on mobility of the analytic situation, speech becomes more than "just words." Speech becomes powerful action, the means by which each of the participants can discharge inner tensions and the means by which each can act upon the other.

Recent work has examined at length the analyst's receptivity, the cognitive and empathic means by which the analyst comes to understand the patient's messages. The motor end of the analyst's activity—the analyst's speech, which includes silence— merits similar scrutiny. Both will be considered in subsequent chapters.

The words an analyst uses are complex in their origins, structures, and effects. Those words arise from more sources than only the content of the patient's associations and affects, their structure contains more than just their manifest messages, and their effects are broader than merely adding to the patient's cognitive knowledge.

As has already been alluded to, the natural tendency of our minds is to think in categories, for instance, to divide with simple clarity inside from outside. Dreams are the prototypical model of formations within the inner world. Spoken words, in contrast, are so clearly communicative that they represent the quintessentially interpersonal. But so neat a division does not survive close examination. Dreams during an analysis have come to be recognized as having communicative as well as discharge functions. Words spoken during an analysis, by the analyst as well as by the analysand, similarly can be recognized as having overdetermined internal functions beyond those of communication.

In the past we have tended to think as if a pure communication uncluttered by hidden private meanings were possible. A patient's words that carried import beyond the immediately relevant were spoken of as transference. An analyst's words that had private inner investments beyond the manifest were again seen as if they were of a separate new process, countertransference.

An extreme of this artificial separation of pure message from hidden forces as carried over to clinical practice was stated most clearly by Loewenstein (1956). He noted three major functions of speech: a speaker may speak about matters, may express what is in the speaker's own self, or may appeal to the addressee. Expressing a presumably ideal model, Loewenstein said, "In his own speech the analyst will exclude both the function of appeal and the expressive function, limiting himself specifically to the cognitive function in relation to facts concerning his present addressee: the patient" (p. 462).

Such tidiness of concept is appealing. Like a journalist, the patient reports the inner world, and like an objective outside observer, the analyst interprets. Unfortunately, as every analyst knows firsthand, such categorized clarity is far from the whole story. Autonomy is always a matter of degree, not of absolutes. The analyst's words are not exempt from the principle of multiple determination. Words spoken by each party in the analysis arise from within that person's intrapsychic world to form a bridge of communication and action to the other person present.

Consideration of the analyst's words offers an opportunity to examine the multiple levels of meanings: those that relate to the world of the analysand, those that relate to the world of the analyst, and those that relate to their connections. Though my focus here will be on the analyst's words at work, those words and that work have as their supraordinate task the analyzing of the analysand. My attention here to the analyst's perspective is meant to define a focus for the current study, not to undo the centrality of the patient's perspective as the ultimate object of analytic concern.

I shall start by presenting several brief instances regarding the analyst's words as a way to view the analyst's working within the analytic process. Next I shall consider the analyst's words from the vantage point of their context in the dyadic analytic situation. After that, I shall focus on the view from the analyst's intrapsychic formation of words and on the power and the limits of the power of words. Division into these separate aspects is artificial. Any clinical instance, whatever it is intended to demonstrate, must include intrinsically all aspects at once. This point, applicable to any analytic discussion, is particularly apt to a consideration of words. Here as within an analysis, the words that clarify by identifying simultaneously betray by abstracting.

ILLUSTRATIONS OF THE ANALYST'S WORDS

Let us begin with a statement so commonplace as to seem unremarkable, one requiring little knowledge of a specific patient or a specific analyst. A patient presents a dream in which the manifest content repudiates an urge, one the patient would prefer to disown. Speaking about the dream, the patient states, "I would *never* do anything so outrageous as what the dream suggests." Acknowledging these protests I say, "You wouldn't even dream of such a thing."

Such a remark is generally recognized as both summarizing a conscious feeling and interpreting its defensive nature, implying the presence of a forbidden wish. For me to say such a thing I need know little about the patient or myself. The simplest grasp of analytic theory informs me enough to provide my choice of words.

My words, nonetheless, are said with purpose, purpose that the patient can both read and distort. Am I suggesting the patient ought to have a different attitude toward emerging impulses? An ideal reply might be that I am only trying to broaden the range of possibilities the patient can consider. Still, such an invitation to reconsideration involves a suggestion. The analyst's refusal to be aware of the possible implicit suggestion can be felt by the patient as a taboo, driving underground concerns such as those of domination and compliance.

Now, a next instance. When I say, to a hysterical woman telling her fears of a supervisor's comments, she is "afraid of a penetrating remark," I offer a preliminary partial interpretation seeming to imply two levels of meanings. On one level I refer to the specific interchange with her superior as threatening and possibly leading to feelings of being assaulted. On a second level I raise a question of a link to issues of sexuality and body damage we have previously addressed.

Yet is not my comment itself "a penetrating remark" in current actuality? To what extent am I the interpreter, only playing back in another language the original words of the patient, and to what extent am I modifying the patient's experience through a new enactment by translating into my own words? How much is in the immediate service of the patient's analyzing and how much goes further? Am I showing my own comfort with vulnerability while secretly reassuring myself that in contrast to the patient *I* am not helpless and weak, that *I* am able to be active? How much of what I said was simply "saying" and how much was enacting? Indeed, can there even exist such a phenomenon as "simply saying" that is not also an action upon the other?

Speaking freely about penetration, I am now acting, intervening within our work. I speak mainly to help get something clear. But at the moment I speak to assist the work, am I also, in the process, trying to resolve on a microscopic level issues of my own, such as ones regarding being subordinate and vulnerable? Was the timing of my remark significantly provoked by an unwitting need to evidence activity, thus showing myself to be one to deny passive vulnerability by speaking up? No matter how well analyzed I am, no matter what degree of self-mastery, at some time it is appropriate for me to speak up, and at that time these questions are unavoidably present.

The answers to these questions matter deeply to the progress of the analytic work. The analyst's music, like the patient's, carries messages as important as those in the manifest words. The patient at work will hear and consider my manifest message and will certainly add her own unconsciously determined meanings to what I say. But equally certainly, the patient's observing ego and empathy will be alert to my buried messages, just as mine are to hers. Even simple remarks carry implied messages beyond the manifest.

Some words an analyst uses develop in the course of analytic work as a private shared shorthand. An outsider would not recognize connotations that both analyst and patient would know well. Yet the analytic situation, no matter how well structured and protected, exists within the context of a larger world. The analyst as well as the patient brings in experiences from the outside. Again I offer a simple instance. More often than I would have suspected, an idiom expressed by one patient returns when I speak of a similar conflict with another patient. For example, I said to one young man that he spoke as if after a lifetime of practice to be a subordinate he now was shocked to find himself a general. He found the comment apt. Privately, I was surprised: military references are not usual for me. On reflection I realized that another patient earlier in the day had contrasted his passivity with the active model of General Patton. Something said by one patient returned in response to a stimulus in a relevant area of another.

Here the words came from what might be called a verbal residue, perhaps a natural grabbing of what lay on top of the pile when I reached for a word. But why that memory at that moment? On watching myself more, I was surprised to discover how far down into the pile I would unwittingly reach, linking words from one patient with another.

Speaking to a different patient, one who lived like a misfit, I commented on how he presented himself to the world, his refusal to "decorate" himself for the world. Once again I was surprised by my choice of words. I was curious about the source of that word "decorate." It struck me as not fitting perfectly. Perhaps I was evidencing my own microscopic identification with the patient as misfit by choosing a phrase that did not fit well. Then I remembered that about fifteen years earlier I had worked with an attractive young woman who also seemed to defy social success. Once, while bemoaning her failure to attract men, she mentioned that a new young man had moved into her apartment building. Approaching her by the pool, he introduced himself and said he needed help to decorate his new apartment. My patient answered by saying she had a girlfriend who was good at that sort of thing.

The "decorating" metaphor had come to my mind with a current patient from an unfinished memory involving an earlier patient I had thought I had forgotten. Again troublesome questions result. How long does the analytic discourse continue? When is a case terminated? More crucially, to whom was I speaking? Was I addressing not only my current patient but also a patient long gone and, I thought, forgotten? When I talk to another person, am I always speaking at some level to myself, unknowingly mindful of all my hidden, present ghosts? Indeed, is this not close to our very definition of transference, now in the analyst? At times these personal forces may be intrusive, at times not. What an analyst does with such matters will influence the course of the work, but such forces cannot validly be denied. The psychology of the analyst is not just a contaminant in an otherwise sterile field. Eccentric distortions can be vastly destructive to the analytic work, but no statement an analyst makes comes into being outside the analyst's mental functions. The analyst's self-mastery is always a matter of degree.

Consider the next pair of vignettes. "It sounds," I said to my patient, "as if when you moved from your parents' home to live with your new bride, you felt you were being traded to the minor leagues." Those words seemed fitting to my patient, a passive-dependent man who, not weaned from his mother's breast until his fourth year of life, was preoccupied with matters of separation. However, my use of a baseball simile surprised and intrigued me.

I had rarely thought of baseball for years, and what thoughts I had were negative. Then I remembered. My father had been a fan of baseball at a time I was most definitely not a fan of my father. Only once had I attended a professional baseball game, dragged as a begrudging teenager against my will by my eager father. It had been a doubleheader. And *minor* league teams! Miserable on that hot summer day, fidgety and bored, I struggled with my fears of a strong father, my disappointment with a weak father, and my adolescent hopelessness about ever being at peace with and apart from my father.

My associations then turned to my professional adolescence, to a study group in which a colleague spoke of "pure" analytic technique. He told of a patient of his, a baseball fanatic, who used baseball terminology when speaking of all areas of his life. Though this colleague knew none of the baseball jargon, he proudly proclaimed that he never acknowledged his ignorance to his patient, never asked that something be explained. Instead, he waited for what he called the transference and interpreted that. Trying to come to terms with my own weaknesses, my own not knowing, I was aware for the first time of feeling sympathy and respect for a baseball fan. My competitiveness was still alive, if slightly muted, in my disdain for my colleague's technique.

Why now? Why had I chosen from my own reservoir of images such a simile to use with a patient preoccupied with maternal matters? I had not been aware of these conflicts in his current associations, and his salient themes had been of mothering, security, and loss. Gradually I recognized that these themes were not the only ones. In the earliest phase of the analysis, when the patient spoke with a detached freedom, I had heard from him of baseball.

As a child the patient had been waited on by both parents, not just his mother, as if he were royalty. Or to be more precise, the son of royalty. Father, a professional man who chose to live in a poor neighborhood, acted like a king. All around deferred to him. The son was clever and quick. Despite overwhelming reinforcement for passivity, he often burst forth in activity. On his insistence his father would join him to play ball, but only on the father's terms: that the son pitch and father be at bat. The place at bat was never shared.

Later in childhood the patient eagerly joined neighborhood ball games. He loved the game, the activity, the excitement. Once, though, he returned home red-faced and out of breath. Father exploded. How dare the boy risk his health, his future, his life by such overexertion? Never again was he to allow himself to get so overheated. After this incident (or what it condensed), the son never again risked facing the terror of his father's rage. He also never again played baseball.

All of this came to my conscious awareness *after* I heard my own comment to my patient. It was after I heard my own words that I recognized a subtle shift in the transference and an insinuation of themes of competition, power struggles, and mastery over body activities into themes of mothering and dependency. The new themes had not been consciously recognized: they had required self-analysis to come into the open.

Was my resistance to hearing this new theme solely neurotic countertransference? Might not my private resistance itself arise from a trial identification with the patient? This matter may be clarified by a comparison. When I presented this incident to colleagues, one posed a question I had neglected to ask myself.

Had not others with whom I worked spoken of baseball? Had my reactions been similar?

Indeed, I had worked at the same time with another patient, a second young man who spoke often of baseball. To the best of my recollection his references had never elicited from me a comparable reaction. This was a man whose father had been substantially absent, off to the wars during the early years of this man's life and remote even after his physical return. This, too, was a man who had to deal with intense ambivalence. However, for this man baseball provided an arena for good fathering, not a source of conflict. "The only times I had my father to myself," he said, "were the few times he took me to the baseball game."

What now is to be made of my reactions, both the "minor league" remark to the first and my comfortable silence when I listened to the second of these men? In each instance my reaction, my words and my silence, had evoked aspects of my own partial identifications, my own private history and psychology. At each of those moments I had not been conscious of the active presence of my self-analysis, yet it is clear that significant forces determining my responses came more than I knew from outside my conscious intent.

THE CONTENT OF THE ANALYST'S WORDS

Let us consider both the dyadic context within which the analyst speaks and then the intrapsychic aspects by which the analyst's words are formed. First we turn to the context of the analyst's words.

The patient and the analyst speak to each other in the context of a collaborative work, each performing different tasks for the common goal, each having an impact on the other. This basic medium of collaboration underlies the apparent asymmetry of the participants (Leavy 1980), the necessary division of labor in the shared work of the patient's analysis.

There is a fundamental similarity for analyst and patient. For both, when activity other than speech is minimized, words become the major medium of action. There are, however, vast differences. During a session the patient speaks and then observes. The analyst, in contrast, observes and then speaks. The patient faces the analyst's abstinence, the patient's words come from inner sources with the least possible external stimulation. In contrast, the analyst's words come in response to a flood of stimuli from the patient. The vastness of the patient's speech pulls the patient from mature logical structure back toward primitive fluidity. The paucity of the analyst's words press in the opposite direction, toward more organized secondary process language.

What is the specific position of the analyst? Reacting to the sense of separation resulting from the patient's regression and maintaining little active speaking contact, the analyst responds with trial identification (Fliess 1942) to keep a feeling of connection.

Manifestly, the analyst speaks to the patient. Before that can be done, the analyst's own inner forces must be dealt with, not in the abstract but in specific relevance to those issues brought to life by the analysis. Most of what the analyst says is so comfortable that its preparation goes unnoticed, like the shifting of gears by an experienced driver. Attention to what is said shows that indeed more has been prepared than the analyst himself knew, as noted in my use of the baseball simile.

Unlike the patient's vocally expressed regression, the analyst's parallel regression takes place unexpressed. Responding to that regression as a signal, the analyst tries to integrate what is going on, to sort out personal forces from those of the patient, and then to offer an interpretation (Olinick et al. 1973). Along the way the analyst's words contribute both to the analyst's own self-analysis and to the manifest clinical work. Thus, these words carry tacit messages.

An interpretation explicitly recognizes unconscious meanings of the patient's associations. In so doing, it implicitly distinguishes forces in the patient from those in the analyst. The powerful message may be that more deeply structured one that states, "No, I am neither you nor your ghosts, yet together, in contact as separate observers, we can recognize and speak of your inner forces and ghosts." Though most often the analyst's self-analytic work preceding interpretation takes place outside conscious awareness, still, the analyst speaks to the analyst's own self as well as to the patient. The private part of that speech is silent. As a result, interpretations of forces within the patient simultaneously expose a model of the analyst's own separate autonomy and mastery. It is likely that this message carried implicitly beyond the manifest message is necessary, though not sufficient for the analytic work.

The interpretation does more than simply provide conceptual links between elements within the patient's fantasies. The message structured within the interpretation shifts both the analyst and the patient from a more conflictual position to a more observing position, a shared observing. The analyst's words move the two from a fantasied joining to a level of respectful contact, the "intimate separation" Stone (1961) described.

For this to occur, the analyst's interventions are available to address the patient subsequent to and along with the analyst's self-addressing. Along with their "mutative" effect (Strachey 1934), there is a second consequence to this implicit structure regarding the power of words. The analyst's self-analysis helps protect the analyst's speech from covert use to maintain power over the patient as an object, whether for narcissistic, aggressive, or sexual power. The analyst's naming of the patient's forces implies the separation of the analyst's self-analysis from that of the patient.

There is a third important function of the analyst's interpretation that derives from the first two, the explication of the patient's psychology and the distinguishing of the analyst's. That third function is the offering of a framework to facilitate further movement in the patient's unfolding work. Responding to the patient's metaphors, the analyst's own metaphors are also offered.

Let us take another example. The following hour occurred near the end of an analysis, after much analytic work had already been done. The patient's first twenty minutes or so were spent speaking of events in which the patient had shown "more backbone." In the course of that I asked a minor question to clarify what was described. The patient's physical position then became

more rigid, and he replied in the formal tone that had been customary earlier in our work. I noted the change and said that he
had just "stiffened" toward me as he had when he tried to protect himself as a child from his father's hits and from his own
urge to hit his father.

The word "stiffened," which I used without conscious selection, gives an instance of the use of a metaphoric word, one that
provides a link between physical sensation and thought, offering a broad range for the patient's response.

The patient's next association appeared to be a manifest
change of subject, though he used my word as a switch word. He
had just met and started to date a new woman. When she rested
her head on his arm, he said, he became aware that his arm
slightly stiffened; he bemoaned his problem with intimacy. Then
he spoke of trouble falling asleep, of trying to masturbate to help
himself fall asleep. He fantasized about the new woman's genitals,
but found himself unable to have an erection. "It just wouldn't
get stiff." From the image of that woman, his mind went back to
the frightening sight of blackness between his mother's legs when
at age 3 or 4 he saw his mother sitting on the toilet. He thus moved
from "stiff" to "not stiff" to uncertainty regarding what is or isn't
there to get stiff. His mind wandered next to an embarrassing
slip he had made when talking to his daughter: he had made a
reversal and spoken of "Aunt Sam and Uncle Jane."

For the remainder of the hour he continued with themes of
gender uncertainty and interpersonal firmness, whether he was
vulnerable to the phallic potency of other men (including me and
his father), whether he was or wanted to be more man or woman.
Derivatives of the metaphor "stiffened" recurred throughout.

When earlier I spoke of "stiffness" I did not engage in a consciously intentional enactment of the transference. My word was
used in an effort to approach the patient's state of mind at the
moment, and the patient then used this word to facilitate further
opening. The metaphor resonates with the body feeling in a manner that permits the patient a choice of the degree of conscious
awareness tolerable; it can provide enough conceptual structure
to assist the patient in extending the range of conscious recall
and experience.

Words have many levels of specificity, and the analyst's words make use of both greater and lesser levels of such specificity of meaning. The simultaneous presence of the patient's individual meanings and of the collaborative context in which those meanings are explored leads to paradoxical aspects in the choice of words. To be sure, elucidating the unconscious requires the analyst to choose words that contain a multiplicity of meanings. Yet either explicit or implicit meanings that refer to the underlying actualities of two people at analytic work need as much specificity as the analyst can achieve. The tasks of addressing the patient's inner worlds and also the collaborative context call on words with different levels of multiplicity of meanings. Though both levels exist simultaneously in any statement, they will be more clear if we consider them separately.

Meanings Regarding the Analysand's Fantasies

Let us take first use of language with a relatively wide range of meanings. I am not referring to the analyst's speaking in the cryptic style of an oracle—as if to imply wisdom unknown to the patient or to disguise ignorance or personal conflicts (Isay 1977), nor do I imply compromise of efforts toward clarity. The analyst must interpret the deepest meanings accessible. An appeal to multiple levels of meanings does not mean avoiding the unconscious; it is not a rationalization for a taboo against talking of conflictual matters.

In trying to expose unconscious matters, we use language to approach experience that cannot be exactly reduced to language. I have in mind what I think Fenichel (1941) meant when he said, "I was once reproached with the use of the words, 'something like,' . . . as indicating that I do not take unconscious fantasies seriously. I deny this. Its use means that the unconscious fantasies are *vague*, and therefore can only be reproduced in words inexactly, always with the addition of 'something like'" (p. 10n).

The lack of absolute precision results both from what it is we try to know and from the limits of knowing. Inner experience is not solely verbal. The patient's associations, even at their most free, are already translations. As previously pointed out, interpretations are translations of translations, having passed through the filter of the analyst. Even empathy and introspection provide a taste of "something like," not the experience of the other's original inner state.

When speaking, the analyst uses the patient's terms, trying to weave them into and around interpretive remarks. When this is successful, the work flows. Exploring the unconscious, the analyst tries to integrate both the patient's words and the analyst's own in order to bring fresh light to the implications of the patient's words. When the analyst is limited to the patient's words, new connections may be made, but there is a serious risk of a mirroring that can become a folie à deux. When the analyst modifies the patient's words, in addition to the risk of distortion there is also the possibility of suggesting new understandings.

This broadening of understanding is facilitated by the use of words with a multiplicity of meanings. Evocative words, those that call forth the hidden voice, are of particular value. A metaphor may come closer to the patient's inner truth than could a detailed black and white verbal map. It has been said that if one tries to be precise, one is bound to be metaphorical. Monet's impressionism captures the sense of shifting light on the cathedral of Rouen as could not be done by any photograph. Greater knowledge of that cathedral comes from combining impression and detail than could come from either source alone. What is sought is, as Yeats put it, a way "where passion and precision are one."

Psychoanalytic consideration has widened the understanding and use of metaphor beyond its narrow usage as a single form of speech. Beginning with Aristotle's reference to metaphor as a transference of a word to a sense different from its significations, Sharpe (1940) emphasized that metaphor fuses sense, experience, and thought in language, thus providing an optimum manner for expressions that displaced the physical to the psychical. Indeed, Sharpe considered speech itself the ultimate metaphor.

In the same vein, Arlow (1979) pointed out that metaphor

economically condenses multiple levels of experience, symbols, and meanings in a statement at once ambiguous and clear. He summarized, "In the psychoanalytic situation the interaction of analyst and analysand is an enterprise of mutual metaphoric stimulation in which the analyst, in a series of *approximate* [emphasis added] objectifications of the patient's unconscious thought processes, supplies the appropriate metaphors upon which the essential reconstructions and insights may be built" (pp. 381–382). It is the quality of *approximation* that mitigates against the use of words with a specificity that narrows rather than broadens, that closes rather than opens. Indeed, Arlow went so far as to link language and transference by stating that transference in the analytic situation is a particularly intense, lived-out metaphor of the patient's neurosis.

The analyst's use of metaphor takes fullest advantage of what Hartmann (1951) called the "principle of multiple appeal." Metaphor offers the patient an opportunity to utilize the analyst's words on any level of psychic functioning, giving easiest access to the multiple determination of the patient's mind.

The vignette cited earlier, in which I used the word "stiff," gives an instance of the patient's making use on many levels of a metaphor offered in a partial interpretation. I include this partial—rather than full, discrete—interpretation because the latter exists as theoretical model, not clinical actuality. Yet again, all interpretations result from step-by-step work within the structure of the analytic situation, including the reverberations of messages already discussed. All interpretations are partial interpretations, and all interpretations are trial interpretations.

Meanings Regarding the Underlying Collaborative Relationship

While all words have many levels of meaning, some tend to more specificity. It is in reference to the context of the two persons sharing collaborative work that greater specificity becomes necessary.

I do not suggest that there exists a "real" relationship that is pure and unencumbered by unconscious meanings. Once again the tendency of our minds to think dualistically misleads us. Disagreements over questions of "therapeutic alliance" have sometimes sounded as if there were *only* unconscious hidden meanings or *only* current external actualities. All levels are real and actual. None exists without the others. Rather, it is the simultaneous presence of all of the many meanings that makes greatest clarity essential when referring to the two selves at work.

When someone engages me in analysis, that person hires me to be a professional assistant in a self-investigation. Analysis demands profound regression. The long-term goal orientation toward insight is let go from immediate view in the shorter-term transference regression. However, even at times of greatest regression, the regression is not all there is to the patient. A general tendency to underestimate the patient's ego strengths ought not obscure the person who is the patient. The patient, though exposing primitive and childlike aspects, is neither a primitive nor a child. Therefore, while our spoken words explore the primitive, they speak to the integrative aspects of the patient.

The analyst's statements inform the analysand not only of interpretive explanations but also of how the analyst views the analytic relationship. In addition to the examples presented, we can think of the analyst's use of the word "we." Beyond the value of such a word in helping effect an ego split in the patient (Sterba 1934), other implications can also be involved.

Let us take another example. The request of an analyst who wishes to hear a dream repeated, "Tell me the dream again," communicates more than concern with the dream. "You" tell "me" can imply a statement of domination and submission, of the analyst's activity and responsibility and the patient's passivity and lack of personal agency. At worst, that could undermine any true analytic process, and at the very least, it could make erroneous any future interpretation of the patient's feelings of submissiveness as transferential.

Thus, at the same time that there is an effort to approach understanding of the patient's meanings, cautious expression is required to guard the neutrality of the collaborative base on which the work toward insight takes place. This caution relieves the work from the artifact of a relationship in which the analyst is the one who "knows." By employing such precision in references to the underlying dyadic context, the analyst protects the transference from covert contamination.

Similarly, words respectful of the immediacy of the analytic experience protect the work. Though many remarks the analyst makes are predictable, they require statement in the immediacy of the moment. Universal basic concepts serve like a compass to expose and map an individual analysis. They orient our words but are not the subject of our words. Basic concepts obscure if they are substituted for observation and relating that refer to the specific territory.

The direction of our search and our words is always toward singularity. Routinized statements corrode genuineness, subverting analytic inquiry in the guise of analytic form. Words said to reconfirm theoretic postures expose underlying closure, while ones that address the specificity, the singularity, of the current unfolding process promote analytic inquiry.

THE INNER FORMATION OF THE ANALYST'S WORDS

Let us move from the analytic dyad and the question of how the analyst's words are adapted to the clinical task and turn to the processes within the analyst, what we might call "the word work." Word work, similar to the familiar concept of dream work, refers to the mechanisms by which deep motivations combine with current pressures to be converted into spoken statements.

In dream work current forces unite with the stream of older and deeper unconscious drive derivatives to find discharge in the special circumstances of sleep, that is, the limitation on discharge through external action and the presence of the need for representation primarily in visual images. In word work the psychological state of the analyst's mind and the conditions for discharge are different: the interpreting analyst's mind works toward greater consciousness rather than toward lesser consciousness as does the dreamer's mind; mobility, though limited, is much less limited; the medium of discharge is speech rather than visual representation; the laws of secondary process must be imposed on the underlying condensations and displacements. Thus, dream work and word work follow different imperatives. But the natures of their compromise formations have similarities. It is in that sense that word work assumes its importance, defining the area of the particular intrapsychic paths the analyst's mental processes take behind and prior to any communication in speech.

Our attention has been called first to the consciously intentional communicative functions of the analyst's words, the manifest message to the other. But words serve, in addition, as intrapsychic compromise formations for the analyst, responding not only to the external demands of the patient's analytic needs but also to the discharge of forces within the analyst. Words are simultaneously both end products of internal processes and communications designed to have effect on the other. Words actualize, evidencing inner as well as outer action.

To understand the development of the analyst's words, we must keep in mind the analyst's private personal intrapsychic functions. Only then can the multiple resonances and reverberations of messages and feelings between analysand and analyst be properly placed.

Evaluation of the patient's needs combines with the analyst's signal response to personal regression, moving the analyst to speak. Deeply rooted motivations sublimated in the urge to do analytic work provide motor force. Discharge is restricted to speech drawn from the large reservoir of words, and effect is determined by the circumstances of the external reality of the state of the analysand and the analysis.

It obviously is impossible in a single study to do justice to the complexity of the psychology of the analyst at work. For brevity's sake, in order to demonstrate the general categories involved in the analyst's internal word work, I shall offer only a programmatic overview of these areas: the analyst's deep motivations, the choice of specific words and the "verbal residue," and the role of words as action, that is, the discharge effect of words on the patient as the analyst's external reality of the moment.

The Analyst's Deep Motivations

The analyst is brought to do analytic work by a broad range of early motivations arising from private urges, personal identifications, and their subsequent mastery and sublimation through growth and insight. Each genetic level provides forces that contribute to work activity, and each of these forces can be examined on a continuum ranging from infantile drive to sublimated aim inhibition. Such unconscious motivations include rescue and healing fantasies, urges to master objects, urges to master conflicts, urges to regressive symbiosis, scopophilia, and so on. Let us take voyeurism as an example.

Voyeurism is part of a paired set of component instincts, exhibitionism and voyeurism. An analyst's original wish to see may have arisen in defense against conflicts over pleasure in being seen, in showing. If the analyst's working curiosity persists as a defensive substitution for forbidden exhibitionistic impulses, the analyst may be inappropriately silent out of a reluctance to be exposed. This specific conflict can account for much of the difficulty in an analyst's struggle over activity and passivity, over how much he speaks. Obviously, the reverse, with inappropriate overactivity, can also occur.

Choice of Words

Now, for the specific words. The analyst's personality and culture contribute to the determination of vocabulary as well as to the tendency to speak more or less. Words used by significant others, including words heard in childhood and adolescence, words read in books, and words heard in an early formal analysis, reappear. The impact of patients, including patients other than an analysand under immediate consideration, has been noted.

The vignettes in which I used the simile of a general to refer to activity or of decorating to refer to ways of relating to others demonstrate the use of verbal images from different patients in the form of day residues. How often do our words carry echoes of the analytic past? With clinical work so central in the analyst's self-analysis, it seems inevitable that patients' private languages would become especially important elements in an analyst's choice of words.

The sense of "day" residue may need revision. The day is a natural unit, the day's memories easily accessible. As a consequence we readily notice associations to seemingly insignificant matters from the immediate past. But the unconscious has no sense of time; the buried is not lost. In the analyst's partial ego regression when at work, old memories can arise as readily as recent ones for the crystallization of images and words. My use of the word "decorate" came across the years quite as easily as my use of a military analogy had come across the hours.

Words as Action

Now, we can turn to the power of speech, the role of speech as action. The analyst speaks for effect; the analytic work is done for purpose. If the analyst were to have no impact on the patient and the analysis (akin to the patient's common fantasy of having no impact on the analyst), then the analyst and the analysis would be meaningless (Poland 1978).

In contrast to the manipulative strategies appropriate to other therapies, the analyst's words are spoken to help understanding. An analyst does not speak to elicit specific responses. Rather, the patient's associations in response to the analyst's words become, themselves, new data. When the work goes well, the patient's subsequent associations often lead to unexpected areas.

In the power of interpretation even our fashion of speaking has effect. The psychoanalytic function of tact deals directly with *how* our words act, the effect on the analysand of the manner in which we choose and deliver our words. The very first vignette cited, which included the analyst's commenting that a patient "would never dream" of a forbidden impulse, gives an example of how vital the tone is to the analyst's message. Spoken with regard for the patient's struggles, the statement is helpful. Spoken with an edge of sarcasm, it ridicules and belittles. Interpretations of transference reactions are undermined if the message itself is not truly respectful and nonprovocative.

The analyst's style of speech can have as significant an impact on the patient as do the words. The patient may react both accurately and with transference distortions to the analyst's manner of speaking. One young man, a heavy drug user, felt that the way I spoke about drugs was contrived and lacked an ease of authenticity. In fact, my language was awkward, because he was describing ways of life I did not know. Two separate themes were consequently exposed. One arose from what he took to be the phoniness, the dishonest posing he inferred from my choice of words. His views of his experiences with his father, whom he considered phony, were clarified from the transference meanings he placed on my speech. The second theme came from his identifying with me as subject, rather than with my being cast like father as object. This line of thought led to his own sense of shame in association with ignorance, weakness, and vulnerability.

All of the analyst's utterances, not just words, act with effect. A small example. At times some previously confusing aspects of the patient's fantasies will fall into place, making sense of something not before clear. For the patient this has an "Aha!" effect. Often the effect is the same for the analyst. Sometimes at such moments I will emit a slight half-laugh of recognition. Reflecting on that sound, I have come to think of it as closely akin to a smile of recognition, the sort of pleased and surprised smile when one suddenly notices an unexpected but very welcome friend.

That sound, never consciously planned, never seems to go unnoticed by the patient. Early in an analysis it is at times heard as if I have laughed *at* the patient, the event taken over by the transference. Later in the analysis such an event is heard by the patient as a validation of a new insight.

In my half-laugh I show both my ignorance and my sense of learning something. In a nonword oral message I tell the patient that I am not ashamed of ignorance but find a pleasure in insight into new connections. The half-laugh, like a verbal partial interpretation, inseparably reveals messages both of expression and cognition, indeed of recognition.

The analyst's silence, too, is a form of statement, often a powerful one. Silence is more than a technique of abstinence. Silence, which cannot say what words can say, can state with great effect some things words cannot. Inappropriate silence by the analyst can be an act of sadism in the guise of analytic form. Appropriate silence at times can be more powerful than the spoken word.

A recent moment in my office offered a painful instance. A young single woman came for her session shortly after she had been told she needed a hysterectomy. Though there was, of course, much to analyze, at that first moment when she faced the horror of what she just had learned, any word of mine would have been irrelevant and demeaning, pulling her from experiencing the enormity of her feelings to the distraction of appreciating me as sympathetic. Among other meanings, this woman heard my silence as my staying in respectful attendance while she, not I, was suffering a massive loss.

Both the analyst's words and the analyst's silence have effects, both are intended to have effects. The analysis of a person is thus crucially different from the analysis of a text, which continues its essentially fixed existence after the interpreter departs. Words about a text or a work of art may alter the way others subsequently see that work. Words in analysis of a person become new parts of that person's experience. As Leavy (1980) summarized, "The history of the analysis is an important part of the patient's current history, and not as merely a parallel to the rest of his experience, but as it both reflects and modifies it" (p. 95). The analyst's words act on the analysand directly.

The Analyst's Eccentric Distortions and His Words

Thus far, for the most part, I have not described clinical vignettes marked by dramatic distorting countertransference. Before commenting on countertransference directly, I will turn to an incident in which my words more markedly reflected a conflict of my own regarding the patient's unfolding work. My patient was an accomplished writer. He spoke naturally with an articulate ease, a subtlety of nuance I admired. One day well into the work he commented on *my* ease with words, *my* articulate skill. It was then I recognized that I had feared humiliation before this patient, a man whose world was peopled by masters in the use of language. To defend myself and to impress the patient in the face of his remarkable verbal facility, I had enacted undercurrents of my own competitive fears and ambitions. Recognition permitted me to step back to allow an important part of the transference to be analyzed. What turned out to be at hand in the patient were intense childhood conflicts over inhibited competitiveness.

Combining some prior observations may permit us to notice connections between the effect of the analyst's words as actions within the analysis and problems of the analyst's eccentric distortions. As already described, the analyst's relation to personal exhibitionistic and voyeuristic impulses can influence how much the analyst speaks.

Consider the patient who does not carry insight into new ways of functioning outside the office. We are familiar with the idea that the analysand identifies with the analyzing function of the analyst. An analyst's inhibition of speech, reluctance to show himself, and undue delay in interpreting also are sources for possible internalization by the patient. In the context of speech as the primary medium of action in analysis, could it be that these inhibitions provide a countertransference model of inhibition in the realm of action? If so, the analyst's inappropriate silence would be a hidden contributor to a patient's inhibition of freedom to act.

COUNTERTRANSFERENCE AND
THE ANALYST'S PSYCHOLOGY

Just as in the past it has been felt that the analyst's words could be purely cognitive without including either affective message or appeal to action, so, too, there has been a belief that the analyst could speak, that is, act within the analysis, with pure objectivity. Any deviation from that purity was termed "countertransference." The word was coined by Freud (1910b) to refer to those forces in the analyst that led him to set aside neutrality toward the patient.

Countertransference, like transference, was seen at first as an interference in analytic work. The uses of both later came to be realized. The inevitability of countertransference was stated most succinctly and elegantly by Viderman (1974): "The transference neurosis does not develop in an emotionally empty space. It can only develop in a space saturated with affects. It is thus that Kant's dove believed that its flight would be easier if it did not encounter the air's resistance. The analytic space is also a distortion of what is inscribed in it and a resistance, but it is because of this distortion and this resistance that something becomes discernible within it. It is through these resistances that the dialectic process of the analysis develops" (p. 472).

Certainly, the analyst can interfere with the course of an analysis; inappropriate functioning can be vastly destructive. Problems have arisen, however, over the use of the word countertransference. Used in a narrow sense, it speaks of the analyst's eccentric intrusions into the analysis; in a broad sense, it speaks of the activity of the analytic instrument, the analyst's entire psychology at work. The word has been used in such a variety of ways as to lose its specificity and communicative value.

Consideration of the analyst's use of words suggests that the psychology of the analyst at work *always* processes and thus necessarily modifies that which is being explored by the patient. Where shall we now draw the line when we speak of the analyst's not setting aside neutrality?

Perhaps the answer lies in the degree to which the analyst facilitates the work, the degree to which he moves it off course. The analyst's own compromise formations while at work can both serve and distort the analytic task, and they can also do both at the same time on different levels.

Recognizing that the analyst's mind must be lent to the service of the analytic work, how shall we measure aptness or distortions? Many scales are possible. For instance, we can size up the analyst's reaction on a continuum, finding gradations from mastered trial identifications at one end to more regressed counteridentifications and overidentifications at the other. Or we can evaluate differentiations in the degree of mastery, the degree of autonomy from personal conflict. Here we can note how open the analyst is for self-analytic scrutiny, how able to modify and correct readings to be ever more true to the patient's. The capacity to analyze is directly related to the capacity to master the counter-transference and to utilize the information garnered from it.

Consciously or unconsciously, the analyst struggles with personal transference forces in an effort to be as true as possible to the patient's work. Self-analysis is an essential part of what goes on when an analyst "analyzes" someone, whether or not that self-analysis occurs on a conscious level. The analyst's self-analysis is not only of benefit to the analyst, but it is vital to the ultimate clinical goal, the patient's analysis. Evidence of the analyst's inner processing and self-analysis are built into his very use and choice of words.

Whatever comes up from a patient is said to be "grist for the mill." Though I believe that anything an analyst thinks or feels is similarly apt for his examination, I do not suggest that just as the patient needs to put all into words so ought the analyst. Eccentric intrusions by the analyst are to be recognized as such. Still, the absence of marked or clear intrusions does not imply the absence of contributions from the working of the analyst's mind.

Clinical analytic work has a double task, the exploration of the patient's mind and the transfer of a technique so that the patient can continue that exploration independently. The words the analyst uses for the first purpose, interpretive explanations in exploring the patient's mind, contain in addition to their explicit message other messages structurally implied within them. These help the analysand achieve the second goal, the internalization by the patient of the technique of self-analyzing. Insight can free the patient from symptoms and inhibitions. The capacity for self-analysis, for autonomously developing further insights, offers the greatest freedom analysis can provide. It is from the implicitly structured deeper messages that the patient learns not only how the analyst views the material, but how the analyst views the analyst's own related conflicts, how the analyst views the analysand–analyst relationship, and most importantly, how a person analyzes.

The Analyst's Slips
—An Addendum to
The Analyst's Words

She was known for her limitless kindness, a woman to whom everyone turned because of her readiness to help, never to refuse. When she came for analysis, she knew how different her public softness was from her private sense of pervasive but shapeless discontent. Quite sophisticated, she spoke from the start of an intellectual knowledge that her tics must be connected to repressed rage. Indeed, with her determined commitment to analyzing, that intellectual knowledge slowly and with difficulty moved to an ever-expanding emotional insight.

In conflict over expressing any of her impulses toward autonomy, she suffered with an underlying fantasy that to have something for herself was to betray others. It was as if there were in the world a finite amount of whatever was good, as if her having more meant someone else's having less (Modell 1965). Her inhibited anger toward others became the leitmotif of our work.

As this theme was repeatedly exposed and explored, first outside the transference and then within, I felt the occasion to interpret, as I had before, what was becoming increasingly clear to both of us. "Here again," I said, "when you have an urge to do it your own way, even start to feel having your own idea, a mind of your own, you feel you are betraying the other person and killing yourself, I mean, the other person."

It was *my* slip that substituted herself for the other as the object of her murderous impulses. We had long ago known that the undoing of herself was *the result* of her pattern, but we had not before directly focused on the self-punishing quality as a derivative wish in its own right. When

I made my slip, I had not been thinkiɩ. consciously of aggression turned against herself.

Hearing my slip, I recognized the vague background of unspoken depression that had never taken full shape as we heard about inhibited anger.

I heard my slip and called her attention to it. She, too, had heard it and felt surprised and initially confused. When I asked about it, she proceeded to speak of fantasies of her own death, fantasies that in the subsequent nights also appeared increasingly in association to and then in the manifest content of her dreams.

My interest now is not in the specifics of her dynamics but rather in the place of my slip of the tongue in our unfolding collaborative inquiry. A model of the analyst's ideal mastery might seem to limit such slips only to parapraxes primarily determined by the analyst's neurotic pressures. Indeed, it is valid to consider that were I not inhibited by a personal conflict, my recognition of this aspect of her psychology that was newer to our attention could have been reflected upon by me and then clearly stated.

The validity of that observation, however, rests in the context of the awesome multiplicity of forces at work during an analysis. So very much presses for expression at once! The effort for technical precision is like the labor of steering while riding on a tidal current. Neurotic transference and countertransference forces are exactly what require good technique; their mastery is the primary aim of analysis.

Yet the goals of expression, exposure, and understanding carry their own forward power for both analyst and analysand. There is no question of an exception to the basic rule of putting it into words. However, issues at times begin to be heard and even understood before they are known to have been heard. In this instance, if it were my own personal repression that had been mainly responsible for my not having addressed more directly the patient's turning her aggression against herself, then it does not seem likely I would have been able to hear and accept consideration of my slip without great resistance.

At times the analyst hears emerging trends unconsciously and preconsciously before turning to them consciously. Any slip of the tongue calls for personal examination. Nevertheless, as Olinick (1980) has noted, often at important moments in analytic progress the analyst's own slips can be heard as expressing themes emerging in the patient, ones that are ready to be noticed but that until then had not been made explicit.

3

The Analyst's Empathy and Pseudo-Empathy

Psychoanalytic technique is a complicated task.
Its tool is the unconscious of the analyst which intuitively
comprehends the unconscious of the patient.
Its aim is to lift this comprehension out of intuition
into scientific clarity. . . . The subject matter, not the
method, of psychoanalysis is irrational.
—FENICHEL

To help a patient know himself or herself, an analyst listens to the patient's words and music, sorts out personal engagement from integration of the patient's messages, and then states back to the patient the understanding that the patient can consider and use toward personal insight. *The engagement of analyst and patient is whole, with interactions going back and forth on all levels in all directions at all times.* Nonetheless, temporary distinguishing of the analyst's receiving, the analyst's personal inner consideration and mastery, and then the analyst's active response facilitates closer examination of the analyst's role in the analytic process.

We are faced with three sets of questions. One is how the analyst knows what to interpret, how the analyst hears messages from the patient that the patient alone cannot hear. This is the question I wish to address in this chapter. Another set of questions involves the problems of how the analyst expresses interpretive feedback to the patient, to which I shall turn in a subsequent chapter on tact. Between the analyst's hearing and the analyst's expression lies the complex inner world of the analyst's own knowledge of psychodynamics and psychopathology as well as the crucial task of the analyst's self-analysis. The essential training and experience leading to an ever-increasing even if ever-insufficient knowledge of psychodynamics are not my present subject. The analyst's self-analysis, on the other hand, is so central to every aspect of the analyst's clinical functioning as to be a part of each clinical issue discussed.

Now, let us turn to the analyst's sensory receptivity, to how the analyst hears that which can then be reflected back to the patient. Freud's radical exposure of the world of the unconscious arose significantly from his close attention to the multiple layers of meanings buried in the words of the patient's free associations. Following from that, the early decades of the century of psychoanalytic work were rich with discoveries primarily resulting from exploring in great depth the multiple levels of meanings revealed in the words and patterns of words patients expressed.

At first slowly, and then almost explosively, attention turned to the subtle interactive psychological engagements between patient and analyst through which significant understandings are communicated behind and beyond manifest words. However, as we address that affective music of interaction, the essential central importance of the patient's free associations should never be thought of as left in the wings. Attention to music alone betrays the patient's truths just as much as does attention to words alone. Understanding requires alert attention to both words and music, even to the interaction between the two.

Growing recognition of the importance of the human field in which the patient's psychology comes to life is an advance that rides on the tide of the zeitgeist. One cannot escape one's times, and our efforts to define and master the concept of empathy take place in a context of historical inevitability. Indeed, the broad theme of reconciling individual identities and needs with group pressures and demands has been in the air for all aspects of Western civilization. In an unfolding beyond self-conscious awareness, psychoanalysis, like other arts and sciences, has naturally expressed its own manifestation of broad historical forces.

Consolidated compromises that were the Victorian world's resolution of many of these individual-in-society conflicts were exploded with Freud's unraveling of his personal unconscious conflicts. Despite his use of Fliess and others, Freud's analysis was primarily a self-analysis. Following naturally from this opening into one person's psychology, the thrust of attention in the first third of the psychoanalytic century was paid to exploring the native qualities of the newly revealed Unconscious. Then, studies in the century's middle third were strongly determined by the recognition that the primitive terrain being explored was controlled by a complex administration (ego psychology), that it could not even be understood outside the context of its influence by and on the rest of the world (object relations).

A one-person theory has been recognized as necessary but insufficient and attention has broadened from focus on symbols and words to efforts to define subtleties of fields of forces in which people in relationships do not have simple, discrete boundaries. The early analyst's clinical question "What do I know that I can interpret?" now requires the additional consideration of "How do I know what I know to interpret?"

The effort to know *how* we know may be new in its prominence, but it is not an entirely new approach. Already in 1915, Freud wrote: "It is a very remarkable thing the *Ucs.* of one human being can react upon that of another, without passing through the *Cs.* This deserves closer investigation ... but, descriptively speaking, the fact is incontestable" (1915a, p. 194). Freud wrote of the mirror and the surgeon as metaphors relevant to analytic technique, yet he was also always keenly sensitive to unspoken emotional communication, even to the point of reflecting on telepathy. (See Pigman [1995] for an incisive and scholarly review of Freud's relation to the concept of empathy.)

ILLUSTRATIONS

The power of the patient's transference and the analyst's own psychology unite to pull the analyst into the impact of the patient's underlying emotions. Thus, all the while listening, the analyst also experiences. To demonstrate the analyst's listening to emotional experience as well as to words, that is, the empathic process as a partial function of the analyst at work, I present three brief clinical vignettes. However, even beyond these instances, all of the clinical episodes mentioned throughout this volume involved my own partial identification with aspects of the patient's unfolding psychology, each coming clear only as sorted out through personal self-analysis. My earlier-cited use of a baseball metaphor and my identification with the man afraid of gaps offer familiar instances of the use of partial identification.

Most often the analyst's psychic work is silent in its development, leaving hidden the activity preceding interpretation. The topographic regression involved, however, may range from covert to manifest. The first incident below is one that will seem familiar to most analysts, serving to reveal a sample of the empathic process working in the silence of the analyst's preconscious activity with very slight regression. The remaining two cases demonstrate ever-increasing degrees of topographic regression by the analyst, the first to the point of conscious affective identification, the second to the point of reverie during the session. Though these may seem more unusual, they still fall within the range of generally successful analyses and are not presented as instances of analytic pathology. The following examples are offered to illustrate, not prove, the basically successful functioning of empathy as a tool for insight.

Case #1

The greatest part of clinical work unfolds within the range of the analyst's quiet, seemingly detached cognitive understanding. I am indebted to Dr. David Raphling for offering this vignette of unusual clarity.

A young woman started an analytic hour ruminating about the analyst's observation during the previous hour that when a man threatened getting too close to her emotionally, she became frightened and attempted to make him lose interest. The woman then began to cry, worrying that if she continued to act this way she would never have a satisfying relationship with a man. She wondered why she acted as she did, why she was afraid of men. Then a dream from the prior night came to mind. She was lying in bed in a bedroom that led into the back yard through a partially open sliding glass door covered by beautiful drapes, also open. She was aroused from sleep by noise and found men loitering outside. Seeing strangers, she wondered whether they were going to break into the house. In her associations to the dream she said that she would be afraid of such openness in her own house, that someone really could break in to rape her, that it was dangerous to live in a crowded city.

The analyst then commented that the patient's arousal reflected her own desires. The danger, he added, was that she could be excited by imagining a man attacking her sexually.

The woman acknowledged the interpretation in an indifferent manner and turned to talking about trivial problems at work. This was followed by her complaints about the troubles she had attempting to get away from work to attend her analytic sessions. Next she insisted that her two morning sessions be changed because she hated getting up so early. Coming to her hours was such a pain that she thought she would quit if the analyst did not change her schedule.

She became silent, and the analyst then said, "You would provoke me so that I would force myself on you like the rapist. The door in the dream opens to the back, back here where I sit." The patient answered by saying that she was afraid she would become too provocative, wondering whether the analyst would ever lose patience with her and really get mad. Her thoughts then went to a childhood memory regarding her observations of a female dog in heat attacked sexually by one male dog after another.

The essential accuracy and usefulness of the analyst's partial interpretation was confirmed by the unfolding of the subsequent analysis of the roots of the passivity, the masochism, the anality, and so on. Our interest here is primarily in *how* the analyst knows what to interpret.

The interpretation of the transference dynamics might seem clearly evident from the manifest material alone. However, as is common, further light is cast by the analyst's self-analysis shortly after the session. Considering the patient's silence after her threat to quit, the analyst recalled a fleeting sense of becoming frustrated and irritated with the patient, a feeling "like shoving an interpretation down her throat." The interpretation next offered was neither shoved nor even charged with aggressive energy. Preconsciously, the analyst had recognized his regressive reaction, understood it, and utilized his new insight in the service of the work.

For many, analytic work may most often flow without this degree of conscious awareness of emotional response by the analyst. But to say that processing goes on out of awareness, as if on automatic pilot, does not mean the processing is not active. Even for those whose style is strongly cognitive, their very logical thinking likely carries with it the useful consequences of underlying feelings within the context of the analyst–patient dyad.

Case #2

The second instance is one in which the course of work was temporarily blocked, only to be reopened by the analyst's understanding, which was gained through a mastered transient identification with one of the patient's important introjects.

The patient was an obsessional young language teacher whose perfectionism blocked him from making important career decisions unless he was 100 percent certain of his wishes. We had done much work that had led to an understanding that his totalism defended against an ambivalence related to old feelings toward his father. These were feelings that had crystallized into an organizing fantasy that for the patient to succeed, to be a man, his father would have to die. However, despite prolonged work, there was no evidence of change in this man's life, no signs of freedom as a result of his having emotionally worked through this constricting conflict.

One day, as the patient seemed caught in a tangle of obsessional associations, my own mind wandered. One thought in my passing fantasies particularly caught my attention: *"I was like that before I died."* It seemed an odd thought to have, but it was not until later that evening that its full impact hit me. At the time, I was not personally depressed nor feeling dead, not especially experiencing concerns of my own with death, loss, or emptiness inside myself. Instead, I realized, I was experiencing an identification with the patient's father imago, an identification I had not before recognized and, therefore, from which I had not yet distinguished myself.

The next day, as the familiar and repetitive context of the hour again arose and as I again felt the impulse to pull away from active engagement with the patient, I once more interpreted the patient's inhibitions as based on his fear that his success would necessitate his father's death. This time, however, I was able to say with more direct clarity that his success in the analysis would necessitate my own death in his life. I added that the fear was a fear of his own wish. And this time the interpretation had a different effect. Instead of responding with more obsessional intellectualizations, the patient burst into tears. An idea I had interpreted before had now been stated with a knowledge from inside the experience rather than academically from outside. The patient moved from obsessing to mourning, going on to work through his childhood ambivalent wishes toward his father.

A patient's working through and an analyst's understanding do not develop from a single interchange. This particular incident demonstrated the relationship of knowledge to timing. I had relatively early formulated the nature of the patient's conflicts, yet it was not until I experienced, understood, and then interpreted that piece of the transference that the work was able to move on. An incident such as this is not a unique moment standing alone out of context, but more likely represents a culmination of very many similar back-and-forth, less evident interchanges in which we together had to work our way toward a level critical for explicit exposure and understanding.

Other aspects of this incident needed to be investigated by me alone, personal questions of why I handled this particular interchange in my own idiosyncratic style. Such questions are inevitable in an analyst's work and are to be treated with genuine and profound respect. However, the seriousness of such personal questions should not be taken to imply a model of the perfect analyst as one with all inner conflicts, inner biases, and characterologic tendencies totally mastered. More mastery is better than less, but perfection is a conceptual ideal, not an aspect of living humanity. Flawless as an analyst might hope to be, the importance of uniting empathic with cognitive sources of knowledge stands clear.

Case #3

This case is yet more marked than the last in that it involves the analyst's transient regression to the point of reverie. Still, the regression was partial, reflected on, and put to clinical use. It is impossible to define precisely how much the regression originated in the pull of the analytic work and how much it was occasioned by my, the analyst's, eccentric personal needs, but in the end the regression was clearly utilized in the service of the analysis. In addition, this interaction demonstrates yet again the impact of the emotional communication of the patient's inner processes on the unconscious of the analyst.

The patient was a Neapolitan beauty, a woman who, when young, had paid a high price for her beauty. From early childhood on she experienced marked sexual overstimulation from men and boys around her, starting with her father. As a result, she lived a life of frantic drivenness, full of urgency but almost devoid of satisfaction.

This woman had a recurrent terrifying fantasy that she would grow bigger and bigger to monstrous proportions. A well-known photograph of an acromegalic giant panicked her, as she feared she too would grow to such freakish proportions. Exploration of this particular terror revealed its links to childhood clitoral masturbation and penis envy (the latter quite a specific and actual fantasy for this woman, not an academic theory). The punishment for masturbating would be to get what she wished—with a vengeance. Just as her masturbation produced clitoral swelling, she feared her clitoris would swell into a penis, her body as a penis equivalent would swell, and her monstrous giantism would be her proper punishment.

The investigation of these issues extended over a period of about three years. There was notable change in her self-image, in her relations to others, and in her capacity to tolerate, master, and integrate her own impulses, yet this change did not become fully clear to me or to us until, in a striking way, I became aware of her readiness to move on to new areas.

One day this woman seemed quite scattered in her associations, once again making it difficult for me to follow her. My mind wandered to the point of reverie, and I had a fantasy that there was a crack in the wall by the picture at the far end of my office. As one might in a dream, I tried to focus all my attention on seeing through to what was beyond the room. Gradually, the room beyond became clear. It was warm, plush, with a rosy glow that seemed to come from a fireplace on the far side of it. Around the fireplace was a group of overstuffed armchairs, all inviting, warm, and receptive. I felt a strong pull to leave my office altogether and to sink into the warm glow of the room beyond.

In retrospect, I was more surprised by the thought that followed, because it seemed a "scientific" association while still in the reverie of the regressive pull. I thought of a paper by Kestenberg (1968), "Outside and Inside, Male and Female." That thought served to alert me. I recognized now that this woman was making a shift from clitoral to vaginal sexual gratification, paralleling a shift in the depth and commitments with which she now could love and hate. It was a shift she had not been able to make in adolescence. Her subsequent work confirmed my new understanding, but the change itself was announced by this particular fantasy.

Once again, there are obvious questions regarding what interfered with my availability to follow the unfolding work by "simple listening," questions that, as always, include the sorting out of self-analytic issues from clinical technical matters. However, while it may be said that it was personal countertransferential distortion that required and shaped this particular circuitous route, it would be fallacious to conclude that a good analysis could and indeed should go without any such detours. I have never known a successful analysis that did not require my ongoing self-analysis.

My central point here lies not in the specific idiosyncrasies of my inner responses, but rather in the use of those responses as an essential source of information about the patient and the unfolding work.

THE EMPATHIC TOOL

Each of these clinical examples demonstrates the presence of unconscious communication within the context of an intimate relationship in which the analyst first was pulled to maintain an emotional connection with the patient while the patient regressed, in which there was then an interference with that personal connection, and in which ultimately the tendency toward an emotional fusion was replaced by a resultant explanatory conscious verbal communication between the two partners now recognized as separate but in contact.

Yet again we note Freud's emphasis on the need for the analyst's evenly suspended attention as a means "to catch the drift of the patient's unconscious with his own unconscious" (1923a,

p. 239). Empathy refers to the process by which the analyst temporarily shares the quality, though not the quantity, of the patient's feelings (Greenson 1960). Empathy arises in the face of felt separation. In order to stay joined with the patient as the patient regresses, the analyst goes along, tolerating a personal, parallel, partial regression, feeling along with the patient what the patient both describes and invokes. Except as personal significant distortions interfere, the analyst's "going along" suspension of disbelief in the patient's blossoming transference is partial, controlled, and reversible, aptly described by Olinick (1980) as "regression in the service of the other" (p. 7). Beyond simple cognitive content information, such a trial identification (Fliess 1942) allows the analyst to approach a knowledge of the processes of the patient's functioning. Clearly, the analysis of the patient requires a spontaneous state of self-analysis for the analyst (Gitelson 1952).

This process of identification is not merely with the patient as narrator but involves the analyst's feeling pulled into identification sometimes with the patient, the patient's feelings and urges, and sometimes with the others in the patient's relationships, those who are the objects of the patient's loves and hates and those who themselves are subjects acting on the patient, whether with love or hate. In part drawing on Deutsch (1926) who had described an analyst's complementary position, Racker (1957) distinguished two broad categories of the analyst's identifications with the patient, concordant and complementary. The concordant identifications are those in which each part of the analyst's personality identifies with the corresponding psychological part of the patient, and the complementary identifications are those in which the analyst identifies with the patient's internal representations of significant others.

While this distinction proves useful for initial examination of an analyst's response to the patient, the actualities of multiple determination leave it inadequate to provide a full examination. Close scrutiny leads to failure of the concordant-complementary split, since subject and object, active and passive, are both present in the unconscious and both readily reversible.

What goes on in the analyst thus becomes a vital part of the primary data the analyst has for understanding what unfolds in the patient. Just as the patient is bound by the basic rule of trying to explore with no exceptions all that comes to mind, so too is the analyst bound by an equivalent rule: the requirement to consider *all* experiences within the analysis for their informational value. While including all personal emotional experiences within the analysis as relevant, the analyst endeavors to sort out that which is informative about the patient and the analytic relationship from that which is mainly informative about the analyst's own self. An analyst's interpretation then represents the final outcome of having heard the patient's words, having scanned and collated the primary data of empathy, and having recognized and mastered the analyst's own regression (Olinick et al. 1973).

General Psychology of the Analyst

To be understood, empathy must be considered within the context of the general psychology of the analyst and then in the specific framework of the analyst's underlying pressures regarding both self and others.

Who the Analyst Is

"Importantly affected by his identity as physician, by his need to be a healer" (McLaughlin 1961, p. 122), the analyst works within a therapeutic context, variously recognized as a diatrophic presence (Spitz 1956), an intention to heal or support the patient (Gitelson 1962), an underlying positive attitude that can be compared to the basic positive transference the patient brings.

In working toward an understanding of who the patient is, the analyst has also some concept of what the patient might become (Loewald 1960). Views of the scope of indications for analysis (Stone 1954) and of possible goals of analysis (Wallerstein 1965) are based on both the theoretic understanding and private personality of the analyst. The analyst's concept of analysis, expectations of the analysand's potential, and indeed the stage of the analyst's own personal and professional life influence the limits of what the analyst can hear.

As has been mentioned, historically, initial attention to countertransference dealt with the concept in a narrow sense, that is, referring to those of the analyst's emotional factors that interfered with the work at hand. Subsequent recognition of the broad implications of the psychology of the analyst at work has brought out important qualifications by which the analyst facilitates the clinical work: underlying functions of intellectually sublimated curiosity, mastered compassion and helpfulness, and an open intrapsychic system of communication (Gitelson 1952). Among the profound characterologic aspects of the analyst, which when tamed can add to integrated work functioning, are such unconscious motivations as infantile rescue fantasies, urges to master objects, pressure to master conflicts on all levels of psychosexual development, pull to regressive symbiosis, scopophilia, and so on.

Self and Object Relationships in the Analyst at Work

Undoubtedly, it was Kohut (1959) who most importantly drew our modern attention to empathy when he defined the analytic process itself as based on and defined by vicarious introspection. Much of the work of the later self psychologists has greatly enriched appreciation of the dynamic interchange in clinical work. Inevitably, enthusiasms have at times led to excesses.

The phrase "empathic response" has gained ready usage to denote the constellation of sensitive and concerned attention to the other person followed by mastered warm, appreciative, responsive behavior. One difficulty with this lumping together of multiple phenomena lies in the consequent tendency to obscure the precision of empathic perception as distinct from the uses to which that perception can be put, as I shall mention in terms of pseudo-empathy. A second problem has arisen from the tendency in clinical discussions for an analyst's emotional warmth to be equated with empathy, when, in fact, warmth and receptivity—like any actions—may be appropriately based on an empathic reading of the patient or may instead be insensitively inappropriate.

Again, to reiterate my earlier discussion, greater clarity comes from dividing this part of the clinical process into its components: "empathy" referring to the specific area of a mode of sensory input, and "tact" referring to those output functions at the motoric end of the work involving the process of interpreting or making other responses. These two components—empathic perception as a sensory input and tact as a motoric form of action, of touching—both derive from the analyst's own underlying conflict in the sphere of object relationships. In this conflict there are pulls for regressive merger of self and object representations, pulls toward reunion and sleep, which have to be integrated with those pressures toward differentiation, such as separation and awakened alertness.

Although there is a regular flow between these pressures in the analyst, technique patterns them into an ordered use. First the analyst's own regressive pulls toward fusion, harking back to an early symbiotic state, are manifest in their aim-inhibited derivative as trial identification, the technical function of empathy. Then the pressures toward individuation and separation are manifest in their derivative technical functions of cognitive mastery and tactful interpretation. The analyst's personal familiarity with inner life is essential to harnessing these forces for the understanding and analysis of the patient's inner experiences with a minimum of distortions.

The restricted mobility, the relaxing quiet, the narrowing of forced attention—these aspects of the analytic situation facilitate partial ego regression in the analyst as well as in the patient. The inner wish to fuse with the analyst's own objects becomes manifest in trial identification. The threatened loss of self leads to movement to a higher level of ego integration, one that attempts to maintain contact while acknowledging essential separateness. The interpretation then invites the patient to join on this more integrated level by collaboratively observing the analyst's message, "No. I am not you, nor am I your ghost. But together the two of us can understand how you and your ghosts came to be as you are."

PSEUDO-EMPATHY

The mind of the analyst at work is a vulnerable tool, an instrument that can easily slip away from the task at hand to work, instead, primarily in the analyst's defense. In order to consider such variations, it is useful to view the empathic function on a continuum of degrees of autonomy from conflict rather than on a simple right-wrong, good-bad, healthy-neurotic dichotomy. This continuum would extend from empathic trial identification with ego mastery to ever more regressed counteridentifications and ultimately primarily eccentric counterresponses.

Working, the analyst makes use of the entire cluster of functions that arise out of the material of underlying motivations, mastered in personal growth and analysis, shaped by training and experience. As the infantile motivation led to the mature aim-inhibited desire and ability to work, so eccentric distortion often represents a regression in the direction of the original work motivation. (Regression in this sense is pathological, in contrast to the nondefensive regression in the service of the work that is part of the empathic capacity.)

A simple, commonplace example may serve as a model of the essential continuity of motivation and work sublimation, with eccentric distortion seen as a step back on that path. A young analyst found himself having difficulty in setting appropriate fees, even in asking to be paid. A patient would withhold regular payment, and the analyst would respond as if only with a sense of sympathy for the patient. He could not allow himself to hear or feel hostility or aggression to himself, putting it aside and hearing only those issues that had to do with the patient's hurting.

An important part of the young analyst's original motivation to become a therapist arose from his wish to heal a depressed mother, a mother whose hurt he experienced himself as having been caused by his own aggression. His therapeutic zeal was tamed as he grew so that he was able to move on to an analyzing position. However, when threatened by the revival of his own primitive guilt, he responded with the reaction formation of accommodating helpfulness. And behind and prior to those acts of helpfulness was the empathic deafness that left him unable to recognize the other's aggression or hostility. They were emotional communications he must have heard unconsciously in order to defend against them, but they were messages he could not allow himself to hear consciously. Here, the pathologic regression follows the line of the underlying work motivation, with the analyst once again fearing his not being a good enough child, his wishing to protect the hurt mother.

There are many forms of distortions that relate specifically to our empathic functions, derivative of motivations arising out of wishes for reunion. Two in particular merit mention because each has at times been reinforced by parochial polemics within historical analytic discourse.

The fear of losing oneself can lead to a perfectionistic rigidity that blocks openness. At times this has led to an inappropriate and disproportionate emphasis on the one-person psychology view of the analytic process, the attempt to eliminate the working of the analyst's mind entirely from the analytic process. A consequent defensive manifestation is that of focusing on content to the exclusion of interactive process, distancing the patient and hiding transference dynamics behind exclusive attention to genetic sources. All then seems safely abstract to the threatened analyst.

An equally destructive defense arises from the analyst's failure to inhibit pressure toward merger of self and other representations, from the analyst's failure to tame inner pressures and needs. Here, the analyst's interest and attention turn so fully to the analyst's part in the intersubjective engagement that the specifics of the patient's dynamics and genetics fade from central importance. At such times, the analyst's honesty becomes a pseudo-honesty, a cover story for the analyst's urgency to express and enact personal needs rather than subjugate them to the immediate professional task. There are many times when it is fitting and appropriate for an analyst to acknowledge a personal part in a clinical interaction. However, exploitative distortion into pseudo-honesty in order to act out the analyst's own personal needs always exposes a defensive empathic deafness, an underlying inability to hear consciously what originates from the patient.

MISUSES OF EMPATHY

Distinguishing the level of empathic reading from the level of active response allows us to notice that not all inappropriate analytic responses necessarily arise from failures of empathy. Each of us knows someone who seems to know just when and how to say precisely the wrong word. Such a person is empathic, however much this empathy is put to the service of neurotic or sadistic needs. To limit empathy to its idealized form ideally applied is tendentious, converting empathy from an operational concept into a shibboleth.

That empathy can be used hatefully is revealed in the sad frequency with which patients come to us suspicious that knowledge of them will be used against them. Demagogues may have a highly developed talent for the reading of others; their empathic understanding is not negated when it is put to the use of their own self-aggrandizement. We are not immune from such maneuvers in clinical work.

I once worked with an artist who suddenly one day announced, to my total surprise, that she had decided to stop our work, that she was giving me two weeks' notice, and that she would not come after that date. It was startling to me, unexpected, coming out of the blue, and I asked what she had in mind, what it was all about, what was going on. I am certain surprise and confusion were audible in my tone. The patient was almost as surprised by my reaction as I had been by her sudden announcement. She said that several years earlier she had told a prior analyst the same thing and that his response was that he was not to be given notice like some maid and that she "could get her fat ass out of there right now." I had not before known how her prior analytic work had ended, but I had had enough experience with other analysands of that same prior analyst to lead me to believe the likely accuracy of her report. That prior analyst's hostile rejection had reenacted for the patient what her history had led her to expect, what her transference had undoubtedly partially provoked. The consequences of the unmastered acting out were very far from helpful.

I could give other instances of analytic sadism that likely were based on the analyst's perceptive reading of the patient's conflicts turned to nontherapeutic use, but it is always too easy to find errors in the work of others rather than in oneself. Over time, I have learned with difficulty, and with shame and guilt, of my own sadistic impulses and behavior. On the whole more neurotic than perverse, more defending than enacting (as I suspect are most analysts), the shame, guilt, and inhibition have been more of a problem for me than has been the destructive acting out. Still, life is always mixed, and I know that my own sadism has been at times manifested with patients in my own way, a way that is most natural to me, that is, with words. When feeling personally threatened, it is too easy for me to become sarcastic, cutting with words. I know I have been so at times with patients.

I think it fair to myself to say that the problem was more evident when I was a beginner, that it now arises less often, and that I more often than not now head it off at the pass, recognizing a sadistic impulse and turning it into a needed personal inner signal, one that can alert me to currents in myself I had earlier not recognized. While with age, if not with experience, the impulse to sarcasm has been attenuated, I always give extra attention to any time a patient speaks of hearing an edge in my voice or words that I had not been aware of hearing myself.

While sadistic behavior is the most dramatic, let us also look at a more modest problematic clinical instance. An analyst may empathically perceive a patient's feeling state and make an active response on the basis of that perception, possibly leading to partial clinical movement. However, if the analyst has a need to hear selectively, such as if the analyst has the need always to see the patient as an innocent victim, never to see the patient as aggressive or hateful except in innocent self-defense, then the patient's perceived feeling state will always be a selective facet, never becoming more fully true to the total psychic state of the patient. This is, of course, equally true in the other direction, if the analyst has a preference for matters of aggression and power and is uncomfortable with matters of closeness, intimacy, and love.

Any tool can be misused as well as profitably used, and the misapplication does not alter the essential validity of the tool. Eternal vigilance really is the price of liberty, and constant self-scrutiny allows the analyst the most that can be gained from the essential analytic tool of empathy. Still, empathy vitalizes, it does not supersede attention to free association. It is by most fully combining attention to both roads to understanding that the analyst has the greatest likelihood of getting ever closer to the truths of the patient's own inner world.

Also, it is good to remember that while empathic perception brings us as close as we can get to a true feeling, we can never have a fully true feeling of what the other experiences because we always process through our own mind and history. Insight is always relative, not perfect; the patient is always an other, not a fully merged part of the self. Communication is not communion. Empathy is valid as a vital and primary source of partial knowledge, not of omniscience.

On "Surmise"

—An Addendum to The Analyst's Empathy

Much psychoanalytic attention has been paid to the question of how the analyst comes to know about the patient that which must be interpreted. Listening to a patient, the analyst forms tentative hypotheses before proceeding. The analyst *surmises* the patient's meanings, testing out those tentative formulations and trying to stay faithful to the patient's import. This need to distinguish what comes from the other from what comes from oneself is so difficult that it is no accident that in everyday conversation the words "imply" and "infer" are so often erroneously interchanged.

Let us look at "surmise," the word we use to speak of inferring or drawing hypotheses on the basis of slight or preliminary evidence. When we surmise, we take hints from what we hear or see or otherwise sense. But it was not always so. "Surmise" comes to us from the French, and before that the Latin. In the French, *sur* is "on," *mise*, the past participle of *mettre*, "to put." Thus, *surmise*, literally, means put onto. Indeed, the intervening old French word was *surmise*, the past participle of *surmettre*, which meant not simply "to put onto" but more specifically "to accuse." It was similar to the Latin from which it in its turn came: *supermittere*, "to throw on."

Therefore, we discover that our word for inferring has developed from our word for implying, in fact from a word even more strong than that, the word for accusing. We may have found a linguistic specimen similar to the law that ontogeny recapitulates phylogeny. Perhaps the development of the word recapitulates psychological development.

With an infant's dawning awareness of others, with infantile reaching out, there is that very early psychological split from the other that led Freud (1915c) to note, "At the very beginning, it seems, the external world, objects, and what is hated are identical" (p. 136). Freud thus described the primitive sense that what is good is on the inside, what is bad is on the outside; this coincides with what Klein later described as the paranoid position.

According to our language, our early way of knowing the other with an awareness of the otherness of the outside was, as Freud suggested, to accuse. Yet with increasing development we become able to do as the colloquial idiom says, to put ourselves into the other's shoes, to size others up for what they, not we, are.

The word surmise reflects our progressive mastery of our self-centered egoism, our ability not simply to accuse or to put what we have onto the other, but to come to a position where we can infer, to come to know from the other.

We cannot simply set aside the psychological history manifest in our language. (As has been noted, language may be structured like the unconscious.) If we try to skip these stages of our own maturation and mastery, if we act as if we could skip this inner growth and discipline of our own, then what confronts us is not *surmettre*, "to put onto," but *surprendre*, using the French word for "to take" rather than "to put." Then the past participle reveals that we were unprepared: instead of *surmise*, we are left with *surprise*.

4

The Analyst's Tact and Pseudo-Tact

Tact consists in knowing how far to go too far.
—Cocteau

Together, analyst and patient construct a unique analytic universe in a manner designed to be maximally shaped by the patient's inner forces and minimally, albeit inevitably partially, by the analyst's. The analyst's neutrality is that attitude that is dedicated to protecting the center-stage positioning of the derivatives of the patient's inner life, dedicated to seeing that the interactive drama serves and aids exposure and exploration of the patient's self.

After considering neutrality we have addressed an analyst's empathy, the perceptive sensitivity with which an analyst hears and reads the patient. A combination of thought and self-analysis are brought to bear—not always consciously—by the analyst who tries to master personal feelings and fantasies elicited and evoked by the patient, all in an effort to augment understanding of the patient. It is then time for the analyst to act and to do so in the way an analyst does best, by speaking to a patient, reporting back the messages and connections heard. We have looked at the variety of forces at play in the analyst's choice of words. Now, let

us focus on the specific issue of technique regarding how the analyst actually addresses the patient.

A patient's sensitivity to hurt is among the most difficult
technical issues confronting us as we ask patients to look at and
reflect on themselves, to question their customary ways of being.
As a result, we are faced with the task of offering observations
that will be insightful yet not too traumatic, of interpreting within
the limits of what the patient can bear.

How can we best get the patient to consider that which is
unpleasant or painful? Historically, we have answered this familiar question theoretically, by saying that we must first address
the resistance, the defensive side of the patient's conflicts. Rely-
ing on a working alliance, we say to the patient, in effect, "You
guard against something because of experiences that have made
it necessary for you to do so. You and I together can try to see
how this has come to be." Thus we invite the patient to effect an
ego split and to join us in a detached observation of inner conflict (Sterba 1934).

However, the subtleties of dealing with narcissism are not
always so simply handled. How much more we ask of a patient
when we ask for a distancing from an experience of gratification
that seems vital to self-respect, that seems essential to the integrity of a sense of self. Then, a patient's distressed reaction can be
both immediately appropriate as well as a result of transference
distortion. Certainly we do not wish to avoid confrontation for
the sake of our own comfort, and equally certainly we do not wish
to provoke gratuitous confrontations to satisfy our own aggression. Yet, we must at times tell a patient things that the patient
does not want to hear. By doing so, we may seem no longer a
helpful other; we ourselves come to be felt as threats. Having to
tell the patient something the patient does not want to hear, we
try to speak in such a manner that our message can be heard, in
such a way that the implication of lack of performance or of felt
belittlement can be integrated without destroying the possibility of further work.

Our own personalities are important determinants of when
we intervene. Our knowledge, our skill, our ability to permit gran-

diosity or devaluation—all influence our comfort in facilitating narcissistic regression and in tolerating the aggression implicit in our interpretive interventions. Whatever way we each may vary, we agree on our model for the manner of intervention: with tact.

In this chapter, I wish to discuss tact in narrow terms as a specific psychoanalytic function. In social and political situations tact is highly valued and can be very useful, despite its being always purposeful, very often self-serving, and at times even grossly exploitative. However, *in psychoanalysis, tact refers to a specific function of the analyst that always has as its goal the ultimate exposure of intrapsychic conflicts and their manifestations in the transference.* Though often present as an analyst's seemingly amorphous background attitude, an analyst's tact is contained by the goals and the limits of the basic psychoanalytic model.

Considered as a function, analytic tact will be defined in terms of process. While a particular statement may be described as tactful, my focus here is on the process leading to such a quality. Tact is a circumscribed analytic technical function dealing with *how* a statement is made, based on an understanding of the patient.

Successfully functioning tact generally is invisible. Aspects come into view mainly at times when tact fails or threatens to fail, when we notice a mistake on our part or when we become concerned with how to pose a difficult statement to a patient.

Highly developed tact is central to the art of analysis, manifest in an experienced clinician's skill in broadening the range accessible to joint therapeutic observation. Here elements of narcissism are interpreted in such a manner of underlying acceptance that the patient not only tolerates the new information but may experience it as enriching.

DEFINITION

Tact is defined as the "ready and delicate sense of what is fitting and proper in dealing with others, so as to avoid giving offense, or win good will; skill or judgment in dealing with men or negotiating difficult or delicate situations; the faculty of saying or doing the right thing at the right time" (*Oxford English Dictionary*).

The employment of tact involves complex interactions among multiple levels in the phenomenologically unitary patient–analyst relationship. Part of the patient may feel narcissistically invested in and vulnerable to the analyst's reaction at the same time that at a deeper level the patient feels an underlying positive basic attachment. At other times, a patient may feel negatively toward the analyst both on more superficial neurotic and on more deep object-related levels, with the patient all the while still feeling a positive attachment to the analytic process. Whatever the level of trust present, it is the security of the willingness of the patient to go on working that permits vulnerability to be tolerated and exposed. On our side, we try to get someone to look along with us at personal narcissism while at the same time trying not to so puncture self-esteem by removing narcissistic gratification that the patient feels devastated and unable to continue. Implicitly we ask a patient to assume an abstinent position vis-à-vis the patient's own self, to forgo customary self-gratification. Such a request can only be made successfully on the basis of the patient's sensing, despite hateful feelings, our willingness to remain in respectful attendance as collaborative work continues.

It is natural to think first of harsh, negative, or aggressive statements when the place of tact comes to mind. However, the need for an appropriately sensitive touch extends to all of an analyst's interventions, including those that address positive as well as negative urges. For instance, obsessional patients often will be familiar with their hostile feelings but much more uncomfortable when confronted by their warm or loving impulses. The need for an analyst's appropriate touch applies whatever the patient's style that is being brought into question.

We ask the patient to tolerate frustration, shame, or other pain that might be felt from exposing frailty and sensitive areas. In return we offer not only hope but also the sustenance of the underlying respect for and gratification from laboring together at a difficult task. Narcissistic defensiveness yields to shared work.

Tact used in this way invites the patient to experience inner conflict and to permit that conflict to become evident in the transference neurosis. Simultaneously, it also allows identification with our style of searching for insight as a means of mastering conflicts. We lay claim to the patient for analysis as we ask the patient to forgo some self-absorption in the service of joint investigation. The pattern is like that of a parent's laying claim to the child. When reacting to a child's unacceptable behavior, a mother or father may say without being demeaning, "*This* is the way *we* do it in *our* family." Here the strengthening of the analytic alliance parallels that of the family alliance.

TACT AND INSIGHT

As a function involving the analyst's activity toward the patient, tact is intimately related to but distinct from another subfunction of the analyst's work ego, empathy. The use of tact is founded on appreciation of the patient's inner workings gained both through cognitive understanding and empathy, the latter involving the analyst's trial identification with the patient. As already described, in the service of gaining knowledge and in an effort to maintain an identificatory link with the patient, the analyst undergoes a partial regression in the service of the other. Responding to this regression as a signal, the analyst integrates the new information, utilizing it as a basis for interpretation.

Tact follows empathy. Empathy is one way we come to know the processes of the patient's mind. Tact is the way we then utilize this information in dealing interpretively with the patient. Empathy might be considered to be on a sensory end of the analyst's functioning as one source of insight. Tact is on the motor end. We learn with empathy and understanding, and we interpret with tact.

Although the question of manners is also at this end of the model of the analyst's work, it is not the same as tact. Styles vary

greatly with individuals and cultures, and an analyst's personal
style becomes part of the baseline of a specific psychoanalytic
situation. There are good analysts whose personal styles may
seem to others to be severely rough yet who function with finely
tuned tactful technique, just as there are very refined analysts
capable of insensitivity and even cruelty. Individuality of style
refers to appropriate baselines of manners, not to an analyst's
subsequent behavioral vicissitudes.

An appreciation of the defensive structure of the patient's
ego bridges issues of timing and tact. Tact is predicated on
understanding, including an empathic alertness to what the
patient can integrate. Interpretations must be made within the
limits of the patient's tolerance, premature interpretations creating stubborn resistances (Loewenstein 1951). Timing and dosage of interpretations are based on cognitive and empathic esti-
mation of how much the patient can take.

The discretion implicit in tact and in proper timing involves
not an avoidance of issues, but rather an appreciation of the order
of unfolding into awareness. For instance, when an obsessional
young male patient tries to prod us into contradicting him, we
may soon recognize the passive homosexual longings behind his
masochism. But no matter how we interpret, tact cannot make
it appropriate to tell something a patient is not yet able to hear.
Unfortunately, complicating this clinically is the analyst's tendency to understimate a patient's strengths.

The goal of tact is to protect and strengthen the other's self-
esteem in such a way that even the self-esteem itself can become
the object of analytic examination. Thus immature narcissism
is made ego-dystonic by valuing the more mature narcissism
achieved in a person's laboring toward introspection and insight
with unrelenting candor.

The use of the function of tact does not imply the magic
power for just the right music or just the right words to overcome
the most obdurate of narcissistic positions. Tact reflects its occurrence in a two-party system: in any duality there are limits to
the range of the "language of love." There may be persons who
cannot respond to the beckoning expressed in the tactful response

however phrased. In addition, there may be idiosyncrasies of idiom that may prove beyond the expectable capabilities of a given analyst.

Still, even apparent tactlessness may be put to good use. Seeming failures of tact are extremely valuable if they are analyzed without masochism and without exhibitionism on the part of the analyst. Also, in the later phases of many analyses, the function of tact does not unfold in a manner that at a conventional first glance would look tactful, but rather in the style of the mutual respect that makes anything but absolute and even brutal honesty unthinkable. Such that may, in fact, signal the ultimate evidence of the functioning of tact.

ORIGINS OF TACT: SEPARATION

The roots of tact can be traced back to early periods of life. Indeed, the origin of the function is reflected in the development of the word. The definition given above is the second one listed by the *Oxford English Dictionary*, which cites 1793 as the earliest example of its use. The first definition given is: "The sense of touch; touch." Traced all the way back to the Latin, the five senses are listed as *"visus, auditus, gustus, odoratus et tactus."* The word is derived from the participle of the Latin *tangere*, to touch.

The issues of narcissism and the roots of tact both arise from the early separation-individuation from the mother–child symbiosis. Primary narcissism refers to that early state. Secondary narcissism is an effort to reestablish the omnipotence of that early union either through the magic of pathology, the adult rationalization of perfectionism, or the sublimation into an ego ideal.

Tact derives from separation experiences. Here the model is literally that of the mother's soothing touch. It extends, of course, beyond touch to all modalities available for the infant's experience of the mothering one in that early phase. In particular, we think of the quality of the analyst's warmth, not the excessive warmth of denied hostility, but the basic readiness of the analyst to be available to understand the patient. The tact of the analyst is a highly refined technical correlate of the physician's historical art of "the laying on of hands."

Tact is one of the integrative functions of the ego. It is based on the mother's acceptance and tolerance of the child's anger and her own sadism as less intense than her basic claim to and bond with the child.

To say that someone "feels hurt" is to refer to a sense of wounded narcissism. The mother–child dyad appears to be experienced originally as a true symbiosis, a unity in which the two parts are as intrinsically integrated as the concave and convex sides of an arc. The gradual differentiation and separation of the mother and child tears at that unity: a rent occurs that is bound to be painful. Though not the only factor in determining outcome, the mother's tolerant response to the child's pulling away is essential for further growth. Her acceptance and appreciation of the child's rejections of her serve as early roots of the analytic function of tact.

Secondary narcissism is a retreat not to the mother, but to a union with an idealized mother imago. Therefore, the mother often experiences its presence in the child as a rejection of her. The child's rejection, aggression, and narcissistic rage must all be dealt with by the mother. In analysis we see the patient's rejection-aggression-hate and we accept it. We may later come to speak to the patient of our own hate (Winnicott 1949), but at first we must accept the destructive in order to allow ourselves and our patients to bring it into view. This acceptance is part of the normal psychology of the analyst, a positive expectation and implicit wish for the patient's growth (Loewald 1960). Thus tact is a technical function deriving from the analyst's care, which itself can be compared as an underlying positive countertransference to the basic positive transference that the patient brings (Greenacre 1954, Stone 1961).

Adequate positive mothering is necessary for the child to bind his own destructive impulses. The harshness of primitive superego precursors can be seen as stemming from the unbound nature of aggression. Our tact lets the patient look at the patient's personal demands, either narcissistic or object-related, id or superego, knowing that the demands will not prove limitless, incapable of being bound.

One particular severely perfectionistic patient had been crippled by a broad range of inhibitions. His analysis revealed pressures arising from his own narcissistic hunger (indeed, his perfectionism served as the adult rationalization of early omnipotence) and ultimately also from the insatiable demands of a malevolent mother introject. One striking point in the course of our work together came when I realized that I was never able to conjure within myself a visual image of how his mother might look. The patient never spoke of his mother's face and, unlike some other patients, never mentioned old photographs. Still, there was one piece of imagery frequently repeated both in the transference and in manifest association to her. Mother "had eyes in the back of her head." This recurrent concept had in it an early view of ominous omniscience. It was never benevolent but always judgmental, critical, and threatening. Sadly but unavoidably, the absence of the friendly face had generalized into an absence of the experience of joy in recognizing the familiar or in being recognized.

Within the conflictual character of his early childhood, there was a weakness of loving mothering available to bind infantile rage. Splitting had been reinforced into the intense ambivalence of the allness (with fantasied perfect idealized union) or nothingness (with the horror of total destruction of inner and outer worlds).

Tact provides the derivative of the mother's smile, of the mother's visual touch. It serves to bind, to integrate, to allow assimilation of new interpretive information, and to permit further opening up. *It is in its ability to expose aggression by implicit holding and containing that the integrative function of tact is mutative.* Again, our very words confirm and make clear what we have worked to know: we describe a person who has benefited from such integrative holding as *intact*, together.

Tact not only follows empathy, it is more complex. Empathy involves a regressive pull in an effort to fuse object and self representations. Tact, in contrast, moves to a higher level of ego functioning by working toward *contact*, that is, union through touching while acknowledging essential separateness. *Tact implies acceptance of differentiation of other and self with mutual respect.* The primitive wish for merger at the start of an analysis matures into a regard for separateness with appreciation of communicative contact by the end of the analysis.

Because of the early nature of matters dealt with in analysis, nonverbal aspects of tact are often more crucial than the verbal. The words matter but the music may matter more. *How* an interpretation is made is at issue. To reiterate an earlier point, analytic neutrality can never mean indifference or disinterest; our underlying acceptance of the patient is vital. This basic positive attitude allows the patient to hear the interpretation that otherwise would be experienced as rejecting. Acceptance implies the analyst's faith in the patient's ultimate understandability.

Thus far tact has been described mainly in terms of what is said. Silence, also, can be tactful. Such silence is not the diplomat's obscuring denial of contradiction or confrontation. Rather it is a silence of acceptance, the patience of waiting or standing by quietly as someone experiences profound affect, be it grief or joy. Silence here is not a separate case or a passive distancing. It is an activity of the analyst, a nonverbal statement of waiting and accepting emotionally. Especially when a person is discovering something painful, it would be wrong to rush into words that which is being felt and pieced together.

ORIGINS OF TACT: LATER STAGES

The basic model described has been that of the loving mother's acceptance of her own frustration of the child and her acceptance of the child's rage so that both narcissism and aggression are tamed.

Later libidinal issues also make a contribution to the development of tact, with the function of tact developed and shaped by contributions in all psychosexual stages. These can be viewed epigenetically, with new experiences added on top of old in relation to the maturation and development of all libidinal drives and object relationships. In each step of progress during life, including adolescent and adult periods, the skill of relating tactfully to others must be enriched and refined. The parent–child interaction during the phase of limit setting around toilet training is a single but obvious example. The possibility of growth and change never ends in life.

An integrated sexual identification also contributes to the development of tact. Beyond the oral level of mothering, femininity itself includes comfort with receptivity. Although male analysts are generally at peace with this part of their feminine identification, they still may be more vulnerable to the old confusion of receptivity with passivity and of passivity with castration.

At times the need to interpret phallic narcissism revives an analyst's own narcissism in regressive reaction to the threat of competition. A comfortable appreciation of the goal of successful analyzing is needed. Narcissistically, this may be made easier by the pleasure of identification with the patient as a growing successful junior; however, even here there is the ever present danger of counteridentification and the development of a private twosome that hides rather than analyzes narcissism. Even a supposedly "unobjectionable" countertransference requires the analyst's self-analytic attention. Analytic tact works to expose and explore, not to obscure.

Mastery of early separation serves as the primary model for the development of tact. Among later factors, the handling of exhibitionism stands out as a secondary model in the genesis of tact. Shame is an emotion shared by each of these levels. On the primary level, shame arises from conflict with the ego ideal, the ego ideal seen as salvaging for the child the lost feelings of omnipotence (Freud 1914), serving as a rescue operation for narcissism (Hartmann and Loewenstein 1962). On a later level, shame is seen as a reaction defending against infantile sexuality, in particular the component instinct of exhibitionism (Freud 1905a).

The goal of analytic tact is not to circumvent or hide shame but rather to permit its analysis. The very experience of being viewed by the analyst may feel disintegrating to a patient with a weak sense of self. Implied in any interpretation is the statement, "I see you, and together we can look at you without adding shame." Some gratification of exhibitionistic urges is probably inevitable, as is some dependency gratification. More painful and therefore more urgent to the patient than such gratification is the narcissistic wound often felt in the realization that the analyst can see something of the patient first, before the patient sees it.

It may well be that while tact is learned, it cannot be taught. We can describe it, but as a basic function related to the taming of instincts, its learning may depend on identification with a suitable model. Professionally, we naturally think first of the importance of the training analyst. The original mothering one was the primary model for tactful sensitivity. Later the father, and still later friends and good teachers (particularly during adolescence), may have gone far in correcting early deficits. But it is in the training analysis that the student analyst has a major opportunity to identify with the use of tact.

In this regard supervisory experiences can also be especially valuable. A young professional person must present work to a relatively senior figure who stands as a partial personification of the younger one's ego ideal. The manner in which the supervisor handles the threatened narcissism of the student may be as important as the academic and technical issues that are taught. Instances in which the mastery of narcissism is avoided by the development of a "mutual appreciation society" result from the avoidance of aggression by the use of pseudo-tact and are always to be regretted.

PSEUDO-TACT

Explaining his success in dealing with Queen Victoria, Disraeli remarked, "I never refuse. I never contradict. I sometimes forget." In the analysis of narcissistic persons there are periods when such a stance may seem necessary as the only one that will permit the work to continue. We are then confronted with the question of what is technically necessary restraint and what instead may be "prudence" in the service of resistance. For no matter the start, all agree that by the end of the work the analyst's position cannot be one of never refusing, never contradicting, sometimes forgetting. Analytic technique was not devised for the protection of the analyst (A. Freud 1954).

As Medlicott (1969) put it,

> Some people mistake weakness for tact. If they are silent when they ought to speak and so feign an agreement they do not feel, they call it being tactful. Cowardice would be a much better name. Tact is an active quality that is not exercised by merely making a dash for cover. Be sure, when you think you are being extremely tactful, that you are not in reality running away from something you ought to face. [p. 626]

Errors in judgment of what the patient can take tend to the side of underestimation of the patient's ego strengths. Analytic tact is not self-defensive but serves to help interpret.

Pseudo-tact on the patient's side is often seen as a resistance of the patient who wants to avoid giving offense. In understanding our patients, we are, of course, concerned with the nature of their object relations, with their awareness of other people's feelings. While, appropriately applied, it is an important aspect of the psychoanalyst's technique, tact is not a function the patient may legitimately use to provide an exception to the need to say whatever comes to mind.

A woman patient, a statuesque beauty, "tactfully" put off for a long time mentioning my being short; she wanted to protect me against feeling a narcissistic wound. Her "tact" was a resistance apart from the reality of my size. She would not have had me notice what she took to be my impotence, defensively projecting her shame in order to avoid noticing her own deeper anguish over her lack of a penis.

A homosexual man "tactfully" avoided noticing derivatives of feminine aspects of my personality, also to spare me the shame he projected onto me. In such instances, pseudo-tact is used as a resistance by the patient, projecting shame in order to guard against the experience of narcissistic wounds.

Pseudo-tact also may be used as a resistance by the analyst. Such an eccentric response is a countertransference resistance designed to avoid the analyst's own sadism. It is often manifest not simply in delicacy, diplomacy, or ingratiation, but more importantly in the avoidance of making transference interpretations. Again it is a fear of giving offense, though here often an indication of the analyst's fear of his own aggression, whether secondary to sadism or to narcissistic rage. One not uncommon manifestation of this arises in a young analyst's difficulty in setting a fee or asking to be paid, such pseudo-tact enacting a fear of personal aggression.

With such resistances there is a regression in the analyst's work motivation. The analyst again may fear not being the good child, with a revival of urgency to rescue the depressive mother. This is commonly experienced, when conscious, as an effort to avoid the patient's rage. Thus pseudo-tact deals with projected rage, some of the reactivation being in response to the analyst's own archaic superego precursors.

The defensive use of tact, that is, of pseudo-tact, dealing with projected shame or projected rage from the analyst confirms the genetic level as that early one when projection is our major defense. At such times the trial identification essential in the functioning of the work ego may shift from a concordant to a complementary mode.

As Racker (1957) noted, "The concordant identification is based on introjection and projection . . . this part of you is I, and . . . this part of me is you. . . . The complementary identifications are produced by the fact that the patient treats the analyst as an internal (projected) object, and in consequence the analyst feels treated as such; that is, he identifies himself with this object" (p. 312).

At such times we may find the appearance of banter, with humor used destructively (Kubie 1971) rather than analytically integrated. Teasing is an activity highly charged with mixed aggressive and sexual investment, and generally it is not an appropriate analytic tool. Yet the process of "teasing something out" may well occur in an aim-inhibited manner, promoting analytic progress by making a point sufficiently dystonic as to bring it into the field of vision of joint observation.

In general, an analyst's failure of tact, the emergence of untamed aggressive impulses, appears as a result of a threat to the analyst's own personal sense of self-integrity. A relevant instance of a parent–child model was presented by a patient who had an opportunity to make manifest the effect of his own splitting. He was the father of twin boys 18 months old. His attitude toward his sons was one of indulgence that went beyond love, but was strikingly based on identification with them. Other than in fantasy, it was only in his relationship with them that he had grand feelings about himself, feeling satisfied, full, and complete.

Customarily, the patient's wife bathed the boys. When for the first time the wife was away, the patient eagerly approached bathing the two children himself. Pleased and proud of himself, he was disconcerted when, bathing the first son, water splashed on the boy's face. The child began to cry but was fairly easily soothed by the still happy father.

With the second son it was different. When his face was splashed and he cried, the father became upset. He wondered whether indeed the splashing were inadvertent or whether instead an unknown sadistic impulse had slipped through. This time around he tried to soothe with inner urgency. The more he tried to calm the child, the more the child screamed until a full-blown temper tantrum developed.

The issue of the handling of our mistakes as analysts has to do with similar attitudes. Competition for narcissistic gratification may be the most common basis for the disruption of the function of tact, interfering with our awareness of the other person's needs. It is the appreciation of our own basic wish for the patient to grow that permits acknowledgment of error and of any implicit sadism without questioning the security of our fundamental trustworthiness.

The later sexual aspects of tact, like those issues of separation and reunion, make their appearance when the function fails
and is reinstinctualized. Resexualization is revealed by the presence of seductiveness in the analyst, a position often present when
we come to think of someone as currently our "favorite patient."
This position may seem comfortable and easy, but it requires
insight and mastery for the analytic process to resume.

When tactfulness is successful, it works silently, autonomously. As such it functions with neutralized energy and tends
not to be observable. Tactlessness arises from regressive rein-
stinctualization of the analyst's functioning.

In order to clarify the process of tact, the extremes of pseudo-
tact and "pure" tact have been defined. In actuality there likely
is a continuum of degrees of neutralization, ranging from the
reaction formation inherent in pseudo-tact to the sublimation
present in tact.

CONCLUSION

In summary, tact has been presented as a specific technical
function of the analyst at work. It refers to a mode of activity that
is mutative by virtue of its integrative nature, binding both narcissism and aggression through underlying maintenance of relatedness and acceptance. It refers to a mode of utilization of knowledge gained both by cognitive understanding and by empathy; it
is directly related to the timing and dosage of interpretations.

Tact represents the technical derivative of the therapeutic
intention of the analyst to facilitate growth. The primary model
of tact is that of good mothering at the time of the child's separation from the original symbiosis. A secondary model of tact is
the parent's handling of the child's sexual exhibitionism with
combined acceptance and limit setting.

Tact is distinguished from pseudo-tact, the latter involving
the protection of the analyst's own narcissism. Reinstinctualized
into seductiveness, this may be used to win the patient's love
rather than to analyze.

Through the use of tact the analyst attempts a reinforcement of mature narcissism implicit in a working analytic alliance so that immature narcissism may be made dystonic and can be observed.

The goal of tact is to protect the other's self-esteem. Tact and analytic progress are mutually interdependent. Interpretations can never be successful if they violate the fundamental integrity of the patient's sense of self, that is, they must not be disintegrative. Nonetheless, the need for tact cannot serve as a rationalization for avoiding difficult interpretations.

IV

MANIFEST
CLINICAL ISSUES

1

The Gift of Laughter: On the Development of a Sense of Humor in Clinical Analysis

He was born with a gift of laughter and a sense that the world was mad.
—SABATINI

In the opening section we considered the dyadic context in which a psychoanalytic struggle toward insight unfolds, turning in the second section to the implications that context holds for an analyst's technique while at work. Now, let us turn from those levels of abstraction to look directly at aspects of clinical practice that could afford us the opportunity to reflect on these matters as actualized in daily work.

Perhaps no area exposes concerns for the presence and importance of an other even while one seems preoccupied with oneself more readily than that of the place of humor in a partnership working toward insight in one of its members. No matter the extent that a patient's humor may serve as an avenue for emotional discharge, just as a dream might; nonetheless the use of humor inevitably implies concern for the effect one has on an other. With that in mind, let us turn now to examine what can be one of the happiest outcomes of analytic work (even if it is rarely an imagined goal at the onset): the development of a sense of humor in an analytic patient.

Sabatini's words above, his opening words describing Scaramouche (1921, p. 3), sketch the portrait of someone we turn to with delight, one enough at peace with himself to keep alive warmth and humor in the face of frustration and pain.

Rare are those who by nature fit Sabatini's description. Yet the capacity for humor linked to wisdom about the world is available in varying degrees to all of us, and one of the special delights of clinical analysis is seeing the liberation and development of such humor in the course of a patient's analytic work. My interest here is in the realization of such a capacity for humor during the course of and through the process of analysis. I shall first try to make clear the nature of that particular developed, perhaps mature, humor that Sabatini described and to which I refer. I shall also address the phrase "the gift of," the implications of the word "gift." I will look at some clinical considerations, a sampling of the range of the development of such a sense of humor in practice. And finally, I will offer some thoughts on the technical questions these matters imply.

THE MATURE SENSE OF HUMOR

The varieties of sense of humor are vast: lesser and greater, drier and broader, sharper and gentler, and so forth. Many sorts of laughter, such as the cruel, the sardonic, and the sadistic, are strongly colored by aggression, while other sorts are markedly charged with sexuality. Such conflictual jokes are familiar in our daily analytic work. They are not, however, what we have in mind when we speak of "the gift of laughter." Rather, we refer to a capacity for sympathetic laughter at oneself and one's place in the world. Humor of this sort does not imply pleasure in pain but reflects a regard for oneself and one's limits despite pain. With such humor there is an acceptance of oneself for what one is, an ease in being amused even if bemused. This humor exposes a mature capacity to acknowledge inner conflict and yet accept oneself with that knowledge, even when it is the knowledge of one's narcissistic limits. Such humor, often linked to an appreciation of irony, requires a self-respecting modesty based on underlying strength and simultaneous recognition of and regard for others.

As I proceed, I shall refer to these specific aspects of what might be called sublimated or instinctually neutralized humor when I speak of the gift of laughter. Such a sense of humor implies sufficient skills of mastery for at least a partial taming of drive urgency, together with a moderation of the narcissistic demands of vanity, a respect for the authenticity of others, and a realization of the grander scale of reality beyond oneself. The quality is of acknowledgment and even acceptance of pain and loss with resignation to depressive hopelessness and hatred.

What I try to define is a *quality* of humor, a way of accepting oneself and the world with neither undue guardedness nor pretentious standing on high places. As with any human functioning, the qualities cannot be known simply from considering manifest behavior. There is no brand of humor or style of wit that in its manifest expression can proclaim itself as integrated and mature. The meanings and the uses of humor within the individual's psychic world, not the outside form, determine the type of humor. Both the appearance and the deeper meanings are always individual and unique.

There likely is a line of development of the sense of humor, one that parallels both psychosexual development and the development of maturity of object relationships. From the child's earliest smile on being satisfied, through sadistic delight in manipulating others, on to the flourishing of pleasure in recognizing the limits of words yet the ability to play with words in riddles and puns, to the aggressive and sexual jokes of adolescence, and so on—the line of development is determined by constitutional drive pressures and by maturing capacity to appreciate otherness, finiteness, and the limits of reality. The adult gift of laughter, as I shall be using the phrase, refers to the relatively mature capacity to acknowledge urges and frustration, hopes and disappointments, with a humor in which bitterness is tamed but not denied.

This is a flower we all recognize on sight even though we have difficulty describing it botanically. Immature and conflictual jokes are familiar to us all. For illustration (and not as a proto-typical model) I offer an example of mature humor. Robert Bak, highly regarded for his analytic skills, was known as a man dedi-cated to the good life. A former analysand of Bak's recalled with warmth a time in his analysis when he had been bemoaning the losses that come with disillusionment. After reviewing them in sad detail, the man had sighed, "There is no Santa Claus." Refer-ring to the then preeminent restaurant in town, Bak answered in a sympathetic tone, "There *is* no Santa Claus . . . but there's al-ways Lutece!"

It is not a perfect world or an ideal world, but we deal with it as best we can and even find delight in that. Such a mature level of delight is the quality now addressed as the gift of laughter.

Freud (1905b) considered jokes at the same early time in his development that he first considered dreams. Later, after he had moved on to appreciation of the structural implications of inner conflict, he returned to take a look at humor (1927). He then addressed the ego's assertion of invulnerability in humor, even while acknowledging the trauma confronting the person. An ex-treme can be seen in the instance of the rogue on the gallows early Monday morning saying, "See how my week begins!" In all uses of humor there is, as Freud (p. 162) said, a "triumph of narcis-sism." Clearly, such an aspect must be present whenever one says, "I can continue to look at myself and the world even in the face of my own destruction." Narcissism itself is at the same time acknowledged and ridiculed with such humor.

Freud (1927) declared that such "triumph of the ego,"

> [one of] the great series of methods which the human mind has constructed in order to evade the compulsion to suffer . . . possesses a dignity . . . by means of which a person refuses to suffer, emphasizes the invincibility of his ego by the real world, victoriously maintains the pleasure principle—and all this, in contrast to other methods having the same purpose, without overstep-ping the bounds of mental health. [p. 163]

Freud made the point that the ability of humor to view danger as tolerable is like that of the parent who reassures the child by saying, "Look! Here is the world, which seems so dangerous! It is nothing but a game for children—just worth making a jest about!" (p. 166). The internalization of such a parental view lies in the superego consoling and protecting the ego, the legacy of benevolent parents.

Roustang (1987) noted that laughter reveals suffering as human, containing the possibility of respect. He linked humor to uncertainty; its toleration, to time and to anguish. "Whereas, according to Kierkegaard, anguish is the kind of freedom which is imposed as an unavoidable possibility, laughter is freedom's possibility to escape from itself" (p. 711).

Chasseguet-Smirgel (1988) addressed humor by considering its links to depression. Agreeing with Kris (1938), she felt that the greatest accomplishment of humor was that of banishing the terror of loss of love. She drew attention to Freud's carrying the roots back to the smile of the "infant at the breast when it is satisfied and satiated and lets go of the breast as it falls asleep" (Freud 1905b, p. 146n2). For Chasseguet-Smirgel (1988), "the humorist is a person trying to be his own loving mother" (p. 205).

THE GIFT OF HUMOR

Discussion of the early good parents reminds us that we have spoken of the *gift* of laughter. For Sabatini, the gift was a God- or nature-given gift, an endowment at birth. Could anyone doubt the existence of a variety of natural endowments, the variable capacities present at birth? It may be too simple even to think of an underlying attribute called a capacity for humor. Rather, an entire range of attributes and functions may have to coalesce to determine both the style and the range of ultimate sensibilities. These attributes include the innate strength of drives, the strength of capacities for self-taming and frustration tolerance, styles of activity/motility, and the capacities for symbol formation and for a range of play with ideas. Yet, as in all other aspects of life, how a natural endowment is realized, indeed whether it even has the opportunity to become actualized, is determined by experience and fate.

Freud (1927), too, called this a gift, "a rare and precious gift" (p. 166). But Freud was emphasizing what was given through experience as the underlying capacities matured and were shaped by the actualities of an individual's life. He thus implied a question that extends to our clinical work: Can this capacity for detached amusement be given by one person to another? In asking this, I do not minimize the individual's constitution. Freud (1927) remarked that "many people are even without the capacity to enjoy humorous pleasure that is presented to them" (p. 166). Perhaps there are some whose humorlessness is beyond repair. Fortunately, clinical analysis most often leads to the appearance of some degree of humor, with endowment and experience uniting for humor to flower.

We are in no position dogmatically to divide this much as constitutional and that much as experiential. Staying respectful of the limits of what is inborn, what is by inheritance given, we still can turn our attention to the more approachable, to what can be changed, that is, how experience can modify the actualization of what is given.

Experience is internalized; the ego grows around precipitates of identifications. A woman known for her wit had a young daughter just learning to speak. The 16-month-old child walked into the living room, bent over, put a piece of bread on her foot, looked up at the adults present, announced "Shoe," and burst out laughing. She not only knew a word and what it represented, but she was able to play with the idea, mocking reality. Hearing the story retold, friends replied, "She comes by it naturally. She has her mother's humor."

No doubt "her mother's humor" includes an inherited constitutional capacity. But equally certain is the importance of identification. We used to speak of primary autonomous spheres of the ego, areas like the capacity for walking and talking, which were thought to develop free of conflict. But no child grows outside the human world, and children walk and talk in the manner of those who raise them. So it seems, too, with humor. A child's humor, or lack of humor, reflects the child's level of development, but it is also expressed in the idiom of the private world in which the child has grown.

Also, it is important to notice that this instance does not seem to be a function of the child's internalizing a comforting mother at a moment of pain. Rather, what has been internalized, what has been identified with, is the way the mother's mind works. The clever little girl has a way of playing with words that is a small replica of the way her mother plays with words. Adding her own talents and freedom, she becomes a new, improved version, not merely a secondhand copy.

The role of identification is sufficiently clear that we even speak of cultural differences in humor, of national styles of humor. We talk of a dry British humor, a pained Jewish gallows humor, an irreverent French humor. (Though unknown to me, theoretically there might even be a Swiss fashion of humor.) Prejudice is present along with generalization when we speak in terms of such large groups, yet the underlying recognition of cultural patterns confirms the role of identification and shared experience in the development of brands of humor.

THE PATIENT'S HUMOR

What does this have to do with clinical analysis? Let us move from vast groups to that small and private two-person group, the clinical analytic dyad. What can an analysis do, what does it do, in terms of the gift of laughter? Might the analytic process not only be a freedom road that liberates from the slavery of inhibition and repetition but also a technique that fosters new ways of viewing oneself, resulting in new uses of humor?

Consideration of the development of a sense of humor during analysis does not suggest that the analytic experience is a laughing matter. Engagement in relentless self-investigation with and before another person demands courage in the face of terrors and uncertainties. Shengold (1981) demonstrated the value of humor even as he emphasized the essentially painful nature of psychoanalytic work. He compared the journey to insight with Freud's tale of a poor man who stowed himself without a ticket on the fast train to Karlsbad. The man was repeatedly caught and repeatedly thrown roughly off the train each time tickets were inspected. At one of the stations near the end of his traumatic trip, he met a friend who asked where he was going. "To Karlsbad," he replied, "if my constitution can stand it."

Moments of humor arise during the analytic journey. When they do, they are as multiply determined as are all other associations: their unconscious and instinctually charged aspects demand analytic attention. However, there are times when the humorous moments appear like unexpected clearings in internal conflicts, moments not mainly defensive but rather exposing new understandings and integrations.

A markedly guarded patient, long crippled by overriding shame, reflected once he was able to view himself more respectfully that he previously "only opened my mouth to change feet." He had been self-deprecating for very long. His new way of expressing his self-observation revealed both pain and respectful sympathy for himself in conflict. His humor, a sign of strength, was a secondary reward from his arduous labor.

There are people whose natural wit becomes inhibited by the development of an acute neurosis, such as depression. Working through the current pathology then exposes a humor already present. Here, analysis does not significantly contribute to developing a capacity for humor. Rather, it clears an interference, exposing what had always been present but temporarily hidden.

Another brief instance was evident in work with a patient who for years had been severely constricted, appearing publicly like a socially proper automaton. After much struggle to understand this quality as it appeared in the transference, she exposed an earlier unseen humor. Begrudgingly acknowledging an interest in our collaborative analytic work, she said, "All right, I'll look at reality, but only as a tourist." A remarkable capacity for subtle wit had been hidden, buried under the rubble of the psychic warfare of her development.

The ability to tolerate uncertainty and ambiguity and the ability to integrate into one's view of oneself and the world the vast mix of contradictory urges, feelings, and ideas are accepted goals of successful character analysis. They are, at the same time, the requisites for the gift of laughter. Mature humor is a reflection of analytic work successfully done.

Before considering the relative impact of the patient's analyzing position, such as the loosening of associations, and of the place of the analyst as a new person in the patient's analyzing experience, let us turn to a few clinical samples, instances intended to be illustrative of a range rather than all-inclusive.

First Illustration—An Initial Unwitting Joke

A first dream of a beginning analytic patient offers a fitting beginning illustration of the development of humor, especially apt because the humor that struck me, as the listener, was at the time of the dream unknown to the patient.

He was a young musician, bright and cultured but something of a snob. Racked by envy and disdain, he was tortured by having a place in his social and professional worlds that was distressingly junior to the position he felt properly his due.

The sense of the dream was of his receiving news of the birth of the son of a colleague. The content of the dream was the name printed on the birth announcement card: Montgomery Fink.

Here were grandeur and abasement, exposed side by side. Although I remained quiet, I remember finding the name then, as now, funny. Pride and humiliation, naked and condensed.

These were the major themes of our subsequent work together. At that first moment I was able to see as humorous what had already been impinging on me in the conflicting currents of the transference. As time went on, and with it very much work, the patient himself came to see many of his own tendencies with increasing acceptance, coming to find his own humor in such circumstances.

This man's dream was at once symptomatic and witty. It was a condensation that was clearly structured like an elegant joke, one that aided the development of distance and increased understanding, an early analytic step in his development of his own mastery and, secondarily, his own sense of humor.

Second Illustration—Freeing of an Already Evident Capacity for Humor

Formal, perfectionistic, rigid obsessional patients often seem humorless, though some reveal a contemptuous sarcasm. Such patients are familiar to us.

There are at times, however, patients who expose from the start a natural humor and wit, but who consider such capacities symptoms rather than strengths.

One young reporter came for analysis paralyzed by indecisiveness. His need for absolutes, his inability to integrate mixed feelings, left him frozen in the face of needed life decisions. It was with embarrassment that his humor was revealed. He felt it to be "silly," the inane humor of a little boy, a humor that showed him as cute but not an adult among adults. At first, the "silly humor" was presented as a symptom to be removed.

As oedipal conflicts were analyzed, as the patient was able to venture beyond his clinging to juniority, was able to be a man among men, he began to value his native wit and whimsy, enjoying rather than squelching them. With his father away at war he had been raised by a mother who did not seem responsive to his budding masculinity. His humor, like his sexuality, were taken as signs of smallness, weakness, qualities to be overcome. Now, feeling more respectful of himself and more secure in the world of adults, he became able to expose his humor in both professional and social circles. He was no longer ashamed of the childlike aspects of his whimsy, and his increased freedom for fantasy allowed him a humor that was often creative.

In this instance, analysis did not so much facilitate the development of an unformed humor; rather, it liberated a sense of humor already substantially developed.

Third Illustration—Growth of Previously Undeveloped Humor

The last patient's humor, though at first defensively devalued, had been present from the start. There are others whose capacities for comfortable humor had never had the freedom to develop, those with depressed characters unable to realize their native humor. What wit that does show through is often bitter. Analysis of the depression, both working through superego pressures and allowing opportunity for mourning when necessary, may reveal an underlying potential for humor atrophied by fixation. With the following woman, the humor that broke through her depression was mainly sadistic. Analysis both helped expose her wit and aided in mastering the conflicts that kept that wit caustic.

A widow of many years consulted me at the time her youngest child was going off to college. She was militantly depressed, convinced she would end up as a bag lady walking the streets. She ate and slept only with great difficulty, was withdrawing from her limited earlier social contacts, and led a life of isolation. She considered killing herself.

As analytic work progressed, first signs of humor had the quality of biting acerbic wit. For instance, she spoke of the House of Ruth (a local charity for abused women) as the House of Medea. As another instance, after mentioning M.A.D.D. (Mothers Against Drunk Driving), she said her own preferred charity was D.A.M., initials she said stood for Mothers Against Dyslexia.

Through analytic work, in which the direct analysis of such humor played only a minor role, her underlying character structure was explored. The youngest child, she had been conceived to cure her mother's depression. The prescription had failed. During childhood she had used a sharp tongue to protect herself against cutthroat competition with two older brothers and also to handle the excitement of overstimulation, her verbal acuity at once both discharging and warding off sexual urges.

She married a controlling and withholding husband who seemed to her to repeat the ungiving qualities of her mother and the stimulating but unavailable aspects of her brothers. When he died young, she gave over her life to raising the three children with whom she was left. She did not become involved with any new men and, by her account, did not masturbate. Despite loneliness and sexual frustration, the years she had her children to herself were generally happy ones.

Sharp-tongued wit was the first face she showed of her humor, but as the analytic work went on the harshness softened. Increasingly, new openings in the work were announced by jokes. When erotic feelings first made their way into the transference, she signaled the fact by telling a joke, the story of two elderly nursing home residents in adjoining wheelchairs. An old woman insisted she could tell an old man's age despite his skepticism. Repeatedly, she challenged him to let her prove her ability. When he finally agreed to let her try, she said she first had to take hold of his penis. After fondling it several minutes, she announced the man was 87 years old. He was astonished by her accuracy and asked how she could tell. "Easy," she answered, "you told me last week."

The humor served to bridge conflicts from displaced areas to the transference; telling the joke had in it the wish to elicit a sexual effect in me. The patient's charged use of humor served as an introduction to and enactment of her sexual and aggressive concerns in the transference. Its analysis made what had been implicit now explicit: whether with me in the transference or with her brothers while growing up, her sexual curiosity and sexual wishes arose in *her*. Sexual urges were her own.

Indeed, the grace with which the patient could use her wit with me was itself seductive. That is, the use of humor, above and beyond the contents of any specific instance, enacted the patient's subtle enticement. Analysis of the sexual nature of the transference, revealed through such humor, exposed underlying sadistic fantasies and impulses, with terrors of helplessness lying behind both.

By the time of termination, the patient not only was no longer depressed but had a broadened social life. She was increasingly known by her friends for her uncommon wit and good humor, which were now generally put to the use of opening herself in life rather than closing herself off. The patient herself, however, knew how easily her humor could fall back to sadistic biting. She came to use that knowledge as a valuable signal for introspection when such regression appeared. Old conflicts no longer interfered with her ability to take and to give pleasure.

The analysis of this woman evidenced the important links between depression and humor focused on by Chasseguet-Smirgel (1988). This woman indeed used humor as a way of becoming her own loving mother.

Fourth Illustration—A Moment of Humor in the Progressive Unfolding of the Transference

The prior clinical example illustrated the broad movement of the patient's sense of humor over the length of an analysis. In this instance I would like to turn to a more narrow movement in the midst of an analysis to demonstrate a shift of identifications in the transference related to the patient's humor.

A 35-year-old writer, whose great social charm was used in the service of intense self-aggrandizing narcissism, came for analysis because of dissatisfaction with his life. After a long period of work it became apparent that he went about his seemingly lighthearted social life in a deadly earnest manner to protect himself against a sense of body fragility that he experienced as dangerously disintegrative.

Early in our work the patient happened across a brief paper I had written defending the therapist's use of humor. As he belittled and resented his father, so he competitively resented my having written, and he belittled my published view as not that of a real or strong analyst. All my efforts to address his narcissism and his competitiveness were long repudiated for implying vulnerability in him or competent strength in me.

Nonetheless, gradually and with undeniable courage, the patient confronted the power of his own vanity. Careful of his appearance, he looked ten years younger than his actual age. Now he admitted that socially he pretended to an age many years younger than he was, trying to cling to an image of idealized youth. By this time, his egotism had given way to recognition of and beginning regard for the otherness of others. Now his charming seductive humor could leave room for early evidences of humor about himself.

During one session he bemoaned the length of analysis and wondered of what use integration would prove to him if it were not obtained until he was 45 years old. Then with a laugh he added, "Because for me, when *I* am 45, I'll actually be 70!" It was apt that his humorous self-observation served to announce his readiness to give up the social facade of eternal youth. This was one of the first times he had been able to laugh at his own foibles.

The complexities of multiple determination make seeming clarities in analysis dangerous. I believe what I have described captures accurately a significant shift in the analysis. However, what serves the resolution of one conflictual level can simultaneously serve the defensive side of a deeper and, one hopes, emerging, conflictual level in the transference. There was a ring of truth in his witty introspection, but there also seemed a beginning effort to identify with me, as in a defensive and detoxifying identification with the aggressor.

The joke expressed both a new insight and a new level of defense. The capacity to look at himself and at his vanities was a major accomplishment for this man. In part, the use of humor manifested an effort to observe himself, perhaps even to identify with my analyzing functions. On the other hand, the process involved a narcissistic bribe to me in order to gain approval and relief from further free association. In the hierarchy of movement in the analytic process, what was worked out on one level served simultaneously to defend against, and thus implicitly expose, what was coming next.

My effort, then, was to respect the genuineness of the self-observation and the creativity of the humor while at the same time questioning the implied appeal for me to like him because he would be, presumably, like me. Attention to the latter proved fruitful, leading to a world of fantasies and memories about the patient's seduction of and by his mother. But the partial mastery evidenced in his half-mocking self-reflection was neither diminished nor undone by the simultaneous effort to turn a partial insight to defensive use.

THE DEVELOPMENT OF HUMOR IN CLINICAL ANALYSIS

The above vignettes have been selected to give a taste of patients' gradual transitions from humorlessness or conflicted humor to more mature senses of humor. Yet the special nature of humor, and particularly the question of "the gift of laughter," may allow us to focus specifically on some aspects of the analytic process. Humor implies in its very nature the presence of an other. Certainly, no drive can exist in actuality outside the context of an implied object; and, just as certainly, no object conceptualization has useful meaningfulness outside the context of drives. The transference presents our model: intrapsychic forces are manifest and open to examination as they become evident in a special and unique dyadic field.

Freud attended from the beginning to both dreams and jokes. Dreams took precedence of attention because they truly seem to offer a "royal road to the unconscious." They seem a very model of intrapsychic processing. Though the significance of dreaming as a form of communication within a transference relationship has been recognized, still dreams maintain their centrality as an inner dynamic whether or not others appear to be immediately involved.

Jokes, a developmentally early level of humor, are different. While wit and mature humor can be private, that is, with oneself as one's own private audience, the origin always implies others. There is an other made to laugh, and private humor has merely developed to the point where parts of oneself can serve as both originator and observer. Unlike dreams, humor cannot be conceived of without uniting both inner forces and intended or imagined impact on others.

Transference is a way of relating: relating as telling, as in associations, and relating as connecting, as in attempting to elicit a feeling or a reaction. The very words used in the talking cure also carry both levels, the content and the emotional action. Humor in the clinical situation inevitably partakes of this double path, the patient's story as a tale told and as an effort to elicit and engage the analyst-other in an enactment. Although in actuality the two are facets of an experiential unity, for convenience we can consider each aspect separately.

The Nature of Words and the Patient's Development of Humor

The analytic situation fosters free association with resulting loosening of rigidities of word meanings and broadening of abilities to play with words. Interpretations open new levels of meaning, extending the previous range of understanding of what was thought and said. Such relaxation of constricted patterns of relating to words, to ideas and fantasies, to reality in general, leads to greater freedom of play of thoughts and feelings and greater ease in seeing both oneself and the world for what they are.

The nature of words as exploited by the nature of analytic listening offers the first push to a developing sense of humor. In listening to both words and music, analysts are particularly alert to the multiple meanings of words. This is no more than another way of saying that they listen for unconscious implications in the manifest messages of patient associations.

As Freud (1905b) made clear in his study of the relation of humor to the unconscious, the experience of humor derives significantly from the economic discharge of tension. We also know that transference is manifest on many levels, not only from past to present and from others to analyst, but centrally within the mind, where transference involves passage of energy from one level to another and from one symbol to another (Loewald 1960). When we hear and interpret any condensation, any displacement, any symbol, we help free energy in the patient's mind.

Words not only make a statement, they also reveal what is hidden behind the statement. The role of metaphor is crucial in clinical communication. The literature is large, but Sharpe (1940) provided an exemplary instance in her attention to biological meanings structured in metaphor. When the analyst hears the implications of puns or of metaphorical meanings of which the patient was not aware and interprets those to the patient, the analyst draws a part of the patient a step away from the experience of the moment into a split position, one of both experiencing and noticing. In making this split (Sterba 1934), patients move to a position of being able to notice conflicts and paradoxes, even ironies. They have the beginning of the ability to laugh at parts of themselves.

Certainly, our common experience is that words give this ability. We groan when we hear simple puns, but the groan, I think, is a sign of great familiarity, even, at times, of affectionate familiarity. The earlier-mentioned little girl who was learning to speak was playing with nascent humor when she recognized that "bread" and "shoe" were different, that the words for those two were not the same as the things spoken of, and that the words could in play be interchanged. The play, the sense of pleasure, comes from the sense of mastery, along with the singular delight that comes from making the unspeakable speakable. As a result, when working analytically, even the most staid analyst with abstinent technique and sober style contributes to patients' developing sense of humor by recognizing the implications of multiple meanings of words, the presence of puns.

The principle of multiple determination has led us to recognize and respect the presence of compromise formation behind any manifest mental function. Freud spoke of "dream work" in his early examination of compromise formation regarding dreams. Paralleling that model, the phrase "word work" has been used above to consider factors involved in the compromise formations behind the choices of words. Increasing understanding of the power and limits of words, strengthened by their being heard by the analyst as tentative associations rather than immutable ultimate facts, leads to the ability to play with words. Toying with the motives behind the compromise formations involved in the processing, the choosing of words, a person is then able to play with words. "Word work" speaks of the compromise formation structured behind words used. As those forces are increasingly recognizable, a person is increasingly able to move to "word play," the economical discharge of mental energy by freer mobility and freer use of words themselves.

The Analyst as an Other in the Analytic Process and the Patient's Development of Humor

As patients learn over time how the analyst's comments reflect an openness of hearing and thinking, they notice new attentiveness to multiple meanings; and when they learn to listen similarly in their own private scanning of their minds, the new looseness and ease of thought can become manifest as a broadening sense of humor. Where beyond the use of words is the analyst in relation to "the gift" of laughter?

A sense of humor, like insight, cannot simply be given. It is not available on prescription. But when transference evocations do not call forth the reaction the patient expected and instead elicit an unexpected reaction such as an interpretation, then the analyst inevitably comes to function as a model for increased freedom for mental play. Thus, the analytic process of transference crystallization and exploration contributes as much as does the structure of words to the capacity for humor.

There are structural similarities between the development from jokes to humor on the one hand and the development of transference in the analytic dyad on the other hand, which may allow each to cast some light on the other. (For this comparison from a different slant, see also Weber 1982.)

Let us first look at jokes. Freud (1905b) emphasized the object relationship implicit in jokes. Focusing on "dirty jokes," he considered their telling to be like the seduction of a woman in the presence of a third person. In this structure he saw the joke teller as a first person with the listener as third. The listener "laughs as though he were the spectator of an act of sexual aggression" (p. 97), the seduced woman serving as absent but implied second person.

The success of such a joke is measured by the listener's reaction, the laughter. Thus, not only are the skill of the telling and the gratification potential of the content essential to the joke's success, the psychology of the listener is also a crucial factor. (That, certainly, is something we all know firsthand, having told jokes with great success to some, only to find the same stories falling flat with others.)

The third person, the listener, must approach the listening from a position of some degree of propriety. He must also be able to share delight in transgressing a prohibition, otherwise he would not find pleasure in the joke. That is to say, he must have a mind that can be both shocked and also illicitly pleased by the urges expressed in the joke. As regards the possible shock, he represents a superego that threatens the joke teller's underlying anxiety, that of unsuccessfully violating taboos. And as regards the possible pleasure, he must have an ego sufficiently integrated to admit to pleasures, even illicit ones, when recognized as "only in a joke," that is, only played in words, not enacted in outer reality.

The teller tells the story and by wit captures the listener into sharing emotionally in the forbidden enactment. When the teller is successful, the listener laughs. In contrast to the joke, mature humor involves taming and internalizing both parts of this process. There is an implicit telling oneself a joke, plus the ability to see the humor in it, whether or not the joke is shared with others.

In the analytic situation patients, the first persons, come to tell the analyst, the third person, about themselves and their relationships with the characters of their life events, the second persons. Simple telling does not an analysis make. Freud remarked that you cannot execute a man by hanging him in effigy; inner conflicts cannot be known and mastered simply by the intellectual discussion of them. If not from the first moment, then very soon the patient works to engage the analyst transferentially, that is, the patient tries to lure the analyst into participating emotionally in the patient's characteristic patterns of relating.

Both joke teller and patient start out as if to offer their listeners the manifest content of stories. And both joke teller and patient work to engage their listeners, trying to draw them actively into the experience of participating and reacting, into sharing forbidden wishes and mutually confirming the badness of authorities feared and flouted.

If the listener is too rigid to tolerate mental play about a taboo, there can be no humorous effect. If the analyst is too rigid to tolerate trial identification, a partial tasting of the patient's processes, similarly there can be no analytic process. Also, if joke listener or analyst is too identified with the views of the tellers, humor and analytic process are lost.

In an analysis, the patient attempts to elicit the supposedly gratifying reaction, akin to the laughter of the person told a joke. It is the frustration of that wish that, in important part, permits further regression and possible insight. Yet, for the sake of understanding, analysts must leave their minds sufficiently open to get the point, to recognize and even feel some of what their patients try to elicit.

As analysts, we put our minds to work in the service of our patients. I repeat for emphasis: our own various conflicts are sufficiently mastered to allow us an integrated functioning in consideration of the reality of the moment, the analytic task with the patient. As the patient begins to regress, we respond with trial identifications as a way of maintaining a connection in the face of psychological separation (Greenson 1960). However, we respond to our personal parallel regression as to a signal, recognizing the separateness of our minds from those of our patients (Olinick et al. 1973). We utilize our understandings of what has occurred within us, both similarities and differences from the patient, as a way of enriching our understanding of what we hear from the patient. Then, no matter the content of our interpretations, our words carry the implicit message, "No, I am not you nor am I your impulses nor am I your ghosts, but as a person who can know the experience of such forces, I can speak of them. Together we can find your urges and your ghosts to be speakable and identifiable. We can give them names." In the process, the patient's pull to shared enactment and the analyst's responsive pressure to merger yield to recognition of essential separateness of the two. Respectful contact across separation replaces frustrated fusion, and the patient (though not he or she alone) is changed in the process. With the successful joke, there is the tale, the invitation to enactment, and the resulting laughter, marking the listener's having been seduced or tricked into sharing the implicit forbidden expression. With the successful analytic moment, the tale and invitation to enactment are sufficiently potent to be experienced by the analyst, but inhibition of enactment permits understanding, interpretation, and insight.

The grand sweep thus summarized takes place on repeated and gradually progressive microscopic levels. This working out and working through with constant sorting out takes place in the confused uncertainties of analytic exploration (an experience belied by the clarity of even the best retrospective case report). It is shared exploration of the dark in many preceding hours that makes the highlights of "good hours" possible. Repeatedly, behind the patient's words the patient acts, exerting a pull to "come along with me, enact with me." Repeatedly, the analyst goes a bit of the way, then steps aside to notice and ultimately to speak of what is going on.

To find a joke funny, the listener must be alert against being taken in and must simultaneously be willing to be taken in. To let the analytic process take hold, we, as analysts, must not only be alert against being taken in; we must also be open enough to be willing in our own privacy to go along emotionally a part of the way. Our fear of enactment cannot be so strong that we hold the line against experiencing emotional engagement. However, rather than offering the patient the comfort of our affective discharge (like the listener's laughter following a joke), we offer understanding. The patient who starts to make a point can thus end by getting the point.

With each small step in and out—experiencing together, observing, and distinguishing—the patient's mind strengthens and eases, allowing more room for looseness and play. In the first illustration above, that of the patient's early dream of a newborn child's being named Montgomery Fink, the patient presented a conflict in neurotic condensation. Coming to the patient's mind as an outside stranger, I first heard the name as a humorous condensation. I laughed to myself when I was with the patient. In the years of our work together, as I joined the patient in a collaborative effort of exploration, for a long time I no longer saw humor in such matters. As the analysis progressed, the patient came to a point where he could accept himself, and himself in his world. Instead of envy and contempt, he came to know humor. There should be no misunderstanding: the price for humor was paid with rage, discomfort, and pain.

As mentioned, the early capacity for jokes develops into the mature internalized sense of humor. This particular shift has a further relevance. In early jokes the teller invites the listener to share an overthrow of the superego. With mature humor, in contrast, taboos and frustrations are observed but dealt with to internal satisfaction. Now, instead of the collusion of an outsider, the speaker turns to an accepting part of the speaker's own self (with or without an other), and finds comfort in the face of pain. Conflictual emotions are tamed. Jokes are steps toward mature humor. They not only express conflictual urges, they also are moments of trial mastery on the road to mature humor.

This developmental shift parallels an analytic shift. Patients present themselves for analysis for the treatment of painful conflicts. However, clinical analysis takes for itself a double goal, the relief of that pain and also the development of the capacity for self-analysis. In analysis one hopes for transfer of the technique so that patients can continue exploration independently.

Mastery through the multiple slight identifications, observations, distinctions, and understandings leads not only to insight but also to a gradual internalization of the analyzing process. As transference is progressively understood and mastered, the patient develops an increasing capacity for self-analysis. As outer jokes grow into inner humor, transference neurosis gives way to self-analytic skill.

The Analyst's Own Sense of Humor and the Patient's Development of Humor

The general question of humor cannot be set aside without at least briefly considering the place of the analyst's own humor in the course of clinical analysis. The thought of one person's exposing a hidden inner world to and with another over years of intimate engagement and finding that other person throughout those years of agony and lightness to seem totally devoid of humor is, at the least, frightening. Yet, with good clinical reasons, including those implied above, the principle of abstinence substantially constricts the appropriateness of the analyst's own direct expression of humor.

What is the role of the analyst's humor? In addition to the factors discussed, can the patient's humor grow by manifest example? Does analysis work in this area exclusively by ego strengthening through insight and the analyzing experience, or are instances of the analyst's own expression of humor, such as that cited in Bak's case, also of value?

If, as seems likely, some degree of the analyst's humor is bound to show through in the course of an analysis, how much of the patient's burgeoning sense of humor is bound to reflect that of the analyst, with unanalyzed or even unanalyzable transferences included? And, as with insight, how much might be colored by identification with the process in the analyst but realized in the patient's own idiosyncratic style?

I do not believe the questions are answerable as posed. Rather, it is more realistic to consider the possible benefits and the dangers inherent when analysts *enact* their own humor. Speech is a form of action, especially powerful in the analytic situation; and humorous speech is emotionally charged and especially potent. The questions for the analyst are the same as they would be for the patient. Why now? What does the particular use of humor mean? What feelings and associations of the analyst are screened from experience by virtue of being discharged into action?

These questions apply to any intervention, and posing them ought not lead to paralysis, a destructive caricature of appropriate abstinence. Yet the questions demand fair consideration. If we use humor to discharge some aspect of our own conflicts, we do not help the development of the patient's insight, mastery, and humor. In that circumstance, we seriously inhibit progress.

Kubie (1971) gave thoughtful and strong warning against the clinician's use of humor, emphasizing especially the aggressive and even sadistic forces often, if not usually, carried by a seemingly funny intervention. As Greenson once remarked, he never said anything clever to a patient that he did not later regret.

Yet acceptance of the need for great caution in approaching the analyst's humor does not imply that all such humor is necessarily technically wrong. Rose (1969) pointed out the model of the Fool as the one who could say to King Lear what Lear could not hear from anyone else. Regardless of how much prior analysis of resistances has been done, some especially painful observations can be made digestible by slight leavening. The caution is that this be in the service of opening, not of enacting and obscuring.

In addition, the analyst's words are always those of an interpretive other, not one who knows the essential truth of the patient's meanings. Thus, a modest humor can mitigate authoritarian tendencies while still striving to keep faith with ruthless candor. Humor is always double-edged in its use. Even seeming modesty, self-deprecating humor, runs the risk of the analyst's warding off emerging negative transferences.

Respecting Kubie's important and accurate caveats, instances of integrated and fitting humor can also be considered. To round out the instances given of the patient's humor, I offer a single example.

> The patient, a 40-year-old professional man, was quite enthusiastic on starting his analytic work. He greatly valued his analysis and me as his analyst. In the early months everything relating to the two of us was seen as good. His wife was for him then the embodiment of evil in the world. During that early period, the patient was pleased by whatever I said, even when I tried to interpret the transferential nature of such idealization.
>
> After some months the patient's delight in me changed to its opposite. Where I had previously been ideal, I now was seen to be seriously flawed in all ways. He now seemed dedicated to the analysis of my defects. Whatever I said, including my efforts to observe the shift, was taken as further evidence of my own character flaws. Any comment I could make was of no avail in getting him to observe himself.
>
> At one point, as he was recounting how seriously limited and disappointing I was, he reflected, "And to think, I used to hang on your every word." I am not now sure whether it was with a laugh or with an exasperated sigh that I spontaneously replied. "And now *I* hang on my every word."

My intervention reflected a moment of my acceptance and acknowledgment of my exasperation, my sense of futility in making contact with the patient's observing capacity in the face of transference conflict. My use of humor stated my acceptance of the limitation of my power to impose observation on his attention, and it did so without anger or accusation aimed at him. It also credited his power to frustrate me. Issues of his power or impotence later proved central in his analytic work. What is noteworthy is that it was with my expression of humor that his passing brief reflectiveness could be extended to a broader reflection of himself in the analytic context. I am not saying that the humor was what made the shift possible for the patient. It certainly exposed my style of coming to grips with my own impotence, whether that sense of impotence arose from my identification with the patient or from my own eccentric difficulties.

My own use of humor was in no way consciously planned or contrived. It happened to be my own style of dealing with an inner conflict within the constraints of the analytic situation. Perhaps the work would have proceeded better had I been able to analyze the personal roots of my frustration so that I could have more steadily interpreted the patient directly. The humor revealed to the patient the fact that I had felt frustrated. Since that exposure was, I believe, substantially devoid of retaliation, it permitted and may even have facilitated the continuation of the work.

There is no perfect, ideal technique. Rather, a tension is always present involving the multiple advantages and disadvantages of any intervention, silence, too, being an active intervention. An analysis is the patient's show, not the analyst's. While the analyst's narcissism and drives must be tamed, it seems unrealistic and even destructive to think an analysis could pass with no aspect of the analyst's humanity ever revealed. Yet, it *is* the patient's show. The manifest analysis of the patient's mind takes place in a matrix of reciprocal self-inquiries (Gardner 1989), but analysis is not a two-person group therapy. Like a very powerful spice, the analyst's humor contributes most when used in exceedingly sparing doses.

More is at stake than the technical principle of abstinence. The principle of the analyst's neutrality is of a broader range than mere technical maneuvers. While the analyst's mind must be open to that of the patient, its clinical use must always be in the service of the patient or else the price is high for both.

Furthermore, we may be experienced by the patient as expressing humor even when we neither intended to do so nor were aware of doing so. Not only the analyst, but the patient, too, listens for multiple meanings. There is more to the patient's mind than merely neurotic distortion, and the patient is able to hear what the analyst says not only with distortion but also with incisive empathic accuracy. Indeed, as an analysis proceeds, that skill is sharpened.

At times an analyst makes a comment, anything from a simple observation to an interpretation, and the patient will laugh, hearing more levels than simply that of which the analyst had been consciously aware. Very often the patient will ascribe conscious intent to the analyst, laughing and asking, "How did you mean that?" Whether noted as such or not, the patient often ascribes humor to the analyst.

The analyst's processing of what goes on takes place unconsciously as well as consciously. The words we use to address the patient, therefore, often carry messages beyond the narrow one immediately intended. The patient, in this instance, is the one to hear the unwitting messages and to move onward as a result. Analytic progress, understanding, mastery, and the growing capacity for humor are contributed to by both parties in the analytic venture.

CLOSING

As analysts we know more of pain and live more with pain than we do with humor. Humor merits recognition, respect, and study. As we respect its development in the patient, we must also be alert to its soothing siren call away from attention to psychic horrors, loss of love and esteem, castration anxiety, death, and nonbeing.

Mature humor offers an opportunity for sustenance and consolation throughout life. Insightful humor not only has its "given" aspects but is itself a gift, a gift the ego gives to itself. It offers self-comfort without denial. Indeed, its mark is precisely its capacity to soothe while at the same time respecting the power of inner conflicts and outer hurts. The facilitating of the development of the patient's capacity for mature humor is one of the happiest and proudest effects of clinical analysis. With humor, as elsewhere, the solitary significance of a person's laboring to self-understanding grows within the sharing of a dyadic universe. And, at the same time, with humor, as elsewhere, the effects of the shared universe of a partnership for insight exist and matter as they are actualized and as they unfold within the privacy of each separate individual.

2

Long and
Interrupted Analyses

Time goes on crutches till love have all his rites.
—SHAKESPEARE

The problem of long analyses is, properly and understandably, of special concern to anyone about to begin treatment. Clinical analysis seems mysterious and uncertain to someone embarking on a personal analytic venture, and the danger of the mystery is compounded by the consulting analyst's inability to state the likely length of the analytic voyage. Stories abound, horror stories often apocryphal, of analyses extending into endless time. Beyond the anticipation of personal unknowns, which demands courage of any new analysand, the existence of analyses that last very many years is of substantial concern not only to prospective patients but to analysts themselves.

Friedman (1994) organized his incisive historical overview of psychoanalysis by defining analysis in terms of the analyst's *attitudes* to the patient and to the analytic task. This vantage proved to be especially fruitful since it took into account both the analyst's practice and theory, including an analyst's unconscious positions as well as conscious principles. Concern with the dyadic context of clinical work makes it valuable to follow that model and question clinical analyses lasting unusually long durations of time from a similar organizing vantage point of the analyst's attitude to the problem.

First, however, we must address the biases and self-interests we bring to the table. Long analyses are of concern to us on many levels, touching questions as broad as our ideals and as specific as our incomes, even as crucial as the very survival of our profession. Therefore, before we narrow our focus down to matters intrinsic to long analyses, it is fitting that we first face the outer pressures and inner predispositions we bring to our topic.

As the exploration of the patient's mind does not exist removed from the clinical context within which it is studied, so too the demands and influences on the analytic partners do not stop at the office walls. Years ago Racker (1968) wrote of the analyst's fantasies about how the way the analyst was working would appear to other analysts. Nowadays, an analyst's worry is not only of the appearance to such projected superego figures but of the appearance to the powers of the actual broad world around. The superego is reinforced by the reality of the general world.

Since its birth, psychoanalysis has repeatedly been declared dead. Ironically, in some ways proclamations of the death of analysis can be a comforting sign that analysis has remained true to itself. There is a historical tension between the demands of the individual and the demands of the group, and psychoanalysis is predicated on respect for the uniqueness of each individual. In the face of intense social upheaval emphasizing the demands of the group, the quiet voice of psychoanalysis finds itself threatened. With Freud, I am confident that the soft voice of reason will not rest without gaining a hearing. Nonetheless, powerful social forces regularly insist that if analysis is not already dead, it *should* be, and long analyses are cited to demonstrate the foolishness of investing in analysis at all.

With the tiger at the gate of analytic practice—indeed, with the tiger often having broken through the gate and having devoured much of the public prestige of psychoanalysis and with it much of the analytic patient population—living in such a world, we all become concerned about public relations. However, our wish to prove our worth to the public, to the government, and to insurers must be recognized for its influence on our thinking. Vital as such concerns are, they must not distort the instrument we wish to protect. Instead, our emotional accommodation or defensiveness must itself be looked at through that very same analytic instrument.

So-called reality is, as always, the best defense and as such it can mask hidden internal personal conflicts. Each of us must examine individually the extent to which valid concerns with our social field rationalize personal biases. Therapeutic zeal and the unmastered guilt from which such zeal grows may combine to evoke disdain when one hears of an analysis lasting very many years.

Over time I have been impressed by the intensity of the reactions long analyses can trigger when mentioned to other colleagues. I have seen usually thoughtful analysts react with an almost reflexive horror when told of an analysis that lasted ten, fifteen, or twenty years. They often took such length to imply at the least stalemate and at the worst exploitation, reacting as if the only real question were whether the practicing analyst were stupid or, instead, a knave.

Interestingly, reports one hears of unusually short analyses do not elicit quite the same emotional reaction, although the same questions are equally appropriate. Prolonged analyses *do* raise questions of "how come?" Concerns of possible stalemates *are* valid. But the emotion of moral indignation and disdain in some analysts when hearing of long analyses conducted by other analysts betrays the active presence of more forces than merely thoughtful analytic curiosity.

Let us, therefore, be suspicious of our own tendencies to defensive or narcissistic moralism. If we approach long analyses with moralistic skepticism, let us also remember Freud's comment that when one is skeptical it is prudent also to be skeptical of one's own skepticism. Let us acknowledge our valid concerns for the future of the field we cherish, but let us set aside for now external political issues.

It was Philip II of Spain who said that undoubtedly the world would be in better shape had *he* been present at the creation. To the extent we can, let us not take at face value those private fantasies that massage our vanity with the secret belief that undoubtedly the analysis at hand would have been shorter had *we* been the analyst.

Let us now approach the questions of unusually long analyses in the frame of mind of analytic inquiry.

GENERAL CONSIDERATIONS REGARDING LONG ANALYSES

The subject of long analyses is as broad as the subject of analysis itself. Therefore, before turning to illustrative case instances, it is appropriate to consider general aspects inherent to all long analyses.

To start, we must remember that in looking at the length of analyses we are seeing manifest behavior, and as with any manifest behavior, the visible functionings arise from a diverse world of hidden meanings. Each analysis is unique. What length of time is fitting and necessary for any particular analysis is a function of that particular patient with that particular analyst at that particular time.

We can find analyses that take long because they need to be long as a result of the patient's character. We can find analyses that drag on because of the analyst's insufficiencies, whether from countertransference interferences or from the inadequacies of contemporary analytic knowledge. These are the troublesome cases of stalemates. But not all long analyses imply stalemates. Some analyses are born long, some achieve longness, and some have longness thrust upon them. We can learn from every case, but no case can set the law explaining all others.

What is it that we mean by "long"? Time, we know, is wondrously relative. A minute is too long for some things and a lifetime too short for others. I recall the story of the dragonfly who late one afternoon said that dragonflies live only twenty-four hours and then added with a sigh, "If only I knew at 9 A.M. what I know now."

How long is too long is relative to how old the field of psychoanalysis is and to how old as individuals we ourselves are—how long our own personal lives and how long our own professional lives have been. Analyses at the start of the century addressed specific symptoms and were measured in months. Decades ago, when I was a beginner, I thought a five-year analysis long. Now that I count among my most successful and satisfying clinical experiences analyses that lasted multiples of that, I find the calendar measurement of little relevance.

Time changes because goals change, and goals have changed because our understanding has grown. We are not so ready to be content with the analysis of circumscribed symptoms as we were before we understood the nature of character structure. This deepening of understanding has produced a clinical problem of modern times not apparent in our early history, a greater concern with how long to continue an analysis.

A patient comes because of pain, because of something that hurts. As the analytic work proceeds, that presenting pain or symptom often eases, and at times does so relatively soon. We are no longer so quick as we might have been in our early days to accept such change as a cure. In the process leading to the respite of symptoms, more pervasive and more subtle constrictions and conflicts are exposed and recognized.

On some occasions, the patient consults us in such distress that, hoping for relief, he accepts our recommendations for analysis. When the pain is lessened, the patient has the right to an informed choice, to reevaluate whether what was originally desired has been gotten and therefore the patient wishes to stop or whether what has already been obtained in the way of insight and mastery leads the patient to want to continue for more.

As analysts, we see the price of neurotic character constrictions and properly interpret resistances. Still, the patient has the right to feel satisfied and to stop without closing off the possibility of the analyst's future availability. The analyst has the paradoxical tasks of serving the patient by actively interpreting the patient's self-limiting defenses and simultaneously respecting the autonomy of the patient, never forgetting that it is the *patient's* analysis, that it is the *patient's* life over which the *patient* has the ultimate responsibility and the last word.

Analysis cannot come in unisize, that marvel of modern marketing where one size fits all. Clothes on a rack are not in themselves too large or too small unless we say for whom. If we are to ask whether an analysis is too large, takes too long, then we must equally ask if it allows too little time either for opening unexplored areas or for working through aspects of already opened areas. The ultimate decision is the patient's. The analyst's obligation is to see that the patient has the opportunity to make the most informed choice possible.

From the dim memory of my early medical training, one basic principle survives across the years. It is that the proper dose of any medicine is *enough*. Enough, and no more. But how much is enough? And enough for whom? If we wonder for an analysis what is long enough, what is too long, then we must ask what it is that we are trying to do. How long a journey should take depends on how far the destination lies. And how is one to decide that?

Consider ourselves. Can there be any analyst who wishes a personal analysis had taken longer? That it accomplished more, all may wish, but that it had taken longer is likely very much less desired. A colleague once jokingly complained that during his analysis his analyst got three tickets for loitering. Yet, can there also be any analyst who has not come face to face with issues later recognized as not adequately confronted and mastered during the formal analysis?

Time from the patient's side implies both the patient's sense of time and the actual time of the patient's phase of life. Emotionally, some patients are always in impulsive rushes while others act as if they have forever in life, with most people combining both approaches. In terms of the patient's life phase, the importance of time is different for a young child, for whom resumption of normal phase development patterns has an urgency that is not the same for those in their forties or fifties.

Yet, while the unconscious is timeless, life is not. Imperative concern for the passage of time must be both relinquished and realistically respected at the same time, despite the logical paradox.

So, in general terms, examination of long analyses implies coming to grips with what is meant by "long" and what is meant by "analysis." As with time, so, too, what analysis means is different for the patient and for the analyst. However, as already noted, the analyst has a professional responsibility. When the analyst recognizes subtle yet pervasive characterologic factors that the patient does not see, the patient taking them for granted as just the way the world is, then it is incumbent upon the analyst to make clear what it is that is seen so that the greater psychoanalytic goal can become genuinely the patient's own.

ILLUSTRATIONS

A Long Analysis Related Primarily to Patient Character Structure

Although there would be no shortage of instances in which I believe that my own unmastered conflicts accounted for clinical delays, for the sake of simplicity in this introductory illustration I have chosen a case in which I think the need for a long duration arose primarily out of the patient's character. This was one analysis in which the patient was troubled by the passage of time, but in which I felt quite clear about the work to be done and consequently very much at ease about my recommendation for continuing across the years. Thus, from the view of my own attitudes, the case presents a baseline, an analysis untroubled by my own anxieties or guilt about keeping the patient too long or about not working well enough with him. Other cases, which I will offer in shorter vignettes, revealed more of my own discomfort over lengthy analyses.

The work with this patient consisted of an interrupted analysis, one moderately long in its own right—over eleven years, but made considerably longer according to the calendar because of an interruption of almost two decades in its middle.

Whenever I hear a case presented, I always wonder why this case was chosen, why not another. I think the reason I found this case more compelling than even longer analyses arose from the coincidence of our terminating at the time I sat to write. No doubt my writing about Mr. A must be part of my own work of letting him go. Yet the question of long analyses implies the question of termination, so the choice seems apt. Whether painting a landscape, writing an essay, educating a child, or analyzing a patient, when to stop is often one of the hardest questions.

Mr. A was referred to me because of acute anxiety shortly after he was graduated from an ivy league college. Uncertain about his plans for the future and frightened when considering any decision, he accepted a position with a government agency and started in analytic work with me. So simple a statement already misleads. Mr. A came for help and would have accepted whatever direction I gave, whether medication or hypnosis or talking. Helping him define his state of feelings, helping him turn an attitude unfamiliar with introspection into one that was self-reflective, was a large part of our beginning work.

It turned out that Mr. A had always been a winner, and indeed an awesome winner. For instance, on his high school varsity baseball team he had been voted the most valuable player, even though he had the lowest batting average of anyone on the team. Everyone knew he was a winner: when time came to apply to colleges, his school counselor told him that despite his average good grades he need apply to only one school because he would certainly be accepted anywhere he chose. I should add that this was not because the family had any special clout. It was part of the establishment but was not of particular prominence or power.

Much of what developed would not surprise you. Since birth, Mr. A had been his mother's special winner, eventually becoming her confidant. When he entered the room, his mother's eyes would shine, at least until she started her later routine of heavy evening drinking. Father was seen as an *almost* successful lawyer, one whose star, somehow, always seemed to be fading.

As the analysis unfolded, with fairly strong and recognizable transference manifestations, the ambivalence of

Mr. A's self-image became clear. He felt himself a natural star and expected to be recognized as such. He imagined that with envy I—whom he initially had privately taken to be gay, weak, and ineffective—used to watch him from my window leaving after sessions, thinking myself fortunate to know him, thinking him the most wonderful and most interesting patient I had ever had the good luck to treat.

However, in contrast, lurking more buried and more agonizing to him, was his sense that behind the marvels of his life was his secret, the terrible deep secret that he had been born with a tiny penis. It was for him a physical actuality that caused great pain as well as the dreadful potential humiliation were the fact to be exposed. He experienced it as a physical not a psychological fact, and it left him privately feeling himself a fraud. He was preoccupied with competition, due always to be the victor but fated always to be secretly terrified.

The analysis progressed in fits and starts as Mr. A increasingly came to recognize the special nature of his relationship to his mother, the seeming collaboration of all three—his mother, his father, and himself—in making a family world in which he was sublime and father was trivial. I followed his lead, and much of our early work focused on his relationship to powerful women.

The combination of the security of the analytic holding environment plus the insight that was achieved led to significant symptomatic improvement. Mr. A became involved with a woman who fit his bill of particulars: she was bright, controlling, powerful, interested in him, and only slightly interested in sexual activity. He felt frustrated but safe. Indeed, he found the frustration exciting and even somewhat satisfying.

However, as the material turned more to male competition, to aggression, to the question of whether I were strong or weak, his anxiety increased. In brief, despite my respectful and even sympathetic but, to me, appropriate interpretations, Mr. A felt the need to run. As he came face to face with the terror of retaliation for oedipal victories over his father, he could not stand the heat. He left analysis and, as I later learned, married his strong woman and left the country for an overseas position.

Our first work had taken about six years. Mr. A had come close to core conflicts, but despite my respect for his defenses, he had to flee. Before he stopped, he and I discussed our differing views of the ending. I respected Mr. A's youth and wish to move on in other areas of his life, but I felt quite comfortable in my opinion that unresolved conflicts would continue to constrict the patient's life, that the price of continuing analysis was likely much less than the price to him of ending. For Mr. A, stopping then left him feeling himself again a winner, though, I then believed, again with the implicit question of fraudulence. I felt he was approaching dangerous territory, land that was frightening but that offered essential gains. He felt that he had gained much and had accomplished all he wanted, and that I was merely caught up with my own perfectionism. So be it. Win some, lose some. Both of us were explicit about our differing views.

Almost twenty years later, Mr. A called to ask whether I would see him for a consultation. Now in his late forties he was suffering from back pain that he thought might be connected to his feeling depressed, and he wondered whether seeing me briefly might help. I recall two particular aspects of that consultation. One was that while he was talking he slipped a candy into his mouth. Thinking he must be quite anxious, I asked if his mouth were dry. "Oh, it's nothing. Just the side effect of the medicine."

When I inquired and then looked surprised on learning that he was taking an antidepressant, he reacted as if he, too, suddenly realized what he had been doing, as if he suddenly realized how much he had been disowning his feelings and trying to handle them as if they were external not-me objects.

The second noteworthy aspect of that first hour back was his revealing that a friend had suggested he call me, that until that suggestion seeing me again had never seemed possible to him. He assumed I would have written him off for having quit, in effect believing that the retaliatory anger he assumed I must have against him would be fatal to our continued relationship. My actual reaction was one of pleasure in seeing him again and a selfish pleasure that I would have the opportunity to know him and work with him at very different points in his life. Indeed, my initial reaction was that this would be a second, a new, analysis, not the continuation of an interrupted work.

Mr. A then entered an analysis that lasted about another five years. As ought not to have surprised me, in some ways he picked up as if our last time together almost twenty years earlier had been only the prior week. In other ways there were important differences, and, I am certain, differences in both of us. Mr. A felt I was much more easy and open, which was undoubtedly generally true. More crucially for Mr. A, the most important change was that his father had died two years earlier.

It is sad to see the peculiar shapes into which we can twist ourselves to avoid recognizing parts of ourselves we ought be able to take for granted. Mr. A had spent much of the time after his father's death taking it in detached stride, albeit with a stride crippled by back pain. He spent much of his first year back on the couch in painful mourning, crying in grief for a father for whom, he was surprised to discover, his heart as well as his back ached.

During the years of analytic interlude, Mr. A had had great professional and financial success, but always as the man in the number two position below a stronger mentor. Despite some spectacular opportunities, he always resisted moving to where he would be the chief, the number one man who would then be vulnerable to the treatment he felt he had given his own father. Also, he thus avoided being forced to reveal his most painful secret, that he really was small. At great personal price he avoided exposing what was hidden, that his penis was actually tiny.

Once again, the analytic work we did—in the context of intense transferential actualizations—would likely seem garden-variety triangular oedipal issues built on the familiar ground of earlier two-person separation experiences and a conflicted sense of gender identity. That it was not unusual does not mean in any way that it was not personally unique, genuine, and intense, leading to great changes and openings for Mr. A.

This time around we came to a point where each of us concluded, separately and together, that it was indeed time to stop. The analysis had lasted well over eleven years of active sessions, but those eleven-plus years spread from the patient's early twenties to his early fifties. Was this a long analysis? How do we measure the time? When Mr. A returned for his second set of sessions, he still felt it had been appropriate for him to have stopped the analysis when he did. By the time of the termination of his analysis, he regretted having interrupted, mourned the losses of what he had missed by spending so much of his life in a repetitive pattern, but accepted that at that earlier time he had not yet been able to proceed.

A Long Analysis Complicated by Analyst's Guilt over Length

Though lengthy, Mr. A's analysis, in retrospect, seems relatively straightforward. While any formal analysis removes one from the routines of life longer than any patient would wish, it also uses less time and explores less than the potential of the analytic tool could offer. The unconscious is timeless, but life, the clock, and the calendar are not. When we give ourselves over to our inner worlds, time flies, yet as Hans Sachs said, having terminated an analysis we find we have scratched the surface of a continent.

With this in mind, having considered long analyses required by some character structures, I turn now to the problem of those long analyses that arise from stalemates, those that continue toward twenty or more years with no end apparent.

One case of my own to which I can refer is one that lasted more than fifteen years of formal analysis, to which years of less intensive consultation were added later. It is the case of Ms. R, a woman already considered in Section II in connection with transference as an original creation. Ms. R, the patient to whom I had peremptorily handed the telephone when the person on the other end did not speak English, was a woman who had survived emotional undermining in her childhood by keeping hidden all evidence that her mind had ideas of its own. Her need not to stir her mother's rage had led to a rare capacity to keep her private mind secret, while her feeling of responsibility for that rage had resulted in a stunning, pervasive sense of guilt. Consequently, as we could understand only in retrospect, the early years of our analytic work dragged on at a snail's pace. Yet what seems most cogent here is that during much of the time with this patient it was *I* who most felt troubled by the passing years. I felt burdened by guilt. I was confused, worried whether I were so interested in this particular patient that I exploited for my own interest and convenience her readiness to accommodate me and stay.

I found myself frequently bringing this issue up to the patient before slowly and finally recognizing that in addition to my own eccentric difficulties my guilt had as part of its source important roots in the patient's transference. Much of what I had felt to be my professional responsibility in watching out for the patient's welfare in the analysis had come, subtly and without my recognition, to manifest the intense denied guilt in the patient's early life.

Ms. R had grown up in the face of what has been called "soul murder," one that went beyond the mother's physical abuse to the more devastating undoing of the patient's sense of authenticity of her self, her right to any mind of her own. The denied guilt of the early family setting, the guilty collaboration of those around who looked the other way when Ms. R was both physically and emotionally abused, and the deeply rooted guilt in the patient's own severely inhibited aggression all combined. But *my* first true realization of them in the shared dynamic processes of the analysis came from struggling with the question of whether *I* was guilty, whether I was hurting the patient by keeping her too long in a possibly stalemated analysis.

In my experience through my own self-analysis and exposure to colleagues I have come to know well, the analyst's basic motivation often relates to pressures to repair maternal loss or depression. As a result, our tendency has been more on the side of neurotic guilt and excess effort to protect the patient than on the side of perverse enactment of exploitation. Certainly both are possible and in varied mixtures. Nonetheless, the guilt an analyst feels when caught in uncommonly long analytic work arises, naturally enough, from both transference and countertransference forces.

Here I would like to digress to make a related point that merits attention in its own right. I want to emphasize strongly a view borne out of long practice that goes against the comfortable delight we all take in the so-called "good hour." Nothing succeeds like success, and we all feel good when analyses go well. We are all human, we all prefer dessert to spinach. Nonetheless, I wish to stress my growing appreciation of what in contrast to the "good hour" might be called the "bad hour." My willingness to continue in long analyses when necessary reflects, in part, my shifting view of what a "good hour" means.

It has been said that an interpretation is a commemorative event. An interpretation permits new unfolding, but it *follows* the hard work that has made it possible. Such is the case with the "good hour." Borrowing Freud's frequent military analogy, I can say that I used to take pleasure in feeling like the general whose contribution led to capturing new territory in order to civilize it. Now, perhaps with the diminishing sense of power associated with age but also with increased experience, I find myself more modest. Rather than with the general, I now feel more identified with the common soldier of World War II, when the infantry slowly and laboriously fought its way across Europe, paying a high price in blood for each new yard gained. The foot soldier's saying then was, "Beyond the river, there's a hill, and beyond the hill, another river."

Wars are won on the ground, a foot at a time, not in the victory parades back at home. *The greatest contribution the analyst can make is in patiently persevering in the clinical psychoanalytic task, undeterred either by the gratifying seductions of seemingly great breakthroughs or by the disheartening discouragements of nagging resistances.*

I once heard a colleague comment that he could analyze anybody in six months but that it often took years to get to those six months. To me it is those years that are the heart of analysis. The credit due the analyst is not that which comes from demonstrating intellectual interpretive virtuosity but that which comes from keeping the faith in the patient's ultimate understandability in the face of frustrating, draining, and corrosive constriction.

But perhaps my fairly clear report of an analysis makes it sound as if, if the work was not simple, at least it was clear all along. That is not true. Whether with my own presentations or with others, no matter the effort to be fair to the clinical work and no matter the talent of the analyst/author, the actual day-to-day clinical struggle never has the clarity of the retrospective writing. For the patient it is not simple to put into words the confusing chaos for which one did not thus far have words. To a lesser extent, the same is true for an analyst at work. I have never lost my suspiciousness of an analyst at work, including myself, who seemed comfortably to understand all that was going on at the moment. Every analysis has, especially in its middle phase, the uncertainty of not knowing where one is going, a feeling that is accentuated in long analyses.

I do not argue for a know-nothing posture nor do I argue against the constant effort to turn what goes on into understanding, to try to help the patient have the words to contain and express what unfolds. But the analyst's confusion in the seeming stalemate of a protracted analysis implies a chronic state of feeling that is present on and off in every authentic analysis.

A Failed Long Analysis

So far the analyses I have presented were, on the whole, successful. Fortunately, that has more often than not been the case. However, more often than not is not the same as always. While failures have been few, they have existed. What is an analyst to do when the work does not seem to move? In the face of an apparent stalemate, the analyst can retire to private self-analytic exploration, make use of a consultant, advise the patient to seek a second opinion, or interrupt the work. I have done them all. I recall one patient in particular with whom I did them all as I worried about the passing months without any emotional movement apparent to me.

In this instance, the patient, a graduate student in mathematics, came regularly, spoke easily, and went through all the analytic routines, but he did so without apparent intensity or attachment. There was not simple obsessional undoing nor were there other clear defenses I could handle analytically. In the only dream recalled, the patient was alone on the top of a tower in a forlorn landscape with no other people around.

I worked hard with this patient, at times even wondering if I were working too hard, if my efforts were a piece of unwitting countertransferential enactment. Whether I were more active or less active seemed to make no difference. The patient came, the patient talked, and still there seemed no emotional engagement, no emotional process unfolding.

I tried hard to confront and master what seemed a hopeless standstill. I wondered about my own contribution, and I did so both privately and then in consultation with others. While I did not tell the patient of the latter, I did discuss with him our mutual concerns about the lack of movement, acknowledging the possibility that I might be contributing significantly to the sense of frustration. I believe I tried everything I could think of, certainly including considering the sense of frustration itself as the crucial manifestation of the transference engagement, with or without my own contribution. Time passed and nothing changed.

After my own consultations with others proved fruitless, I suggested to the patient that he see someone else for consultation while we continued. Perhaps there was simply something in the patient's chemistry that did not click with mine but that would with someone else. He certainly was entitled to get his work done.

After several sessions, the consultant told the patient that what he was doing with me was what, given his history and character, he had to do, that it would be the same with someone other than me, that he might as well continue with me, carrying on the work. The patient and I continued for about another year, again with no apparent change.

The patient's career moved, then, in such a way that it was appropriate for him to transfer to another city. He decided to make that change, and several others at the same time, including such personally significant shifts as shaving off his beard and switching from the use of his first to his middle name. He was determined to become a new man. I learned this later when, by surprising accident, I happened to cross his path at a public event in his new city and he decided to talk with me for a few minutes. As that new man in the new city, he had begun a new analysis with a well-known analyst, one whose work I happen to know and greatly respect. The new analysis, he told me, lasted two years before the new analyst told the patient he was not analyzable and all efforts at formal analysis ended.

Should I have saved the patient time, labor, and money by telling him the same years earlier? *Could* I have told him the same? I have never told an other that that one was unanalyzable, though I have told people that I did not believe they could get their analytic work done with *me*. I have had my own share of failures. I have interrupted what felt like a stalemated analysis with the suggestion that the patient work with someone else, not with me, never assuming that because work did not go well with me it might not succeed better with someone else. I am aware that my continuing hope for the patient at those times implies a sense of limitlessness to the potential powers of psychoanalysis. While in general I accept that analysis is not appropriate for everyone, I always wonder whether further understanding, personal growth, and advances in theory might not make analytic intervention of more use.

In considering long analyses and the analyst's attitude of apt responsibility, one must also recognize the need for the analyst's modesty when feeling it is time to tell a patient that stopping analysis is more appropriate than continuing with more years of work. The analyst's desire to avoid overtreating must be balanced by a caution about colluding in a system that would maintain a patient's constrictions. I believe the patient is entitled to the analyst's absolute candor in spelling out impressions and recommendations. However, as uncomfortable as I may be about long analyses, I am much more uncomfortable about taking a stance that would limit someone else's potential.

If all I have said seems ambiguous or insufficiently clear, of this I feel certain. Life is not general, it is specific. What always matters is each specific person in unique individuality. My own view is that this is the ultimate context in which the length or the brevity of any analysis must be placed. Just as the individual patient's uniqueness must always be respected, the uniqueness of the analytic match, the pairing of the two idiosyncratic partners, must also be respected, and conclusions come to about another person's life must always be offered with modesty and a certain tentativeness.

ENVOY

A few words must be added in closing. I have taken a segment of our large subject hoping to suggest some of the broad implications of the topic. Clearly, I believe the analyst must feel free to work with a patient in an analysis as long as that patient requires. Still, the implicit difficult question remains of when to stop.

In considering the analyst's own attitudes about long analyses, I have emphasized the need for the analyst not to accept guilt at face level, respecting the value of continuing. However, with the intention not of negating what I have said but of complicating it, I would like to end with a brief statement in support of closure, even when it may seem that more can be gained by continuing formal analytic work. Some things that cannot be accomplished with someone else can be accomplished and realized alone.

In his paper on transience, Freud (1916) noted that acceptance of death and decay was felt by some to negate the value of beauty. He added that the ultimate return of spring after winter led one to be able to accept personal transience while maintaining appreciation of beauty and values arising from recognition of long-term growth beyond one's own existence.

For the analyst to act as if he could always be available, forever there, denies the patient the opportunity to deal with the reality of termination, the realities of death and of loss. There is some analytic work the patient can only do alone, after the analysis has ended. Appropriate as they are at times, long analyses ought not be used as collusive efforts to deny the limitations of ourselves and of what analysis can alter, and in a sense to enact the implication of the magical power of analysis and fantasy over termination and death.

I stop while knowing that what I have said is a fragment, interrupted rather than completed. Every focused discussion—inside a clinical analysis or out—is always only a part of the infinitely complex universe of phenomenological reality. As much as we seek principles related to long analyses, we must recall that what we find are not ultimate laws of science or nature but are the principles we can put to use to try to expand our understandings as we move from one unique particular analytic experience to another.

3

Pilgrimage:
The Place of Action in
Extending Insight

And smale foweles maken melodye
That slepen al the nyght with open ye
(So priketh hem nature in hir corages);
Thanne longen folk to goon on pilgrimages.
—CHAUCER

People grow in many ways, using an endless variety of experiences for learning and self-mastery. Although nothing has yet been devised to challenge the specificity of psychoanalysis for helping one master fixations that inhibit continued growth, for working toward insight, it is fitting to remember that formal analysis is not the sole route to emotional self-knowledge and personal integration.

The personal pilgrimage in its modern secular form represents a pattern of action that also can serve as an organizer for resolving conflict and for psychic growth. Although action has frequently been thought of in its destructive face of acting out—removing urges from examination by discharging them—action can also represent efforts to expose and explore internal conflicts, aiding in their mastery by catalyzing working out and consolidation, or working through. As a search made manifest, the personal pilgrimage is particularly valuable in the task of mastering inner struggles resulting from identifications passed down through generations. I turn to such pilgrimages now in order to examine an instance of growth toward and with insight outside of the usual clinical setting.

The importance of pilgrimages is evidenced by the pervasiveness of the phenomenon throughout history and among a wide range of cultures. While I shall focus on a contemporary secular form, it is worth first noting the phenomenon's general background.

A pilgrimage has been defined as "a journey to some distant place, sacred and venerable for some reason, undertaken for devotional purposes" (Webster's *New Twentieth Century Dictionary of the English Language*). In addition to travels religious in nature, the pilgrimage has referred to any major journey in life, extending even to the journey of life itself from birth to death. Psychoanalysis, too, is at times experienced by patients as a pilgrimage, with symbolic references to journeys, trips, and expeditions common in dreams and free associations.

The ancient Greeks made pilgrimages to Eleusis and Delphi, the Indians to Benares and the Ganges, the Chinese to Mount Tai, the Japanese to Uji-yamada Taisha. In more recent Western civilization, Jews made an annual pilgrimage to Jerusalem at the time of Passover, with the journey to modern Jerusalem and Israel distinguished by a special name, *aliya*, a going up. Christian pilgrimages to holy places, immortalized by Chaucer in his *Canterbury Tales*, reached a peak during the time of the crusades, and since 1800 popes have continued to name special years as holy years for pilgrimages to Rome. To Moslems, a pilgrimage to Mecca represents the consummate life goal; they even adopt a new title, *haji*, in recognition of completion of the trip. Such a brief sampling in no way exhausts the list; rather, it hints at the ubiquity of the occurrence.

Certain characteristics are common to all pilgrimages. The pilgrimage is a journey that is difficult, demanding work and sacrifice, and usually covering long distances. It often has a religious context, its goal an act of devotion, a forgiveness of sins, or a personal change to a new level of integrity, whether a higher level of self-integration or even a new specifically physical body integration, as in the curing of a disease. The outcome is a shift in the sense of one's self, at times in relation to unassimilated introjects, at times in the strengthened relation of the ego to the superego.

My focus here is on the role of action in the struggle to integrate previously unmastered identifications—to assimilate them into one's sense of self. There is simultaneously an effort to establish one's self as an individual and to fit one's self into a continuity of generations, an effort to master unconscious identifications and conflicts. The child completes the work of mastery that the parent had not achieved, thus making the continuity from one generation to another more conflict-free.

The pilgrimages I am considering here are made to sites of special traditional importance. I do not have in mind travel undertaken while one is a patient in analysis or journeys to the scenes of one's childhood. The latter are familiar enough both during and apart from analysis and have been well described by Novey (1968) in *The Second Look*. I am referring to those difficult journeys some people take in the face of inner resistance to sites of importance in the historic tradition of the individual in an effort to master internal conflicts, including generational conflicts acquired by identification.

ILLUSTRATIONS

Ben

When the time came to arrange for his oldest son's bar mitzvah, Ben was already well established in a successful law firm. The anticipated event, however, revived issues that had last been active during Ben's analysis several years earlier. At that time he had shown marked anxiety over success, an anxiety found to be related to his early ambivalence regarding his now long-dead father. This time, however, the stress of dealing with the implications of a developmental change in his son led Ben to confront old issues revived at a time when his formal analysis and analyst were no longer on the scene.

In the face of renewed anxiety and in response to social pressures, Ben made a decision that was at once both defensively determined and creative. Rather than arrange the expected bar mitzvah party for the extended family, Ben decided to take his son and immediate family to celebrate the bar mitzvah in Israel. He went on a pilgrimage.

To many at the time, the journey seemed an act of defiance, a turning away from family attachments at a time when greater family closeness seemed called for. However, on closer examination, Ben recognized that this outer defiance covered over an inner attitude of submission. Ben's father had once said that he considered the most important event of his lifetime—other than the births of his children—to be the reestablishment of Israel. Now Ben offered his son's bar mitzvah as a tribute to the father. In this act, it was as if Ben were assuring the internalized father that he was not overthrowing him but rather symbolically was letting grandfather be father to the young boy. Thus Ben acted as if removing himself from competition with each of the other generations.

The trip's importance for dealing with revived oedipal conflicts was underscored by the emergence of a forgotten memory of Ben's own bar mitzvah. A few months before that event, the father of one of Ben's friends died abruptly in the midst of the friend's bar mitzvah. As a lad, Ben was terrified lest the same thing happen to his own father. Now Ben feared for himself. An important factor for the decision to go to Israel, to offer son to father, was the presence of the fear of retaliation, the fear that the son's growth now threatened Ben's own life.

The journey served another purpose beyond the defensive avoidance of competition growing out of a positive oedipal complex. Ben also idealized his father and longed to be accepted and loved by him. The submission to and identification with father's values, which was implicit in the trip, expressed the longing for approval and love from the good father.

As the time for departure approached, Ben became increasingly anxious, rationalizing his fears in terms of external dangers and expenses. Another aspect of his motivation then became clear. A terror, mixed with fascination, gripped him as if he was about to approach a forbidden scene. Although he recognized that early primal-scene fantasies were being awakened, Ben nevertheless still felt unsatisfied with his understanding of his wish to make pilgrimage.

On arrival in Jerusalem, he had difficulty expressing his feelings, using words like "uncanny" and "magical," but admitting that they were inadequate. Though others on the trip described him at the time as seeming happier than they had ever known him to be, he did not appear manic, driven, or expansive. He was content. The Israeli landscape held a particular fascination for him. The sight of the domed yellow stone buildings of Jerusalem left him feeling suffused with a warm delight he could not explain. In a postcard to a friend at home, he described his Jerusalem hotel as having "a room with a déjà view."

Ben could not explain one further observation. He was extremely moved by hearing Hebrew spoken in the native sections of town, particularly by children at play and women shopping. Because the Hebrew he had heard at religious services during childhood had a very different sound, Sephardic Hebrew as a spoken language was strange to him. Yet it sounded uncannily familiar.

When the journey was over, Ben noticed that his emotional tie to Israel felt stronger and less defensive. He was less argumentative though no less firm in his views when Middle East politics were discussed. His inner relation to his father changed. Deaths within his social circle no longer elicited unsettling dreams of his dead father. Indeed, there seemed to be as great a change as had occurred years earlier during his formal analysis. Father was less idealized and

more respected. Ben's own sense of self-knowledge was more
solid; he felt and seemed less provocative, less compliant,
more sturdy.

Ben's understanding of the changes evoked by his trip
focused mainly on his father. He felt he had concluded,
through his journey, an unfulfilled task of his father. In
actuality, the father had been a man of modest success, but
one who never felt he had lived up to the standards of his
own father. Ben's grandfather had been a businessman of
achievement within his community, but haughty, arrogant,
and demanding. The father's idealization of the grandfather
had left the father feeling inadequate, never quite successful.

Israel symbolized the father's greatest ideals. In making the pilgrimage, Ben felt he worked through conflicts
passed to him from previous generations. He felt he also
achieved a solution that freed him from demands passed
through the generations. That is, in a creative manner, by
joining with his son and making an *aliya*, a going up to
Israel, Ben felt he symbolically satisfied a central one of his
father's unmastered conflicts and did so in a way that integrated continuity among generations. Ben thus felt that he
had worked through oedipal issues for himself without alien-
ating himself defensively from his heritage.

Ben had not given any attention to early preoedipal
issues when he considered the trip. Nor had he discussed
concerns about his mother and issues of reunion with the
good mother. He noticed his fascination with the Israeli
landscape and the sounds of Hebrew speech, but he
had no explanation for the depth of his feelings in these
areas.

His son's coming of age reawakened in Ben multiple
conflicts from his own earlier developmental levels, the son's
bar mitzvah primarily reviving oedipal issues that previously
had settled into stable personal compromises. Now, however, Ben was able to face the reappearance of old father–
son conflicts with the greater inner resources of a maturity
enhanced by a capacity for self-analysis that grew out of

prior formal analysis. The personal pilgrimage provided Ben the context of a journey he was able to utilize as he had his earlier psychoanalytic journey for the sake of insight and self-mastery.

Michael Arlen

An uncommonly detailed and revealing account of the inner movement that may accompany a pilgrimage is provided by Michael Arlen in his sensitive memoir *Passage to Ararat* (1975). In this touching and beautifully crafted volume, Arlen traces his personal search for the meaning of Armenian experiences, his journey serving as the context for the unfolding of familial conflicts over Armenian identity as they continued to be alive in his own buried internal conflicts.

As he studied and learned of the history of Armenia, of the Armenian people, Arlen also learned of himself. To exemplify the way in which outer pilgrimages may serve inner journeys of self-enlightenment, I have abstracted highlights of the personal parts of Arlen's account.

Although Arlen's father was Armenian, he worked hard to maintain first an English and later an American identity. He came to live as if he had no connection with Armenia. Even the language was erased: at least at home, where the growing son could observe, the father never spoke Armenian.

Arlen had not realized that he himself was in any way Armenian until he was 9. He and his family thought of themselves as English and spoke only English. Confronted by prejudices at school, the young boy became aware of a shadowy sense of being connected with Armenians, a sense that seemed reinforced by his father's determination to go beyond any such identity. When young Arlen asked his mother whether they were Armenian, she replied, "Of course not. . . . Your father's family have Armenian blood, but he is English and so are you" (p. 6).

As a boy, however, young Arlen had little curiosity about his Armenian background. On the whole he felt it to be bad, somehow frightening. He knew he loved his father, but despite that love, he also knew he hated his father, blaming him for the subtle background fear he felt.

Arlen was in his twenties when his father died. Partially in deference to the mother's Greek background, the funeral was held in a Greek Orthodox rather than an Armenian church. As mother said of the father, "All his life, he wanted to be free of the Armenians" (p. 12).

Arlen was aware of feeling a mixture of relief and longing for the lost father. Like his father, Arlen became a writer, though working in a different genre. Where the father had been a leading novelist, Arlen became, primarily, a successful cultural critic and essayist. In the years after his father's death, Arlen dreamed of a recurrent theme. "Sometimes he [Father] called to me and I couldn't hear what he was saying. Sometimes he merely stood apart—a solitary and somehow disapproving figure. We were still strangers" (p. 12).

Shortly after he turned 40, long after his mother, too, was dead, Arlen was invited to address an Armenian group. By that time he felt his own identity as an American to be well established: his wife was American, his children were American, his life and his career were American. Yet a confrontation with a group of Armenians nineteen years after his father's death triggered the forces that ultimately led to the pilgrimage.

Arlen felt simultaneous curiosity, attraction, and repulsion about a group that seemed both familiar and strange. The more he investigated, the more he became aware of a keen ambivalence. He felt himself disliking much about the Armenians and wishing strongly to repudiate any connection with them. What troubled him most was the characterization of Armenians as passive, sufferers in a victim role. At first he was able to allow himself to be close only to active, successful Armenians. "I know that somewhere there exists a different type of Armenian, a prosperous, vigorous, robust type of Armenian, who does not live in dark rooms and weep about the past" (p. 24).

He read what he could of Armenian history but found himself comfortable only in the context of aggressive Armenian heroes. One in particular had the same name as his father. The sense of passivity and weakness he had resented in his father was opened for reconsideration. "Tigran smiling from the turret of a tank! Tigran among the nightingales!" (p. 40). In the context of strength and tenderness, there was a hint of the possibility of father as not just literary, not just effete, not just gentle.

The first stage of the journey was in the reading; the second was in a trip to Fresno to see an Armenian colony. Curiosity fused with the apparent wish to find Armenians to be strong and not weak, a wish to learn more of what father was actually like. But this trip was inadequate to satisfy his curiosity, to help him to master his ambivalence. The need to travel to the source was clear.

On the night before Arlen embarked on his pilgrimage, his trip to Armenia, he dreamed he was a child traveling with his father to an isolated airport. In the dream father climbed the steps to the doorway of a lonely large plane and motioned for the son to follow. As the son reached the top step, father entered the plane. Standing on the step, the son put his head inside to see only empty darkness.

Arlen woke and thought he saw his father's face looking at him. He then realized it was his own face, a mirror reflection of himself. Both his fusion with father and his loss—his separation from his father—were evident as he departed on his journey.

Unlike Ben who had found himself so moved on arrival in his familial homeland, Arlen felt repelled. He did the usual sight-seeing and tried to make contact with native Armenians, but it was as if he were frozen. He withdrew to his room, surrounding himself with Armenian books. Again he seemed to struggle against an identification with Armenia, against an Armenia seen as weak and passive, against an Armenian heritage that his father, too, had tried to renounce.

Once more the highlights of his readings were those sections that revealed Armenians of strength, the powerful fathers, "these terrible Armenians" (p. 77). His dreams now had at their center a dread of being lost, combined with a persistent search. The anxiety in these dreams was of a feeling of being kept away or kept apart. As he read, he struggled inwardly in his self-analysis. Long-buried feelings came to the surface: first a shame, then an anger. He realized the extent to which he had always hated being an Armenian, and for this he blamed his father. Though he remembered as a child resenting his father for being too authoritarian, he now felt betrayed by a father who gave him over to European values, to European hate of Armenians.

Where Ben had had a self-analytic capacity resulting from his prior formal analysis, Arlen had the benefit of a personal, newfound friend, a local Armenian who served as a personal guide and secret sharer. As Arlen struggled, he was accompanied by Sarkis, a sympathetic other who maintained a respectful understanding of a fellow Armenian's turmoil. It was Sarkis who offered the needed interpretations that lighted Arlen's path toward insight, and in particular the recognition that Arlen's battle with Armenia and Armenians was at its heart a manifestation of his conflict with his father.

With his shame of his repudiated identification with the weak Armenians now in the open, Arlen tried to understand his father's nonaggressive, passive reaction formation. He spoke contemptuously of those Armenians who "accepted subservience" (p. 135). In response to that remark, Sarkis offered the crucial interpretation: "I know what you want. You want to tear down your father" (p. 136).

A flood of feelings burst into the open. Old love for his father. Old respect. Childhood rage. Compassion and fury. The voice of an other brought forth the emotions against which Arlen had been struggling. His own face had once been indistinguishable from his father's when he was half asleep; now it was a portrait of a successful eighteenth-century Armenian merchant that merged with his father's image.

Over the next days, feelings of strength and weakness began to fuse, the passive, weak man merging with the active, powerful one. "And it came to me then and there that, all along, the two sets of mannerisms had been a variant of a single response—this cool, 'un-Armenian' control and the shrill, 'Armenian' excitability. They were twin symptoms, one bursting wildly outward, the other absorbed coldly inward" (p. 142).

Arlen came to peace with the prior sense of helplessness about Armenians. In this he seemed to master his own ambivalence, no longer splitting good and bad fathers. The mastery led to an ability to see strength in forbearance. He tried to reconstruct his father's own experiences, the father's personal proximity to the massacres. The father's anxieties, previously the cause of such pain, were now cause for respect. Arlen recognized father's wish to protect his son and the dreadful price father paid in the service of the son. "There was also something about it of the story of the man and the fox: The man who, for fear of being caught with the contraband, clutches the animal so close beneath his shirt that the animal tears at his stomach" (p. 189).

With this Arlen was able to mourn his father, to cry, to know his father's face. "I used to think that what he had wanted of me had been hard. But what he had wanted of himself turned out to have been literally unspeakable" (p. 191). Arlen understood his father's silent self-hatred and the extent to which the silence was his father's effort to protect him.

Early in his stay, Arlen had visited a key Armenian monument without being able to make an emotional connection. At the end of the trip, Arlen returned to the monument. There he had a sense of the feel of his father's hand in his. Throughout his childhood the feel had been one of being pulled. Now it was a sense of being released. "But here his hand was again. I felt that I held it in mine. I felt that somehow I had brought him here—to this place. I didn't know what else I felt or knew, but I wept, large tears streaming down my face" (p. 255).

It was at the end of the journey that Arlen was able to recall and understand a key dream his father had once told him. The father had dreamed of *his* father, saying, "You know, he was just as I remembered him as a boy. Except his hair was white—but very thick. He wore a frock coat and steel-rimmed spectacles. He stood at the end of our road speaking to me, calling. But he was speaking in Armenian, and I couldn't understand a word" (p. 292).

The entire memoir relates to Arlen's attachment to his father. Aside from evidence of his trusting dependence on his wife, only once is there a shift from man to woman, possibly from references of his father to those of his mother. He spoke of the exhausted dignity, the nobility of the long-suffering Armenian peasant woman, and made references to the impact of the scenery (the latter of which I will soon discuss in terms of their connection with mother).

When Arlen left Armenia, he was proud. After his journey, he still felt himself an American, but now with Armenian kin. In the context of a pilgrimage, he had extended his self-analysis through an analysis of his father's buried conflicts.

DISCUSSION

Not all pilgrimages are as successful as the two instances described above, chosen for the clarity with which they demonstrate the inner activity that paralleled the outer journey. Often, such trips are made defensively as magical gestures to obscure anxiety and obviate the need for difficult emotional work. So familiar is the pattern of travel, often frenzied and urgent, as a way of avoiding inner difficulties, that caution is always necessary in evaluating supposed pilgrimages. It is likely that the vast majority of such travels are flights from confrontation with intrapsychic conflicts, with most pilgrimages acting as religious practices designed to ward off superego threats by submissive atonement, expiating superego pressures rather than transforming them through ego growth.

By contrast, these pilgrimages give evidence of an integrated action as part of a flight *toward* a conflict. Here, action is adaptive for growth, serving not primarily as a discharge of energy but rather to crystallize personality change.

Some common characteristics in successful pilgrimages of the type under discussion may be noted. Much introspection, much analytic work had already been done. The journeys represented efforts to further mastery of inner conflicts by forcing their realization through activity. Inner pressures to master and to integrate were dominant. Nonetheless, these integrative functions did not go unchallenged. Both travelers felt keen ambivalence over making the trip. Resistances were evident in dragging heels and the reluctance to go. Externally realistic issues of time, money, and the needs of others were used to rationalize the fear of awakening sleeping dogs. But the trips were made. In each instance the resistances seemed to center on reluctance to submit to an identification with a familial heritage felt in some way to be bad. The badness was easily seen in oedipal terms: fears of passivity and castration anxiety. For each, the activity of making the trip betokened submission to the frightening father, and, for each, the success of the pilgrimage involved a resolution of oedipal conflicts within the context of traditional heritage. There was an opening up of personal freedom while coming to peace with earlier generations. Through this inner work, ego growth was extended, the punitive superego softened by a newly structured ego ideal.

With possible, extremely rare, exceptions, the task of mastering the oedipal complex is not simply to renounce primary oedipal objects, but to do so in a way that simultaneously permits individual autonomy together with maintenance of valued traditional continuity. An example of a failure in this regard was described by Rangell (1975), writing of the split between Jung and Freud: "The son had freed himself from the father but had separated himself from his heritage as well. The price was high, for both" (p. 88).

In adult life the revival of the oedipal conflict is complicated by the realization of the actuality and inevitability of death. As a result, the wish to triumph over the father and to destroy him is muted by the son's identification with the father, resulting in a wish to tame and remove the father's dangerous retaliatory power while, at the same time, keeping the image of the benign father alive. Recognition of mortality mutes the parricidal urge.

Successful resolution of oedipal conflicts requires, therefore, acknowledgment of early identifications. This is necessary along with acceptance of one's murderous urges, not as an obscuring reaction formation. Freedom depends on comfort with the knowledge of both parricidal urges and recognition of the parent within. And both aspects, the hate and the love, were actualized in the pilgrimages presented here.

The pilgrims agonized over their urges to repudiate important ties, their urges to submit to early objects (both for anaclitic dependent gratification and, defensively, to undo aggression), and their urges genuinely to come to peace with old ghosts. The pilgrimage is given its peculiarly religious flavor by the pressure to convert a threatening superego into a loving ego ideal in dedication to that ideal.

Both travelers came to recognize that what had troubled them was a father's conflict that had been "swallowed whole." By making the journey, each felt he had for once satisfied the father's unresolved pressure and thus put that internalized father to rest. Each felt he had resolved a part of both his own and his internalized father's oedipal conflicts.

We are familiar with the extent to which children identify with the unconscious conflicts of their parents. To be free to resolve his own inner battles, the child must come to grips with pressures unwittingly "borrowed" from parents, borrowed in the sense of Freud's (1923b) discussion of "borrowed guilt" as "the product of an identification with some other person who was once the object of an erotic cathexis" (p. 50n). The pilgrimage, wherein the person travels to the sites of his traditional roots, serves uniquely well to facilitate the working through of this portion of inner struggles.

Preoedipal Issues

While both cases clearly demonstrate oedipal concerns, I believe we can infer many of the preoedipal roots. The superego as a cohesive complex of functions rules over the ego out of its derivation from the resolution of the oedipal conflict. It grows, however, from earlier roots onto which the postoedipal structure is grafted. Freud (1930) wrote that "the original infantile stage of conscience . . . is not given up after the introjection into the super-ego, but persists alongside of it and behind it" (p. 126). With the ego ideal the child takes to himself those aspirations he feels would "restore the lost Shangri-La of the relations with the all-giving mother" (Murray 1964, p. 478).

The pilgrimage thus represents the longing for reunion with the early good mother. This is partially evidenced in the strong regressive pull, the pull to return to the source, seen in both Ben and Arlen. It is likely that this also accounts for the powerful and deep effects of the sight of the landscape on the travelers.

It is not surprising that forces deriving from preverbal periods should be those forces the pilgrims themselves could understand least well, consciously. Ben was able to consider the urge to journey as a repetition of primal-scene strivings. It seems likely that the voyeurism of primal-scene wishes is common to the urge to go back and see for oneself.

Pacella (1975), in considering the déjà vu phenomenon, developed the relationship of distance perception to the experience of the child at the breast, with the distant viewing related to the view of the mother's facial configuration. He quoted Greenacre, who "noted that the mother's face as beautiful landscape is quite clearly produced in dreams" (p. 311). The impact of the landscape on the pilgrims evidenced the touching of early mother–child symbiotic feelings. Here was Mother Earth.

Déjà vu was presented by Pacella as a defense against castration anxiety by means of a controlled regression—one searches for the good omnipotent mother, with landscape symbolizing mother. It is probable that similar regressive pulls also provide a motivation for undertaking pilgrimages. The crucial difference lies in the state of mental functioning. The mind of the pilgrim works in a sublimating manner to master conflict through active integration rather than solely through transient passive regression to symbiotic wishes.

There are dangers in efforts to reunite with an idealized maternal imago. The psychologic success of these journeys distinguishes them from those instances in which conflicts are resolved through the development of manic defenses. Ego and superego did not join for a euphoric alliance; rather, there was an exposure of hidden aspects of both ego ideal and archaic superego precursors. The outcome, as a consequence, was not one of urgency with constriction, but of new freedom of inner communication.

Action

In the pilgrimage, a current life event triggers an inner conflict, which awakens and has attached to it childhood issues that had been dormant. Each new phase in life presents the opportunity for reworking previous conflicts; the epigenetic developmental process allows for new creative solutions to earlier problems. Ben provides an example. His son's entry into adolescence revived for him his own oedipal conflicts. The current and the infantile threats united to demand psychic activity; the pilgrimage was the creative solution.

The pilgrimage continues the adaptive function of early play. As Waelder (1933) wrote of play, so, here too, there "is a pressure exerted by unfinished processes" with "a striving to assimilate" (p. 216). Action is utilized to assist mastery. Like child's play, the attempt is to master inner forces triggered by external reality. Like child's play, the activity is autoplastic rather than alloplastic, using the behavior to enact the drama, not with the goal of changing the external world, but of resolving internal conflicts (Peller 1954).

Postoedipal play presages the adult pilgrimage. Primary oedipal issues are fear of punishment and concerns with sibling relations. In the postoedipal period, efforts to aid detachment from oedipal ties produce games based on the fantasy of belonging to a group of brothers, with the formula, "I am not alone; there is a group of us." This theme continues in the adult revival, and contributes to the pressure to maintain communal ties.

Thus we see that both journeys actualized the psychic conflicts symbolically and metaphorically. Having first objectified the problem, the act of pilgrimage then facilitated resolution of the internal conflicts, catalyzing the sublimating psychic changes. The significance of the early issues of union and separation may account for the particular importance of action in these cases, the action aiding mastery of forces originating in preverbal experience.

The action of the pilgrimage would therefore be similar to the adaptive role of action promoting psychic change in analysis (Wheelis 1950), serving not only as a discharge for energy but also as crystallizing personality change.

Action is necessarily multiply determined. In these illustrations, both defensive forces and those seeking gratification of unconscious oedipal and preoedipal wishes were present. But action was also taken in the service of integrative functions; action and its effects were available to the scrutiny of already strong self-observing functions. Action, thus, was utilized to confront threatening situations and to promote self-analysis. The result was a stepwise interdigitation of action and insight, each responding to and extending the possibility of the other. Action contributed to both working out and working through of inner conflicts.

The crucial factor in successful pilgrimages is the strength of the capacity to observe oneself and ruthlessly reflect on what is seen. The familiar trip taken as a defensive flight from inner conflict manifests ego weakness and may end in psychic constriction. By contrast, the successful personal pilgrimage favors mastery of conflict by the creative use of enactment of fantasy, promoting personal freedom within an acceptance of ties with other generations.

The struggle for insight and self-mastery always unfolds in the lonely theater of one's inner world and, simultaneously and paradoxically, in the interactions with the broader theater of the human world within the context of which that inner theater exists.

V

Closing Reflections, Opening Glimpses

1
Self-Analysis

*The only true voyage of discovery, the only
real rejuvenating experience, would be not to visit
strange lands but to possess other eyes.*
—Proust

I have considered the interactive context in which a person's
struggle toward insight unfolds as well as the place of an introspective person in the world of action manifested in a personal
pilgrimage. Here I turn to the question of self-analysis, those
labors toward insight that appear to be solitary.

How can one come to have a new understanding of one's
own mind, even of one's own blind spots? So regularly do we see
what we expect to see that we must labor to see afresh, to see
with other, new eyes. And as that is true for how we see outward,
it is more so for how we see when we look within. Too often our
self-portraits are like the delightful images painted by court artists, portrayals of loveliness with an occasional beauty mark intended to mask the idealization. Contented, we call the beauty
mark "insight."

Clinical analysis offers a way to move beyond such self-
serving reflections, a way to aim toward greater truth. In a formal analysis self-serving reflection is corrected as the image is
refracted through another's eyes. A patient comes to someone

else, an analyst, and tries, as always, to structure the present so as to refind the past. The analyst, meanwhile, attempts to avoid conventional and predictable reactions, holding, instead, to a position of candid and nonself-serving description of what unfolds. In such a way are the analyst's eyes put in the service of the patient, the analyst's eyes becoming the needed "other eyes" until the patient is able to develop personal ways of looking within afresh.

What other eyes are available for a person alone so that inner vision can yield to re-vision, so that re-vision can lead on to insight? Without the benefit of "other eyes," is such a thing as self-analysis truly possible? And if, as I believe, it is, then how can it come about? Before turning to the sources of "new eyes" in self-analysis, I want to address background questions that relate to both clinical and self-analyses.

WHAT IS ANALYSIS?

First, what do we even mean by "analysis"? Whether two people are involved or one person is alone, just what *is* analysis and how does it differ from what is *non*analytic? If we do not consider this, then every rationalization can be presented in the guise of analysis and called a beauty mark. We cannot determine that analytic work *has* been done unless at other times we can say that it has *not* been done. To consider a new idea to be the result of analysis, we must see it as an idea that had not been known before and that became knowable only with difficulty, through work.

This is, of course, already well known to us in our clinical experience. We may struggle to define analysis behaviorally (for instance, in terms of a patient's lying down on a daily basis and saying what comes to mind to a technically appropriate interpreter sitting out of view), or we may define analysis conceptually (for instance, in terms of an analyst's working on the basis of concepts of the unconscious, transference, and interpretation). But when we sit among colleagues to examine a case that is said to be ready for termination, no matter how technique is defined and no matter how good the analyst's technique may have been, we ask whether core issues have indeed been touched, whether "real analytic work" has been accomplished.

The problem is the same with self-analysis. The proof is in the outcome. Both clinical analysis and self-analysis must demonstrate genuine inner change and outer opening subsequent to emotional work before one can say that *analysis* has taken place. Self-absorption is not self-reflection, and self-reflection is not, by itself, self-analysis.

When Proust's Marcel spoke of feeling happy, he described his state of being. When he wrote that his sometime lover Albertine had been responsive, he reflected on the immediate source of his pleasure. When he let his mind move on to his childhood longings for his mother's kiss, he extended and deepened his reflections. And when, *laboring hard against considerable inner resistances*, he managed to open the universe of memories and ghosts, struggling for candor about his own loving and lustful, envious and hateful urges, he extended his reflections to a breadth as well as depth that permitted him major new freedoms and choices in his personality, in the entire structure of his life. There is a continuum from conscious awareness of a feeling to reflection to deeper reflection to profound opening of buried memories with increasingly candid and even merciless self-exposure. Also, steps along the continuum from emotional awareness through levels of reflection to deep insight take increasing levels of work, that is, the expenditure of energy despite increasing discomfort. For one to say analysis has gone on, hard work has to have been done. An understanding that was not emotionally available before must follow the inner labor of overcoming prior defense. If the process seems easy and ends with a tone of self-congratulations, we question what work has been done.

It has been said that an understanding is a place where the mind comes to rest. One, and especially someone intellectually bright and psychologically sophisticated like an analyst, can easily satisfy oneself that a comfortable conclusion based on self-reflection is the result of a piece of self-analysis. Whether in clinical analysis or in self-analysis, insight and understanding are always partial, and what is proclaimed to be self-analysis is always open to the question of how far it has actually gone beyond self-satisfying self-reflection. Respecting the continuum of psychological depth, our question about analytic work now becomes how much and in what ways an insight is authentic and how much and in what ways the same insight serves to protect against deeper exposure.

Recognition of the importance of degree when considering self-knowledge and self-mastery exposes a further problem that is similar yet different in clinical analysis and self-analysis. If analysis is always a question of degree, then when is one finished?

In clinical analysis the question of termination is complex. There is always the temptation for a patient to quit while moderately ahead but still wishing to feel safe. Such defensive retreats require interpretation rather than enactment. Nonetheless, a time arrives in a clinical analysis when analysand and analyst agree that central issues have been mastered and it is time to stop.

What of self-analysis? At first glance there would seem to be no termination in self-analysis. Yet when we turn to those specimens of self-analysis we most often examine—the resolution of eccentric engagements by analysts at work—we see that they are relatively well-defined instances with beginnings, middles, and ends. This is so for each example of an analyst's self-analysis while at work, even if each clinical analysis carries with it, as I believe it does, a continuing series of reciprocal patient and analyst self-inquiries.

In clinical analysis we are aware of work that remains undone even when there is a successful termination. Aiming at the least for analysis of the core neurosis, we also try to aim higher, attempting to analyze as much of the character structure as we can. Even with success, we never presume to have analyzed *all* of the character.

How does this apply to self-analysis? Beyond the analyst's self-analysis of circumscribed episodes, such as countertransferential engagements, we are left with the vexing question of character analysis. We all are limited by and partially blind to our characters. In self-analysis we are faced with the distinction between segmental analysis and character analysis. Can a self-analysis go so far as to yield character changes?

What remains untouched by the bits and pieces of self-analysis? When we limit ourselves to repeated fragments of self-analysis, we may master crises but end up like Eugene O'Neill's father, spending our lives playing the same old familiar role over and over. Regrettably, the tennis coach was right when he said, "Practice makes permanent." Without the benefit of reflections from another person in regular attendance, self-analysis runs the risk of becoming a series of never-ending reruns, a sophisticated version of a neurotic symptom.

With the model of the analyst at work as our major focus for studying self-analysis, we fall short of answering whether self-analysis can lead to significant character analysis. We await multiple longitudinal studies that could demonstrate clear alteration in character beyond repeated small steps. Until we have such data, in recognition of the power of the repetition compulsion, we must be cautious about the defensive nature of self-analytic conclusions. As Gardner (1991) observed, the main business of self-inquiry may be trading yesterday's illusions for today's.

Caution in evaluating analytic gains does not imply nihilism. Both clinical analysis and self-analysis *do* take place and both *do* work. Let us now turn to the particular dilemma of "self" in self-analysis.

COMPARISONS BETWEEN SELF-ANALYSIS AND CLINICAL ANALYSIS

So far in our field, vignettes offered by analysts at work have been the main building blocks of our understanding. Deutsch, Fliess, Gitelson, and Racker in the early years and Calder, McLaughlin, Jacobs, Gardner, Silber, and Sonnenberg more recently have been among the major contributors in this area. Perhaps none since Freud has so consistently and so productively focused on self-analysis as has Eifermann. Rather than adding another

clinical vignette of my own, I think there may be more use in stating briefly how an aspect of my character colors my views as I
turn to the question of self-analysis.

After a life of curiosity about myself and others I have found
one major thread running through every aspect of my life and
my thought—the marvel of otherness. With more than mere curiosity, rather with an amazement linked to intense and permanent puzzlement, I am taken by the question of what it is like to
be somebody else, what it means to be an other. Indeed, after
following this theme to its professional application, I have come
to believe that *the fundamental principle from which all other principles of clinical analytic technique derive is regard for otherness,
from in the marrow an analyst's deep respect for the uniqueness of
the patient's self as an authentic other.* Similarly, I find that in self-
analysis, *looking at oneself as an other while remaining dedicated
to truth with ruthless candor is the highest respect that one can
pay oneself.*

My own life has been both as representative of the universal and simultaneously as idiosyncratic as all others. Whether I
start with my earliest infantile memories, move to the later sexual
and hateful unfolding of my oedipal struggles, or continue up
until this very moment when I walk in the warm afternoon sun
of maturity chilled by the dusky cool shadow of nonbeing always
at my side—whatever the level and whatever the inner forces, I
see that the struggle to recognize the essential separateness of
people, the essential uniqueness of others, is always present. The
uncanny realization of being alive, and alive as *one* person and
not someone else, the mind-spinning awareness that I am another
person's "other"—these senses of self and otherness color every
moment of my life. For me, grasping reality always requires a
stretch to try to realize what self and otherness mean, to struggle
to contain with great difficulty the awareness that, while you and
I share the same world, we have different and equally valid realities.

Back to our immediate concern, we ask whether and how a
self-analysis can exist, indeed, whether a self can exist, apart from
a universe of others. We ask how there can be a *self*-analysis
without the presence of others, and, as an unavoidable parallel,

how there could be a dyadic clinical analysis without having at its center one soul's *self*-analysis in the presence of but apart from the analyst/other. Unfortunately, we use the same language to talk of our private worlds and our public interactive worlds, at times misleading ourselves into thinking the two are identical. At times we even foolishly sound as if we can know someone else in the same way we know ourselves.

In contrast, as has already been mentioned, Anna Freud (1981) suggested that insight and understanding be distinguished. She suggested reserving "insight" for the kind of awareness one can have of oneself and "understanding" for the very different level of grasping one can have of another. Expressing no quaint daintiness of semantics, she cut to the center of our analytic plight. When we say that we analyze a patient and when we say that one analyzes oneself, do we even use the same word in both instances or are we using a single word-symbol to stand for two importantly different meanings? "Analyzing," the search for inner truth in oneself, and "analyzing," the professional technician's efforts to help another in the other's own search, are not identical. In the sense of true knowing rather than knowing about, analyzing refers to the self-knowledge that arises within.

In appreciation of the private nature of inner experience and self-knowledge, as has been noted, the only person in an analysis an analyst can analyze is himself. Certainly it is legitimate to say that an analyst analyzes the patient, but one must keep aware that this implies a different technical use of the word "analyze." Anna Freud's distinction between *insight* and *understanding* reminds us to distinguish the world of inner emotional experience from the professional tasks involved in approaching another's inner world.

As understanding of another and insight into oneself differ, so also the processes leading to those distinct states differ. In a clinical analysis, the patient takes the analyst at first as a distinctly other person, but with growing investment in transference actualizations the analyst/other comes to seem as if a part of the patient's own self, an actor of those emotions and expectations that derive from the patient's inner drama. With the aid of the

analyst's interpretations the patient comes to re-cognize, to realize anew, that the analyst is, indeed, an other, not part of the
patient's mind.

In a self-analysis, by contrast, one must be open to oneself
but also aim for the candor to see that self as if it were an other.
And just as in clinical analysis the processes of the dyadic interchange must themselves come to be the object of study, so also
in a self-analysis must the subject of one's own analyzing submit
to the scrutiny of self-investigative skepticism.

How can one develop the ability to see oneself with increasing candor? What "other eyes" can be adopted so one can extend
vision to one's own blind spots? At present, we are learning much
about the clinical two-person interchange from studying the
analyst's self-analysis. Paradoxically, the study of interaction and
internalization in dyadic clinical work may yet teach us much
about how "other eyes" are taken in in self-analysis.

The search for knowledge of the inner workings of one
person's mind is the ultimate similarity between self-analysis and
clinical analysis. But behind that similarity lies an essential difference. The paradox that discomforts our usual orderly way of
thinking is that *inner emotional experience is unique and internal
even when one is sharing a moment with an other, and at the same
time one lives within the network of human connection even when
one appears to be alone.* The seemingly self-evident difference
between the solitude of self-analysis and the shared intimacy in
two-person clinical work is not so simple as at first appears. In
clinical work, although the patient invests the relationship with
private meanings, the patient's mind functions in the privacy of
inner emotional experience. Although there may be a longing for
merger, probably in both patient and analyst, and although there
may be fantasies of merger, perhaps also in both, the two clinical partners remain separate people.

The fantasy of fusion is not the actuality. Clinical success
brings with it the realization that intimacy exists within a framework of essential separateness, the "intimate separation" Stone
(1961) described. The two analytic partners come to share respect
for the essential otherness, the unique individuality, the authen-

ticity, of each for the other. The mutual respect of two separate people connected in shared contact but apart in selves replaces fantasied symbiosis.

In self-analysis, the person alone is not quite so totally alone as at first might appear. Just as dyadic analysis is more inwardly private and solitary than its two-person interactive context may suggest, so also a self-analysis unfolds more within the fabric of human connections than the ostensible individuality suggests. One lives in the context of current external life engagements and internal reflections of earlier engagements. Offering a poignant fragment of his own self-analysis, Silber (1991) noted, "When I work upon my dreams I feel I am in the company of analysts." Nonetheless, the complication in self-analysis is the apparent absence of a single, clearly defined other as coparticipant.

Consideration of self and otherness leaves us with the question of how much clinical analysis is actually a patient's self-analysis undertaken in a setting structured to make possible the contributions of an expert assistant in attendance. With regard to self-analysis the question becomes: How much is *not* really being done by one mind in solitude but subtly depends on and draws from external assistance?

THE PLACE OF OTHERS IN SELF-ANALYSIS

How do engagements with others contribute to the "new eyes" of objectivity that make original discoveries possible in self-analysis? As in clinical analysis, so is it in self-analysis. An other is needed for two main functions: first, to provide a supportive structure, and, second, to provide the interpretations that can come from an other's views.

Supportive Others in Self-Analysis

The following examples are illustrative fragments that were crucial parts of active self-analyses. Were it feasible to spell them out more fully, each would fit our criteria of inner labor followed by inner and outer growth. I have selected narrow aspects of experiences only for the sake of offering illustrations.

The search for the sources of "other eyes" leads directly to one's learning from others. While learning implicitly raises the question of teachers, education and self-analysis are not the same. An analyst provides the analytic situation in which an analysis can unfold and the interpretive tools that help open doors through which a patient can proceed. In like manner, what at times appears to be teaching may also provide an emotional holding environment as well as new ways of looking that are necessary to self-analysis.

Taking in the Eyes of a Teacher

Since all contributors to one's self-analysis can be considered teachers, I shall start with an experience involving an actual teacher, in this instance a teacher from relatively late in my life, the chief of the department of psychiatry where I had my formal training.

During the first week of my psychiatric residency, I met with my new chief, who asked me how I would like to spend my time in training. Thinking in terms of formal requirements for board certification, I began, "Well, for my three years. . . ." He looked confused and interrupted me. "What do you mean, three years?" It was my turn to be confused since I was sure that he knew them full well, but I stated the requirements for certification. I have thought of the incident often and I am certain he appeared genuine in his surprise when he answered back, "Are *you* telling *me* that *you're* the kind of guy who would let a bunch of old men in another city tell *you* what *you* are going to do with *your* life?" I felt abashed as I was forced to recognize that yes, I *was* telling him exactly that. But I did not know what I was telling him until *he* told *me*.

That brief interchange was of pivotal importance to me in coming to recognize what has been called my own agency, the sense that I am the one living my own life, the realization of my proprietorship of this life and of my responsibility for whatever choices I make. Is that a new insight? A clinical analysis would certainly take credit for such an internal shift. Is this not, then, part of a self-analysis? Coming to my new realization required recognizing my earlier ways of seeing my place in the world and appreciating how those earlier views had developed in order for me to move beyond them. As McLaughlin (1988) wrote, "No fresh and mutative insight occurs in our work excepting as some previous and compelling insight, i.e., some former understanding of one's self by which one has lived, is worked over and discounted" (p. 374). My experience with a teacher offered the vision through new eyes that widened my own view of myself in the world as I proceeded with my self-analytic work.

Taking in the Eyes behind the Eyes of a Teacher

At times others who contribute to our self-analyses are not only those we know we see but also that flood of many whom we do not know we see when they approach us through others. Having just quoted him, I shall turn to my involvement with McLaughlin to show the presence of others hidden behind an apparent other in the facilitation of inner growth.

In the discussion of Ben in the last chapter, I focused on children's identification with the unconscious conflicts within their parents, and on how values and conflicts are thus transmitted as traditions across generations. The grandfather Ben never knew suffered from inner conflicts developed in his relationship with *his* parents, conflicts that Ben's father internalized and spent his life struggling to master, conflicts that Ben—yet another generation later—also labored to put to rest.

In my professional career, McLaughlin's intellectual engagement and emotional encouragement have clearly influenced my own thinking and questioning. Transforming competitiveness into support, he has helped me venture to explore. For the sake of my present point I cite, out of context, two sentences about his own life that McLaughlin (1988) had occasion to publish. He wrote: "I had lost my physician father in the great flu epidemic shortly after my birth. . . . At the same time I was fortunate in having frequent contact with a paternal outdoorsman uncle, a journeyman carpenter and ingenious craftsman, who summered with us and taught me much until his abrupt and permanent departure to the west coast in my early adolescence" (p. 378).

I have no doubt that McLaughlin's uncle's warm light is reflected in the prism of McLaughlin's personality. It is probable that "ingenious craftsman" was vital in forming the skills that in the next generation were realized in an ingenious psychological craftsman who was able to help me gain some bits of mastery of myself in my own effort to develop my craft. Our paths are lit, colored, and influenced from within our personal reservoirs by the traces of ghosts we could never know we knew. The selves we hope to analyze and the skillful parts of our selves that do the analyzing have in them both assimilated and unassimilated others. Our selves *are* the others at the same time that they most keenly are ourselves, *not* the others.

Interpretive Others in Self-Analysis

Let us move from the nourishing and educational to those relationships that might be deemed more interpretively informative.

We are most readily open to taking in from those in whom we are most emotionally invested. Those most close not only have greatest access to seeing us most fully but also greatest opportunity to speak to us when our defenses are down. Spouses, children, parents, patients, friends, and enemies—all have ways of looking at us and opportunities to tell us more of what they see of us than we may wish to hear at any moment. Similarly, in those moments when we relax our control and open ourselves, as when engaged with reading, theater, and music, we allow ourselves to be vulnerable to learning more about our worlds and ourselves than we might have expected.

Analytic patients are central contributors to an analyst's continuing self-analysis. This is not only because repeated engagements within regressive states of emotion provide the opportunities and demands for repeated self-analysis. In addition, patients have their own perceptive capacities and repeatedly inform an analyst of aspects of the analyst's self that the analyst would prefer not to know. Analysands are, thus, primary contributors to their analysts' own analyses. However, since this area has been the most common focus of previous study, I shall here merely acknowledge it and move to other sources of other eyes.

Others as Contributors—Children and Segmental Focus

A primary (I sometimes think *the* primary) category of facilitators of self-analysis is that of one's children. If patients contribute to the self-analysis of analysts by their impact from the firing line of daily work, then one's children are even more potent, knowing their parents from having grown up *behind* the lines. Also, one's identification with and investment in one's children is greater than that with and in one's patients.

One demand for self-analysis comes each time one faces one's own child's confrontation with the pressures of moving to a new life phase. Indeed, growing older as one's child grows older and reworking developmental crises as one's child confronts that child's first edition of those crises may well provide the major opportunity for carrying self-analysis beyond the narrow into broad reaches of character structure.

As my children have grown, as each has found an original way of resolving developmental issues I had thought I dealt with sufficiently in the past, I have regularly been forced to question and to alter prior private conclusions. As a result, in the process of reworking earlier self-analysis I have had to learn ever again the importance of degree rather than absolutes when considering insight. Cherishing insight, one comes to realize that what one cherishes is always tentative; one comes to have increasing respect for the tentativeness of one's convictions.

Children often serve as our most useful, if at times most painful, interpreters. For an example, I turn to an early moment in my son's growth, one of the initial steps in his move from infancy to independence.

When my son was about 3 he and I engaged in a defining power struggle. Full of a growing sense of himself, he challenged usual rules beyond tolerable limits and repeatedly did so to such a point that I sent him to his room. Still defiant, he left his room. I carried him back. Again he left, and again I carried him back. The back and forth continued several times until I was sitting on the floor at his doorway holding him in while he pushed to come out. Exasperated, I told him that if he left his room one more time, I would spank him. He left.

Forcefully, I picked him up and announced, "All right, that's it! I'm going to pull your pants down and spank you." And just as clearly he answered, "If you have to spank me, then spank me. But you don't have to pull my pants down."

It would be difficult and a bit embarassing to try to estimate how many times in my life I have been in the position of apologizing to my children. I *did* spank my son, though after his words I spanked lightly, half apologetically, and never spanked him again. I certainly did *not* pull his pants down. Instead, I found myself confused (a choice state for self-analysis), wondering about old conventions, wondering about myself both as current father and as former son. The incident set off considerable private discomfort and anguished extension of my insight into previously hidden aspects of myself and my relationship with my own body and with my father, both in connection with my years as a boy and as I had later come to experience myself in the world.

Others as Contributors—Children and Characterologic Focus

The question has been raised whether self-analysis can extend beyond specific areas of symptoms to character issues. I turn to a second instance of a child's contributions. My daughter has equally contributed to the painful extension of my self-awareness. I choose one terse example. It was a time when she was central in forcing me to see—and fragilely master—narcissistic pressures.

It was a time when my narcissism was running rampant, a time I was newly in private practice and impressed with myself as a "promising young doctor." Then 5, my daughter was fed up with my undoubtedly pompous lectures. One time that she must have found one time too many, she heard me out and then answered simply but forcefully, "You don't know everything just because you're a doctor."

Again, on the surface that might seem to be an ordinary if apt comment not related to the question of self-analysis. But in the context of the vulnerability of intimacy, it was as powerful as any interpretation of resistance I had ever heard in my formal analysis and its effect was to force me to take a pained new look at myself. My readiness for self-analysis must also have been present, but that too is always a matter of degree.

Nothing of true value that I have learned about myself would I ever, at the time, have chosen to learn. In self-analysis we take our breakthroughs where we find them and we find them when we are most vulnerable in our attachments. Each of my children has helped me learn more about myself and my unconscious dynamics than I can specify. I have learned much from each even if it then took me a long time to forgive them for having enlightened me.

Much is made in the analytic literature of the role of the parents, especially the father, in introducing principles of reality to the growing child. More notice is due to the extent to which the growing child introduces principles of reality to the still growing parent. This offers a new level of meaning to the poet's observation that the child is father of the man.

Others as Contributors—Nonfamily Members

Friends and enemies, those we love and those we hate, even strangers to whom we open ourselves—all help us look into ourselves in ways we otherwise could not. Greenson said that he believed analysts' needs included having good spouses and good analytic friends, friends who could listen to one's concerns with a friendship enriched by analytic wisdom. I refer back to the fragment of self-analysis by Michael Arlen detailed in the last chapter. After all the preliminary introspection and struggling, it was finally a tour guide who offered Arlen the crucial interpretation he was at last able to hear. "I know what you want. You want to tear your father down."

Undoubtedly there were others, most likely especially Arlen's wife, who had provided important help as Arlen proceeded to this turning point. But the guide turned out to be the right person with the right understanding and the right words at the right moment. He became a guide on both of Arlen's journeys, the inner as well as the outer. As a helpful escort on the outer journey, the guide offered the immediate personal connection that facilitated the unfolding self-analysis. In that context it was the guide, an other, who could put into interpretive words what had to be said for Arlen to open his eyes to self-knowledge.

Others as Contributors—New Sensations Contributing to Reworking

Others once removed can also serve important functions, their effects delivered by their creative products. New experiences can also elicit sensations that trigger memories, the new sensations thereby introducing the possibility of new understandings. Two categories of experiences particularly contribute to self-analysis: experience of changes as part of aging and aesthetic experiences.

As we age we have renewed opportunities to view the inner landscape with new eyes. Recently, at a time of uncommon exhaustion and without immediately visible prospects for a vacation, I had a day of disheartening fatigue. I love my work, but at the end of that difficult day I turned to my wife and said I would love never to work again.

In bed that night, at a time of relaxed reflection, my mind turned to my father during those early years of my life when I had considered him my enemy. Not able to defeat him in the multiple ways I then wished, I had often consoled myself with a private attitude of disdain for him.

Now older than my then young father, I found myself thinking back to my childhood during the 1930s. The world, I later learned, was in a terrible depression, but the circumstances of my life were all I had ever known and I took them to be the essence of normality. My father had three jobs. One was his regular daytime work; a second was on weeknights, far across town; for the third, he worked behind a counter in yet another remote section of the city. At the time I had convinced myself I was glad the old man was always out of the house, but privately I felt hurt, rejected, and furious. I was certain he preferred being at work to being at home. As far as I could see he was having the time of his life.

In the years between that childhood and the tired moment of my own reflection upon that childhood, I had had two conventionally successful analyses. But it was not until I was fifteen years older than my father had ever lived to be that I came to realize that my father must have felt then something akin to what I felt now. I came to recognize how I had distorted my view of my father, how much, sadly, I had blamed him for what undoubtedly had been his effort to protect me from having to see his fatigue and unhappiness. At that moment, very late in my life, I came to appreciate parts of my father I had previously labored to repudiate. And, at that moment, I came to be able to extend my own self-analysis to levels and areas into which I had not before had access. A small step in my own natural development had enabled me to re-view how I saw myself and how I saw others who had mattered to me deeply in my life.

Others as Contributors—An Immediate Sensation Contributing to Reworking

Before moving to the last major category, that of aesthetic experiences, I share a hint of self-analysis in *status nascendi*. At work now, while writing, I have been constantly distracted as each point has revived yet further questions and further observations in my mind. For just one instance, I am struck by how often I have turned in my writing to examine ambivalent struggles with my father and with his later stand-ins. Seeing that, I then notice how uncommon it has been for me to choose to write of matters touching on my mother. As a result, I have been able to realize only now how a self-analytic broadening in this regard likely was influential in shaping the second chapter in Section II on transference as an original creation. While at work on that chapter, I found myself turning my attention from Freud, whose self-analysis of his involvement with his mother was limited, to Proust, whose relationship to his mother was central to his self-analysis.

I shall not speak more of myself other than to notice how work—the process of writing about matters I already had considered—forces to my attention areas I had not as openly considered, questions of possible resistance that demand further self-scrutiny. General reflection broadens the vista for further self-reflection.

Others as Contributors—Aesthetic Experiences

The final category of contributing others, that of aesthetic experience, is so broad and vital as to merit full study in its own right. Here, it can only be given token and modest acknowledgment. What gives art its power? Sensitive involvement with reading, drama, music, and visual art can open inner emotional areas that had been closed. Willing suspension of disbelief is a literary description akin to what we clinically think of as partial regression. Walls between inside and outside weaken, reality testing is relaxed. In such a state one is particularly receptive to engagement with the creative works of others.

I once worked with an obsessional young man who was consumed by the intensity of his hatred and buried adoration for his industrialist father. A transference neurosis crystallized, and we labored hard to try to expose how his passions colored his views of himself and his world. Our progress was slow.

One day everything seemed to change, loosen, and open. The previous night, like many such previous nights, he had watched television. That evening, however, *Death of a Salesman* was shown. The young man had never seen the play before and its impact was explosive. The father whom he had described as detestable was suddenly reconsidered, even seen with sympathy. Tears brought forth the until then hidden longing to be loved by his father. Hate and love, previously compartmentalized from each other, were now felt together. No doubt, prior analytic work had contributed to his receptivity when he saw the play. However, it is equally doubtless that continuing analytic work would have maintained its snail's pace had it not been for the overwhelming power of the experience of great art. Great art can move greatly.

We frequently learn, from ourselves and from our patients, about times when a book, drama, work of music, or other art had vast personal importance. Although I have known of analysts who, based on that experience, have suggested particular books or movies to their patients, I have never known instances when such prescriptions were of notable value.

In this context, play is relevant as a personal art form. Play—adult play as well as child's—offers the opportunity not only for discharge but also for bringing hidden conflicts to where they can be seen with new insight. In the context of relationships with others, unconscious fantasies can be brought forth that then can be seen and analyzed, one's eyes strengthened and enriched by others' eyes.

IN CLOSING

The analytic endeavor, whether in a dyadic clinical setting or in a self-analysis, requires effort to extend insight into areas previously kept in the dark. Earlier limited vision into oneself is extended with the assistance of an other, someone available to help one see what one could not see for oneself.

Every clinical analysis unfolds within the framework of the pair of resonating and interactive self-analyses, the patient's manifest one and the analyst's more silent one. Similarly, every individual self-analysis is nurtured by the communicative and interactive interplay between the individual and the human world of which he is a part.

True self-analysis is always a struggle against inner defensive forces, never the simple delight of self-admiration. Its outcome—the freedom that comes from insight and self-mastery—is always partial, always vulnerable to continued scrutiny.

The seemingly lonely task of self-analysis opens within the matrix of connection to others in the world, others known and not known to be known, others as close at hand as one's spouse and children and friends and enemies, and as far removed as the presences hidden in the inner lives of other people and their work.

The appeal of simple dualisms can mislead us. The two major errors into which we fall when considering self-analysis are, first, those of making a subject–object split—that is, thinking that self and other exist apart from a relationship—and, second, failing to make a subject–object split—that is, feeling as if the other is part of the self and the self part of the other.

Each view, that one is separate, *apart from* others, and that one is *a part of* others, is, of course, correct. Though separateness and connectedness seem contradictory, they are both true and both true at the same time.

To be a person is always to be alone and simultaneously to be in relationship to others. The loneliness of self-analysis unfolds in the fabric of otherness. And the interactive engagement of clinical analysis always matters as it is taken in, translated, and digested within the inner life of each patient's private and unique existence.

2

Continuing Questions

Good reasons must, of force, give place to better.
—SHAKESPEARE, *Julius Caesar* iv,3

I n conclusion, to start . . .
   In clinical work the analyst never has the last word. Having described some of my experiences in practice and the thinking that has grown out of those experiences, it is proper now to emphasize that my closing does not imply the last word. Questions remain.

   I have in this work stepped back from the valid familiar guidelines of therapy—such as interpretation of resistances, the significance of dreams, and the like—in order to look afresh at the human engagements that unfold as the manifest clinical work progresses. My focus of attention implies no diminution of the importance of the theoretical and technical complexities conventionally covered in studies on psychoanalytic practice.

   However, having addressed underlying aspects of clinical work, what are some of the main questions that remain? While many arise in any point of the compass to which one turns, I want to single out one theme that continues to demand particular notice. It is the problem of how parts connect, how the parts

within an individual's intrapsychic world communicate and interact, and how the clinical partners, each of whom has such a
complex personal inner universe, also communicate and interact. How can we best conceptualize and comprehend the multiplicity of levels of interaction and engagement, both inner and
outer? I turn to two interrelated faces, that of subjectivity and
that of meaning.

SUBJECTIVITY AND INTERSUBJECTIVITY

Psychoanalytic understanding originated in the exploration
of a single mind, first in Freud's self-analysis and subsequently
in the analyses of the minds of the myriad of patients who made
use of the psychoanalytic tool toward insight. Experience has
exposed the importance of the interaction of the minds of both
partners in the clinical endeavor in effecting and shaping what
came to be learned about the patient's mind. Attention to the
depth psychology of the patient's mind that preoccupied workers in the early part of the twentieth century has by the end of
the century turned to similar preoccupation with the multiple
subjectivities involved in clinical work.

"The id" was the concept most in the air one hundred years
ago, "the ego" fifty years ago, "empathy" twenty-five years ago,
and "intersubjectivity" today. On each occasion, a new discovery vastly enriched understanding. After a while, in the enthusi-
asm to explore the implications of that understanding, application of the concept broadened, at times spreading like a new
religion growing beyond immediate relevance and applicability.
Eventually, what was solid and valid in each idea was incorporated into basic analytic understanding, although there have always been small parochial groups who continued to keep their
favored concept as their primary organizing principle.

During the period of rapid growth of each new idea, the
central words themselves expanded in meaning beyond consistent specificity. We are in such a period now, with current enthusiasms for the word "intersubjectivity." The vital importance of the

patient's subjectivity, of the analyst's subjectivity, and of the interaction between them is by now firmly established. That interaction *between* two parties, two separate "subjects," can be called "intersubjectivity." Another activity I shall shortly describe, that *within* a unified emotional field containing two parties, two "subjects," can also be termed "intersubjectivity." The distinction between these different meanings and the relationships of these conceptualizations are of great importance. Quick and easy use of the word "intersubjectivity" may obscure more than it clarifies.

The questions that remain are not only central to psychoanalytic understanding but are fundamental questions that have puzzled mankind since the start of reflective thought. What is a person and how do persons connect? What is uniquely individual and what shared? Indeed, what does sharing mean if all experience is unique, individual, and internal even when it arises in the context of others engaged in the actions of the same experience?

Exploring the one-person psychology of a patient's mind, we learned the value of attending to the two-person psychology of the minds of both the analyst and the patient. In what ways is that two-person psychology an interaction of separate individuals, and in what ways is it a function of a new dyadic universe, a unity in which each of the two is only a contributing part?

From a phenomenological view, an analysis unfolds in the experience created in the immediacy of the present. Attention to the past has been so compelling that we have tended to forget that analyst and analysand live in a *current* engagement in which the present freshly defines the intruding and influencing past. From this angle people are seen to exist as alive in context, or, as it has been described, as beings-in-the-world. From this angle an interpretation addresses the dynamic quality of *where* a person is in an unfolding universe, in contrast to the static diagnosis of *who* a person is as seen descriptively from apart. Now, transference is seen not simply as the past's distortion of the present but also as the current engagement in which shadows of the past are cogent as current original actualities. Now, not only may meaning be discovered but also meaning is created through the very acts of engagement and interpretation.

This sense of the essential unity of experience may become more clear if you follow with me a few steps as I trace the personal path along which my own thinking has come. When I was young I used to believe that the most miraculous discovery in the history of science was the discovery of air. Air was everywhere, the very stuff of space, but since everyone existed within the universe of space, I wondered how somebody would ever have thought that something was there filling the space. When I shared my amazement with one older and wiser, he reminded me of the wind. When leaves rustled, when something inert moved as if of its own accord, when it moved as no one would have expected, people wondered why and realized that something unseen but active had to be inferred, something they called air.

When I grew older and more curious of what it means to be a person, I came to the belief that the most miraculous discovery in the history of human science was that of the existence of an active unconscious. Again, who would ever have thought that something unseen and unseeable was there? And again I came to recognize that, as with air, the discovery had been inevitable. Effects of the unconscious, of unexpected ways of feeling and behaving, could be seen. Here, too, an invisible actor had to be inferred.

The existence of air and the existence of an active unconscious were realized because people were forced to consider why the world did not function as they would have expected. It was recognition of the discrepancy between their expectations and the resistance of the forces of nature to fulfilling those expectations that made great discoveries necessary and possible.

From the physical and the human universes, my curiosity turned to the clinical. Free association, were it truly free, would logically lead uninterruptedly to broad and perhaps even easy understandings. But clinical experience shows that insight does not fall freely like unimpeded cascades. It flows, instead, in unexpected currents, running through rough rapids and standing in seemingly stagnant side pools. Once again it is a resistance, a force that frustrates expectation, which compels recognition of the presence of hidden forces. As with air and as with the unconscious, it is the variation from what would seem expectable that signals the presence of something unseen. Resistance is the name we give this particular frustration of clinical expectation.

The frustration of expectation is one way an observer recognizes the presence of a distinction. However, there is another aspect quite as important as the role of expectation. It is the principle of the essential unity of phenomena, the fact that actuality is not segmented and compartmentalized in the way our minds dissect to permit cognitive thinking. Despite the need to abstract processes from their integrated, unitary setting in order for our minds to focus on them, it is only when what has been abstracted is returned to its natural context that understanding can approach more full validity.

While focused study of air and of the unconscious have taught us much, we have also learned that air exists and matters as it is *in*, a part *of*, not apart *from* the world. We have learned that the unconscious exists *in*, a part *of*, not apart *from*, mental life. And recognition of the interchange between patient and analyst has revealed that resistance is a name for a process alive and defined *within* a shared engagement in a unified clinical field. Resistance never simply "is," a force existing in its own inner right (for which we have the name "intrapsychic defense"), but is always part of a whole, created by being seen and named as such by someone who is a part *of* the clinical universe.

Customary analytic theorizing always implies a subject–object split. The two clinical partners are separate individuals interacting with each other, trying to influence each other, observing each other. Whether one's orientation is shaped by depth psychology or by object relations, the subject–object split is implicit even while concerns for subjectivity are active. Now, however, we are faced with the problem of how each separate subjectivity may, all at the same time but from a different angle of view, also be a resultant of the intersubjectivity constructed in the immediate clinical universe.

The need to define and distinguish the multi-leveled interactions of two participants, each with personal subjectivities, from the unfolding in shared-common engagement of the unique clinical universe is a basic problem. The clinical psychoanalytic universe likely offers us the best laboratory yet conceived for exploring this problem. Yet, as we proceed, it is prudent to be alert to the seductive ease with which the word "intersubjectivity" can obscure differences between the unconscious interaction of separate persons and the unitary construction of shared experience in which the persons are unified parts.

As is often the case, the whole is more than merely the sum of its parts. One- and two-person psychologies must both be respected at the same time that the vantage point of the dyadic unity is added to our multiple points of view. Indeed, it may be more logical not to divide relational points of view into three categories of one-person, two-person, and unitary dyad. Rather, the relational views can be seen from either *person-separate* or *person-unified* considerations, with the person-separate then examined from one-person or two-person angles. Ultimately, all three dimensions must be included to approach full comprehension.

Clarification of these differing points of view stands before us, a task whose success always depends on our respecting the importance of the other points of view even though to our dualistic minds they seem to be in logical conflict. Progress, as always, demands our remaining alert to the temptation of easy answers, to the lure of parochial allegiance to partial visions.

MEANING

It is meaning that bridges these philosophical questions with daily clinical practice. It is with meaning that drive is actualized in experience and that experience is internalized, shaping desire. And it is through the communication of meanings that the inner dynamics of one person are exposed and explored in interactive exchange with another, all in the dyadic universe shaped by both. It seems possible that meaning may be the basic unit of the clinical experience, the identifiable molecule that is itself composed of the various atoms that represent the multiple aspects of intrapsychic structure and of experienced life.

Psychoanalysis has been a study of human meaning. Long before he made his revolutionary leaps of analytic insight, Freud's genius was already evident in a remarkable way. As a doctor treating patients with medical complaints, he went against medical tradition and spent long periods of time listening, searching for the meanings behind his patient's symptoms. Through all the vicissitudes of analytic history and changing theories, the exploration for meanings has remained cardinal to the clinical task. In that sense, a bibliography of the psychoanalytic consideration of meaning would be synonymous with the entire corpus of analytic literature.

Crucial to the meaning of meaning is the implication of connection, the linking of some levels of observations and understandings to other levels beyond them, to other significances. Aiming for levels of connection beyond ready access and conscious awareness defines the psychoanalytic attitude. While there is no such thing as *full* understanding, whatever the levels attained, essential to the idea of meaning is the implication of connection, of linkage between separate levels, both those within a person and those between persons.

Meanings reflect all levels of mental and emotional functioning, the psychological and the physical as underlying and impinging on the psychological. Since its birth, psychoanalysis has been concerned with the body, with the biological roots of meaning. This aspect of meaning was pivotal in Freud's work on dreams, in his early case histories, and in *Three Essays on Sexuality* (1905a). Ella Freeman Sharpe's (1940) observations on biological roots of metaphor stand as a subsequent exemplary model of this attention to aspects of mental representations and meanings shaped by underlying biology. Inherent psychosexual reflections in symptoms and in language have been recognized as core aspects not only of symptom formation but of all symbol formation.

With increasing regard for the significance of the objects of drives, with increasing realization of the import of communication, new complexities have been added to our grasp of meanings. Meanings are at once *both* private and public, that is, they are both individually internal and at the same time communicative.

A patient says something but without knowing it, or without knowing that he or she knows it, what is said appears to mean something more. What is manifest implies what is latent. Is that implication only built into what is said, or is the supposedly deeper meaning created when the other hears the message as having something more in it? While neat lines are at times drawn between what is implied and what is inferred (as described in the chapter "On Surmise"), in actuality meaning is exposed, and even created, as a combination of both. The analytic situation that is designed to facilitate maximum exposure of the patient's hidden meanings as evident in associations and in transferences also simultaneously provides a unique dyadic universe that influences and colors the unfolding shapes of those meanings. To what extent in clinical work is the past reconstructed and to what extent is it newly constructed?

The pulls between past influence and present actuality, and between innate structure and outer engagement, are united in the understanding of any clinical moment. Attending to the nature of meaning allows us to approach our familiar debates from a fresh vantage point. We already know that certain characteristics are innate to meaning. Primary is that meaning changes. Meaning changes across time, and it changes across relationships.

In terms of time, what someone means at one moment may well not be the same as the meaning as it is recalled at the next moment, and still different when reflected on at yet another moment. We are all partially in the position of the poet who was asked the meaning of a passage in his poem. He replied, "God and I *both* knew what it meant once. Now, God alone knows!"

Insight, the grasping of meanings, varies with the shifting perspective of time. The history of meanings developed over time in an analysis influences the understanding of a meaning in the immediate moment, just as a moment's new understanding can cast light on and change prior understandings. Meanings arrived at in the course of analysis can be revised in memory as new and broader meanings are synthesized over time, with differing and even conflicting meanings abiding at the same time.

As there is variation across time, so is there a change in meaning as it moves from one person to another, that is, through the very act of communicating. When a patient speaks of feeling understood, when a patient has the impression that a meaning has successfully crossed to the analyst/other, the patient often has a sense of feeling touched, of being in emotional contact. Yet understanding, comforting as it may be, is always partial, always approximate, and always falling short.

Theory can inform the analyst of possibilities of meaning, never of specific meanings in the immediacy of an interchange. When an analyst is unduly influenced—rather than informed of possibilities—by theory, such an error constricts what the analyst may continue to suppose is valid investigation. Such missteps are sad in clinical practice, but are amusingly exemplified in the mirror of the theater. Stoppard (1967), in his play *Rosencrantz and Guildenstern Are Dead,* provided a sharp caricature of someone getting the manifest meaning but missing the emotional significance. He has Rosencrantz say of Hamlet: "To sum up: Your father, whom you love, dies. You are his heir. You come back to find that hardly was the corpse cold before his young brother popped onto his throne and into his sheets, thereby offending both legal and natural practice. Now why, exactly, are you behaving in this extraordinary manner?" (p. 51).

Our appreciations of our patients' meanings are customarily better than that, but even when sufficient for extending understanding they are never total. One person's inner meaning is unique and can only be approached, never fully known, by another person. It is as if each of us is a walking drama sharing the stage with others, each the center of his own walking drama. Each of us has languages both in common and unique. Understanding may be great enough to be mutative, but it can never be complete.

To complicate matters yet more, even though meaning is spoken of as singular, it must be recognized to be inevitably multiple, not only a network rather than a logical point of content, but also a layer of internal and interpersonal networks, all interacting, all coming together in one discrete, meaningful instant.

Also, out of convenience and the habit of convention, we speak of meaning as if it were a thing. Yet we are aware that any mental structure, though relatively stable, is essentially a function that changes slowly over time. Meaning is similarly best recognized as a process that unfolds over time even though seen in a single snapshot as if it were static. The noun "meaning" serves as shorthand for the implication of the unfolding verb "to mean." A meaning, an intention, is caught on the run, seen as if it were static though actually a process in motion, shifting even as it is seen, heard, or conceived.

Just as "meaning" must be recognized as a verb, so must it be recognized as at once active and passive. Meanings are both self-reflective and other-reflective. Self-reflectively, they evidence the multiple inner contexts of the person expressing the meaning, and they reflect the structure of the manifest form in which they are expressed, whether in language or in other behavior. Other-reflectively, they reflect not only the speaker's expectation of the other's reaction that colors the expression, but also the shape imposed by the hearer/interpreter/reactive-other in the unique dyadic pair of the moment. In its actualization and realization, meaning changes the expresser, the hearer, and the meaning itself in the act of being expressed and in the act of being heard.

As we seek meanings, as we name them, what makes us accept that the meanings identified have the ring of truth behind them, the power and immediacy of the experience of psychic reality? Then, if a meaning rings true at one moment, how long can that moment last, how long does that truth last? To speak properly of a meaning we need to identify its location in time both within the shifting intrapersonal context and within the moving interpersonal clinical universe.

We also ask what makes a meaning meaningful, alive rather than academic. In addition to the power of an emotional significance that commands attention to some meanings as more urgent than others, there is also the issue of the hearer's selectivity. The analyst selectively notices. The analyst's putting something into words, naming something, interpreting—these may identify a meaning, they may actuate a meaning, they may institute a meaning, they may modify a meaning, they may even undo a meaning.

IN CLOSING

It seems likely that outside help with our questions may come from the study of aesthetics, the science that examines interaction of form and content, of emotional shapes and transmissions, within and between people. Still, what we gain from allied disciplines are mainly hints, beneficial as they are. As we continue to struggle toward better understanding of the interplay between meaning and subjectivity, close scrutiny of the specificities of individual clinical analytic moments and their depths offers us the best light in our efforts to push back the darkness.

Hans Sachs said that when we have completed an analysis we have scratched the surface of a continent. Yet a time comes when, recognizing the inevitable incompleteness of what has been accomplished, analyst and patient know it is time to go their separate ways. For us too this is such a time.

APPENDIX

At Work

*The chief contests of wit among . . . handicraftsmen
arise from a mutual endeavour to exalt one trade
by depreciating another. . . . A blacksmith was
lately pleasing himself at his anvil, with observing
that, though his trade was hot and sooty, laborious
and unhealthy, yet he had the honour of living by
his hammer, he got his bread like a man, and if his
son should rise in the world . . . no body could
reproach him that his father was a taylor.*
—JOHNSON

Some years ago, when I had not yet as fully thought through the principles implicit in clinical work, I was asked to write a description of how I functioned in my office, including something about such routine mechanics as the handling of fees and missed sessions and such issues as how I thought my background, both professional and personal, might influence the ways I work. While what I then wrote was necessarily a small fragment of who I am and how I work, it offered a glimpse into the picture I had of myself. So private a description must be of dubious accuracy, and so I hold it apart from the general text, which is closer to my understanding of the clinical process. However, as a slanted glimpse of who it is who has offered such clinical reflections, I append the following, unchanged from its original form except for appropriate editorial corrections.

To help an other know that one's self, to know that one's own mind and how it works, and through that to help that person increase inner peace and widen the range of possible actions in the outer world—the goals of analysis are not modest. The task of achieving these goals is pervaded with subtle conflictual pulls.

One central conflict results from the differing directions and opposing feelings these paradoxical aims stir within the analyst's own self. Helping leads to lending a hand, whereas for one to know oneself calls for the helper to avoid intrusiveness. The helpful attitude is often associated with psychotherapy; the exposure and exploration of unconscious fantasies requires a more manifestly abstinent attitude from the assistant. This paradox, the need to restrict helpful activity in the short term in order to be more helpful in the long term, exists within me, an analyst at work.

When I look back over how I have practiced in my office over the past decades, I realize that even when I conduct insight psychotherapy, psychoanalytic psychology serves as my organizing basic science. As a result, my orientation is always psychoanalytic.

Does the work aim toward making the unconscious conscious? Is that done by facilitating the crystallization of the transference? Are the clues that are inherent in that transference process—in dreams, in free associations, plus in the resistance—all utilized to bring into the open underground currents within the patient? Is the effort to achieve mastery through insight? These traditional defining characteristics of psychoanalysis are the ones most vital for my view and, I hope, to my work.

There are solid reasons for the conventions of psychoanalytic technique, reasons born out of what are by now generations of clinical experience. These conventions are all in the service of the ultimate analytic goal; they are not the ends in themselves. Whether one maintains a baseline stance that seems warm or cool, close or distant, will definitely influence the nature of the unfolding process. What determines the psychoanalytic work is the issue of what is then done with those factors, whether their effects are exposed and explored for the patient's meanings, or whether they are allowed to stand as if in a background "reality" beyond exploration.

This does not suggest, to me, that any intervention is acceptable or useful if only it is examined subsequently. There is, rather, the implication that the fundamental task is to expose, explore, and identify the forces and workings of the patient's inner world.

There are differences between psychotherapy and psychoanalysis; there are significant effects from the differing range of techniques. In my practice, I always try to work toward an analytic goal of exploration and insight. My techniques, to the extent I can be aware, are always in the service of that goal.

As a result, my work experience is best described as psychoanalysis and insight therapy. I do not conduct other forms of psychotherapy, limiting myself and my interests to those efforts in which help is based on the effort to understand. My patients, therefore, are not "in psychiatric hands" or "under psychiatric care." They are all in analytic self-investigation, with a psychoanalyst in attending assistance.

For the rest of this chapter, I limit myself to psychoanalysis, the vast majority of my practice. Reviewing what has gone on in my office through the years, rather than what I thought would go on or theorized should go on, reveals to me that some individuals with whom I worked on a twice-weekly basis developed intense and relatively clearly crystallized transference neuroses. These were people often unsophisticated about analytic matters. Yet, from their own fresh psychologic-mindedness, they developed complex transference processes that, with increasingly free associations and dream analyses, they were able to understand in a manner that connected their past and current lives.

These people have been exceptions and exceptional, but they have been there. For the most part, my experience has been that more full transference regression and utilization require the continuity of daily sessions and the ambiguity that comes from greater levels of analytic abstinence and the use of the couch.

A law student consulted me because of problems he had making decisions. He felt he could never make a full commitment to a career because mixed feelings destroyed "total" certainty. Socially, too, he doubted the possibility of his finding "total" true love. He had "given up the idealistic ideas of things going well in marriage" and did not "want to impose" himself on anyone. He had few friends and got along poorly with his parents, though he was said to be just like his father.

The most striking qualities at the beginning of our work were his humorlessness (that when analyzed later revealed an uncommon dry appreciation of irony), verbal caution, and intense shame. He appeared markedly anxious, felt fragmented, was clearly perfectionistic, and was afraid of being dependent. The shame and obsessional effort to protect against loss of control was striking even in setting the original arrangements for an analysis. When I described these, he tried to negotiate on each point (for instance, he wanted three sessions per week rather than four), reinforcing his demand by the pressure of external forces. My response was to interpret the sense of danger rather than to negotiate.

During the series of consultative sessions, the patient reported a dream of selecting neckties and wanting to steal an ashtray. He then began to smoke and recalled an earlier dream that his grandfather died of cancer caused by the patient's smoking.

Much of his early position in the analysis seemed a passive masochistic presentation to me, the analyst, in what later came to be understood as paternal transference. He repeatedly attempted to mold the relationship in "seduction of the aggressor," that is, I was to be made to feel guilty and then to react with retaliatory punishment. An example was the suffering I was said to cause by my fee and office location. Though he had no external financial problems, he walked daily the several miles to and from his appointment in order to save carfare, presumably to minimize his father's financial suffering.

Exploring the implications of this was like picking up a point on a net and discovering unexpected complex threads leading in many directions. What is central at the moment is not the story of the patient's psychodynamics, but the technique that aided their discovery.

Though I noticed incipient feelings of guilt in response to the patient's maneuvers, I took these as significant data for understanding the unfolding associations, not as requirements for me to alter the way I work.

The need to be flexible in technique does not mean that anything goes; flexibility does not betray my primary concern to understand the patient's expectations and fantasies. As a psychoanalytic technician, I have on the whole clear ideas of what works and what does not. While I am comfortable being silent or saying, "No," that silence or that statement, like all others, is not made capriciously or simply as evidence of my power. Rather, appropriate technique is needed in order to protect and to promote the analytic work. The analytic goal of mastery through insight takes priority over quick comfort for either the patient or me, the analyst.

In one way or another, every patient who has ever consulted me did so because something hurt. And each wanted to feel better, whether simply to relieve pain or to achieve power felt to be missing. Each came to a doctor for help. No matter what was the patient's appreciation of analysis as a technique in the service of insight, no patient was simply involved in an academic research project.

The word "doctor" requires clarification. I do not use it to imply anything about the question of lay analysis. I do use it to suggest that the analyst has a professional therapeutic responsibility to the patient, that a clinical analysis can never be an applied analysis addressed to a living human being as if the patient were nothing more than a text or a work of art. The destructive consequences of therapeutic zeal demand that the analyst master personal rescue fantasies, sadism, and the urge to have power over another person. The issue is not whether the analyst be a physician, but that the analyst have worked through the crucial implications of therapeutic responsibility in inviting an other to put oneself at risk.

When I commit myself to analytic work with someone and explain that the way the work proceeds is for that person to try to follow the basic rule of free association, I am implicitly advising that many important executive ego functions be set aside during the analytic work. It is then my responsibility to watch them for the patient while the patient is vulnerable. In such a situation, matters that would otherwise be simple become complicated. My changing the schedule or raising a fee, for instance, must of course be explored analytically for the meaning to the patient. No matter the roots of the patient's attitudes—be they compliant, defiant, or whatever—I must, in addition to analytic exploration, watch out for the patient's interest. When someone is analytically exposed, I am not only trying to listen in order to interpret, I am also a temporary guardian of those ego functions that are set aside along with the censoring functions.

Privately, I feel a personal pride at being a part of the psychoanalytic movement, a movement that combines what I think are the best of liberating and civilizing effects. Yet I feel very strongly that I, the analyst, am there at work for the sake of the analysis, which exists for the sake of the patient. In some small manner, each analysis results in greater psychoanalytic knowledge. Still, it is primary that the analysis is there for the patient; the patient is not there for the sake of psychoanalysis.

The most I have to offer someone in my office is that unique psychoanalytic tool that assists that person to be ever more open to the inner world and to broaden knowledge of personal urges, feelings, and fantasies. Thus, the practice of abstinence, my withholding of sought-after help or other response, is not arbitrary. I do not define myself as an analyst either on the basis of the level of abstinence I achieve or the level of deep infantile sexual interpretations I offer. I am an analyst at work to the extent that I use the analytic tool to help an other come to know oneself, come to approach oneself with an attitude of ruthlessly open-minded introspection.

It is here that I find the second of the major sets of responsibilities I feel in my practice. I am a guardian of the analysis. A friendly ear, an opportunity for ventilation and catharsis, helpful advice, simple or not so simple compassion—all of these can be obtained many places in the world outside an analyst's office. Nowhere else, however, can someone obtain a psychoanalysis.

For me, the early voice of authority was that of my father calling out, "Who's watching the store?" By now that voice in my own superego has been tamed to the softer tone of an ego-ideal. The message that voice speaks is now more of values than of threat, but it remains the message of the commitment to "watch the store." Despite the temptations to the contrary, and especially those presented by the patient in the form of seductions and narcissistic bribes, it is I, the analyst, who must continuously watch the analytic store.

Analytic practice carries with it a frighteningly broad series of occupational hazards, to which no one is immune. Chief among these are the analyst's belief that the analyst could live the patient's life better than the patient can, and the analyst's belief that the analyst is engaged in an academic research project that is unrelated to how the patient's life proceeds. Both excessive helpfulness and disowning of analytic responsibility subvert the analytic task.

For me, analytic technique is one in which I try to structure a fairly comfortable and standard basic relationship, the psychoanalytic situation, in which the patient is permitted and at times encouraged to let loose and to allow increasingly open experience and verbal expression of all impulses, feelings, and fantasies. The couch, the daily sessions, and the minimization of external stimuli and unpredictable changes are all means, not ends in themselves. They are designed to facilitate that regression by which the patient can best see and describe the varied forces acting within.

I try to speak as little or as much as seems necessary to permit and aid the furthering of that opening up. I am essentially always behind the patient.

A bright but very frightened woman stated soon after the initial consultations that she would never be able to use the couch. She said she would do what she could sitting up but would accept as just another in the long line of personally disappointing limitations in her life whatever it was she would lose by having an analysis that did not include the use of the couch. In fact, for close to a year, she worked hard and well while sitting face to face. Her fears of loss of control, the history behind those fears, and the revival of those fears in relationship to me all came before us. That did not make it easy for her to use the couch. However, she was a woman of genuine courage (as I find anyone genuinely courageous who presents for psychoanalytic investigation), and the time eventually came when she realized that she had to move to the couch. She saw it as necessary not because she now understood why she had been afraid, but because she came to recognize she would never see through the fear without confronting it.

One day, long after further work had been accomplished, she reflected on all that had gone before. She found humor in the irony. She was afraid, she said, to allow me to be out of her view, behind her, because she never realized nor believed that I was in fact behind her. Raised by a mother who always knew what was best, who had eyes in the back of her head for seeing and knowing what the young girl was thinking and doing, she felt the couch manifested what was for her a major danger of analysis, the dreadful experience of having another person know more of what she was thinking than she did herself.

It is true that I often hear a hidden message before the patient recognizes it, but I cannot hear it before the patient says it. No matter how much it may seem otherwise to the patient at first, I am always behind the patient.

Before going on to follow issues as they arise in the course of an analysis, there is more to say of what I have in mind from the beginning. The need to say this first is, itself, a statement of my understanding of analytic work. I am not only an outside assistant to the patient, but I am one who does the work in part by utilizing my own psychology to construct a collaborative medium onto which the patient's inner world can be drawn. My ultimate responsibility is to protect and aid the analysis, my purpose deriving from my awareness that it is the capacity for mastery through insight that analysis has to offer the patient.

My overview of analysis, my own psychology of who and how I am, all inform my actual practice. I believe that each person—whether psychotic, Republican, Jewish, poetic, or whatever—does, acts, and lives life in that person's unique and idiosyncratic style because it is the best way of getting along in the world as that person sees it. I believe that what analysis uniquely offers is the specially developed occasion in which one can learn how it happens that the world is seen as it is and in which one can thereby widen the range of inner vision and outer potential action.

I try to structure a receptive but neutral setting that will allow the patient to expose private patterns of relating and experiencing. I use my own psychology not to suggest or to inspire, but to hear the patient's words, learn from the patient's music, and then interpret back that which I hear for the patient's consideration.

Thus, the broad goals of analysis and the general responsibilities of the analyst that I have described are neither abstractions demanding perfectionism nor moralistic imperatives. They are the conscious aspects of the structure that determines the specifics of my daily work. Let us now turn to how I put these into practice.

I am reminded of the time the International Psychoanalytic Congress met in Jerusalem during a mind-searing heat wave. Retreating to my air-conditioned hotel room one afternoon, I happened to hear the English language news broadcast. "Was this the hottest it has ever been here?" the newsman asked. The weatherman's answer was precise: "It was the hottest we have records for, but how can I say it was never hotter before?"

My concern here is with how I work, but like that weatherman, all I can knowingly tell is what I have in my field of vision, how I think I work. This is not an obsessional point but an essential psychoanalytic view. Unconscious forces may be mastered, but they are always alive and potentially active. Perhaps now the best approach is to address some of the specifics of my analytic practice.

When someone calls me, even if for an analysis, I start with a consultation that lasts anywhere from one to several sessions. I consider the interruptions of the sessions to be the arbitrary

effect of the rate at which the clock moves, a rate totally uncon-
nected with the speed at which the patient opens up. I start by
hearing as much as I can about whatever the patient cares to bring
up. In this, I am determined not only not to prejudice the unfolding of the patient's ideas and pattern of relating in order to
observe them better, but also to demonstrate my wares, namely,
the practice of helping an other come to observe that other's mind
as seen both in content and in interactional patterns.

My preference is to have the consultation extend over a brief
period of time. I especially want to note how this other person
responds to the consultative experience with me, to what extent
the patient seems inclined to chew something over or to allow
my presence or my comments to reflect themselves in an active
inner reworking.

After I have a relatively strong sense of the matters with
which the patient is struggling, I note that it would be helpful if
I could briefly hear an overview of the person's life. I am interested in a general though short biographical survey in order to
get the broadest sense of the context in which the patient lives
and in which the troubles have arisen. Though I do not take a
finely detailed history, I do want to know whom the patient considers to be the major life characters and how the patient initially
portrays them. Also, it is helpful to hear of any earlier life inci-
dents felt by the patient to be of relevance. All of this, naturally,
not only informs me but also informs the patient, particularly
reinforcing the idea that the past and present are connected and
that past experiences may continue to live in the present.

Having come to my own conclusions, I then feel it my turn
to tell the person consulting me what I think. I state the major
themes that I think I have heard. I comment on whether I feel
there is value in the patient's undertaking formal self-investigative
work at this time, whether or not (and sometimes not) I think
that the patient and I can work together, and what I consider the
various options in terms of the differences between psychotherapy and psychoanalysis.

A word is in order about analyzability. I have read many
studies that labor to define the specific cues that are broadly and

covertly subsumed in the analyst's intuition, the sense of whether someone is likely to make use of a psychoanalytic venture. Gross matters are, of course, easy. The problem is to move beyond such easy dramatic indications and contraindications.

On reflection, I notice how often the question of analyzability turned out to be the question of the analysis itself. What would have seemed to be unanalyzable was precisely what required analyzing. I do not have an inordinately high opinion of the ability to predict what will be around the corner. Patients who seemed to be choice candidates for analysis have, at times, turned out to be the most stickily intractable, with dreadfully difficult negative therapeutic reactions. On the other hand, I can think of those about whom one would not have started out feeling too optimistic but who have subsequently developed and analyzed fairly classical transference neuroses. In contrast to some severe criteria for analyzability, I do not consider the presence of psychopathology a contraindication to psychoanalysis.

I believe I should say whatever I learn from the patient that I think the patient can make use of. I also feel it is my task to say what needs to be said about how to proceed. I have heard it said that the basic rule is best communicated by action rather than words, by attention. Generally, this is an attitude of wishing to avoid "rules," as if the basic rule were an evidence of power orientation rather than a neutral informed statement of how the work is likely best to unfold.

My own view is that the analyst's neutrality does do away with enactments of domination, but that such true neutrality does not involve the analyst's going underground. For me, the analyst who orchestrates an analysand's direction, no matter how subtly, is manipulating. I see no room in analysis for tricks hidden up the analyst's sleeve.

My model is Freud's—the blind archaeologist. The analysand and I are engaged in a collaborative endeavor in which I am the expert hired hand. Thus, it is inconceivable to me that the analyst would not instruct the patient in what the patient needs to know about how an analysis works. With words that vary from patient to patient, I generally say that the way that works best is for the patient to try to put into words all thoughts, feelings, body feelings, dreams, ideas, or whatever as they come up. And, I add, all of this should be said aloud, whether it seems relevant or irrelevant, important or unimportant, polite, rude, or whatever imaginable. Occasionally I add that if the answers to the questions on which the person is reflecting could be provided by simple logic or reasoning, they would long since have been known. I have never seen anyone in consultation who had not been doing hard psychological work long before turning to me.

This view of the basic rule leads naturally to one facet of the issue of resistance. If a rule is something imposed, then failure to follow the rule is a form of defiance or subversion of the residing authority. Resistance, long recognized as the clinical manifestation within the analytic dyad of conflict and defense on the intrapsychic level, is of the essence of the analytic process. It is not insubordination.

Two additional points are significant. First, empathy is a vital part of the analyst's work. The wish both to correct a mistakenly rigid and intellectualized picture of the analytic model and, more fairly, to notice the humanly dyadic nature of the analytic process has contributed to clarification of the importance of empathy. However, current preoccupation with empathy has at times obscured the importance of free association. To be analytically informed and accurate, empathic perceptions must be combined with what is learned by attention to the content of free associations. Both are essential for validity in determining unconscious fantasies.

Second, there is also a fundamental rule for the analyst. Just as the patient has no exceptions to the basic rule, the analyst also must consider all experiences within the analysis for their informational value. Observations of what passes within me are vital data that I examine to sort out what they tell me of myself from what they tell me of the patient. Nothing that goes through my own mind or feelings can be dismissed out of hand.

As analyst, I both effect and affect the analytic work. My present attention to myself results not simply from a wish to express how I work, but rather my sense that I as analyst am a vital tool in effecting the analysis. My personality and technique effect, that is, make possible, the basic work; my personality and style affect the tone of the unfolding work.

It is as a collaborator that I can invite the patient to tolerate regression and exposure for the sake of our common goal. It is as someone with technical expertise and at times greater experience in analytic introspection that I can often hear the hidden messages from the patient, sort out my own contributions to them, and report back to the patient that which I hear. These points emphasize a concept I feel essential to analytic work: *If analysis is a journey, the transference–countertransference engagement is the train, not the destination!*

The spontaneously unfolding transference provides the primary and crucial set of data about the patient's inner life. The consciously and unconsciously experienced fantasies, feelings, urges, and inhibitions provide the heart of the difficult analytic work; hearing about displaced relationships is peripheral.

Early in the analytic work, I find such "talking about" informative for bringing to open life the transference neurosis. Late in the analytic work, I find myself sitting considerably more on the sidelines while I listen to the patient's growing self-analytic functions in action. But the central part of the analytic work takes place in the area of the transference, which is what I think Freud meant when he observed that one cannot execute a man by hanging him in effigy. Transference is not the end point for cure, effected simply by the dynamics of a corrective interpersonal experience. It is rather the means by which underlying genetic roots can be known—emotionally and intellectually—and mastered.

A young accountant briefly alluded to earlier opened his analytic work in an unusually dramatic fashion. Its very exaggeration shows how the transference at times takes shape, how I at times observe it, and how at those times when I work well I utilize my experience of the transference in the service of insight rather than primarily in the service of my own comfort.

This man had been sent for analysis by his wife, who in the course of her own analysis concluded she could not continue living with him unless he changed.

When he consulted me he appeared incredibly controlled, detached, and rigid. Although a professional, he was ruled by such totalistic perfectionism as almost never to be able to effect any simple action. The purchase of an unfinished bookcase involved more than a six-month city-wide search and accumulation of files to determine which was the best bookcase to buy in the entire metropolitan area. He was bright and talented enough to have had a modicum of professional success, despite the fact that completion of any project always required another person to do the final write-up.

At the outset, the patient appeared formal, precise, cooperative, and proper, a person greatly concerned with "bookkeeping" balances in his contacts with others. He was not on a first-name basis with any of his colleagues and his obsessive control and perfectionism were robbing him of apparent satisfaction in any area of his life.

In his first session, the patient spoke of his background, a barren one as an only child on an isolated southern rural farm. During that first hour, I had a momentary sense of complete freedom and power, a sense that I could schedule his appointments with any frequency, any timing I chose, that I could shift his hours as I wished, all with no concern for his reactions. In a crazy way it was a fantasy that he would be an "ideal patient" (reflecting what was later understood as his concept of his parents' image of an "ideal child"), that is, one who was no threat, no challenge, no problem, no burden. It was a feeling that there would be no future demands or complications, that the analysis would be easy and effortless, even if inconsequential. There was even a sense that the patient would allow me absolute importance without my ever having to be confronted by his being accommodating or compliant, simply with a sense that he did not matter. This brief flight of fantasy during our interchange was followed by a second shift in my mood, a strong wave of sleepiness.

During the course of the analysis that followed, all of my reactions became comprehensible in terms of his early development, and it is the fact that such subsequent under-standing took place, not the details of his life, that is cogent here.

Much time was spent by the patient's making moun-tains out of molehills, speaking of trivial details with exquis-ite precision. Minutiae of daily life and of professional projects were offered endlessly. I found it harder and harder to follow him, feeling increasingly impotent, in striking con-trast to my feelings in the first session. I felt the patient and his analysis becoming more and more remote. At times I thought he came for the sole purpose of driving me crazy, but it was difficult to hold onto even that fantasy version of attachment. I fought to stay awake during the hours, feel-ing as if I were simply filling time and were totally irrelevant in the analysis. He appeared neither satisfied nor dissatis-fied as he dragged on.

Once again, my private theoretical speculations at the time, including those regarding issues of aggression, are not cogent here. These, too, later came to be understood, but for about a half year the situation I have described continued.

The patient droned on. I began to feel I could take it no longer. One day, outside the hour, I had the fantasy of the patient getting away from me altogether, of his leaving this world, and of my reaching out and grabbing him by his foot to pull him back.

I mentioned, as a complaint to a colleague about the patient I was to see the next hour, my thought of pulling the patient back by his foot. The patient then came in, and re-ported a dream in which his mother was arranging his father's body in a coffin. (Actually, both parents were then living.) In the long and complex dream, the patient found one detail especially confusing. In the coffin, one of the father's feet was broken at the ankle and bent back, "as if someone had grabbed hold of his foot and pulled him back." The moment was for me eerily uncanny.

The taste of the earlier detachment returned from time to time, but it was never again the same, never again so total.

That dream became the text for the dreams of the next few years of analytic work, with new dreams generally connecting by some detail to that crucial first dream. Indeed, the patient's analysis and life story unfolded in broad reference to that dream. The only element that was never understood, and that continued to puzzle the patient, was why the foot was bent back. Phallic and castration issues were explored, but the specific symbol never lost its mystery.

Anecdotal vignettes can demonstrate, but they bear their own hazards. This uncanny transference–countertransference phenomenon was attached to a dream that turned out to be the skeleton on which subsequent analytic work was fleshed out. In this analysis, it was precisely such an uncanny experience that announced a crucial shift in the transference. I believe it reasonable that the patient's move evidenced some subterranean, essential work already done. This "turning point" (the "twisted foot" comment I made to a colleague and the simultaneous parallel image in the patient's dream) may well have represented a shared preconscious and unconscious understanding in which the patient and I were about to become attuned to the meaning of his massive affective resistance.

The vignette demonstrates an extreme. Most analyses progress within a narrower compass of experiencing and understanding, yet all include unconscious and preconscious components. Conscious mastery is essential and is certainly the desired end point, but it does not exist in detached cognitive isolation. The ability to interpret requires attention to pattern, content, and details of associations and also to the emotional forces evoked and elicited in the analyst.

I sense that my personality, my style, and also my understanding of proper analytic technique all limit my functioning at work to a fairly narrow range. Yet there are some patients who know me as cold and remote, and others who feel I am warm and personal. To some, I have seemed hopelessly detached, even emotionally absent; to others, I have seemed ever present. In some important way, each has been right.

I participate with each patient in structuring an analytic situation and in trying to do the analytic work. However, unless I interfere with some grievous personal intrusion that is fatal to a significant segment of the analytic work, neither my proper technique nor my errors determine the basic course of the analysis. The nature of each unfolding analysis is overwhelmingly determined by the power of the patient's transference forces.

Life in the middle phase of an analysis has very little of the clarity retrospectively imposed by case reports. Ambiguity, paradox, and even seeming amorphousness abound. Never able to grasp consciously more than a fragment of the forces at work, I find that I have to pressure myself against the tendency to premature closure, to false understanding. I do not feel I owe it to some inner perfectionistic pressure to be instantly understanding, but I still do feel I must always try to understand.

Tolerance for feeling lost at sea is essential, particularly in the middle phase of an analysis. Here my conscience has been a difficult adversary. Repeatedly, I find myself in the position of stupidly not understanding, of trying to understand but missing the point. The great ally of that enemy is the professional community's perfectionistic proclamation of standards of excellence, standards that at times seem to suggest that somewhere someone knows exactly the right word to say in each situation, that my own confusion is evidence of inexcusably sloppy inadequacies on my part. (Knowing that such a professional perfectionism somewhere "out there" is both a projection of a part of my own superego and a partial external fact, I am sadly aware how often I have played the game, participating in competitively doing the same unto others.)

My own great ally in the face of such perfectionism is honesty. Honesty here is not simply a personal value but is a benefit of the reality principle. It makes life incredibly easier. I am quite content to have patients conclude in the course of their work with me that "dumb but honest" is my fitting motto.

I tried to work analytically one time with a woman who was simply too much for me. Believing that I could hang in with her to get the work done, I tried to continue despite the presence of a flood of primitive forces that was more than I could handle. Finally, I told the patient so. She said, with some indignation, that she thought the analyst was supposed to be able to take anything. I answered that at the moment I was not too clear about that, but that I knew what was going on was more than *I* could take. If the forces at play were what had to be dealt with, then there could be no question she was entitled to have them dealt with and my own limits' interference with the work did not mean that the work ought not proceed. Feeling unable to be of analytic use to her, I suggested she consult a colleague who could be of benefit.

I am not happy about this vignette, but the postscript is also to the point. A year or two later I received a telephone call from a woman requesting a consultation. I was so startled when this woman identified herself on the phone that I blurted out the question of where she received my name. I recognized her as my prior patient's best friend. The lady on the phone laughed. She said that her friend had made the referral, telling her all about how the work had gone but adding that I could be trusted as honest.

In general, I find I make several sorts of mistakes. The type that often troubles the patient the most—when what I have to say is both slower and more imprecise than either the patient or I would prefer—is that from which I feel the least guilt.

The other categories of my mistakes are those arising from ignorance or from intrusions of unmastered personal conflicts and needs. Ignorance is a troublesome enemy. I am distressed at the frequency with which I hear people speak of how little is known by and about psychoanalysis. There is already more known than any one person could learn in a lifetime. That is a fact, not an excuse. It certainly offers no help to the patient tangled in a subtlety of psychopathology that I do not yet understand and that someone else would. The other category, that of eccentric countertransferential distortions on my part, is like a chronic plague: repeatedly fought, never eradicated.

Whatever the source of my error, the primary cure is candid clarification. Once seen, it must be acknowledged, to myself but not necessarily immediately to the other. The aim of analytic technique is always analytic understanding, not simply making me, the analyst, feel good or less guilty. If an acknowledgment would interfere with an unfolding understanding of the patient's significances, then it must be deferred. The effort is to analyze anxiety, not obscure it. Acknowledgment does not mean confession, exhibitionism, or revelation of my personal fantasies. The formal work in the office is the patient's analysis.

These issues of ambiguity and error are most relevant to my activity particularly during the middle phase. I try to follow the patient, but I also try to interpret what I hear and what I think is going on. What I anticipate the patient will make of my interpretations is for me of minor importance; what the patient makes of them is centrally important. The possibility of a patient's finding what I say as implying something peculiar does not inhibit me. Tact involves respecting the patient's underlying equal validity, equal to mine. It does not mean demonstrating what a sensitive, nice chap I am, one who would never risk hurting anyone's feelings.

Knowing that whatever I hear has been processed within me, and therefore knowing that whatever I interpret cannot be totally precise to the patient's meanings, I try not to offer interpretations *ex cathedra*. Most interpretations are trial interpretations aimed at getting ever closer to whatever forces are unfolding from the patient.

Yet there are frequently times, often when issues of domination and submission are being dealt with, when the patient acts and feels as if I, unlike the imago of the parent, must not be too definitive. There are times when a patient tries to slip around issues without ever experiencing the feelings that would accompany a forbidden confrontation. There are times when for many reasons the patient works subtly to keep me from speaking clearly. When something seems clear to me, I try to say it clearly, not with, "I wonder whether" or "What about . . . ?" or "Do you think, maybe?" but in simple declarative sentences. There is, of course, the danger of engaging in a power struggle. I do not have the right or analytic reason to start such an issue, but if that is what the patient is engaged in, I have neither the right nor the inclination to avoid it.

Also, despite the need for appropriate silence on my part, there are times I speak up to avoid misunderstandings. After a while all patients catch on to my frequent lack of response to questions, to my silence, as a useful analytic technique rather than as evidence of my capricious or arbitrary nature. However, especially in the earlier parts of an analysis, silence generally is taken as communicating assent.

No rule holds up across the board in the face of individual unconscious meanings. For several years into an analysis, my silence was felt by one young person as indicating unspeakable contempt and criticism. Indeed, that has proved analytically to be at least as commonly attributed to silence as communication of assent. While I make statements as called for to clarify, I try not to speak merely to avoid having disagreeable motives or feelings ascribed to me.

Regarding the inevitable question of what to interpret, I find the old saw of interpreting what is on the surface to be generally useless and at times wrong. As I discussed this matter in great detail in an earlier section I shall summarize here only that its uselessness arises from the frequency with which one finds very much on the surface—the saying offers no help in choosing, and its wrongness comes from its implicit bias toward the conscious and away from the unconscious. If I as the analyst will not aim toward the deep water of the unconscious, who will?

The two major guidelines I use to help me choose what to interpret are those of affect and transference. Every statement I, the analyst, make involves a choice. Free association is the technique for the patient to attempt. If I randomly accept all messages as being of equal importance, I trivialize all significance. I prefer to comment on messages that include affective experience or defense against the experience of that feeling by the patient. My motto is to go in the direction of anxiety. Interpretation of symbols as such seems to me sterile and intellectual, usually without power for the patient.

The other guideline for interpretation is that of the transference. This does not mean that I pounce on the transference implications of everything the patient says. Indeed, that strikes me as an effective way to interfere with the crystallization of an intense transference neurosis. I do try to conceive of what patterns the patient describes outside the analysis in terms of how they relate to what occurs within the transference–countertransference relationship. For me, that relationship is the living biopsy specimen of the patient's forces and patterns.

The question of interpretation also demands attention to the relationship of resistance and drive. I am not entirely comfortable with the word "resistance." It seems a fine word when used to name a clear process, such as in the phrase "inner resistance," but for that we have the word "defense." Resistance is traditionally and properly used to refer to the manifestation of that inner defense in the analytic context. As such, it is a useful, indeed vital, signal of the presence of a not yet fully exposed conflict, and as such a signal, it is to be welcomed as a harbinger that something is working its way into the open.

However, the word readily lends itself to only a part of its meaning, that of a signal that goes unrecognized. Then there is the sense that the patient is frustrating the analysis and me. Reaction to such felt frustration without analytic processing is a countertransferential intrusion. Unrecognized, resistance becomes a hook that captures the analyst on unrecognized ambition, a personal urge for power or control. Recognized, resistance is a valued friend. Without resistance there is no analytic work, but recognized, resistance is the cutting edge of progress, the primary road to clinical analysis. Resistance brings forth central analytic questions, "How come this?" and "Why now?"

Consistently, my theme is that of attending to the meanings revealed by the process of the unfolding transference forces. It is in that sense that I try to attend to process in the context of content, to content in the context of process.

It is also in that context that I consider the question of the central importance of dreams in analysis. There can be no doubt that dreams are the royal road to the unconscious, but a clinical analysis is not a royal journey. In a clinical analysis, one leaves the royal road for the mud and the underbrush, returning from time to time to the high ground to extend the view. Brilliant views, like that of Moses looking over the Promised Land, are wondrously impressive, but they are no substitute for the struggle to capture new territory. Working to expose a clearing, getting lost and then finding new paths, revealing the intensities of one's struggles in the actuality of the analytic experience—it is the transference neurosis and its resolution that provide the crucial road in clinical psychoanalysis.

There are, of course, times I get a glimpse of an unfolding pattern before the patient has come to recognize it. If I feel it to be clear, I state what I see to the patient. Interpretation of resistance may come first, but I do not believe the discoveries of ego psychology are properly used if they are put in the service of avoiding deep meanings. An analysis should expose and examine hidden horrors and ghosts, not sidestep them. The depth to aim for is always the most the patient can take, a depth often underestimated by both analyst and patient.

The unfolding dialectic of the analysis in the context of the analytic dyad gives each interpretation a double quality. Work had to proceed before an interpretation could be offered. In that sense, interpretations are, as Laurence Hall spoke of them, commemorative events. Yet they open new ground at the same time that they consolidate the old. I am not in accord with those current theories that would seem to minimize the importance of interpretation. It is not enough that I understand something that is going on within the patient; I have to share that knowledge with the patient. Although they are commemorative events, interpretations are essential parts of the ongoing war, not dispensable subsequent memorial ceremonies. Working out and working through take place in stepwise fashion, even if small step by small step.

I have addressed the major themes of analytic work: active unconscious forces and fantasies, their exposure within the transference neurosis in an analytic situation, interpretation of resistances and unconscious forces so as to expose the unconscious to conscious mastery. But the daily work also proceeds in the presence of routine problems of everyday analytic life. Fees, schedule changes, missed sessions, acting out, and so on are the stuff of daily work. I make errors, but my routine handling of such issues is determined by how I understand each of them in the context of the broad themes I have described. An example is that of the patient's actions outside the analysis. Early on in the work, especially as I try to help the development of the transference neurosis, I am alert to outside action for its possible implications of the patient's defending against emotional intensity by diluting our relationship, carrying out part of the feelings and urges "out there" rather than "in here." When I see such a process occurring, I point it out to the patient. Enactment can be a powerful defense against experiencing and remembering.

It is not always so, however. As the work is proceeding, what might seem to be acting out may turn instead into enacting in the service of extending insight and actualizing growth. An analysis is not a verbal chess game. Insight that does not extend the range of a person's potential in life is not true insight. Therefore, I value action not only with the phobic patient who must be assisted to confront anxiety but with anyone who seems to be exploring, who is working in the service of insight and growth. I value action in such cases and avoid interpreting all as acting out.

With the passing years I find myself ever more at ease. I find it less often necessary or appropriate to vary my basic routines. On reflection, I think this arises from increasing respect for the analytic process, not simply from personal aging. For instance, I do not lightly or frequently change a patient's hours or cancel an appointment.

When it comes to money, which is always an area of important private meaning to each patient, I try to maintain a predictable consistency. I earn my living by selling my analytic services. I charge by units of time, though it is the service that I sell, not my time. Once my time is committed, the patient is responsible for paying for it whether or not the patient uses it. I do not see myself as having either the right or even the inclination to decide when a session should be "excused" or not. While within the context of the analytic regression the patient exposes a personal side that is childlike, it is an adult exposing that facet of the personality, not a child. The patient's validity is equal to mine, with the patient having as much responsibility for the patient's life as I have for mine.

The list of such routine issues of analytic practice is far from exhausted. My wish, without possibly touching every imaginable base, is to demonstrate that the appropriate criteria of how to handle such matters as they arise are those determinants that are realistic, honest, and will protect the continued course of the analytic work.

Just as no two analyses are alike, no two terminations are the same. Some analyses have a classical shape with a clear transference neurosis and a well-defined termination phase heralded by termination dreams and marked by intense recapitulation of previously worked-through conflicts. Many are less clearly demarcated, though in each the heart of the transference neurosis has been exposed and explicitly explored before an authentic termination arises. I prefer to call things by clear names: termination, stopping, and quitting are each called what they are, with an effort to avoid any glossing over.

My focus in this appendix has been on myself at work. That focus has distorted attention, turning it away from the patient and the analysis proper to that segment in which I am most apparent. In the whole picture of a clinical analysis, my own contribution is less noticeable, more a part of the background canvas on which a tableau of the patient's inner life is painted.

I return to where I began this book, acknowledging those who have taught and influenced me. Here I have consciously restrained myself and mentioned only Freud, whose combined genius and humanity have created the language in which the rest write sentences. When I start to refer to others, I am flooded by a list, such a fond list—that I fear to forget one—that I worry who should go first, who could go second. I am a product of my teachers, of prior writers, my times, and my patients, as well as myself.

Yet at this last moment, at the bottom line, I, like all analysts, am in my office daily, alone with one other person with whom and for whom I work and to whose struggle toward insight I am responsible.

References

Abrams, S. (1981). Insight: the Teiresian gift. *Psychoanalytic Study of the Child* 36: 251–270. New Haven, CT: Yale University Press.

Arlen, M. (1975). *Passage to Ararat*. New York: Farrar, Straus & Giroux.

Arlow, J. A. (1979). Metaphor and the psychoanalytic situation. *Psychoanalytic Quarterly* 48: 363–385.

Bibring, E. (1937). On the theory of the results of psycho-analysis. *International Journal of Psycho-Analysis* 18: 170–189.

Bird, B. (1957). The curse of insight. *Bulletin of the Philadelphia Association for Psychoanalysis* 7: 101–104.

Boesky, D. (1990). *Psychic surface*. Discussion at panel on The Analytic Surface, meeting of the American Psychoanalytic Association, New York, May.

Brenner, C. (1982). *The Mind in Conflict*. New York: International Universities Press.

Calef, V. (1987). The process in psychoanalysis. *Dialogue, A Journal of Psychoanalytic Perspectives* 7: 11–21.

Chasseguet-Smirgel, J. (1988). The triumph of humor. In *Fantasy, Myth, and Reality: Essays in Honor of Jacob A. Arlow, M.D.*, ed. H. P. Blum, Y. Kramer, A. K. Richards, and A. D. Richards, pp. 197–213. Madison, CT: International Universities Press.

Chaucer, G. (1960). *The Canterbury Tales*. London: Penguin Books.

Deutsch, H. (1926). Okkulte Vorgäng während der Psychoanalyse. *Imago* 12: 418–433.

Fenichel, O. (1941). *Problems of Psychoanalytic Technique*. New York: Psychoanalytic Quarterly, Inc.

Fliess, R. (1942). The metapsychology of the analyst. *Psychoanalytic Quarterly* 11: 211–227.

Friedman, L. (1985). Potentiality shrouded: how the newer theories work. *Psychoanalytic Quarterly* 54: 379–414.

——— (1994). Ferrum, ignis, and medicina: return to the crucible. Plenary presentation at Annual Meeting of the American Psychoanalytic Association, Philadelphia, May.

Freud, A. (1954). Problems of technique in adult analysis. *Bulletin of the Philadelphia Association for Psychoanalysis* 4: 44–70.

——— (1981). Insight. Its presence and absence as a factor in normal development. *Psychoanalytic Study of the Child* 36: 241–249. New Haven, CT: Yale University Press.

Freud, S. (1900). The interpretation of dreams. *Standard Edition* 4/5: 1–626.

——— (1901). Fragment of an analysis of a case of hysteria: prefatory remarks. *Standard Edition* 7: 7–14.

——— (1905a). Three essays on the theory of sexuality. *Standard Edition* 7: 125–243.

——— (1905b). Jokes and their relation to the unconscious. *Standard Edition* 8: 3–236.

——— (1905c). Fragment of an analysis of a case of hysteria. *Standard Edition* 7: 3–122.

——— (1910a). 'Wild' psycho-analysis. *Standard Edition* 11: 219–227.

——— (1910b). The future prospects of psycho-analytic therapy. *Standard Edition* 11: 139–151.

—— (1911). The handling of dream-interpretation in psycho-analysis. *Standard Edition* 12: 89–96.

—— (1914). On the history of the psycho-analytic movement. *Standard Edition* 14: 3–66.

—— (1915a). The unconscious. *Standard Edition* 14: 159–215.

—— (1915b). Observations on transference-love. *Standard Edition* 12: 157–171.

—— (1915c). Instincts and their vicissitudes. *Standard Edition* 14: 109–140.

—— (1916). On transience. *Standard Edition* 14: 303–307.

—— (1919). Lines of advance in psycho-analytic therapy. *Standard Edition* 17: 157–168.

—— (1923a). Two encyclopaedia articles. *Standard Edition* 18: 235–259.

—— (1923b). The ego and the id. *Standard Edition* 19: 3–66.

—— (1927). Humour. *Standard Edition* 21: 159–166.

—— (1930). Civilization and its discontents. *Standard Edition* 21: 59–145.

Gardner, M. R. (1989). *Self Inquiry*. Hillsdale, NJ/London: Analytic Press.

—— (1991). Presentation at panel on *Self Observation, Self Analysis, and Reanalysis* at annual meeting of American Psychoanalytic Association, New York City, December.

Gitelson, M. (1952). The emotional position of the analyst in the psychoanalytic situation. *International Journal of Psycho-Analysis* 33: 1–10.

—— (1962). The curative factors in psycho-analysis. *International Journal of Psycho-Analysis* 43: 194–205.

Gray, P. (1986). On helping analysands observe intrapsychic activity. In *Psychoanalysis: The Science of Mental Conflict—Essays in Honor of Charles Brenner*, ed. A. Richards and M. Willick, pp. 245–262. Hillsdale, NJ: Analytic Press.

Greenacre, P. (1954). The role of transference. *Journal of the American Psychoanalytic Association* 2: 671–684.

Greenson, R. R. (1960). Empathy and its vicissitudes. *International Journal of Psycho-Analysis* 41: 418–424.

Hartmann, H. (1951). Technical implications of ego psychology. *Psychoanalytic Quarterly* 20: 31–43.

Hartmann, H., and Loewenstein, R. (1962). Notes on the super-ego. *Psychoanalytic Study of the Child* 17: 42–81. New York: International Universities Press.

Hatcher, R. L. (1973). Insight and self-observation. *Journal of the American Psychoanalytic Association* 21: 377–398.

Isay, R. A. (1977). Ambiguity in speech. *Journal of the American Psychoanalytic Association* 25: 427–452.

Jacobs, T. J. (1991). *The Use of the Self: Countertransference and Communication in the Analytic Situation*. Madison, CT: International Universities Press.

Joseph, E. D. (1986). Psychoanalytic concepts of insight. In *Psychoanalysis: The Science of Mental Conflict*, ed. A. D. Richards and M. S. Willick, pp. 263–280. Hillsdale, NJ: Analytic Press.

Kestenberg, J. (1968). Outside and inside, male and female. *Journal of the American Psychoanalytic Association* 16: 457–520.

Kohut, H. (1959). Introspection, empathy, and psychoanalysis. *Journal of the American Psychoanalytic Association* 7: 459–483.

Kris, E. (1938). Ego development and the comic. In *Psychoanalytic Explorations in Art*, pp. 204–216. New York: International Universities Press, 1952.

——— (1956). On some vicissitudes of insight in psychoanalysis. In *Selected Papers*. New Haven, CT: Yale University Press.

Kubie, L. S. (1971). The destructive potential of humor in psychotherapy. *American Journal of Psychiatry* 127: 861–866.

Laplanche, J., and Pontalis, J.-B. (1973). *The Language of Psycho-Analysis*. New York: Norton.

Leavy, S. A. (1980). *The Psychoanalytic Dialogue*. New Haven and London: Yale University Press.

Levy, S. T., and Inderbitzen, L. B. (1990). The analytic surface and the theory of technique. *Journal of the American Psychoanalytic Association* 38: 371–392.

Loewald, H. W. (1960). On the therapeutic action of psychoanalysis. *International Journal of Psycho-Analysis* 41: 16–33.

Loewenstein, R. M. (1951). The problem of interpretation. *Psychoanalytic Quarterly* 20: 1–14.

—— (1956). Some remarks on the role of speech in psychoanalytic technique. *International Journal of Psycho-Analysis* 37: 460–468.

McLaughlin, J. T. (1961). The analyst and the Hippocratic oath. *Journal of the American Psychoanalytic Association* 9: 106–123.

—— (1988). The analyst's insights. *Psychoanalytic Quarterly* 57: 370–389.

Medlicott, F. (1969). In *The International Dictionary of Thoughts*, ed. J. Bradley et al. Chicago: Ferguson.

Meyerson, P. (1965). Modes of insight. *Journal of the American Psychoanalytic Association* 13: 771–792.

Michels, R. (1986). Oedipus and insight. *Psychoanalytic Quarterly* 55: 599–617.

Modell, A. H. (1965). On having the right to a life: an aspect of the superego's development. *International Journal of Psycho-Analysis* 46: 323–331.

—— (1968). *Object Love and Reality*. New York: International Universities Press.

Murray, J. (1964). Narcissism and the ego ideal. *Journal of the American Psychoanalytic Association* 12: 477–511.

Nacht, S. (1965). Interference between transference and countertransference. In *Drives, Affects, Behavior*, vol. 2, ed. M. Schur, pp. 315–322. New York: International Universities Press.

Novey, S. (1968). *The Second Look*. Baltimore: The Johns Hopkins University Press.

Olinick, S. L. (1980). *The Psychotherapeutic Instrument*. New York/London: Jason Aronson.

——, Poland, W. S., Grigg, K. A., and Granatir, W. L. (1973). The psychoanalytic work ego: process and interpretation. *International Journal of Psycho-Analysis* 54: 143–151.

Pacella, B. (1975). Early ego development and the déjà vu. *Journal of the American Psychoanalytic Association* 23: 300–318.

Paniagua, C. (1985). A methodological approach to surface material. *International Review of Psycho-Analysis* 12: 311–325.

———— (1989). Patient's surface, clinical surface and workable surface. Presented at the Congress of The International Psychoanalytic Association, Rome, July.

Peller, L. (1954). Libidinal phases, ego development, and play. *Psychoanalytic Study of the Child* 9: 178–198. New York: International Universities Press.

Pigman, G. W. (1995). Freud and the history of empathy. *International Journal of Psycho-Analysis* 76: 237–256.

Poland, W. S. (1978). On the analyst's responsibility: an editorial. *Journal of the Philadelphia Association for Psychoanalysis* 4: 187–196.

Proust, M. (1913–1927). *Remembrance of Things Past*. Trans. C. K. S. Moncrieff, T. Kilmartin, and A. Mayor. New York: Random House, 1981.

Racker, H. (1957). The meanings and uses of countertransference. *Psychoanalytic Quarterly* 26: 303–357.

———— (1968). *Transference and Countertransference*. New York: International Universities Press.

Rangell, L. (1975). Psychoanalysis and the process of change. *International Journal of Psycho-Analysis* 56: 87–98.

Read, A. W. (1989). Perspective on the English language. In Profiles: Allen Walker Read, by M. Stacey. *The New Yorker*, September 4, p. 64.

Reid, J., and Finesinger, J. (1952). The role of insight in psychotherapy. *American Journal of Psychiatry* 108: 726–734.

Richfield, J. (1954). An analysis of the concept of insight. *Psychoanalytic Quarterly* 23: 390–408.

Rizzuto, A. M. (1985). The function of the analyst's memory in the analytic process. Paper presented at the meeting of the American Psychoanalytic Association, Denver, May.

Rose, G. J. (1969). *King Lear* and the use of humor in treatment. *Journal of the American Psychoanalytic Association* 17: 927–940.

Roustang, F. (1983). *Psychoanalysis Never Lets Go*. Baltimore and London: The Johns Hopkins University Press.

———— (1987). How do you make a paranoiac laugh? *Modern Language Notes* 102: 707–718.

Sabatini, R. (1921). *Scaramouche: A Romance of the French Revolution*. Boston/New York: Houghton Mifflin.

Shapiro, T. (1990). Unconscious fantasy: introduction. *Journal of the American Psychoanalytic Association* 38: 39–46.

Sharpe, E. F. (1940). Psycho-physical problems revealed in language: an examination of metaphor. In *Collected Papers on Psycho-Analysis*. London: Hogarth, 1950.

Shengold, L. (1981). Insight as metaphor. *Psychoanalytic Study of the Child* 36: 289–306. New Haven, CT: Yale University Press.

——— (1989). *Soul Murder: The Effect of Childhood Abuse and Deprivation*. New Haven, CT: Yale University Press.

Silber, A. (1991). Presentation at panel on *Self Observation, Self Analysis, and Reanalysis* at the meeting of the American Psychoanalytic Association, New York, December.

Southwood, H. M. (1974). The communicative relationship. *International Journal of Psycho-Analysis* 55: 417–423.

Spitz, R. A. (1956). Countertransference: comments on its varying role in the analytic situation. *Journal of the American Psychoanalytic Association* 4: 256–265.

Stein, C. (1983). Unpublished discussion at the Franco-American Psychoanalytic Encounter, Paris, April.

Sterba, R. (1934). The fate of the ego in analytic therapy. *International Journal of Psycho-Analysis* 15: 117–126

Stone, L. (1954). The widening scope of indications for psychoanalysis. *Journal of the American Psychoanalytic Association* 2: 567–594.

——— (1961). *The Psychoanalytic Situation: An Examination of Its Developmental and Essential Nature*. New York: International Universities Press.

Stoppard, T. (1967). *Rosencrantz & Guildenstern Are Dead*. New York: Grove.

Strachey, J. (1934). The nature of the therapeutic action of psychoanalysis. Reprinted. *International Journal of Psycho-Analysis* 50: 275–292, 1969.

Viderman, S. (1974). Interpretation in the analytical space. *International Review of Psycho-Analysis* 1: 467–480.

———— (1979). The analytic space: meaning and problems. *Psychoanalytic Quarterly* 48: 257–291.

Viederman, M. (1991). The real person of the analyst and his role in the process of psychoanalytic cure. *Journal of the American Psychoanalytic Association* 39: 451–490.

Waelder, R. (1933). The psychoanalytic theory of play. *Psychoanalytic Quarterly* 2: 108–224.

Wallerstein, R. S. (1965). The goals of psychoanalysis: a survey of analytic viewpoints. *Journal of the American Psychoanalytic Association* 13: 748–770.

Weber, S. (1982). *The Legend of Freud*. Minneapolis: University of Minnesota Press.

Wheelis, A. (1950), The place of action in personality change. *Psychiatry* 13: 135–148.

Winnicott, D. W. (1949). Hate in the countertransference. *International Journal of Psycho-Analysis* 30: 69–74.

————(1953). Transitional objects and transitional phenomena. *International Journal of Psycho-Analysis* 34: 89–97.

Index

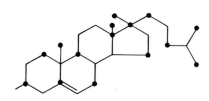

ORGANIC CHEMISTRY
OF SECONDARY
PLANT METABOLISM

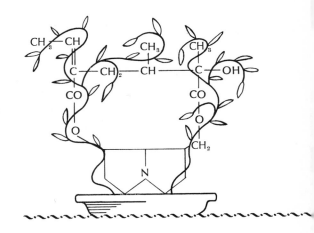

Organic Chemistry of Secondary Plant Metabolism

T. A. GEISSMAN

University of California, Los Angeles

D. H. G. CROUT

University of Exeter

Freeman, Cooper & Company

1736 Stockton Street, San Francisco, California 94133

Preface

This book is intended to help introduce to upper-division undergraduate and graduate students in organic chemistry an area of the subject that is rarely presented in undergraduate chemistry courses. Although the study of the organic compounds of nature engages the attention of many chemists and represents a major area of investigation, students of organic chemistry often encounter it only in specialized courses and seminars, and then, in many cases, only if they have chosen the field for specialization. Moreover, despite the fact that there exists a vast literature devoted principally or entirely to the chemistry of naturally occurring compounds, there are few books or monographs of moderate length that provide an overall view of the field and introduce the student to the classes of compounds that nature provides and to the unifying concepts that bind them together into a coherent whole. The authors, and doubtless other teachers of organic chemistry as well, have frequently been asked by inquiring students to suggest to them a general textbook that will introduce them to this field of study. There are many excellent books about separate classes of naturally occurring compounds, but there are few of a less specialized nature. It is the hope of the authors that this book will serve as a means by which the inquiring student can survey the area, be led to further study of one of its parts, and perceive the relationship of the various parts to each other.

Although there is no doubt that a sound education in the theory and principles of organic chemistry is an essential and proper preparation for the study of naturally occurring organic compounds, natural products chemistry is more than a body of exercises in structure elucidation and methods of synthesis. There are many aspects of natural products chemistry that deserve a special emphasis that is not likely to be encountered in a conventional course in organic chemistry. Biosynthesis, metabolic origins and fates, cellular transformations, physiological and other biological properties of natural substances are topics that are peculiar to this class of compounds.

v

Natural products are, of course, organic compounds. Some of them are of a simple and quite unexceptional structure, while others are of complex, even bizarre, constitution. Their chemical properties, the transformations they undergo, the methods used for their synthesis can be dealt with in terms of general principles that may bear no necessary relationship to their origins. Carbonium ion rearrangements, stereospecific cyclizations, nucleophilic substitution reactions, oxidations and reductions, and many of the characteristic reactions of functional groups find many striking and instructive examples in the chemistry of natural products. Yet many of these may be regarded as illustrative of principles which the competent student in a properly presented course in organic chemistry can learn with little or no acquaintance with compounds of natural origin. Thus, while it is valuable to use the chemistry of natural products as an instructional medium for enlarging upon organic chemical principles that are known in other contexts, they are not indispensable for this purpose. Their greatest importance lies in the metabolic processes by which they are formed, in the genetic individuality that they express, and in the added dimensions of special fascination that they add to the subject of organic chemistry and to related fields of scientific inquiry.

The field of natural products chemistry is immense both in the almost limitless scope of the compound types that it embraces and in the literature that documents its progress. Specialized works, many of them in many volumes, describe the chemistry of separate classes of compounds: steroids, terpenes, alkaloids, polyphenols, sugars, carotenoids, fatty acids, and so on. Compounds of special classes of organisms—lichens, bacteria, fungi, higher plants—are treated in special monographs. Many specialized periodical journals are devoted to or include articles on one or another class of natural products. Because of the great size of these areas of investigation, and because many individual topics are adequately treated in special monographs and books, this textbook has had to be limited in its coverage. We have chosen to stress those aspects of the subject that the student is not likely to find in a general organic chemistry course in which compounds of natural origin are occasionally brought into the discussion. Certain classes of compounds are treated superficially, others scarcely at all: steroids, certain classes of antibiotic compounds, carotenoids, some kinds of alkaloids, and those carbohydrates that are properly classed as "natural products" are discussed briefly or tangentially. Most of these subjects can be studied with comprehension and understanding by the student who has developed a familiarity with the kinds of metabolic processes that are involved in their formation and interconversions. We have resisted the attempt to avoid the criticism that we have neglected to include one or another topic of special interest to one or another individual. We cannot pretend that what we have included is what is "most important," nor that topics that are omitted are less interesting than what is included. We do believe, however, that the general principles of the chemistry of natural products that are described and illustrated in this book will furnish a foundation upon which the student may build a more detailed and extensive familiarity with one or more of the individual classes that make up the compounds of nature.

Reading references to the topics discussed in this book are given in the form of books and review articles that cover large segments of the subject, and certain current research communications that are particularly germane to important points in the discussion. In all cases, the articles cited will be found to contain numerous references to the original articles from which the results described in the text have been taken. We must ask the indulgence of those of our colleagues whose findings have been described without specific reference to their work in individual citations.

It is to be hoped that if this book is used in a formal course of instruction, the instructor will enlarge upon such topics as the methods of isolation, separation and purification of natural products; individual examples of structure diagnosis and elucidation; methods of partial and total synthesis; physiological properties; biological applications of naturally occurring compounds in medicine, agriculture; and so on.

One of the still incompletely developed but potentially valuable areas of inquiry in which the chemistry of natural products will in time be found to play a conspicuous role is in the study of systematic and evolutionary relationships in the world of living organisms. Growing interest in recent years in the application of chemical data to the problems of plant taxonomy and phylogeny has been formalized by the development of an area of investigation known by the terms chemotaxonomy, or chemosystematics. Although many allusions to this aspect of natural products chemistry are to be found in this book, because of the formative state of its present development few attempts have been made to expand upon it in detail. But in order that the reader will always be aware of the importance of the relationship between a natural organic compound and the source from which it comes, all references to plants are given with the use of the genus, species, and family names. It should be emphasized that all studies of natural products should, so far as possible, be placed in the context of the identity and classification of the plant or other organism under study, and careful identification, description, and naming of the living object of study should accompany the description of the chemical results. The chemistry of natural products of plant origin is both organic chemistry and plant biochemistry.

It is the hope of the authors that this book will excite the interest of the students who read it to participate in further discovery in this exciting and significant area of biological science.

T. A. Geissman
University of California, Los Angeles
D. H. G. Crout
University of Exeter

April, 1969

Contents

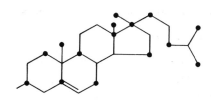

ORGANIC CHEMISTRY

OF SECONDARY

PLANT METABOLISM

▌ CHAPTER

REFERENCES FOR FURTHER READING

Books, monographs and reviews of the principal areas of natural products chemistry.

1. *The Terpenes*, 5 Vols., J. L. Simonsen with L. N. Owen, D. H. R. Barton, and W. C. J. Ross, Cambridge University Press, Cambridge, 1949-1957.

2. *Chemistry of Carbon Compounds*, (E. H. Rodd), Second Edition Edited by S. Coffey. Vol. I, 1964, and continuing.

Vol. IF: Saccharides (Carbohydrates)	Vol. IID, E: Steroids
Vol. IIB: Monocylic Terpenes, Carotenoids	Vol. IVC (1st Ed.): Alkaloids
Vol. IIC: Polycyclic Compounds	

3. *The Chemistry of Natural Products*, K. W. Bentley, Ed., Interscience, New York:

   Vol. I (1957): The Alkaloids, K. W. Bentley

   Vol. II (1959): Mono- and Sesquiterpenoids, P. de Mayo

   Vol. III (1959): Higher Terpenoids, P. de Mayo

   Vol. IV (1960): The Natural Pigments, K. W. Bentley

4. *The Alkaloids*, 11 Vols., R. H. F. Manske and H. L. Holmes, Eds., Academic Press, New York, 1950 and continuing.

5. *Steroids*, L. F. Fieser and M. Fieser. Reinhold, New York, 1959.

6. *The Pfizer Handbook of Microbial Metabolites*, M. W. Miller, McGraw-Hill, N. Y., 1961.

7. *Chemistry of Lichen Substances*, Y. Asahina and S. Shibata, Japan Soc. Promotion of Science, Tokyo, 1954.

8. *Konstitution und Vorkommen der Organischen Pflanzenstoffe*, W. Karrer, Birkhauser, Basel, 1959.

9. *Biogenesis of Antibiotic Substances*, V. Zanek and Z. Hostalek, Czech. Acad. Sciences, Prague, 1965.

10. *Chemistry of Flavonoid Compounds*, T. A. Geissman, Ed., Pergamon, Oxford, 1962.

11. *Progress in the Chemistry of Organic Natural Products*, L. Zechmeister, Ed., Springer Verlag, Vienna. Annual compendia of review monographs on various aspects of natural products chemistry.

12. *Comprehensive Biochemistry*, M. Florkin and E. H. Stotz, Eds., Elsevier, Amsterdam, 1963. Volumes 5-11, *Chemistry of Biological Compounds*.

13. *Encyclopedia of Plant Physiology*, W. Ruhland, Ed., Springer Verlag, Berlin, 1958. Volume X, *The Metabolism of Secondary Plant Products*.

14. *Modern Methods of Plant Analysis*, 4 Vols., K. Paech and M. V. Tracey, Eds., Springer Verlag, Berlin, 1955.

15. *Annual Index of the Reports on Plant Chemistry*, T. Kariyone, Ed., Hirokawa Publ. Co., Tokyo. An annual volume of which the years 1957-1962 are now published.

16. *Recent Advances in Phytochemistry*, T. J. Mabry, R. E. Alston, and V. C. Runeckles, Eds., Appleton-Century-Crofts, 1968. Volume I of a series.

17. *Comparative Phytochemistry*, T. Swain, Ed., Academic Press, New York, 1966.

18. *Chemotaxonomie der Pflanzen*, R. Hegnauer, Birkhauser, Basel, 1962 and continuing. A series, covering all plant families.

19. *Plant Taxonomy*, V. H. Heywood, St. Martin's Press, New York, 1968.

Background and Character of Natural Products Chemistry

1.1 Introduction

The world of nature abounds in organic compounds of nearly every conceivable structural class, the study of which constitutes a fascinating and fruitful area of scientific investigation. The cells of living organisms—plants, fungi, bacteria, lichens, insects, and higher animals—are the sites of intricate and complex synthetic activities that result in the formation of a remarkable array of organic compounds, many of them of great practical importance to mankind.

The compounds discussed in this book are principally those found in the higher (green) plants; it is in this class of living things that the broadest spectrum of synthetic capabilities is found. Synthesis in plants is the more striking because the starting materials are the simple substances water, carbon dioxide, nitrogen (both elemental and in inorganic salts), phosphorus compounds, and a number of inorganic salts in small amounts.

The primary synthetic process of nature is photosynthesis, by which green plants utilize the energy of the sun for the production of organic compounds from carbon dioxide. The initial products of photosynthesis are carbohydrates, further metabolic alterations of which lead to the formation of a pool of organic compounds of low molecular weights and simple structures. Among these are the common sugars, low-molecular-weight carboxylic acids and amino acids. These simple and universally distributed substances are formed in and enter into transformations that are described as *primary metabolic processes*. They form the synthetic starting materials for specific, genetically controlled, enzymatically catalyzed reactions that lead to the complex compounds that characterize the *secondary metabolism* of plants.

A summary outline of the chemical classes with which this book will deal is given in Fig. 1-1.

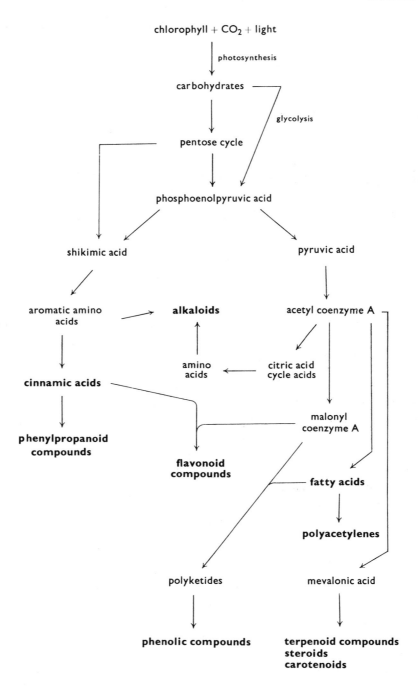

Fig. 1-1. Products of Secondary Plant Metabolism.

The principal reasons for emphasizing the chemistry of plant metabolism are these:

1. The variety of chemical structures found in the organic constituents of plants is so wide that accounts of the proofs of their structures, their synthesis, and the transformations that they undergo provide almost unlimited possibilities for instructive discussion.

2. Because of the wealth of information that is now at hand, the study of plant chemistry can be directed both to those aspects of chemical behavior that are of special interest to the organic chemist, and to matters of fundamental biological importance as well. Paths of biosynthesis, both in the hypothetical but often compelling terms of structural comparison and reconstruction, and in terms of the experimentally verified pathways revealed by the use of isotopic labeling of precursors and intermediates, are now beginning to be understood.

3. Studies of the chemical constitution of plants are beginning to be of substantial value in making it possible to discern and refine evolutionary and systematic (i.e., taxonomic) relationships.

Thus, the study of plant chemistry (or, in a larger sense, natural products chemistry) affords a view of nature that extends from chemistry into related areas of scientific inquiry. It is to these areas that the study of the chemistry of living organisms can be expected to make increasingly useful contributions.

1.2 Primary and Secondary Metabolites

The term "natural products" is recognized by the chemist as meaning those secondary metabolites, usually of relatively complex structure, which are of more restricted distribution and more characteristic of specific botanical sources than are the compounds produced by primary metabolic processes. Compounds ordinarily regarded as the products of the primary metabolism of plants comprise such relatively simple and universally distributed substances as the low molecular weight carboxylic acids of the citric acid cycle, the twenty or so amino acids that make up the majority of the proteins, the common fats and lipids, the common sugars and sugar derivatives.

It is not complexity of structure alone that distinguishes the "natural products" of the organic chemist from those compounds that have traditionally been the province of the biochemist, but rather a degree of uniqueness of the secondary metabolites, some of which are found only in a single plant species, and many of which are characteristic of restricted groups (i.e., a genus or family) of plants. Primary metabolites, on the other hand, are nearly universal in their distribution; they are the products of and participants in the cellular activities of nearly all living things, from single-celled organisms to man. It will, however, be apparent that there are no sharp lines delimiting either class of compounds. While such common amino acids as glycine, alanine, tryptophan, and so on, would not ordinarily be categorized by the term natural products, other amino acids, not found as constituents of proteins but wide-spread in the plant kingdom, such as pipecolic acid, the hypoglycins, β-uracil-3-alanine, stizolobic acid, and many others have found their way into the literature through the studies of the natural products chemist. The chemistry and metabolic transformations of glucose, fructose, the pentoses, and the common polysaccharides have formed a major area of biochemical research; yet such closely related but rare sugars as cladinose, oleandrose, desosamine, and others found as components of antibiotic compounds and of unique steroidal glycosides, have the qualities of uniqueness and infrequency of occurrence that have brought them under the scrutiny of organic chemists. Some illustrative examples are given in Fig. 1-2.

A general characteristic of "natural products" is that few of them have a clearly recognized function in the metabolic activities of the organisms in which they are found. Thus, alkaloids, most of the phenolic compounds of plants, terpenes, sugars of unique and specialized structure, the "rare" amino acids, appear to play no essential role in the cellular economy. This is not to say that they do not enter into metabolic activity, for they are degraded, reduced, acylated, alkylated, and oxidized. But it is not possible in the present state of our knowledge to say that they are indispensable to the plant in which they occur; many plants do not contain alkaloids, or flavones, or certain kinds of terpenes; and in many cases two plants of closely related (or even of the same) species may contain quite different amounts or different representatives of one or another of these classes of compounds.

It is improper, however, to accept the conclusion, as has often been done, that the secondary plant products are "flotsam on the metabolic beach," or to say that they are "functionless anomalies" or simply the "end products" of metabolism. Our inability to ascribe a metabolic function to these compounds may mean only that if they have one we have not yet discovered it. It is only necessary to recall, for example, that shikimic acid (see Eq. 2-49, Chap. 2) was, as recently as about 1950, recorded in monographs and textbooks as an obscure compound that occurred only in the Asiatic plant *Illicium religiosum*; and that within the lifetime of many readers of this book, squalene (see Eq. 11-2, Chap. 11) was known only as an unusual triterpene found in shark liver oil. Both shikimic acid and squalene are now known to be among the most universally distributed and fundamental participants in the metabolic activities of living plants (and in the case of squalene, of animals). It is likely that many of the organic compounds now regarded as "natural products" will in time be recognized as possessing important biological functions. One of the most useful contributions to knowledge that the organic chemist can be expected to make will come from his continuing studies of naturally occurring compounds as biological entities whose origins, transformations, and fate in the living organism

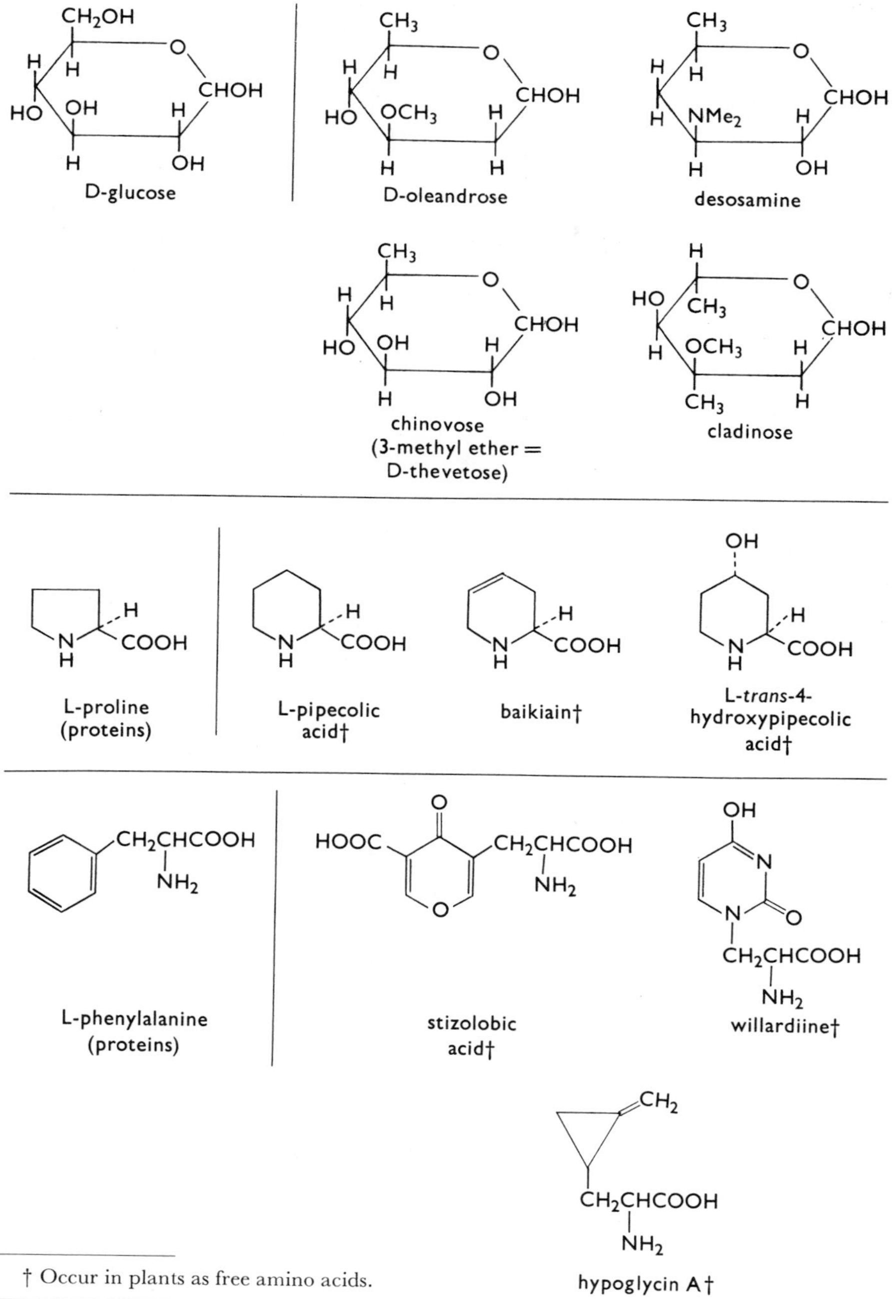

D-glucose

D-oleandrose

desosamine

chinovose
(3-methyl ether =
D-thevetose)

cladinose

L-proline
(proteins)

L-pipecolic
acid†

baikiain†

L-*trans*-4-
hydroxypipecolic
acid†

L-phenylalanine
(proteins)

stizolobic
acid†

willardiine†

hypoglycin A†

† Occur in plants as free amino acids.

Fig. 1-2. Some Typical Primary Metabolites and Structurally Analogous Secondary Metabolic Products of Plants and Microorganisms.

may in time provide clues to the meaning and importance of their existence in nature.

The development of a teleological attitude and approach to the study of naturally occurring compounds has been slow, principally, perhaps, because the primary concern of the organic chemist has properly been the discovery of novel compounds and the establishment of their chemical constitution. An understanding of biological function can come only with the accumulation of a good deal more information than is gained from the isolation of a single new compound from a single source. With the development in recent years of such new and powerful tools as refined separation procedures and rapid and reliable physical methods for identification and structure determination it is to be expected that many new naturally occurring compounds will be discovered, and—what may eventually prove to be as important—it will be possible to discover the presence of known compounds in unsuspected sources, just as shikimic acid is now known to occur widely in plants of all kinds and not only in plants of the genus *Illicium*.

1.3   Historical Background

The study of naturally occurring compounds from plants has progressed to its present state of development by passage through several distinct stages. In the *first phase*, in the early years of the nineteenth century, when organic chemistry was developing from an empirical science that lacked an established theoretical structure, chemists stood on the verge of a vast and unexplored domain in which each discovery of a new compound from nature was to provide in time a unique opportunity for studying further the problems of chemical constitution. New compounds of all kinds were the fuel for the fires of early discovery, and those obtained from natural sources were no less valuable than those produced in laboratories. Such beliefs and controversies as those surrounding the question of a "vital force" that was supposed to control the chemical processes in living things may have influenced but did not seriously deter the continued examination of nature, and organic compounds of many kinds accumulated in the hands of the chemists. The earliest accomplishments were what in our present state of sophistication we take for granted and regard as no more than preliminary to the attack on structural problems. These were the isolation, purification, and elemental analysis of individual compounds.

Numerous naturally occurring compounds were known by the end of the first quarter of the nineteenth century. Scheele (1742–1786), whose curiosity led him to examine natural materials of many kinds, from human body fluids to the vegetable materials that lay readily at hand, isolated oxalic, lactic, tartaric, citric, gallic, uric and malic acids, glycerol, phosphoric acid (from bones), as well as many inorganic compounds. Sertürner discovered morphine in 1817, and Pelletier and Caventou isolated strychnine, brucine, quinine, cinchonine, and caffeine (1818–1821).

It is significant that by far the largest number of natural products discovered (that is, isolated in a pure state) up to about 1860 were compounds that we recognize at once as those that have conspicuous physiological properties, and, indeed, include many valuable medicinals. In addition to the alkaloids isolated by Sertürner and by Pelletier and Caventou, all of which were from familiar vegetable drugs, the following natural plant substances were isolated during these years:

SOME NATURALLY OCCURRING COMPOUNDS DISCOVERED IN THE EARLY 1800's

Year	Compound	Discovered by
1817	morphine	Sertürner
1817	narcotine	Robiquet
1818	strychnine	Pelletier and Caventou
1819	brucine	Pelletier and Caventou
1820	quinine	Pelletier and Caventou
1820	cinchonine	Pelletier and Caventou
1821	caffeine	Pelletier and Caventou
1824	taurine	Gmelin
1827	coniine	Giesecke
1828	nicotine	Posselt and Riemann
1831	atropine	Hesse
1832	codeine	Robiquet
1834	creatine	Chevreul
1834	cinnamic acid	Dumas and Peligot
1837	amygdalin	Liebig and Wöhler
1839	salicin	Piria
1841	borneol	Pelouze
1845	camphor	Bouchardat
1846	tyrosine	Liebig
1848	papaverine	Merck
1859	cocaine	Niemann

It is obvious from this brief chronology that most of the early investigations of natural compounds were centered around those materials—mostly vegetable drugs with recognized poisonous or medicinal properties, or fragrant oils and food flavoring materials—that were readily accessible as articles of commerce or were used in one way or another by man. It was not until about 1835 that correct analyses were possible for most of these compounds, and even later that correct molecular formulas were assigned to them. Since theories of chemical constitution and concepts of molecular structure did not develop until the latter part of the nineteenth century, little progress was made in the study of these compounds, most of which are, it will be seen, of quite complex structure. Investigators of the time could do little more than establish the molecular composition and describe the characteristic reactions of the compounds in empirical terms.

By the time chemical theory had progressed to a stage at which concepts of molecular structure began to develop, a mass of experimental data had accumulated, and the application of structural theories to the existing empirical knowledge led to rapid advances in the establishment of the structures of many natural products. During this *second phase* of the development of natural products chemistry the isolation and description of new natural compounds continued, but the chief concern of the organic chemist now became the application of the developing structural concepts to the proof of the structures of the known compounds, and the confirmation of structure by total synthesis. Indeed, by about 1870 most of the medicinally important vegetable drugs had yielded their principal active constituents as pure, crystalline compounds, and there began a long period during which the search for and isolation of new compounds became of secondary importance to structural investigations on this backlog of available materials.

The less complex compounds were conquered in a relatively short time. Coniine was synthesized in 1886, atropine in 1901, nicotine in 1904, cocaine in 1885 (partial synthesis), papaverine in 1909. Strychnine, morphine, and quinine proved to be more recalcitrant, and hundreds of papers are to be found in the literature, representing the work of numerous investigators over many decades, as testimony to the difficulties presented by these complex polycyclic structures. The correct structure for quinine was proposed in 1908, but morphine did not succumb until 1923 and strychnine until 1946. The total syntheses of these alkaloids were not accomplished until very recently.

The history of the investigation of natural products of other kinds parallels that just described for the nitrogenous plant principles. Terpene chemistry began with investigations of the many essential oils that have been used by man, chiefly as perfumes and to some extent as flavoring materials in food, from the most remote times. Turpentine and many plant oils and essences were known to the ancients, and more were introduced into use by the alchemists. The period from about 1810 to 1870 saw the isolation of many pure organic compounds from these materials: simple terpenes, camphor, borneol, and others. With the development of structural theory and experimental technics in the latter half of the nineteenth century there began the investigations of the constitution of these principles, and by the turn of the century the work of such celebrated organic chemists as Baeyer, Perkin, Wallach, Bredt, Wagner, Harries, and others had established the basic structures of many of the more accessible of the terpenes. The synthesis of many of the simpler terpenes was soon accomplished, chiefly after the advent of the Grignard reagent. Present-day investigations of the chemistry of the simple terpenes consist largely in the solution of the remaining questions of stereochemistry, the study of the many novel chemical transformations of these compounds, and the development of improved methods for their synthesis. Pioneering work continues, for the immense area of the chemistry of higher (C_{15} to C_{40}) terpenoid and steroid compounds continues to provide limitless opportunities for important advances in organic chemistry.

By the early years of the present century many basic tools had been assembled, in the form of reagents and synthetic and diagnostic methods, for the investigation of structure; and in the last two decades these have been augmented by the development of the powerful physical methods that are widely used today. Ultraviolet and infrared spectroscopy, nuclear magnetic resonance, mass spectrometry, and X-ray crystallography are now capable of providing in a matter of hours information that once required the painstaking efforts of months or years to acquire by the classical procedures of oxidation, cleavage, reduction, etc. The determination of structure has lost the characteristic of a pioneering achievement and has become, if not routine, at least accessible to the competent organic chemist.

It is becoming clear that new goals and purposes are now being added to the study of natural products, and a new phase of inquiry is beginning. The determination of the complete structure of an organic compound and the synthesis of the compound was once the principal goal of the organic chemist. If the compound was one with exceptional practical importance—a medicinally useful drug, an insecticide, and so on—the synthesis of derivatives and analogs which it was hoped would be more active was often a secondary aim, one whose by-products, the development of new reagents and synthetic procedures, have enriched organic chemistry. Present-day research in natural products chemistry ranges far beyond the limits of the search for drugs or other compounds with practical uses, and even beyond the challenge presented by an unknown structure of a new compound. The structures of naturally occurring compounds are often reflections of genetic individuality, and many of them are now recognized as valuable indicators of the relationships between the living organisms from which they are derived and of the chemical transformations that take place in the cell.

1.4 Principal Pathways of Biosynthesis

Microorganisms, plants, and animals are extraordinarily complex structures. The products of their metabolic activities cannot be categorized in simple terms; yet several principal pathways of their synthetic capabilities can be described. Each of these is ramified in many ways, and in the chapters to follow, variations on these fundamental themes will be encountered. The chief pathways outlined in the scheme of Fig. 1-1 are further elaborated in Fig. 1-3, in which specific examples of a number of kinds of naturally occurring compounds are shown as the products of the several main channels of synthesis.

Standing at the head of this network of direct and interlinked patterns of synthesis are three primary compounds: acetic acid, as its coenzyme A ester (Sec. 2.8, Chap. 3); shikimic acid (Sec. 2.12, Chap. 5); γ,γ-dimethylallyl alcohol, as its pyrophosphate ester (Sec. 2.17, Chap. 8).

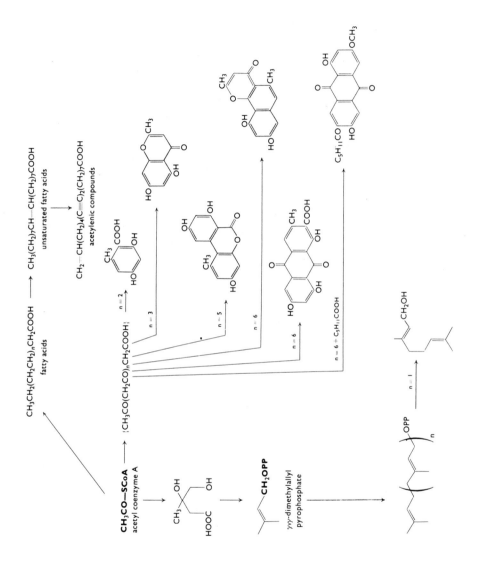

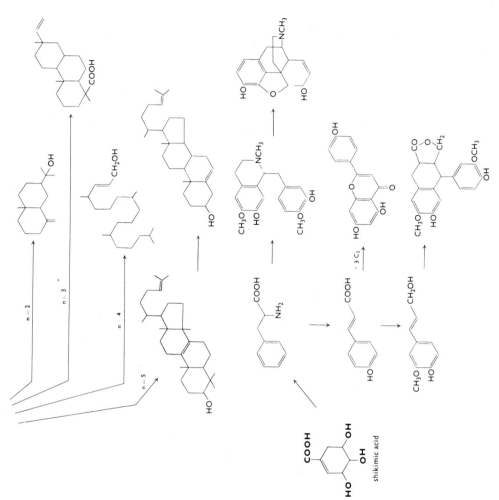

Fig. 1-3. Principal Pathways of Synthesis in Secondary Metabolism.

It will be apparent as the discussion develops that most of the chemical transformations that take place in the living organism occur by routes predictable on the
grounds of rational mechanistic and structural considerations. Yet it is probable
that most of these reactions are mediated by the catalytic action of enzymes. It is a
fundamental premise in the study of biosynthetic processes that they follow courses
that are consistent with structural considerations, and occur by way of "normal"
mechanisms, the role of the enzyme being either (a) to catalyze a reaction to a
degree sufficient to increase its rate over those of competing reactions, or (b) to
direct, by specific stereochemical control, the course of a reaction to one rather than
to another, equally likely, product. For these reasons, it will seldom be necessary to
invoke the role of the enzyme in the discussion of the reactions to be described, for
the *capacity* of a precursor to react along the path described will be inherent in its
structure. However, there are many cases in which a part of the enzyme—the prosthetic group, or coenzyme—participates in a reaction in a manner that can be
explicitly represented by the formation of an intermediate substrate-prosthetic
group combination. In such cases, the synthetic steps will include explicit formulation of the role of the prosthetic group. Examples of this are to be found in those
reactions which require enzymes of which thiamin pyrophosphate is the prosthetic
group (Secs. 2.6, 2.8).

It will be noted in the discussions in this book that a great many of the biosynthetic transformations described belong to simple and well-known categories of
reactions. Among these are the following:

1. Carbon-carbon bond formation by reaction of a nucleophilic methylene
grouping with the electrophilic carbon atom of a ketone, an ester, carbon dioxide,
an allylic ester, or a methylsulfonium ion (Eq. 1-1);

2. Carbon-carbon bond formation by oxidation (Eq. 1-2);

3. Introduction of oxygen by oxidation of C—H bonds (Eq. 1-3) or by direct
epoxidation of a carbon-carbon double bond (Eq. 1-4);

4. Oxidation-reduction of carbon-oxygen and carbon-carbon bonds (Eq. 1-5);

5. Decarboxylation of β-keto carboxylic acids (Eq. 1-6);

6. Alkylation and acylation of nucleophilic nitrogen and oxygen atoms
(Eq. 1-7).

When these processes occur as part of a sequence of biosynthetic steps it may
be presumed that they are mediated by specific enzymes. Yet our knowledge of the
intimate details of the way enzymes participate in many of these reactions is very
imperfect. It is possible to conclude in many cases that in acid-base catalyzed
reactions the role of the enzyme is to act as an acceptor and donor of protons. In
other cases it is known that a metal ion is essential to the action of the enzyme, and
it may be assumed that the metal acts as the site of formation of a metal-enzyme-
substrate complex at which the reaction occurs. But it is only rarely that the

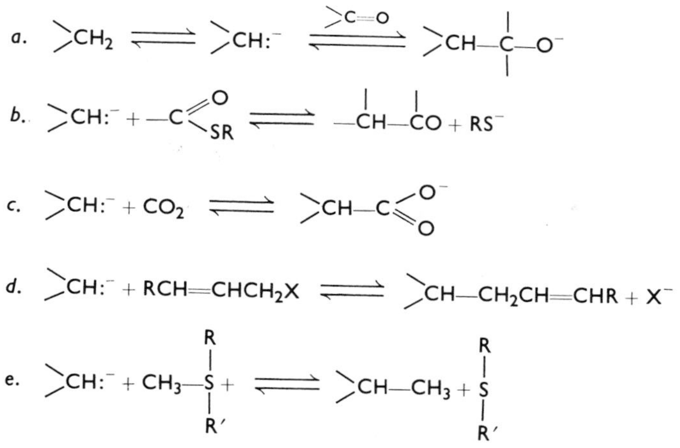

a. $\quad >CH_2 \rightleftharpoons >CH:^- \overset{>C=O}{\rightleftharpoons} >CH-\overset{|}{\underset{|}{C}}-O^-$

b. $\quad >CH:^- + -C\overset{O}{\underset{SR}{\diagdown}} \rightleftharpoons -\overset{|}{\underset{|}{CH}}-\overset{|}{\underset{|}{C}}O + RS^-$

c. $\quad >CH:^- + CO_2 \rightleftharpoons >CH-C\overset{O^-}{\underset{O}{\diagdown}}$

d. $\quad >CH:^- + RCH=CHCH_2X \rightleftharpoons >CH-CH_2CH=CHR + X^-$

e. $\quad >CH:^- + CH_3-\overset{R}{\underset{R'}{S}}+ \rightleftharpoons >CH-CH_3 + \overset{R}{\underset{R'}{S}}$ [Eq. 1-1]

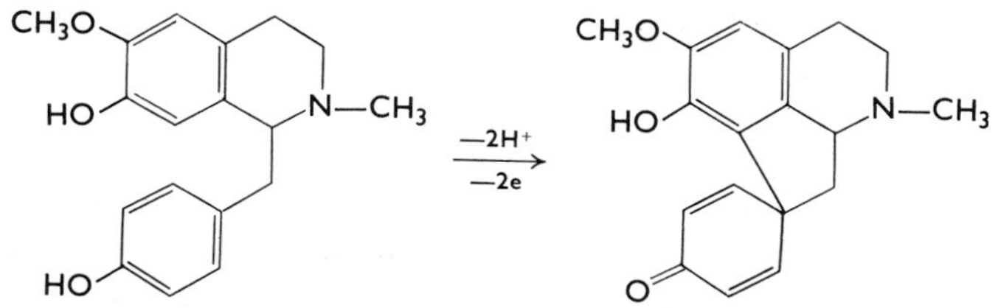

[Eq. 1-2]

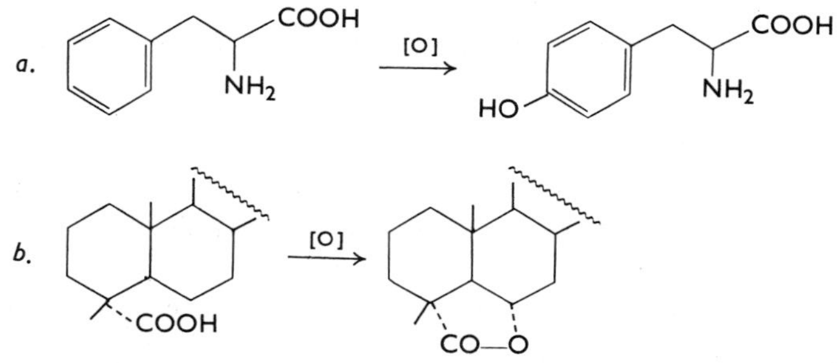

[Eq. 1-3]

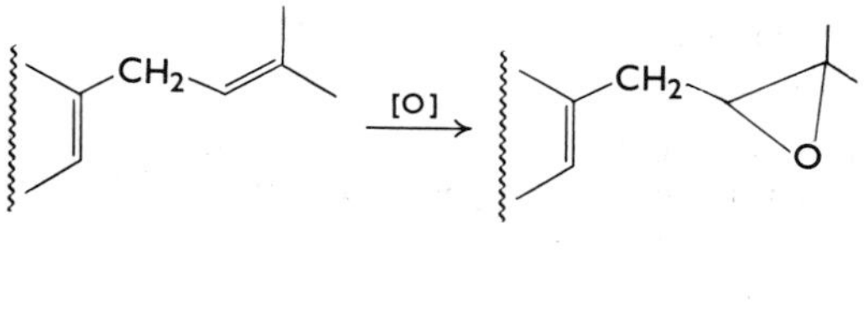

[Eq. 1-4]

a.

$$CH_2=CH \text{ (structures with OH and O)}$$

b. $CH_3(CH_2)_7CH_2CH_2(CH_2)_7COOH \longrightarrow CH_3(CH_2)_7CH{=}CH(CH_2)_7COOH \longrightarrow$

$$CH_3(CH_2)_4CH{=}CHCH_2CH{=}CH(CH_2)_7COOH \qquad \text{[Eq. 1-5]}$$

$$\text{----}COCH_2COOH \longrightarrow \text{---} COCH_3 + CO_2 \qquad \text{[Eq. 1-6]}$$

a. $-O^- + RCH{=}CHCH_2X \longrightarrow -OCH_2CH{=}CHR + X^-$

b. $-O^- + CH_3C\overset{\displaystyle O}{\underset{\displaystyle SR}{\big<}} \longrightarrow -OCOCH_3 + RS^-$

c. $\displaystyle {>}NH + CH_3\!\!-\!\!\overset{\displaystyle R}{\underset{\displaystyle R'}{\overset{|}{\underset{|}{S^+}}}} \longrightarrow {>}N\!\!-\!\!CH_3 + R\!\!-\!\!S\!\!-\!\!R' \qquad \text{[Eq. 1-7]}$

specific sites and structural environments of the "active centers" of enzyme action can be described. For these reasons it is seldom that an attempt will be made here to discuss the pathways of biosynthesis described in the following chapters in terms of explicit enzymatic mechanisms.

1.5 Botanical Classification

The botanical classification of plants relates to the activities of the organic chemist in two principal ways:

1. A recognition of relationships between plants and plant groups can guide him in a search for organic compounds of special kinds, for certain groups of plants (families, genera) are often characterized by particular (often unique) classes of compounds.

2. His study of naturally occurring plant constituents may enlarge his (and the botanist's) understanding of the relationships of plants to one another, and provide information of value in the study of their classification and evolution.

Although the study of the chemistry of plants selected at random or for other reasons* is not without importance, there can be no doubt that the addition of the

---

* Reasons why a plant may excite a chemist's interest are many, and among them may be a plant's toxicity to human or animal life, its medicinal value, its possession of unusual pigments or exudates, its physiological activity of various kinds, and so on.

added dimension of a knowledge of botanical systematization can greatly increase the chemist's pleasure and satisfaction in his studies and can provide him with the opportunity to contribute to progress in peripheral areas of scientific inquiry.

The ordering of plants into systematic schemes of classification is as old as man's awareness of nature, and in its simplest forms is practiced by everyone. The common names by which familiar plants are known are a form of plant taxonomy. Anyone can recognize the difference between grasses and trees, and, in the latter, between an oak and a pine. Most of our common descriptive plant names designate related groups, often families or genera: lilies, grasses, legumes, roses, orchids, daisies. Gross differences as exist between such groups are apparent to casual observation; but to recognize and describe the differences between a fir and a spruce, a chrysanthemum and a sunflower, a hollyhock and a hibiscus, or between the numerous species of grasses requires attention to detail, the establishment of criteria for distinction, and the development of a descriptive terminology by means of which individual differences can be expressed. The systematic arrangement of plants according to established criteria is described by the term *plant taxonomy*. The immediate practical purpose of a taxonomic scheme is to provide a means for identifying plants and for developing a rational arrangement into which plants can be grouped according to the similarities which exist between them. Taxonomic schemes are based principally upon characters that can be recognized by visual examination, that is, morphological characters. The ultimate goal of taxonomy, however, is the construction of an arrangement that goes beyond simple description and will reflect evolutionary relationships in the plant world. In progress toward the attainment of these goals taxonomists utilize the resources of all areas of science that bear upon the growth, development and evolution of plants. Morphology, physiology, cytology and genetics, ecology, geology, paleontology, and, in more recent years, chemistry all contribute to the taxonomist's interpretations of the relationships between the plants he studies. The contributions of chemistry to this complex of information are of comparatively recent origin, but promise to add a valuable dimension to the total picture of a plant's relationship to its ancestors and contemporaries.

It is not the intention of the authors to attempt to discuss in detail the principles and concepts of taxonomy; but, being aware that the average student of chemistry has little or no acquaintance with botanical relationships and plant classification, present here a brief outline of the way in which a plant may be described in terms of its position in a taxonomic scheme.

Classification is couched in terms that place the plant within certain major groups, starting with the largest and most inclusive (e.g., the plant kingdom) and proceeding by successive refinement of the criteria used in the description to the individual specimen (e.g., *Eriophyllum staechadifolium* Lag. subspecies *artemisiaefolium* (Less.) Macbr.). The following scheme describes the principal divisions into which plants are arranged.

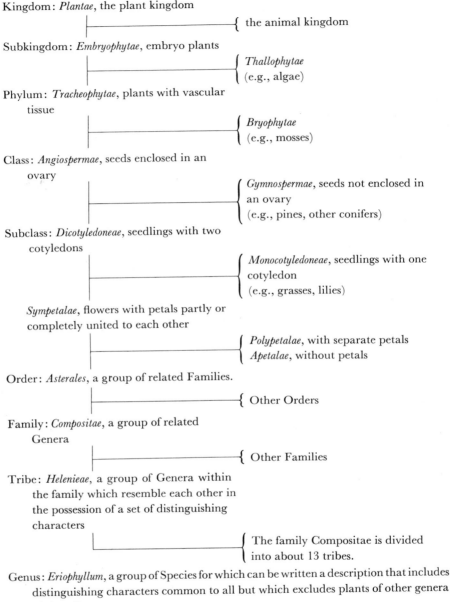

Kingdom: *Plantae*, the plant kingdom

{ the animal kingdom

Subkingdom: *Embryophytae*, embryo plants

{ *Thallophytae*
(e.g., algae)

Phylum: *Tracheophytae*, plants with vascular
tissue

{ *Bryophytae*
(e.g., mosses)

Class: *Angiospermae*, seeds enclosed in an
ovary

{ *Gymnospermae*, seeds not enclosed in
an ovary
(e.g., pines, other conifers)

Subclass: *Dicotyledoneae*, seedlings with two
cotyledons

{ *Monocotyledoneae*, seedlings with one
cotyledon
(e.g., grasses, lilies)

Sympetalae, flowers with petals partly or
completely united to each other

{ *Polypetalae*, with separate petals
Apetalae, without petals

Order: *Asterales*, a group of related Families.

{ Other Orders

Family: *Compositae*, a group of related
Genera

{ Other Families

Tribe: *Helenieae*, a group of Genera within
the family which resemble each other in
the possession of a set of distinguishing
characters

{ The family Compositae is divided
into about 13 tribes.

Genus: *Eriophyllum*, a group of Species for which can be written a description that includes
distinguishing characters common to all but which excludes plants of other genera
of the tribe.

Species: *staechadifolium* Lag., a group of individual plants or populations of like plants
which possess a number of characters in common but which are distinguished from
other, similar, species by these characters.

Subspecies or Variety: *artemisiaefolium* (Less.) Macbr., plants which are not clearly
separable from the typical species but which, in this example, possess leaves that
differ in the degree of division into lobes from those of the typical species.

The individual plant specimen, then, would be described by the terms *Eriophyllum staechadifolium* Lag. var. (or ssp.) *artemisiaefolium* (Less.) Macbr., tribe *Helenieae*, fam. Compositae. It is seldom necessary to specify higher categories (Order, etc.) in naming a plant, but it is often important and always useful to name the tribe and family to which it belongs.

The names (as abbreviations) attached to this botanical name are those of botanists in whose judgment the plant was originally designated as a separate species or subspecies. In the above example, "Lag." is the abbreviation for the name of Mariano Lagasca y Segura, a Spanish botanist of the early nineteenth century, who first named the plant *E. staechadifolium*.*

A distinguished taxonomist has said that it is too easy an assumption that "taxonomy is a cut-and-dried affair, with everything in its own neat pigeon-hole. Nothing could be farther from the truth: taxonomy is very much a matter of personal opinion." Nevertheless, the botanically concerned organic chemist must be aware that the "personal opinions" are those of skilled and experienced botanists and are supported by a wealth of evidence drawn from many sources.

The organic chemist can play a role in the development of plant taxonomy by providing new information that is beyond the reach of visual observation. The chemical constituents of plants are "characters" whose value cannot be less than (although it may not exceed) that of the physical characteristics of flower structure or leaf shape or plant habit. Chemical taxonomy is not a revision but an extension of traditional taxonomy, and it is to be expected that it will in time assume a prominent role in the study of plant systematics and evolution.

Because of the intimate relationship between plant chemistry and allied areas of botanical science, the greatest value will be derived from studies of naturally occurring compounds only if the plants that are brought under study are carefully and completely identified and described. Existing schemes of classification must, of course, be used, despite the fact that there are occasionally differences of taxonomic opinion or imprecision in the identification of a plant specimen. For this reason it is strongly to be recommended that each plant brought under study be preserved as a properly mounted specimen in a recognized specimen museum (a herbarium) so that it may be referred to when necessary.

The plants of the world and of its many regions (continents, countries, states, even restricted locales) are described in books and manuals known as "floras." The organic chemist who is inclined to the study of the plant world is well advised to acquaint himself with the plants of the region from which his materials are drawn by a study of the flora of the area of his interest. Even a little knowledge of botany will be found to be an excellent thing.

---

* Less. and Macbr. stand, respectively, for Christian Lessing, a German botanist, and James Macbride, an American, both of whose judgments regarding the classification of this plant are recorded in the appearance of their names (as "authorities") in the plant's present name.

II CHAPTER

REFERENCES FOR FURTHER READING

1. Articles by A. L. Lehinger, D. I. Arnon, J. A. Bassham in *The Living Cell,* readings from Scientific American, W. H. Freeman and Co., San Francisco, 1965.
2. The Biogenesis of Carbohydrates, in *Biogenesis of Natural Compounds,* P. Bernfeld, Ed., Pergamon Press, 1963.
3. The Carbon Reduction Cycle in Photosynthesis, A. A. Benson, in *Encyclopedia of Biochemistry,* R. J. Williams and E. M. Lansford, Jr., Eds., Reinhold Publishing Co., 1967.
4. E. M. Kosower, *Molecular Biochemistry,* McGraw-Hill, 1962.
5. J. D. Bu'lock, *The Biosynthesis of Natural Products,* McGraw-Hill, 1965.
6. G. N. Cohen, *Biosynthesis of Small Molecules,* in the series *Modern Perspectives in Biology,* Harper & Row, Inc., New York, 1967.

CHAPTER **II**

Primary Metabolic Processes

2.1 Photosynthesis

The series of chemical transformations that constitute the synthetic apparatus of higher (green) plants starts with the reduction of carbon dioxide, the ultimate source of the carbon that finds its way into the myriad organic compounds that are found in living organisms. The reduction of carbon dioxide is brought about by the agency of the energy provided by sunlight, with the initial formation of phosphorylated sugars, simple sugar derivatives, and low-molecular weight organic compounds related to the principal routes of carbohydrate metabolism. The overall process may be represented by the following equation (Eq. 2-1):

$$x CO_2 + x H_2O + energy \longrightarrow (CH_2O)_x + x O_2 \qquad \text{[Eq. 2-1]}$$

The details of the chemistry involved in this simple expression represent an extraordinarily complex web of reactions, brought about by a catalytic mechanism that resides in the photosynthetic elements of green plants and includes chlorophyll, the principal catalytic component, which is a magnesium-containing porphyrin; catalytic enzymes of various kinds; and a host of minor cellular constituents, all of which make up the organized structure of the photosynthetic apparatus.

The course of the reactions by which carbon dioxide is converted into its reduction products is now known in substantial detail. It was worked out by painstaking experiments in which radioactive (^{14}C) carbon dioxide was provided to living, chlorophyll-containing organisms (green leaves of higher plants and green, photosynthetic algae), and the products of the earliest steps in the reaction sequence isolated and identified by chromatographic techniques.

In a typical experiment, a suspension of the green, single-celled alga *Scenedesmus obliquus* was illuminated and exposed to carbon dioxide containing $^{14}CO_2$ (or

$H^{14}CO_3^-$). After a short period of time (which varied with the individual experiment) the cell suspension was poured into hot alcohol, which terminated cellular activity and extracted from the tissue the organic compounds that were present. Analysis of the resulting mixture, principally by paper chromatography, and measurement of the amounts of radioactivity in each of the constituents, disclosed the fate of the administered carbon dioxide.

The incorporation of carbon dioxide into the organic components of a photosynthesizing plant tissue is extraordinarily rapid: rates of incorporation of more than 0.5 mg of CO_2 per gram of leaf tissue per minute have been observed. In early experiments in which this technique was used it was found that after but 30 seconds of photosynthesis (using algae), more than 20 radioactive compounds could be discerned on a paper chromatogram* of the alcoholic extract. As the time allowed for photosynthesis was shortened, the number of radioactive products was reduced, and it became clear at length that the first stable and recognizable compound into which carbon dioxide was incorporated was 3-phosphoglyceric acid. In Table 2-1 are shown some representative results of altering the length of time that photosynthesis is allowed to proceed:

Table 2-1.

Period of exposure of CO_2 to Scenedesmus	^{14}C-labeled products observed
30 sec	alanine, serine, glycine, glutamic acid, malic acid, citric acid, aspartic acid, sucrose, phosphoenol pyruvic acid, hexose phosphates, triose phosphate, phosphoglyceric acid.
10 sec	alanine, malic acid, aspartic acid, triose phosphate, hexose phosphates, phosphoenol pyruvic acid, phosphoglyceric acid.
5 sec	alanine, malic acid, triose phosphate, hexose phosphates, phosphoenol pyruvic acid, phosphoglyceric acid.

Further experiments disclosed the following:

a) 3-phosphoglyceric acid formed in the presence of $^{14}CO_2$ is initially labeled in the —COOH group only.

b) 3-phosphoglyceric is the product of a light-independent (dark) reaction in which ribulose-1,5-diphosphate acts as the carbon dioxide acceptor.

---

* Detection and determination of radioactivity in chromatographically separated compounds can be performed in a number of ways. A simple qualitative method is to place the developed chromatogram in contact with the emulsion surface of a sensitive photographic film. The radioactive spots appear as black areas on the developed film, and can be compared with the original paper chromatogram after the latter is sprayed with suitable color-forming reagents.

c) the overall material balance of the incorporation process shows that three molecules of carbon dioxide are reduced to yield one molecule of 3-phosphoglyceric acid (3-PGA) (Eq. 2-2); thus

$$3 \, CO_2 + 10 \, [H] \longrightarrow C_3H_6O_4 + 2 \, H_2O$$ [Eq. 2-2]

2.2 Reduction of Carbon Dioxide

Where and in what way does the "reduction" of carbon dioxide occur in the carbon fixation process? Since the reduction of carbon dioxide to carbohydrates (or to their equivalents in oxidation level) is in effect a reversal of the oxidation of carbohydrates to carbon dioxide and water, a process in which energy is liberated, the answer to our question can be found in the answer to the equivalent question: how is energy used in the conversion of carbon dioxide to phosphoglyceric acid?

Studies of the kind just described have led to the discovery that the key reaction in which carbon dioxide is incorporated is the carboxylation of the five-carbon atom compound ribulose-1,5-diphosphate to yield an unstable six-carbon-atom compound. The latter undergoes cleavage to two molecules of 3-PGA (Eq. 2-3):

[Eq. 2-3]

ribulose-1,5-diphosphate†   unstable C_6 intermediate   two 3-phosphoglyceric acid

† In this and discussions to follow, the symbol —OP will be used for the phosphate grouping

$$(-O-\overset{\overset{O}{\|}}{\underset{\underset{OH}{|}}{P}}-OH, \text{ or an ionized form}), \text{ and } -OPP \text{ for the pyrophosphate grouping}$$

$$(-O-\overset{\overset{O}{\|}}{\underset{\underset{OH}{|}}{P}}-O-\overset{\overset{O}{\|}}{\underset{\underset{OH}{|}}{P}}-OH).$$ It is also to be noted here that these groupings, strongly acidic moieties,

are undoubtedly ionized at physiological pH, and thus could be more exactly represented as

$$-\overset{\overset{O}{\|}}{\underset{\underset{OH}{|}}{P}}-O^- \text{ and } -\overset{\overset{O}{\|}}{\underset{\underset{OH}{|}}{P}}-O-\overset{\overset{O}{\|}}{\underset{\underset{OH}{|}}{P}}-O^-.$$ Yet, for uniformity in the discussion, when these groups are written

in full the unionized form will ordinarily be used.

Similarly P_i and PP_i will be used to represent the phosphate and pyrophosphate ions.

The reaction of 3-PGA with carbon dioxide is clearly a nucleophilic attack by C-2 of the ribulose diphosphate upon the carbon atom of CO_2. Since C-2 in ribulose-1,5-diphosphate is not nucleophilic, a mechanism for this reaction must provide for the availability of electrons at the C-2 position of the ketose phosphate. The following reaction scheme satisfies this requirement (Eq. 2-4):

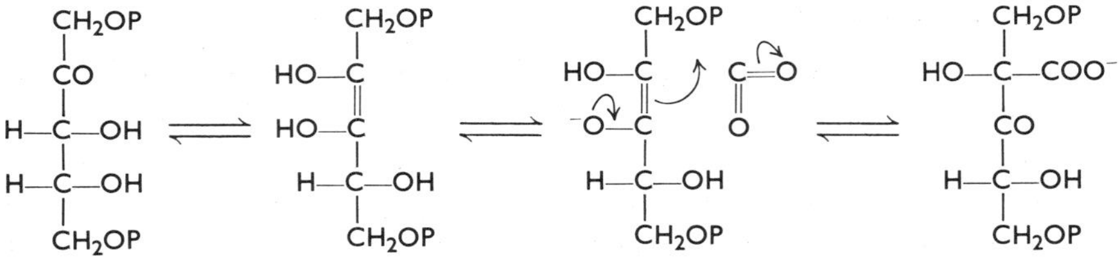

$$
\begin{array}{cccc}
\text{CH}_2\text{OP} & \text{CH}_2\text{OP} & \text{CH}_2\text{OP} & \text{CH}_2\text{OP} \\
| & | & | & | \\
\text{CO} & \text{HO}\!-\!\text{C} & \text{HO}\!-\!\text{C}\quad\text{C}\!=\!\text{O} & \text{HO}\!-\!\text{C}\!-\!\text{COO}^- \\
| & \| & \| \quad \quad | & | \\
\text{H}\!-\!\text{C}\!-\!\text{OH} \rightleftharpoons & \text{HO}\!-\!\text{C} \rightleftharpoons & {}^-\text{O}\!-\!\text{C}\quad\text{O} \rightleftharpoons & \text{CO} \\
| & | & | & | \\
\text{H}\!-\!\text{C}\!-\!\text{OH} & \text{H}\!-\!\text{C}\!-\!\text{OH} & \text{H}\!-\!\text{C}\!-\!\text{OH} & \text{H}\!-\!\text{C}\!-\!\text{OH} \\
| & | & | & | \\
\text{CH}_2\text{OP} & \text{CH}_2\text{OP} & \text{CH}_2\text{OP} & \text{CH}_2\text{OP}
\end{array}
$$

[Eq. 2-4]

Base-catalyzed cleavage of the intermediate six-carbon-atom compound offers no conceptual problem, and may be formulated as follows (Eq. 2-5):

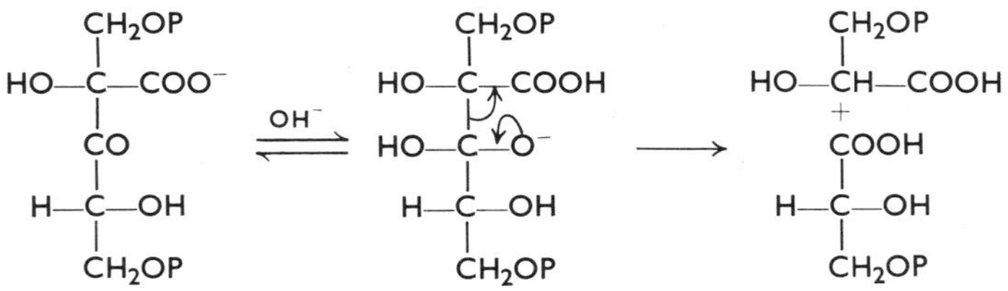

$$
\begin{array}{ccc}
\text{CH}_2\text{OP} & \text{CH}_2\text{OP} & \text{CH}_2\text{OP} \\
| & | & | \\
\text{HO}\!-\!\text{C}\!-\!\text{COO}^- & \text{HO}\!-\!\text{C}\quad\text{COOH} & \text{HO}\!-\!\text{CH}\!-\!\text{COOH} \\
| & | & + \\
\text{CO} & \text{HO}\!-\!\text{C}\!-\!\text{O}^- & \text{COOH} \\
| & | & | \\
\text{H}\!-\!\text{C}\!-\!\text{OH} & \text{H}\!-\!\text{C}\!-\!\text{OH} & \text{H}\!-\!\text{C}\!-\!\text{OH} \\
| & | & | \\
\text{CH}_2\text{OP} & \text{CH}_2\text{OP} & \text{CH}_2\text{OP}
\end{array}
$$

$\xrightarrow{\text{OH}^-}$ $\longrightarrow$ [Eq. 2-5]

It should always be borne in mind that these reactions, like nearly all of those that will be discussed in this book that occur in the living cell, are mediated by enzymes. Many of these individual enzymes—for example, that which catalyzes the addition of carbon dioxide to ribulose-1,5-diphosphate—have been isolated from plant tissues, purified, and studied in *in vitro* experiments. In this book, however, attention will of necessity be directed principally to the transformations of the organic substrates whose reactions are mediated by specific enzymes, and no extended description of the enzymes themselves will be given. In certain cases, the coenzyme, or prosthetic group, of an enzyme participates in the reaction in a way that permits a description of the precise manner in which it acts; in such cases, the complete formulation will be given.

2.3   The Role of Light and Chlorophyll in Carbon Dioxide Fixation

The utilization of the energy of sunlight for the reduction of carbon dioxide is accomplished by processes that can be summarized in the following diagram (Fig. 2-1):

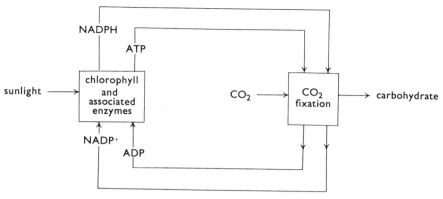

Fig. 2-1.

The role of chlorophyll and the accessory factors found in the chloroplasts is in (a) the formation of the reduced coenzyme NADPH (p. 51) from its oxidized form, NADP$^+$ (Eq. 2-6) and (b) the phosphorylation of adenosine diphosphate (ADP) (Eq. 2-7). Both of these reactions require energy, and both of them utilize the energy of light through the agency of the photosynthetic apparatus.

a.   NADP$^+$ +   H$^+$ + 2e $\xrightleftharpoons{\text{energy}}$ NADPH

        triphosphopyridine   reduced
           nucleotide   triphosphopyridine
                                   nucleotide

nicotinamide   (NADP$^+$)

CONH$_2$

CHCHOHCHCHCH$_2$O—P—O—P—O—CH$_2$CHCHOHCHOHCH

          OP   OH   OH

ribose   adenosine

2e,H$^+$

CONH$_2$ (NADH)   [Eq. 2-6]

ribose—P—P—adenosine

P

b.   ADP   +   P$_i$ $\underset{\longleftarrow}{\overset{energy}{\longrightarrow}}$ ATP

     adenosine   inorganic   adenosine
    diphosphate   phosphate   triphosphate

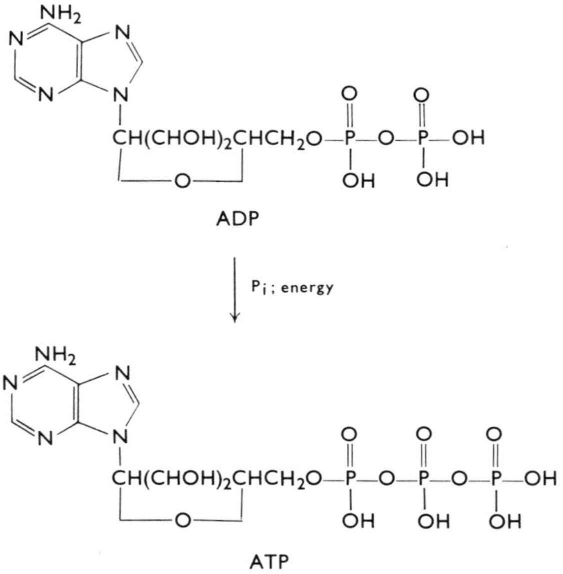

ADP

P$_i$; energy

ATP   [Eq. 2-7]

The role of NADPH and ATP will be discerned in the total scheme of the carbon fixation cycle to be described in the following sections. The process can be described by examining the fate of 3-PGA as it proceeds through the steps that comprise the complete cycle of CO_2 fixation and 3-PGA regeneration. An overall representation of this cycle is the following (Eq. 2-8):

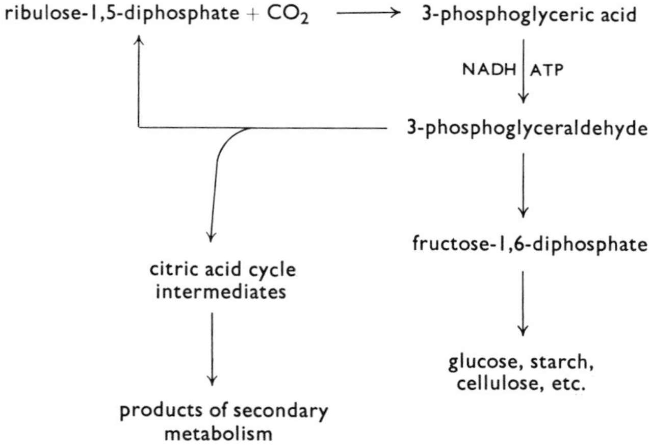

[Eq. 2-8]

A material balance on the carbon fixation cycle can be represented in the following form (Eq. 2-9):

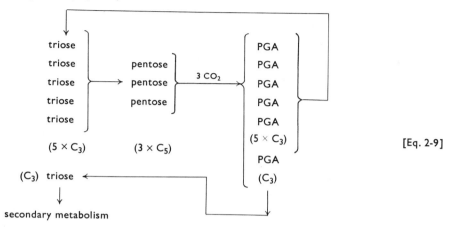

[Eq. 2-9]

It is clear from Eq. 2-9 that the complete cycle yields a net profit of one three-carbon compound at the cost of three molecules of CO_2 (Eq. 2-10):

$$3\ CO_2 + 12[H] \longrightarrow C_3H_6O_3 + 3\ H_2O$$
triose

[Eq. 2-10]

The three-carbon-atom compound is available for further reactions at the level of primary metabolism and for transformation into the compounds produced in the secondary metabolic processes of the plant.

2.4 Carbohydrate Transformations in the Fixation Cycle

The routes by which 3-PGA is converted into triose, and triose is converted into pentose involve transformations that can first of all be represented by a re-statement of Eq. 2-10 in more explicit terms (Eq. 2-11):

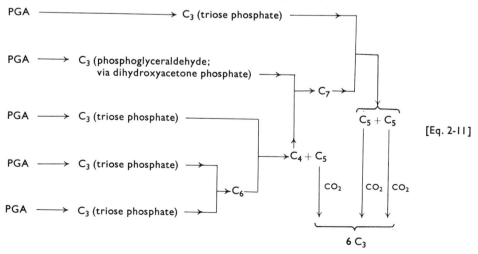

[Eq. 2-11]

and in summary:

a. $C_3 + C_3 \longrightarrow C_6$

b. $C_6 + C_3 \longrightarrow C_4 + C_5$

c. $C_4 + C_3 \longrightarrow C_7$ [Eq. 2-12]

d. $C_7 + C_3 \longrightarrow C_5 + C_5$

sum: $C_6 + 3\,C_3 \longrightarrow 3\,C_5 \xrightarrow{3\,CO_2} 3\,\{C_6\} \longrightarrow 6\,C_3$

The initial reaction in this complex of reactions is the reduction of glyceric acid to glyceraldehyde* (Eq. 2-13):

$$
\begin{array}{c}
\text{COOH} \\
|\\
\text{CHOH} \\
|\\
\text{CH}_2\text{OP}
\end{array}
\xrightarrow[\text{ATP; NADPH}]{\substack{\text{triose phosphate}\\\text{dehydrogenase}}}
\begin{array}{c}
\text{CHO} \\
|\\
\text{CHOH} \\
|\\
\text{CH}_2\text{OP}
\end{array}
$$
                                                                                          [Eq. 2-13]

Reaction *a* of Eq. 2-12, catalyzed by the enzyme aldolase, leads to fructose-1,6-diphosphate and hence to fructose-6-phosphate (Eq. 2-14):

$$
\begin{array}{c}
\text{CHO} \\
|\\
\text{CHOH} \\
|\\
\text{CH}_2\text{OP} \\
\text{3-phosphoglycer-}\\
\text{aldehyde}
\end{array}
\underset{\longleftarrow}{\overset{\substack{\text{phosphotriose}\\\text{isomerase}}}{\longrightarrow}}
\begin{array}{c}
\text{CH}_2\text{OH} \\
|\\
\text{C}=\text{O} \\
|\\
\text{CH}_2\text{OP} \\
\text{dihydroxyacetone}\\
\text{phosphate}
\end{array}
$$

$$\downarrow \text{aldolase}$$

$$
\begin{array}{c}
\text{CH}_2\text{OP} \\
|\\
\text{CO} \\
|\\
\text{CHOH} \\
|\\
\text{CHOH} \\
|\\
\text{CHOH} \\
|\\
\text{CH}_2\text{OP} \\
\text{fructose-1,6-}\\
\text{diphosphate}
\end{array}
\underset{\longleftarrow}{\overset{\text{phosphatase}}{\longrightarrow}}
\begin{array}{c}
\text{CH}_2\text{OH} \\
|\\
\text{CO} \\
|\\
\text{CHOH} \\
|\\
\text{CHOH} \\
|\\
\text{CHOH} \\
|\\
\text{CH}_2\text{OP} \\
\text{fructose-6-}\\
\text{phosphate}
\end{array}
$$
                                                                                          [Eq. 2-14]

* For convenience, the compounds will occasionally be referred to as their free, non-phosphorylated forms; i.e., triose instead of triose phosphate, etc.

The formation of a tetrose and a pentose (reaction *b*, Eq. 2-12) takes place by the transfer of carbon atoms 1 and 2 of fructose-6-phosphate to a triose by the action of the enzyme transketolase (Eq. 2-15):

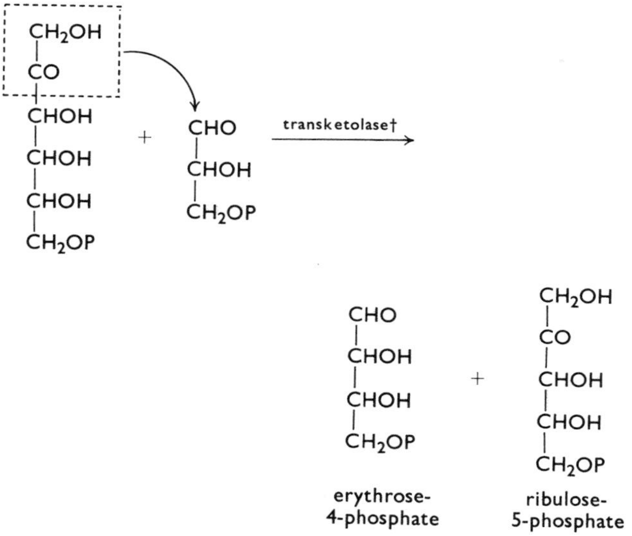

$$
\begin{array}{c}
\boxed{\begin{array}{c} CH_2OH \\ | \\ CO \end{array}} \\
| \\
CHOH \\
| \\
CHOH \quad + \quad
\begin{array}{c} CHO \\ | \\ CHOH \\ | \\ CH_2OP \end{array}
\quad \xrightarrow{\;transketolase\dagger\;} \\
| \\
CHOH \\
| \\
CH_2OP
\end{array}
$$

$$
\begin{array}{c}
CHO \\ | \\ CHOH \\ | \\ CHOH \\ | \\ CH_2OP
\end{array}
\quad + \quad
\begin{array}{c}
CH_2OH \\ | \\ CO \\ | \\ CHOH \\ | \\ CHOH \\ | \\ CH_2OP
\end{array}
\qquad \text{[Eq. 2-15]}
$$

$$
\begin{array}{cc}
\text{erythrose-} & \text{ribulose-} \\
\text{4-phosphate} & \text{5-phosphate}
\end{array}
$$

† For the nature of the transketolase reaction, see Sec. 2-5 and Eq. 2-19.

The combination of erythrose-4-phosphate with triose phosphate (reaction *c*, Eq. 2-12) now occurs with the aid of the enzyme aldolase (Eq. 2-16):

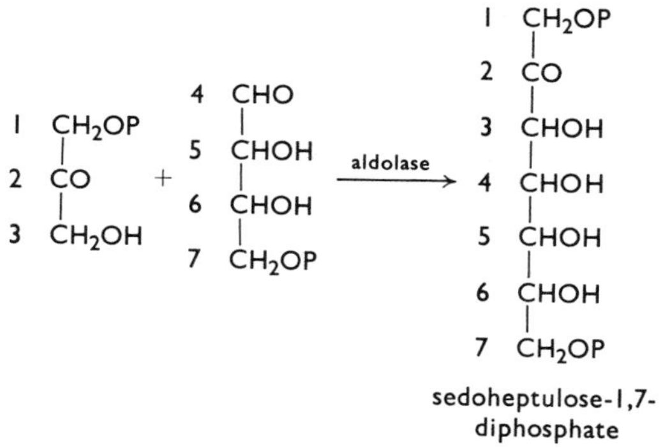

$$
\begin{array}{c}
1 \; CH_2OP \\ | \\ 2 \; CO \\ | \\ 3 \; CH_2OH
\end{array}
\;+\;
\begin{array}{c}
4 \; CHO \\ | \\ 5 \; CHOH \\ | \\ 6 \; CHOH \\ | \\ 7 \; CH_2OP
\end{array}
\;\xrightarrow{\;aldolase\;}\;
\begin{array}{c}
1 \; CH_2OP \\ | \\ 2 \; CO \\ | \\ 3 \; CHOH \\ | \\ 4 \; CHOH \\ | \\ 5 \; CHOH \\ | \\ 6 \; CHOH \\ | \\ 7 \; CH_2OP
\end{array}
\qquad \text{[Eq. 2-16]}
$$

$$
\text{sedoheptulose-1,7-}
$$
$$
\text{diphosphate}
$$

Finally, the transfer of carbon atoms 1 and 2 of sedoheptulose to a molecule of triose, with the enzyme transketolase (reaction *d*, Eq. 2-12), leads to two molecules of pentose (Eq. 2-17):

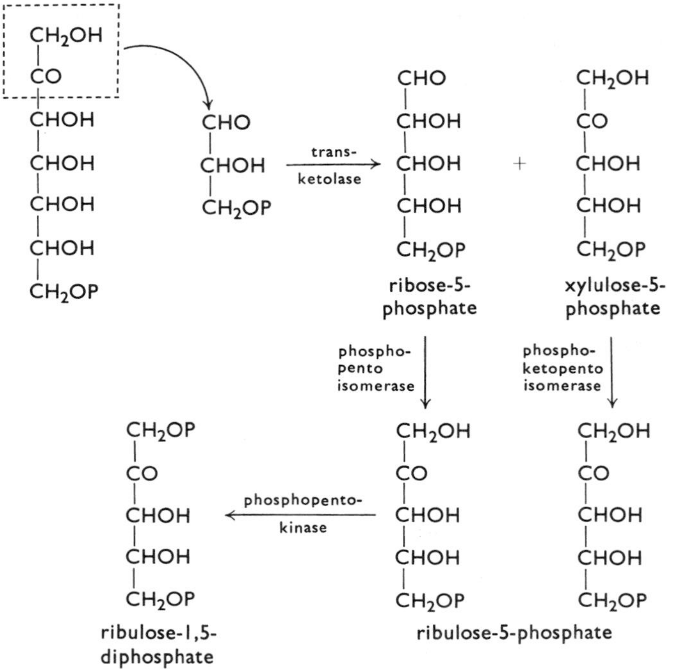

CH$_2$OH
|
CO
|
CHOH   CHO   CHO   CH$_2$OH
| | | |
CHOH   CHOH   trans-→   CHOH   +   CO
| | ketolase | |
CHOH   CH$_2$OP   CHOH   CHOH
| | |
CHOH   CH$_2$OP   CHOH
| |
CH$_2$OP   ribose-5-   CH$_2$OP
                                   phosphate   xylulose-5-
                                                 phosphate

                              phospho-   phospho-
                              pento   ketopento
                              isomerase   isomerase

CH$_2$OP   CH$_2$OH   CH$_2$OH
| | |
CO   CO   CO
| phosphopento- | |
CHOH   ←──────────────   CHOH   CHOH   [Eq. 2-17]
| kinase | |
CHOH   CHOH   CHOH
| | |
CH$_2$OP   CH$_2$OP   CH$_2$OP
ribulose-1,5-   ribulose-5-phosphate
diphosphate

The sum of the reactions a, b, c, and d of Eq. 2-10 provide the three molecules of ribulose-1,5-diphosphate which then accept carbon dioxide in the fixation step (Eq. 2-3).*

2.5   The Transketolase Reaction

The transfer of the unit HOCH$_2$CO— from sedoheptulose to triose (Eq. 2-17) and from hexose to triose (Eq. 2-15) is catalyzed by an enzyme of which the participating prosthetic group is thiamin pyrophosphate (Fig. 2-2):

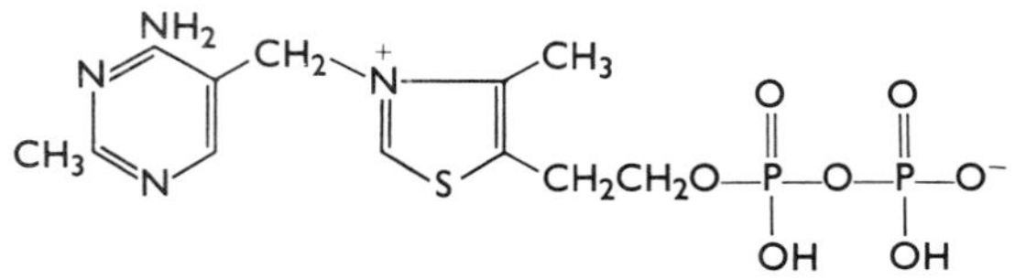

Fig. 2-2. Thiamin pyrophosphate.

* Further details of these reactions and the role of chlorophyll in the cellular reactions leading to NADP reduction and phosphorylation will be found in the references at the beginning of this chapter.

Thiamin pyrophosphate participates in two transfer reactions that are of fundamental importance in primary metabolic reactions. The transfer involved in the transketolase reaction may be loosely described as proceeding by the conversion of the $HOCH_2CO$— grouping of a ketose into "active glycolaldehyde," a fragment having the character described by the expression $(HOCH_2—\ddot{C}{=}O)^-$. It is clear that such a fragment (which is not a real substance, but a representational device) can add to the aldehyde group of an aldose in the following way (Eq. 2-18):

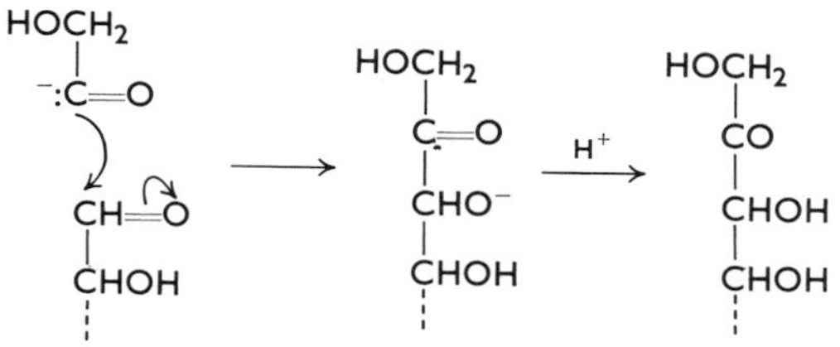

[Eq. 2-18]

The actual identity of the "active glycolaldehyde" is in fact not greatly different from that of the hypothetical two-carbon fragment shown in Eq. 2-18; it differs from the latter in that it exists in combination with thiamin pyrophosphate, and is transferred to the aldehyde group with concomitant or subsequent loss of the co-enzyme moiety. The total reaction scheme can be formulated as follows (Eq. 2-19):*

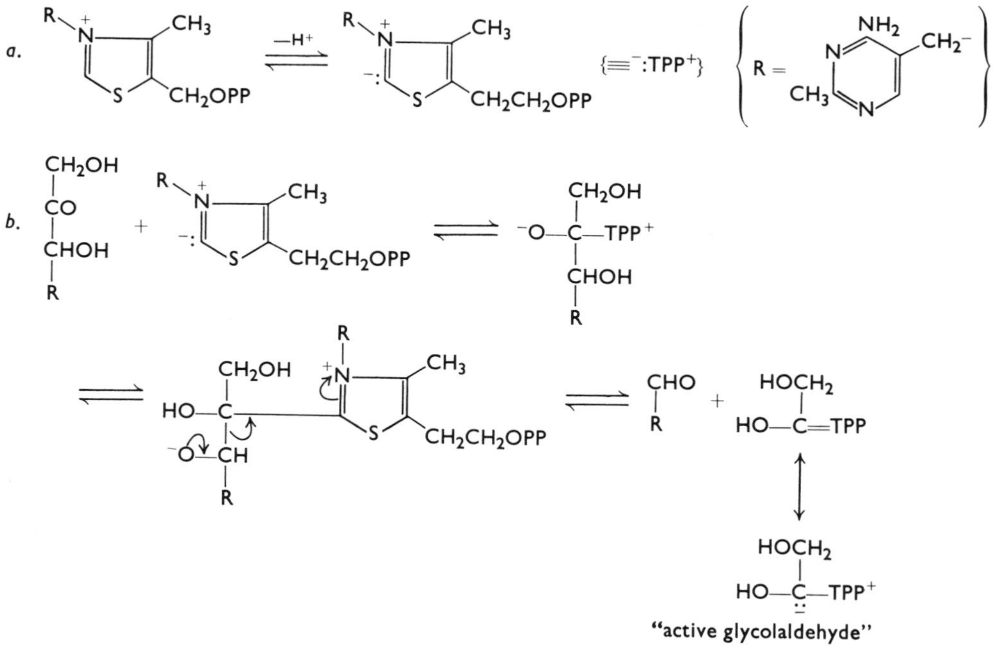

"active glycolaldehyde"

* In this formulation only the thiazole grouping will be written; and the abbreviations $HTPP^+$ and $^-:TPP^+$ will be used for the intact coenzyme and its deprotonated form. See Eq. 2-19 for details.

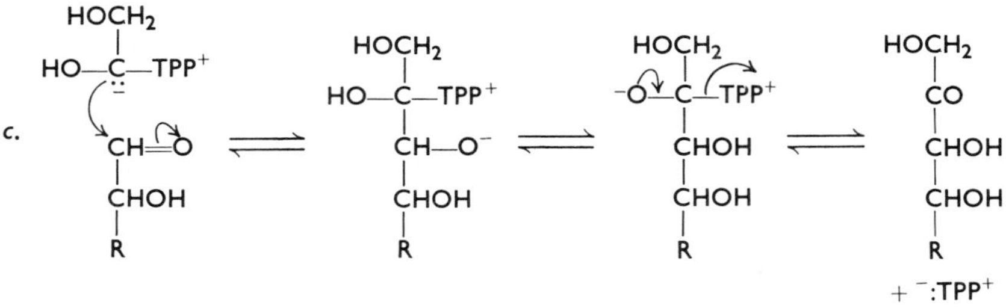

$c.$

$$
\begin{array}{ccc}
\underset{\substack{|\\ \text{HO}\text{---}\text{C}\text{---}\text{TPP}^+ \\ | \\ \text{CH}\overset{\curvearrowright}{=\!\!=}\text{O} \\ | \\ \text{CHOH} \\ | \\ \text{R}}}{\overset{\text{HOCH}_2}{}} & \rightleftharpoons & \underset{\substack{|\\ \text{HO}\text{---}\text{C}\text{---}\text{TPP}^+ \\ | \\ \text{CH}\text{---}\text{O}^- \\ | \\ \text{CHOH} \\ | \\ \text{R}}}{\overset{\text{HOCH}_2}{}} & \rightleftharpoons & \underset{\substack{|\\ -\text{O}\!\!\curvearrowleft\!\!\text{C}\!\!\curvearrowright\!\!\text{TPP}^+ \\ | \\ \text{CHOH} \\ | \\ \text{CHOH} \\ | \\ \text{R}}}{\overset{\text{HOCH}_2}{}} & \rightleftharpoons & \underset{\substack{|\\ \text{CO} \\ | \\ \text{CHOH} \\ | \\ \text{CHOH} \\ | \\ \text{R}}}{\overset{\text{HOCH}_2}{}}
\end{array}
$$

[Eq. 2-19]

$+ \; ^-\!:\text{TPP}^+$

It will be seen from the events formulated in Eq. 2-19 that TPP acts as an "operator" and enters and leaves the reaction sequence without undergoing an overall change. Its behavior in this respect resembles that of the cyanide ion in bringing about the benzoin condensation (Eq. 2-20):

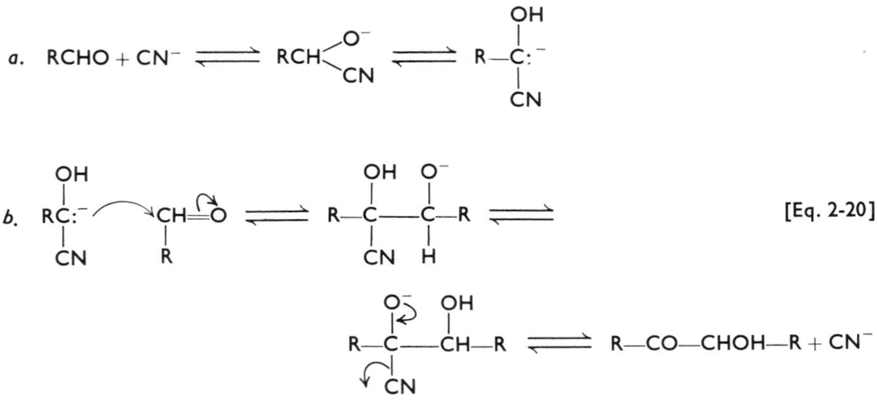

$a.$ $\text{RCHO} + \text{CN}^- \rightleftharpoons \text{RCH}\!\!<^{\text{O}^-}_{\text{CN}} \rightleftharpoons \text{R}\text{---}\underset{\substack{|\\ \text{CN}}}{\overset{\substack{\text{OH} \\ |}}{\text{C}}}\!:^-$

$b.$ $\underset{\substack{|\\ \text{CN}}}{\overset{\substack{\text{OH} \\ |}}{\text{R}\text{C}}}:^- \; \overset{\curvearrowright}{} \; \text{CH}\overset{\curvearrowright}{=\!\!=}\text{O} \rightleftharpoons \text{R}\text{---}\underset{\substack{|\\ \text{CN}}}{\overset{\substack{\text{OH} \\ |}}{\text{C}}}\text{---}\underset{\substack{|\\ \text{H}}}{\overset{\substack{\text{O}^- \\ |}}{\text{C}}}\text{---}\text{R} \rightleftharpoons$ [Eq. 2-20]

 $\text{R}\text{---}\underset{\substack{\curvearrowleft\\ \text{CN}}}{\overset{\substack{\text{O}\overset{\curvearrowleft}{}\\ ||}}{\text{C}}}\text{---}\underset{}{\overset{\substack{\text{OH} \\ |}}{\text{CH}}}\text{---}\text{R} \rightleftharpoons \text{R}\text{---}\text{CO}\text{---}\text{CHOH}\text{---}\text{R} + \text{CN}^-$

2.6   Thiamin

Thiamin pyrophosphate (also known as cocarboxylase) plays its role in the transketolase reaction and in the decarboxylation of pyruvic acid (Sec. 2.8) by virtue of the peculiar stabilization of the zwitterion formed by loss of the proton at C-2 (Eq. 2-21):

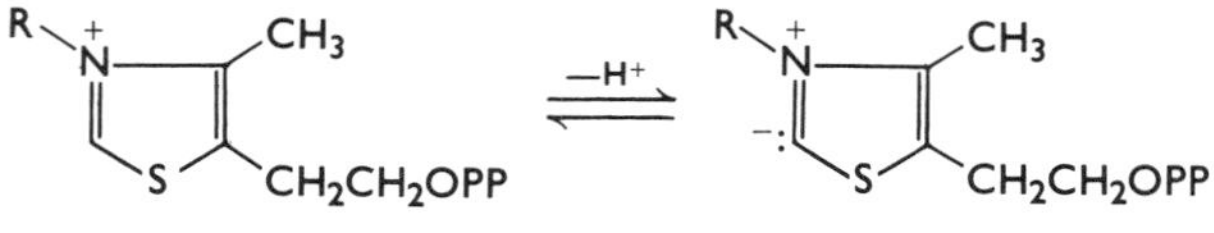

$$
\underset{\substack{\text{S} \\ \\ \text{CH}_2\text{CH}_2\text{OPP}}}{\overset{\text{R}\diagdown \overset{+}{\text{N}}\diagup \text{CH}_3}{}} \quad \underset{-:}{\overset{-\text{H}^+}{\rightleftharpoons}} \quad \underset{\substack{\text{S} \\ \\ \text{CH}_2\text{CH}_2\text{OPP}}}{\overset{\text{R}\diagdown \overset{+}{\text{N}}\diagup \text{CH}_3}{}}
$$

[Eq. 2-21]

There is a considerable body of evidence to support the view that the $^-\!:\text{TPP}^+$ zwitterion is readily formed. Thiazolium salts, for example, 3,4-dimethylthiazolium bromide (Eq. 2-22), undergo ready exchange with deuterium oxide with the introduction of one deuterium atom at C-2:

$$[\text{Eq. 2-22}]$$

Moreover, 2-acylthiazolium salts are active acylating agents (Eq. 2-23):

$$[\text{Eq. 2-23}]$$

The ready (i.e., fast) acylation of methanol with 2-benzoyl-4-methylthiazole methiodide (Eq. 2-23) reflects the low activation energy associated with the stability of a transition state in which the $-\overset{+}{\underset{|}{N}}=\overset{|}{C}:^-$ structure is involved. Additional evidence of a related nature includes the rapid decarboxylation of thiazole-2-carboxylic acids.*

2.7   Three-carbon Compounds of Primary Metabolism

Triose phosphate and phosphoglyceric acid, and the carbohydrates of the pentose phosphate cycle, all of which are important participants in the photosynthetic fixation of carbon dioxide, are key compounds in primary metabolic processes of the plant. By transformations at the primary metabolic level they lead to pyruvic acid, phosphoenolpyruvic acid, and acetyl coenzyme A. These, as we shall see, form the principal building blocks for most of the elaborate secondary metabolites of living plants.

Phosphoglyceraldehyde and its isomer, dihydroxyacetone phosphate, are formed in photosynthetic carbon dioxide fixation and by the breakdown of sugars.** Since carbohydrates are formed from these three-carbon-atom compounds, and also give rise to them by metabolic breakdown, chemical interrelationships at this small-compound level can be discussed from either point of view. It will be con-

---

* Pyridinium-2-carboxylic acids are also readily decarboxylated. Relevant to this matter is also the Hammick reaction of pyridine-2-carboxylic acid, which may be referred to (see *Quart. Rev., Chem. Soc.*, **5**, 131 (1951)).

** Since green plants are photoautotrophic, all of their organic constituents derive ultimately from CO_2 *via* PGA. Nevertheless, synthetic and catabolic breakdown processes apart from photosynthesis provide additional routes by which simple compounds are formed in the cell, and must be recognized as sources of the participants in the metabolic processes of the plant.

venient to consider carbohydrate breakdown as a point from which to view a complex of chemical transformations that will be seen to be central to later discussion of the biosynthesis of natural compounds. Glucose serves the living organism in two ways: it is a source of energy for growth, activity and reproduction; and it is the precursor of a pool of starting materials which are drawn upon for the synthetic activities of the cells. Glucose breakdown occurs in several ways, but our chief interest here will be in the oxidative metabolism called respiration.

The oxidative breakdown of glucose proceeds in the manner represented in the following scheme (Eq. 2-24):*

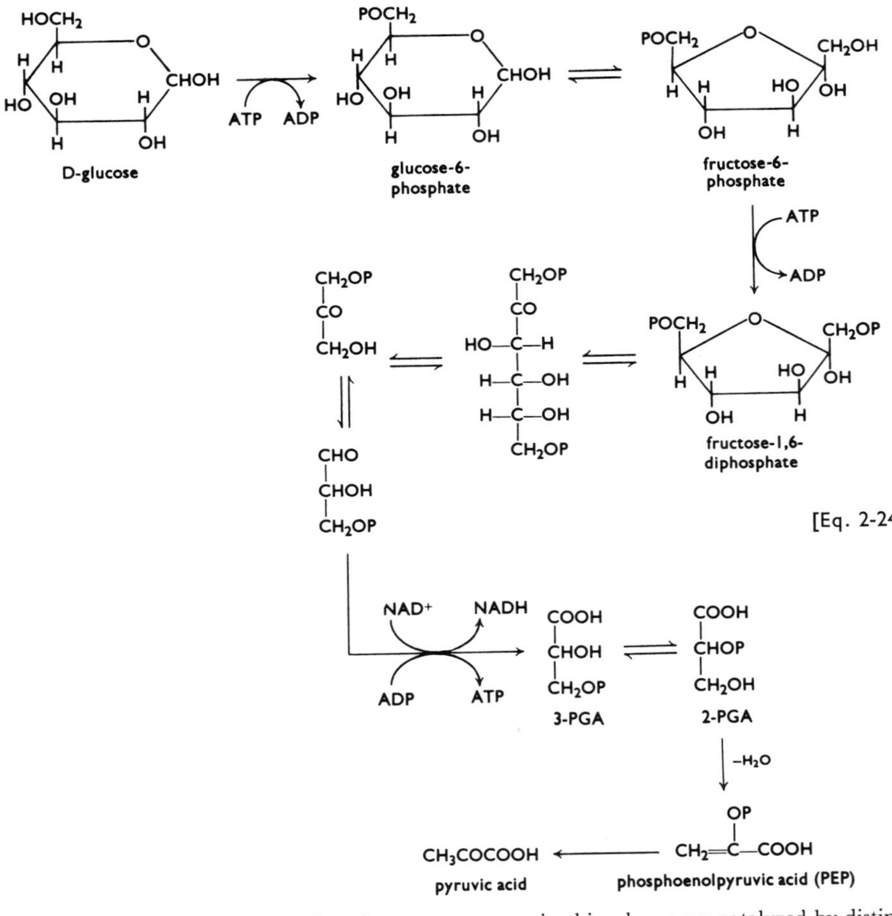

[Eq. 2-24]

* It is to be borne in mind that the separate stages in this scheme are catalyzed by distinct enzymes, all of which, in the case of glucose breakdown, have been isolated and characterized. While these enzymes are indispensable participants in the reaction sequence they seldom need explicit identification when attention is being directed to the reactions they catalyze, and they will be described only when their mechanistic roles call for explicit discussion.

It is to be noticed that 3-phosphoglyceric acid (3-PGA) is a product of glucose breakdown as well as a product of carbon dioxide assimilation. Its importance is further emphasized by its close relationship with two compounds whose key roles in biosynthesis will soon become apparent: pyruvic acid and phosphoenol-pyruvic acid (PEP).

The enzymatically catalyzed decarboxylation of pyruvic acid leads to the formation of *acetyl coenzyme A*, the starting point for three reaction sequences of far-reaching significance:

1. the citric acid cycle for the complete oxidation of pyruvic acid, with the concomitant formation of ATP, α-keto acids and, with associated reactions of nitrogen metabolism, amino acids;
2. the formation of polyketide chains of —CH_2—CO— units; and
3. the formation of β-hydroxy-β-methylglutaric acid, mevalonic acid, and eventually the terpenes and steroids.

These processes have been briefly represented as a part of the general scheme of Fig. 1-1 (Chap. 1), and are outlined in somewhat greater detail in Fig. 2-3 (see also Fig. 1-3).

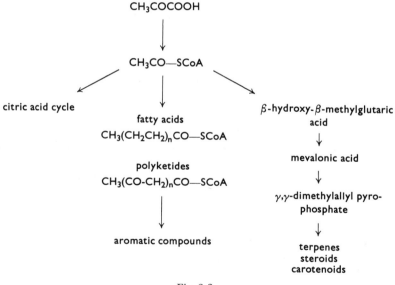

Fig. 2-3.

The special importance of acetyl coenzyme A in the biosynthetic processes of secondary plant metabolism is such that it is of interest to examine in detail the reactions by which it is formed and the chemical properties that account for the remarkable versatility with which it enters into cellular transformations.

2.8   Acetyl Coenzyme A

Acetyl coenzyme A is a complex thioester of acetic acid, with the following total structure* (Fig. 2-4):

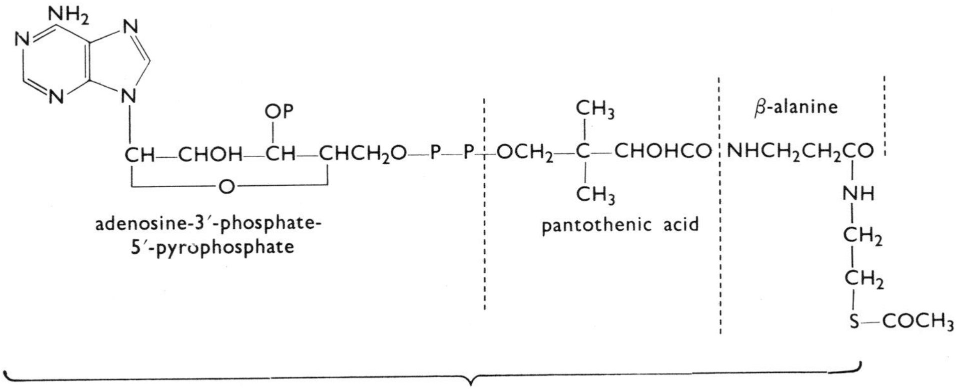

Fig. 2-4. Acetyl coenzyme A.

The usual way of representing this complex compound is CH_3CO—SCoA, in which —SCoA represents the whole of the structure shown attached to —$COCH_3$ in Fig. 2-4.

Acetyl coenzyme A is formed by several routes, that which is most relevant to the carbohydrate metabolic cycle being by way of the oxidative decarboxylation of pyruvic acid with the aid of thiamin pyrophosphate acting as a cofactor in the enzymatically catalyzed reaction.

Thiamin pyrophosphate (TPP), the prosthetic group of transketolase (Sec. 2.5) as well as α-ketodecarboxylase, catalyzes the reaction shown in Eq. 2-25 in a series

$$CH_3COCOOH + CoA-SH + NAD^+ \longrightarrow CH_3CO-SCoA + CO_2 + NADH + H^+$$

[Eq. 2-25]

of stages that are represented as follows. The oxidative decarboxylation with the formation of acetyl CoA may be dissected into the steps: (a) decarboxylation of pyruvic acid to yield an intermediate at the oxidation level of acetaldehyde (Eq. 2-26); (b) the oxidation of this intermediate by the disulfide (—S—S—) grouping of thioctic (lipoic) acid, with concomitant reduction of —S—S— to

* Nearly all of the "biological" compounds that are encountered in this chapter contain ionizable groups (amino, carboxyl, phosphate, etc.), and thus can exist in various states of protonation, depending upon pH. The selection of any one of these ionization states for representation in a formula is arbitrary, and so it will be convenient to select but one of the possible ionic states for the structures that are written.

(—SH)$_2$ (Eq. 2-27); and (c) the combination of the resulting acetyl derivative with CoA—SH to yield acetyl CoA (Eq. 2-28):

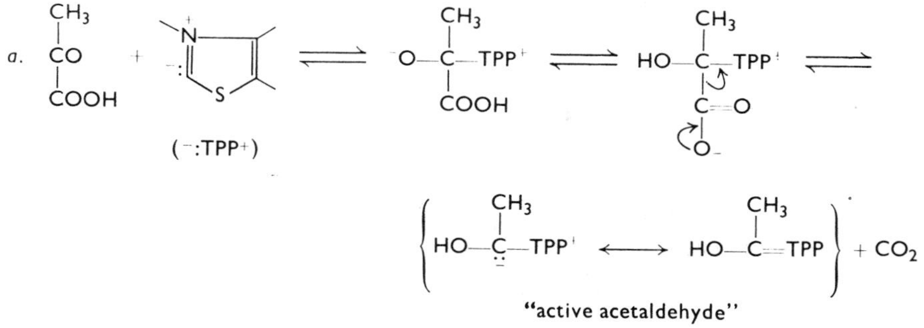

a.

$$
\begin{array}{c} CH_3 \\ | \\ CO \\ | \\ COOH \end{array}
\;+\;
(\text{—:TPP+})
\;\rightleftharpoons\;
\begin{array}{c} CH_3 \\ | \\ O\text{—}C\text{—TPP}^+ \\ | \\ COOH \end{array}
\;\rightleftharpoons\;
\begin{array}{c} CH_3 \\ | \\ HO\text{—}C\text{—TPP}^+ \\ | \\ C\text{=}O \\ | \\ O_- \end{array}
\;\rightleftharpoons\;
$$

$$
\left\{
\begin{array}{c} CH_3 \\ | \\ HO\text{—}C\text{—TPP}^+ \end{array}
\;\longleftrightarrow\;
\begin{array}{c} CH_3 \\ | \\ HO\text{—}C\text{=}\text{=TPP} \end{array}
\right\}
+\; CO_2
$$

"active acetaldehyde"

[Eq. 2-26]

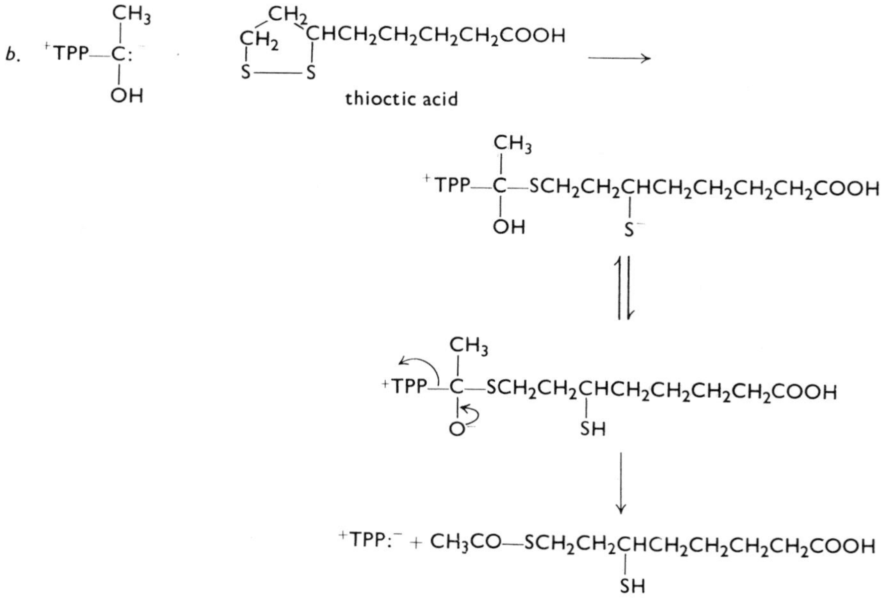

b.

$$
\begin{array}{c} CH_3 \\ | \\ {}^+TPP\text{—}C\text{:}^- \\ | \\ OH \end{array}
\qquad
\begin{array}{c} CH_2 \\ CH_2 \quad CHCH_2CH_2CH_2CH_2COOH \\ | \quad\quad | \\ S\text{——}S \end{array}
\;\longrightarrow\;
$$

thioctic acid

$$
\begin{array}{c} CH_3 \\ | \\ {}^+TPP\text{—}C\text{—SCH}_2CH_2CHCH_2CH_2CH_2CH_2COOH \\ | \quad\quad\quad\quad\quad | \\ OH \quad\quad\quad\quad\quad\quad S^- \end{array}
$$

$$
\begin{array}{c} CH_3 \\ | \\ {}^+TPP\text{—}C\text{—SCH}_2CH_2CHCH_2CH_2CH_2CH_2COOH \\ | \quad\quad\quad\quad\quad | \\ O^- \quad\quad\quad\quad\quad\quad SH \end{array}
$$

$$
{}^+TPP\text{:}^- + CH_3CO\text{—SCH}_2CH_2CHCH_2CH_2CH_2CH_2COOH \\ \phantom{{}^+TPP\text{:}^- + CH_3CO\text{—SCH}_2CH_2}\ \ | \\ SH
$$

[Eq. 2-27]

c.

$$
CH_3CO\text{—SCH}_2CH_2CH(CH_2)_4COOH \\ | \\ SH
$$

CoA—SH

$$
CH_3CO\text{—SCoA} + HSCH_2CH_2CH(CH_2)_4COOH \\ | \\ SH
$$

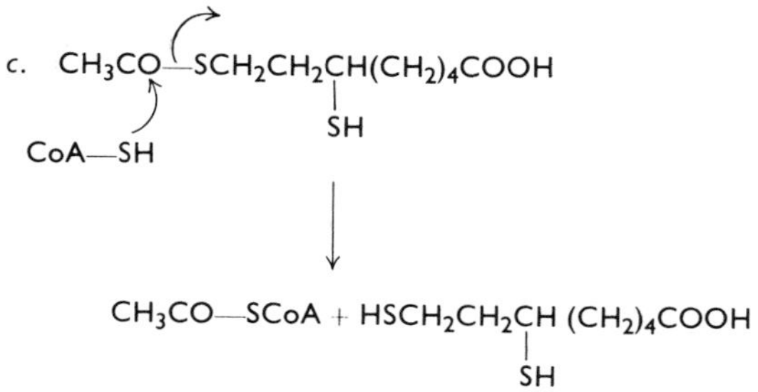

[Eq. 2-28]

Reaction step (a) (Eq. 2-26) involves the attack of the nucleophilic 2-thia-zolium ion upon the carbonyl group of pyruvic acid. It will be noted that a similar attack of $^-$:TTP$^+$ upon a carbonyl group occurs in the transketolase reaction (Eq. 2-19b). The subsequent loss of CO_2, with generation of the resonance-stabilized $CH_3C(OH)$=TPP, completes this stage of the reaction.

In step (b), the nucleophilic "active acetaldehyde" attacks the disulfide link-age with the formation of the carbon-sulfur bond. Displacement of $^-$:TTP$^+$ re-generates this coenzyme for further reaction (Eq. 2-27).

Finally, the exchange reaction takes place in which CoA—SH displaces the acetyl group from the S-acetyl derivative of the dihydrothioctic acid (Eq. 2-28).

The last step of this series of reactions, and that in which the actual oxidation (of the *oxidative* decarboxylation) occurs, is the conversion of the reduced thioctic acid to the disulfide form (Eq. 2-29):

$$d. \quad HSCH_2CH_2CH(CH_2)_4COOH \xrightarrow[\quad NAD^+ \quad NADH \quad]{} \begin{array}{c} CH_2 \\ CH_2 \quad CH(CH_2)_4COOH \\ | \qquad | \\ S\text{——}S \end{array} \qquad \text{[Eq. 2-29]}$$
$$\qquad\qquad\quad\; SH$$

The condensed summary of the series of reactions shown in Eqs. 2-24 to 2-27 is the following* (Eq. 2-30):

$$a. \quad RCOCOOH + {}^+TPP{:}^- \longrightarrow R\overset{..}{C}(OH)\text{—}TPP^+ + CO_2$$

$$b. \quad R\overset{..}{C}(OH)\text{—}TPP^+ + Thioct\text{—}S_2 \longrightarrow RCO\text{—}S\text{—}ThioctSH + {}^+TPP{:}^-$$

$$c. \quad RCO\text{—}S\text{—}ThioctSH + CoA\text{—}SH \longrightarrow RCO\text{—}SCoA + Thioct(SH)_2$$

$$d. \quad Thioct(SH)_2 + NAD^+ \longrightarrow Thioct\text{—}S_2 + NADH \qquad\qquad \text{[Eq. 2-30]}$$

Acetyl coenzyme A is an extraordinarily versatile reagent. It possesses two reactive functional centers:

a) The acetyl methyl group, which by removal of a proton is converted into the highly nucleophilic carbon anion (Eq. 2-31):

$$CH_3CO\text{—}SCoA + B{:} \; \rightleftharpoons \; {:}CH_2CO\text{—}SCoA + BH\dagger \qquad\qquad \text{[Eq. 2-31]}$$

† The symbol B:$^-$ is a conventional device for representing a proton acceptor, perhaps a basic site in a protein (enzyme) molecule.

* It may be noted that acetyl CoA can also be formed in other ways; for example, by way of the series:

$$ATP + acetate \longrightarrow AMP\text{—}acetyl + PP_i;$$

$$AMP\text{—}acetyl + CoA\text{—}SH \longrightarrow acetyl \; CoA + AMP$$

b) the carbonyl groups of thioacids and their derivatives are extraordinarily reactive. Even thioacetic acid (CH_3COSH) reacts with amines at ordinary temperatures to yield N-acetyl derivatives. Thus, acetyl CoA is an active acylating agent; it undergoes self-condensation in a reaction similar to the Claisen condensation (Eq. 2-32) and is undoubtedly the agent that is responsible for the formation of N- and O-acetates in living systems (Eq. 2-33, 2-34):

$$2\ CH_3CO{-}SCoA \longrightarrow CH_3COCH_2CO{-}SCoA + CoA{-}SH \qquad \text{[Eq. 2-32]}$$

$$RNH_2 + CH_3CO{-}SCoA \longrightarrow RNHCOCH_3 + CoA{-}SH \qquad \text{[Eq. 2-33]}$$

$$ROH + CH_3CO{-}SCoA \longrightarrow ROCOCH_3 + CoA{-}SH \qquad \text{[Eq. 2-34]}$$

Our concerns with acetyl coenzyme A will be with reactions of both of these types: those in which it acts as the nucleophilic reagent (Eq. 2-31), and those in which it accepts nucleophilic attack at the carbonyl group (Eqs. 2-32, 2-33, 2-34).

2.9 The Citric Acid Cycle

One important consequence of the conversion of pyruvic acid into acetyl coenzyme A is the complete oxidation of pyruvic acid (and thus of glucose, from which it derives) to carbon dioxide and water. The fruits of this oxidation are several:

a) energy provided by the oxidation is conserved for metabolic use, principally by the generation of ATP;

b) numerous low-molecular weight organic acids (succinic, malic, citric, α-keto acids) are provided by the reactions involved in the oxidative breakdown of pyruvic acid. Many of these are stable compounds, found widely distributed as normal plant constituents; others are important intermediates in further biosynthetic processes;

c) the α-keto acids formed in pyruvate breakdown are the precursors which, by amination, provide a number of important amino acids.

d) acetyl coenzyme A is formed in the first stage of pyruvate breakdown.

The cycle of reactions in which pyruvic acid is oxidized is known as the citric acid cycle;* it may be described in three stages:

1. the conversion of pyruvic acid into acetyl coenzyme A (Eq. 2-35);
2. the condensation of acetyl CoA with oxaloacetic acid to yield citric acid (Eq. 2-36);
3. transformations of citric acid leading to the production of CO_2, ATP, the various low-molecular weight acids of the cycle, and eventual regeneration of oxaloacetic acid, which condenses with pyruvic acid to continue the cycle (Eq. 2-37).

* Also, the "Krebs cycle" and the "tricarboxylic acid cycle."

Stage 1:

$$CH_3COCOOH \longrightarrow CH_3CO—SCoA$$ [Eq. 2-35]

(Eqs. 2-26 to 2-29)

Stage 2:

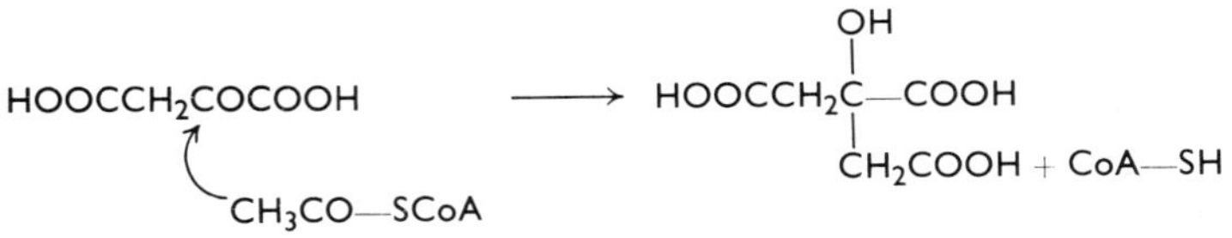

$$HOOCCH_2COCOOH \longrightarrow HOOCCH_2\overset{\overset{\displaystyle OH}{|}}{C}—COOH$$ [Eq. 2-36]

$$CH_3CO—SCoA \qquad\qquad CH_2COOH + CoA—SH$$

Stage 3:

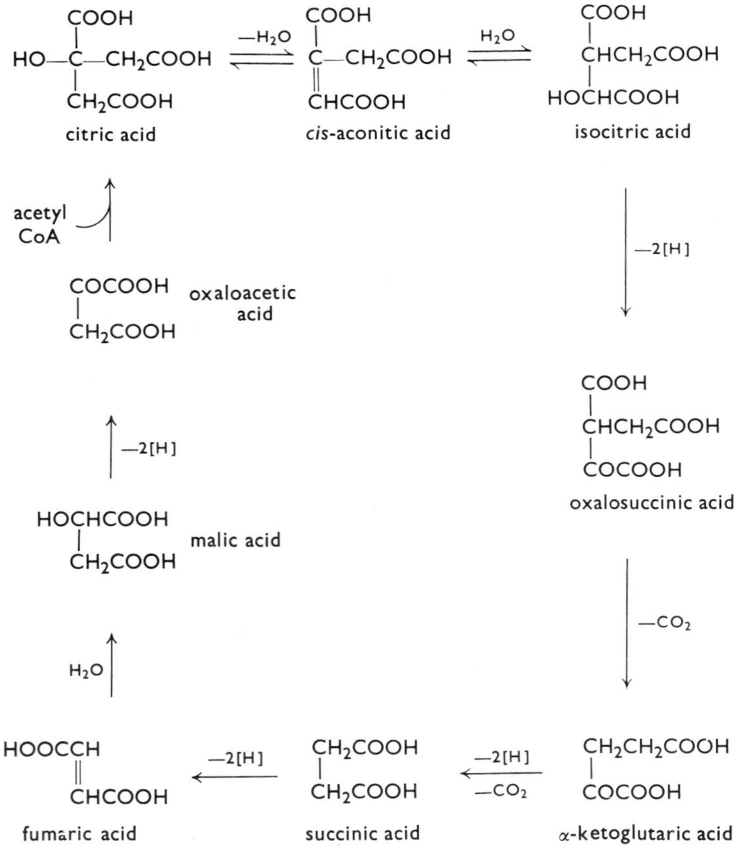

The Citric Acid Cycle

The summary of these reactions leads to the result that for each complete turn of the cycle one molecule of acetic acid is converted into carbon dioxide and water according to the following equations (Eqs. 2-38, 2-39):

$$CH_3COOH + 3\,H_2O \longrightarrow 3\,CO_2 + 8[H] \qquad\qquad\qquad \text{[Eq. 2-38]}$$

$$8[H] + 4[O] \longrightarrow 4\,H_2O \qquad\qquad\qquad\qquad\qquad \text{[Eq. 2-39]}$$

The energy provided by the oxidation of acetic acid is utilized in the generation of adenosine triphosphate in an overall process that is summarized in the following expression (Eq. 2-40):

$$CH_3CO{-}SCoA + 2\,O_2 + 12\,ADP + 12\,P_i \longrightarrow 2\,CO_2 + CoA{-}SH + 12\,ATP \quad \text{[Eq. 2-40]}$$

The function and importance of ATP in cellular metabolism cannot be categorized in a single statement. Its participation in many of the reactions that constitute what may be broadly designated as "biosynthesis" will become apparent as it appears in many of the reactions that will be described in chapters to follow.

2.10 Carbohydrates in Cellular Processes

Besides their participation in the reactions of photosynthetic carbon fixation, and, through oxidative breakdown, in the energy-yielding reactions of cellular metabolism, carbohydrates play important roles in cellular processes of many kinds, and are found widely distributed in nature as stable end products of plant biosynthesis. Although the extensive field of the organic chemistry of carbohydrates will not be dealt with in detail in this book, certain aspects of carbohydrate chemistry are of special relevance to natural products chemistry.

Simple sugars and the polysaccharides formed by their polymerization are familiar natural substances. Glucose, fructose, sucrose, cellulose, starch, poly-aldoses, polyuronic acids occur widely in nature. Combinations of sugars—most commonly glucose—with naturally occurring phenolic compounds in the form of glycosides are directly relevant to our present purposes. The widespread natural occurrence of polysaccharides and glycosides indicates that there exists in plants a general process for the attachment of a sugar residue to oxygen, such as that of a phenolic or alcoholic hydroxyl group (to produce a glycoside) or of another sugar (to produce a di- or polysaccharide).

The compound most generally involved in reactions of this kind is uridine di-phosphoglucose (UDP-glucose, or UDPG), which is a glucose donor in the process called transglycosylation. The structure of UDPG is shown in Fig. 2-5:

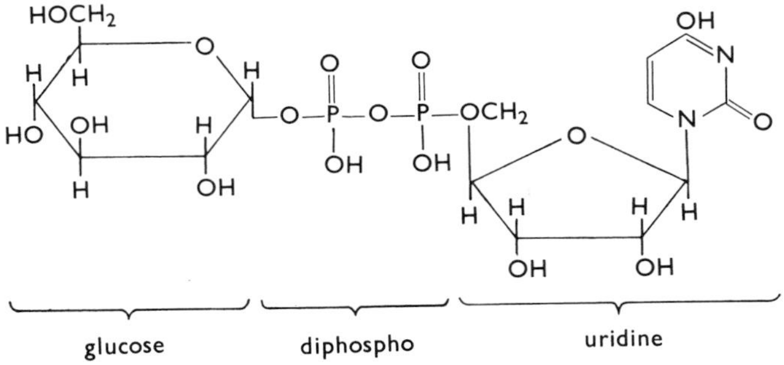

Fig. 2-5. Uridine diphosphoglucose (UDPG).

Other, similarly constituted, compounds consisting of combinations of the same general type (Fig. 2-6) are known; but UDPG will be used as the typical representative of this class of tranglycosylating agents.

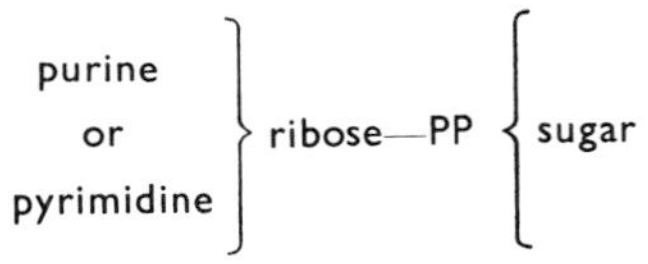

Fig. 2-6. Compounds of the UDPG Type.

The glucose transfer reaction proceeds by nucleophilic attack of the oxygen atom of, for example, a phenolic hydroxyl group upon the UDPG, with displacement of the uridine diphosphate grouping (Eq. 2-41):

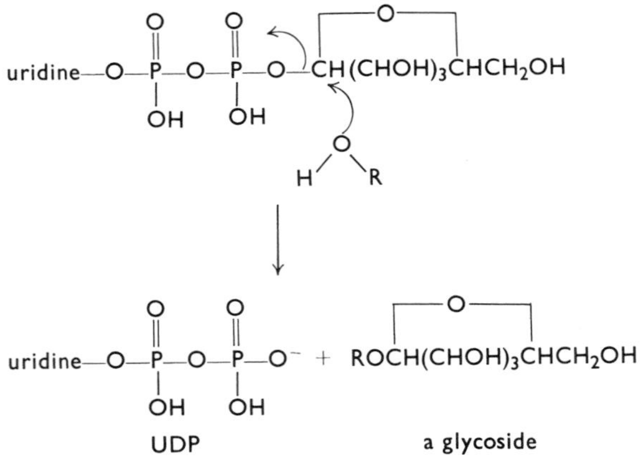

[Eq. 2-41]

It will be seen in Eq. 2-41, and again in numerous other cases in the pages to follow, that nature utilizes a mechanistic principle that is of wide application in all areas of organic reactions: the displacement of a "leaving group" that is the anion of a strong acid. In Eq. 2-41 this is the group uridine pyrophosphate. In the phosphorylation of glucose the leaving group is adenosine diphosphate; and in examples to be discussed in later chapters, the pyrophosphate ion is itself the leaving group (for instance, Sec. 2.9; and in the following example).

Indeed, the formation of UDP-glucose is brought about by a reaction in which pyrophosphate is the leaving group. The reaction of uridine triphosphate with glucose-1-phosphate as the nucleophile results in the following displacement (Eq. 2-42):

$$
\text{uridine—O—P(=O)(OH)—O—P(=O)(OH)—O—P(=O)(OH)—OH}
$$
$$
\text{glucose—O—P(=O)(OH)—O}^-
$$
$$
\longrightarrow \quad \text{UDPG} + \text{PP}_i \qquad\qquad \text{[Eq. 2-42]}
$$

The glycosylation reaction of Eq. 2-41 illustrates another well known principle of the nucleophilic displacement reaction, namely, the inversion of configuration of the carbon atom at which displacement occurs. UDP-glucose, which, as was described in the foregoing paragraph (Eq. 2-42), is formed from glucose-1-phosphate, has an α-oriented bond between the 1-position of the glucose residue and the UDP grouping. Displacement of UDP by nucleophilic attack at C-1 of the sugar residue results in inversion of configuration at C-1 and the formation of a β-glucopyranoside (Eq. 2-43):

$$
\text{(glucose ring structure)} \quad \longrightarrow \quad \text{(β-glucopyranoside)} \; + \; \text{UDP} \qquad \text{[Eq. 2-43]}
$$

a β-glucopyranoside

The sugar nucleotides have other functions in cellular transformations of carbohydrates. Transformations of the sugar, while it is attached to the nucleotide, can lead to oxidation, epimerization and other reactions, with the formation of new sugar nucleotides.

In Eq. 2-44 are shown in outline form a number of typical transformations of this kind:

$$
\text{UDP-glucose}
\begin{cases}
\xrightarrow[\text{(NAD$^+$)}]{\text{oxidize at C-6}} \text{UDP-glucuronic acid} \xrightarrow{-CO_2} \text{UDP-xylose} \\[2ex]
\xrightarrow[\text{at C-4}]{\text{epimerize}} \text{UDP-galactose} \\[2ex]
\xrightarrow[\text{galactose-1-phosphate}]{\text{reaction with}} \text{UDP-galactose} + \text{glucose-1-phosphate}
\end{cases}
\qquad \text{[Eq. 2-44]}
$$

2.11   Other Carbohydrates of Common Occurrence

The three- to seven-carbon-atom aldoses and ketoses that have appeared in the above sections may be regarded as the sugars of the primary metabolic processes. They are involved in photosynthesis and in the metabolism of glucose, and thus belong to the area of primary metabolic processes that are common to living cells of many kinds. Nature affords, in addition to these common sugars, a wide variety of derived carbohydrates that are simple structural modifications of these. Glycuronic acids (such as galacturonic acid, found in pectins), amino sugars (such as N-acetyl-glucosamine, a constituent of chitin), deoxy sugars (such as deoxyribose, found in the nucleic acids), N-methylated, O-methylated sugars of many kinds, abound in

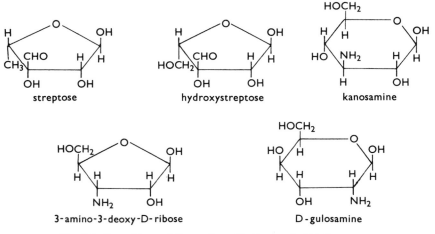

Fig. 2-7. Some Unusual Sugars from *Streptomyces* Antibiotics.

nature. Sugars of the latter kinds are characteristic of certain of the antibiotic compounds produced by microorganisms. For example, the sugars streptose, hydroxystreptose, kanosamine, 3-deoxy-3-amino-D-ribose, D-gulosamine are a few examples of unusual carbohydrates found (in combined form) in various *Streptomyces* antibiotics (Fig. 2-7).

2.12 Phosphoenolpyruvic Acid and Shikimic Acid

The key position occupied by pyruvic acid in cellular metabolism depends upon the importance in biosynthetic processes of two compounds: phosphoenolpyruvic acid, a product of the oxidative breakdown of glucose; and acetyl coenzyme A, a principal source of which is the oxidative decarboxylation of pyruvic acid, as described in an earlier section. A summary of the process of glycolysis, in which glucose is degraded to three-carbon-atom compounds anaerobically (leading to lactic acid or ethanol) and aerobically (leading to pyruvic acid and, eventually, to carbon dioxide and water), is given in the following scheme (Eq. 2-45):

glucose ⇅ glucose-6-phosphate ⇌ glucose-1-phosphate ⇅ glycogen

glucose-6-phosphate ⇅ fructose-6-phosphate ⇌ fructose-1,6-diphosphate

fructose-1,6-diphosphate ⇅ glyceraldehyde-3-phosphate

dihydroxyacetone phosphate ⇌ glyceraldehyde-3-phosphate

glyceraldehyde-3-phosphate ⇅ 1,3-diphosphoglyceric acid ⇅ 3-phosphoglyceric acid ⇅ 2-phosphoglyceric acid ⇅ phosphoenolpyruvic acid

phosphoenolpyruvic acid → $CH_3COCOOH$ (pyruvic acid)

$CH_3COCOOH$ (pyruvic acid) → $CH_3CHOHCOOH$ (lactic acid)

$CH_3COCOOH$ (pyruvic acid) → CH_3CHO ⇅ CH_3CH_2OH

$CH_3COCOOH$ (pyruvic acid) → $CH_3CO—SCoA$ → citric acid cycle

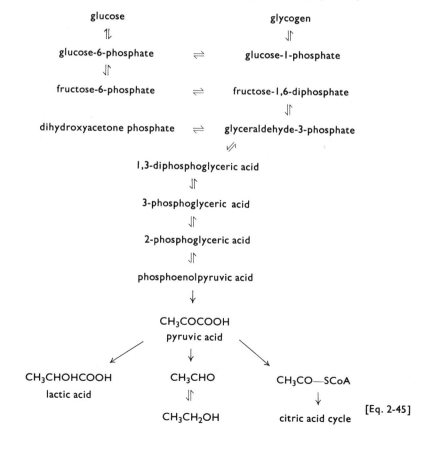

[Eq. 2-45]

Phosphoenolpyruvic acid, the product of the glycolytic cleavage reaction and subsequent oxidation of the three-carbon-atom cleavage product, is a participant in a number of reactions that occur at both the primary and secondary levels of metabolism. A reaction that provides for an incorporation of carbon dioxide into organic combination is the carboxylation of phosphoenolpyruvic acid with concomitant reduction, to yield malic acid (Eq. 2-46):

$$CO_2 + CH_2\!\!=\!\!\overset{\displaystyle OP}{\underset{\displaystyle |}{C}}\!\!-\!\!COOH \longrightarrow \{HOOCCH_2COCOOH\} \longrightarrow HOOCCH_2\overset{\displaystyle OH}{\underset{\displaystyle |}{C}}HCOOH$$

[Eq. 2-46]

The reduction is catalyzed by an enzyme which provides, as the reducing agent, the reduced triphosphopyridine nucleotide, NADPH.

It is to be noted that nucleophilic attack on the phosphorus atom of the phosphate group can provide for the generation of anionic character at the carbon atom of PEP (Eq. 2-47):

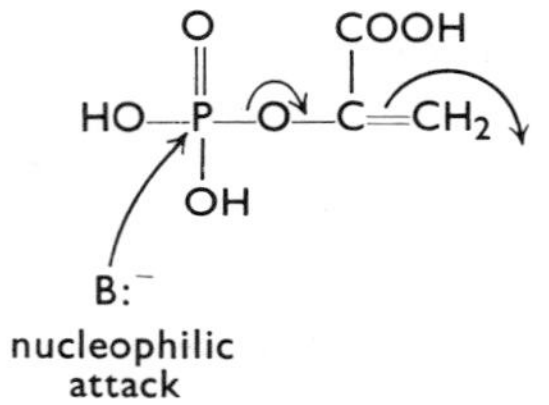

[Eq. 2-47]

nucleophilic
attack

When carbon dioxide (probably in combination with another cofactor, biotin) is the electrophilic acceptor, carboxylation of PEP occurs to yield oxaloacetic acid. Although this reaction represents a minor pathway for the incorporation of carbon dioxide into organic combination, it provides a prototype for a mode of behavior of phosphoenolpyruvic acid that will be encountered again. The overall process is shown in Eq. 2-48:

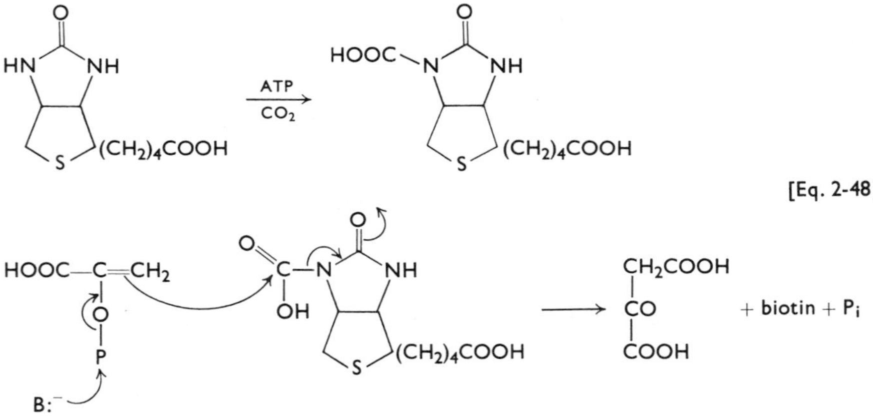

[Eq. 2-48]

The nucleophilic character of PEP finds expression in other ways, and its combination with the electrophilic aldehyde carbon atom of erythrose-4-phosphate is a reaction of far reaching importance in biological synthesis. The following (Eq. 2-49) is a summary expression of the genesis of shikimic and prephenic acids, the central compounds produced by this condensation; further discussion of these reactions, with additional details of shikimic acid synthesis, will be deferred until Chapter 5.

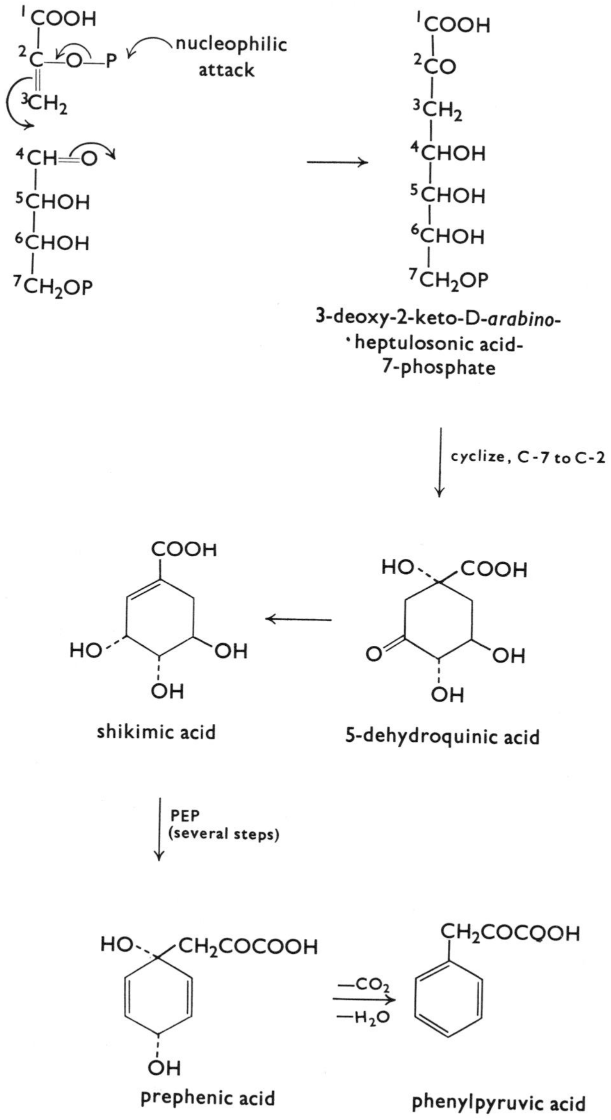

3-deoxy-2-keto-D-*arabino*-
heptulosonic acid-
7-phosphate

cyclize, C-7 to C-2

shikimic acid   5-dehydroquinic acid

PEP
(several steps)

prephenic acid   phenylpyruvic acid

$-CO_2$
$-H_2O$

[Eq. 2-49]

2.13 Summary

This chapter has dealt so far with several of the central processes by which living organisms (for the most part, chlorophyll-containing plants) produce, in primary metabolic processes, a number of reactive compounds which serve as the raw materials for further synthesis. In summary, these processes are:

1. photosynthesis

phosphoglyceric acid
ATP
carbohydrates
reduced pyridine nucleotides

2. glycolysis and the citric acid cycle

ATP
pyruvic acid (and its enol phosphate)
acetyl coenzyme A
citric, α-ketoglutaric, malic, succinic, fumaric, oxaloacetic acids

3. pentose phosphate cycle

aldopentoses
ketopentoses
other sugars

4. reactions of phosphoenolpyruvic acid

shikimic, prephenic acids

2.14 "One-carbon" Metabolism

The universal occurrence, in naturally occurring organic compounds of all kinds of methyl groups linked to carbon, oxygen, and nitrogen, as well as the demonstration that one-carbon units are introduced into the skeletal framework of many compounds, indicates the operation of a mechanism by which a single carbon atom may be transferred from a donor to an acceptor molecule.

Single-carbon-atom metabolism is a topic that embraces a wide range of biological processes: the provision of single-carbon atoms in the skeletal framework of purines and pyrimidines; the formation of some of the N-methylated components of the phospholipids; the detoxification by methylation of certain drugs or endogenous metabolites; N-, C-, and O-methylations of many naturally occurring phenolic and amino compounds. Our concern will be principally with three of these processes:

1. the formation of phenolic ethers
2. the formation of N-methylated amines
3. the formation of C-methylated phenols and ketones.

The principal agent involved in the transfer of methyl groups to nucleophilic centers is S-adenosylmethionine (Fig. 2-8).

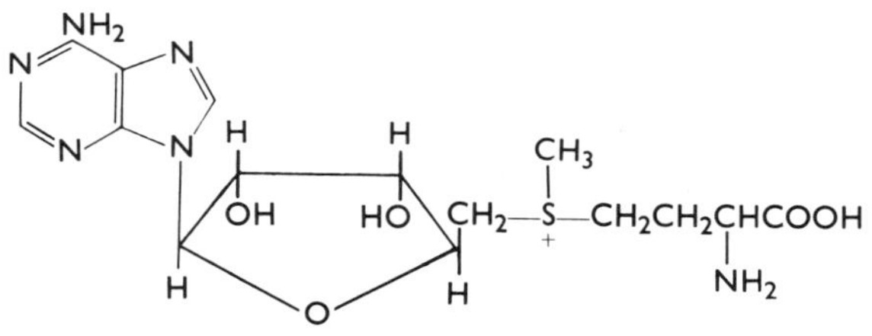

Fig. 2-8. S-Adenosylmethionine.

It is apparent that this sulfonium compound possesses the characteristics necessary for it to act as an alkylating (methylating) agent. Attack of a nucleophile (such as the nitrogen or oxygen of an amine or a phenoxide ion, or the carbon atom *ortho* or *para* to anionic oxygen) results in displacement of the sulfide grouping and transfer of methyl to the anionic center (Eq. 2-50):

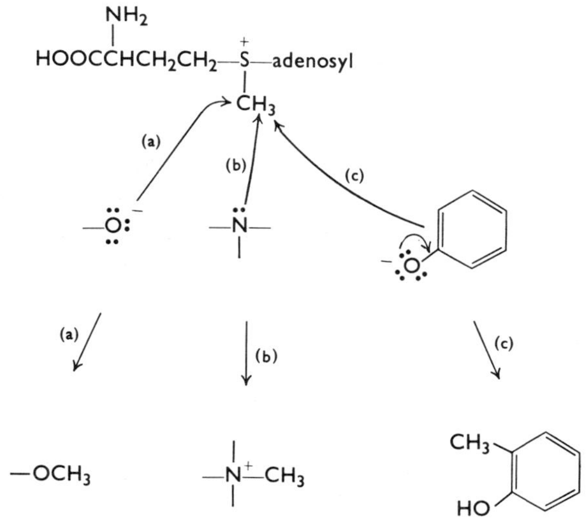

[Eq. 2-50]

The reactions formulated above are "methyl transfer" reactions, and will be reintroduced in later chapters when they are again encountered. Of immediate interest is the genesis of the methyl group from primary metabolic sources. The agent to and from which single-carbon atoms are transferred is folic acid (a generic term for a group of pteridine derivatives which differ in the terminal substituent, R, of the benzoic acid unit) (Fig. 2-9):

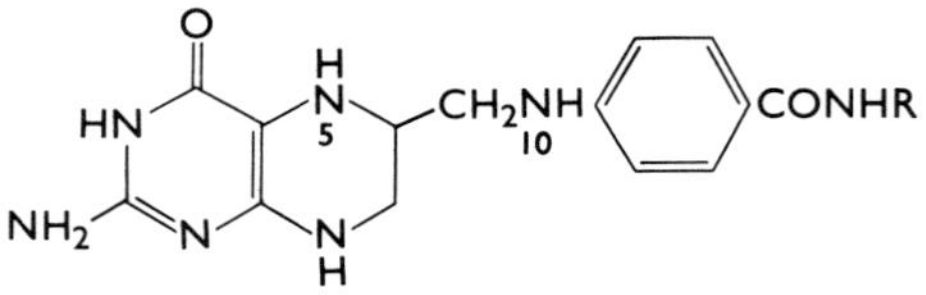

Fig. 2-9. A Tetrahydrofolic Acid (R = glutamyl or polyglutamyl).

The conversion of tetrahydrofolic acid to a methyl donor takes place by way of the formylation of the 5- or 10-positions (between which a formyl group can be transferred in an equilibrium reaction), reduction of the —CHO group, through —CH$_2$OH, to —CH$_3$, and eventual transfer of the —CH$_3$ group from position 5 to homocysteine (Eq. 2-51):

$$\underset{\text{homocysteine}}{HSCH_2CH_2\underset{\underset{NH_2}{|}}{C}HCOOH} \xrightarrow[\substack{\text{tetrahydro-}\\ \text{folic acid}}]{\text{N-methyl-}} \underset{\text{methionine}}{CH_3SCH_2CH_2\underset{\underset{NH_2}{|}}{C}HCOOH} \qquad [\text{Eq. 2-51}]$$

The available sources of the single-carbon atom unit are many: formic acid, formaldehyde, ethanol, serine, glycine and histidine have all been shown, by isotopic labeling experiments, to lead to N-formyl- and thence to N-methyltetrahydrofolic acid.

In experimental studies of the origin of methyl groups in naturally occurring organic compounds by use of isotopically labeled precursors, formate and methionine are most commonly used. In the examples to be discussed later on, it will be seen that $^{14}CH_3$-methionine is a specific source of the methyl groups in many methoxy and methylated amino compounds, with the formation of specifically labeled $^{14}CH_3O$— and $^{14}CH_3$—$\overset{|}{N}$— derivatives.

2.15   Phosphorylation; Adenosine Triphosphate (ATP)

Most natural processes of transformation of organic compounds by synthesis, degradation and structural alteration proceed under the catalytic influence of enzymes. Although the exact role of the protein components of enzymes in increasing the rates of the reactions they catalyze cannot usually be described in detail, many enzymes possess as integral structural elements relatively small molecular entities known as "cofactors," "prosthetic groups," or "coenzymes," the roles of which can be defined with considerable exactness. The prosthetic groups participate in the relevant chemical reaction of the substrate in ways that can be explicitly described in terms of specific structural representation. For example, when the pyridine nucleotides (NAD, NADP) participate in electron transfer, or oxidation-reduction, they undergo oxidation or reduction (Eq. 2-52):

$$\text{sugar—pyrophosphate—purine} \quad \rightleftharpoons \quad \text{sugar—pyrophosphate—purine}$$

$$(\text{NAD}^+) \qquad\qquad (\text{NADH})$$

or:

substrate + coenzyme $\rightleftharpoons$ oxidized substrate + reduced coenzyme   [Eq. 2-52]

A great many distinct oxidation-reduction enzymes are known which carry out this electron-transfer reaction through the agency of NAD or NADP. Among these are lactic dehydrogenase, 3-phosphoglyceraldehyde dehydrogenase, malic acid dehydrogenase. It is not within the design of this book to describe these or other reactions with details of the enzymes that catalyze them. Rather, it is sufficient for our purposes to make clear that while an overall reaction is under the influence of enzymatic catalysis, there is often a discrete and definable entity, the coenzyme or prosthetic group, involved in the reaction in a way that can be expressed in terms of specific structural changes.

Other prosthetic groups that act in similarly describable ways in oxidation-reduction reactions are the flavin nucleotides and the iron atom in the cytochromes.* Besides the electron-transfer coenzymes, we have already encountered several important coenzymes with other functions. Thiamin pyrophosphate, tetrahydrofolic acid and coenzyme A have been discussed in earlier sections.

A universal participant in the chemical reactions of the living cell is adenosine triphosphate (ATP). In combination with enzyme catalysts, ATP and its less highly phosphorylated congeners, adenosine mono- and di-phosphate (AMP, ADP), engage in transphosphorylation reactions, in which phosphate residues are transferred from one site to another. ATP provides the driving force by means of which many of the essential chemical reactions of the living cell are enabled to proceed under conditions of equilibria which are favorable for the formation to a useful degree of the products of the reaction.

The actions of the adenosine phosphates can be described in terms of energy relationships, in which the relative bond energies of the linkages between phosphate groups and the atoms to which they are bound can be expressed in terms of the free

* It should, however, be pointed out that not all enzymes are known to possess definable prosthetic groups.

energy change that occurs in the formation of breaking (as in hydrolysis or alcoho-
lysis) of the bond. They may also be described in terms comparable to those used in
describing the behavior of derivatives of carboxylic acids; in particular, esters and
acid anhydrides. It is implicit in the description of the relative extent of the reaction
of an ester and an anhydride, with, for example, an alcohol or water, that the position of the equilibrium depends upon the free energy change in the reaction. The
reactions shown in Eqs. 2-53a and 2-54b proceed to equilibrium states in which the

$$\text{(a)} \quad CH_3C\overset{O}{\underset{OR}{\diagup}} + R'OH \rightleftharpoons CH_3C\overset{O}{\underset{OR'}{\diagup}} + ROH \qquad \text{[Eq. 2-53]}$$

$$\text{(b)} \quad \begin{matrix} CH_3C\overset{O}{\diagup} \\ CH_3C\underset{O}{\diagdown} \end{matrix} O + R'OH \rightleftharpoons CH_3C\overset{O}{\underset{OR'}{\diagup}} + CH_3COOH \qquad \text{[Eq. 2-54]}$$

equilibrium constants are (a) near unity and (b) very large. In the usual terminology reaction (b) goes "essentially to completion." This is equivalent to saying that
the standard free energy decrease in the first reaction is very small (in the neighborhood of zero), while that in the second reaction is large. In the usual (but to some
objectionable) terminology of biochemical discussion, the ester is said to have a
"low-energy" O-acyl bond, and the anhydride a "high-energy" O-acyl bond.

In the same terms, simple phosphate esters have low-energy O—P bonds,
while pyrophosphates and triphosphates, such as ATP, have high-energy O—P
bonds. These high energy bonds are often designated by a special symbol: O ~ P.
Thus, ATP may be represented as follows (Fig. 2-10):*

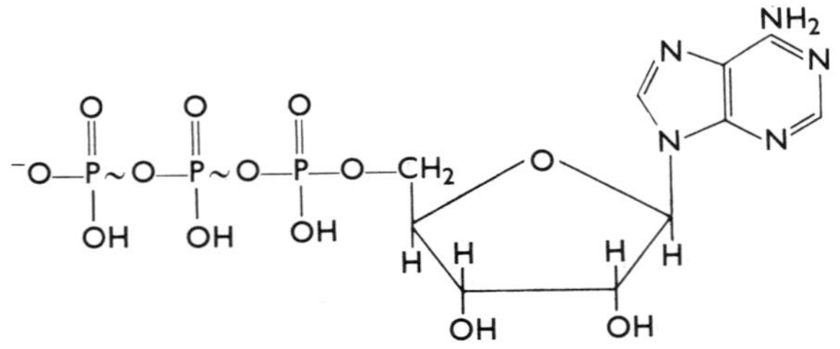

Fig. 2-10. Adenosine triphosphate (ATP).

ATP is thus a polyphosphoric anhydride, and is an active phosphorylating agent.
The degree to which an alcohol (for example, D-glucopyranose) is phosphorylated
will depend upon the relative free energies of solvolysis of the O—P bonds in

* It was pointed out earlier that the representation of the ionic character of such a polyprotic
acid is arbitrary, for the degree of ionization depends upon the pH of the medium. At physiological
pH, ATP is probably ionized to a greater degree than that shown.

glucose-6-phosphate and in ATP. In fact, the equilibrium of Eq. 2-55 lies to the right to such a degree as to make it permissible to represent the reaction with the use simply of an arrow →.

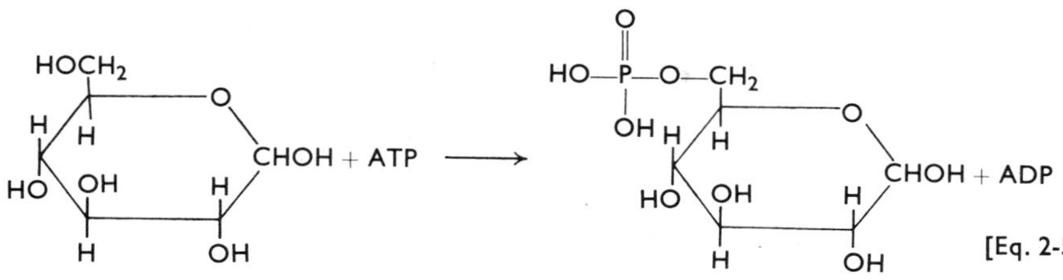

glucose-6-phosphate

[Eq. 2-55]

The transfer of "high-energy" phosphate to AMP and ADP—that is, the generation of ATP—is therefore a way in which the energy of chemical change can be preserved in a form available for the synthetic reactions that take place in the living cell. A simple reaction that illustrates how some of the energy of oxidation might find its way into ATP bond energy can be found in the oxidation of 3-phosphoglyceraldehyde to 3-phosphoglyceric acid (Eq. 2-56):

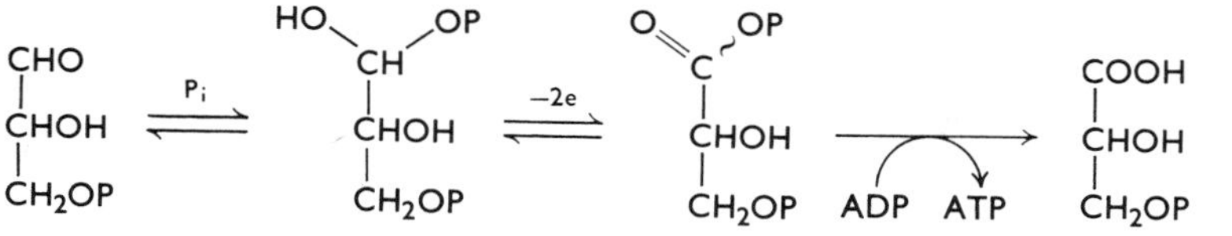

a phosphate ester

a phosphoric anhydride

[Eq. 2-56]

The conversion of the "low-energy bond" of the 1,3-diphosphoglyceraldehyde, represented here as the 1-phosphorylated hydrate of the aldehyde, into the "high-energy" $O \sim P$ bond of the glyceric-phosphoric anhydride permits the latter, acting as a phosphorylating agent, to transfer its phosphate grouping to ADP, with the formation of ATP. While this reaction scheme is oversimplified in omitting from discrete inclusion the $NAD^+ \rightleftharpoons NADH$ reaction involved in the dehydrogenation step, it represents the essential means by which energy derived from the oxidation is "stored" in ATP and made available for synthetic uses. The overall reaction can be written as in Eq. 2-57:

glyceraldehyde-3-phosphate + P_i + NAD^+ + ADP $\rightleftharpoons$

3-phosphoglyceric acid + NADH + ATP   [Eq. 2-57]

Further transformation of 3-PGA, by way of its isomerization into 2-phospho-glyceric acid, to yield phosphoenol pyruvic acid (PEP) generates a new reactive ("high energy") $O \sim P$ bond (Eq. 2-58):

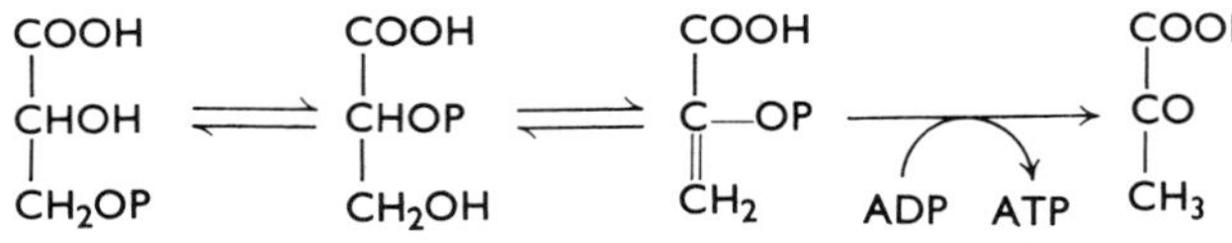

$$
\begin{array}{ccccc}
\text{COOH} & \text{COOH} & \text{COOH} & & \text{COOH} \\
| & | & | & & | \\
\text{CHOH} \rightleftharpoons & \text{CHOP} \rightleftharpoons & \text{C—OP} \longrightarrow & & \text{CO} \\
| & | & \| & & | \\
\text{CH}_2\text{OP} & \text{CH}_2\text{OH} & \text{CH}_2 & \text{ADP ATP} & \text{CH}_3
\end{array}
\qquad \text{[Eq. 2-58]}
$$

Comparable oxidations result in the generation of ATP in analogous ways (Eqs. 2-59, 2-60, 2-61):

a. isocitric acid $+ NAD^+ + P_i + ADP \rightleftharpoons$

α-ketoglutaric acid $+ NADH + ATP$ [Eq. 2-59]

b. malic acid $+ NAD^+ + ADP \rightleftharpoons$ oxaloacetic acid $+ NADH + ATP$ [Eq. 2-60]

c. α-ketoglutaric acid $+ NAD^+ + CoA—SH \rightleftharpoons$

succinyl—CoA $+ NADH + CO_2;$ [Eq. 2-61]

succinyl—CoA $+ ADP + P_i \rightleftharpoons$ succinic acid $+ ATP + CoA—SH$

Complete oxidation of acetyl CoA through the citric acid cycle yields ATP in an amount related to the large energy production by so extensive an oxidative degradation (Eq. 2-62):

$CH_3CO—SCoA + 2 O_2 + 12 ADP + 12 P_i \longrightarrow 2 CO_2 + CoA—SH + 12 ATP$ [Eq. 2-62]

All reactions of these kinds, and numerous others not described, can be represented by the summary expression (Eq. 2-63):

ADP $+$ inorganic phosphate $\xrightarrow[\text{energy}]{\text{oxidation}}$ ATP   [Eq. 2-63]

Reoxidation of NADH to NAD^+, ultimately, through accessory enzymes, by molecular oxygen, yields ATP in ways that are not understood in all details because of the multiplicity of enzymes and co-factors involved in the reaction chain. An overall expression may be written to represent the processes in a general form

(Eq. 2-64) where X and Y represent groups that are often of unknown identity, perhaps parts of enzyme (protein) molecules or their associated prosthetic groups.

$$NADH + FAD\dagger + H^+ + X \rightleftharpoons NAD^+ \sim X + FADH$$

$$NAD^+ \sim X + Y \rightleftharpoons NAD^+ + X \sim Y \qquad \vdots [O]$$

$$X \sim Y + P_i \rightleftharpoons X + Y \sim P$$

$$FAD + H_2O$$

$$Y \sim P + ADP \rightleftharpoons Y + ATP \qquad\qquad\qquad\qquad \text{[Eq. 2-64]}$$

---

† FAD, flavin adenine dinucleotide, is a hydrogen (electron) acceptor in the chain leading at length to oxygen.

2.16   Phosphates in Nucleophilic Displacement Reactions

The importance of phosphorylation in cellular metabolism lies in the fact that the pyrophosphate group

$$\begin{array}{ccc} & O & O \\ & \parallel & \parallel \\ -O- & P-O- & P-OH \\ & | & | \\ & OH & OH \end{array}$$

is an effective leaving group in nucleophilic displacement reactions, certain of which are among the most fundamental reactions of secondary plant metabolism.

Consider, for example, the generalized displacement reaction (Eq. 2-65):

$$Y: + R:X \rightleftharpoons Y:R + :X \qquad\qquad\qquad\qquad \text{[Eq. 2-65]}$$

It is well known that the rate and conditions of equilibrium of this reaction depend upon the nature of all three entities, R, X and Y. In general, the ionizability of X as X^-, or its capacity for acting as a leaving group in heterolytic cleavage of the R—X bond is one of the most important factors in determining the rate of a reaction of this class. With a given nucleophile Y: and a given group R, the rate of the reaction will be slower if :X is a highly nucleophilic species and fast when it is poorly nucleophilic (toward carbon, if R—X is a carbon-X bond). Although there are exceptions to the generalization, the better leaving groups :X are conjugate bases of strong acids HX; that is, :X are weak bases. Both phosphoric and pyrophosphoric acids are strong acids; thus, the ions $H_2O_3PO^-$ (phosphate) and $H_3O_6P_2O^-$ (pyrophosphate) resemble in their tendency to undergo displacement as :X in Eq. 2-65 such leaving groups as halide ion and the anions of sulfonic acids. Phosphates and, in particular, pyrophosphates may be regarded as the biological counterparts of sulfonic esters (Eq. 2-66):

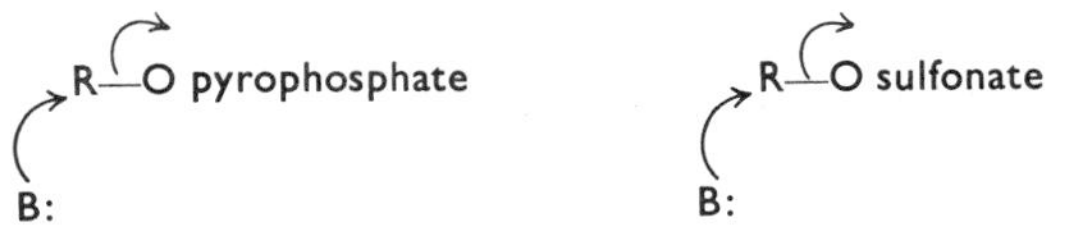

$$\text{R} \overset{\curvearrowright}{\underset{\underset{\text{B:}}{\curvearrowleft}}{\text{O}}} \text{pyrophosphate} \qquad \text{R} \overset{\curvearrowright}{\underset{\underset{\text{B:}}{\curvearrowleft}}{\text{O}}} \text{sulfonate} \qquad\qquad [\text{Eq. 2-66}]$$

It will thus be apparent that the ability of ATP to phosphorylate an alcoholic hydroxyl group provides a means by which the alkyl group of ROH can alkylate a nucleophilic center (Eq. 2-67):

$a.$ adenosyl—OPPP + ROH $\longrightarrow$ ROP + adenosyl—OPP
             (ATP)   (ADP)

$b.$ Y:$^-$ + R—OP $\longrightarrow$ Y:R + OP$^-$ (= P$_i$)   [Eq. 2-67]

One example of the phosphorylation of an alcoholic hydroxyl group by ATP has already been mentioned: the conversion of glucose into glucose-6-phosphate, the starting point for glycolytic degradation. This process and others of a similar nature are key reactions in what has been termed primary cellular metabolism; and although they are of importance in this realm they do not bear directly upon most of the secondary metabolic transformations with which we shall be concerned.

2.17   Mevalonic Acid and Pentenyl Pyrophosphates

The most important processes involving ATP in the realm of secondary plant metabolism are those in which acetyl coenzyme A is converted in a series of stages to 3,3-dimethylallyl pyrophosphate, and the utilization of the latter as an effective alkylating agent for carbon and oxygen. The reactions of 3,3-dimethylallyl pyrophosphate and its double-bond isomer, 3-methyl-3-butenyl pyrophosphate (also called "isopentenyl pyrophosphate"), will be dealt with in later chapters; the formation of these compounds is at or close to the level of primary metabolism and is appropriately discussed here.

The complete process by which the isopentenyl esters are formed is outlined in Eq. 2-68:*

---

* Because the principal emphasis in this book is upon the secondary products of the metabolism of plants, the source of acetyl coenzyme A has been described as the primary processes of metabolism at the level of photosynthesis and glycolysis. Acetyl coenzyme A can, however, be formed in other ways, one important route being the breakdown of fatty acids. In organisms in which the ingestion of fats, proteins and carbohydrates provides the principal sources of metabolic energy there are, then, several routes to acetyl coenzyme A. Indeed, the formation of acetyl CoA can also occur by the breakdown of fats in green plants, but since this is effectively a "recovery" of acetyl CoA that was the original source of the fat the process has not been considered in this chapter, but will be dealt with in the discussion of fatty acid synthesis.

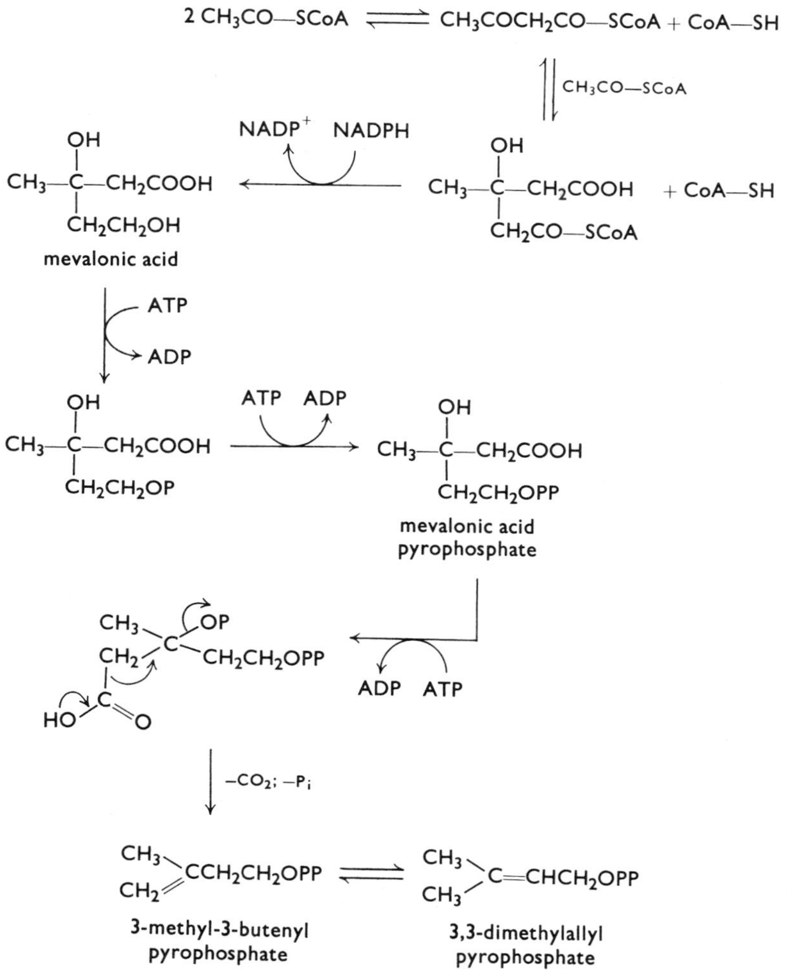

$$2\ CH_3CO{-}SCoA \rightleftharpoons CH_3COCH_2CO{-}SCoA + CoA{-}SH$$

$$\Big\Uparrow CH_3CO{-}SCoA$$

mevalonic acid

$$\begin{array}{c} OH \\ | \\ CH_3{-}C{-}CH_2COOH \\ | \\ CH_2CH_2OH \end{array} \xleftarrow[\;\;NADP^+\quad NADPH\;\;]{} \begin{array}{c} OH \\ | \\ CH_3{-}C{-}CH_2COOH \\ | \\ CH_2CO{-}SCoA \end{array} + CoA{-}SH$$

ATP → ADP

$$\begin{array}{c} OH \\ | \\ CH_3{-}C{-}CH_2COOH \\ | \\ CH_2CH_2OP \end{array} \xrightarrow[\;\;ATP\quad ADP\;\;]{} \begin{array}{c} OH \\ | \\ CH_3{-}C{-}CH_2COOH \\ | \\ CH_2CH_2OPP \end{array}$$

mevalonic acid
pyrophosphate

$$\begin{array}{c} CH_3 \\ \quad \diagdown \; OP \\ CH_2 {-} C {-} CH_2CH_2OPP \\ | \\ C \\ HO \diagup \;\diagdown O \end{array} \xleftarrow[\;\;ADP\quad ATP\;\;]{}$$

$-CO_2; -P_i$

$$\begin{array}{c} CH_3 \diagdown \\ \qquad C\,CH_2CH_2OPP \\ CH_2 \diagup \end{array} \rightleftharpoons \begin{array}{c} CH_3 \diagdown \\ \qquad C{=}CHCH_2OPP \\ CH_3 \diagup \end{array} \qquad\qquad \text{[Eq. 2-68]}$$

3-methyl-3-butenyl   3,3-dimethylallyl
pyrophosphate   pyrophosphate

3,3-Dimethylallyl pyrophosphate is a reactive substrate in nucleophilic displacement and an effective alkylating agent. It reacts with nucleophilic centers of several types in a manner that can be expressed by the following general equation (Eq. 2-69):

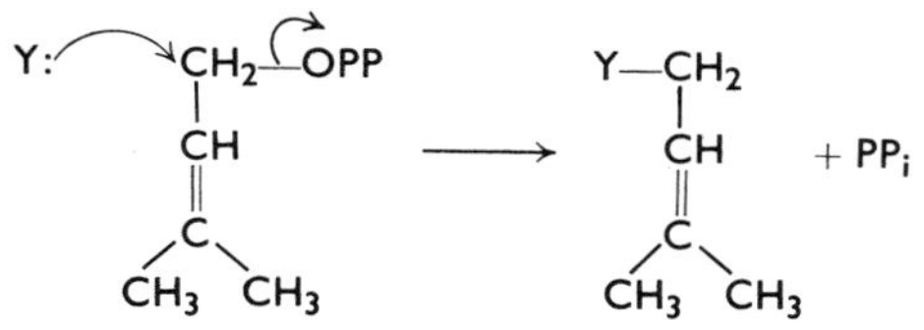

$$\begin{array}{c} Y{:} \overset{\frown}{} CH_2{-}OPP \\ | \\ CH \\ \| \\ C \\ CH_3 \;\; CH_3 \end{array} \longrightarrow \begin{array}{c} Y{-}CH_2 \\ | \\ CH \\ \| \\ C \\ CH_3 \;\; CH_3 \end{array} + PP_i \qquad\qquad \text{[Eq. 2-69]}$$

A number of examples of this reaction, in which Y: may be the nucleophilic center on oxygen or carbon (or a carbon-carbon double bond) will be encountered in the discussion to follow.

It is interesting to note that while O- and C-dimethylallyl derivatives, formed according to Eq. 2-69, are common among naturally occurring compounds, N-dimethylallyl derivatives are not. The reason for this may be that at pH values at which the pyrophosphate group is in the state of ionization requisite to its acting as the leaving group, OPP⁻, the necessary amino group is in a protonated, and thus non-nucleophilic, condition. Further, ion-pair combinations such as

$$R-NH_3^+\Big\}^-O-\overset{\overset{\displaystyle O}{\|}}{\underset{\underset{\displaystyle OH}{|}}{P}}-O\text{-----}$$

may prevent access of the amine to the site of nucleophilic displacement.

The sequence of reactions shown in Eq. 2-68 is of central importance to the vast field of biosynthesis embracing the terpenes, the steroids and the carotenoids. The role of the five-carbon-atom pyrophosphates will be considered in greater depth when terpenoid biosynthesis is described in a later chapter.

2.18 Summary

The reactions described in this chapter give rise in the living plant cell to a relatively small number of extraordinarily simple but often very reactive molecules; but from this handful ·of structural building blocks come thousands of organic molecules, many of them of complex structures, most of them fascinating subjects of study by the organic and biological chemist.

Reference to Fig. 2-3 will serve to recapitulate the ways in which these building blocks participate in the formation of the secondary plant products. Not shown explicitly in the outline embodied in this Figure, but playing vital roles in biosynthetic pathways sketched there, are the accessory substances ATP, S-adenosylmethionine, UDP-glucose, the pentenyl pyrophosphates, phosphoenolpyruvic acid, and the host of specific enzymes and coenzymes which act not only to catalyze these reactions but also direct their stereochemistry, and in many cases select one of several equally probable routes by which a given precursor can undergo further transformation.

III CHAPTER

REFERENCES FOR FURTHER READING

1. J. D. Bu'Lock, *The Biogenesis of Natural Acetylenes,* in Comparative Phytochemistry, T. Swain, Ed., Academic Press, New York, 1966.
2. Sir Ewart R. H. Jones, *Natural Polyacetylenes and their Precursors,* Chemistry in Britain, 2, (1966), 6.
3. J. D. Bu'Lock, *The Biosynthesis of Natural Products,* McGraw-Hill, Ltd., London, New York, 1965.
4. J. D. Bu'Lock, *The Origin of Naturally Occurring Acetylenes,* J. Chem. Soc., 1967, 332.
5. K. L. Mikolajczak, C. R. Smith, Jr., M. O. Bagby, and I. A. Wolff, *A New Type of Naturally Occurring Polyunsaturated Fatty Acid (Crepenynic Acid),* J. Org. Chem., 29, (1964), 318.
6. J. C. Craig and M. Moyle, *The Synthesis of Acetylenes from Enol Phosphates,* Proc. Chem. Soc., (1962), 149.
7. R. W. Bradshaw, A. C. Day, Sir Ewart R. H. Jones, C. B. Page, and V. Thaller, *A Synthesis of Crepenynic Acid,* Chem. Comm., (1967), 1055.
8. H. K. Black and B. C. L. Weedon, *The Synthesis of Erythrogenic (Isanic) and Other Acetylenic Acids,* J. Chem. Soc., (1953), 1785.
9. N. A. Sorensen, *The Taxonomic Significance of Acetylenic Compounds,* in Recent Advances in Phytochemistry, T. J. Mabry, Ed., Appleton-Century-Crofts, New York, 1968.
10. K. P. Strickland, *The Biogenesis of Lipids,* in Biogenesis of Natural Compounds, 2nd Ed., P. Bernfeld, Ed., Pergamon, Oxford, 1967.
11. F. Bohlmann and H. Schulz, *The Formation of Poly-ynes in Cell-free Homogenates,* Tetrahedron Letters, (1968), 4795.
12. A. T. James, *Biosynthesis of Unsaturated Acids by Plants,* Chemistry in Britain, 4, No. 11, (1968), 484.

CHAPTER III

Compounds Formed by Linear Combination of Two-Carbon Units

3.1 Fatty Acid Biosynthesis: General Considerations

The two-carbon-atom unit of acetic acid, in its biosynthetically active form, acetyl coenzyme A, is of central importance in plant biochemistry, for it is the starting point for two main routes of plant biosynthesis. In both of these pathways, the two functional characteristics of the acetyl group are involved:

a. the activation of the α-hydrogen atoms of the acetyl methyl group in such a way as to permit the development of anionic character at the carbon atom. The abstraction of the proton, shown in Eq. 3-1, may be presumed to occur by the action of a basic site in the enzyme taking part in the synthetic process:

$$CH_3CO—SCoA \xrightarrow{-H^+} {}^-:CH_2CO—SCoA \qquad [\text{Eq. 3-1}]$$

b. the exceptional electrophilic character of the carbonyl group of the thiolester, which provides a point of attack by nucleophiles; in the case under discussion in this chapter, by the anionic carbon atom of the deprotonated ester (Eq. 3-2):

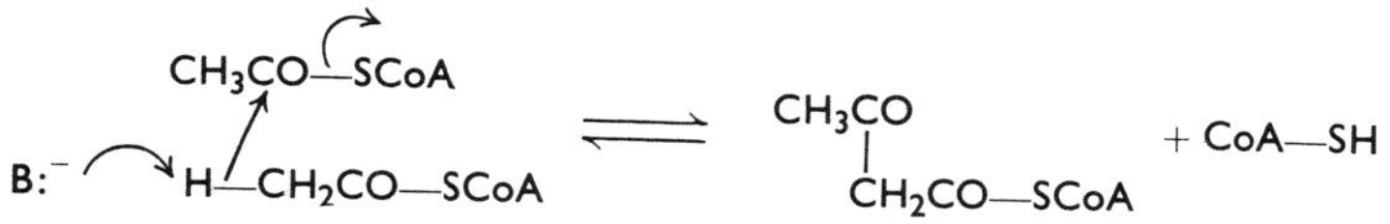

$$
\begin{array}{c}
CH_3CO—SCoA \\
B:^- \quad H—CH_2CO—SCoA
\end{array}
\rightleftharpoons
\begin{array}{c}
CH_3CO \\
CH_2CO—SCoA
\end{array}
+ CoA—SH \qquad [\text{Eq. 3-2}]
$$

The electrophilic character of the carbonyl group of the thiolester resembles that of a ketone carbonyl group rather than that of an oxygen ester. The electrophilic character (i.e., electron deficiency) of the oxygen ester carbonyl group is reduced by the charge delocalization symbolized in the following expression (Eq. 3-3):

$$
CH_3—\overset{\overset{\displaystyle O}{\|}}{C}—OR \longleftrightarrow CH_3—\overset{\overset{\displaystyle O^-}{|}}{C}{=}\overset{+}{O}R \qquad [\text{Eq. 3-3}]
$$

In the thiolester, the diminished tendency for participation of the $3s/3p$ electrons of sulfur in such charge delocalization, coupled perhaps with the large nuclear charge on sulfur, results in a retention of carbonyl character in the —CO—S— group, with the result that carbonyl addition reactions occur through lower energy transition states than in the less reactive oxygen esters.

The simple Claisen-like condensation shown in Eq. 3-2 does indeed occur in nature, and provides the starting point for another route of acetate metabolism— that leading to terpenoid synthesis to be discussed later in Chapter 8. The continuation of the process, as shown in Eq. 3-4, appears to provide a plausible mechanism for the further stepwise addition of C_2 units; this process, coupled with reduction of —CH_2CO— to —CH_2CH_2— as the chain growth proceeds, would appear to lead at length to the common long-chain fatty acids.

$$CH_3COCH_2CO—SCoA$$
$$CH_3CO—SCoA \longrightarrow CH_3COCH_2COCH_2CO—SCoA + CoA—SH$$

[Eq. 3-4]

For the eventual formation of a fatty acid of the general type $CH_3(CH_2)_nCOOH$, the condensation shown in Eq. 3-4 must be followed by reduction steps to convert —CH_2CO— units to —CH_2CH_2—. This process is in fact a reversal of a route of fatty acid degradation, first discovered by Knoop in 1904, and for many years regarded as an acceptable explanation for fatty acid biosynthesis by its operation in the reverse manner. The breakdown of fatty acids by β-oxidation, with the successive removal of C_2 fragments proceeds through the following stages (Eq. 3-5):

$$RCH_2CH_2COOH \xrightarrow[\substack{ATP \\ (1)}]{CoA—SH} RCH_2CH_2CO—SCoA$$

$$(2) \quad \substack{FAD\dagger \\ \\ FADH}$$

$$\underset{\underset{RCHCH_2CO—SCoA}{OH}}{} \xrightleftharpoons[(3)]{H_2O} RCH{=}CHCO—SCoA$$

$$(4) \quad \substack{NAD^+ \\ \\ NADH}$$

$$RCOCH_2CO—SCoA \xrightleftharpoons[(5)]{CoA—SH} RCO—SCoA + CH_3CO—SCoA$$

[Eq. 3-5]

_____

† FADH, mentioned briefly in Eq. 2-64, is one of the coenzymes of the electron-transfer chain which, acting in concert with NAD and the cytochromes, provides a means for the eventual reduction of oxygen by a substrate undergoing oxidation.

_____

The first stage of the degradation process provides a new fatty acid-CoA and a molecule of acetyl-CoA. It is clear that this is a source of acetyl-CoA in organisms in which fats are ingested as food, and from fats present in "storage depots."

The formation of long chain fatty acids by the reversal of the process shown in Eq. 3-5 does not, however, appear to be a major source of such long-chain acids as palmitic, stearic, etc. Experiments with the purified enzymes that operate in the individual steps of this series have demonstrated that the equilibria shown in Eq. 3-5 strongly favor the route toward breakdown of a fatty acid rather than the reverse path of synthesis; and that the process of synthesis does not proceed efficiently past the step of addition of one or two C_2 units. The reason for this may be the essential irreversibility of the step (2) in Eq. 3-5; in any case, the actual route by which fatty acid biosynthesis occurs is now known, and will be seen to consist essentially of the reactions of Eq. 3-5 modified in two important respects: the participation of CO_2, and the provision of the necessary enzymatic reducing systems.

3.2 Malonyl Coenzyme A in Chain Extension

Present knowledge of the true course of fatty acid biosynthesis followed the recognition in the course of *in vitro* studies with isolated enzymes that the complete system for fatty acid synthesis requires carbon dioxide (or bicarbonate) in addition to ATP, NADH, and magnesium ion. It was of special importance that carbon dioxide, essential to the synthetic process, was not incorporated into the final fatty acid, as shown by the use of radioactive carbon dioxide.

The intervention of carbon dioxide in fatty acid synthesis is now known to involve the initial carboxylation of acetyl coenzyme A to yield malonyl coenzyme A. It is apparent that the doubly-activated methylene group of the malonic acid derivative is much more readily converted into the nucleophilic α-carbon anion than is that of the acetic acid ester, with a consequent enhancement of the Claisen-like condensation reaction. The summary process of C_2 chain extension by this mechanism is shown in Eq. 3-6; details of some of the steps are given farther on:

$$
\begin{array}{c}
& & \overset{\displaystyle *COOH}{\underset{\displaystyle |}{}} \\
CH_3CO\!-\!SCoA & \xrightarrow[\text{biotin-enzyme}]{*CO_2,\ ATP} & CH_2CO\!-\!SCoA
\end{array}
$$

$$
\xrightarrow{\ RCH_2CO-SCoA\ }
$$

$$
\begin{array}{c}
\overset{\displaystyle OH}{\underset{\displaystyle |}{}} \\
RCH_2CHCH_2CO\!-\!SCoA \longleftarrow RCH_2COCH_2CO\!-\!SCoA
\end{array}
\qquad \text{[Eq. 3-6]}
$$

$$
RCH_2CH\!=\!CHCO\!-\!SCoA \longrightarrow RCH_2CH_2CH_2CO\!-\!SCoA
$$

$$
\xdashrightarrow[\text{above}]{\text{as}} RCH_2(CH_2CH_2)_nCOOH
$$

The carboxylation (or carbonation) of acetyl CoA is catalyzed by an enzyme, of which biotin is the prosthetic group, that is directly involved in the transfer of CO_2 to acetyl CoA. The role of biotin depends upon its transformation into an intermediate N-carboxylic acid, perhaps as the O-phosphorylated imidazoline (Eq. 3-7):

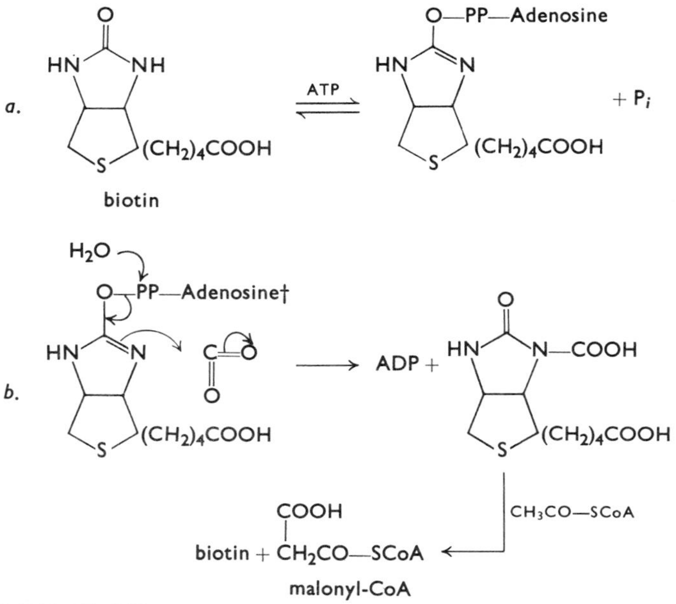

[Eq. 3-7]

† The attacking nucleophile shown in this step is chosen arbitrarily as the water molecule. In the intact cellular system it may be that the actual attacking species is a nucleophilic site in the protein portion of the enzyme.

The condensation of malonyl CoA with the carbonyl group of an acyl CoA is accompanied by loss of CO_2. It seems likely that the generation of anionic character at the —CH_2— group of malonyl CoA is concomitant with decarboxylation, and that the acylated malonic acid does not appear as a discrete intermediate in the reaction sequence (Eq. 3-8):

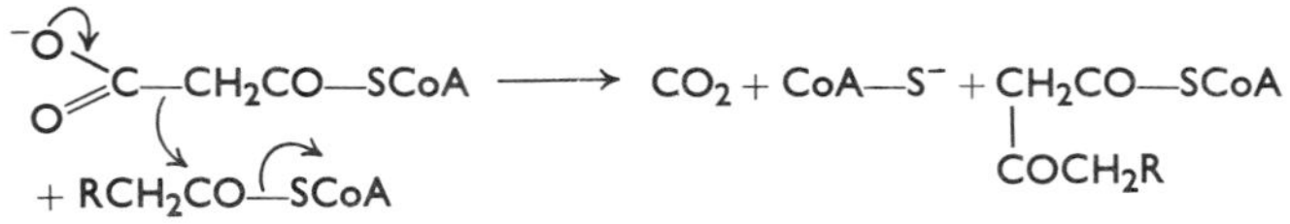

[Eq. 3-8]

A complete scheme of the synthetic pathway to fatty acids, modeled after the step shown in Eq. 3-8, has been elaborated by Lynen, with the added refinement that the process of successive addition of the malonyl CoA to the growing

$R(CH_2)_nCO$—SCoA chain occurs on a special carrier enzyme (i.e., protein) known as "fatty acid synthetase." Both the malonyl CoA and the acyl CoA are converted into thiolesters of a sulfhydryl-containing group of the protein molecule and react in a way exemplified by that shown in Eq. 3-8, with the difference that the reacting entities are ---CO—S-enzyme rather than ---CO—SCoA thiolesters. The complete cycle can now be represented as in Eq. 3-9:

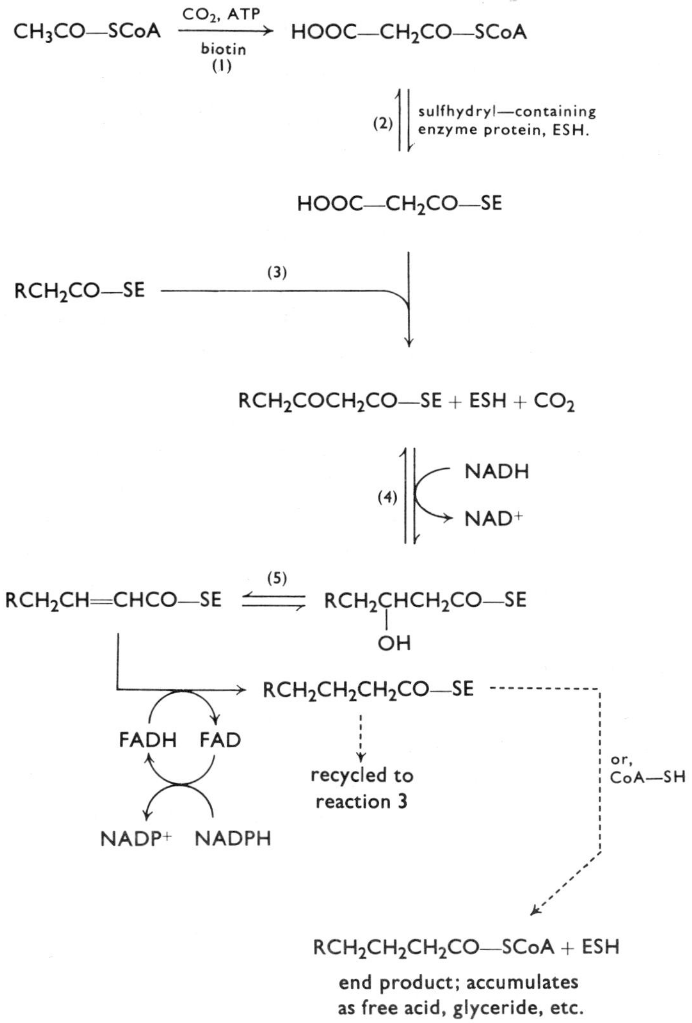

$$CH_3CO\text{—}SCoA \xrightarrow[\substack{\text{biotin} \\ (1)}]{CO_2, ATP} HOOC\text{—}CH_2CO\text{—}SCoA$$

(2) $\quad$ sulfhydryl—containing enzyme protein, ESH.

$$HOOC\text{—}CH_2CO\text{—}SE$$

$$RCH_2CO\text{—}SE \xrightarrow{\quad (3) \quad}$$

$$RCH_2COCH_2CO\text{—}SE + ESH + CO_2$$

(4) $\quad$ NADH $\to$ NAD+

$$RCH_2CH{=}CHCO\text{—}SE \overset{(5)}{\rightleftharpoons} RCH_2\underset{OH}{C}HCH_2CO\text{—}SE$$

$$RCH_2CH_2CH_2CO\text{—}SE \dashrightarrow$$

FADH FAD

recycled to reaction 3

or, CoA—SH

NADP+ NADPH

$$RCH_2CH_2CH_2CO\text{—}SCoA + ESH \qquad \text{[Eq. 3-9]}$$

end product; accumulates as free acid, glyceride, etc.

The reactions of the cycle shown in Eq. 3-9 are written with a generalized acyl CoA (RCH_2CO—SCoA or RCH_2CO—SE). It is to be expected that the addition of C_2 units can occur with "starter" groups other than acetyl or the $(C_2)_n$ intermediates in the chain extension process. That this is so has been amply demonstrated. With the use of purified, cell-free enzyme preparations, incorporation of propionyl, isobutyryl, isovaleryl, and α-methylbutyryl CoA esters into long-chain fatty acids occurs (Table 3-1):

Table 3-1.

Starter, as acyl-CoA	Principal Acid Formed	
CH_3CH_2COOH	$CH_3CH_2(CH_2CH_2)_7COOH$	(C_{17})
CH_3 CH_3 $CHCOOH$	$(CH_3)_2CH(CH_2CH_2)_7COOH$	(C_{18})
$CH_3CH_2CHCOOH$ $\vert$ CH_3	$CH_3CH_2CH(CH_2CH_2)_6COOH$ $\vert$ CH_3	(C_{17})
CH_3COOH	$CH_3(CH_2CH_2)_7COOH$	(C_{16})

Additional evidence of other kinds will be presented in later chapters to support the view that chain extension can occur by the addition of C_2 units to a wide variety of "starter" units.

It has long been recognized that the common fatty acids, most of which occur in nature in ester combination,* contain even numbers of carbon atoms. They are represented by the general constitution $CH_3(CH_2)_nCOOH$, where n = 2 or multiples of 2, of which palmitic (n = 14) and stearic (n = 16) acids are by far the most abundant of the saturated acids. Equally common, moreover, are long-chain acids containing double bonds; these are discussed in the following section.

3.3 Unsaturated Fatty Acids

Nature affords a large number of fatty acids** of an extraordinary diversity of structure. Unsaturated acids, hydroxy acids, keto acids, and acids containing two or more of these functions are widespread in plant and animal organisms. Although many unsaturated fatty acids possess certain marked structural similarities (Table 3-2), it is clear that there is no single pattern that characterizes the known acids (Table 3-3).

* Fatty acids, both saturated and unsaturated (Sec. 3-3), occur in ester combination with glycerol (fats, oils); long-chain alcohols (waxes); sugar derivatives (glycolipids); and certain phosphorus-containing molecules (phospholipids, sphingolipids).

** The term "fatty acids" used in this context refers principally to acids containing long (most C_{12} to C_{18}) chains of carbon atoms derived by the acetate-malonate route described in foregoing sections. Used in the generic sense, the term includes such derived structures as unsaturated, hydroxylated, etc., compounds.

Table 3-2. Some Naturally Occurring Δ^9-Alkenoic Acids

Name	Structure
gadoleic	$CH_3(CH_2)_9CH{=}CH(CH_2)_7COOH$
oleic	$CH_3(CH_2)_7CH{=}CH(CH_2)_7COOH$
palmitoleic	$CH_3(CH_2)_5CH{=}CH(CH_2)_7COOH$
myristoleic	$CH_3(CH_2)_3CH{=}CH(CH_2)_7COOH$
Δ^9-undecenoic	$CH_3CH{=}CH(CH_2)_7COOH$
Δ^9-decenoic	$H{-}CH{=}CH(CH_2)_7COOH$

Table 3-3. Naturally Occurring Alkenoic Acids with Unsaturation Other Than Δ^9

Common Name	Systematic Name
linderic	Δ^4-dodecenoic acid
lauroleic	Δ^5-dodecenoic acid
tsuzuic	Δ^4-tetradecenoic acid
petroselinic	Δ^6-octadecenoic acid
vaccenic	Δ^{11}-octadecenoic acid

Similar variations in the positions of double bonds are observed in di- and trienic acids (Table 3-4):

Table 3-4. Some Polyunsaturated Naturally Occurring Fatty Acids

Number of carbon atoms	Positions of double-bonds ($COOH = 1$)
C_{18}	9, 12
	9, 12, 15
	9, 11, 13
C_{20}	8, 11
	11, 14
	5, 8, 11
	8, 11, 14
	5, 8, 11, 14
	5, 8, 11, 14, 17
C_{22}	10, 13
	7, 10, 13
	7, 10, 13, 16
	4, 7, 10, 13, 16
	7, 10, 13, 16, 19
	4, 7, 10, 13, 16, 19
C_{24}	9, 12, 15, 18

The evidence now available indicates that the unsaturated fatty acids can arise by more than one biosynthetic route, although, as will be shown in the discussion to follow, the desaturation of the corresponding alkanoic acid, and further desaturation in subsequent steps, appears to be the commonest pathway. Yeast cells, and enzymes present in cell free extracts prepared from yeast, can convert stearic acid into oleic acid with the (added) cofactors NADP and adenine nucleotides, and in the presence of molecular oxygen (Eq. 3-10).

$$CH_3(CH_2)_{16}COOH \xrightarrow[\text{CoA-SH}]{\text{ATP}} CH_3(CH_2)_{16}CO\text{—}SCoA \xrightarrow{\text{enzyme-SH}}$$

$$CH_3(CH_2)_{16}CO\text{—}SE \xrightarrow[\substack{\text{2) hydrolysis} \\ \text{or transfer} \\ \text{to ROH}}]{\text{1) NADP}^+; \text{O}_2} CH_3(CH_2)_7CH \overset{c}{=} CH(CH_2)_7COOH(or\text{—}COOR).$$

[Eq. 3-10]

The interesting suggestion has been made by Hendrickson that the hydrogen abstraction may occur in a stereospecifically oriented RCO—SCoA peroxide, attached to the enzyme surface in a manner indicated in Fig. 3-1.

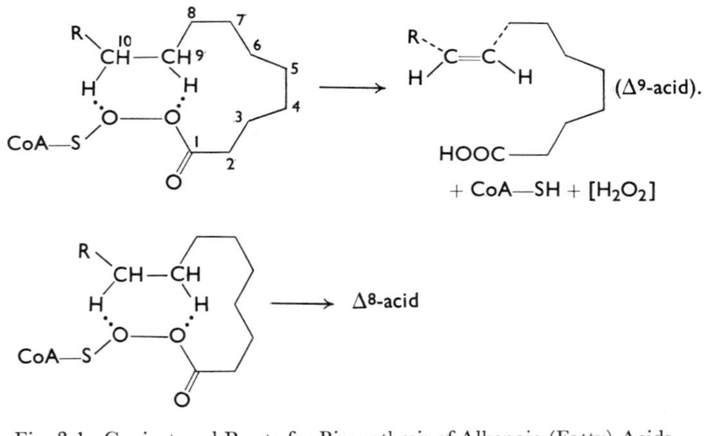

Fig. 3-1. Conjectured Route for Biosynthesis of Alkenoic (Fatty) Acids.

It is clear from the two cases pictured in Fig. 3-1 that other modes of folding of the alkanoic acid upon an enzyme surface could be devised to produce unsaturation at other points in the carbon chain. It is significant to note that the double bonds in the Δ^9-alkenoic acids are *cis*. This suggests that, whatever the nature of the site at which dehydrogenation occurs, the process occurs at an enzyme surface to which the acid is fixed during the desaturation step.

Unsaturated fatty acid synthesis can also occur by an alternative course in which the double bond is introduced by way of an initial β-keto acid. The following course has been reported to occur in *Clostridium* and in certain plant tissues (Eq. 3-11)

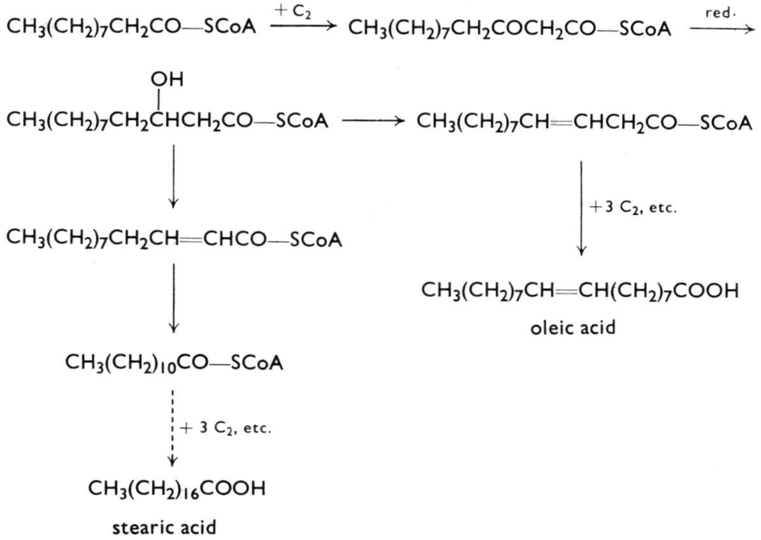

$$CH_3(CH_2)_7CH_2CO\text{—}SCoA \xrightarrow{+C_2} CH_3(CH_2)_7CH_2COCH_2CO\text{—}SCoA \xrightarrow{red.}$$

$$\underset{\overset{|}{CH_3(CH_2)_7CH_2CHCH_2CO\text{—}SCoA}}{OH} \longrightarrow CH_3(CH_2)_7CH\text{=}CHCH_2CO\text{—}SCoA$$

$$CH_3(CH_2)_7CH_2CH\text{=}CHCO\text{—}SCoA \qquad\qquad \Big|+3\ C_2,\ etc.$$

$$CH_3(CH_2)_7CH\text{=}CH(CH_2)_7COOH$$
oleic acid

$$CH_3(CH_2)_{10}CO\text{—}SCoA$$

$$\vdots + 3\ C_2,\ etc.$$

[Eq. 3-11]

$$CH_3(CH_2)_{16}COOH$$
stearic acid

It is curious that oleic acid (with the *cis*-configuration of the double bond) is formed in this reaction; the α,β-unsaturated acids formed in the normal process of chain extension are *trans* unsaturated acids. Just what respective roles these two pathways (Eq. 3-10 and Eq. 3-11) play in oleic acid biosynthesis is not known. It is probable that the desaturation pathway is the more prevalent route in most organisms.

3.4 Polyunsaturated Acids

It is noteworthy that the commonest of the known dienic, trienic, and tetraenic acids contain the double bonds in isolated (i.e., non-conjugated) array, as the repeating unit $(CH\text{=}CH\text{—}CH_2)_{2,\ 3\ or\ 4}$. For example:

linoleic	$CH_3(CH_2)_4CH\text{=}CHCH_2CH\text{=}CH(CH_2)_7COOH$	C_{18}
linolenic	$CH_3(CH_2CH\text{=}CH)_3(CH_2)_7COOH$	C_{18}
γ-linoleic	$CH_3(CH_2)_4(CH\text{=}CHCH_2)_3(CH_2)_3COOH$	C_{18}
arachidonic	$CH_3(CH_2)_4(CH\text{=}CHCH_2)_4(CH_2)_2COOH$	C_{20}

Animal feeding experiments with the use of ^{14}C-labeled acids have shown some of the ways in which unsaturated fatty acids are formed and undergo interconversion. The conversion of palmitic and stearic acids into palmitoleic and oleic acids, respectively, according to Eq. 3-10, has been known for many years. More recent experiments have demonstrated the further desaturation of oleic acid into linoleic acid, and other changes, including those represented in Eq. 3-12:

$$CH_3(CH_2)_4CH=CHCH_2CH=CH(CH_2)_7\overset{*}{C}OOH \quad (\overset{*}{C}={}^{14}C)$$

1-^{14}C-linoleic acid

in the rat

$$CH_3(CH_2)_4(CH=CHCH_2)_3CH_2CH_2CH_2\overset{*}{C}OOH$$

γ-linolenic acid

C$_2$ (malonyl-CoA)

$$CH_3(CH_2)_4(CH=CHCH_2)_4\overset{*}{C}H_2CH_2COOH$$

3-^{14}C-arachidonic acid

and:

$$CH_3(CH_2)_4(CH=CHCH_2)_2(CH_2)_6COOH$$

linoleic acid (no ^{14}C)

$$CH_3\overset{*}{C}OOH$$

$$CH_3(CH_2)_4(CH=CHCH_2)_4CH_2CH_2\overset{*}{C}OOH$$ [Eq. 3-12]

1-^{14}C-arachidonic acid

Fatty acids containing triple bonds and allenic double bonds will be discussed in following sections.

3.5 Branched-chain Fatty Acids

Nature affords a striking array of fatty acids with branched chains, the substituent groups being simple alkyl groups (e.g., methyl) or what appear to be the long-chain residues of other fatty acids. Branched chain acids occur in wool fat, in small amounts in animal body fats and milk fats, and are the characteristic fatty acid constituents of the lipid coatings of various bacilli.

Corynomycolic acid is found in *Corynebacterium diphtheriae*, along with its unsaturated analog, corynomycolenic acid. The structures of these acids (Fig. 3-2)

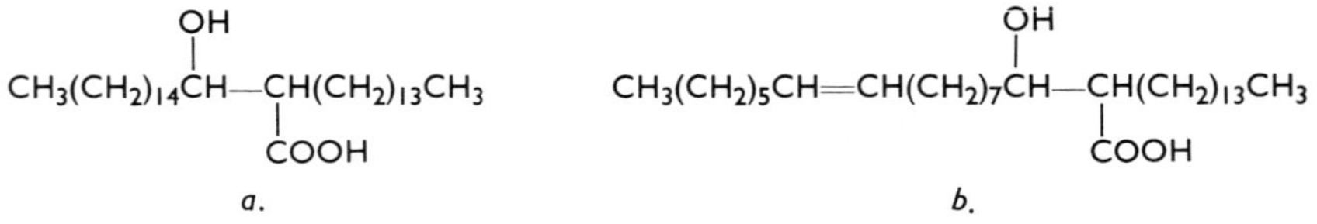

$$CH_3(CH_2)_{14}\underset{\underset{COOH}{|}}{\overset{\overset{OH}{|}}{C}H}-CH(CH_2)_{13}CH_3 \qquad CH_3(CH_2)_5CH=CH(CH_2)_7\underset{\underset{COOH}{|}}{\overset{\overset{OH}{|}}{C}H}-CH(CH_2)_{13}CH_3$$

a.   b.

Fig. 3-2. Corynomycolic acid *a*; Corynomycolenic acid *b*.

strongly suggest their origin by the acylation of (in the case of corynomycolic acid) palmitic acid (presumably as the substituted malonyl CoA) with palmitic acid (presumably as the CoA ester). This has been confirmed by experiments in which palmitic acid-1-^{14}C was provided to the living organism and the corynomycolic acid isolated and degraded. The labeling pattern was in agreement with the anticipated biosynthetic pathway (Eq. 3-13):

$$CH_3(CH_2)_{14}\overset{*}{C}O—SCoA$$

$$CH_3(CH_2)_{13}CH_2CO—SCoA \longrightarrow \begin{array}{c} CH_3(CH_2)_{14}CO \\ | \\ CH_3(CH_2)_{13}CHCO—SCoA \end{array} \longrightarrow$$

$$\begin{array}{c} CH_3(CH_2)_{14}\overset{*}{C}HOH \\ | \quad * \\ CH_3(CH_2)_{13}CHCOOH \end{array} \qquad \text{corynomycolic acid} \qquad [\text{Eq. 3-13}]$$

$$\underset{-CO_2}{\overset{\text{oxidize;}}{\Big\downarrow}} \text{(location of }^{14}C\text{)}$$

$$\overset{*}{C}O_2 + CH_3(CH_2)_{14}\overset{*}{C}O(CH_2)_{14}CH_3$$

Tuberculostearic acid (10-methylstearic acid) is formed by the methylation of 9,10-octadecenoic (oleic) acid, the methyl group being provided by a one-carbon source (formate or methionine) (Eq. 3-14). The nature of this alkylation reaction is obscure although the suggestion has been made (Bu'Lock) that the biological process may involve the reaction between the olefinic double bond of the acid and an ylid derived from S-adenosylmethionine. Related reactions could lead to the known cyclopropane- and cyclopropene-derived fatty acids (Eq. 3-14). Although the derivation of sterculic acid could be rationally derived by the analogous process shown in Eq. 3-15a, this does not appear to be the course that is followed in nature. It has been shown by experimental means that the cyclopropene-derived acid is actually formed by desaturation of the corresponding cyclopropane. The latter is formed by the alkylation of the alkenoic acid by methionine (Eq. 3-15b).

$$\overset{+}{>}S—CH_3 \xrightarrow{-H^+} \left. \begin{array}{c} \overset{+}{>}S—CH_2:^- \\ \\ —CH=CH— \end{array} \right\} \longrightarrow \begin{array}{c} :CH_2^- \\ | \\ —CH—\overset{+}{CH}— \end{array}$$

$$\underset{}{\overset{H^+;}{\Big\downarrow}} \text{(NADH?)}$$

$$\begin{array}{c} \quad\; CH_2 \\ \diagup \;\;\;\; \diagdown \\ ^{12}\overset{}{C}H—CH^{11} \end{array} \qquad \begin{array}{c} CH_3 \\ | \\ —CH—CH_2— \\ ^{10}\quad\;\; 9 \end{array}$$

lactobacillic acid   tuberculostearic
(from vaccenic acid,   acid
$CH_3(CH_2)_5CH=CH(CH_2)_9COOH)$ (from oleic acid)   [Eq. 3-14]

a. If an acetylenic acid instead of an ethylenic acid were used as in Equation 14, above, the product would be a cyclopropene derivative by way of the formally equivalent course:

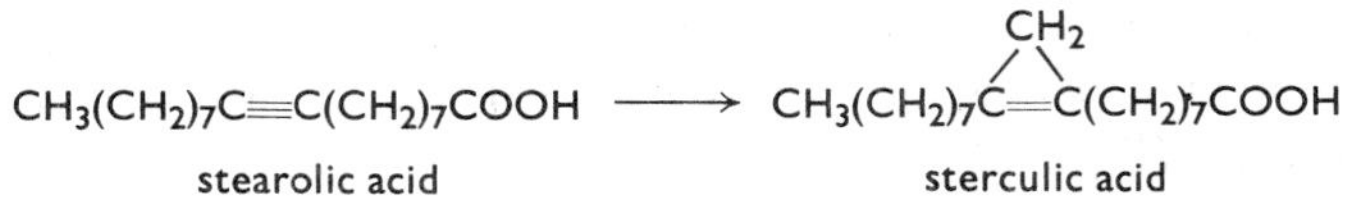

$$CH_3(CH_2)_7C\equiv C(CH_2)_7COOH \longrightarrow CH_3(CH_2)_7\overset{\displaystyle CH_2}{\overbrace{C=C}}(CH_2)_7COOH$$

stearolic acid   sterculic acid

b. however, the following course has been established for the biosynthesis of sterculic acid in Malvaceae:

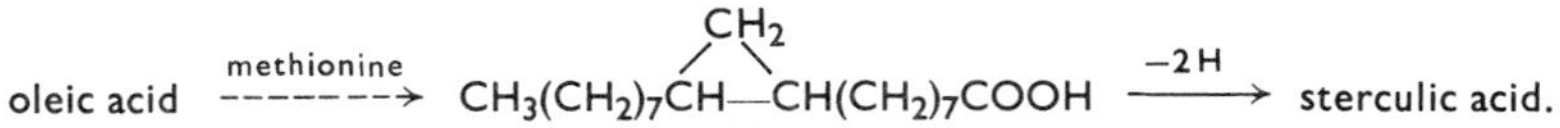

$$\text{oleic acid} \xrightarrow{\text{methionine}} CH_3(CH_2)_7\overset{\displaystyle CH_2}{\overbrace{CH-CH}}(CH_2)_7COOH \xrightarrow{-2H} \text{sterculic acid.}$$

[Eq. 3-15]

3.6   The Problem of the Origin of Carbon-linked Methyl Groups

The presence of $-\overset{|}{C}H-CH_3$ groups in compounds of which the apparent origin is the linear combination of C_2 units is not always readily accounted for. There are two* well established origins of such carbon-methyl groups: (a) by carbon-methylation of the active $-CH_2-$ groups in the polyketide (poly-β-carbonyl) chain during the course of chain extension (Eq. 3-16); and (b) the incorporation of propionic acid units (as methylmalonyl CoA) into the growing chain (Eq. 3-17):

$$a. \quad ----COCH_2CO---- + \overset{|}{-\underset{+}{S}}-CH_3 \longrightarrow ----CO\overset{\displaystyle CH_3}{\overset{|}{C}}HCO---- \qquad [\text{Eq. 3-16}]$$

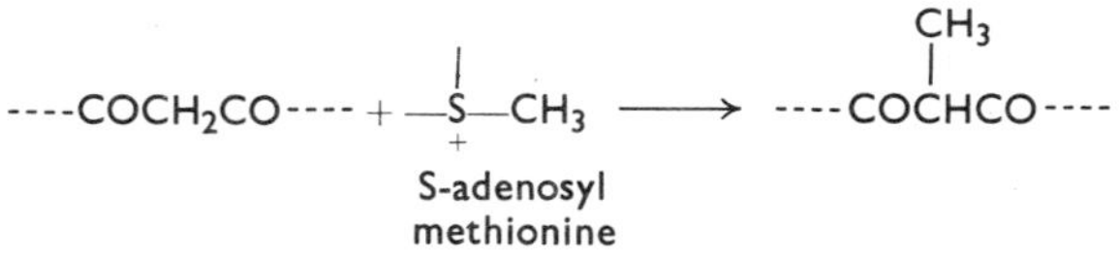

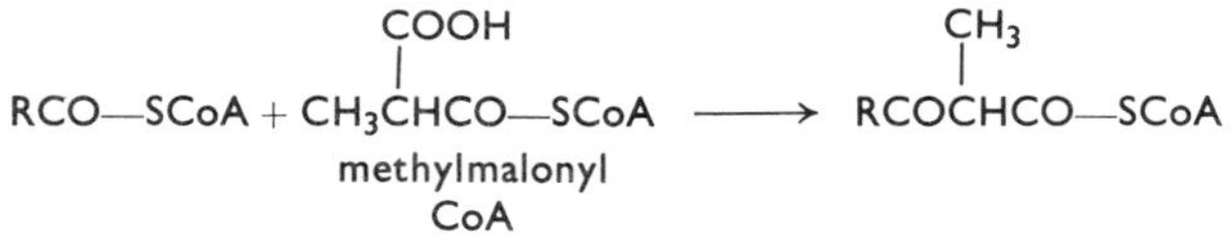

S-adenosyl
methionine

$$b. \quad RCO-SCoA + CH_3\overset{\displaystyle COOH}{\overset{|}{C}}HCO-SCoA \longrightarrow RCO\overset{\displaystyle CH_3}{\overset{|}{C}}HCO-SCoA \qquad [\text{Eq. 3-17}]$$

methylmalonyl
CoA

The incorporation of propionyl units in biosynthesis is well substantiated, the best known examples being found in a group of compounds elaborated in microorganisms (*Streptomyces* spp.). One such compound is erythromycin (Fig. 3-3); labeling experiments have shown that the C_3 units outlined in the formula have their

---

* Besides the one by which tuberculostearic acid is derived; this origin is probably of uncommon occurrence.

origin in the incorporation of propionic acid (Eq. 3-17) and not by the C-methylation of an acetate-malonate-derived chain (Eq. 3-16):

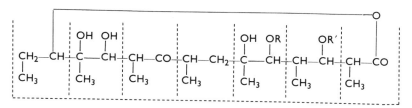

Fig. 3-3. Erythromycin (R = desosamine residue; R′ = cladinose residue).

The incorporation of propionic acid into certain fatty acids bearing methyl groups as substituents is, while not common in nature, well established as a natural process. The simplest example is α-methylvaleric acid, a metabolic produced by the helminth *Ascaris lumbricoides*. Feeding experiments using ^{14}C-labeled propionic acid disclosed that the six carbon atoms of α-methylvaleric acid are derived by the condensation of two molecules of propionate, presumably by way of propionyl-CoA and methylmalonyl-CoA (Eq. 3-17*a*):

$$CH_3CH_2CO—SCoA + CH_3CHCO—SCoA \longrightarrow$$
$$| $$
$$COOH$$

$$\underset{\displaystyle |}{\overset{\displaystyle CH_3}{}} \quad\quad\quad\quad \underset{\displaystyle |}{\overset{\displaystyle CH_3}{}}$$
$$CH_3CH_2COCHCO—SCoA \longrightarrow CH_3CH_2CH_2CHCOOH \quad\quad [Eq. 3-17a]$$

Mycolipenic acid (Fig. 3-4), the structure of which is established by the reactions described in Eqs. 3-18 and 3-19, has also been shown by labeling experiments to be derived by the combination of 9 acetate and 3 propionate units and not by the alternate route involving C-methylation of a poly-β-keto progenitor.

$$CH_3(CH_2)_{17}CHCH_2CHCH=CCOOH$$
$$\quad\quad\quad | \quad\quad | \quad\quad |$$
$$\quad\quad\quad CH_3 \quad CH_3 \quad CH_3$$

mycolipenic acid

$$\downarrow \text{ oxidize at } C=C$$

$$CH_3(CH_2)_{17}CHCH_2CHCOOH$$
$$\quad\quad\quad | \quad\quad |$$
$$\quad\quad\quad CH_3 \quad CH_3$$

Fig. 3-4. Mycolipenic acid.

Synthesis of mycolipenic acid

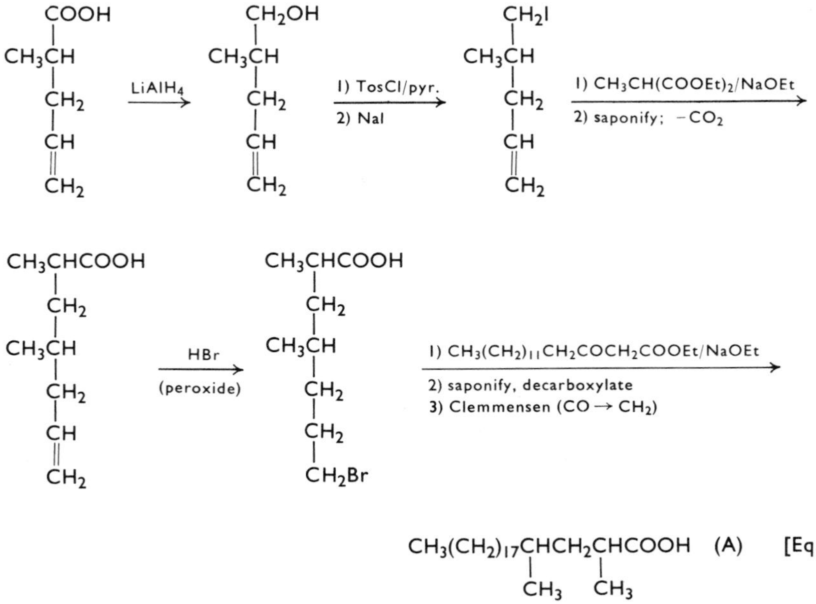

$$\underset{\substack{|\\CH_2}}{\overset{\substack{COOH\\|\\CH_3CH\\|\\CH_2\\|\\CH}}{}} \xrightarrow{\text{LiAlH}_4} \underset{\substack{|\\CH_2}}{\overset{\substack{CH_2OH\\|\\CH_3CH\\|\\CH_2\\|\\CH}}{}} \xrightarrow[\text{2) NaI}]{\text{1) TosCl/pyr.}} \underset{\substack{|\\CH_2}}{\overset{\substack{CH_2I\\|\\CH_3CH\\|\\CH_2\\|\\CH}}{}} \xrightarrow[\text{2) saponify; }-CO_2]{\text{1) CH}_3\text{CH(COOEt)}_2/\text{NaOEt}}$$

$$\underset{\substack{|\\CH_2}}{\overset{\substack{CH_3CHCOOH\\|\\CH_2\\|\\CH_3CH\\|\\CH_2\\|\\CH}}{}} \xrightarrow[\text{(peroxide)}]{\text{HBr}} \underset{\substack{|\\CH_2Br}}{\overset{\substack{CH_3CHCOOH\\|\\CH_2\\|\\CH_3CH\\|\\CH_2\\|\\CH_2}}{}} \xrightarrow[\substack{\text{2) saponify, decarboxylate}\\\text{3) Clemmensen (CO}\rightarrow\text{CH}_2)}]{\text{1) CH}_3(\text{CH}_2)_{11}\text{CH}_2\text{COCH}_2\text{COOEt/NaOEt}}$$

$$\underset{\substack{|\\CH_3\ \ CH_3}}{CH_3(CH_2)_{17}CHCH_2CHCOOH} \quad (A) \qquad [Eq.\ 3\text{-}18]$$

(degradation product of
mycolipenic acid, Fig. 3-4).

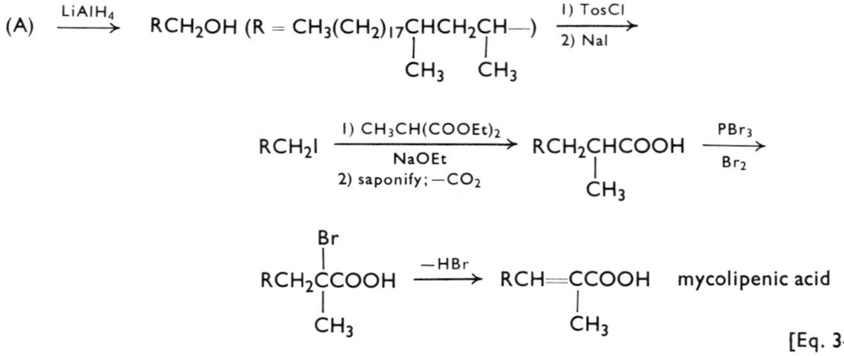

$$(A) \xrightarrow{\text{LiAlH}_4} RCH_2OH\ (R = \underset{\substack{|\ \ \ \ \ |\\CH_3\ \ CH_3}}{CH_3(CH_2)_{17}CHCH_2CH-}) \xrightarrow[\text{2) NaI}]{\text{1) TosCl}}$$

$$RCH_2I \xrightarrow[\substack{\text{NaOEt}\\\text{2) saponify;}-CO_2}]{\text{1) CH}_3\text{CH(COOEt)}_2} \underset{\substack{|\\CH_3}}{RCH_2CHCOOH} \xrightarrow[\text{Br}_2]{\text{PBr}_3}$$

$$\underset{\substack{|\\CH_3}}{\overset{\substack{Br\\|}}{RCH_2CCOOH}} \xrightarrow{-HBr} \underset{\substack{|\\CH_3}}{RCH=CCOOH} \quad \text{mycolipenic acid}$$

$$[Eq.\ 3\text{-}19]$$

3.7 Acetylenic Compounds of Polyketide Origin

Naturally occurring acetylenic compounds (-ynes, poly-ynes, ene-ynes, polyene-ynes) and compounds derived from them (Sec. 3.10) are widespread in living organisms of many kinds. They are especially common in plants of the families Compositae and Umbelliferae and in fungi of the class Basidiomycetes, but are not confined to these.

The plant *Ongokea gore* (fam. Olacaceae) contains several acetylenic acids whose relationship to such acids as oleic and stearolic (Sec. 3.8) is evident from their possession of the unit $-(CH_2)_7COOH$ (Fig. 3-5).

$$CH_2\!\!=\!\!CH(CH_2)_4C\!\!\equiv\!\!C-C\!\!\equiv\!\!C(CH_2)_7COOH$$

isanic (erythrogenic) acid

$$CH_3(CH_2)_5C\!\!\equiv\!\!C-C\!\!\equiv\!\!C(CH_2)_7COOH$$

$$CH_3(CH_2)_3CH\overset{c}{=\!\!=}CH-C\!\!\equiv\!\!C-C\!\!\equiv\!\!C(CH_2)_7COOH$$

$$CH_2\!\!=\!\!CH(CH_2)_2CH\overset{c}{=\!\!=}CH-C\!\!\equiv\!\!C-C\!\!\equiv\!\!C(CH_2)_7COOH$$

† The symbol $-CH\overset{c}{=\!\!=}CH-$ designates the *cis* configuration at the double bond; the *trans* is written $-CH\overset{t}{=\!\!=}CH-$.

Fig. 3-5. Acetylenic Acids of *Ongokea gore*.

The detection, isolation, and structure determination of polyunsaturated, acetylenic compounds has been aided in recent years by the development of chromatographic methods of separation and purification, and of physical methods (UV, IR, NMR, mass spectrometry) of structure investigation. In the past twenty years the number of known naturally occurring acetylenic compounds has risen from a mere dozen or so to the presently known 300-odd, and continuing investigations are adding to this number.

The refinements of isolation methods have made possible the intensive study of the occurrence of polyacetylenes in single plants and restricted groups of closely related plants. For example, from five members of the genus *Dahlia* have been isolated 30 polyacetylenes. From studies of this kind has come a rich source of information with which to investigate chemotaxonomic and biosynthetic relationships.

Although physical methods of study of the structure of polyunsaturated compounds have afforded so rich a fund of experience that the spectral properties of new compounds often provide sufficient information to reveal the structure, degradation, synthesis, and interconversions still play important parts in structure proof. The synthesis of polyacetylenes is often accomplished with the use of an oxidative coupling procedure which permits the joining of two acetylenic compounds according to the general scheme (Eq. 3-20).

$$RC\!\!\equiv\!\!CH + HC\!\!\equiv\!\!CR' \longrightarrow R-C\!\!\equiv\!\!C-C\!\!\equiv\!\!C-R'$$ [Eq. 3-20]

A representative example of this technique, along with details of corollary steps in the overall process, is found in the total synthesis of isanic acid (Fig. 3-5), (Eq. 3-21):

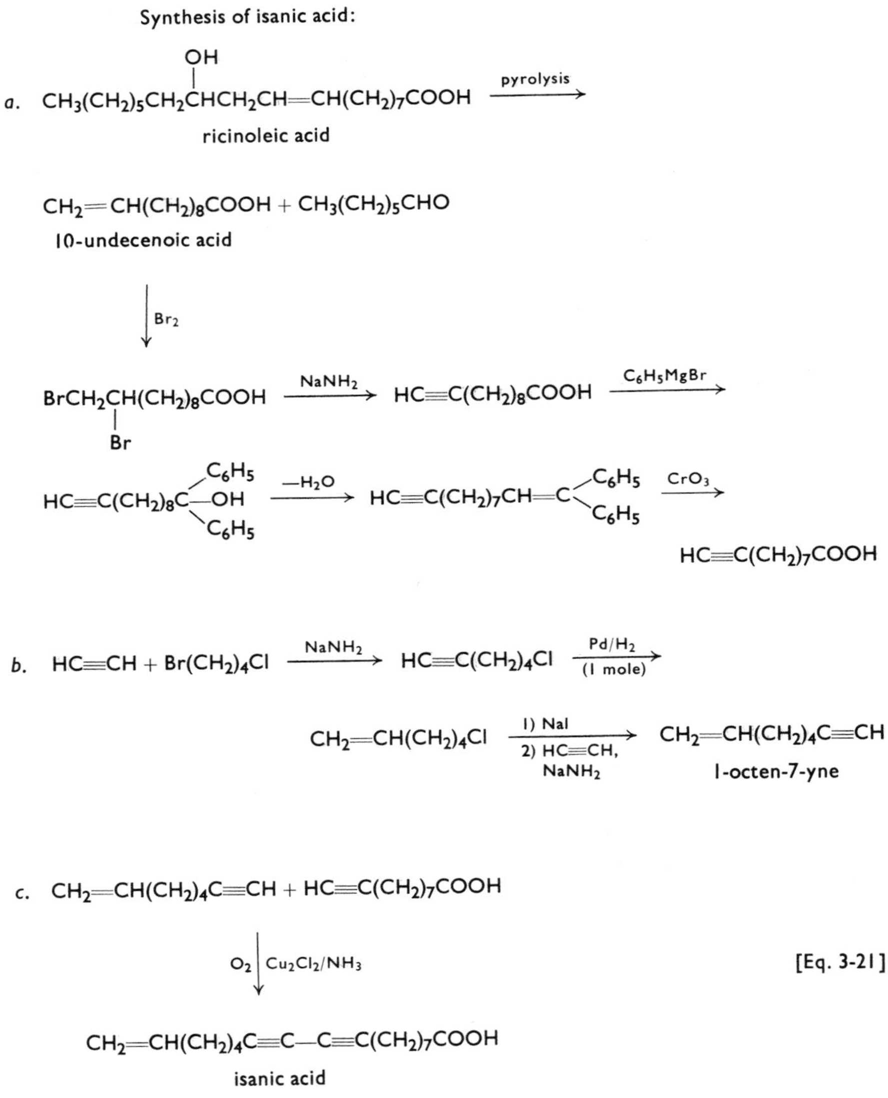

Synthesis of isanic acid:

$$\overset{\text{OH}}{a. \quad CH_3(CH_2)_5CH_2\overset{|}{C}HCH_2CH=CH(CH_2)_7COOH} \xrightarrow{\text{pyrolysis}}$$

ricinoleic acid

$$CH_2=CH(CH_2)_8COOH + CH_3(CH_2)_5CHO$$

10-undecenoic acid

$$\downarrow \text{Br}_2$$

$$\underset{\overset{|}{Br}}{BrCH_2CH(CH_2)_8COOH} \xrightarrow{\text{NaNH}_2} HC\equiv C(CH_2)_8COOH \xrightarrow{\text{C}_6\text{H}_5\text{MgBr}}$$

$$HC\equiv C(CH_2)_8\overset{\overset{C_6H_5}{|}}{\underset{C_6H_5}{C}}-OH \xrightarrow{-H_2O} HC\equiv C(CH_2)_7CH=C\overset{C_6H_5}{\underset{C_6H_5}{<}} \xrightarrow{\text{CrO}_3}$$

$$HC\equiv C(CH_2)_7COOH$$

$$b. \quad HC\equiv CH + Br(CH_2)_4Cl \xrightarrow{\text{NaNH}_2} HC\equiv C(CH_2)_4Cl \xrightarrow[\text{(1 mole)}]{\text{Pd/H}_2}$$

$$CH_2=CH(CH_2)_4Cl \xrightarrow[\substack{\text{2) HC}\equiv\text{CH,}\\\text{NaNH}_2}]{\text{1) NaI}} CH_2=CH(CH_2)_4C\equiv CH$$

1-octen-7-yne

$$c. \quad CH_2=CH(CH_2)_4C\equiv CH + HC\equiv C(CH_2)_7COOH$$

$$O_2 \Big| Cu_2Cl_2/NH_3 \qquad\qquad\qquad\qquad\qquad \text{[Eq. 3-21]}$$

$$CH_2=CH(CH_2)_4C\equiv C-C\equiv C(CH_2)_7COOH$$

isanic acid

One of the simplest of the acetylenic fatty acids, and one that will be seen in what follows to play a key role in the biosynthetic pathway, is crepenynic acid, first isolated along with linoleic acid, from the seeds of *Crepis foetida* (fam. Compositae).

The structure of crepenynic acid, which is a 12,13-dehydrolinolenic acid, was established by the method shown in Eq. 3-22:

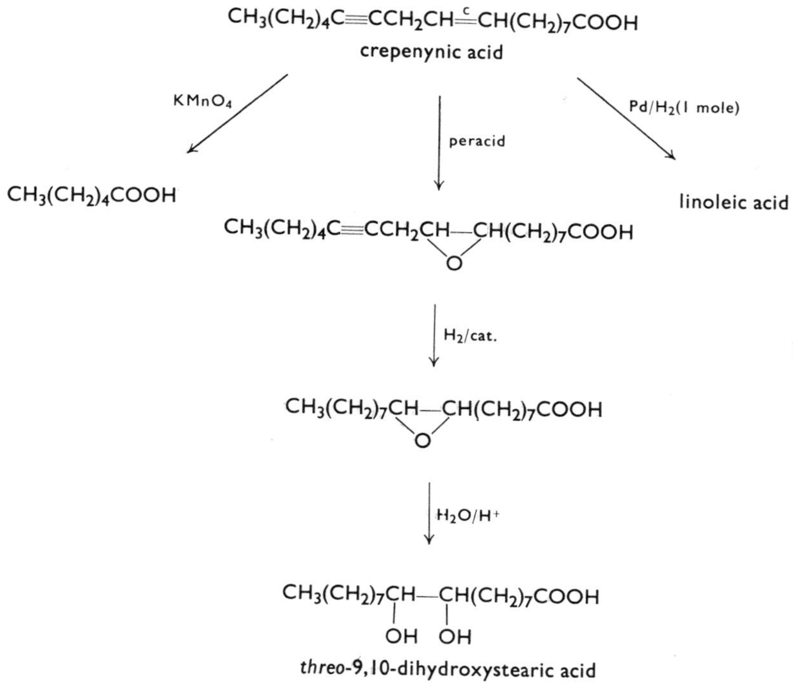

$$CH_3(CH_2)_4C{\equiv}CCH_2CH{\overset{c}{=}}CH(CH_2)_7COOH$$

crepenynic acid

KMnO$_4$ peracid   Pd/H$_2$(I mole)

$$CH_3(CH_2)_4COOH$$

linoleic acid

$$CH_3(CH_2)_4C{\equiv}CCH_2CH{-}CH(CH_2)_7COOH$$
$$\underset{O}{\diagdown\diagup}$$

H$_2$/cat.   [Eq. 3-22]

$$CH_3(CH_2)_7CH{-}CH(CH_2)_7COOH$$
$$\underset{O}{\diagdown\diagup}$$

H$_2$O/H$^+$

$$CH_3(CH_2)_7CH{-}CH(CH_2)_7COOH$$
$$\quad\quad\quad\ OH\ \ OH$$

threo-9,10-dihydroxystearic acid

Since studies of the biosynthetic role of crepenynic acid required the radioactive (^{14}C) compound, a total synthesis of the acid was carried out as shown in Eq. 3-23:

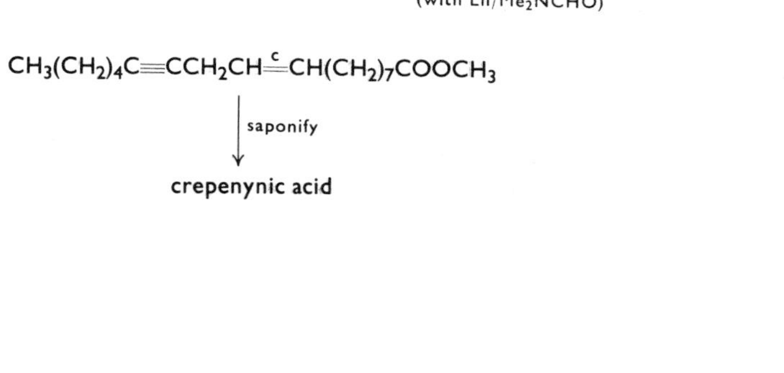

$$CH_3(CH_2)_4C{\equiv}CH \xrightarrow[\text{Li/NH}_3]{\text{ethylene oxide}} CH_3(CH_2)_4C{\equiv}CCH_2CH_2OH \xrightarrow{\text{PBr}_3}$$

$$CH_3(CH_2)_4C{\equiv}CCH_2CH_2Br \xrightarrow[\text{2) BuLi}]{\text{1) (C}_6\text{H}_5)_3\text{P}}$$

$$CH_3(CH_2)_4C{\equiv}CCH_2CH{=}P(C_6H_5)_3 \xrightarrow[\text{(with LiI/Me}_2\text{NCHO)}]{(CH_2)_7\overset{\text{CHO}}{\underset{\text{COOCH}_3}{<}}}$$ [Eq. 3-23]

$$CH_3(CH_2)_4C{\equiv}CCH_2CH{\overset{c}{=}}CH(CH_2)_7COOCH_3$$

saponify

crepenynic acid

The acetylenic compounds from *Dahlia* species include both oxygenated compounds and hydrocarbons, and vary in total chain length from C_{13} to C_{17}. It is noteworthy that the hydrocarbons of this group contain an odd number of carbon atoms (C_{13}, C_{17}), while the even-numbered members (C_{14}, C_{16}) possess an oxygenated terminal group. In Table 3-5 are given some of these polyacetylenes:

Table 3-5. Some Naturally Occurring Polyacetylenes of *Dahlia* spp

C_{13}: *a.* $CH_3(C\equiv C)_4CH\overset{c}{=}CH-CH=CH_2$

     b. $CH_3CH\overset{t}{=}CH(C\equiv C)_4CH=CH_2$

C_{14}: *c.* $CH_3(C\equiv C)_3CH\overset{t}{=}CH-CH\overset{t}{=}CHCH_2CH_2CH_2OH$

     d. $CH_3CH\overset{t}{=}CH(C\equiv C)_2CH\overset{t}{=}CH-CH\overset{t}{=}CHCH_2CH_2CH_2OH$

C_{16}: *e.* $CH_3CH\overset{t}{=}CH(C\equiv C)_2CH\overset{t}{=}CH-CH\overset{t}{=}CH(CH_2)_4CH_2OH$

     f. $CH_3-CH\overset{t}{=}CH-CH\overset{t}{=}CHC\equiv C-CH_2CH\overset{c}{=}CH(CH_2)_5CH_2OH$

     g. $CH_3CH\overset{t}{=}CH(C\equiv C)_2CH_2CH\overset{c}{=}CH(CH_2)_5COOH$

C_{17}: *h.* $CH_3(C\equiv C)_3CH\overset{t}{=}CH-CH\overset{t}{=}CH(CH_2)_4CH=CH_2$

     i. $CH_3(C\equiv C)_3CH\overset{t}{=}CH-CH\overset{t}{=}CH-CH(CH_2)_3CH=CH_2$
$$\underset{OAc}{|}$$

     j. $CH_3CH\overset{t}{=}CH(C\equiv C)_2CH\overset{t}{=}CH-CH\overset{t}{=}CH(CH_2)_4CH=CH_2$

The structures of compounds (f) and (g) of Table 3-5 reveal some interesting and suggestive features. They possess the $C\equiv C-C-C\overset{c}{=}C$ grouping in the C-7/C-11 position ($CH_2OH = 1$), corresponding to the C-9/C-13 positions in a C_{18} compound such as crepenynic and linoleic acids. The presence of the 7,8-*cis*-double bond suggests that these compounds arose as the result of later modification of a precursor derived by initial desaturation of the kind known to occur in the change stearic acid $\rightarrow$ oleic acid. Crepenynic acid can be regarded as the product of further desaturation at 12,13- of linoleic acid; and it is noteworthy that linoleic and crepenynic acids occur together in the seed fats of *Crepis foetida*.

A plausible biosynthetic scheme leading to the acetylenes of *Dahlia* species is the following (Fig. 3-6):*

acetate-malonate -------> stearic acid ⟶ oleic acid ⟶ linoleic acid ⟶

$$CH_3(CH_2)_4C{\equiv}CCH_2CH{=}CH(CH_2)_7COOH \xrightarrow[\text{(as CoA ester)}]{-C_2 \text{ by } \beta\text{-oxidation}}$$
crepenynic acid

$$CH_3(CH_2)_4C{\equiv}CCH_2CH{=}CH(CH_2)_5CO{-}SCoA$$

↓ reduction

$$CH_3(CH_2)_4C{\equiv}CCH_2CH{=}CH(CH_2)_5CH_2OH$$

↓ further desaturation

$$CH_3CH{=}CH{-}CH{=}CH{-}C{\equiv}C{-}CH_2{-}CH{=}CH(CH_2)_5CH_2OH$$
(f), Table 3-5.

↓

$$CH_3CH{=}C{-}C{\equiv}C{-}C{\equiv}C{-}CH_2{-}CH{=}CH(CH_2)_5COOH$$
(g), Table 3-5.

Fig. 3-6. Some Plausible Biosynthetic Relationships Between Fatty Acids and Polyacetylenes of *Dahlia* Species.

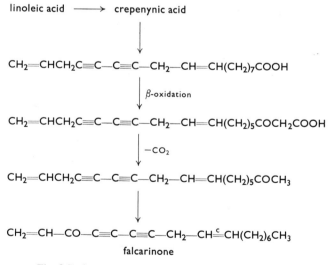

linoleic acid ⟶ crepenynic acid

↓

$$CH_2{=}CHCH_2C{\equiv}C{-}C{\equiv}C{-}CH_2{-}CH{=}CH(CH_2)_7COOH$$

↓ β-oxidation

$$CH_2{=}CHCH_2C{\equiv}C{-}C{\equiv}C{-}CH_2{-}CH{=}CH(CH_2)_5COCH_2COOH$$

↓ −CO₂

$$CH_2{=}CHCH_2C{\equiv}C{-}C{\equiv}C{-}CH_2{-}CH{=}CH(CH_2)_5COCH_3$$

↓

$$CH_2{=}CH{-}CO{-}C{\equiv}C{-}C{\equiv}C{-}CH_2{-}CH{\overset{c}{=}}CH(CH_2)_6CH_3$$
falcarinone

Fig. 3-7. Suggested Biosynthetic Origin of Falcarinone.

* Alternative corollary schemes, essentially equivalent in concept, based upon palmitic acid and an intermediate 7,8-alkenoic acid (rather than 9,10-) are possible.

The process of chain-shortening by way of β-oxidation could also lead to a C_{17} compound by loss of carbon dioxide from the β-keto acid that is first formed. A widely distributed polyacetylene, falcarinone, found in a number of plants, including some of the Compositae, possesses a structure the derivation of which by a process resembling that of Fig. 3-6 has been proposed as shown in Fig. 3-7.

3.8 Biosynthetic Origins of Polyacetylenes: Labeling Experiments

In the foregoing discussion, biosynthetic pathways are modeled upon structural relationships of compounds that occur together in one plant or in plants that are closely related by botanical (taxonomic) criteria. Proposals of this kind often carry the weight of compelling consistency and have much predictive value. Their principal importance, however, is in providing a hypothesis which can be put to specific experimental test. Several kinds of experimental study can give the information that is needed to demonstrate the operation of a specific pathway of biosynthesis. One of these is the administration to the living organism of a suspected precursor, appropriately labeled with an isotopic marker, followed by isolation of the product and its systematic degradation to locate the position of the labeled atom or atoms. A second method, not often realizable in a complex organism such as a higher plant, is the isolation of the separate enzyme systems that catalyze individual steps in the biosynthetic sequence and demonstrating, again with the use of labeled compounds, that the postulated series of reactions occur. A third method, related to the second, and likewise not widely applicable to higher organisms, is the discovery or formation (e.g., by suitable irradiation) of mutants in which one or another of the stages in the reaction sequence is blocked, followed by the demonstration that intermediates in the series of transformations accumulate, and that the provision of the compound whose synthesis is blocked will permit subsequent steps to take place.

The first of these methods is the one commonly used in studies of biosynthesis in higher plants. Its application to the polyacetylenes has established that these compounds are formed by way of the acetate (polyketide) pathway by the linear combination of C_2 units.

The plant *Santalum acuminata* (fam. Santalaceae) contains a number of acetylenic acids; the close structural relationships between these compounds can be seen from their structures (Tables 3-6):

Table 3-6. ACETYLENIC ACIDS OF *Santalum acuminata*.

a.	$CH_3CH_2CH_2CH_2CH_2CH_2CH=CH-C\equiv C(CH_2)_7COOH$
b.	$CH_3CH_2CH_2CH_2CH=CH-CH=CH-C\equiv C(CH_2)_7COOH$
c.	$CH_3CH_2CH_2CH_2CH=CH-C\equiv C-C\equiv C(CH_2)_7COOH$
d.	$CH_3CH_2CH=CH-CH=CH-C\equiv C-C\equiv C(CH_2)_7COOH$
e.	$CH_3CH_2CH=CH-C\equiv C-C\equiv C-C\equiv C(CH_2)_7COOH$
f.	$CH_2=CH-CH=CH-C\equiv C-C\equiv C-C\equiv C(CH_2)_7COOH$

The acetylenic acids of *S. acuminata* to which ^{14}COOH-labeled acetate was fed were isolated and degraded by oxidation, and the radioactivity of the oxidation products measured. The results showed the labeling pattern to be expected for synthesis by the usual fatty acid pathway; that is, by the linear combination of "acetate" units (Eq. 3-24).

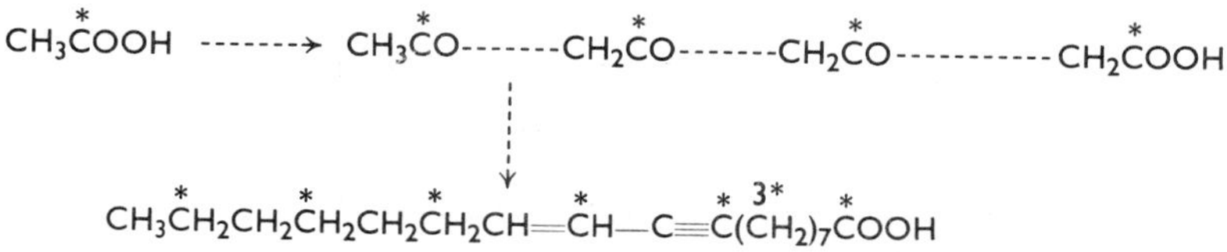

$$\overset{*}{CH_3}COOH \dashrightarrow CH_3\overset{*}{C}O\text{------}CH_2\overset{*}{C}O\text{------}CH_2\overset{*}{C}O\text{----------}CH_2\overset{*}{C}OOH$$

$$CH_3CH_2\overset{*}{C}H_2CH_2\overset{*}{C}H_2CH_2\overset{*}{C}H=\overset{*}{C}H-\overset{*}{C}\equiv\overset{3*}{C}(CH_2)_7\overset{*}{C}OOH$$
[Eq. 3-24]

(*a*), Table 3-6

Oxidation of acids (c) and (e) (Table 3-6) gave results that can be represented as in Fig. 3-8:

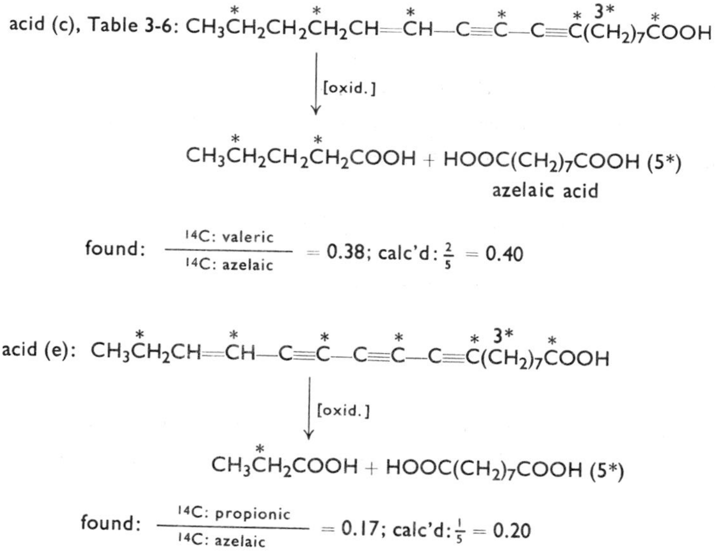

acid (c), Table 3-6: $CH_3CH_2CH_2\overset{*}{C}H_2CH=\overset{*}{C}H-C\equiv\overset{*}{C}-C\equiv\overset{*}{C}(CH_2)_7\overset{*}{C}OOH$ with 3* on the sixth carbon

|[oxid.]|

$$CH_3CH_2\overset{*}{C}H_2\overset{*}{C}H_2COOH + HOOC(CH_2)_7COOH \; (5*)$$
azelaic acid

found: $\dfrac{^{14}C:\text{valeric}}{^{14}C:\text{azelaic}} = 0.38$; calc'd: $\dfrac{2}{5} = 0.40$

acid (e): $\overset{*}{CH_3}CH_2CH=\overset{*}{C}H-C\equiv\overset{*}{C}-C\equiv\overset{*}{C}-C\equiv\overset{3*}{C}(CH_2)_7\overset{*}{C}OOH$

|[oxid.]|

$$CH_3\overset{*}{C}H_2COOH + HOOC(CH_2)_7COOH \; (5*)$$

found: $\dfrac{^{14}C:\text{propionic}}{^{14}C:\text{azelaic}} = 0.17$; calc'd: $\dfrac{1}{5} = 0.20$

Fig. 3-8. Degradation of Labeled Acids from *Santalum acuminata*.

These results, strongly supported by the occurrence of the $-C\equiv C(CH_2)_7COOH$ unit in these acids, suggest that the biosynthetic pathway proceeds by way of the stages stearic → oleic → stearolic → further desaturation to give the end products.

Nemotinic acid, an allenic-acetylenic constituent of the basidiomycetic fungus *Poria corticola* (Fr.) Cke. has the structure shown in Fig. 3-9, with the labeling pattern indicated in the acid produced when the fungus is grown in the presence of acetate-1-^{14}C. The presence of ^{14}C at the terminal position of the carbon chain,

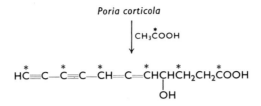

Fig. 3-9. Incorporation of ^{14}C in *Poria corticola*.

coupled with the regular alternation of labeled carbon over the remainder of the structure, indicates that another kind of degradation occurs in this biosynthesis: the loss of the carbon atom which must originally have been the CH_3— group of a terminal CH_3CO--- unit. The fact that nemotinic acid is a C_{11} compound is consistent with this conclusion.

The ω-oxidation of a terminal methyl group has been demonstrated experimentally with the use of the fungus *Merulius lacrimans* (Jacq.) Fr. When 1-^{14}C-dehydromatricaria ester was supplied to a culture of the fungus, the dicarboxylic acid shown in Eq. 3-25 was produced:

$$CH_3C{\equiv}C-C{\equiv}C-C{\equiv}C-CH\overset{t}{=}\overset{*}{C}HCOOCH_3$$

Merulius lacrimans

$$HOOC-C{\equiv}C-C{\equiv}C-C{\equiv}C-CH\overset{t}{=}\overset{*}{C}HCOOH \qquad\qquad \text{[Eq. 3-25]}$$

Dehydromatricarinol, and thus presumably dehydromatricaria ester, has been shown to be formed by the acetate-malonate pathway (Eq. 3-26):

$$CH_3CO-SCoA + 4\ \underset{\underset{COOH}{|}}{CH_2}CO-SCoA$$

$$CH_3C{\equiv}C-C{\equiv}C-C{\equiv}C-CH{=}CHCH_2OH \qquad\qquad \text{[Eq. 3-26]}$$

acetate ⟵ 4 malonate ⟶

dehydromatricarianol

The loss of the terminal methyl group, a presumed step in the biosynthesis of nemotinic acid (Fig. 3-9) has been demonstrated in the fungus *Coprinus quadrifolius* Pk. with the use of 1-^{14}C-dehydromatricaria ester. The triol produced by the fungus in cultures to which the labeled ester was added has the structure shown in Eq. 3-27; it is evident that this experiment shows two of the biosynthetic processes earlier alluded to: the loss of the terminal carbon atom, probably by oxidation (as in Eq. 3-26) and decarboxylation; and reduction of the carboxyl group. The hydroxylation of the double bond, perhaps by way of an intermediate epoxide, is an unexceptional step and needs no extended comment.

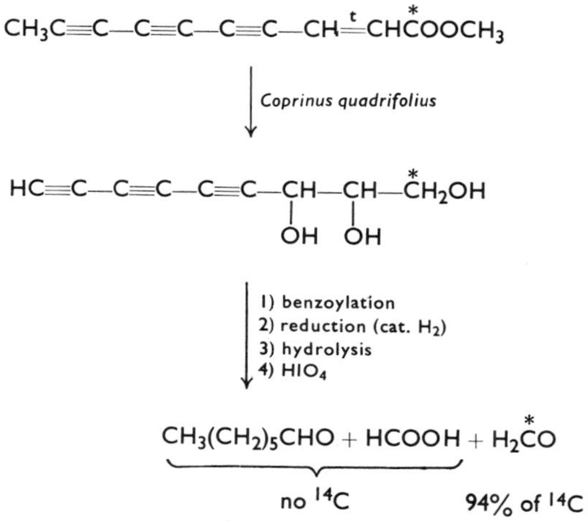

$$CH_3C≡C-C≡C-C≡C-CH \overset{t}{=} CH\overset{*}{C}OOCH_3$$

Coprinus quadrifolius

$$HC≡C-C≡C-C≡C-\underset{OH}{CH}-\underset{OH}{CH}-\overset{*}{C}H_2OH$$

1) benzoylation
2) reduction (cat. H$_2$)
3) hydrolysis
4) HIO$_4$

$$CH_3(CH_2)_5CHO + HCOOH + H_2\overset{*}{C}O \qquad\qquad [Eq.\ 3\text{-}27]$$

$$\underbrace{CH_3(CH_2)_5CHO + HCOOH}_{no\ ^{14}C} \qquad 94\%\ of\ ^{14}C$$

The reduction —COOH→ —CH$_2$OH has also been observed in the transformation shown in Eq. 3-28, when 1-^{14}C-dehydromatricaria ester was fed to a culture of the fungus *Melanoleuca grammopodium* (Bull. ex Fr.) Pat. (synonym, *Tricholoma grammopodium* (Bull. ex Fr.) Quél.).

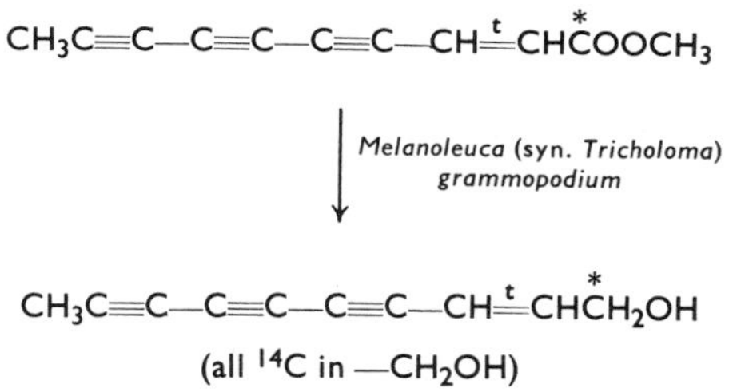

$$CH_3C≡C-C≡C-C≡C-CH \overset{t}{=} CH\overset{*}{C}OOCH_3$$

Melanoleuca (syn. Tricholoma)
grammopodium

$$CH_3C≡C-C≡C-C≡C-CH \overset{t}{=} CH\overset{*}{C}H_2OH \qquad\qquad [Eq.\ 3\text{-}28]$$

(all ^{14}C in —CH$_2$OH)

Experiments with cell-free extracts of *C. quadrifolius* have further shown the decarboxylation of the unit —C≡C—COOH to —C≡CH. When the (non-naturally occurring) C_8 acid shown in Eq. 3-29 was added to the fungus culture, the decarboxylated alcohol was formed:

$$HOCH_2CH=CH-C\equiv C-C\equiv C-COOH$$

added to | cell-free extract of *Coprinus quadrifolius*

$$HOCH_2CH=CH-C\equiv C-C\equiv CH$$ [Eq. 3-29]

Finally, the use of $2\text{-}^{14}C$-acetate ($\overset{*}{C}H_3COOH$) has shown that the terminal —CH_2OH group in the tetraynic tetrahydroxy compound produced by *Fistulina hepatica* has its origin in the —CH_3 group of acetate (Eq. 3-30):

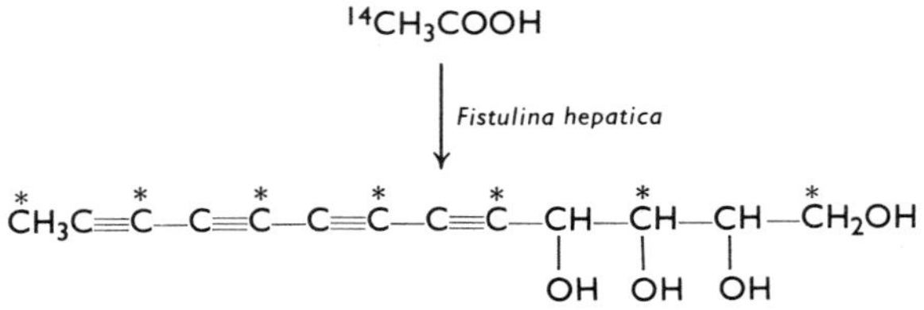

$$^{14}CH_3COOH$$

Fistulina hepatica

$$\overset{*}{C}H_3C\equiv\overset{*}{C}-\overset{*}{C}\equiv\overset{*}{C}-\overset{*}{C}\equiv\overset{*}{C}-\overset{*}{C}\equiv\overset{*}{C}-CH-\overset{*}{C}H-CH-\overset{*}{C}H_2OH$$

$$\underset{OH\ \ OH\ \ OH}{}$$ [Eq. 3-30]

It seems evident that the precursor that leads to this C_{13}-tetrol is a C_{14} compound composed of seven C_2 units, from which a terminal (unlabeled) carbon atom was lost in the synthetic process.

Acetylenic compounds other than straight-chain hydrocarbons, acids and alcohols are also produced by plants. Cyclization of a terminal group of six carbon atoms leads to the aromatic triyne, shown in Eq. 3-31, a constituent of plants of the family Compositae. Its labeling pattern, when it is produced by the $1\text{-}^{14}C$-acetate-fed plant, shows that it is formed from seven C_2-units with the loss of the terminal —$\overset{*}{C}OOH$ group:

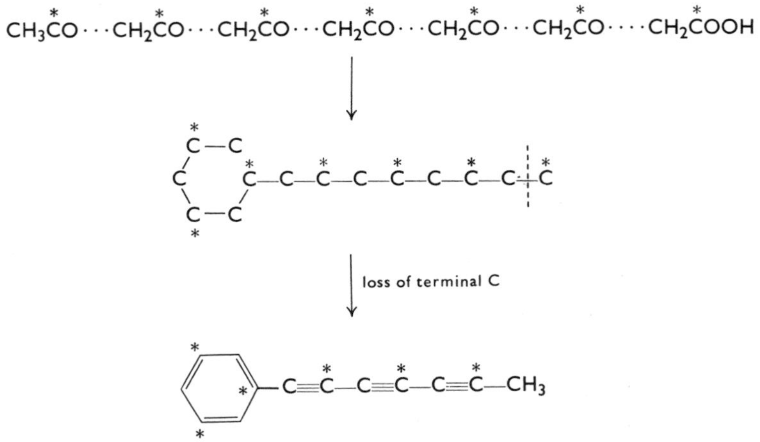

$$CH_3\overset{*}{C}O\cdots CH_2\overset{*}{C}O\cdots CH_2\overset{*}{C}O\cdots CH_2\overset{*}{C}O\cdots CH_2\overset{*}{C}O\cdots CH_2\overset{*}{C}O\cdots\cdot CH_2\overset{*}{C}OOH$$

loss of terminal C

[Eq. 3-31]

A labeling experiment in which 10-^{14}C-oleic acid was administered to the fungus *Tricholoma grammopodium* has given convincing confirmation of the overall pathway to polyacetylenes, and strongly supports the hypothesis of sequential dehydrogenation of a precursor fatty acid. The results of this study are outlined in Eq. 3-32, to which is added the outline of a possible sequence of stages through which the overall transformation is effected.

$$CH_3(CH_2)_7\overset{*}{C}H\overset{c}{=}CH(CH_2)_7COOH$$
10-^{14}C-oleic acid

Tricholoma | *grammopodium*
↓

$$CH_3(CH_2)_4CH=CHCH_2\overset{*}{C}H\overset{c}{=}CH(CH_2)_7COOH$$
↓

$$CH_3(CH_2)_4C\equiv CCH_2\overset{*}{C}H\overset{c}{=}CH(CH_2)_7COOH$$
↓

$$CH_3CH_2CH_2CH=CH—C\equiv CCH_2\overset{*}{C}H\overset{c}{=}CH(CH_2)_7COOH$$
Δ^{14}-crepenynic acid

−8 C atoms
↓

$$CH_3C\equiv C—C\equiv C—C\equiv C—CH\overset{t}{\underset{}{=}}\overset{*}{C}HCOOH$$
2-^{14}C-dehydromatricaria acid

Possible biosynthetic pathway:

acetate/malonate ⟶ stearic ⟶ oleic ⟶
linoleic ⟶ crepenynic ⟶ Δ^{14}-crepenynic
↓

$$CH_3CH_2CH_2C\equiv C—C\equiv CCH_2CH=CH(CH_2)_7COOH$$
↓

$$CH_3CH=CH—C\equiv C—C\equiv CCH_2CH=CH(CH_2)_7COOH$$
↓

$$CH_3C\equiv C—C\equiv C—C\equiv CCH_2CH=CH(CH_2)_7COOH$$

3 β-oxidations
↓

$$CH_3C\equiv C—C\equiv C—C\equiv CCH_2CH\overset{c}{=}CHCH_2COOH$$

rearrange to conjugation of C=C
↓

$$CH_3C\equiv C—C\equiv C—C\equiv C—CH\overset{t}{=}CHCH_2CH_2COOH$$

β-oxidation
↓

$$CH_3C\equiv C—C\equiv C—C\equiv C—CH=CHCOOH$$ [Eq. 3-32]
dehydromatricaria acid

It will be noticed that in the proposed biosynthetic pathway of Eq. 3-32 the rearrangement of the system —C≡C—CH$_2$—CH=CH— to the conjugated —C≡C—CH=CHCH$_2$— is assumed to follow three β-oxidation steps, and is then followed by a final β-oxidation. This assumption is made for the purpose of accommodating in the general pathway the formation of the polyacetylenes shown in Eq. 3-33, both of which are known in nature:

$$CH_3C≡C—C≡C—C≡CCH_2CH \overset{c}{=} CH(CH_2)_3COOH$$

$$HOOCC≡C—C≡C—C≡CCH_2CH \overset{c}{=} CH(CH_2)_3COOH \text{ (known)} \qquad \text{[Eq. 3-33]}$$

$$HC≡C—C≡C—CH=C—CH—CH \overset{c}{=} CH—CH \overset{t}{=} CHCH_2COOH \text{ (known)}$$

A hydroxylated enynoic acid from a *Helichrysum* species (fam. Compositae) seems also to derive from crepenynic acid (Eq. 3-34). It will be noted that allylic isomerization of the double bond converts it from the *cis* configuration, characteristic of the oleic, crepenynic, etc., types, to the *trans* configuration.

$$CH_3CH_2CH_2CH_2CH_2C≡CCH_2CH \overset{c}{=} CH(CH_2)_7COOH$$
crepenynic acid

$$\left\{ CH_3CH_2CH_2CH_2CH_2C≡CCHCH \overset{c}{=} CH(CH_2)_7COOH \right\}$$
$$\underset{OH}{|}$$

anionotropic | rearrangement

$$CH_3CH_2CH_2CH_2CH_2C≡C—CH \overset{t}{=} CHCH(CH_2)_7COOH \qquad \text{[Eq. 3-34]}$$
$$\underset{OH}{|}$$

(known in *Helichrysum* spp.)

The labeling experiments described in the foregoing paragraphs were performed with the use of intact organisms, in most cases fungi. The ultimate description of a course of biosynthesis will be possible only when each step of the pathway of structural elaboration can be isolated and studied as a separate event. Such a goal will be reached when the separate participating units in a chain of enzyme systems are separated and examined as discrete entities.

Relatively little progress has been made toward reaching this goal, but in a few cases partial success has been recorded. Cell-free preparations of the leaves of *Chrysanthemum flosculosum* L. have been found to have the capacity for carrying out the overall conversion of oleic acid (^{3}H-labeled compounds were used) into the final tri-yne-diene ketal shown as the final product (*g*) in Eq. 3-35. Separation of leaf homogenates into particulate and non-particulate (i.e., supernatant) fractions gave some indication that enzymes responsible for separate steps in the sequence *a–g* (Eq. 3-35) were in some cases bound to cellular elements, in others dissociable into soluble units. Further studies of this kind may be expected to elucidate such pathways as that shown in Eq. 3-35 in complete detail.

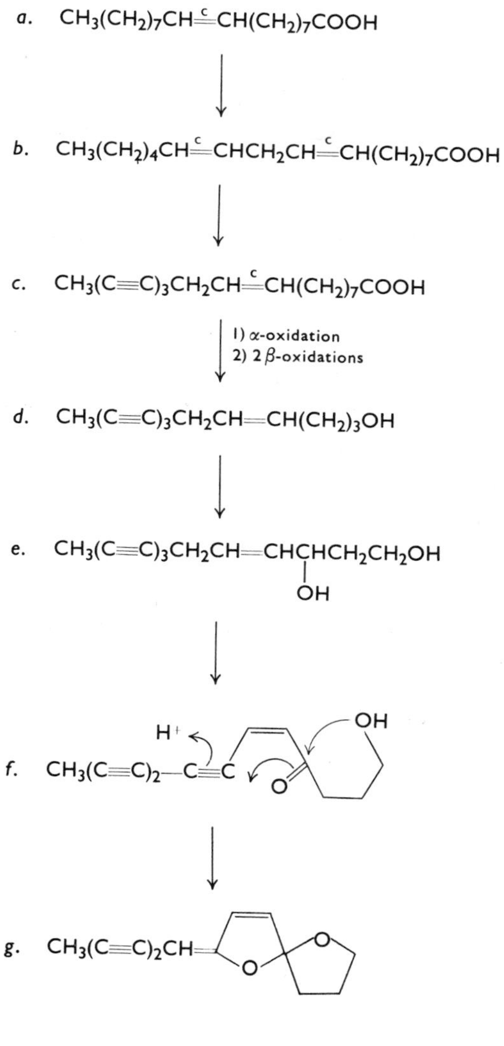

a. $CH_3(CH_2)_7CH \overset{c}{=} CH(CH_2)_7COOH$

b. $CH_3(CH_2)_4CH \overset{c}{=} CHCH_2CH \overset{c}{=} CH(CH_2)_7COOH$

c. $CH_3(C \equiv C)_3CH_2CH \overset{c}{=} CH(CH_2)_7COOH$

$\quad$ 1) α-oxidation
$\quad$ 2) 2 β-oxidations

d. $CH_3(C \equiv C)_3CH_2CH = CH(CH_2)_3OH$

e. $CH_3(C \equiv C)_3CH_2CH = CHCHCH_2CH_2OH$
$\qquad\qquad\qquad\qquad\qquad\quad | $
$\qquad\qquad\qquad\qquad\qquad OH$

f. $CH_3(C \equiv C)_2 - C \equiv C$

g. $CH_3(C \equiv C)_2CH =$

[Eq. 3-35]

3.9 Alternative Hypotheses for the Genesis of Triple Bonds

The desaturation hypothesis so satisfactorily supported by experiments of the kind just described appears to be adequate as a means for the introduction of double and triple bonds into carbon chains. There are, however, other readily conceivable ways in which a triple bond could be formed, one of which has received support from the success of analogous reactions on model systems. Enol phosphates have been found to undergo a ready elimination reaction with the formation of the carbon-carbon triple bond (Eq. 3-36):

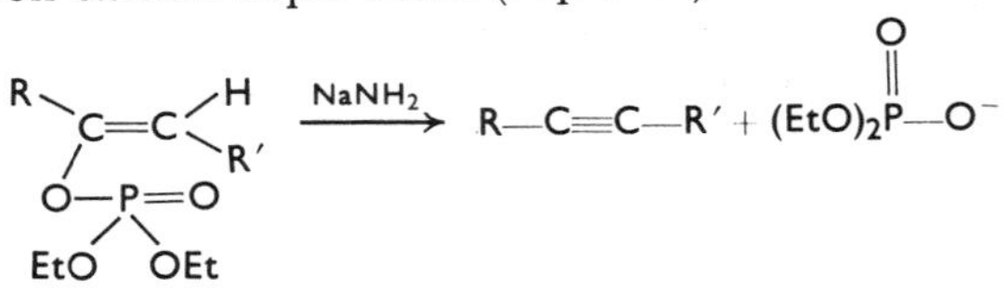

$$R-C\underset{\substack{|\\O-P=O\\ /\quad\backslash\\ EtO\quad OEt}}{C}=C\overset{H}{\underset{R'}{}} \xrightarrow{NaNH_2} R-C\equiv C-R' + (EtO)_2\overset{\overset{O}{\|}}{P}-O^- \qquad [Eq.\ 3-36]$$

This is an inviting hypothesis, for it has a direct relationship to the genesis of the carbon chain by extension of a polyketide, phosphorylation of the enol form of which would provide the substrate for the reaction of Eq 3-37:

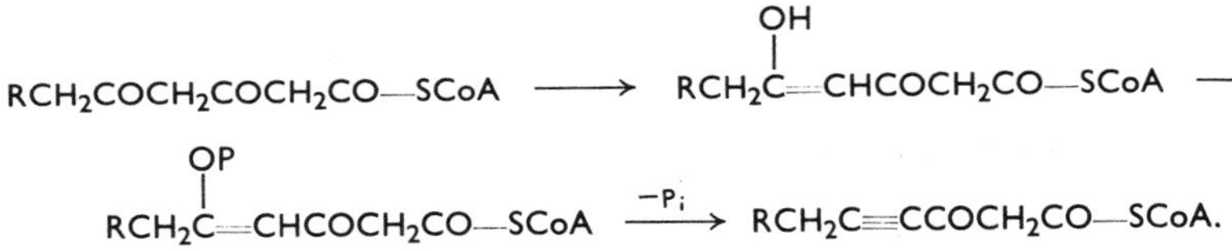

$$RCH_2COCH_2COCH_2CO-SCoA \longrightarrow RCH_2\overset{\overset{OH}{|}}{C}=CHCOCH_2CO-SCoA \longrightarrow$$

$$RCH_2\overset{\overset{OP}{|}}{C}=CHCOCH_2CO-SCoA \xrightarrow{-P_i} RCH_2C\equiv CCOCH_2CO-SCoA. \quad [Eq.\ 3-37]$$

There is, however, no more support for this mechanistic route to acetylenes than that the model experiments suggest its feasibility. The desaturation route described in the foregoing discussion, on the other hand, is supported by the compelling evidence of direct experimental study with isotopically marked precursors.

3.10 Modified Polyacetylenes—Thiophene Derivatives

Plants of the genus *Tagetes* (fam. Compositae) contain a group of related compounds that possess thienyl groups, the most striking of which is terthienyl itself. Some examples of these are given in Table 3-7:

Table 3-7. THIOPHENES FROM COMPOSITAE.

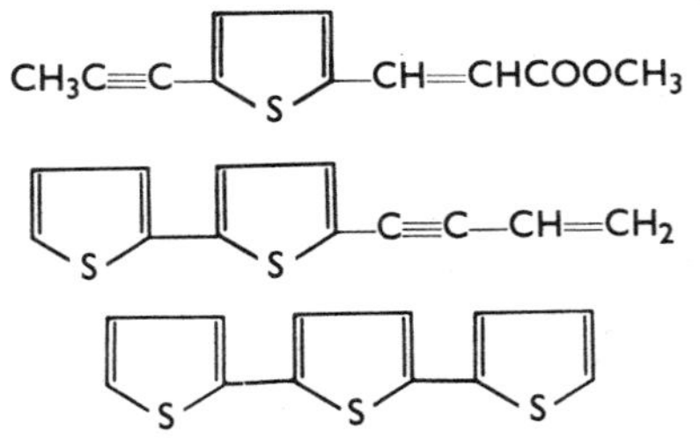

The genesis of these from a diacetylene and hydrogen sulfide (Eq. 3-38) offers a satisfactory explanation for their presence, particularly since they occur in a plant family of which polyacetylenes are characteristic constituents. In support of this view is the isolation from a number of species of *Anthemis* (fam. Compositae) of several thiomethyl ethers that may be regarded as having derived from the first addition reaction shown in Eq. 3-38. Several examples of these unusual sulfur-containing compounds, all of them closely related to the dehydromatricaria esters (both the 2-*cis* and 2-*trans* forms are present), are given in Table 3-8:

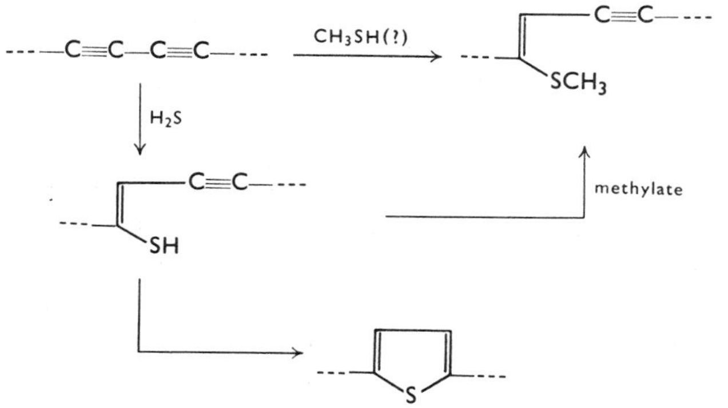

[Eq. 3-38]

Table 3-8. THIOETHERS FROM *Anthemis* SPECIES.

A. tinctoria L.	$CH_3—C(SCH_3)\overset{t}{=}CH—C\equiv C—C\equiv C—CH\overset{c}{=}CHCOOCH_3$
A. carpatica Willd.	$CH_3C\equiv C—C\equiv C—C(SCH_3)\overset{t}{=}CH—CH\overset{c}{=}CHCOOCH_3$
A. cota L.	$CH_3C\equiv C—C(SCH_3)\overset{t}{=}CH—C\equiv C—CH\overset{t}{=}CHCOOCH_3$
A. carpatica L.	

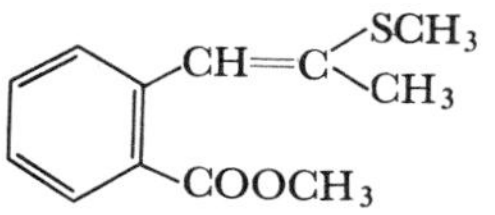

The absence of thiophene derivatives from these *Anthemis* constituents suggests that the sulfur compound that adds to the triple bond is CH_3SH rather than H_2S.

3.11   Chain Extension by C_2 Addition to α-Keto Acids

Studies of the biosynthesis of the mustard oil glycosides (thioglucosides)* have revealed that the general course of their formation can be represented by the following equation (Eq. 3-39):

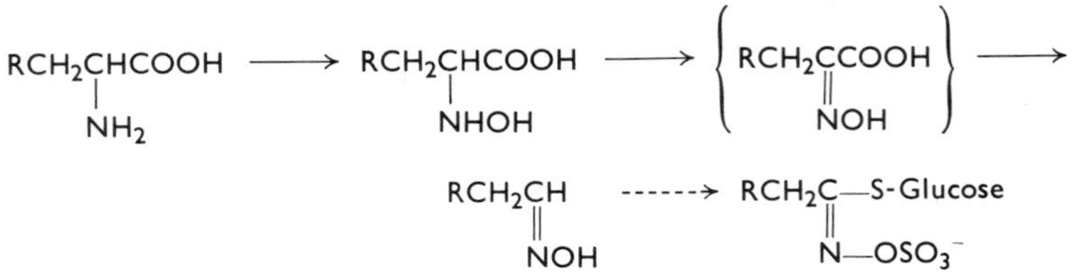

$$RCH_2\underset{\underset{NH_2}{|}}{C}HCOOH \longrightarrow RCH_2\underset{\underset{NHOH}{|}}{C}HCOOH \longrightarrow \left\{ RCH_2\underset{\underset{NOH}{\|}}{C}COOH \right\} \longrightarrow$$

[Eq. 3-39]

$$RCH_2\underset{\underset{NOH}{\|}}{C}H \dashrightarrow RCH_2\underset{\underset{N-OSO_3^-}{\|}}{C}-S\text{-Glucose}$$

an R-glucosinolate

Feeding experiments with appropriately labeled precursors have shown that the nitrogen of the glycoside is that of a precursor amino acid, and that the necessary precursor amino acids for certain of these glycosides are formed by chain extension of lower homologs.

Two examples will be considered. Glucotropaeolin and gluconasturtiin have the structures shown in Eq. 3-40, where the labeling pattern produced by the administration of ^{14}C-phenylalanines to the appropriate plants is also indicated.

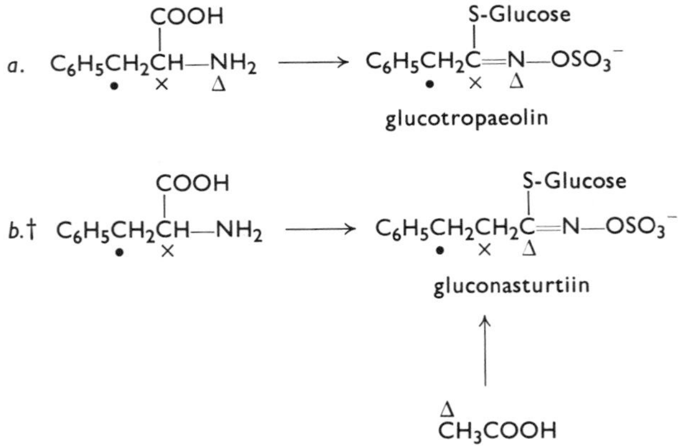

$$a. \quad C_6H_5CH_2\underset{\bullet \quad \times \quad \Delta}{C}\underset{\underset{NH_2}{|}}{H}\overset{\overset{COOH}{|}}{} \longrightarrow C_6H_5CH_2\underset{\bullet \quad \times \quad \Delta}{C}=N-OSO_3^-$$

glucotropaeolin

[Eq. 3-40]

$$b.\dagger \quad C_6H_5CH_2\underset{\bullet \quad \times}{C}\underset{\underset{NH_2}{|}}{H}\overset{\overset{COOH}{|}}{} \longrightarrow C_6H_5CH_2CH_2\underset{\bullet \quad \times \quad \Delta}{C}=N-OSO_3^-$$

gluconasturtiin

$$\uparrow$$

$$\underset{CH_3COOH}{\overset{\Delta}{}}$$

† See also Eq. 3-41.

* The general term "glycosinolate" has been proposed for these compounds, of the general formula

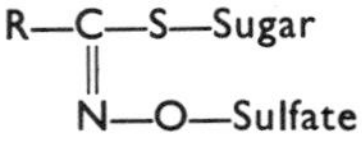

$$R-\underset{\underset{N-O-Sulfate}{\|}}{C}-S-Sugar$$

Two observations relevant to the processes dealt with in this chapter are the following:

a. the nitrogen atom of the aglucone (the thiohydroxamic acid) is derived directly from the amino nitrogen of the amino acid;

b. when the requisite amino acid is an uncommon one, it can be synthesized in the plant by condensation of acetyl coenzyme A (perhaps via malonyl coenzyme A) with an α-keto acid. The latter may be the keto acid directly related to a common amino acid.

The synthesis of β-phenylethyl glucosinolate (gluconasturtiin) requires the uncommon amino acid, 4-phenyl-2-aminobutanoic acid (Eqs. 3-40, 3-41). The latter is synthesized in the plant by addition of a two-carbon fragment to phenylpyruvic acid (Eq. 3-41).

$$C_6H_5CH_2\underset{\underset{NH_2}{|}}{CH}COOH \;\rightleftharpoons\; C_6H_5CH_2COCOOH \xrightarrow{\{CH_3CO-SCoA\}\dagger}$$

$$C_6H_5CH_2\underset{\underset{COOH}{|}}{\overset{\overset{OH}{|}}{C}}-CH_2CO-SCoA \xrightarrow{-H_2O} C_6H_5CH_2\underset{\underset{COOH}{|}}{C}=CHCOOH \xrightleftharpoons{H_2O}$$

$$C_6H_5CH_2\underset{\underset{COOH}{|}}{CH}-\overset{\overset{OH}{|}}{CH}-COOH \xrightleftharpoons{(ox.)} C_6H_5CH_2\underset{\underset{COOH}{|}}{CH}COCOOH \xrightarrow{-CO_2} \qquad\qquad \text{[Eq. 3-41]}$$

$$C_6H_5CH_2CH_2COCOOH \xrightleftharpoons[\text{amination}]{\text{trans-}} C_6H_5CH_2CH_2\underset{\underset{NH_2}{|}}{CH}COOH \xdashrightarrow{\substack{\text{cf. Eq.}\\ \text{3-40b.}}}$$

$$C_6H_5CH_2CH_2C\overset{\displaystyle{S\text{-Glucose}}}{\underset{\displaystyle{N-OSO_3^-}}{\big\backslash}}$$

gluconasturtiin

---

† Perhaps as $HOOCCH_2CO-SCoA$.

It will be noted that the aldol-like addition of the C_2 unit to the α-carbonyl group bears a close relationship to the reaction in which β-hydroxy-β-methylglutaric acid is formed from acetoacetic acid and acetic acid (as their thiol esters).

The reactions shown in Eq. 3-41 have not been widely observed in nature, but it appears likely that, in view of the simplicity of the reaction course and the prevalence of the requisite reactant types, other amino acids of the uncommon types may be formed by a similar route.

IV CHAPTER

REFERENCES FOR FURTHER READING

1. A. J. Birch, *Some Pathways in Biosynthesis*, Proc. Chem. Soc., (1962), 3.
2. S. Shibata, *Chemistry and Biosynthesis of Some Fungal Metabolites*, Chemistry in Britain, 3, (1967), 110.
3. Y. Asahina and S. Shibata, *Chemistry of Lichen Substances*, Japan Soc. for Promotion of Science, Tokyo, 1954.
4. J. H. Richards and J. B. Hendrickson, *The Biosynthesis of Steroids, Terpenes and Acetogenins*, W. A. Benjamin, Inc. New York, 1964.
5. H. Grisebach, *Biosynthetic Patterns in Microorganisms and Higher Plants*, John Wiley and Sons, Inc., New York, 1967.
6. A. R. Burnett and R. H. Thomson, *Biogenesis of Anthraquinones in Rubiaceae*, Chem. Comm., (1967), 1125.
7. R. W. Rickards, *The Biosynthesis of Phenolic Compounds from Activated Acetic Acid Units*, in Recent Developments in the Chemistry of Natural Phenolic Compounds, W. D. Ollis, Ed., Pergamon Press, Oxford, 1961.
8. E. Leistner and M. H. Zenk, *Incorporation of Shikimic Acid into 1,2-Dihydroxyanthraquinone in Rubia tinctorum L.*, Tetrahedron Letters, (1967), 475.
9. A. J. Birch and F. W. Donovan, *Studies in Relation to Biosynthesis* (I), Austr. J. Chem., 6, (1953), 360.
10. T. A. Geissman, *The Biosynthesis of Phenolic Plant Products*, in Biogenesis of Natural Compounds, 2nd Ed., P. Bernfeld, Ed., Pergamon Press, Oxford, 1967.
11. R. Bentley and J. G. Keil, *The Role of Acetate and Malonate in the Biosynthesis of Penicillic Acid.*, Proc. Chem. Soc., (1961), 111.

Compounds Formed by Cyclization of Polyketide Chains

4.1 The Acetate Hypothesis

The "acetate hypothesis" of the natural formation of compounds containing aromatic (usually phenolic) nuclei had its origin in straightforward considerations of the possible reaction paths of a poly-β-keto compound of the following general structure:

$$RCOCH_2COCH_2COCH_2COOR'$$

The presence in this hypothetical substance of the doubly-activated —CH_2— groups and reactive carbonyl groups makes possible two kinds of reactions, both leading to cyclization and both being examples of condensations of the general aldol type.

1. Intramolecular aldolization (Eq. 4-1):

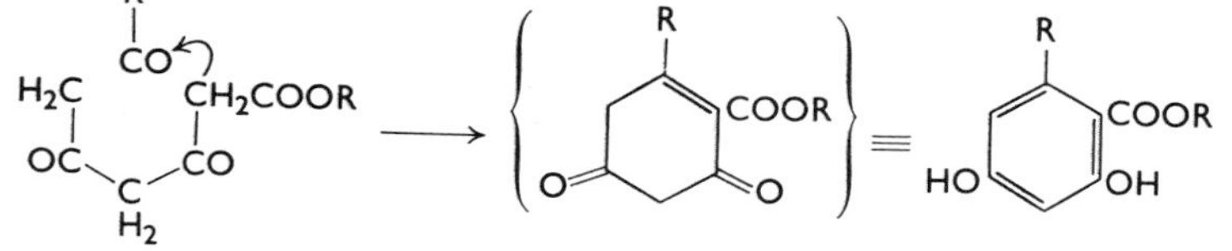

[Eq. 4-1]

2. Intramolecular carbon acylation of the Claisen-condensation type (Eq. 4-2):

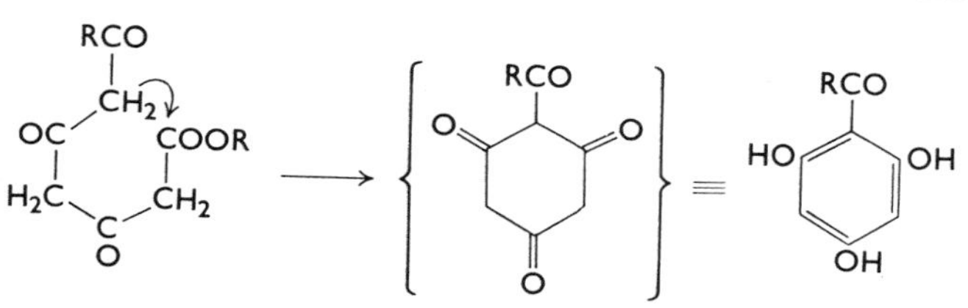

[Eq. 4-2]

The products of both kinds of reaction are polyhydroxybenzene derivatives: in one case, a resorcinol carboxylic acid; in the other, an acylphloroglucinol.

The first expression of the hypothesis by Collie (1907), as it related to the biogenesis of naturally occurring phenolic compounds, was based not only upon the obvious mechanistic plausibility of the concept but also upon experimental demonstration. When dehydracetic acid, formed from acetoacetic ester (Eq. 4-3), was treated with alkali, orsellinic acid was formed (Eq. 4-4):

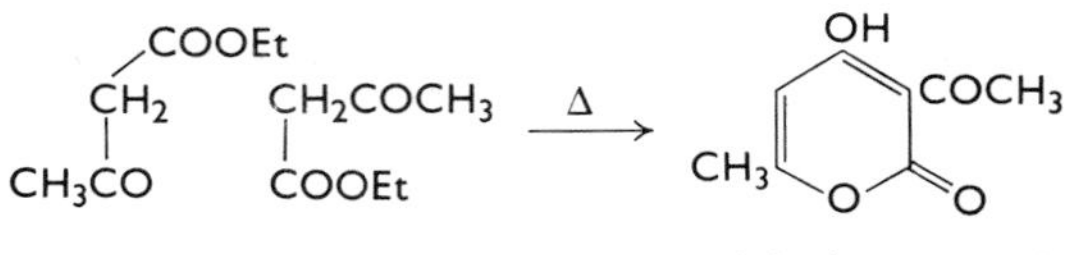

dehydracetic acid   [Eq. 4-3]

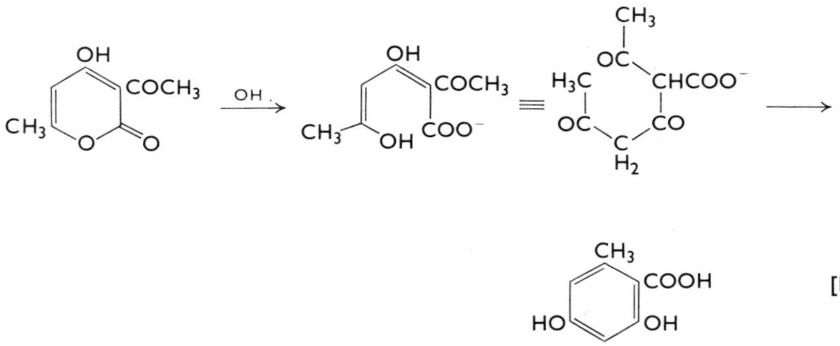

orsellinic acid   [Eq. 4-4]

Similarly, diacetylacetone was found to undergo a comparable base-catalyzed intramolecular aldolization to yield a naphthalene derivative (Eq. 4-5):

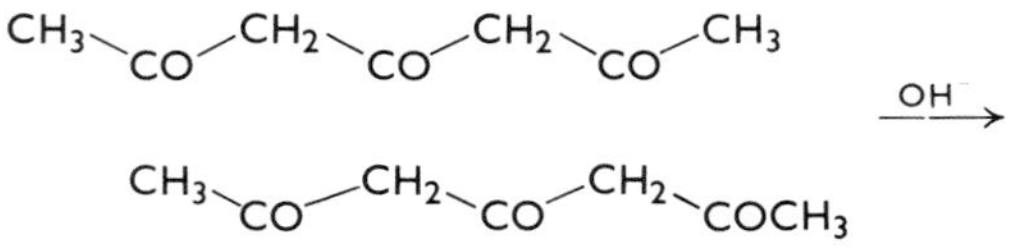

diacetylacetone (2 molecules)

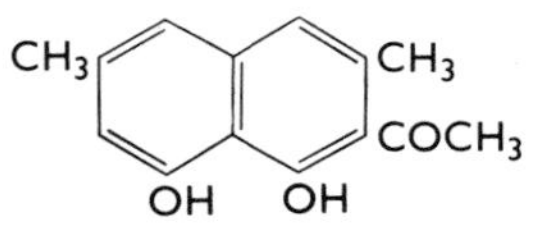

                                                                                              [Eq. 4-5]

The occurrence in nature of orsellinic acid and of hydroxylated napthalenes similar in general structure to that produced from diacetylacetone led Collie to suggest that natural polyphenols might owe their origin to the cyclization of precursors derived from acetic acid. Since at that time little was known about such now familiar subjects as fatty acid synthesis and breakdown, and the vital role of acetate and its thiolesters in metabolic processes, the acetate hypothesis remained a purely formal expression that lay undeveloped and unexploited until 1953, when Birch and Donovan gave renewed expression to the idea, bringing to its support an impressive body of structural argument and experimental evidence. The validity of the hypothesis was first assessed on two grounds:

1. the statistical weight of the evidence of a large number of structures of natural compounds, most of which could be correlated with the central concept of the cyclization of a linear poly-β-keto chain; and
2. its predictive value in permitting the selection of a correct structure from among two or more proposed for a given compound, and in correcting the structures of compounds which had been erroneously formulated.

Although the validity of the hypothesis—now more properly described by the term "the acetate-malonate pathway" of synthesis—was at length firmly established by the use of isotopically labeled compounds in experiments with living organisms, certain of the structural arguments that were first put forward in its support deserve special review here. Indeed, in many theories of biosynthesis the structural arguments have always been and continue to be valuable in planning the experimental approach with labeled compounds, and in most instances the labeling experiments have confirmed predictions based upon the grounds provided by the hypothesis.

4.2 Structural Correlations

Nature affords many compounds whose structures accord accurately with their derivation by the cyclization of a two-carbon-derived poly-β-keto (hereinafter usually called "polyketide") chain. In Fig. 4-1 are listed a selected number of these, chosen to represent a range of structures derived by application of the hypothesis in its simplest expression. Numerous secondary transformations—the addition and removal of oxygen functions (OH, OCH_3), the introduction of alkyl substituents, the oxidation of substituent groups (e.g., $CH_3 \rightarrow CH_2OH \rightarrow CHO \rightarrow COOH$), the loss of CO_2 from a terminal —$COCH_2COOH$ group—will be the subjects of later discussion.

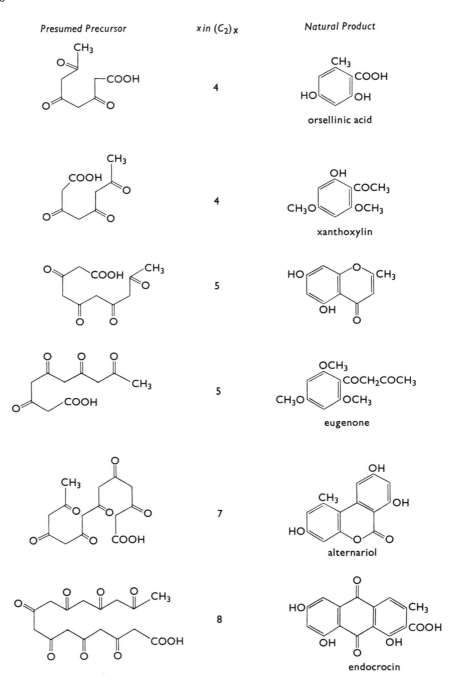

Fig. 4-1. Naturally Occurring Compounds Conforming to the Acetate Hypothesis.

4.3 Structure of Eleutherinol

One of the first successful applications of the concept was in its application to the revision of the structure of eleutherinol, a chromone found along with several related compounds in the plant *Eleutherine bulbosa* (fam. Iridaceae). Earlier investigations of the chemistry of eleutherinol had led to the conclusion that its structure was the following (Fig. 4-2):

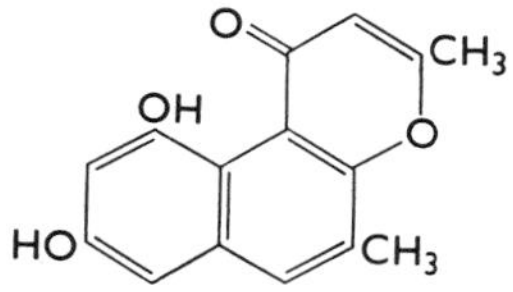

Fig. 4-2. First Structure Proposed for Eleutherinol.

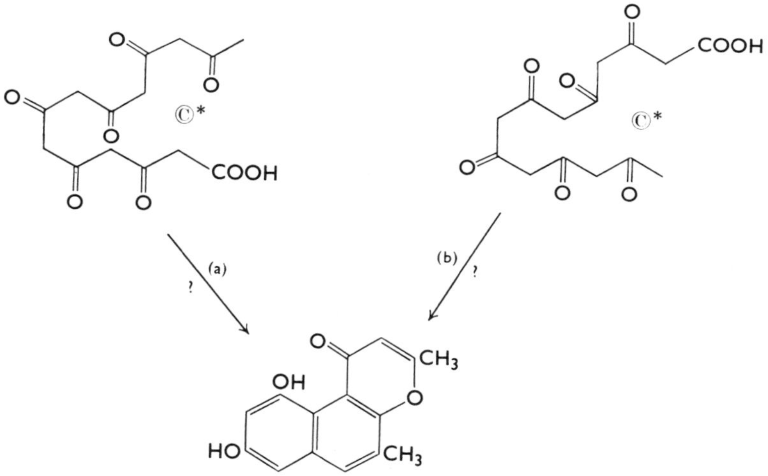

ⓒ* = C$_1$-fragment from one-carbon-atom source

Fig. 4-3. Derivation of Earlier (Incorrect) Structure for Eleutherinol on the Acetate Hypothesis.

This conclusion was based in part upon the alkaline degradation of eleutherinol to a naphthol to which was assigned the structure shown in Eq. 4-6:

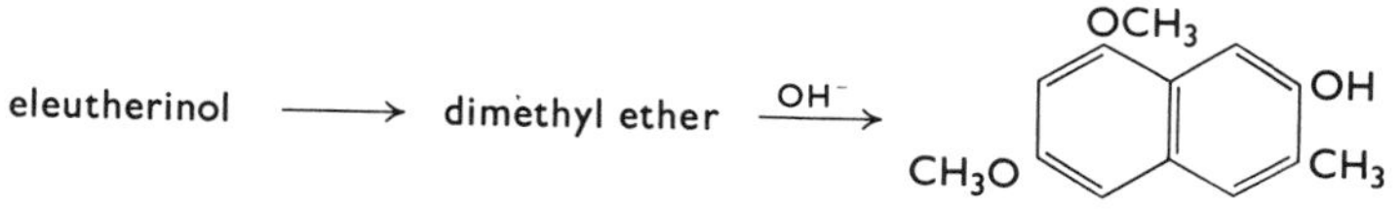

structure assigned to the naphthol formed by degradation of eleutherinol dimethyl ether

[Eq. 4-6]

It will be apparent from Fig. 4-3 that the structure first assigned to eleutherinol cannot be simply constructed from —CH_2CO— units arranged in a head-to-tail fashion. In both (a) and (b) an "extra" carbon atom must be added; and both suffer from the unusual requirement that a —CH_3 group of eleutherinol be formed by the reduction of —COOH. Moreover, for (a) to serve as the progenitor an extensive revision of the pattern of oxygenation is required. It will be seen from the examples of Fig. 4-1 that one of the most striking features of the acetate hypothesis is that the pattern of oxygenation of the natural product conforms exactly to that of the sequence of —CO— groups in the polyketide precursor.

An alternative to the structure shown in Fig. 4-2 is that shown in Eq. 4-7. It will be seen that the revised structure requires that the naphthol derived from eleutherinol dimethyl ether (Eq. 4-8) have a structure different from that shown in Eq. 4-6. A reevaluation of the earlier experimental evidence led to the conclusion that the naphthol could indeed have the structure required for the revised formula (Eq. 4-8), and this was confirmed by its synthesis (Eq. 4-9).

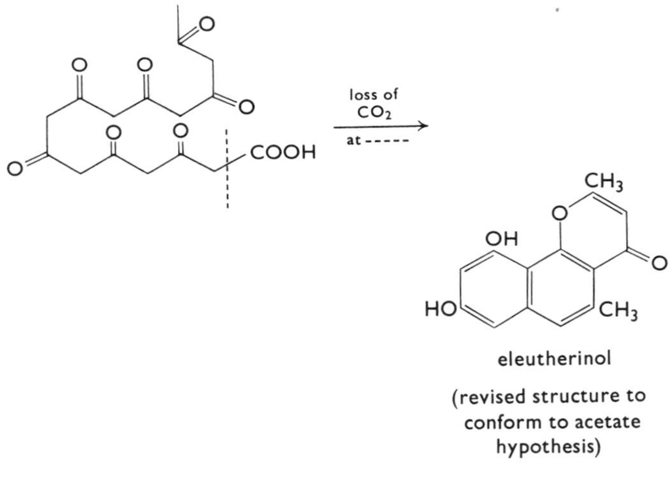

eleutherinol

(revised structure to
conform to acetate
hypothesis)

[Eq. 4-7]

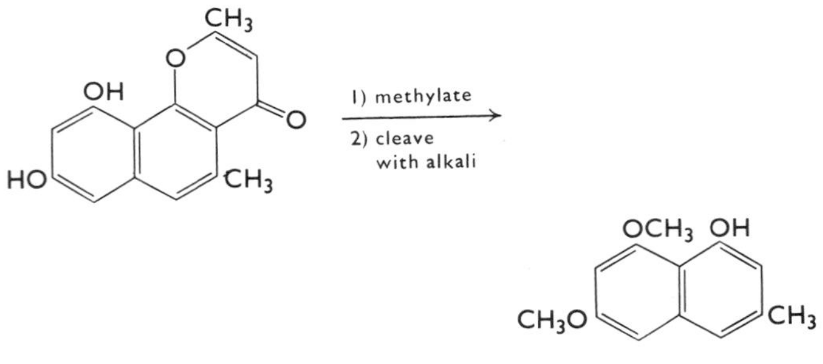

1) methylate

2) cleave
   with alkali

[Eq. 4-8]

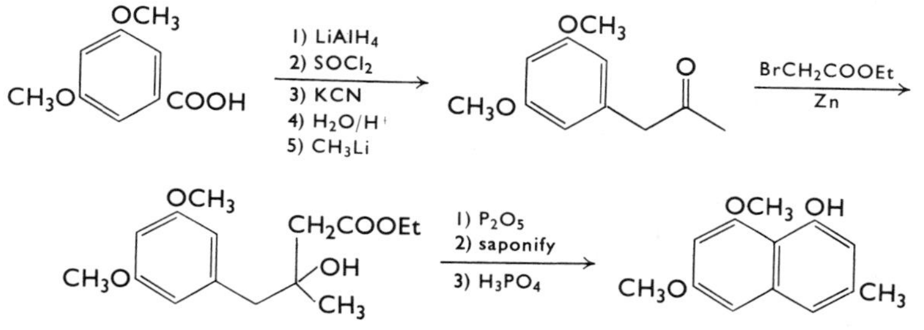

[Eq. 4-9]

m.p. 82°
(naphthol from
eleutherinol (Eq. 4-8)
had m.p. 82-4°)

Final confirmation of the revised structure for eleutherinol was achieved by a synthesis of the chromone from the synthetic naphthol. In Eq. 4-10 another synthesis of the naphthol is represented, along with its conversion into eleutherinol.

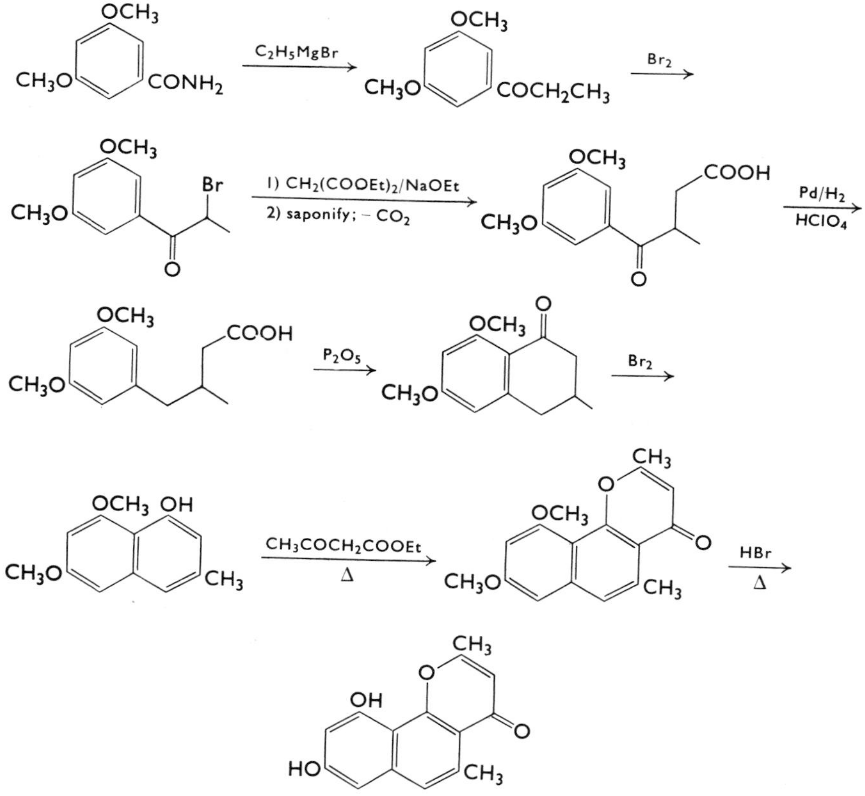

eleutherinol
(identical with natural
compound)

[Eq. 4-10]

4.4 Structure of Nalgiovensin

This early demonstration of the predictive value of the acetate hypothesis was followed by several others. Nalgiovensin, an anthraquinone derivative produced by the fungus *Penicillium nalgiovensis* Lax., was formulated in early studies as one of the three compounds shown in Fig. 4-4. Of these, the one possessing the side-chain —$CH_2CH(OH)CH_3$ could be derived most directly from a regular polyketide chain, and that this was indeed the correct structure was established experimentally.

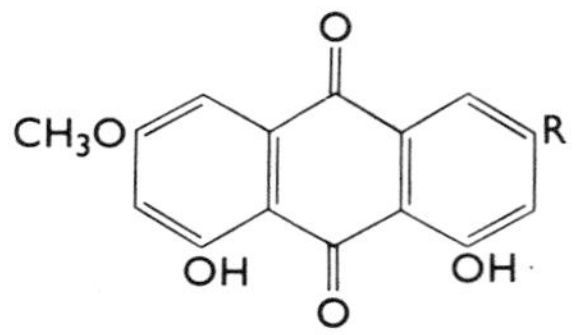

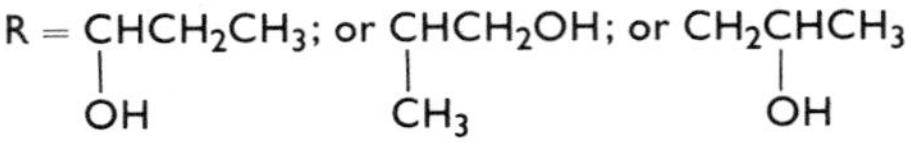

R = $\underset{OH}{CHCH_2CH_3}$; or $\underset{CH_3}{CHCH_2OH}$; or $\underset{OH}{CH_2CHCH_3}$

(a)   (b)   (c)

Derivation of (c) by acetate hypothesis:

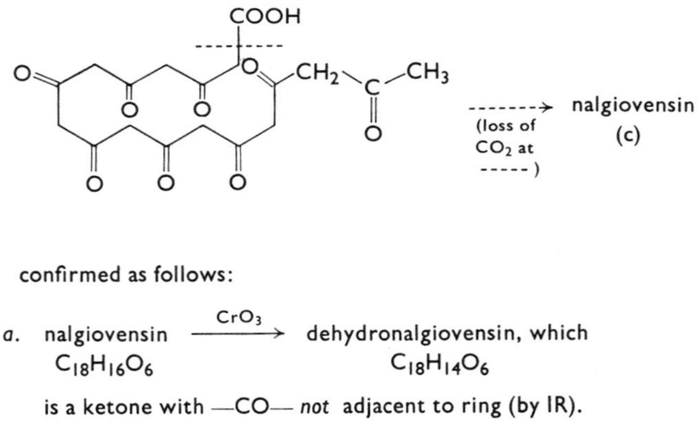

confirmed as follows:

a. nalgiovensin $\xrightarrow{CrO_3}$ dehydronalgiovensin, which
 $C_{18}H_{16}O_6$ $C_{18}H_{14}O_6$

 is a ketone with —CO— *not* adjacent to ring (by IR).

b. nalgiovensin $\xrightarrow[\text{2) oxidation}]{\text{1) HI}}$ $CH_3COOH + CH_3CH_2COOH$
$\phantom{b.\ nalgiovensin\ \xrightarrow{aaaaaa}\ }$ $CH_3CH_2CH_2COOH$

Fig. 4-4. Structure of Nalgiovensin.

It will be seen that the side-chains (a) and (b) in Fig. 4-4 do not bear so immediate and direct a relationship to the polyketide precursor as does (c).

4.5   The Structure of Sorigenin

α- and β-Sorinin, two compounds isolated from *Rhamnus japonicus* (fam. Rhamnaceae), are primeverosides of the naphthalenic lactones shown in Fig. 4-5:

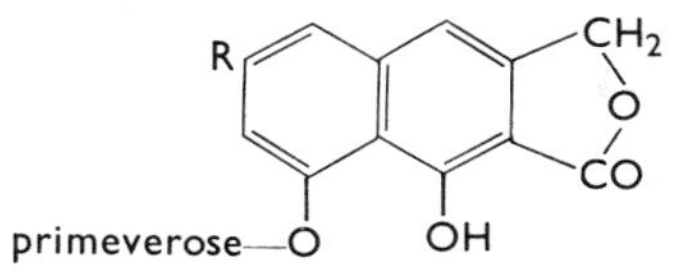

(primeverose = 6-[β-D-xylopyranosido]-D-glucose)

R = CH₃O   α-sorinin
R = H   β-sorinin

Fig. 4-5. α- and β-Sorinin.

β-Sorigenin, prepared by hydrolytic removal of the sugar residue, was at first assigned the structure shown in Fig. 4-6. It is evident that the derivation of this structure from a regular polyketide chain would require extensive secondary transformations of an unusual kind. The positions of the hydroxyl groups on the nucleus are not consonant with the placing of the carbonyl groups in one of the possible polyketide chains from which it may be presumed to be derived (Fig. 4-6a):

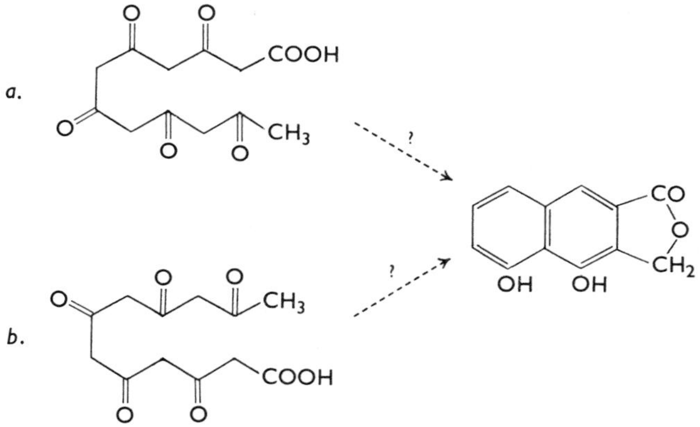

Fig. 4-6. Early (Incorrect) Formulation of β-Sorigenin, and the Question of its Origin.

If this difficulty were to be surmounted by another kind of cyclization (Fig. 4-6b), a new objection arises: in order to form the lactone ring in a β-sorigenin of the structure shown, the —CO— group would be formed from —CH₃, and the —CH₂— group from —COOH.

These objectionable features are easily removed by the revision of the structure of β-sorigenin to one in which the position of the lactone ring is the reverse of that shown in Fig. 4-6. The revised structure (see Fig. 4-5) is now derivable from a regular polyketide chain with two secondary modifications: the removal of an oxygen at the position indicated in Fig. 4-7 and oxidation of —CH₃ to —CH₂OH, a process which it will be shown in subsequent discussion is commonplace in nature.

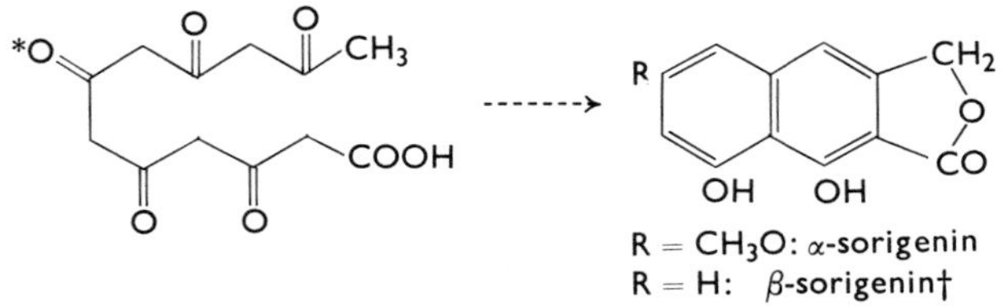

R = CH₃O: α-sorigenin
R = H: β-sorigenin†

† By removal of oxygen marked * in formula.

Fig. 4-7. Structure and Polyketide Origin of Sorigenins.

Substantiation of the structure of β-sorigenin was readily achieved by hydroxymethylation of a naphthol derivative that had previously been obtained in another study. The synthetic lactone was not identical with β-sorigenin dimethyl ether. That it was, however, the compound otherwise identical but with the "reversed" lactone was demonstrated by reduction of both lactones to the same glycol (Eq. 4-11).

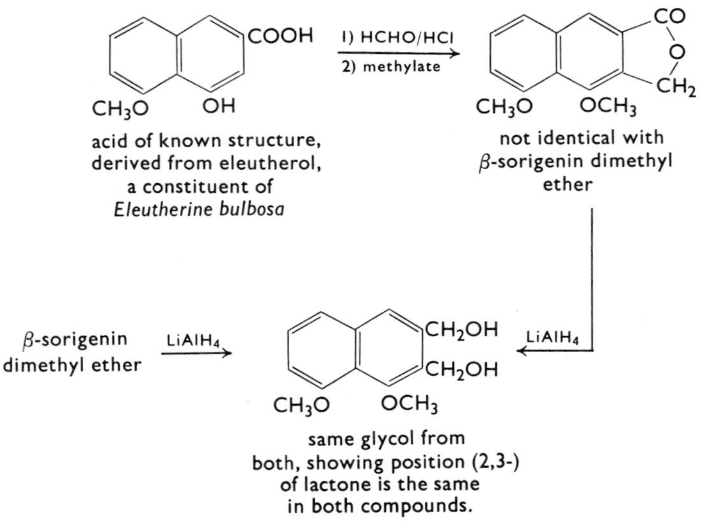

acid of known structure,
derived from eleutherol,
a constituent of
Eleutherine bulbosa

not identical with
β-sorigenin dimethyl
ether

β-sorigenin
dimethyl ether

same glycol from
both, showing position (2,3-)
of lactone is the same
in both compounds.

[Eq. 4-11]

Additional evidence for the orientation of the lactone ring in both α- and β-sorigenin is found in the infrared spectra of the compounds, both of which show carbonyl absorption at 1727 cm^{-1}. The two phthalides in Fig. 4-8 show the infrared absorptions given in the figure. It is clear that the phthalide in which the hydroxyl group and the lactone carbonyl group are in the 1,2 relationship corresponds in IR absorption with the natural compounds.

Fig. 4-8. Infrared Absorption of Model Phthalides.

4.6   Confirmation of the Acetate Hypothesis by Labeling Experiments

The early hypothesis that compounds formed by the linear combination of C_2-units that were derived ultimately from acetic acid received its first direct confirmation by the observation that 6-methylsalicylic acid formed by *Penicillium griseofulvum* to which 1-^{14}C-acetate had been fed was labeled at the positions predicted by the hypothesis (Eq. 4-12):

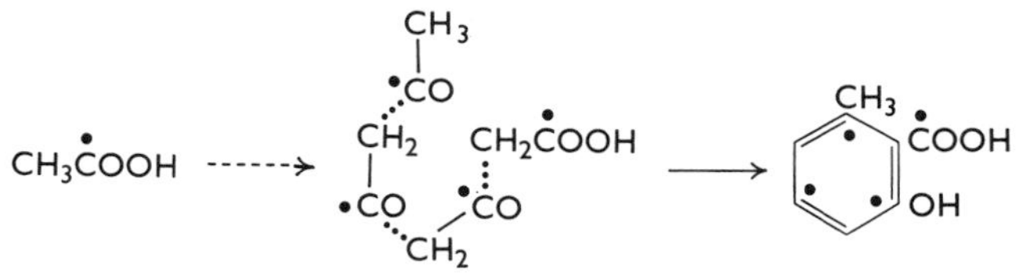

[Eq. 4-12]

Orsellinic acid, a common constituent of many lichen compounds (Sec. 4-2) and a metabolite of several fungi, is produced from acetate in the same manner, with the difference that the oxygen that is lost in the formation of 6-methylsalicylic acid is retained in orsellinic acid. The latter is, indeed, one of the examples of complete conformity with the acetate hypothesis in which no secondary metabolic alterations occur (Fig. 4-1). Experiments on the biogenesis of orsellinic acid carried out with the use of acetic acid labeled with ^{14}C and ^{18}O gave another important result. While the ^{18}O/^{14}C ratio for the oxygen atoms attached to the nucleus (phenolic OH) is one half that of the acetic acid fed, the ^{18}O/^{14}C ratio in the carboxyl group shows that there is present only 25% of the original ^{18}O content (relative to ^{14}C). This shows that additional ^{16}O was introduced into the carboxyl group, probably by hydrolysis of the coenzyme A ester as the final step (Eq. 4-13).

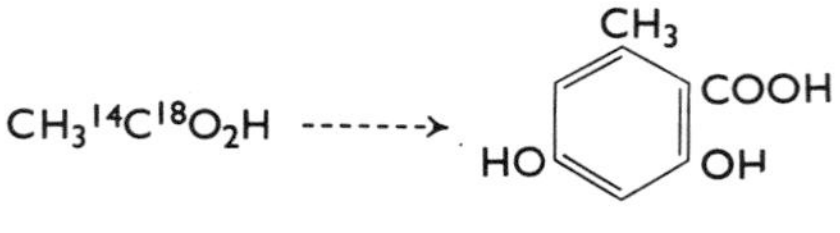

$$CH_3{}^{14}C^{18}O_2H \dashrightarrow$$

  a. C—O groupings in ring had $^{18}O/^{14}C$ ratio one half that of $CH_3{}^{14}C^{18}O_2H$ fed.
  b. COOH group contained one-quarter the amount of ^{18}O present in $CH_3{}^{14}C^{18}O_2H$ used, probably as the consequence of the introduction of ^{16}O by hydrolysis of CO—SCoA ester.

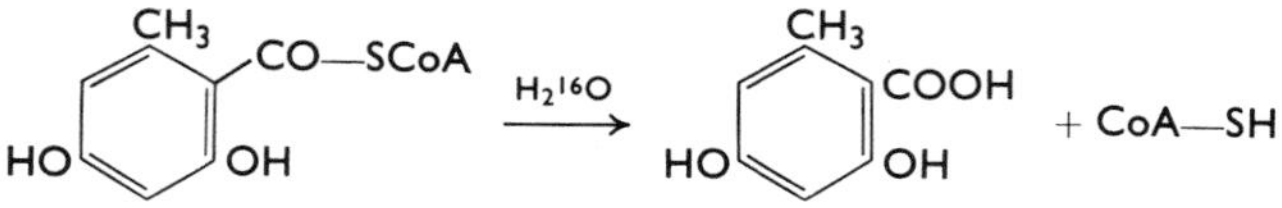

$$\xrightarrow{H_2{}^{16}O} \qquad + CoA{-}SH \qquad [Eq. 4\text{-}13]$$

During this early phase of the study of compounds that appeared to be derived from acetic acid, numerous studies were carried out to show that the acetate hypothesis did indeed provide a satisfactory explanation of their biosynthesis. In Fig. 4-9 are summarized the results obtained from a selected few of such experiments, in which the fate of the labeled precursor is shown.

  a. 3-hydroxyphthalic acid
      $CH_3\overset{\bullet}{C}OOH$

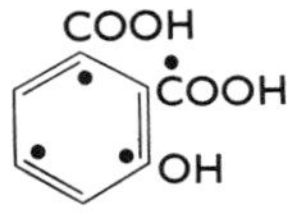

(*Penicillium islandicum*)

  b. 5-hydroxy-2-methyl-
      chromanone
      $CH_3\overset{\bullet}{C}OOH$

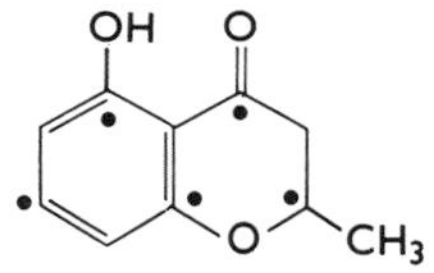

(*Daldinia concentrica*)

  c. curvularin
      $CH_3\overset{\bullet}{C}OOH$

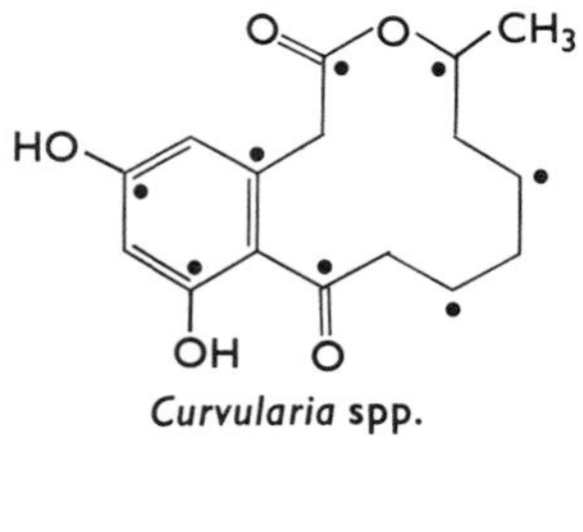

Curvularia spp.

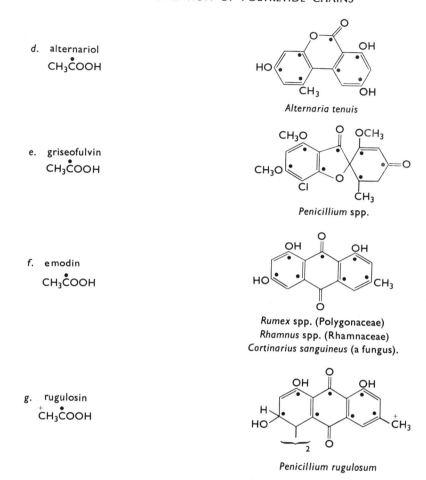

d. alternariol
CH₃COOH

Alternaria tenuis

e. griseofulvin
CH₃COOH

Penicillium spp.

f. emodin
CH₃COOH

Rumex spp. (Polygonaceae)
Rhamnus spp. (Rhamnaceae)
Cortinarius sanguineus (a fungus).

g. rugulosin
CH₃COOH

Penicillium rugulosum

Fig. 4-9. Labeling Patterns in Some Natural Compounds Formed in the Presence of ¹⁴C-labeled Acetate.

4.7 The Acetate-Malonate Pathway

In some of the early experiments in which ^{14}C-labeled acetic acid was fed to plants and fungi it was occasionally noticed that the "starting" end derived from the first acetic acid unit in the sequence CH_3CO---CH_2CO---CH_2CO--- was labeled to a somewhat greater extent than the remainder of the C_2 units. Although the reason for this slight imbalance in the labeling of a chain that appeared to be constructed from identical units was not understood for some years, the observation did suggest that there was some distinction between the initial C_2 unit and those that made up the balance of the assembly.

The explanation for these results became clear when it was discovered that the building of the C_2—C_2—C_2--- polyketide chain took place by the attachment of malonyl units rather than acetyl units to the "starter" acetyl group. This assembly process has been described in Chapter 3 in the discussion of fatty acid synthesis. The formation of polyketide chains differs from the synthesis of fatty acids in an important respect: in fatty acid synthesis the sequentially formed $RCOCH_2CO$—$SCoA$ intermediates are reduced to RCH_2CH_2CO—$SCoA$ before attachment of the next C_2 unit; in biosynthesis via the polyketide route, the $RCOCH_2COCH_2$---CO—$SCoA$ chain remains intact until cyclization occurs.

How the highly reactive poly-β-keto chain is stabilized until the assembly is complete and ready for cyclization is not known with certainty. It is highly probable that it exists as the poly-enol (Fig. 4-10), which may be stabilized by hydrogen bonding to a suitably oriented enzyme surface or by chelation with metal ions.

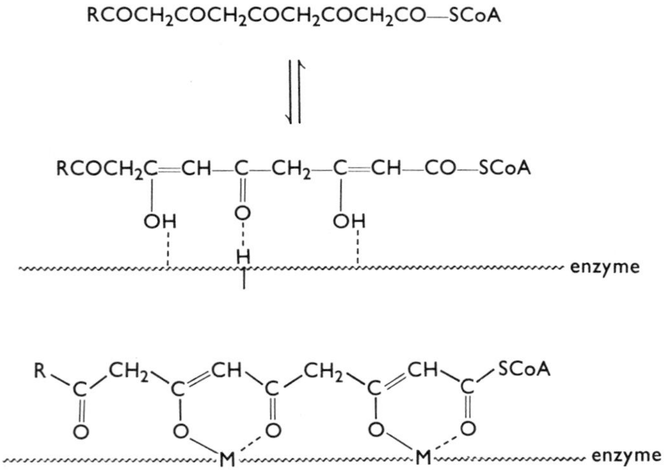

Fig. 4-10. Possible Stabilization of Poly-β-keto Chain by Attachment in Enol Form to Enzyme through H-bonds or Metal Chelation.

Experimental evidence for the acetate-malonate (rather than the acetate-acetate) course for the condensation leading to polyketides was obtained soon after the existence and significance of malonyl CoA was recognized.

When *Penicillium urticae* was grown in the presence of diethyl 2-^{14}C-malonate, the 6-methylsalicylic acid that was formed was unlabeled in the CH_3—C portion of the molecule; all of the radioactivity was found in the carbon dioxide formed upon Kuhn-Roth oxidation, and none in the acetic acid (Eq. 4-14a):

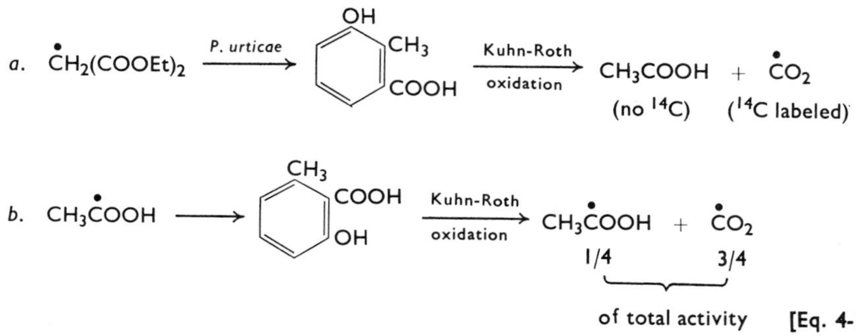

a. $\overset{\bullet}{C}H_2(COOEt)_2$ $\xrightarrow{P.\ urticae}$ [benzene ring with OH, CH_3, COOH substituents] $\xrightarrow[\text{oxidation}]{\text{Kuhn-Roth}}$ CH_3COOH + $\overset{\bullet}{C}O_2$

(no ^{14}C)   (^{14}C labeled)

b. $CH_3\overset{\bullet}{C}OOH$ $\longrightarrow$ [benzene ring with CH_3, COOH, OH substituents] $\xrightarrow[\text{oxidation}]{\text{Kuhn-Roth}}$ $CH_3\overset{\bullet}{C}OOH$ + $\overset{\bullet}{C}O_2$

$\underbrace{\quad 1/4 \qquad\qquad 3/4 \quad}$

of total activity   [Eq. 4-14]

It will be recalled that when 1-^{14}C-acetate is fed, about one-fourth of the radio-activity is found in the acetic acid and three-fourths in the carbon dioxide (Eq. 4-14b).

A detailed study of the labeling pattern in penicillic acid, a metabolic product produced by *Penicillium cyclopium*, provided excellent evidence for the acetate-malonate route of polyketide biosynthesis. Penicillic acid is a product of secondary transformation of orsellinic acid according to the scheme shown in Eq. 4-15. The results of the feeding of suitably labeled precursors to the fungus are shown in the equation. The source of the atoms comprising the skeleton of penicillic acid is shown by 1-^{14}C-acetate labeling.

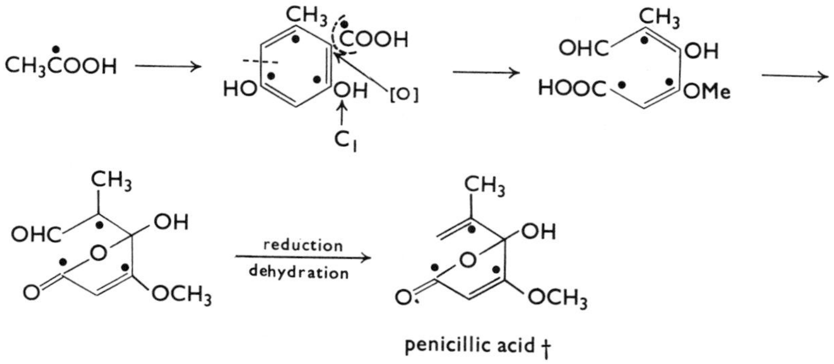

$CH_3\overset{\bullet}{C}OOH$ $\longrightarrow$ [structure with CH₃, COOH, HO, OH, C₁] $\xrightarrow{[O]}$ [structure with CH₃, OHC, OH, HOOC, OMe] $\longrightarrow$

[structure with CH₃, OHC, OH, O, OCH₃] $\xrightarrow[\text{dehydration}]{\text{reduction}}$ [structure with CH₃, OH, O, OCH₃]

penicillic acid †

Thus:

[structure: $^7CH_3$, positions 5, 4, 6 COOH, HO 3, 2, OH]

$\longrightarrow$

[structure: 7 CH₃, 5, 4, OH, O 6, O 3, 2, OCH₃]

[Eq. 4-15]

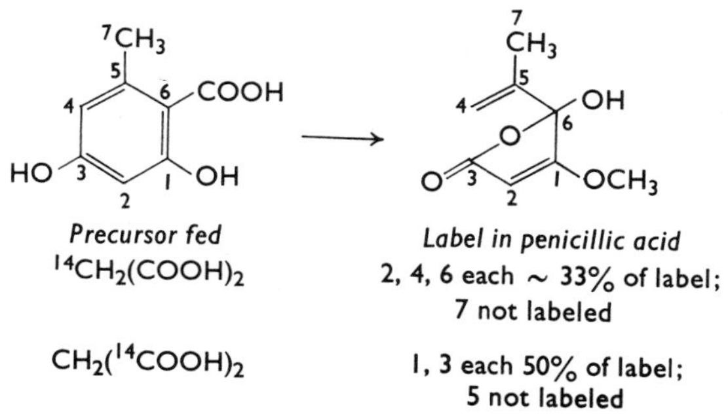

Precursor fed
$^{14}CH_2(COOH)_2$

Label in penicillic acid
2, 4, 6 each ~ 33% of label;
7 not labeled

$CH_2(^{14}COOH)_2$

1, 3 each 50% of label;
5 not labeled

† See Chapter 15

These findings show decisively that an acetate "starter" group reacts with malonate units to assemble the chain which forms the final orsellinic acid—penicillic acid structure.

4.8 "Starter Units" Other than Acetate

The compounds described in the foregoing sections are "acetate" derived; that is, they are formed by the addition of C_2 units, in the form of malonyl coenzyme A, with concomitant loss of CO_2, to an initial acetyl coenzyme A. The addition of C_2 units to "starting" coenzyme A esters of the general type RCO—SCoA is a well recognized biosynthetic process which, it will be at once apparent, can lead to a wide variety of polyketide-derived compounds of an extraordinary diversity of structure.

One of the clearest cases of this kind, and one that provides in addition a most persuasive demonstration of the intermediate polyketide chain, is found in a group of constituents of Tigaso oil, produced from *Campnosperma* species (fam. Anacardiaceae). These compounds appear to be produced from long-chain fatty acids by chain extension with C_2 units. Campnospermonol (Fig. 4-11c), a phenol, is evidently the product of dehydration of the cyclohexenone derivative (Fig. 4-11b). The latter is clearly the simple aldol related to the modified polyketide precursor formed from oleic acid (presumably as oleyl CoA) and malonyl CoA (Fig. 4-11a):

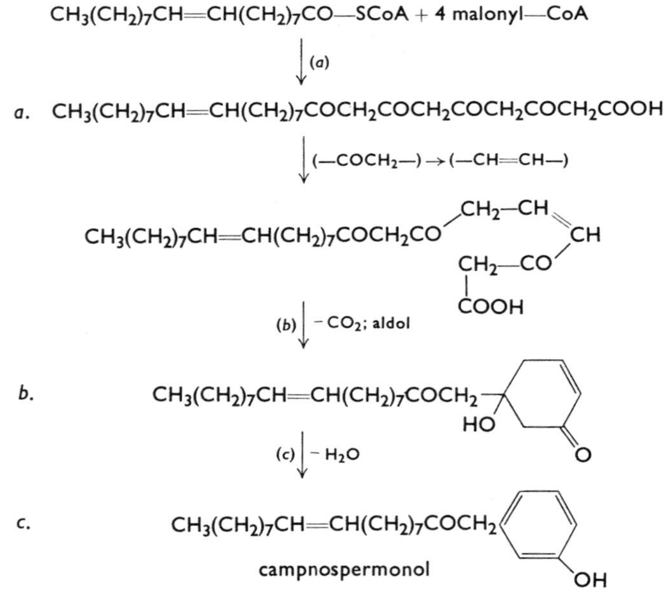

$$CH_3(CH_2)_7CH{=}CH(CH_2)_7CO{-}SCoA + 4\ malonyl{-}CoA$$

$$\downarrow (a)$$

a. $CH_3(CH_2)_7CH{=}CH(CH_2)_7COCH_2COCH_2COCH_2COCH_2COOH$

$$\downarrow (-COCH_2-)\rightarrow(-CH{=}CH-)$$

$CH_3(CH_2)_7CH{=}CH(CH_2)_7COCH_2CO$

$$(b)\ \Big\downarrow\ -CO_2;\ aldol$$

b. $CH_3(CH_2)_7CH{=}CH(CH_2)_7COCH_2$

$$(c)\ \Big\downarrow\ -H_2O$$

c. $CH_3(CH_2)_7CH{=}CH(CH_2)_7COCH_2$

campnospermonol

Fig. 4-11. Biosynthesis of *Campnosperma* Compounds. Compounds (b) and (c) are Present in Tigaso Oil.

Other anacardiaceous plants are characterized by a closely allied class of compounds, the relationship of which to a common course of biosynthesis is a striking demonstration of the close relationship between botanical affinity and unique chemical constitution. Several of these compounds, along with a suggested course of biosynthesis, are shown in Fig. 4-12 and Eq. 4-16.

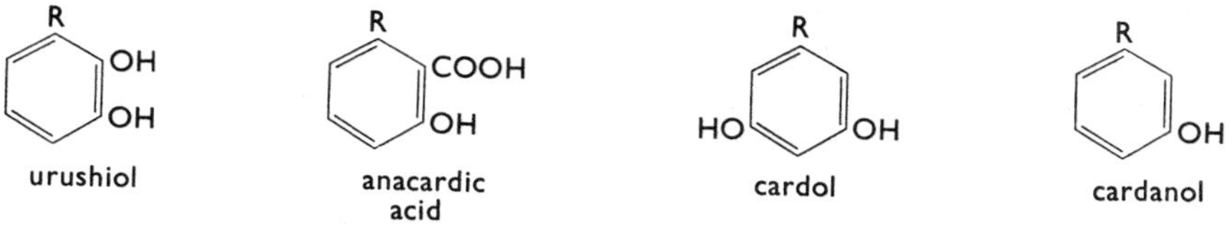

R = *n*-C$_{15}$: The natural compounds are difficultly separable mixtures which possess *cis*-$\Delta 8$, $\Delta 8:11$ and $\Delta 8:11:14$ unsaturation in the C$_{15}$ side chain. Thus, they represent the residual portions of a palmitoleic starter unit, or of the corresponding dienic, trienic acids, with unsaturation in the typical linoleic and linolenic pattern.

Fig. 4-12. Typical Phenols from Plants of the Family Anacardiaceae.

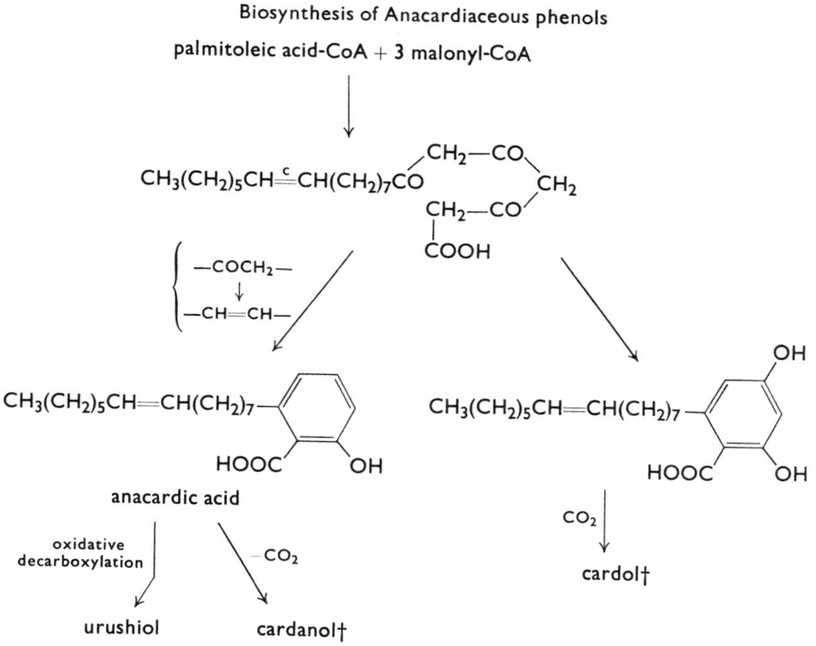

Biosynthesis of Anacardiaceous phenols

palmitoleic acid-CoA + 3 malonyl-CoA

[Eq. 4-16]

† Alternatively, loss of CO_2 may occur at the polyketide stage prior to cyclization, or may be concomitant with cyclization.

Further known modifications of structure in the anacardiaceous phenols include compounds with C_{17} and C_{19} side-chains, and compounds that possess 4-alkyl- (or -alkenyl or -alkadienyl) catechol structures.

Structure proof of the naturally occurring compounds of these classes has often been difficult because of their occurrence as mixtures (Fig. 4-12). Gross structural details have been easily ascertained by hydrogenation of the side-chain unsaturation and identification of the resulting alkylated catechols or phenols as the dimethyl ethers. Oxidative (e.g., ozonolytic) degradation of the unsaturated side chains served to locate the positions of unsaturation. Many of these compounds, in particular urushiol, the toxic principle of the common anacardiaceous plant *Rhus toxicodendron* L., or poison ivy, are powerful vesicants and produce a severe dermatitis when they come into contact with the skin.

4.9 Lichen Compounds

Lichens, which are symbionts consisting of a fungus and an alga growing together in a composite structure, produce an extraordinary range of organic compounds of a wide variety of structural types. The commonest of the lichen compounds are the depsides and depsidones, of which lecanoric acid and gyrophoric acid represent the simplest of the class (Fig. 4-13):

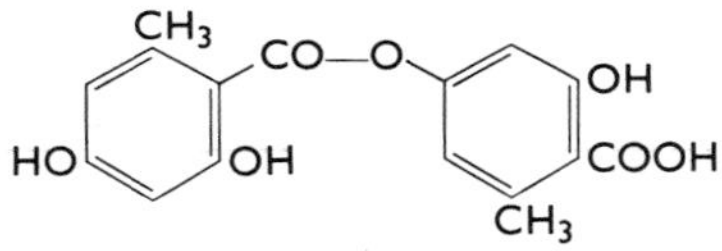

lecanoric acid

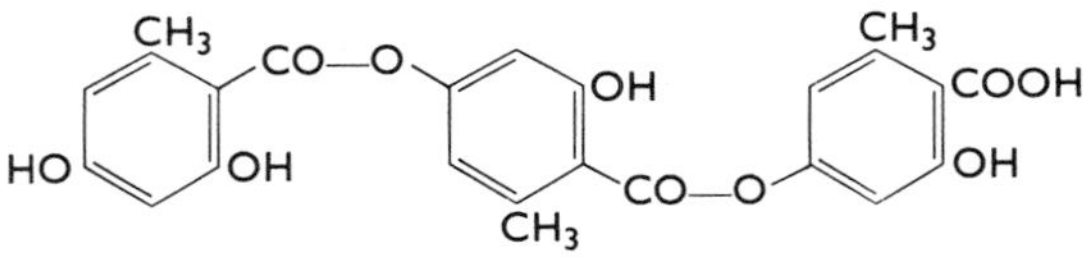

gyrophoric acid

Fig. 4-13. Acetate-malonate-derived Depsides.

It will be seen that lecanoric acid is simply the ester formed by the O-acylation of one molecule of orsellinic acid by another. Gyrophoric acid is the corresponding triester. It was pointed out in Sec. 4.6 that orsellinic acid is formed in a sequence that ends in a terminal hydrolysis of a derivative, presumably the coenzyme A ester. It is apparent that an orsellinic acid-CoA could serve as an effective esterifying species which, by reaction with the phenolic hydroxyl group of another, will yield lecanoric acid. The formation of gyrophoric acid can be explained in the same way (Eq. 4-17):

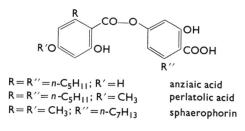

$$\text{[Eq. 4-17]}$$

The study of biosynthesis in lichens is experimentally difficult, in part because of their very slow rate of growth. Nevertheless, labeling experiments have been performed in a number of cases, with results that confirm the expectation that the orsellinic acid units of lecanoric and gyrophoric acids are derived by the acetate-malonate pathway.

Lichen depsides display a range of structural variation that provides excellent examples of what appears, but has not been proved to be, the use of a variety of starter units and modes of cyclization. Some simple alkyl homologs of lecanoric acid are shown in Fig. 4-14. It is apparent that these can be constructed by chain extension of an alkanoic acid by malonate units (Eq. 4-18a). It is equally apparent that the derivation of these depsides could as well be accounted for by the partial and selective reduction of the distal portion of a polyketide chain (Eq. 4-18b and c).

$R = R'' = n\text{-}C_5H_{11}; R' = H$ anziaic acid
$R = R'' = n\text{-}C_5H_{11}; R' = CH_3$ perlatolic acid
$R = R' = CH_3; R'' = n\text{-}C_7H_{13}$ sphaerophorin

Fig. 4-14. Some Representative Lichen Depsides.

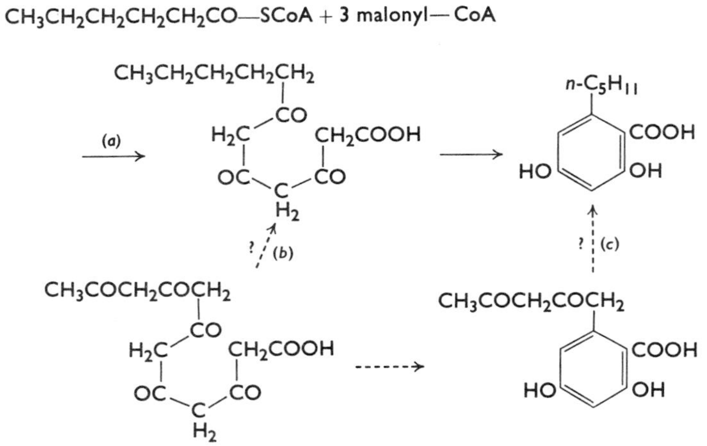

$$CH_3CH_2CH_2CH_2CH_2CO—SCoA + 3 \text{ malonyl—CoA}$$

[Eq. 4-18]

Anziaic acid is probably formed by route a of Eq. 4-18, in which hexanoyl CoA is extended by three C_2 units derived from malonate. The addition of four malonate units to the C_6 acid leads to an alkyl polyketide precursor whose cyclization leaves one carbonyl group outside of the benzene ring. The resulting depside thus contains a C-alkanoyl orsellinic acid. The lichen depside olivetoric acid contains both C-alkyl and C-alkanoyl orsellinic acid units in its structure (Fig. 4-15):

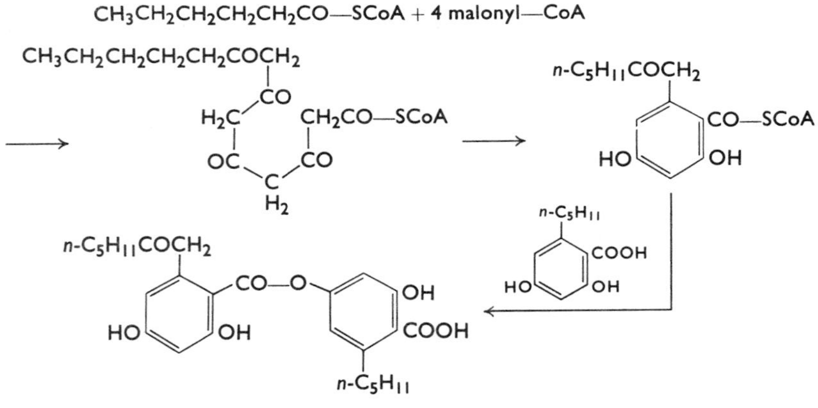

$$CH_3CH_2CH_2CH_2CH_2CO—SCoA + 4 \text{ malonyl—CoA}$$

olivetoric acid

Fig. 4-15. Probable Course for the Biosynthesis of Olivetoric Acid.

The secondary metabolic products of lichens are probably those of the fungal partner of the symbiotic pair, the alga providing the photosynthetic apparatus for the production of the primary metabolites required for synthesis. Although there are only a few examples of the separation and separate culture of the individual symbionts, in the several instances where this has been accomplished it has been observed that the fungus, grown in separate culture, has produced compounds (but none of them depsides) originally isolated from the lichen. Depsides and depsidones (Chap. 14) are peculiar to lichens, and it appears that the algal partner is in some unexplained way necessary for the coupling of the two phenolic units (i.e., orsellinic acid → lecanoric acid). Indeed, when the fungal partners of several depside-producing lichens were grown in isolated culture, no depsides were formed; instead, the "monomeric" acids (e.g., orsellinic acid) were produced by the fungus although the complete system—the lichen—contained no free orsellinic acid.

4.10 Anthraquinones

Both lichens and fungi produce anthraquinones, most of which represent model examples of the cyclization of extended polyketide systems. An example is endocrocin (Fig. 4-1) in which the complete pattern of oxygenation of the precursor is retained in the final product.

In the preceding section there were described the depsides derived from the addition of three and four malonate units to an initial hexanoic acid starter unit (e.g., olivetoric acid, Fig. 4-15). The lichen anthraquinone solorinic acid (Fig. 4-16) is evidently the product of further extension of the chain derived from the hexanoyl starter, with addition of seven C_2 units:

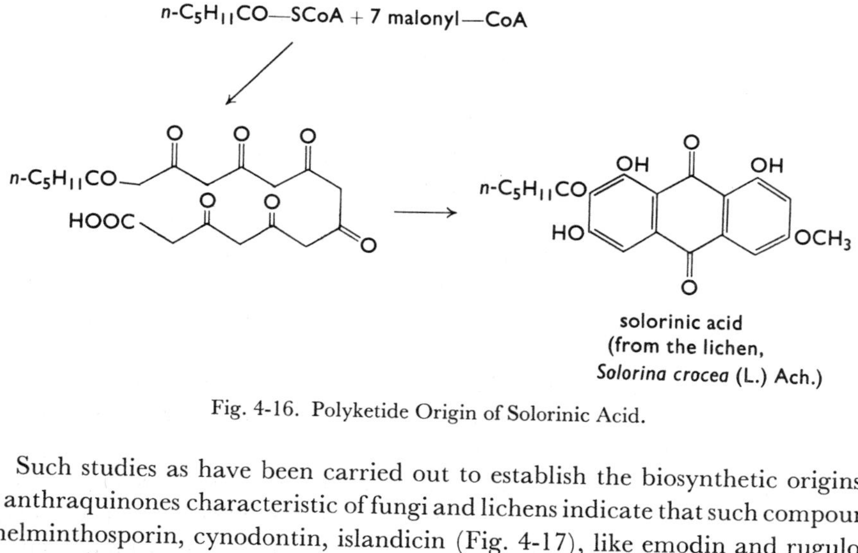

$$n\text{-}C_5H_{11}CO\text{—}SCoA + 7\ \text{malonyl—CoA}$$

solorinic acid
(from the lichen,
Solorina crocea (L.) Ach.)

Fig. 4-16. Polyketide Origin of Solorinic Acid.

Such studies as have been carried out to establish the biosynthetic origins of the anthraquinones characteristic of fungi and lichens indicate that such compounds as helminthosporin, cynodontin, islandicin (Fig. 4-17), like emodin and rugulosin (Fig. 4-9), are formed by the acetate-malonate pathway. A significant result that emerges from some of these investigations is that oxygen (as nuclear hydroxyl groups) often appears in "unexpected" positions and is often lacking in "expected"

using CH₃C̈OOH:

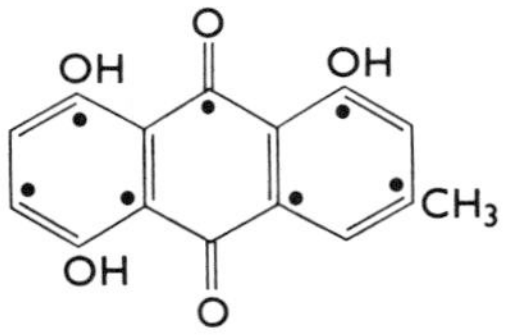

helminthosporin
(*Helminthosporium gramineum*)

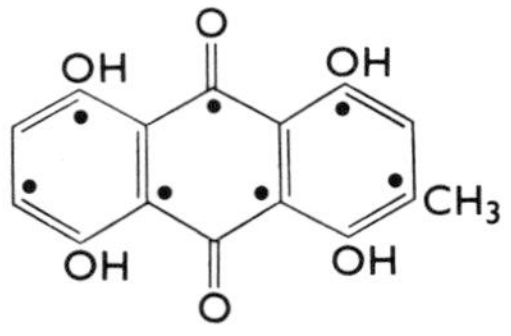

cynodontin
(*Pyrenochaeta terrestris*)

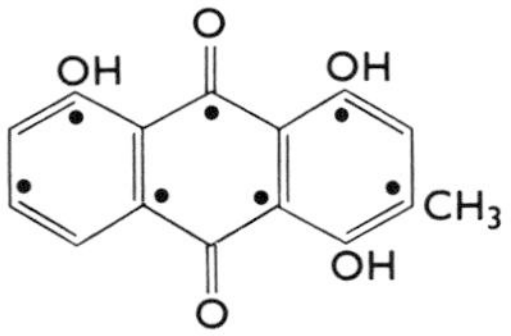

islandicin
(*Penicillium islandicum*)

Fig. 4-17. Fungal Anthraquinones with Hydroxyl Groups in Other Positions than Expected for Acetate-Malonate Origin.

positions. It is to be noted that because of the practical difficulties in identifying by degradation procedures all of the labeled atoms in compounds as complex as anthraquinones of these kinds, certain of the experimental procedures that have been used were designed to ascertain only whether a particular radioactivity predicted by the theory corresponded with a single degradation. For example, helminthosporin, produced by a fungus growing on a medium containing carboxyl-labeled acetate, would, according to the acetate hypothesis, contain the distribution of label shown in Fig. 4-17. Kuhn-Roth oxidation yields acetic acid, which should contain one-seventh of the radioactivity of the quinone. The experimental finding was in perfect agreement with this expectation: helminthosporin with a specific activity of 2770×10^2 (arbitrary units) was oxidized by the Kuhn-Roth procedure to give acetic acid having a specific activity of 399×10^2. The ratio of activities is $2770/399 = 6.95$.

The removal of oxygen in the biosynthesis of fungal anthraquinones is readily rationalized, for the process —COCH₂— → —CH=CH— is widely encountered in biosynthesis by the acetate-malonate pathway. A simple example is the occurrence of 6-methylsalicyclic acid and orsellinic acid, the carbon labeling patterns of which are identical. Because of the prevalence of this reductive step in phenolic biosynthesis of the kind that has been described there is a disarming facility in erecting conjectures as to the biosynthesis of a compound whose origin has not been studied with the use of tracer methods. A noteworthy case in point is found in certain anthraquinones found in higher plants.

Certain genera of the plant families Verbenaceae, Rubiaceae, and Bignoniaceae contain the simple anthraquinone, 2-methylanthraquinone (Fig. 4-18):

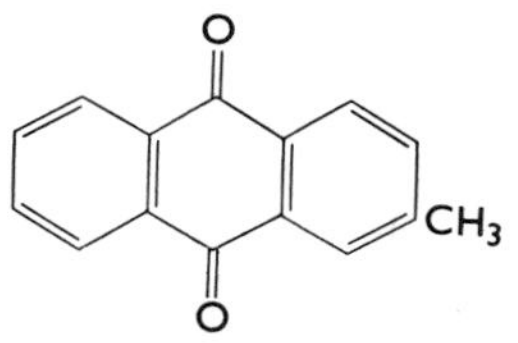

Fig. 4-18. 2-Methylanthraquinone.

The relationship of this quinone to emodin (Fig. 4-9) is obvious: they differ only in the three phenolic hydroxyl groups present in the latter. 2-Methylanthraquinone is not, however, acetate-derived (except in small part, as will be indicated below). A clue as to its probable biosynthesis is found in the observation that accompanying it in the plant (teak; fam. Verbenaceae) are the β,β-dimethylallylnaphthoquinone and the corresponding naphthol shown in Fig. 4-19 (a, b). Further, several species of *Galium* and *Rubia* (fam. Rubiaceae) contain anthraquinones along with one or more of the naphthalene derivatives shown in Fig. 4-19.

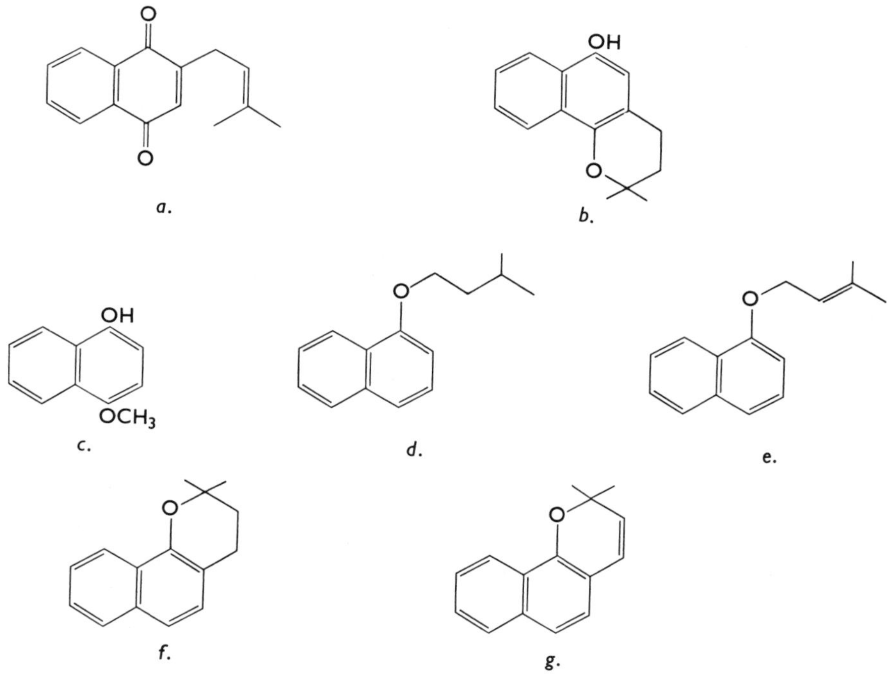

Fig. 4-19. Naphthalene Derivatives Accompanying Anthraquinones in *Verbenaceae* (a, b) and *Rubiaceae* (c, d, e, f, g).

The *in vitro*, acid-catalyzed cyclization of 2-(γ,γ-dimethylallyl)-1,4-naphtho-quinone (Fig. 4-19a) to 2-methylanthraquinone, although proceeding under con-ditions that are far from physiological, does suggest that a similar cyclization can occur in the plant, and that naphthalene derivatives such as those in Fig. 4-19 (and others that are not shown) disclose the pattern of biosynthesis. The isopentyl frag-ment is derived from acetate by a pathway that is quite distinct from that described by the term "acetate-malonate pathway" as it has been used in this chapter. The naphthalene nucleus, too, is not "acetate derived," but has its origin (in part) in shikimic acid (Sec. 5.2). These conclusions derive from the following experiments with labeled precursors.

Alizarin is an anthraquinone found in the roots of madder (*Rubia tinctorum*). When 2-^{14}C-acetate was fed to madder plants, the alizarin isolated was radioactive but the incorporation of radioactivity was only 0.0069%.* Degradation of the alizarin showed that ring A contained no radioactivity, all of the label being found in rings B and C (but not located). Radioactive shikimic acid (1,6-^{14}C) was incor-porated to the extent of 0.77%, and all of the radioactivity was found in ring A (Fig. 4-20).

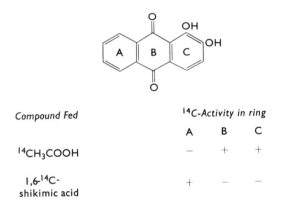

Compound Fed	^{14}C-Activity in ring		
	A	B	C
[14]CH$_3$COOH	−	+	+
1,6-^{14}C-shikimic acid	+	−	−

Fig. 4-20. Incorporation of Radioactivity into Alizarin in *Rubia tinctorum*.

Rubia tinctorum elaborates other anthraquinones as well, and in another experi-ment pseudopurpurin was isolated from plants that had been fed with 2-^{14}C-mevalonic acid. The labeling pattern of the quinone is shown in Fig. 4-21; and in Eq. 4-19 derivation of ring C from mevalonic acid is shown in brief form (a more extensive discussion of mevalonic acid metabolism will be found in a later chapter).

* Because of the active participation of acetate in the primary metabolic cycles, some incorpora-tion of activity is to be expected in most constituents of a plant to which it is fed.

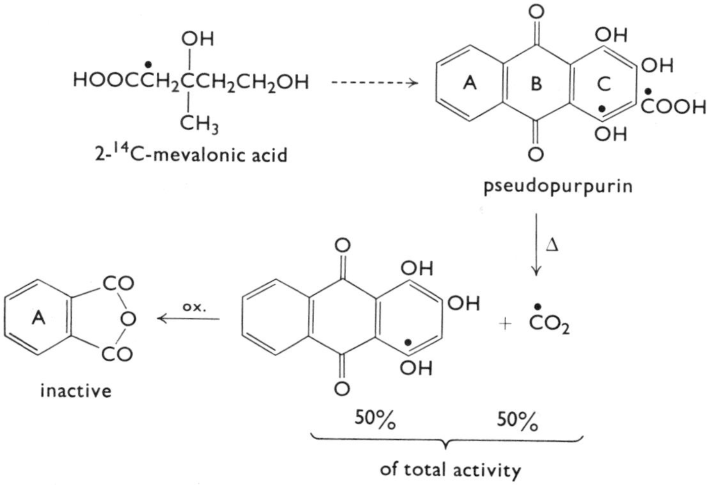

Fig. 4-21. Incorporation of Radioactivity from Mevalonic Acid into Pseudopurpurin in *Rubia tinctorum*.

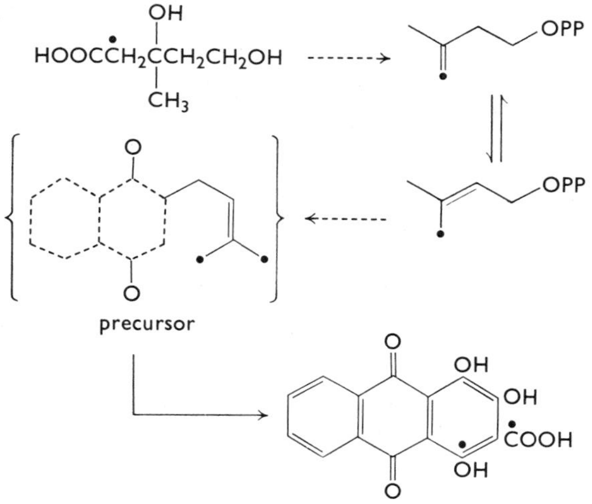

[Eq. 4-19]

These experiments do not, of course, show the manner in which the hydroxyl groups are introduced into the ring. An additional observation made in this study is illuminating, for it supports the view that alizarin is also mevalonate-derived (C-ring). The pseudopurpurin isolated had over twice the specific activity of the alizarin isolated from the same experiment. This suggests that pseudopurpurin is closer to the precursor (mevalonic acid) in the synthetic pathway than is alizarin, the latter being formed by loss of the carbon atom that is present as the —COOH group in pseudopurpurin. Rubiadin, 1,3-dihydroxy-2-methylanthraquinone, isolated at the same time, had a slightly higher specific activity than the pseudo-purpurin and three times that of alizarin.*

These experiments using higher plants suggest that fungal metabolism and the metabolism of the green plants may differ fundamentally in respect to the synthesis of anthraquinones. Indeed, it has been suggested that perhaps the synthesis of fungal anthraquinones may also proceed by a pathway involving shikimic acid rather than, as has been indicated in earlier sections of this chapter, by the acetate-malonate pathway. While this seems unlikely, it will be recalled that conclusions regarding the origin of fungal anthraquinones were in most cases based upon an incomplete identification of all of the skeletal carbon atoms. It is clear that there is room for further investigation of this point.

4.11   Introduction of Additional Substituents into Compounds Derived by the Acetate Pathway. Carbon Alkylation

The compounds listed in Figs. 4-1 and 4-9 follow the acetate hypothesis in a "regular" way; those in Fig. 4-1 retain all of the oxygen atoms of the polyketide precursor (save those consumed in ring closures), while those of Fig. 4-9 have undergone one or more reductive changes in which $-CH_2CO-$ units have altered to $-CH=CH-$ or $-CH_2CH_2-$. In all of the examples in these figures, however, the carbon skeleton of the chain of C_2 units remains and no additional groups are present. These compounds are, however, exceptional and represent a class that is far outnumbered by acetate-derived compounds that have been modified by further substitution.

The principal variations found in the polyketide-derived compounds of nature arise from the introduction, by carbon alkylation, of methyl groups and groups derived from the γ,γ-dimethylallyl grouping. The latter will be dealt with in a later chapter. Carbon-methylated compounds are commonplace among natural products. The source of the methyl groups is methionine (and, through the one-carbon metabolic pathways, formic acid). The methyl transfer reaction from S-adenosyl-methionine to an anionic carbon (or oxygen or nitrogen) atom has been formulated earlier (Eq. 2-50), and represents a mechanistically unexceptional reaction. Some typical examples of C-methylated, acetate-derived compounds are presented in Fig. 4-22. It will be noted that alkylation has occurred at carbon which, in the polyketide chain, is flanked by activating (carbonyl) groups; that is at the methylene groups of $-COCH_2CO-$.

---

* Further discussion of biosynthesis involving mevalonic acid and shikimic acid will be deferred until later chapters.

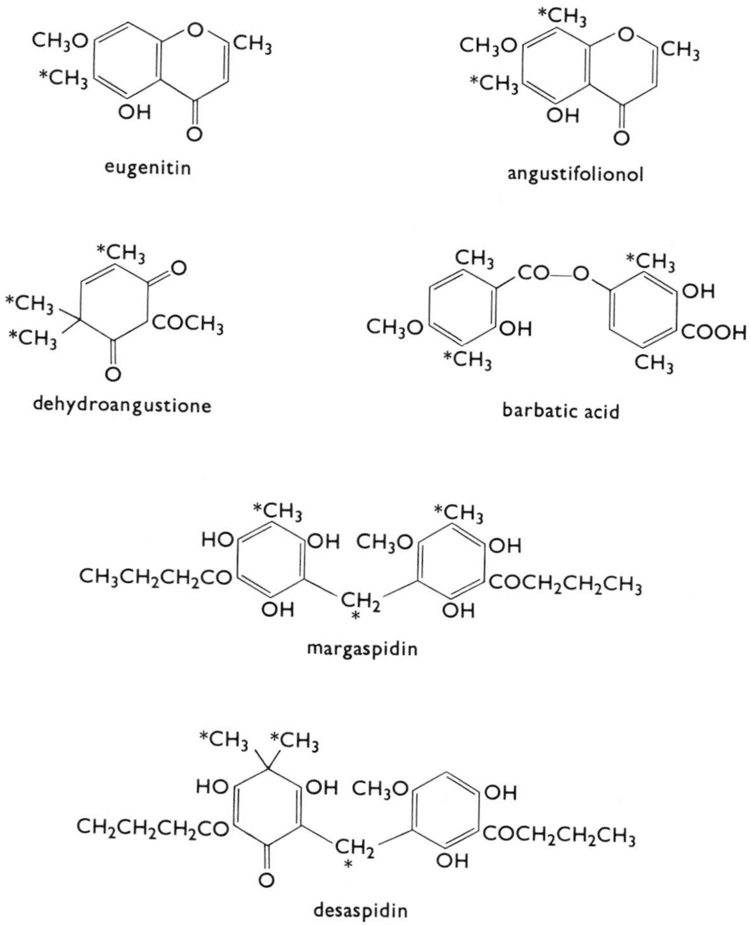

Fig. 4-22. Some Carbon-methylated Compounds of Acetate (Polyketide) Origin. "Extra" Methyl Groups Marked by *.

Since carbon-alkylation of phenols, and in particular of polyhydric phenols, is a well known reaction, it is not immediately obvious whether the introduction of the carbon-linked substituent occurs at the polyketide or the aromatic stage. That the former reaction occurs has been established in some cases; whether alkylation at the phenol stage also occurs cannot be ruled out.

An early demonstration of carbon-methylation by a one-carbon source (^{14}C-formic acid was used in the experiment) is found in studies on the biosynthesis of the fungal metabolite sclerotiorin (Eq. 4-20). When ^{14}C-acetic acid and ^{14}C-formic acid were supplied to the fungus (*Penicillium multicolor*), the labeling pattern observed was as shown in the following scheme (Eq. 4-20):

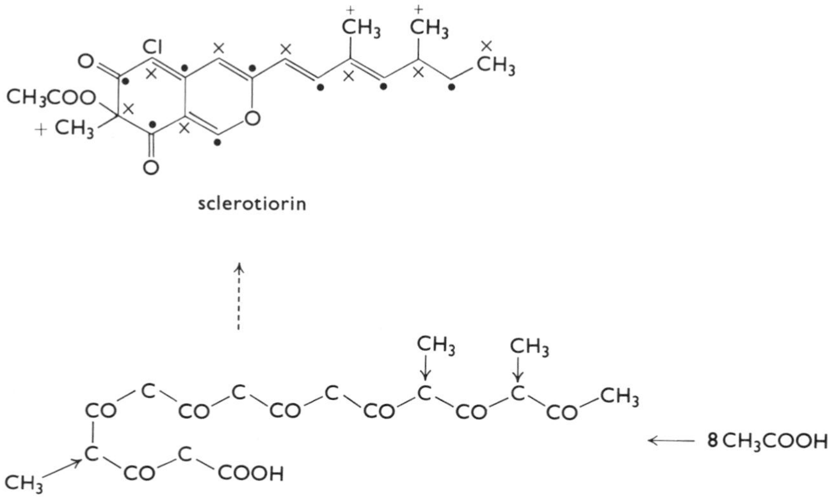

sclerotiorin

⟵ 8 CH$_3$COOH

$\bullet$ from CH$_3\overset{\bullet}{C}$OOH

$\times$ from $\overset{\times}{C}$H$_3$COOH

$+$ from H$\overset{+}{C}$OOH

[Eq. 4-20]

Citrinin, also acetate-derived, contains three "extra" one-carbon groups (two —CH$_3$, one —COOH), all of them derived from methionine (or, less efficiently, from formate) (Eq. 4-21). It is of special interest to note that propionate was found not to be utilized in the biosynthesis of citrinin, for *a priori* considerations would permit the assumption that the grouping ----CHCO---- could represent a unit of

$$\overset{|}{\underset{CH_3}{}}$$

propionic acid.

⟵ 5 CH$_3$COOH

citrinin

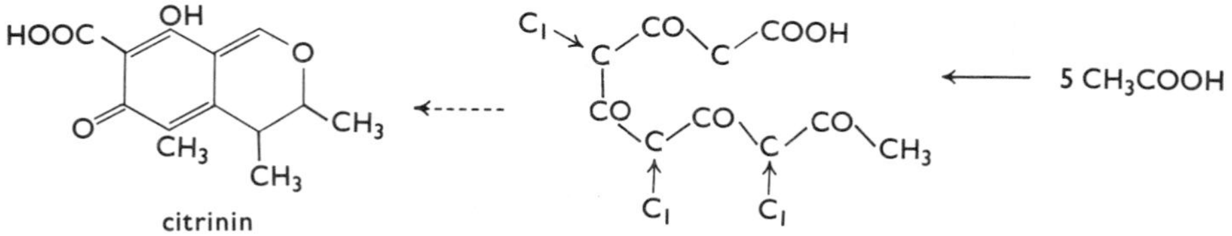

C$_I$ from ^{14}C-methionine or ^{14}C-formate.

[Eq. 4-21]

4.12 Carbon Alkylation in Lichen Compounds

Although lichen depsides represent a group of compounds in which one can discern a variety of structural modifications arising from what appears clearly to be an initial substitution of a one-carbon fragment into an acetate-derived precursor, proof of this has been difficult to obtain because of the relative difficulties of performing feeding experiments with these slow-growing organisms. Recently, however, several successful demonstrations of lichen biosynthesis have been achieved.

Some typical depsides containing "extra" carbon atoms are shown in Fig. 4-23.

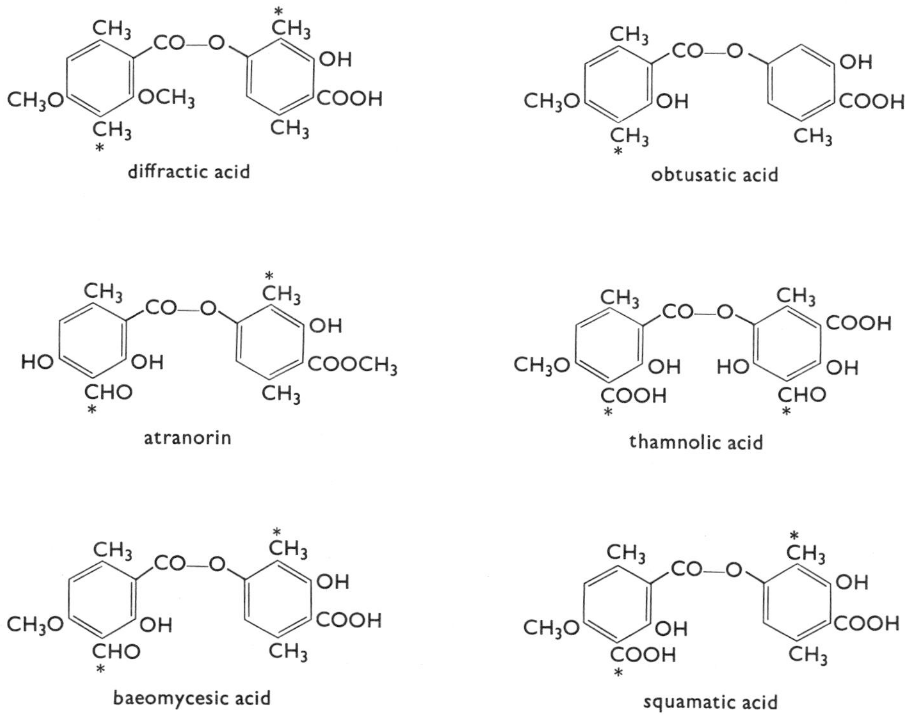

Fig. 4-23. Some Lichen Depsides Containing "Extra" One-carbon Substituents (*).

Atranorin is of special interest, for successful experiments on its biosynthesis in the thalli of the lichen *Parmelia tinctorum* have shown the origins of the formyl group and the "extra" methyl group, and in addition have provided evidence that carbon-methylation does not occur after aromatization has been completed. When $1\text{-}^{14}C$-acetate and ^{14}C-formate were provided to the lichen, labeled lecanoric acid and atranorin were produced. The labeling pattern found by degradation is shown in Eq. 4-22.

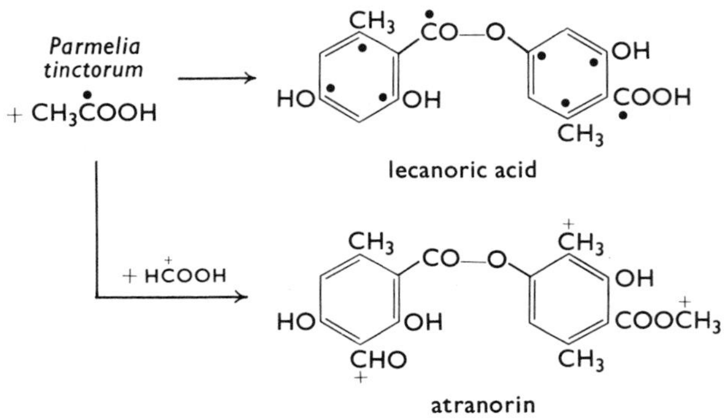

lecanoric acid

[Eq. 4-22]

atranorin

When labeled orsellinic acid was fed to the lichen, radioactive lecanoric acid was formed, but the atranorin produced at the same time was inactive (Eq. 4-23):

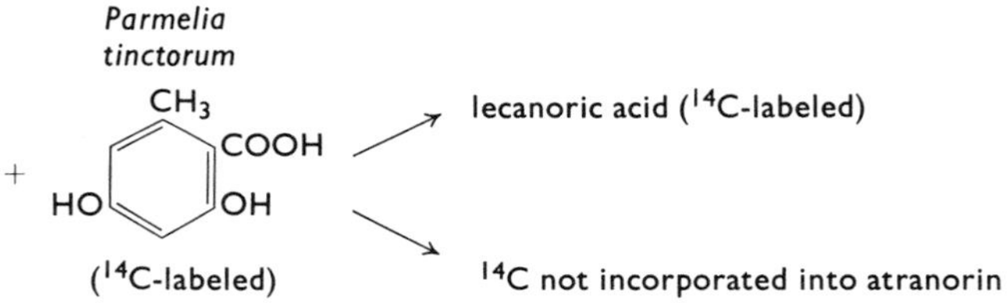

lecanoric acid (^{14}C-labeled)

^{14}C not incorporated into atranorin   [Eq. 4-23]

This result shows that the additional one-carbon substituents (CHO and CH_3) in atranorin are not introduced into preformed orsellinic acid or into lecanoric acid. It is the conclusion from these observations that in this lichen, alkylation (methylation) occurs at the polyketide stage, prior to cyclization to orsellinic acid.

4.13   Usnic Acid

A widely distributed constituent in lichens of a number of genera is usnic acid, a compound of great practical and theoretical interest. Its formation by oxidative coupling of two molecules of methylphloracetophenone will be considered in a later chapter; its relevance to the present discussion lies in the formation of the acetophenone derivative and in other aspects of the metabolism of the lichen in which it is found.

Usnea diffracta contains both usnic acid and diffractic acid (Eq. 4-24).

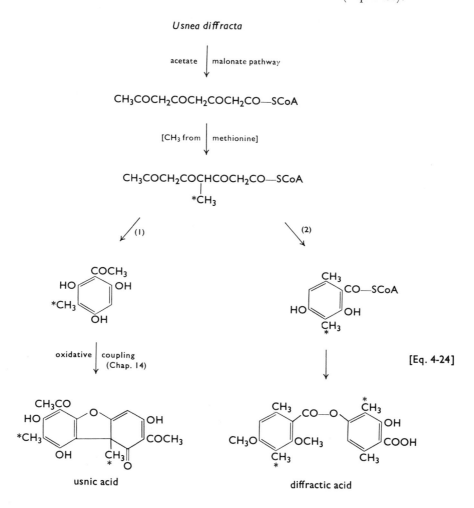

usnic acid   diffractic acid

It will be seen that the fundamental chain, consisting of four head-to-tail-linked —CH_2CO— units, cyclizes in the lichen in two ways to produce (1) the aceto-phenone derivative that gives usnic acid by oxidative coupling, and to produce (2) the orsellinic acid derivative that leads to diffractic acid, a depside. The "extra" methyl groups in usnic acid and diffractic acid are located on the same (i.e., cor-responding) carbon atoms in these two compounds, and can be regarded as having been introduced into the polyketide precursor prior to cyclization (Eq. 4-24). The biosynthesis of usnic acid is appropriately discussed in respect to the reaction that causes the linking of the two C_9-units, and will be deferred until Chapter 14.

4.14 Methylenebisphloroglucinols of Ferns

A class of compounds typically elaborated by ferns (for example, *Dryopteris* spp.) consists of two acyl-malonyl-derived, methylated phloroglucinol units coupled through a —CH₂— group. In Fig. 4-24 are shown some examples of these compounds.

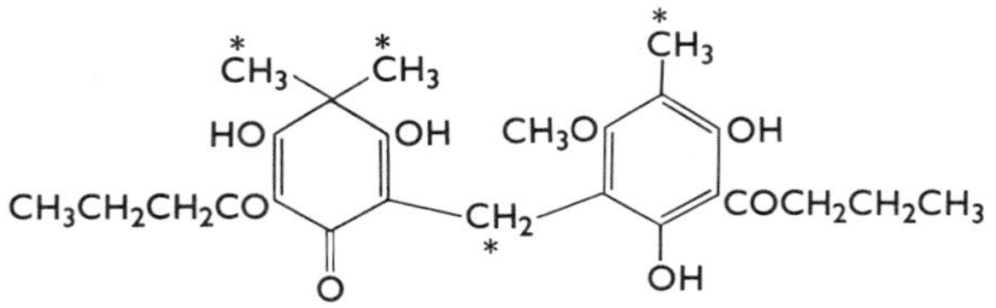

p-aspidin

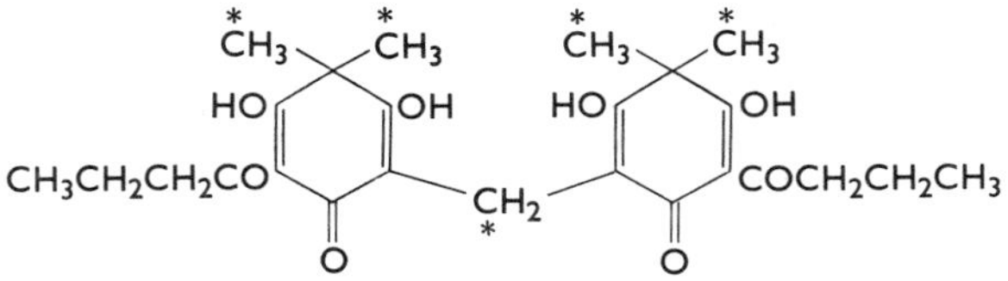

albaspidin

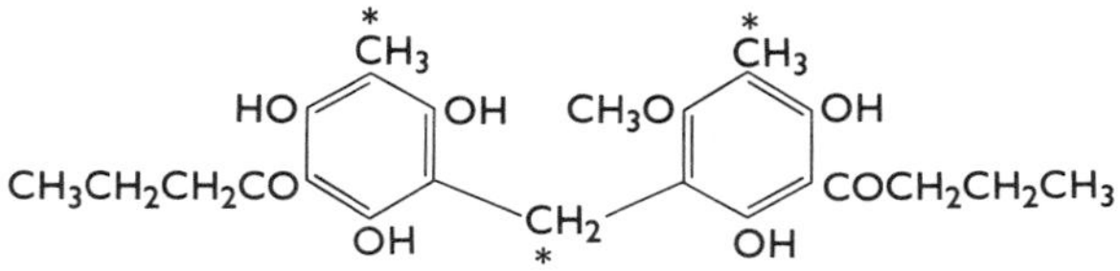

margaspidin

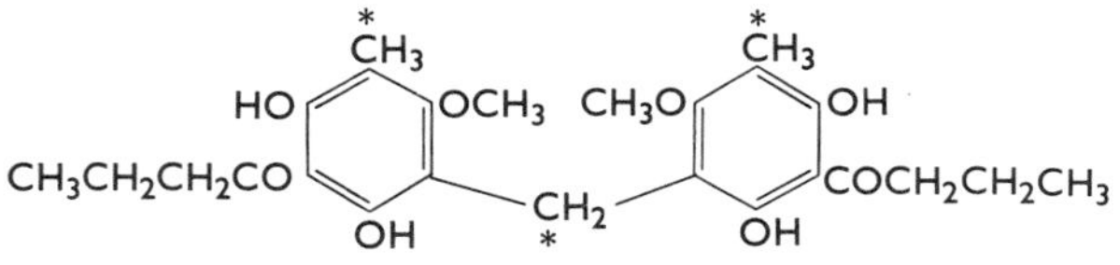

methylenebisaspidinol

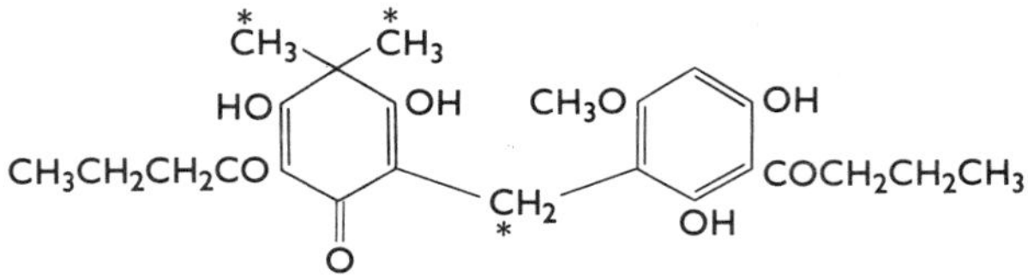

desaspidin

(*CH₃ = "extra" methyl groups from C₁-source)

Fig. 4-24. Methylenebisphloroglucinols of Ferns.

The origin of the aromatic or quinonoid nuclei of these compounds is readily rationalized on the hypothesis developed in the foregoing pages, and might be represented as in Eq. 4-25.

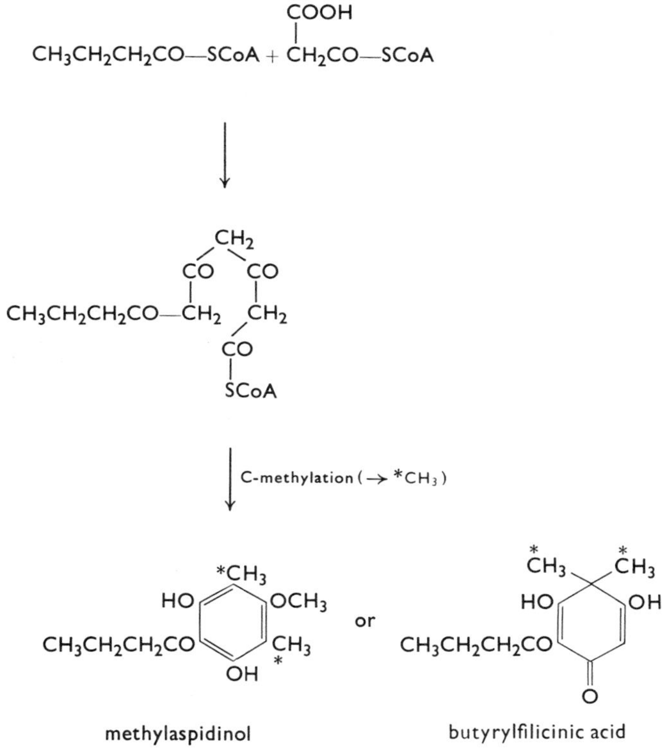

$$CH_3CH_2CH_2CO-SCoA + \overset{\displaystyle COOH}{\underset{}{CH_2CO-SCoA}}$$

$$\downarrow$$

CH$_2$
CO   CO
CH$_3$CH$_2$CH$_2$CO—CH$_2$ CH$_2$
CO
SCoA

$$\downarrow \text{C-methylation} (\rightarrow *CH_3)$$

*CH$_3$
HO   OCH$_3$
CH$_3$CH$_2$CH$_2$CO   CH$_3$ or
OH   *

*CH$_3$ *CH$_3$
HO   OH
CH$_3$CH$_2$CH$_2$CO
O
[Eq. 4-25]

methylaspidinol   butyrylfilicinic acid

There has, however, been adduced experimental evidence that the actual biosynthetic route to the phloroglucinols of the methylaspidinol type is not the direct pathway shown in Eq. 4-25, but is in fact a variant of this.

First of all, experiments in which labeled methionine has been used have demonstrated that the methyl groups of the rings and the methylene group that connects the rings are derived from methionine, presumably by carbon-alkylation at the polyketide stage.

The linking of the two rings through the —CH$_2$— group can be formulated as in Eq. 4-26, in which an oxidation step provides the means for formation of the carbon-carbon bond. The source of the bridging —CH$_2$— group is seen to be a methyl group derived originally from methionine. (It should be noted that the reactions shown in Eq. 4-26 may be equally well represented for a monomethyl ether of the original acylphloroglucinol, for the —CH_3 group involved in the oxidative coupling is flanked by two hydroxyl groups, either of which may participate in the reaction as it is written.)

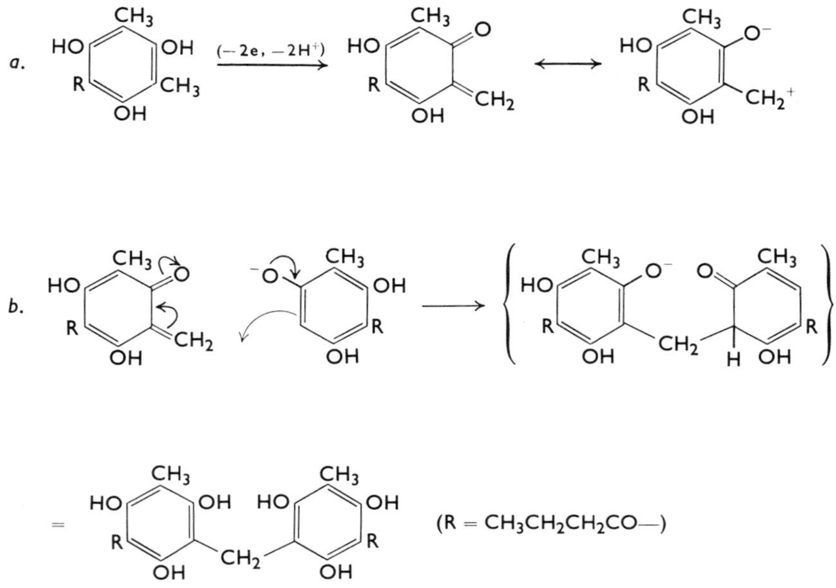

$(R = CH_3CH_2CH_2CO—)$

(*Note:* An equivalent sequence, starting with

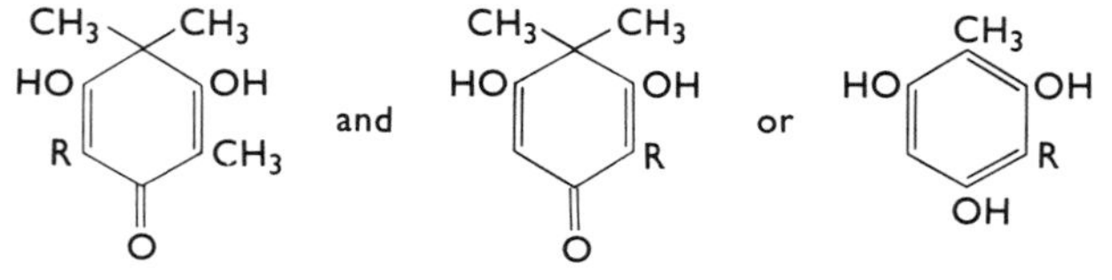

can be formulated in the same way)

[Eq. 4-26]

When 1-^{14}C-butyric acid was provided to tubers of the fern *Dryopteris marginalis* with the aim of demonstrating the biosynthetic route shown in Eq. 4-25, a surprising result was obtained. Although, as was anticipated, the two phloroglucinol rings of the margaspidin and desaspidin isolated from the plant were equally labeled, only one-half (instead of all) of the radioactivity was located at the carbonyl group of the butyryl residue. The remaining half of the activity was located in the phloro-glucinol ring (Eq. 4-27):

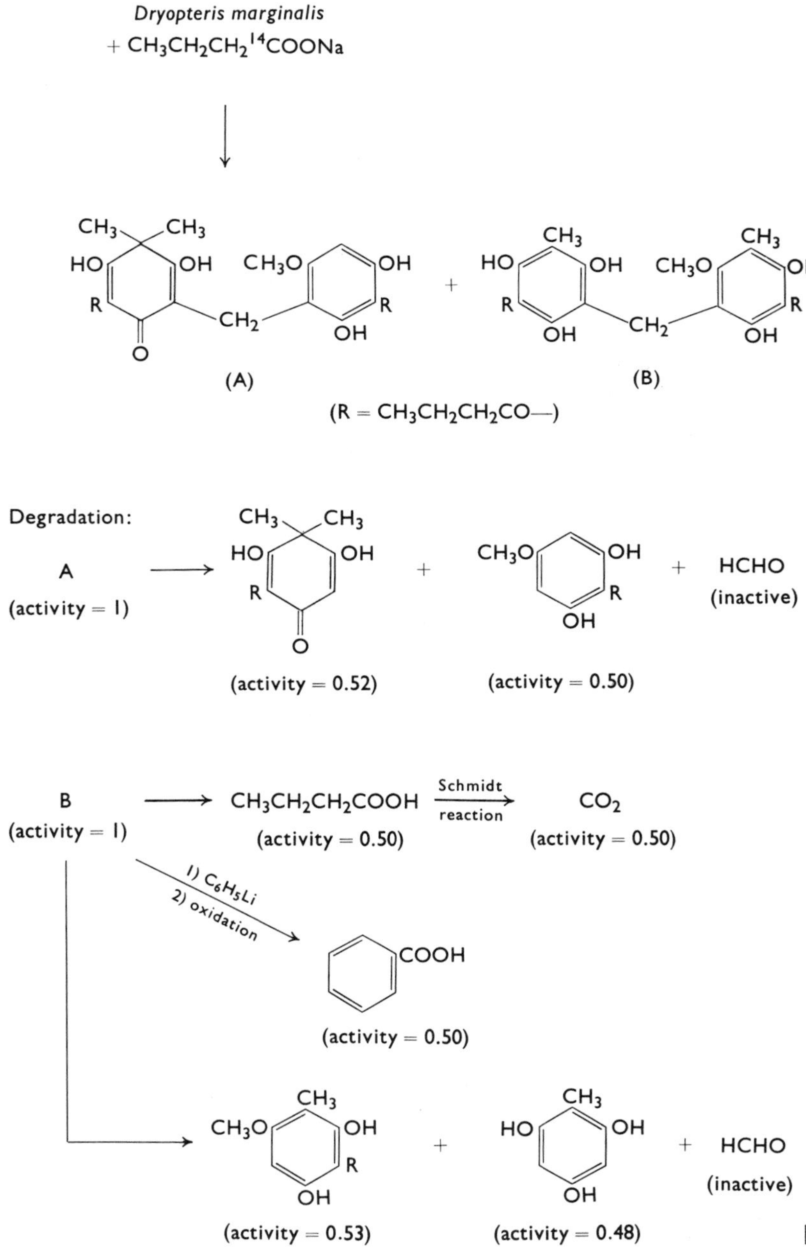

Dryopteris marginalis
$+ CH_3CH_2CH_2{}^{14}COONa$

(A)

(B)

$(R = CH_3CH_2CH_2CO—)$

Degradation:

A
(activity = 1)

(activity = 0.52)   (activity = 0.50)   HCHO (inactive)

B
(activity = 1) $CH_3CH_2CH_2COOH$ $\xrightarrow[\text{reaction}]{\text{Schmidt}}$ CO_2

(activity = 0.50)   (activity = 0.50)

1) C_6H_5Li
2) oxidation

COOH

(activity = 0.50)

(activity = 0.53)   (activity = 0.48)   HCHO (inactive)   [Eq. 4-27]

Further degradation by ozonolysis of margaspidin showed that the activity was distributed as indicated in Eq. 4-28.

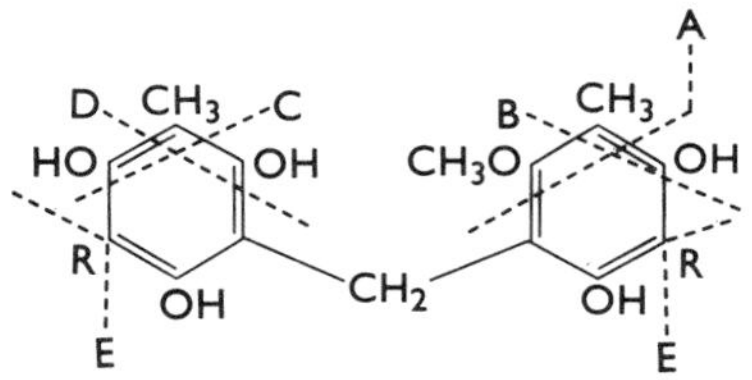

$(R = CH_3CH_2CH_2CO—)$

(activity = 1)

O_3

	activity	source
CH_3COOCH_3	0.21	A
$[CH_3COCOOH]$		

CH_3COOH	0.02	B, C, D
$CH_3CH_2CH_2COOH$	0.25	E

Thus, distribution of ^{14}C:

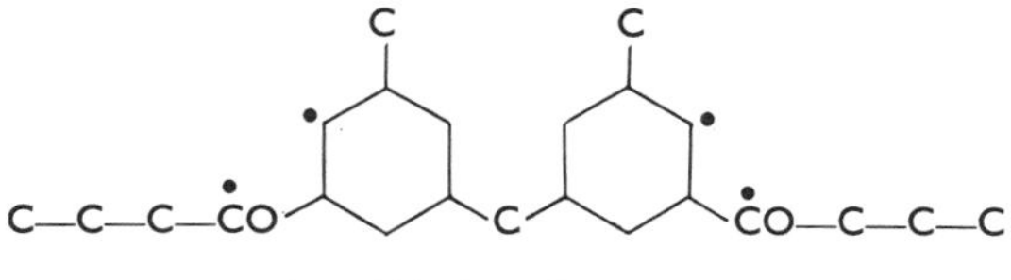

(• = 1/4 of total activity)

[Eq. 4-28]

This result leads to the conclusion that the biosynthesis of each of the aromatic rings proceeds by the linkage of two four-carbon units and final addition of a two-carbon unit. A suggested scheme is shown in Eq. 4-29.

Suggested biosynthesis of the phloroglucinol rings of margaspidin

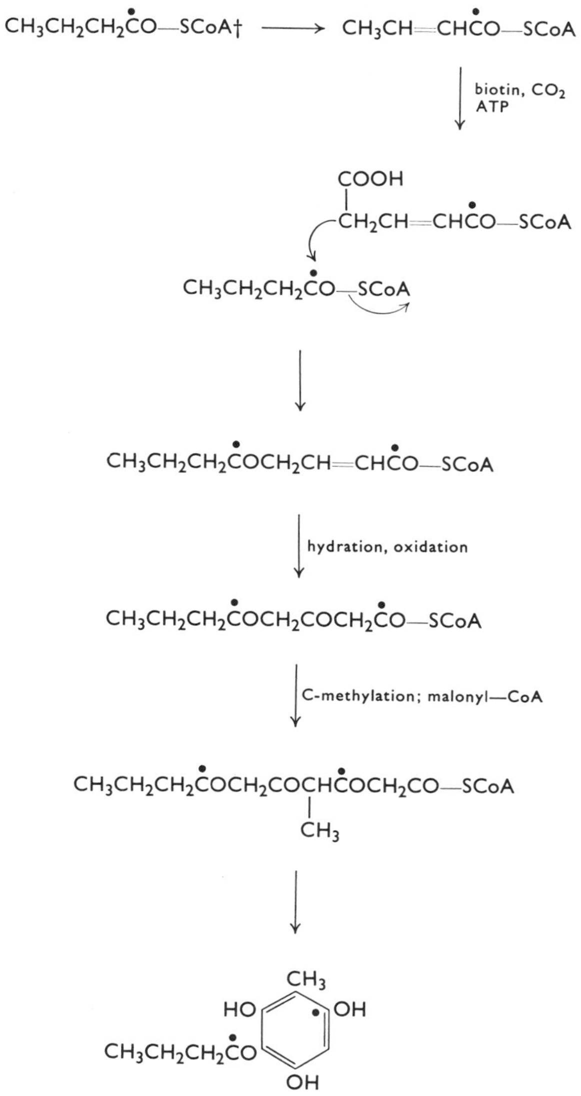

$$CH_3CH_2CH_2\overset{\bullet}{C}O\text{—}SCoA\dagger \longrightarrow CH_3CH\text{=}CH\overset{\bullet}{C}O\text{—}SCoA$$

biotin, CO_2
ATP

$$\underset{CH_3CH_2CH_2\overset{\bullet}{C}O\text{—}SCoA}{\overset{\overset{COOH}{|}}{CH_2CH\text{=}CH\overset{\bullet}{C}O\text{—}SCoA}}$$

$$CH_3CH_2CH_2\overset{\bullet}{C}OCH_2CH\text{=}CH\overset{\bullet}{C}O\text{—}SCoA$$

hydration, oxidation

$$CH_3CH_2CH_2\overset{\bullet}{C}OCH_2CO CH_2\overset{\bullet}{C}O\text{—}SCoA$$

C-methylation; malonyl—CoA

$$\underset{\overset{|}{CH_3}}{CH_3CH_2CH_2\overset{\bullet}{C}OCH_2CO\overset{\bullet}{C}HCOCH_2CO\text{—}SCoA}$$

[Eq. 4-29]

† - - - CO—SCoA is adopted arbitrarily, although the reactions shown may occur in an enzyme-bound complex, - - - - CO—SEnzyme.

The course shown in Eq. 4-29 finds analogy in the known carboxylation of β-methylcrotonyl-CoA (in the presence of ATP and biotin) to give HOOCCH₂C=CHCO—SCoA. The validity and generality of this unusual course

$$HOOCCH_2C(CH_3){=}CHCO{-}SCoA$$

of biosynthesis remain to be confirmed and extended by further study.

4.15 Further Alteration of One-carbon Substituents

The occurrence in nature of groups of closely related compounds that differ in the degree of oxidation of a one-carbon substituent suggests that the pathway

$$CH_3 \longrightarrow CH_2OH \longrightarrow CHO \longrightarrow COOH$$

is a common biosynthetic sequence. In Fig. 4-25 are shown some examples of compounds, derived by the acetate-malonate pathway, which have been further modified by secondary alterations. The labeling patterns shown in the figure reveal the origins and indicate the manner in which metabolic alterations have taken place.

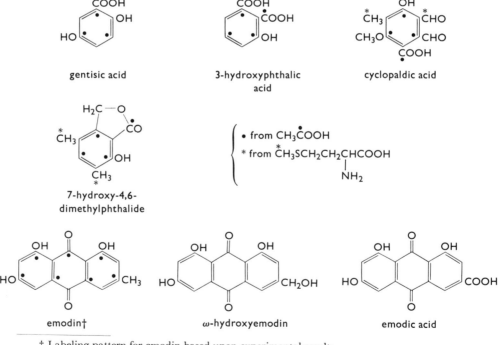

gentisic acid

3-hydroxyphthalic acid

cyclopaldic acid

7-hydroxy-4,6-dimethylphthalide

• from CH₃COOH
* from CH₃SCH₂CH₂CHCOOH
                             |
                            NH₂

emodin†

ω-hydroxyemodin

emodic acid

† Labeling pattern for emodin based upon experimental results.

Fig. 4-25. Compounds of Acetate-malonate Origin with Modified Carbon-linked Substituents.

The distribution of ^{14}C from $CH_3{}^{14}COOH$ in gentisic acid shows that the hydroxyl group *ortho* to the carboxyl group occupies the position at which COOH appears in orsellinic (or 6-methylsalicyclic) acid. The oxidative removal of —COOH can be accounted for by assuming an electrophilic attack of oxygen (conveniently represented as the protonated species OH^+) in the manner shown in Eq. 4-30a. An analogous pathway may be adduced for the biosynthesis of hydroquinone, which occurs in nature as the glucoside arbutin, and is known to be a product of the metabolism of phenylalanine and tyrosine (Chap. 5). Since these aromatic amino acids are also the progenitors of *p*-hydroxybenzoic acid, the pathway shown in Eq. 4-30b is a plausible one.

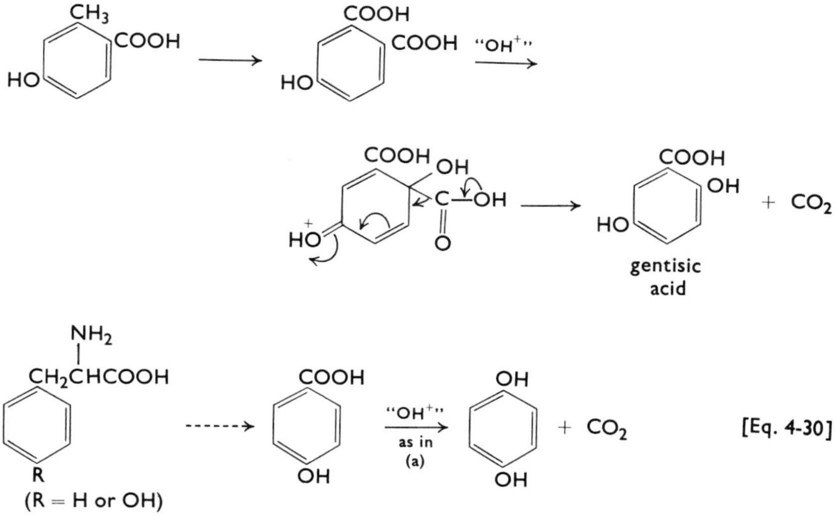

Suggested routes for biosynthesis of

a. gentisic acid (*via* acetate pathway) and
b. hydroquinone (from tyrosine, *via* shikimic acid pathway)

4.16 Termination of Polyketide Chains by Non-acetate-derived Units

The presence at some point in the process of polyketide chain extension of the terminal unit —$COCH_2CO$—S—X (where X is —CoA or part of an enzyme) provides for the final attachment of fragments of various kinds by a concluding displacement of —SX by nucleophilic attack. One such nucleophilic grouping is an amino residue, and polyketide-derived compounds with terminal amino-acid-derived structures are known in nature.

Two fungal metabolites that illustrate this possible biosynthetic process are tenuazonic acid (from *Alternaria tenuis*) and erythroskyrin (from *Penicillium islandicum*). In Fig. 4-26 are shown the structures of these compounds along with an indication of their probable origins.

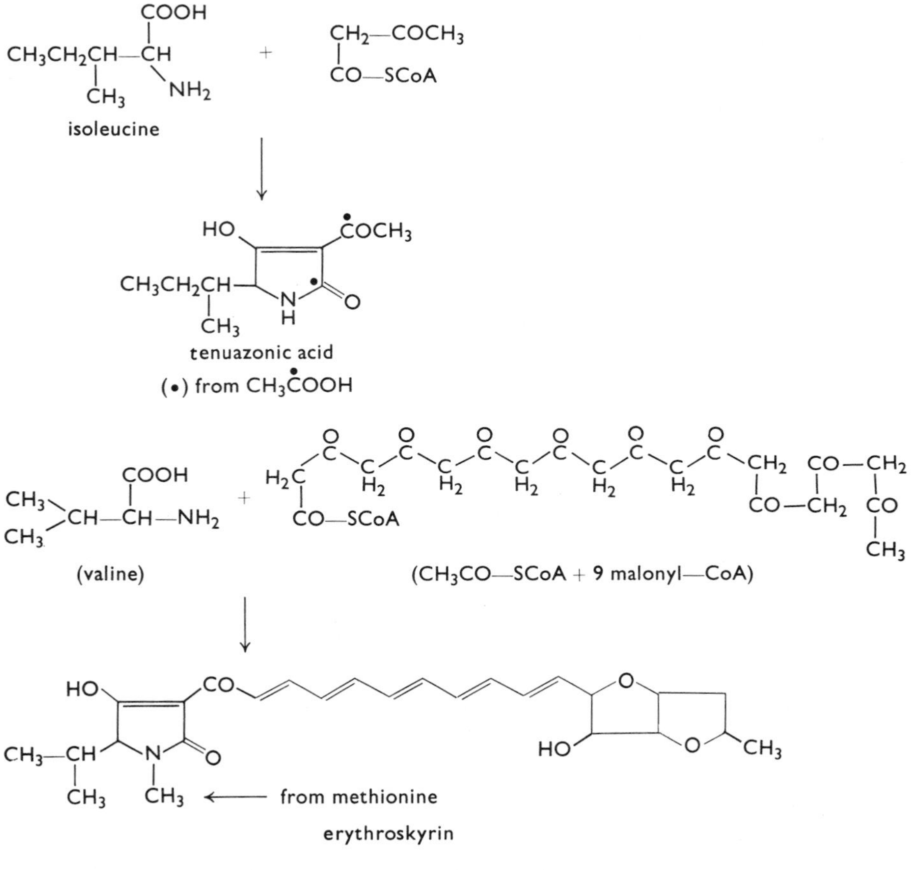

Fig. 4-26. Tenuazonic Acid and Erythroskyrin.

Although the origins of tenuazonic acid and erythroskyrin are known from the experimentally established labeling patterns, the details of the steps in which the final coupling reactions occur can only be surmised. The formation of the amide linkage offers no difficulty, for the reaction of the —CO—SX grouping with the amino group can lead to the formation of the —CO—NH—·bond. The ring closure, with attachment of the —COOH group of the amino acid to the —CH$_2$— group of the polyketide chain is a C-acylation of the latter. It may be assumed that the amino acid acts in the form of an acyl derivative (an "activated" amino acid), comparable to that involved in protein synthesis. The reactive species may be the amino acid-AMP shown in Eq. 4-31, where the behavior of the nucleophilic —NH$_2$ and —CH$_2$— groups are compared.

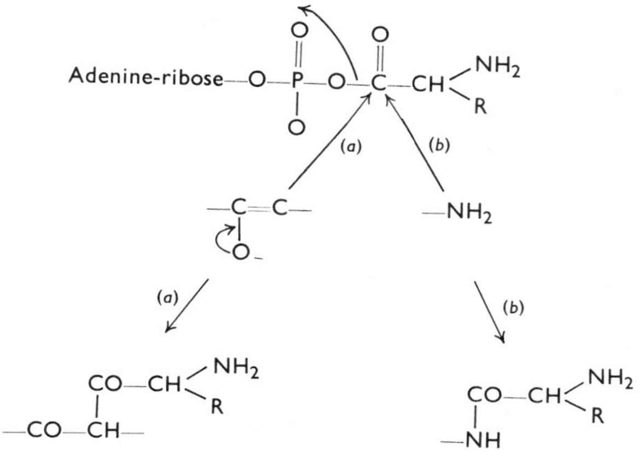

[Eq. 4-31]

Whether in erythroskyrin the —N—C— or the —C—C— bond between valine and the polyketide chain is formed first cannot be suggested from the above conjectures.

4.17 Structural Alteration Subsequent to Cyclization of the Polyketide Chain

In Sec. 4.6 is found a description of the biosynthetic origin of the non-aromatic, acetate-derived compound penicillic acid, a compound formed by an oxidative ring opening of orsellinic acid. Labeling experiments have shown that the fungal metabolite patulin owes its origin to a similar process (Eq. 4-32):

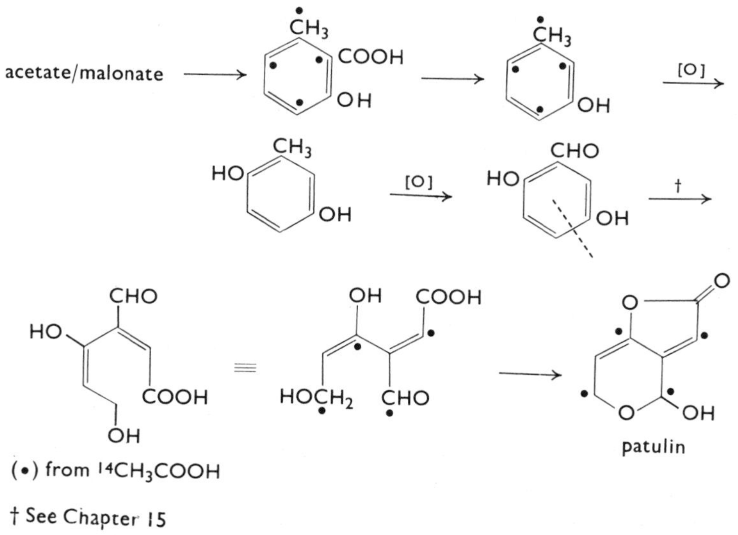

[Eq. 4-32]

patulin

(•) from $^{14}CH_3COOH$

† See Chapter 15

Ring-opening of an orsellinic acid derivative formed by introduction of a one-carbon substituent may account for the formation of a group of seven-membered ring compounds of which stipitatonic acid is representative (Eq. 4-33):

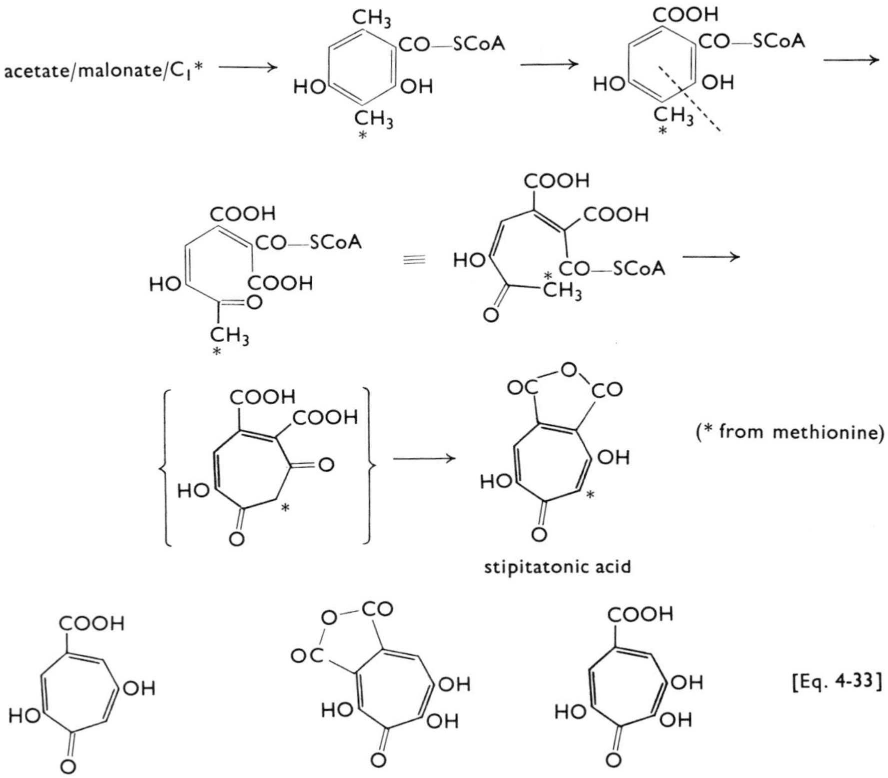

stipitatonic acid

(* from methionine)

stipitatic acid   puberulonic acid   puberulic acid   [Eq. 4-33]

(derived by variants of above pathway)

4.18   Summary

The general picture of polyketide formation by the acetate-malonate pathway, followed by reductions, alkylations, and cyclizations in various mechanistically and stereochemically satisfactory ways is firmly established by experimental proofs of several kinds. Variants in the scheme include alteration of substituents by secondary (mostly oxidative) processes, the starting of the chain with an acyl-CoA other than acetyl-CoA, attachment of terminal units that originate from non-acetate pathways, and deep-seated terminal changes that involve oxidative ring openings and reclosures. The introduction, by alkylation or acylation of the active $-CH_2-$

groups of the polyketide chain, of substituents other than CH_3 is a source of further variation that has not been covered in this chapter, for the substituents most commonly found are derivatives of the five-carbon unit derived from mevalonic acid. This subject will be discussed in Chapter 8. In the chapters to follow the terms acetate-derived, acetate-malonate pathway, acetate hypothesis will be used without further elaboration to refer to structures and structural units that owe their origin to processes of the kind described in the foregoing pages. The extension by malonate units of acyl-CoA "starters" formed by a pathway starting from shikimic acid represents a biosynthetic route to an extraordinarily wide variety of naturally occurring compounds. This will be the subject of the next chapter.

V CHAPTER

5.1 Structural Characteristics of Shikimic-derived Compounds
5.2 Shikimic Acid
5.3 Phenylalanine and Cinnamic Acids
5.4 The Cinnamic Acids
5.5 Chlorogenic Acid and Other Quinic Acid Esters
5.6 Compounds of the Class C_6–C_1
5.7 Benzaldehyde and Benzyl Alcohol Derivatives
5.8 Simple Phenols (C_6 Compounds)
5.9 Compounds of the Class C_6–C_2
5.10 Compounds of the C_6–C_3 Class: Phenylpropanoid Compounds
5.11 Lignans and Lignin
5.12 Chemistry and Stereochemistry of Lignans

REFERENCES FOR FURTHER READING

1. M. R. Young and A. C. Neish, *Properties of the Ammonia Lyases Deaminating Phenylalanine and Related Compounds in Triticum aestivum and Pteridium aquilinium,* Phytochemistry, *5,* (1966), 1121.
2. S. Z. El-Basyouni, D. Chen, R. K. Ibrahim, A. C. Neish, and G. H. N. Towers, *The Biosynthesis of Hydroxybenzoic Acids,* Phytochemistry, 3, (1961), 485.
3. M. H. Zenk, *Pathways of Salicyl Alcohol and Salicin Formation in Salix purpurea L.,* Phytochemistry, 6, (1967), 245.
4. H. Erdtman, *Lignans,* in Modern Methods of Plant Analysis, K. Paech and M. V. Tracey, Eds., Springer Verlag, Berlin, 1955.
5. F. F. Nord and W. J. Schubert, *The Biogenesis of Lignins,* in Biogenesis of Natural Compounds, 2nd Ed., P. Bernfeld, Ed., Pergamon Press, Oxford, 1967.
6. E. Haslam, *The Biosynthesis of Gallic Acid,* in Recent Developments in the Chemistry of Natural Phenolic Compounds, W. D. Ollis, Ed., Pergamon Press, Oxford, 1961.
7. A. W. Schrecker, and J. L. Hartwell, *Application of Tosylate Reductions and Molecular Rotations to the Stereochemistry of Lignans,* J. Amer. Chem. Soc., *77,* (1955), 432.
8. A. J. Birch, B. Milligan, E. Smith, and R. N. Speake, *Some Stereochemical Studies of Lignans,* J. Chem. Soc., (1958), 4471.

Compounds Derived from Shikimic Acid

5.1 Structural Characteristics of Shikimic-derived Compounds

Shikimic acid, first isolated as a constituent of an Asian plant, *Illicium* spp. (fam. Illiciaceae), is now recognized as a compound that is the starting point for a vast array of naturally occurring compounds of many classes. Its occurrence as a discrete plant constituent has been widely observed only in recent years, but there is no doubt that it is a universal metabolite of higher plants and of non-mammalian organisms of many kinds.

Shikimic acid is the precursor of most plant constituents that contain aromatic rings other than those formed by the acetate pathway. As will be seen in the sections to follow, there is in most instances a clear structural pattern that permits a recognition of shikimic-derived compounds. This is in the pattern of hydroxylation of the aromatic ring. In acetate-derived compounds, the phenolic hydroxyl groups are characteristically *meta* disposed; that is, the polyphenols are typically resorcinol or phloroglucinol derivatives. In shikimic-derived aromatic compounds the patterns of the aromatic hydroxyl groups are characteristically those of catechol (1,2) or pyrogallol (1,2,3). Monohydric phenols of shikimic origin are characteristically *p*-hydroxy compounds.

In Fig. 5-1 are shown a number of compounds of the kind whose chemistry and biosynthetic origins will be considered in the discussions to come. A variety of structural types is represented, including examples ranging from simple benzene derivatives, to compounds of the type Ar—C—C—C, and finally to those whose origin is through the extension of the Ar—C—C—CO—SCoA "starter" unit by acetate fragments. It is to be noted that these various compounds can be regarded as possessing a C₆—C—C—C unit; or as being derived from this by the loss of carbon atoms from the C₃-side chain; or by extension of the side chain by the addition of carbon atoms (usually C₂ units).

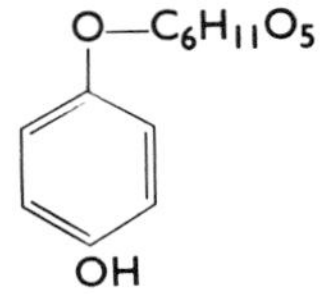
O—C6H11O5
OH

arbutin
(hydroquinone
β-D-glucopyranoside)

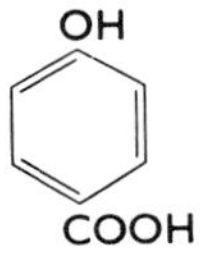
OH
COOH

p-hydroxybenzoic
acid

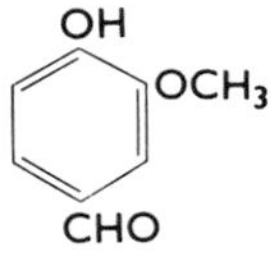
OH
OCH3
CHO

vanillin

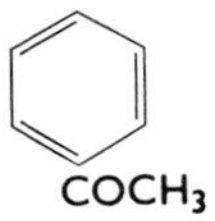
COCH3

acetophenone

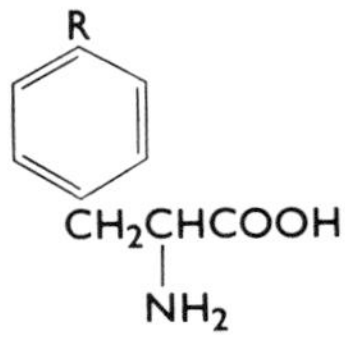
R
CH2CHCOOH
NH2

R = H, phenylalanine
R = OH, tyrosine

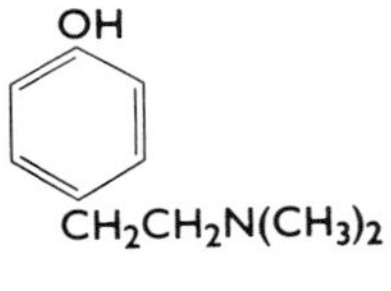
OH
CH2CH2N(CH3)2

hordenine

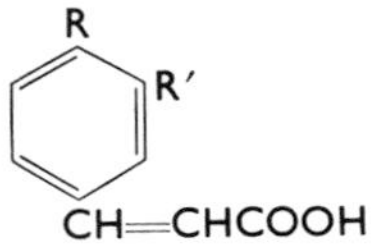
R
R′
CH=CHCOOH

(R = R′ = H), cinnamic acid
(R = OH, R′ = H), *p*-coumaric acid
(R = R′ = OH), caffeic acid
(R = OH, R′ = OCH_3), ferulic acid

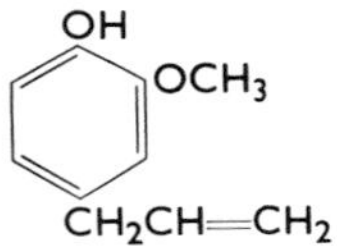
OH
OCH3
CH2CH=CH2

eugenol

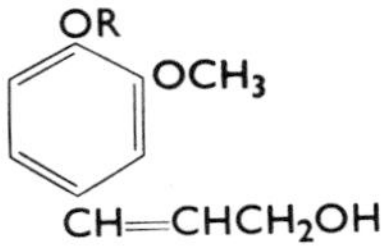
OR
OCH3
CH=CHCH2OH

(R = H), coniferyl alcohol
(R = β-D-glucopyranosyl),
coniferin

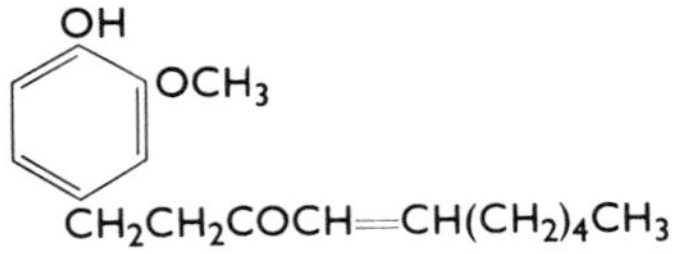
OH
OCH3
CH2CH2COCH=CH(CH2)4CH3

shogaol

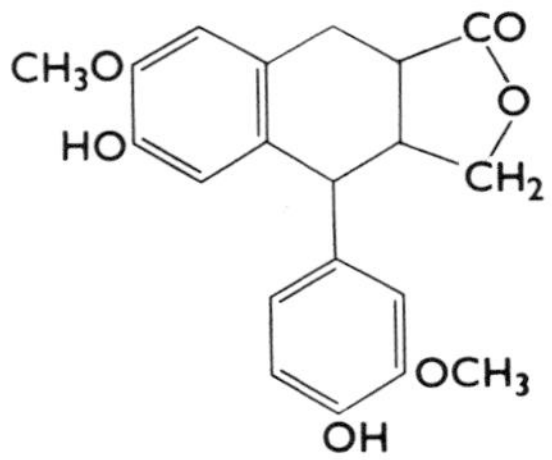
CH3O
HO
CO
O
CH2
OCH3
OH

conidendrin

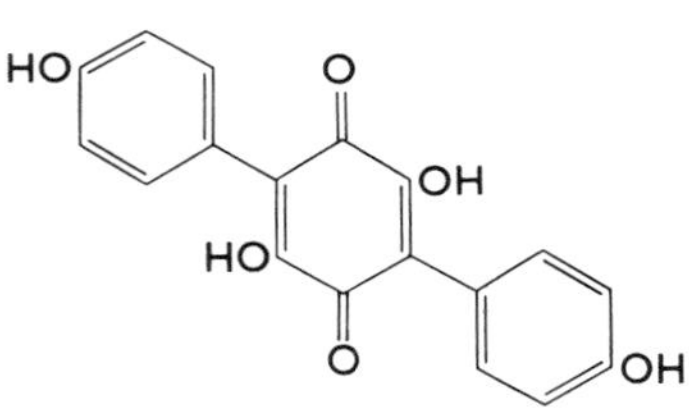
HO
O
OH
HO
O
OH

atromentin

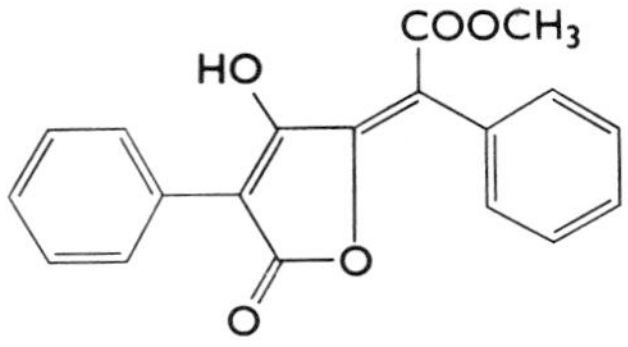
COOCH3
HO
O
O

vulpinic acid

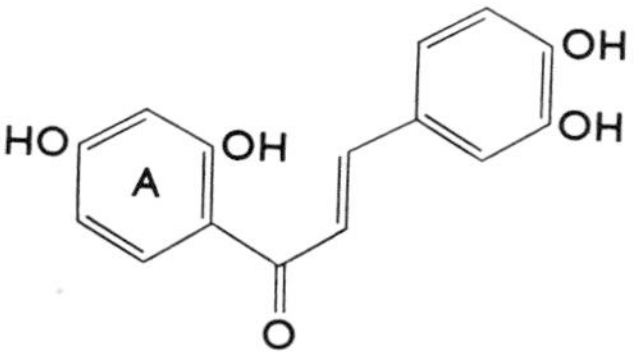

butein†

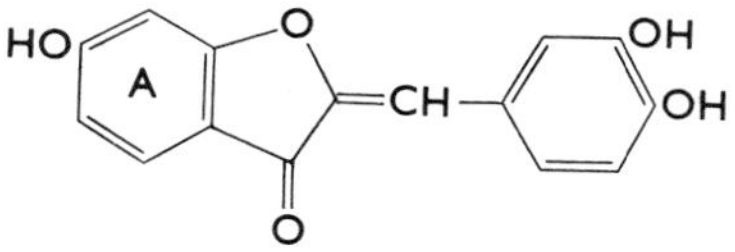

sulfuretin†

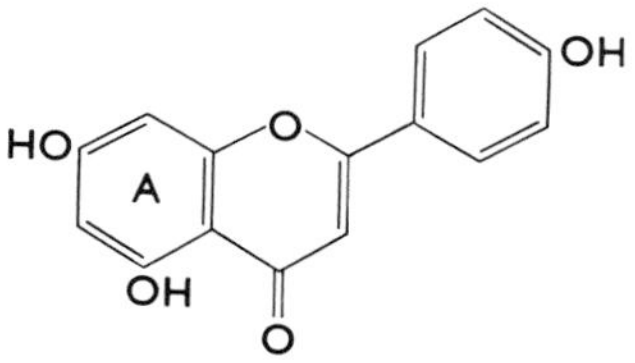

apigenin†

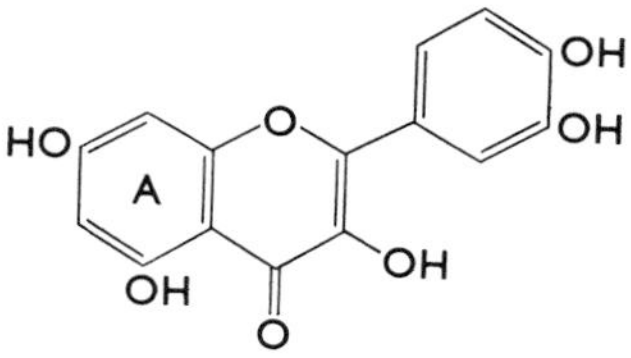

quercetin†

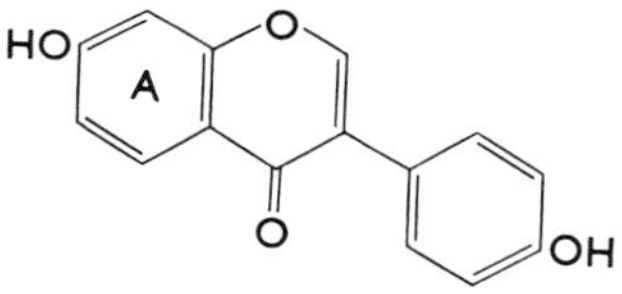

daidzein†

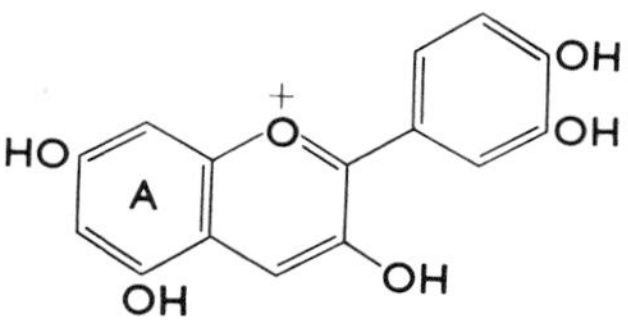

cyanidin†

† Ring A acetate-derived. These compounds are nearly always present in nature as glycosides.

Fig. 5-1. Some Representative Shikimic Acid-derived Naturally Occurring Compounds.

The central unit in the biosynthesis of shikimic acid-derived compounds is the nine-carbon entity represented by phenylalanine, cinnamic acid, and their derivatives (Fig. 5-1). The generation of this structural unit will be described in the following sections.

5.2 Shikimic Acid

The discovery by B. D. Davis and his co-workers of the central role of shikimic acid in metabolic processes leading to the aromatic amino acids and, subsequently, to C_9 compounds derived from these, represented a major advance in understanding of biosynthesis in living organisms.

The formation of shikimic acid proceeds from the three- and four-carbon atom precursors phosphoenolpyruvic acid and erythrose-4-phosphate through a series of steps that have been represented in summary form in Eq. 2-49 and are given in further detail in Eq. 5-1.

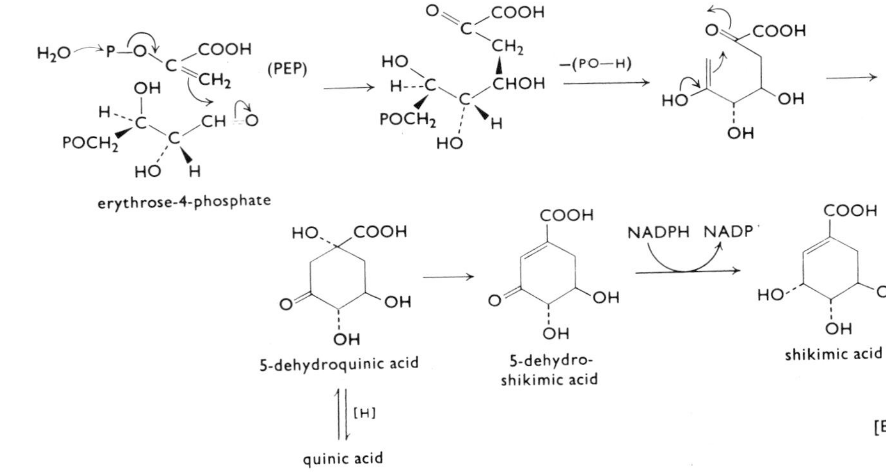
(PEP)
erythrose-4-phosphate
−(PO—H)
NADPH NADP⁺
5-dehydroquinic acid
5-dehydro-shikimic acid
shikimic acid
[H]
quinic acid

[Eq. 5-1]

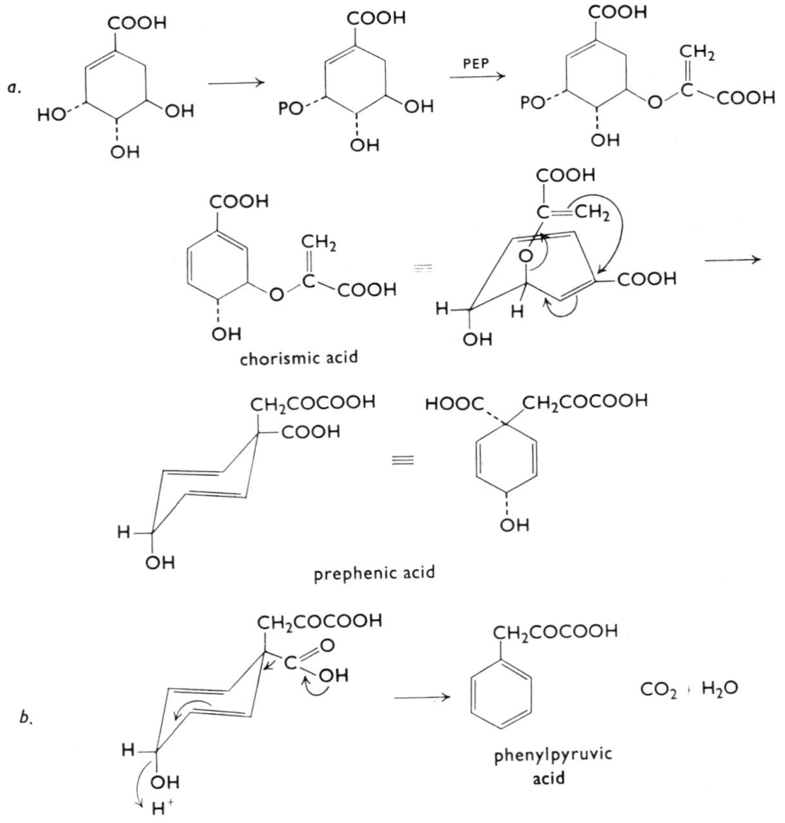
a.
PEP
−[HOP]
chorismic acid
prephenic acid
b.
phenylpyruvic acid
CO₂ + H₂O

[Eq. 5-2]

Further reaction of shikimic acid with phosphoenolpyruvic acid, followed by the transformations shown in Eq. 5-2*a*, leads by way of the intermediate chorismic acid to prephenic acid and thence (Eq. 5-2*b*) to phenylpyruvic acid. Reductive amination of phenylpyruvic acid to form phenylalanine provides this important amino acid as the starting point for a remarkably diversified network of further synthesis.

Chorismic acid is the immediate progenitor not only of prephenic acid but also of anthranilic acid. It was first isolated from a mutant strain of *Aerobacter aerogenes* which when grown in the absence of tryptophan accumulates anthranilic acid, but when grown with excess added tryptophan accumulates a new compound which could be isolated and characterized. This compound, chorismic acid, was found to have the composition $C_{10}H_{10}O_6$, and an ultraviolet absorption spectrum that was very like that of 3,4-dihydrobenzoic acid. Pyrolytic decomposition of chorismic acid yielded *p*-hydroxybenzoic acid, phenylpyruvic acid, and pyruvic acid, while hydrolysis of dihydrochorismic acid yielded *trans*-4,5-dihydroxy-1-cyclohexene-1-carboxylic acid and pyruvic acid. Ozonolysis of the cyclohexenecarboxylic acid yielded (+)-β,β'-dihydroxyadipic acid, of known configuration. These transformations are shown in Eq. 5-3:

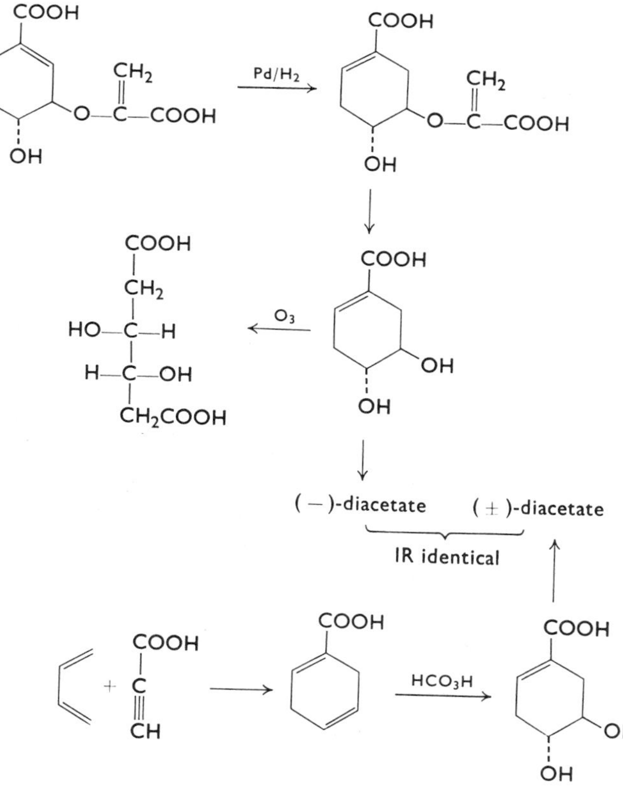

[Eq. 5-3]

A detailed interpretation of the NMR spectrum of chorismic acid led to conclusions that were in complete accord with the structure that is shown.

5.3 Phenylalanine and Cinnamic Acids

Prephenic and phenylpyruvic acids (Eq. 5-2) are the precursors of phenylalanine, a compound important as a universal constituent of proteins, as a precursor for an extensive class of alkaloids, and, as the compound that stands at the head of the biosynthetic sequence that leads to compounds of the C_6—C—C—C class.

The importance of cinnamic acid and its 4-hydroxy-(p-coumaric), 3,4-dihydroxy-(caffeic), 4-hydroxy-3-methoxy-(ferulic), and 4-hydroxy-3,5-dimethoxy-(sinapic) derivatives as plant constituents and as probable progenitors for compounds of the C_6—C_3 type has long been recognized. The manner in which the —CH=CHCOOH grouping is formed from the —CH_2CH(NH_2)COOH or —CH_2COCOOH groupings has become clear only in recent years.

Early theories proposed to account for the formation of cinnamic acids from arylpyruvic acids or β-arylalanines included such proposals as the sequence shown in Eq. 5-4.

$$ArCH_2COCOOH \underset{\text{amination}}{\overset{\text{reductive}}{\rightleftharpoons}} ArCH_2\overset{\overset{\displaystyle NH_2}{|}}{C}HCOOH$$

$$2[H]\updownarrow$$

$$ArCH_2\underset{\underset{\displaystyle OH}{|}}{C}HCOOH \overset{-H_2O}{\rightleftharpoons} ArCH=CHCOOH \qquad \text{[Eq. 5-4]}$$

Although the reduction of phenylpyruvic acid to phenyllactic acid is a reaction that has its parallel in the malic-oxaloacetic and isocitric-oxalosuccinic equilibria, the ready dehydration of the α-hydroxy acid is less likely to represent a major pathway to the unsaturated acid.

What is probably the major route to cinnamic acids from phenylalanine was revealed when it was found that plant tissues contain enzyme systems capable of catalyzing the removal of the elements of ammonia from phenylalanine and tyrosine, with the formation of cinnamic and p-coumaric acids (Eq. 5-5):

R = H, phenylalanine ⟶ cinnamic acid

R = OH, tyrosine ⟶ p-coumaric acid

[Eq. 5-5]

L-Phenylalanine ammonia lyase (PAL) appears to be widely distributed in plants, while L-tyrosine ammonia lyase (TAL) is found principally in grasses (fam. Gramineae).

These ammonia lyases are stereospecific; they deaminate the natural L-acids but are inactive toward the D-acids. Their structural specificity is not absolute, however, for PAL can convert various substituted (fluoro-, hydroxy-, hydroxymethoxy-) L-phenylalanines into the corresponding cinnamic acids. TAL is a different enzyme from PAL, but neither has been purified to the point at which it can be stated with assurance that the activities are completely separable.

The ammonia-lyase reaction is direct and unaccompanied by other structural change. When ^{14}C-labeled tyrosine was acted upon by TAL from rice seedlings the p-coumaric acid that was formed had the same specific activity as the amino acid used as the substrate.

5.4 The Cinnamic Acids

The cinnamic acids provided by the action of ammonia-lyases form the starting point from which an enormous number of secondary metabolic processes begin.

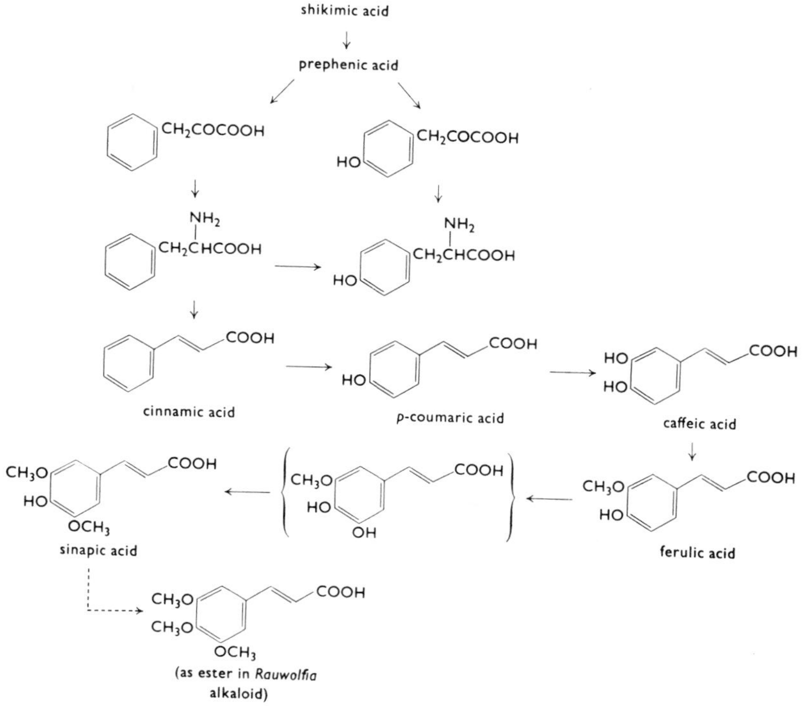

Fig. 5-2.

The common cinnamic acids of higher plants, most of which occur as esters of sugars and quinic acid or as glycosides (at the phenolic hydroxyl groups), are those shown in Fig. 5-2. The interrelationships shown in this figure have been established by experiments with living plants with the use of labeled compounds.

5.5 Chlorogenic Acid and Other Quinic Acid Esters

Caffeic acid is widely distributed in higher plants in the form of its esters with quinic acid; the 3-O-caffeyolquinic acid is known as chlorogenic acid (Fig. 5-3), so called because of its reaction with amino acids under oxidative conditions to form a green compound (of uncertain structure). Other substituted cinnamoylquinic acids

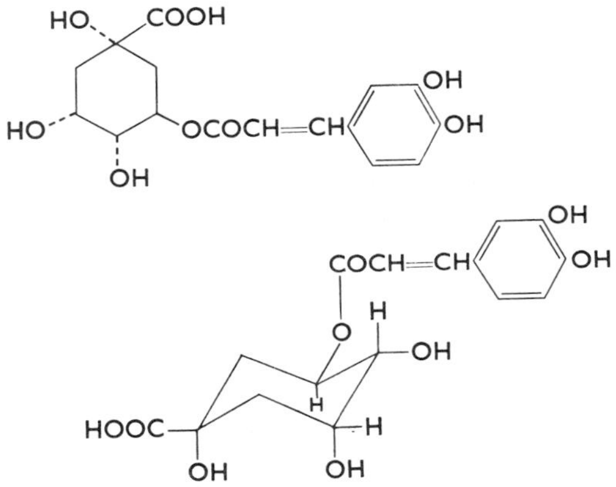

Fig. 5-3. Chlorogenic acid.

are also known in nature (for example, the p-coumaroyl and cinnamoyl esters), and experimental evidence has been adduced to show that these esters are the direct precursors of chlorogenic acid, aromatic hydroxylation taking place on the esterified cinnamic acid residue. The formation of chlorogenic acid in higher plants from phenylalanine (or cinnamic acid) has been established by experiments in which ^{14}C-labeled precursors were used. There is no doubt that aromatic hydroxylation is a common metabolic process.

Cinnamoylquinic acids are evidently end products; they accumulate in the plant, and although there is some reason to believe that they undergo metabolic alteration they do not appear to lie on the main pathway that leads to C_6—C_3 compounds of other kinds. It may be assumed that the esterification reaction by which the cinnamoyl residue is linked to the quinic acid hydroxyl group involves the CoA ester of cinnamic acid. This ester (and that of p-coumaric, and perhaps other congeners as well) represents a starting point for cinnamic acid metabolism of many kinds: ester formation, β-oxidation, reduction to the aldehyde and alcohol, and extension by reaction with malonyl CoA units to form compounds of classes that may be represented by C_6—$C_3(C_2)_n$. In Fig. 5-4 is shown in schematic form a chart of the metabolic transformations of the C_6—C_3 unit as a precursor for compounds of a variety of classes.

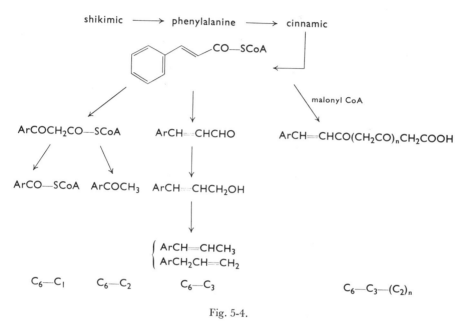

Fig. 5-4.

5.6 Compounds of the Class C_6–C_1

Benzoic acid and substituted (hydroxylated) benzoic acids are widely distributed in higher plants, where they usually occur as esters (at —COOH) or glycosides (at phenolic —OH). Benzoic acid is found in esterified form in cocaine, and salicylic acid occurs as the methyl ester in oil of wintergreen. In Fig. 5-5 are shown some of the common naturally occurring benzoic acid derivatives.

Of the acids shown in Fig. 5-5, gallic acid appears to be derived principally from the cyclohexanecarboxylic acids at the shikimic-quinic level, but has also been found to be formed from phenylalanine. Protocatechuic acid can be formed by degradation of phenylalanine and by hydroxylation of p-hydroxybenzoic acid. Feeding experiments in a plant (*Geranium pyrenaicum*) using ^{14}C-labeled compounds have shown that D-glucose is a better precursor for the formation of gallic acid than phenylalanine. Experiments with fungi have shown that gallic acid can be formed from 5-dehydroshikimic acid.

The direct hydroxylation of protocatechuic acid to gallic acid, although rare, is not unknown, for when ^{14}C-protocatechuic acid was fed to *Pelargonium hortorum* (fam. Geraniaceae), radioactive gallic acid was formed. In Fig. 5-6 are shown the biosynthetic relationships between shikimic, pyrocatechuic, and gallic acids; it is

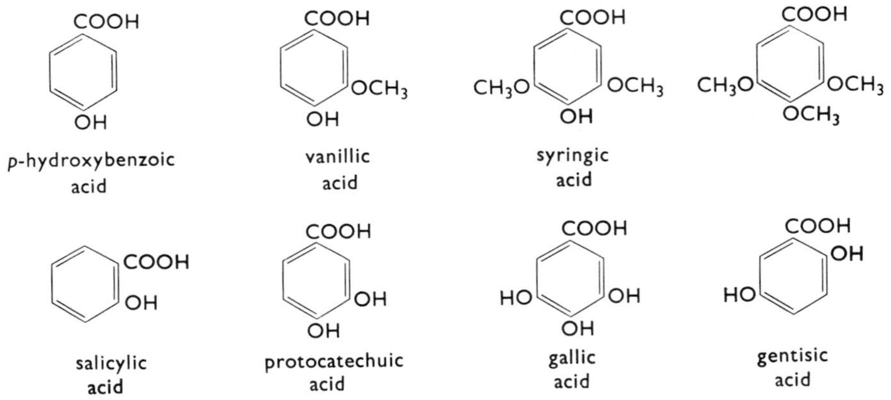

p-hydroxybenzoic acid

vanillic acid

syringic acid

salicylic acid

protocatechuic acid

gallic acid

gentisic acid

Fig. 5-5. Naturally Occurring Benzoic Acid Derivatives.

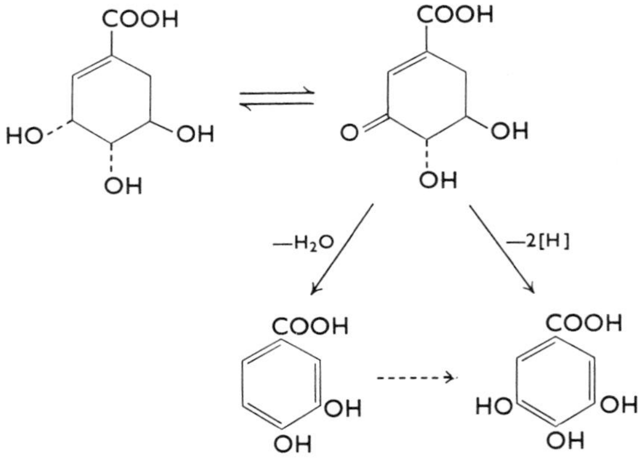

Fig. 5-6. Biosynthesis of Gallic Acid.

clear that only minor metabolic alterations in 5-dehydroshikimic acid are necessary to produce the aromatic compounds.

Salicylic, *o*-pyrocatechuic, *p*-hydroxybenzoic, gentisic, vanillic, and syringic acids have all been found to be produced from 3-^{14}C-phenylalanine or 3-^{14}C-cinnamic acid, with the expected retention of the label in the carboxyl group of the benzoic acid derivative. Similarly, ferulic and sinapic acids can be converted by the loss of two carbon atoms into vanillic and syringic acids. It thus appears that the process shown in Eq. 5-6 is a general metabolic pathway. The assumption that the degradation leads to the initial formation of a benzoic acid-CoA derivative is arbitrary but mechanistically very probable. The formation of benzoyl-labeled cocaine in *Erythroxylum coca* plants fed with 3-^{14}C-phenylalanine is in accord with this, for the benzoyl CoA would be an effective benzoylating agent.

[Eq. 5-6]

Finally, hydroxylation of the aromatic ring is known to occur, for ^{14}C-benzoic acid, fed to *Gaultheria procumbens* (fam. Ericaceae) and *Primula acaulis* (fam. Primulaceae), was converted into salicyclic, *o*-pyrocatechuic, gentisic, and *p*-hydroxybenzoic acids. Whether CoA-ester formation precedes these hydroxylations is not known, but there appears to be no obligatory relationship between the nuclear hydroxylation reaction and the condition—free or esterified—of the carboxyl group. Indeed, it would appear on mechanistic grounds that nuclear hydroxylation would proceed faster in the anionic form of the acid than in its CoA ester.

5.7 Benzaldehyde and Benzyl Alcohol Derivatives

The first glucoside isolated from a natural source was salicin (in species of the family Salicaceae, (willows, poplars), and in other families). Salicin is the β-D-glucopyranoside (at phenolic —OH) of salicyl alcohol. The isomeric glucoside (at —CH$_2$OH) is also known in nature but is less common. The related aldehyde helicin is also found in nature, sometimes, but not always, along with salicin.

The question of the biosynthesis of salicyl alcohol is a multiple one. Is it formed by the acetate pathway, and thus related to the acids of the orsellinic group; or is it formed by degradation of a precursor derived by the shikimic acid-phenylalanine pathway? Is the —CH$_2$OH (or —CHO in helicin) group the result of the reduction of —COOH (or —CO—SCoA); or is it the product of oxidation of a methyl group? Finally, at what point in the biosynthetic path is glucosylation accomplished?

Salicyl alcohol is formed in *Salix purpurea* leaf tissue *via* the phenylalanine-cinnamic acid pathway, for ^{14}C-phenylalanine and ^{14}C-cinnamic acid were far more efficiently incorporated into salicyl alcohol than were labeled glucose or acetic acid. (It is curious that when labeled glucose and acetic acid were fed to the plant no activity was found in the salicyl alcohol, for it would be expected that these would provide, by degradation and resynthesis, some of the fragments for shikimic acid synthesis.)

Salicylic acid, benzoic acid and benzyl alcohol (all ^{14}C-labeled) were all incorporated into salicyl alcohol in *Salix*, but the most effective precursor was 3-^{14}C-*o*-coumaric acid. The biosynthesis of salicin does not proceed by a series of steps of which the final stage is the glycosylation of salicyl alcohol, for when the latter was fed, the product was largely the glucoside of the —CH$_2$OH grouping. A summary of the probable course of salicin (and helicin) biosynthesis, embodying in part the degradation reaction shown in Eq. 5-6, is given in Eq. 5-7

salicin   helicin

[Eq. 5-7]

5.8   Simple Phenols (C$_6$ Compounds)

Relatively few compounds containing only the six carbon atoms of the benzene ring are known in nature. The commonest are arbutin (hydroquinone β-D-glucopyranoside) and its methyl ether. Arbutin is derived by way of the shikimic acid-phenylalanine pathway, for administration of ^{14}C-labeled phenylalanine, cinnamic acid, tyrosine, and shikimic acid to leaves of *Pyrus communis* (pear; fam. Rosaceae) led to the formation of ^{14}C-labeled arbutin, while ^{14}C-labeled acetate, pyruvate and succinate were not utilized. The formation of arbutin from ^{14}C-phenylalanine in *Grevillea robusta* (fam. Proteaceae) confirmed this finding.

The formation of arbutin from phenylalanine may proceed by way of *p*-coumaric acid and *p*-hydroxybenzoic acid, and thence to hydroquinone by the oxidative decarboxylation reaction suggested in Eq. 4-30.

Antiarol (3,4,5-trimethoxyphenol), found in the plant *Antiaria toxicaria* (fam. Moraceae), is related to gallic acid in the same way that hydroquinone methyl ether is related to *p*-hydroxybenzoic acid. Nothing is known about the biosynthesis of antiarol, but it may be suggested that the 1,3,4,5-tetrahydroxylation pattern is produced by oxidative decarboxylation of gallic (or syringic) acid.

5.9 Compounds of the Class C_6—C_2

Derivatives of β-phenylethylamine, many of them familiar alkaloids, are derived from phenylalanine and tyrosine, presumably by a decarboxylation of the amino acid followed (or preceded) by minor modifications such as N-methylation (by methionine) and oxidation (as in the formation of ephedrine and epinephrine). Since the biosynthesis of compounds of this class presents no unusual features in its gross aspects, no detailed discussion is needed.

A class of C_6—C_2 compounds that arises from C_6—C_3 precursors by the process of β-oxidation, followed by decarboxylation of the resulting β-keto acid, are the acetophenone derivatives of which pungenoside, picein, and androsin are typical (Eq. 5-9). That these are derived by the shikimic acid pathway is suggested by the 4- and 3,4-hydroxylation, and this has been substantiated in the case of pungenoside (pungenin 3-glucoside) by feeding labeled compounds to *Picea pungens*. L-Phenylalanine, 3,4-dihydroxycinnamic acid (caffeic acid), and cinnamic acid were incorporated into pungenin, while phenylacetic acid, mandelic acid, and 3-hydroxytyramine (dopamine) were ineffective. Acetate was not effectively incorporated. Experiments with specifically labeled cinnamic acids showed clearly that the —$COCH_3$ group of pungenin is derived from the —CH=CH— carbon atoms of cinnamic acid by a process that may be briefly represented by the sequence

$$—CH=CHCOOH \longrightarrow —COCH_2COOH \longrightarrow —COCH_3 + CO_2 \qquad [Eq.\ 5\text{-}8]$$

$$[Eq.\ 5\text{-}9]$$

pungenoside

picein

androsin

Paeonol and xanthoxyletin are, respectively 2-hydroxy-4-methoxy-acetophenone and 2-hydroxy-4,6-dimethoxyacetophenone, a pattern that indicates their derivation by the acetate-malonate pathway. The biosynthetic origin of acetophenone, found in the root of *Stirlingia latifolia* (fam. Proteaceae) is not obvious, for in the absence of hydroxyl groups no clue is present. It is most probable that acetophenone is shikimic (i.e., cinnamic) acid-derived, for the occurrence in nature of unsubstituted phenyl groups in compounds of shikimic origin is frequent.

The phenolic ketone zingerone, although not of the C_6—C_2 class, is clearly derived by an analogous route (Eq. 5-10).

C_6—CH=CHCO—SCoA† + malonyl—CoA

$\downarrow$

C_6—CH$_2$CH$_2$COCH$_2$CO—SCoA††

$\downarrow$

C_6—CH$_2$CH$_2$COCH$_2$COOH

$\downarrow$

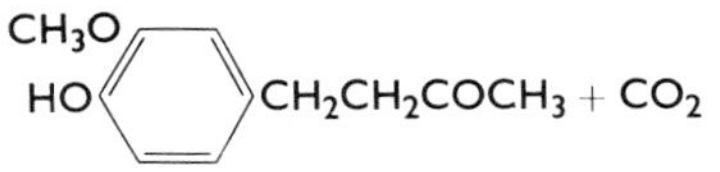

CH$_3$O
HO — CH$_2$CH$_2$COCH$_3$ + CO$_2$ [Eq. 5-10]

zingerone

---

† The symbol C_6 is used for the aromatic ring when it is not known at which stage in the biosynthetic sequence the hydroxylation pattern is established.

†† The stage at which reduction of CH=CH to —CH$_2$CH$_2$— occurs cannot be assumed with certainty.

It will be recalled that certain polyacetylenes containing terminal —COCH$_3$ groups (Chap. 3) arise by way of the decarboxylation of a polyketide-derived β-keto acid. The foregoing observations, coupled with the occurrence in nature of many alkyl methyl ketones, indicate that the formation and decarboxylation of β-keto acids is a common metabolic process.

5.10 Compounds of the C_6—C_3 Class: Phenylpropanoid Compounds

The fundamental importance of the reaction sequence shikimic acid → prephenic acid → phenylalanine → cinnamic acid, and the widespread occurrence in nature of cinnamic acids and their biodegradation products, leads to the conclusion that the many natural compounds containing three-carbon side-chains attached to phenolic nuclei are reduction products of the cinnamic acids.

Nature affords examples of nearly all of the levels of oxidation of the three-carbon side chain of the C_6—C_3 class; a number of examples of naturally occurring compounds are shown in Fig. 5-7.

Little more is known about the biosynthesis of the compounds of this class than can be discerned from the close structural analogies that are evident. In particular, the frequent occurrence of 4-hydroxy and 3,4-dihydroxy groups (or methyl ethers of these) is the hallmark of the phenylpropanoid class of compounds. Thus, while their origin through the shikimic-prephenic-phenylalanine (or tyrosine)- cinnamic (or *p*-coumaric) pathway can be assumed, the pathways by which the various reduction levels are reached must await further experimental study.

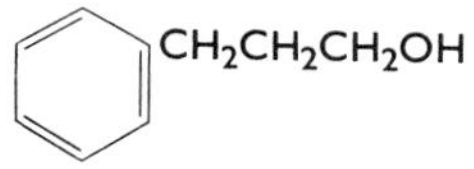

hydrocinnamyl alcohol

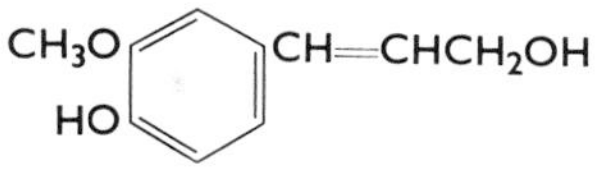

coniferyl alcohol

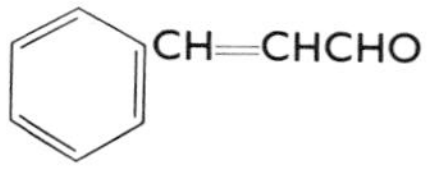

cinnamaldehyde

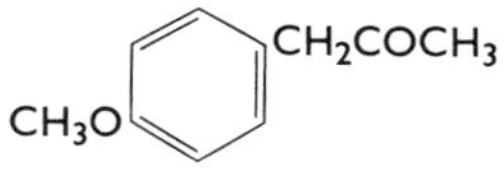

anise ketone

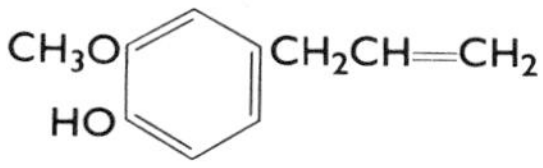

eugenol

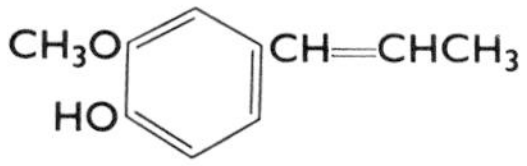

isoeugenol

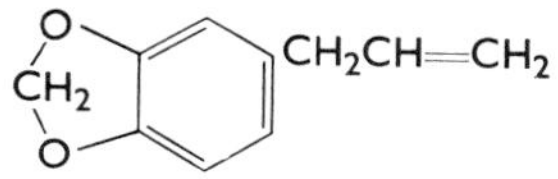

safrole

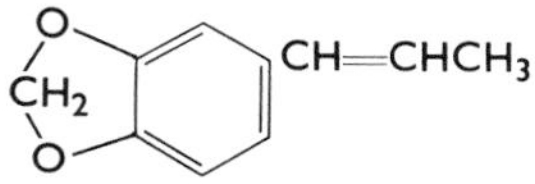

isosafrole

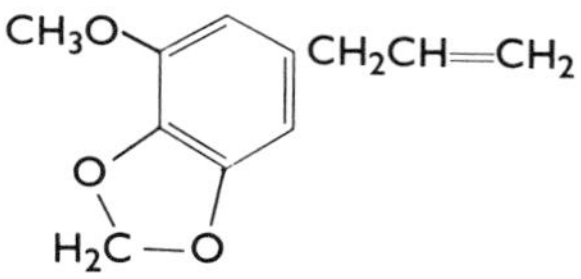

myristicin

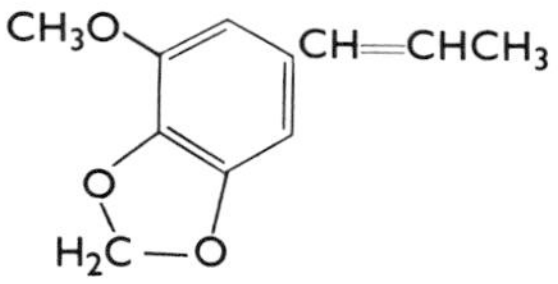

isomyristicin

Fig. 5-7. Naturally Occurring C_6—C_3 Compounds with Various Oxidation States of C_3.

It is, however, significant that in certain cases the allyl and propenyl isomers occur together in the same plant. For example, safrole and isosafrole have both been found in *Cananga odorata* (fam. Anonaceae), and myristicin and isomyristicin can occur together in *Myristica fragrans* (fam. Myristicaceae).

The isomerization of the allyl side chain to the propenyl side chain can be accomplished in the laboratory; but, as might be expected from the relatively inactive character of the —CH_2— group adjacent to the aromatic ring, this isomerization is effected only by rather vigorous treatment with strong alkali. It is highly improbable that a direct prototropic isomerization takes place in the plant, and thus it is likely that the allyl-propenyl pairs are independently formed.

The reduction of the cinnamic acid side chain through the steps

$$-CH{=}CHCOSCoA \longrightarrow -CH{=}CHCHO \longrightarrow -CH{=}CHCH_2OH$$

has an obvious parallel in the formation of mevalonic acid from β-methyl-β-hydroxyglutaric acid. In the latter case, the last stages of the generation of the isoprenoid building unit (Sec. 2.18) is the pyrophosphorylation of the alcoholic hydroxyl group. If the cinnamyl alcohol shown above were similarly converted into the pyrophosphate, the resulting ester would be highly susceptible to nucleophilic attack. It is well recognized that many biological reductions occur by a mechanism which is in effect an attack by a hydride ion donated by NADH or NADPH. Reduction of a cinnamyl pyrophosphate could occur in two ways, corresponding to (a) direct nucleophilic displacement of pyrophosphate or (b) allylic displacement. Alternatively, if the reaction proceeded by (c) an S_N1 mechanism, the manner of formation of the allyl or propenyl isomers is at once apparent, for the charge-delocalized ion could accept a hydride ion at either of the allylic positions (Eq. 5-11):

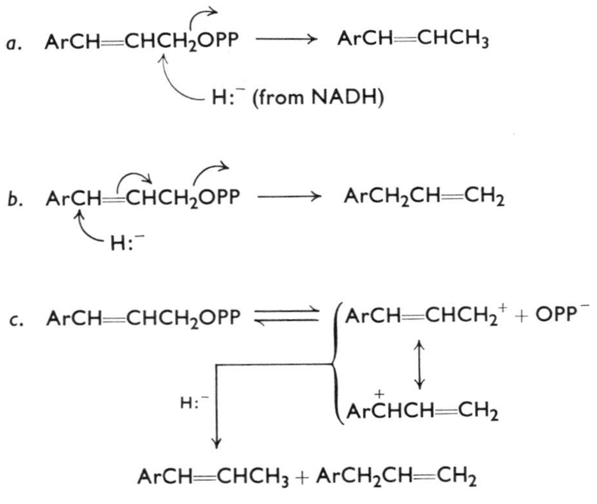

a. $ArCH{=}CHCH_2OPP \longrightarrow ArCH{=}CHCH_3$

$H{:}^-$ (from NADH)

b. $ArCH{=}CHCH_2OPP \longrightarrow ArCH_2CH{=}CH_2$

$H{:}^-$

c. $ArCH{=}CHCH_2OPP \rightleftharpoons \left(ArCH{=}CHCH_2^+ + OPP^- \right.$

$\left. Ar\overset{+}{C}HCH{=}CH_2 \right)$

$H{:}^-$

[Eq. 5-11]

$ArCH{=}CHCH_3 + ArCH_2CH{=}CH_2$

5.11 Lignans and Lignin

The lignans and lignin are a widely distributed class of phenylpropanoid compounds whose structures clearly support the view that they are formed in nature by the oxidative dimerization or polymerization of C_6—C_3 units. In Fig. 5-8 are given some typical examples of natural lignans, along with a formal representation of the way in which the lignan carbon skeleton is formed.

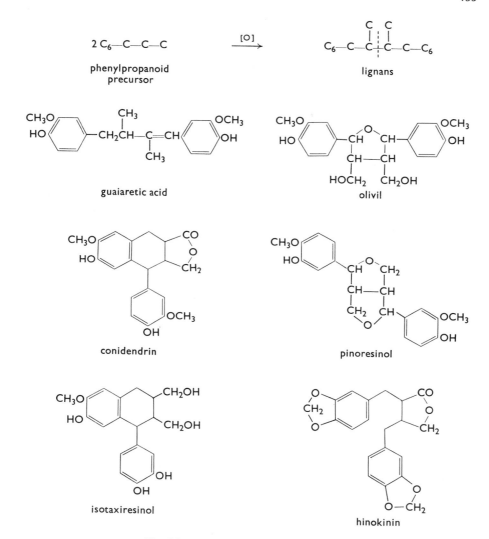

Fig. 5-8. Some Representative Lignans.*

The phenylpropanoid route (shikimic acid → phenylalanine (or tyrosine) → cinnamic (or *p*-coumaric) acid → lignans and lignin) can be inferred on several substantial grounds:

1. By far the greatest number of the known lignans possess the 3,4-dioxygenated substitution pattern shown in Fig. 5-8.

* The stereochemistry of some selected examples will be discussed in the text.

2. Lignans have been found to be formed by the oxidation of coniferyl alcohol *in vitro* by the action of enzyme preparations, under conditions that simulate the physiological conditions that obtain in living cells.

3. Labeled C_6—C_3 compounds (phenylalanine, tyrosine, cinnamic and *p*-coumaric acids, coniferyl alcohol) have been fed to living plants, with the formation of radioactive lignin labeled in the expected position(s).

Because of the structural complexity of lignin, which is a high molecular weight polymer, the probability that authentic "native" lignin has not been obtained as a pure compound, and the uncertainty as to whether "artificial" lignins (formed by *in vitro* enzymatic oxidations of coniferyl alcohol) are structurally identical with natural lignin, the conclusion that lignans lie directly on the biosynthetic pathway to lignin cannot be said to have been established with certainty. There is, however, little doubt that the oxidative processes that lead from "monomeric" C_6—C_3 compounds to the dimeric and trimeric products and ultimately to lignin represent the natural course of lignin biosynthesis.

The central role in lignan and lignin biosynthesis appears to be played by coniferyl alcohol and its glucoside, coniferin (Fig. 5-9).

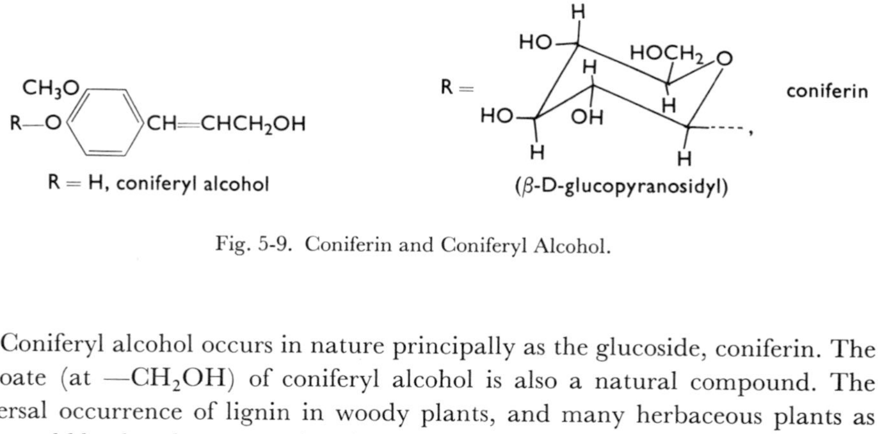

Fig. 5-9. Coniferin and Coniferyl Alcohol.

Coniferyl alcohol occurs in nature principally as the glucoside, coniferin. The benzoate (at —CH_2OH) of coniferyl alcohol is also a natural compound. The universal occurrence of lignin in woody plants, and many herbaceous plants as well, would lead to the expectation that coniferin is equally widely distributed. The fact that coniferin has not been widely observed in nature may be because of its high metabolic activity, with the result that only very small pools of the compound are present in the tissues of growing plants, or simply due to the fact that it has been overlooked in studies aimed at the isolation of other compounds. The limited (reported) occurrence of coniferin in nature may be compared with the infrequency with which shikimic acid was reported as a plant constituent prior to the recognition of its central role in secondary plant metabolism.

Coniferin, the glucoside, is a stable, relatively unreactive compound; its participation in the metabolic changes to be described in the following discussion follows its hydrolysis* to the highly reactive coniferyl alcohol (Eq. 5-12):

Shikimic acid pathway ⟶

[Eq. 5-12]

Lignans appear structurally, and have been shown experimentally, to be oxidative dimers of coniferyl alcohol. Enzymatic oxidation of coniferyl alcohol *in vitro* leads to lignans and related oxidation products as well as to polymeric materials having many of the characteristics of natural lignin. By altering the experimental conditions of the coniferyl alcohol-oxidase reaction and interrupting it at stages prior to the formation of the final polymer, numerous "intermediates" have been isolated and characterized.

The precise mechanism of the phenol oxidations that lead to these products is not certain (see Chap. 14). The prevailing view that the reaction involves the formation and coupling of an intermediate free radical has some experimental support; and the alternative, that a two-electron oxidation, leading to an electron-deficient "onium" ion, provides the reactive intermediate offers an equally rational view of the overall process. These questions, which are involved in oxidative coupling reactions in a wide variety of compound classes and are not easily resolvable, will be dealt with separately in another section. For present purposes the two-electron course will be selected for its convenience to illustrate the reactions to be discussed; if a one-electron intermediate is indeed the reactive species, the formulations can be modified accordingly. For additional convenience in representation, a simplified reactant, a *p*-hydroxystyrene prototype, will be used in the examples, for it will be seen that the *p*-hydroxystyrene system is the relevant structure in most of the reactions to be described (Eq. 5-13):

[Eq. 5-13]

* The hydrolysis of coniferin in the cell would, of course, be an enzymatic process. It must be recognized, however, that the coniferyl alcohol involved in the transformations to be described might be used prior to its glucosylation, coniferin formation being a final—and terminal—step.

The nature of the oxidative coupling reaction is most clearly represented by the formation of guaiaretic acid (Fig. 5-8), one of the simplest of the lignans (Eq. 5-14):

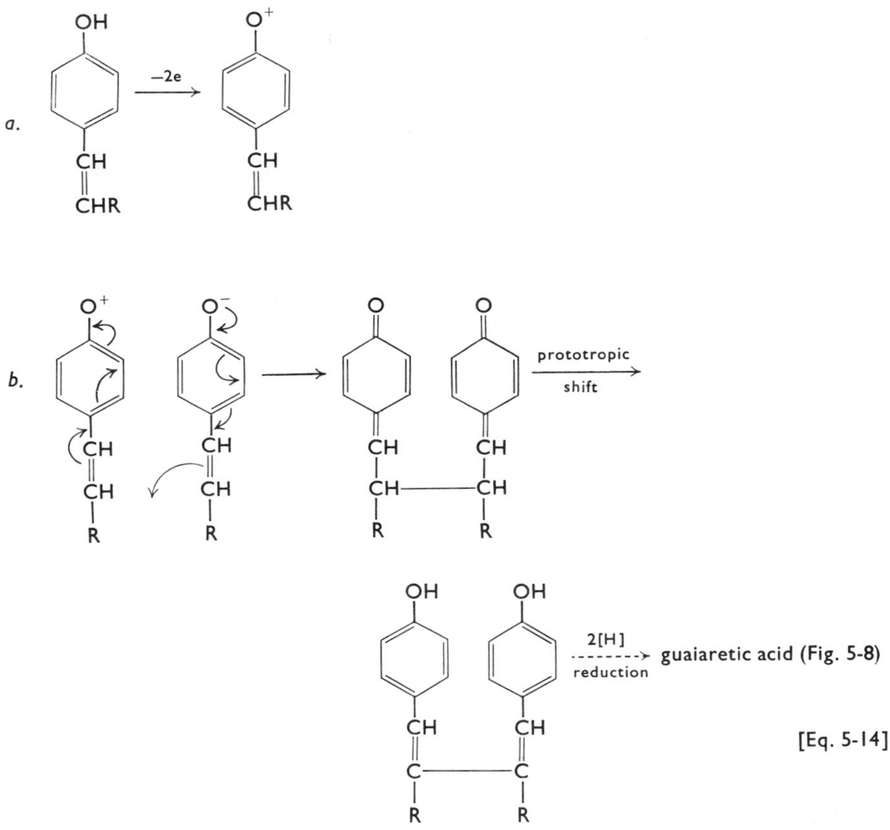

a.

$$\text{(structure: 4-hydroxy benzene with CH=CHR)} \xrightarrow{-2e} \text{(structure: O}^+ \text{ benzene with CH=CHR)}$$

b.

(oxidative coupling structures) $\longrightarrow$ (bis-quinonemethine structures) $\xrightarrow[\text{shift}]{\text{prototropic}}$

(bis-phenol structure with OH groups, CH, C—C, R) $\xrightarrow[\text{reduction}]{2[H]}$ guaiaretic acid (Fig. 5-8)

[Eq. 5-14]

e.g., $HO\text{—}\bigcirc\text{—}CH{=}CHR$ represents $CH_3O\text{, }HO\text{—}\bigcirc\text{—}CH{=}CHCH_3$

(Note: An additional reduction stage leading to nordihydroguaiaretic acid as the final product, can also occur, possibly at the stage of the bis-quinonemethine:

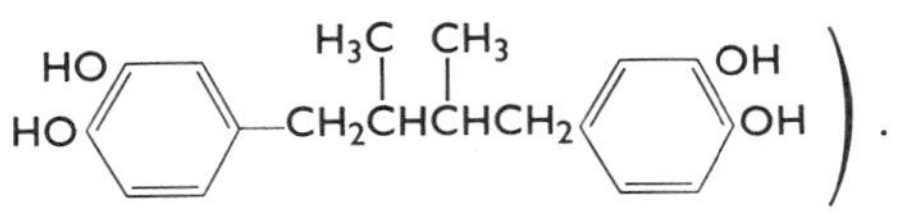

$$\begin{array}{c} HO \\ HO \end{array}\text{—}\bigcirc\text{—}CH_2\overset{H_3C}{\underset{}{C}}H\overset{CH_3}{\underset{}{C}}HCH_2\text{—}\bigcirc\begin{array}{c} OH \\ OH \end{array}\Bigg).$$

nordihydroguaiaretic acid.

The furan-derived lignans, olivil and pinoresinol, are at the oxidation level of the two-electron stage; that is, they can be derived by direct combination of un-oxidized coniferyl alcohol with the intermediate shown in Eq. 5-14a (Eq. 5-15);

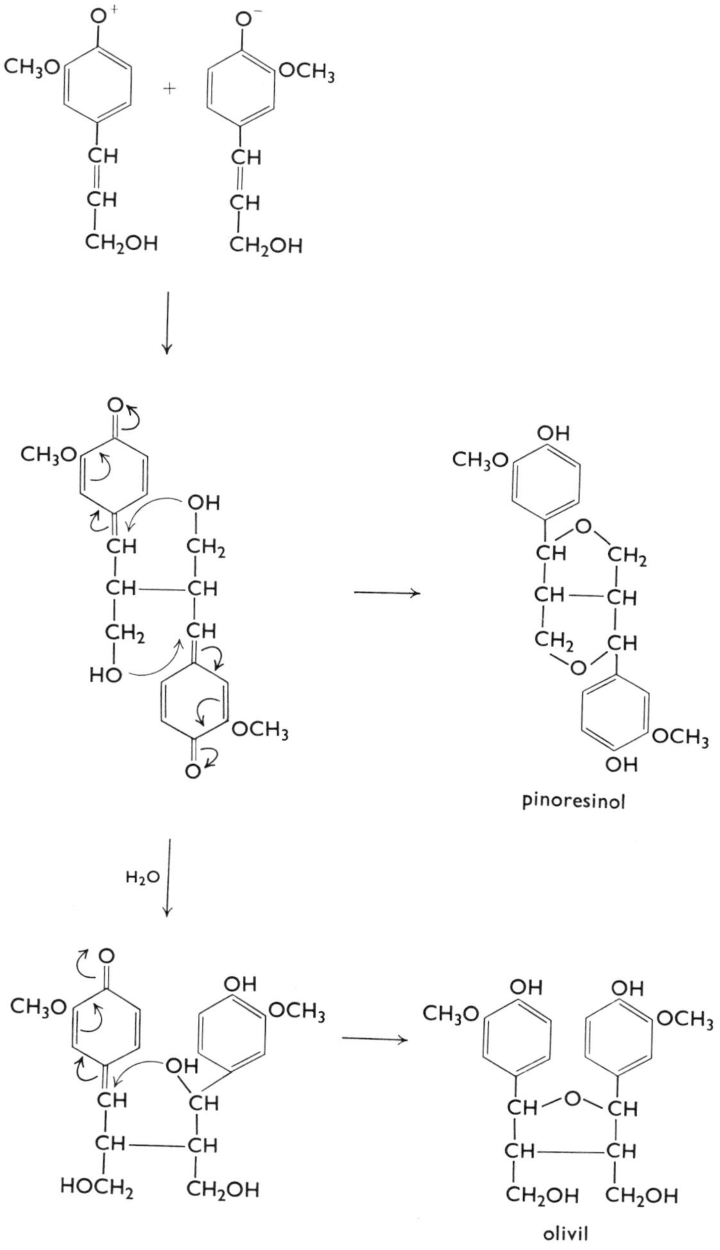

pinoresinol

[Eq. 5-15]

olivil

Because of charge (or electron) delocalization in the oxidized intermediates, electrophilic character is present at the positions *ortho* and *para* to the 4-hydroxyl group. Coupling can thus take place as in Eq. 5-16, to give a product that has been isolated as a discrete compound in *in vitro* oxidation experiments.

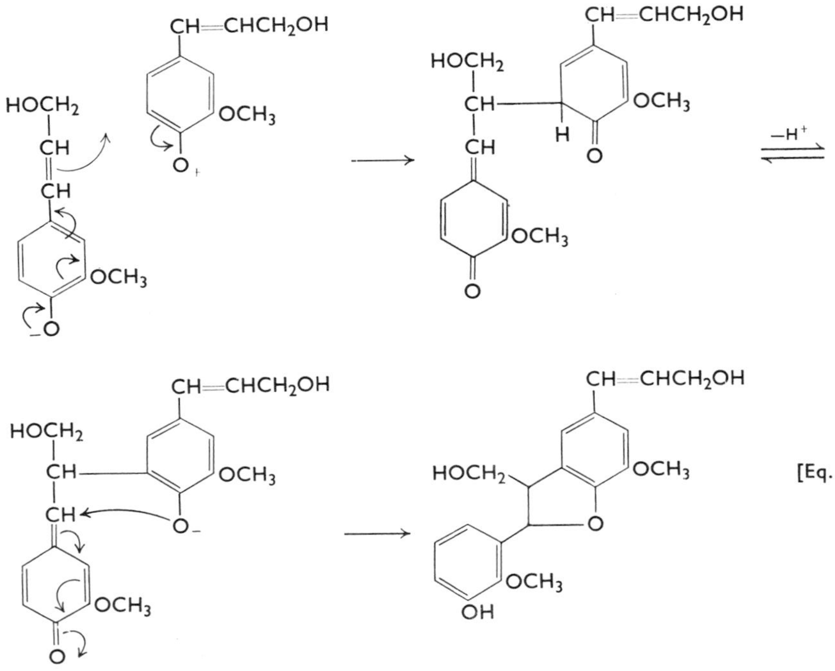

[Eq. 5-16]

Lignin, which according to this hypothesis, is a polymer formed by repetitions of the oxidative steps illustrated in the foregoing examples, is a complex, high molecular weight substance for the structure of which only an illustrative fragment can be formulated. Indeed, it is reasonable to suppose that because of the variety of ways in which each successive oxidative coupling step can occur, lignins in the same or different plants may possess structures that, although having essentially the same gross features, differ in detail. The precise role of enzymes in lignin formation is not known, except for the high probability that plant oxidases or peroxidases are involved in the electron-transfer steps.

Depending upon their botanical source, lignins may be constructed principally of coniferyl alcohol (i.e., 3-methoxy-4-hydroxyphenyl) units, or may include syringyl alcohol (i.e., 3,5-dimethoxy-4-hydroxyphenyl) units. Lignins of the former class are characteristic of conifers and other gymnosperms (e.g., pine, spruce, fir, etc.), while the syringyl unit is found in the lignins of angiosperms (e.g., maple, oak, elm, etc.).

A structure proposed as a representation of a part of a lignin molecule is shown in Fig. 5-10; it should be borne in mind that so large a portion of a lignin has not yet been characterized in complete detail.

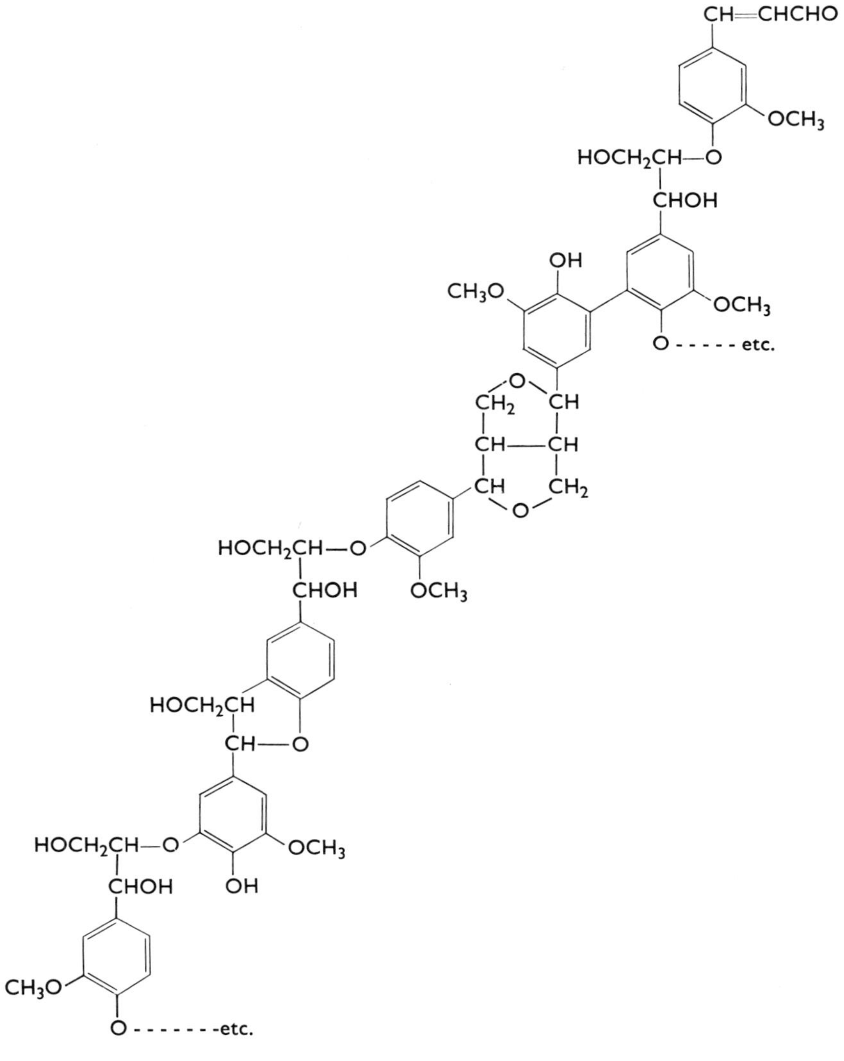

Fig. 5-10. Idealized Structure of a Portion of the Lignin Molecule.

A more detailed discussion of the phenol oxidation processes outlined above is to be found in Chapter 14.

5.12 Chemistry and Stereochemistry of Lignans

Among the naturally occurring lignans are found compounds that contain as many as four asymmetric carbon atoms.

$(-)$-Guaiaretic acid serves as a reference compound for one center of asymmetry. The absolute configuration of this carbon atom is shown in Eq. 5-17, where the procedure used for establishing the configuration is outlined.

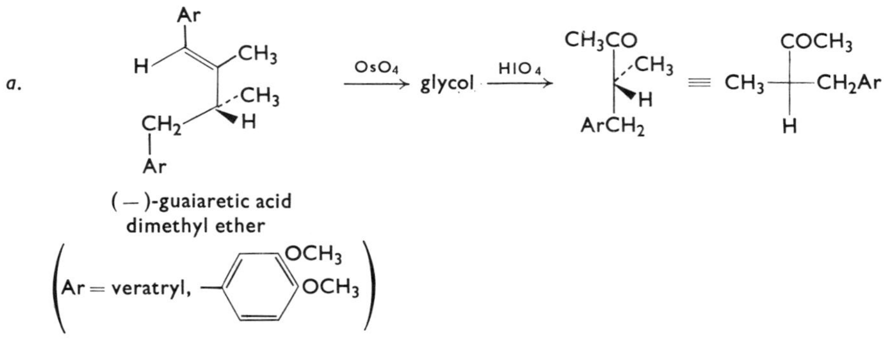

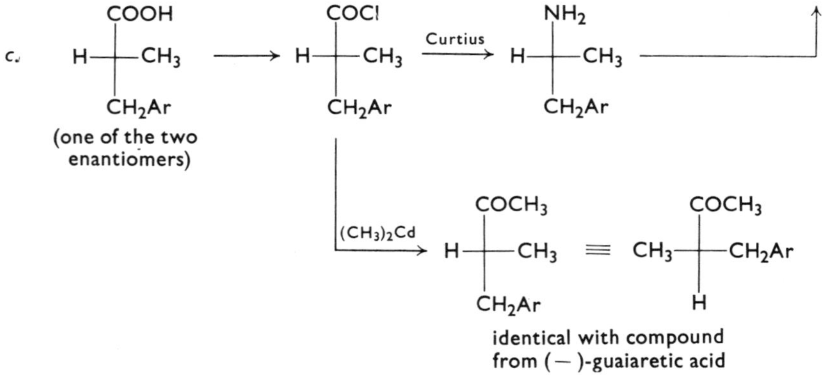

a.

$(-)$-guaiaretic acid
dimethyl ether

$\left(Ar = \text{veratryl,} \right.$ $\left. \right)$

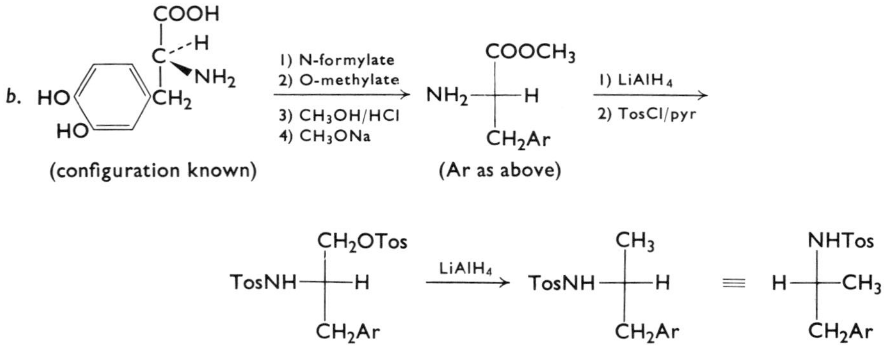

b. (configuration known) → (Ar as above)

c. (one of the two enantiomers)

[Eq. 5-17]

identical with compound
from $(-)$-guaiaretic acid

The establishment of the absolute configuration of the asymmetric carbon atom in (−)-guaiaretic acid permits the assignment of the configuration of the dihydro compounds formed by hydrogenation of (−)-guaiaretic acid. One of these is the *meso* form; the other, optically active, has the configuration shown in Eq. 5-18. The natural lignans (−)-matairesinol and (−)-arctigenin (and its glucoside, arctiin) can also be directly correlated with dihydroguaiaretic acid by the reactions shown in Eq. 5-18.

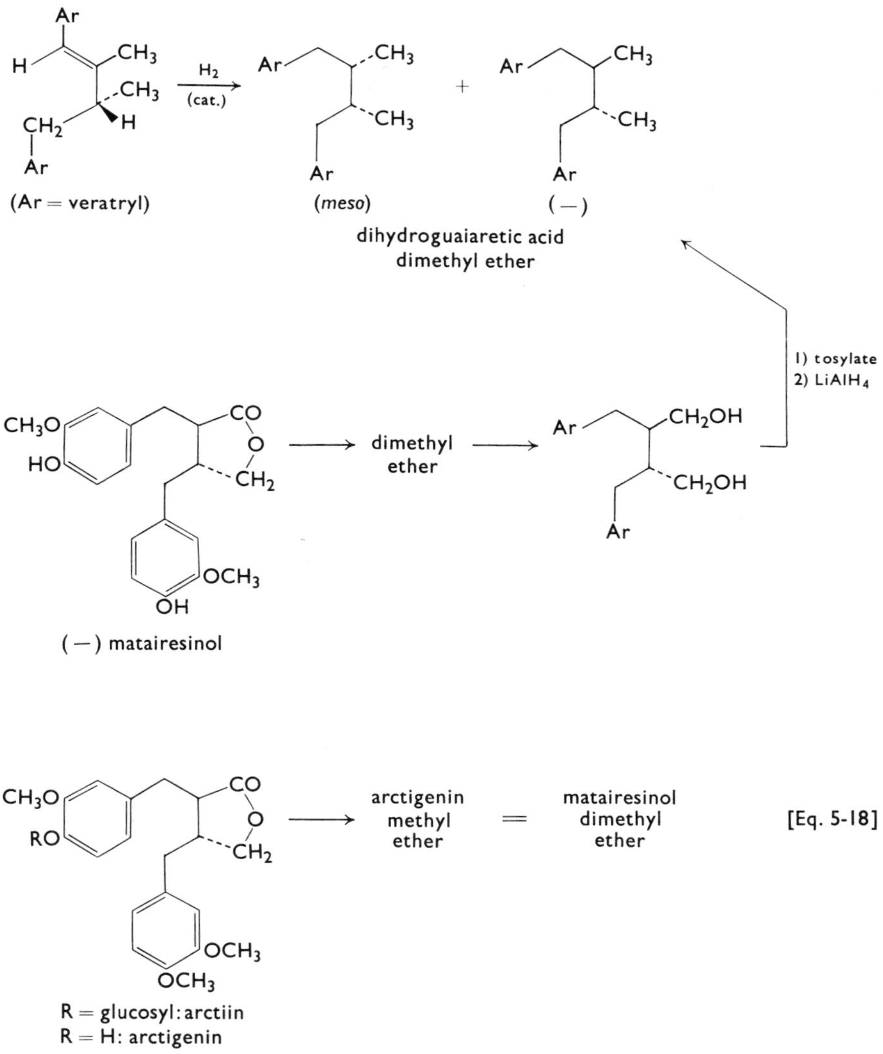
H2 (cat.)
(Ar = veratryl)
(meso)
(−)
dihydroguaiaretic acid dimethyl ether
1) tosylate
2) LiAlH4
dimethyl ether
(−) matairesinol
arctigenin methyl ether
=
matairesinol dimethyl ether
R = glucosyl: arctiin
R = H: arctigenin

[Eq. 5-18]

α-Conidendrin is a lignan formed in abundance in conifers. Its structure and stereochemistry were established by the interrelationships described in Eq. 5-19. (+)-Lariciresinol, a lignan containing a tetrahydrofuran ring, is converted by acid-catalyzed cyclization to (+)-isolariciresinol, and by catalytic hydrogenation (hydrogenolysis of the ArCH—O— linkages) to the diol obtained from matairesinol:*

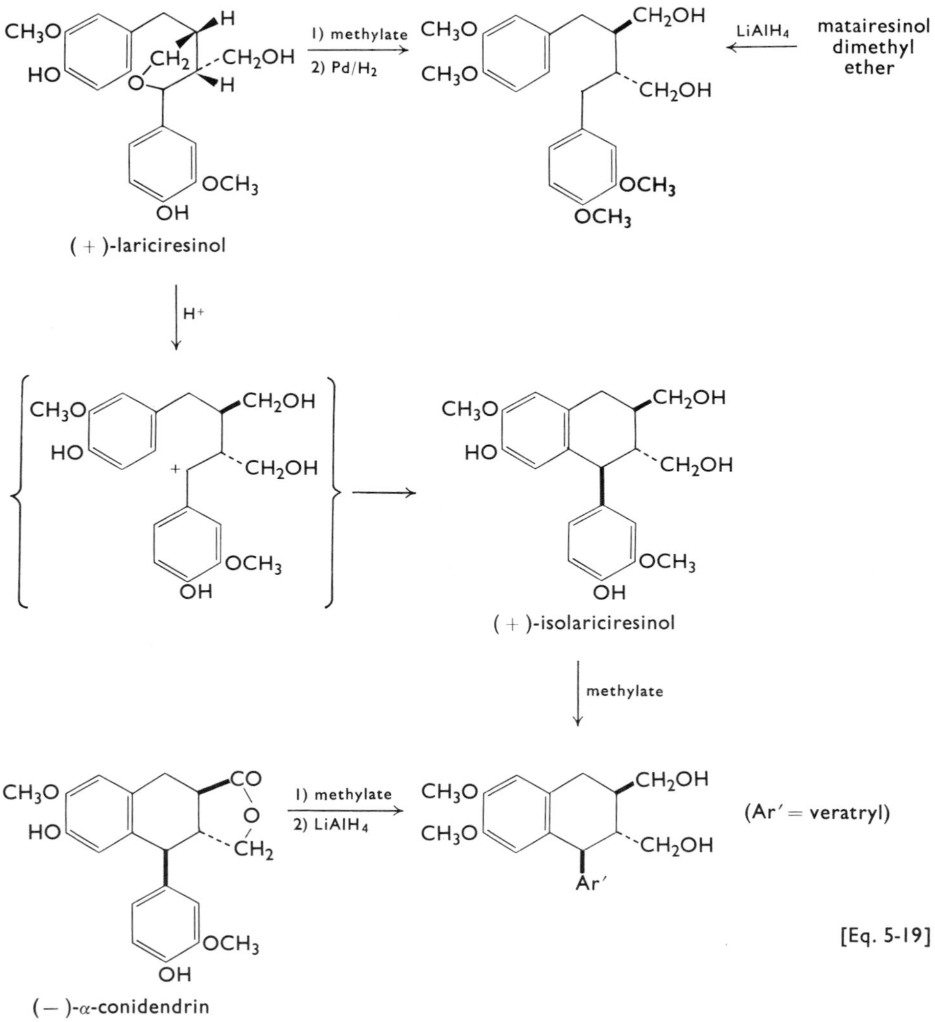

[Eq. 5-19]

* Most of the transformations described here were performed with the O-methylated compounds, or final comparisons were made with O-methylated products.

An added confirmation of these relationships was obtained when it was observed that oxidation of arctigenin acetate (Eq. 5-18) with lead tetraacetate brought about an oxidative ring closure to give a compound which, upon deacetylation and O-methylation, yielded conidendrin methyl ether.

Although the foregoing experimental results reveal a common stereochemistry at the 2,3, and 4 positions of the 4-aryl-1,2,3,4-tetrahydronaphthalene ring, it does not follow that the stereochemistry of all the lignans fits a common pattern. Stereoisomeric lignans occur, often in the same plant.

Two lignans isolated from the heartwood of *Guaiacum officinalis* L. (fam. Zygophyllaceae) are the tetrahydrofurans shown in Fig. 5-11:*

THFG-A and THFG-B dimethyl ethers (DME) from *Guaiacum officinalis* L.

(Ar = veratryl)

galgravin ≡ THFG—A—DME   (−)-galbelgin

from *Galbulimima belgraveana*

Fig. 5-11.

THFG-A-DME and THFG-B-DME are optically inactive (*meso*) compounds and one of them is identical with galgravin, a *meso* tetrahydrofuran, isolated along with galbelgin, an optically active isomer, from *Galbulimima belgraveana* (F. Muell.) Sprague (fam. Himantandraceae) (Fig. 5-11).

The configurations of the *Galbulimima* compounds and of the THFG compounds are shown by the transformations described in Eq. 5-20 and Eq. 5-21. Partial reductive cleavage of galgravin and galbelgin gave isomeric carbinols (C and C′ in Eq. 5-20), which when cyclized by the action of mineral acid gave isomeric tetralin derivatives. That from galgravin (called isogalbulin) is necessarily a pair of enantiomorphs (since the starting material was not asymmetric), while (−)-galbelgin gave an optically active product, (−)-galbulin. The structure and stereo-

* The compounds occur as methoxyphenols, but they were isolated and examined as the methylated compounds (veratryl derivatives), and will be dealt with here as these dimethyl ethers (DME).

chemistry of (−)-galbulin was established by its preparation from isolariciresinol in the manner shown in Eq. 5-20.

The stereochemistry of galgravin, the *meso* isomer, was suggested by the observation that upon dehydrogenation by heating it with palladium it was converted into a 4-arylnaphthalene. THFG-B-DME, on the other hand, lost four

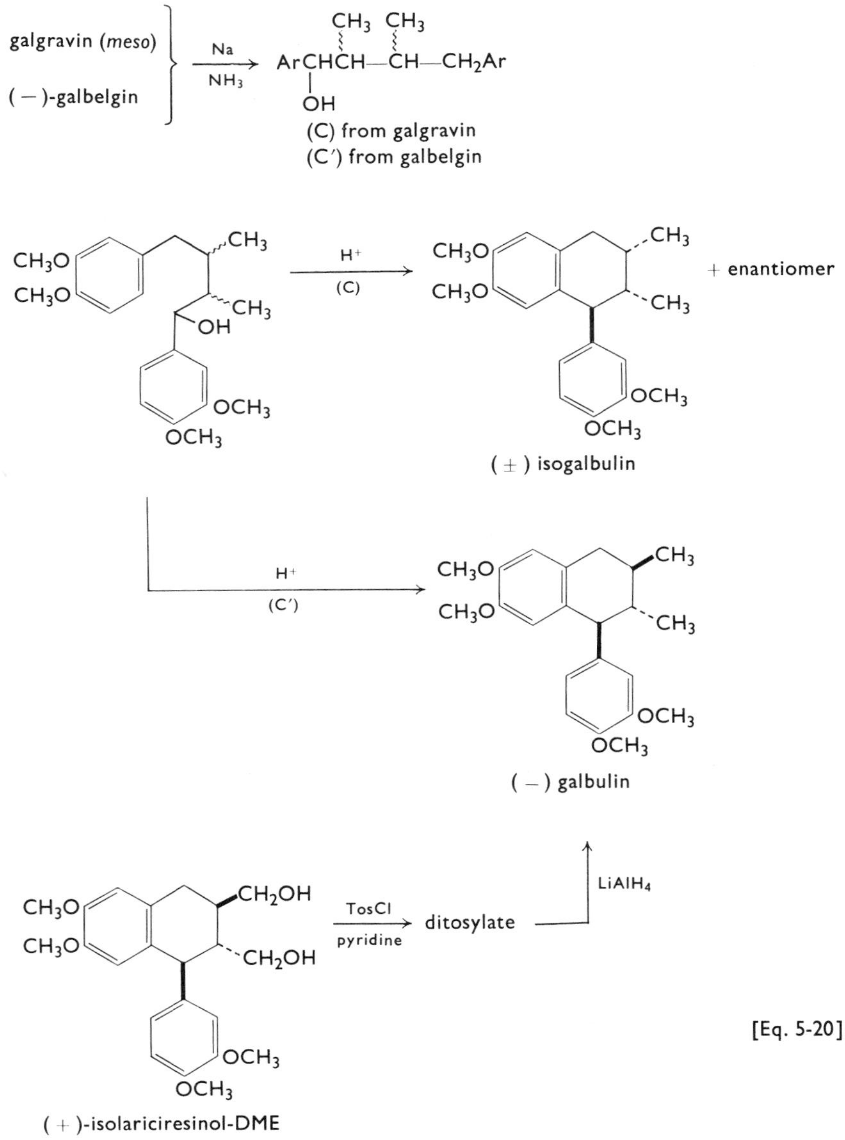

[Eq. 5-20]

hydrogen atoms to give the furan derivative (Eq. 5-21). This furan, also prepared synthetically, could be reduced catalytically to THFG-B-DME.

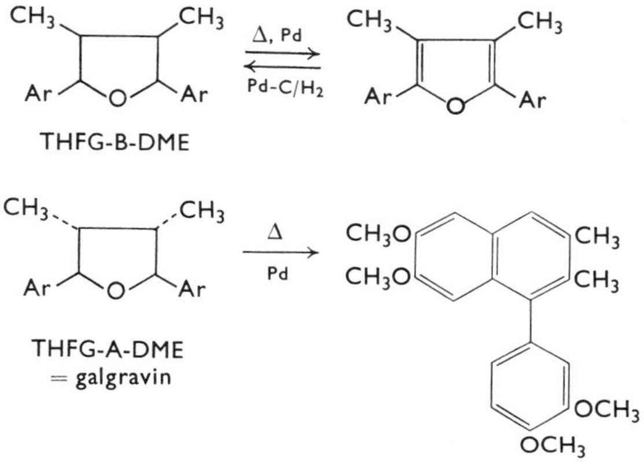

[Eq. 5-21]

Finally, it was observed that neither galgravin nor (−)-galbelgin was isomerized when heated with perchlóric acid (short of secondary cyclization reactions) (Eq. 5-22):

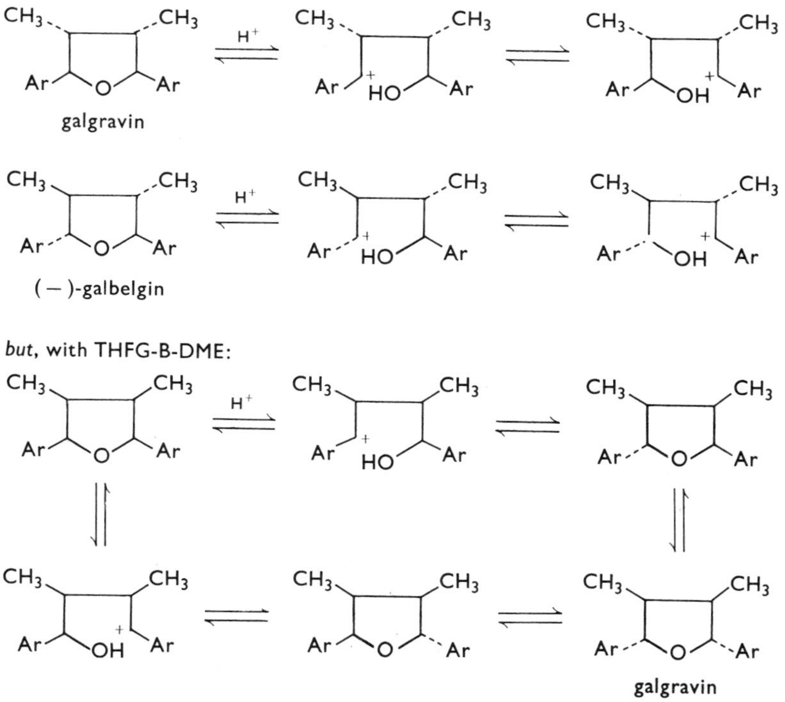

but, with THFG-B-DME:

[Eq. 5-22]

Since THFG-B-DME is isomerized to galgravin under these conditions, the 2,3-*trans*-4,5-*trans* configuration for galgravin, and the 2,3-*cis*-4,5-*cis* configuration for THFG-B-DME are indicated. The reversible, acid-catalyzed ring-opening, ring-closure would be expected to lead to isomerization of the 2,3-*cis* arrangement to the more stable 2,3-*trans* arrangement of Ar and CH$_3$. In THFG-B-DME this isomerization is observed. These results indicate that ($-$)-galbelgin possesses the stereochemistry shown in the foregoing equations, rather than the alternatives shown in Eq. 5-23.

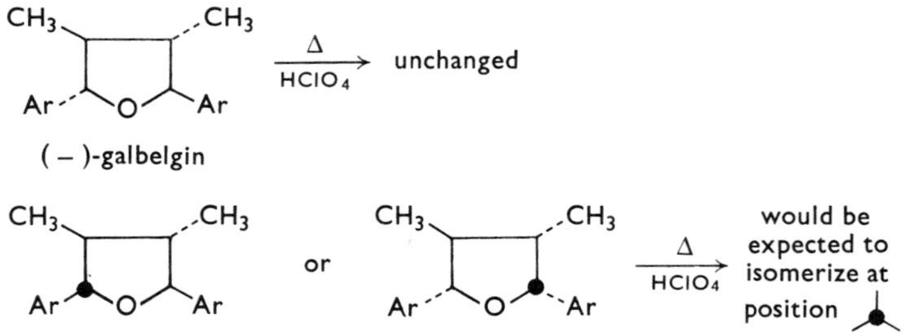

For reasons similar to those advanced for the retention of the *trans*-2,3 relationships in the tetrahydrofuran derivatives, the 4-aryltetralins formed by ring closures such as lariciresinol → isolariciresinol (Eq. 5-19), and those leading to galbulin and isogalbulin (Eq. 5-20), proceed with the formation of 3,4-*trans* substituted tetralins. The formation of 4-aryl-tetralins in nature, however, does not invariably lead to the same stereochemical result, for natural lignans are known that possess 3,4-*cis*-disposed substituents. An example is podophyllotoxin, a compound of special interest because of its activity as a tumor-damaging agent (Fig. 5-12).

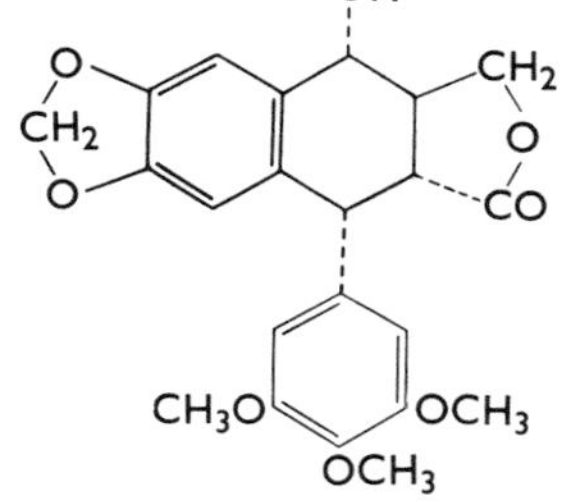

podophyllotoxin

Fig. 5-12.

VI CHAPTER

~~~~~~

REFERENCES FOR FURTHER READING

1. E. von Rudolff and E. Jorgensen, *The Biosynthesis of Pinosylvin in the Sapwood of Pinus resinosa* Ait., Phytochemistry, *2*, (1963), 297.
2. G. Billek and H. Kindl, *Biosynthesis of Plant Stilbenes. Formation of Ring A of Hydrangenol,* Monatshefte, *93*, (1962), 814.
3. R. K. Ibrahim and G. H. N. Towers, *Biosynthesis of Hydrangenol from* [14]*C-Labeled Compounds,* Can. J. Biochem. Physiol., *40*, (1962), 449.
4. O. R. Gottlieb and W. B. Mors, *The Chemistry of Rosewood (Aniba* spp.), J. Amer. Chem. Soc., *80*, (1958), 2263.

Extension of the Phenylpropanoid Unit: C_6-C_3-$(C_2)_x$ Compounds

6.1 Phenyl Alkyl Ketones; Acids

The extension of the C_6—C_3 unit, acting as a "starter" in acyl CoA-malonyl CoA syntheses, leads to the formation in nature of a large and structurally varied group of compounds, most of them of the general class represented by C_6—C_3—$(C_2)_n$.

The simplest example of this class is the ketone, zingerone, the active principle of ginger, *Zingiber officinalis* (fam. Zingiberaceae). Although the biosynthetic origin of zingerone has not been established by the obvious feeding experiments, the presence of the 4-hydroxy-3-methoxyphenyl group clearly suggests its shikimic acid origin. The course of its biosynthesis can be surmised in broad terms only, for the point at which the (presumable) progenitor, cinnamic acid, is reduced and hydroxylated cannot be decided on arbitrary grounds (Eq. 6-1).

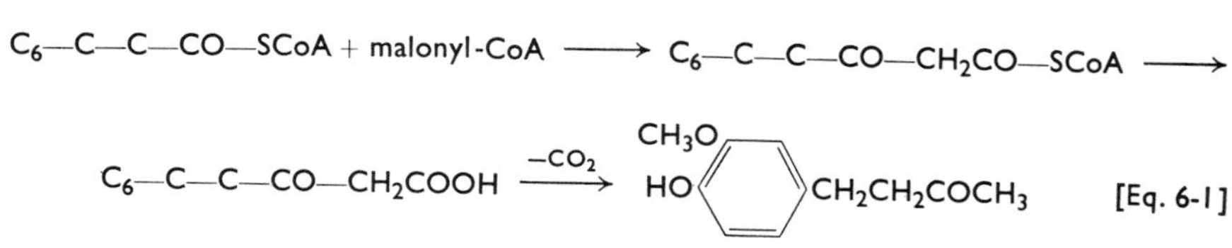

$$C_6\text{—C—C—CO—SCoA} + \text{malonyl-CoA} \longrightarrow C_6\text{—C—C—CO—CH}_2\text{CO—SCoA} \longrightarrow$$

$$C_6\text{—C—C—CO—CH}_2\text{COOH} \xrightarrow{-CO_2} \text{HO}\underset{\text{CH}_3\text{O}}{\bigcirc}\text{CH}_2\text{CH}_2\text{COCH}_3 \qquad \text{[Eq. 6-1]}$$

zingerone

The intermediate formation of a similar C_6—C_3—C_2 precursor can be discerned in the structure of curcumin, the red pigment found in the root of *Curcuma tinctoria* (fam. Zingiberaceae). The probable manner of its biosynthesis is shown in Eq. 6-2, with the provision that the step in which the hydroxylation pattern is established cannot be stated with assurance.

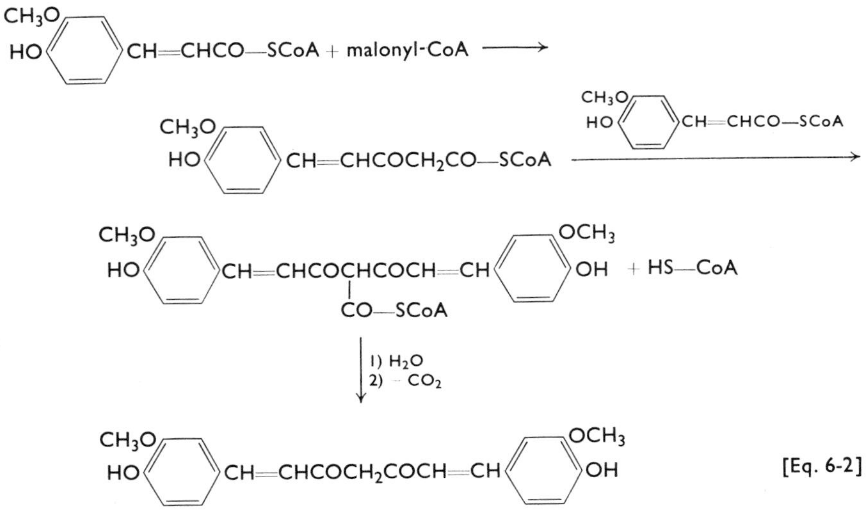

$$CH_3O—C_6H_3(HO)—CH{=}CHCO—SCoA + malonyl\text{-}CoA \longrightarrow$$

$$CH_3O—C_6H_3(HO)—CH{=}CHCOCH_2CO—SCoA \xrightarrow{\quad CH_3O—C_6H_3(HO)—CH{=}CHCO—SCoA \quad}$$

$$CH_3O—C_6H_3(HO)—CH{=}CHCOCHCOCH{=}CH—C_6H_3(OCH_3)OH + HS—CoA$$
$$\underset{CO—SCoA}{|}$$

1) H_2O
2) $- CO_2$

$$CH_3O—C_6H_3(HO)—CH{=}CHCOCH_2COCH{=}CH—C_6H_3(OCH_3)OH \qquad [Eq.\ 6\text{-}2]$$

curcumin

Piperic acid, the acyl constituent of the pungent principle of pepper, and chavicic acid, a geometrical isomer of piperic acid, are also found in pepper (*Piper nigrum*, fam. Piperaceae). The natural flavor principles, piperine and chavicine, are the corresponding amides of these acids with piperidine (Fig. 6-1). The origin of

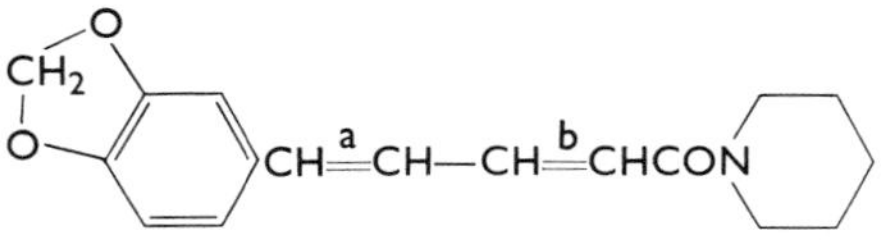

piperine (a, b = *trans*)
chavicine (a, b = *cis*)

Fig. 6-1. Flavor Principles of *Piper* Species.

piperic and chavicic acids is evidently that shown in Eq. 6-3; again, the 3,4-position of the methylenedioxy ring is typical of the compounds of the phenylpropanoid class.

$$ArCH{=}CHCO—SCoA + malonyl\text{-}CoA \longrightarrow$$

$$ArCH{=}CHCOCH_2CO—SCoA \longrightarrow ArCH{=}CH—CH{=}CHCO—SCoA \longrightarrow$$

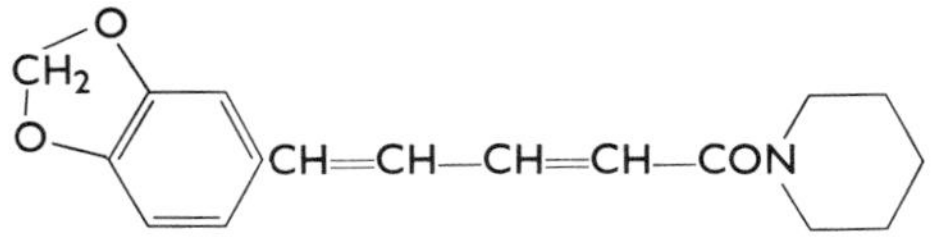

[Eq. 6-3]

piperine (chavicine)

6.2   Constituents of Coto Bark and Kawa Root

The extension of the C_6—C_3 unit by additional C_2 fragments leads to the formation in coto bark (fam. Lauraceae) of several compounds whose structures provide an illuminating example of the various ways in which a common precursor may cyclize. Coto bark (and a related plant material called paracoto bark*) contain the compounds shown in Fig. 6-2.

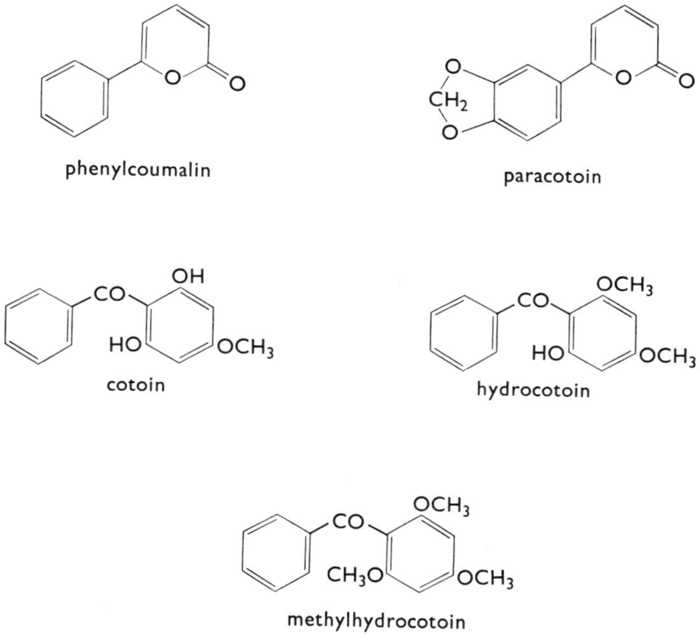

phenylcoumalin

paracotoin

cotoin

hydrocotoin

methylhydrocotoin

Fig. 6-2. Constituents of Coto Barks.

The structures of these compounds raise some questions that cannot be answered categorically. Paracotoin, with the 3,4-methylenedioxyphenyl group, appears to be of shikimic acid origin and a member of the class of phenylpropanoid compounds, many of which are characterized by the 3,4-dioxygenated aryl group. Its origin may be outlined as in Eq. 6-4, in which the sequence of events in which the side chain is altered is necessarily arbitrary.

* The precise botanical designation of these (South American) plants, for a long time obscure, has now been clarified. Coto is *Aniba coto* (Rusby) Kostermans; and paracoto is *A. pseudocoto* (Rusby) Kostermans.

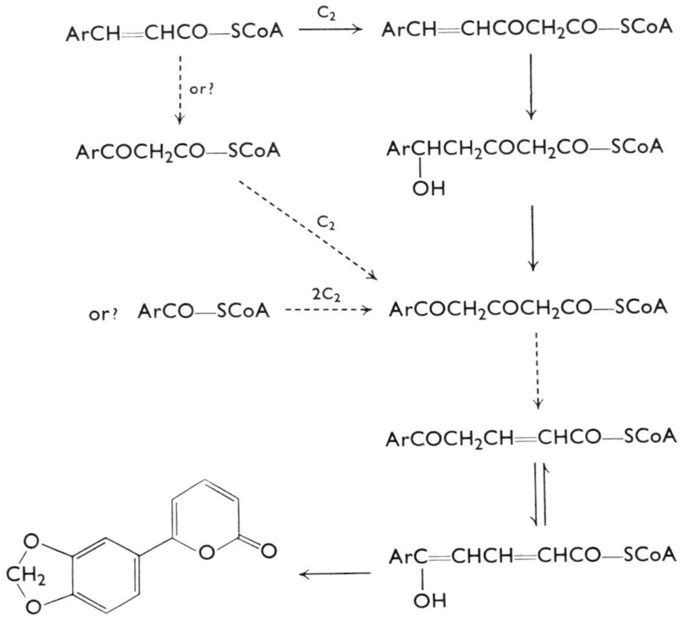

$$ArCH{=}CHCO{-}SCoA \xrightarrow{\ C_2\ } ArCH{=}CHCOCH_2CO{-}SCoA$$

$$\Big\downarrow \text{or?}$$

$$ArCOCH_2CO{-}SCoA \qquad\qquad \underset{\overset{|}{OH}}{ArCHCH_2COCH_2CO{-}SCoA}$$

$$\text{or? } ArCO{-}SCoA \xrightarrow{\ \ 2C_2\ \ } ArCOCH_2COCH_2CO{-}SCoA$$

$$ArCOCH_2CH{=}CHCO{-}SCoA$$

$$\underset{\overset{|}{OH}}{ArC{=}CHCH{=}CHCO{-}SCoA} \qquad\qquad \text{[Eq. 6-4]}$$

It is noteworthy, however, that most of the compounds from coto bark possess two common features: they contain unsubstituted phenyl groups; and they contain the unit $C_6H_5CO{-}$, to which is added two or three two-carbon units (Eq. 6-5):

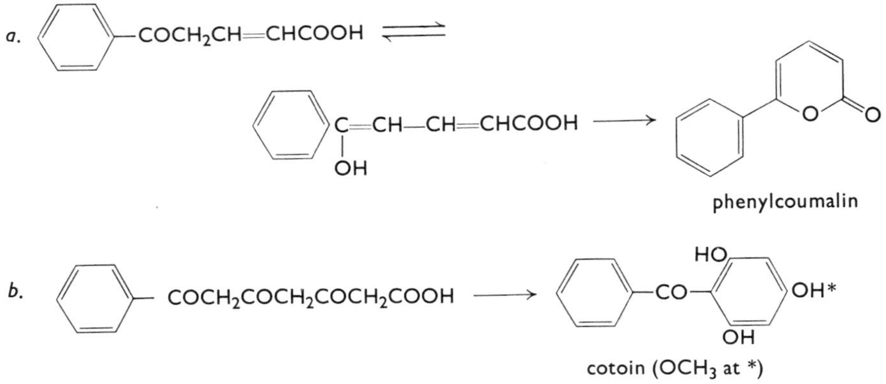

a. $\text{Ph}{-}COCH_2CH{=}CHCOOH \rightleftharpoons$

$$\underset{\overset{|}{OH}}{\text{Ph}{-}C{=}CH{-}CH{=}CHCOOH} \longrightarrow \text{phenylcoumalin}$$

phenylcoumalin

b. $\text{Ph}{-}COCH_2COCH_2COCH_2COOH \longrightarrow$ cotoin (OCH$_3$ at *)

cotoin (OCH$_3$ at *)

[Eq. 6-5]

It is clear that two possible biosynthetic courses must be considered for the coto bark compounds: one in which an original cinnamyl-CoA unit has at some later stage undergone the change $ArCH{=}CHCO{-}{-}{-} \rightarrow ArCOCH_2CO{-}{-}{-}$; and the other, in which a benzoyl-CoA starter unit, and not a $C_6{-}C_3$ unit, has occupied the starting point of the synthetic sequence.

The probable availability in secondary metabolic processes of the benzoyl group (as the CoA derivative) is supported by the frequent natural occurrence of benzoyl derivatives. In Fig. 6-3 are shown, for illustration, a few examples:

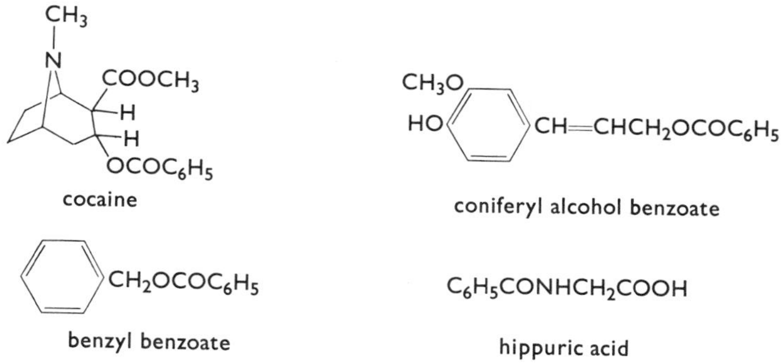

cocaine

coniferyl alcohol benzoate

benzyl benzoate

hippuric acid

Fig. 6-3. Some Naturally Occurring Benzoyl Derivatives.

The natural origin of the C_6-C_1 fragment by degradation of a shikimic-derived progenitor has been discussed (Sec. 5.6). Thus, the question of the biosynthesis of the coto bark compounds resolves itself into a question of the point in the synthetic process at which the carbonyl group adjacent to the aromatic ring is formed. There is at present no basis for a clear decision on which of the three alternative pathways shown in Eq. 6-4 is the natural process, although it will be shown below that a likely course is by way of an aryl-CO-SCoA "starter."

Another member of the family Piperaceae, *Piper methysticum* (Kawa), is characterized by the presence of a group of compounds which, like piperic acid, appear to arise by the addition of C_2 fragments to a cinnamoyl precursor (Fig. 6-4):

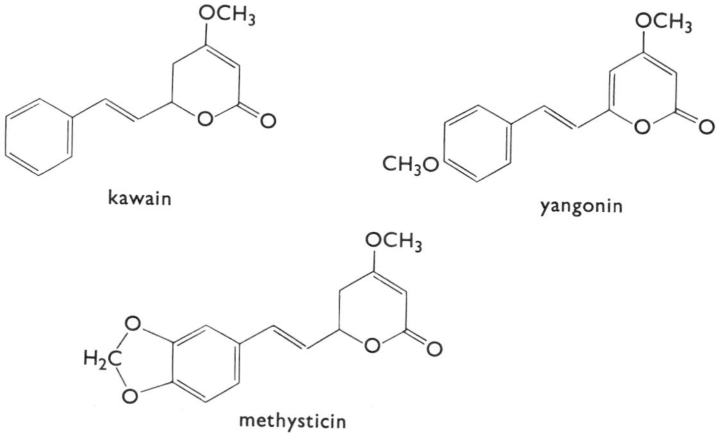

kawain

yangonin

methysticin

Fig. 6-4. Compounds of *Piper methysticum*.

An inspection of the structures of the Kawa pyrones discloses that they can be regarded as cyclized forms of precursors formed by extension of a cinnamic acid (or piperic acid) starter unit by increments of C_2 units (Eq. 6-6):

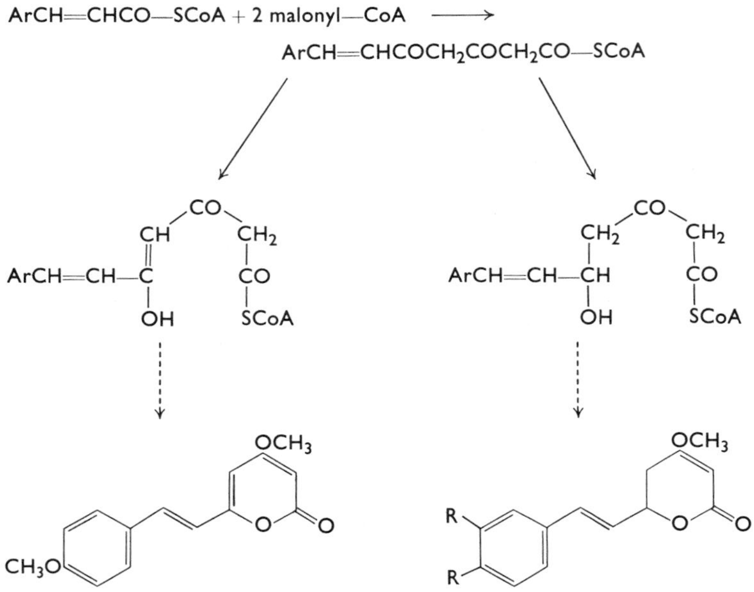

$$ArCH{=}CHCO{-}SCoA + 2\ malonyl{-}CoA \longrightarrow$$

$$ArCH{=}CHCOCH_2COCH_2CO{-}SCoA$$

yangonin

(kawain (R = R = H).
methysticin (R, R = OCH$_2$O).   [Eq. 6-6]

It is of interest to note that pyrones of other types occur in *Aniba* species other than those designated as "coto" (Sec. 6-2). These *Aniba* pyrones are those shown in Fig. 6-5. The presence of paracotoin (Fig. 6-2) and 4-methoxyparacotoin (Fig. 6-5)

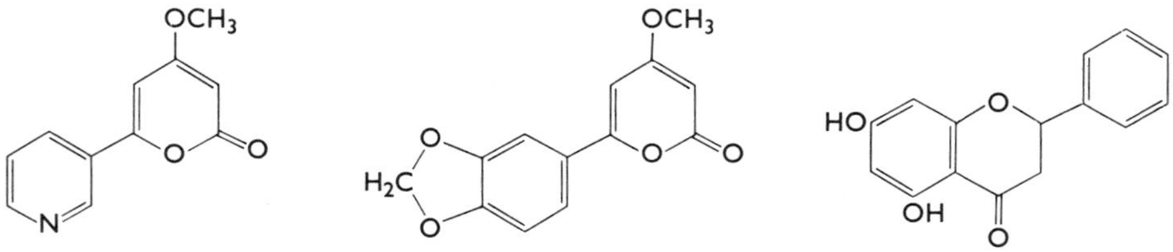

anibine   4-methoxyparacotoin   pinocembrin

Fig. 6-5. Pyrones of *Aniba rosaeodora* Ducke.

in more than one *Aniba* species suggests that these lauraceous plants possess the capability of utilizing an aryl-CO-SCoA unit as a starting point to which, by addition of —CH_2CO— fragments, the pyrone ring is added. The alternative suggestion, that the starting point is Aryl CH=CHCO—SCoA, is not to be arbitrarily dismissed (see Eq. 6-4); but an argument in favor of the aryl-CO-SCoA route is found in the presence in *Aniba* of the pyridine derivative, anibine (Fig. 6-5). The widespread occurrence in nature of nicotinic acid, and the absence in nature of β-3-pyridylacrylic acid and 3-pyridylalanine, strongly suggests that anibine is formed as shown in Eq. 6-7a, and not as in Eq. 6-7b:

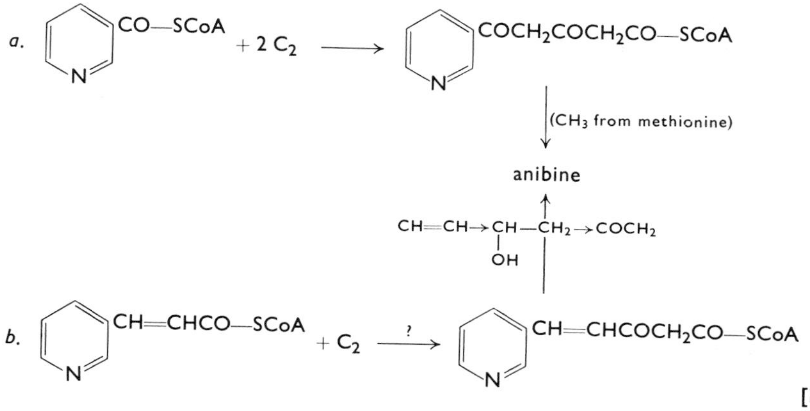

[Eq. 6-7]

The presence of pinocembrin (see Chap. 7) along with the pyrones in *Aniba* shows, however, that a precursor of the type

$$ArCH=CHCO(CH_2CO)_2CH_2CO—SCoA$$

is present at some point in the biosynthetic pathway, for the structure of pinocembrin is uniquely constructed of the units shown in Eq. 6-8:

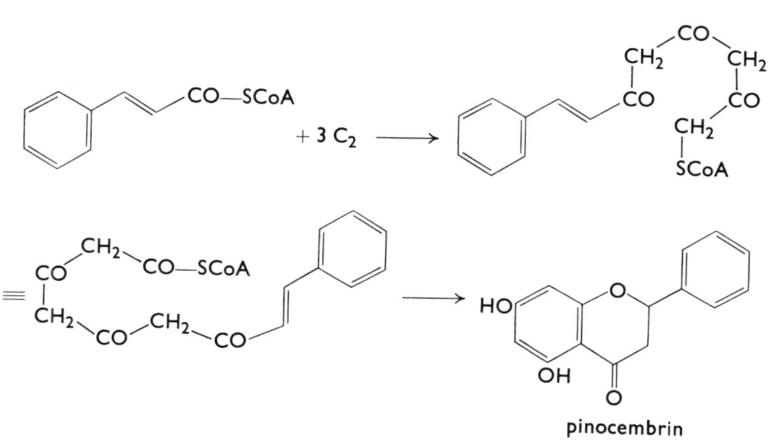

pinocembrin [Eq. 6-8]

An alternative course, in which the starter unit is C_6H_5CO—SCoA, and the steps —$COCH_2$— → —$CHOHCH_2$— → —CH=CH— intervene, cannot, of course, be dismissed; but, in view of what is known about flavonoid biosynthesis (Chap. 7), this is a less likely route.*

6.3 Structures of the Kawa Root Pyrones

Kawain, methysticin and yangonin are written as 4-methoxy-α-pyrones (Fig. 6-4). Yangonin was until recently regarded as possessing the 2-methoxy-γ-pyrone structure, a view that was based upon a synthesis that involved a final methylation of the tautomeric 4-hydroxy-α-pyrone ⇌ 2-hydroxy-γ-pyrone, a step that is not unambiguous.

The structure of kawain has been established by the total synthesis shown in Eq. 6-9:

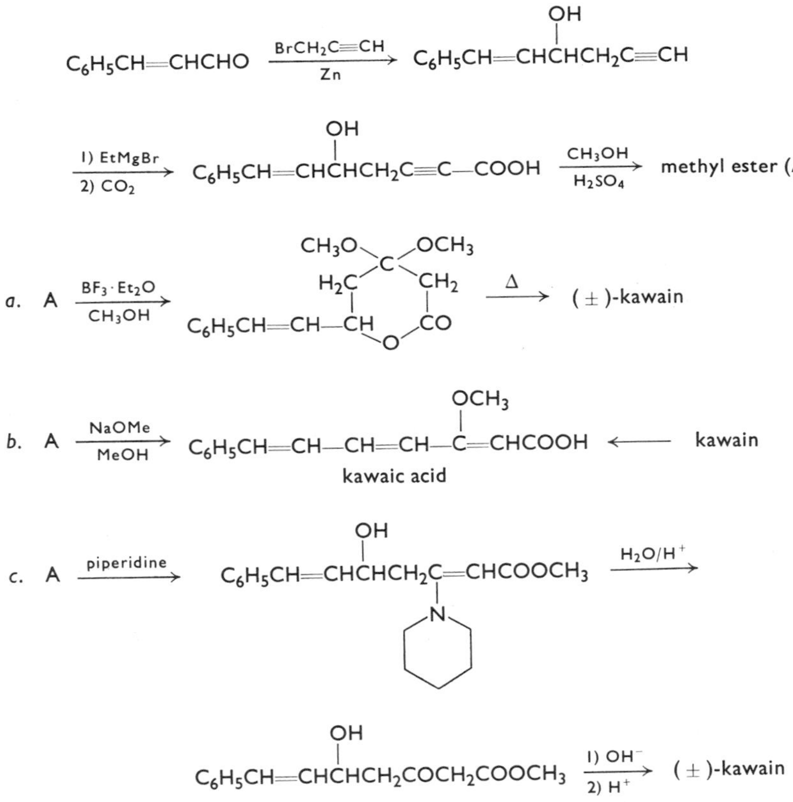

[Eq. 6-9]

* The above arguments lead to the question of whether 3-β-pyridylalanine is indeed a natural substance which it may be expected will in time be isolated (perhaps from an *Aniba* species?).

To discover a way to dispel the ambiguity in the structure of yangonin, model α- and γ-pyrones have been prepared and studied. Methylation of the lactone of 5-hydroxy-3-oxohex-4-enoic acid ("triacetic acid lactone") with diazomethane gave the two isomeric lactones shown in Eq. 6-10. One of these readily formed a crystalline hydrochloride; the other underwent a Diels-Alder reaction with diethyl acetylenedicarboxylate to yield (after saponification) 5-methoxy-3-methylphthalic acid.

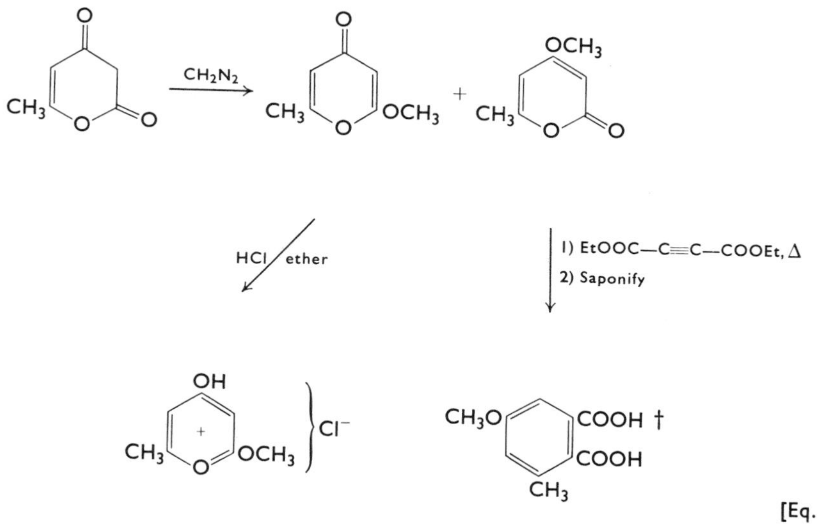

[Eq. 6-10]

† via

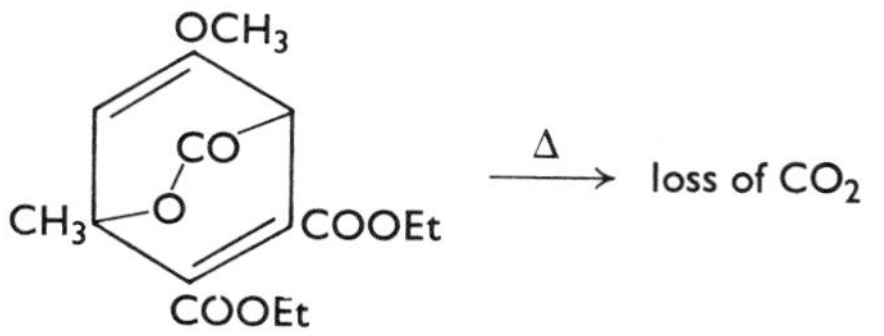

The chemical properties of the simple pyrones shown in Eq. 6-10 characterized them beyond doubt, and made it possible to use them as reliable models for spectroscopic studies. In Table 6-1 are listed the characteristic carbonyl and enol-ether (C—O) bonds in the infrared spectra of the model lactones and of yangonin. It is clear from these data that yangonin is the 4-methoxy-α-pyrone, and that the older 2-methoxy-γ-pyrone structure for this compound is excluded.

Table 6-1. Infrared Spectra of Some α- and γ-Pyrones

Compound	Type	C=O and C—O (cm^{-1})	
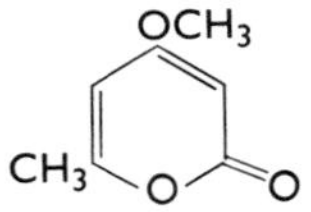	α-	1722, 1736	1250, 1265
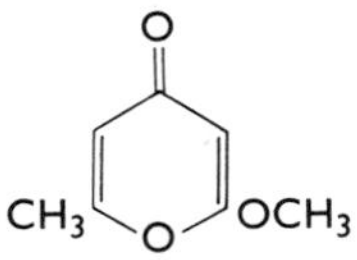	γ-	1677, 1692	1260
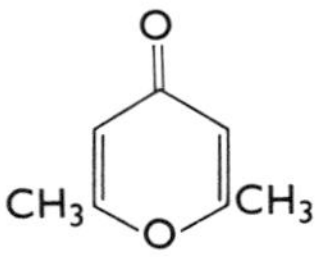	γ-	1672	—
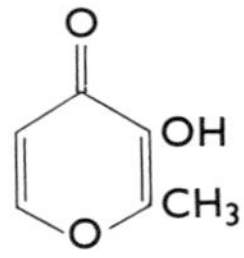	γ-	1656	—
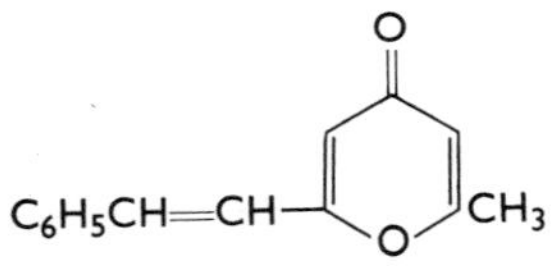	γ-	1665	—
Yangonin†	α-	1720	1250
Anibine††	α-	1732	—
4-Methoxyparacotoin ††	α-	1738	—
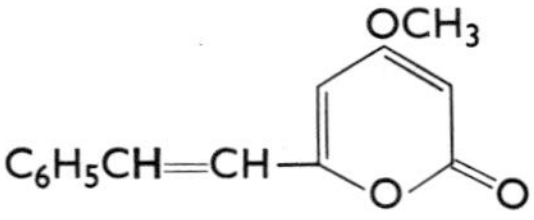	α-	1724	—

† See Eq. 6-6.
†† Fig. 6-5.

6.4 Stilbenes and Dihydroisocoumarins

The naturally occurring polyhydroxy (and -methoxy) stilbenes constitute a group of compounds that provide further examples of the process of addition of polyketide chains to C_6—C_3 starter units. Closely related to the naturally occurring stilbenes is the isocoumarin derivative hydrangenol (Fig. 6-6):

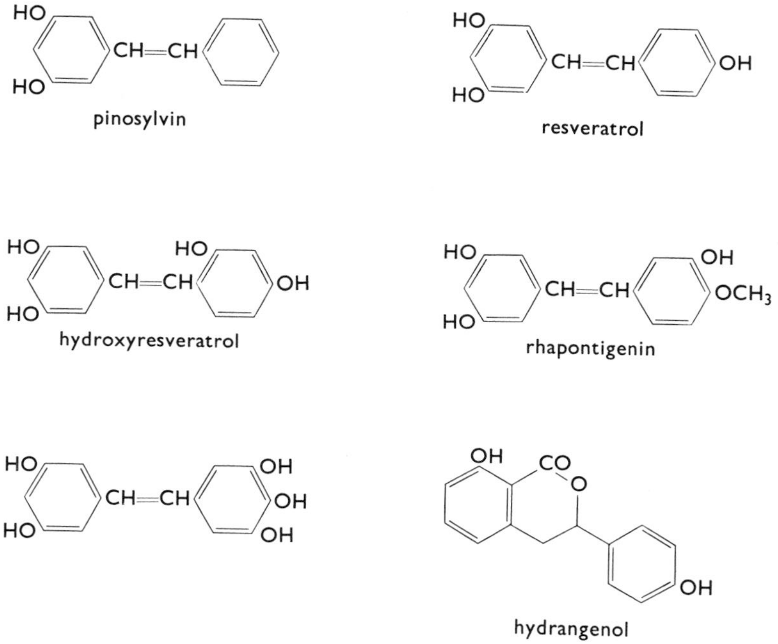

Fig. 6-6. Some Naturally Occurring Polyhydroxy Stilbenes.

The hydroxylation pattern of the left-hand rings of the stilbenes shown in Fig. 6-6 is typical of that of rings derived by the cyclization of poly-β-keto chains, while that of the second ring of resveratrol, rhapontigenin and 3,5,3′,4′,5′-pentahydroxystilbene is characteristically phenylpropanoid. The biogenetic origin of these stilbenes is strongly suggested by these features, and can be represented as in Eq. 6-11a. An alternative possibility, shown in Eq. 6-11b, is that pinosylvin is constructed by appropriate cyclization (and reduction of —CO— groups) of a chain composed completely of C_2 units.

a.

$$CH=CH-CO \quad\quad CH_2 \xrightarrow{\text{cyclize; } CO_2} \quad CH=CH \quad OH$$

e.g., pinosylvin

b.

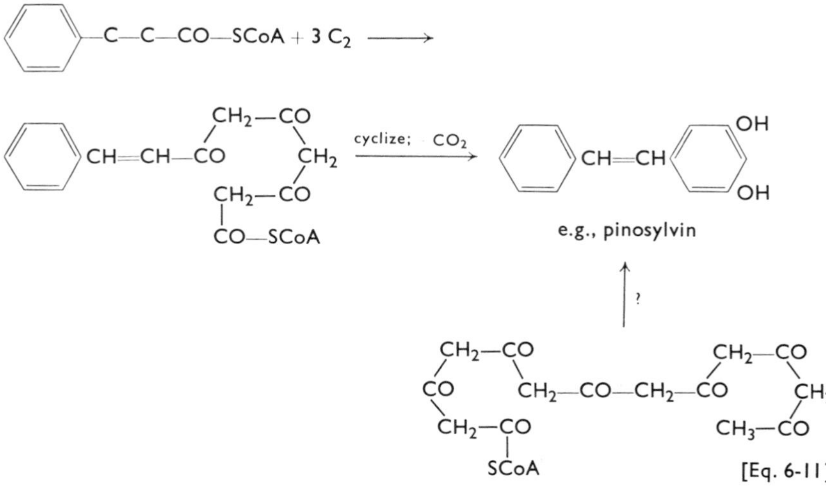

[Eq. 6-11]

The dihydroisocoumarin hydrangenol is structurally related to the stilbenes; it may be regarded as representing the product of cyclization of a $C_6-C_3-(C_2)_3$ precursor without loss of CO_2 (Eq. 6-12):

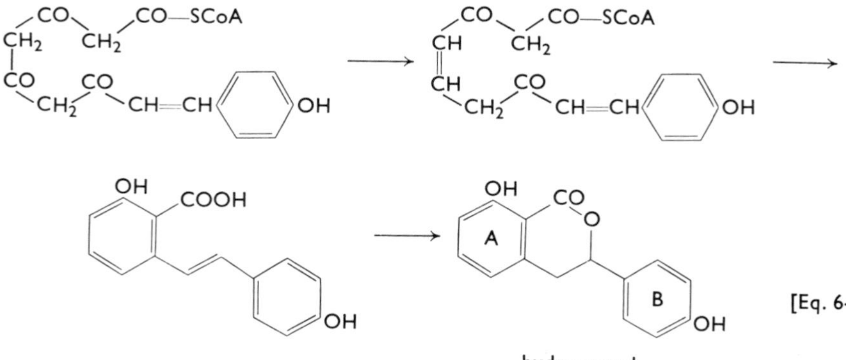

[Eq. 6-12]

hydrangenol

It will be noted that if Eq. 6-11*b* were to represent stilbene biosynthesis, there is no relationship of this course to the biosynthesis of hydrangenol corresponding to that between Eq. 6-11*a* and Eq. 6-12.

Feeding experiments have established that pinosylvin is indeed synthesized by *Pinus resinosa* Ait. (red pine) by the route outlined in Eq. 6-11*a*. The administration of 1-^{14}C-acetic acid, G-^{14}C-glucose, G-^{14}C-phenylalanine, and 1-^{14}C-phenyl-alanine to wounded red pine branches gave labeled pinosylvin and pinosylvin monoethyl ether. Degradation of the methylated pinosylvin (and its methyl ether) to benzoic acid and 3,5-dimethoxybenzoic acid showed that the incorporation of label was in complete accord with the scheme of Eq. 6-11a. The degradation results also showed that the terminal carbon atom (as —COOH) was lost in the course of the biosynthesis as shown in Eq. 6-11a.

Feeding experiments with *Hydrangea macrophylla* (fam. Saxifragaceae) have also confirmed that hydrangenol is constructed from C_6—C_3 + 3 C_2 units as outlined in Eq. 6-12.

The co-occurrence in many pine species of pinosylvin and chrysin and pinocembrin, coupled with the feeding experiments described above, show that the assembly of the C_6—C_3—C_2—C_2—C_2 precursor can be followed by subsequent events of more than one kind. The course of flavonoid biosynthesis will be described in the chapter to follow.

VII CHAPTER

REFERENCES FOR FURTHER READING

1. T. A. Geissman, Ed., *The Chemistry of Flavonoid Compounds*. Pergamon Press, Oxford, 1962.
2. J. H. Richards and J. B. Hendrickson, *The Biogenesis of Steroids, Terpenes and Aceto-genins*. W. A. Benjamin, Inc., New York, 1964.
3. J. D. Bu'Lock, *The Biosynthesis of Natural Products*, McGraw-Hill, Ltd., London, New York, 1965.
4. *Bio-organic Chemistry*, readings from Scientific American, W. H. Freeman and Co., San Francisco, 1968.
5. H. Grisebach, *Biosynthetic Patterns in Micro-organisms and Higher Plants*, John Wiley and Sons, Inc., New York, 1967.
6. J. B. Harborne, *The Evolution of Flavonoid Pigments in Plants*, in Comparative Phytochemistry, T. Swain, Ed., Academic Press, New York, 1966.
7. T. A. Geissman, *The Biosynthesis of Phenolic Plant Products*, in Biogenesis of Natural Compounds, 2nd Ed., P. Bernfeld, Ed., Pergamon Press, Oxford, 1967.
8. J. B. Harborne, Ed., *The Biochemistry of Phenolic Compounds*, Academic Press, London, 1964.
9. Edmon Wong, *The Role of Chalcones and Flavanones in Flavonoid Biosynthesis*, Phytochemistry, 7, (1968), 1751.
10. W. D. Ollis, K. L. Ormand, and I. O. Sutherland, *The Oxidative Rearrangement of Chalcones by Thallic Acetate*, Chem. Comm., (1968), 1237.
11. W. D. Ollis and O. R. Gottlieb, *Biogenetic Relations Involving the Neoflavanoids and their Congeners*, Chem. Comm., (1968), 1396.

Flavonoid Compounds

7.1 Classes of Flavonoid Compounds

One of the largest classes of naturally occurring phenolic compounds, the flavonoid compounds, provide many illuminating examples of the techniques used in the study of natural products. Their distribution in nature, their chemotaxonomic usefulness, the methods used in their isolation and purification, the determination of their structures and stereochemistry, and the methods used for their synthesis and interconversion provide a wide view of an important area of organic chemistry.

Flavonoid compounds are C_{15} compounds (exclusive of O-alkyl groups and secondary substitution) composed of two phenolic nuclei connected by a three-carbon unit. The A-ring is characteristically of the phloroglucinol or resorcinol hydroxylation pattern, and the B-ring usually 4-, 3,4-, or 3,4,5-hydroxylated. Other hydroxylation patterns are known, but these can usually be seen to be super-imposed upon the basic pattern described.

In Fig. 7-1 are shown these fundamental structural features.

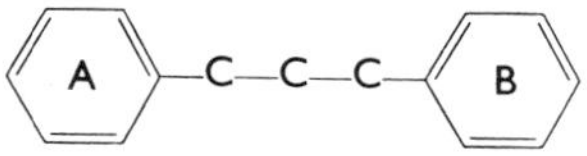

Fundamental flavonoid skeleton

A-ring: characteristically phloroglucinol or resorcinol substitution pattern:

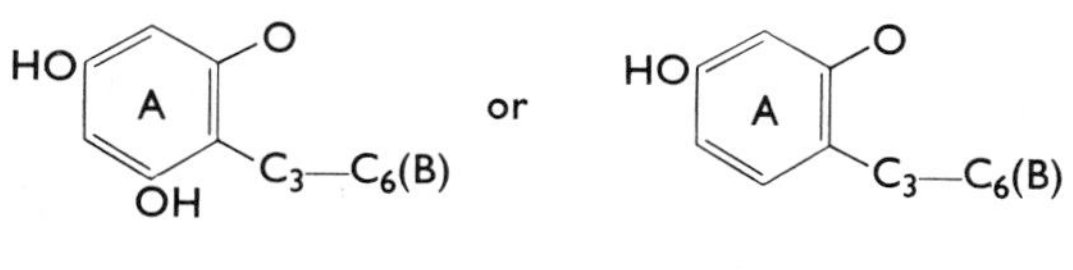

continued...

but is often further hydroxylated:

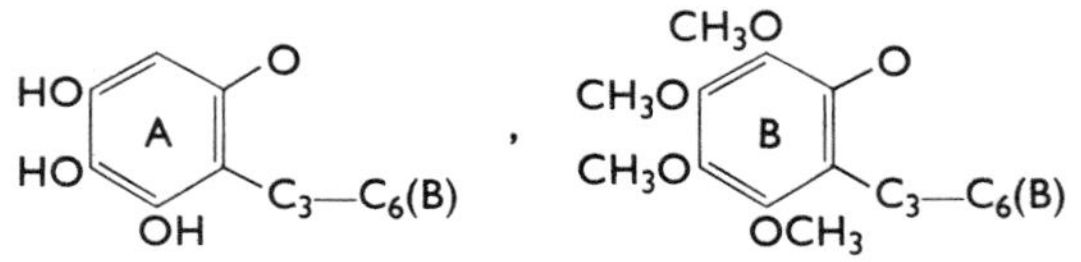

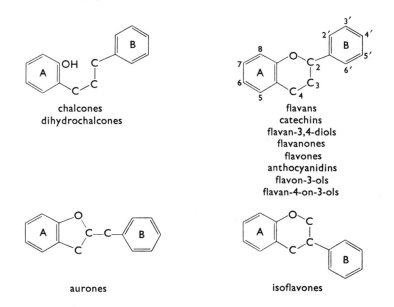

B-ring: characteristically 4-, 3,4-, 3,4,5-hydroxylated:

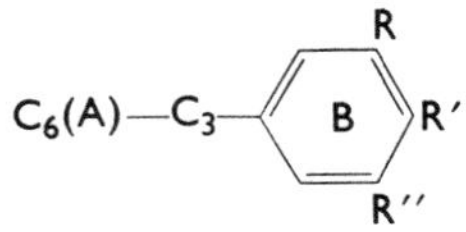

R = R'' = H, R' = OH
R = H, R' = R'' = OH
R = R' = R'' = OH
(also, R = R' = R'' = H)

but may bear a 2'-hydroxyl group as well:

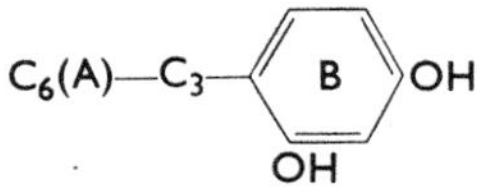

Fig. 7-1.

The central three-carbon fragment, with the attached B-ring, commonly occurs in four forms (Fig. 7-2):

chalcones
dihydrochalcones

flavans
catechins
flavan-3,4-diols
flavanones
flavones
anthocyanidins
flavon-3-ols
flavan-4-on-3-ols

aurones

isoflavones

Fig. 7-2. Common Flavonoid Types.

The oxidation level of the three-carbon portion of the flavonoid molecules can be represented by the formal relationships shown in the following summary. It will be noted that the A-ring always possesses a hydroxyl group so situated as to provide for the formation of the heterocyclic ring in the tricyclic compounds. In the bicyclic chalcones and hydrochalcones the hydroxyl group of the A-ring persists.

$$A—CH_2CH_2CHOH—B \longrightarrow \text{flavans}$$

$$A—CH_2\underset{\overset{|}{OH}}{CH}CHOH—B \longrightarrow \text{catechins}$$

$$A—COCH_2CH_2—B \longrightarrow \text{hydrochalcones}$$

$$A—COCH_2CHOH—B \longrightarrow \text{flavanones, chalcones}$$

$$A—COCH_2CO—B \longrightarrow \text{flavones}$$

$$A—CH_2COCO—B \longrightarrow \text{anthocyanins}$$

$$A—COCOCH_2—B \longrightarrow \text{aurones}$$

$$A—COC\underset{\overset{|}{OH}}{H}CHOH—B \longrightarrow \text{3-hydroxyflavanones}$$

$$A—COCOC\underset{\overset{|}{OH}}{H}—B \longrightarrow \text{flavonols}$$

In the sections to follow, representative compounds of these structural types will be described in detail with respect to their occurrence and chemical properties.

7.2 Dihydrochalcones

Although dihydrochalcones are rare in nature, one member of the class, phlorizin, is a well known and important compound, and is a common constituent of the root bark (and other parts) of certain members of the family Rosaceae, in particular the pomaceous fruits (pears, apples). Phlorizin has long been important in pharmacological studies for it has the unique ability to produce a diabetes-like condition, a glucosuria that appears to be the result of impaired reabsorption of glucose by the kidney tubules.

Phlorizin is the β-D-glucoside of phloretin, to which it is converted by acid hydrolysis. The structure of phloretin is readily demonstrated by its decomposition by strong alkali into phloroglucinol and p-hydroxyhydrocinnamic acid (phloretic acid). If the glucoside, phlorizin, is decomposed with alkali in the same manner, the glucose residue is not removed and phloroglucinol β-D-glucoside is produced. Finally, the position of the glucose residue is established by the reactions shown in Eq. 7-1; the interaction of the acetoxyl group with the —COCH$_2$CH$_2$Ar unit shows that the glucose unit must have been attached at the 2'-position in phlorizin.

Glycosylation of a hydroxyl group *ortho* (or *peri*) to a carbonyl group is not common in nature, chiefly because of the effective hydrogen bonding between —OH and O=C in this relationship. The presence of hydroxyl groups in the 2,6-positions relative to the carbonyl group renders one of them reactive and glycosylation can occur.

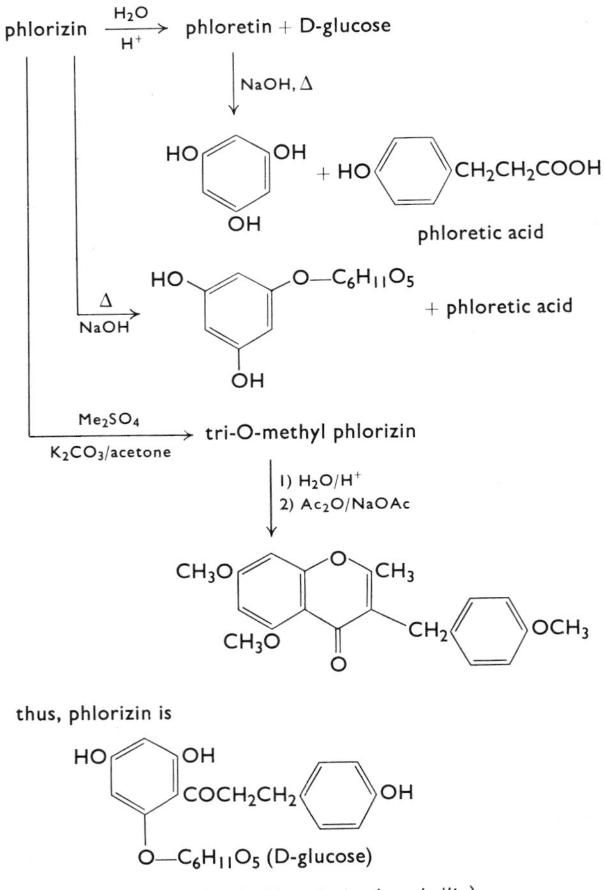

thus, phlorizin is

(The L-rhamnoside of phloretin is *glycyphyllin*)

[Eq. 7-1]

7.3 Chalcones

Polyhydroxychalcones are found in numerous plants, but their distribution in nature is far from common (Fig. 7-3). The principal reasons for this is that chalcones are readily isomerized to flavanones in the equilibrium shown in Eq. 7-2. When the chalcone is 2′,6′-dihydroxylated, the isomeric flavanone bears a 5-

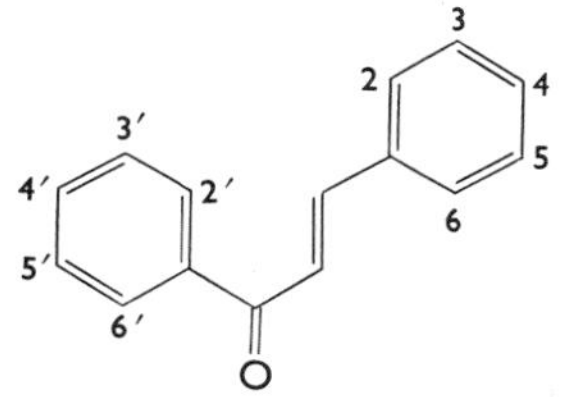

marein: 2',3',4',3,4 penta OH (4'-glucoside)
coreopsin: 2',4',3,4 tetra OH (4'-glucoside)
stillopsin: 2',4',5',3,4 penta OH (?-glucoside)
lanceolin: 2',4',3,4-tetra OH-3'-OMe (?-glucoside)

All of these are found in species of *Coreopsis*.

Fig. 7-3. Some Naturally Occurring Chalcones.

hydroxyl group, and the stabilizing influence of the 4-carbonyl-5-hydroxyl hydrogen bonding causes the chalcone-flavanone equilibrium to lie largely on the side of the flavanone. Thus, chalcones that occur in nature are those that possess 2',4'-hydroxyl groups or 2'-hydroxy-6'-glycosyloxy groups.*

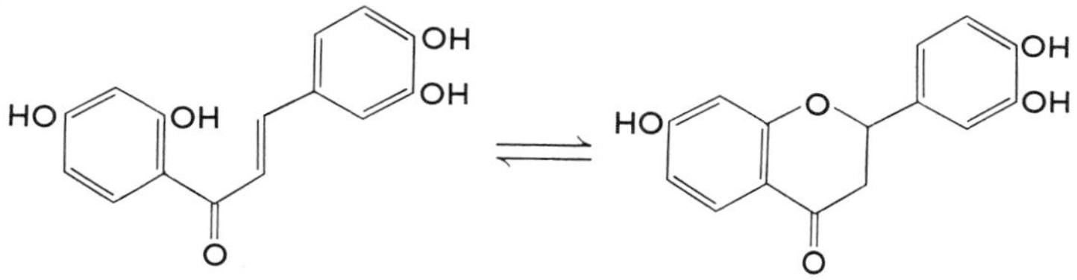

buteint   butin
(both isolable, stable)

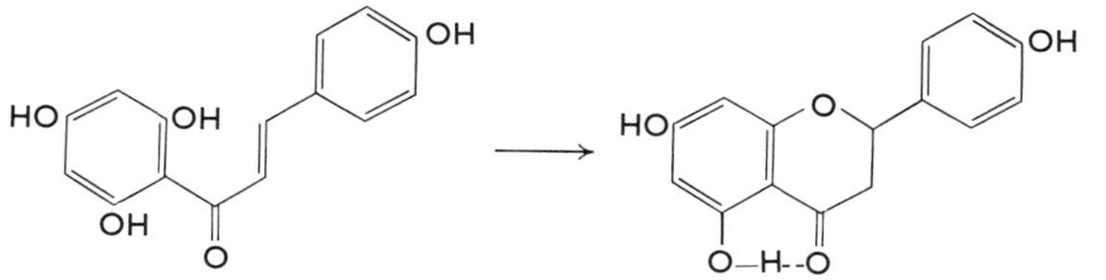

2',4',6',4-tetrahydroxychalcone   naringenin   [Eq. 7-2]
(unstable)   (stabilized by OH - - - O=C bond)

---

† Butein occurs naturally as the 4'-glucoside, coreopsin.

---

* The numbering of substituted chalcones is such that "A-ring" substituents bear primed numbers; thus, the 6'-hydroxyl group of a 2',6'-dihydroxychalcone becomes the 5-hydroxyl group of the isomeric flavanone.

Isosalipurposide is the glucoside of the chalcone corresponding to naringenin 5-D-glucoside. The aglucon of the chalcone is not naturally occurring, nor are 2',4',6'-trihydroxylated chalcone glucosides in which the glucose residue is at the 4'-position (Eq. 7-3):

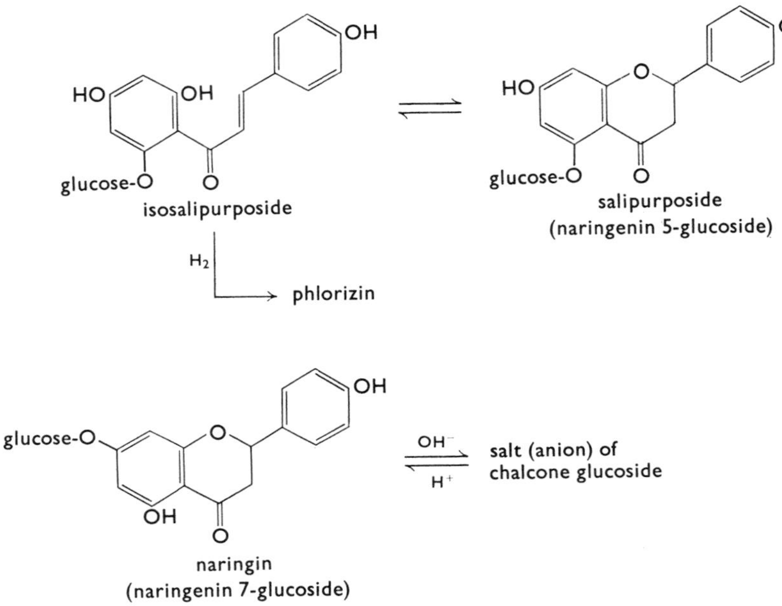

Chalcones (and their glycosides) occur naturally in a far more limited range of structure than most other classes of flavonoid compounds for all of the (potential) chalcones that possess the phloroglucinol nucleus with free 2' and 6' hydroxyl groups are found in the flavanone form. In Fig. 7-3 are shown several chalcones found in plants, chiefly as the pigments of yellow flower petals, and in most, but not all, cases in plants of the Heliantheae tribe, Coreopsidinae subtribe, of the family Compositae.

7.4 Carthamin

The safflower, *Carthamus tinctorius* L. (fam. Compositae), contains a yellow flower pigment which, as the flower ages, turns red. Extracts of the flower also redden, with the formation of a red pigment. The red pigment, first called carthamin,* is a glycoside, and when hydrolyzed with aqueous phosphoric acid gives rise to two isomeric compounds, carthamidin and isocarthamidin.

---

* The red pigment is now referred to as "carthamone."

Carthamidin and isocarthamidin have been shown to be the isomeric flavanones shown in Eq. 7-4a by the synthesis of the fully methylated compounds and demethylation to the tetrahydroxy flavanones:

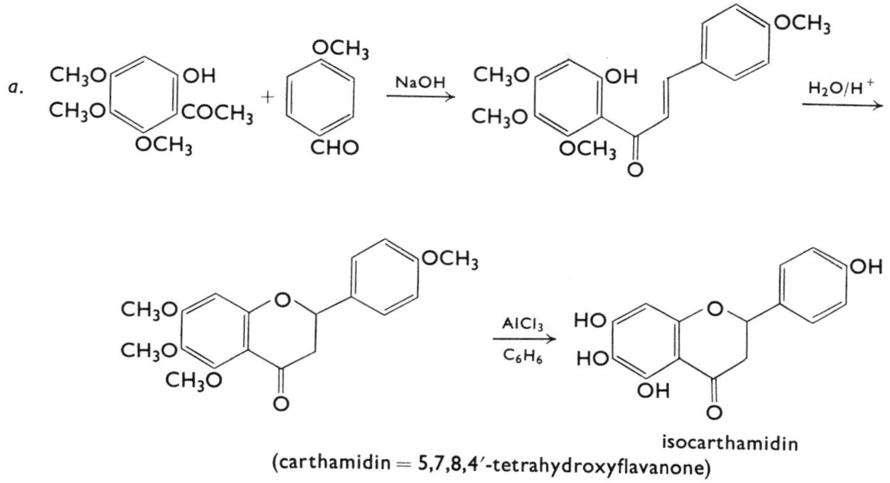

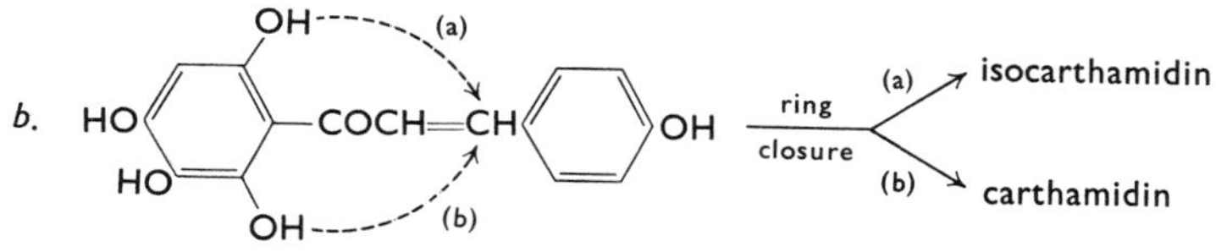

(carthamidin = 5,7,8,4'-tetrahydroxyflavanone)

[Eq. 7-4]

The formation of the two flavanones from a single precursor is readily accounted for by the transformation shown in Eq. 7-4b; the intermediate chalcone can cyclize by addition of either the 2'- or the 6'-hydroxyl group to the double bond.

Although carthamidin and isocarthamidin are flavanones, carthamone cannot be the corresponding chalcone from which the flavanones are produced by removal of the sugar and acid-catalyzed C-ring closure. Carthamone is red, and the polyhydroxychalcones are yellow to orange-yellow compounds; for example, coreopsin (Fig. 7-3), a typical representative of the class, has its long-wavelength absorption maximum at 385 mμ.

It is now to be recalled that the yellow safflower blossoms contain a pigment which turns red upon injuring (i.e., macerating) the petals, or upon ageing of the flower. This yellow precursor is now regarded as a chalcone glucoside which undergoes oxidation to the red quinonoid glycoside (carthamone). The formation of the flavanones in the hydrolysis of carthamone must be ascribed to the reduction of the quinone, probably by the glucose released in the hydrolysis (Eq. 7-5):

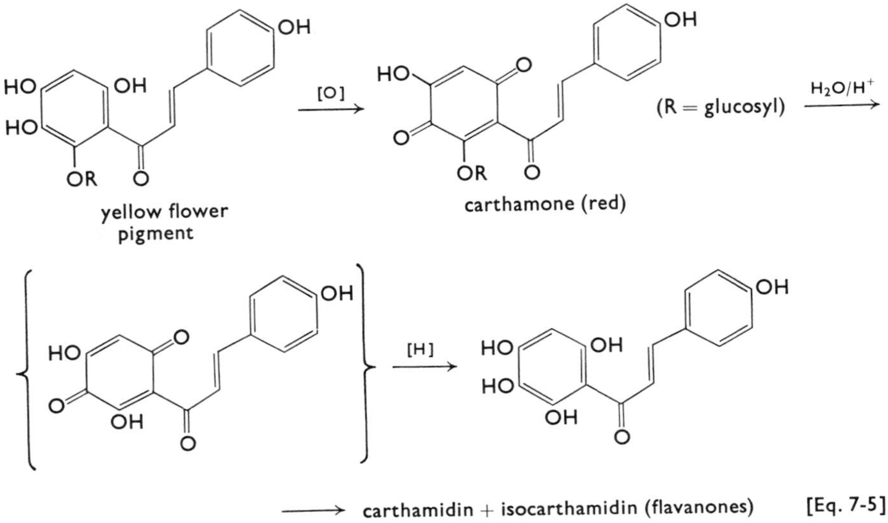

yellow flower pigment

carthamone (red)

$(R = glucosyl)$

$\xrightarrow{H_2O/H^+}$

$\xrightarrow{[H]}$

⟶ carthamidin + isocarthamidin (flavanones)   [Eq. 7-5]

An early alternative proposal, discarded in the light of later studies, was that what was then called carthamin (the red pigment) was the quinonoid "enol" of the chalcone (Eq. 7-6).

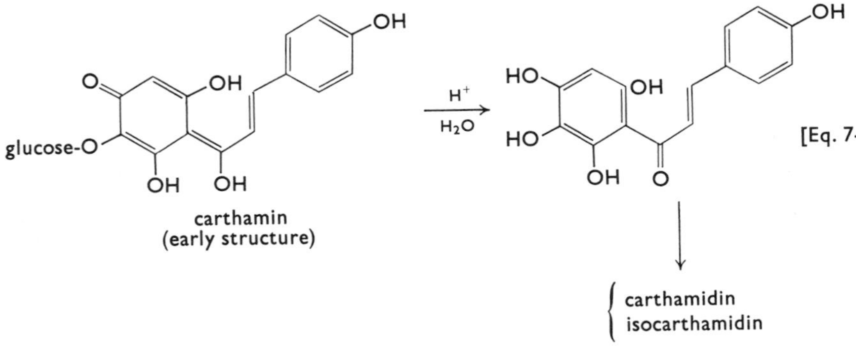

$\xrightarrow[H_2O]{H^+}$

[Eq. 7-6]

carthamin
(early structure)

{ carthamidin
  isocarthamidin

While this suggestion has the merit of explaining the ready formation of the flavanones by hydrolysis of the red precursor, the structure of the "enolic" chalcone is unacceptable. The recent experiments, showing that carthamone (the red pigment) is converted by reduction with sulfur dioxide into the yellow chalcone, and that the latter can be reoxidized to carthamone, substantiate the structural conclusions described in the foregoing account.

7.5 Flavans

Flavans are not common plant constituents. Indeed, only one example of the class has been found as a naturally occurring compound. The complex phenolic constituents of the resinous exudate of the Australian liliaceous plant genus *Xanthorrhoea* include a variety of flavonoid compounds, the separation and purification of which is difficult. Methylation (with methyl sulfate and potassium carbonate in acetone) of a crude resin from *X. preissii* yielded several flavonoid compounds, one of which was 4′,5,7-trimethoxyflavan (numbering system shown in Fig. 7-2), the structure of which was demonstrated by interpretation of the nuclear magnetic resonance spectrum and by mass spectrometry. Reduction of the flavan with sodium and ethanol in liquid ammonia and methylation of the resulting phenol yielded the known 1-*p*-methoxyphenyl-3-(2,4,6-trimethoxyphenyl)-propane (Eq. 7-7).

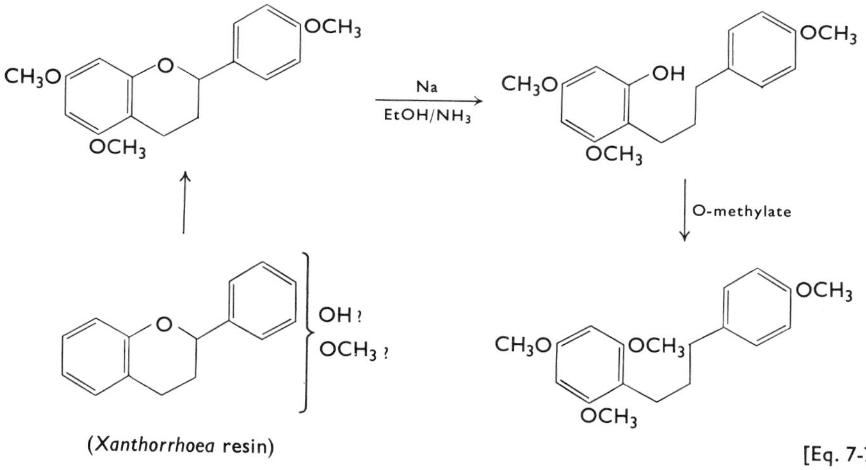

(*Xanthorrhoea* resin)

[Eq. 7-7]

The degree of methylation (if any) of the tri-hydroxy/methoxy compound in the plant is unknown.

7.6 Flavanones

Flavanones (usually as glycosides) are widely distributed in nature. They are not uniquely characteristic of any plant group, and are found in wood, leaves, and flowers. They are common to many woody tissues and are frequent constituents of flower petals. Flavanone glycosides are prominent constituents of members of the genus *Prunus* (fam. Rosaceae) and of citrus fruits; two of the commonest are glycosides of naringenin and hesperetin, found in grapefruit and oranges. Several representative flavanones are shown in Fig. 7-4.

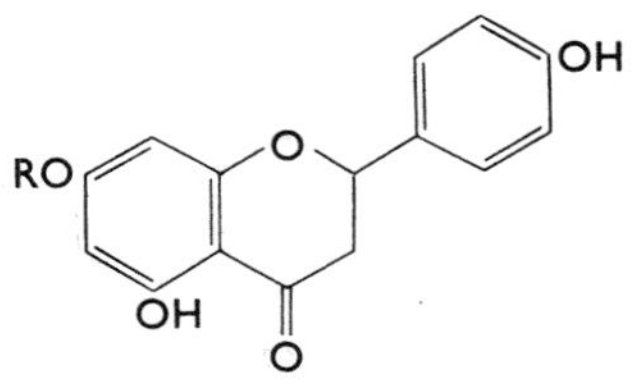

R = H, naringenin
R = A*, naringin

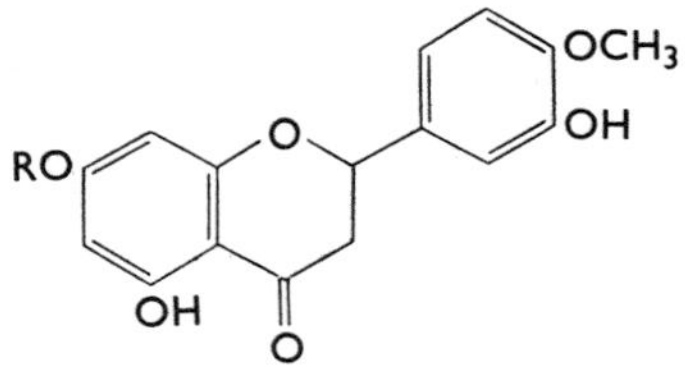

R = H, hesperetin
R = A*, hesperidin
R = B*, neohesperidin

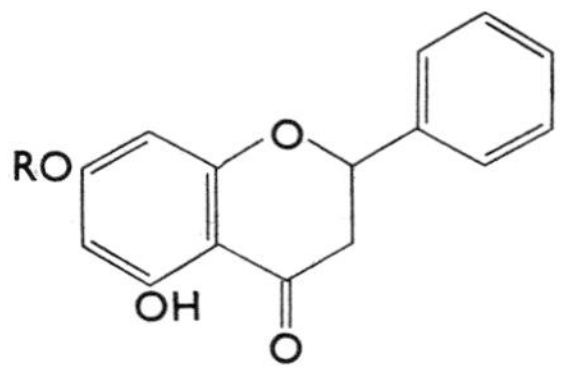

R = H, pinocembrin
R = CH₃, pinostrobin

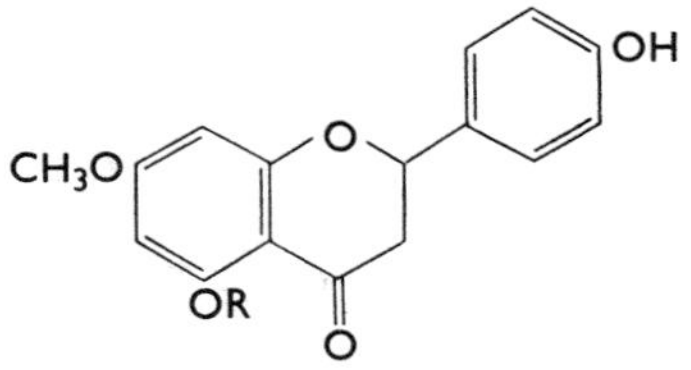

R = H, sakuranetin
R = I-glucosyl, sakuranin

Sugar residues:

A =

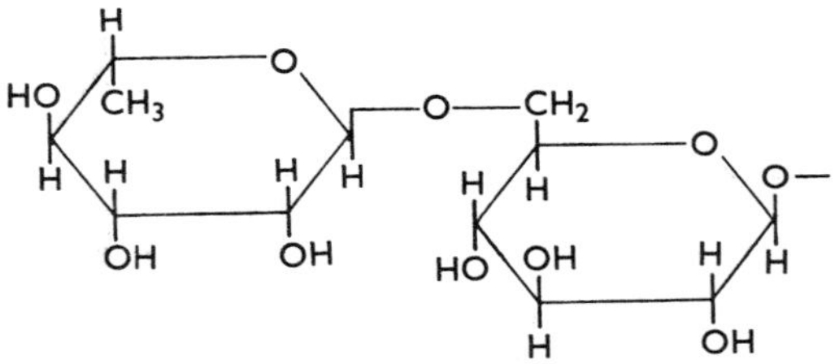

rutinose = 6-O-(α-L-rhamnopyranosyl)-D-glucopyranose

B =

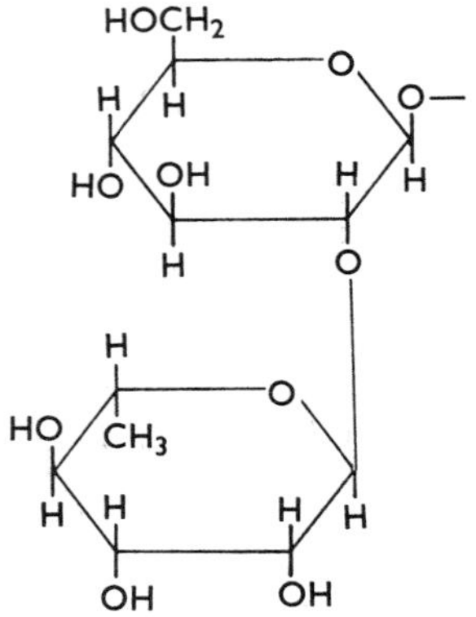

neohesperidose = 2-O-(α-L-rhamnopyranosyl)-D-glucopyranose

Fig. 7-4. Representative Natural Flavanones.

Flavanones lacking a 5-hydroxyl group are readily isomerized to chalcones by solution in alkali and acidification. When the 5-hydroxyl group is present, acidification of the alkaline solution results in reformation of the flavanone (see Sec. 7.3).

The proof of structure of flavanones is readily accomplished by classical methods. The polyhydroxyflavanones are easily recognizable by the deep colors (red, magenta, purple) that result when the flavanone is reduced with magnesium and hydrochloric acid in ethanol solution. Although this color test is not uniquely diagnostic of the flavanones (flavon-3-ols and flavanon-3-ols give similar colors), when it is taken in conjunction with spectral characteristics,* analytical data, and the formation of simple derivatives (O-methyl and O-acetyl derivatives), the recognition of a flavanone can usually be made with confidence. The principal problems in establishing the structure of a flavanone are (a) the position of linkage of the sugar residue, if the compound is a glycoside; and (b) the positions of nuclear hydroxyl and methoxyl groups of the A- and B-rings.

Flavanones and chalcones are degraded by alkaline hydrolysis to the benzoic acid derivative that comprises the B-ring and, depending upon the conditions, to the phenol comprising the A-ring (e.g., phloroglucinol) or to the corresponding acetophenone. An alternate course of degradation of a chalcone is that leading to the A-ring unit and a cinnamic acid derived from the C_3—C_6(B) portion of the molecule. In Eq. 7-8 are illustrated some typical degradations of the kind described.

Another useful device for establishing the structure of a flavanone involves the dehydrogenation of the 2,3-bond, with the formation of a flavone. Since flavanones

liquiritigenin

[Eq. 7-8]

homoeriodictyol

ferulic acid

* Flavanones have ultraviolet absorption spectra that are little influenced by the number and position of hydroxyl groups. The spectra are similar to those of polyhydroxyacetophenones.

are often difficult to synthesize, while flavones offer no problems, this procedure is a valuable one (Eq. 7-9):

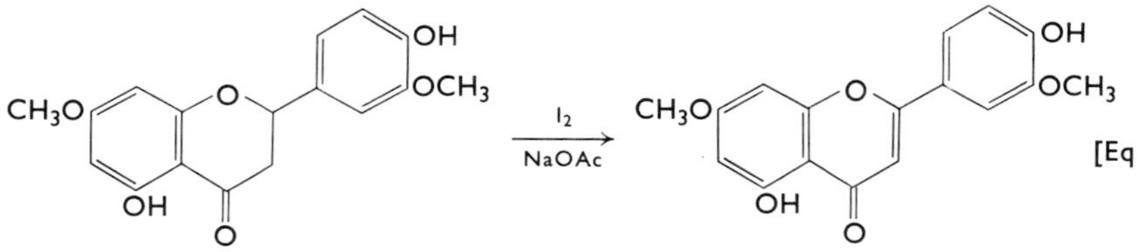

[Eq. 7-9]

Classical methods (i.e., degradation, interconversion, synthesis) of structure proof of flavonoid compounds are being superseded by physical diagnostic procedures, of which nuclear magnetic resonance is presently the most informative. The protons at the 2- and 3-positions show characteristic chemical shifts and coupling patterns which differentiate flavanone structures sharply from those of flavones, chalcones, etc. The aromatic substitution patterns can usually be recognized by the chemical shifts and coupling patterns (o-, m-, or p-coupling) of the A- and B-ring protons.

7.7   Flavones

Apigenin and luteolin are widely distributed in nature and represent the fundamental substitution pattern derived (as will be shown in a later section) from the combination of a C_6—C_3-derived fragment with acetate units:

$$(B)C_6—C_3 + 3\ C_2 \longrightarrow (B)C_6—C_3—C_6(A)$$

Nearly every possible pattern and degree of nuclear hydroxylation is known in nature, from flavone itself to nobiletin 5,6,7,8,3',4'-hexamethoxyflavone.* In Fig. 7-5 are shown some representative natural flavones. Most hydroxyflavones occur as glycosides; those in which only methoxyl or methylenedioxy substituents are present cannot, of course, be glycosylated and occur as the free compounds in the plant tissues.

Flavones are readily cleaved by alkali, yielding diacylmethanes or, depending upon the conditions of the reaction, the benzoic acid derived from the B-ring and

---

* Seven hydroxyl (or methoxyl) groups are found in some flavonols, in which an additional oxygen atom is present at C-3. These are considered in a section to follow.

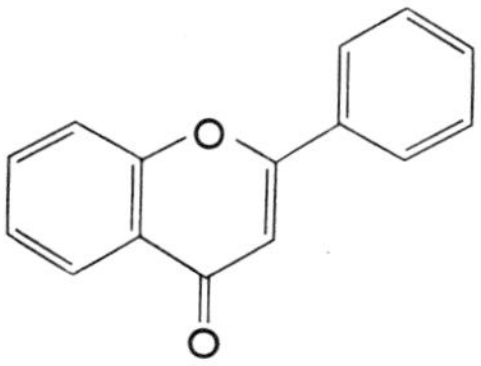

Fig. 7-5. Representative Natural Flavones.

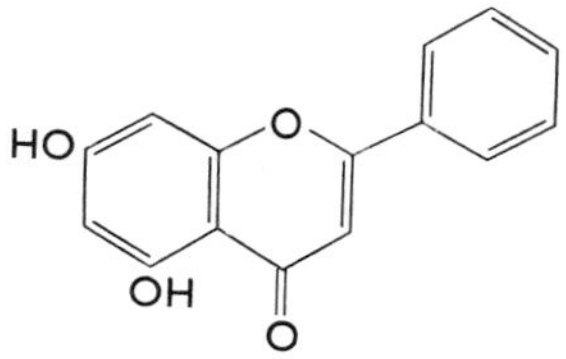

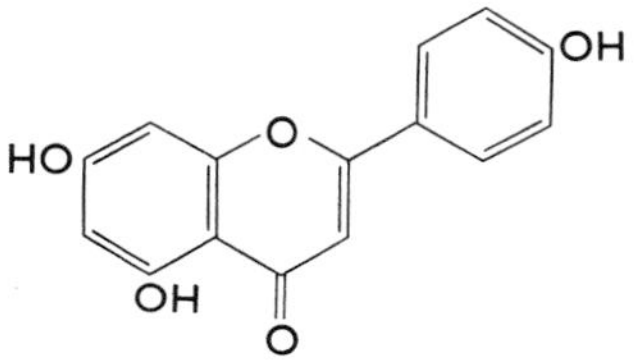

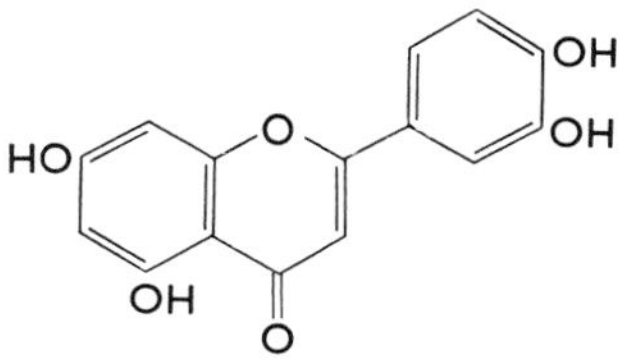

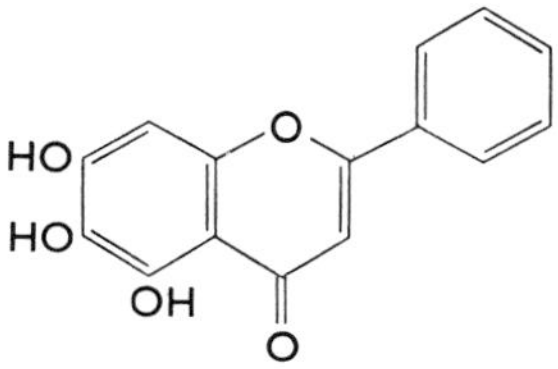

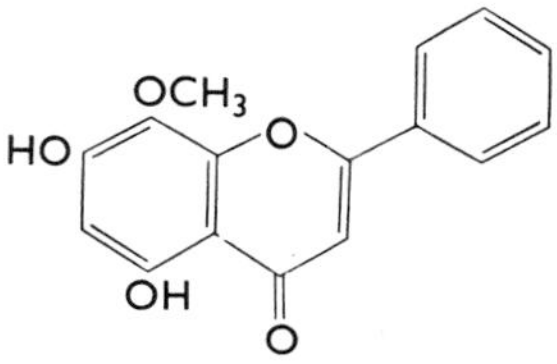

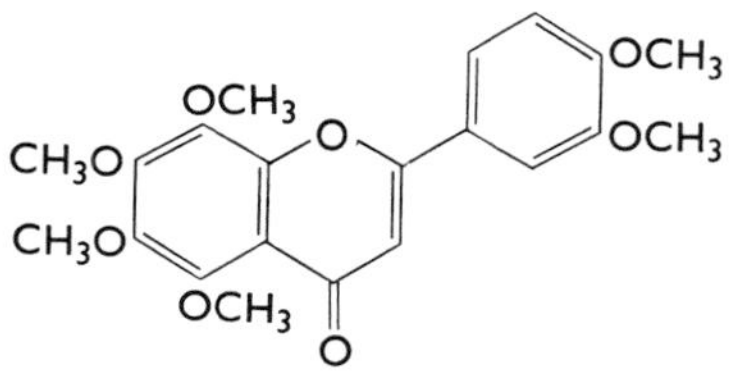

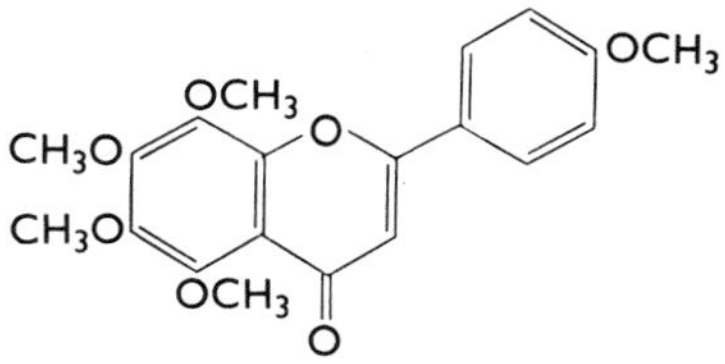

the *o*-hydroxyacetophenone representing the A-ring. The reaction is illustrated in Eq. 7-10:

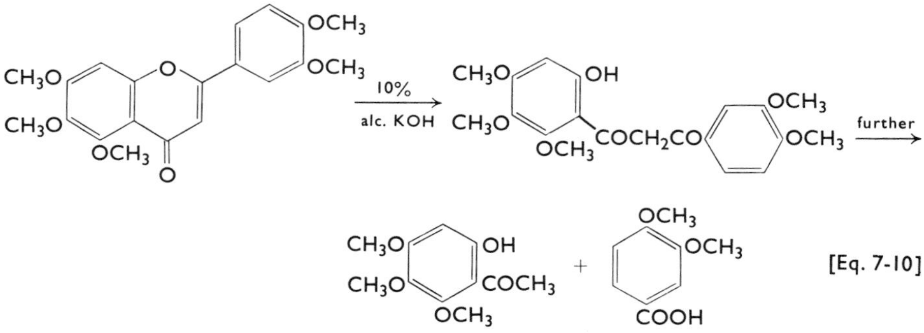

[Eq. 7-10]

The diacylmethanes derived from flavones as in Eq. 7-10 are readily recognizable degradation products. Their bright yellow color indicates that they exist in the enolic form. They are readily synthesized from the corresponding acetophenones and substituted benzoic acid esters (Eq. 7-11*a*), or from the *o*-acyloxyacetophenones, as shown in Eq. 7-11*b*. Since the *o*-hydroxydiacylmethanes are readily converted into the flavones by acid-catalyzed ring closure, these procedures constitute a useful method of flavone synthesis.

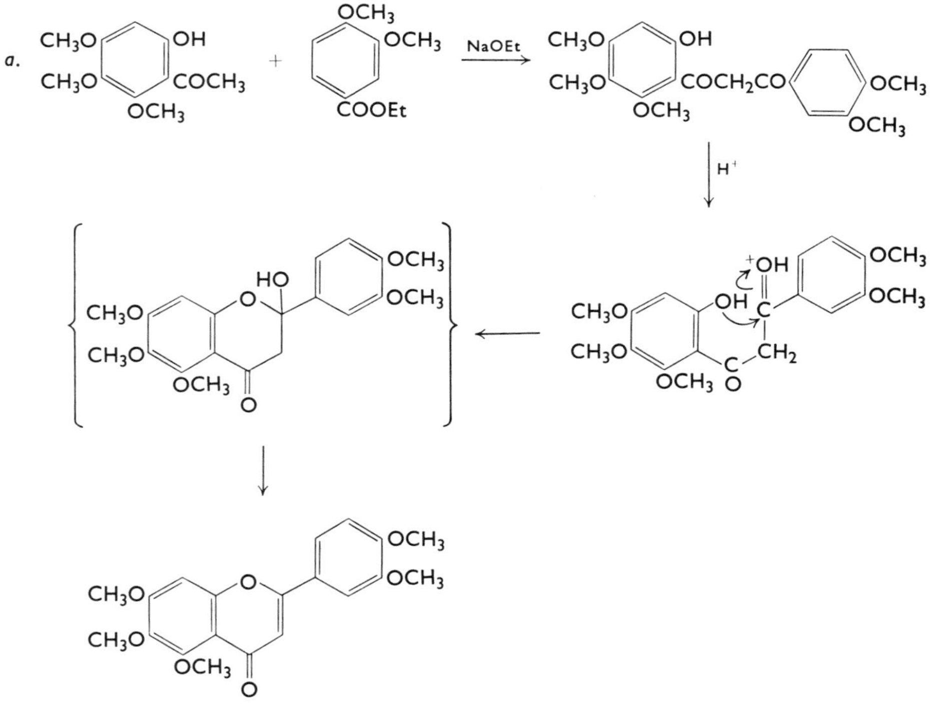

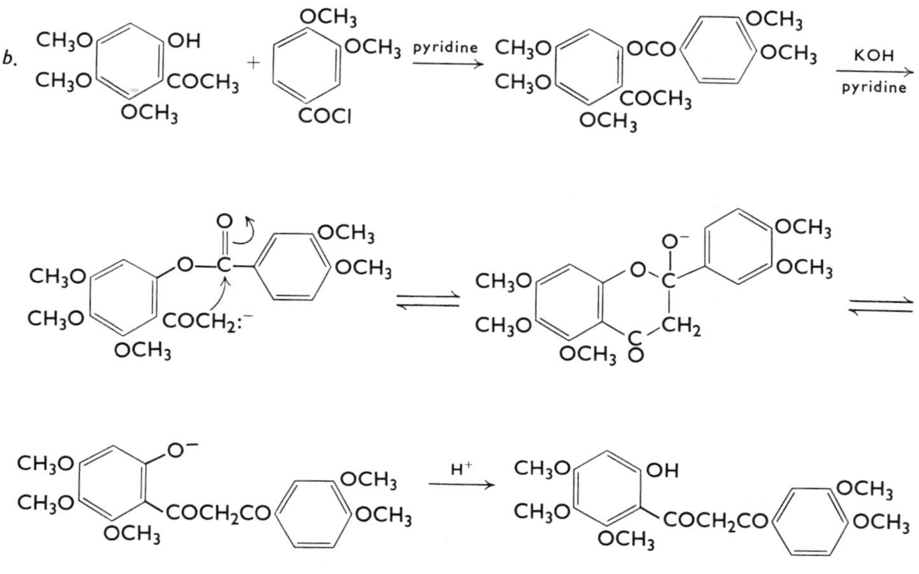

[Eq. 7-11]

Flavones are stable to strong acids and their ethers can be readily dealkylated by treatment with HI or HBr, or with aluminum chloride in an inert solvent. Rearrangements are often observed, however, during such demethylations, for strong acid can cause ring opening of a flavone to the diacylmethane, followed by ring closure in another way. For example, the demethylation of 5,8-dimethoxyflavone with HBr in acetic acid leads to the formation of 5,6-dihydroxyflavone (Eq. 7-12a). In special cases, more profound changes may occur (Eq. 7-12b):

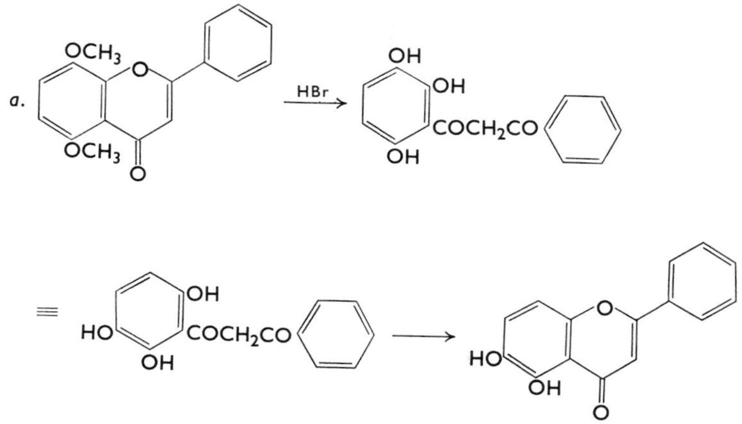

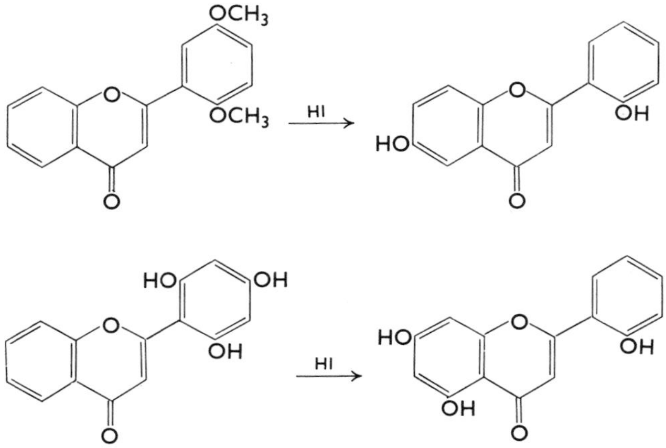

[Eq. 7-12]

When the A-ring of the polymethoxyflavone is for example, phloroglucinol-derived, no isomerization of the kind shown in Eq. 7-12*a* can occur.

Demethylation of the 5-methoxy group in polymethoxyflavones occurs readily under mild conditions, so that 5-hydroxy-polymethoxyflavones are easily prepared.

Although flavones can be prepared by the oxidation (with sodium acetate-iodine) of flavanones, the reverse route—reduction of flavones to flavanones—is not of general usefulness. Eriodictyol (3′,4′,5,7-tetrahydroxyflavanone) has been prepared by the catalytic hydrogenation of luteolin (Fig. 7-5), but the method is not of wide application.

7.8   Flavonols (3-Hydroxyflavones)

Flavonols are common constituents of higher plants, and occur in a wide variety of hydroxylation patterns. The simplest natural flavonol is galangin, 3,5,7-trihydroxyflavone; the most elaborate, hibiscetin, is 3,5,7,8,3′,4′,5′-heptahydroxyflavone. The typical $C_6(A)$—C_3—$C_6(B)$ hydroxylation pattern, in which $C_6(A)$ is phloroglucinol-derived, and ring B is 4- or 3,4-dihydroxylated, is found in the two commonest flavonols, kaempferol and quercetin (Fig. 7-6):

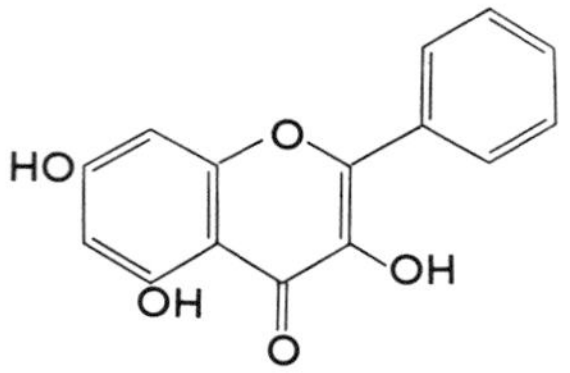

galangin 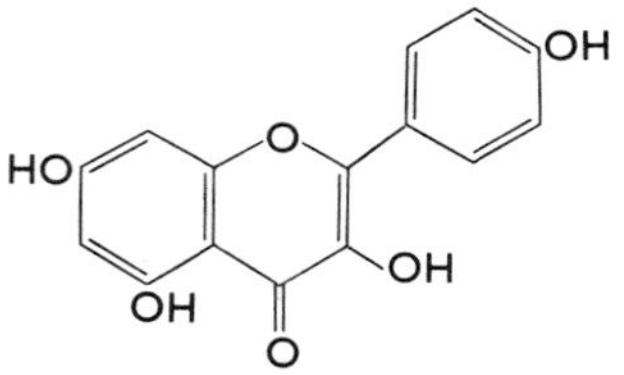   kaempferol

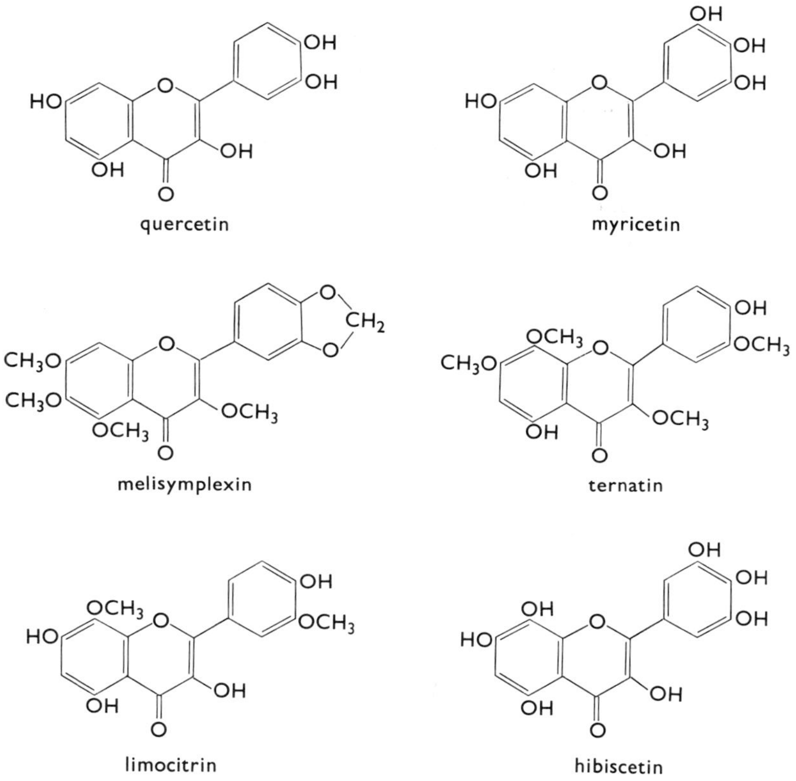

Fig. 7-6. Representative Natural Flavonols.

Hydroxyflavonols, like hydroxyflavones, usually occur in plants as glycosides. Flavonols most commonly occur as 3-glycosides, but glycosylation at other positions (chiefly at 7-OH) is not uncommon.

Although flavones, flavonols, and flavanones are so generally distributed through the families of higher plants that there are no clear chemotaxomic relationships to be discerned, several correlations appear. It is characteristic of plants of the family Rutaceae that polymethoxyflavones occur in many of its genera. The genus *Melicope* contains melisymplexin and ternatin (Fig. 7-6), as well as several related polymethoxy- and methylenedioxy-containing flavones; and the genus *Citrus* contains nobiletin, tangeretin (Fig. 7-5) and 3',4',5,6,7-pentamethoxyflavone (Eq. 7-10). It has been noted in an earlier chapter that the source of these O-methyl groups (and, as will be described later on, of methylenedioxy groups) is the system in which methionine acts as the methyl donor. It appears that the Rutaceae possess an active methylating mechanism.

Pinoquercetin and pinomyricetin are the 6-methyl analogues of quercetin and myricetin (Fig. 7-6). Carbon-methylation of polyketides has been discussed in Chapter 3. It has not been established in all cases whether the introduction of the carbon-methyl groups occurs at the polyketide stage or after the phloroglucinol structure has been established. Although the C-alkylation of β-diketones is a commonplace process, the C-alkylation of polyhydroxybenzenes—in particular, phloroglucinols—is also a well known reaction. The methylation of quercetin with methyl iodide in ethanolic alkali yields 6-methylquercetin-3′,4′,3,7-tetra-O-methyl ether, demethylation of which with HI yields the naturally occurring pinoquercetin (Eq. 7-13):

pinoquercetin   [Eq. 7-13]

Corollary evidence suggests, however, that the biological C-methylation that leads to pinoquercetin and pinomyricetin occurs at the polyketide stage prior to formation of the aromatic A-ring.

The determination of the structure of flavonols follows the general procedures outlined for flavones, and includes alkaline cleavage of the O-methylated compounds. Quercetin pentamethyl ether is cleaved by alcoholic alkali to veratric acid and α,2,4,6-tetramethoxyacetophenone. The points of attachment of sugars in the glycosides are ascertained by (a) methylation of the phenolic hydroxyl groups, (b) hydrolysis of the resulting methylated glycoside, and (c) identification of the monohydroxypolymethoxyflavone so formed. 3-Hydroxyflavones are usually recognizable by the ease with which stable complexes are formed with aluminum or zirconium salts, and with boric acid. Such complexes show brilliant fluorescence under ultraviolet light and are readily recognized; for example, on paper chromatograms. Numerous other chromatographic and spectroscopic methods have been devised to diagnose the structures of polyhydroxyflavones with the aim of locating the positions of the hydroxyl and methoxyl groups. These are described in special monographs and will not be discussed here.

7.9 Catechins. Stereochemistry of Flavonoid Compounds

Flavones and chalcones possess no asymmetric carbon atoms and thus (except for possible questions of *cis-trans* isomerism in chalcones) present no stereochemical problems. Flavanones contain one center of asymmetry and can exist in (+) and (−) forms. Most natural flavanones are levorotatory and possess the S-configuration. The stereochemistry of the flavanones and the 3-hydroxyflavanones (dihydroflavonols) has been established by methods in which the stereochemistry of the catechins is involved. (+)-Catechin and (−)-epicatechin are diastereomers differing in the disposition of the 2-aryl and 3-hydroxyl group (Fig. 7-7).

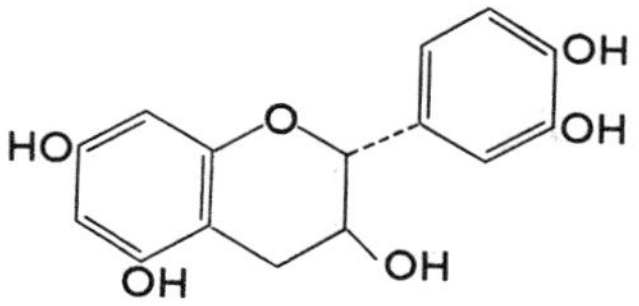

(+)-catechin

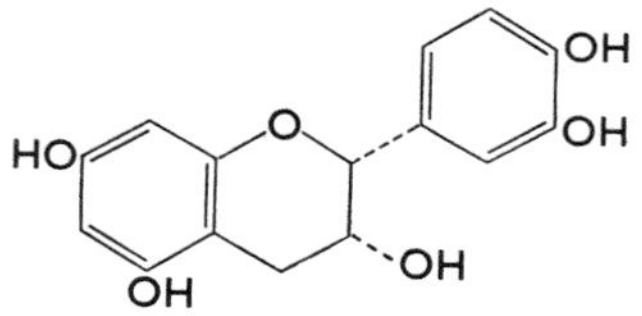

(−)-epicatechin

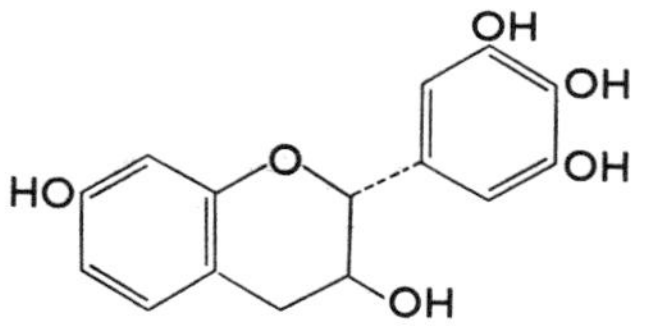

(−)-robinetinidol

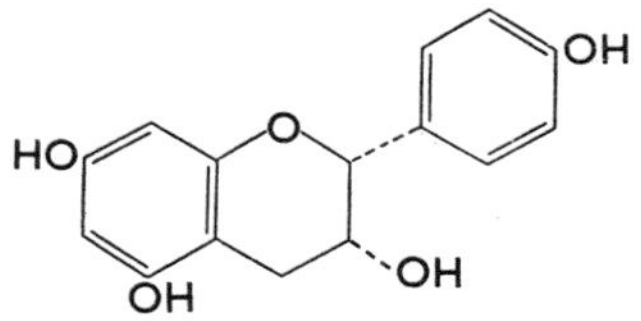

(−)-epiafzelechin

Fig. 7-7. Representative Natural Flavan-3-ols.

The gross structure of the catechins was established by conventional methods: (a) alkali fusion yielded phloroglucinol and 3,4-dihydroxybenzoic acid (protocatechuic acid); and (b) vigorous reduction of catechin tetramethyl ether,* followed by methylation of the resulting phenol, yielded 1-(2,4,6-trimethoxyphenyl)-3-(3,4-dimethoxyphenyl)propane. Although these observations could be accommodated by the three structures shown in Eq. 7-14*a*, the flavan structure of epicatechin was proved by its preparation (as the (±)-form) by catalytic reduction of cyanidin chloride.

* The formation of a pentaacetate and the methylation of but four (phenolic) hydroxyl groups shows that one of the hydroxyl groups is nonphenolic.

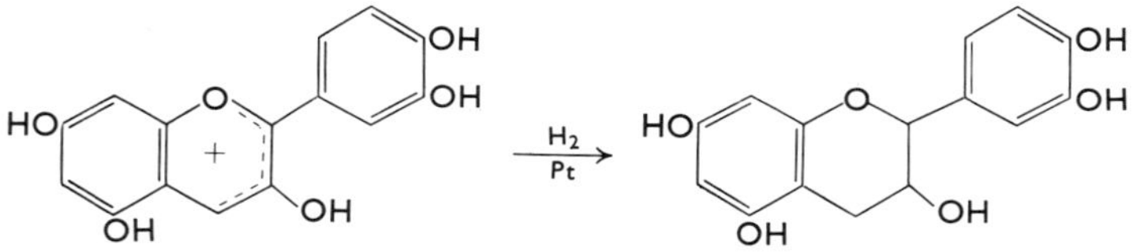

cyanidin (cation)   (±)-epicatechin

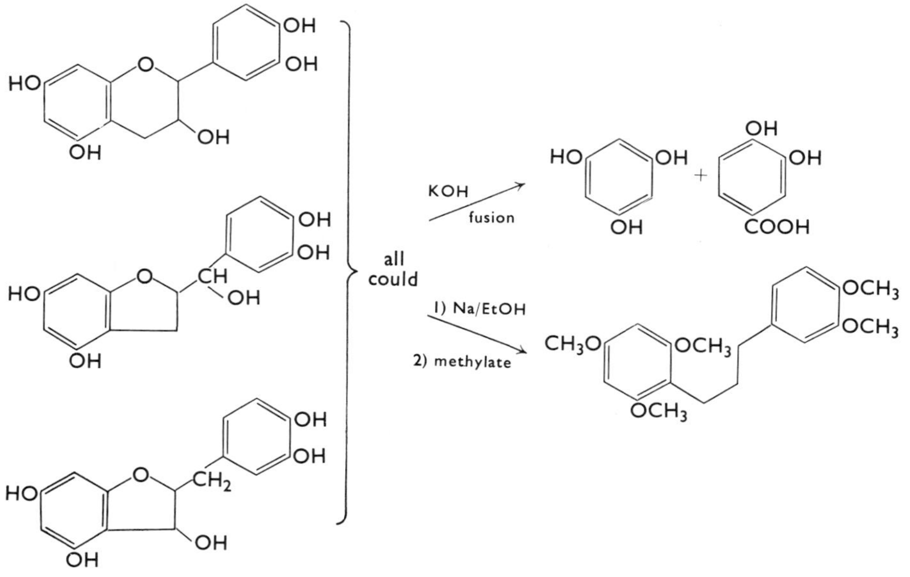

[Eq. 7-14]

Reduction of (+)-catechin tetramethyl ether and (−)-epicatechin tetra-methyl ether with sodium and ethanol in liquid ammonia, followed by methylation of the resulting phenols, yielded the enantiomeric 1-(3,4-dimethoxyphenyl)-3-(2,4,6-trimethoxyphenyl)-2-propanols (Eq. 7-15).

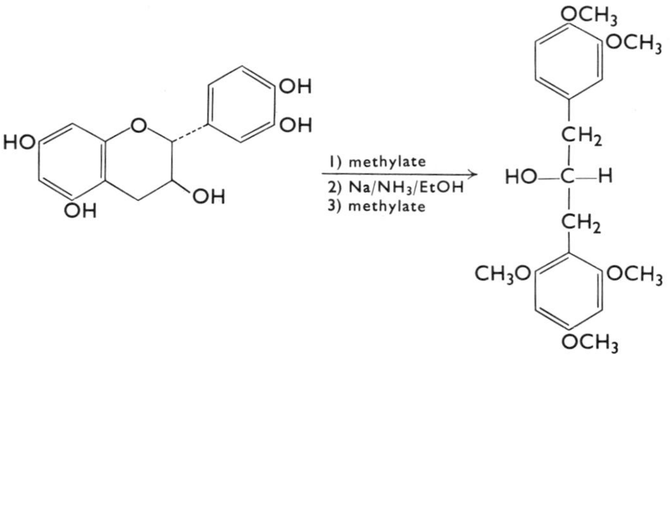

b.

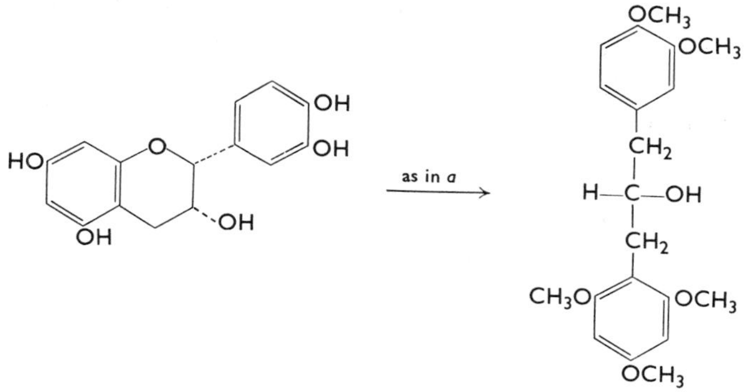

as in a

[Eq. 7-15]

This demonstrated that these two catechins have opposite configurations at C-3 and thus the same configuration at C-2. Although the formation of epicatechin by the reduction of cyanidin is evidence that epicatechin possesses the 2,3-*cis* configuration, the result is not unambiguous for catalytic hydrogenation is not always certainly *cis*.

Further evidence for the configurations of catechin and epicatechin is found in the reactions of the 3-tosyl derivatives of the respective tetramethyl ethers with hydrazine. Epicatechin tetramethyl ether 3-tosylate reacts with hydrazine to eliminate H-OTos and give the 2-arylflav-2-ene, a result in accord with the *trans* diaxial disposition of the hydrogen at C-2 and the tosyloxy group at C-3 (Eq. 7-16):

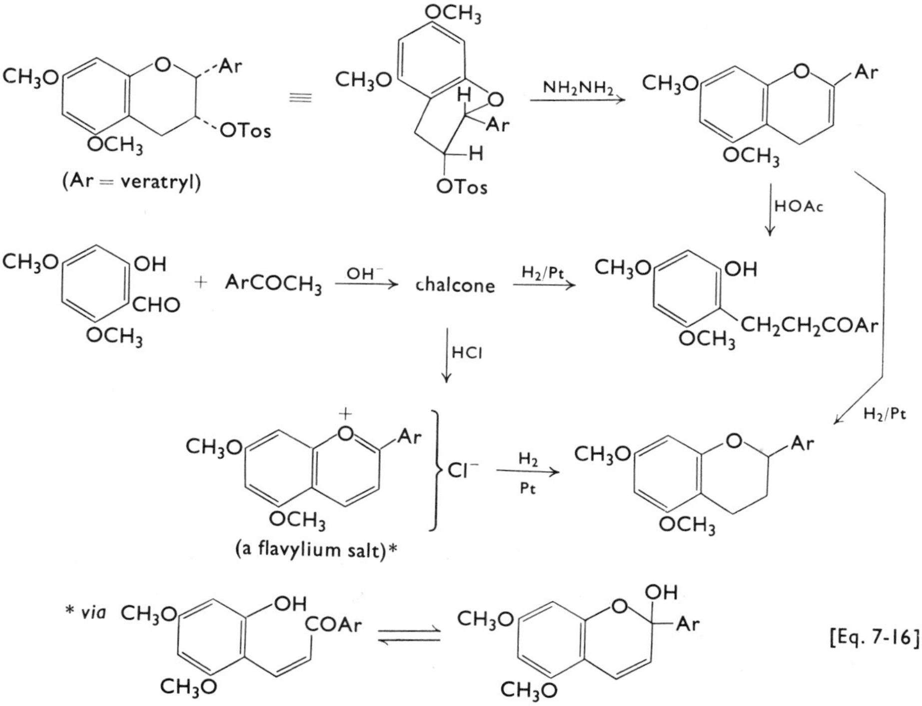

(Ar = veratryl)

NH_2NH_2

HOAc

$+ ArCOCH_3$ $\xrightarrow{OH^-}$ chalcone $\xrightarrow{H_2/Pt}$

HCl

H_2/Pt

$\left. \right\} Cl^-$ $\xrightarrow[Pt]{H_2}$

(a flavylium salt)*

* via

[Eq. 7-16]

On the other hand, the 3-tosylate of catechin tetramethyl ether does not undergo a simple 2,3-elimination reaction. Instead, elimination of TosOH is accompanied by migration of the 2-aryl group to the 3-position, with formation of the 3-arylflav-2-ene. This reaction, along with the structure proof of the 3-arylflavene, is shown in Eq. 7-17:

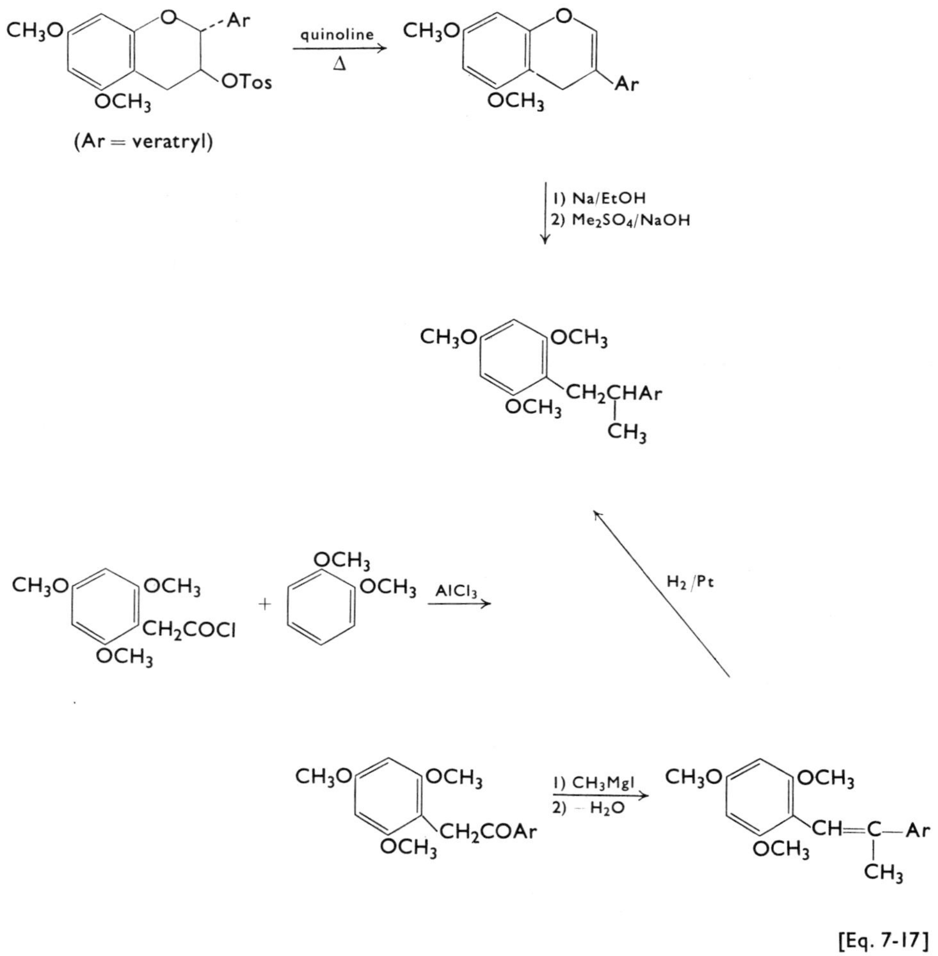

(Ar = veratryl)

[Eq. 7-17]

The transformations described by Eqs. 7-16 and 7-17 show the relative configurations of catechin and epicatechin. The absolute configurations were established by the degradation shown in Eq. 7-18, in which the configuration of the 3-OH group was fixed. Ozonolysis of (+)-catechin destroyed the phenolic rings and gave an α,β-dihydroxyglutaric acid whose configuration was established by relating it to 2-deoxy-D-ribose:

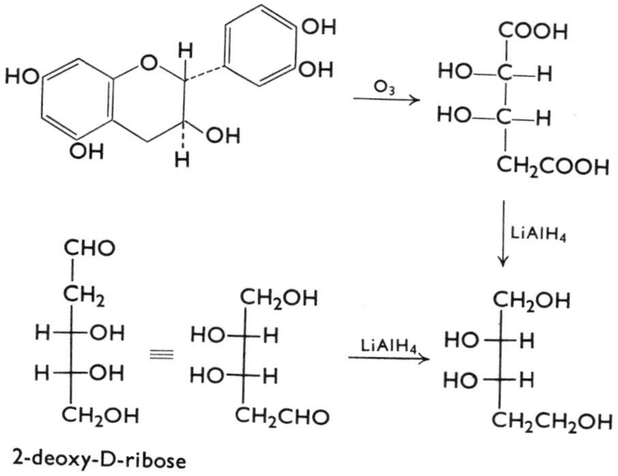

[Eq. 7-18]

The same series of reactions carried out with $(-)$-epicatechin yielded the tetraol derived from 2-deoxy-D-xylose.

The absolute configurations of the levorotatory natural flavanones have not all been established in separate experiments, but are regarded as being the same by comparisons of optical rotatory dispersions. The 2S configuration of $(-)$-hesperetin was demonstrated by ozonolysis, with the formation of malic acid, characterized as L-$(-)$-malamide (Eq. 7-19):

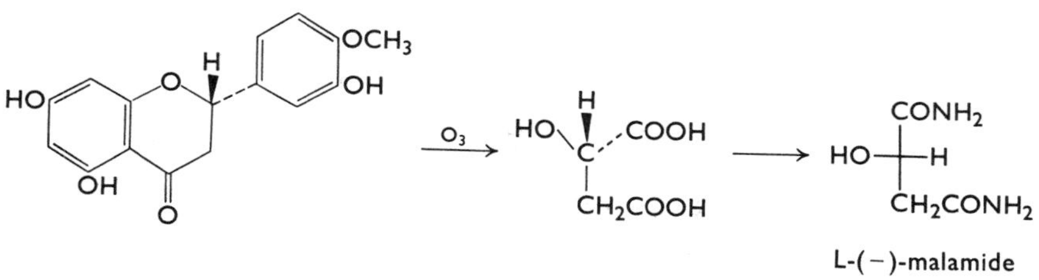

L-$(-)$-malamide

[Eq. 7-19]

The naturally occurring dihydroflavonols (3-hydroxyflavanones) possess the *trans*-2,3 configuration as in $(+)$-catechin. For example, $(+)$-dihydroquercetin tetramethyl ether has been converted into $(+)$-catechin tetramethyl ether by catalytic reduction. It is to be noted that the 4-hydroxyl group of a flavan-3,4-diol (to which the 3-hydroxyflavanone is first reduced) is a benzylic hydroxyl group and is subject to hydrogenolysis. Further, the α-orientation of the 2-aryl group in (+)-fustin and (+)-dihydrorobinetin has been demonstrated by the removal of the 3-hydroxyl group and formation of the levorotatory flavanones. These inter-relationships are illustrated in Eq. 7-20:

a.

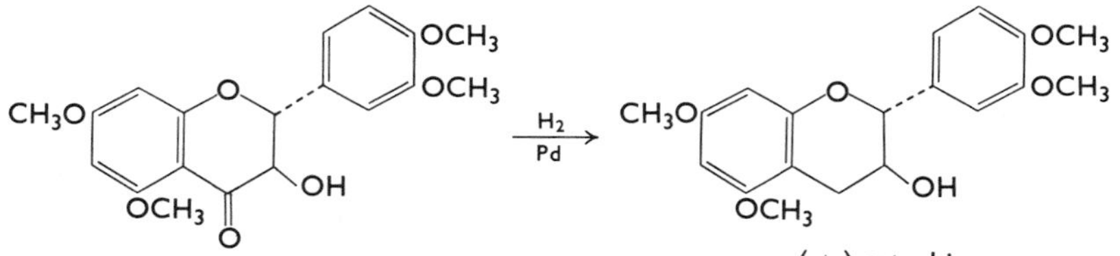

$\xrightarrow[\text{Pd}]{\text{H}_2}$

(+)-dihydroquercetin†
tetramethyl ether

(+)-catechin
tetramethyl ether

† Also named taxifolin.

b.

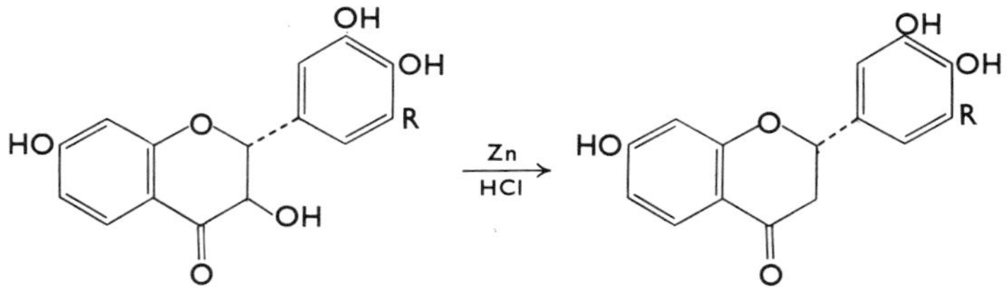

$\xrightarrow[\text{HCl}]{\text{Zn}}$

R = H, (+)-fustin
R = OH, (+)-dihydrorobinetin

R = H, (−)-butin
R = OH, (−)-robtin

[Eq. 7-20]

Certain of the chemical properties of the dihydroflavonols are in accord with these structural assignments. Thus, dihydroquercetin and dihydrokaempferol cannot be dehydrated to yield the corresponding flavones (luteolin and apigenin). Instead, they are readily dehydrogenated to yield the corresponding flavonols (quercetin and kaempferol). The conformation of the dihydroflavonols is thus most probably 2(ax)H:3(ax)H, as shown in Eq. 7-21:

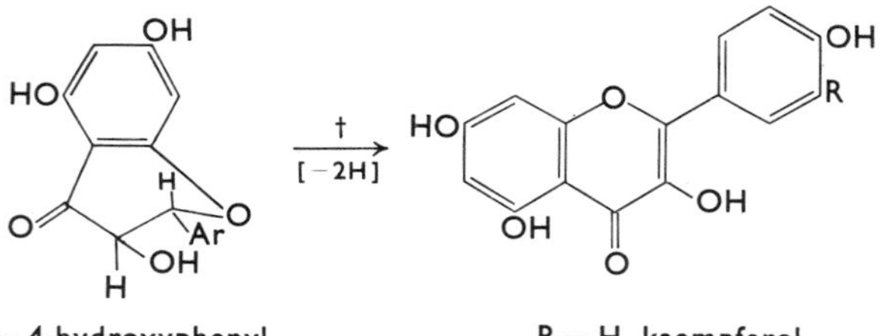

$\xrightarrow[\text{[−2H]}]{\dagger}$

Ar = 4-hydroxyphenyl,
 = dihydrokaempferol
Ar = 3,4-dihydroxyphenyl,
 = dihydroquercetin

R = H, kaempferol
R = OH, quercetin

[Eq. 7-21]

† Under various conditions, probably involving air oxidation.

7.10 Anthocyanidins and Proanthocyanidins

The most conspicuous natural flavonoid compounds are the anthocyanins, for these constitute the principal red, violet and blue pigments of plants, chiefly as the coloring matters of flowers and fruits. Anthocyanins are glycosides of anthocyanidins, which are polyhydroxyflavylium (2-arylbenzopyrilium) salts. By far the majority of the natural anthocyanins are glycosides (at the 3- or the 3,5-positions) of a limited number of anthocyanidins (Fig. 7-8):

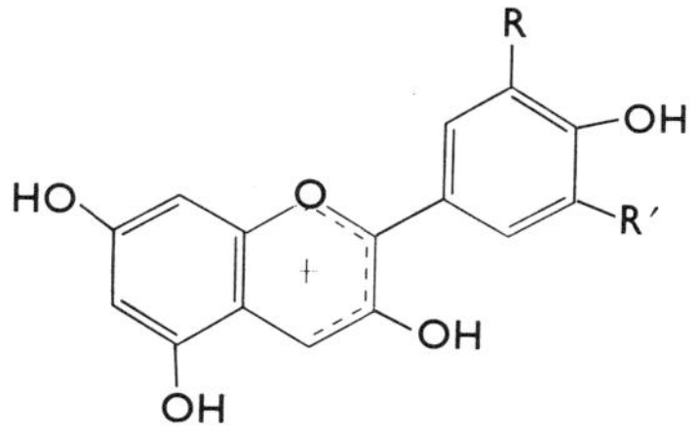

R = R′ = H, pelargonidin
R = H, R′ = OH, cyanidin
R = R′ = OH, delphinidin
R = H, R′ = OCH$_3$, peonidin
R = R′ = OCH$_3$, malvidin
R = OH, R′ = OCH$_3$, petunidin

Fig. 7-8. The Principal Natural Anthocyanidins.

The structure proof of the anthocyanidins was first accomplished by degradation methods similar to those outlined in foregoing sections for other flavonoid compounds, but was later established more firmly by total synthesis. The synthesis of cyanidin chloride is shown in Eq. 7-22:

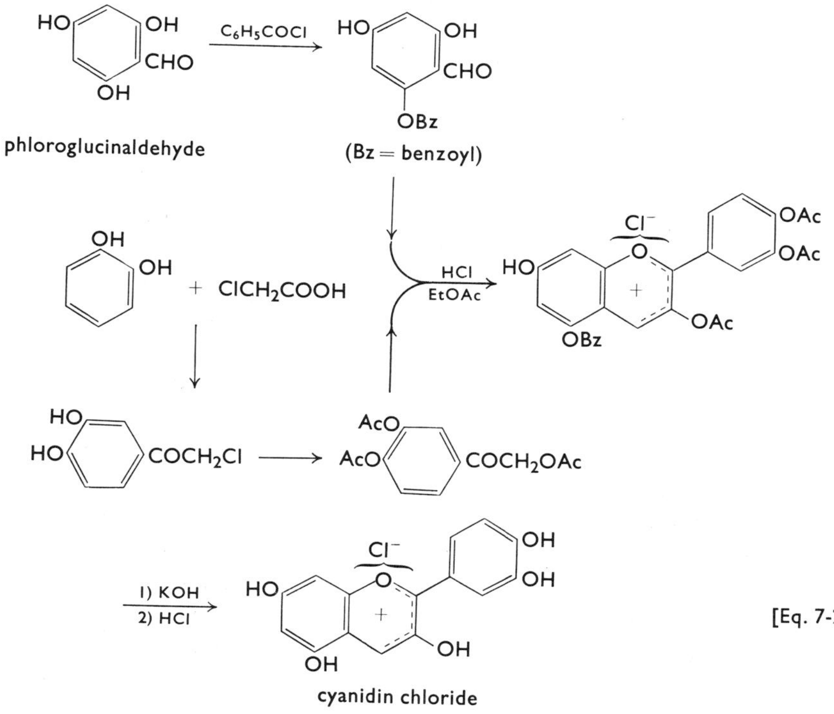

phloroglucinaldehyde

(Bz = benzoyl)

cyanidin chloride

[Eq. 7-22]

By the use of appropriately substituted (i.e., glycosylated) analogues of the reactants shown in Eq. 7-22 the natural anthocyanins have been synthesized in the same manner.

Anthocyanidins are also formed when flavan-3,4-diols are heated under strongly acidic conditions (Eq. 7-23). The reaction is complex and the yields of the flavylium salts are low; and in addition it is to be noted that the reaction involves an oxidation, for simple dehydration of the flavandiol leads, not to an anthocyanidin but to a 3-flaven-3-ol (a "leucoanthocyanidin").

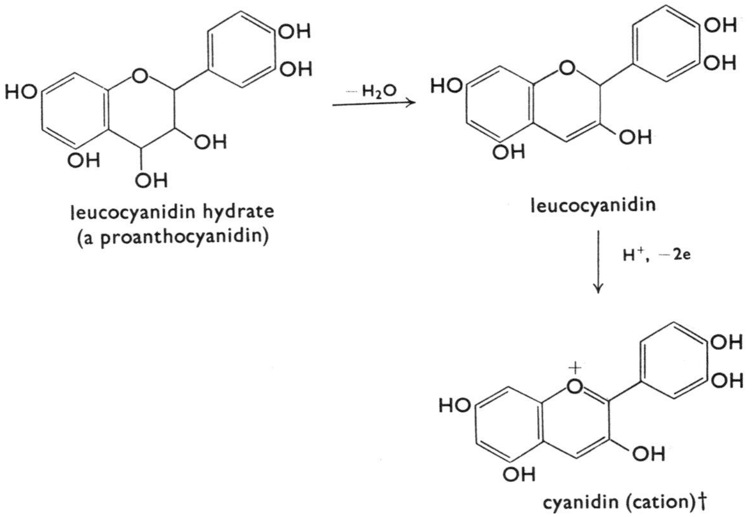

leucocyanidin hydrate
(a proanthocyanidin)

leucocyanidin

$H^+, -2e$

cyanidin (cation)†

[Eq. 7-23]

† Charge localized representation corresponding to charge delocalized representation of Fig. 7-8.

Although flavan-3,4-diols are well known naturally occurring compounds, there is no persuasive evidence that they lie on the biosynthetic pathway leading to the anthocyanins. Indeed, the first compound of the class to be isolated from a natural source is melacacidin, 3,4,7,8,3',4'-hexahydroxyflavan, which does not correspond in hydroxylation pattern with a known anthocyanidin. The co-occurrence of anthocyanins and the correspondingly substituted flavan-3,4-diols is not general and when it is observed may be ascribed to parallel courses of synthesis from a common precursor.

The immediate precursor of an anthocyanin (that is, at the same oxidation level) is a 2-flaven-3,4-diol or a 3-flaven-2,3-diol. Examples of the former of these are known as synthetic compounds. The reduction of acetylated rutin (quercetin 3-rutinoside) with lithium aluminum hydride and subsequent reaction of the product with HCl yields cyanidin 3-rutinoside, indicating that the reaction proceeds through the 2-flaven-3,4-diol as shown in Eq. 7-24.

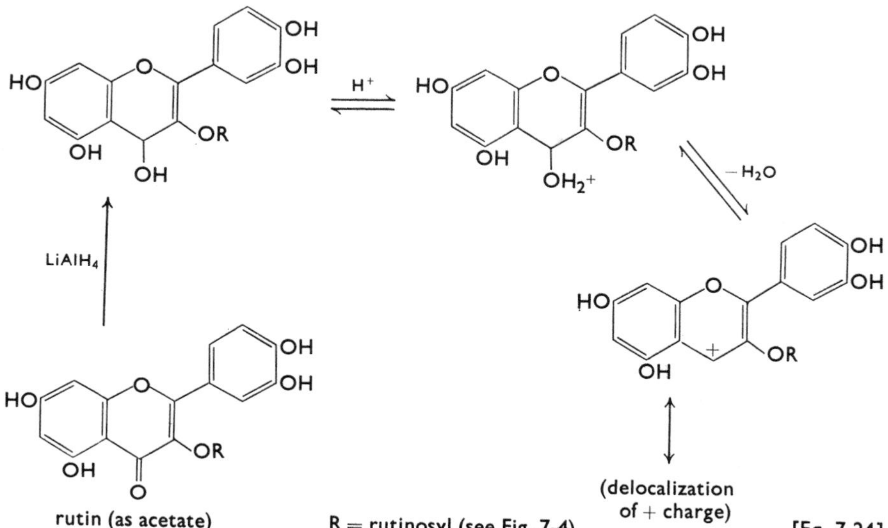

rutin (as acetate)   R = rutinosyl (see Fig. 7-4)   (delocalization of + charge)   [Eq. 7-24]

7.11 Complex Proanthocyanidins*

Many plants, chiefly but not exclusively those of the woody habit, contain mixtures of complex flavonoid compounds which are colorless and are converted by acid hydrolysis into anthocyanidins and catechins. These substances are often of high molecular weight and of ill-defined structure. They are astringent to the taste and have the ability to tan leather. Indeed, the so-called "condensed tannins" belong to this class of substances. It is probable that the true tannins, which are high-molecular weight compounds, are produced by a multiple condensation of C_{15}-"monomers," and some support for this concept is found in the isolation of the least complex members of the polymeric series, namely, the dimers.

Proanthocyanidins containing 30 carbon atoms have been isolated from a number of plant sources. A typical compound of this type has been shown to have the following characteristics:

a. it forms an octamethyl ether and a deca-acetate.
b. the octamethyl ether forms a diacetate.
c. upon mild acid hydrolysis, catechin and epicatechin are formed.
d. treatment with strong acid yields cyanidin.

* The term "proanthocyanidin" is not structurally explicit, but is based solely upon the experimental observation that compounds of this class yield true anthocyanidins (e.g., cyanidin) upon treatment with strong acids.

These properties suggest that the C_{30} compound is composed of a molecule of a catechin (or epicatechin) with a flavan-3,4-diol. There are several ways in which such a combination might be effected, bearing in mind that the resulting "dimer" is readily dissociated by very mild acidic hydrolysis, the simplest of which is ether formation between the catechin and flavan-3,4-diol. Another mode of combination, and the one which experimental evidence supports, is by substitution of the flavan-3,4-diol into the phloroglucinol nucleus by the acid-catalyzed condensation shown in Eq. 7-25.

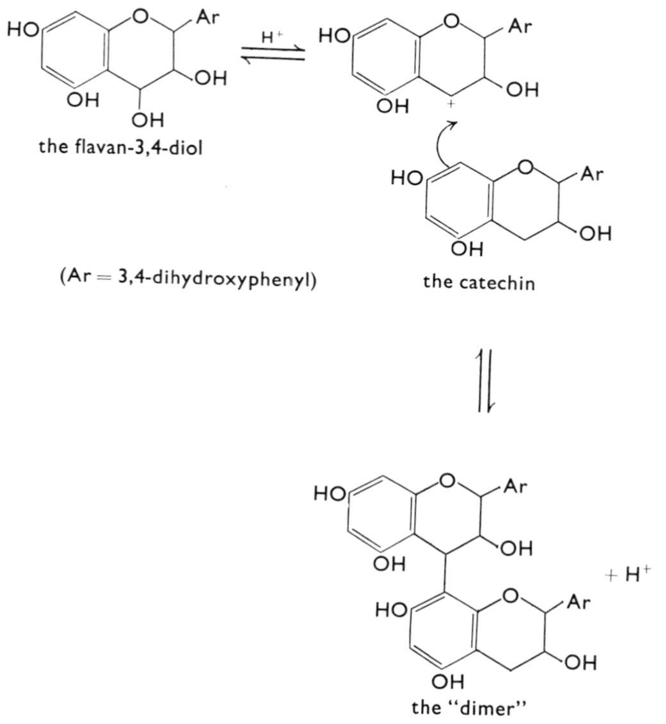

the flavan-3,4-diol

(Ar = 3,4-dihydroxyphenyl)

the catechin

+ H⁺

[Eq. 7-25]

the "dimer"

It is clear that the reversibility of the acid-catalyzed reactions shown in Eq. 7-25 provides for the regeneration from the dimer of the catechin and the flavan-diol, the latter of which can then lead to the formation of the anthocyanidin.

It is suggested the higher condensed tannins are formed in the same way, with the difference that if the first condensation takes place between two flavandiols (from the 4-position of one to the 8-position of the other), the resulting "dimer" retains the flavan-3,4-diol structure and is capable of further condensation of the same kind. On this theory, a condensed tannin may be represented as in Eq. 7-26 (with the provision that the condensation may occur at the 6-position, which is equivalent to the 8-position in the reaction pictured; or that the native polymers possess both 4–6 and 4–8 unions).

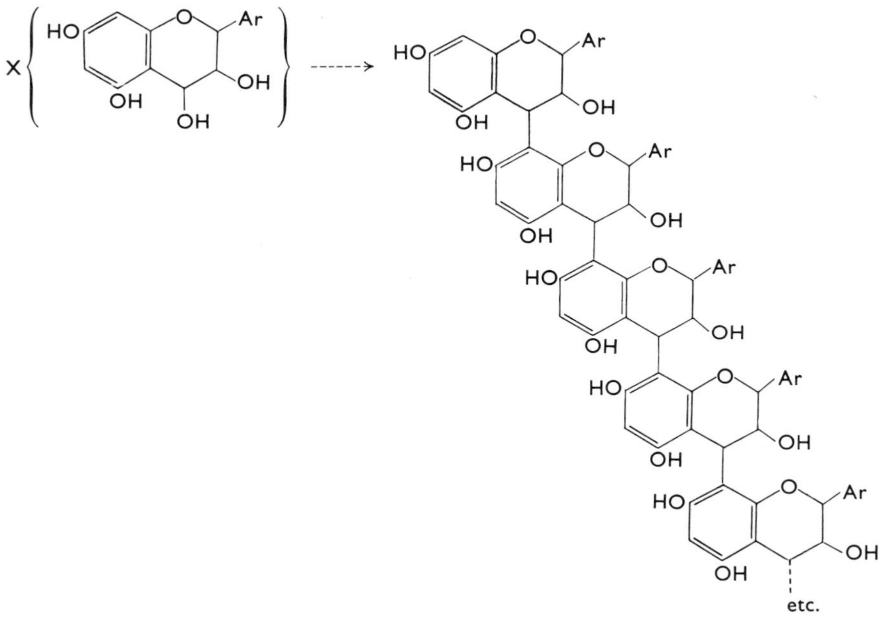

[Eq. 7-26]

Experimental support for these concepts has been found in the observation that flavan-3,4-diols condense with phloroglucinol under very mildly acidic conditions to give 4-(2,4,6-trihydroxyphenyl)-flavan-3-ols.

7.12 Aurones

A class of flavonoid compounds less widely distributed in nature than the flavan-derived groups contain a five-membered heterocyclic ring. The aurones, or 2-benzalcoumaran-3-ones, are typified by sulfuretin, related in hydroxylation pattern to butein, the chalcone. Indeed, it is probably of biogenetic significance to note that most aurones are accompanied in their natural sources by the chalcones of corresponding hydroxyl substitution. The reason for this may be that aurones are formed directly from chalcones by a simple oxidative ring closure. The formation of sulfuretin from butein occurs readily under ordinary conditions—even in alcoholic solutions exposed to air. The probable course of this oxidation is shown in Eq. 7-27:

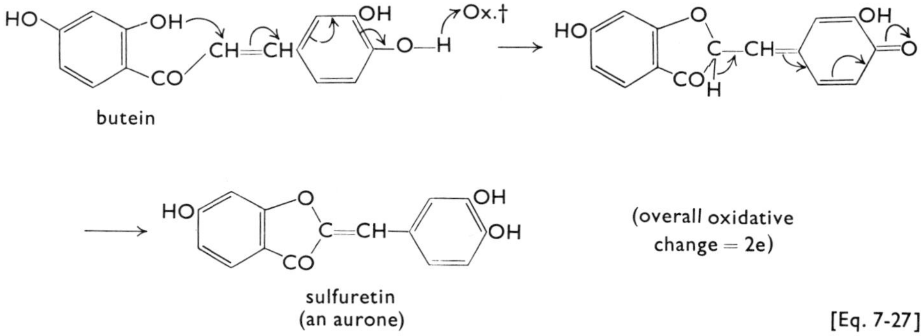

butein

(overall oxidative change = 2e)

sulfuretin
(an aurone)

[Eq. 7-27]

† An oxidant, perhaps enzymatic in the biological reaction; or oxygen in the *in vitro* reaction.

It has been observed that tissue preparations (petal meal) of aurone-containing flowers are capable of catalyzing the chalcone $\rightarrow$ aurone conversion, a process that is inhibited by cyanide.

7.13 Isoflavonoid Compounds

Isoflavones possess "rearranged" flavonoid skeletons, the B-ring being attached to the 3-position of the central ring. A variety of modifications of the isoflavonoid structure lead to a large class of compounds that includes isoflavones, isoflavanones, 3-arylcoumarins, rotenone and its congeners, and the desoxybenzoin, angolensin (Fig. 7-9).

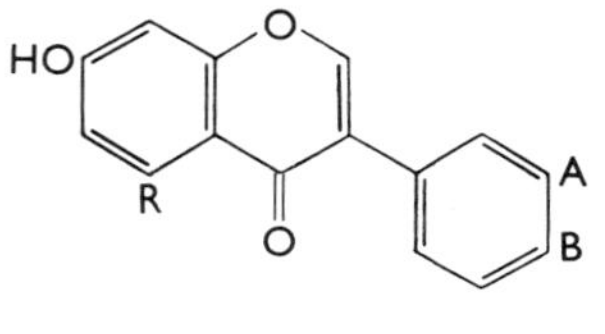

R = H; A = H; B = OH: daidzein
R = H; A = H; B = OCH$_3$: formononetin
R = H; A—B = —OCH$_2$O—: ψ-baptigenin
R = OH; A = H; B = OH: genistein
R = OH; A = H; B = OCH$_3$: biochanin-A
R = OH; A = B = OH: orobol

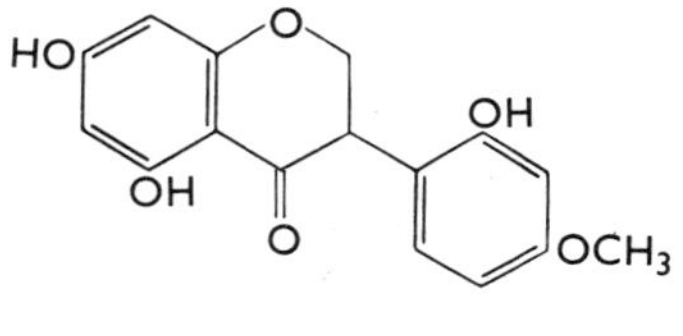

ferrerein
homoferrerein (2′—OCH$_3$)

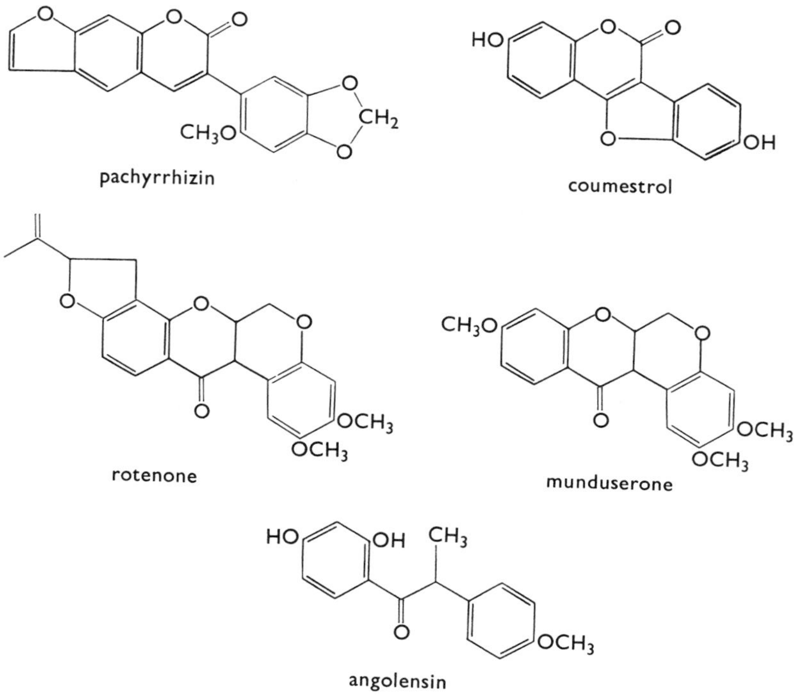

pachyrrhizin

coumestrol

rotenone

munduserone

angolensin

Fig. 7-9. Representative Natural Isoflavonoid Compounds.

The isoflavonoid compounds are common constituents of plants of the family Leguminosae, and all of the compounds shown in Fig. 7-9 are found in plants belonging to this family. Although isoflavonoid compounds are not sharply confined to the legumes, the great preponderance of their distribution in this family strongly suggests that the taxonomic classification of these plants is coupled with a common enzymatic capability for bringing about a unique structural transformation. We shall see in the discussion to follow that isoflavonoid compounds are indeed members of the $C_6(A)$—C_3—$C_6(B)$ class in which the $C_6(B)$-aryl group has migrated in the course of biosynthesis.

The methods used for the structure proof of isoflavonoid compounds cannot be encompassed in a brief discussion because of the great variety of compound types represented by this class. Physical methods of study now find application to problems which in earlier years were attacked by degradation procedures. Because of the position of the aryl group at the 3-position of the chromone ring, the ultraviolet spectra of isoflavones are not strongly influenced by substitution in the B-ring and are of somewhat less diagnostic value than are the spectra of flavones, flavonols, chalcones, and aurones. Infrared spectra are of limited predictive and analytical value in isoflavonoid structure determination and there is little that can be said of its general application to the problems of flavonoid structure proof. Because of the charge delocalization in the chromone ring, and the effective hydrogen bonding between the 5-hydroxyl group and the 4-carbonyl group, the stretching frequencies of the latter are at much lower values than those of aryl ketones of conventional kinds.

A few examples are given in the following table:

Table 7-1. C=O Stretching Frequencies of
Some Flavonoid Compounds

flavone	1649 cm^{-1}
3-hydroxyflavone	1615 cm^{-1}
5-hydroxyflavone	1652 cm^{-1}
7-hydroxyflavone	1625 cm^{-1}
flavanone	1680 cm^{-1}
5-hydroxyflavanone	1648 cm^{-1}
5,7,3′,4′-tetrahydroxyflavanone	1620 cm^{-1}
5,7,3′,4′-tetraacetoxyflavanone	1680 cm^{-1}
3,5,7,3′,4′-pentamethoxyflavone	1627 cm^{-1}
3,5,7,3′,4′-pentaacetoxyflavone	1640 cm^{-1}

It will be noted that the fully acetylated polyhydroxyflavones show carbonyl stretching frequencies very similar to those of the non-hydroxylated compounds. A similar observation is made in the case of ultraviolet absorption spectra: the complete acetylation of a polyhydroxyflavonoid compound causes its UV absorption spectrum to resemble closely that of the parent (non-hydroxylated) compound. For example, penta-O-acetylquercetin gives a UV absorption spectrum very nearly that of flavone itself, or of tetra-O-acetylluteolin; the UV spectrum of tetra-O-acetylbutein is not unlike that of benzalacetophenone; and so on. The reasons for the effect of O-acetylation are easy to see, for the auxochromic effect of a hydroxyl group upon a suitably located carbonyl group (Eq. 7-28) is nullified by the opposing effect of the acyl group.

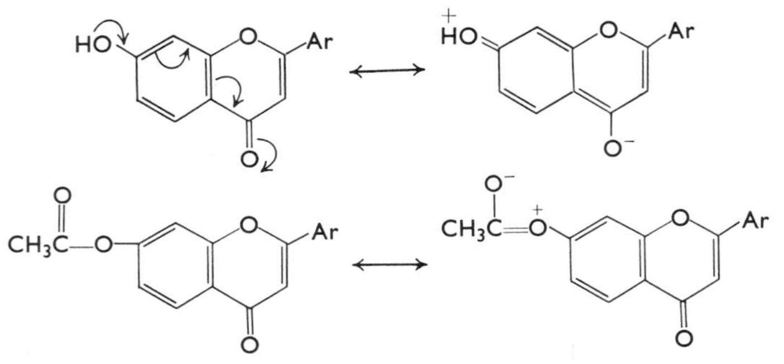

[Eq. 7-28]

Isoflavones are usually stable to acids; like pyrones of other kinds, protonation of the carbonyl oxygen atom yields a resonance stabilized pyrylium salt that undergoes further attack under drastic conditions only. Alkaline hydrolysis of isoflavones, on the other hand, proceeds readily, with cleavage of the heterocyclic ring. Treatment with concentrated alkali under vigorous conditions ("alkali fusion") decomposes the isoflavone into the phloroglucinol (or resorcinol) portion corresponding to ring A, and a substituted phenylacetic acid, from ring B and the C-3 and C-4 carbon atoms. Alkaline hydrolysis under milder conditions yields formic acid (from C-2) and a desoxybenzoin. These reactions are illustrated with the example shown in Eq. 7-29:

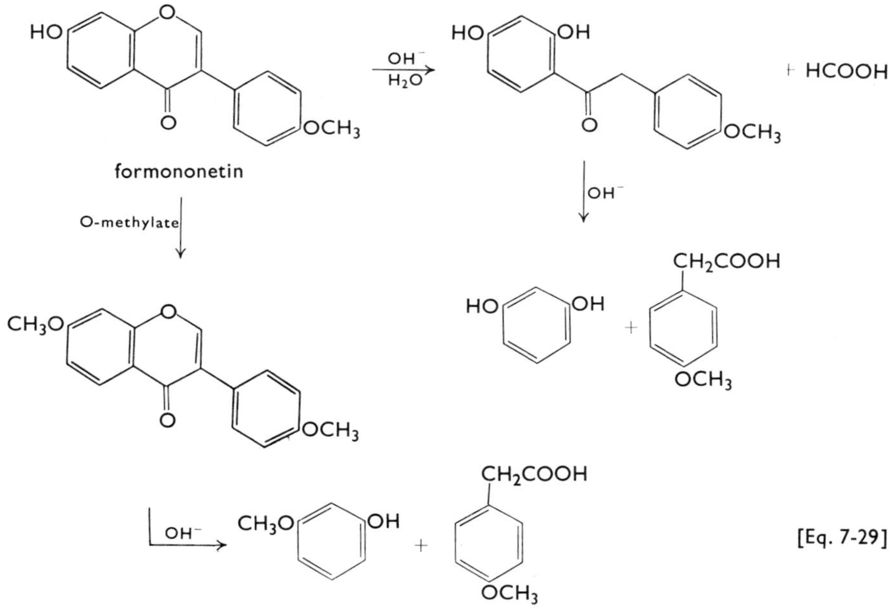

[Eq. 7-29]

It should be noted that the degradation reactions shown in Eq. 7-29 do not in themselves distinguish between the structure shown for formononetin and the alternative 5-hydroxy-4'-methoxy compound. A distinction between the 7- and 5-positions for the hydroxyl group can be made by spectral measurements, for the formation of stable chelated complexes with heavy metals (e.g., aluminum) causes a marked shift in the ultraviolet absorption maximum in 5-hydroxy-4-carbonyl flavonoid compounds when aluminum chloride is added to an alcoholic solution of the compound. No such spectral shift occurs in the case of formononetin.

The synthesis of isoflavones is readily accomplished by what is effectively a reversal of the cleavage shown in Eq. 7-29. The introduction of a formyl group at the —CH$_2$— group of a suitably substituted deoxybenzoin yields a compound which cyclizes readily to the isoflavone. The formyl group may be introduced by the reaction of the deoxybenzoin with ethyl formate and sodium; with ethyl orthoformate; or with dimethylformamide and phosphorus oxychloride. An alternative procedure is to introduce the ethoxalyl grouping, a procedure that requires a later decarboxylation of the isoflavone-2-carboxylic acid that is formed upon ring closure. The two methods are outlined in a generalized formulation in Eq. 7-30; since the three methods of formylation involve intermediates which differ in certain details of their structures the reaction shown in Eq. 7-30 is written in terms of an arbitrary C-formyl intermediate; it will be clear that the use of ethyl orthoformate would probably proceed through the ethyl ether of the enolic form of the C-formyl compound.

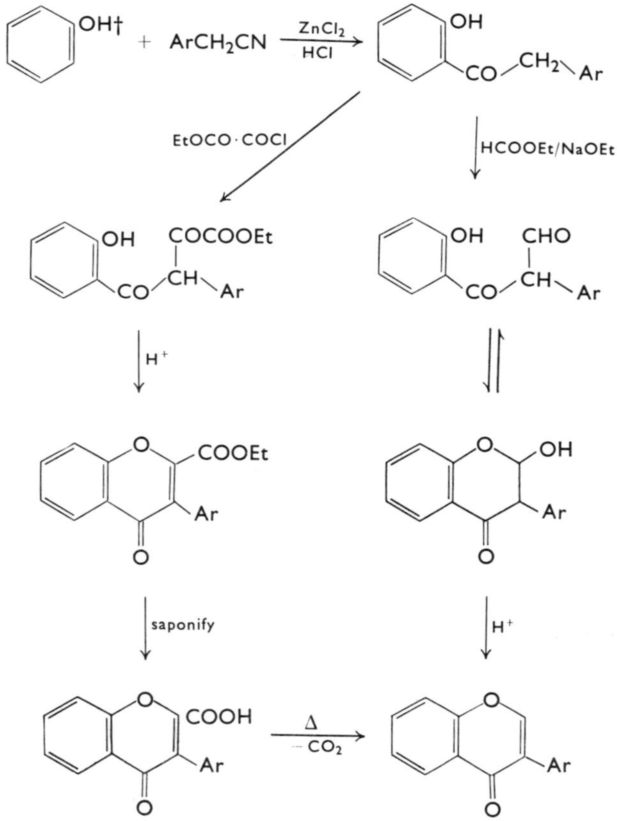

[Eq. 7-30]

---

† Although only the *o*-hydroxyl group is shown in this model synthesis, the Hoesch reaction with which most isoflavone syntheses start is performed with a resorcinol, phloroglucinol, or other polyhydroxy phenol.

7.14 Biosynthesis of Flavonoid Compounds

The general course of biosynthesis of the C_6—C_3—C_6 carbon skeleton of flavonoid compounds is now understood, and can be represented by the expression

$$C_6\text{---}C_3 \quad + \quad 3\,C_2 \quad \longrightarrow \quad C_6\text{---}C_3\text{---}(C_2)_3 \quad \longrightarrow \quad C_6(B)\text{---}C_3\text{---}C_6(A)$$

(phenylpropanoid)   (acetate)

An early observation that suggested that a C_6—C_3 fragment was a precursor of the C_{15} flavonoid molecule was made in the course of chemical-genetic studies of the petal pigments of snapdragons. Colored varieties contain flavonoid pigments of various kinds, but an albino mutant was found to have no C_{15} flavonoid compounds but did contain cinnamic acids (e.g., p-coumaric). The inference that the genetic block in the albino mutation prevented the extension of the C_6—C_3 unit by six carbon atoms, as shown in Eq. 7-31, is now confirmed by direct evidence obtained from experiments with isotopically labeled compounds.

When uniformly-labeled ^{14}C-phenylalanine was administered to buckwheat plants, the quercetin (present in the plant as the 3-rutinoside, rutin) that was formed was found to contain the radioactive label only in the C_3—C_6(B) portion of the molecule; the C_6(A) ring was unlabeled (Eq. 7-32).

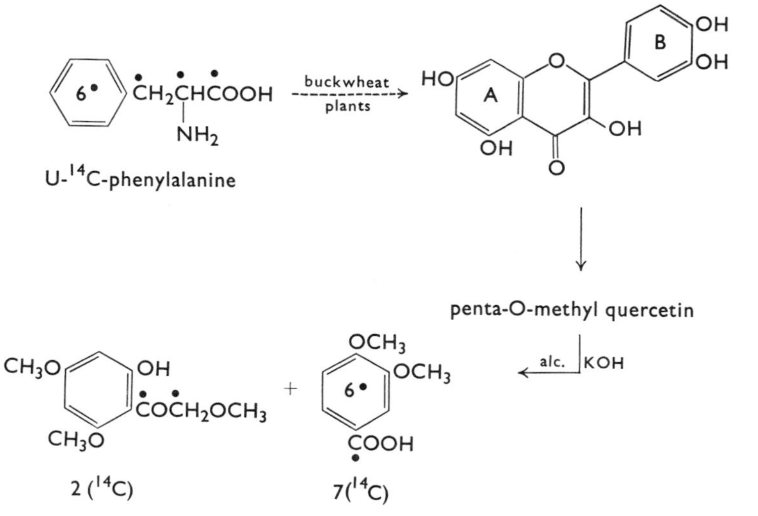

[Eq. 7-32]

Other feeding experiments showed that various phenylpropanoid compounds can serve as effective precursors of the C_3—C_6(B) portion of the flavonoid (quercetin) molecule: shikimic acid, phenylalanine, p-coumaric, cinnamic and caffeic acids were all incorporated, but tyrosine, ferulic, sinapic and m-methoxycinnamic acids were incorporated much less efficiently.* The most revealing results of these studies were that the C_6—C—C—C unit of phenylalanine, cinnamic acid and p-coumaric acid was introduced into quercetin as a unit. The use of specifically ^{14}C-labeled compounds showed that the quercetin that was formed bore the label as shown in Eq. 7-33a:

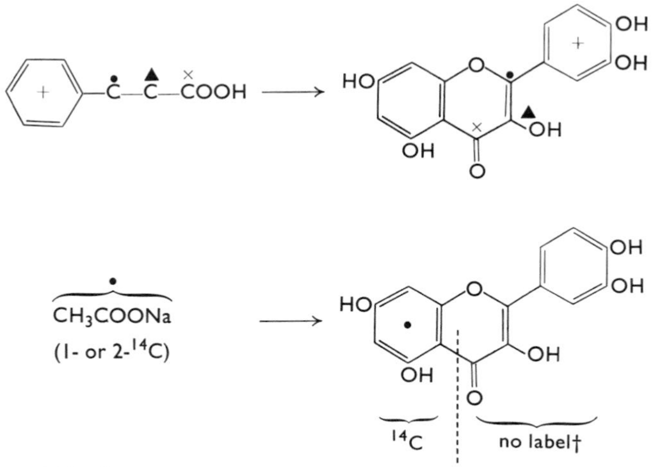

$$[Eq. 7-33]$$

† Except for slight randomization as a result of entrance of ^{14}C-acetate into general metabolic pools.

Labeled sodium acetate was, as expected, incorporated only into the C_6(A) portion of the quercetin molecule (Eq. 7-33b).

The incorporation of acetate into the flavonoid molecule proceeds according to the acetate hypothesis. Specifically labeled (1-^{14}C- and 2-^{14}C-) acetate was found to be incorporated into cyanidin (in red cabbage seedlings) in the manner shown in Eq. 7-34, in which the probable acyclic precursor is indicated.

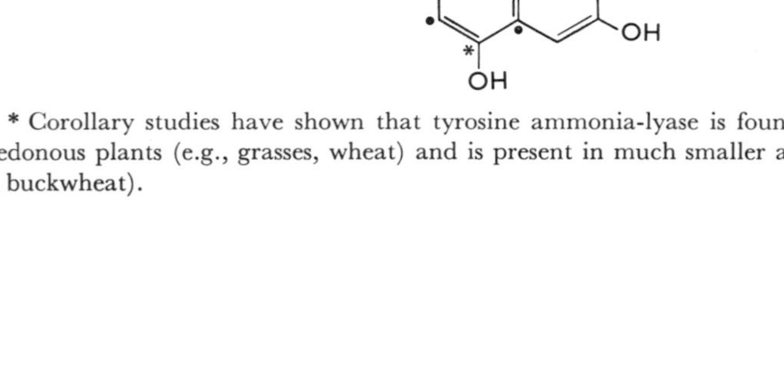

$$[Eq. 7-34]$$

* Corollary studies have shown that tyrosine ammonia-lyase is found principally in monocotyledonous plants (e.g., grasses, wheat) and is present in much smaller amounts in dicotyledons (e.g., buckwheat).

The results of the experiments just described, and others of a similar kind, lead to the conclusion that the formation of the C_6—C_3—C_6 unit proceeds by a route that has its counterparts in numerous other biosyntheses that follow the acetate pathway. In the case of flavonoid biosynthesis, the two pathways, one leading through shikimic acid to phenylalanine and cinnamic (or p-coumaric) acid, the other the acetate-malonate pathway, combine to give the final natural compounds. The complete process is outlined in Eq. 7-35:

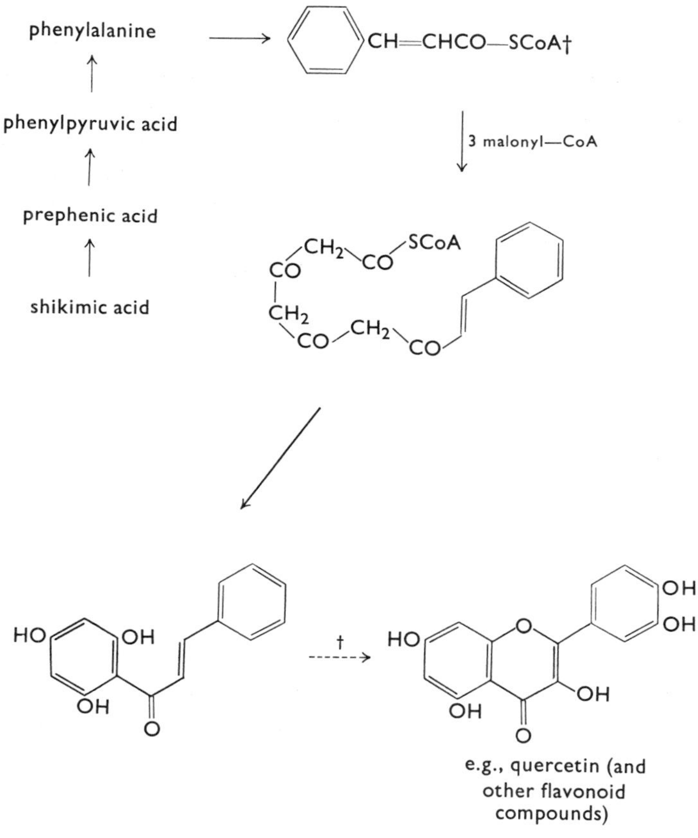

e.g., quercetin (and other flavonoid compounds)

[Eq. 7-35]

---

† The exact point in the total reaction sequence at which the p- or 3,4-hydroxyl groups are introduced is not known with certainty. See text for further comment.

The assumption that the initial C_{15} stage of flavonoid biosynthesis is a chalcone is strongly supported (but not proved) by the following observations:

a. cinnamic acids are effective precursors for *in vivo* flavonoid biosynthesis;

b. the chalcone is the immediate product of the extension of the C_6—C_3 unit by malonyl CoA units;

c. chalcones, appropriately labeled with ^{14}C, are effective precursors of flavonoid compounds of other kinds.

The exact nature of the B-ring of the initial chalcone that lies on the pathway to a flavone that possesses 4'- or 3',4'-hydroxyl groups is not known with certainty. That is, the point at which B-ring hydroxylation occurs has not been firmly established. A number of experimental facts can be adduced:

a. phenylalanine is a good precursor of flavonoid compounds with various degrees of B-ring substitution. It is also a good precursor of caffeic acid (in tobacco seedlings). This shows that hydroxylation can occur at the C_6—C_3 stage.

b. cinnamic and *p*-coumaric acids are better than caffeic acid as precursors of quercetin (in buckwheat plants). But because caffeic acid is quite unstable toward oxidative degradation, this observation is not a compelling argument against dihydroxylation at the cinnamic acid stage.

c. ferulic acid (3-methoxy-4-hydroxycinnamic acid) is incorporated into tricin, 5,7,4'-trihydroxy-3',5'-dimethoxyflavone, showing that cinnamic or *p*-coumaric acid is not an obligatory precursor for the chain-extension stage.

d. since there is no compelling evidence for the *removal* of hydroxyl groups from aromatic rings in flavonoid biosynthesis, the occurrence in nature of B-ring-unsubstituted (i.e., 2-phenyl-) flavones shows that cinnamic acid itself can serve as the C_6—C_3 starter unit.

e. many plants are known to contain cinnamic acids whose substitution patterns do not correspond with the co-occurring flavonoid constituents. For instance, ferulic acid is more widely occurring than flavonoid compounds with 3-OCH_3-4-OH B-rings.

Experiments designed to resolve these questions have not given unequivocal answers. It appears that the hydroxylation of aromatic rings can take place in compounds of various degrees of structural complexity.

7.15 Isoflavone Biosynthesis

The biosynthesis of isoflavones begins in the same manner as that of flavonoid compounds of other kinds: by the union of a C_6—C_3 precursor (phenylalanine and its congeners) with six carbon atoms from acetic acid. The formation of the isoflavone (3-arylchromone) structure has been shown by labeling experiments to proceed by a rearrangement of the $C_6(B)$ aryl group, probably at the flavanone stage, from the 2- to the 3-position (Eq. 7-36):

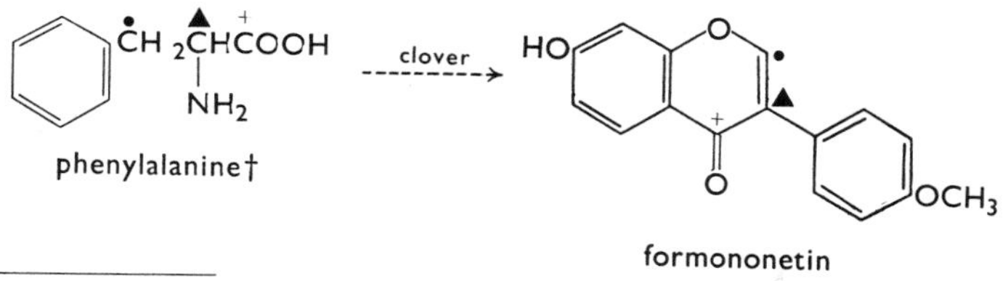

[Eq. 7-36]

formononetin

† Cinnamic acid is incorporated in the same way. The A-ring is derived from acetate, as shown by feeding experiments with ^{14}C-acetate.

Neither the mechanism of the rearrangement nor the exact identity of the compound in which it occurs are known in detail. There are, however, certain facts that argue against some of the possible courses for the reaction; and certain other considerations lead to suggestions as to what the natural course may be.

Dihydroflavonols do not appear to be the natural precursors of the isoflavones. Although 3,7,4'-trihydroxyflavanone (garbanzol) is incorporated into biochanin-A with specific retention of the ^{14}C-label, the incorporation occurs to a very small extent, and is much less efficient than that of phenylalanine. That the rearrangement would occur by a mechanism outlined in Eq. 7-37 is in any case unlikely, for the generation of electron-deficiency at the carbon atom α- to a carbonyl group is energetically disadvantageous.

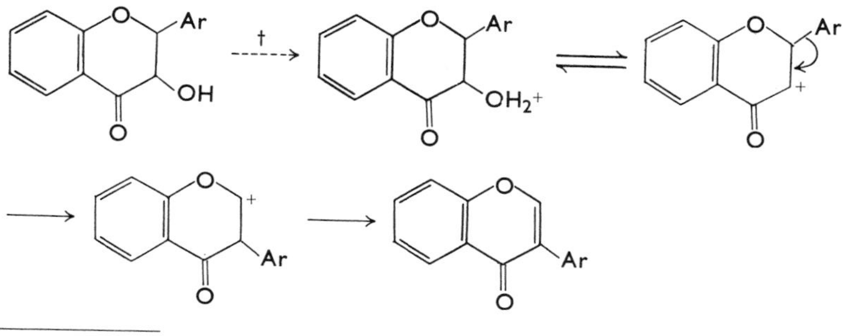

[Eq. 7-37]

† The use of protonation to assist the dissociation of the 3-OH group is an arbitrary device. The biological equivalent process might be pyrophosphorylation of 3-OH.

Nearly any alternative mechanism based upon the same precursor would be arbitrary and probably awkward. There is, however, a reasonable pathway that has the advantage of being related to other changes that occur in the heterocyclic ring. This is an oxidative process that can lead to rearrangement only, or to oxidation without rearrangement, and serves to accommodate a variety of flavonoid compounds within the framework of a single concept. This is discussed in the following section.

7.16 Oxidation in the C₃-fragment of Flavonoid Compounds

The progression in the oxidation level of the C_3 portion of the flavonoid molecule from that of the flavanone to that of the flavonol* is summarized in Eq. 7-38:

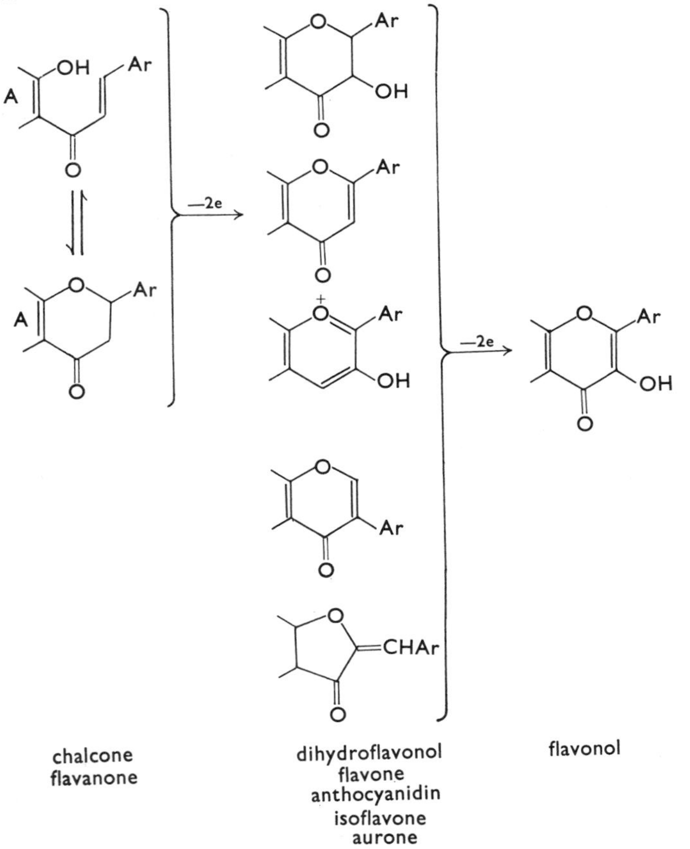

$$-2e \qquad -2e$$

chalcone
flavanone

dihydroflavonol
flavone
anthocyanidin
isoflavone
aurone

flavonol

[Eq. 7-38]

The conversion of chalcones into aurones has already been alluded to (Sec. 7.12). It will be noted that flavones, dihydroflavonols and isoflavones are at the same oxidation level; and it is also to be observed that it is possible to devise a means for generating flavones and isoflavones (Eq. 7-37) from dihydroflavonols, although it has been argued above that the reactions shown in Eq. 7-37 are mechanistically unattractive.

Biological oxidation processes of many kinds occur commonly in nature. The detailed mechanisms (in structural or in enzymatic terms) of many of them are not

* Reduction processes, which must be assumed to be responsible for conversion of the chalcone-flavanone stage to the catechin and flavan-3,4-diol stages, may be assumed to occur by the agency of the usual hydrogen-transfer systems of the cell, coupled in appropriate instances with loss of the elements of water.

known in detail, but it is possible and convenient to regard some of them as events which are initiated by an arbitrarily formulated oxidant described by the symbol OH^+.* The alternative device of extracting two electrons from the compound undergoing oxidation is an equally convenient (and mechanistically non-committal device). It will be recalled that the course proposed (Eq. 7-27) for the oxidation of a chalcone to an aurone is formulated in this way.

If the assumption be made that oxidative attack occurs on the enolic form of the flavanone, the formation of the dihydroflavonol, the flavone and the isoflavone can be formulated in a rational way. It should be noted that because these reactions are undoubtedly enzyme-mediated, alternative fates of a common intermediate can be ascribed to the enzyme specificity that reflects the genetic individuality of the organism. Thus, the fact that isoflavones are less widely encountered than flavones need not imply that their biosynthetic origins are unrelated. The proposed scheme of flavanone oxidation is shown in Eq. 7-39.

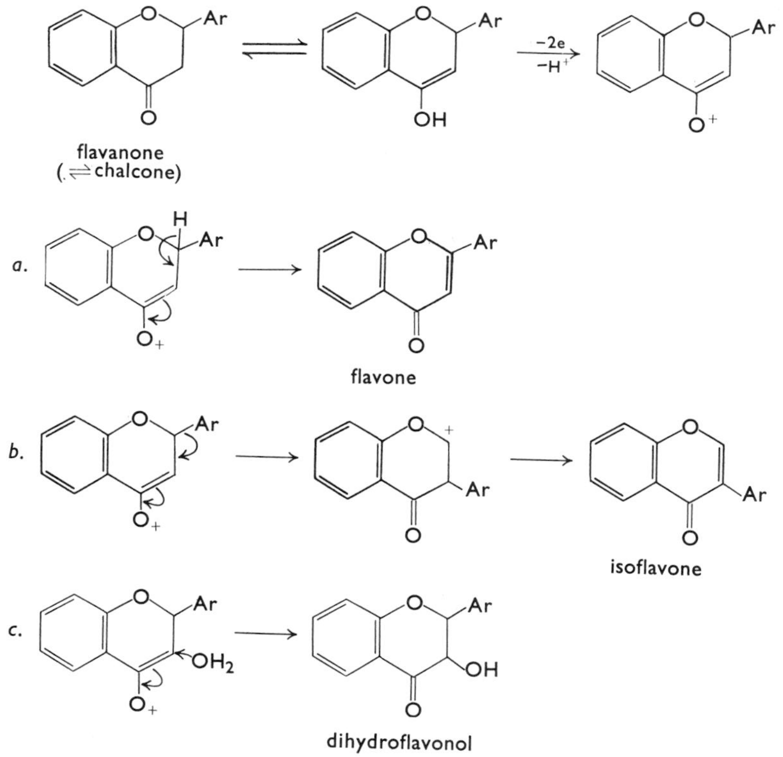

flavanone
($\rightleftharpoons$ chalcone)

a.

flavone

b.

isoflavone

c.

[Eq. 7-39]

dihydroflavonol

* It is to be emphasized again that this is at the present time an artificial device. It has the virtue of being consonant with the fact that in many oxidations in which oxygen is introduced, the oxygen atom is derived from molecular oxygen and not from water. It is to be noted that "OH^+" is the protonated oxygen atom.

It will be noted that the formation of the dihydroflavonol (Eq. 7-39c) would be expected to lead to the observed 2,3-*trans* relationship of the aryl and hydroxyl groups.

Further oxidation of the dihydroflavonol to the flavonol can be formulated in a manner corresponding to the course shown in this scheme. It is perhaps significant that in at least one case (*Antirrhinum majus*, snapdragon), flowers lacking anthocyanins contain flavones but no flavonols. Anthocyanin-pigmented flowers contain flavonols, and the flavonols and anthocyanins possess the same pattern of hydroxylation. It appears from this observation that the flavonols and anthocyanins are derived from a common precursor; and since anthocyanins and dihydroflavonols are at the same oxidation level, the latter may be the common precursor (Eq. 7-40).

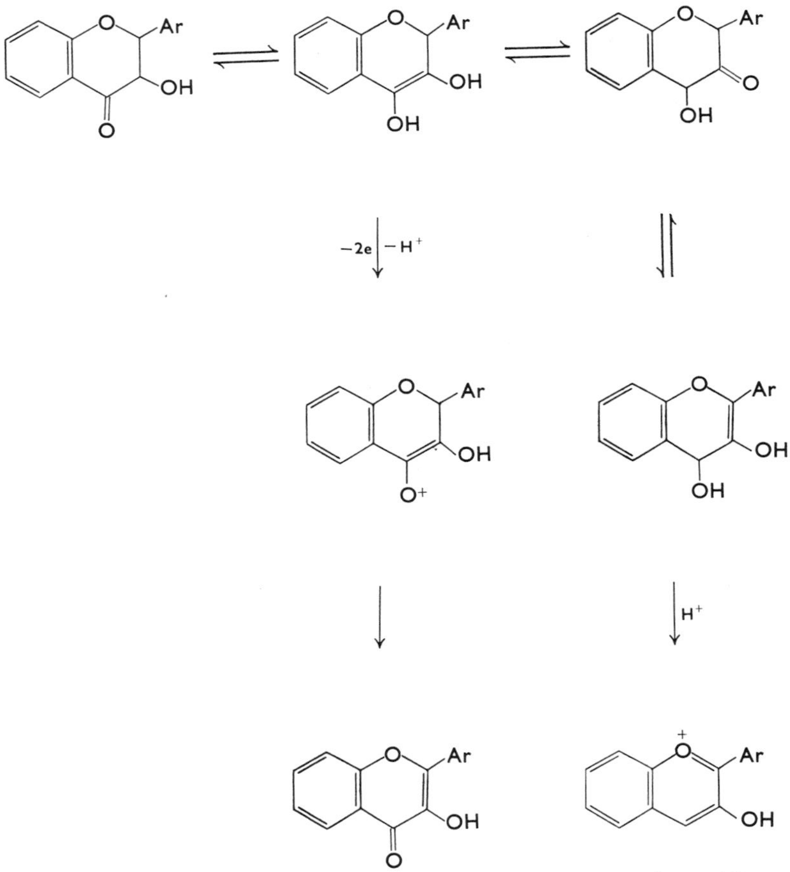

flavonol   anthocyanidin   [Eq. 7-40]

These conjectures have not yet been substantiated in detail by experimental study. Indeed, two recent investigations have led to results that lend some support for the view that isoflavone biosynthesis proceeds from the chalcone without the intermediacy of the (isomeric) flavanone. In one of these studies, a chalcone (2',4',4-trihydroxychalcone) and its isomeric flavanone were fed to clover seedlings in the following way: (a) ^{14}C-chalcone + inactive flavanone; and (b) ^{14}C-flavanone + inactive chalcone. The isoflavones isolated from feeding (a) had higher specific activities than those from feeding (b).

Model oxidation experiments with the use of thallic acetate have shown that chalcones can be converted into isoflavones by a reaction of which one plausible interpretation is that it proceeds by way of the —OTl(OAc)$_2$ derivative of an enol form of a derivative of the dihydrochalcone. It is clear that this course bears a strong mechanistic resemblance to that outlined in Eq. 7-39.

7.17 Coumestrol; 3-Arylcoumarins

The modified 3-arylcoumarin, coumestrol (Fig. 7-9), can be readily derived by further modification along the pathway proposed for isoflavone synthesis (Eq. 7-41):

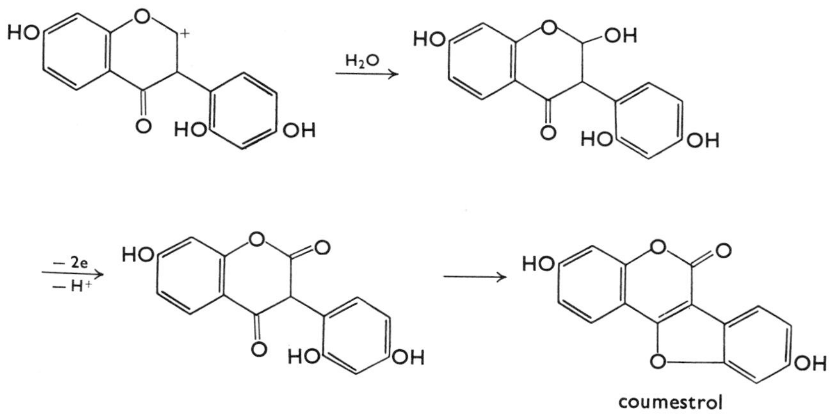

coumestrol

[Eq. 7-41]

It is interesting to find that coumestrol can be synthesized by the oxidation of a 3-methoxy-2',4',7-trihydroxyflavylium salt with alkaline hydrogen peroxide. A possible course for this reaction is shown in Eq. 7-42; and the significant feature of this transformation is that what is regarded as the B-ring of the flavylium salt is found as the A-ring of the resulting coumarin:

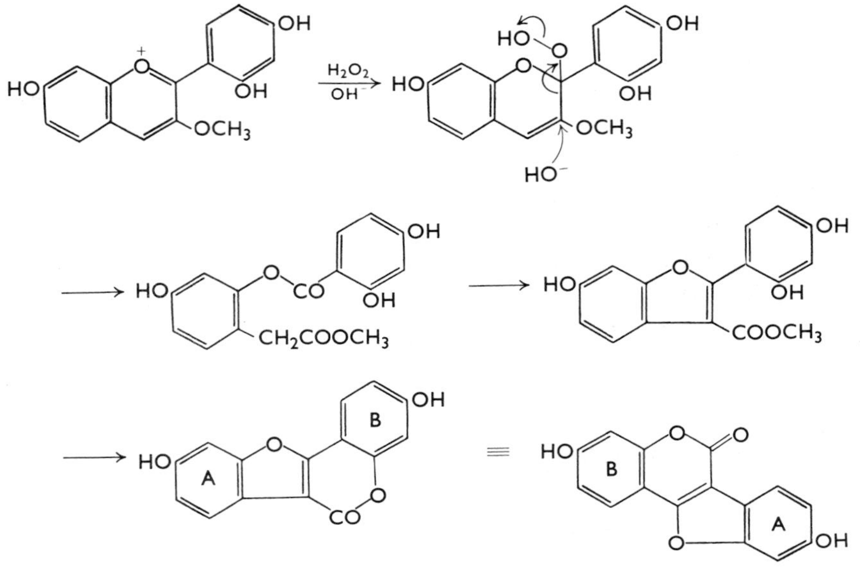

[Eq. 7-42]

The possibility that coumestrol is formed in the plant by a transformation like that shown in Eq. 7-42 was shown to be untenable when feeding experiments demonstrated that the biosynthesis of coumestrol follows the same pathway as that leading to isoflavones (Eq. 7-43):

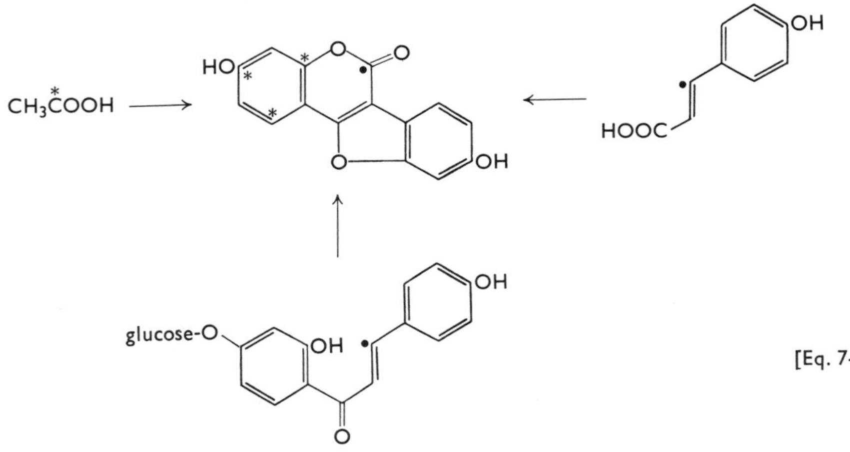

[Eq. 7-43]

Biosynthesis of coumestrol in *Medicago sativa* L. (alfalfa)

It is interesting and probably biosynthetically significant that 3-arylcoumarins of the coumestrol type and isoflavones are both typical constituents of plants of the Leguminosae, a fact which suggests that the migration of the aryl group leads to a precursor common to both classes of compounds.

7.18 Neoflavanoid Compounds

Besides the 2-arylchroman and 3-arylchroman derivatives (e.g., flavones and isoflavones), a group of 4-arylchroman derivatives (and some biosynthetically related compounds—see below) have recently been found to occur in nature, most of them in species of *Dalbergia* and *Machaerium* (fam. Leguminosae). Representative compounds of this group, the relationship between which will be considered in what follows, are shown in Fig. 7-10.

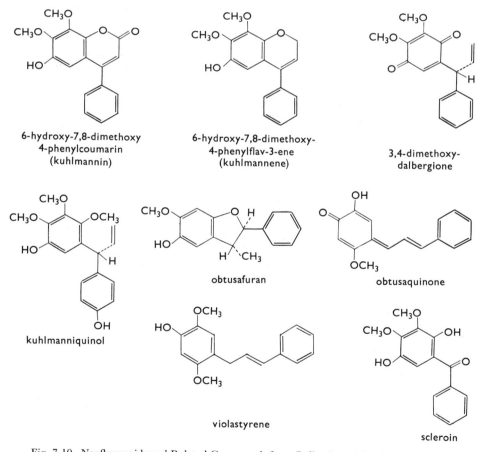

6-hydroxy-7,8-dimethoxy 4-phenylcoumarin (kuhlmannin)

6-hydroxy-7,8-dimethoxy- 4-phenylflav-3-ene (kuhlmannene)

3,4-dimethoxy- dalbergione

kuhlmanniquinol

obtusafuran

obtusaquinone

violastyrene

scleroin

Fig. 7-10. Neoflavanoids and Related Compounds from *Dalbergia* and *Machaerium* Species.

The occurrence in the family Leguminosae of flavones, isoflavones and 3-aryl-coumarins, and the 4-arylchroman derivatives such as those in Fig. 7-10 might lead to facile conclusions regarding the biosynthetic origins of the latter group. For example, since isoflavones are known to arise by a $2 \rightarrow 3$ aryl migration in a C_6—C_3—C_6 precursor, it is tempting to assume that a second aryl migration $(3 \rightarrow 4)$ occurs to lead to the 4-arylchroman group of compounds. But the discovery of cinnamylphenols (e.g. violastyrene), the related dehydro compounds

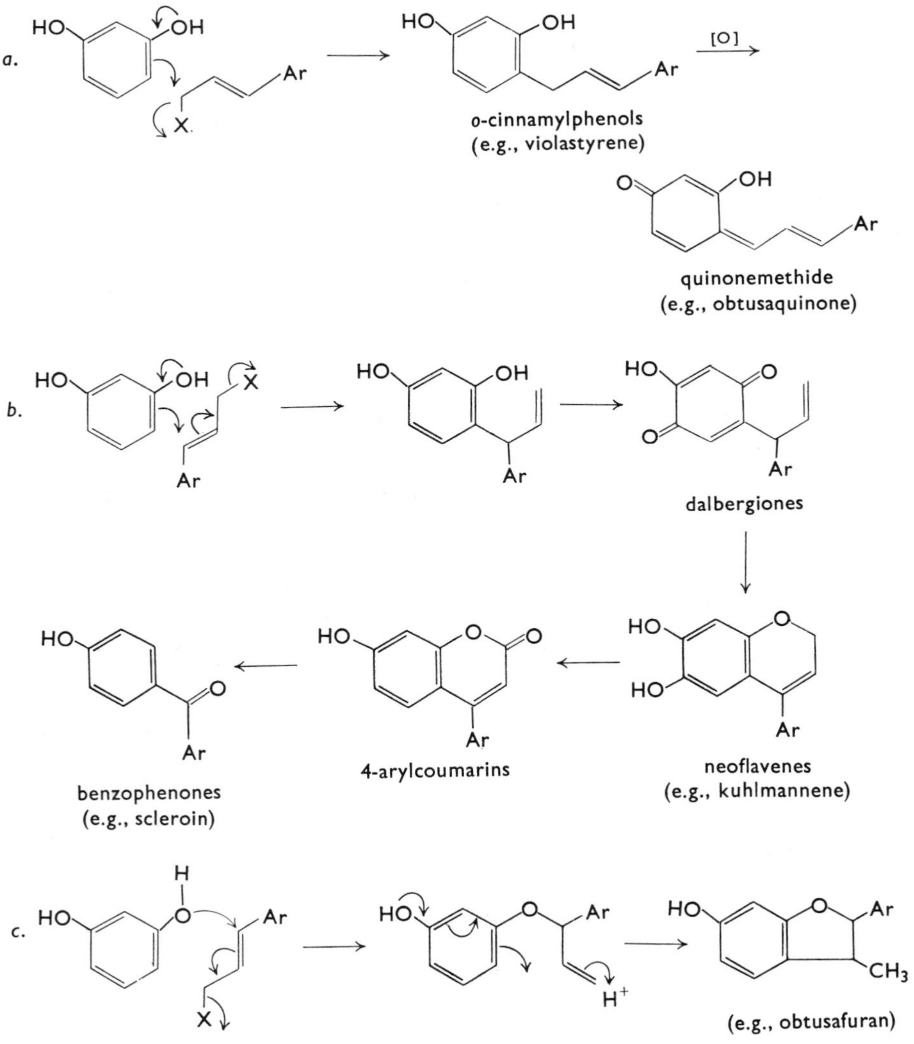

Fig. 7-11. Suggested Biosynthetic Routes to Compounds of *Dalbergia* and *Machaerium* Species.

(e.g., obtusaquinone), and the benzofuran obtusafuran in plants of the same genus (*Dalbergia*) in which the 4-arylchroman derivatives occur suggests another and more persuasive possibility.

Although the biosynthetic origins of the *Dalbergia* constituents have not been established by the appropriate feeding experiments with labeled precursors, the generalized scheme shown in Fig. 7-11 has been proposed to account for the formation of these compounds. In this scheme, the two reacting components are (a)

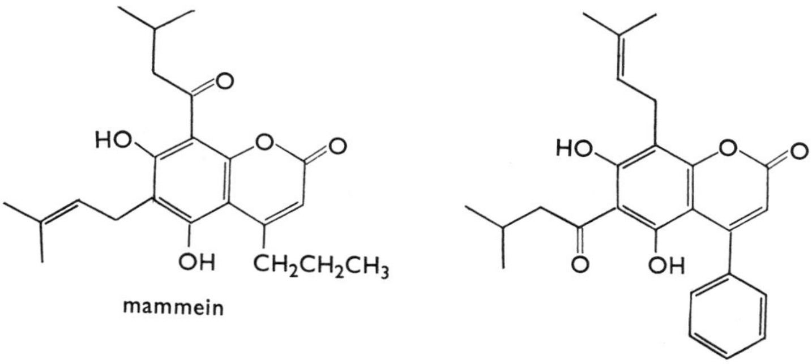

Fig. 7-12. 4-Substituted Coumarins of *Mammea* Species.

a phenol, presumably acetate- (i.e., polyketide-) derived; and (b) a cinnamyl unit in which the displaceable group X shown in the figure may be regarded as a phosphorylated hydroxyl group. In the reactions shown in Fig. 7-11, only the groups directly relevant to the principal reactions (e.g., only the necessary hydroxyl groups of the phenolic unit) are shown, although the natural substrate is undoubtedly a polyhydroxylated phenol.

It will be seen that this scheme accounts in a very satisfactory way for the formation of this group of compounds. The central concept in all of the pathways shown is the mechanistically acceptable nucleophilic attack (by oxygen or carbon of the phenol) upon the cinnamyl pyrophosphate. It will be recalled that the suggestion made earlier (Eq. 5-11) for the formation of the natural allyl- and propenyl-phenols involves the mechanistically related reaction: nucleophilic attack by NADH (or other enzymatic H:$^-$ donor) upon a cinnamyl pyrophosphate.

Experiments to establish the validity of these conjectures are still to be performed. Despite the overall consistency and persuasive character of this proposal, certain observations that have been made suggest that there are alternative routes for the synthesis of one or another of the compounds in question that cannot be overlooked. For example, the compounds mammein and the related 4-phenyl-coumarin derivative (Fig. 7-12) occur together in the plant *Mammea americana* L. (fam. Guttiferae). The biosynthesis of mammein is quite readily accounted for by the condensation of a phenol with what is obviously the acetate-derived 3-keto-hexanoic acid. Is the 4-phenylcoumarin formed by way of a similar condensation involving benzoylacetic acid, or is it formed by a route similar to that shown in Fig. 7-11? Neither the striking fact of co-occurrence nor the weight of a satisfactory conjecture is sufficient to resolve this question.

7.19 Summary

Although the biosynthesis of some classes of flavonoid compounds has not been proved by direct experiment, sufficient information has been accumulated to support the view that the synthetic pathway of all of the C_6—C_3—C_6 compounds of this class proceeds by a common course up to the formation of a chalcone. The subsequent stages, leading to the various kinds of flavonoid compounds, involve alteration of the oxidation level of the C_3 portion of the molecule, often in ways that appear to be directed by genetically controlled enzymatic processes that possess chemotaxonomic and phylogenetic significance. Chemical-genetic studies have shown that hydroxylation patterns, oxidation levels, and positions of O-methylation and glycosylation are under specific genetic control, often subject to variation in easily recognized mendelian ratios. These discoveries are not, of course, a cause for surprise, for the relationship between genes and enzymes is now a generally recognized tenet in biology.

Other features of flavonoid molecules that have not been discussed in this chapter, because they reflect more general processes that are not unique to compounds of the flavonoid class, are the hydroxylation of aromatic rings, C- and O-alkylation, and glycosylation, the oxidative coupling of flavones to biflavonyls, the formation of methylenedioxy groupings, and the inclusion of substituents derived by other (e.g., mevalonic acid) pathways. Some of these have been discussed in earlier sections and others will be considered in later chapters.

VIII CHAPTER

REFERENCES FOR FURTHER READING

1. L. Ruzicka, *History of the Isoprene Rule*, Proc. Chem. Soc., (1959), 341.
2. F. Lynen and U. Henning, *The Biological Route to Natural Rubber*, Angew. Chem. (Intl. Edn.) May, (1961), p. 9.
3. J. W. Cornforth, *Terpenoid Biosynthesis*, Chemistry in Britain, 4, (1968), 102.
4. D. Arigoni, *Steric Aspects of the Biosynthesis of Terpenes and Steroids*, Biochemical Society Symposia, No. 19, p. 32; Cambridge Univ. Press, 1960.
5. F. W. Hefendehl, E. W. Underhill, and E. von Rudloff, *The Biosynthesis of the Oxygenated Monoterpenes in Mint*, Phytochemistry, 6, (1967), 823.
6. H.-G. Floss and U. Mothes, *On the Biosynthesis of Furocoumarins in Pimpinella magna*, Phytochemistry, 5, (1966), 161.
7. G. E. Risinger and H. D. Durst, *On the Mechanism of the Reductive Dimerization of Farnesyl Pyrophosphate*, Tetrahedron Letters, (1968), 3133.
8. J. H. Richards and J. B. Hendrickson, *The Biosynthesis of Steroids, Terpenes and Aceto-genins*, W. A. Benjamin, Inc., New York, 1964.
9. K. Sisido, T. Kageyama, H. Mera and K. Utimoto, *Synthesis of Boshnia-Lactone and Stereoisomers*, Tetrahedron Letters, (1967), 1553.
10. G. Büchi and R. E. Manning, *The Structure of Verbenalin*, Tetrahedron, 18, (1962), 1049.
11. D. A. Whiting, *Iridoids*, in Chemistry of Carbon Compounds, 2nd Ed., S. Coffey, ed., Vol. II B, pp. 208-214; Elsevier, New York, 1968.
12. D. V. Banthorpe and D. Baxendale, *The Biosynthesis of (—)- and (+)-Camphor*, Chem. Comm., (1968), 1553.
13. R. B. Clayton, *Biosynthesis of Sterols, Steroids and Terpenoids*, Quart. Rev. (Chem. Soc.) 19, (1965), Pt. 1, p. 168, Pt. 2, p. 201.

Terpenoid Compounds

8.1 Introduction

The largest and structurally the most various class of naturally occurring organic products of secondary plant metabolism includes the terpenes and the allied sesqui-, di-, tri-, and poly-terpenoid compounds. The terpenes, and in particular the lower, volatile members of the class, have been known from antiquity, having been isolated from plants and used for a variety of human purposes (although seldom as pure compounds) since pre-Christian times. Their volatility, which made them easily discoverable in fragrant plant materials and at the same time readily obtainable by simple distillation of leaves, wood, and blossoms, lent to them the term "essential" oils. A large number of plant "essences" are known and used for such purposes as the flavoring of foods, perfumery, medicinals, and adjuvants of various kinds. Although many essential oils are terpenoid compounds, the term is not uniquely definitive of this class, for such other essences as oil of wintergreen and other non-terpenoid foliage and flower perfumes are also volatile and odorous.

The terpenes hold a special place in organic chemistry. Their ready accessibility, their abundance, the ease with which they can be isolated, their relatively simple gross composition, and the remarkable and fascinating transformations that they were found to undergo made them favorite objects for study by organic chemists during the later 1800's and the early years of the present century. During this period the chemistry of terpenoid compounds claimed the attention of many chemists, whose familiar names are found throughout any account of organic chemistry: Wallach, Perkin, Tiemann, Baeyer, Bredt, Meerwein, Treibs, and many others; and in more recent years, Ruzicka, Barton, Jones, and numerous of their contemporaries. The early studies led by the early 1900's to the establishment

233

of the gross structures of most of the common terpenes, and later investigations, continuing to the present time, have added many of the details of the stereo-chemistry, reactions, rearrangements and biosynthesis of these interesting compounds. Terpenoid chemistry, with which may be included the chemistry of steroids and carotenoids, now represents a major division of the field of organic chemistry and of natural products.

Most terpenoid compounds occur free in plant tissues, uncombined with other substances; but many of them are found as glycosides, esters of organic acids, and in some cases in combination with proteins. The lower members of the class (C_{10} and C_{15} compounds) can often be obtained from the fresh or dried plant by steam distillation, while higher members (C_{20} and above) are usually isolated by extraction with solvents and separated and purified by crystallization, distillation, and chromatography.

8.2   The Isoprene Rule

Terpenoid compounds are related by a common origin and a common structural relationship. As their compositions (C_{10}, C_{15}, C_{20}, C_{30}, etc.) suggest, they are composed of multiples of a five-carbon-atom unit, and as the discussion of their structures will show, this unit has the isopentyl carbon skeleton. Because in the early years of the study of terpenes the hydrocarbon isoprene was encountered as a product of pyrolytic decomposition of many of them, the terpenes were regarded as being composed of "isoprene units." For this reason, terpenoid compounds are often referred to as "isoprenoid" compounds. Although many terpenes possess structures that can be dissected formally into five-carbon units with the isoprene skeleton, it is now known that terpenoid compounds are not derived from isoprene itself,

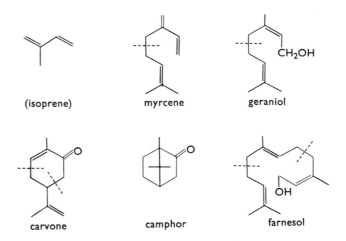

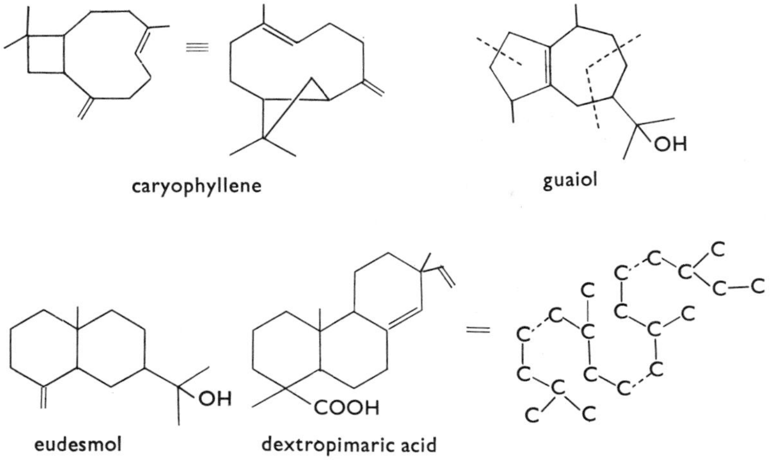

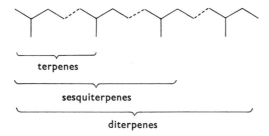

caryophyllene   guaiol

eudesmol   dextropimaric acid

Fig. 8-1. Some Typical Isoprenoid Compounds.

nor is isoprene a naturally occurring compound. In Fig. 8-1 are shown some terpenoid compounds that "follow" the isoprene rule; that is, their structures can be regarded as being composed of two, three or four isoprene units combined head-to-tail (Fig. 8-2):

terpenes

sesquiterpenes

diterpenes

Fig. 8-2. The "Regular" Isoprene Rule.

The isoprene rule is a summary of structural relationships, and when it was first introduced was exemplified by compounds, most of which were "regular." As time went on, more and more terpenoid compounds were discovered whose structures departed from, or "violated," the rule. It was soon recognized that the "irregular" structures could be brought into conformance with the fundamental hypothesis by postulating a rearrangement of the regular head-to-tail isoprenoid skeleton, usually following or concomitant with cyclization, or by the partial degradation of the molecule with the loss of one or more carbon atoms of the original, regular array.

The modern expression of these relationships is called the *biogenetic isoprene rule*, and takes into account the fact that the compound that is finally formed in the plant, while having its origin in a regular isoprenoid precursor, may have undergone later alteration in structure during its elaboration into the end product that is finally isolated. In view of what is now known about the course of terpenoid biosynthesis it is usually more meaningful to view the process of structural elaboration in terms of the actual processes of secondary plant metabolism than to invoke a formal rule. Nevertheless, the terms "isoprenoid" and "isoprene rule" are convenient summaries of structural information and are widely used.

8.3 Classification of Terpenoid Compounds

The principal classes of naturally occurring terpenoid compounds are the following:

hemiterpenes	C_5
terpenes	C_{10}
sesquiterpenes	C_{15}
diterpenes	C_{20}
triterpenes	C_{30}
tetraterpenes	C_{40}
polyterpenes	$(C_5)_n$

Several important classes of compounds, including steroids (which are ordinarily treated as a special class of compounds), are derived from the triterpenes by degradation of the original C_{30} molecule to compounds with as few as twenty carbon atoms, a circumstance that indicates that caution must be observed in assessing the biogenetic origin of a compound from its gross composition and other suggestive structural features. At least one class of triterpene-derived C_{20} compounds, to be discussed in the sequel (Chap. 12), can be accommodated to a diterpenoid origin but are in fact known to be derived from a C_{30} precursor.

8.4 Hemiterpenes

From a biogenetic standpoint the simplest members of the terpenoid compounds are those that contain only the five carbon atoms of the basic isoprene unit. Compounds of this class are only rarely encountered in nature as stable, isolable metabolic end products; but that they exist in living cells as highly reactive substances is well established. Indeed, two hemiterpenoid compounds are ubiquitous in living organisms and, as will be seen in what follows, represent the fundamental isoprene unit in terpenoid biosynthesis. These compounds are the alcohols, γ-γ-dimethylallyl alcohol and 3-methyl-3-buten-1-ol (Fig. 8-3). These alcohols are not known as discrete (i.e., isolable) plant constituents; they occur in nature as their

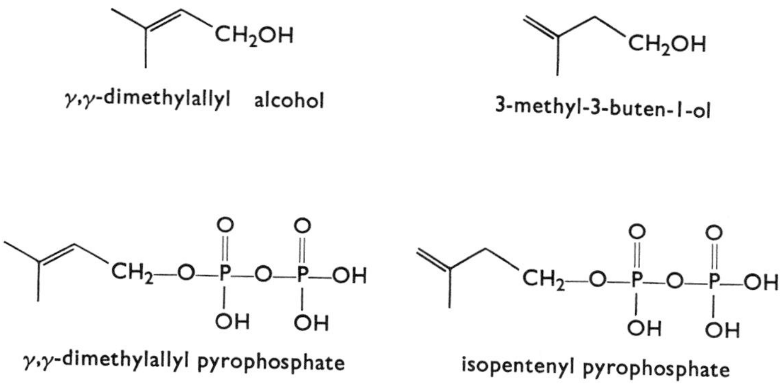

γ,γ-dimethylallyl alcohol

3-methyl-3-buten-1-ol

γ,γ-dimethylallyl pyrophosphate

isopentenyl pyrophosphate

Fig. 8-3. The Fundamental Hemiterpenes.

pyrophosphate esters, the presence of which in metabolizing tissue and in cell extracts has been well established. Although the most extensive studies of these compounds have been carried out in systems other than those derived from green plants, principally because of their role in steroid biosynthesis, it is nevertheless certain that they are ubiquitous participants in secondary metabolism of nearly all living cells.

Evidence for the occurrence of these hemiterpenoid compounds in higher plants is found in two observations: (1) the universal occurrence in plants of compounds for which the five-carbon pyrophosphates are precursors; and (2) the appearance of the dimethylallyl group (and simple derived forms of it) as a part of the structure of many natural products. The γ,γ-dimethylallyl, or prenyl,* unit is found in compounds of a wide variety of types, most of them phenols, as a C- or O-linked substituent. This alkylation process has been described earlier (Fig. 2-56) and needs no additional comment.

* The term "prenyl" for the $(CH_3)_2C{=}CHCH_2{-}$ group is a convenient one, and will be used here. The companion acyl grouping, $(CH_3)_2C{=}CHCO{-}$, is referred to as "senecioyl."

A number of examples of C- and O-prenylated compounds are shown in Fig. 8-4:

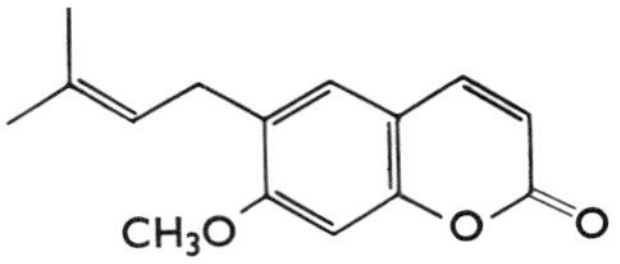

suberosin

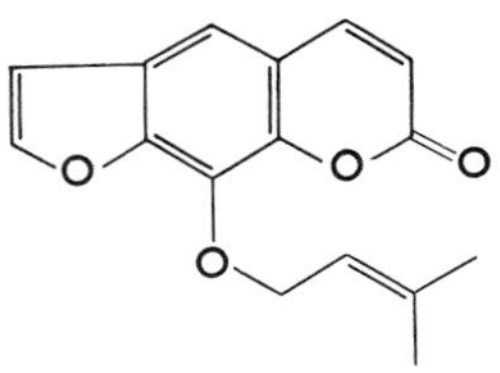

imperatorin

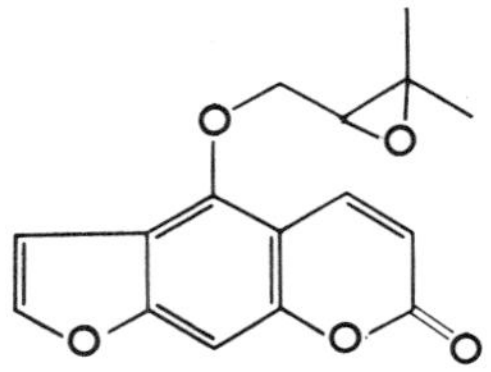

oxypeucedanin

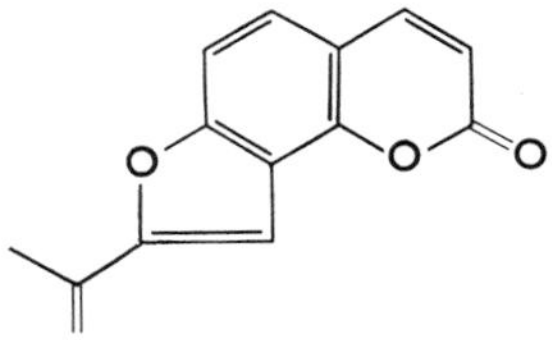

oroselone

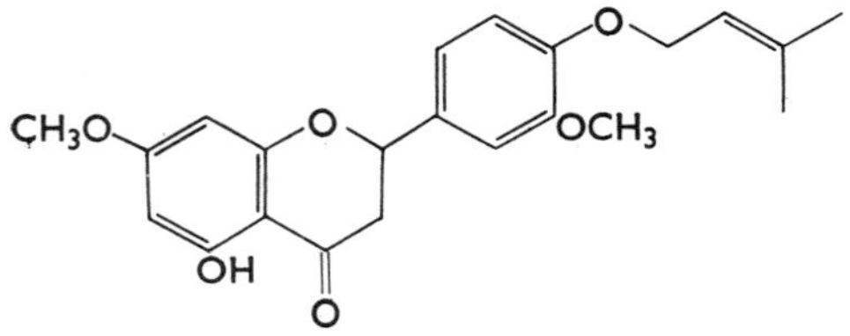

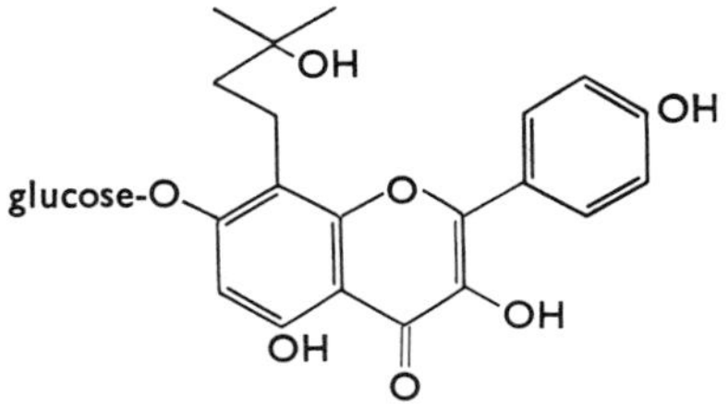

amurensin

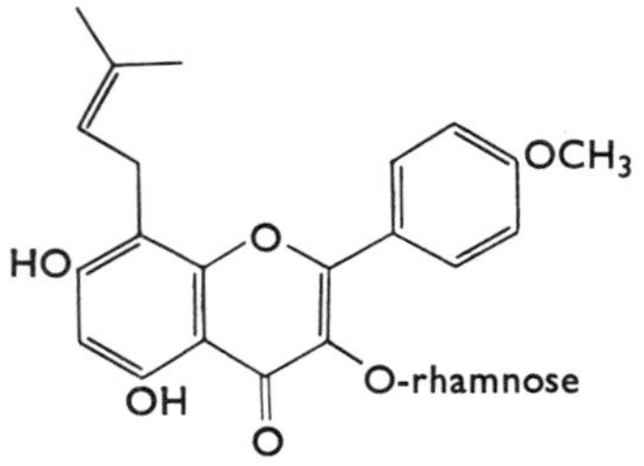

icariside-II

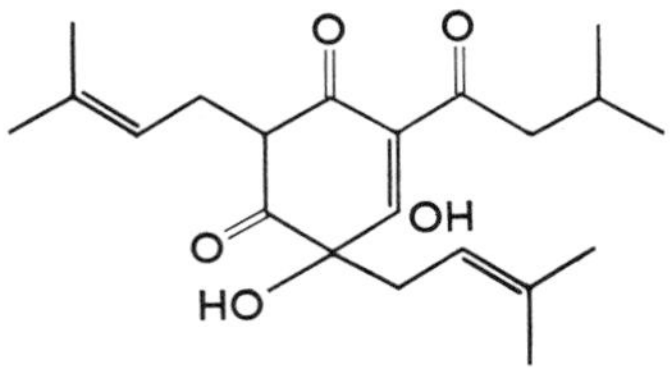

humulone

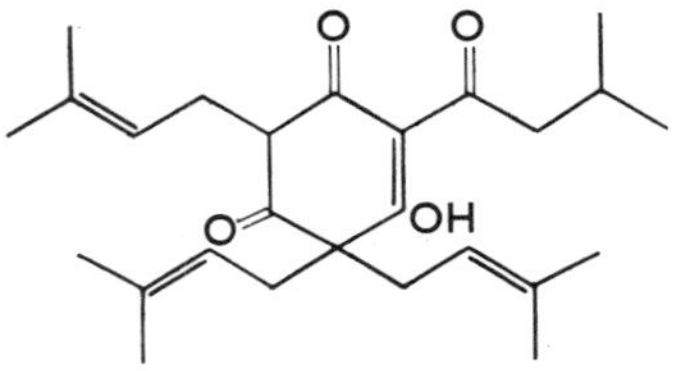

lupulone

Fig. 8-4. Natural Compounds with Prenyl and Modified Prenyl Substituents.

It is apparent from the structures of the compounds shown in Fig. 8-4 that the $(CH_3)_2C{=}CHCH_2{-}$ fragment is available as an electrophilic agent which can be transferred to oxygen or carbon by nucleophilic attack. The pyrophosphate esters (Fig. 8-3) clearly fulfil the requirements for a reaction of this kind.

It is also to be noted that there occur in nature a number of five-carbon compounds (both free and combined, for example in ester linkage) whose structures are isoprenoid in respect to their carbon skeletons. Some of these are the compounds shown in Fig. 8-5:

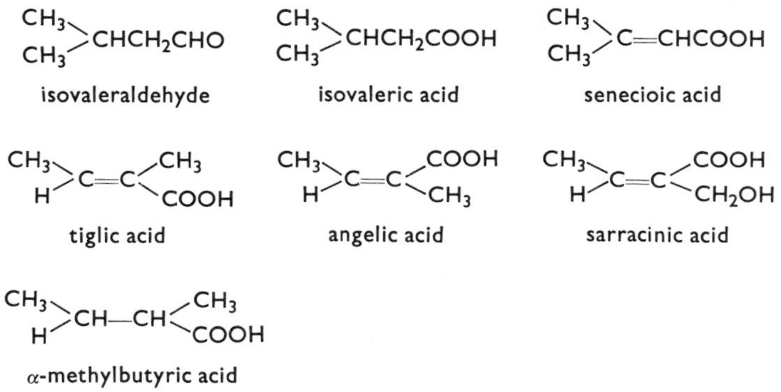

Fig. 8-5. Five-carbon Compounds of Natural Occurrence.

All of these compounds possess isoprenoid carbon skeletons, but it is to be noted that there is a sharp difference in the oxygenation pattern of isovaleric acid and senecioic acid on the one hand, and tiglic, angelic, and sarracinic acids on the other. The former compounds are simply and directly derivable from the prenyl group without alteration in the terminal $(CH_3)_2C{-}$ group. Tiglic acid and its analogues, however, possess a carboxyl group in a position that corresponds to one of the methyl groups of the prenyl group. It is now known that tiglic and angelic acids are not isoprenoid in origin, but are derived from the amino acid isoleucine by a process described briefly as follows (Eq. 8-1):

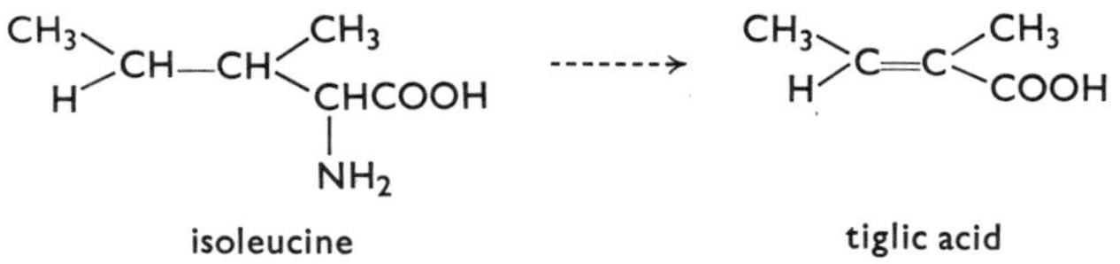

[Eq. 8-1]

These structurally isoprenoid but biogenetically non-isoprenoid compounds will be discussed in greater detail in Chapter 13.

8.5   Biosynthetic Origin of the Isoprenoid Structure

The discovery of the role of mevalonic acid (3-methyl-3,5-dihydroxypentanoic acid) in the biosynthesis of steroidal compounds opened the way to the researches that at length elucidated the pathways leading to the synthesis of terpenoid compounds of all kinds. Mevalonic acid, a six-carbon-atom compound derived by the condensation of three molecules of acetic acid, is the essential and universal progenitor of terpenoid compounds, giving rise to the "isoprene unit" by simultaneous loss of water and carbon dioxide.

The condensation of two molecules of acetyl coenzyme A to yield acetoacetyl coenzyme A is a step that appears to be identical with the first stage in the pathway leading to acetate-derived poly-β-keto compounds and to the products of cyclization of the polyketide chain, or, with intermediate reduction-dehydration-reduction steps, to fatty acids. Terpenoid metabolism, however, departs from this pathway at an early stage, and, by an aldol-like condensation of acetyl CoA with the acetoacetic acid derivative, leads to β-hydroxy-β-methylglutaryl CoA. Reduction of this gives mevalonic acid (Eq. 8-2):

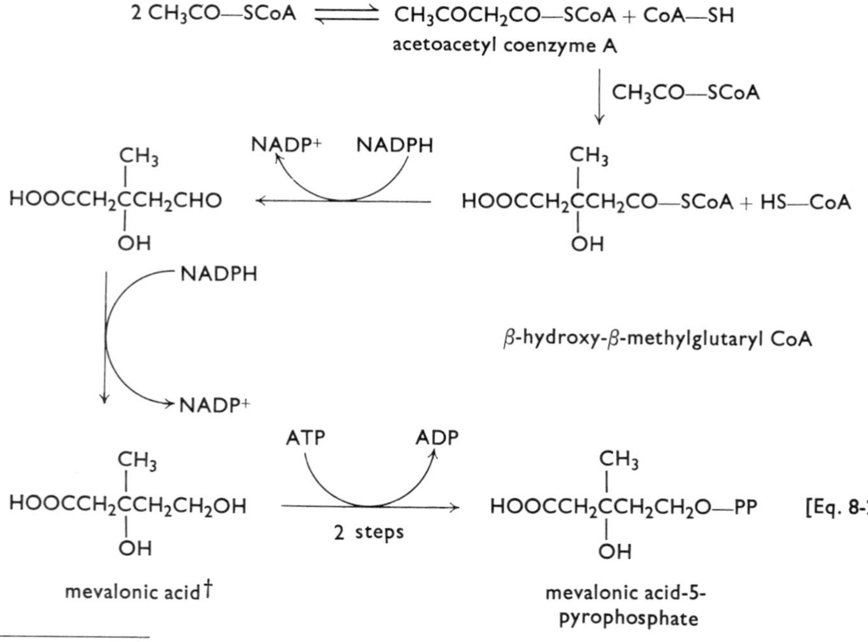

$$2 \text{ CH}_3\text{CO—SCoA} \rightleftharpoons \text{CH}_3\text{COCH}_2\text{CO—SCoA} + \text{CoA—SH}$$

acetoacetyl coenzyme A

$$\downarrow \text{CH}_3\text{CO—SCoA}$$

β-hydroxy-β-methylglutaryl CoA

[Eq. 8-2]

mevalonic acid†   mevalonic acid-5-
                                                   pyrophosphate

---

† The absolute configuration of mevalonic acid is the following:

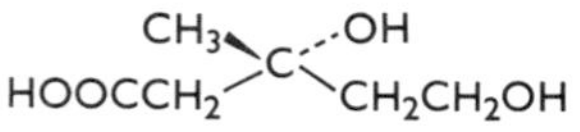

(R)-mevalonic acid

Phosphorylation of mevalonic acid (by ATP) gives, by way of the 5-phosphate, mevalonic acid-5-pyrophosphate (Eq. 8-2). This is the immediate precursor of the five-carbon ("isoprene") units shown in Fig. 8-3. It is probable that the loss of the hydroxyl group in the concerted decarboxylation-dehydration shown in Eq. 8-3 is aided by a phosphorylation of the tertiary hydroxyl group:

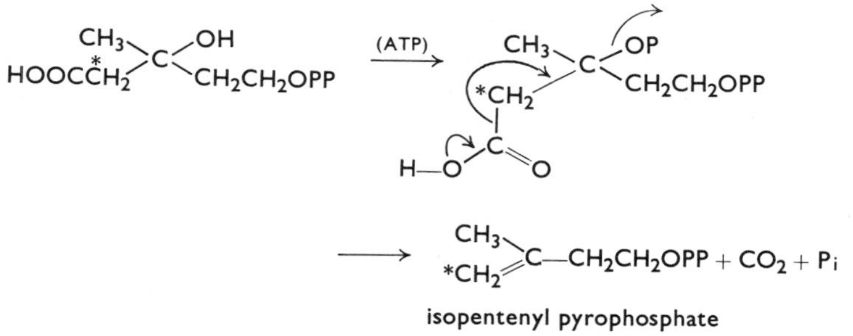

$$isopentenyl \ pyrophosphate$$

Isopentenyl pyrophosphate is the biogenetic isoprene unit. Its participation in isoprenoid biosynthesis (and its conversion into the active prenylating agent) is dependent upon an enzyme-catalyzed prototropy, by which it is converted into an equilibrium mixture of the isopentenyl and the dimethylallyl esters (Eq. 8-4):

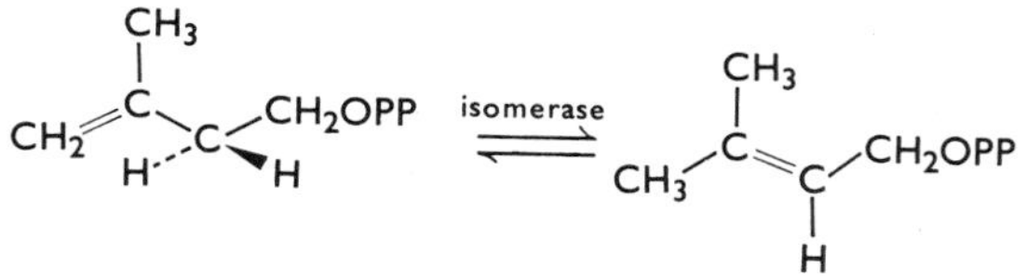

[Eq. 8-4]

The prototropy of Eq. 8-4 is stereospecific: the methyl group derived from the $=CH_2$ group of the isopentenyl ester appears *trans* to the $-CH_2CH_2OPP$ grouping. This stereospecificity permits a distinction between the methyl groups of dimethylallyl pyrophosphate when this is derived from a specifically labeled precursor. For example, if $2\text{-}^{14}C$-mevalonic acid (C-2 is marked in Eq. 8-3) is used in a feeding experiment, the $=CH_2$, and thus one of the $-CH_3$ groups of the allyl pyrophosphate, will be labeled. Consequently, if the final product of the plant metabolism contains a *gem*-dimethyl group, only one of the seemingly equivalent methyl groups will bear the isotopic label (Eq. 8-5):

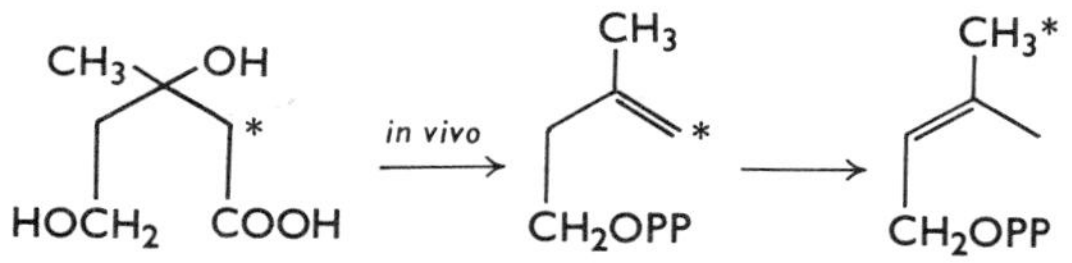

[Eq. 8-5]

8.6 Dimethylallyl Pyrophosphate as an Alkylating Agent

Dimethylallyl pyrophosphate is ideally constituted to serve as an electrophilic agent for the transfer of the dimethylallyl unit to a nucleophilic center. Not only does it possess the highly reactive allylic system, but the pyrophosphate group is an excellent leaving (displaceable) group in the nucleophilic displacement reaction.

Whether the transfer of the dimethylallyl group to a nucleophilic center is S_N1 in type (i.e., proceeds through a discrete $(CH_3)_2C=CHCH_2^+$ ion), or is S_N2 in type cannot be stated with certainty. Even were evidence to be adduced concerning the preference for one of these courses over the other in conventional solvent media, the fact that the biological alkylation reaction occurs under the influence (and therefore at the surface) of an enzyme would render the usual arguments regarding the details of mechanism rather meaningless. We shall take the arbitrary view (in formulating reactions) that the reaction is S_N2 in type, and show the displacement as a one-step process, partly because of convenience in exposition but partly because this is as likely a course as another. An alternative route, common to many enzyme reactions, that a double displacement occurs, with a $(CH_3)_2C=CHCH_2$-enzyme intermediate, can also be regarded as a possible course. These various mechanisms, all of which lead to the same result, are shown in Eq. 8-6:

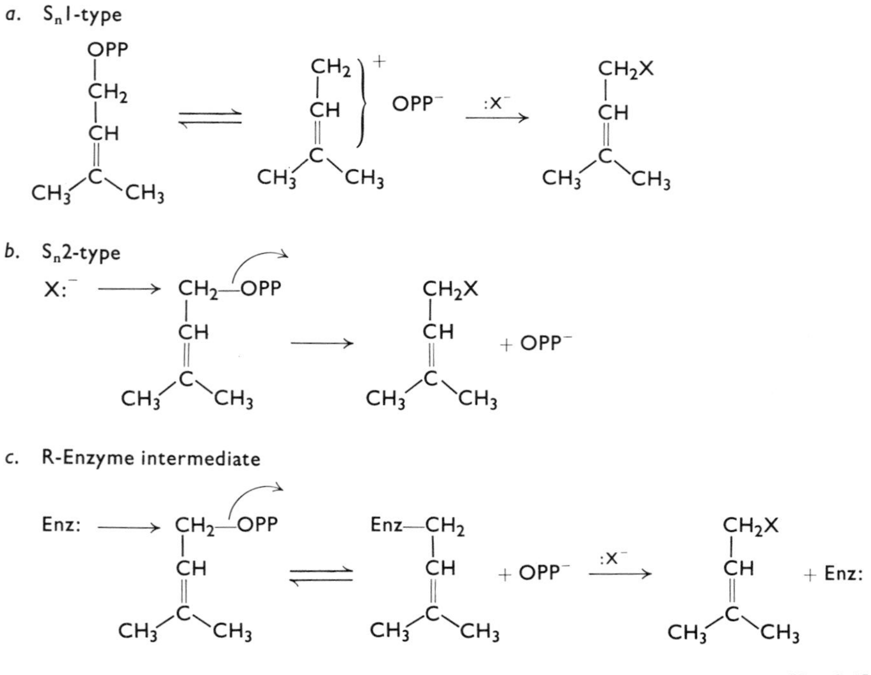

a. S_n1-type

b. S_n2-type

c. R-Enzyme intermediate

[Eq. 8-6]

The prenylation of phenolic oxygen atoms or phenolic nuclei follows a conventional course. Whether the prenylation of acetate-derived phenolic nuclei occurs at the polyketide stage or after cyclization-aromatization is not known with certainty. There is, however, no mechanistic objection to C-alkylation of phenols, for this is a well known process. Indeed, the existence of C-prenylated coumarins (such as suberosin, Fig. 8-4) argues for prenylation of the fully constituted phenol, for simple coumarins of the type exemplified by suberosin are C_6—C_3 compounds, derived by the shikimic-phenylalanine (or tyrosine) pathway, and thus do not stem from a polyketide precursor. It must be recognized, however, that although suberosin is probably formed by C-prenylation of the phenol, this is not necessarily evidence that C-prenylated flavonoid compounds, in which the prenylated aromatic ring derives from an acetate-derived polyketide, are formed in the same way. The nucleophilic character of the (deprotonated) methylene group of —COCH$_2$CO— is well known, and it is clearly possible for C-alkylation to occur at this point in the biosynthetic process.

The alkylating ability of dimethylallyl pyrophosphate is responsible for the key reaction in terpenoid biosynthesis. In this case the nucleophile is the terminal double bond of the isopentenyl pyrophosphate, the overall reaction resulting in the union of two C_5 residues with the formation of a carbon-carbon bond (Eq. 8-7):

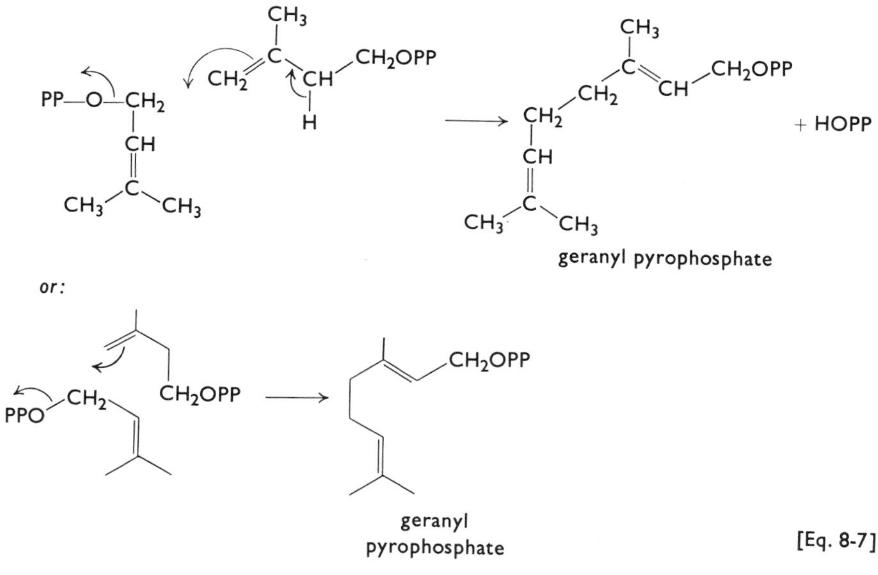

[Eq. 8-7]

The product of the step shown in Eq. 8-7 is geranyl pyrophosphate, the ester of one of the commonest of naturally occurring terpenoid compounds, geraniol (and its geometric isomer, nerol).

Geranyl pyrophosphate is also an alkylating agent; it possesses the same reactive allyl pyrophosphate structure as the five-carbon precursor, and can act as a
reagent capable of transferring the geranyl group to a nucleophile. Numerous O-
and C-geranyl compounds are known as natural products; some examples are given
in Fig. 8-6.

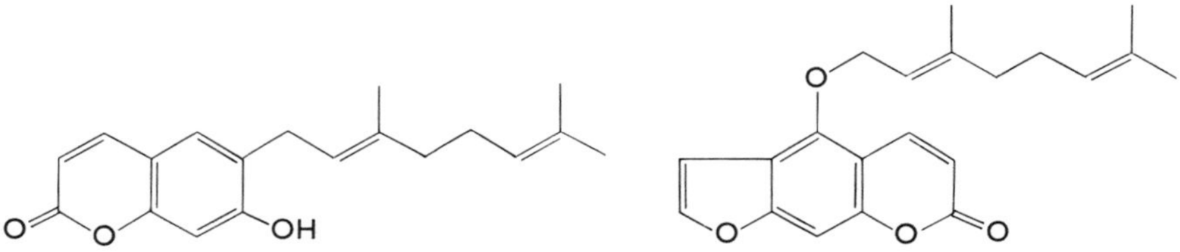

ostruthin   bergamottin

Fig. 8-6. Natural O- and C-geranyl Derivatives.

Extension of the geranyl unit by addition of an isopentenyl unit, in the manner
illustrated in Eq. 8-7, gives rise to the C_{15} compound, farnesyl pyrophosphate; and
continuation of the process yields the C_{20} compound, geranylgeranyl pyrophosphate, the progenitor of the diterpenes (Eq. 8-8):

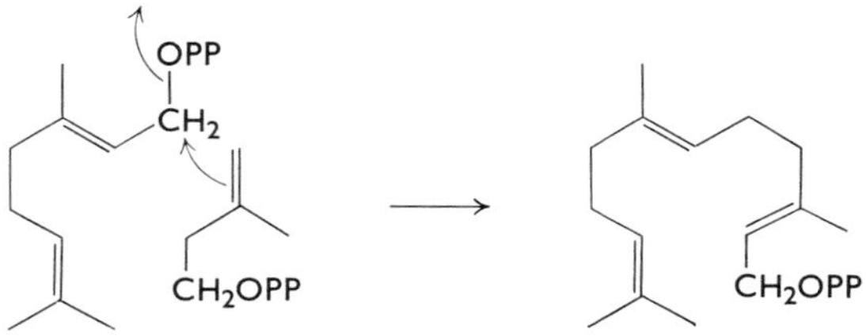

geranyl pyrophosphate   farnesyl pyrophosphate
+ isopentenyl pyrophosphate

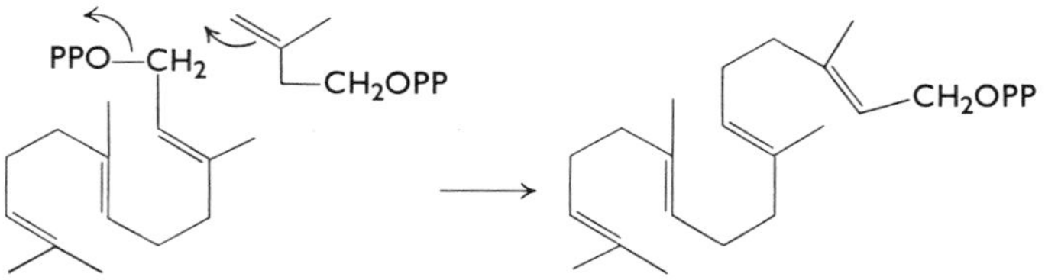

farnesyl pyrophosphate   geranylgeranyl
+ isopentenyl pyrophosphate   pyrophosphate   [Eq. 8-8]

It is clear that the processes shown in Eqs. 8-7 and 8-8 can continue, for each product retains the allyl pyrophosphate terminal unit. Moreover, the intermediate
esters are potential alkylating agents. In Fig. 8-7 are shown some natural compounds that possess these polyprenyl groups as substituents.

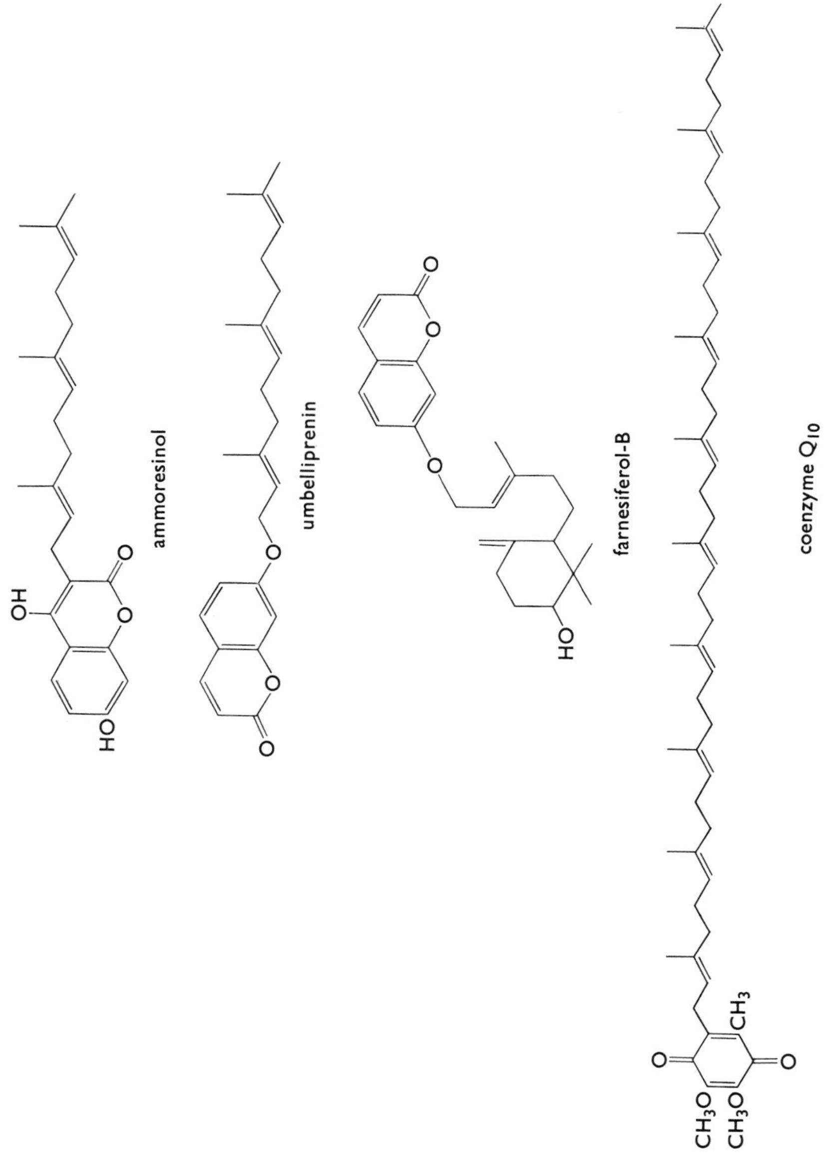

Fig. 8-7. Natural Compounds with Polyprenyl Substituents.

The further elaboration of the C_{10}, C_{15}, C_{20}, and so on, products of these initial C_5—C_5—C_5---- condensations into the terpenes of natural occurrence will be described in sections to follow.

8.7   Monoterpenes

The biosynthetic pathway to the terpenes that proceeds from mevalonic acid in the manner just described has received ample support from studies with iso-topically labeled compounds. The use of labeled acetic acid and mevalonic acid, fed to fungi and higher plants,* has yielded findings that establish this route of bio-synthesis for terpenes and the derived steroids.

An early study of terpene biosynthesis in *Eucalyptus citriodora* Hook. (fam. Myrtaceae) showed that acetate was incorporated into citronellal in a manner that was in accord with the operation of the acetate-mevalonate pathway (Eq. 8-9):

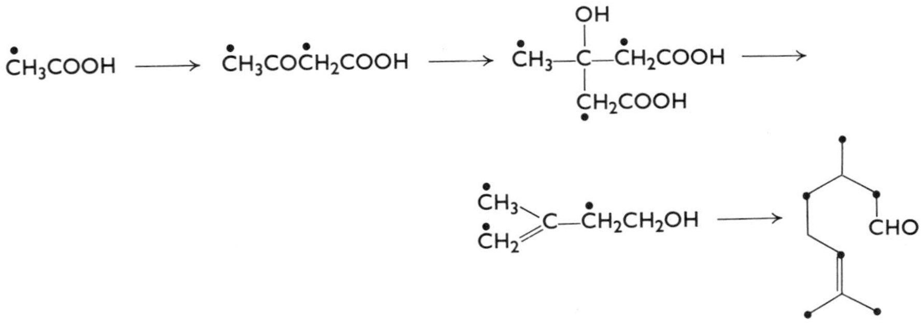

[Eq. 8-9]

Degradation of the citronellal formed from the labeled acetate showed that the pattern of ^{14}C distribution in the terpene corresponded with that shown in Eq. 8-9.

The incorporation of 2-^{14}C-mevalonic acid into cineol in *Eucalyptus globulus* Lab. confirmed this result (Eq. 8-10):

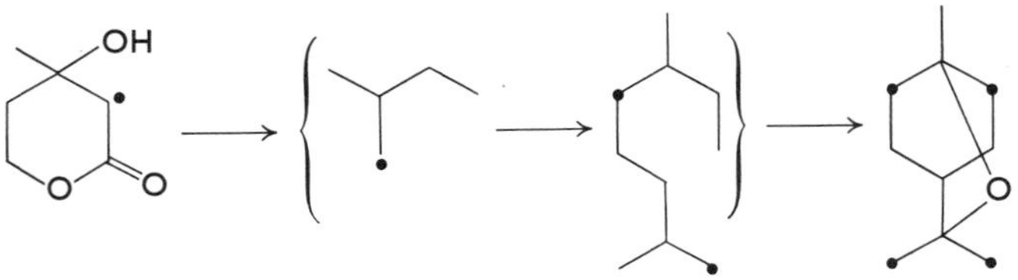

[Eq. 8-10]

1,8-cineole †

† The positions marked • in cineole are symmetrically disposed and cannot be individually distinguished.

* And, in the study of steroid biosynthesis, administered to animal subjects, and also studied in yeast and in isolated tissue (e.g., liver slices).

The principal route from acetate, through mevalonate, to the five-carbon pyrophosphate esters, and to the acyclic and monocyclic terpenes is described by the initial stages shown in Eqs. 8-9 and 8-10, ring closures to the monocyclic compounds probably (but not in all cases certainly) proceeding by way of ionic mechanisms which find their counterparts in mechanistically unexceptional acid-catalyzed cyclization reactions (Eq. 8-11a).

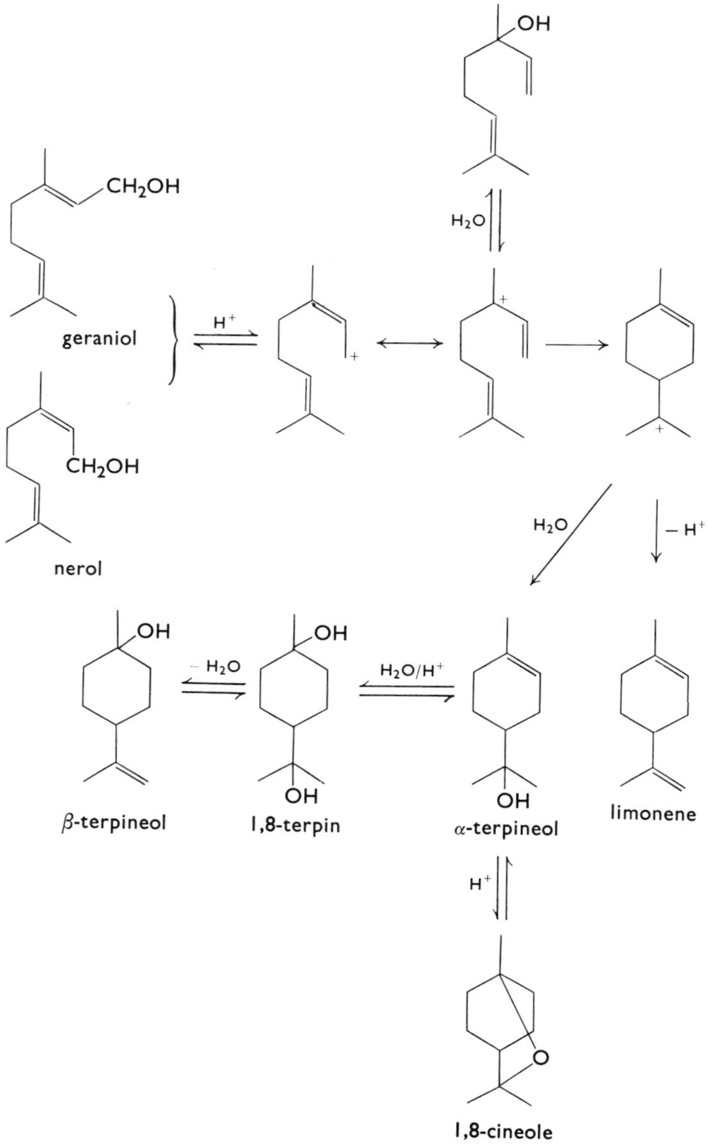

b.†

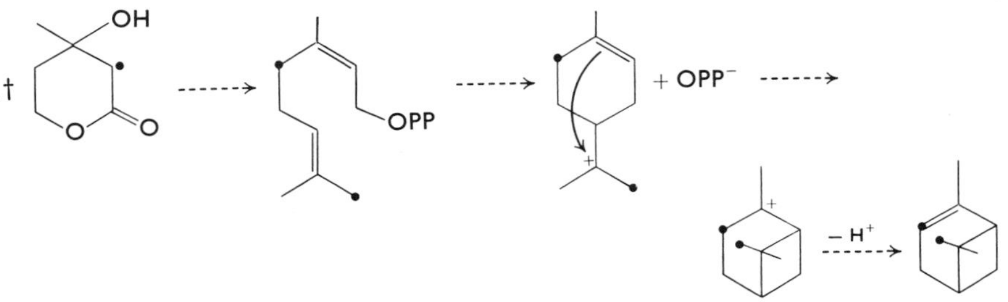
OH
O
O
OPP
+ OPP⁻
– H⁺

c.

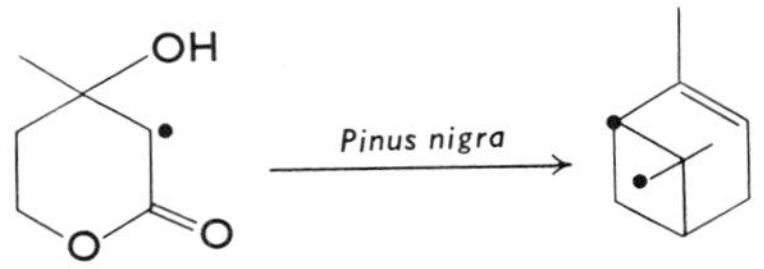
OH
O
O
Pinus nigra

α-pinene

d.

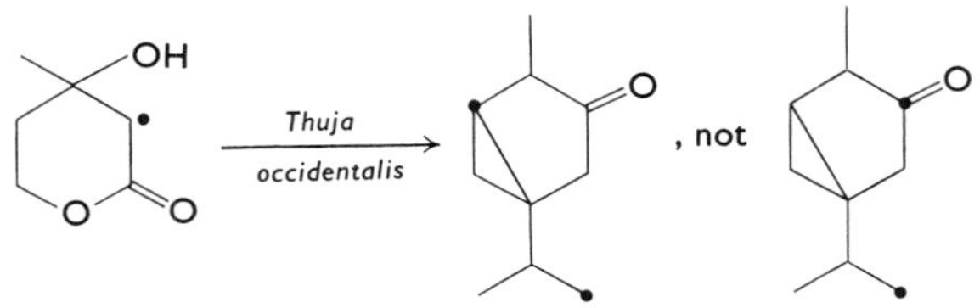
OH
O
O
Thuja
occidentalis
O
, not
O

thujone

† *Note*: Although only one of the *gem*-dimethyl groups is shown to bear the label, this is not experimentally demonstrable in these cases.

e.

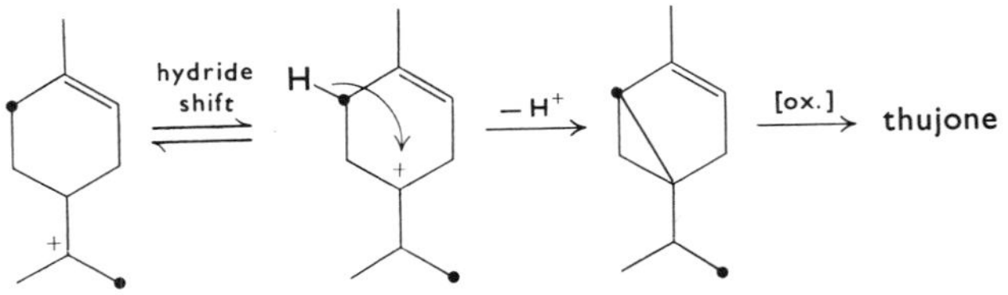
hydride
shift
H
– H⁺
[ox.]
thujone

f.

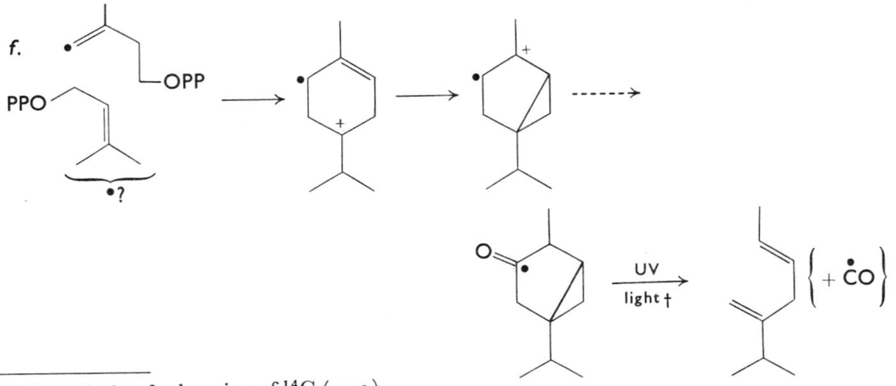
OPP
PPO
•?
O
UV
light †
+ CO

(activity 100) (activity < 1)

† degradation for location of ^{14}C (= •).

[Eq. 8-11]

Certain experimental results on the biosynthesis of bicyclic monoterpenes indicate that what would appear to be straightforward and conventional pathways of synthesis through cationic intermediates may in fact not be valid. For example, the biosynthesis of α-pinene by the pathways so far described could be anticipated to follow the course shown in Eq. 8-11b. Feeding experiments in *Pinus* species with the use of 2-^{14}C-mevalonate have revealed the labeling pattern shown in Eq. 8-11c. A similar situation was encountered in the study of the synthesis of thujone in *Thuja occidentalis* (Eq. 8-11d) where the ring label is not found in the position that would be anticipated were the process of secondary ring closure one that involved direct attack of the double bond upon the C-4 (carbonium) carbon atom.

These "abnormal" labeling patterns can be rationalized by postulating an attack of the carbonium center upon the allylic —CH$_2$— group of the ring (Eq. 8-11e); but it must be borne in mind that the labeling result above does not establish the details of the mechanism involved.

Indeed, the manner of incorporation of mevalonic acid into thujone, as described in the foregoing discussion, a quite unexpected one, is subject to some doubt, for other investigators have obtained different results. In another study, when 2-^{14}C-mevalonic acid was fed to specimens of the genera *Thuja*, *Juniperus* (fam. Cupressaceae) and *Tanacetum* (fam. Compositae), the thujone isolated in every case contained the label at the carbonyl carbon atom, as would be expected were the mechanistically "normal" course shown in Eq. 8-11f followed in the synthesis. The degradation of the labeled thujone gave the further surprising result that no label was found in the isopropyl group. This suggests that the labeled isopropenyl pyrophosphate (from labeled mevalonate) condenses with *unlabeled* dimethylallyl pyrophosphate (from a large metabolic pool) before undergoing double-bond migration.

In a parallel study of the biosynthesis of camphor, essentially the same results were obtained. Feeding of 2-^{14}C-mevalonic acid to *Artemisia*, *Chrysanthemum* (fam. Compositae) and *Salvia* (fam. Labiatae) species yielded (depending upon the species) both (−)- and (+)-camphor. Degradation of the camphor showed that the label was almost exclusively at C-6 (CH_2) and not at C-2 (C=O). The scheme of biosynthesis, which includes the formation of thujone (in other plants) is outlined in Eq. 8-11g. It will be seen that the results with camphor along with those described for thujone, are in agreement with the conclusion that the dimethylallyl partner in the initial $C_5 + C_5 \rightarrow C_{10}$ condensation is unlabeled.

It was suggested that the earlier results described in the earlier paragraph (showing *no* label in the thujone carbonyl group) could have been due to isomerization of *labeled* isopentenyl pyrophosphate (^{14}C-I) into *labeled* dimethylallyl pyrophosphate (^{14}C-II) and subsequent condensation of ^{14}C-II with *unlabeled* I from the metabolic pool. This would give thujone with no label at C=O but with label elsewhere in the molecule.

8.8 Mycophenolic Acid. Degradation of the Isoprenoid Unit. Benzofurans

A terpenoid (in part) compound that provides in a single example a number of features of biosynthetic processes is mycophenolic acid, in which a terpenoid side chain is found in combination with a modified, acetate-derived phenolic ring. When mycophenolic acid is formed (by *Penicillium brevi-compactum* Dierckx) in the presence of 1-^{14}C-acetate, the labeling pattern is that shown in Eq. 8-12a; when 2-^{14}C-mevalonic acid is used, the pattern is that in Eq. 8-12b.

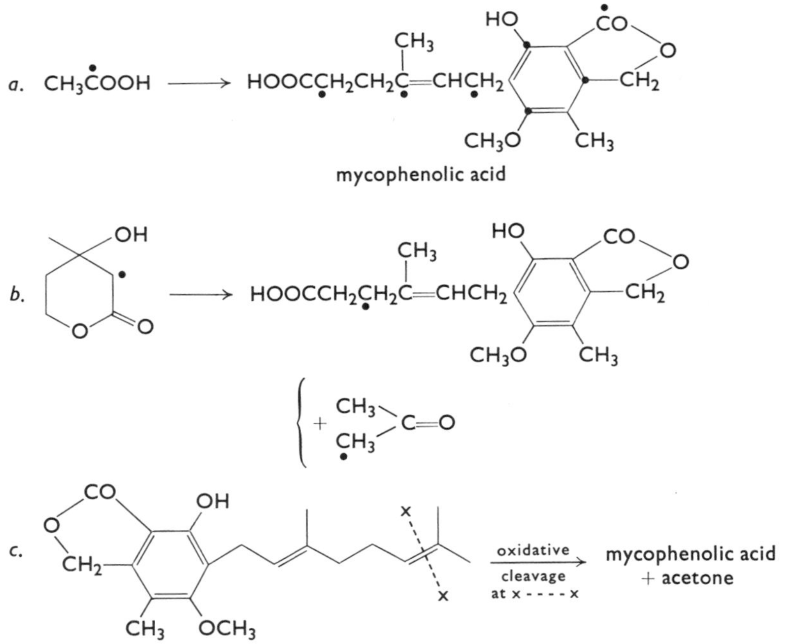

[Eq. 8-12]

It is significant that when 2-^{14}C-mevalonate is fed, no label appears in the ring, showing that mevalonic acid is not degraded to acetic acid (except perhaps to a small extent by random metabolic destruction to fragments which reenter metabolic cycles). The methoxyl and nuclear methyl groups are derived from methionine. The genesis of mycophenolic acid from a geranyl-substituted precursor, by oxidative removal of the terminal isopropylidene group, is shown in Eq. 8-12c; this view is supported by the isolation from a 2-^{14}C-mevalonate-fed culture of the fungus of labeled mycophenolic acid and labeled acetone of approximately equal specific activities.

An additional result deriving from these studies is of special relevance to the biosynthetic role of mevalonic acid. It will be noted that the mycophenolic acid shown in Eq. 8-12b is labeled only at the —CH$_2$— group, and not at the adjacent —CH$_3$ group. This shows that the two terminal carbon atoms of the isopentenyl pyrophosphate retain their identity, and that the labeled =CH$_2$ group of this precursor, derived from C-2 of mevalonic acid, becomes the —CH$_2$— group of the C$_{10}$ compound resulting from the dimethylallyl-isopentenyl combination shown in Eq. 8-7.

Finally, another common biosynthetic process has its parallel in the chain degradation process shown in Eq. 8-12c. It will be noted that imperatorin, oxypeucedanin (Fig. 8-4) and bergamottin (Fig. 8-6) are benzofuran derivatives. It is also to be seen that oroselone (Fig. 8-4) contains an isopropenylfurano ring. The suggestion from these observations that the furan ring of these compounds is derived from a hemiterpenoid side chain has indeed been shown to be correct. Certain structural correlations provided the first indication of this biosynthetic pathway. Besides the common occurrence of 3-isopropylfuran derivatives (such as oroselone), nature provides many examples of compounds in which the oxidation of the iso-C$_5$ chain is already started. One example is oxypeucedanin (Fig. 8-4), and other examples support the concept. In Fig. 8-8 are shown only the furano portions of a number of naturally occurring compounds. These show a variety of stages in the secondary elaborations of an α-(o-hydroxyphenyl)-γ,γ-dimethylallyl unit.

It is clear, and it has upon occasion been suggested, that the two carbon atoms of the furano unit could represent a modified C$_2$ (e.g., acetate) unit. That the origin of this ring is, however, isoprenoid (i.e., from a hemiterpenoid substituent) has been established by feeding experiments. When *Pimpinella magna* (fam. Umbelliferae) was grown with the administration of 1-^{14}C-cinnamic acid and 4-^{14}C-mevalonic acid (separate experiments), the furanocoumarins* were found to be labeled in a way

---

* The wide distribution of furanocoumarins and coumarins containing isoprenoid C$_5$-units in other combination (e.g., as prenyl ethers) in the family Umbelliferae is an excellent example of a chemotaxonomic characteristic. These compounds, while not unique to this plant family, are characteristic components of many of its genera. Most of the coumarins of Fig. 8-4 are found in the family Umbelliferae.

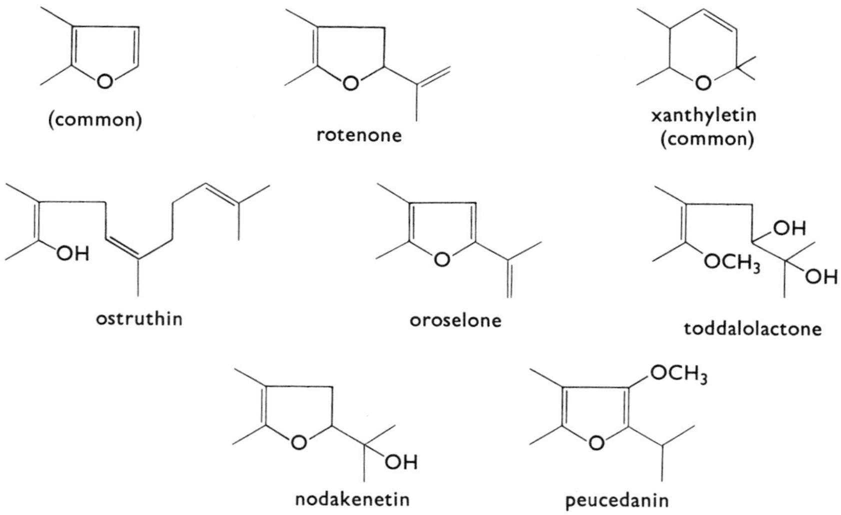
(common)
rotenone
xanthyletin
(common)
OH
ostruthin
oroselone
OH
OCH3
OH
toddalolactone
OCH3
OH
nodakenetin
peucedanin

Fig. 8-8. Alterations of the Dimethylallyl Unit.

that showed that (a) the coumarin portion of the molecule is derived from the cinnamic acid and (b) the furan ring is derived from mevalonic acid. An outline of the scheme of biosynthesis deduced from these experiments is shown (with respect to origin of the carbon atoms) in Eq. 8-13:

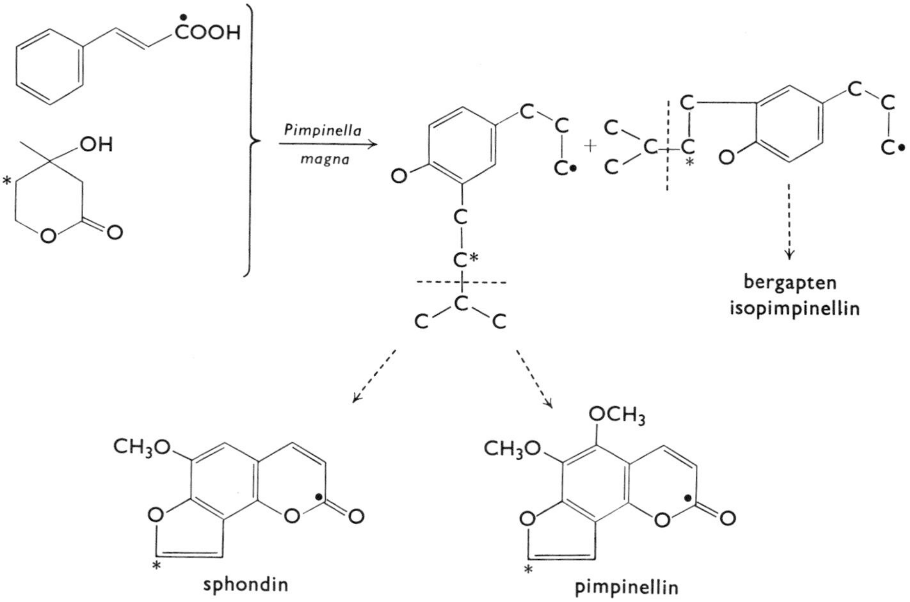
COOH
OH
O
Pimpinella
magna
bergapten
isopimpinellin
CH3O
O
OCH3
CH3O
sphondin
pimpinellin

isopimpinellin   bergapten   isobergapten

(also present; were radioactive but were not degraded to locate the label)   [Eq. 8-13]

8.9 Monoterpenes with Irregular Isoprenoid Skeletons

Although the majority of the natural monoterpenes are formed by the initial union of the isoprene units head-to-tail, there are some exceptions that invite discussion. Departures from the isoprene rule may arise as a result of (a) the combination of isoprene units in other than head-to-tail linkage, (b) alteration of the regular skeleton by degradation (bond cleavage or loss of one or more carbon atoms), or (c) rearrangement. It is not always possible to decide, in the absence of direct experimental evidence, upon one or another of the alternative explanations for an "abnormal" structure.

Artemisia ketone, found in *Artemisia annua* L. and *Santolina chamaecyparis* L. (both of the fam. Compositae) has the structure shown in Fig. 8-9. Also present in *S. chamaecyparis* is the hydrocarbon of corresponding structure; and a structurally related compound is found (as an ester) in *Chrysanthemum* species (also Compositae) in chrysanthemic acid.

Labeling experiments have shown that the compounds of Fig. 8-9 are mevalonate-derived, and the question that remains is the nature of the biochemical

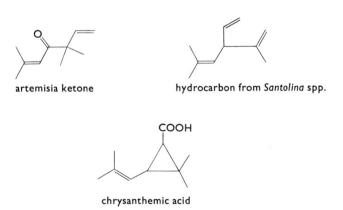

artemisia ketone   hydrocarbon from *Santolina* spp.

chrysanthemic acid

Fig. 8-9. Structurally Related Compounds from Compositae.

reaction in which the two C_5 residues are joined. It is clear that all three compounds can be related to a single progenitor (Eq. 8-14):

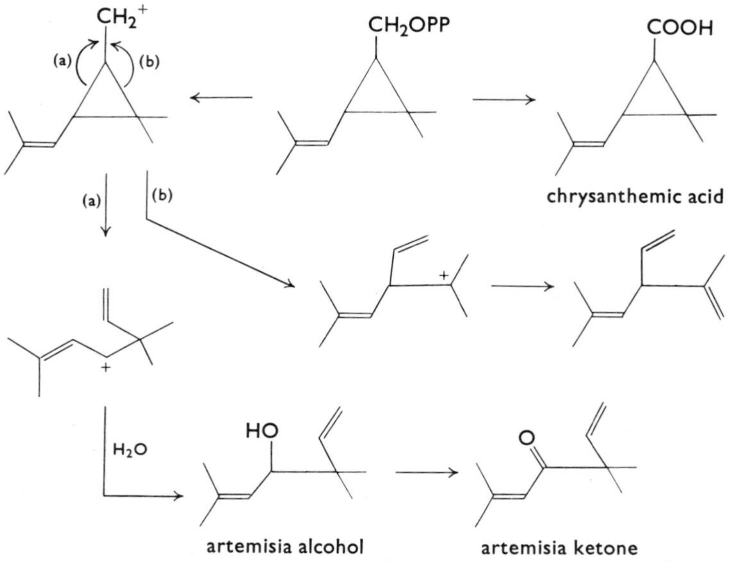
CH_2^+
(a)
(b)
CH_2OPP
COOH
chrysanthemic acid
(a)
(b)
+
+
H_2O
HO
O
artemisia alcohol
artemisia ketone

[Eq. 8-14]

The question of the mechanism of the reaction resolves itself into that of the manner of formation of the cyclopropane-derived pyrophosphate ester shown as the central participant in the processes of Eq. 8-14.

A simple and direct route to this central compound is that formulated in Eq. 8-15; it requires only the assumption that the α-elimination, leading to a carbene, occurs in nature.

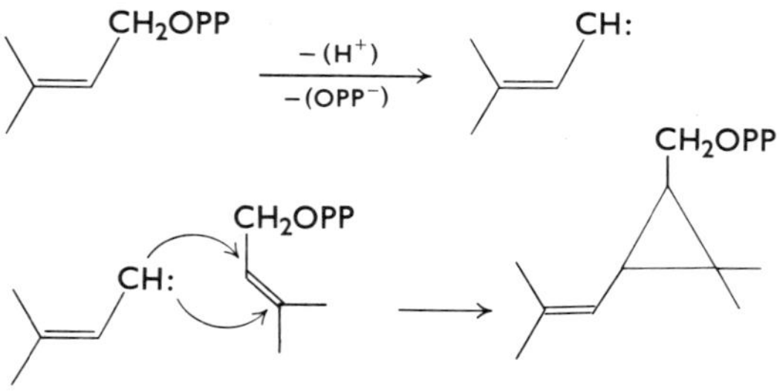
CH_2OPP
$-(H^+)$
$-(OPP^-)$
CH:
CH_2OPP
CH_2OPP
CH:

[Eq. 8-15]

The α-elimination reaction and the addition of carbenes to olefinic double bonds are well known reactions. Whether they in fact occur in nature is still open to conjecture.

An alternative course is suggested by observations that have been made in the course of studies of the biosynthesis of squalene (see Chapter 11). It has been suggested that thiamin pyrophosphate (TPP) plays a role in the coupling of two farnesyl pyrophosphate units in a tail-to-tail manner. A possible role of TPP in the reactions discussed here can be invoked, as shown in Eq. 8-16. It will be seen that these steps involve an *overall* process that is equivalent only to the displacement of pyrophosphate (Eq. 8-16*a*); but the process, which is without doubt enzyme-mediated, may be accelerated with the participation of TPP as in Eq. 8-16*b*:

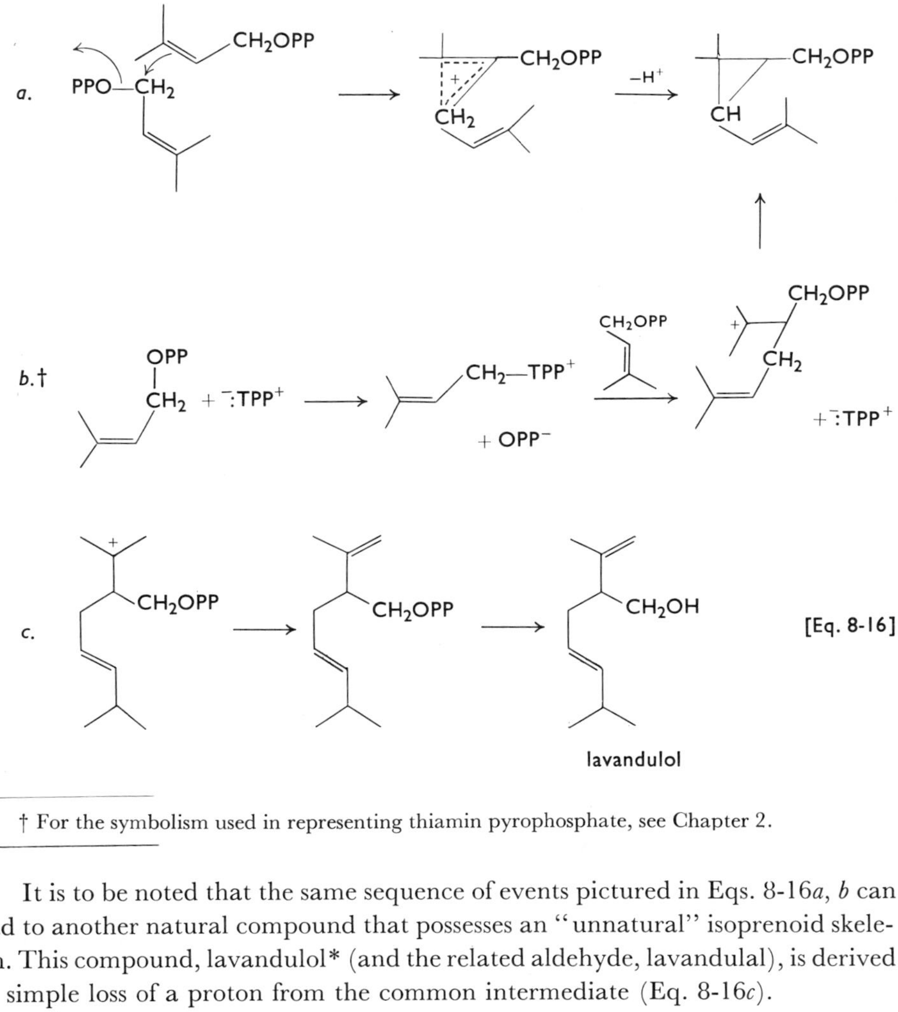

lavandulol

[Eq. 8-16]

---

† For the symbolism used in representing thiamin pyrophosphate, see Chapter 2.

It is to be noted that the same sequence of events pictured in Eqs. 8-16*a*, *b* can lead to another natural compound that possesses an "unnatural" isoprenoid skeleton. This compound, lavandulol* (and the related aldehyde, lavandulal), is derived by simple loss of a proton from the common intermediate (Eq. 8-16*c*).

* From lavender oil, *Lavandula officinalis* L. (fam. Labiatae), which also contains a number of other terpenes of "regular" isoprenoid structures. The Labiatae (mint family) are notably rich in terpenoid compounds.

8.10 Further Evidence on the Biosynthetic Route to Terpenes

Numerous early studies on the terpenoid constituents of *Eucalyptus*, *Pinus*, and *Mentha* species with the use of ^{14}C-labeled carbon dioxide, acetic acid, and mevalonic acid established the overall features of the biosynthetic pathway:

acetate ⟶ mevalonate ⟶ geranyl pyrophosphate ⟶ monoterpenes.

Recent, more detailed studies have enlarged the picture by providing evidence for some of the later stages in which the monocyclic and bicyclic terpenes are formed.

When *Mentha piperita* L. (fam. Labiatae) plants were fed with ^{14}C-labeled acetate, mevalonate, and carbon dioxide, the observed incorporation of radioactivity into the terpenes led to the conclusions that (a) acetate and mevalonate are incorporated as such and not by way of prior metabolic degradation to CO_2; (b) carbon dioxide incorporation takes place only in the light; (c) acetate is incorporated at the same rate in darkness and in light; and (d) carbon dioxide is incorporated in the light at a higher rate than is acetate.

Analysis (by vapor-phase chromatography) of the terpenes formed in plants exposed to ^{14}C-carbon dioxide at different total periods of exposure led to the proposed scheme of biosynthesis shown in Fig. 8-10. The biosynthesis of the mint terpenes is regarded as proceeding by way of piperitone and perhaps pulegone, leading finally to the mixture of terpenes which include menthone, isomenthone, menthofuran and menthol. An earlier suggestion (put forward on the basis of studies that did not involve the use of radioactive precursors) that piperitenone was the common precursor of all of the *Mentha* terpenes, was not substantiated by the labeling experiments. The scheme shown in Fig. 8-10 is to be regarded as still imperfect in detail, but it probably represents a reasonably valid picture of the main routes of monoterpene synthesis in the plant.

8.11 Derived Terpenoid Compounds. Iridoids

A widely distributed class of natural substances, not terpenoid compounds in the usual meaning of that term, but of mevalonate origin and isoprenoid in carbon skeleton, is that called the "iridoid" compounds. The name is a generic term derived from the names iridomyrmecin, iridolactone and iridodial, compounds isolated from species of *Iridomyrmex*, a genus of ants, in which they occur as defensive secretions. Iridoid compounds are widely found in plants, usually, but not invariably, as glucosides. They are cyclopentane derivatives possessing a common basic structural pattern but differing in details. In Fig. 8-11 are shown some representative compounds of the class.

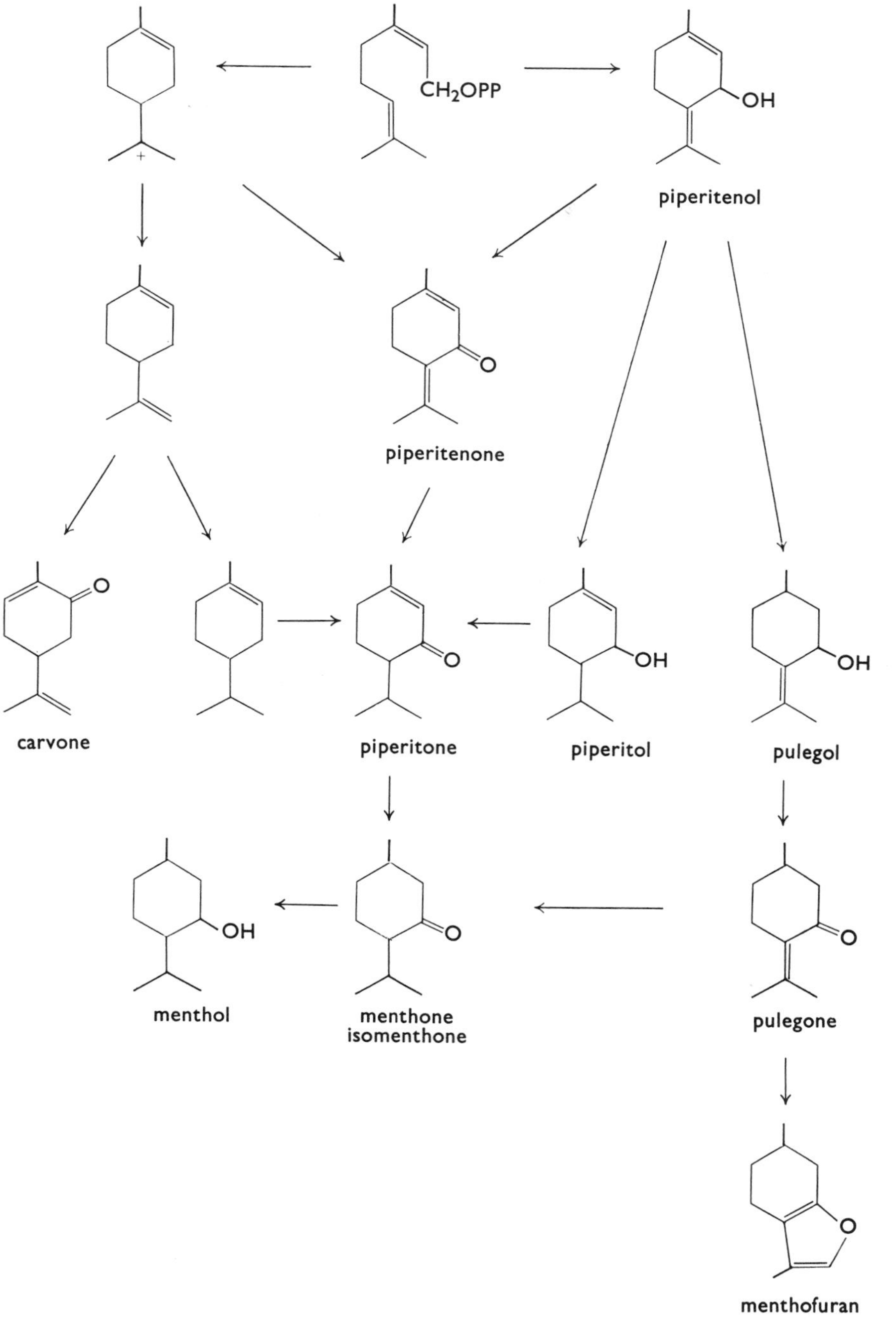

Fig. 8-10. Proposed Biosynthetic Pathway in *Mentha*.

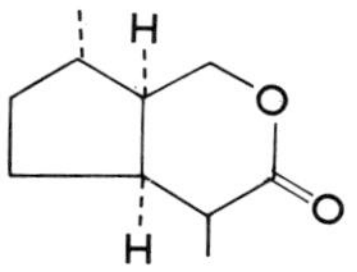

iridomyrmecin† 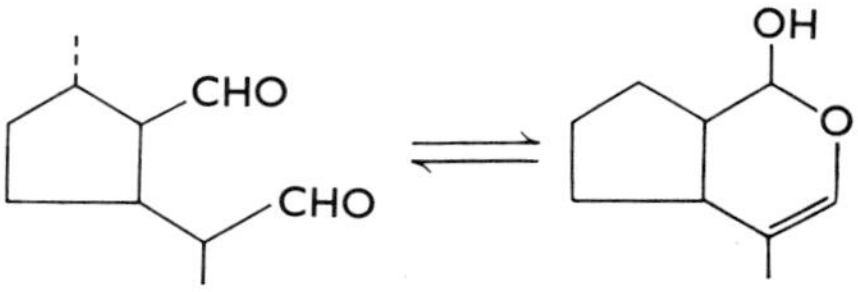   iridodial†

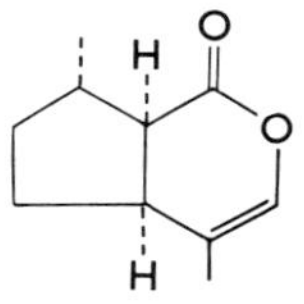

nepetalactone 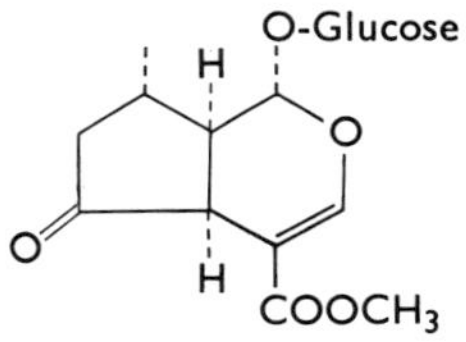   verbenalin

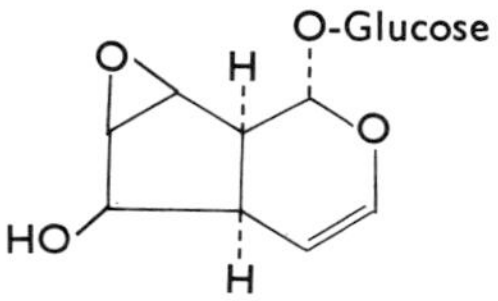

unedoside 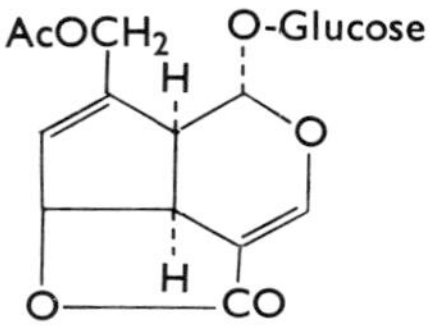   asperuloside

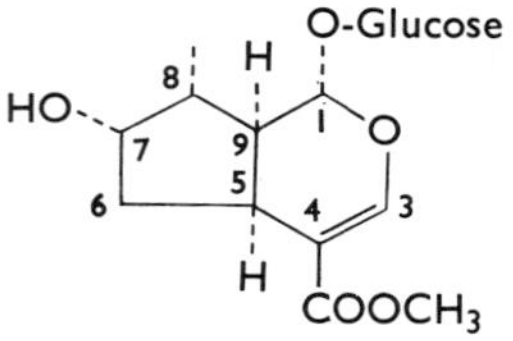

loganin 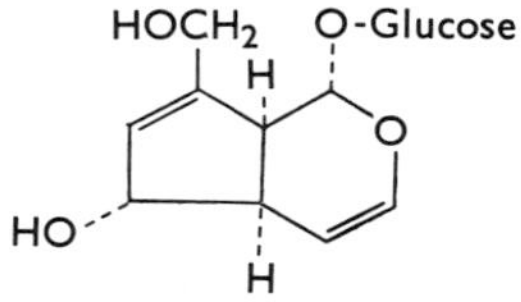   aucubin

† From ants (*Iridomyrmex* spp.); others are plant products, representing six different plant families.

Fig. 8-11. Iridoid Compounds.

It has been demonstrated by experiments with appropriately labeled precursors that the iridoid compounds are terpenoid, and conform to the biogenetic isoprene rule. For example, when 1-^{3}H-geraniol was fed to *Menyanthes trifoliata* (fam. Menyanthaceae; related to the fam. Gentianaceae), radioactive loganin was formed with good incorporation of radioactivity. The feeding of 2-^{14}C-geraniol yielded ^{14}C-labeled loganin, and geraniol labeled with ^{14}C at the C-3 methyl group yielded ^{14}C-loganin in which the activity was largely (85%) in the methyl group at C-8 (see Fig. 8-11).

An early intimation that the iridoid compounds were constructed from a regular C_{10} isoprenoid precursor came from a laboratory synthesis of iridodial from citronellal in the manner shown in Eq. 8-17:

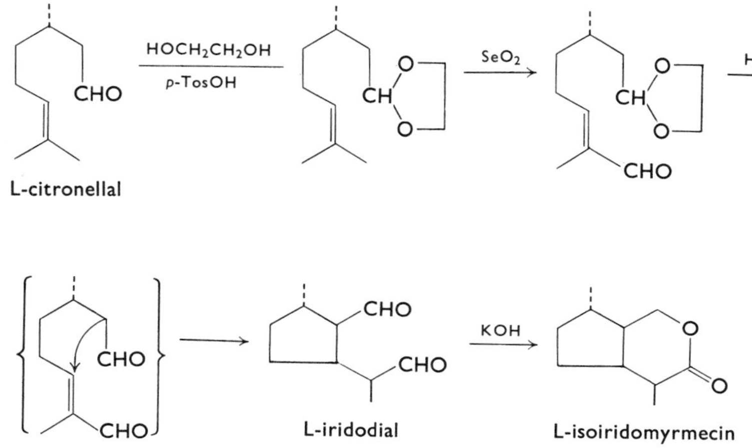

Although the exact details of the natural ring closure corresponding to the Michael reaction of the synthetic series are not known, the structural analogy between citronellal, the iridoids, and the synthetic route is so strong that it may be presumed that the natural process resembles in its main features the sequence shown in Eq. 8-17. In any case, the labeling experiment that showed that the C-3 methyl group of the terpenoid precursor becomes the C-8 methyl group of loganin is in complete accord with this concept.

8.12   Loganin

A discussion of the chemistry of the plant iridoid compounds is most appropriately presented with the use of loganin as the example, for, as will be shown in greater detail in a later chapter, loganin plays an important part in the biosynthesis of an important group of indole and isoquinoline alkaloids, in the structures of which the loganin molecule is incorporated essentially in its entirety (Chapter 19). It is of interest also to note that loganin is found in *Strychnos nux-vomica* (fam. Loganiaceae), the source of an important group of indole alkaloids, as well as in *Menyanthes* spp. (see above).

The chemical transformations leading to the gross structure of loganin are shown in Eq. 8-18.

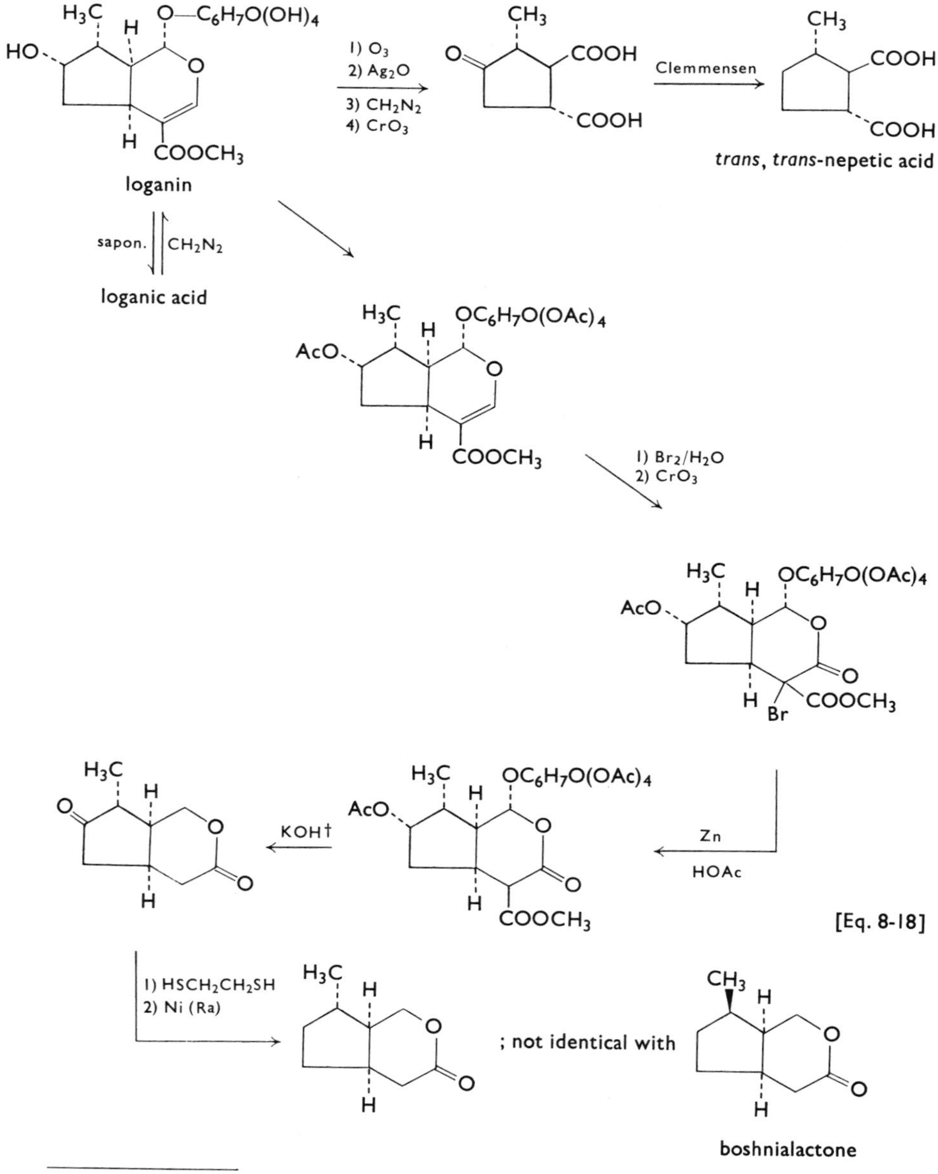

loganin

1) O₃
2) Ag₂O
3) CH₂N₂
4) CrO₃

Clemmensen

trans, trans-nepetic acid

sapon. ‖ CH₂N₂

loganic acid

1) Br₂/H₂O
2) CrO₃

[Eq. 8-18]

KOH†

Zn
HOAc

1) HSCH₂CH₂SH
2) Ni (Ra)

; not identical with

boshnialactone

† Possibly via

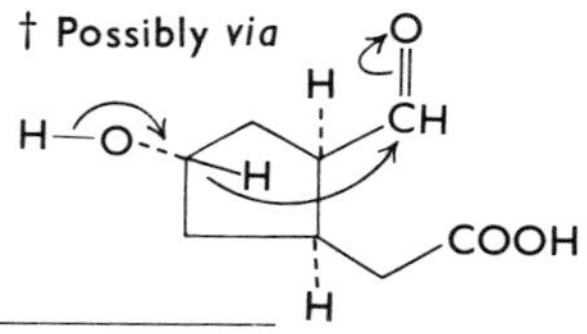

Loganin is a β-D-glucoside. It contains an esterified carboxyl group, for it can be saponified to an acid which upon reconversion into the methyl ester regenerates loganin. Finally, the carbomethoxy (or methoxycarbonyl) group is present in the system —O—C=C—COOCH$_3$ for its ultraviolet absorption spectrum shows a λ_{max} (237 mμ; log ϵ 4.0) in agreement with those of model compounds containing this grouping.

Ozonolysis of penta-O-acetyl loganin, followed by a further mild oxidation, esterification with diazomethane, and oxidation with chromic acid gave a keto ester (which was not a β-keto ester) and which was reduced (Clemmensen) to 3-methylcyclopentane-1,2-dicarboxylic acid. The latter was found to be identical with *trans, trans*-nepetic acid, first obtained by degradation of nepetalactone (Fig. 8-11). Because of the nature of the reactions involved in this series of transformations the stereochemistry of loganin is not defined by that of the dicarboxylic acid.

Definition of the remainder of the loganin structure was achieved by its transformation into a saturated lactone (Eq. 8-18) which proved to be different from boshnialactone, first isolated from the plant *Boschniakia rossica* Hult. (fam. Orobanchaceae).*

Boshnialactone has been synthesized in a way that established the stereochemistry shown in Eq. 8-18. Alkylation of 5-methyl-2-carboethoxycyclopentanone (Eq. 8-19a) with ethyl bromoacetate, followed by saponification and decarboxylation, gave 3-methyl-2-oxocyclopentanecarboxylic acid (Eq. 8-19b), the ethyl ester of which was converted by means of the Wittig reagent to the corresponding methylene derivative (Eq. 8-19c), which was a mixture of the two isomers at $>$CH—CH$_3$.

The mixture of isomers (Eq. 8-19c) was subjected to hydroboration with a dialkylboron (R$_2$BH), which reacted preferentially with the *cis* compound to give as the principal product the lactone Eq. 8-19d. This was the ($\pm$)-form of the natural boshnialactone, the structure and stereochemistry of which are defined by these reactions. It will be apparent from the reactions outlined in Eq. 8-19 that the stereochemical assignments are based in large part upon the stereochemical control of the attack of the hydroboration reagent upon the exocyclic methylene group. Attack upon the *cis* ester (Eq. 8-19c) from the side opposite to the two projecting groups (—CH$_3$ and —CH$_2$COOEt) is what would be expected, and defines the stereochemistry of boshnialactone.

It will be seen from the reactions described in Eqs. 8-18 and 8-19 that loganin has the stereochemistry shown in Eq. 8-18. Further evidence for this stereochemistry is found in correlations between other iridoids and between loganin and verbenalin.

---

* Boshnialactone, like nepetalactone, has the unusual property of being attractive to members of the cat family. Nepetalactone is the active principle of catnip.

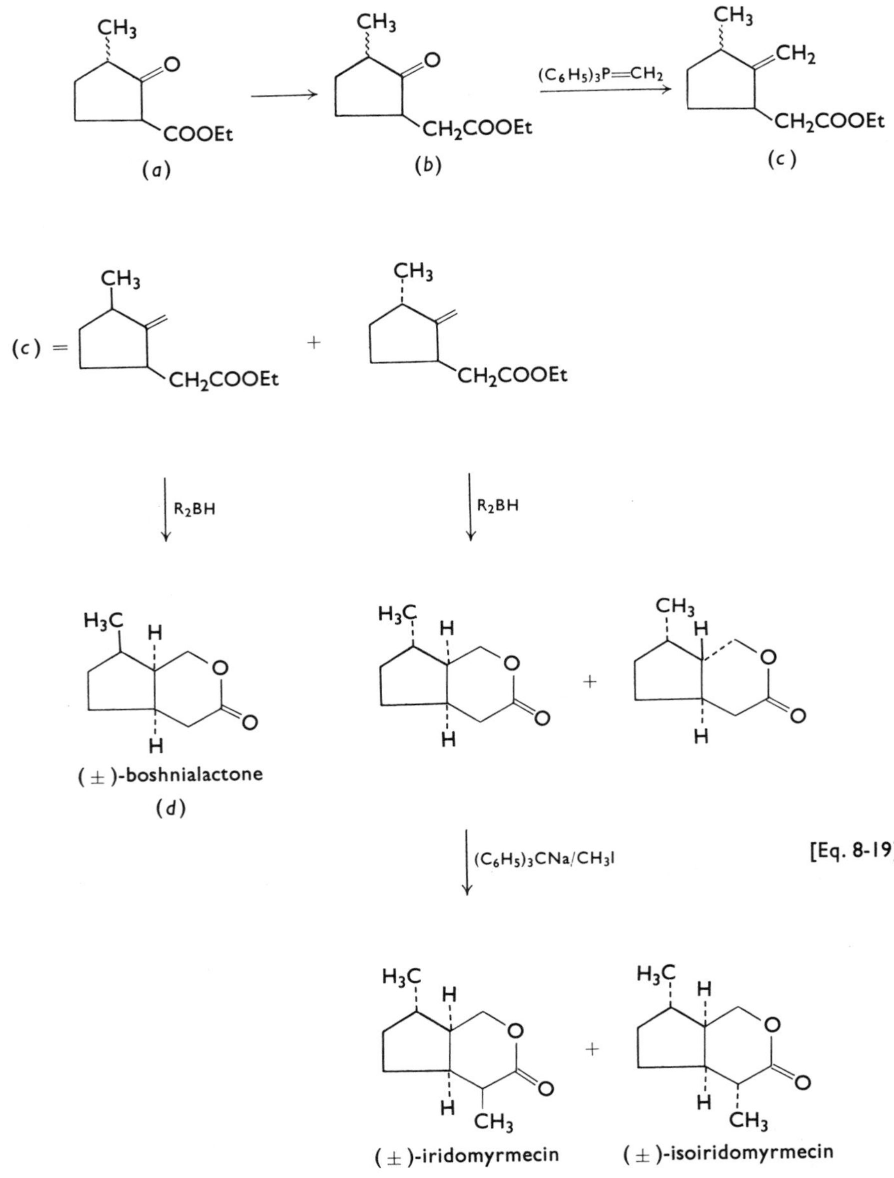

(a)   (b)   (c)

$(C_6H_5)_3P{=}CH_2$

(c) =

+

R_2BH R_2BH

(±)-boshnialactone

(d)

+

$(C_6H_5)_3CNa/CH_3I$ [Eq. 8-19]

(±)-iridomyrmecin   (±)-isoiridomyrmecin

Verbenalin has the structure and stereochemistry shown in Fig. 8-11 and Eq. 8-20. Part of the evidence for the *cis* ring fusion and for the configuration of the methyl group is found in the conversion of verbenalin into (+)-iridomyrmecin and into nepetalinic acid (Eq. 8-20b). Verbenalin and loganin have both been converted into the same dehydro derivative by elimination of the hydroxyl group by removal of CH_3SO_3H from the isomeric mesylates (Eq. 8-20a):

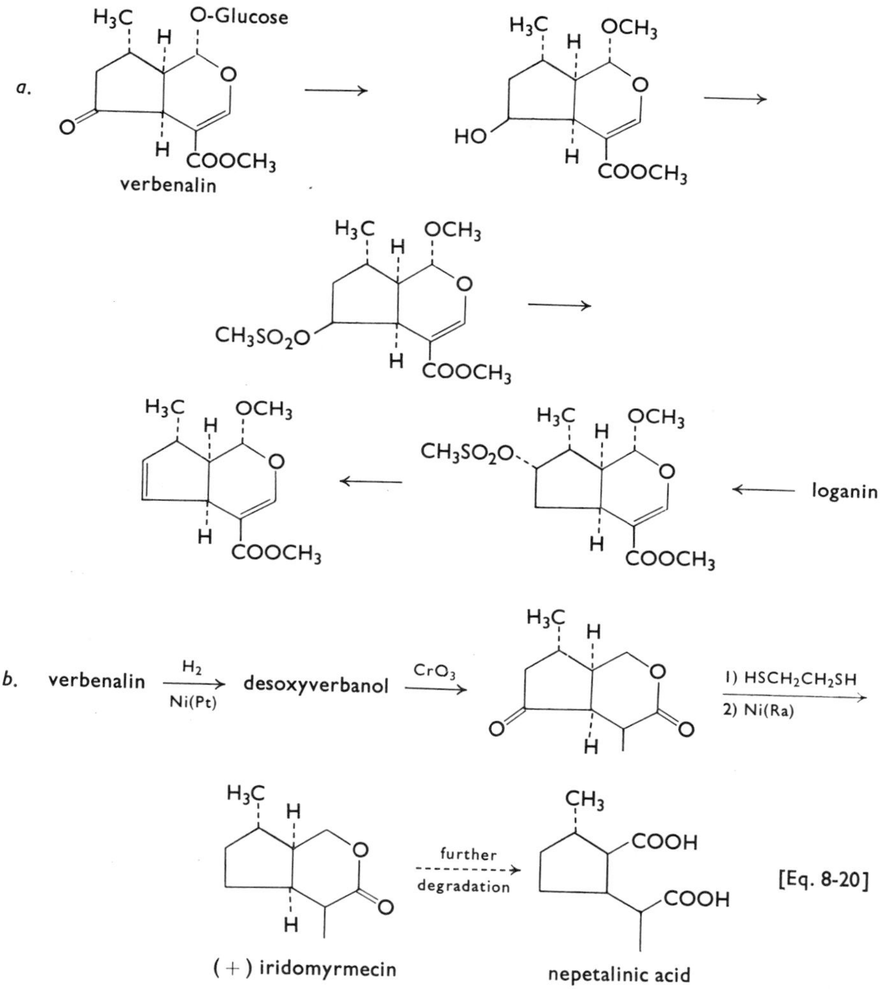

verbenalin

loganin

b. verbenalin $\xrightarrow[Ni(Pt)]{H_2}$ desoxyverbanol $\xrightarrow{CrO_3}$ $\xrightarrow[2) Ni(Ra)]{1) HSCH_2CH_2SH}$

(+) iridomyrmecin

$\xrightarrow[\text{degradation}]{\text{further}}$

nepetalinic acid

[Eq. 8-20]

Numerous correlations similar to those described in the preceding discussion have established that the iridoid compounds are characterized by a common stereochemistry, as shown in the structures pictured in the above equations and in Fig. 8-11. Two variations in the fundamental terpenoid (i.e., modified isoprenoid) structure are found in the iridoid compounds aucubin and unedoside (Fig. 8-11). Nothing is yet known about the manner or the step in the biosynthesis in which the carbon atom attached to C-4 in loganin is lost in these compounds, although it appears very likely that the key step is a decarboxylation of a carboxylic acid.

8.13 Further Alteration of the Isoprenoid Structure. Modified Iridoid Compounds (Secoiridoids)

A group of compounds that are typical of (but not unique to) members of the plant family Gentianaceae are characterized by an alteration of the iridoid structure that results from cleavage of the cyclopentane ring. Some typical members of this class, known as "secoiridoids," are shown in Fig. 8-12.

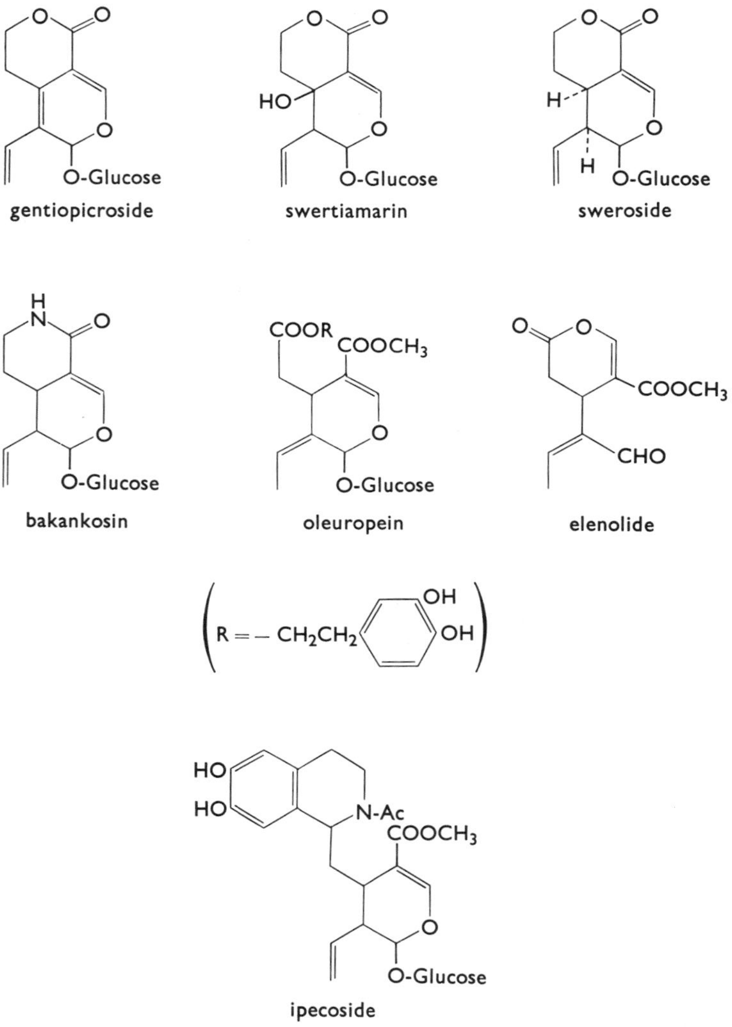

Fig. 8-12. Secoiridoid Compounds.

Loganic acid (the acid corresponding to the methyl ester, loganin) and gentiopicroside occur together in the plant *Swertia caroliniensis* (fam. Gentianaceae), and feeding experiments with the use of $2\text{-}^{14}\text{C}$-mevalonic acid have shown that both compounds are of mevalonate (i.e., isoprenoid) origin. The relative incorporations of label into loganic acid and gentiopicroside were consistent with the view that loganin is the precursor of gentiopicroside. The cleavage of the cyclopentane ring and the reorganization of the resulting product into the ring systems of sweroside and elenolide are shown in Eq. 8-21.

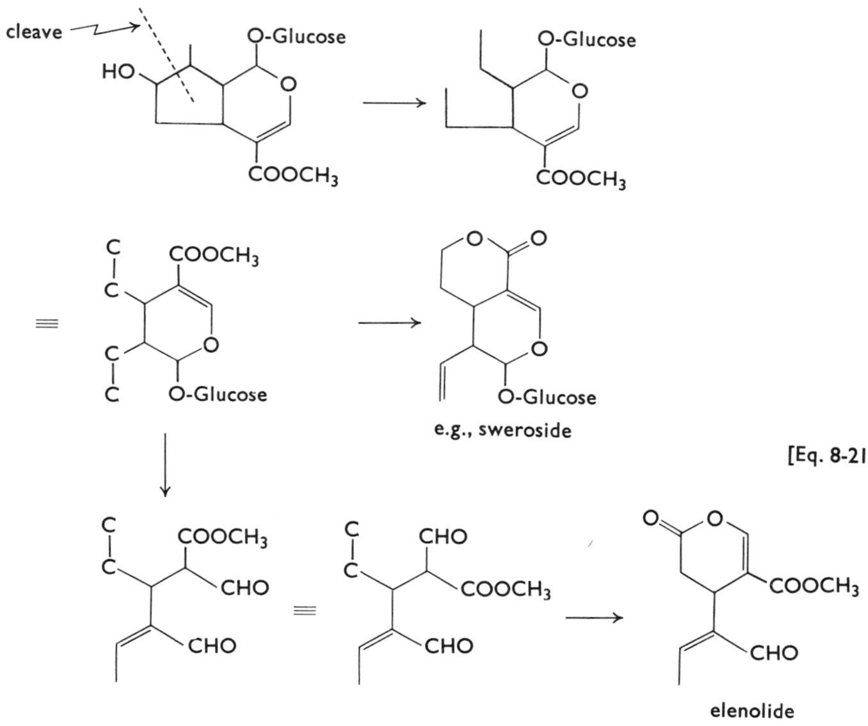

e.g., sweroside

[Eq. 8-21]

elenolide

The introduction of nitrogen to produce such compounds as bakankosin needs no special comment. The formation of ipecoside proceeds by way of a biosynthetic pathway that will be discussed in greater detail in a later chapter.

8.14 Summary Comment

The fundamental biosynthetic pathway acetate → mevalonate → isopentenyl and dimethylallyl pyrophosphates → geranyl pyrophosphate, is the start of a synthetic route that ramifies into a number of subsequent pathways. The products of these are the acyclic monoterpenes; the mono-, bi- and tri-cyclic terpenes; the carbon- and oxygen-linked isoprenoid substituents of phenolic compounds; and, by ring closure and subsequent cleavage, compounds in which the original head-to-tail isoprenoid skeleton is not at once apparent but the mevalonate origin of which is firmly established by the use of isotopically labeled precursors in studies with living organisms.

A great deal remains to be learned about the secondary details of mono-terpenoid synthesis, for the wide variety of oxidation levels found in these ten-carbon compounds show that higher plants possess many mechanisms for the dehydrogenation and oxygenation of organic compounds, few of which are under-stood in more than a superficial way. The facility with which synthetic sequences can be formulated on paper is disarming, for in only a few cases can the separate steps of such "biosynthetic" series be substantiated by experiment. For a complete understanding of the biosynthesis of a compound such as, for example, gentio-picroside, a great deal must be learned about the countless individual reactions that occur in living cells.

IX CHAPTER

REFERENCES FOR FURTHER READING

1. W. Parker, J. S. Roberts, and R. Ramage, *Sesquiterpene Biogenesis,* Quart. Rev. (Chem. Soc.), *21,* (1967), 331.

2. J. B. Hendrickson, *Stereochemical Implications in Sesquiterpene Biogenesis,* Tetrahedron, *7,* (1959), 82.

3. E. D. Brown, M. D. Solomon, J. K. Sutherland, and A. Torre, *A Possible Intermediate in Sesquiterpene Biosynthesis,* Chem. Comm., (1967), 111.

4. P. Yates, *Cedrene and Cedrol,* in Structure Determination, W. A. Benjamin, Inc., New York, 1967.

5. D. A. Archer and R. H. Thomson, *The Structure of Perezone,* Chem. Comm., (1965), 354.

6. F. Walls, J. Padilla, P. Joseph-Nathan, F. Giral, and J. Romo, *The Structures of α- and β-Pipitzols,* Tetrahedron Letters, (1965), 1577.

7. W. Herz, *Pseudoguaianolides in Compositae,* in Recent Advances in Phytochemistry, T. J. Mabry, Ed., Appleton-Century-Crofts, New York, 1968.

Sesquiterpenes

9.1 Introduction

Sesquiterpenoid compounds contain fifteen carbon atoms in an isoprenoid or modified (e.g., by rearrangement) isoprenoid structure. They are among the most universally distributed naturally occurring compounds, and, because they occur in so wide a range of structural variation, have provided an almost limitless field of chemical investigation. Moreover, because of the fortunate circumstance that there is often a close relationship between botanical origin and structural characteristics, they often provide useful examples of chemotaxonomic relationships. As will be seen from the discussion to follow, many sesquiterpenes fall into structurally delimited groups, each of which can be regarded as having a common origin in a unique ionic precursor; thus, clear boundaries often exist between separate classes of these compounds, the limits of which frequently define corresponding botanical classes. Indeed, as the study of the sesquiterpenes has developed through the years, there have repeatedly been discovered new compounds whose existence could be predicted (or anticipated) on the grounds of a theoretical relationship to compounds already known. The compelling unity of the origins of sesquiterpenoid compounds from a relatively few and structurally simple modifications of a single precursor is most impressive, and persuades one to accept the view that many of the conjectures concerning their origins are substantially correct.

In this chapter will be described some sesquiterpenoid compounds that have been selected to show some of the principal structural classes, some of the unique structural alterations that occur during their biosynthesis, and some of the relationships that provide an insight into the genetic factors that govern their formation.

9.2 Farnesol and Acyclic Sesquiterpenes

The formation of farnesyl pyrophosphate by the reaction of geranyl pyrophosphate with isopentenyl pyrophosphate has been described (Chap. 8, Eq. 8-8). Farnesol (or its pyrophosphate ester) may be regarded as existing in two forms, corresponding to geraniol and nerol, differing in the geometry of the 2,3-double bond. The third possible isomer at this terminal unit, nerolidol, is the tertiary alcohol corresponding to linaloöl (Fig. 9-1). Both farnesol and nerolidol are naturally occurring constituents of numerous essential oils.

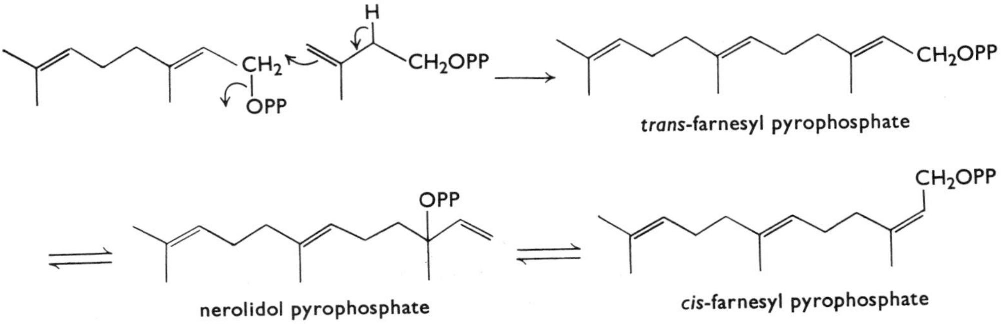

Fig. 9-1. Farnesol and Nerolidol.

The establishment of the structure of farnesol, and its synthesis, are outlined in Eq. 9-1. The reactions described, while unexceptional, are characteristic of those used in studies of the acyclic mono- and sesquiterpenoids.

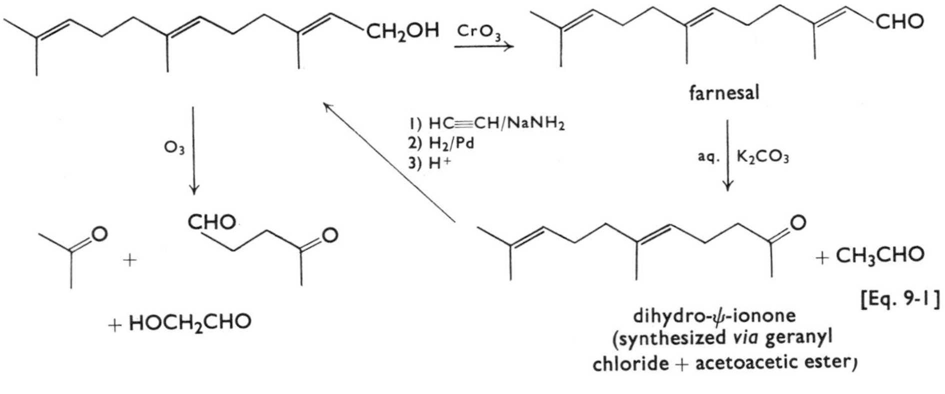

[Eq. 9-1]

Although farnesol and nerolidol are the only known acyclic sesquiterpene alcohols, a number of acyclic (i.e. non-carbocyclic) sesquiterpenes, clearly derived from farnesol, are found in nature. The simplest of these are the farnesenes, products of the simple dehydration of farnesol (or elimination of pyrophosphoric acid from the pyrophosphate ester). Dehydration of farnesol (or nerolidol) under acidic conditions yields chiefly β-farnesene, the sesquiterpene corresponding to the terpene, myrcene. β-Farnesene occurs in nature and until very recently was the only known naturally occurring acyclic sesquiterpene hydrocarbon. α-Farnesene is of limited occurrence, and is known as the only sesquiterpene in the waxy coating of a variety of apple, and as the sole constituent of the Dufour's gland of the myrmecine ant, *Aphaenogaster longiceps* (F. Sm.). Ultraviolet absorption and NMR data both suggest that the natural α-farnesene is the *trans* compound (Fig. 9-2), a conclusion reached by comparison of relevant values with the known *cis*- and *trans*-β-ocimenes.

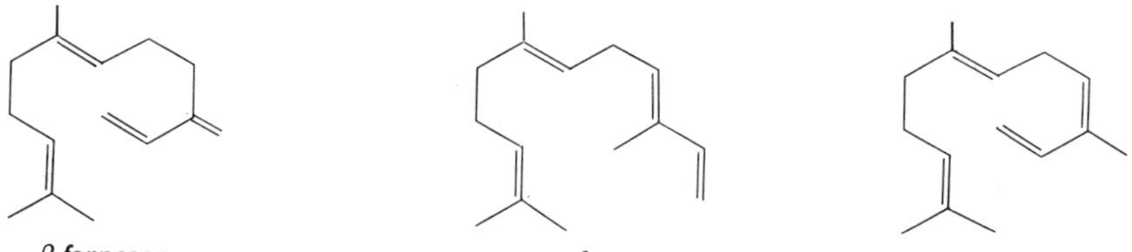

β-farnesene
UV λ_{max} 225 mμ (ϵ 16600)

trans-α-farnesene
obs. UV λ_{max} 232 mμ (ϵ 36400)

cis-α-farnesene

cis-β-ocimene 237 mμ (ϵ 21000)

trans-β-ocimene 232 mμ (ϵ 27600)

NMR —C$\underline{H}$=CH$_2$: α-farnesene δ6.30 ppm
trans-ocimene 6.30 ppm
cis-ocimene 6.73 ppm

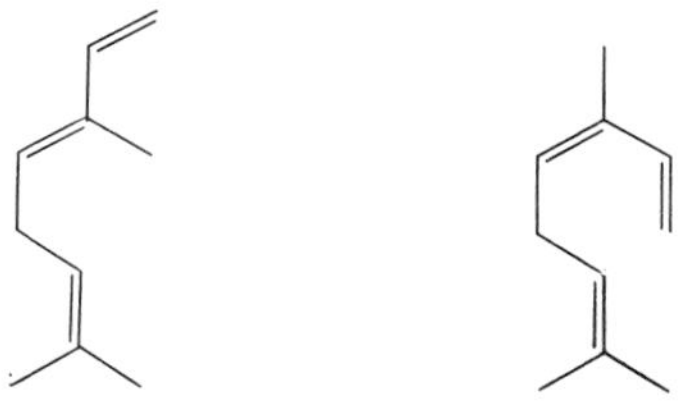

trans-

cis-

β-ocimenes

Fig. 9-2. α- and β-Farnesenes.

9.3 Dendrolasin, Ipomeamarone, and Related Compounds

The formicine ant, *Dendrolasius fuliginosus*, produces as a defensive secretion a sesquiterpenoid furan, dendrolasin, with the structure shown in Eq. 9-2. The same compound is also found in a plant source, namely, in the fusel oils produced by the fermentation of the sweet potato, *Ipomoea batata* (fam. Convolvulaceae). The spectral properties and the results of ozonolysis of dendrolasin led to the assignment of the structure shown, and this was confirmed by its synthesis from geraniol by the steps described in the equation.

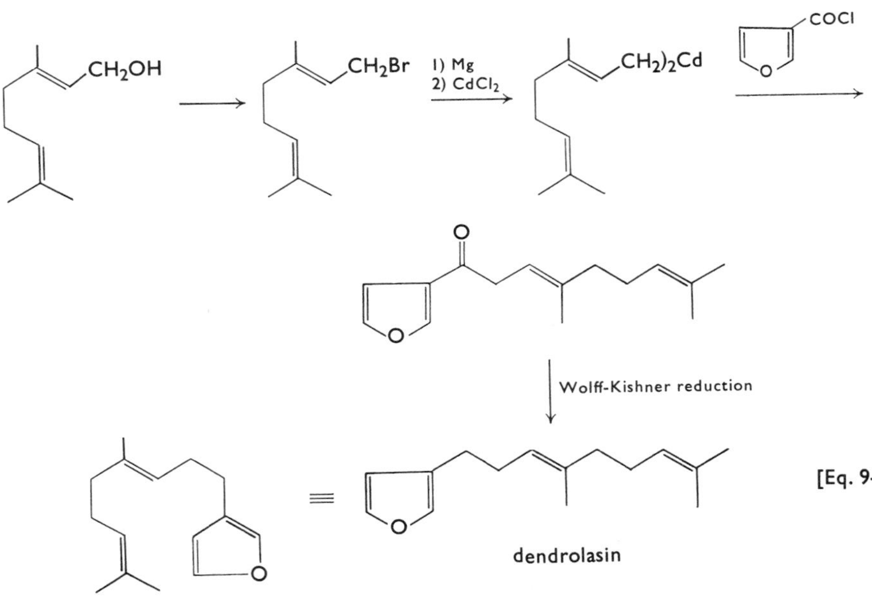

[Eq. 9-2]

dendrolasin

The occurrence of dendrolasin in the fermentation products of the sweet potato takes on special interest in view of the remarkable chemical effects of infection of the sweet potato by the black-rot fungus, *Ceratocystis fimbriatum* (*Ceratostomella fimbriata*). The infected tissue is found to contain a group of related terpenoid compounds, not found in the healthy plant, which include the C_{15} compound, ipomeamarone, and what are evidently degradation products of this (Fig. 9-3). It is

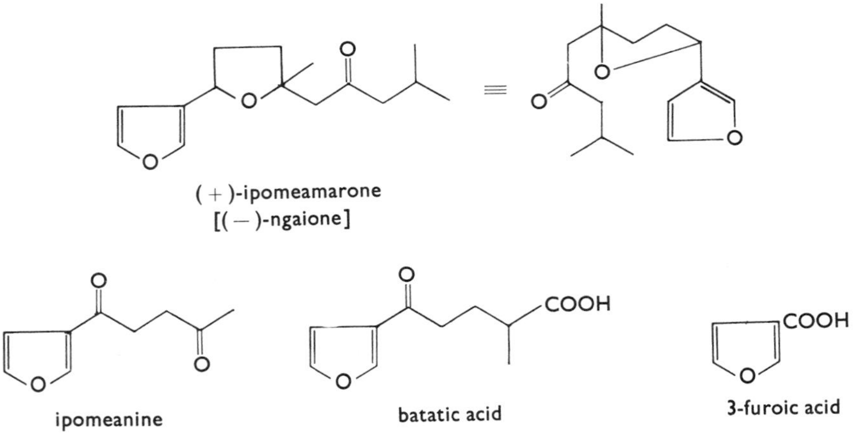

(+)-ipomeamarone
[(−)-ngaione]

ipomeanine   batatic acid   3-furoic acid

Fig. 9-3. Products Formed in Black-rotted Sweet Potato.

believed that ipomeamarone is a product of the metabolism, not of the fungus, but of the host, and it has been suggested that it is formed as a protective measure against

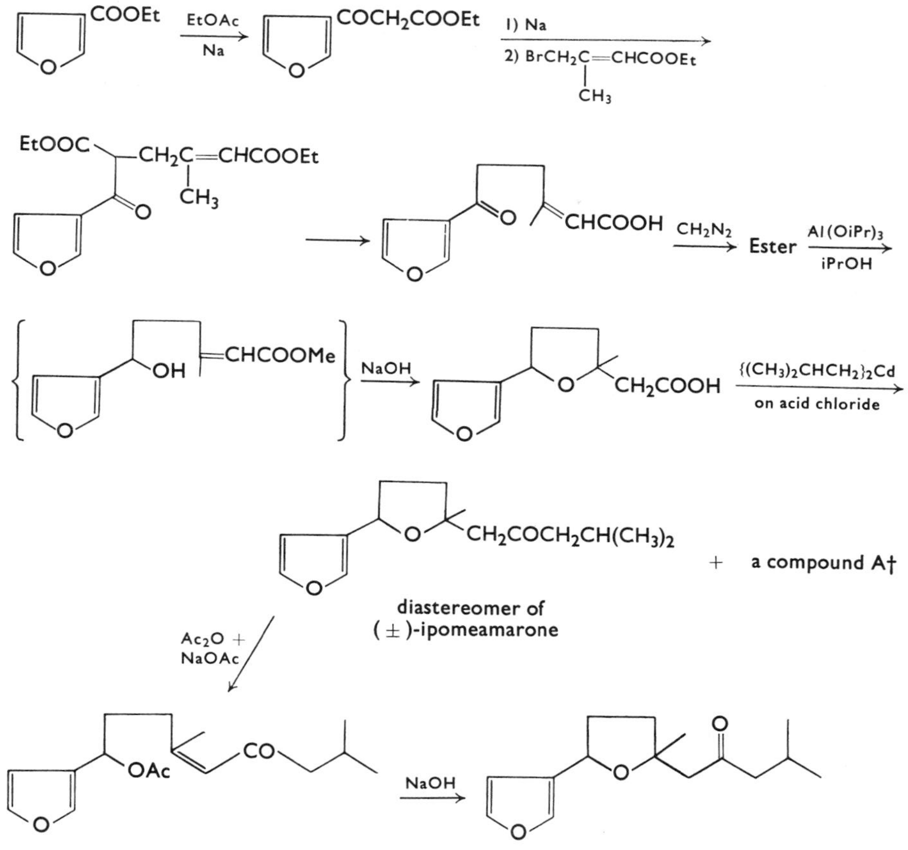

diastereomer of
(±)-ipomeamarone

Ac₂O +
NaOAc

+ a compound A†

(±)-ipomeamarone [Eq. 9-3]

---

† Compound A

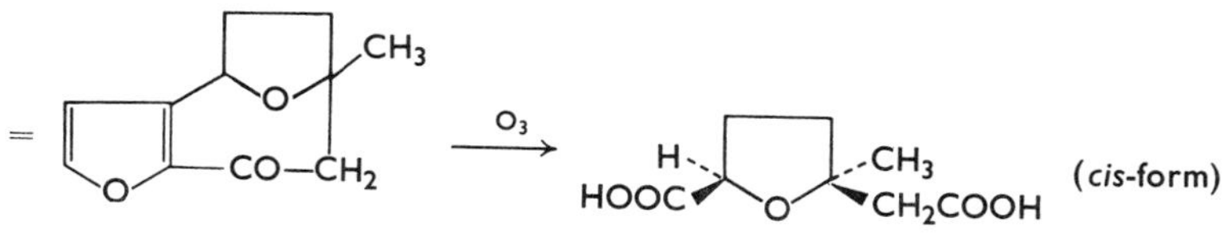

O₃ → (cis-form)

Thus, the conclusion is that the diastereomer of (±)-ipomeamarone is the *trans* form, and thus that ipomeamarone has the following stereochemistry:

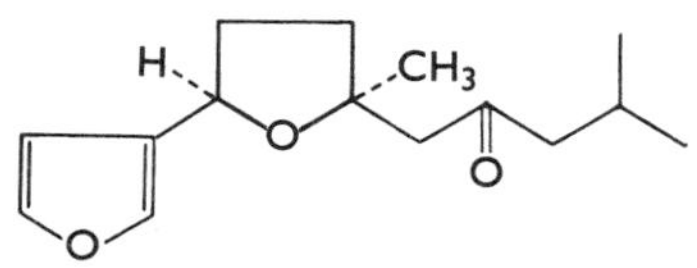

---

the infecting organism. Ipomeamarone is dextrorotatory. It is of interest to note that the enantiomorphic compound, $(-)$-ngaione, is found as a normal constituent in the New Zealand tree *Myoporum lactum* Forst. (fam. Myoporaceae). A synthesis of $(\pm)$-ipomeamarone $(=(\pm)$-ngaione) is described by the steps formulated in Eq. 9-3.

The action of sodium acetate-acetic anhydride upon ipomeamarone to produce the tetrahydrofuran-ring opened acetate is a reaction related to the reversal of a Michael addition. The saponification of this acetate is followed by reclosure of the tetrahydrofuran ring to give what appears to be the more stable of the two possible configurations; the product is $(\pm)$-ipomeamarone.

The biosynthetic origin of ipomeamarone has been studied with the use of ^{14}C-labeled acetate and mevalonic acid. Labeled ipomeamarone is produced, but the positions of the labeled carbon atoms have not been determined. In view of the adherence of the carbon skeleton to the regular isoprene rule, it is more than likely that ipomeamarone is a "regular" terpenoid compound.

9.4 Cyclic Sesquiterpenes

Cyclization of farnesol (as the pyrophosphate) can be viewed as proceeding by way of two intermediate carbonium ions, depending upon whether the precursor is *trans, trans* or *trans, cis*-farnesol (Eq. 9-4):

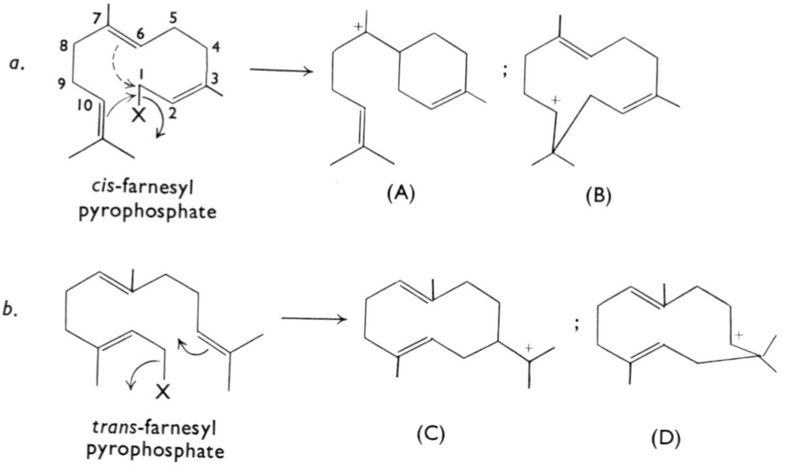

a.

cis-farnesyl
pyrophosphate   (A)   (B)

[Eq. 9-4]

b.

trans-farnesyl
pyrophosphate   (C)   (D)

Loss of a proton from the carbonium ion intermediate* A (Eq. 9-4) leads directly to γ-bisabolene, one of the most widely distributed of natural sesqui-

---

* The ionic intermediates will ordinarily be represented as the classical carbonium ions with localized charges so situated as to accommodate the reaction under discussion.

terpenes. Secondary alterations in the structure (double-bond isomerization, oxidation) give rise to the well known compounds γ-curcumene, turmerone, lanceol, and atlantone (Eq. 9-5a):

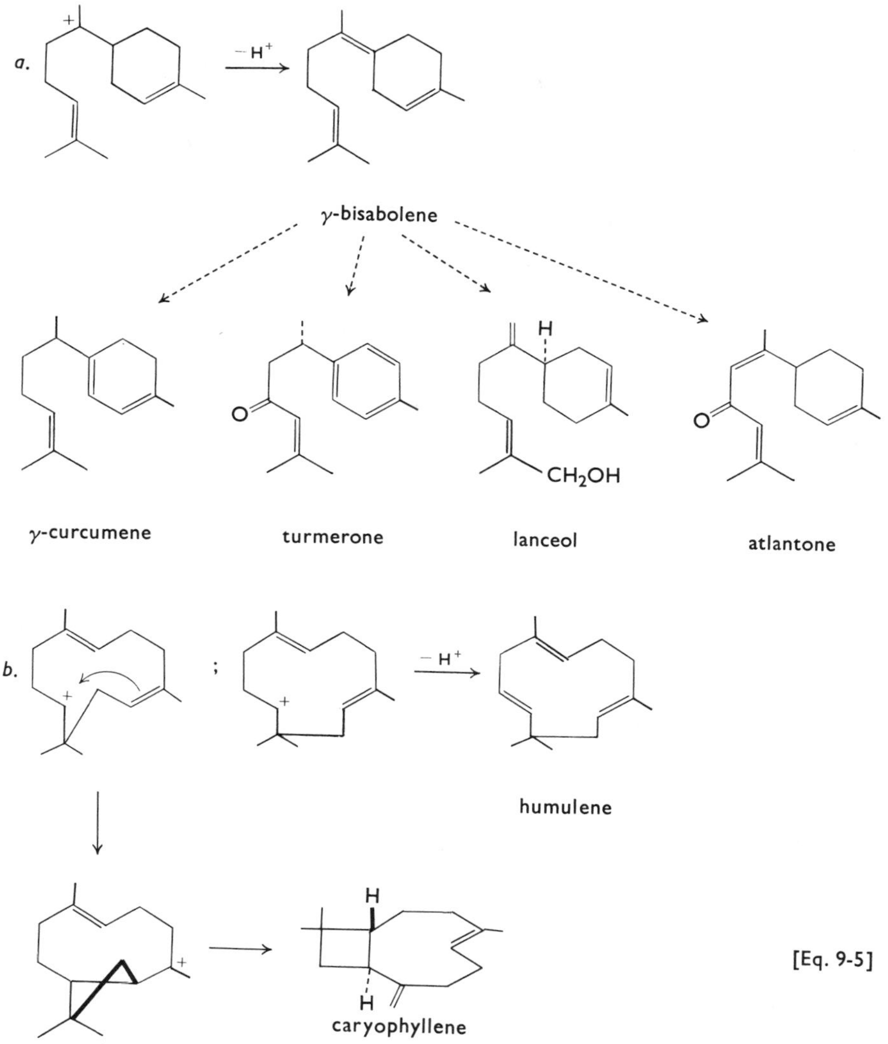

γ-bisabolene

γ-curcumene   turmerone   lanceol   atlantone

humulene

caryophyllene

[Eq. 9-5]

The carbonium ions B and D can be transformed by deprotonation or by attack of the 2,3-double bond to give the well known sesquiterpene hydrocarbons, humulene and caryophyllene (Eq. 9-5b).

By utilizing the four possible isomers of farnesol (*cis, cis*; *cis, trans*; *trans, cis*; and *trans, trans*), with appropriate skeletal rearrangements following the initial cycliza-tions, it is possible to account, at least on paper, for the formation of the large number of known sesquiterpenoid compounds. An extensive account of schemes of biogenesis based upon these principles will not be given here, for excellent reviews of this subject are available. One example, given to illustrate the manner in which such biosynthetic proposals are devised, is that of the suggested route of bio-synthesis of the tricyclic sesquiterpene, cedrene (to which are related cedrol and shellolic acid). The synthetic pathway is assumed to start with the formation of the ion derived by protonation of γ-bisabolene, followed by the changes shown in Eq. 9-6:

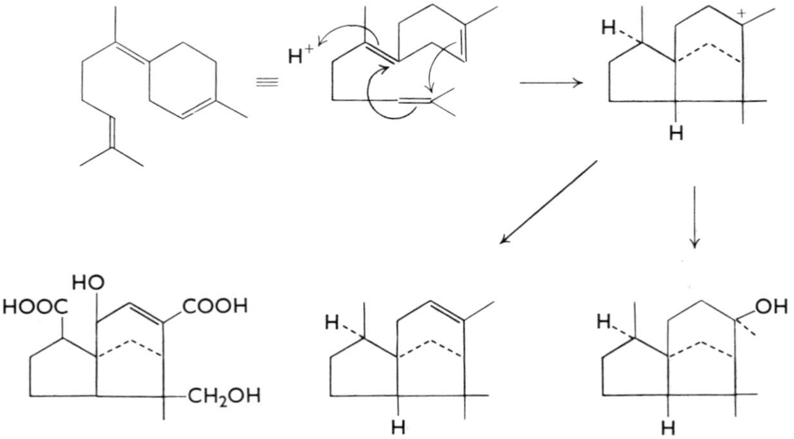

shellolic acid   cedrene †   cedrol   [Eq. 9-6]

_____

† Cedrene can also be drawn

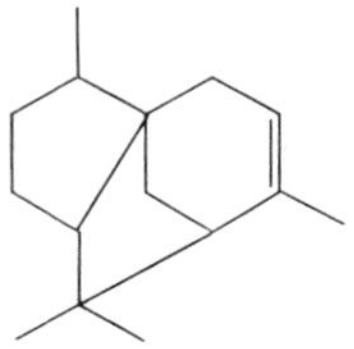

which shows more clearly the regular isoprenoid skeleton.

_____

The cedrane* ring system is of particular interest because of its generation by an *in vitro* transformation of a sesquiterpenoid quinone, perezone.

_____

* The ending -ane is used to denote the basic saturated hydrocarbon that possesses the ring system of the natural prototype.

9.5 Perezone

Perezone is an orange pigment found in plants of the genus *Perezia* (fam. Compositae). Early studies of perezone led to the conclusion that its structure was that shown as *a* in Fig. 9-4; but this was later shown to be incorrect. The NMR spectrum of perezone shows a signal for the methyl group on the quinone ring which is not a singlet as would be expected for structure *a* (Fig. 9-4), but is a well-defined doublet at δ 2.06 ppm with a coupling constant of about 1.8 cps. The single proton (δ 6.47) of the quinone ring also shows spin-spin coupling and appears as a quartet

(*a*) perezone (incorrect)   (*b*) perezone (correct)

Fig. 9-4. The Structure of Perezone.

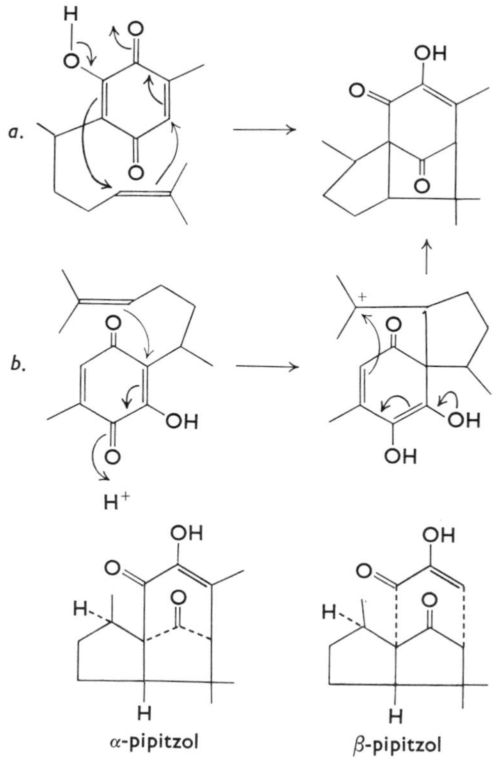

α-pipitzol   β-pipitzol

[Eq. 9-7]

with $J = 1.8$ cps. It is evident that the proton and the methyl group are adjacent and display allylic coupling; thus, the correct structure of perezone is b (Fig. 9-4).

These conclusions were supported by the study of the NMR spectrum of a synthetic compound having the structure of dihydro-a, in which the methyl and hydroxyl groups are in adjacent positions on the ring. The NMR spectrum of this compound was found to be almost identical with that of dihydroperezone, with the important exception that the signals for the quinonoid methyl group and ring hydrogen atom were sharp singlets at δ 1.95 and 6.5 ppm, respectively.

When perezone is heated or subjected to the action of sulfuric acid it undergoes rearrangement to a mixture of α- and β-pipitzols. Pipitzol is also a natural product, occurring in *Perezia* species as the mixture of the α- and β-compounds.

The pipitzols are stereoisomers having the cedrane-derived structures shown in Eq. 9-7. The mechanism of formation of the pipitzols from perezone has been formulated as shown in Eq. 9-7a; an alternative route, in which acid catalysis is invoked, is also shown (Eq. 9-7b):

It is of interest and perhaps of biosynthetic significance that the stereochemistry of α-pipitzol is the same as that of cedrene. It will be noticed that perezone could arise from α-pipitzol by the route formulated in Eq. 9-8. There is, however, no compelling reason to assume that perezone is formed in nature *via* a roundabout pathway which leads from a bisabolene-derived precursor, to a cedrene-derived intermediate and thence, as in Eq. 9-8, to perezone.

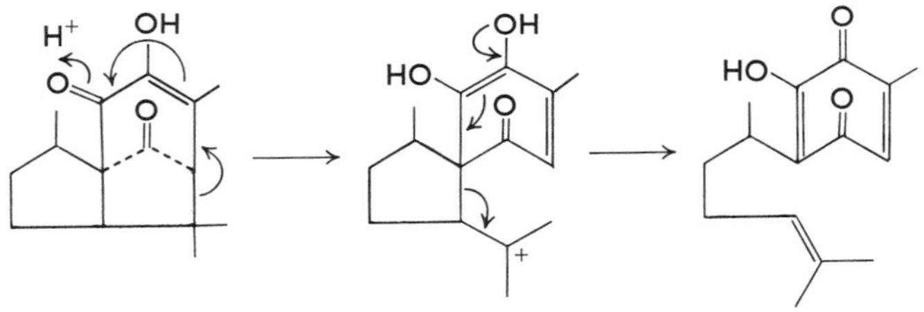

α-pipitzol   perezone   [Eq. 9-8]

9.6 Products Arising from *trans, trans*-Farnesol

2,3-*trans*-Farnesyl pyrophosphate may undergo solvolytic ring closure by the route shown in Eq. 9-4b. When the immediate carbonium ion is written in the symbolism of non-classical ions, it is easy to see that three kinds of sesquiterpenes may result from the common intermediate (Eq. 9-9). Naturally occurring compounds of all of these classes are well known; typical examples, corresponding to Eq. 9-9a, b, and c are (a) germacrone (and compounds to be discussed below); (b) humulene and zerumbone; and (c) maaliol (in which a subsequent cyclization has occurred to give the tricyclic compound):

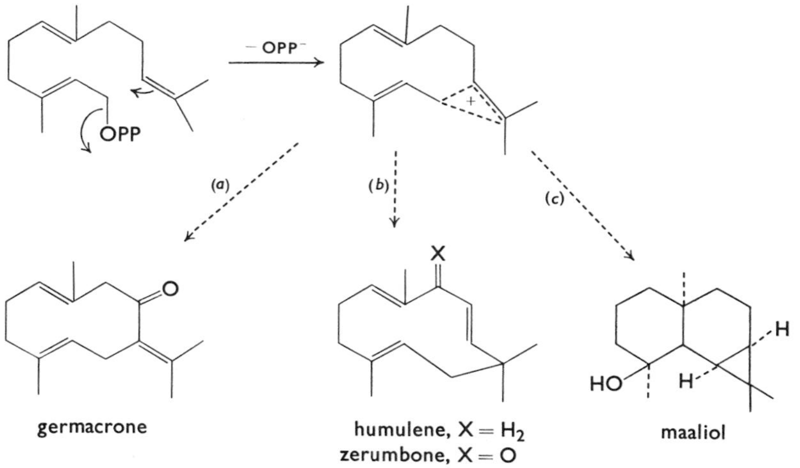
– OPP⁻
OPP
(a)
(b)
(c)
X
O
H
HO
H
germacrone
humulene, X = H2
zerumbone, X = O
maaliol

[Eq. 9-9]

The product of the initial ring closure shown in Eq. 9-9 appears most commonly to proceed to further products by way of the cyclodecadiene. The isopropyl group, which in this form carries the positive charge, can accept a hydroxyl group to give the side chain —C(OH)$(CH_3)_2$ found in a number of sesquiterpene alcohols, among them the compounds guaiol, bulnesol, occidol, and occidentalol (Fig. 9-5).

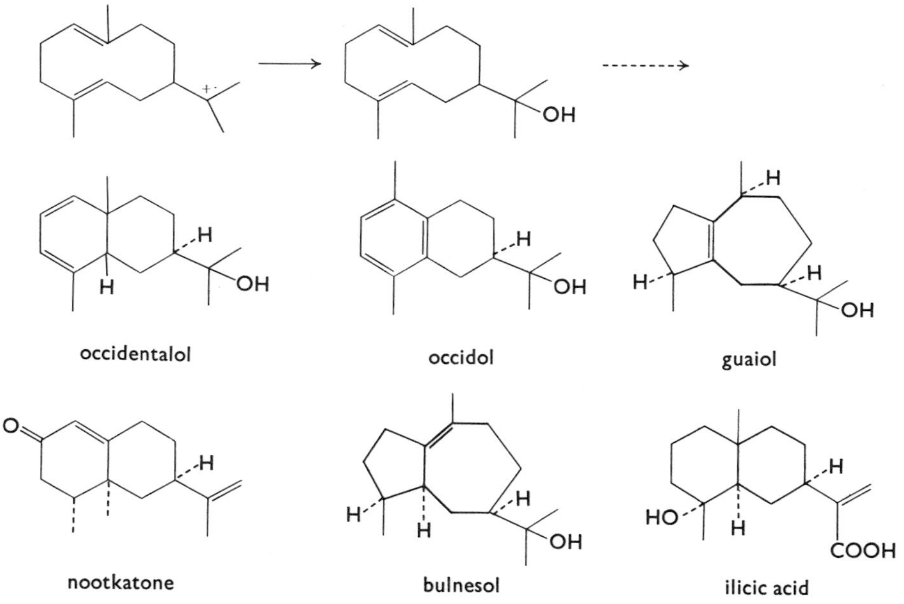
OH
H
H
OH
occidentalol
H
OH
occidol
H
H
H
OH
guaiol
O
H
nootkatone
H
H
H
OH
bulnesol
H
HO
H
COOH
ilicic acid

Fig. 9-5. Alteration of —$C^+(CH_3)_2$ Side Chain.

Loss of a proton from the $-\overset{+}{C}(CH_3)_2$ group to give the isopropenyl side chain, or oxidation to give a carboxylic acid are other courses open to the tertiary carbonium ion. Examples of these are shown in Fig. 9-5. It will be seen that the compounds shown in this figure possess various kinds of ring systems, belong to more than one stereochemical class, and in some cases have rearranged (and thus "irregular") carbon skeletons. Some of these features will be discussed in the following sections.

9.7 Bicyclic Compounds Derived from Farnesol

The intermediate cyclodecadiene (Fig. 9-5), with both double bonds in the *trans* configuration, can assume any of several conformations (Eq. 9-10), although the all-chair conformations *a* and *b* would appear to be sterically the most favorable and, indeed, can be shown to lead to the most commonly encountered compounds. Nevertheless, conformations *c*, *d*, and *e* are in principle capable of existence. Cyclization by transannular interaction of the double bonds, initiated by electrophilic attack (e.g., by a proton donor; i.e., $X = H$ in Eq. 9-10) leads in the various ways shown in the equation to perhydronaphthalenes (eudesmane derivatives) and perhydroazulenes (guaiane derivatives) with stereochemistry of various kinds. Examples of naturally occurring compounds of most of these types are known.

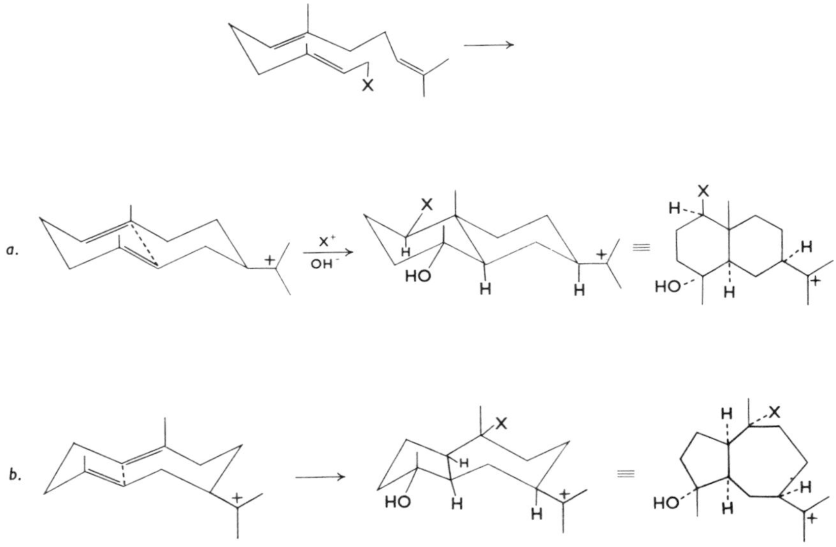

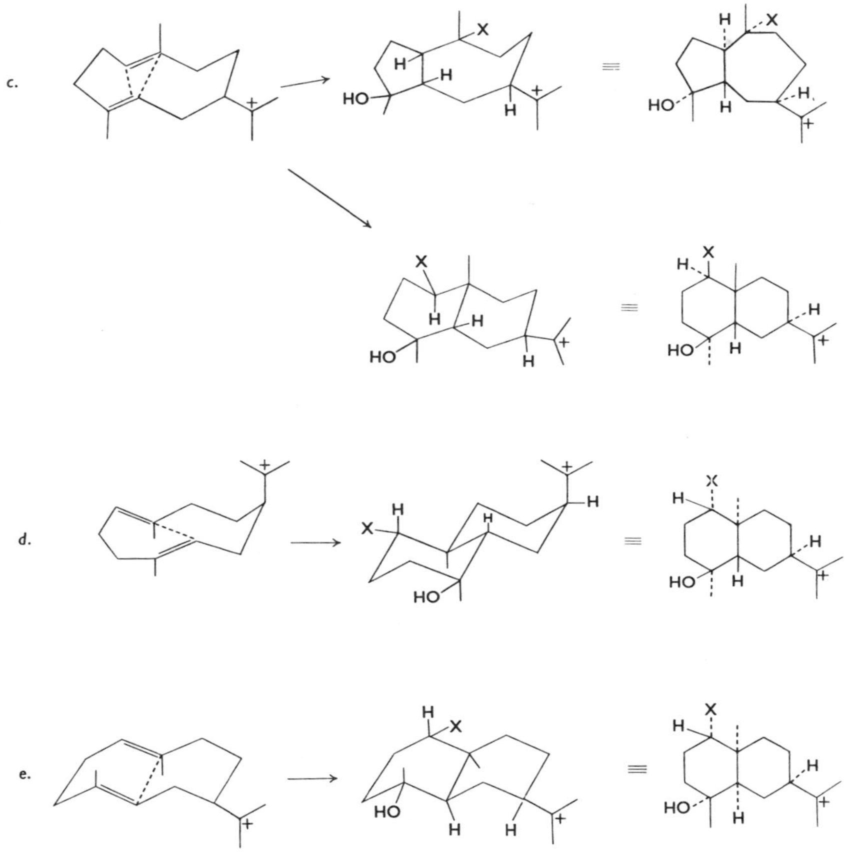

[Eq. 9-10]

It should be added here, without further comment, that it is possible to make further assumptions concerning both the configuration (i.e., one or both double bonds *cis*) and conformation of a cyclodecadiene intermediate derived from the one shown in Eq. 9-10, and thus to write proposed biosynthetic routes for many more sesquiterpene types. Speculations and proposals of these kinds may be found in the review articles cited at the beginning of this chapter.

9.8 Sesquiterpene Lactones

A large, structurally varied, and botanically closely allied class of sesquiter-penes is a group of lactones found distributed throughout plants of the family Compositae. In these compounds the isopropyl side chain has been modified to the oxidation state of a carboxylic acid. Introduction of oxygen into the ring provides the hydroxyl group with which the carboxyl group interacts to form the lactone ring.

The manner and stage of the biosynthetic steps in which the side-chain oxidation occurs are not known, for the necessary studies of the course of synthesis in living plants have not been performed. It is possible, however, to propose certain plausible conjectures, based upon known biosynthetic processes, to account for the formation of the several kinds of lactone rings that are found in this group of compounds.

It is clear at the outset that the change of the isopropenyl group (equivalent to the initial isopropyl carbonium ion) to the carboxylic acid or lactone is an oxidation process. Oxidation is, of course, a common metabolic process that can take a wide variety of forms, from simple dehydrogenation of saturated linkages ($-CH_2CH_2- \rightarrow CH=CH \rightarrow C\equiv C$; $CHOH \rightarrow C=O$) to more complex reactions in which oxygen is introduced into organic molecules. In the latter category are many reactions that are readily interpretable in terms of an initial epoxidation; or, what is chemically, if not biologically, equivalent, attack of what may be regarded as protonated oxygen upon a carbon-carbon double bond. These courses are outlined in formal terms in Eq. 9-11:

$$
\begin{array}{ccc}
-\overset{|}{C}=\overset{|}{C}- & \xrightarrow{\text{"HO}^+\text{"}} & -\overset{+}{\underset{|}{C}}-\overset{\overset{OH}{|}}{\underset{|}{C}}- \\
\end{array}
$$

$$\text{"O-donor"} \qquad \qquad H_2O$$

$$
\begin{array}{cccccc}
-\overset{O}{\overset{/\backslash}{\underset{|}{C}-\underset{|}{C}}}- & \underset{-H^+}{\overset{H^+}{\rightleftharpoons}} & -\overset{\overset{H}{|}\ \overset{+}{O}\ }{\overset{/\backslash}{\underset{|}{C}-\underset{|}{C}}}- & \xrightarrow{H_2O} & -\overset{\overset{OH}{|}}{\underset{|}{C}}-\overset{\overset{OH}{|}}{\underset{|}{C}}- & \qquad \text{[Eq. 9-11]}
\end{array}
$$

It will be recalled that among the examples of compounds containing O- and C-prenyl side chains (Chap. 8) there are numerous examples of epoxides and the glycols corresponding to them. It is apparent that the supposition that initial epoxidation (or attack of the hydroxonium ion, OH^+) of a carbon-carbon double bond can provide an acceptable starting point for hypotheses of many biological oxidations.

The application of this concept to the formation of the carboxyl group of the sesquiterpene lactones provides a versatile and satisfactory explanation for the biosynthesis of the numerous oxidation states of the isopropyl residue. This scheme is given in Eq. 9-12.

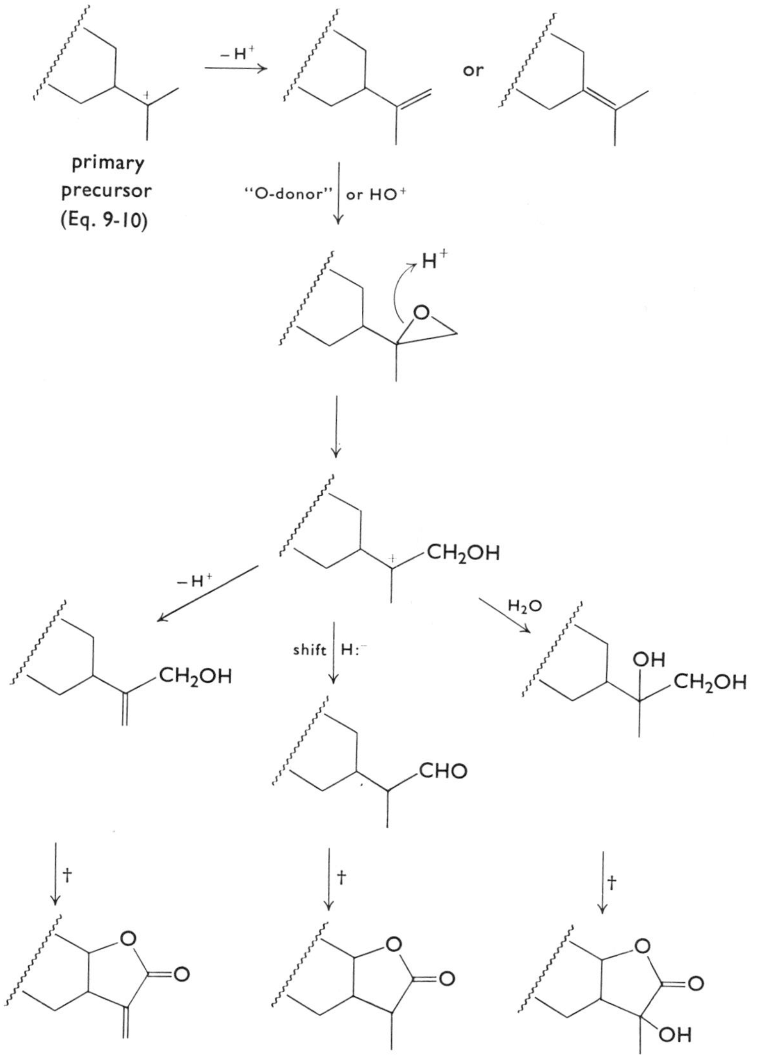

$$[\text{Eq. 9-12}]$$

† Following introduction of oxygen into the ring, and further oxidation.

A number of facts support this overall concept.* One of the most persuasive is the presence in a single plant source of a series of compounds in which the progress

* Little can be said with respect to the mechanistic details of the primary oxidation step, for the enzymatic processes that provide what is in effect peroxidic oxygen are not yet known with certainty. The symbol OH+ is a convenient but arbitrary device.

of oxidation from the alcohol, as the initial product, to the lactone, as the end product, can be seen. Costus oil (from *Saussurea Lappa*, fam. Compositae) contains a group of compounds in whose structures (Eq. 9-13) can be seen the progression of oxidative change outlined in part in Eq. 9-12:

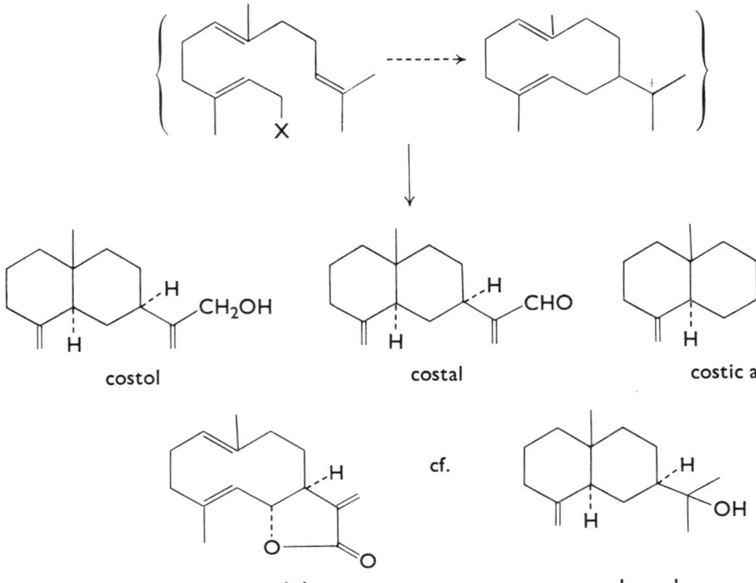

costol   costal   costic acid

costunolide   cf.   eudesmol   [Eq. 9-13]

With the establishment of the lactone ring (as in costunolide, Eq. 9-13), by the oxygenation of the ring, subsequent changes in (a) the manner in which the cyclodecadienolide (germacranolide)* ring is altered by cyclization, and (b) the introduction of oxygen and double bonds into the ring system gives rise to the formation in nature of a large number of lactones of this general class. A number of sesquiterpene lactones showing the kinds of secondary alterations that are known are shown in Fig. 9-6.

The probable biogenesis of these compounds can be indicated only in general terms. The stereochemical requirements that have been discussed (some of which are those shown in Eq. 9-10) often suggest the configurations that the final products possess; and, conversely, when the final configurations are determined by experimental methods, the nature of the precursor can often be inferred.

---

* The ending "-olide" is a generic term for lactones of the kind exemplified by costunolide. The word "germacranolide" is derived from that of the 10-ring sesquiterpene, germacrone. Similarly, "eudesmanolides" (also called "santanolides") are 6/6 ring compounds (perhydronaphthalenes), and "guaianolides" are 5/7 ring compounds (perhydroazulenes).

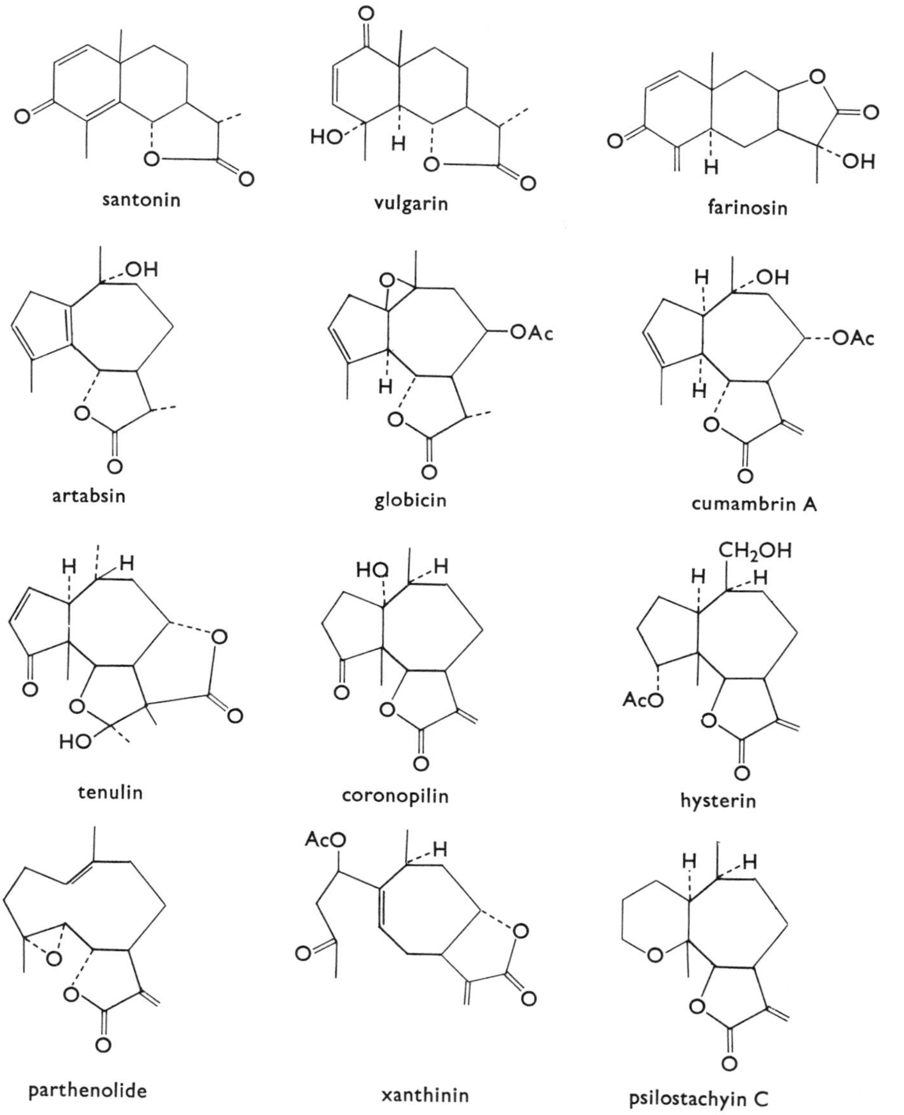

Fig. 9-6. Naturally Occurring Sesquiterpene Lactones.

In Eq. 9-14 is shown a detailed (and hypothetical) course for the synthesis of a number of compounds that appear to arise by cyclization of the precursor shown in Eq. 9-10a. The stereochemistry of these naturally occurring compounds is known, and it will be seen that it is consistent with the views expressed in the foregoing discussion.

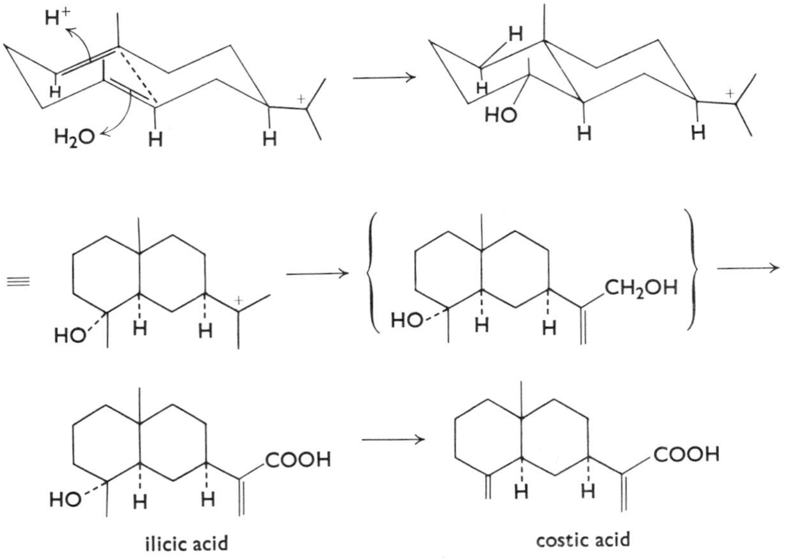

ilicic acid   costic acid   [Eq. 9-14]

9.9 Co-occurrence of Structurally Related Compounds

In the earlier years of speculation upon the biosynthetic origins of naturally occurring compounds, before the development of modern methods of investigation, one of the useful guides to conjecture was the comparison of the structures of a group of compounds found in a single plant or in plants having a close botanical relationship. This device is still useful, for despite the success of isotopic tracer methods in elucidating biosynthetic pathways, many details of the structures and origins of natural compounds remain to be firmly established. It is helpful and for the most part probably valid to inspect the structures of co-occurring compounds and to attempt to perceive therefrom their biosynthetic interrelationships. Enough is now known about the principal routes of biosynthesis to permit the conclusion that a group of closely related compounds occurring in a single plant are all derived by secondary alteration of a common progenitor. Consequently, to be able to construct a hypothesis based upon the principle of a common precursor and its alteration by mechanistically acceptable steps is to provide a compelling argument for the biosynthetic processes that are proposed. Indeed, this principle is frequently of great value in predicting the structures of new compounds derived from sources that are the same as or closely allied to those from which compounds of known structure have already been obtained.

The coniferous plant *Thujopsis dolabrata* (fam. Cupressaceae) has yielded a large number of terpenoid compounds, the comparison of whose structures provides illustrations of some of the biosynthetical relationships that have been discussed above. In Fig. 9-7 are assembled the compounds found in this plant by several investigators.

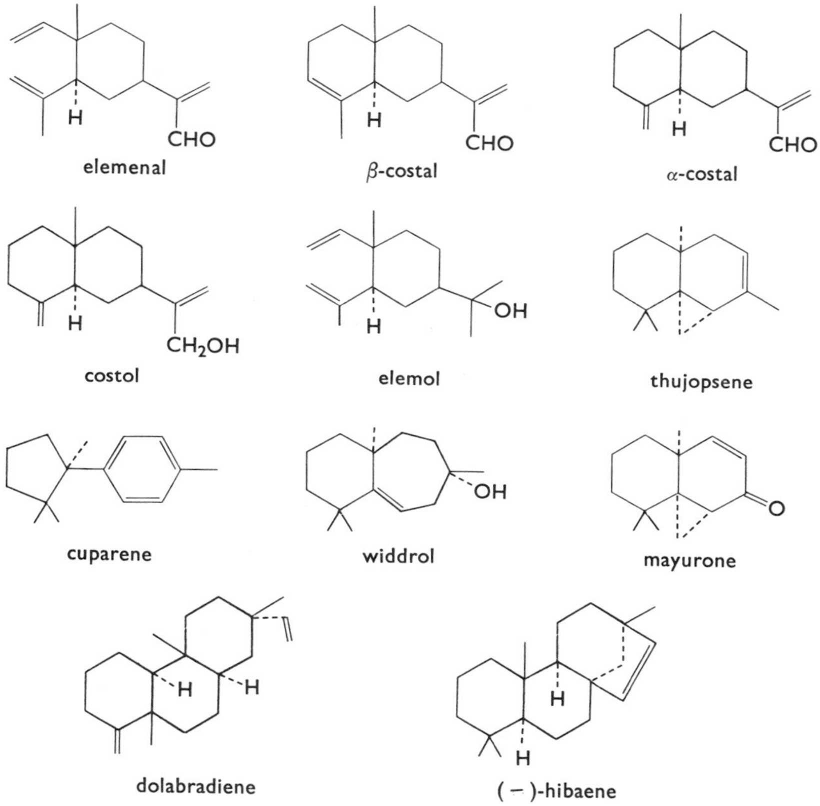

elemenal

β-costal

α-costal

costol

elemol

thujopsene

cuparene

widdrol

mayurone

dolabradiene

(−)-hibaene

Fig. 9-7. Terpenoid Constituents of *Thujopsis dolabrata*.

It is seen that *T. dolabrata* contains sesquiterpenes of five structural types: elemane, eudesmane, thujopsane, widdrane, and cuparane, in addition to diter- penes (Chap. 10) containing an unrearranged (hibaene) and a rearranged (dolar- bradiene) skeleton. In Eq. 9-15 is shown in partial detail a rational scheme for the generation of several of the structural classes mentioned, starting from γ-bisabolene. The genesis of the eudesmane structure has been discussed in foregoing sections.

The presence of these numerous sesquiterpenes and diterpenes in *T. dolabrata* is evidence of an active terpenoid metabolism, and of the presence of a number of specific enzyme systems capable of directing the many divergent, stereochemically distinct, reaction pathways.

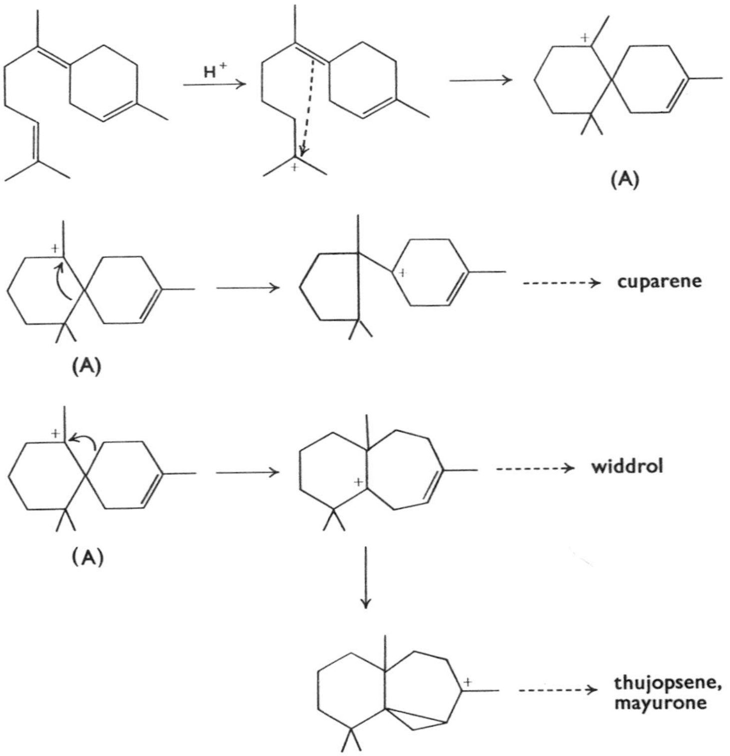

(A)

--------→ cuparene

(A)

--------→ widdrol

(A)

--------→ thujopsene,
             mayurone

[Eq. 9-15]

It is clear that the chemist's examination of the constituents of plant materials should be as complete and exhaustive as possible, for the greater the number of compounds that can be obtained from a single plant, the greater the likelihood that their structures will disclose information of biochemical significance. It is, for example, unlikely that the structure of a *single* compound isolated from a *single* plant species will provide positive evidence concerning pathways of biosynthesis, although it may often provide a basis for interesting conjecture as to its origin.

X CHAPTER

10.1 Acyclic Diterpenes
10.2 Monocyclic Diterpenes
10.3 Bicyclic Diterpenes
10.4 Polycyclic Diterpenes
10.5 Modification of Substituent Groups
10.6 Aromatic and Quinonoid Diterpenes
10.7 Miscellaneous Structural Modifications

REFERENCES FOR FURTHER READING

1. D. Arigoni; J. H. Richards, and J. B. Hendrickson; L. Ruzicka; J. D. Bu'Lock; J. W. Cornforth; R. B. Clayton, have been referred to in preceding chapters, and are pertinent to this chapter as well.
2. G. Ponsinet, G. Ourisson, and A. C. Oehlschlager, *Systematic Aspects of the Distribution [in plants] of Di-and Triterpenes,* in Recent Advances in Phytochemistry, T. J. Mabry, Ed., Appleton-Century-Crofts, New York, 1968.
3. H. J. Nicholas, *The Biogenesis of Terpenes in Plants,* in Biogenesis of Natural Compounds, 2nd Ed., P. Bernfeld, Ed., Pergamon Press, Oxford, 1967.
4. G. Weissmann, *The Distribution of Terpenoids,* in Comparative Phytochemistry, T. Swain, Ed., Academic Press, New York, 1966.
5. G. A. Ellestad, B. Green, A. Harris, W. B. Whalley, and H. Smith *Rosenonolactone,* J. Chem. Soc., (1965), 7246.
6. C. Djerassi, B. Green, W. B. Whalley, and C. G. DeGrazia, *The Absolute Configuration of Rosenono- and Rosolo-lactone,* J. Chem. Soc., (1966), 624.
7. B. E. Cross and K. Norton, *The Role of Gibberellins A-13, and A-14 in the Biosynthesis of Gibberellic Acid,* Tetrahedron Letters, (1966), 6003.
8. H. Kakisawa and Y. Inouye, *Total Synthesis of Tanshinone-I, Tanshinone-II, and Cryptotanshinone,* Chem. Comm., (1968), no. 21, 1327.

Diterpenoid Compounds

10.1 Acyclic Diterpenes

Combination of four C_5-pyrophosphate units in the manner already described leads to a C_{20} compound. In its simplest form, as the direct product of the tetramerization process, this is "regularly" isoprenoid, consisting of four head-to-tail-linked units (Eq. 10-1).

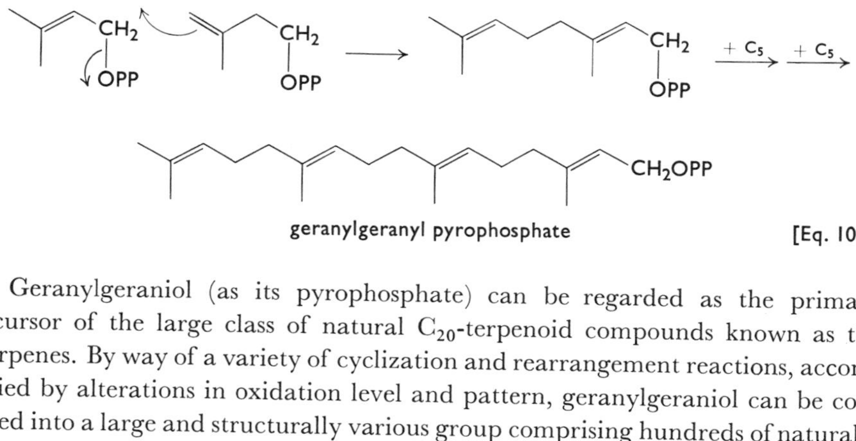

geranylgeranyl pyrophosphate

[Eq. 10-1]

Geranylgeraniol (as its pyrophosphate) can be regarded as the primary precursor of the large class of natural C_{20}-terpenoid compounds known as the diterpenes. By way of a variety of cyclization and rearrangement reactions, accompanied by alterations in oxidation level and pattern, geranylgeraniol can be converted into a large and structurally various group comprising hundreds of naturally occurring compounds that are widely distributed in higher plants and fungi.

Acyclic diterpenes (i.e., C_{20} compounds corresponding to ocimene, geraniol, farnesene, farnesol, etc.) are rare in nature. Evidently the multiply unsaturated precursor, to which are available a number of ways in which the double bonds can interact, is strongly predisposed to cyclization reactions, and seldom survives as an open-chain compound. Geranyllinalool has been discovered as a constituent of oil

291

of jasmine; phytol is universally distributed in green plants as a component of the chlorophyll molecule, in which it is present in ester combination, and as component parts of vitamins E and K (Fig. 10-1):

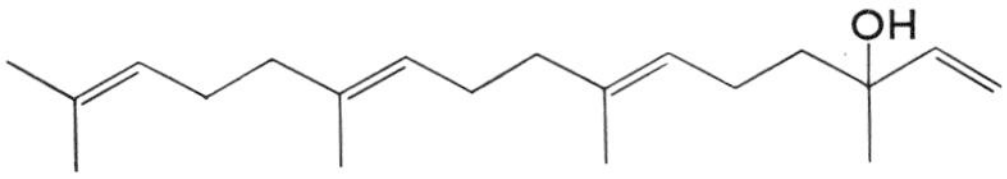

geranyllinaloöl

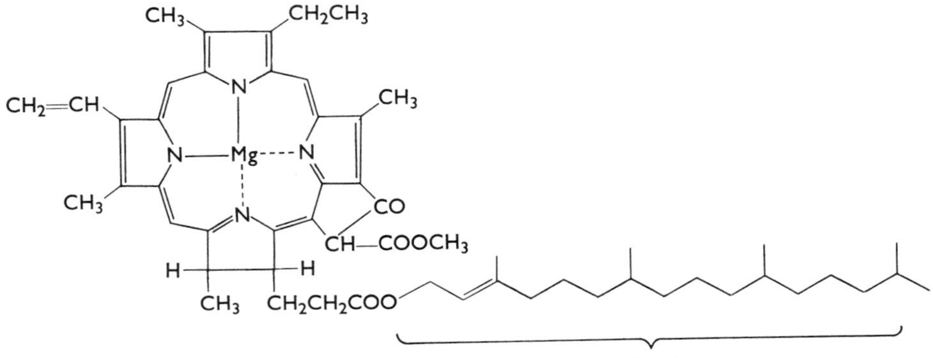

phytol

chlorophyll a

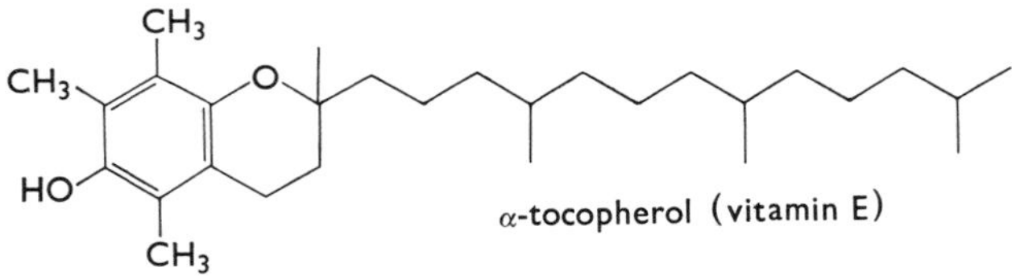

α-tocopherol (vitamin E)

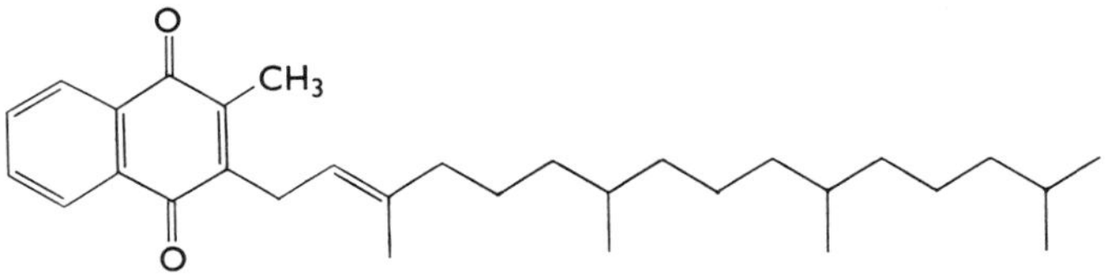

vitamin K₁

Fig. 10-1. Compounds Containing Diterpenoid Units.

The origin of phytol is undoubtedly by way of the mevalonate pathway of terpenoid biosynthesis. It has been shown that corn seedlings can utilize geranylgeraniol and geranyllinaloöl (tritium-labeled) in the synthesis of the phytol residue of chlorophyll. The manner and enzymatic mechanisms of the reduction of the double bonds of geranylgeraniol to form the mono-unsaturated phytol are not known in detail, but it can be assumed that the reduction takes place at a late stage, following the primary condensations of the isopentenyl units. Whether reduction of the double bonds takes place before or after the C_{20} unit is combined in the chlorophyll, vitamin E, or vitamin K molecules is not known.

10.2 Monocyclic Diterpenes

The most widely known and important of the monocyclic C_{20} isoprenoid compounds of nature is vitamin A_1, or retinol. Retinol does not occur in plants, but is a common constituent of vertebrate animal organisms, in which it is formed by the cleavage of C_{40}-carotenoids. Retinol (principally in the form of esters with fatty acids) is produced by the oxidative cleavage of carotenoids that possess at least one β-ionone-derived ring; the process is believed to take place in the intestine, and the retinol formed is stored in the liver and in fatty tissue (Eq. 10-2).

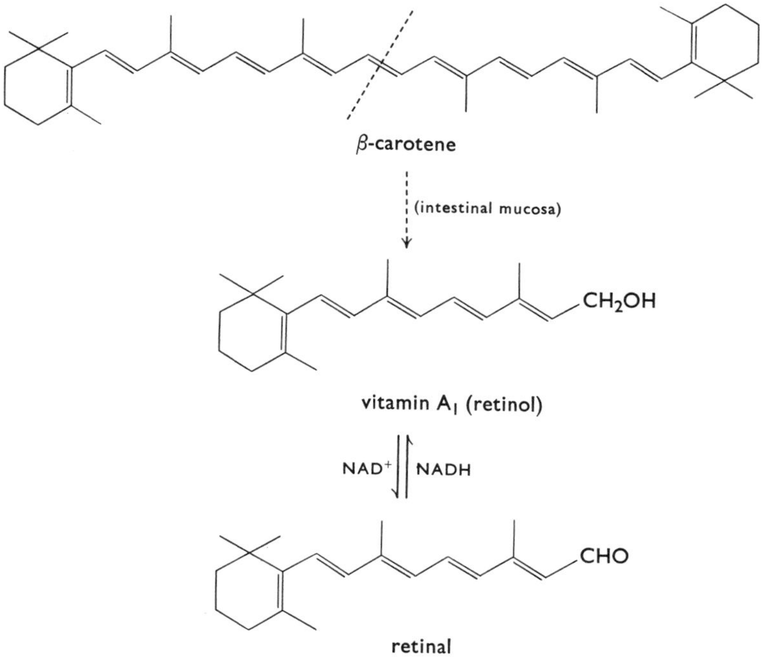

β-carotene

(intestinal mucosa)

vitamin A₁ (retinol)

NAD⁺ NADH

retinal

[Eq. 10-2]

Of the several known physiological actions of retinol in its role as a vitamin, the most thoroughly investigated and best understood is in the process of vision. A chromoprotein, rhodopsin ("visual purple"), found in the vertebrate retina, consists of a combination of a protein, opsin, with 11-*cis*-retinal. Upon illumination of the retina, a nerve impulse is generated and the rhodopsin undergoes a sequence of changes which result ultimately in the dissociation of retinal (now the all *trans* isomer) from the opsin, with a consequent "bleaching" of the visual pigment. Reconstitution of the visual pigment by the action of enzyme systems of the retina is brought about by isomerization of all-*trans* retinal to the 11-*cis* compound and recombination with opsin. The pigment is then prepared for another visual event.

The exhaustion of the visual pigment of the retinal rods by exposure to light, and the need for adequate supplies of vitamin A to maintain the capacity for vision under low light intensity ("night vision"), account for the known observations that adaptation to night vision after exposure to light is a measurably slow process, and one result of vitamin A deficiency is "night blindness."

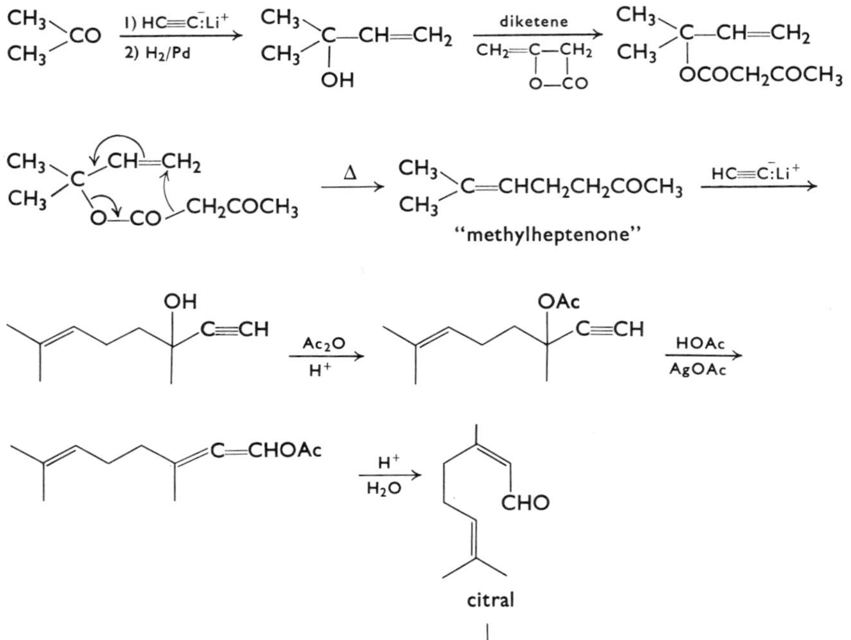

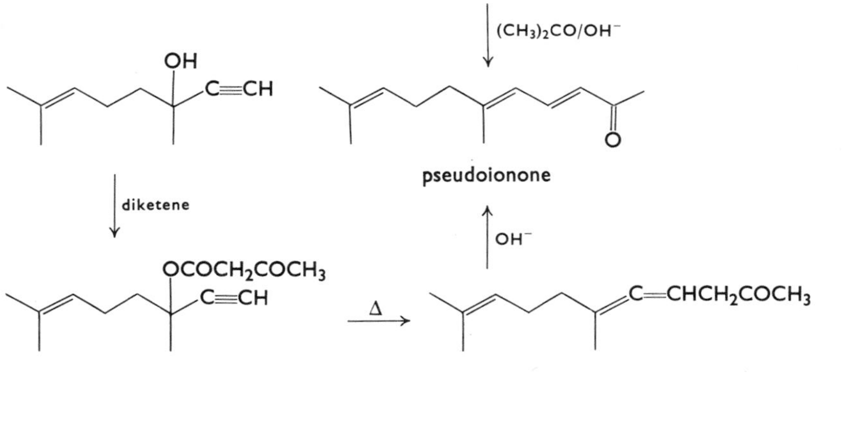

c.

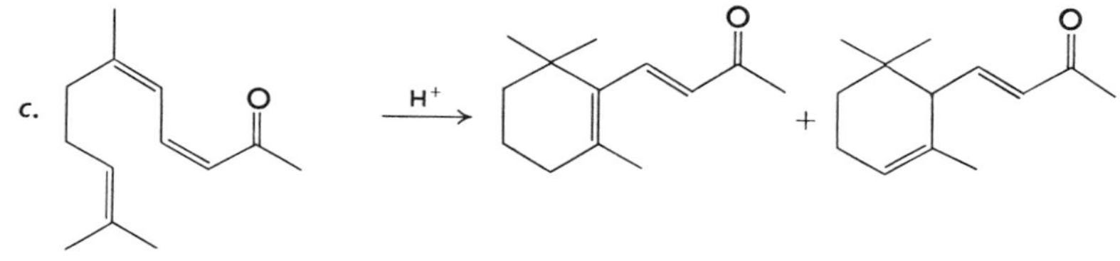

$$[Eq. 10-3]$$

pseudoionone   β-ionone   α-ionone

Vitamin A has been synthesized in a number of ways, and is now prepared commercially in large quantities to fill the needs of both human and animal nutrition. One synthesis is shown below. β-Ionone, synthesized from citral or from dehydrolinalool (Eq. 10-3) is converted to the C_{14} aldehyde (Eq. 10-4a) by means of the Darzens reaction. Condensation of the C_{14} aldehyde with the six-carbon acetylenic alcohol (Eq. 10-4b) leads to an intermediate which by controlled hydrogenation and dehydration gives all-*trans* retinol (Eq. 10-4c).

a.

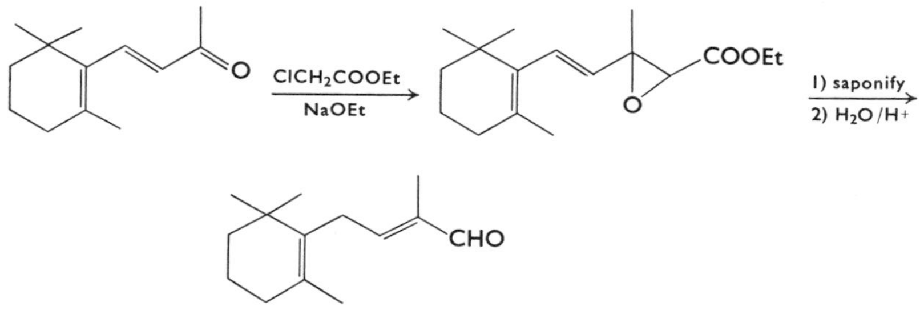

$$\xrightarrow[\text{NaOEt}]{\text{ClCH}_2\text{COOEt}}$$

$$\xrightarrow[\text{2) H}_2\text{O/H}^+]{\text{1) saponify}}$$

(I)

b. $CH_3COCH{=}CH_2 + HC{\equiv}C{:}^-Li^+ \longrightarrow HC{\equiv}C{-}\underset{\underset{CH_3}{|}}{\overset{\overset{OH}{|}}{C}}{-}CH{=}CH_2 \xrightarrow{H^+}$

$$HC{\equiv}C{-}\underset{\underset{CH_3}{|}}{C}{=}CHCH_2OH \xrightarrow{EtMgBr} BrMgC{\equiv}C{-}\underset{\underset{CH_3}{|}}{C}{=}CHCH_2OMgBr$$

(II)

c. I + II $\longrightarrow$

$$\xrightarrow[\substack{\text{2) Ac}_2\text{O} \\ \text{3) I}_2}]{\text{1) H}_2\text{/Pd}}$$

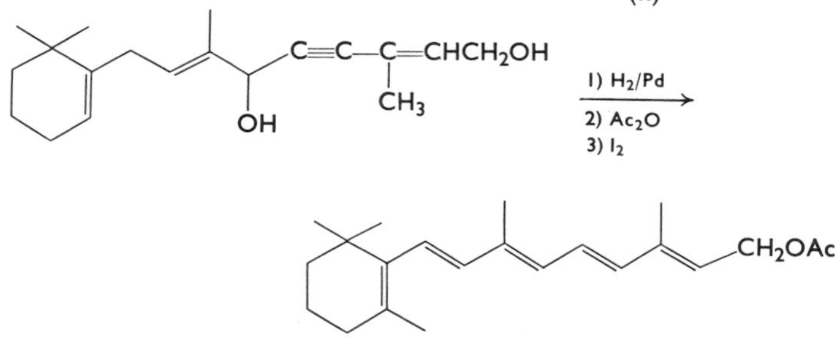

vitamin A₁ acetate $$[Eq. 10-4]$$

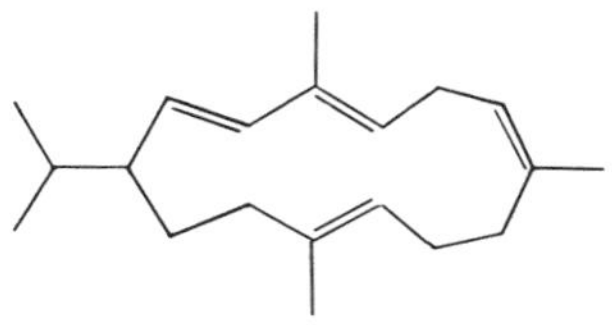

cembrene† 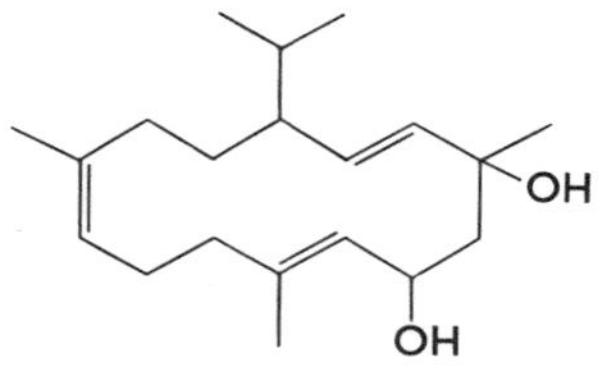   4,8,13-duvatriene-1,3-diol††

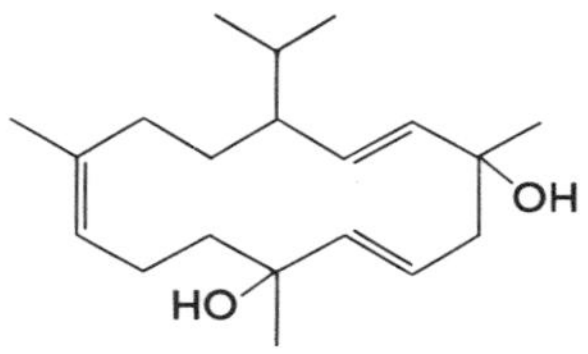

3,8,13-duvatriene-1,5-diol†† 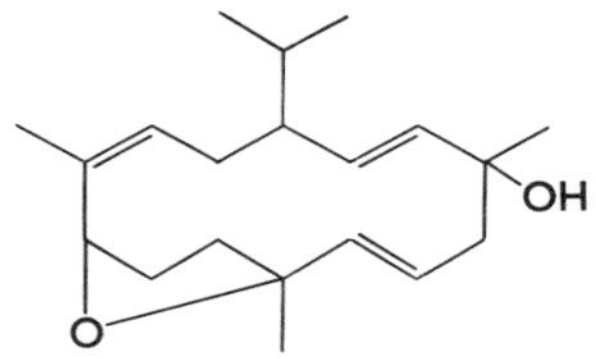   5,8-oxido-3,9,13-duva-
                                             triene-1-ol††

Fig. 10-2.

† from *Pinus* species.
†† from tobacco.

The formation of sesquiterpenes containing ten-membered rings by the cyclization of farnesyl pyrophosphate (Chap. 9) finds its parallel in the case of the diterpenes. As would be expected from stereochemical considerations, the fourteen-
membered rings formed in the latter case are infrequent in nature, and only a few
are known. Cembrene, a constituent of the oleoresin of *Pinus albicaulis*, and a group of
closely related compounds found in tobacco smoke and in flue-cured tobacco leaves,
representatives of this group of monocyclic diterpenes, have been assigned the
structures shown in Fig. 10-2. The biogenesis of these compounds from geranyl-

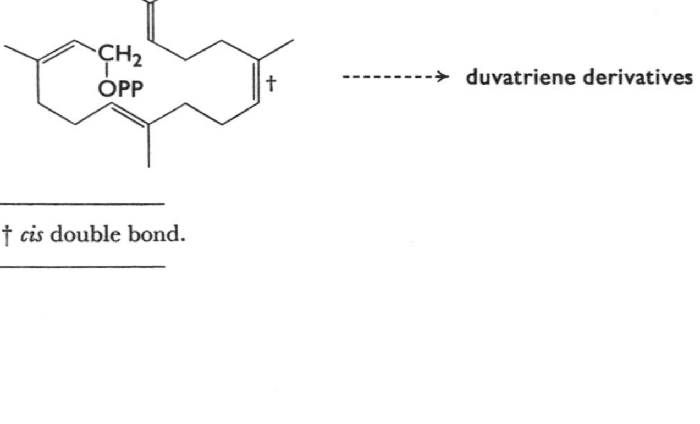

--------→ cembrene

--------→ duvatriene derivatives   [Eq. 10-5]

† *cis* double bond.

geranyl pyrophosphate can be represented in general terms as in Eq. 10-5; it will be noted that the formation of these compounds requires the presence of a *cis* configuration at one or another of the "inner" double bonds in the C_{20} precursor.

10.3 Bicyclic Diterpenes

The most common cyclizations of geranylgeraniol are initiated by electrophilic attack upon the terminal double bond, accompanied by stereoelectronically controlled, concerted ring closure. The process, which will be considered in further detail when triterpenoid and steroid synthesis is discussed, leads to a cationic intermediate which, by subsequent loss of a proton, capture of a nucleophile, further cyclization, or methyl migration, can lead to a wide variety of naturally occurring diterpenoid compounds.

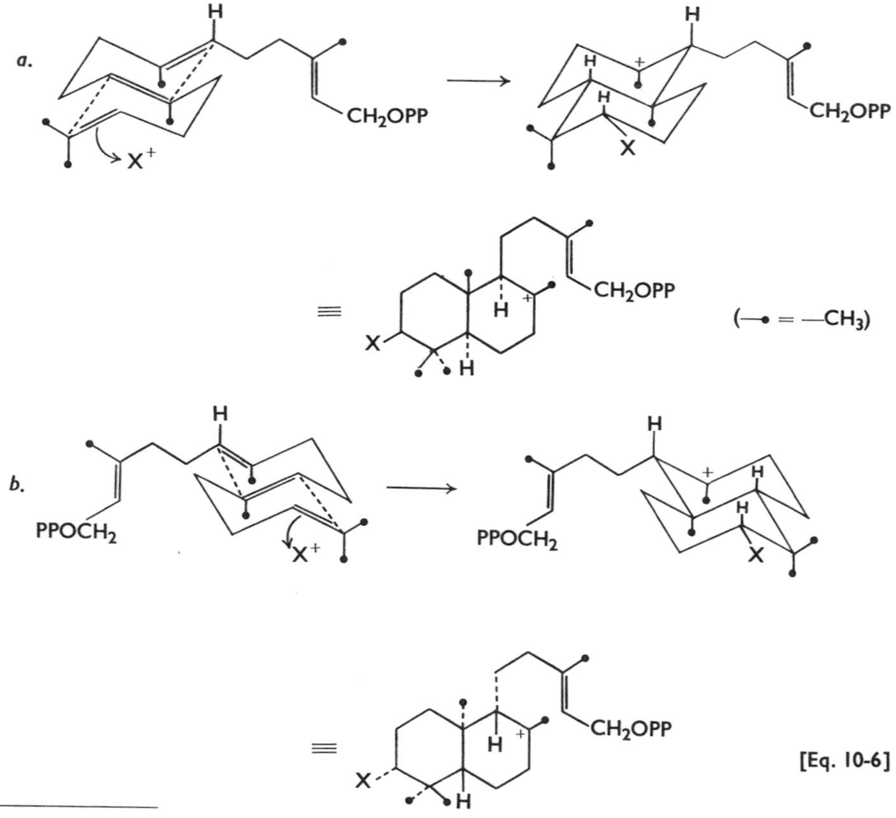

[Eq. 10-6]

Note: If X represents OH, the true biological process may in fact be a cyclization initiated by electrophilic attack upon an initial 2,3-epoxide. See the discussion of squalene cyclization, Chapter 11.

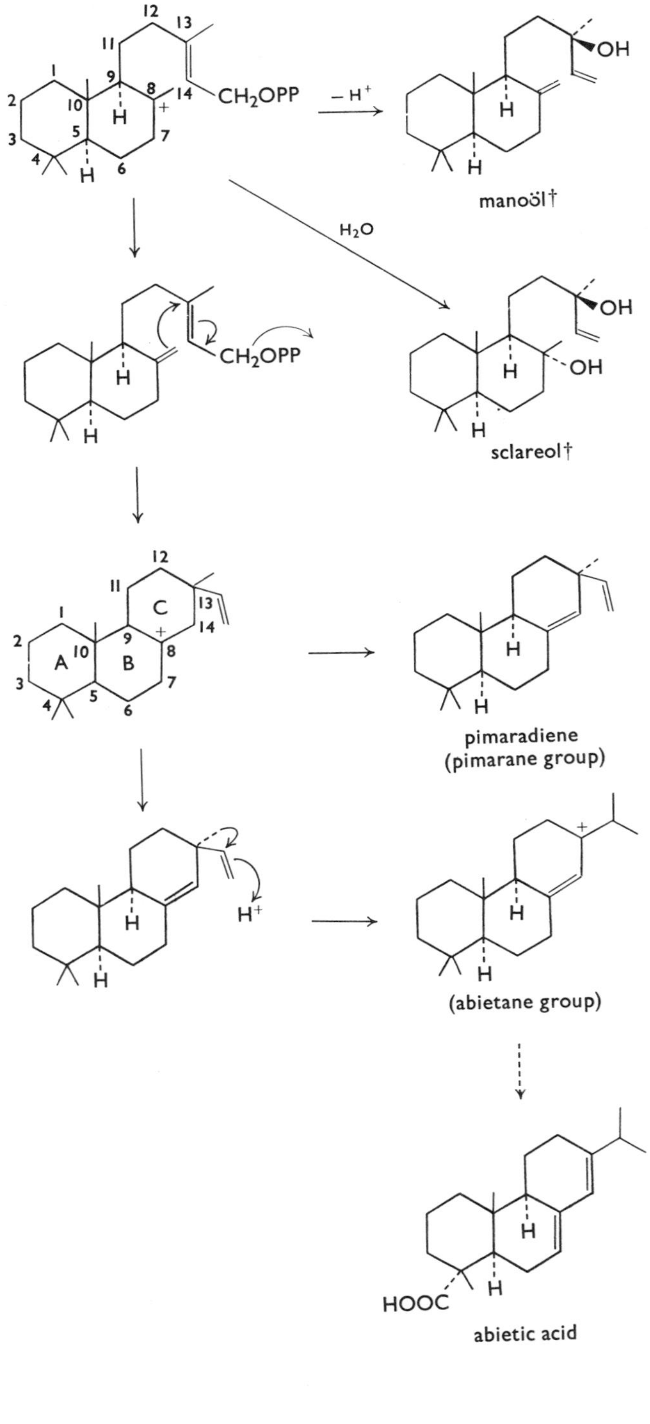
CH2OPP
− H+
OH
manoöl†
H2O
OH
OH
sclareol†
CH2OPP
A
B
C
pimaradiene
(pimarane group)
H+
(abietane group)
HOOC
abietic acid

[Eq. 10-7]

The initial cyclization is shown in diagrammatic form in Eq. 10-6. Two (enantiomeric) intermediates can arise by appropriate disposition upon an enzyme surface, both of which, it can be seen, have identical relative stereochemical features.

The *trans-anti-trans* configuration of the A/B rings of the bicyclic cation produced in this cyclization is clearly the consequence of the chair-like conformation of the folded chain of the precursor.

Further possible transformations of the initial cation are many, and nature affords examples of a wide variety of diterpenes that can be derived by conventional rearrangement processes. In the equations below are shown outlines of some of the changes that lead to known naturally occurring diterpenoid compounds. It will be noted that while the ring closure to form the bicyclic ring system proceeds in a consistent manner to produce a *trans* A/B ring junction, and a *trans* relationship between the C-9 hydrogen atom and the C-10 methyl group, the stereochemistry of the substituents that eventually make up the C-ring and its attached groups is not ordained by the same kind of stereoelectronic requirements. Thus, compounds are known with both configurations at C-13, and with corresponding variations in the stereochemistry of tricyclic (A, B, C rings) and tetracyclic (A, B, C and bridged-C rings) diterpenes.

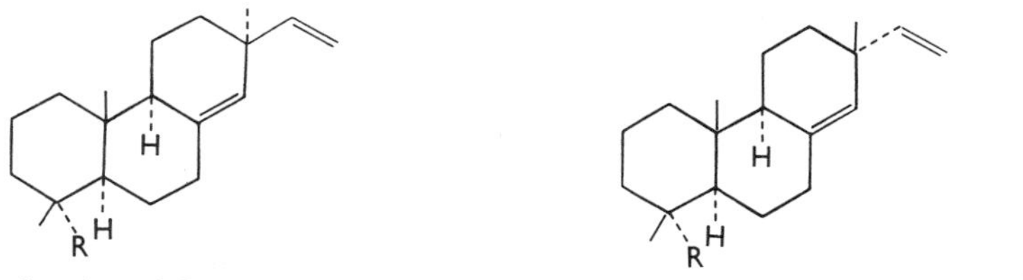

pimaric acid, R = COOH
pimaradiene, R = CH₃

sandaracopimaric acid, R = COOH
sandaracopimaradiene, R = CH₃

Fig. 10-3.

In Eq. 10-7 are shown examples of further transformations of the hypothetical bicyclic precursor formed by the ring closures of Eq. 10-6. The formation of manoöl and sclareol are unexceptional and represent familiar reactions of a carbonium ion. Reaction of the methylene group at C-8 with the developing carbonium ion formed by solvolysis of the —OPP grouping leads to formation of the third (C) ring. Further unexceptional transformations of this intermediate can give rise to pimaradiene, abietic acid, and numerous related compounds.

◄   † A hydrolysis of the allylic pyrophosphate to produce the tertiary alcohol occurs in final stages of this overall transformation. Cf. the structure of linaloöl.

Pimaric acid and sandaracopimaric acid (Fig. 10-3) are examples of compounds formed by cyclization processes which are identical up to the point at which the C ring is formed. The last cyclization occurs in the two possible ways to produce diastereomeric compounds which possess opposite configurations at C-13.

10.4 Polycyclic Diterpenes

Reaction of the double bond of the C-13 vinyl side chain with the carbonium carbon atom at C-8 leads to a wide variety of tetra- (and penta-) cyclic compounds, in which ring C is further modified. In Fig. 10-4 are shown a representative group of polycyclic compounds that appear to be formed in this way. The cyclization process that, it is believed, leads to the series represented by kaurene (and others with an α-oriented C-10 methyl group) is diagrammed in Eq. 10-8.

In Eq. 10-8a it will be seen that addition of the C-13 vinyl group to the carbonium center at C-8 leads to an intermediate which is shown in the equation as a, the classical carbonium ion formed by the process formulated; and b, the non-classical ion which, as it is formulated, is a representation of the several classical

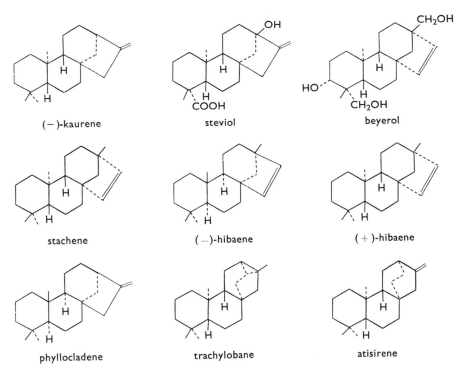

Fig. 10-4. Tetracyclic and Pentacyclic Diterpenes.

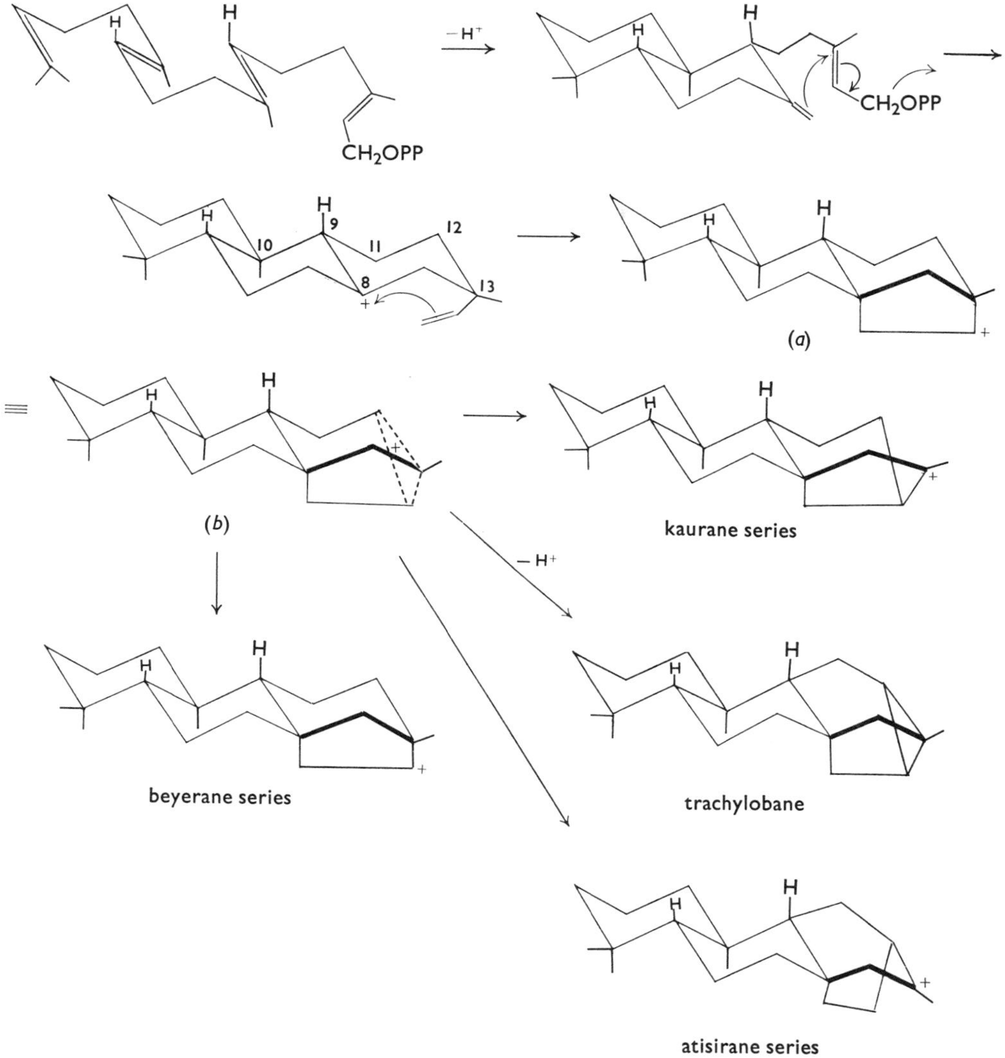

(a)

(b)

kaurane series

beyerane series

trachylobane

atisirane series

[Eq. 10-8]

forms that lead to the four ring systems shown: the tetracyclic kaurane, beyerane and atisirane series, and the pentacyclic trachylobane series. Specific examples of known naturally occurring diterpenoid compounds belonging to these classes are shown in Fig. 10-4.

It will be seen that the changes shown in Eq. 10-8 are in complete accord with the stereochemical disposition of the various reacting centers. It is noteworthy, then, that phyllocladene, which is "enantiomeric" with kaurene in the A/B ring

[Eq. 10-9]

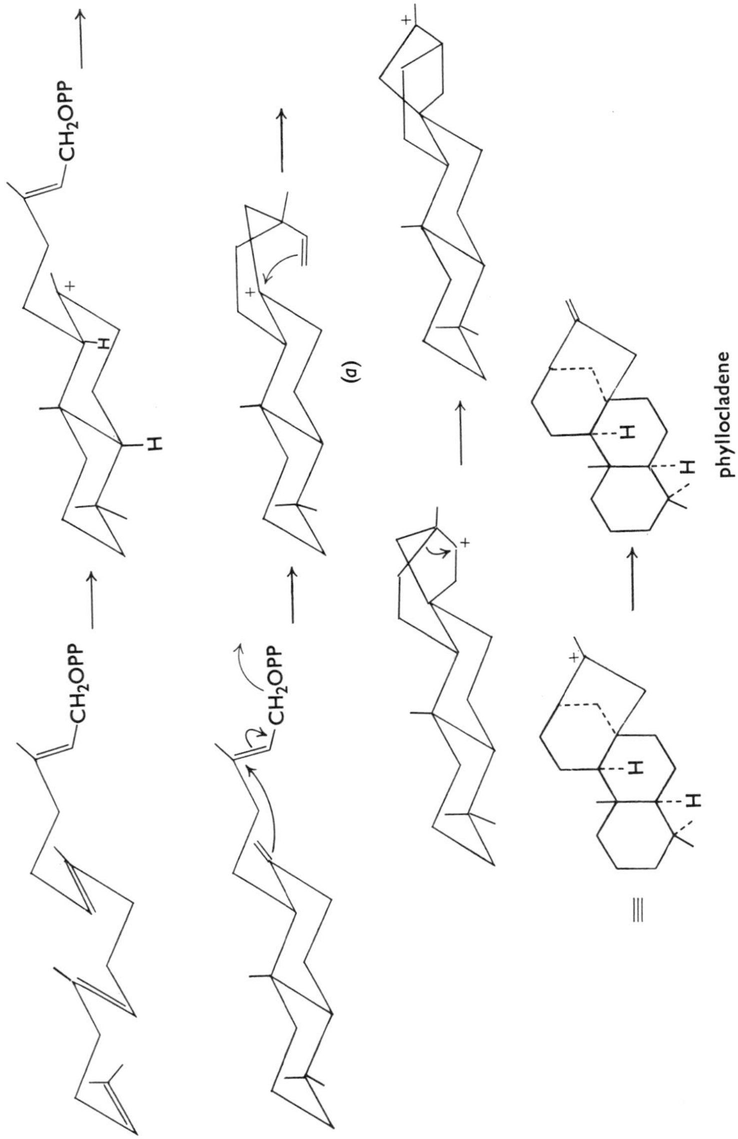

phyllocladene

(Eq. 10-9a)   rimuene

[Eq. 10-10]

portion of the molecule, possesses the same (*not* the enantiomeric) C/D ring stereo-chemistry as kaurene. The biosynthesis of phyllocladene can be formulated as in Eq. 10-9. It will be noted that the "kaurene-like" stereochemistry of the C/D rings is the consequence of the stereochemistry at C-13.

Were the cyclizations of geranylgeraniol that lead to phyllocladene and to kaurene the exact opposite in all respects, one would expect the C/D rings of kaurene to be enantiomeric to those of phyllocladene. But since the precursors of kaurene and phyllocladene have opposite configurations at C-4, C-10, C-8, and C-9, but the same configuration at C-13, the observed stereochemistry shown in Eq. 10-8 and Eq. 10-9 is the result. Examples are known, however, in which completely enantiomeric compounds exist in nature. The structures of (+)-hibaene and (−)-hibaene are shown in Fig. 10-4; these are enantiomeric at all asymmetric centers.

Numerous changes of other kinds occur in nature, for the carbonium ion (Eq. 10-9a) has open to it courses other than those so far described. The origin of the hydrocarbon rimuene (Eq. 10-10) can be accounted for by the following shifts: $9\alpha H \rightarrow$ C-8; $10\beta CH_3 \rightarrow 9\beta$; $5\alpha H \rightarrow 10\alpha$; and finally loss of $6\beta H$ to form the 5,6-double bond (α and β have the usual configurational meanings).

Dolabradiene appears to be formed by a process that resembles that which leads to rimuene, with the difference that the electron-deficient center formed by the migration of $5\alpha H$ to C-10 is followed by the shift of the $4\alpha CH_3$ group rather than by the loss of the C-6 proton. This process is shown in Eq. 10-11, and should be compared with Eq. 10-10.

An example of extensive modification of the original skeleton to produce a diterpenoid whose structure departs widely from the "regular" isoprenoid arrangement is found in pleuromutilin (Eq. 10-12). Pleuromutilin, a glycollic ester formed

dolabradiene

[Eq. 10-11]

by a number of fungi (e.g., *Pleurotus mutilis* (Fr.) Gillet = *Omphalina mutila* (Fr.)
P. D. Orton; *Clitopilus passeckerianus* (Pilat) Sing.), when produced by fungus grown
in the presence of ^{14}C-labeled sodium acetate and ^{14}C-labeled mevalonate, was
found to be labeled as would be predicted from its origin by the mevalonate
pathway.

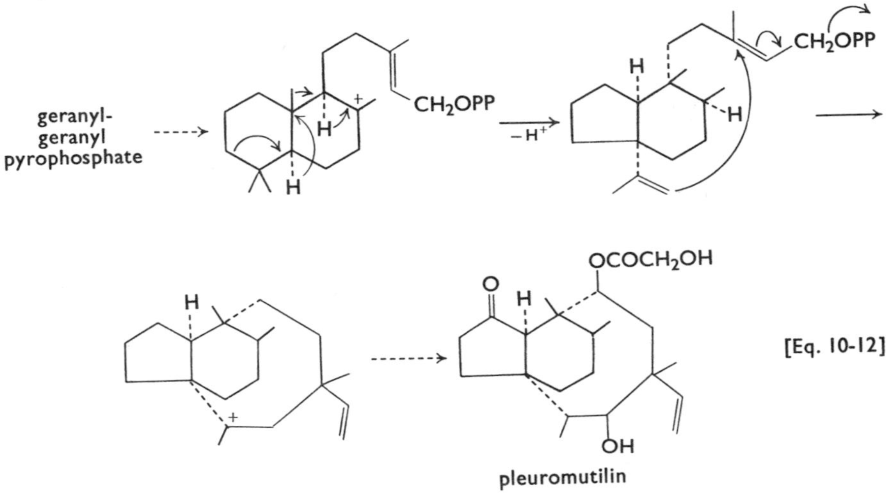

pleuromutilin

[Eq. 10-12]

10.5   Modification of Substituent Groups

Most of the diterpenes described in the foregoing sections possess but few
functional groups; for the most part, they possess the unaltered methyl groups and
terminal vinyl group of the original geranylgeraniol or geranyllinaloöl from which
they are formed. Nature provides, however, many diterpenoid compounds in which
extensive modification—usually by oxidation—of the original skeleton and substituents has taken place. Abietic acid (Eq. 10-7), and corresponding C-4 carboxylic
acids derived from the pimarane skeleton (Fig. 10-3) are well known and widely
distributed compounds. Cativic acid and agathic acid possess carboxyl groups
formed by oxidation of the terminal —CH$_2$OH group. The other compounds
shown in Fig. 10-5 show progressively greater degrees of oxygenation, with pikropolin as the most highly oxidized example with eight oxygen atoms (seven, if the
acetyl group is not counted).

Isorosenolic acid (Fig. 10-5) is produced by a fungus (*Trichothecium roseum*
Link.), an organism which also produces a number of related compounds, among
them rosenonolactone. The structure, stereochemistry and probable biosynthetic
origin of rosenonolactone are shown in Eq. 10-13.

The steps shown in brackets in Eq. 10-13 are conjectural; the stage in the biosynthesis at which the methyl group at C-4 is oxidized to —COOH is not known.

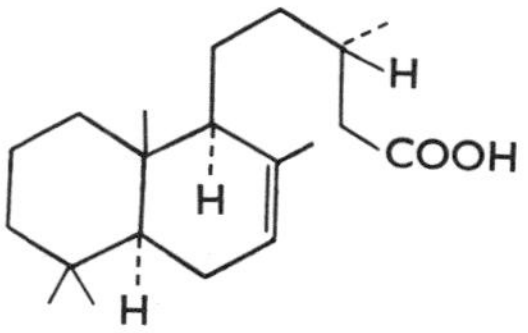

cativic acid

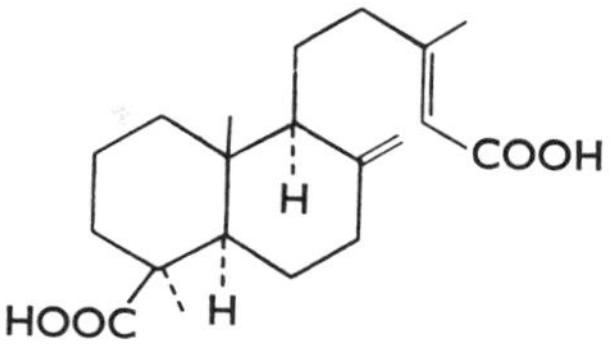

agathic acid

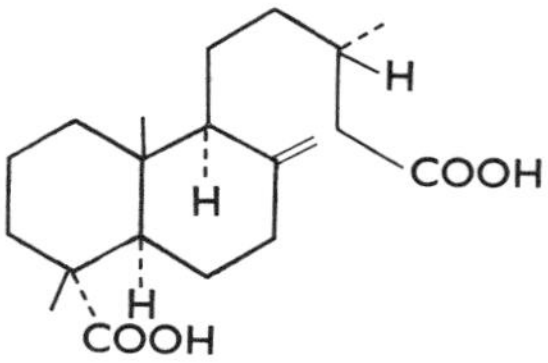

pinifolic acid

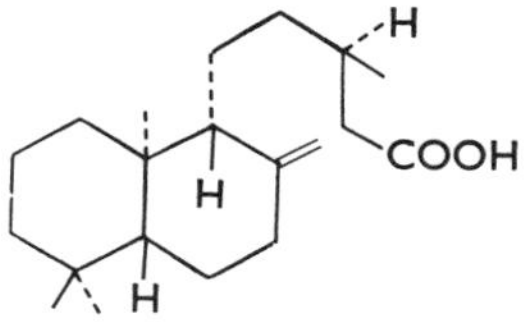

eperuic acid

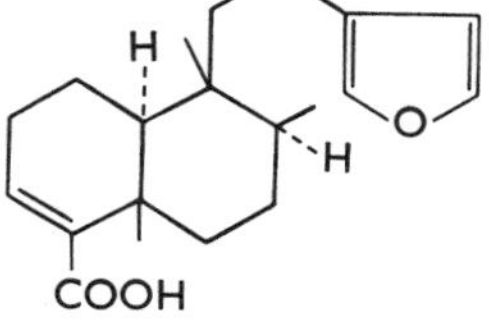

hardwickiic acid

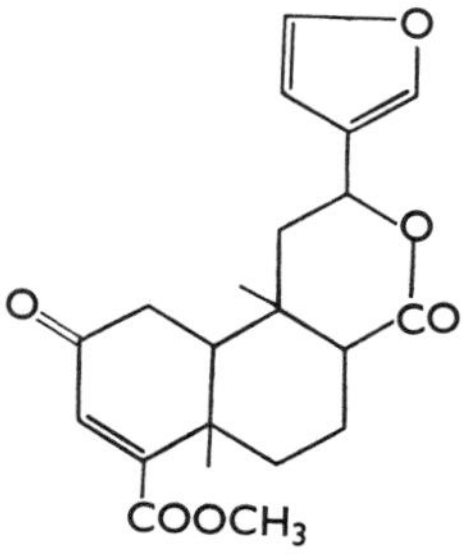

tinophyllone

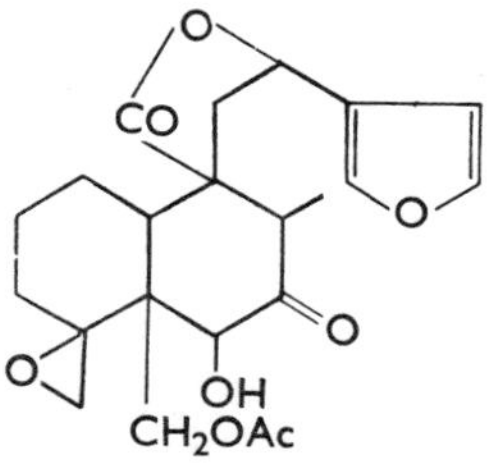

pikropolin

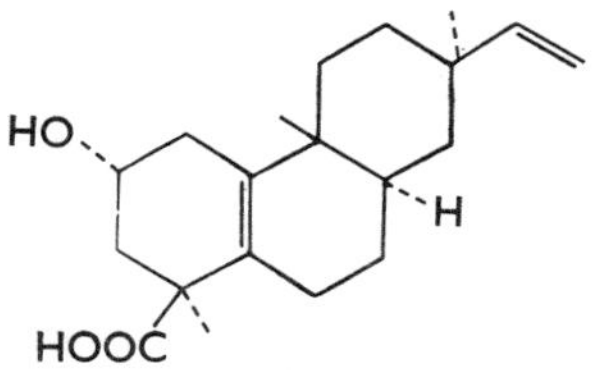

isorosenolic acid

Fig. 10-5.

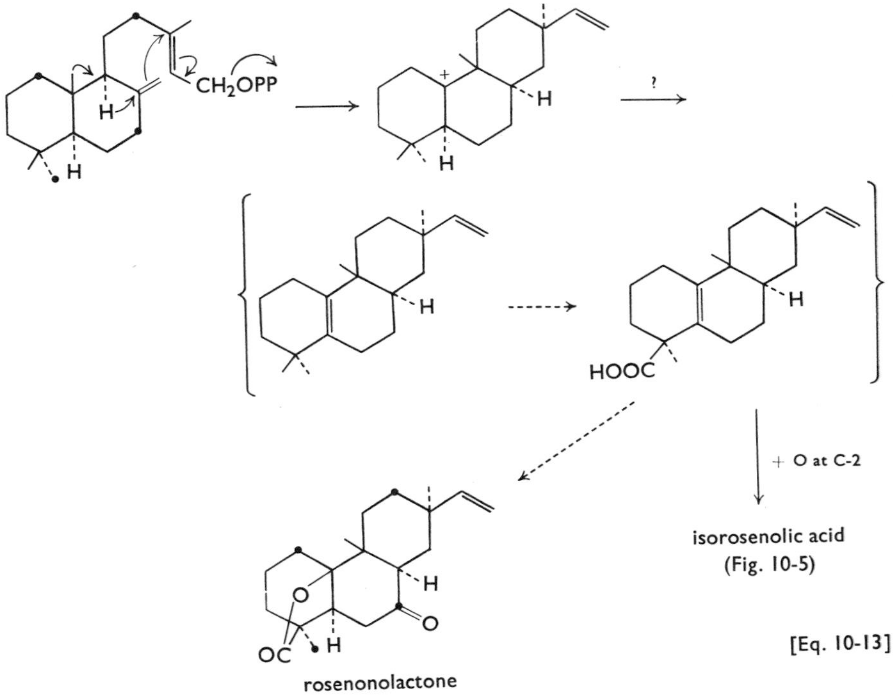
CH2OPP
?
HOOC
+ O at C-2
isorosenolic acid
(Fig. 10-5)
OC
rosenonolactone

[Eq. 10-13]

(carbon atoms marked • are from 2-^{14}C-mevalonate)

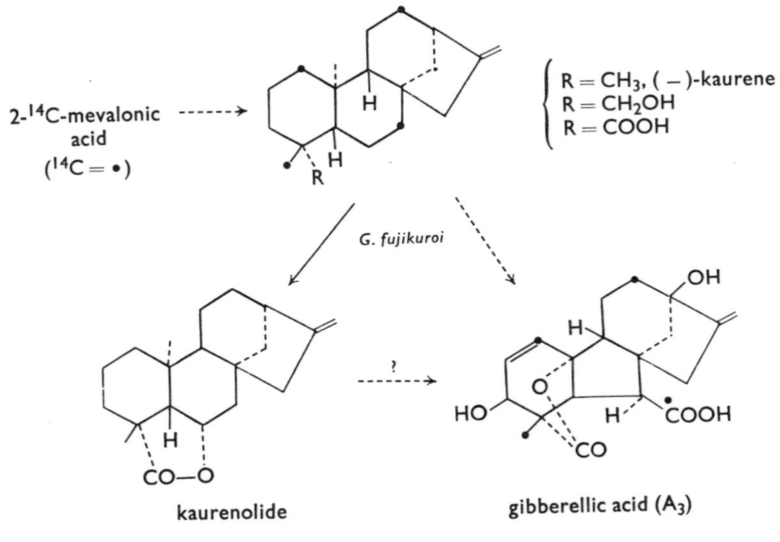
2-14C-mevalonic acid
(14C = •)
R = CH3, (–)-kaurene
R = CH2OH
R = COOH
G. fujikuroi
?
CO—O
kaurenolide
OH
HO
COOH
CO
gibberellic acid (A3)

[Eq. 10-14]

Gibberellic acid, an important plant-growth regulating substance, is also the product of alteration of a diterpenoid precursor. Indeed, experiments have shown that the fungus *Gibberella fujikuroi* is capable of transforming (−)-kaurene and several kaurene derivatives (the -19-oic acid and -19-ol) into gibberellic acid (Eq. 10-14).*

When kaurene, kauren-19-oic acid and kauren-19-ol, labeled with ^{14}C at the carbon atom of the $=CH_2$ group, are fed to *G. fujikuroi*, radioactive gibberellic acid is formed. In the case of the kaurene feeding, degradation of the gibberellic acid showed that there had been no alteration in the position of labeling.

Gibberellic acid formed by the fungus fed with 2-^{14}C-mevalonic acid is labeled in a manner that is in complete agreement with the origin shown in Eq. 10-14. Two significant facts are to be noted from this scheme: (1) the β-oriented methyl group of kaurene (and thus the 4-methyl group of gibberellic acid) is labeled, but the lactone carbonyl group of gibberellic acid contains no label. This is a further demonstration of the stereospecificity of isoprenoid synthesis; and (2) the carboxyl group of gibberellic acid is labeled, showing that it represents the carbon atom of C-7 of kaurene, which is extruded when the B-ring undergoes contraction (by a benzilic acid rearrangement-like reaction).

The contraction of the B-ring evidently proceeds by way of successive oxidations at the C-6 and C-7 positions. Several compounds, probably intermediates in this sequence, are found in the fungus cultures; one of these, kaurenolide, is shown in Eq. 10-14.

The alteration of diterpenoid precursors by oxidation processes, similar to those which lead to the "gibberellins," is not confined to *Gibberella* nor to only a few plants. It is now believed that gibberellic acid (or other growth regulating compounds of closely allied structures) is a widespread—perhaps universal—constituent of higher plants and plays a role as one of the plant "hormones" that act to control and regulate growth and development. An analogous compound, although not a "gibberellin," in which oxidative opening of the B-ring has taken place is enmein, a constituent of *Isodon* (= *Plectranthus*) *trichocarpus* Kudo (fam. Labiatae). In enmein the B-ring has been opened, and the methyl group at C-10 oxidized to —CH_2OH.** The structure of enmein and its relationship to the presumed diterpenoid precursor are shown in Eq. 10-15. This scheme serves only to show the structural and stereochemical relationship between enmein and (−)-kaurene; nothing is known about the details of the numerous oxidation steps that are

---

* Over twenty "gibberellins", which are related to gibberellic acid in possessing the same fundamental ring system but various degrees of functional alteration, are known in nature. Some have been isolated from the fungus, some from higher plants.

**In gibberellic acid this methyl group has been lost, possibly by way of the sequence $CH_3 \rightarrow CH_2OH \rightarrow CHO \rightarrow COOH \rightarrow$ loss of CO_2.

involved in the overall transformation of a diterpenoid precursor to so highly
oxidized a final product.

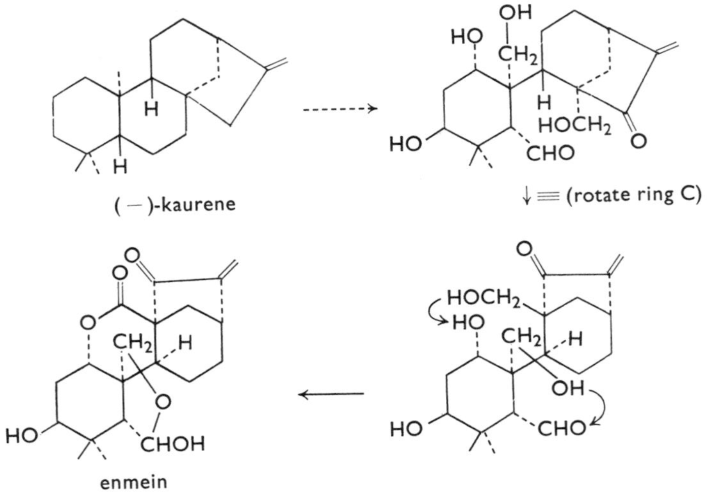

(—)-kaurene   ↓ ≡ (rotate ring C)

enmein   [Eq. 10-15]

10.6 Aromatic and Quinonoid Diterpenes

Aromatization of diterpenes of the abietane group provides a number of
naturally occurring compounds containing benzenoid A- or C-rings, and some in
which further oxidation produces a quinonoid C-ring.

Podocarpic acid (Fig. 10-6) is abundant in plants of the genus *Podocarpus*, a
conifer of the Southern Hemisphere. While not a diterpene in the usual meaning of
the term, podocarpic acid is probably of mevalonate-isoprenoid origin, the isopropyl group having been lost in the course of metabolic alteration. It will be noted
that in podocarpic acid it is the β-oriented (axial) methyl group that has undergone
oxidation to —COOH, while abietic acid (Eq. 10-7) bears an α-COOH at C-4.

Cryptojaponol and royleanone (Fig. 10-6) represent diterpenes in which aromatization or quinonoidization of the C-ring has occurred. These compounds
present no unexceptional structural features, and their biosynthesis appears to be
obvious. It is, however, of interest to note that royleanone is found in *Plectranthus*
species (fam. Labiatae); and other members of this plant family also contain diterpenoid quinones. This botanical-chemical relationship suggests that the ability
to dehydrogenate (i.e., oxidize) the C-ring of the abietane-derived diterpenes is a
genetical characteristic of this plant family, and can be regarded as a chemotaxonomic feature of potential usefulness in plant systematics.

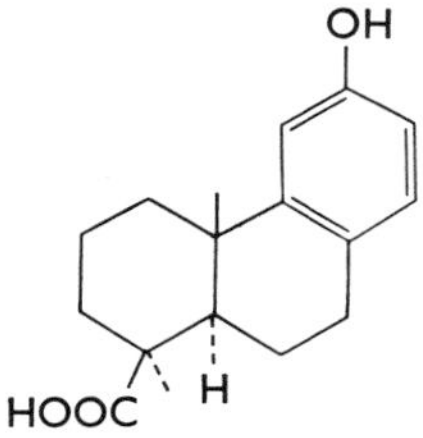

podocarpic acid[1]

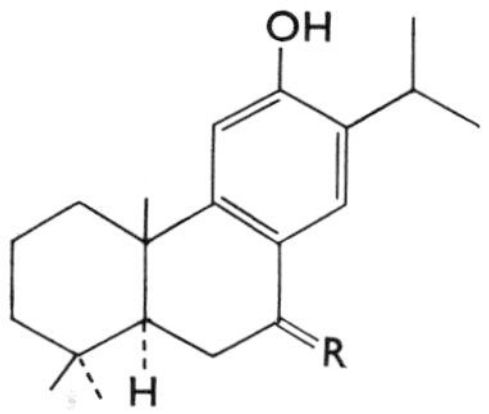

(R = H$_2$) ferruginol[1]
(R = O) sugiol[2]

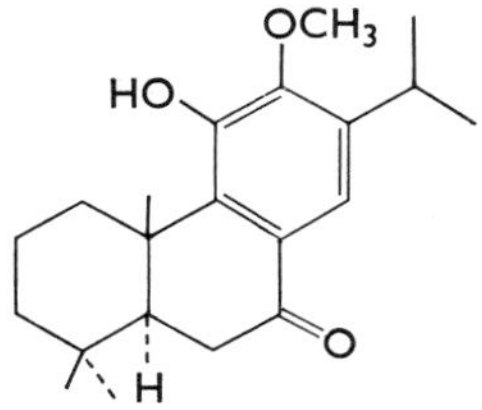

cryptojaponol[2]

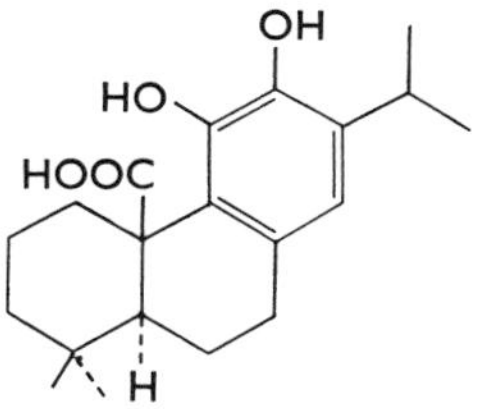

carnosic acid[3]

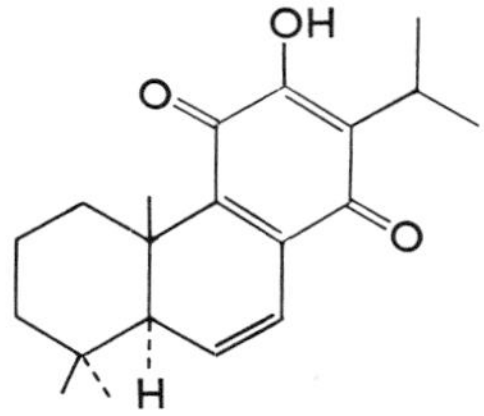

royleanone[4]

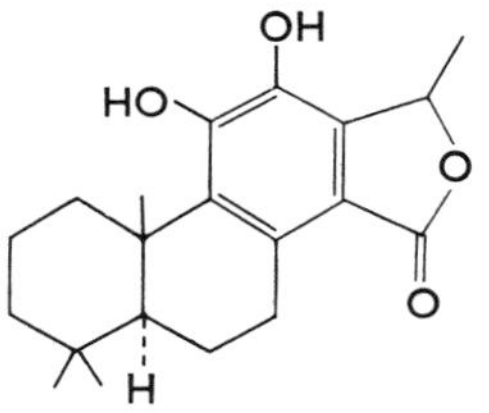

picrosalvin[5]

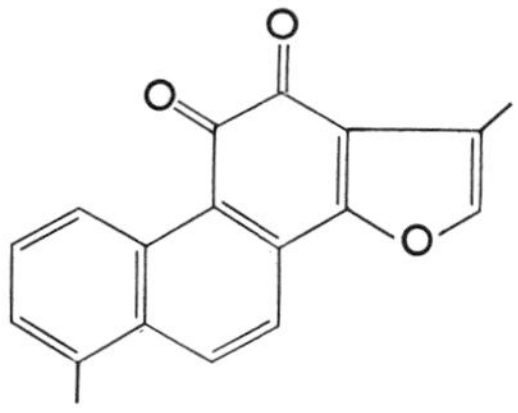

tanshinone I[6]

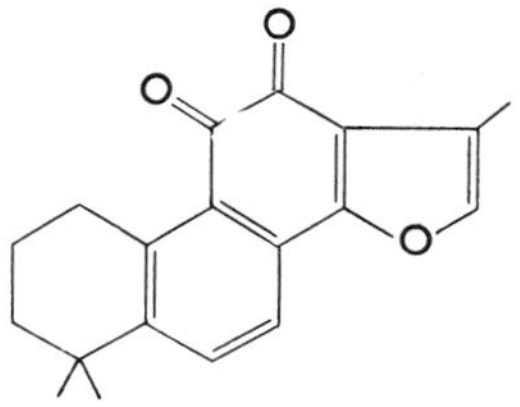

tanshinone II[6]

from coniferous plants: (1) *Podocarpus* spp.; (2) *Cryptomeria* spp.
from Labiatae: (3) *Rosmarinus officinalis*; (4) *Plectranthus* spp.
(5) *Salvia officinalis*; (6) *Salvia miltorrhiza*.

Fig. 10-6.

The botanical sources of the compounds shown in Fig. 10-6 are indicated in the figure; the predominance of constituents of the Labiatae (mint family) is apparent. It should be emphasized, however, that the fact of C-ring aromatization alone cannot be taken as an indication of botanical affinity, for it would be improper to assume, for example, a close relationship between such coniferous plants as *Podocarpus* and plants of the mint family solely on the basis of the chemical similarities seen in the structures of Fig. 10-6.

10.7 Miscellaneous Structural Modifications

The examples of modified diterpenes described in the preceding sections represent only a few of the many variations that Nature plays upon the theme of structural alteration.

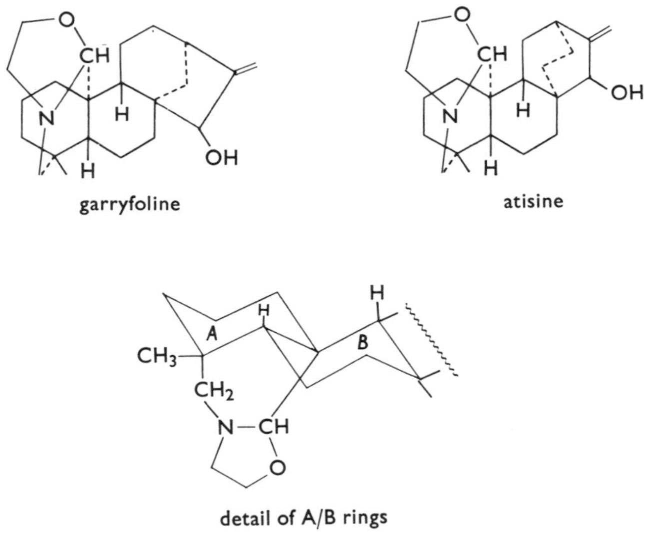

garryfoline   atisine

detail of A/B rings

Fig. 10-7. Diterpenoid Alkaloids.

The introduction of nitrogen into an altered diterpenoid molecule gives rise to a compound of the alkaloid class, and a number of diterpenoid alkaloids occur in nature. Atisine and garryfoline (Fig. 10-7) are representative of the class, which also includes alkaloids (e.g., delphinine) of more complex structures which appear to be formed by further intramolecular rearrangements within the original diterpenoid skeleton.

Atisine (from *Aconitum* spp., fam. Ranunculaceae) and delphinine (from *Delphinium* spp., fam. Ranunculaceae) are closely related botanically as well as chemically. The *Garrya* (fam. Garryaceae) alkaloids are found in a plant family not closely allied to that in which atisine occurs. It will be noted that garryfoline and atisine differ principally in the C/D ring system. The former possesses a kaurene-like structure, the latter, the atisirane ring system (see Fig. 10-4 and Eq. 10-8).

XI CHAPTER

〜〜〜〜〜〜〜〜〜〜〜〜〜〜〜〜〜〜〜〜〜〜〜〜〜〜〜〜〜〜〜〜〜〜〜〜〜

REFERENCES FOR FURTHER READING

1. D. Arigoni; L. Ruzicka; R. B. Clayton; J. H. Richards, and J. B. Hendrickson, referred to in previous chapters.

2. G. E. Risinger and H. D. Durst, *On the Mechanism of the Reductive Dimerization of Farnesyl Pyrophosphate*, Tetrahedron Letters, (1968), 3133.

3. G. Ourisson, P. Crabbe, and O. Rodig, *Tetracyclic Triterpenes*, Holden-Day, San Francisco, 1964.

4. A. Chawla and Sukh Dev, *A New Class of Triterpene from Ailanthus malabaricus, DC.*, Tetrahedron Letters, (1967), 4837.

5. W. Lawrie, J. McLean, P. L. Pauson, and J. Watson, *The Biosynthesis of Eburicoic Acid from Sesquiterpene Precursors*, J. Chem. Soc., (1967), 2002. (Contains references to previous studies on terpenoid biosynthesis.)

Higher Terpenoids

11.1 Introduction

The story of the development of an understanding of the biosynthesis of higher (in particular, tri-) terpenes is intimately related to that of the biosynthesis of steroidal compounds, in particular the important compound cholesterol. Because of its wide occurrence in animal organisms, and its close structural relationship (indeed, as is now known, its role as a progenitor) to the many physiologically important steroids of human metabolism, cholesterol has been the object of intensive inquiry for the last three decades.

By 1950 it had become reasonably certain that cholesterol was synthesized from acetic acid (as well as from such other low-molecular weight compounds as ethanol, pyruvic acid, isovaleric acid, leucine, and others), and shortly thereafter the recognition that the side chain of cholesterol was isoprenoid in pattern led to the suggestion that cholesterol was biogenetically a member of the group of polyisoprenoid compounds.

An early proposal that squalene, then a rare hydrocarbon known only as a constituent of shark (*Squalus* species) liver oil, is a cholesterol precursor was elaborated into the suggestion that cholesterol was formed by the cyclization of squalene with the loss of three carbon atoms (methyl groups). The first proposal for this course of biosynthesis is shown in Eq. 11-1*a*. Experiments with labeled squalene and labeled acetate, using mice and rat liver tissue, soon showed that labeled squalene is indeed formed from 1-^{14}C- or 2-^{14}C-acetate, and that ^{14}C-squalene is incorporated into cholesterol with remarkably high efficiency.

Parallel studies during this period of inquiry on the structure of the triterpene alcohol, lanosterol, led to the suggestion that squalene is the precursor of lanosterol, which in turn is converted into cholesterol. Finally, complete degradation of the

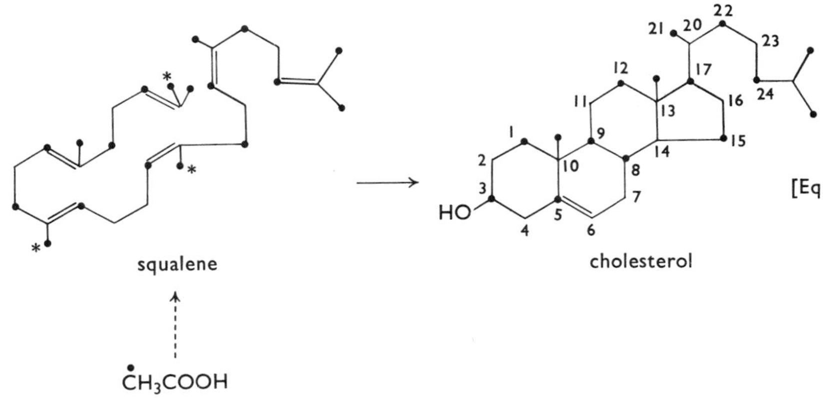

[Eq. 11-1a]

First proposal for squalene cyclization to cholesterol. It was assumed that the methyl groups marked * were lost in the course of the cyclization. Note that if this manner of cyclization were correct, carbon atoms marked • in cholesterol would be derived from CH₃ of acetate, and C-7 and C-13 would be derived from COOH of acetate.

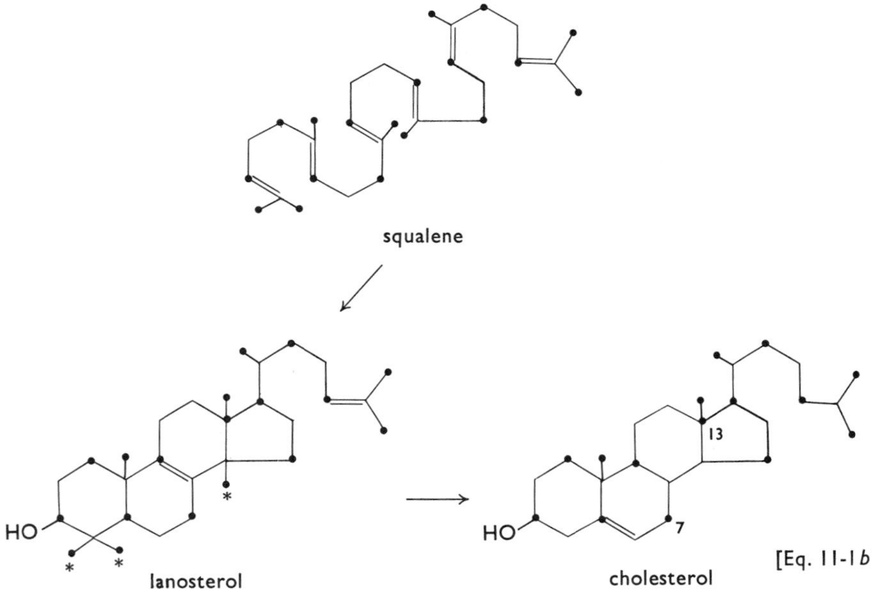

[Eq. 11-1b]

Correct cyclization scheme for squalene → lanosterol → cholesterol, with labeling pattern expected (and experimentally verified) from methyl-labeled acetate. Note that, in contrast to scheme of Eq. 11-1a, C-7 and C-13 are from CH₃ of acetate. The methyl groups marked * are lost in the transformation of lanosterol into cholesterol.

cholesterol formed from ^{14}C-acetate led to the identification of all the carbon atoms of the sterol. Although the side chain of cholesterol is labeled in strict accord with a "normal" isoprenoid origin, the latter studies showed that *both* C-11 and C-12 carbon atoms of cholesterol are derived from —COOH of acetate, the methyl groups of acetate appearing at C-7 and C-13.

These results reinforced the proposal that squalene was the precursor of cholesterol, but that the manner of cyclization was not that shown in Eq. 11-1*a*, but was in fact that shown in Eq. 11-1*b*. The above findings are summarized in the structural representations, with labeling patterns (from acetate) shown. It is clear from the results of the degradation of the labeled cholesterol that the hypothesis of its biosynthesis according to Eq. 11-1*b* is fully in accord with experimental findings.

11.2 Squalene

As a result of the exhaustive studies on the biosynthesis of steroids and triterpenes, it is now recognized that squalene, once an exotic hydrocarbon known only in one natural source, is a universal metabolite. Its conversion by cyclizations of several kinds into triterpenoid compounds forms the body of a hypothesis of biosynthesis into which can be accommodated the large number of naturally occurring triterpenes (Sec. 11.3 and following).

Squalene itself consists of two farnesyl residues combined tail-to-tail (Eq. 11-2).* The genesis of squalene by the mevalonate → geranyl pyrophosphate → farnesyl pyrophosphate → squalene pathway, the early stages of which are those discussed in detail in Chapters 8, 9, and 10, has been firmly established by isotopic tracer experiments and need not be further discussed here. Two remaining features of squalene biosynthesis remain to be examined: (1) the manner in which the two farnesyl residues are joined tail-to-tail at the —CH$_2$OPP ends of the chains; and (2) certain details of the stereochemistry of squalene.

2 farnesyl pyrophosphate   squalene   [Eq. 11-2]

* The synthesis of carotenoids, C$_{40}$-compounds consisting of two isoprenoid C$_{20}$-units joined tail-to-tail, presumably takes place by way of a similar union of two molecules of geranylgeranyl pyrophosphate.

A series of detailed and admirably executed experiments designed to examine the details of the process in which the tail-to-tail farnesyl-farnesyl coupling occurs led to the discovery that in the reaction $RCH_2OPP + RCH_2OPP \rightarrow RCH_2—CH_2R$ (RCH_2 = farnesyl), one of the four hydrogen atoms of the $—CH_2CH_2—$ grouping is derived from the coenzyme, NADH. When 1,1-dideuterofarnesyl pyrophosphate is converted into squalene,* the resulting squalene contains three deuterium atoms and one hydrogen atom in this central unit (Eq. 11-3a). When NAD^2H is used with farnesyl pyrophosphate, the central unit of the squalene is $—CH_2CHD—$ (Eq. 11-3b):

(R = geranyl)   [Eq. 11-3]

The exact mechanism of this coupling reaction remains to be determined; what coenzymes (if any) are involved, and whether intermediate farnesyl-enzyme compounds are formed is not known with certainty. Several plausible conjectures have been put forward. In one (Eq. 11-4a), it is proposed that the initial reaction is that between farnesyl pyrophosphate and nerolidol pyrophosphate, in which the phosphate aids the primary displacement reaction by the nucleophilic assistance shown in the equation. A final reduction in which NADH provides a nucleophilic $H:^-$ to complete the reaction, with displacement (S_N2') of the pyrophosphate ion, yields squalene in which one of the four hydrogen atoms of the central $—CH_2CH_2—$ unit is derived from the pyridine nucleotide.

In a second proposal, the intervention of thiamin pyrophosphate has been invoked.** The course of the coupling reaction is shown in Eq. 11-4b. It is seen that here, too, the final reductive displacement of TPP provides for the introduction of the hydrogen atom from the reducing enzyme (NADH).

Other schemes than those of Eq. 11-4 have been suggested, but it is not possible at this time to draw final conclusions regarding this step of the synthesis.

---

* Experiments of the kind described were performed with the aid of liver enzyme systems ("squalene synthetase"), in which the enzyme(s) is attached to particulate fractions of the cellular material.

** Evidence has been obtained that TPP is a required cofactor for squalene (and carotenoid) biosynthesis.

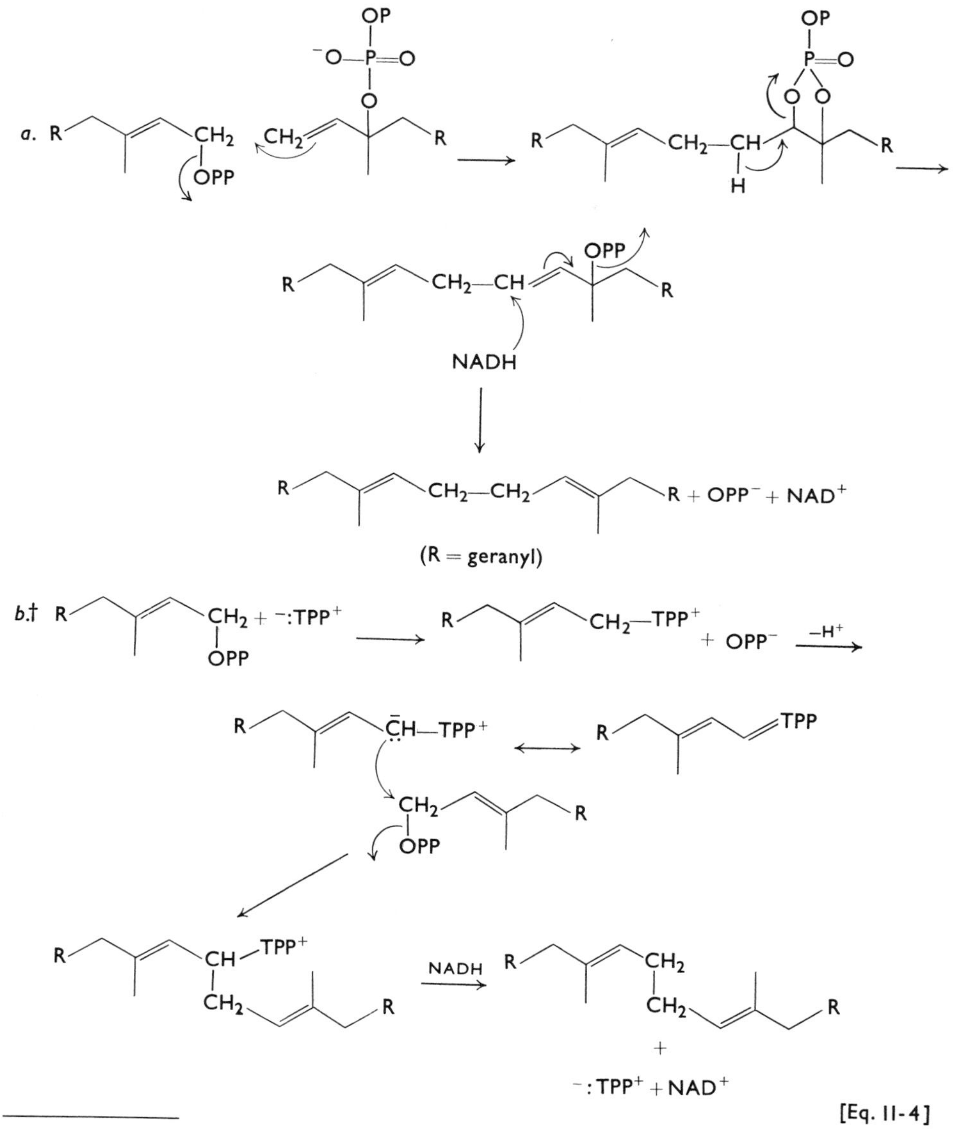

$(R = \text{geranyl})$

$$-:TPP^+ + NAD^+$$

[Eq. 11-4]

---

† For the conventional symbolism used here for thiamin pyrophosphate ($-$:TTP$^+$), see Chapter 2.

11.3 Cyclization of Squalene

In the cyclization of squalene formulated in Eq. 11-1b, the lanosterol produced bears methyl groups in positions different from those in which they occur on the

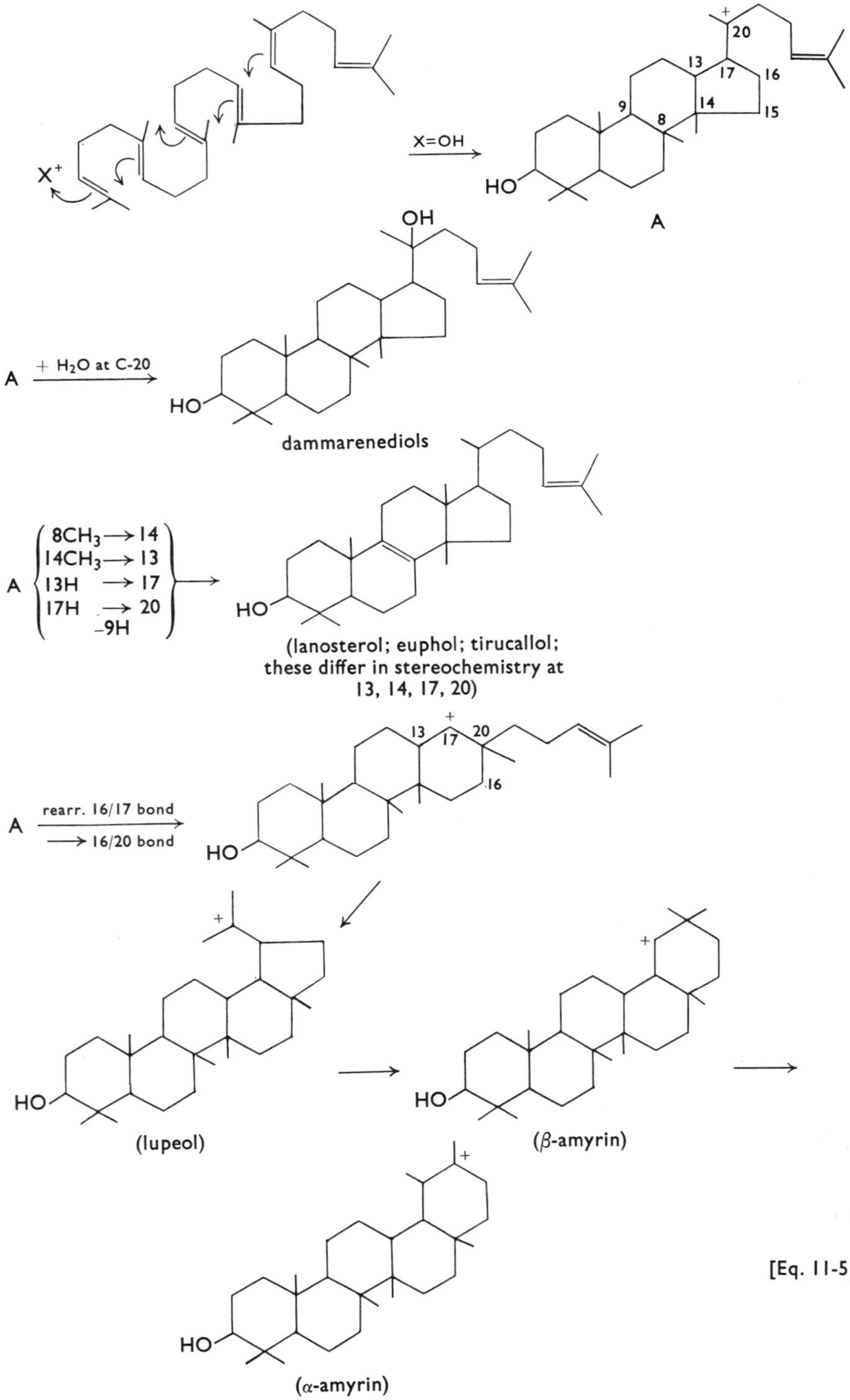

$$X = OH$$

A

A $\xrightarrow{+ \text{ H}_2\text{O at C-20}}$

dammarenediols

A $\left\{ \begin{array}{l} 8\text{CH}_3 \longrightarrow 14 \\ 14\text{CH}_3 \longrightarrow 13 \\ 13\text{H} \longrightarrow 17 \\ 17\text{H} \longrightarrow 20 \\ \phantom{17\text{H}} -9\text{H} \end{array} \right\} \longrightarrow$

(lanosterol; euphol; tirucallol;
these differ in stereochemistry at
13, 14, 17, 20)

A $\xrightarrow[\longrightarrow \text{16/20 bond}]{\text{rearr. 16/17 bond}}$

(lupeol)   (β-amyrin) $\longrightarrow$

[Eq. 11-5]

(α-amyrin)

folded squalene chain. Thus, lanosterol is not a "regular" isoprenoid compound, and must clearly have been formed by a reaction in which methyl group migration has taken place.

A hypothesis, developed by Ruzicka and the Swiss school of organic chemists, that accounted for the formation of lanosterol and at the same time for the transformation of squalene into the large number of triterpenes of many other structural types, is described in the sections to follow. This hypothesis, in the expression of which the isoprenoid squalene is transformed by mechanistically rational processes into the irregular (non-isoprenoid, in the strict sense) structures of many triterpenes, is in accord with what is called the "biogenetic isoprene rule." In contrast to the classical isoprene rule, the biogenetic isoprene rule permits the inclusion in the isoprenoid (or terpenoid) class, of naturally occurring compounds whose skeletons do not consist of discrete isoprene units. It carries the clear implication, however, that such irregular compounds are derived by the mevalonate → geraniol → farnesol pathway.

Although the full expression of the squalene cyclization process must be stated in explicit stereochemical terms, and will be so presented below, it will be useful first to examine the process without stereochemical detail and with carbonium ions expressed in simple, classical forms. In Eq. 11-5 is shown the cyclization of squalene as initiated by an attack of an electrophilic reagent, X^+, with the consequences described by the carbonium-ion initiated rearrangements depicted.

This scheme shows the manner of formation of five widely distributed classes of triterpenoid compounds; for each of the skeletal types shown there are known numerous natural compounds in which additional secondary alterations have occurred. Among these are oxidations, introduction of unsaturation, loss of methyl groups, etc. Examples will be presented in the discussion to follow.

11.4 Lanosterol

Natural squalene is presumed to occur as the all-*trans* form. Its cyclization by electrophile-initiated attack (X^+ in Eq. 11-5) can take more than one stereochemical course depending upon how the chain is folded, presumably by the stereospecific influence of an enzyme surface at which the cyclization occurs. In order to arrive at the configuration that lanosterol is known to possess, it is sufficient to suppose that squalene is folded in the manner shown in Eq. 11-6; that is, with the potential carbocyclic rings in the chair (A)-boat (B)-chair (C)-boat (D) manner. It will be seen that this arrangement leads uniquely to the stereochemistry written for the initial carbonium ion intermediate. Stereospecific 1,2-migrations initiated by the electron-deficient center at C-20 then produce lanosterol, the loss of the C-9 proton being the final step.

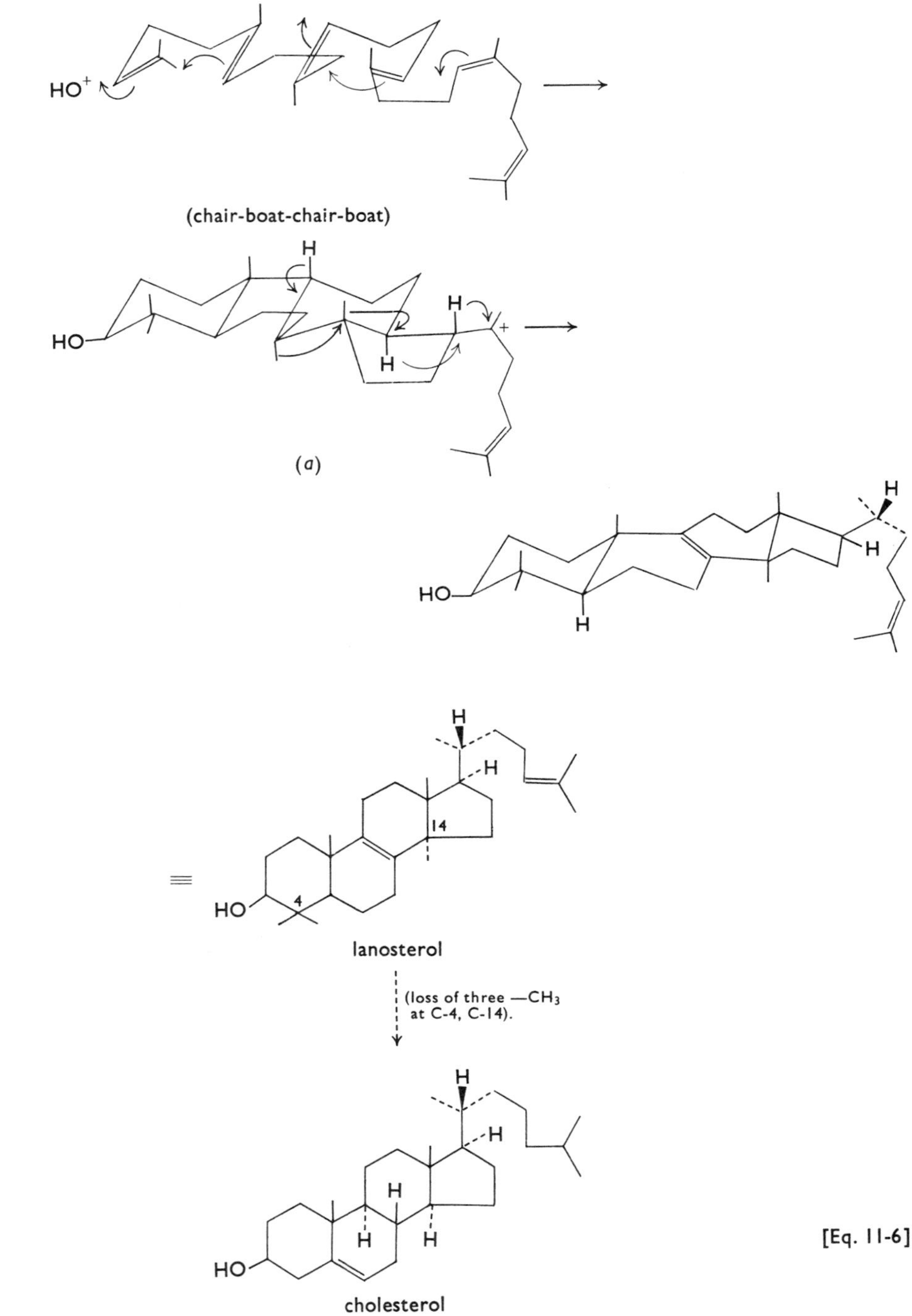

(chair-boat-chair-boat)

(a)

lanosterol

(loss of three —CH₃ at C-4, C-14).

cholesterol

[Eq. 11-6]

The formation of cholesterol from lanosterol follows from the removal of the three methyl groups at C-4 and C-14, their elimination taking place by oxidation to —COOH and loss of CO_2. Experiments with lanosterol formed from $2\text{-}^{14}C\text{-}CH_3COOH$ show that cholesterol formation is accompanied by the loss of $^{14}CO_2$. When lanosterol from $1\text{-}^{14}C\text{-}CH_3COOH$ is transformed into cholesterol, $^{14}CO_2$ is not formed.

11.5   The Euphol Series

Folding the squalene chain in the chair-chair-chair-boat conformation leads to a stereochemistry in the derived terpenes which differs from that of lanosterol (Eq. 11-7).

In Eq. 11-7 the initial cyclization product (the intermediate cation) is shown as the non-classical bridged carbonium ion (a), and is rewritten in the form (b), in which coordination of water at the positive center leads to dammarenediols. Two

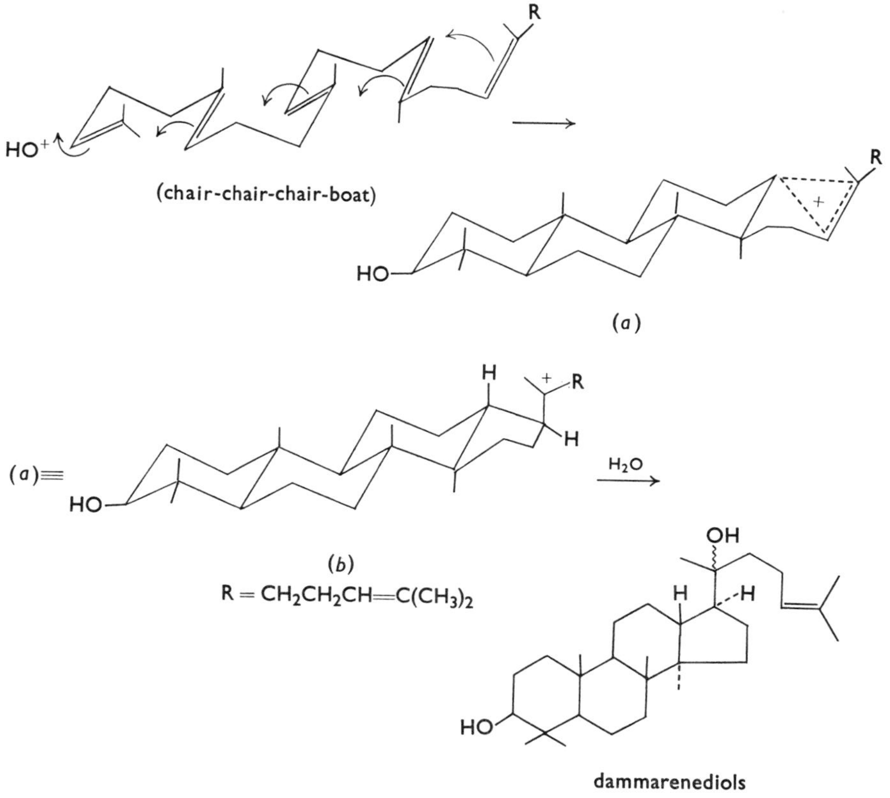

(chair-chair-chair-boat)

(a)

$(a)\equiv$

(b)

$R = CH_2CH_2CH{=}C(CH_3)_2$

dammarenediols

[Eq. 11-7]

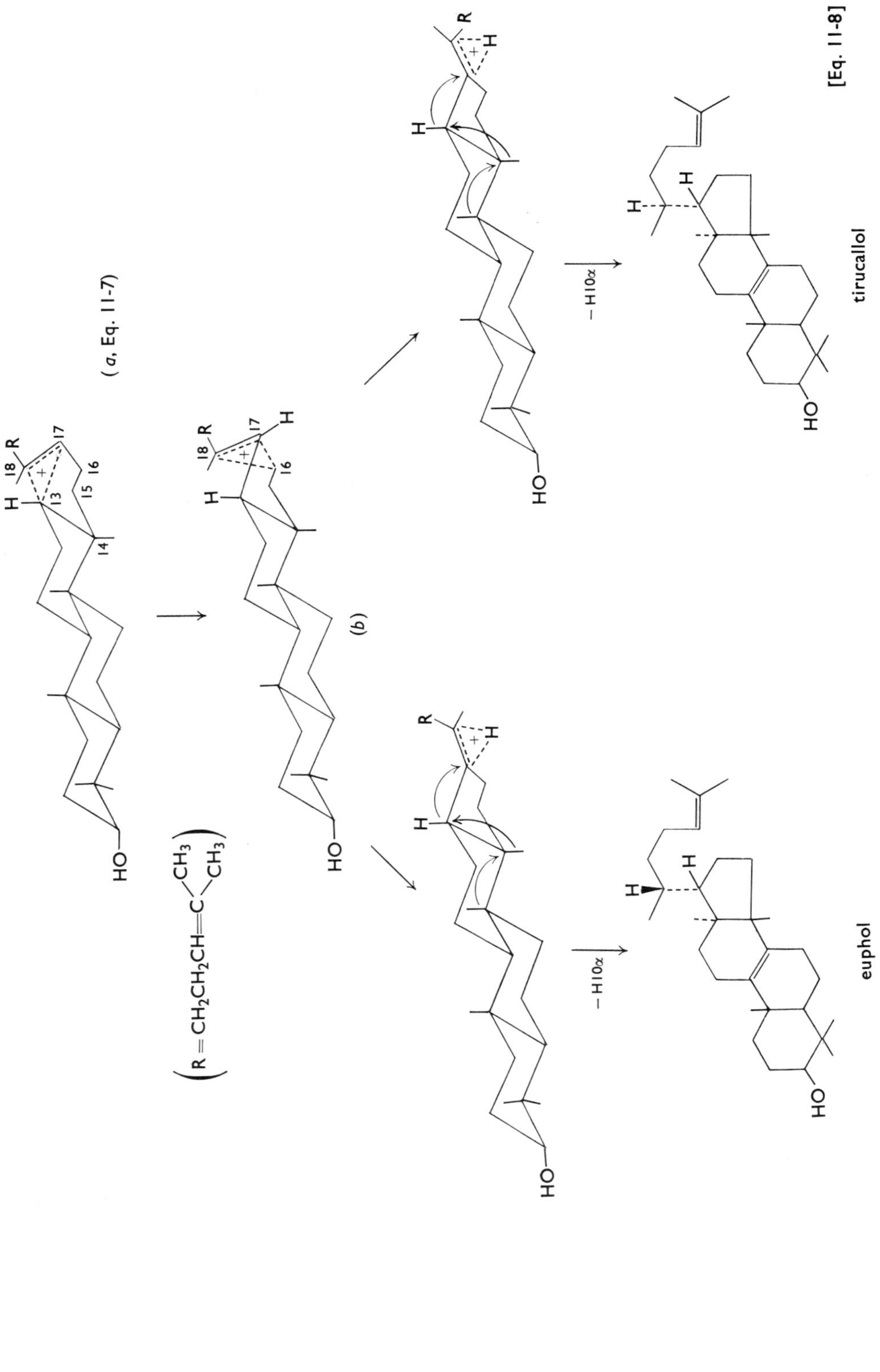

$\left(R = CH_2CH_2CH = C \begin{smallmatrix} CH_3 \\ CH_3 \end{smallmatrix} \right)$

(a, Eq. 11-7)

(b)

− H10α

tirucallol

− H10α

euphol

[Eq. 11-8]

dammarenediols, differing in the configuration at C-20, are known, from which it is concluded that the cyclization process does not uniquely define the stereochemistry at this center.

The remainder of the molecule, it will be seen, is not of the same configuration as lanosterol (or of its immediate ionic precursor), for in the dammarane skeleton the methyl groups are C-8β and C-14α. Lanosterol, on the other hand, (by methyl shifts) is derived from a C-8α/C-14β precursor. The difference between the configurations of these two ring systems is the result of the two different manners in which squalene is folded in the cyclization stage.

If the carbonium ion precursor (Eq. 11-7a) of the dammarane series undergoes the concerted methyl migrations shown in Eq. 11-8, the carbon skeleton is changed into one resembling that of lanosterol, except that the C-13/C-14 configurations are reversed. Two configurations of the carbonium ions center (at C-17/C-18) are possible, and give rise to two isomeric (at C-20 in the final compounds) triterpenes, euphol, and tirucallol. Euphol is a constituent of many species of *Euphorbia* (fam. Euphorbiaceae); and it is of interest to note that euphol and tirucallol are often found together in a single species.

Euphol (or tirucallol) appears to be of fundamental importance as a precursor of a large and widely distributed class of compounds which it is believed are derived by degradation of the D-ring and side chain. These compounds will be discussed in detail in Chapter 12.

11.6 Transformation of the C-9 Carbonium Ion

The sequence of events leading to lanosterol involves as the terminal step the loss of the C-9 hydrogen atom with generation of the 8,9-double bond (Eq. 11-9a). Parkeol and cycloartenol, naturally occurring triterpenes, are isomeric with lanosterol, and all three compounds are identical at all centers save one: parkeol is the $\Delta^{9\,(11)}$ isomer, lanosterol the $\Delta^{8,\,9}$ compound, and cycloartenol contains a cyclopropane ring (Fig. 11-1).

In Eq. 11-9 is shown the relationship between lanosterol, parkeol, and cycloartenol in terms of the intermediate *a* which was shown in Eq. 11-6. By the shifts pictured in Eq. 11-9, all three of these triterpenes are derived in a mechanistically acceptable manner. The carbonium ion *c* of Eq. 11-9 might be regarded as the common intermediate to which the three compounds can be related, although it cannot be concluded that *c* is a discrete precursor of the compounds to which it is formally related. Indeed, parkeol, cycloartenol, and lanosterol are found in different natural sources: lanosterol as a component of the grease (or fat) of sheep's wool, and in yeast; parkeol in *Butyrospermum parkii* (fam. Sapotaceae); and cycloartenol in *Strychnos nux-vomica* (fam. Loganiaceae) and several *Euphorbia* spp., and the corresponding 3-ketone in *Artocarpus integrifolia* (fam. Moraceae). These observations indicate that the manner in which the reactions of Eq. 11-9 occur are under specific enzymatic control. Were the intermediate *c* common to all three triterpenes it might be expected that two or all of them would be formed simultaneously.

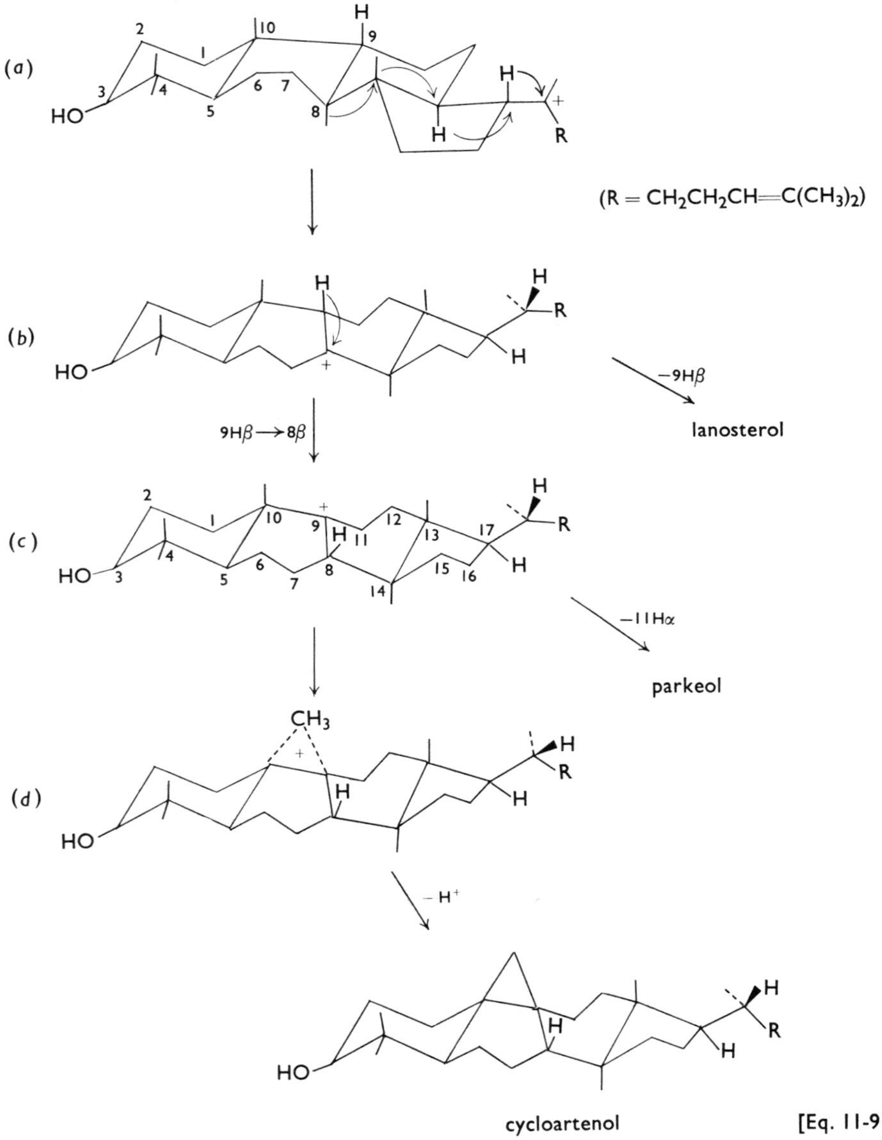

$(R = CH_2CH_2CH{=}C(CH_3)_2)$

[Eq. 11-9]

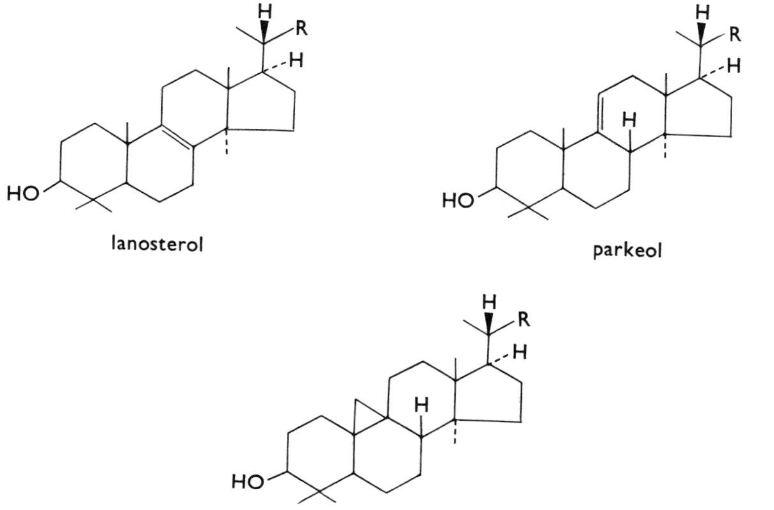

lanosterol   parkeol

cycloartenol

Fig. 11-1.

11.7 Pentacyclic Triterpenes

If the carbonium ion intermediate formed in the initial squalene cyclization reacts further with the terminal double bond of the side chain, a fifth ring is formed. A number of possible hydrogen and methyl migrations can ensue with the formation of a large class of pentacyclic compounds. The derivation of several of these, without stereochemical detail, is shown in the accompanying equations.

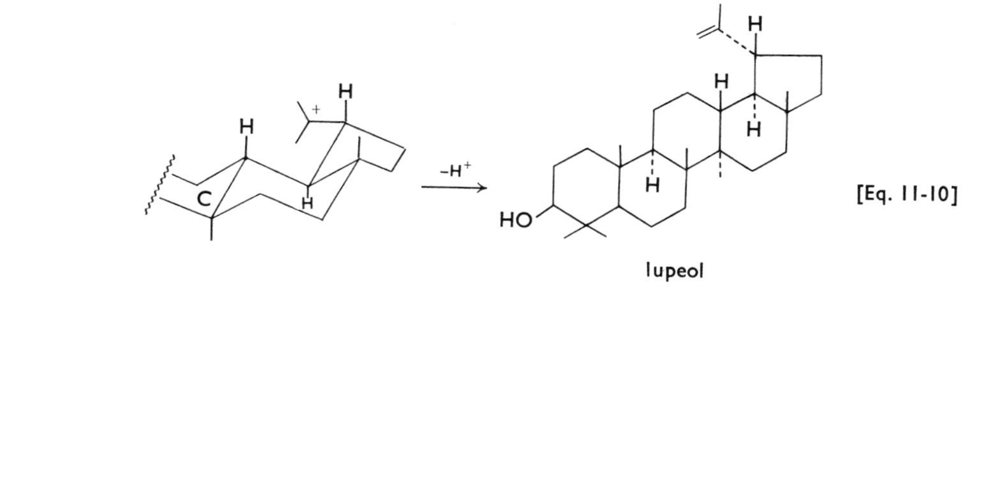

(b, Eq. 11-8)

$-H^+$ [Eq. 11-10]

lupeol

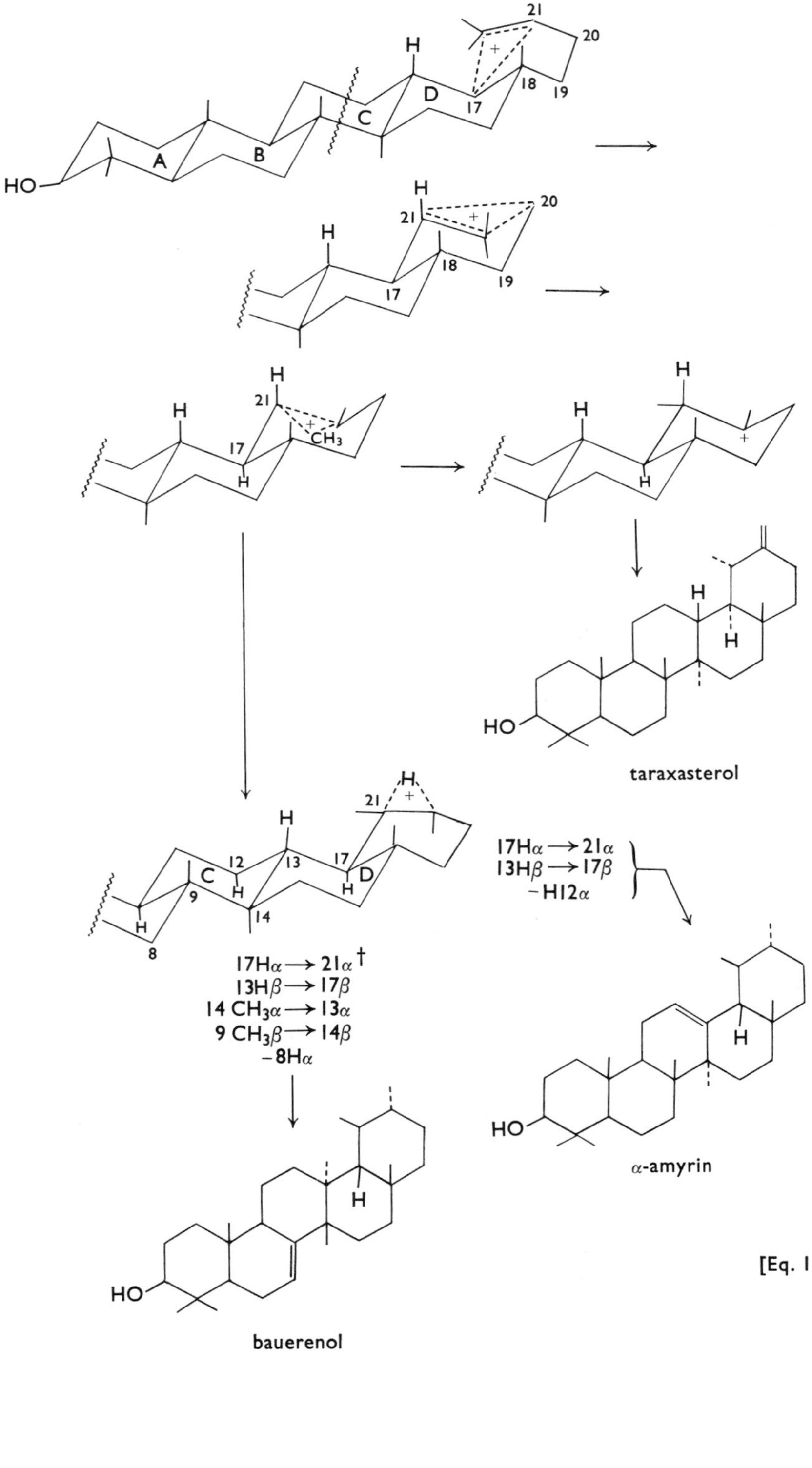

taraxasterol

$17H\alpha \longrightarrow 21\alpha$
$13H\beta \longrightarrow 17\beta$
$-H12\alpha$

$17H\alpha \longrightarrow 21\alpha$†
$13H\beta \longrightarrow 17\beta$
$14\ CH_3\alpha \longrightarrow 13\alpha$
$9\ CH_3\beta \longrightarrow 14\beta$
$-8H\alpha$

α-amyrin

[Eq. 11-11]

bauerenol

In Eq. 11-10 is represented the derivation of the pentacyclic triterpene, lupeol. The starting ion is the chair (A)-chair (B)-chair (C) precursor of the dammarane-euphane series. Interaction of the terminal double bond with the carbonium center at C-16/17/18 leads, through the changes shown, to lupeol. The stereochemistry of the compound follows from the biosynthetic pathway described, and is in fact as it is shown in the equation.

In Eq. 11-11 is shown a different mode of interaction of the side chain double bond with the carbonium center. The sequence of changes shown, leading to taraxa-sterol, α-amyrin, and bauerenol, are but a few of the many that can be formulated in a stereospecific and rational way to lead to most of the known pentacyclic triterpenes.

11.8 Simultaneous Cyclization from Both Ends of the Squalene Chain

Although most triterpenoid compounds are formed by a cyclization process started by electrophilic attack at one end of the folded molecule, it is possible for

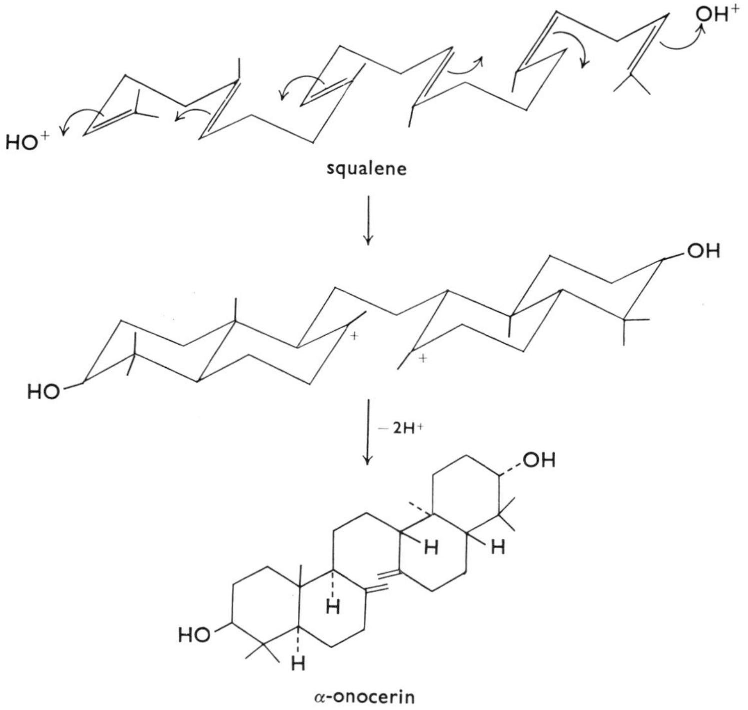

squalene

α-onocerin

[Eq. 11-12]

---

† *Note*: The numbering used to describe these shifts differs somewhat from that ordinarily used for these ring systems.

attack to occur at both ends with cyclization proceeding inward from both terminal —CH=C(CH$_3$)$_2$ groups. The triterpene onocerin possesses the structure shown in Eq. 11-12, where its formation from squalene is shown. It will be noted that the molecule of onocerin is symmetrical about an axis passing between the carbon atoms of the central —CH$_2$CH$_2$— grouping.

11.9   The Electrophilic Cyclizing Agent

Although most of the squalene cyclizations described in the foregoing pages result in the formation of compounds possessing an equatorial hydroxyl group at the 3-position, it will be recalled (Chap. 10) that cyclizations in the diterpene class are often initiated by protons, with the formation of compounds in which the A-ring (cf. Eq. 11-11) contains no oxygen. This kind of cyclization is, while uncommon in the triterpenes, not unknown; the tricyclic triterpene ambrein (Fig. 11-2) is a hydrocarbon, the genesis of which appears to be by way of a cyclization of squalene resembling that leading to onocerin but stopping short of completion.

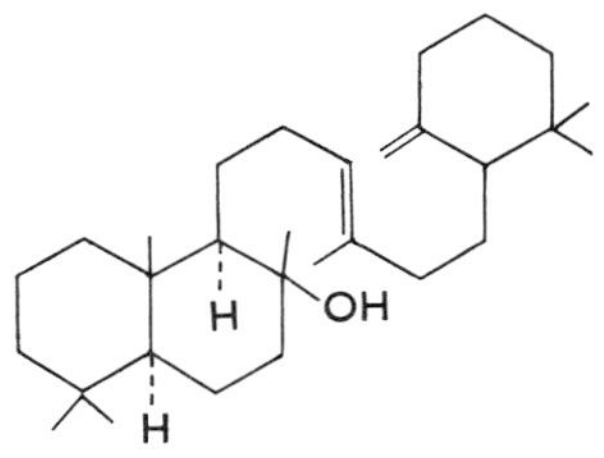

ambrein

Fig. 11-2.

The cyclizations leading to the 3-hydroxylated triterpenes are often formulated as proceeding by electrophilic attack of a species written as HO$^+$, which is simply a protonated oxygen atom. This is a formal device, for this ionic species is not a recognized component of cellular systems; nevertheless, because HO$^+$ (or some biochemical equivalent of HO$^+$) accounts so well for the postulates of the biogenetic rule it has been generally accepted as a rational means of representing the initiator of the reactions described above. Moreover, molecular oxygen is necessary for the reaction, and appears in the 3-OH group.

The exact description of the oxygen donor has not yet been provided. It would appear doubtful that a species, so far described for convenience as HO$^+$, actually exists. The alternative formulations as "enzyme-O$_2$" or "enzyme-O$^+$" have at present the virtue chiefly of leaving vague that which cannot be described more explicitly. Much remains to be learned about the steps that intervene between the precursor that possesses the terminal double bond and the final cyclized product of the reaction.

It is clear, however, that there are other, mechanistically as acceptable, means of initiating cyclizations with the introduction of oxygen, and evidence is accumulating that the cyclization reaction follows the formation of an initial epoxide (Eq. 11-13a).

It is clear from Eq. 11-13 that the carbonium ion formed by attack of a species HO^+, the protonated epoxide derived from this, and the protonated form of an epoxide derived in quite another way are all mechanistically equivalent insofar as the cyclization is concerned. The question that they pose is essentially this: is the true electrophile the proton, acting upon an epoxide formed by an independent pathway; or is the protonated epoxide, formed by attack of HO^+, the initial species?

Nature provides a great many examples of epoxides, well known as stable and isolable natural products, and of compounds (e.g., glycols and ketones) whose biosynthesis is readily explained as proceeding from an initial epoxide (for example, Eq. 11-13b). Are these epoxides formed by attack of "HO^+" upon a carbon-carbon

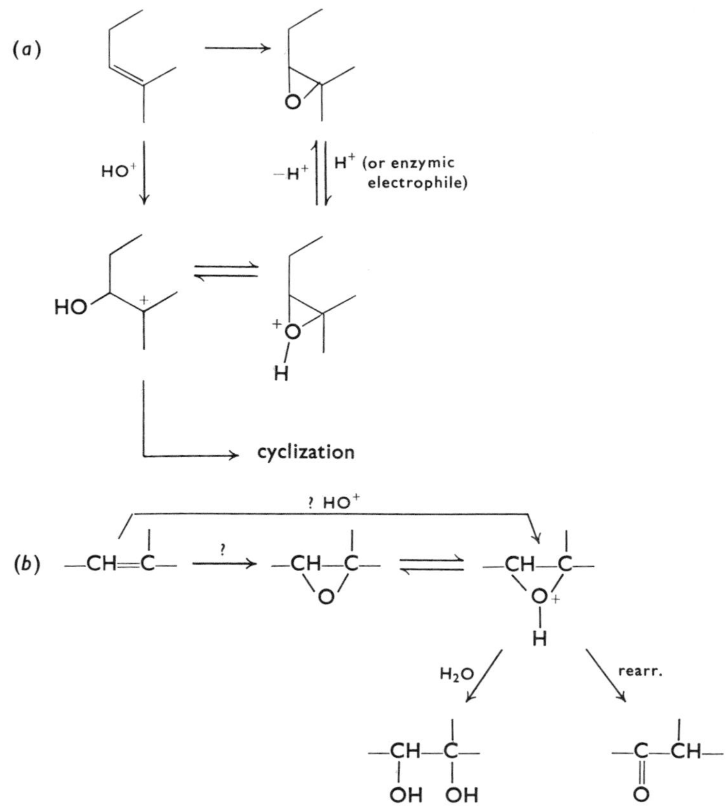

[Eq. 11-13]

double bond, followed by proton exchange; or by direct epoxidation to yield at once the unprotonated epoxide? The question is basically not one of the essential mechanism of the electrophilic cyclization reaction, but one of the precise manner in which oxygen is introduced into the double bond at which cyclization is initiated.

Evidence has been adduced that there exist separate (and experimentally separable) enzyme systems that perform the steps (a) introduction of oxygen at the terminal double bond of squalene, and (b) cyclization by electrophile-initiated attack upon the epoxide function. It would appear from observations of this kind that cyclization is not a necessary concomitant of epoxidation, as might be expected if the first species to appear were the protonated epoxide.

11.10 Secondary Alterations of Triterpenes

Triterpenes undergo secondary alteration by way of many unexceptional reactions such as the introduction of additional hydroxyl groups, the oxidation of secondary alcoholic functions to ketones, the addition and reductive removal of unsaturated linkages. Skeletal modification by the removal of methyl groups has been discussed above in the section dealing with the lanosterol-cholesterol conversion. Many reactions that reflect parts of these pathways can be recognized by the

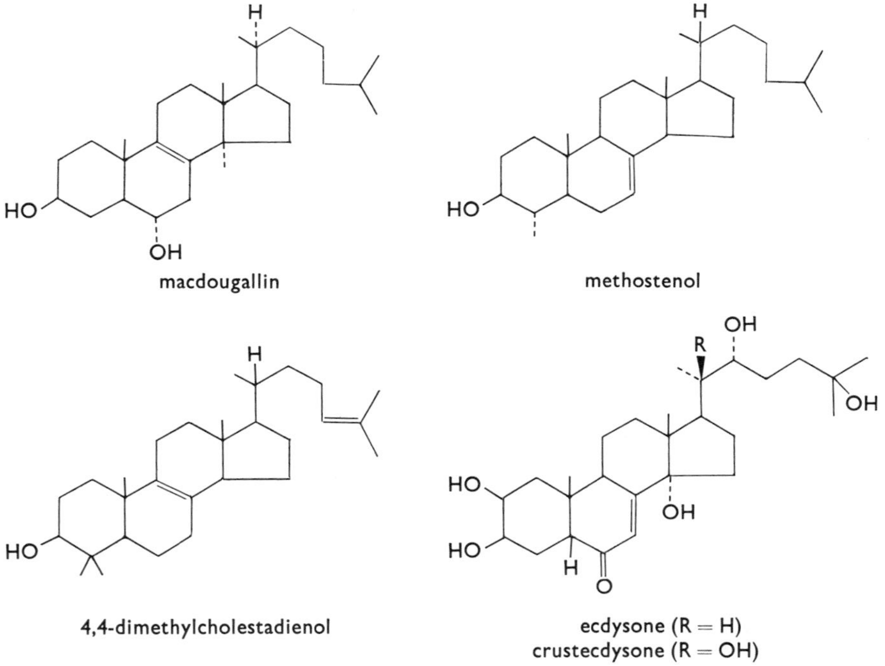

macdougallin

methostenol

4,4-dimethylcholestadienol

ecdysone (R = H)
crustecdysone (R = OH)

Fig. 11-3.

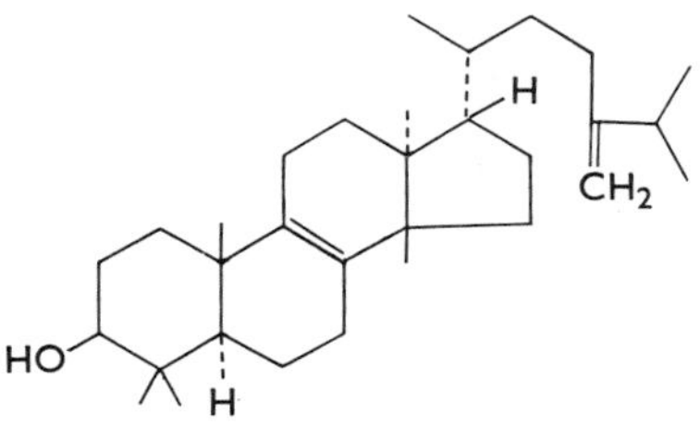

euphorbol

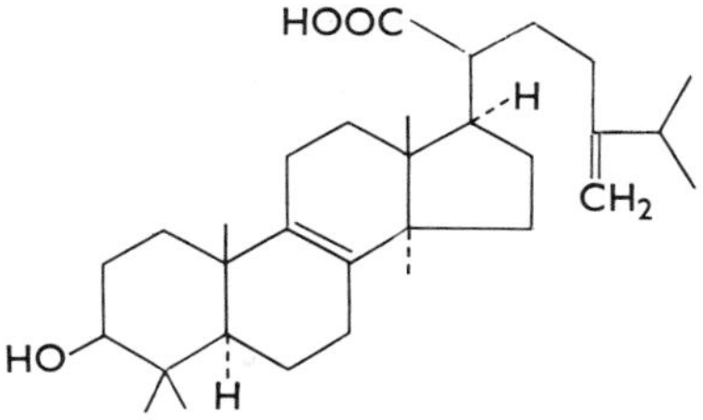

eburicoic acid

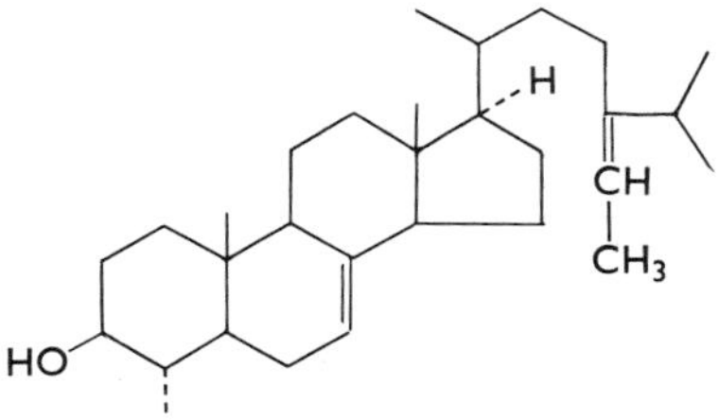

citrostadienol

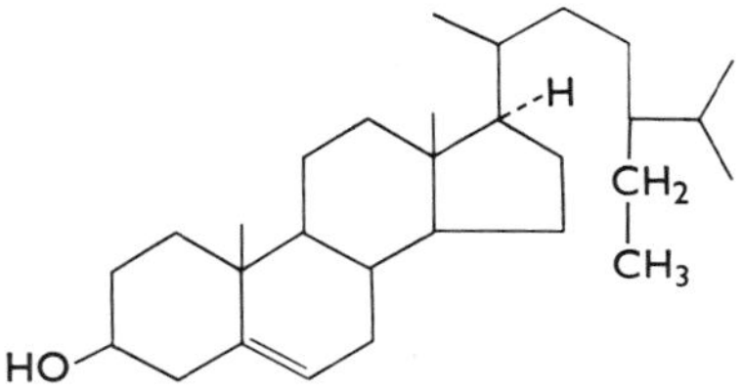

β-sitosterol

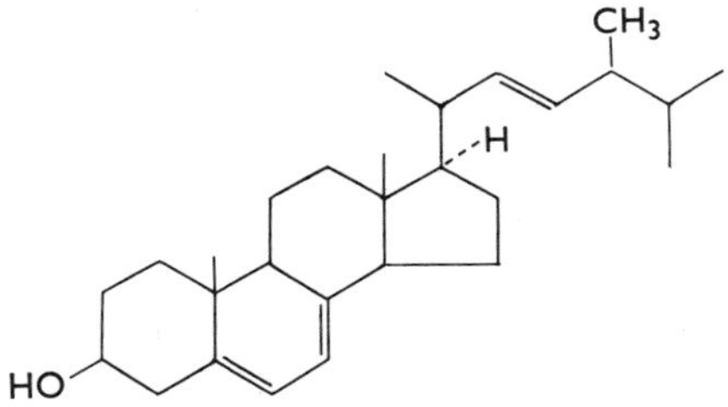

ergosterol

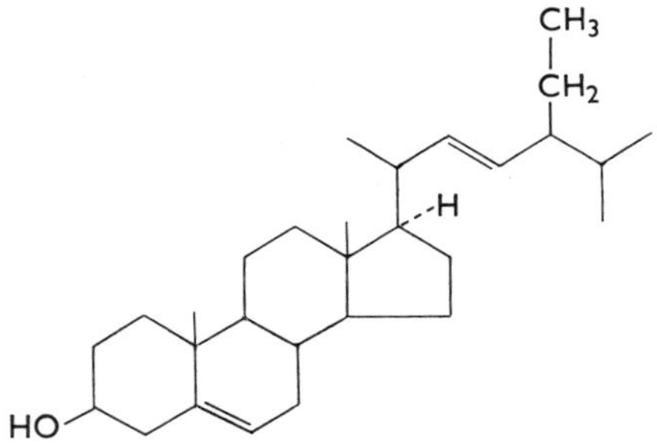

stigmasterol

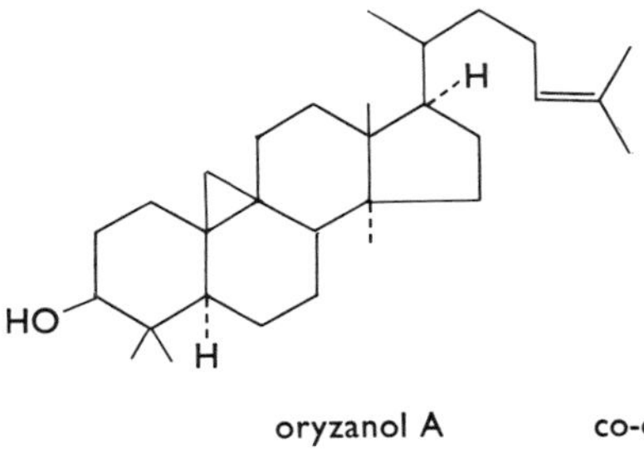

oryzanol A

co-occurs with

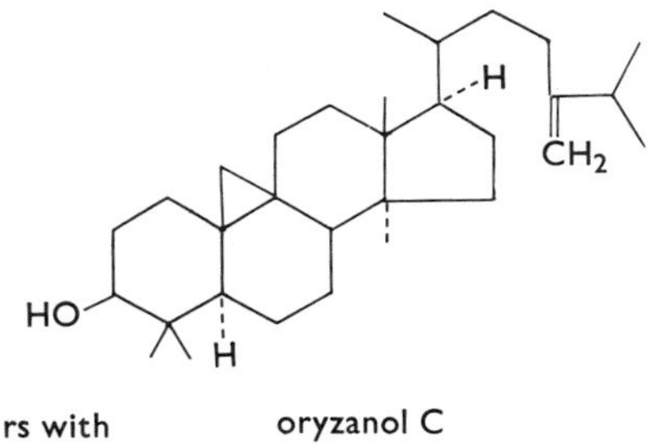

oryzanol C
(as ferulic acid ester)

Fig. 11-4. Representative Triterpenes and Sterols with C-24 Carbon Substituents.

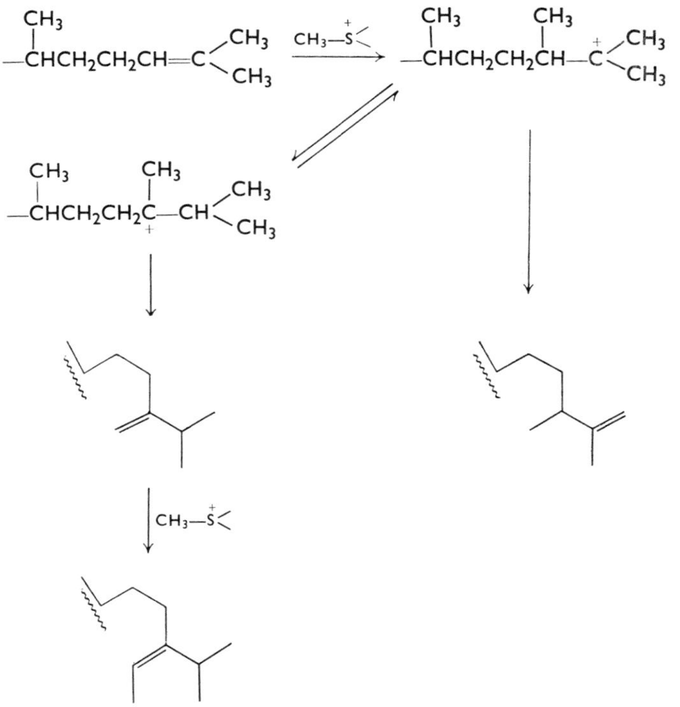

$$CH_3\text{—}S^+\text{—}$$

Structures for reaction scheme (Eq. 11-14):

$$-\underset{|}{CH}CH_2CH_2CH=C\overset{CH_3}{\underset{CH_3}{\diagdown}} \qquad \overset{CH_3}{|} \qquad -\underset{|}{CH}CH_2CH_2\underset{|}{CH}-C\overset{+}{\underset{CH_3}{\diagdown CH_3}}$$

(with CH_3 substituent labels)

$$-\underset{CH_3}{|}CH\ CH_2CH_2\overset{CH_3}{\underset{+}{C}}-CH\overset{CH_3}{\underset{CH_3}{\diagdown}}$$

$$CH_3\text{—}S^+<$$

[Eq. 11-14]

occurrence in nature of such compounds as macdougallin, in which only the 4,4-dimethyl groups have been lost; methostenol, in which one C-4 methyl group and the C-14 methyl group are lost; and 4,4-dimethylcholestadienol, in which the C-14 methyl group is missing.

A group of highly modified steroid compounds of great biological interest and importance is represented by the compound ecdysone, a hormone important in the regulation of the molting of insects. Ecdysone and numerous compounds of related structure (and comparable biological activity) occur in both plants and animals (insects) (Fig. 11-3).

One of the commonest kinds of structural elaboration superimposed upon the fundamental C_{30} skeleton is the addition of "extra" carbon atoms to lead to compounds that contain 31 and 32 carbon atoms.

Examples of compounds of these classes are euphorbol, eburicoic acid, citrostadienol; and, in the steroids, ergosterol, sitosterol, and stigmasterol* (Fig. 11-4).

Experiments carried out with the aid of labeled precursors have shown that the "extra" carbon atoms at C-24 in these compounds are derived from methionine

* The steroids are not, of course C_{31} and C_{32} compounds, but the "extra" carbon atoms are located in the same position as in the modified triterpenes and are undoubtedly introduced in the same way.

(or formate). The second carbon atom of the ethyl or ethylidene group (e.g., citro-stadienol and stigmasterol) is also derived from these one-carbon sources.

The addition of the carbon atom from the methyl donor may be compared with the similar addition of carbon atoms to the alkenoic acids (Chap. 3) and may be formulated in general terms as in Eq. 11-14. The addition of a second methyl group to a C-24 methylene compound to give the C-24 ethylidene or ethyl derivatives can occur by a second alkylation of the same kind.

11.11 Degradation of Triterpenes

The commonest metabolic degradation of triterpenes is that of the demethylation of lanosterol to give cholesterol, and has been discussed above. A large number

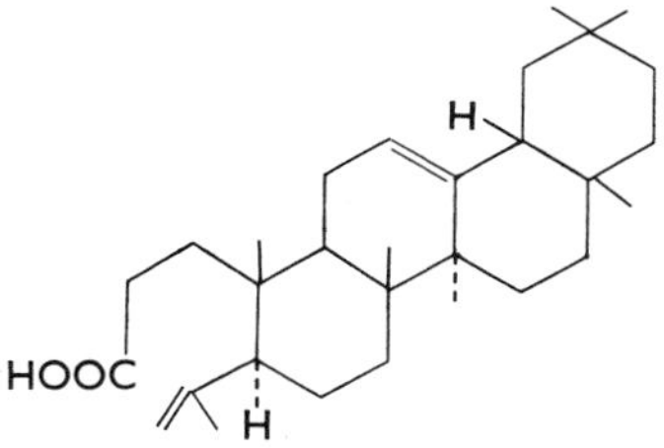

(a) nyctanthic acid

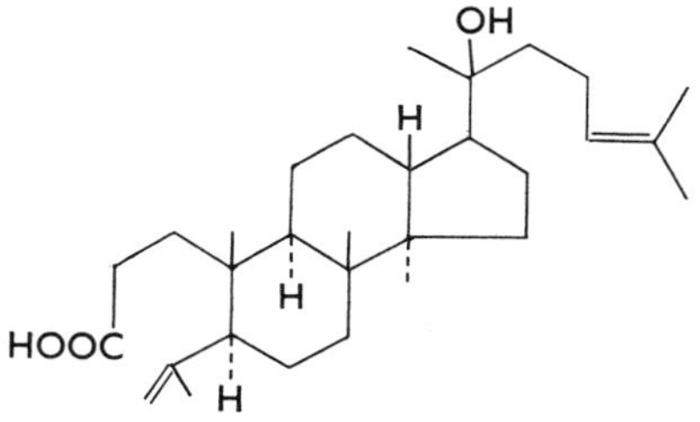

(b) dammarenolic acid

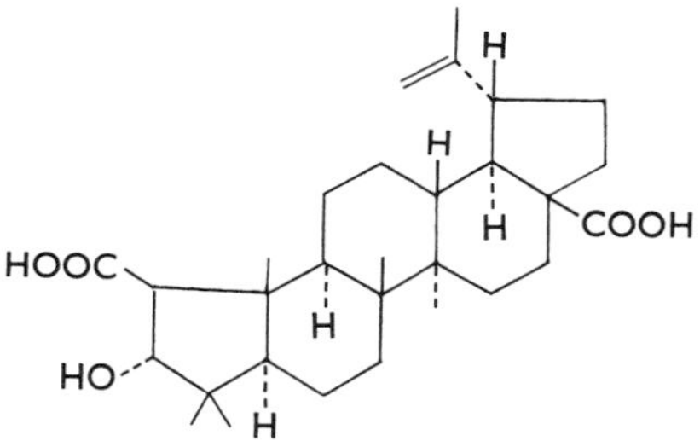

(c) ceanothic acid

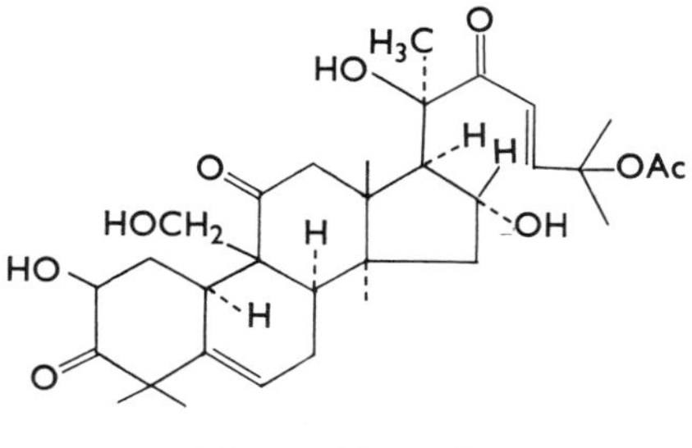

(d) cucurbitacin A

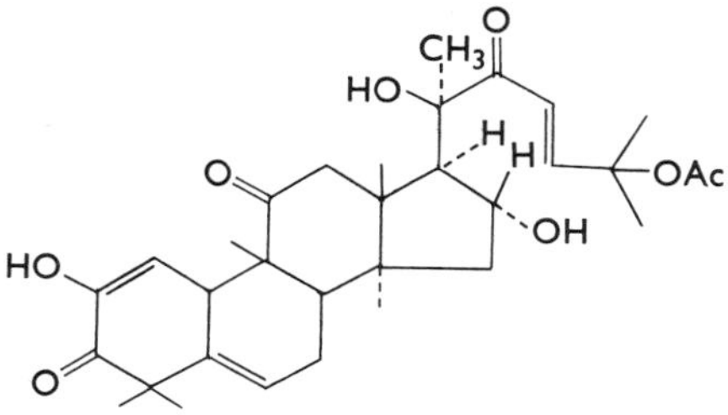

(e) cucurbitacin E

Fig. 11-5.

of compounds of various gross structures, all of which are regarded as degraded triterpenes, occur in nature. One group of these will be described in Chapter 12; several other examples are those discussed here.

Opening of the A-ring by oxidation is a natural process which in its simplest form is expressed by the compounds nyctanthic acid and dammarenolic acid (Fig. 11-5a, b). It will be seen later (Chap. 12) that this process may represent the initial stage in a more extensive alteration of the A-ring portion of the molecule.

A reaction that results in oxidative alteration of the A-ring is expressed in the structure of ceanothic acid in which the A-ring has been contracted, presumably by a reaction of the benzilic acid-rearrangement type, to a five-membered ring (Fig. 11-5c). A rearrangement of this kind would be expected to follow the formation of a 2,3-diketone in ring A of a precursor. Numerous compounds of this kind are known, although the co-occurrence in nature of the associated 6-ring diketones and 5-ring dicarboxylic acids cannot be cited in direct support of this conjecture. The cucurbitacins, a group of closely related triterpenes found in the members of the Cucurbitaceae (gourd or melon family) are characterized by extensive oxidation, including oxidation at C-2 and C-3 of the A-ring. Two cucurbitacins are shown in Fig. 11-5d, e as examples of the class.

Further discussion of degraded triterpenes will be found in the following chapter.

11.12 Markownikov Cyclization

It will be noted that the closure of the C-ring in the cyclization of squalene (Eq. 11-15) takes place in a manner that is different from what would be expected on mechanistic grounds, for the "intermediate"* shown in Eq. 11-15 is a secondary carbonium ion, and not the tertiary ion that might have been expected.

The course that might have been predicted on mechanistic grounds is that shown in Eq. 11-16, in which, with formation of a five-membered C-ring, Markownikov-cyclization occurs.

This mode of cyclization is rare in nature, but is known in the compound malabaricol (from *Ailanthus malabaricus* DC., fam. Simaroubaceae).

It is of particular interest to note that when synthetic 2,3-oxidosqualene is cyclized under non-enzymic conditions, cyclization follows (in part) the Markownikov pathway, and a compound possessing the malabaricol skeleton is formed. This shows that the role of the enzyme(s) that control squalene cyclization in living

---

* The "intermediate" is shown to clarify the discussion, but it is probable that the complete cyclization takes place in a smooth and concerted fashion and that no such discrete intermediate exists.

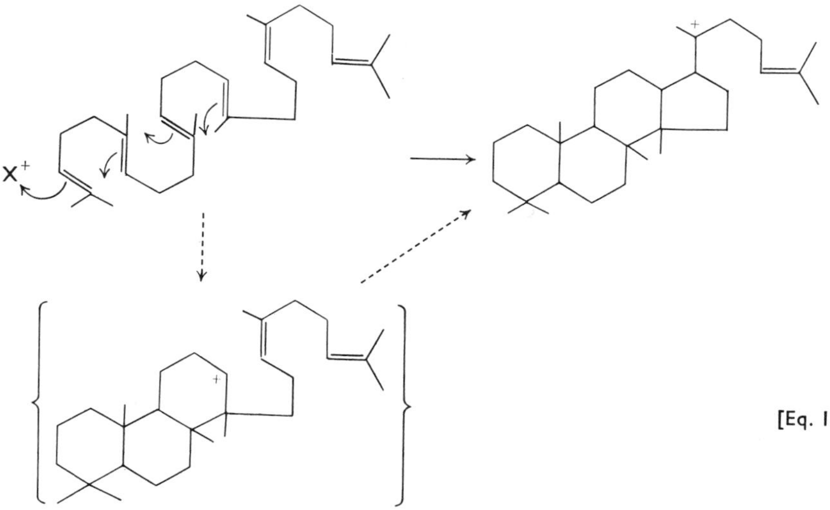

[Eq. 11-15]

organisms is of critical importance in directing the molecular architecture of the products. It will already have been noted that enzymatic control in the folding of the squalene chain (lanostane and euphane series) is a dominant factor in the natural process.

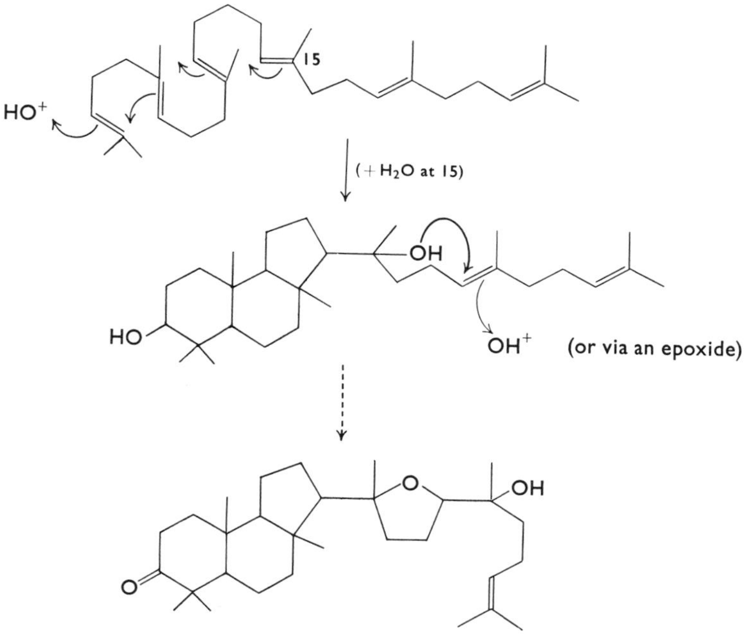

malabaricol

[Eq. 11-16]

XII CHAPTER

REFERENCES FOR FURTHER READING

1. A. J. Birch, D. J. Collins, S. Muhammed, and J. P. Turnbull, *The Structure of Flindissol*, J. Chem. Soc., (1963), 2762.
2. G. J. W. Breen, E. Ritchie, W. T. L. Sidwell, and W. C. Taylor, *Triterpenoids from Leaves of Flindersia bourjotiana*, Austr. J. Chem., *19*, (1966), 455.
3. C. W. L. Bevan, D. E. U. Ekong, T. G. Halsall, and P. Toft, *The Structure of Turraeanthin*, J. Chem. Soc., (1967), 820.
4. D. Lavie and M. K. Jain, *Tetranortriterpenoids from Melia azadirachta L.*, Chem Comm., (1967), 278.
5. D. H. R. Barton, S. K. Prahan, S. Sternhell, and J. F. Templeton, *The Constitution of Limonin and Related Bitter Principles,* J. Chem. Soc., (1961), 255.
6. D. L. Dreyer, *Limonoid Bitter Principles,* Fortschr. Chem. Org. Naturstoffe, L. Zechmeister, Ed., *26*, (1968).
7. D. L. Dreyer, *A Biogenetic Proposal for the Simaroubaceous Bitter Principles,* Experientia, *20*, (1964), 297.
8. J. Moron and J. Polonsky, *On the Triterpenoid Origin of the Simaroubaceous Bitter Principles,* Tetrahedron Letters, (1968), 385.
9. D. E. U. Ekong and E. O. Olagbemi, *Correlation of Gedunin, Methyl Angolensate, and Andirobin,* J. Chem. Soc., (1966), 944.

CHAPTER XII

Metabolic Degradation
of Triterpenes

12.1 Introduction

An extraordinary confluence of chemical and botanical characteristics is found in a group of naturally occurring compounds that occur in three closely allied plant families and which display in their structures a pattern of chemical alteration of a triterpene precursor that leads, evidently by successively greater degrees of biological oxidation, to compounds in which the structural features of the ultimate precursor can scarcely be discerned. These compounds, known under the general terms limonoids, meliacins,* and simaroubalides, are found, respectively, in the plant families Rutaceae, Meliaceae, and Simaroubaceae. The close relationships that exist between the structures of these compounds and certain of their triterpenoid precursors, affords striking evidence of the botanical affinities between these three plant families, affinities that had been recognized by botanists on nonchemical grounds.

Allied to these three classes of compounds, and often occurring along with them in plants of the same family (and often in the same plant) is a group of compounds in which the process of oxidative alteration of the triterpene precursor has just begun, with the introduction of oxygen into the C-17 side chain. It is possible to trace, by inspection of these compounds, starting from an intact (i.e., C_{30}) tetracyclic triterpene and proceeding to the most extensively altered structures, a compelling route of biosynthesis in which nearly all of the steps can be illustrated by well known natural products. In the sections to follow this biosynthetic pathway will be traced. The starting triterpene for most of the compounds of these classes is

---

* Some authors prefer to consider meliacins and limonoids in one class, for which the latter term is used, because of their common possession of a particular type of D-ring modification.

probably tirucallol (Chap. 11), although in those compounds in which asymmetry at C-20 is lost there is no way of knowing whether the precursor is tirucallol or euphol.

12.2   Alteration of the C-17 Side Chain

Numerous triterpenes are known in which oxygen functions are present in the side chain. Some examples have been mentioned earlier; and in Fig. 12-1 are given a number of further illustrations (in which stereochemical details, which will be dealt with later, are omitted, and only the D-ring is shown).

Very few definitive experiments (i.e., with isotopic tracers) have been carried out to define the course of the many secondary elaborations of triterpenes. The present views of the biosynthesis of the extensively degraded triterpenoid compounds discussed in this chapter are based largely upon two lines of argument:

1. comparisons between the structures of compounds belonging to a single class and, ideally, found within a sharply delimited area of the plant kingdom; for example, within a single species, genus, tribe, or family.

Such structural comparisons provide persuasive evidence for interrelationships between compounds within one class or in closely comparable classes when they disclose stereochemical as well as gross structural similarities.

2. the recognition that the compounds in question can be derived by a rational series of changes that start from a compound whose presence in the plants can be assumed with confidence, through a series of structural alterations of each of which specific examples are known in the plant group in question in the form of known naturally occurring compounds. In some cases (notably in those under consideration here) exact laboratory (i.e., in non-biological systems) analogies are known for the individual transformations in the sequence of degradations or alterations.

Although the biosynthesis of triterpenes and steroids has now been established in detail by experiments with the use of labeled compounds in living systems, it will be recalled that the early concepts in which squalene was the progenitor of lanosterol, and lanosterol of cholesterol, formed the conceptual basis for the later experiments which corroborated the hypothesis. Although the two modes of initial coiling of the squalene chain (Eq. 11-1) were not equivalent, as labeling studies showed, the one which is now accepted as being correct was the one which was recognized as that from which the hypothesis of the "biogenetic" isoprene rule was constructed. That is to say, the concepts of triterpene biosynthesis that are now generally held were first derived by considerations such as those of point 2 above and found to have general application to the field of triterpenes, with all of their diversity of structure. Indeed, there are many terpenoid compounds whose biosynthesis has never been

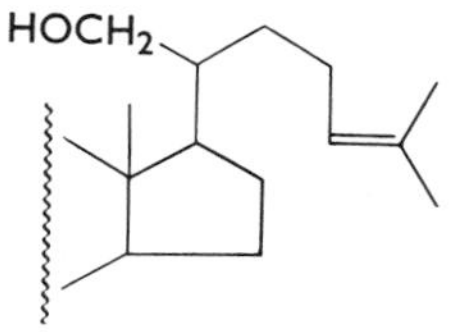

21-hydroxylanostadienone

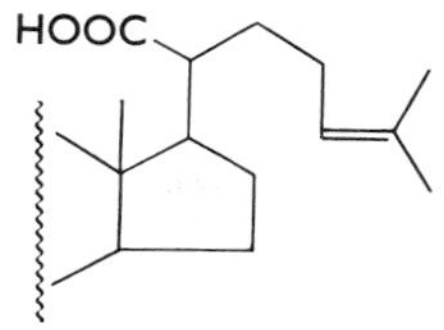

pinicolic acid

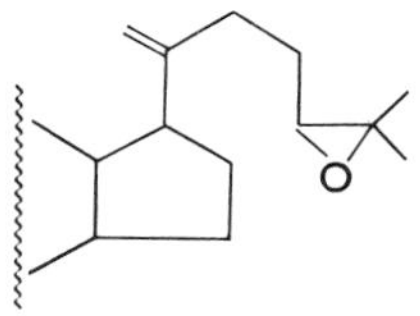

aglaiol

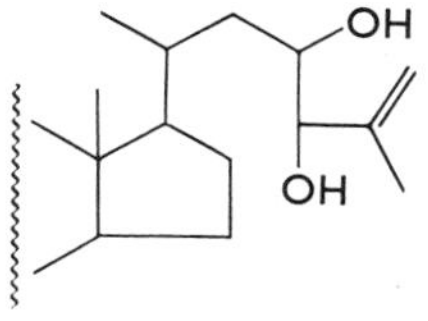

bourjotinolone B

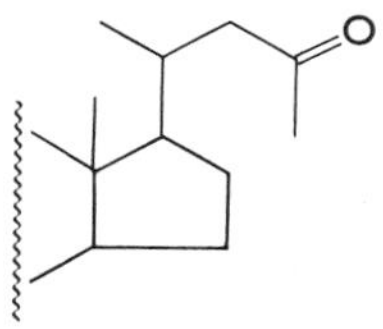

bourjotone
(side chain degraded)

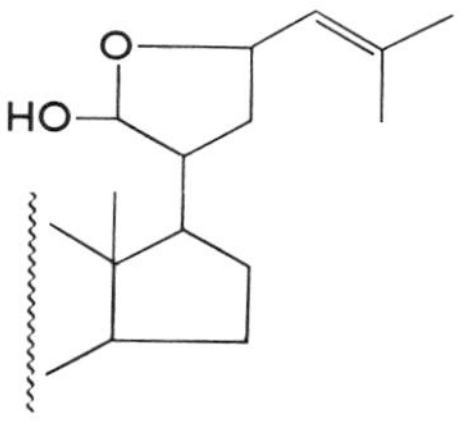

flindissol

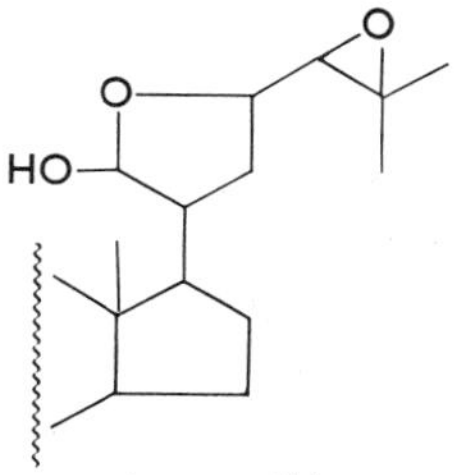

turreanthin
melianone

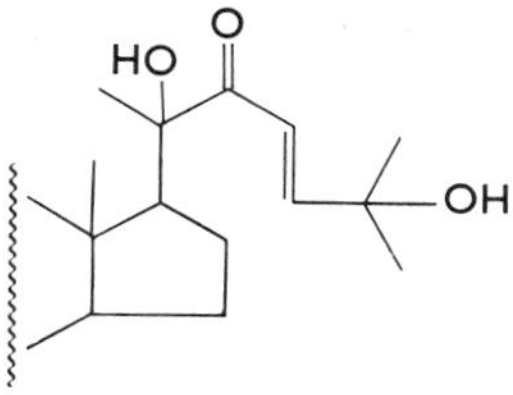

cucurbitacins

Fig. 12-1. Partial Structures of some Triterpenes with Oxygenated Side Chains.

established by the necessary experiments, but which are assumed to be formed by the pathways applicable to members of their class because of the agreement between the requirements of the hypothesis and the structure and stereochemistry they are known to possess.

It is an obvious extension to this kind of argument that the biogenetic hypothesis is a powerful tool in the determination of structure. Although it is often found that predictions (especially of stereochemical details) violate the expectations of the hypothesis, such apparently aberrant findings frequently provide a basis for further refinement of the theory. It is to be emphasized that biogenetic theory does not provide unequivocal answers to questions of structure and stereochemistry; rather, it often does no more than provide the most likely assumption which it is the task of the experimentalist to prove or disprove.

12.3 Flindissol and Turraeanthin

Flindissol is a triterpene found in the plant *Flindersia dissosperma* and *F. maculosa* (fam. Rutaceae). It possesses a number of structural features that, it will be seen as this discussion develops, are of special biogenetic significance. These features are (a) the extensively oxidized side chain which contains the furanoid ring; (b) the 7,8-double bond; and (c) the euphol-tirucallol configuration of the skeletal framework of the molecule.

Flindissol contains the side chain shown in Fig. 12-1, and has the complete structure shown in Eq. 12-1, in which are also outlined certain of the transformations that demonstrate those structural features that are relevant to this discussion. Flindissone lactone, the keto lactone, is formed by the oxidation of flindissol (which is a cyclic hemiacetal), with chromic acid. Since the oxygen atom of the lactone ring is allylically disposed with respect to the double bond of the side chain, treatment of flindissone lactone with hydrogen and platinum resulted in both hydrogenation and hydrogenolysis. One of the products was an acid, recognized as dihydro-α-elemolic acid, the stereochemistry of which was known to be that of a tirucallane derivative.

The 7,8-position of the double bond in the B-ring was established by the appearance in the nuclear magnetic resonance spectrum of flindissone lactone signals for two vinyl protons, one of which is that of the isobutenyl group; and by the isomerization (with HCl) of flindissone lactone into the $\Delta^{8,9}$ compound, isoflindissone lactone.

Turraeanthin occurs in *Turraeanthus africanus*, a plant of the family Meliaceae. It will be seen in the discussions to follow that the family Rutaceae, to which *Flindersia* belongs, and the family Meliaceae are characterized by the presence of two groups of triterpenoid compounds which are characterized by an extensively modified and unusual C/D side chain system. It will be shown that there is a strong likelihood that this structural feature owes its derivation to a series of transformations starting with a modified tirucallol such as flindissol; consequently, the presence of flindissol in a rutaceous plant and of turraeanthin in a meliaceous plant takes on special significance.

Turraeanthin has the structure shown in Eq. 12-2, and the proof of its constitution is most easily expressed by showing its transformation into flindissone lactone

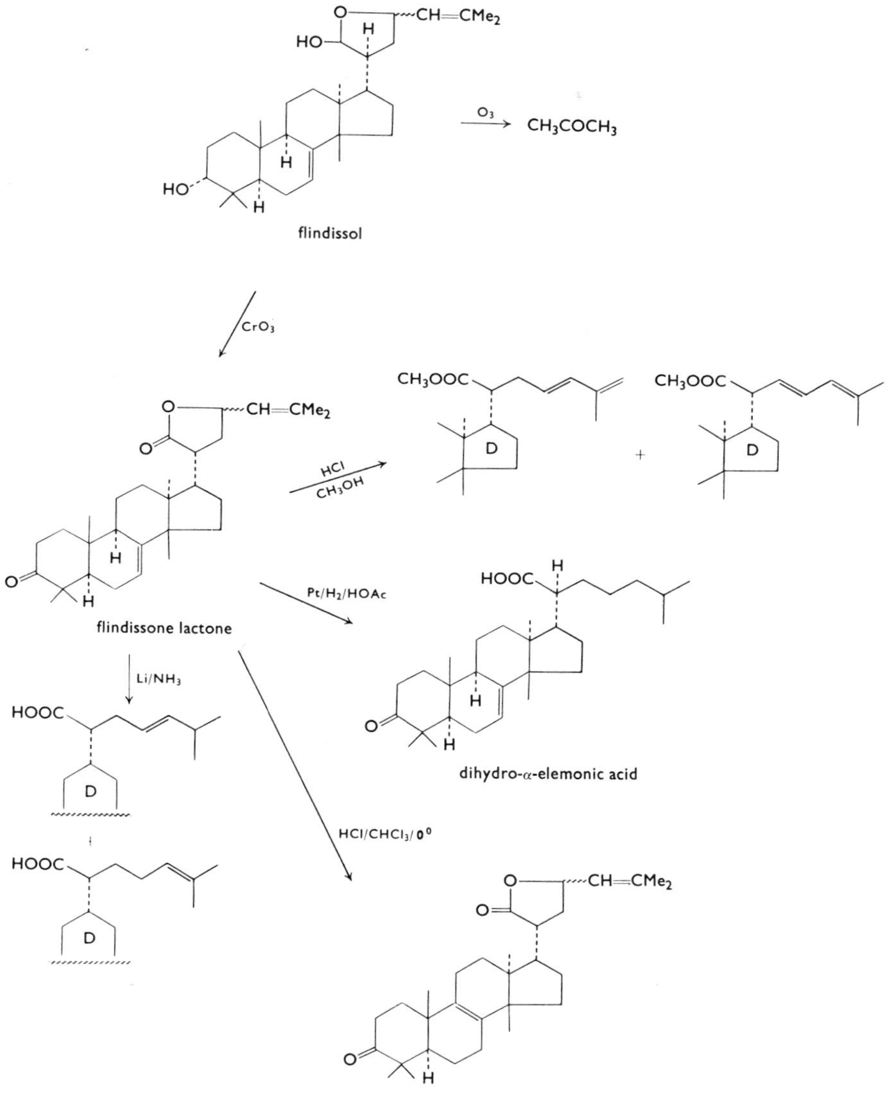
CH=CMe2
HO
H
O3
CH3COCH3
flindissol
CrO3
CH3OOC
D
HCl
CH3OH
flindissone lactone
Pt/H2/HOAc
HOOC
dihydro-α-elemonic acid
Li/NH3
HCl/CHCl3/0°
isoflindissone lactone

[Eq. 12-1]

by the steps given in Eq. 12-2. Additional studies on turraeanthin employed physical methods that were somewhat more refined than those available at the time flindissol was investigated. All of the evidence confirmed the structural and stereochemical details shown in the equations. It will be noted that the 3-hydroxyl group in flindissol is 3α (axial) while in turraeanthin it is 3β (equatorial). Since the expected "biogenetic" configuration of this hydroxyl group is 3β, it is possible that flindissol is formed by the reactions, 3β-OH → 3-keto → 3α-OH, the last reduction being effected under specific enzymatic stereo-control.

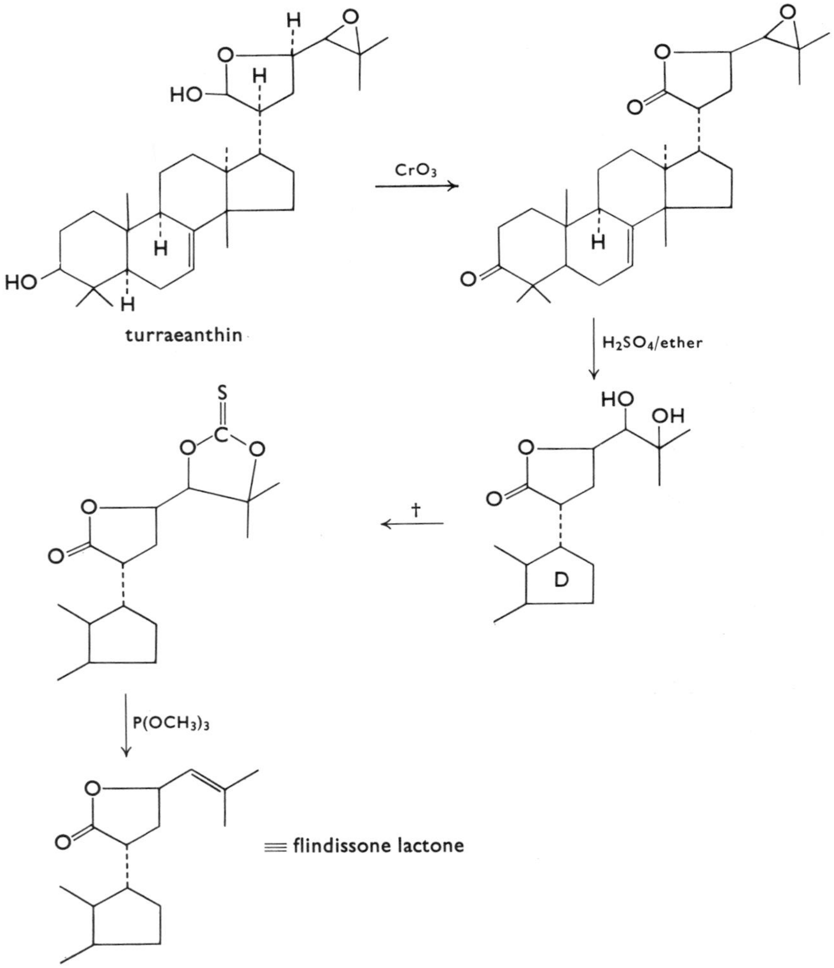

turraeanthin

CrO₃

H₂SO₄/ether

†

D

≡ flindissone lactone

P(OCH₃)₃

+ S=P(OCH₃)₃ + CO₂   [Eq. 12-2]

† Reagent: thiocarbonyldiimidazole.

Melianone, the 3-keto compound corresponding to turraeanthin, and bourjotino-lone (Fig. 12-1) occur, respectively in a *Melia* (Meliaceae) and a *Flindersia* (Ruta-ceae); they, too, are stereochemically members of the tirucall-7-ene group of triterpenes.

12.4 Constituents of *Melia azadirachta* L.

Melia azadirachta L. provides a group of compounds that illustrate further stages in a degradative sequence of which flindissol, turraeanthin and melianone furnish examples of the early stages.

The genus *Melia* (fam. Meliaceae) has been intensively studied over many years by numerous investigators. All parts of the tree—leaves, fruits, flowers, wood, and bark—have been studied at one time or another, and an extensive list of terpenoid compounds have been isolated and studied. In recent years, following the elucidation of the structures of certain analogous compounds from the related families Rutaceae and Simaroubaceae, renewed interest in *Melia* (commonly called nim, or nimb) has developed, with the isolation of many new compounds which, it will be seen, furnish excellent illustrations of the biosynthetic transforma-tions with which this chapter is concerned.

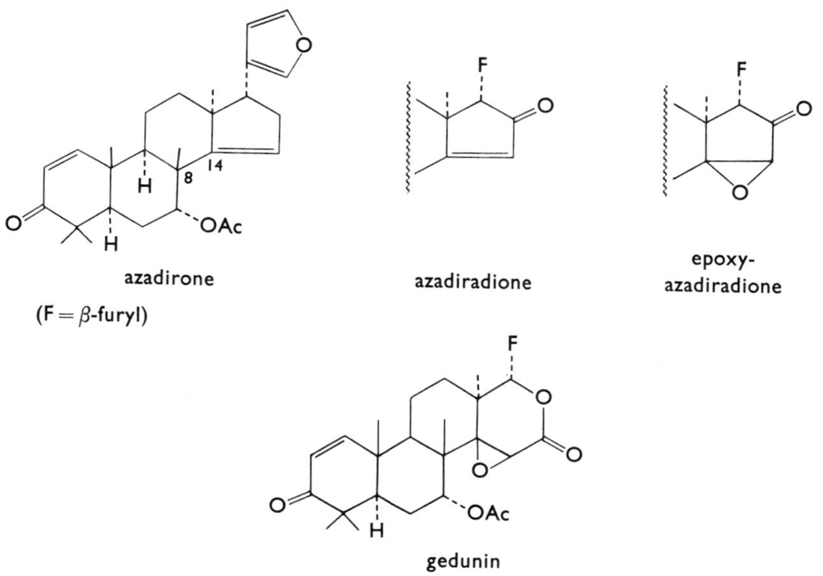

Fig. 12-2. Some Compounds of *Melia azadirachta*.

The simplest of the degraded triterpenes of *M. azadirachta* and one of the more recently discovered constituents, is azadirone. Accompanying azadirone (in the seed oil) are azadiradione, epoxyazadiradione, and a number of other compounds, to be described further on, including gedunin (Fig. 12-2).

Three features of the structures of these compounds are to be noted: (a) they possess a rearranged tirucallane (or euphane) skeleton, in which the methyl group originally at 14β is found at 8β. The methyl groups at 10β and 13α, and the side chain at 17α are as in tirucallol; (b) the side chain has lost the terminal isobutyl grouping, leaving the furan ring. This will be seen to represent a degradation step that appears to be foreshadowed in the structures of the flindissol and turraeanthin side chains; and, finally, an oxygen substituent has been introduced at C-7. The α (rather than β) configuration of the —OAc substituent in this position will be seen to have significant bearing on the (probable) course of the biosynthesis of these compounds (see Eq. 12-8). The further alteration of the D-ring to form gedunin will be considered below.

12.5   Formation of the 8β-Methyl-$\Delta^{14,15}$ Structure

The hypothesis that such compounds as azadirone, gedunin, etc. arise from tirucallol (or euphol) as the result of extensive metabolic alteration cannot yet be established by citing specific instances of each metabolic reaction that occurs. The hypothesis rests chiefly upon the persuasive consistency between the structure and stereochemistry of each of the many compounds that can be visualized as representing the individual stages of a process of degradation, and upon specific examples of many of the postulated steps that can be carried out experimentally.

The change of the tirucall-7-ene structure found in flindissol into the 8β-methyl-$\Delta^{14,15}$ framework of azadirone finds a striking parallel in the oxidation of dihydrobutyrospermol acetate with chromic acid (Eq. 12-3). It will be seen that the demand of the oxidant for the electrons of the 7,8-double bond creates an electron-deficient center at C-8, bringing about migration of the β-methyl group from C-14 to C-8 and ultimate loss of the C-15 proton to produce the structure and stereo-chemistry found in azadirone. It is also evident that a simple biochemical model that can be proposed for this change is that shown in the partial formulation in Eq. 12-4, in which an initial 7,8-α-epoxide, or α-attack of HO$^+$, brings about the same sequence of events. It will be recalled that the same kind of oxidation—the electrophilic attack upon a 2,3-epoxide—is proposed to account for the oxidative cyclization of squalene.

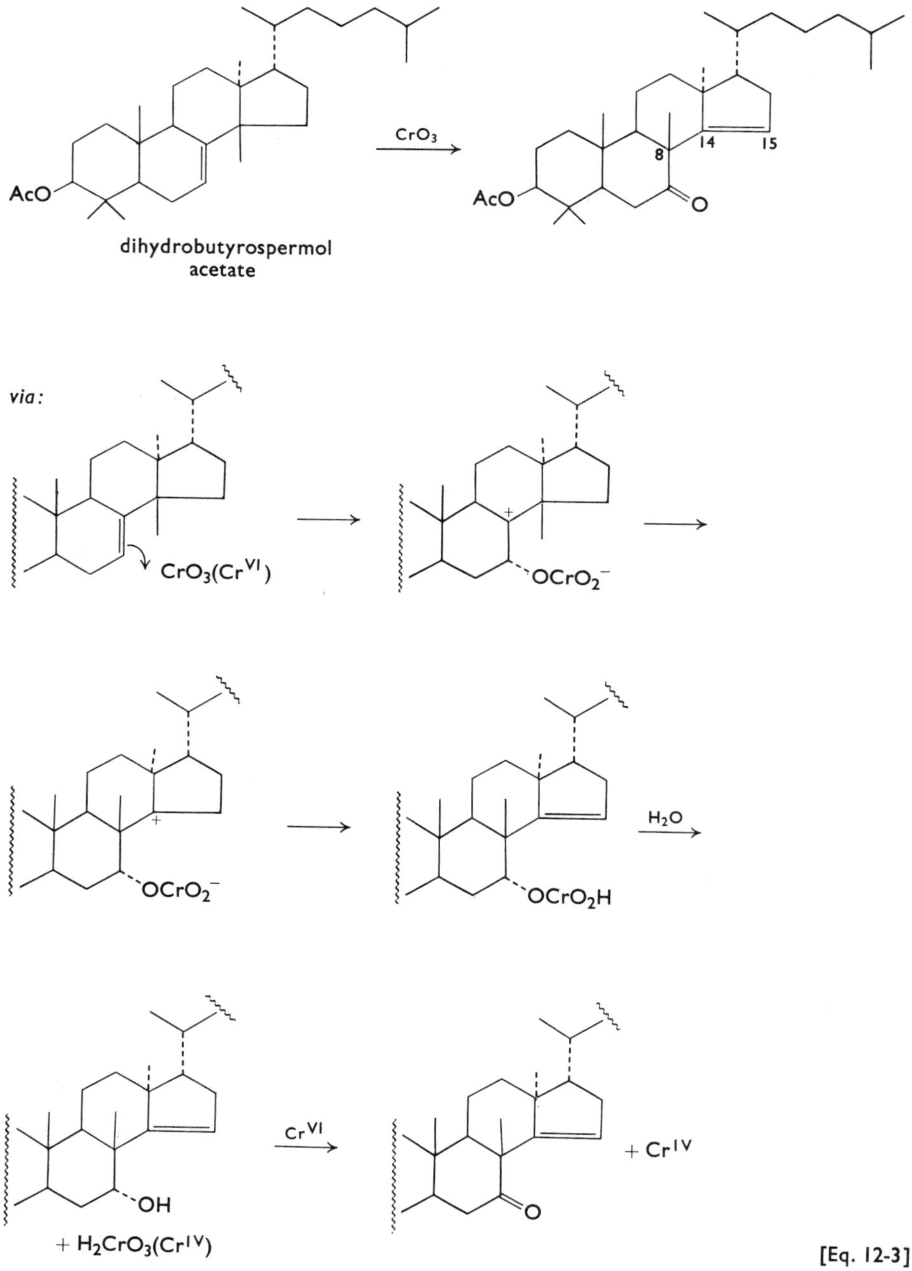

dihydrobutyrospermol
acetate

via:

[Eq. 12-3]

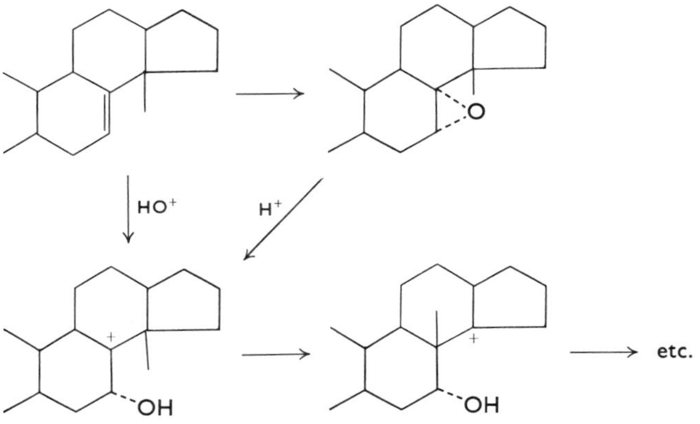

[Eq. 12-4]

12.6 Side Chain Alteration

The change in the side chain of flindissol or turraeanthin to form the β-furyl substituent found in the *Melia* compounds can be formulated as in the reactions shown in Eq. 12-5.

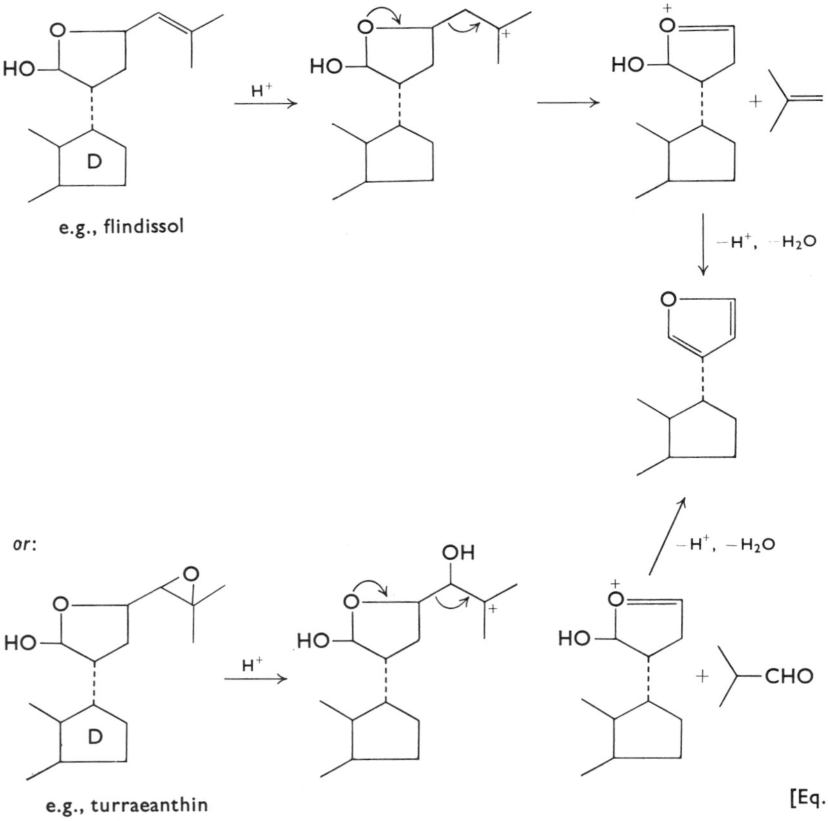

e.g., flindissol

or:

e.g., turraeanthin

[Eq. 12-5]

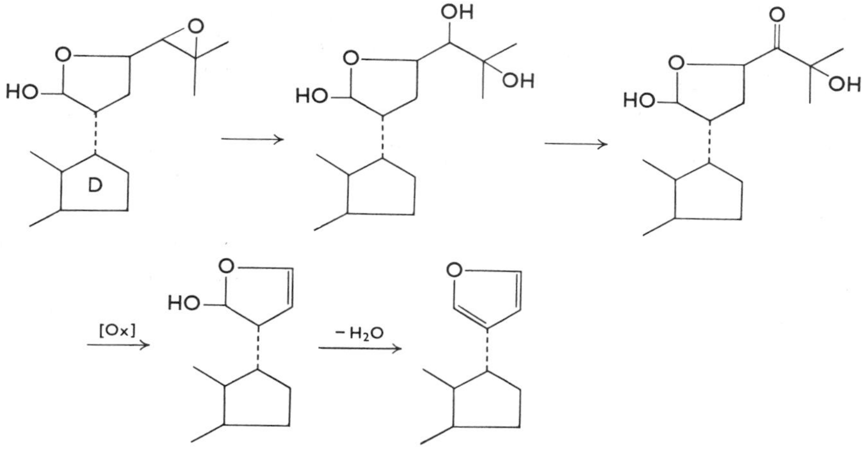

$$+(CH_3)_2C\text{—}COOH \qquad\qquad\qquad\qquad\qquad\qquad [Eq.\ 12\text{-}6]$$
$$\underset{OH}{|}$$

Alternative proposals have been made. For example, the generation of the β-furyl substituent from a hydroxyketone formed by further oxidation of tur-raeanthin (as the 24,25-glycol) has been suggested to take place as in Eq. 12-6, the final step being an oxidative cleavage. It will be seen that these several routes are mechanistically possible, and there is at present no firm basis for selecting one as more likely than another.

The prevalence of the 17-β-furyl substituent in compounds present in Ruta-ceae (limonoids) and Meliaceae(meliacins), and the occurrence of such compounds as the bourjotinolones, flindissol, turraeanthin, and melianone (Fig. 12-1) in plants of these families, provides a compelling argument for the biosynthetic pathway described.

An alternate form of side chain alteration, in which the furan ring is not elaborated but its elements persist in a γ-lactone, is found in simarolide (Fig. 12-5).

12.7   Khivorin and Khivol

Khivorin, from plants of the genus *Khaya*, is a meliacin in which ring D has undergone an oxidative cleavage (and reclosure by lactonization) to form the structure typical of the large class of compounds of the Meliaceae, has the structure shown in Fig. 12-3. It will be seen that the principal structural features that have been discussed so far are present: the 17-β furyl group; and the 7-αOAc-8β methyl groups derived from a tirucall-7-ene that has undergone oxidation as in Eqs. 12-3 or 12-4.

The D-ring of khivorin is like that of gedunin (Fig. 12-2), a constituent of several meliaceous plants; and it will be recalled that gedunin is accompanied in

Melia azadirachta by azadirone, azadiradione, and epoxyazadiradione (Fig. 12-2). *Khaya* species, too, contain numerous compounds in which these same structural relationships can be discerned. Some of these are shown in Fig. 12-3. The occurrence of groups of compounds related in so clearly ordered a structural sequence and in the same plant species leads compellingly to the conclusion that they represent points on a biosynthetic pathway. The whole sequence, expressed in terms of a type structure, but starting specifically from tirucallol, can be represented by the stages shown in Eq. 12-7.* While the exact sequence shown here is in part arbitrary (for example, epoxidation at C15/16 may precede the introduction of the C-16 keto group; cf., anthothecol), it marshals the known facts that have been described in the foregoing sections.

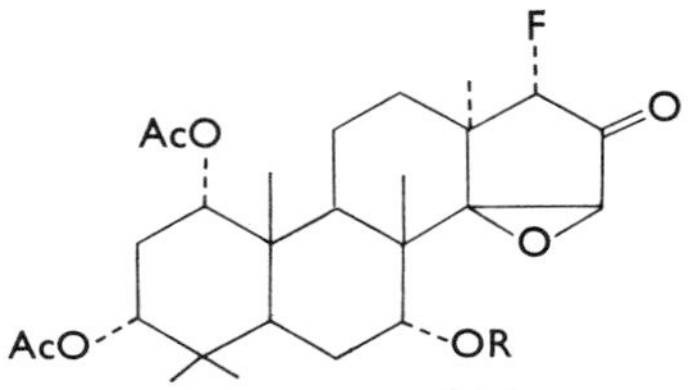

R = H, grandifolione
(*K. grandifolia*)

R = Ac, khayanthone
(*K. anthotheca*)

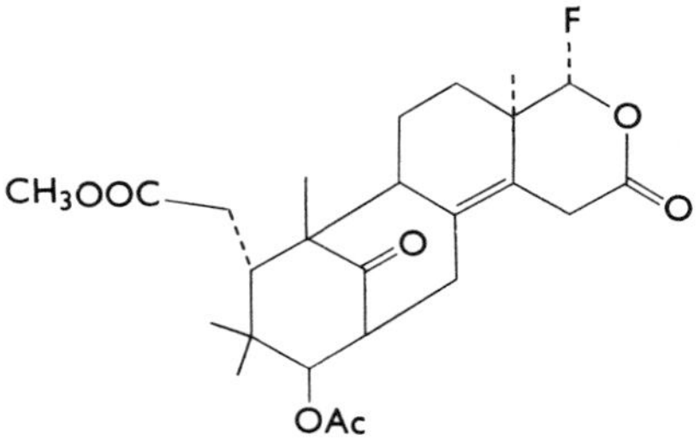

grandifoliolin
(*K. grandifolia*)

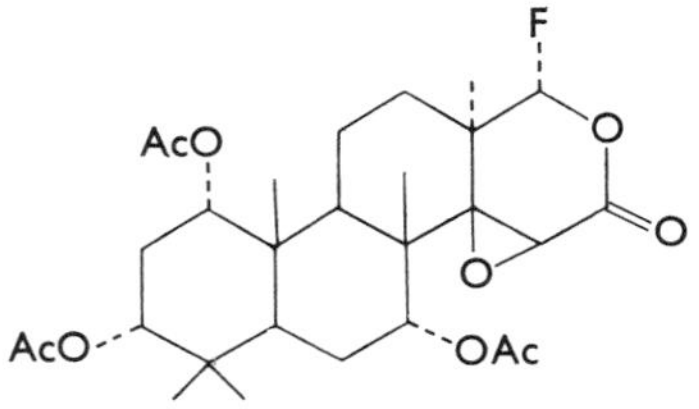

khivorin
(*K. ivorensis*)
(*K. grandifolia*)
(*K. sengalensis*)

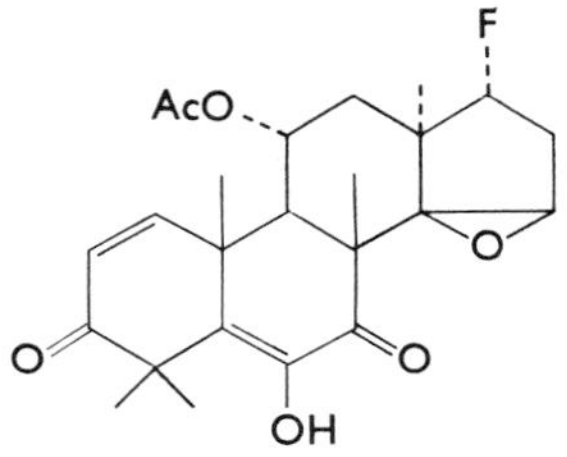

anthothecol
(*K. anthotheca*)

Fig. 12-3. Constituents of *Khaya* Species.

* The progenitor of compounds of these types is often said to be euphol, but since euphol and tirucallol differ only in the configuration at C-20, this reference point is lost in the 17-furyl compound.

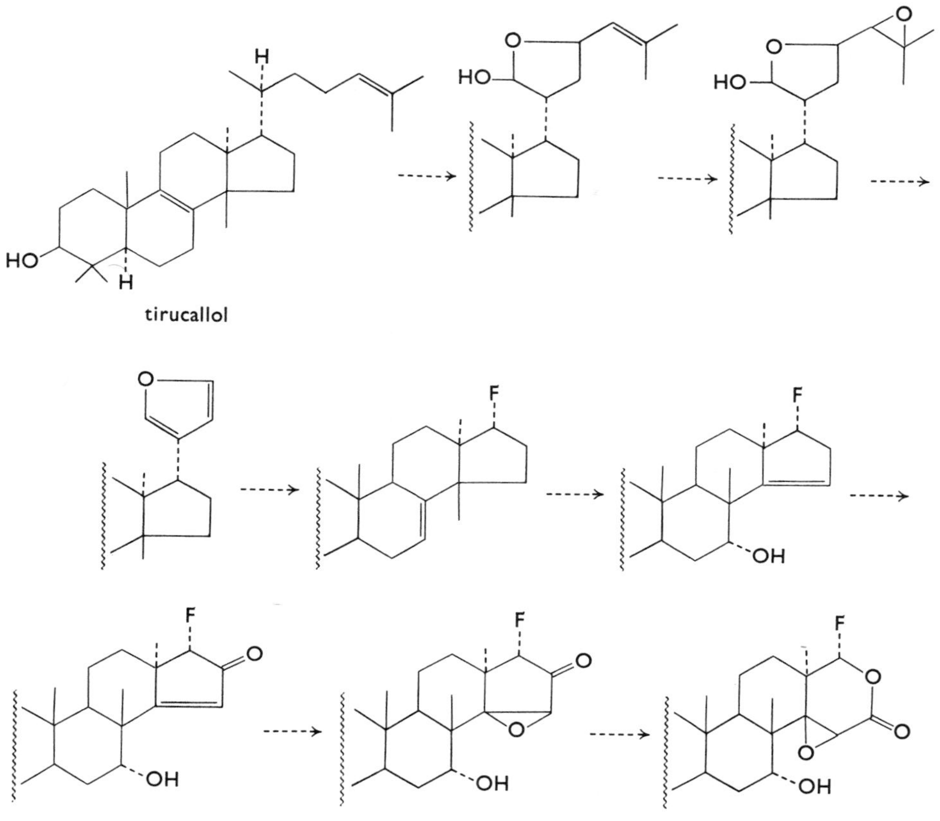

tirucallol

[Eq. 12-7]

The reaction of khivorin ($C_{32}H_{24}O_{10}$) with alkali results in a smooth decomposition and the formation of two products, khivol ($C_{21}H_{32}O_5$) and furan-3-aldehyde. Since khivorin is a triacetate, the change $C_{32} \rightarrow C_{21} + C_5$ shows that khivol and furan-3-aldehyde contain all of the structural carbon atoms of the original compound. The same kind of hydrolytic degradation takes place upon treatment of gedunin (Fig. 12-2) and limonin (Sec. 12-8) with alkali under comparable conditions. Khivol is a δ-lactone; and the formation of furan-3-aldehyde shows that the decomposition involves the C- and D-rings of khivorin.

The reaction is stereospecific with respect to the configuration at C-7, for the C-7 hydroxyl group must be α-disposed. The epimeric compounds which contain a C-7βOH group do not undergo the cleavage. These factors can be accommodated with the formulation shown in Eq. 12-8; the products (khivol, merolimonol, etc.) which contain the δ-lactone ring D have the stereochemistry shown in the equation.

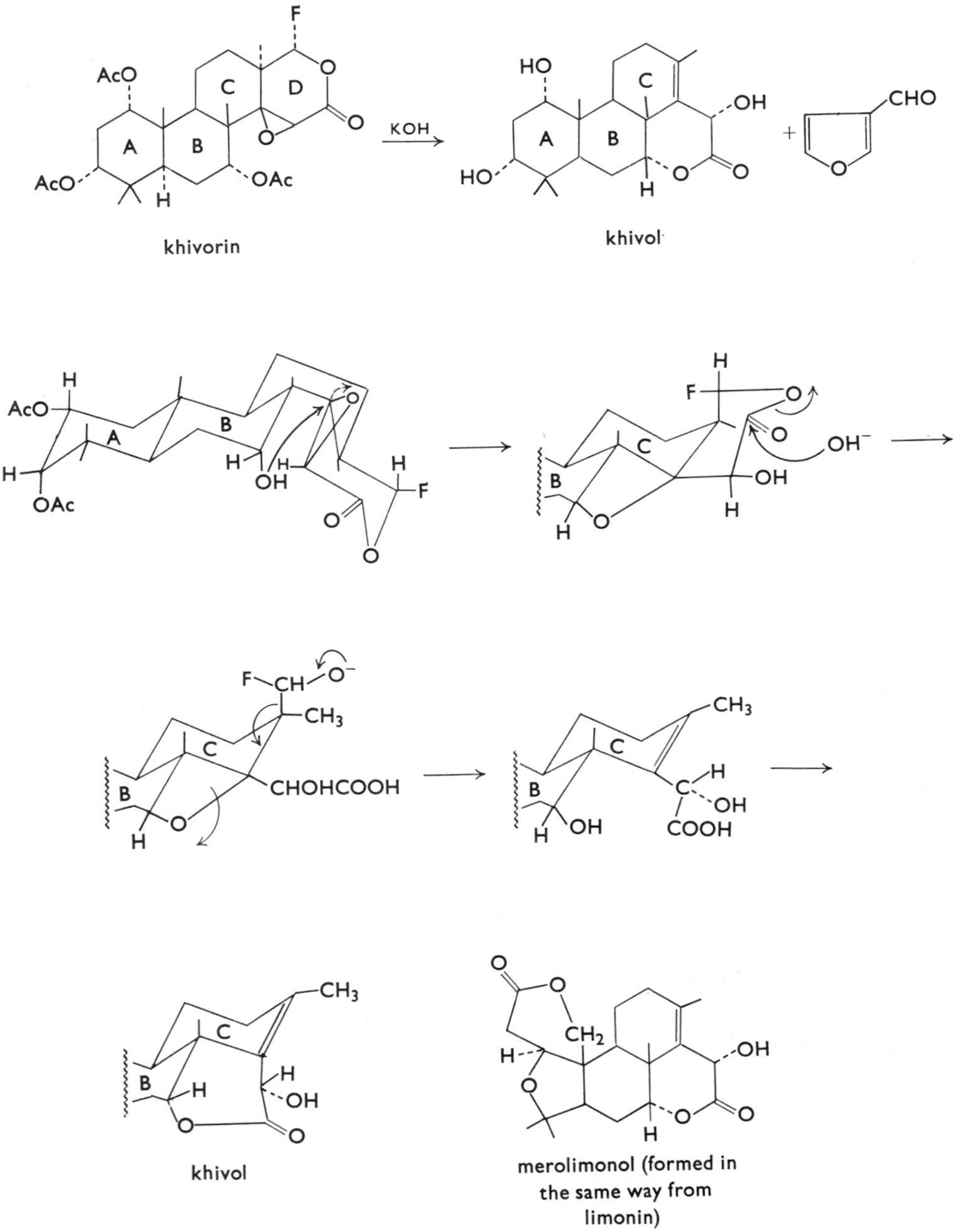

khivorin

$\xrightarrow{\text{KOH}}$

khivol

khivol

merolimonol (formed in
the same way from
limonin)

[Eq. 12-8]

12.8 Limonin and Limonoids

Limonin, a bitter principle found in citrus fruits (fam. Rutaceae), differs from such compounds as khivorin, gedunin, and other "meliacins" in having an A-ring altered by oxidative ring opening. Limonin is usually accompanied in the plants in which it is found by several other compounds of closely allied structures. Nomilin and obacunone possess intact C-10 methyl groups, while in limonin this group, as part of the lactone ring, is in the —CH$_2$OH oxidation state.

Veprisone, from *Vepris bilocularis* (also fam. Rutaceae) resembles nomilin except that the fragments of the opened A-ring are closed to an ether instead of a lactone, the carboxyl group so released appearing as a methyl ester (Fig. 12-4).

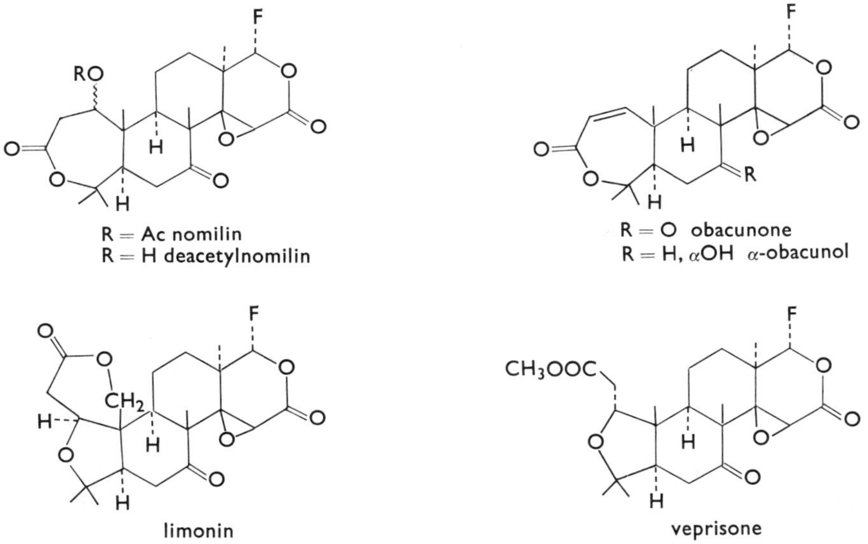

R = Ac nomilin
R = H deacetylnomilin

R = O obacunone
R = H, αOH α-obacunol

limonin

veprisone

Fig. 12-4. Some Limonoid Compounds of Rutaceae.

This kind of A-ring opening recalls the structures of nyctanthic and dammarenolic acids (Chap. 11); and it is easy to see that the A-ring lactones of nomilin and its congeners are equivalent to these triterpene acids, according to the relationship shown in Eq. 12-9. These equations are written with the use of the unsaturated acid so that the relationships to obacunone, obacunoic acid (also known in the Rutaceae), and nomilin are more direct.

The compounds that have been considered to this point are recognized as falling into two chief groups: those occurring in the family Meliaceae, with an intact A-ring, and those found in the Rutaceae, the limonoids, in which the A-ring has been opened in an oxidative cleavage reaction. Both classes are identically constituted at the B-, C-, and D-ring portions of the molecules.

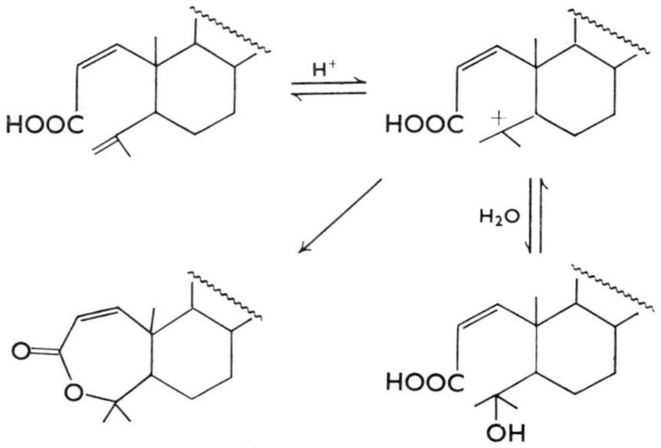

obacunone   obacunoic acid

[Eq. 12-9]

12.9   Compounds of the Simaroubaceae

The family Simaroubaceae consists of about 20 genera of tropical and sub-tropical trees and shrubs. Plants of this family are very little differentiated from the Rutaceae, and this close botanical affinity is reflected in the chemistry of the family. The Simaroubaceae are found to contain a class of compounds, the simaroubalides, that are closely allied to the meliacins and limonoids, clearly derived from a tri-terpenoid precursor and evidently representing additional stages in the same overall pathway.

The simaroubalides are represented by the examples shown in Fig. 12-5. It will be seen that these compounds resemble khivol and merolimonol in the structure of the C- and D-rings. The carbon atoms of the δ-lactone (C-ring) represent the C-15 and C-16 atoms of an original triterpenoid (e.g., tirucallol) precursor.

Although the khivorin → khivol (or limonin → merolimonol) change could be regarded as the model for the biosynthetic reactions that lead to the simarou-balides from, presumably, a β-furyl-substituted lactone of the gedunin or khivorin type, it will be recalled that the transformation of khivorin into khivol is carried out by the agency of hot alcoholic alkali, conditions which scarcely simulate a cellular process. For this reason it is worth while to seek an alternative process for the degradation that leads to loss of the β-furyl grouping (or its equivalent).

It will be noted from the structures given in Fig. 12-5 that all of the simarou-balides, with the sole exception of simarolide, possess an oxygen function (usually —OH) at C-12. Simarolide, which lacks the C-12 oxygen atom, retains the carbon atoms corresponding to the furan-3-aldehyde that is lost in the course of the khivorin → khivol change.

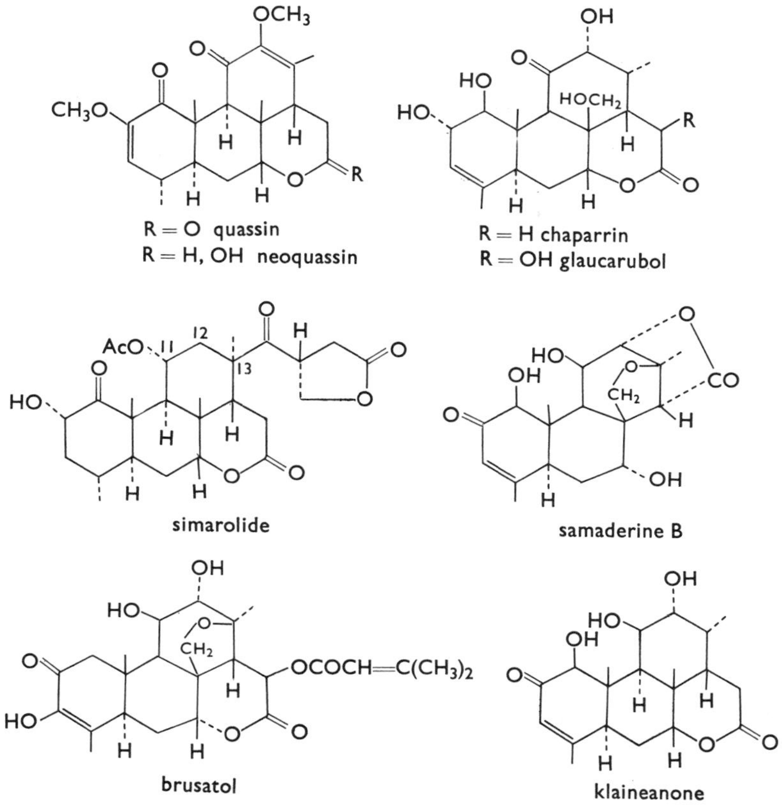

Fig. 12.5. Lactones of Simaroubaceae.

Equation 12-10 shows a possible way in which the degradation can take place by a reaction in which the C-12 oxygen (as a carbonyl group) takes part. There is, of course, insufficient evidence to express this change explicitly in terms of known compounds, but it will be seen that a simarolide-like precursor is ideally constituted to play the desired role in the degradation.

The cleavage of the β-hydroxyketone shown in the sequence of Eq. 12-10 represents a well known type of reaction. Alternatively, if the —CHOH group of the side chain becomes >CO before cleavage, the precursor is the corresponding β-diketone, the cleavage of which would also occur readily.

Conjectures such as these are based only upon mechanistic feasibility and structural relationships, and remain to be established by substantial evidence.

Four simaroubalides—chaparrin, glaucarubol, cedroniline, and samaderine C —all of which contain the dihydroxylated A-ring shown for chaparrin in Fig. 12-5,

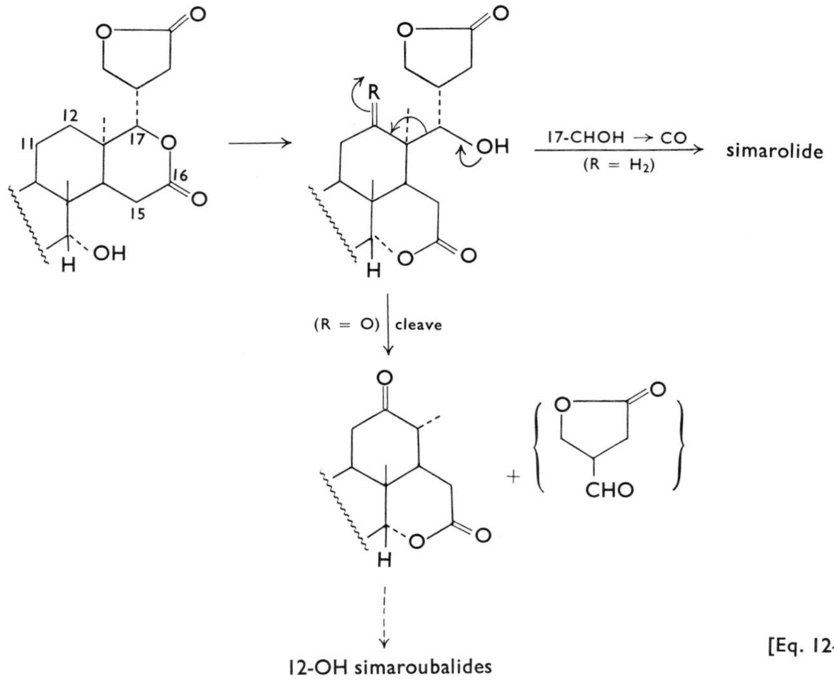

12-OH simaroubalides

[Eq. 12-10]

undergo ready aromatization under extraordinarily mild conditions. Upon treatment with dilute aqueous mineral acid at reflux temperatures the C-10 methyl group migrates to C-1 and the A-ring is transformed into 1,4-dimethylbenzene

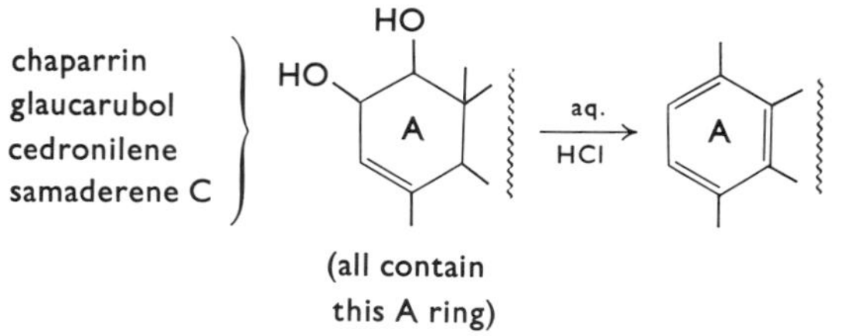

chaparrin
glaucarubol
cedronilene
samaderene C

(all contain
this A ring)

[Eq. 12-11]

(Eq. 12-11). This change has proved to be a useful diagnostic indication of the presence of an A-ring of the indicated structure.

12.10 Biosynthesis of the Simaroubalides

Speculations on the biosynthesis of the simaroubalides have included several proposals, quite disparate in type. For example, the hypotheses have been advanced that these compounds arise (a) by a coupling of two C_{10} precursors (in a manner not specified) to produce the C_{20} compound (e.g., chaparrin, glaucarubol are C_{20}

compounds); (b) from a pimaradiene-like precursor, with rearrangement of the C_2-fragment at C-13 to the C-14 position; and (c) by degradation of a triterpene precursor of the euphol or tirucallol type.

Hypothesis (b) would be difficult to accept, for the stereochemical requirements would have required highly unusual changes in the configuration of parts of the backbone of the molecules. Hypothesis (c), which has been assumed in the discussion of this chapter, has been substantiated by labeling experiments with ^{14}C-mevalonic acid and seedlings of *Simarouba glauca*. The results are shown in summary form in Eq. 12-12.

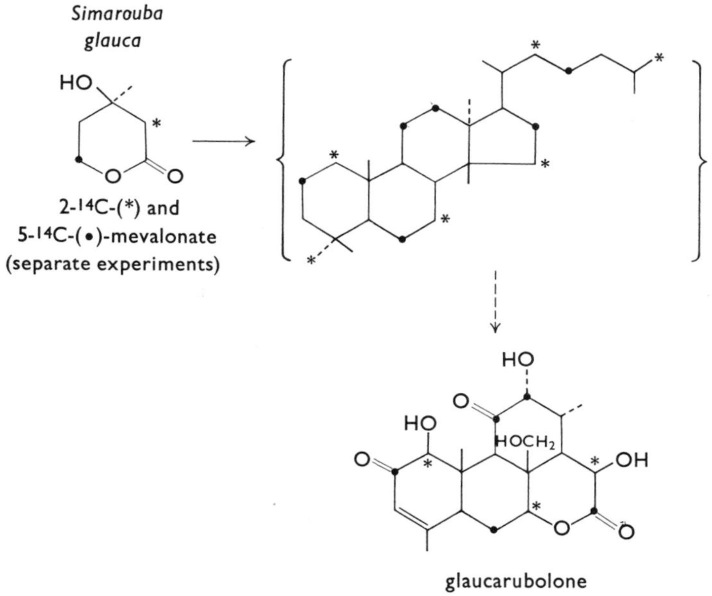

Simarouba glauca

2-14C-(*) and
5-14C-(•)-mevalonate
(separate experiments)

glaucarubolone

[Eq. 12-12]

It is seen that the indicated labeling pattern of the glaucarubolone, with which the results of degradation experiments were in agreement, is in accord with the pattern of biosynthesis that has been developed in this and previous chapters.

12.11 Other Metabolic Degradations

Numerous compounds, particularly among the meliacins, are formed by further metabolic degradations and alterations of the fundamental (i.e., the gedunin type) molecular structure. Oxidative opening of the A-ring has been seen to lead to limonoid compounds; further degradation of the lactone ring of, for example, glaucarubol, leads to compounds that possess a γ-lactone. An example is samaderene B (Fig. 12-5); and others similar to this are known.

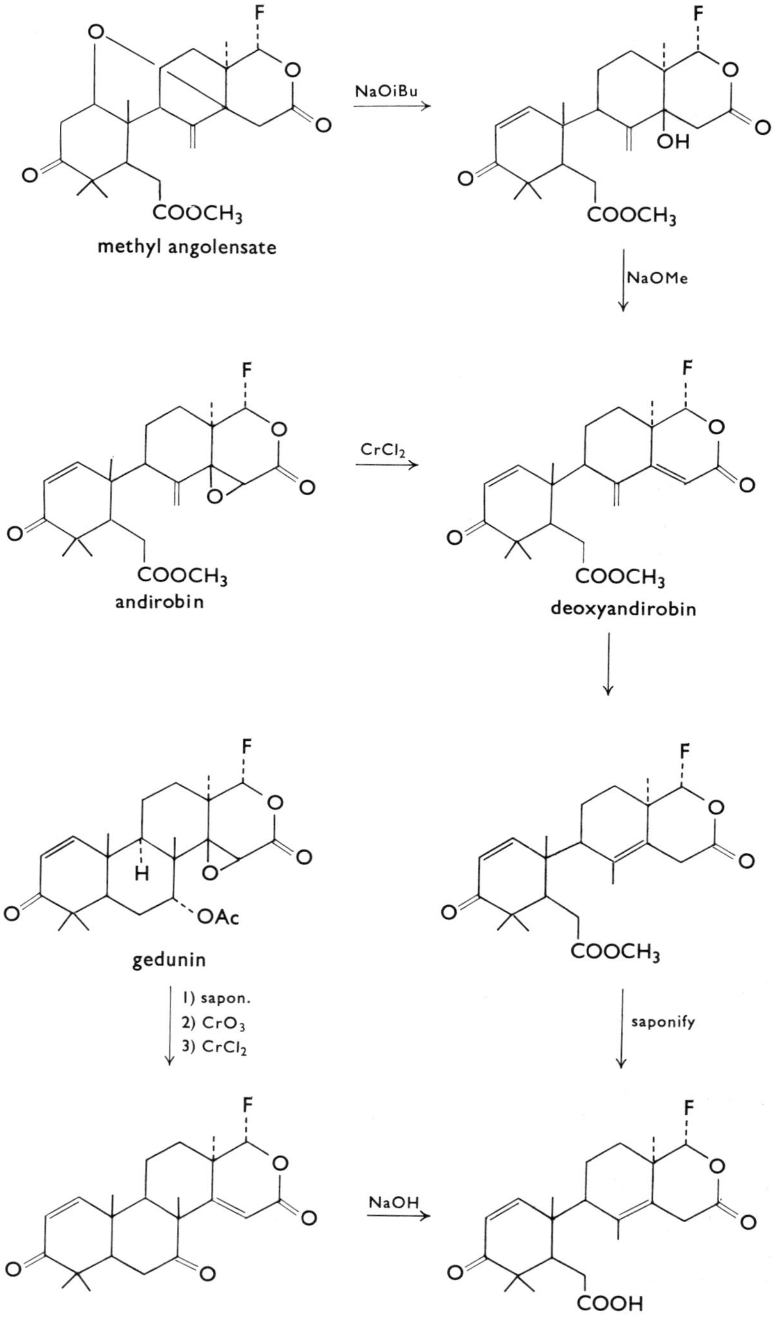

methyl angolensate

NaOiBu

NaOMe

andirobin

CrCl₂

deoxyandirobin

gedunin

1) sapon.
2) CrO₃
3) CrCl₂

saponify

NaOH

[Eq. 12-13]

Opening of the B-ring leads to compounds represented by methyl angolensate and andirobin (both in plants of the family Meliaceae) (Fig. 12-6).

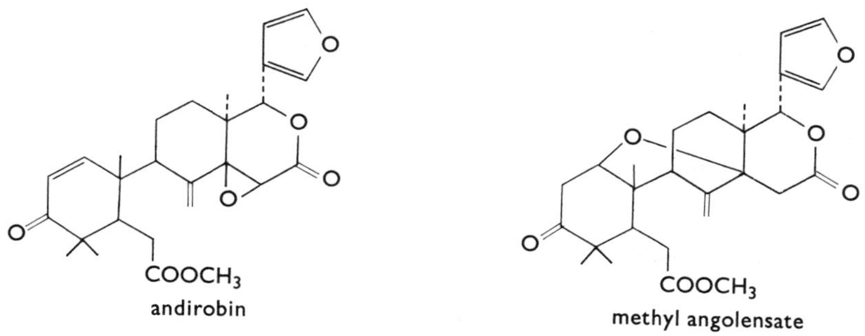

Fig. 12-6. Meliacins with Opened B Rings.

The relationships between andirobin, methyl angolensate, and the well known meliacin, gedunin, have been established by the experimental results shown in the equations of Eq. 12-13. These interconversions establish the stereochemical identity of these compounds at the relevant positions (i.e., those positions that have proved to be valuable in considerations of biosynthetic origins) and reinforce the conclusions reached earlier concerning the intimate biosynthetic relationship of the constituents of the plant family in which they are found.

Salannin and nimbin, constituents of nim oil (*Melia azadirachta*) represent oxidative degradations of other kinds. In these compounds the C-ring is opened with formation of a carboxylic acid (which occurs naturally as the methyl ester), and in addition one of the two methyl groups (the α-CH$_3$) is oxidized (Fig. 12-7).

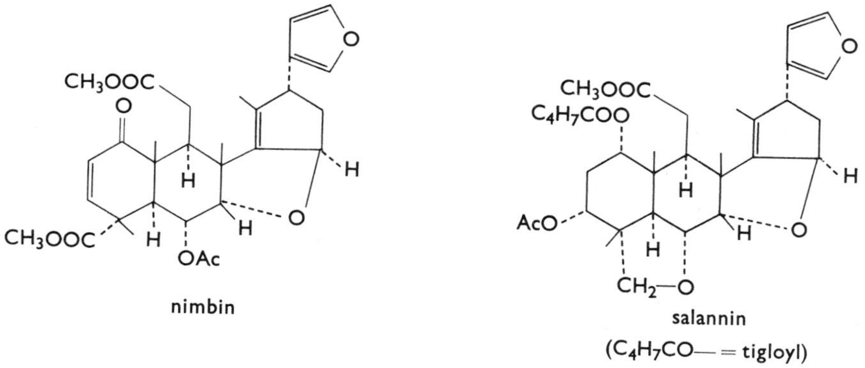

Fig. 12-7. Meliacins with Opened C Rings.

It is especially significant to note that it is the C-4 α-methyl group which is oxidized to form nimbin and salannin. Reference to Eq. 12-12 will show that it is the C-4 α-methyl group (which is labeled from 2-^{14}C-mevalonate) which is lost in the formation of glaucarubolone, a 4-methyl compound. It is reasonable to assume that the biosynthetic change from the 4,4-dimethyl precursor (e.g., tirucallol) to the 4-methyl simaroubalides proceeds by oxidation of the C-4 α-methyl group to —COOH, and decarboxylation; this represents another link between the meliaceous and the simaroubaceous compounds.

12.12 Mexicanolide and Swietenine

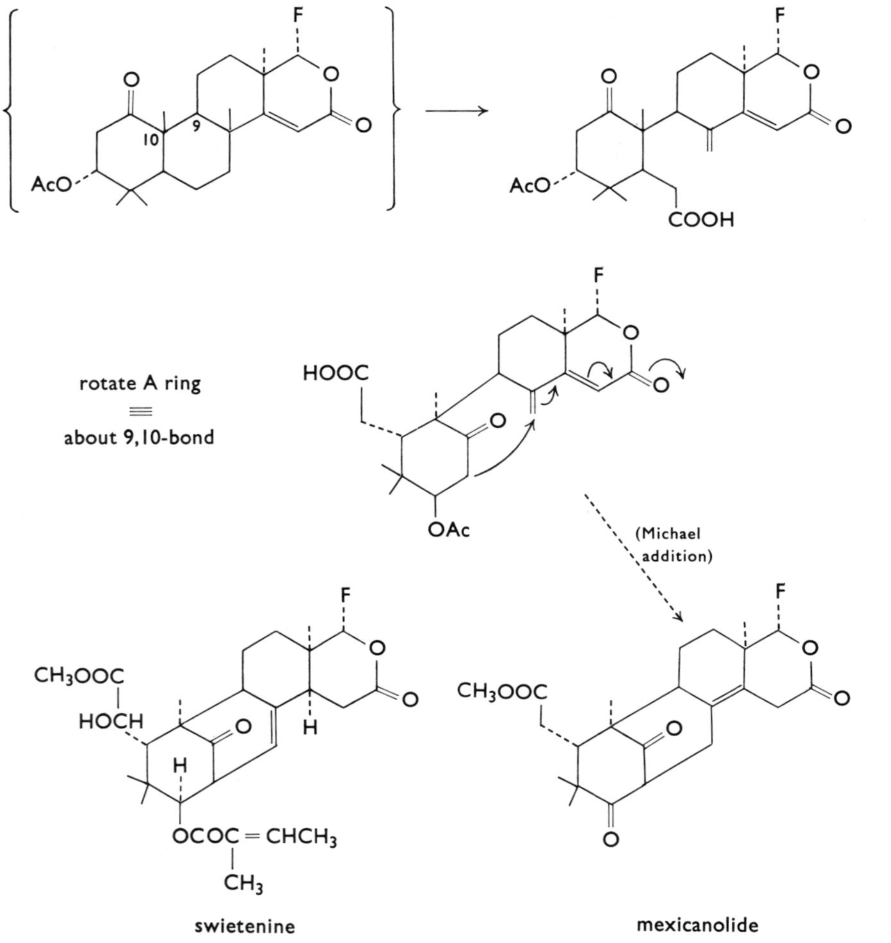

rotate A ring
≡
about 9,10-bond

(Michael addition)

swietenine

mexicanolide

[Eq. 12-14]

An unusual secondary change, following opening of the B-ring, occurs in the formation of swietenine (from *Swietenia macrophylla*, fam. Meliaceae) and mexicanolide (from *Cedrela mexicana*, fam. Meliaceae). The bicyclo-A/B-ring system is formed by a Michael addition following opening of the B-ring of a precursor of the general meliacin type.

The structures of mexicanolide and swietenine are shown, along with a description of the manner of their formation, in Eq. 12-14. It will be seen that an intermediate of the andirobin type, except for a double bond in place of the epoxide ring, provides a straightforward route for the ring closure of the 1-keto precursor shown in the equation.

12.13 Summary

The discussion in this chapter has emphasized the remarkable unity in the chemistry of the secondary metabolic reactions of a group of plants of close botanical affinity. It would be redundant to elaborate further upon what these observations render obvious, namely, that the genetic constitutions of the Rutaceae, Meliaceae, and Simaroubaceae must be regarded as having much in common. The genetic diversity that is revealed by the changes in morphology that lead to separate familial status are likewise revealed in secondary alterations superimposed upon a metabolism that leads to groups of compounds that have many points of structural identity, but which differ in the final stages of metabolism.

It is of interest to note that the family Burseraceae is regarded as belonging to the group of related plants in which the Meliaceae, etc., are found, and to wonder whether these structural relationships extend into this family. So far no meliacins, limonoids, or simaroubalides have been found in plants of the Burseraceae, although one genus of this family is a source of a group of triterpenoids that have long been known and extensively investigated. Manila elemi resin from *Canarium* species, contains elemolic and elemonic acids (see Eq. 12-1). It is perhaps significant that these acids belong to the tirucallol series.

**CHAPTER**

REFERENCES FOR FURTHER READING

1. M. J. Coon, W. G. Robinson, and B. K. Bachhawat, *Enzymic Studies on the Biological Degradation of the Branched Chain Amino Acids,* Symp. on Amino Acid Metabolism, Johns Hopkins Press, (1955), 431.

2. W. G. Robinson, B. K. Bachhawat, and M. J. Coon, *Tiglyl Coenzyme A and α-Methylacetoacetyl Coenzyme A, Intermediates in the Enzymic Degradation of Isoleucine,* J. Biol. Chem., *218,* (1956), 391.

3. E. Leete and J. B. Murrill, *Biosynthesis of the Tiglic Acid Moiety of Meteloidine,* Tetrahedron Letters, (1967), 1727.

4. D. H. G. Crout, *Biosynthesis of the Angelate Component of Heliosupine,* J. Chem. Soc., (1967), 1233.

5. D. H. G. Crout, *Biosynthesis of Echimidinic Acid,* J. Chem. Soc., (1966), 1968.

7. D. H. G. Crout, M. H. Benn, H. Imaseki, and T. A. Geissman, *The Biosynthesis of Seneciphyllic Acid,* Phytochemistry, *5,* (1966), 1.

8. C. K. Atal, R. S. Sawhney, C. C. J. Culvenor, and L. W. Smith, *Nilgirine, a New Crotalaria Alkaloid Lacking the 1'-Carbon Atom,* Tetrahedron Letters, (1968), 5605.

Isoprenoid Compounds of Non-mevalonate Origin

13.1 Introduction

Nature affords numerous compounds which, judging from their carbon skeletons, might be (and often have been) assumed to be of isoprenoid (i.e., mevalonic acid) origin. Among these are certain low-molecular weight organic acids, most of

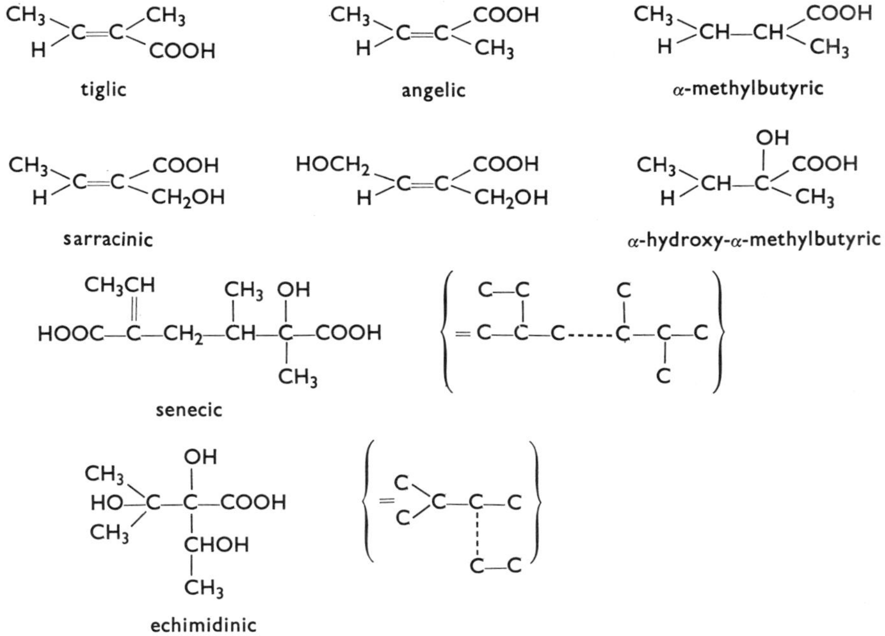

$$\underset{H}{\overset{CH_3}{>}}C=C\underset{COOH}{\overset{CH_3}{<}}$$

tiglic

$$\underset{H}{\overset{CH_3}{>}}C=C\underset{CH_3}{\overset{COOH}{<}}$$

angelic

$$\underset{H}{\overset{CH_3}{>}}CH-CH\underset{CH_3}{\overset{COOH}{<}}$$

α-methylbutyric

$$\underset{H}{\overset{CH_3}{>}}C=C\underset{CH_2OH}{\overset{COOH}{<}}$$

sarracinic

$$\underset{H}{\overset{HOCH_2}{>}}C=C\underset{CH_2OH}{\overset{COOH}{<}}$$

$$\underset{H}{\overset{CH_3}{>}}CH-\overset{\overset{\displaystyle OH}{|}}{C}\underset{CH_3}{\overset{COOH}{<}}$$

α-hydroxy-α-methylbutyric

$$\underset{}{HOOC-\overset{\overset{\displaystyle CH_3CH}{\|}}{C}-CH_2-\overset{\overset{\displaystyle CH_3}{|}}{CH}-\overset{\overset{\displaystyle OH}{|}}{\underset{\underset{\displaystyle CH_3}{|}}{C}}-COOH}$$

senecic

$$\left\{ =C-\overset{\overset{\displaystyle C-C}{|}}{C}-C\text{-----}\overset{\overset{\displaystyle C}{|}}{\underset{\underset{\displaystyle C}{|}}{C}}-C-C \right\}$$

$$\underset{CH_3}{\overset{CH_3}{>}}\overset{}{\underset{}{C}}\text{—}\overset{\overset{\displaystyle OH}{|}}{C}-COOH$$
$$\underset{\underset{\displaystyle CH_3}{|}}{CHOH}$$

echimidinic

$$\left\{ \underset{C}{\overset{C}{>}}C-C-C \atop \underset{\underset{\displaystyle C-C}{\vdots}}{} \right\}$$

Fig. 13-1. Naturally Occurring Low-Molecular Weight Organic Acids of Isoprenoid Structure.

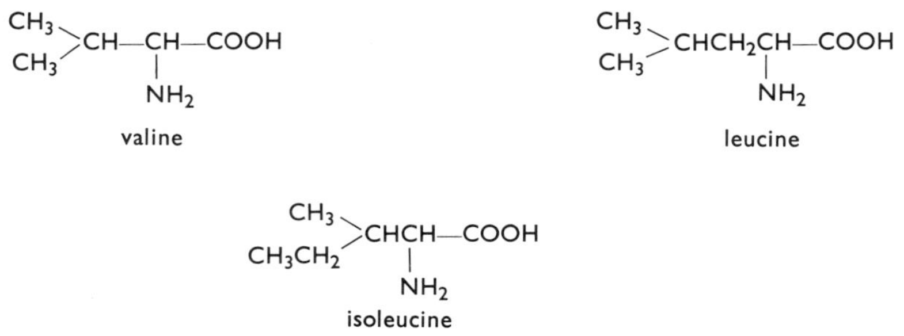

$$CH_3 \backslash CH{-}CH{-}COOH$$
$$CH_3 \diagup \quad\quad |$$
$$NH_2$$

valine

$$CH_3 \backslash CHCH_2CH{-}COOH$$
$$CH_3 \diagup \quad\quad\quad |$$
$$NH_2$$

leucine

$$CH_3 \backslash CHCH{-}COOH$$
$$CH_3CH_2 \diagup \quad |$$
$$NH_2$$

isoleucine

Fig. 13-2. Amino Acids of "Isoprenoid" Structure.

them of five carbon atoms, usually found in plants in esterified form, and a group of C_{10} acids found principally as components of alkaloids which are hydroxypyr-rolizidine esters. In Fig. 13-1 are shown some of these acids, the biosynthetic origins of which are discussed in the following sections.

The isoprenoid carbon skeleton of these acids is evident. Senecic acid appears to be constructed of two isoprenoid C_5 units; but it is clear that the manner in which they are joined is abnormal: they are joined neither head-to-tail, nor in the manner in which artemisia ketone (Chap. 8) is constructed.

Recent evidence indicates that these acids are not isoprenoid, and are derived, not from mevalonic acid, but from amino acids. Several of the aliphatic amino acids contain the essential structural element of the isoprenoid compounds; these are valine, leucine, and isoleucine (Fig. 13-2).

The formation of tiglic acid from isoleucine in animal tissues has been demonstrated experimentally. Its biosynthesis can be formulated in structural terms as in Eq.13-1. A comparable scheme can be devised to show how β,β-dimethylacrylic acid (senecioic acid) is derived from leucine; but it should be recalled that senecioic acid is the immediate product of the mevalonic acid pathway by way of γ,γ-dimethylallyl alcohol, of which it is the direct oxidation product. Consequently, the readiness with which a scheme of synthesis can be constructed is not always a reliable basis for conjecture.

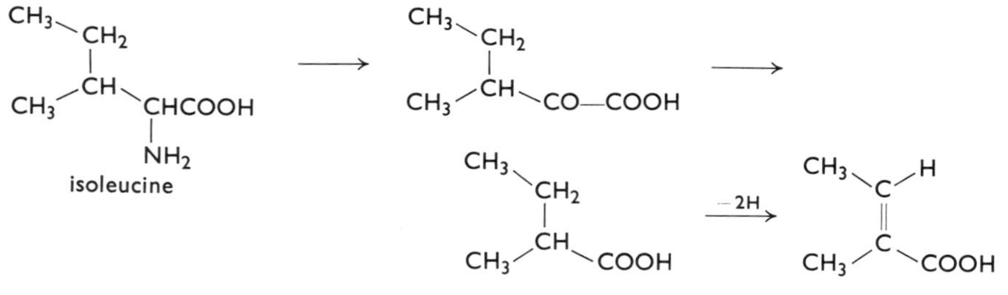

[Eq. 13-1]

13.2 Angelic and Tiglic Acids

Angelic and tiglic acids are found widely in higher plants,* usually in ester combination. It is apparent that their carbon skeletons are isoprenoid, but their structures differ significantly from what would be expected if they were of mevalonate origin. The carboxyl group corresponds to one of the methyl groups at the "head" of the isoprenoid unit; and the "tail" of the prenyl unit, normally oxygenated, appears in angelic and tiglic acids as a methyl group. Thus, for these acids to have been of mevalonate origin, extensive alteration of the oxidation pattern of the precursor would have had to occur.

Angelic and tiglic acids have often been classified as C_5 "terpenoid" compounds, but until recently there has been little evidence for their origin in nature. One suggestion that has been made is that these acids originate by way of the biosynthetic sequence shown in Eq. 13-2.

$$2\ CH_3CO\!-\!SCoA \longrightarrow CH_3COCH_2CO\!-\!SCoA \xrightarrow[\text{(methionine)}]{-CH_3\ \text{donor}}$$

$$\underset{\underset{CH_3COCHCO\!-\!SCoA}{|}}{CH_3} \longrightarrow \underset{\underset{CH_3CH\!-\!CHCO\!-\!SCoA}{|\quad\ \ |}}{OH\ \ CH_3} \xrightarrow{-H_2O}$$

angelic (or tiglic) acid   [Eq. 13-2]

Recent experimental evidence has shown that angelic and tiglic acids are not "terpenoid," nor are they formed according to Eq. 13-2, but are indeed the products of amino acid metabolism.

Datura meteloides (fam. Solanaceae) contains alkaloids which consist of tropanes esterified at the 3-position by tiglic acid. When ^{14}C-isoleucine is fed to *D. meteloides* plants, the alkaloids isolated are radioactive, all of the activity being found in the

Datura meteloides
fed with 2-^{14}C-
isoleucine
(* = ^{14}C)

saponify

[Eq. 13-3]

---

* Since angelic acid is easily isomerized to tiglic acid by the action of alkali or acid, caution must be observed, when tiglic acid is isolated from a natural ester, in concluding that it, and not angelic acid, is the true natural product.

tigloyl grouping. When 2-^{14}C-($\pm$)-isoleucine was fed, the isolated tiglic acid was labeled at the carboxyl group only (Eq. 13-3). These results are in agreement with the general scheme outlined in Eq. 13-1.

Glaucarubolone (see Sec. 12.10), the simaroubalide of *Simarouba glauca*, occurs in the plant as an ester of α-hydroxy-α-methylbutyric acid (at the C-15 hydroxyl group). Experiments have demonstrated that this acid, too, is derived from isoleucine.

13.3   Echimidinic Acid

Cynoglossum officinale L. (fam. Boraginaceae) contains the pyrrolizidine alkaloid heliosupine, which consists of the dihydroxypyrrolizidine, heliotridine, in ester combination with angelic and echimidinic acids. When *C. officinale* was grown with administration of uniformly-labeled ^{14}C-L-isoleucine and with 2-^{14}C-acetate, it was found that the incorporation of radioactivity into heliosupine was ten times more efficient with the amino acid than with acetate. Periodate oxidation of the alkaloid cleaved the echimidinic acid residue and yielded 7-angeloylheliotridine. All of the radioactivity was found in the 7-angeloylheliotridine, and the angelic acid derived from this upon saponification contained all of the radioactivity (Eq. 13-4). These results showed that isoleucine is utilized exclusively for the elaboration of the angelic acid, none of its radioactivity being incorporated into the pyrrolizidine or the echimidinic acid portions of the alkaloid.

When *C. officinale* was fed 4-^{14}C-valine the incorporation of radioactivity into the heliosupine was again far more efficient than when ^{14}C-acetate was used. Substantially all of the radioactivity was found in the two terminal methyl groups of the echimidinic acid residue (Eq. 13-5).

Echimidinic acid contains two carbon atoms more than the five derived from valine. These carbon atoms are undoubtedly acetate-derived, and may be introduced into the α-keto acid derived from valine as indicated in Eq. 13-6, in which the source of the two carbon fragment is the nucleophilic "active acetaldehyde" combined with thiamin pyrophosphate (TPP; see Chap. 2).

Although the biosynthetic process shown in Eq. 13-6 is plausible, an alternative course is equally so. The condensation of α-hydroxyisobutyric acid with acetyl coenzyme A (Eq. 13-7) leads to the same product as the reaction shown in Eq. 13-6, and provides as plausible a pathway to echimidinic acid. The choice between these pathways could probably be made by appropriate labeling experiments. The introduction of acetate by way of the pathway shown in Eq. 13-6 would require the initial conversion of acetate into pyruvate. Introduction of acetate according to Eq. 13-7 would be direct. Thus, the administration of doubly-labeled (e.g., ^{14}C and

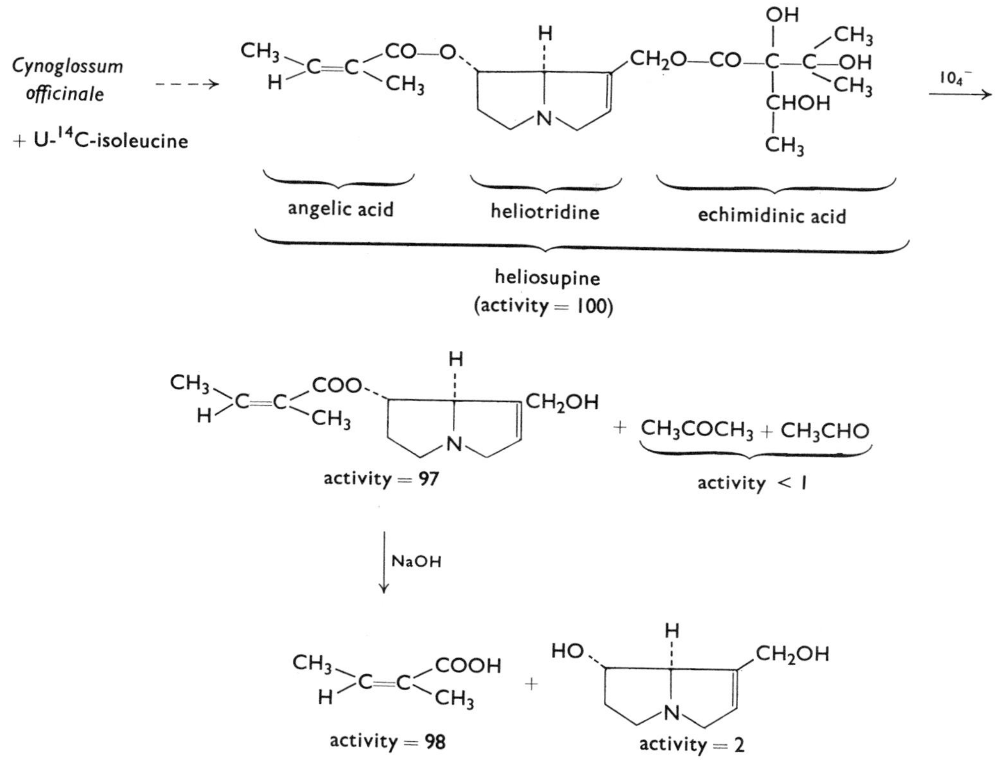

$$\text{Cynoglossum officinale} + \text{U-}^{14}\text{C-isoleucine} \dashrightarrow$$

angelic acid   heliotridine   echimidinic acid

heliosupine
(activity = 100)

$$\xrightarrow{IO_4^-}$$

activity = 97 $+ \; CH_3COCH_3 + CH_3CHO$

activity < 1

NaOH

activity = 98 $+$ activity = 2

[Eq. 13-4]

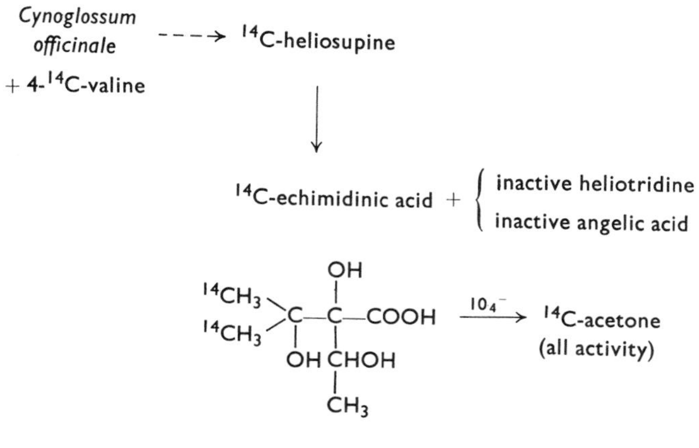

$$\text{Cynoglossum officinale} + \text{4-}^{14}\text{C-valine} \dashrightarrow \;^{14}\text{C-heliosupine}$$

$$^{14}\text{C-echimidinic acid} + \begin{cases} \text{inactive heliotridine} \\ \text{inactive angelic acid} \end{cases}$$

$$\xrightarrow{IO_4^-} \;^{14}\text{C-acetone}$$
(all activity)

[Eq. 13-5]

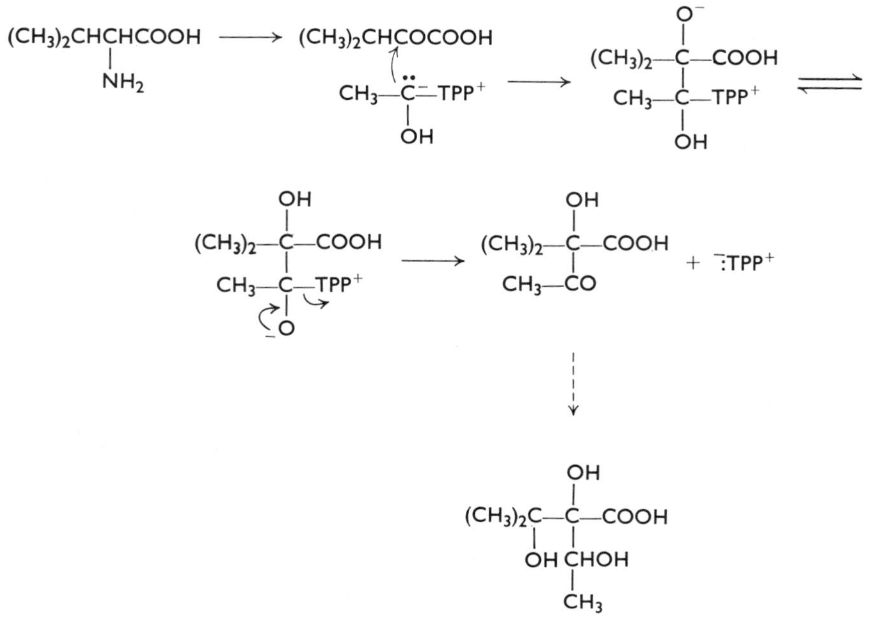

$$(CH_3)_2CHCHCOOH \longrightarrow (CH_3)_2CHCOCOOH$$

$$\underset{NH_2}{|}$$

$$CH_3-\overset{\cdot\cdot}{C}=TPP^+$$

$$\underset{OH}{|}$$

$$(CH_3)_2-\overset{\overset{\displaystyle O^-}{|}}{C}-COOH$$

$$CH_3-\overset{|}{C}-TPP^+ \quad \rightleftharpoons$$

$$\underset{OH}{|}$$

$$(CH_3)_2-\overset{\overset{\displaystyle OH}{|}}{C}-COOH \longrightarrow (CH_3)_2-\overset{\overset{\displaystyle OH}{|}}{C}-COOH \quad + \quad {}^-\!:TPP^+$$

$$CH_3-\overset{|}{C}-TPP^+ \qquad\qquad CH_3-CO$$

$$\overset{|}{\underset{O^-}{C}}$$

$$(CH_3)_2C-\overset{\overset{\displaystyle OH}{|}}{C}-COOH$$

$$\overset{|}{OH}\ \overset{|}{CHOH}$$

$$\underset{CH_3}{|}$$

echimidinic acid   [Eq. 13-6]

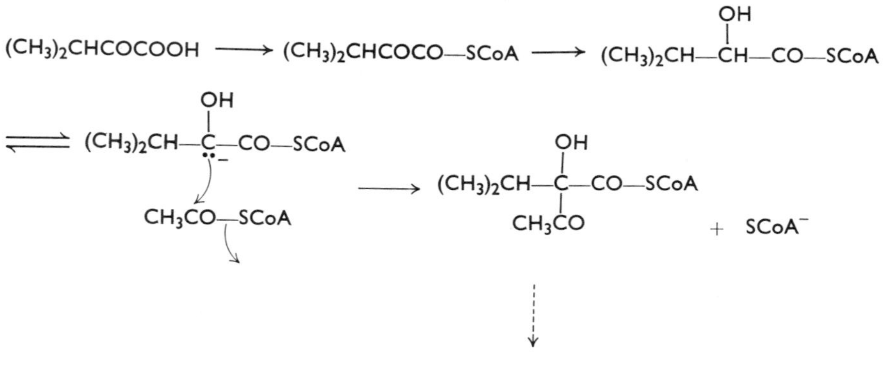

$$(CH_3)_2CHCOCOOH \longrightarrow (CH_3)_2CHCOCO-SCoA \longrightarrow (CH_3)_2CH-\overset{\overset{\displaystyle OH}{|}}{CH}-CO-SCoA$$

$$\rightleftharpoons (CH_3)_2CH-\overset{\overset{\displaystyle OH}{|}}{\underset{\displaystyle \cdot\cdot^-}{C}}-CO-SCoA$$

$$CH_3CO-SCoA$$

$$\longrightarrow (CH_3)_2CH-\overset{\overset{\displaystyle OH}{|}}{C}-CO-SCoA$$

$$CH_3CO$$

$$+ \quad SCoA^-$$

echimidinic acid

[Eq. 13-7]

Note: In the reactions shown in Eq. 13-6 the free acids are represented; in Eq. 13-7 their CoA thioesters are written. These are arbitrary distinctions, for there is no evidence upon which to make a choice. Since echimidinic (and other acids of the class under discussion) occur in nature in esterified form, it is probable that the CoA derivative is formed at some point in the reaction sequence.

---

^{13}C labeled) acetate would be expected to yield echimidinic acid with an un-changed isotope ratio if the pathway were that of Eq. 13-7. If the route of Eq. 13-6 were followed, the scrambling of isotope that would occur in the formation of pyruvate from acetate in the citric acid cycle would be discerned in an altered isotope ratio. Such experiments remain to be carried out.

13.4 Senecioic Acid

Senecioic acid is widely distributed in nature, occurring as a component of many naturally occurring compounds. Because of the direct route by which senecioic acid could be derived either from leucine (cf. Eq. 13-1) or from γ,γ-dimethylallyl alcohol (i.e., from mevalonate) it would be hazardous to attempt to generalize upon the manner of its biosynthesis. Indeed, it is possible that the senecioic acid found in natural sources is derived from leucine in some cases, from mevalonate in others. This is a question which appears unlikely to be answerable by a single or even a few specific labeling experiments.

Senecioic acid derives its name from the genus *Senecio* (fam. Compositae), in which numerous pyrrolizidine alkaloids occur, but the occurrence of senecioic acid as an esterified component in *Senecio* alkaloids is rare; most of these alkaloids con-tain acids that are not structurally related to senecioic acid, and as will be shown below, are amino acid-derived.

It is perhaps significant that the pyrrolizidine alkaloid dicrotaline is an ester of the dibasic acid dicrotalic acid. This acid is β-methyl-β-hydroxyglutaric acid, the principal intermediate in the acetate $\rightarrow$ mevalonate pathway. That dicrotalic acid is formed by the condensation of acetyl CoA with acetoacetyl CoA has not been established, but it would be a reasonable assumption that it is formed in this way. Senecioic acid, then, can be regarded as the product of the mevalonate path-way, on which dicrotalic acid is an intermediate stage. It is thus possible to suggest that the low molecular weight acids are derived by both pathways: angelic, sarracinic, etc., from amino acids, and senecioic and dicrotalic by way of acetate $\rightarrow$ acetoacetate, etc.

13.5 The C$_{10}$ Dibasic Acids of Pyrrolizidine Alkaloids

The *Senecio* alkaloids are most commonly composed of a dihydroxypyrrolizidine esterified with a ten-carbon dibasic acid to form a cyclic diester. Several typical examples are shown in Fig. 13-3. The C$_{10}$ acids of the senecic acid series appear to be composed of two C$_5$ units, each of which is of the isoprenoid type (see Fig. 13-1). Indeed, the "isoprene rule" has occasionally been invoked as a predictive hypo-thesis by investigators in studies on the constitution of acids of this class. Such as-sumptions have proved unfortunate and misleading, for it has now been established that these acids are not isoprenoid, but owe their origin to amino acids.

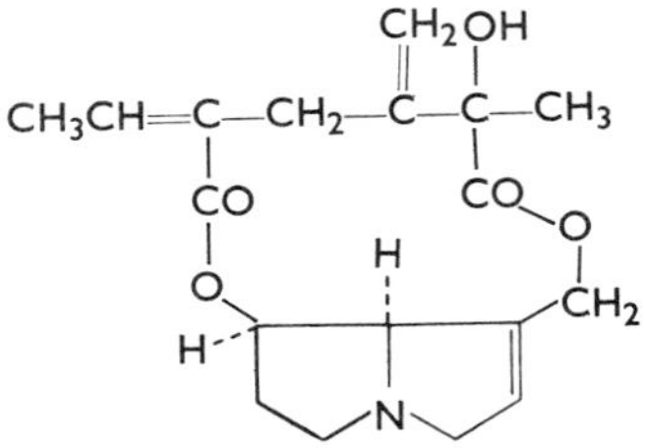

$$CH_3CH{=}C{-}CH_2{-}\overset{\displaystyle CH_2OH}{\underset{\displaystyle CO}{C}}{-}\overset{}{\underset{}{C}}{-}CH_3$$

seneciphylline

$\left\{\begin{array}{l}\text{seneciphyllic acid}\\ \text{retronecine}\end{array}\right.$

$$CH_3CH{=}C{-}CH_2{-}CH{-}C{-}CH_2OH$$

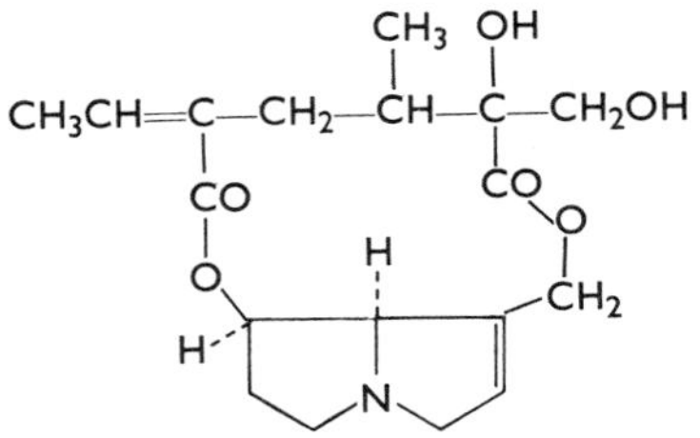

retrorsine

$\left\{\begin{array}{l}\text{retronecic acid}\\ \text{retronecine}\end{array}\right.$

$$CH_3CH{=}C{-}CH_2{-}CH{-}C{-}CH_3$$

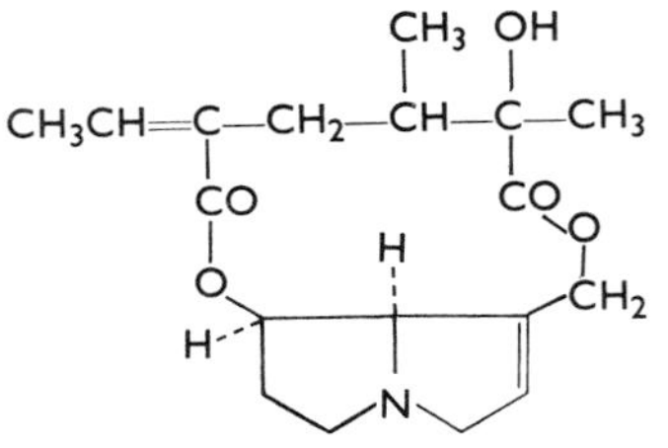

senecionione

$\left\{\begin{array}{l}\text{senecic acid}\\ \text{retronecine}\end{array}\right.$

Fig. 13-3. Typical *Senecio* Alkaloids.

Senecio douglasii DC., in which seneciphylline is the principal alkaloid, incorporates radioactivity into the alkaloids when administered ^{14}C-labeled acetate, but the efficiency of incorporation is very low. Moreover, alkaloid produced by acetate-fed plants is nearly equally labeled in the retronecine portion and in the seneciphyllic acid portion of the molecule, a clear demonstration that ^{14}C from acetate is incorporated as a "general" label as a result of the entrance of the acetate into the metabolic cycles of the plant.

When ^{14}C-labeled isoleucine was fed, incorporation was about twenty times that observed for acetate feeding. Nearly all of the radioactivity of the alkaloid was found in the acid and very little in the retronecine. These results indicated that isoleucine was a precursor of seneciphyllic acid and was incorporated without extensive prior degradation. ^{14}C-Labeled threonine was also an excellent precursor of seneciphyllic acid, and, as in the case of isoleucine, very little label was found in the retronecine.

Additional feeding experiments with the use of ^{14}C-labeled methionine and aspartic acid, coupled with careful degradations of the seneciphyllic acid to locate the positions of labeling, gave additional information about the origin of the ten

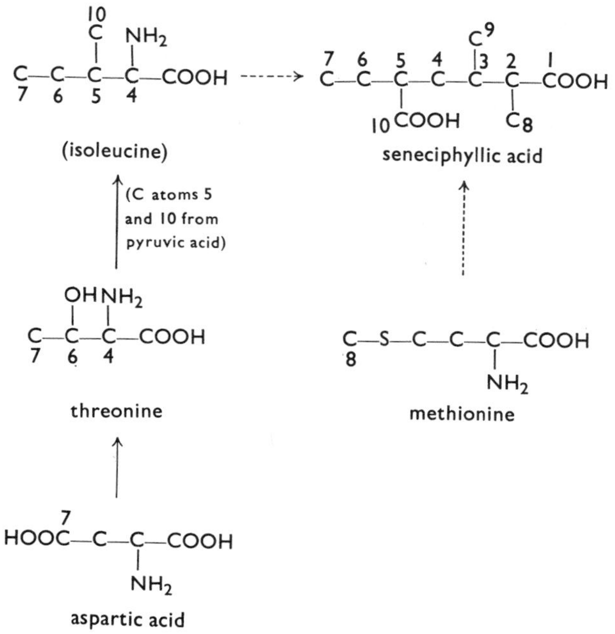

$$
\begin{array}{c}
\overset{10}{C}\ NH_2 \\
| \quad | \\
C-C-C-C-COOH \\
7\ 6\ 5\ 4
\end{array}
\quad\dashrightarrow\quad
\begin{array}{c}
\overset{9}{C} \\
7\ 6\ 5\ 4\ |3\ 2\ 1 \\
C-C-C-C-C-C-COOH \\
\underset{10}{}COOH \quad \underset{8}{}C
\end{array}
$$

(isoleucine)   seneciphyllic acid

↑ (C atoms 5 and 10 from pyruvic acid)

$$
\begin{array}{c}
OH\ NH_2 \\
|\ \ | \\
C-C-C-COOH \\
7\ 6\ 4
\end{array}
\qquad\qquad
\begin{array}{c}
C-S-C-C-C-COOH \\
8 \qquad\quad | \\
NH_2
\end{array}
$$

threonine   methionine

↑

$$
\begin{array}{c}
7 \\
HOOC-C-C-COOH \\
| \\
NH_2
\end{array}
$$

aspartic acid

[Eq. 13-8]

Note: Numbering is chosen to show the origins of the carbon atoms of seneciphyllic acid.

carbon atoms of the acid. The summary of these experiments can be represented by the scheme in Eq. 13-8, in which the origins of the carbon atoms of seneciphyllic acid are expressed in terms of the precursors mentioned above.

It is of special significance that nilgirine, an alkaloid of a *Crotalaria* species, contains an acid of the senecionine type which lacks the carbon atom numbered 8 in Eq. 13-8. If this carbon atom (in seneciphyllic acid) is indeed derived from a one-carbon donor, its absence in nilgirine can easily be accounted for by the omission of this step in the process of biosynthesis. The picture of the biosynthesis of seneciphyllic acid is not complete, for the origins of carbon atoms numbered 1, 2, 3, and 9 are not yet known with certainty. The experimental results do establish, however, the amino acid origin of seneciphyllic acid (and, presumably, of senecic, retronecic, etc., and other acids of the same carbon skeleton) and demonstrate that these acids are not isoprenoid in origin.

13.6 Summary

The experimental findings described in this chapter, which show that the "isoprenoid" compounds tiglic, echimidinic, α-hydroxy-α-methylbutyric, and seneciphyllic acids are actually derived by metabolic alteration of amino acid precursors, point out the caution that must be observed in assuming biosynthetic origins on structural similarities alone. It is clear that α-amino acids, probably in most cases by way of their α-keto analogues, are capable of serving as synthetic starting points for the formation of numerous non-nitrogenous compounds.* It may be anticipated that further examples of biosynthetic processes similar to those described in this chapter will be encountered as studies of this field continue.

* The role of phenylalanine and tyrosine in the biosynthesis of non-nitrogenous naturally occurring compounds has been discussed in earlier chapters.

XIV CHAPTER

REFERENCES FOR FURTHER READING

D. H. R. Barton and T. Cohen, *Festschrift A. Stoll,* Birkhauser, Basle, (1957), 117.

C. H. Hassall and A. I. Scott in *Recent Developments in the Chemistry of Natural Phenolic Compounds,* W. D. Ollis, Ed., Pergamon Press, Oxford, (1961), 119.

B. C. Saunders, A. G. Holmes-Siedle, and B. P. Stark, *Peroxidase,* Butterworths, London, 1964.

A. I. Scott, *Oxidative Coupling of Phenols,* Quart. Rev. (Chem. Soc.) *19,* (1965), 1.

W. I. Taylor and A. R. Battersby, *Oxidative Coupling of Phenols,* Edward Arnold Ltd., London; Marcel Dekker Inc., New York, 1967. (This is a recent book which covers in detail many aspects of the oxidative coupling of phenols.)

Oxidative Coupling of Phenols

14.1 Introduction

In the construction of more complex metabolites from simpler phenolic compounds, nature makes extensive use of oxidative coupling processes in which new C—C or C—O bonds are formed between phenolic precursors. The basic type of reaction involved is illustrated by the laboratory analogies given in Eq. 14-1.

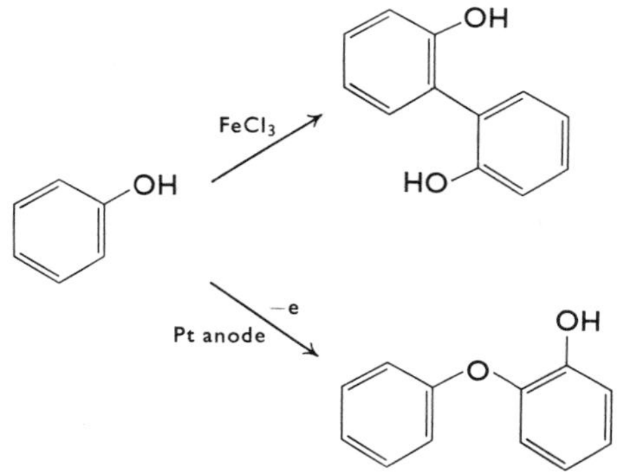

[Eq. 14-1]

At its inception, the idea that oxidative coupling processes might occur in nature was based on the recognition that many natural products bore structural features which were strikingly similar to those produced in certain laboratory oxidations of phenolic substrates. To illustrate this similarity, the structures of some compounds formed in representative laboratory oxidations (Fig. 14-1) may be compared with those of a selection of natural products containing coupled phenolic nuclei (Fig. 14-2).

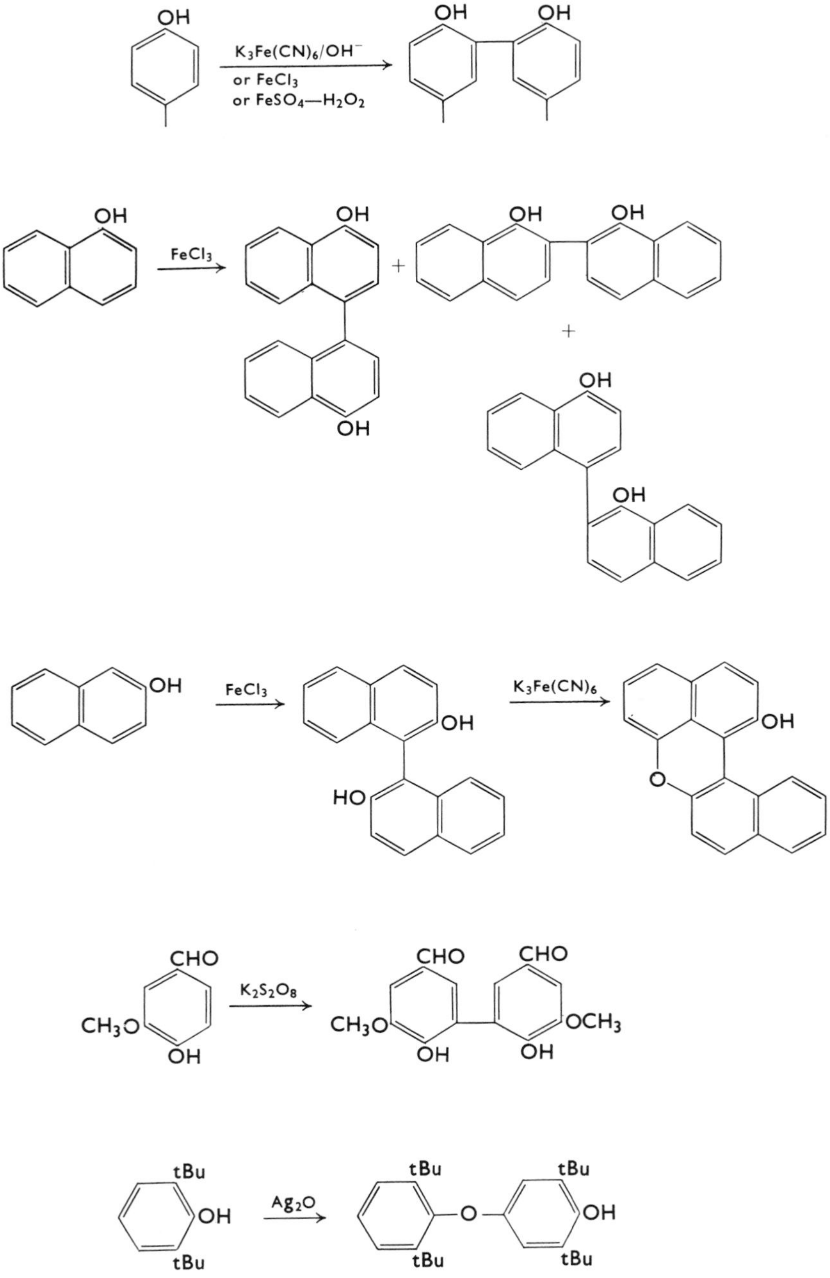

Fig. 14-1. Examples of Oxidative Phenol Coupling Reactions.

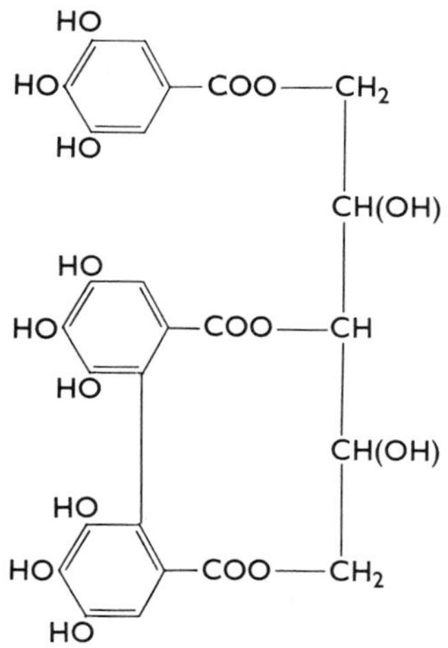

corilagin

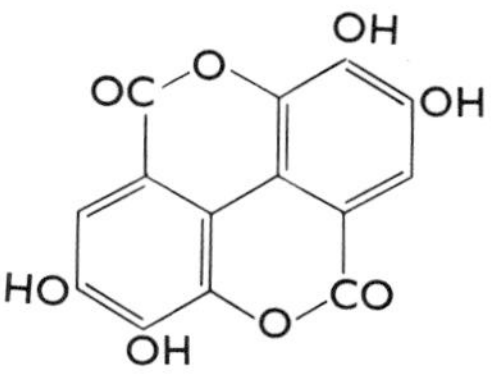

ellagic acid

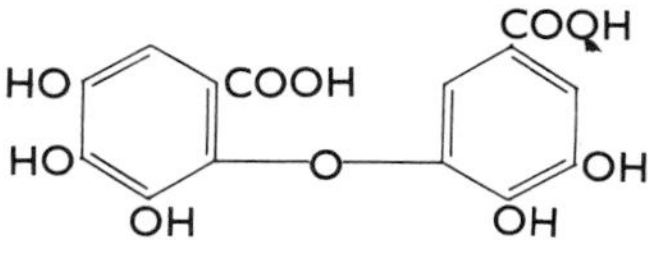

dehydrodigallic acid

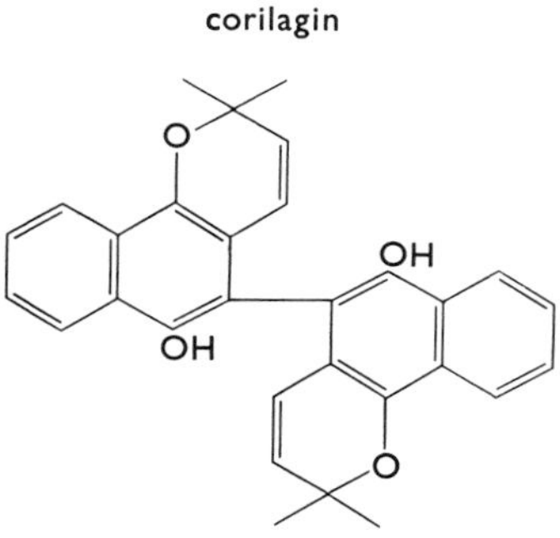

tectol

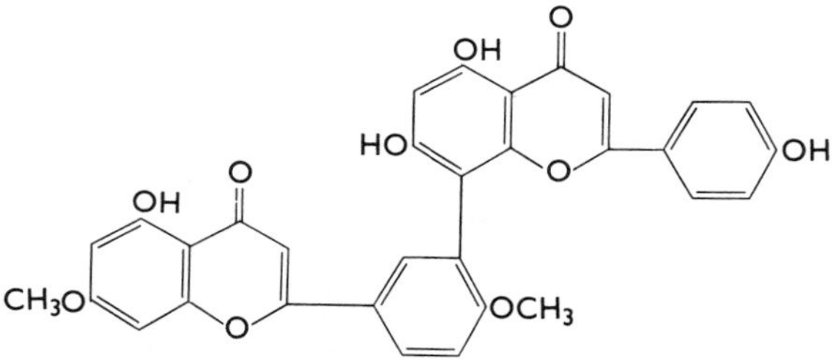

ginkgetin

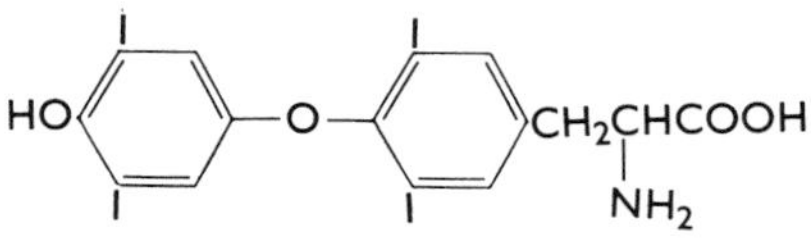

thyroxine

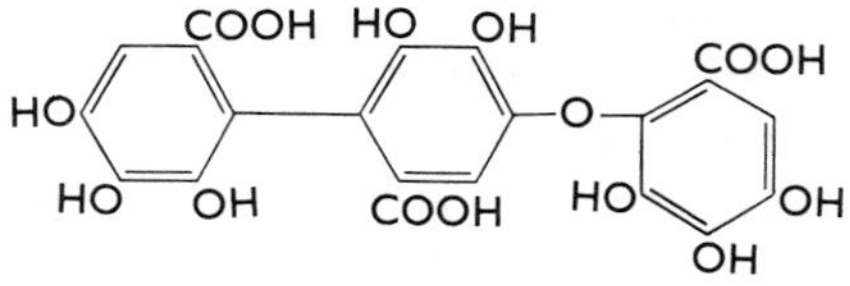

valonic acid

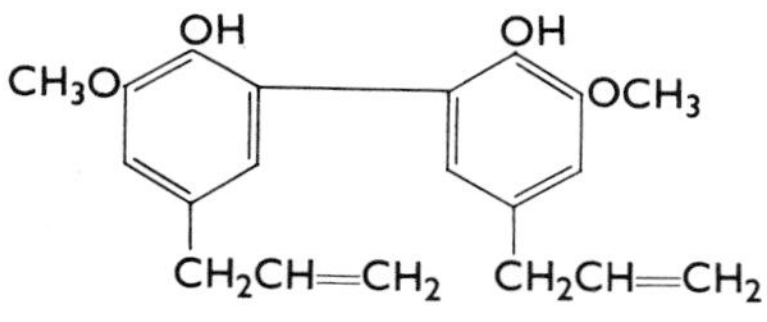

dehydrodieugenol

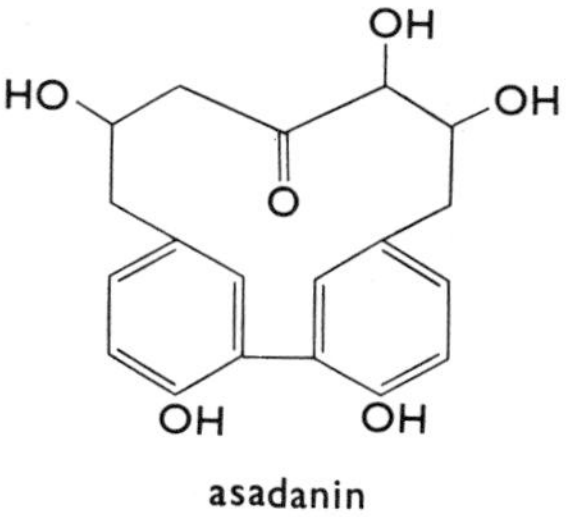

asadanin

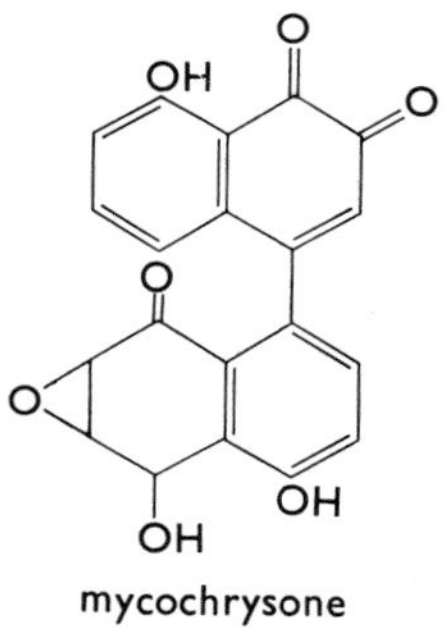

mycochrysone

Fig. 14-2. Some Natural Products Containing Coupled Phenolic Nuclei.

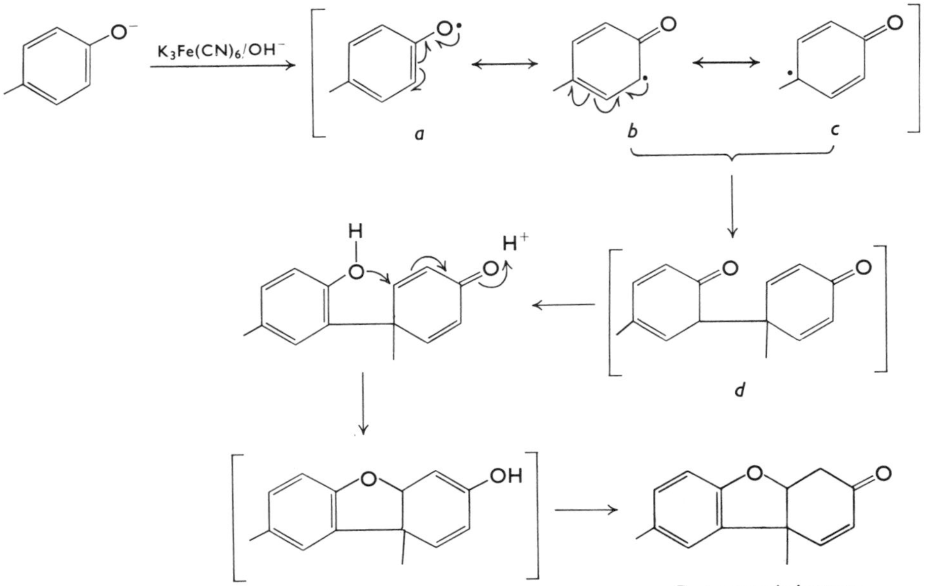

(n.b. Following the usual convention, fishooks (⤳) and arrows (→) are used to indicate the movement of single electrons and electron pairs, respectively.) [Eq. 14-2]

Although the concept of oxidative coupling is of long standing, the systematic investigation of such reactions in relation to biosynthetic pathways stems from a seminal investigation, by Barton and Cohen, of Pummerer's ketone, a compound produced from *p*-cresol by oxidation with potassium ferricyanide in alkaline solution. After demonstrating that the structure originally proposed for this compound was incorrect, Barton and Cohen put forward a revised structure, and pointed out that its genesis could be explained by a mechanism which was of general application in the field of oxidative phenol coupling. According to this mechanism (Eq. 14-2), the coupling process is considered to be initiated by removal of an electron from the *p*-cresolate anion to give a radical species (Eq. 14-2*a*) which by delocalization of the unpaired electron can give rise to further mesomeric forms (Eq. 14-2*b* and *c*). Dimerization of the *ortho* and *para* radical species furnishes the bond between the *p*-cresol units.

It will be noted that the primary product of the coupling step (Eq. 14-2*d*) has a dienone structure. When a hydrogen atom is present at the coupled positions (as in Eq. 14-1), aromatization of the intermediate can take place. When one of these positions is substituted, as in *p*-cresol (Eq. 14-2), aromatization of the corresponding nucleus is not possible and the intermediate is locked in the dienone form, unless further reactions supervene.

The mechanism just described illustrates several features which are considered to be important in phenol coupling reactions. (a) The substrate must contain free phenolic groups, since phenol ethers are not oxidized under comparable conditions. (b) Coupling must occur either at the phenolic oxygen or at positions *ortho* or *para* to the hydroxyl function. This experimental observation is in accord with the presumed intermediacy of free radical species, since both simple resonance theory and more refined wave mechanical calculations indicate that the unpaired electron density at the *meta* position will be very low. Electron spin resonance (e.s.r.) spectroscopy presents the same picture of high electron spin density at the positions *ortho* and *para* to the phenolic hydroxyl and low density at the *meta* position (Fig. 14-3). (c) The mechanism postulates the *dimerization* of two radical species (Eq. 14-2) and

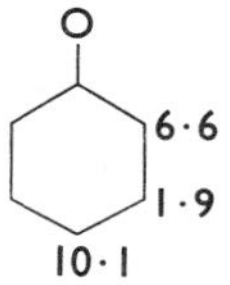

Fig. 14-3. Electron Spin Density in the Phenolate Radical, as determined by Electron Spin Resonance Spectrometry.

not a radical insertion into an unoxidized molecule (Eq. 14-3) or any other coupling reaction involving dissimilar species. Postulates (a) and (b) are based on experi-

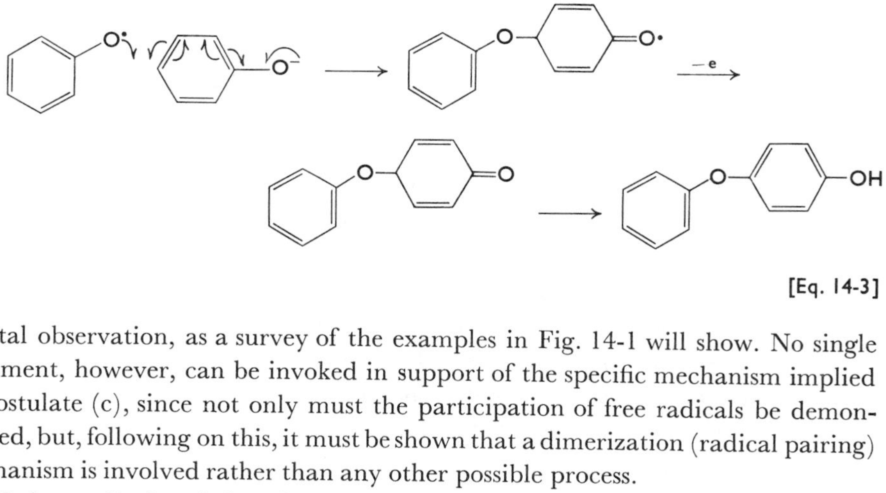

[Eq. 14-3]

mental observation, as a survey of the examples in Fig. 14-1 will show. No single argument, however, can be invoked in support of the specific mechanism implied in postulate (c), since not only must the participation of free radicals be demonstrated, but, following on this, it must be shown that a dimerization (radical pairing) mechanism is involved rather than any other possible process.

It is usually found that the reagents most effective in promoting a particular oxidation are those whose change in oxidation state during the reaction equals the change in oxidation state of the substrate. This observation can be used to support the radical mechanism, since the majority of the reagents used to promote phenol oxidations in the laboratory (Fig. 14-4) act by a unit change in oxidation state and therefore probably operate by removing single electrons from phenolate anions. This leads us to expect that free radicals will be the primary products of the oxidation process. More direct evidence, although based on fewer experimental observations, has come from experiments in which, with the aid of e.s.r. spectroscopy, the transient formation of free radicals in phenol oxidations has been directly observed.

Reagent	Oxidation State	
	Oxidized Form	Reduced Form
$K_3Fe(CN)_6$	+ 3	+ 2
$FeCl_3$	+ 3	+ 2
$CuSO_4$	+ 2	+ 1
$Ce(SO_4)_2$ $(Ce_2(NH_4)_2(SO_4)_3)$	+ 4	+ 3
NH_4VO_3	+ 5	+ 4
Ag_2O	+ 1	0
PbO_2	+ 4	+ 2
MnO_2	+ 4	+ 2
$Pb(OAc)_4$†		
$FeSO_4$-H_2O_2†		
Anodic Oxidation (Pt anode)		

Fig. 14-4. Reagents which bring about Phenol Coupling Reactions.

† The active species in oxidations brought about by these reagents are probably acetate radicals ($CH_3COO\cdot$) and hydroxyl radicals ($HO\cdot$) respectively.

Evidence for a radical pairing mechanism (Eq. 14-2), as opposed to a radical insertion mechanism (as in Eq. 14-3, for example), is indicated by the absence of crossed products both in the oxidation of a mixture of 2,6-dimethoxyphenol and 2,6-dimethylphenol (Eq. 14-4a) and in the oxidation of p-cresol in the presence of a large excess of veratrole (o-dimethoxybenzene) (Eq. 14-4b). In each of these reactions, a radical insertion mechanism should not require the presence of a free phenolic group in the molecule under attack. Coupling with a strongly activated aromatic nucleus, as in veratrole (Eq. 14-4b), would therefore have been anticipated if such a mechanism were in operation.

In spite of what has been said, it should be pointed out that the coupling reactions discussed in this chapter, together with those to be described in Chapter 18,

[Eq. 14-4]

can all be explained in a mechanistically acceptable manner by invoking "onium" ions as intermediates instead of free radicals (Chap. 5). The coupling process on this view would be regarded as an electrophilic substitution reaction (Eq. 14-5).

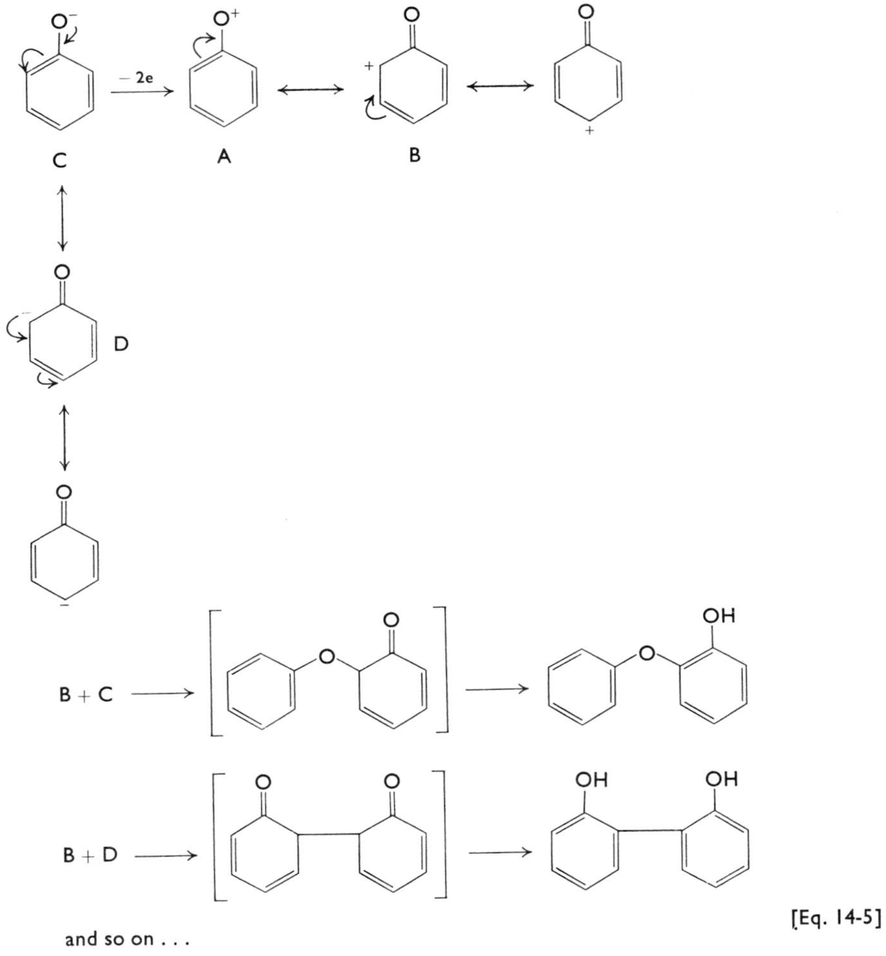

[Eq. 14-5]

and so on . . .

Although there is little direct evidence to support this suggestion, it is nevertheless found that in model studies, better results are sometimes obtained in simulating biological coupling processes, when reactions are used which must certainly proceed through cationic intermediates. Occasionally, such reactions are successful when the analogous coupling reactions involving one-electron oxidizing agents fail altogether, or proceed only in very low yield. Finally, there is no guarantee that all phenol coupling processes in nature proceed by one and the same mechanism. However, since the weight of evidence at the moment favors the radical coupling theory, this representation will be used here, with the *caveat* that alternative mechanisms involving "onium" ion intermediates can also be written, and may indeed be found in time to represent the actual process.

14.2 Enzymes Catalyzing Phenol Oxidations

The very wide distribution of peroxidase,* an enzyme capable of catalyzing the oxidation of many phenolic substrates, pays eloquent testimony to the importance of phenol oxidations in metabolic processes. Peroxidase has been found in many plant species, in animals, fungi, bacteria, and viruses. Peroxidase is remarkably non-specific in its action; besides phenolic compounds it is able to catalyze the oxidation of amines, various heterocyclic compounds (e.g. ascorbic acid and indole), and even inorganic species such as iodide ion. Slightly different varieties of the enzyme have been isolated in crystalline form from various sources including milk, animal leucocytes, and yeast. The most intensively investigated preparation, however, is horseradish peroxidase (H.R.P.). This brown, crystalline enzyme has a molecular weight of 40,000 and has as its prosthetic group, protohaematin IX (Fig. 14-5) which contains ferric iron in complexed form. Four of the six coordination positions of the iron atom are occupied by nitrogen atoms of the

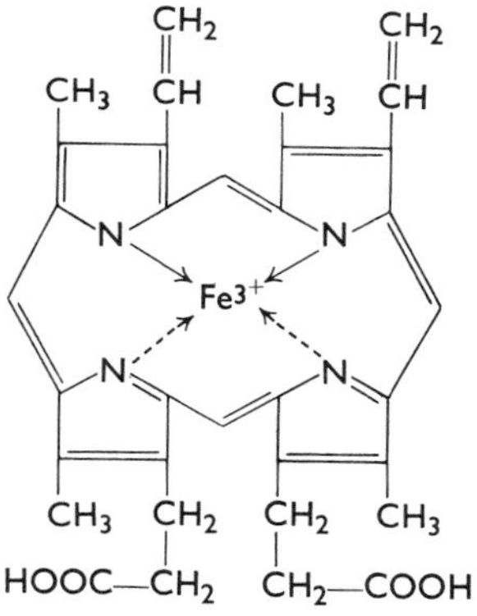

Fig. 14-5. Protohaematin IX.

porphyrin nucleus, a fifth is occupied by a group in the polypeptide chain, and the sixth can be occupied by water, cyanide ion, or the hydroperoxy ion, as in the active form of the enzyme. The prosthetic group is therefore structurally similar to the ferricyanide ion, $Fe(CN)_6^{3-}$, which is the reagent most widely used for promoting phenol oxidations in the laboratory.

---

* For convenience, the name "peroxidase" is used for a group of enzymes which are closely related in action and structure.

For its action, peroxidase, as its name implies, requires hydrogen peroxide as a cofactor. This is ultimately reduced to water at the end of the oxidation sequence.

Many of the oxidations effected by the reagents listed in Fig. 14-4 can be carried out with equal facility using the peroxidase-hydrogen peroxide system. Ferricyanide, for example, can be replaced by H.R.P.-hydrogen peroxide in the oxidation of *p*-cresol to Pummerer's ketone (Eq. 14-2). The mechanism by which peroxidase operates is complex and not fully understood. Two factors, however, emphasize the similarity with ferricyanide; first, the unit change in the oxidation state of the iron atom during the reaction, and second, the demonstrable presence of free radicals in oxidations catalyzed by H.R.P.

An additional important aspect of peroxidase action is its ability to catalyze the hydroxylation of aromatic substrates. Substitution takes place *ortho* or *para* to existing hydroxyl groups, if these are present, as can be seen from the examples in Fig. 14-6.

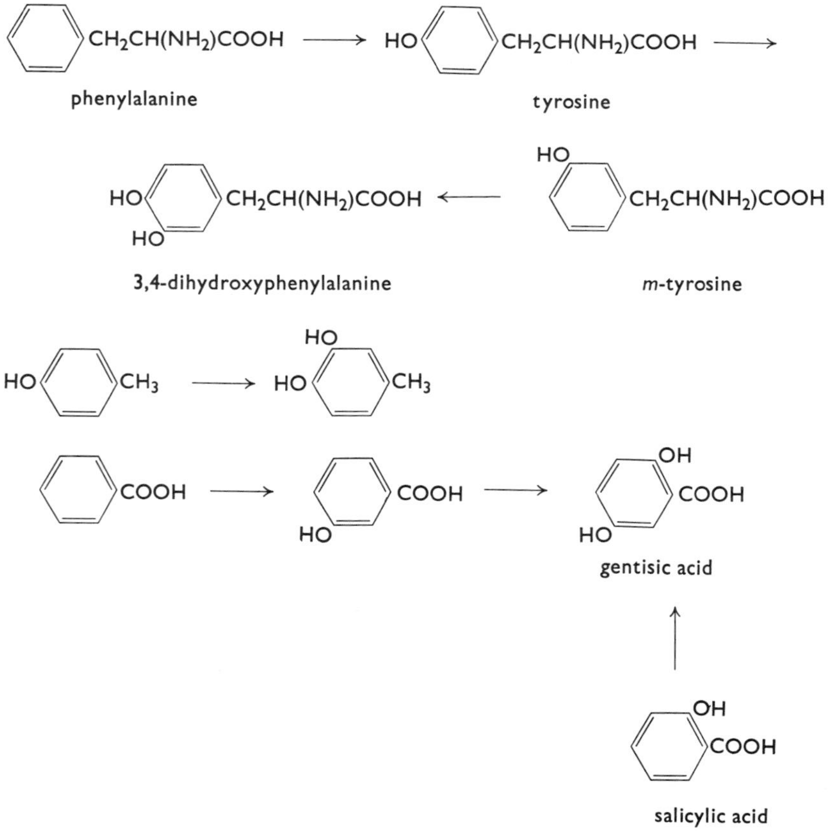

Fig. 14-6. Hydroxylations Catalyzed by Horseradish Peroxidase-Hydrogen Peroxide *in vitro.*

Another widely distributed group of enzymes capable of catalyzing oxidative phenol coupling reactions, are the laccases. These contain divalent copper which is reduced to the monovalent state during the reaction and reoxidized back to the divalent state at the expense of molecular oxygen. Like peroxidase, the laccases are very non-specific; the products formed from the oxidation of phenols resemble those obtained using peroxidase, which points to a similarity in the mode of action of the two enzymes.

Final mention should be made of the tyrosinases, which also have a very wide distribution. These enzymes, like the laccases, contain protein-bound copper, probably in the cuprous state, and are also able to catalyze oxidative coupling reactions. Like peroxidase, but unlike laccase, tyrosinase can catalyze the hydroxylation of aromatic substrates, specifically *ortho*-hydroxylation of monohydric phenols.

14.3   Usnic Acid

The analysis, by Barton and Cohen, of the formation of Pummerer's ketone from *p*-cresol, generated a renewed interest in oxidative phenol coupling as a probable biosynthetic process. This interest was consolidated by a simple synthesis, modeled on the same reaction, of usnic acid (Chap. 4), in which the key step was the oxidative coupling of two molecules of methylphloracetophenone (Eq. 14-6). The pathway of usnic acid biosynthesis was later dovetailed into this synthetic framework in an aesthetically satisfactory manner by the demonstration, in a series of experiments whose main features are set out in Eq. 14-7, that various lichen species are able to convert specifically labeled methylphloracetophenone into correspondingly labeled usnic acid.

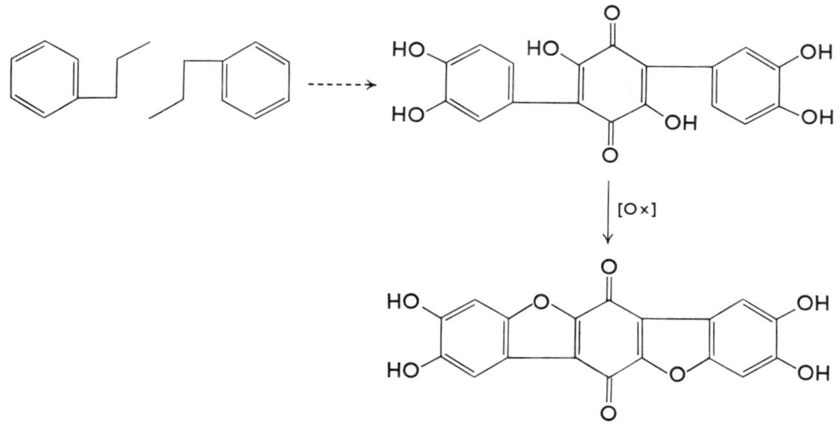

thelephoric acid

Fig. 14-7.

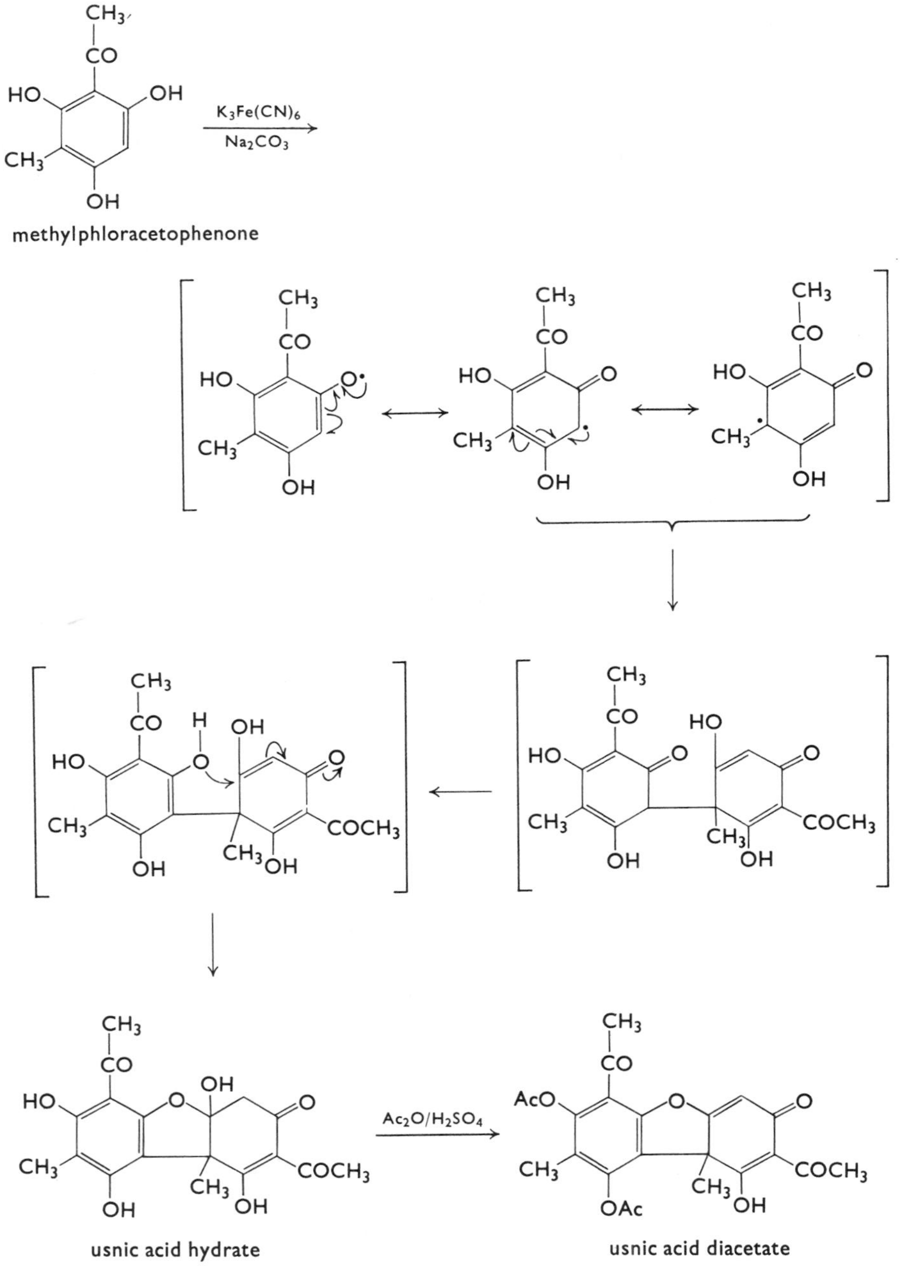
K3Fe(CN)6
Na2CO3
methylphloracetophenone
Ac2O/H2SO4
usnic acid hydrate
usnic acid diacetate

[Eq. 14-6]

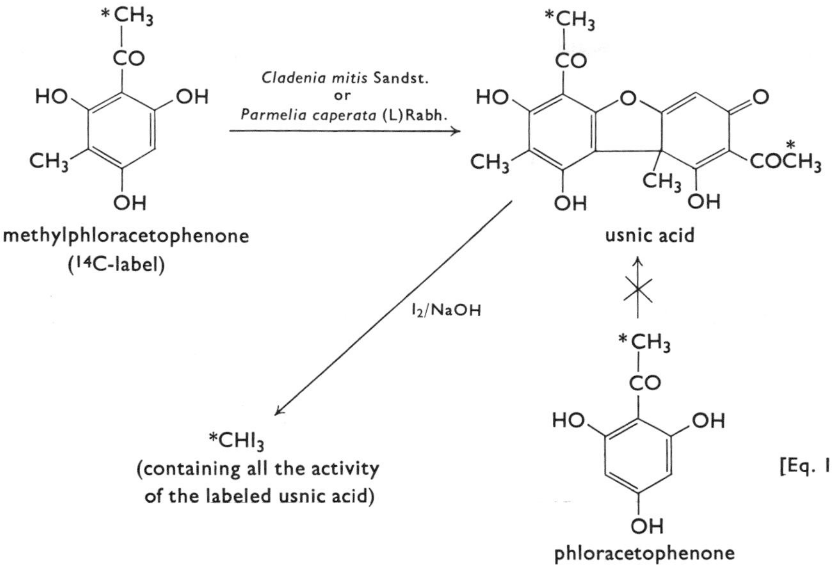

*CH3
CO
HO
OH
CH3
OH
methylphloracetophenone
(14C-label)
Cladenia mitis Sandst.
or
Parmelia caperata (L)Rabh.
*CH3
CO
HO
O
O
CH3
COCH3
CH3
OH
OH
usnic acid
I2/NaOH
*CHI3
(containing all the activity
of the labeled usnic acid)
*CH3
CO
HO
OH
OH
phloracetophenone

[Eq. 14-7]

Usnic acid occurs naturally in both optically active forms and also as the racemate. It is of some significance, therefore, that the oxidation of methylphloracetophenone with H.R.P.-hydrogen peroxide gives usnic acid hydrate (Eq. 14-6) in optically inactive form. Indeed, the formation of optically active products in H.R.P.-catalyzed phenol oxidations *in vitro*, has never been observed, an indication that the isolated system acts primarily to produce phenolate radicals which undergo subsequent coupling without further intervention by the enzyme. The optical activity of many of the products formed in nature by oxidative coupling processes argues for a close association of substrate and enzyme in the crucial coupling step.

The dibenzofuran structures in a further lichen metabolite, thelephoric acid (Fig. 14-7), may also arise through an oxidative O—C coupling step, but the terphenyl skeleton itself is probably derived by the dimerization of two C_6-C_3 units of shikimate origin, in the manner illustrated (Chapter 15).

14.4 Griseofulvin

The elegant synthesis of usnic acid just described, was based on a conjectural biosynthetic pathway which was later established by appropriate tracer experiments. A similar situation developed with griseofulvin, an important metabolite produced by a number of *Penicillium* species. Griseofulvin first aroused interest because of its remarkable fungistatic properties, which gave it great potential medical and commercial importance.

The unique structure of griseofulvin, based on the specially designated "grisan" skeleton (Fig. 14-8), emerged from an extended series of investigations.

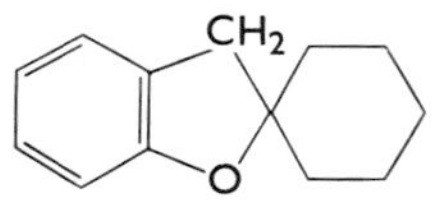

Fig. 14-8. The Grisan Skeleton.

Some of the key degradations in this work are summarized in Fig. 14-9.

The crucial step in the first reported laboratory synthesis of griseofulvin (Eq. 14-8), was the formation of the spirodienone intermediate, dehydrogriseofulvin, by intramolecular oxidative coupling of the benzophenone, griseophenone A, a reaction which was again suggested by the probable biosynthetic pathway.

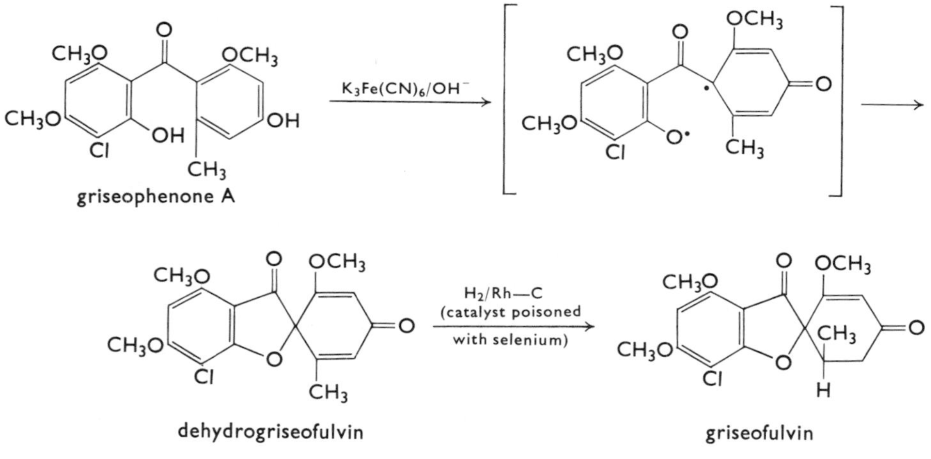

[Eq. 14-8]

A close parallel between the laboratory synthesis of griseofulvin and the biosynthetic pathway is strongly suggested by the isolation of both griseophenone A and dehydrogriseofulvin (Eq. 14-8) from strains of *Penicillium patulum* Bain. Preceding steps in the pathway were indicated by the isolation of the more rudimentary benzophenones, griseophenones B and C. The whole series is known, from appropriate tracer experiments, to stem from an original polyketide precursor. When the various strands of evidence are drawn together, the overall outline of griseofulvin biosynthesis shown in Eq. 14-9, emerges. Although this pathway lacks rigorous proof—only the first and last steps have been the subject of experimental test by tracer techniques—its general validity is widely accepted.

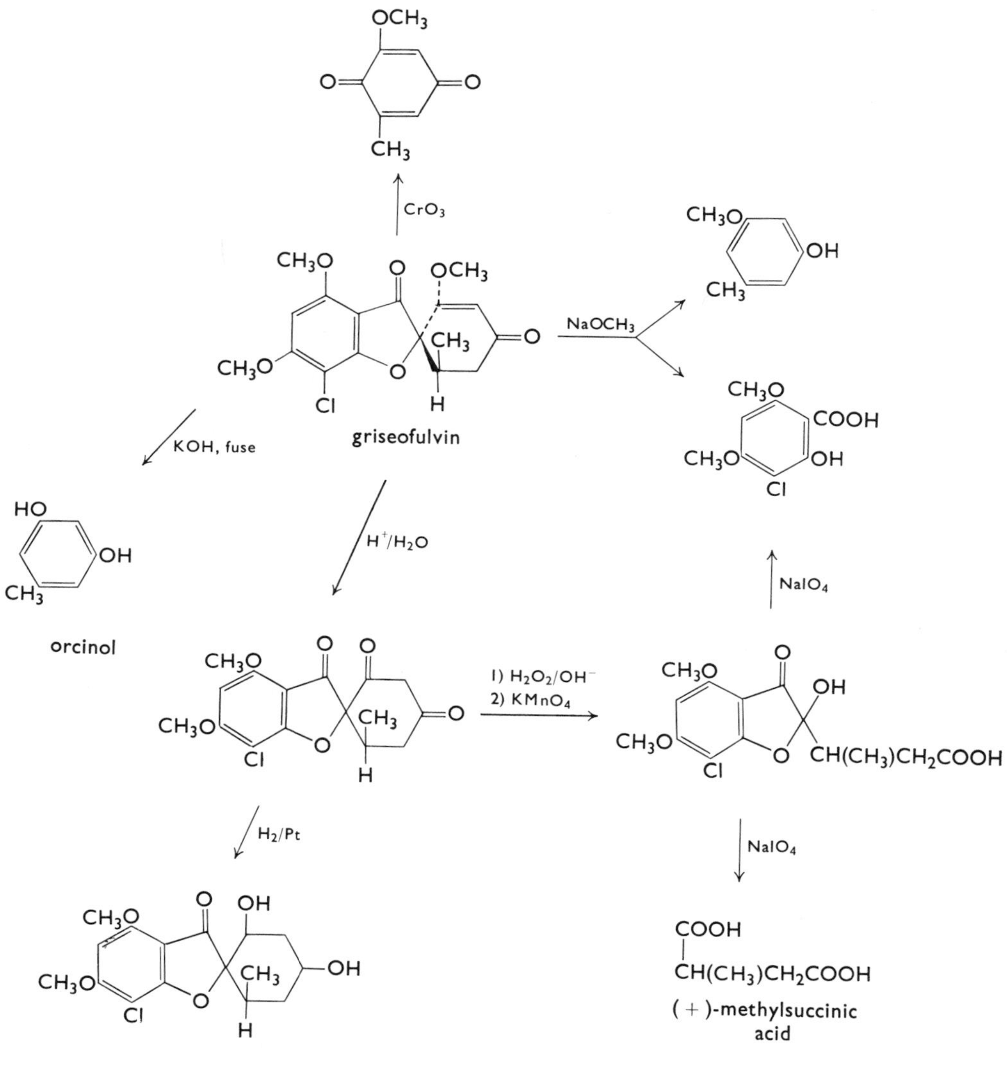

Fig. 14-9. Griseofulvin: Structure Proof.

When a strain of *Penicillium patulum* was grown in a medium deficient in chloride, the amounts of griseofulvin and griseophenones A and B produced were very small, and griseophenone C accumulated. If the chloride deficiency was maintained, a further compound, griseoxanthone C, was produced at the expense of griseophenone C. In the laboratory griseoxanthone C could be obtained from griseophenone C by the methods indicated in Eq. 14-10.

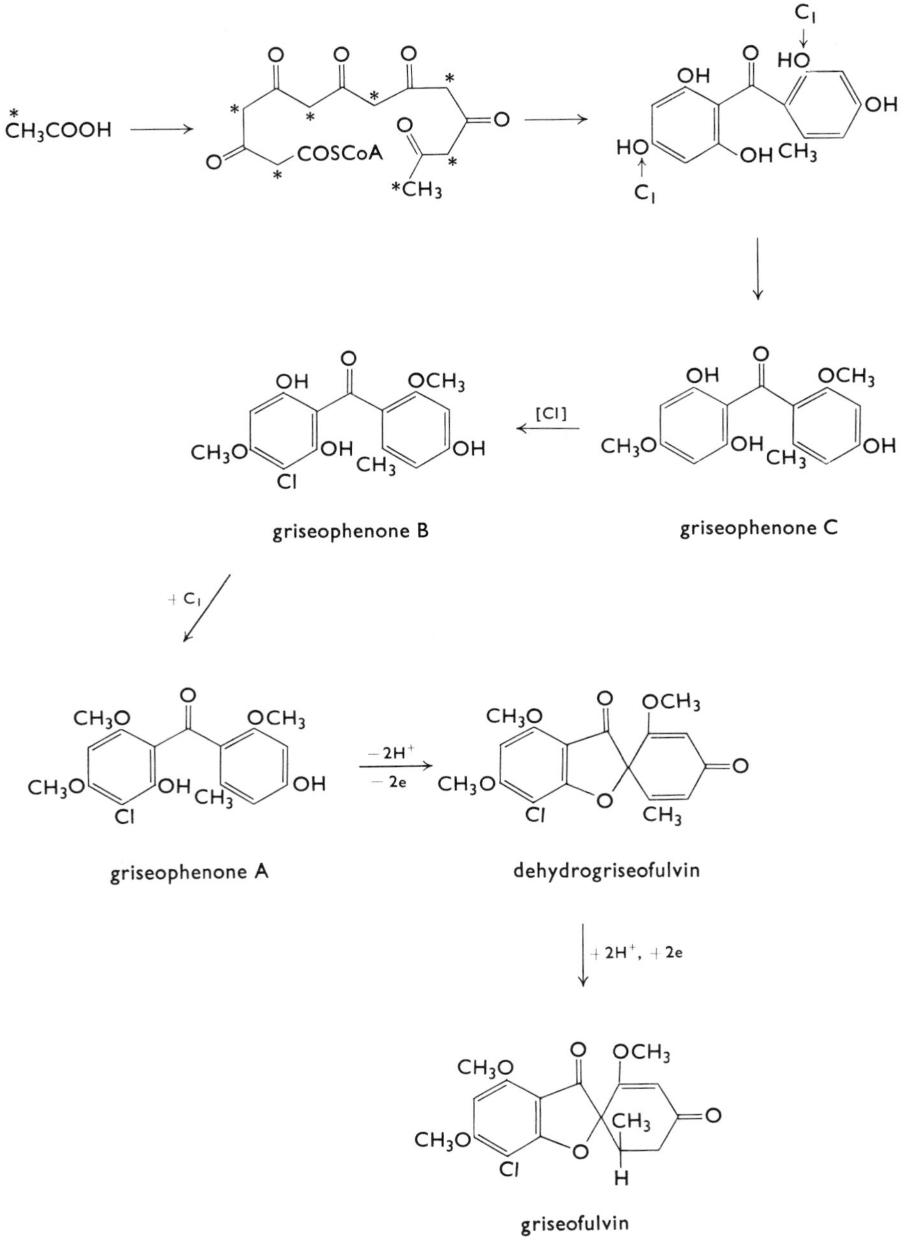

griseophenone B

[Cl]

griseophenone C

+ C₁

griseophenone A

$-2H^+$
$-2e$

dehydrogriseofulvin

$+2H^+, +2e$

griseofulvin

[Eq. 14-9]

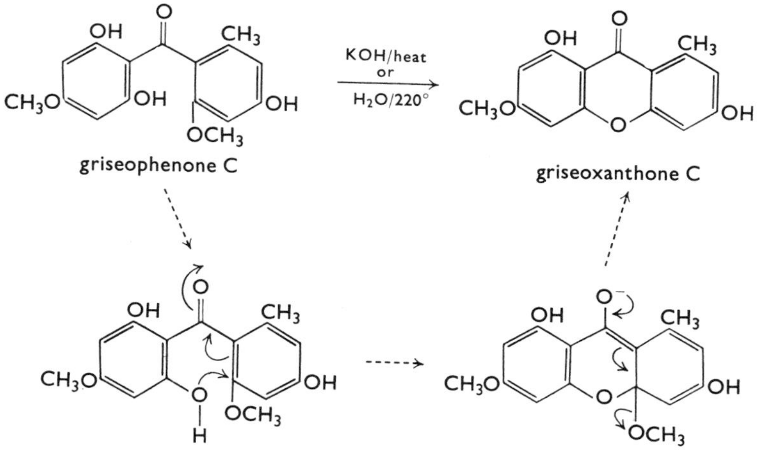

griseophenone C

griseoxanthone C

[Eq. 14-10]

Formation of the oxygen bridge in griseoxanthone C by a radical coupling process would transgress the *ortho-para* orientation rule discussed earlier. The complementary evidence of the laboratory conversion therefore suggests a "demethoxylation" or perhaps a dehydration mechanism for this step (Eq. 14-10, dotted arrows). In nature, a process of this kind would be greatly facilitated by phosphorylation of the phenolic hydroxyl group to be eliminated, since a phosphate or pyrophosphate anion would be far superior to the methoxyl or hydroxyl anion as a leaving group. The ring closure mechanism shown in Eq. 14-10 will be referred to later in connection with the biosynthesis of the fungal xanthones.

14.5 Spirodienones and Related Metabolites of *Aspergillus terreus*

An excellent example of the persuasiveness of laboratory conversions in suggesting biosynthetic pathways is illustrated by the sequence of metabolites set out in Eq. 14-11. These are all found in various strains of *Aspergillus terreus* Thom.* (with the single exception of dechlorogeodoxin, which has not yet been found in nature).

The manner in which the fungus brings about the various changes in the mode of coupling of the carbocyclic rings is strongly suggested by the laboratory conversions indicated in this scheme, which also serves to delineate the probable biosynthetic sequence. The formation of the spiro-lactone bridge in the last step may represent an exception to the normal radical coupling process. Ferricyanide was not effective in bringing about this reaction, whereas lead dioxide gave the required

---

* Sulochrin, dechlorogeodin, and asterric acid are also produced by *Oospora-sulphurea ochracea* v. Beyma, and *Penicillium frequentans* Westl. Dihydrogeodin, geodin, and erdin are also produced by *Penicillium estinogenum* Komatsu and Abe.

products dechlorogeodoxin and geodoxin, respectively, in high yields. Since lead
dioxide does not appear to be able to oxidize carboxyl groups to radical species, the
mechanism of this step may be better represented as attack of a carboxylate anion
on a phenoxonium cation (Eq. 14-12a) rather than as an intramolecular radical
pairing process (Eq. 14-12b).

Mutant No.	Dihydrogeodin	Geodin	Geodin hydrate	Geodoxin
258	+	+	−	−
78	+	+	+	−
"Wild type"	+	+	+	+

+ = appearance of metabolite.

− = non-appearance of metabolite.

Fig. 14-10. Metabolites Produced by Various Strains of *Aspergillus terreus*.

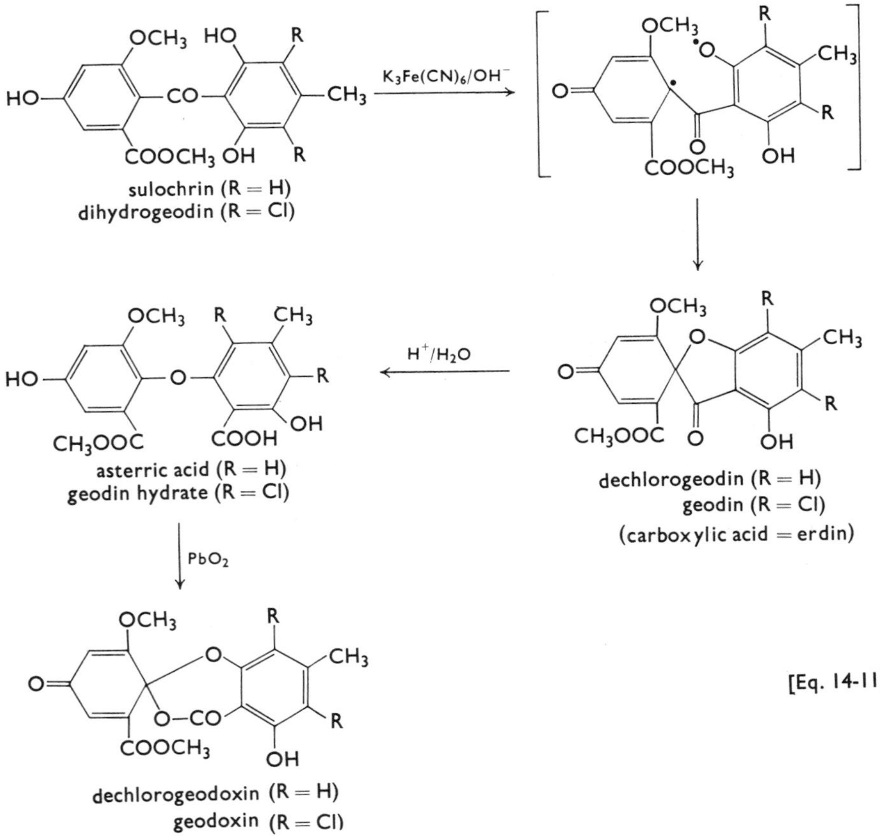

[Eq. 14-11]

[Eq. 14-12]

Evidence for the validity of the proposed biosynthetic sequence has been obtained from studies with mutant strains of *Aspergillus terreus*. The "wild type" fungus was induced to mutate under the influence of ultraviolet light or chemical mutagens. Individual mutant strains were then cultured and analyzed for their metabolite content. The results of one such series of experiments are set out in Fig. 14-10. By making the simple assumption that a metabolite is always accompanied by its precursors,* the biosynthetic sequence; dihydrogeodin → geodin → geodin hydrate → geodoxin, becomes clear.

14.6 Xanthones

The structures of the seventy or so xanthones which have so far been isolated from higher plants, pose an interesting problem when an attempt is made to correlate the various structural types in terms of a uniform pathway of biosynthesis. The wide distribution of xanthones among plant families of more than a dozen different taxonomic orders (most important of which are the families Guttiferae and Gentianaceae) is reflected in a corresponding diversity in the hydroxylation pattern of the basic xanthone framework (Fig. 14-11a). Representative structures are shown in Fig. 14-11. Two clear facts emerge from a statistical survey of the hydroxylation patterns. Firstly, in the great majority of xanthones, one ring (arbitrarily designated ring A) has a clear 1,3,5 oxygenation pattern analogous to the archetypal hydroxylation pattern in ring A of the flavonoids (Chap. 7). Secondly, the substitution pattern of ring B is the source of the great variation in this group, since a coherent

* Although this statement might appear to be a truism, in practice it is frequently found that because the equilibrium concentration of a biosynthetic intermediate in a living system is very low, its existence is not directly observable. Further, in certain pathways, a series of steps may take place with the intermediate bound to an enzyme throughout (cf. fatty acid biosynthesis, Chap. 3). Such intermediates may therefore never appear in free form.

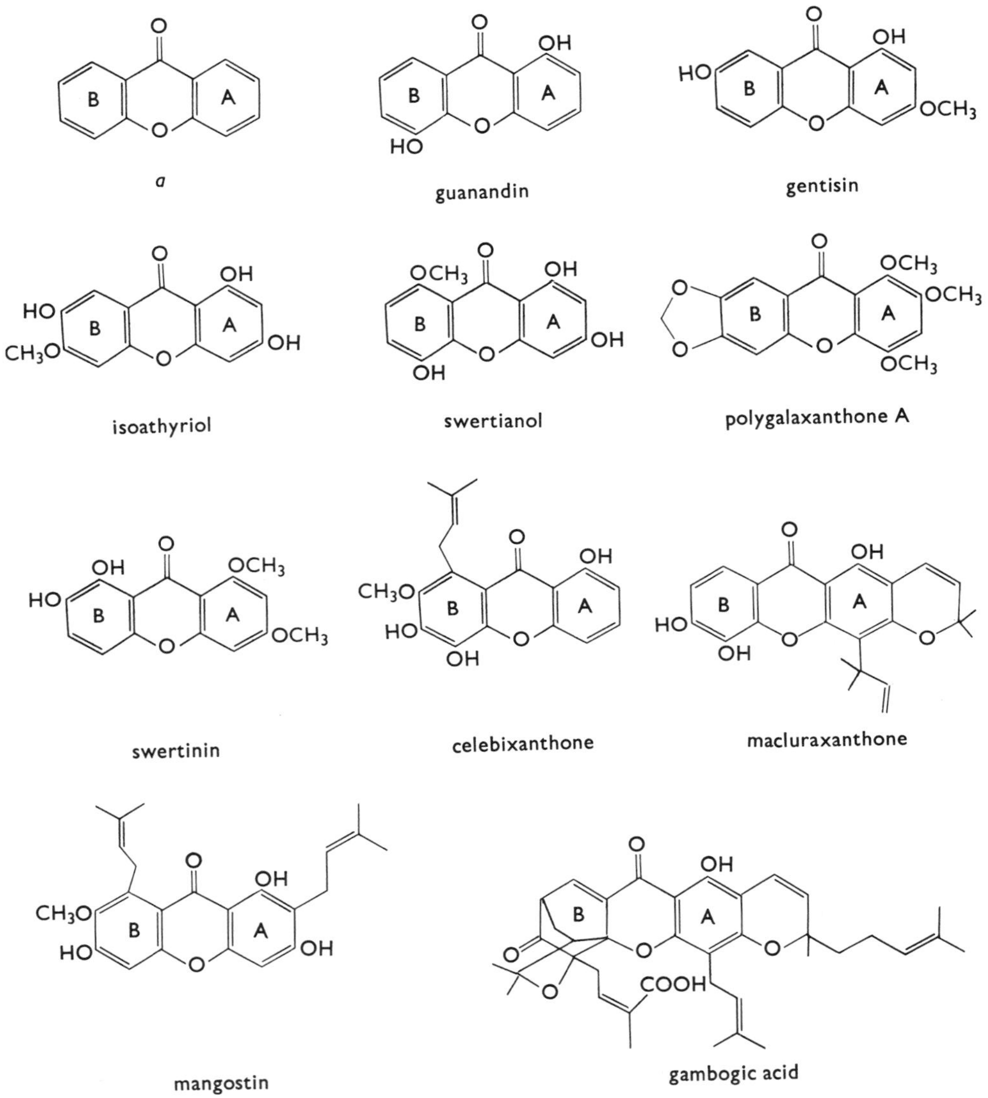

Fig. 14-11. Some Xanthones from Higher Plants.†

_____

† Various secondary processes, which have been described elsewhere, such as the introduction of O—CH₃ groups (Chap. 2), the introduction of isoprenoid side chains (Chap. 8), and the formation of methylenedioxy bridges (Chap. 15), are evident in the biosynthesis of the plant xanthones. These processes are widely observed in the biosynthesis of polyphenolic compounds, and do not require any further discussion here.

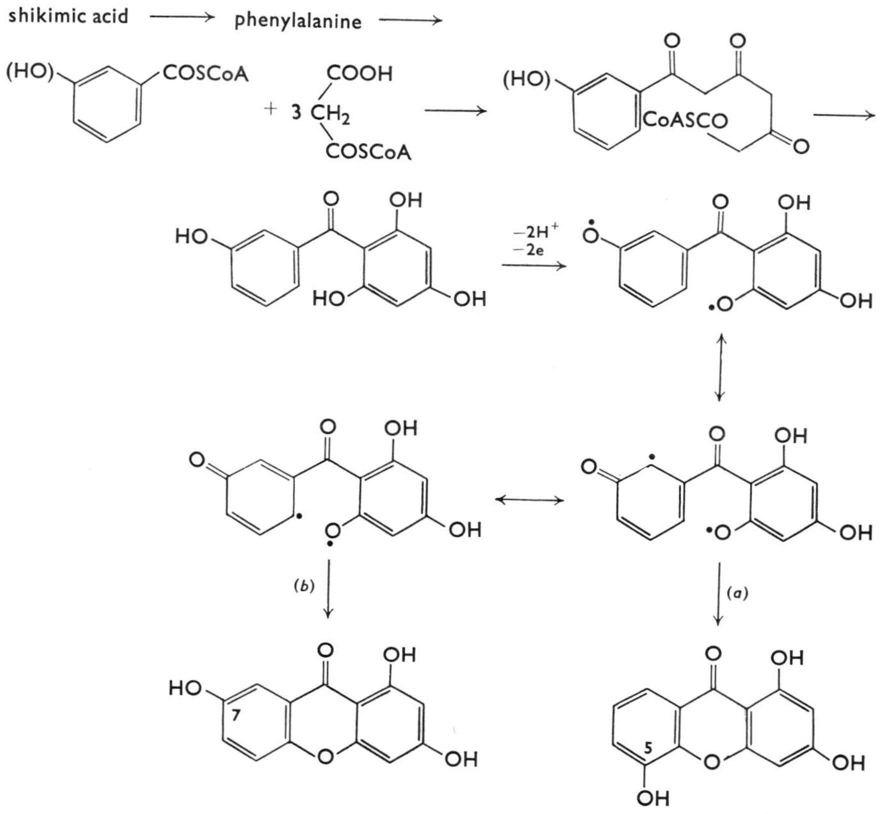

shikimic acid ⟶ phenylalanine ⟶

[Eq. 14-13]

pattern of oxygenation is not found, even among members of the same family. (The forty-nine xanthones isolated from plants of the Guttiferae family, for example, include no less than sixteen different oxygenation types.) However, one clear trend emerges from an analysis of the oxygenation pattern of ring B: the tendency for the oxygen substituents to have an *ortho* or *para* relationship, as opposed to the predominantly *meta* relationship in ring A.

Although lacking the benefit of full experimental corroboration, the pathway of biosynthesis of plant xanthones shown in Eq. 14-13 can accommodate, in a reasonable manner, the observations just made.

The extension of a C_6-C_1 aromatic acid (as the coenzyme A ester), by condensation with three active acetate (malonate) units, is analogous to the corresponding extension of a C_6-C_3 (cinnamyl) unit in the biosynthesis of the flavonoids (Chap. 7). Although the 1,3,5 oxygenation pattern of ring A emerges automatically from this pathway, the chronology of the hydroxylation of ring B cannot be as readily predicted. The introduction of additional hydroxyl groups may precede cyclization; equally this may represent a terminal step in the pathway, taking place after ring closure. No experimental evidence is yet available which would help to clarify this problem. Either possibility would be consistent with accepted ideas regarding the usual mode of hydroxylation of pre-formed aromatic compounds in nature, which suggest that the orientation rules of electrophilic substitution are followed. (The *ortho-para* hydroxylation of phenolic substrates by H.R.P.-hydrogen peroxide illustrates this tendency, which is widely manifested in aromatic compounds derived from shikimic acid.)

In the context of the general theme of this chapter, the important feature of the pathway is the cyclization step resulting in the formation of the heterocyclic ring. The possibility that such a process might occur by an oxidative phenol coupling process is amply supported by analogous laboratory cyclizations such as the one shown in Eq. 14-14.

$$\text{[Eq. 14-14]}$$

The coupling steps illustrated in Eq. 14-13 impose the requirement for a phenolic hydroxyl group to be present at the *meta* position in the aromatic ring postulated to arise from shikimic acid. This hydroxyl group finally appears at either position 5 or 7 in the completed xanthone structure, depending on whether the coupling step proceeds through an *ortho* (Eq. 14-13a) or *para* (Eq. 14-13b) dienone intermediate. The mechanism of Eq. 14-13 therefore leads to the expectation that a phenolic hydroxyl group (or a derived substituent such as methoxy, methylenedioxy, glucosyloxy, etc.) will be present at one of the corresponding positions in the naturally occurring xanthones. A structural survey will show that this expectation is fulfilled in all of the known xanthones of higher plants.

The available evidence to support the pathway of Eq. 14-13 is summarized in Eq. 14-15. An experiment in which labeled phenylalanine was fed to *Gentiana lutea* L. (fam. Gentianaceae) gave radioactive gentisin in which the activity was located predominantly in ring B. A complementary experiment in which carboxyl-labeled acetate was fed gave gentisin labeled predominantly in the oxygenated positions of ring A. It will be noted that these results serve only to support the proposition that the aromatic rings in the xanthones of higher plants are derived from shikimic acid, and acetate, respectively. They do not, in themselves, provide evidence for the individual steps outlined in Eq. 14-13, which must still be regarded as purely speculative.

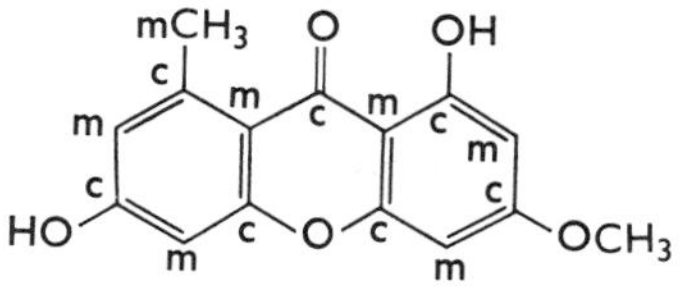

griseoxanthone C
(c: from acetate carboxyl
m: from acetate methyl)

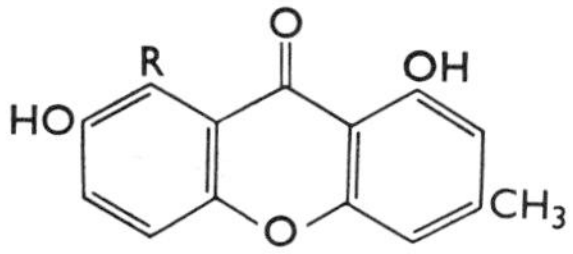

pinsellin (R = COOMe)
pinsellic acid (R = COOH)

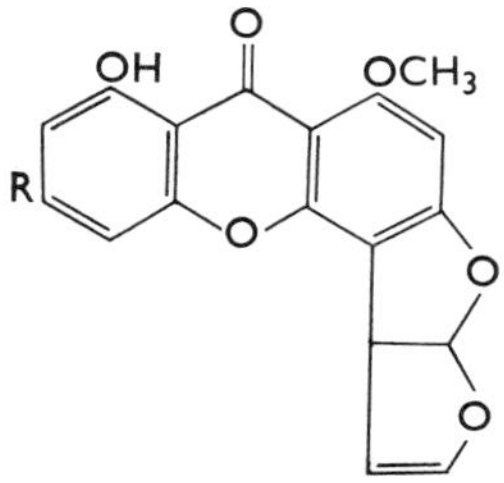

sterigmatocystin (R = H)
6-methoxysterigmatocystin (R = OMe)

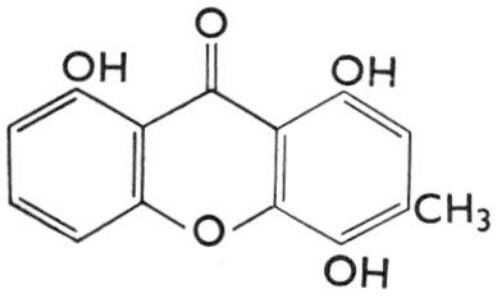

ravenelin

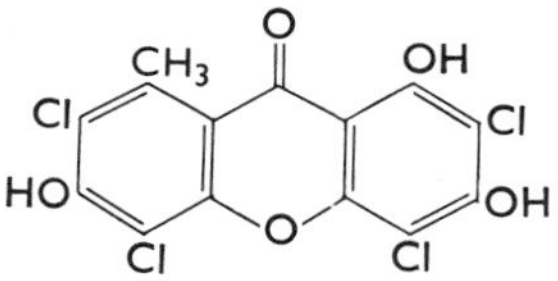

thiophanic acid

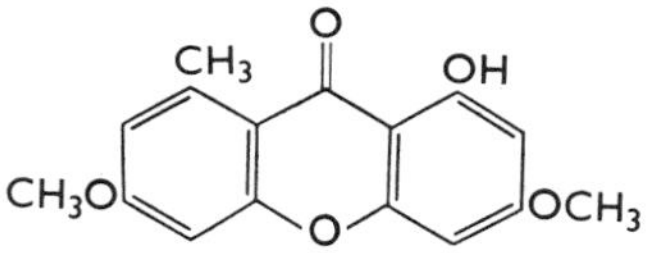

lichexanthone

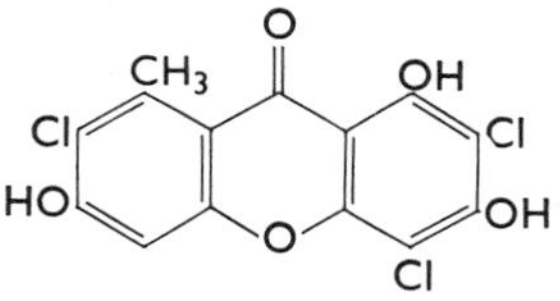

arthothelin

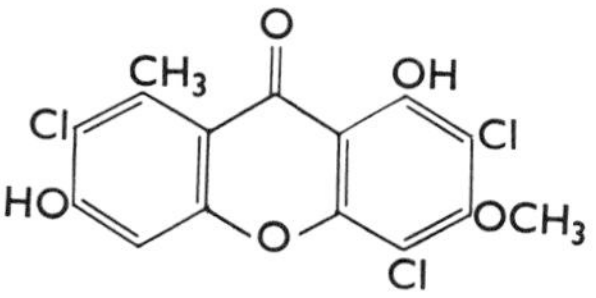

thuringion

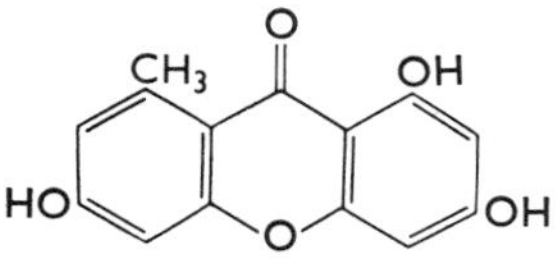

norlichexanthone

Fig. 14-12. Fungal and Lichen Xanthones.

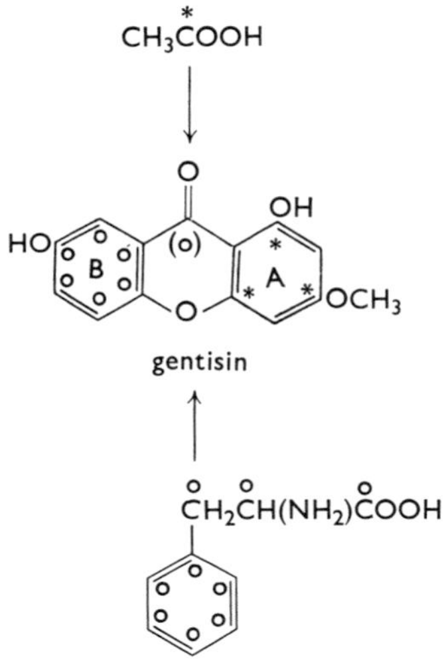

$$\overset{*}{CH_3}COOH$$

gentisin

$$\overset{o}{C}H_2\overset{o}{C}H(NH_2)\overset{o}{C}OOH$$

[Eq. 14-15]

When we turn to the xanthones of fungal or lichen origin (all the known examples at the time of writing are shown in Fig. 14-12), a very different picture emerges. The majority of these compounds do not exhibit an oxygenation pattern which would suggest that the heterocyclic ring is closed by a phenol oxidation process. Instead, the pattern of substitution is more in accord with a dehydration pathway such as that described for the laboratory conversion of griseophenone C into griseoxanthone C (Eq. 14-10). The different oxygenation pattern is attributable to a biogenesis of the fungal and lichen xanthones from a fully polyketide precursor, as implied for griseoxanthone C, by its co-occurrence with griseophenone C, griseofulvin and related metabolites, in *Penicillium* species. The probable origins of the various carbon atoms in griseoxanthone C are indicated in Fig. 14-12.

14.7 The Ergot Pigments and Sulochrin

The fungus *Claviceps purpurea* (Fr.) Tul. (ergot), a specific parasite of rye, has acquired great notoriety because of the toxicity of the lysergic acid derivatives (Chap. 19) which it produces. The fungus is also characterized by the production of a group of dimeric pigments, comprised of xanthone monomer units in which one ring has lost its aromatic character and has undergone further oxidative modification. The formation of the two representative metabolites, secalonic acid A and ergoflavin (Fig. 14-13), is readily rationalized as the *ortho-ortho* and *para-para* coupling respectively, of identical monomeric units. The stage of elaboration of the monomeric unit at which coupling takes place has not been determined.

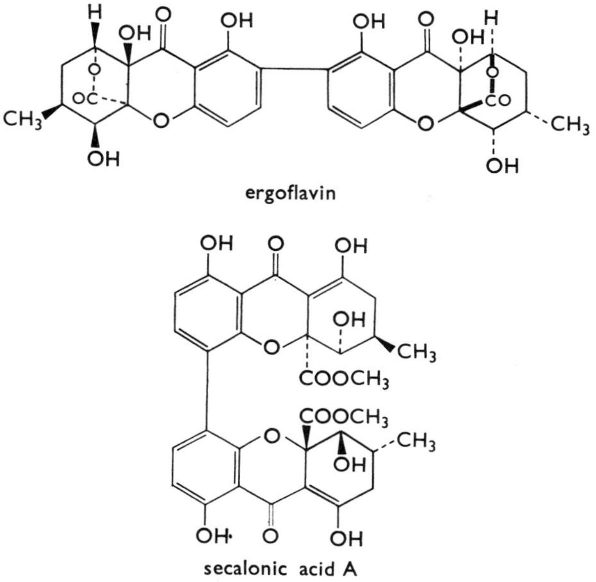

ergoflavin

secalonic acid A

Fig. 14-13. Ergot Pigments.

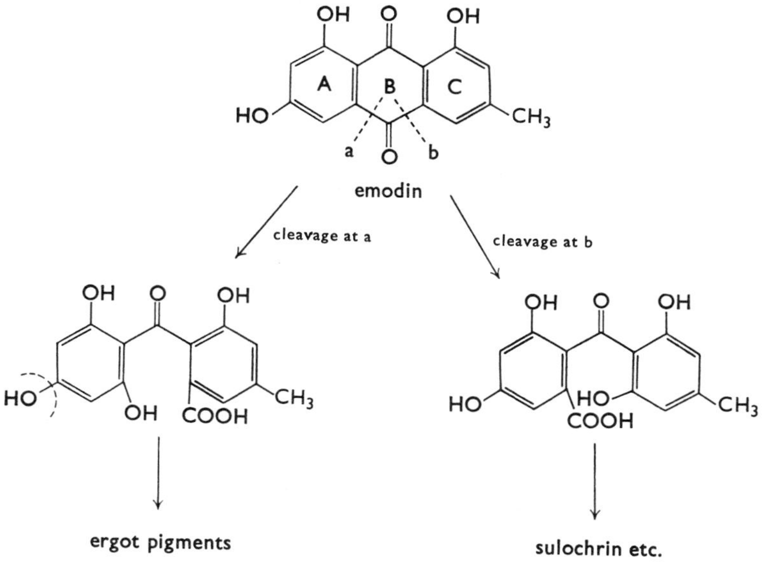

emodin

cleavage at a

cleavage at b

ergot pigments

sulochrin etc.

[Eq. 14-16]

The biosynthetic pathways leading to the ergot pigments and to sulochrin (Eq. 14-11) have been drawn together in a remarkable way by evidence which suggests that biogenetically these metabolites are mutually related to the anthraquinone emodin, a metabolite of *Penicillium islandicum* Sopp., and several other species of fungi. The suggested interrelationships are illustrated in Eq. 14-16, in which the key step in the biosynthesis of both the ergot pigments and sulochrin is seen to be the oxidative cleavage of the anthraquinone nucleus. Fission of ring B at the bond attached to the methyl substituted ring leads to the sulochrin skeleton, whereas cleavage at the other ring junction leads to the monomer unit of the ergot pigments.

The latter conversions have received support from experiments in which biosynthetically labeled emodin* was converted into sulochrin and into ergot pigments, by *Penicillium frequentans* and various *Claviceps* species, respectively.

It should be emphasized that the pathways outlined in Eq. 14-16 are multistep processes, and that nothing is known about the order in which the various individual transformations take place. (For example, a phenolic hydroxyl group must be removed from ring A in emodin at some point in the pathway leading to the ergot pigments; this might occur at any stage in the sequence.) Eq. 14-16 is only intended to give an impression of the overall process.

14.8 Lignans

Lignan biosynthesis illustrates an important extension of the coupling processes so far considered in that two C_6-C_3 units of shikimate origin are joined at the β carbon atom of the side chain. In the general discussion of lignan chemistry given in Chapter 5, the various ways in which cinnamyl alcohols are elaborated to completed lignan structures were discussed in terms of intermediate "onium" ions as the primary products of the oxidation step. The radical pairing mechanism serves equally well to explain the coupling reaction, and is here illustrated by a typical laboratory conversion, modeled on the probable biosynthetic pathway, in which sinapyl alcohol undergoes coupling to furnish ($\pm$)-syringaresinol (Eq. 14-17). As in the "onium" ion mechanism, the presence of the conjugated side chain permits delocalization of the unpaired electron to the β carbon atom, with the result that coupling with other radicals can take place at this position.

---

* The necessity for carrying out a total laboratory synthesis of a complex metabolite in labeled form can sometimes be avoided by making use of the existing biosynthetic machinery in a suitable organism. The emodin required for the experiments under discussion, for example, was obtained by growing *Penicillium islandicum* in the presence of ^{14}C-acetate and harvesting the resulting labeled metabolite.

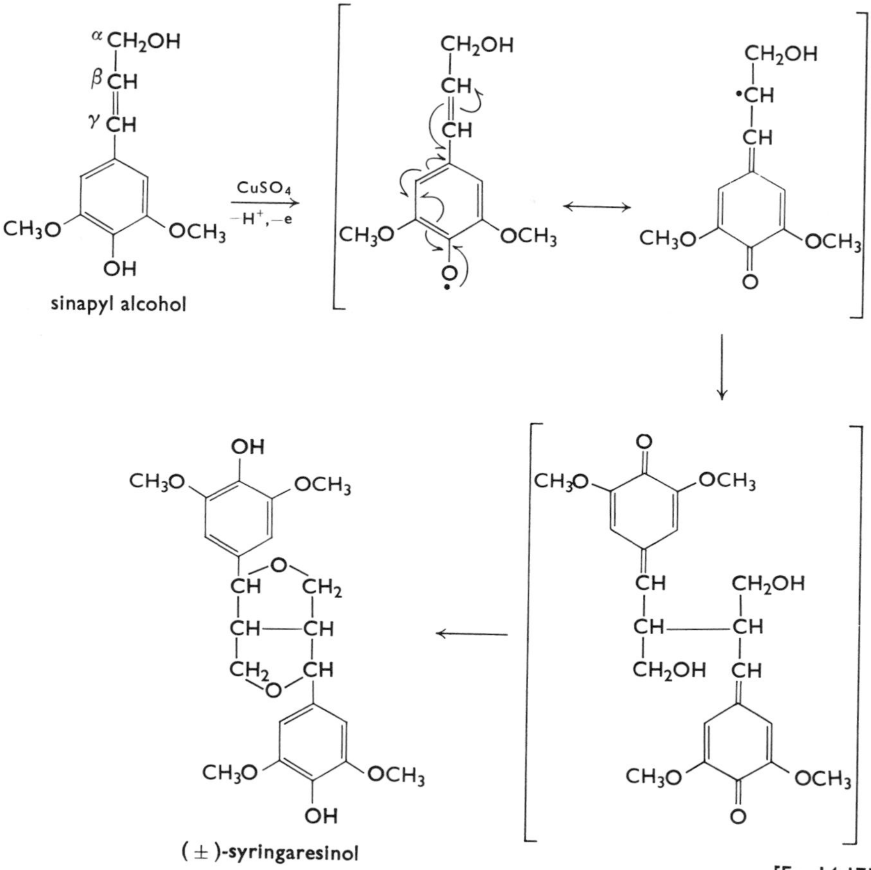

[Eq. 14-17]

14.9 Lignin

If the relative importance of phenol coupling reactions in nature were to be judged solely on the quantity of phenolics oxidized *per annum*, then lignin formation would easily overshadow all other processes. Lignin has already been described in Chapter 5 as a complex polymer composed mainly of C_6-C_3 units derived from coniferyl and sinapyl alcohols. (Sinapyl alcohol (cf. Eq. 14-17) gives rise to the syringyl residues noted to be characteristic of angiosperm lignin, page 158.) Lignin can be regarded as nature's version of the reinforcing steel used in modern building construction, as it provides the strength needed to support the vertical growth of plants and trees, and is therefore of fundamental importance to their survival.

The highly stereospecific course of lignan biosynthesis was emphasized in

Chapter 5. By contrast, the related structures in lignin are apparently formed without the benefit of asymmetric control, since no degradation product has ever been obtained in optically active form. Nevertheless, the structural elements found in the lignans are also represented in lignin, together with the interunitary linkages which knit together the individual subunits into a highly ramified polymeric network (cf. Fig. 5-10).

The lack of optical activity has led to the suggestion that lignin formation is under enzymatic control only during the initial oxidation of the C_6-C_3 precursors. The phenolate radicals produced are presumed to undergo further coupling in a purely "chemical" manner, which serves to explain the reasonably successful outcome of attempts to simulate the formation of lignin under laboratory conditions.

The enzyme currently believed to be responsible for natural lignification is peroxidase. Accordingly, "laboratory" lignin is prepared by the carefully controlled addition of dilute solutions of peroxidase and hydrogen peroxide to a stirred solution of the appropriate mixture of cinnamyl alcohols. Evidence bearing on lignin formation *in vivo* can then be obtained (a) by isolating and identifying low molecular weight intermediates of the polymerization process, and (b) by degrading the polymeric product and comparing the results with those obtained from the similar degradation of natural lignin. However, conclusions drawn from comparisons between the natural and the synthetic material must be tempered by the realization that no extraction procedure has yet been devised which guarantees the isolation of natural lignin in an unaltered form.

Of the many phenol coupling processes which occur in nature, the examples so far discussed, have, for various reasons, been the most intensively investigated. Many further examples can be discerned in a wide range of natural products, although the evidence for the participation of phenol oxidation reactions in their biosynthesis rests largely on structural analysis, or on laboratory studies of the one-electron oxidation of model compounds. Some of the more important classes of compound will be briefly discussed.

14.10 Depsides and Depsidones

The common occurrence of both depsides and the corresponding depsidones (Chap. 4) in different lichen species, and occasionally in one and the same species, provides circumstantial evidence to support the pathway of depsidone formation illustrated by the laboratory synthesis of diploicin shown in Eq. 14-18. In this scheme, the depsidone structure is fabricated directly, by intramolecular oxidative coupling of the corresponding depside.

The structure of a related metabolite, picrolichenic acid (Eq. 14-19), is of particular interest in that the normal coupling reaction which would lead to a

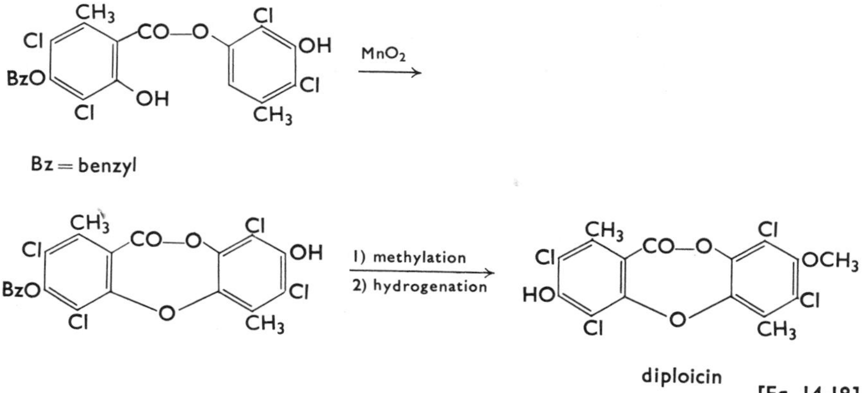

Bz = benzyl

diploicin

[Eq. 14-18]

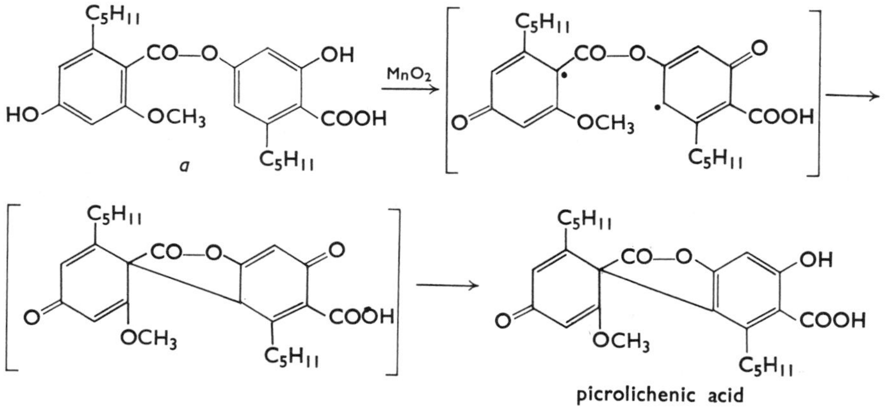

picrolichenic acid

[Eq. 14-19]

depsidone structure has been blocked by methylation; instead, an alternative mode of coupling, leading to a spirodienone, has intervened. A synthesis of picrolichenic acid from the model depside (Eq. 14-19a), based on the probable biosynthetic pathway, has been successfully accomplished in the laboratory by the method shown.

14.11   Bisnaphthalene Derivatives

A bisnaphthalene derivative of fungal origin, mycochrysone, showing clear structural evidence of an oxidative coupling step in its biosynthesis, was illustrated at the beginning of this chapter (Fig. 14-2). The metabolites of *Daldinia concentrica*

(Bolt.) Ces. et de Not. shown in Eq. 14-20, are related in a manner which is particularly suggestive of the indicated biosynthetic pathway. Extended quinone structures of the type found in the final metabolite in this sequence, are often produced by the further oxidation of intermediate p,p'-diphenols in oxidative coupling reactions.

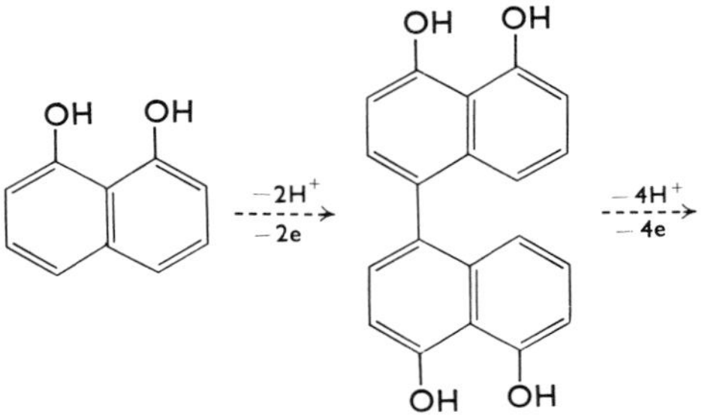

$$[\text{Eq. 14-20}]$$

14.12   Bisanthraquinones

Far more common than naphthalene derivatives, are the anthraquinones and bisanthraquinones produced by many fungal species. Various strains of *Penicillium islandicum* Sopp. are particularly rich in pigments, including the structurally related pairs shown in Fig. 14-14. However, a note of caution should be sounded against

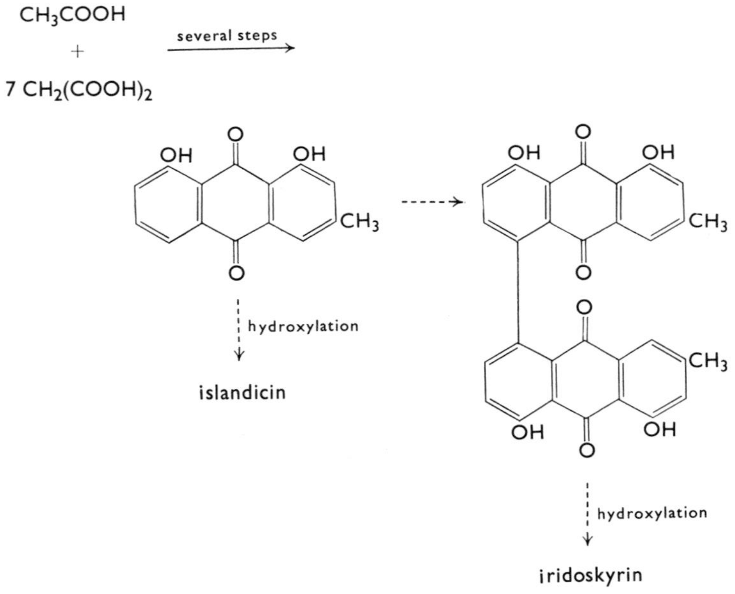

$$[\text{Eq. 14-21}]$$

CH_3COOH

$+$

$7\ CH_2(COOH)_2$

several steps

hydroxylation

islandicin

hydroxylation

iridoskyrin

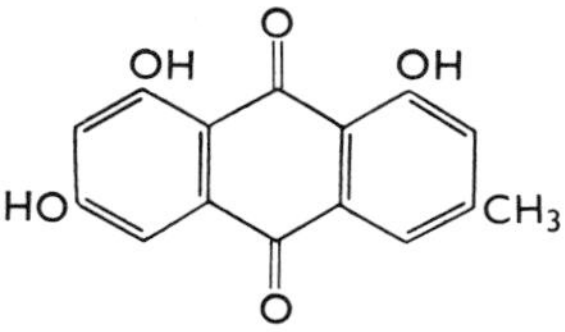

emodin

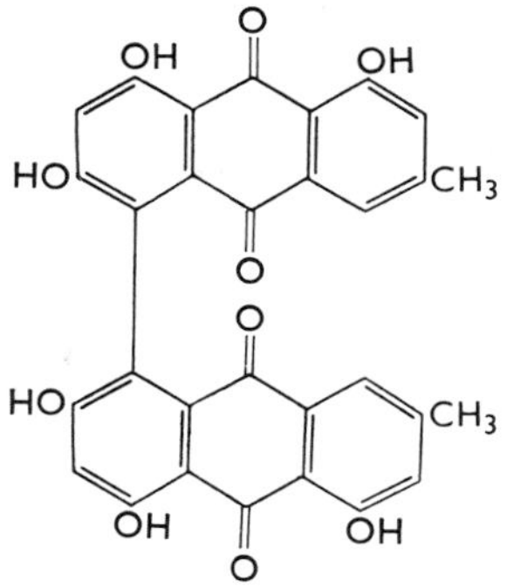

skyrin

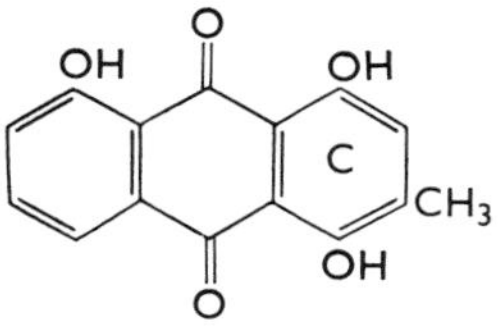

islandicin

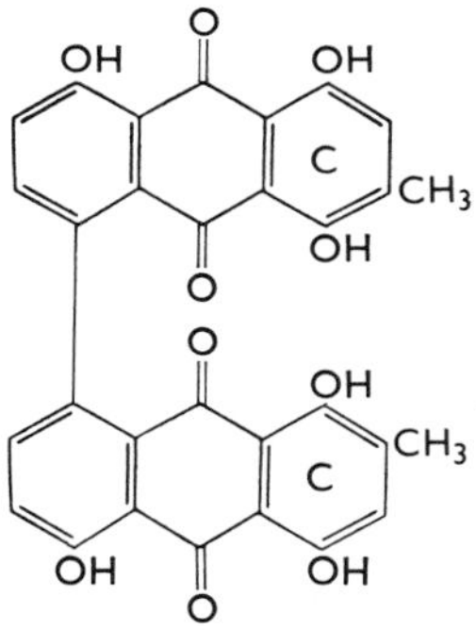

iridoskyrin

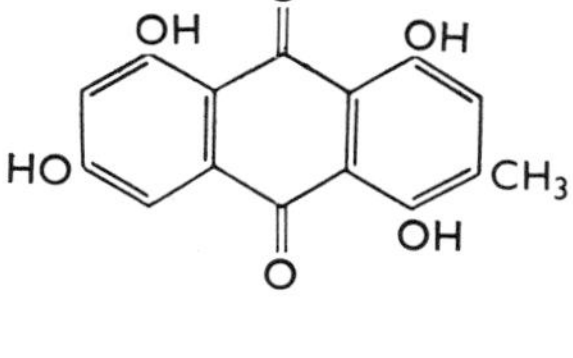

catenarin

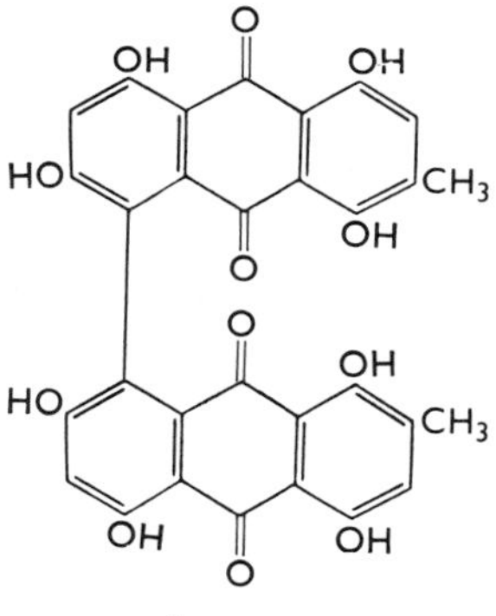

dicatenarin

Fig. 14-14. Fungal Anthraquinones and Bisanthraquinones.

making the obvious assumption that these compounds always bear a precursor-product relationship to one another. In a careful analysis of the radioactivity-time curves of islandicin and iridoskyrin, biosynthesized in the presence of ^{14}C-acetate, it was found that the specific activities of the two metabolites rose and fell in parallel, a situation which could not have arisen if islandicin were an obligatory precursor of iridoskyrin. Such a result suggests that there is a branch at some stage in the biosynthetic pathway. An obvious point at which this could occur is in the timing of the insertion of the "extra" hydroxyl group in ring C, *ortho* to the methyl substituent. (This is the only hydroxyl group which would not arise automatically during cyclization of the hypothetical polyketide precursor (Chap. 4).) If the hydroxylation step took place at a late stage in the pathway, islandicin and iridoskyrin would represent terminal products of metabolism, related through a common progenitor (Eq. 14-21).

14.13 Bisterpenoids

Although the majority of phenols participating in oxidative coupling processes arise by either the polyketide or shikimic acid pathways, in a few instances they appear to be formed from intermediates of terpenoid origin.

Thus, gossypol, the toxic pigment of cottonseed (*Gosspyium hirsutum* L. fam. Malvaceae), evidently arises through the dimerization of a phenolic sesquiterpene precursor, as indicated in Eq. 14-22.

A recent investigation of the tropical tree *Thespesia populnea* Corr. (fam. Malvaceae) has revealed an alternative source of gossypol, but with the interesting

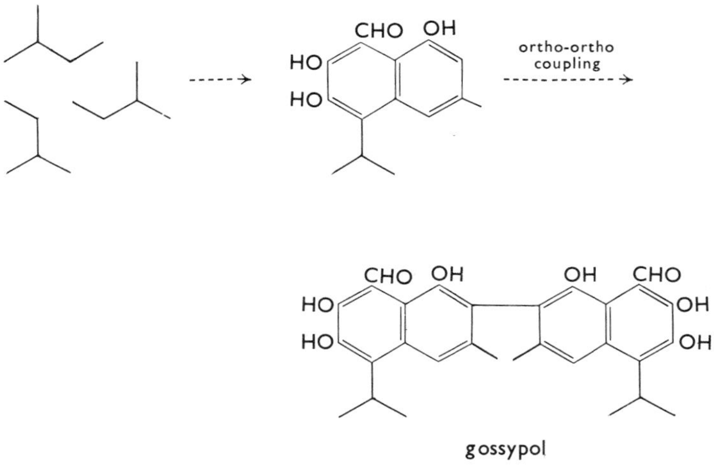

[Eq. 14-22]

gossypol

difference that the product isolated from this source is optically active ($[\alpha]_D^{19} + 445°$ in chloroform), whereas the cottonseed pigment is produced as the inactive racemate. The optical activity of the *Thespesia* gossypol must arise through restricted rotation about the bond joining the naphthalene nuclei—a further illustration of high stereospecificity in a biosynthetic coupling reaction.

14.14 Purpurogallin

Many plants produce growths known as "galls" in response to infestation by insects or fungi. A number of these such as the "Pineapple" gall produced by the aphis *Adelges abietes* L. on the bark of *Abies excelsa* de Cond. (fam. Pinaceae) and the "Cherry" gall produced by *Dryophanta taschenbergii* Schulz. on the leaves of *Quercus sessiliflora* Sal. (fam. Fagaceae), have been found to contain glucosides of purpurogallin. This compound is produced by the oxidation of pyrogallol with ferricyanide, H.R.P., laccase or tyrosinase, according to Eq. 14-23, which also shows the probable mechanism of the reaction.

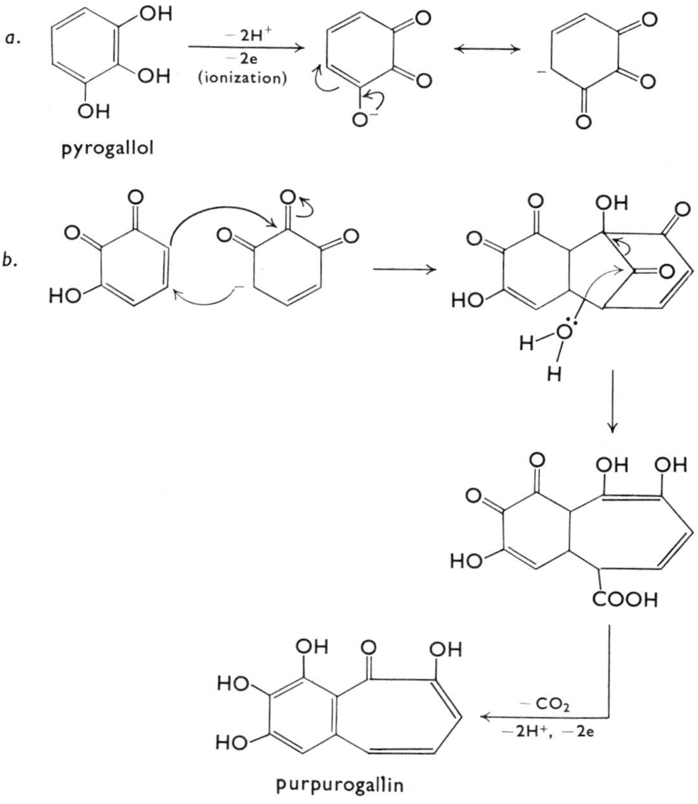

[Eq. 14-23]

Although not strictly a phenol coupling process of the kind considered so far, this reaction is of some importance as it forms the basis of a commonly used method for estimating peroxidase, and also on occasion laccase and tyrosinase, activity. The yellow purpurogallin, produced by the enzyme sample under standard conditions, is extracted and estimated colorimetrically.

The reaction sequence shown in Eq. 14-23 is of further significance, in that it illustrates a mechanism that may be of importance in oxidative coupling reactions in which *ortho* or *para* quinones participate, either as substrates or intermediates. This mechanism involves the addition of an anion to the double bond of the quinone system, as shown in Eq. 14-24. Unless there is positive evidence to the contrary, this mechanism must always be considered as an alternative to the radical pairing mechanism in oxidations which involve the formation of new C—C or

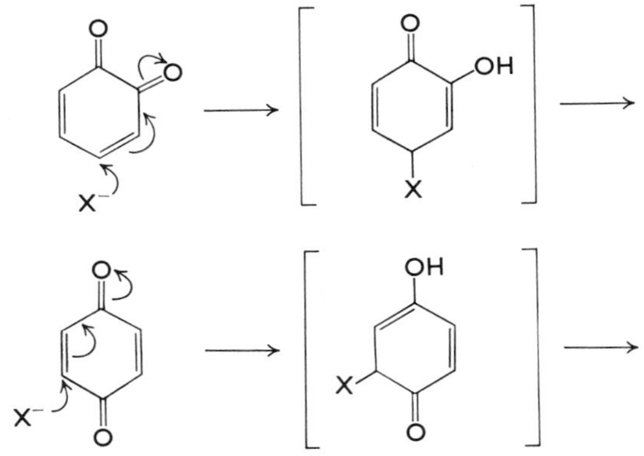

[Eq. 14-24]

C—O bonds in compounds having either an *ortho* or *para*-quinone nucleus (or the corresponding catechol or hydroquinone structures from which the corresponding quinones could arise by oxidation). It is further evident that the quinone may be regarded as the two-electron oxidation product of a hydroquinone.

14.15 Summary

Sufficient examples have been given in this chapter to demonstrate the importance of oxidative coupling processes as a means of constructing complex phenolic metabolites in nature. The story is by no means complete, however, since the part played by phenol coupling processes in alkaloid biosynthesis has not yet been touched upon. The intense activity in this field in recent years has yielded a rich harvest of results which warrant the separate treatment given in Chapter 18.

XV CHAPTER

REFERENCES FOR FURTHER READING

1. D. H. R. Barton, G. W. Kirby, and J. B. Taylor, *On the Origin of Methylenedioxy Groups in Nature*, Proc. Chem. Soc., (1962), 340.
2. D. H. R. Barton, R. H. Hesse, and G. W. Kirby, *The Origin of the "Berberine Carbon"*, Proc. Chem. Soc., (1963), 267.
3. L. Crombie, C. L. Green, and D. A. Whiting, *Biosynthesis of Rotenoids: The Origin of C-6 and C-6a*, J. Chem. Soc. (C), (1968), 3029.
4. L. J. Goad, *Aspects of Phytosterol Biosynthesis* in Terpenoids in Plants, J. B. Pridham, Ed., Academic Press, London and New York, (1967), 159.
5. J. P. Ferris, R. D. Gerwe, and G. R. Gapski, *Detoxication Mechanisms II. The Iron Catalysed Dealkylation of Trimethylamine Oxide*, J. Amer. Chem. Soc., 89, (1967), 5270.
6. W. C. Evans, *The Microbiological Degradation of Aromatic Compounds*, J. Gen. Microbiol. 32, (1963), 177.
7. R. Bentley and I. M. Campbell, *Secondary Metabolism of Fungi* in Comprehensive Biochemistry, M. Florkin and E. H. Stotz, Eds., Elsevier, Amsterdam, London and New York, (1968), 415.
8. H. E. Müller, H. Rösler, A. Wohlpart, H. Wyler, M. E. Wilcox, H. Frohofer, T. J. Mabry, and A. S. Dreiding, *Biogenesis of Betalaines. Biotransformation of DOPA and Tyrosine into the Betalamic Acid Portion of Betanin*, Helv. Chim. Acta, 51, (1968), 1470.

CHAPTER XV

Miscellaneous Oxidative Processes

15.1 Introduction

This chapter deals with two minor pathways of secondary metabolism: the oxidative modification of O, C, and N-methyl functions, and the oxidative fission of aromatic rings.

The transfer of the S-methyl group of methionine to a biological intermediate has been encountered many times in previous chapters. The process of trans-methylation, however, should not be regarded as a biosynthetic *cul de sac*, since further reactions may take place, leading to modification of the methyl function in ways which often obscure its origin as the S-methyl group of methionine. In the limiting case, oxidative transformation may even lead to a reversal of the methyla-tion process itself, since biological demethylation is well established as a minor pathway of secondary metabolism.

15.2 Origin of the Methylenedioxy Group

The methylenedioxy group is a common feature in many natural products containing aromatic rings derived from shikimic acid. It is of frequent occurrence in flavonoids (Chap. 7), and it will be seen to be equally common in various groups of alkaloids derived from aromatic amino acids (Chap. 18).

The most obvious derivation of the methylenedioxy system would be by con-densation of formaldehyde with a 1,2-dihydroxybenzene (catechol) nucleus as indicated in Eq. 15-1.

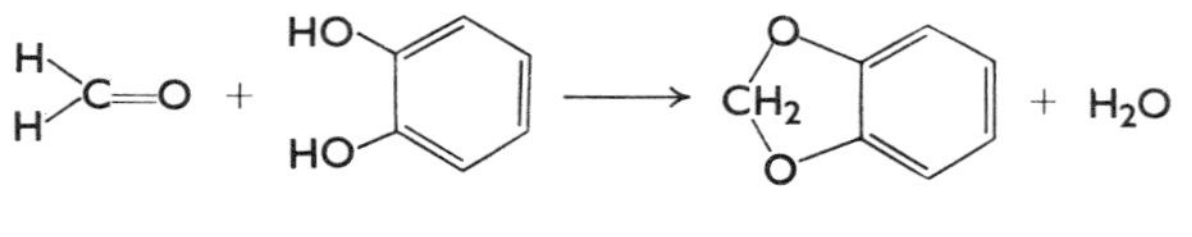

[Eq. 15-1]

However, an alternative suggestion to be considered is that the methylenedioxy system could arise by oxidative ring closure of an *o*-methoxyphenol, as shown in Eq. 15-2.

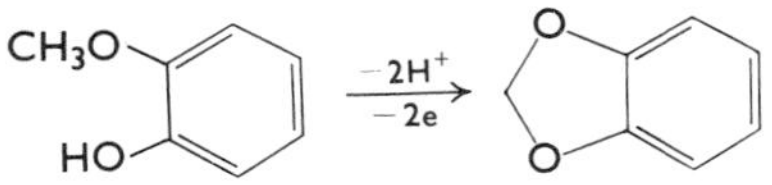

[Eq. 15-2]

It will be noted that an experiment to test the latter hypothesis must be very carefully designed, since it must distinguish between the pathway shown, and an equivalent overall process involving demethylation to a catechol structure and synthesis of the methylenedioxy system *de novo*.

Provision has been made for discriminating between these possibilities in feeding experiments, by using substrates labeled in both the methyl group of an *o*-methoxyphenol precursor and at some other reference point in the molecule.

Experiments relating to the biosynthesis of the daffodil alkaloid haemanthamine (Eq. 15-3) will serve as an illustration of this technique. The postulated

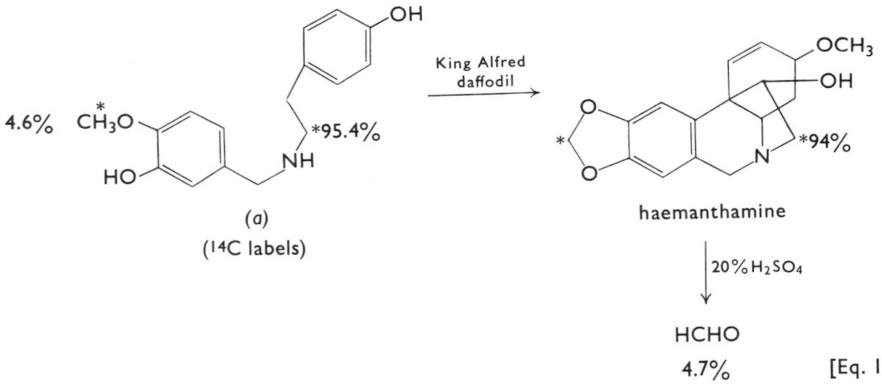

[Eq. 15-3]

precursor (Eq. 15-3*a*) was labeled in the methyl carbon and in the carbon chain, with the relative activities shown. Radioactive haemanthamine, isolated after feeding this precursor to King Alfred daffodils, was hydrolyzed to give the methylenedioxy carbon atom as formaldehyde which contained 4.7% of the total activity. The remaining activity (94%) was found at the expected position adjacent to the nitrogen function. This evidence clearly shows that the methyl group in the precursor was converted directly into the methylenedioxy group of haemanthamine. Demethylation, followed by resynthesis from the consequently labeled C_1 pool, would inevitably have led to a dilution of the label. A number of similar experiments have given identical results and leave little doubt as to the generality of the pathway shown in Eq. 15-2.

The mechanism of the cyclization reaction is not at all clear since speculation is hampered by the lack of a suitable laboratory analogy. Related processes involving N-methyl groups, to be described below, probably involve dehydrogenation to a Schiff base intermediate, followed by nucleophilic addition, and an analogous mechanism may apply in the O-methyl case, as indicated in Eq. 15-4.

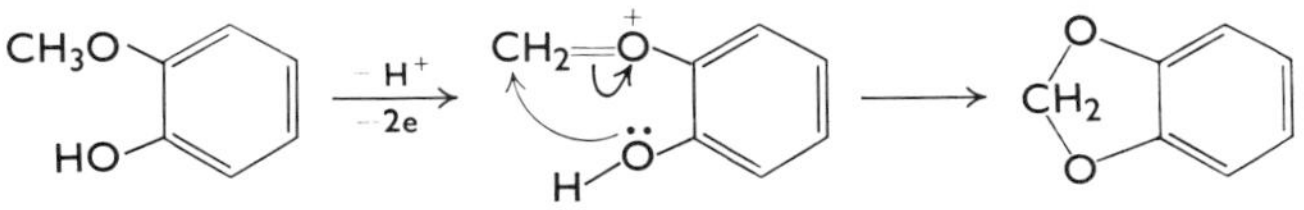

[Eq. 15-4]

15.3   The "Berberine Bridge"

Alkaloids of a large class derived from tyrosine have structures which are based on the simple benzylisoquinoline system shown in Fig. 15-1. By a variety of chemical transformations, the benzylisoquinoline skeleton is elaborated in nature into a

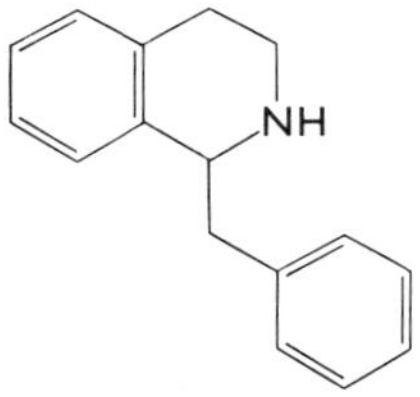

Fig. 15-1.

number of related alkaloid structures, many of which are described in Chapter 18.

In the structure of berberine (Fig. 15-2) we note a significant development in the form of an additional carbon atom (circled) which is not present in the proto- type structure (Fig. 15-1). This additional carbon atom, which constitutes the so- called "berberine bridge", is the characteristic feature of a group known as the

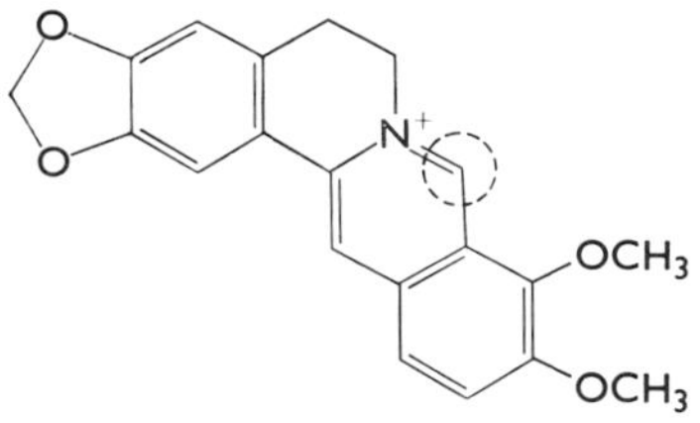

berberine

Fig. 15-2.

protoberberine alkaloids. These occur in several plant families, but are particularly characteristic of the genus *Berberis* (fam. Berberidaceae) and of a number of genera of the family Papaveraceae.

Early proposals for the formation of the "berberine bridge" were based on a Mannich-type ring closure, with formaldehyde as the source of the additional carbon atom, as shown in Eq. 15-5. (Only the structural features essential to the reaction are shown in the formulae.)

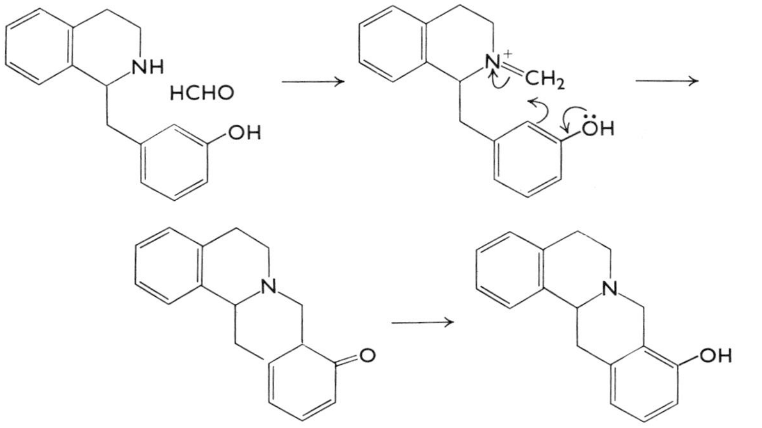

[Eq. 15-5]

An alternative pathway, by way of oxidative cyclization of an N-methyl precursor in a manner analogous to the formation of the methylenedioxy system, is illustrated in Eq. 15-6.

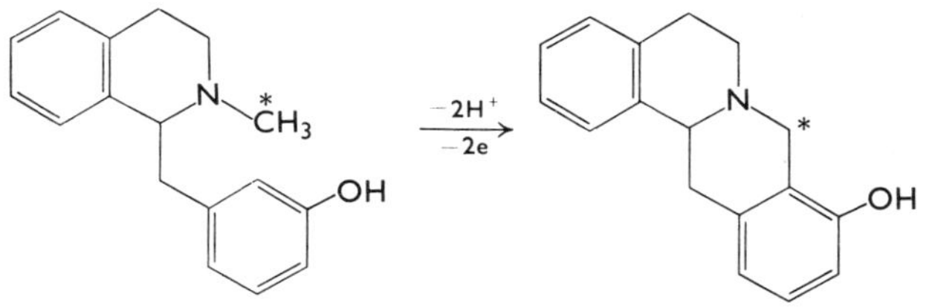

[Eq. 15-6]

The latter pathway is now known to be correct as the result of double labeling experiments similar to those used in the studies of the formation of the methylenedioxy system. The essential experimental results obtained in a typical investigation are summarized in Eq. 15-7.

Once again, we can only speculate as to the mechanism of this reaction; however, a pathway involving dehydrogenation to a quaternary Schiff base intermediate followed by anion addition, as shown in Eq. 15-8, would appear to be the most attractive possibility at present.

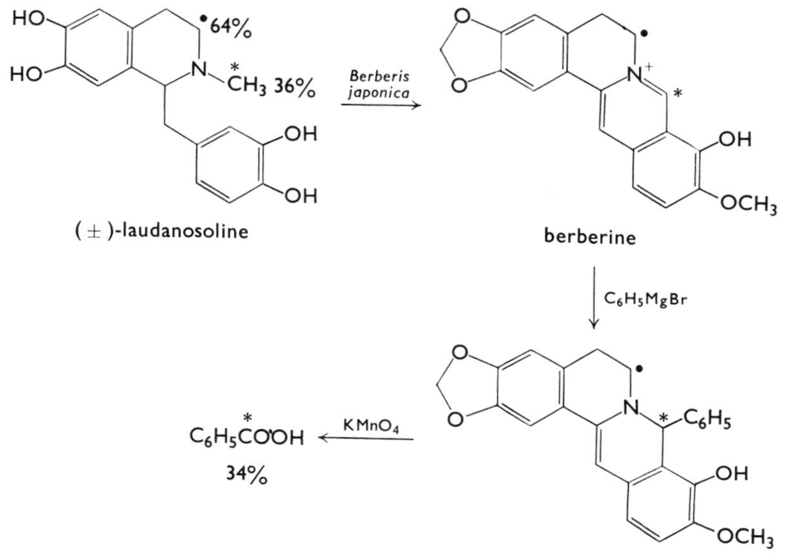

(±)-laudanosoline

berberine

[Eq. 15-7]

berberine

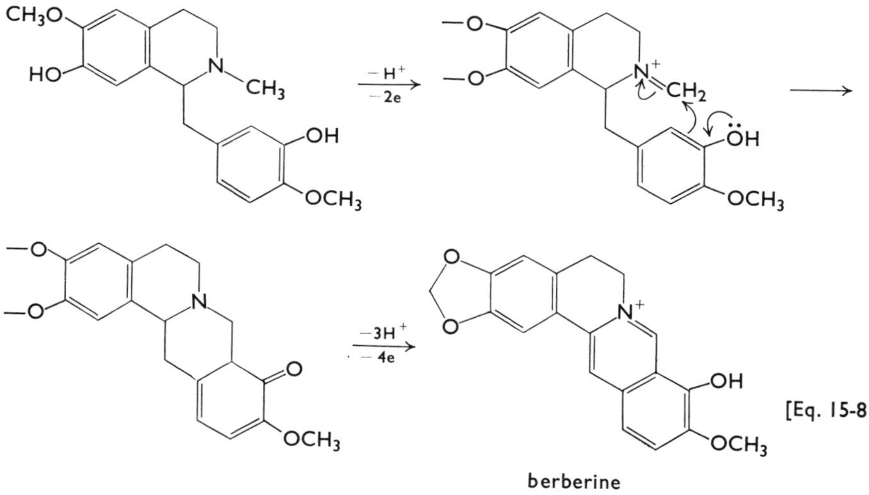

[Eq. 15-8]

15.4 Cyclization of O-methyl Groups on to Carbon

A limited number of secondary metabolites appear to be formed by pathways involving the oxidative cyclization of O-methyl groups on to carbon. Thus we can discern in the structure of the rotenoids, as exemplified by rotenone (Eq. 15-9), the basic carbon skeleton of an isoflavone (Chap. 7), modified by the presence of an

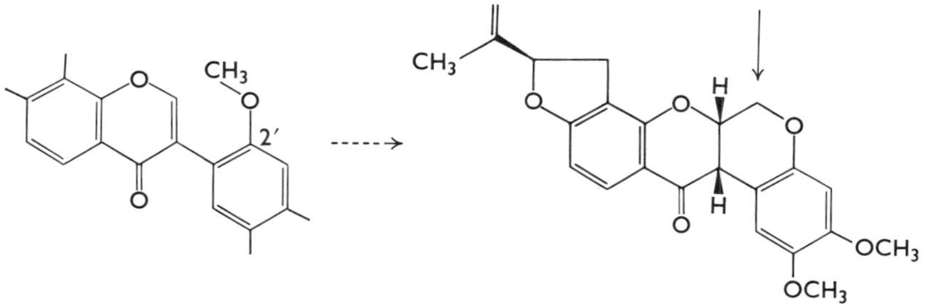

2'-methoxyisoflavone   rotenone   [Eq. 15-9]

additional carbon atom (arrowed), which has been shown by radiotracer experiments to be furnished by the S-methyl group of methionine. This result strongly
suggests that the pathway of rotenone biosynthesis involves at some point the cyclization of a 2'-methoxyl group in an isoflavone precursor, as shown. Although such a
process is capable of more than one mechanistic interpretation, its relevance to
rotenoid biosynthesis is underlined by the observation that in certain leguminous
plants, rotenoids often occur together with isoflavones bearing the required 2'-
methoxy substituent.

Peltogynol, a flavonoid compound found in *Peltogyne porphyrocardia* Griseb. ex
Benth. (fam. Leguminosae) and cissampareine, a bisbenzylisoquinoline alkaloid*
from *Cissampelos pareira* L. (fam. Menispermaceae), Fig. 15-3, represent two further
classes of natural product containing structural elements (circled) which probably
arise in an analogous manner.

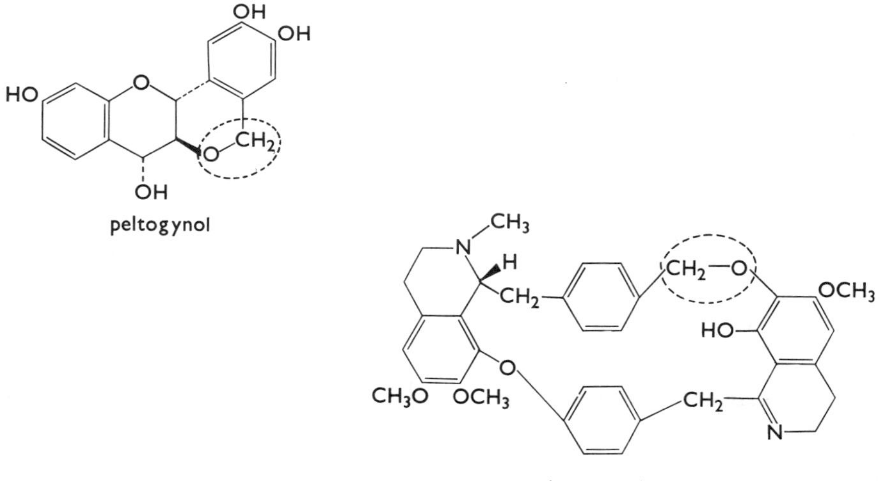

peltogynol

cissampareine

Fig. 15-3.

* Bisbenzylisoquinoline alkaloids are discussed in greater detail in Chapter 18.

It is of interest to note that in the laboratory the substitution of an O-methyl group into an aromatic ring has been accomplished by photochemical means.

15.5   The Oxidative Modification of C-methyl Groups

The methyl group of the ethyl side chain in barnol (a *Penicillium* metabolite), the central methylene group of the *Dryopteris* fern constituents such as *p*-aspidin (Chap. 4), and the ethylidene appendage in the C-17 side chain of certain plant sterols such as fucosterol (Eq. 15-10) (cf. Chap. 11), have all been shown to be provided by the S-methyl group of methionine.

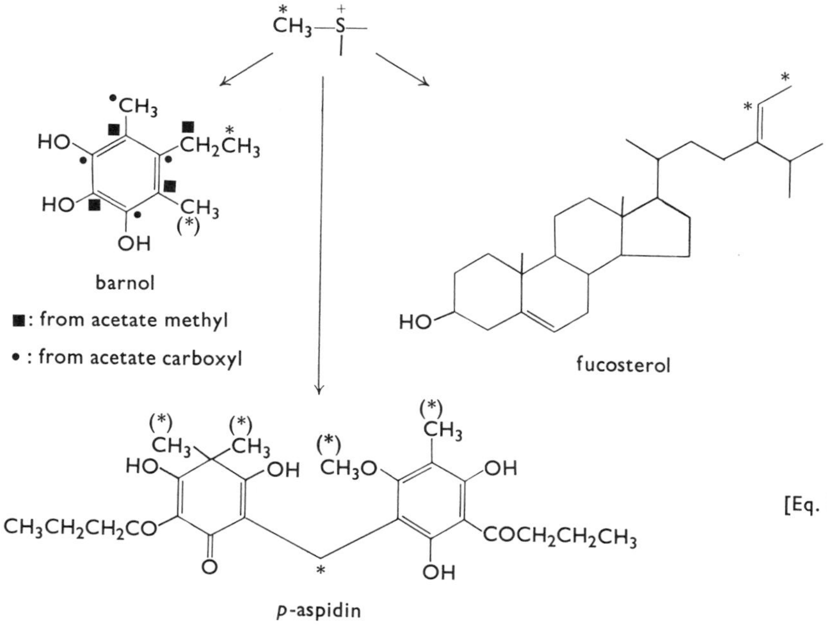

barnol

■: from acetate methyl

●: from acetate carboxyl

fucosterol

p-aspidin

[Eq. 15-10]

(Groups marked (*) arise by transmethylation in the usual way and are not considered here.)

Unless we are to postulate a mechanism for transmethylation quite different from the one generally accepted, we must account in some way for the development of nucleophilic character at the C-1 methyl group of the phenol, (Eq. 15-11*a*), from which barnol is presumably derived. This could be achieved through oxidation to a quinone methine species, with NADP$^+$ as the hydride ion acceptor (Chap. 2), followed by ionization of the enolic hydroxyl function and charge delocalization as shown. It will be noted that since barnol is basically of polyketide origin, the methyl group postulated to undergo oxidative modification is derived from the methyl

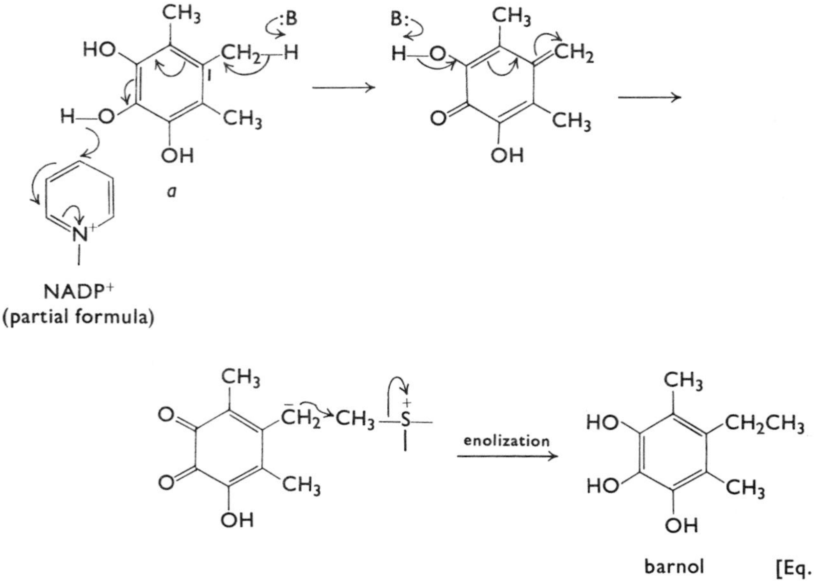

NADP⁺
(partial formula)

a

barnol   [Eq. 15-11]

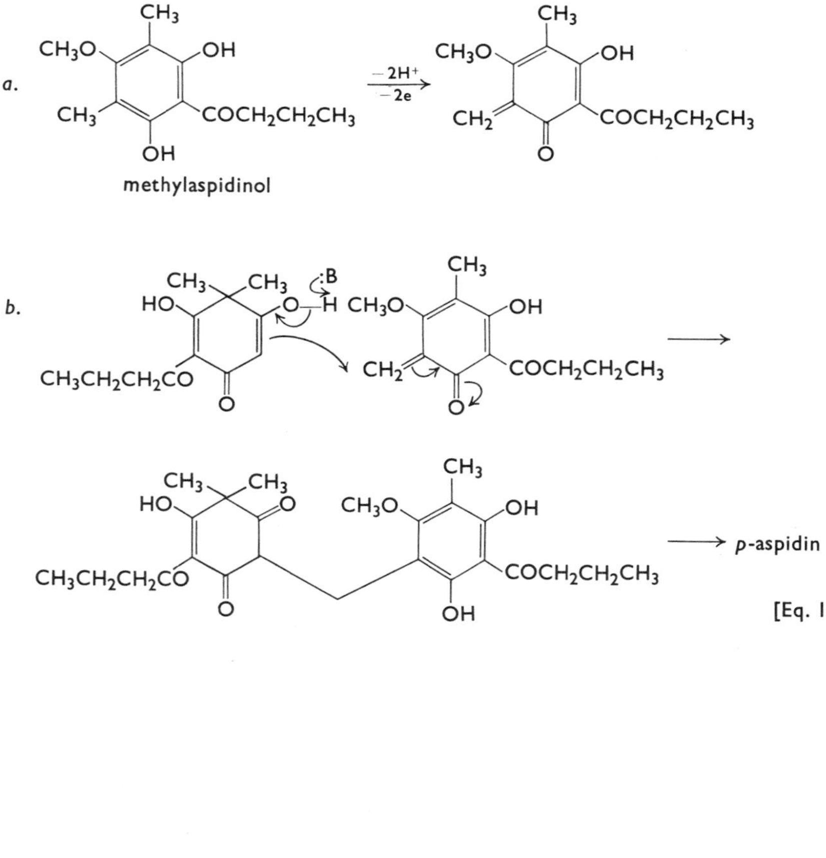

a.

methylaspidinol

b.

p-aspidin

[Eq. 15-12]

group of acetic acid and not from methionine. Nevertheless, this pathway is included here because of its obvious affinity with the various other processes discussed.

The formation of *p*-aspidin can be explained by postulating a similar oxidation
of methylaspidinol to an *o*-quinonemethine species, followed by Michael addition
of the appropriate anion, as indicated in Eq. 15-12.

The observation that this type of coupling can be catalyzed by peroxidase
(Chap. 14), provides a further example of the versatility of this remarkable enzyme.

The formation of the ethylidene side chain in fucosterol and related compounds
(cf. Chap. 11) is readily rationalized in terms of the usual transmethylation
mechanism, if it is accepted that an olefinic double bond can act as the nucleophile, as shown in Eq. 15-13.

The occurrence of plant sterols with side chains having a methylene substituent as in the postulated intermediate Eq. 15-13*a*, is evidence in support of the
proposed mechanism.

It will be noted that the sequence given in Eq. 15-13 does not involve a formal
oxidation step, since the precursor is already at the requisite oxidation level. However, its relationship to the other processes discussed will be evident.

It cannot be too strongly emphasized that the details of the mechanisms proposed for the modification of O-, N-, and C-methyl groups in the preceding sections
are almost entirely speculative. Many alternative mechanisms, involving other

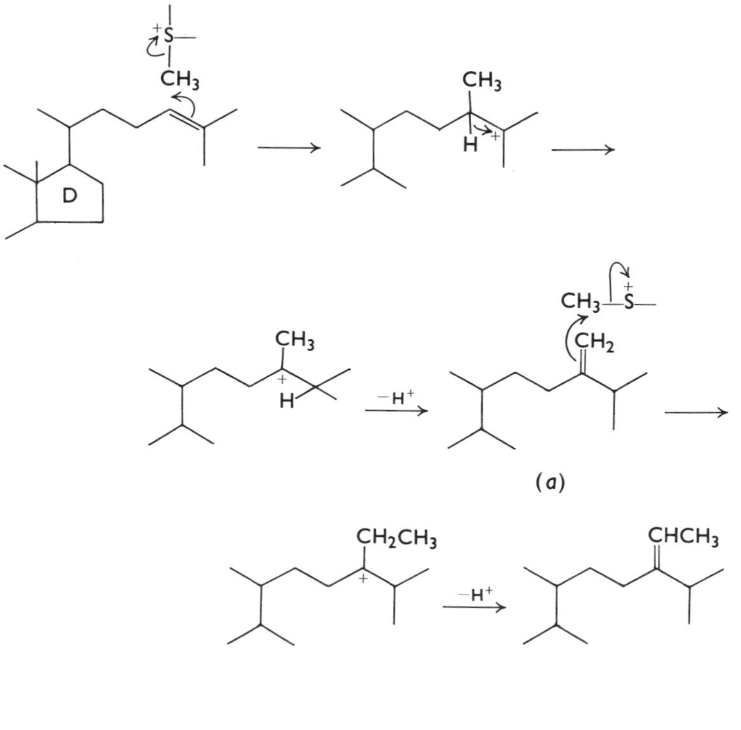

(*a*)

[Eq. 15-13]

intermediates (such as free radicals) can be written with equal justification, since there is essentially no data available which would allow a decision to be made between the various possibilities.

15.6 Demethylation

It will be evident that the oxidative sequence:

$$\text{>N—CH}_3 \longrightarrow \text{>}\overset{+}{\text{N}}\text{=CH}_2$$

can easily lead to loss of the methyl function altogether, by the intervention of a further hydrolytic step:

$$\text{>N}^+\text{=CH}_2 \xrightarrow[-\text{H}^+]{+\text{ H}_2\text{O}} \text{>NH} + \text{HCHO}$$

A mechanism of this kind may account for a number of established biological N-demethylation processes. As an example we may quote the conversion of nicotine into nornicotine in tobacco plants (Eq. 15-14).

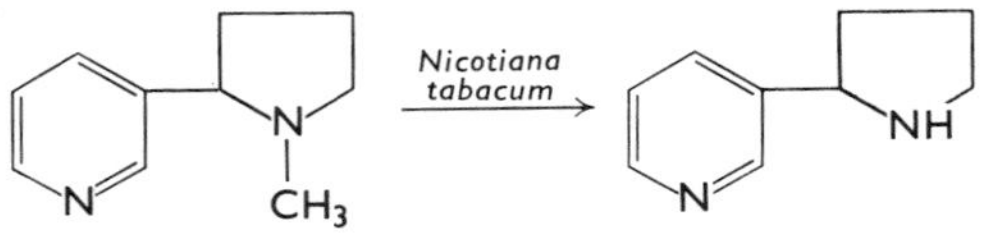

nicotine   nornicotine   [Eq. 15-14]

a.

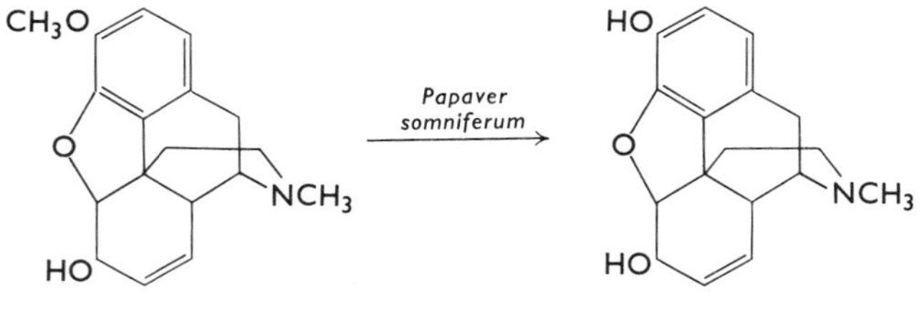

codeine   morphine

b.   [Eq. 15-15]

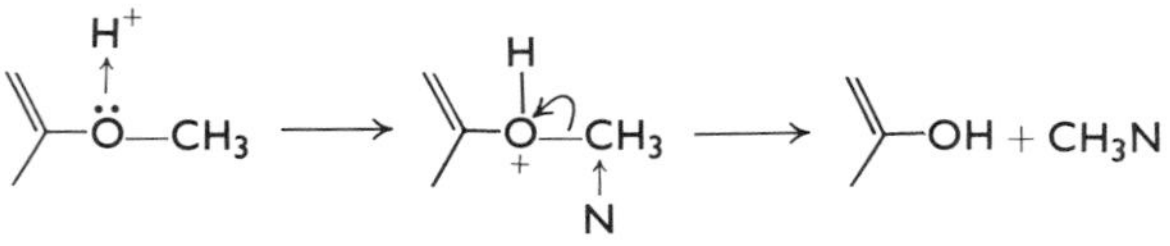

N = nucleophilic center in an enzyme or coenzyme. (n.b. In nature, the proton might be replaced by a metal ion in free or complexed form)

A number of laboratory methods are available for effecting N-demethylation by mechanisms involving nucleophilic displacement (e.g. the von Braun and Herzig-Meyer degradations). However, with respect to the natural process, the evidence available from enzymatic studies is more in accord with a dehydrogenation-hydrolysis sequence.

O-Demethylation is also an established biological process, although it has been only occasionally observed. An example for which there is firm experimental evidence is the conversion of codeine into morphine (Eq. 15-15a), which represents the final step of morphine biosynthesis in the opium poppy, *Papaver somniferum* L. (fam. Papaveraceae). (Preceding steps in morphine biosynthesis are discussed in Chapter 18.)

O-Demethylation of phenol methyl ethers can readily be effected in the laboratory with the aid of either proton acids (HBr, HI) or Lewis acids ($AlCl_3$) and it is very probable that a mechanism involving acid catalysis is operative in the equivalent biological process (Eq. 15-15b).

The oxidative loss of C-methyl groups, whether these are derived from methionine or by any other pathway (cf. cholesterol biosynthesis, Chap. 11) is best rationalized by the partial sequence shown in Eq. 15-16.

$$-C-CH_3 \longrightarrow -C-CH_2OH \longrightarrow -C-CHO \longrightarrow -C-COOH \longrightarrow$$

$$-CH + CO_2 \qquad \text{[Eq. 15-16]}$$

Although we again cannot be sure of the precise mechanism involved in each of these oxidative steps, the actual sequence is well established as a biological process.

15.7 Oxidative Cleavage of Aromatic Systems

Oxidative ring cleavage is an important process in the metabolism of aromatic compounds. Ultimately, by a continuation of the degradative process, low molecular weight compounds are produced which can enter the citric acid cycle and thus by their oxidation provide energy for the maintenance of cellular activity. Many different enzyme systems are active in degradations of this kind; two which have been investigated in bacterial species, operate on catechol in the manner indicated in Eq. 15-17.

It will be noted that the initial oxidative step in both transformations leads to a two-electron change in the oxidation state of each carbon atom affected.

Occasionally the products of related ring cleavage reactions are diverted into pathways leading to the formation of secondary metabolites, as will be seen from the following examples.

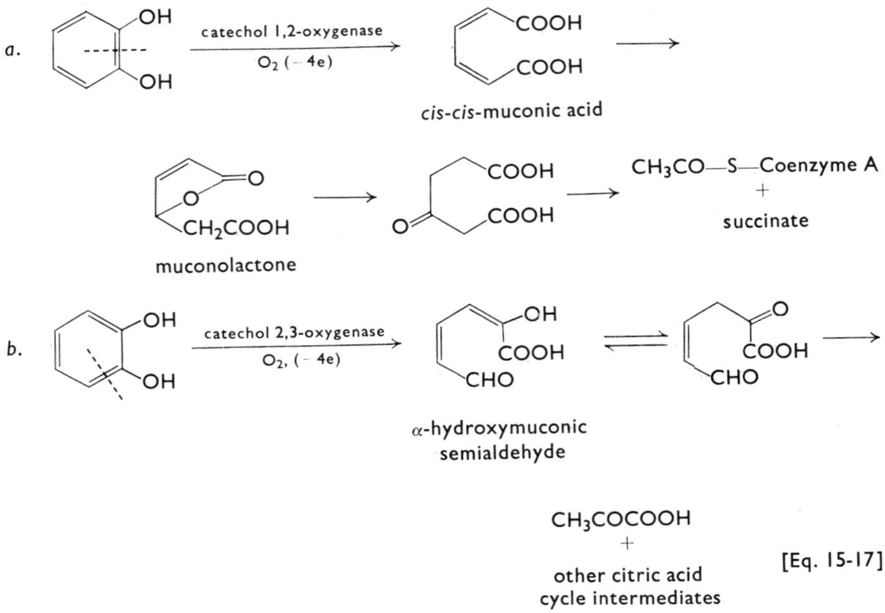

a.   catechol 1,2-oxygenase / O_2 (– 4e)   COOH / COOH

cis-cis-muconic acid

muconolactone (CH₂COOH)   →   COOH / COOH CH_3CO—S—Coenzyme A + succinate

b.   catechol 2,3-oxygenase / O_2, (– 4e)   OH / COOH / CHO ⇌ COOH / CHO

α-hydroxymuconic
semialdehyde

$CH_3COCOOH$
+
other citric acid
cycle intermediates

[Eq. 15-17]

15.8 Patulin

The structure of patulin (Eq. 15-18), a well-known metabolite of *Penicillium patulum*, is particularly suggestive of a biogenesis from a benzenoid precursor by way of oxidative ring cleavage and recyclization. The co-metabolites *m*-cresol, *m*-hydroxybenzyl alcohol and toluquinol have served as valuable clues in the elucidation of the pathway of patulin biosynthesis, which is now known to follow the course illustrated.

An experimental technique used in establishing this pathway is of special interest in that deuterium was employed as a tracer in incorporation studies, the progress of the isotope being followed by mass spectrometry. The labeled precursor, 2,4,6-²H-*m*-cresol, was converted with very high efficiency into patulin as shown in Eq. 15-19. Since the fragmentation pattern of patulin in the mass spectrometer is known, the application of this technique served not only to determine the overall incorporation of the isotope, but also to show its location at the expected positions in the product. (It will be noted that one deuterium atom must be lost in the hydroxylation step of the pathway shown in Eq. 15-18.)

As in the catechol oxidations described above, the initial ring-cleavage step can be interpreted as a two-electron oxidation of each carbon atom involved.

It will be noted that the presence of both *m*-hydroxybenzyl alcohol and toluquinol in *P. patulum* introduces an element of ambiguity into this pathway, in that in the absence of further data it cannot be stated with certainty whether nuclear hydroxylation of *m*-cresol precedes oxidation of the methyl side chain or *vice-versa* (Eq. 15-18).

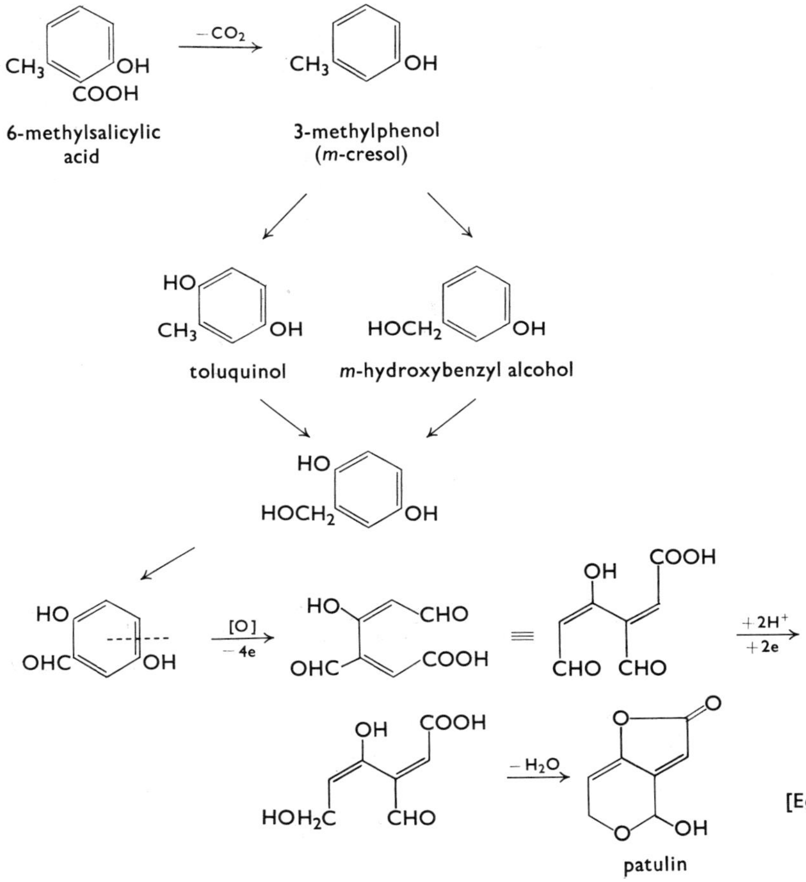

6-methylsalicylic acid
3-methylphenol (m-cresol)
toluquinol
m-hydroxybenzyl alcohol
patulin

[Eq. 15-18]

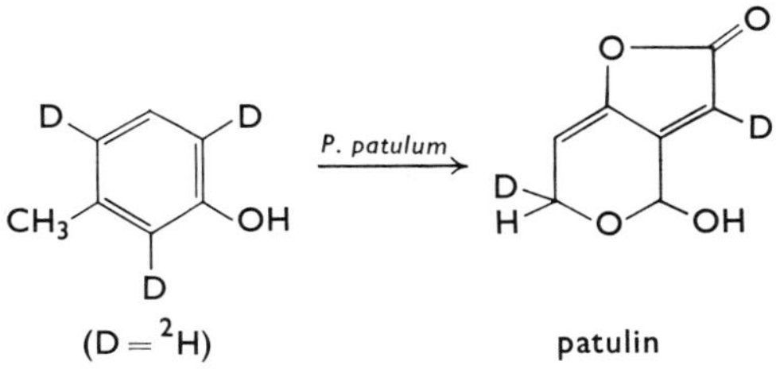

P. patulum
(D = ²H)
patulin

[Eq. 15-19]

15.9 Penicillic Acid

Penicillic acid, a metabolite of various *Penicillium* species, arises by a pathway involving oxidative cleavage of orsellinic acid. Although the intervening steps have not been investigated, they are readily explicable in terms of the simple processes indicated in Eq. 15-20. (The initial oxidative decarboxylation step (a) has a precedent in the biosynthesis of arbutin, page 131.)

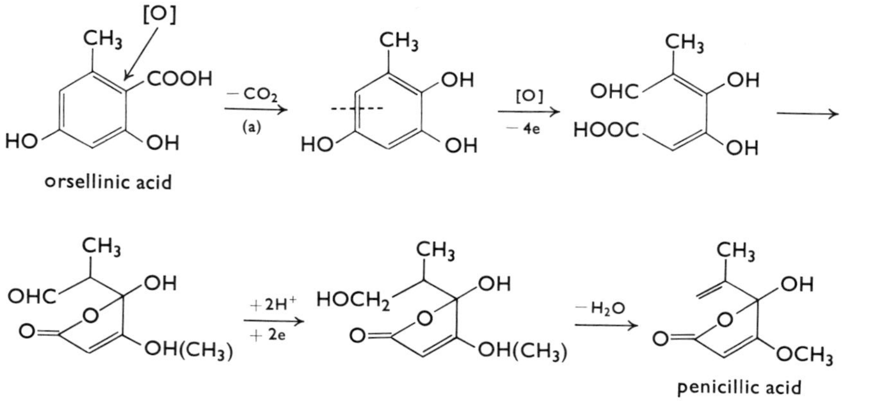

orsellinic acid

penicillic acid

[Eq. 15-20]

15.10 Terphenyl Derivatives and Related Metabolites

Mention was made in Chapter 14 of the terphenyl derivatives produced by various lichen species. The probable formation of these compounds can be illustrated by reference to volucrisporin. Phenylalanine and phenyllactic acid were efficiently converted into volucrisporin in *Volucrispora aurantiaca* Haskins, which suggests the pathway of biosynthesis shown in Eq. 15-21.

The insertion of the *meta*-hydroxyl group at an early stage is not an arbitrary suggestion, since it has been shown that *m*-tyrosine is also a reasonably effective precursor of volucrisporin. This could enter the biosynthetic pathway by way of transamination* as shown in Eq. 15-21*a*.

The introduction of terphenyl derivatives into the present discussion is prompted by their probable relationship to a small class of compounds with the carbon skeleton C_6—C—C—C—C—C_6, which could arise from them by ring cleavage.

$$
\begin{array}{c}
C_6\text{—C—C—C—C—}C_6 \\
| \qquad\quad | \\
C \qquad\quad C
\end{array}
$$

* Transamination is discussed in detail in Chapter 16.

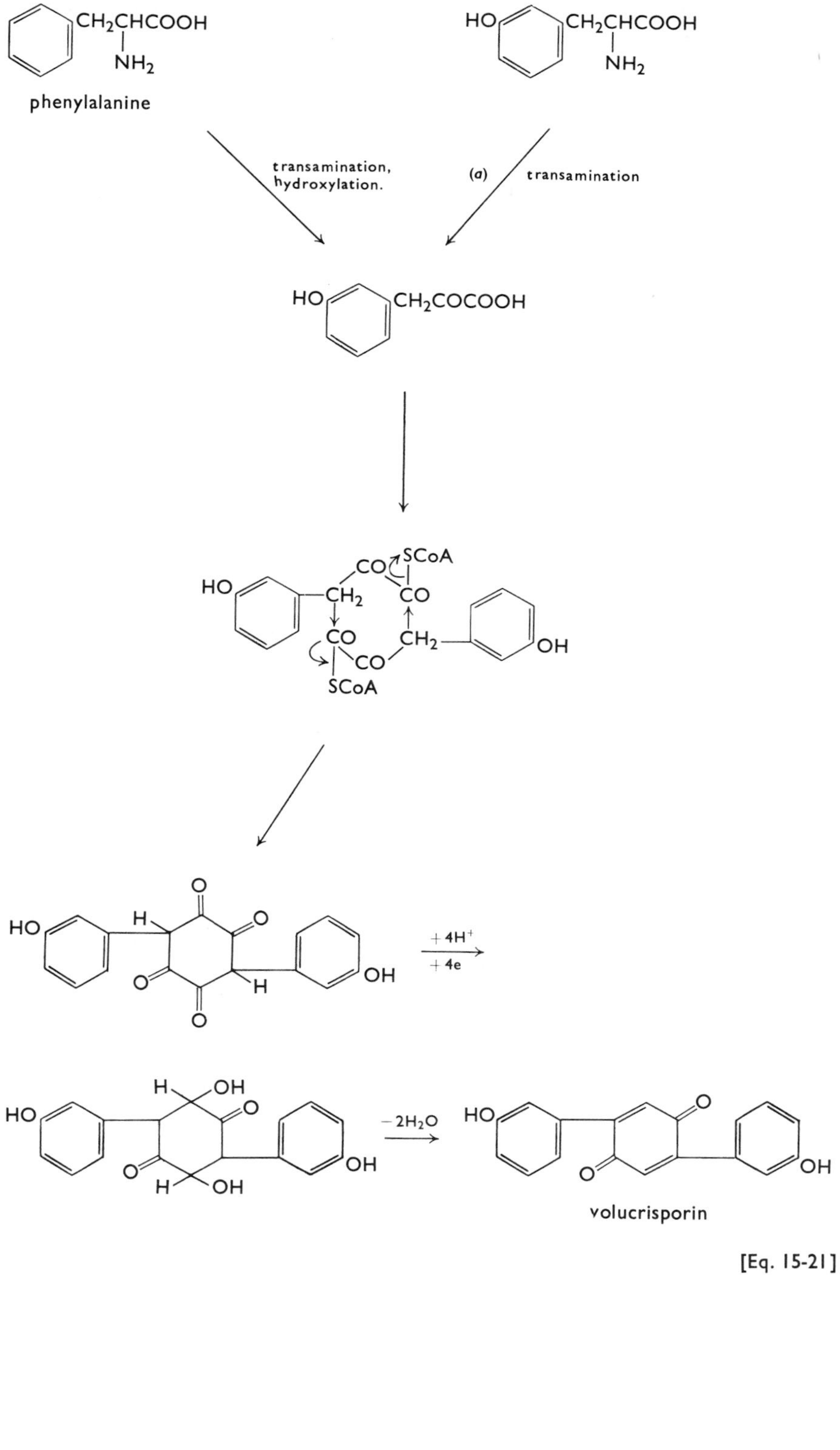
CH2CHCOOH
NH2
phenylalanine
HO
CH2CHCOOH
NH2
transamination,
hydroxylation.
(a)
transamination
HO
CH2COCOOH
CO
SCoA
HO
CH2
CO
CO
CH2
OH
CO
SCoA
HO
H
O
O
O
O
H
OH
+4H+
+4e
HO
H
OH
O
O
H
OH
OH
−2H2O
HO
O
O
OH
volucrisporin

[Eq. 15-21]

The four representatives shown in Fig. 15-4 co-occur in *Candellariella vitellina*.

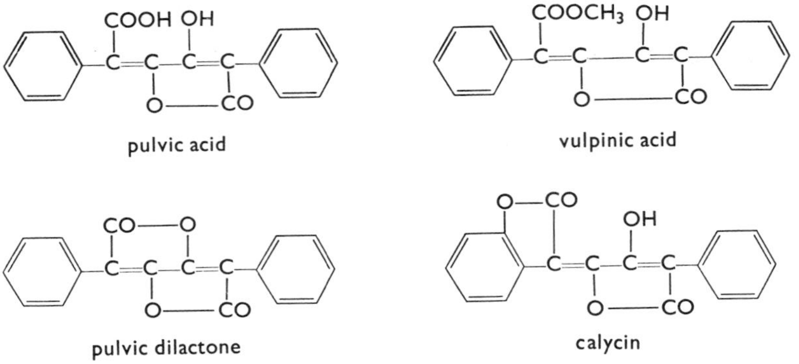

pulvic acid

vulpinic acid

pulvic dilactone

calycin

Fig. 15-4.

A very obvious route to these metabolites is by way of oxidative fission of a terphenyl precursor such as polyporic acid, as shown in Eq. 15-22.

The experimental evidence for such a pathway is based on the observation that $1\text{-}^{14}C$-phenylalanine when fed to *Evernia vulpina*, gave labeled vulpinic acid (Eq. 15-22) with the radioactivity distributed equally between the four carbon atoms indicated. This is precisely the result expected for a biosynthetic pathway involving oxidative cleavage of polyporic acid at one or other of the equivalent positions (a) or (b) as shown.

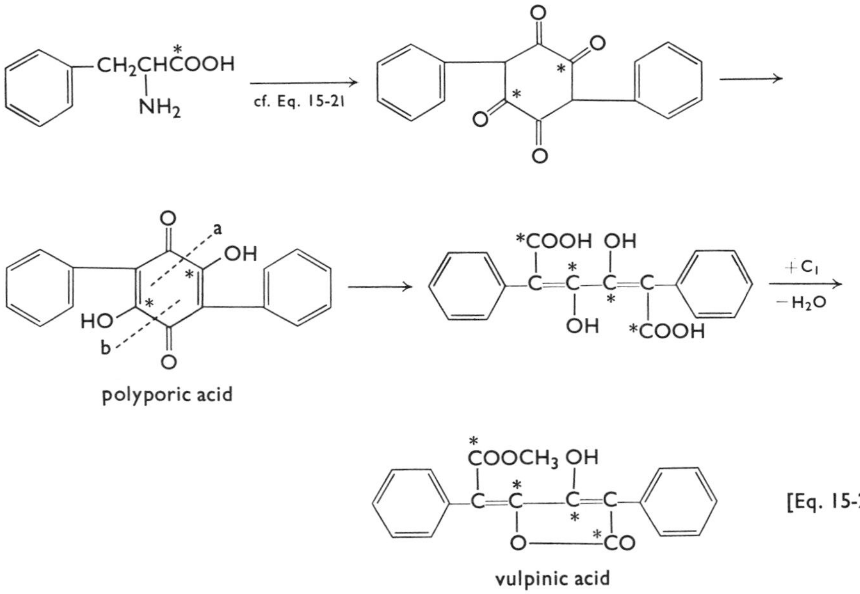

cf. Eq. 15-21

polyporic acid

$+ C_1$
$- H_2O$

[Eq. 15-22]

vulpinic acid

15.11 The Betalaines

The betalaines comprise a series of nitrogenous pigments which may be either red-violet (the betacyanins) or yellow (the betaxanthins). The betalaines have one of the most sharply defined distributions of any class of secondary metabolite, since they appear to be entirely confined to families of the order *Centrospermae*.

The most familiar betacyanin is betanin (Eq. 15-23), the pigment of red beet (*Beta vulgaris* L.; fam. Chenopodiaceae), and of a number of other species. Betanin is a glycoside, giving on hydrolysis glucose, and betanidin, which has been shown to be the aglycone in the majority of betacyanins investigated.

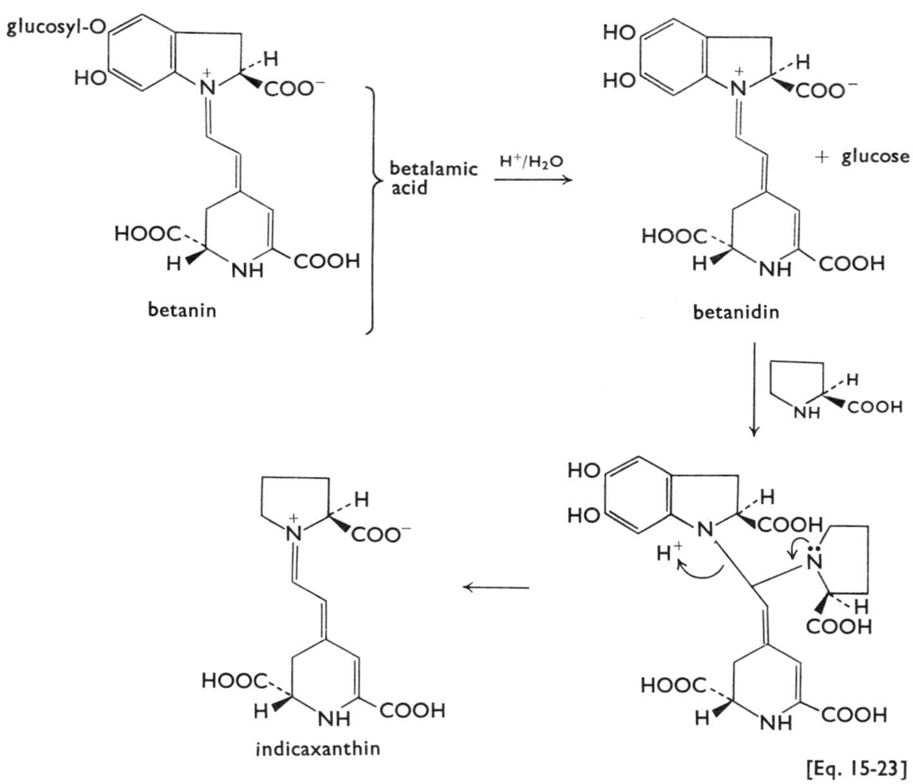

[Eq. 15-23]

The yellow colour of the betaxanthins denotes the presence of a chromophore less conjugated than that of the betacyanins. Thus in the representative pigment indicaxanthin (from *Opuntia ficus-indica* Mill; fam. Cactaceae), the indolic portion of betanin is replaced by a proline residue. The evidence for the structure of indicaxanthin rests to a large extent on the partial synthesis from betanin illustrated in Eq. 15-23.

The indolic portion of betanin has an obvious derivation from an intermediate of the shikimic acid-tyrosine pathway. The derivation of the remaining (betalamic acid) portion of the molecule is less obvious, but suggestions that it might arise by ring fission and recyclization of an aromatic amino acid precursor have received strong support from experiments with species of *Opuntia* (fam. Cactaceae). Thus 3,4-dihydroxyphenylalanine (DOPA), labeled with carbon 14, was shown to be incorporated almost exclusively into the betalamic acid portion of betanin in these species (cf. Eq. 15-23).

The pathway from DOPA to betanin is readily rationalized by the mechanism shown in Eq. 15-24, in which the cleavage step is identical to that brought about by catechol 2,3-oxygenase (Eq. 15-17).

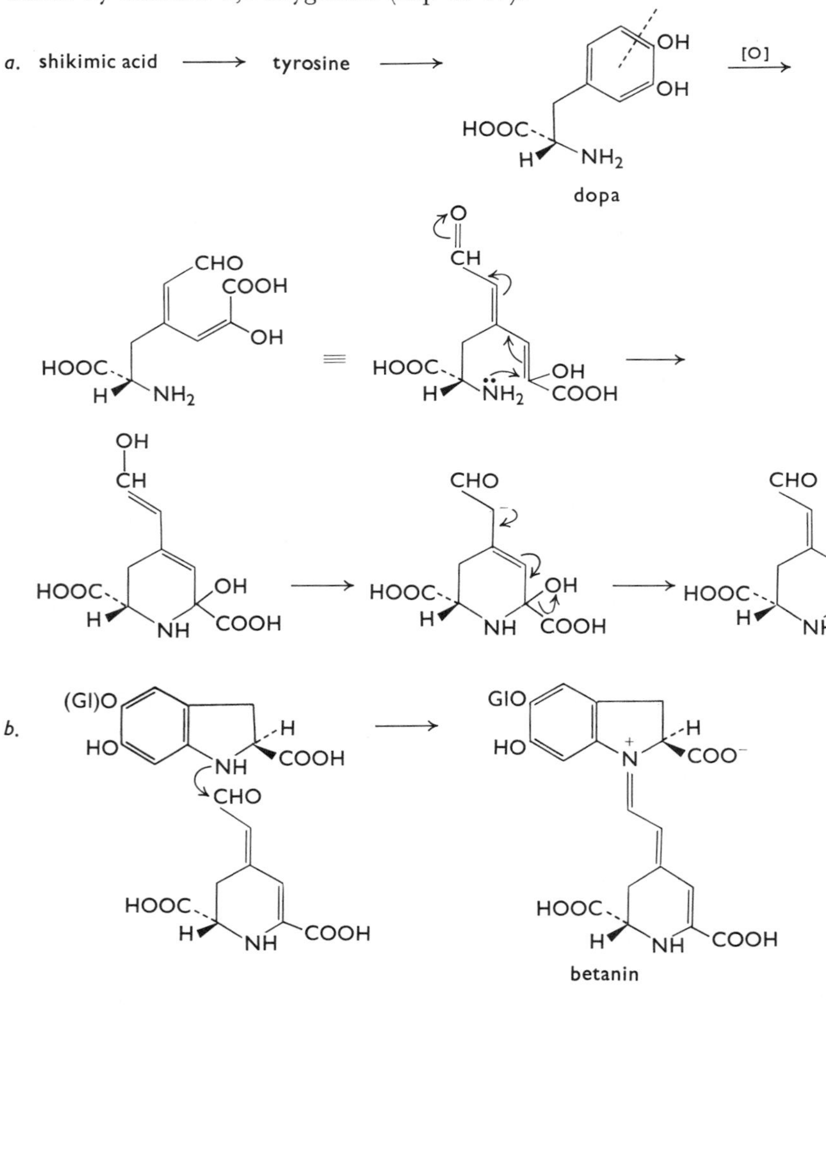

a. shikimic acid $\longrightarrow$ tyrosine $\longrightarrow$ dopa $\xrightarrow{[O]}$

b. [Eq. 15-24]

betanin

The low and therefore probably non-specific incorporation of DOPA into the indolic portion of the molecule is unexpected, since a pathway involving quinone addition as shown in Eq. 15-25 is strongly indicated on theoretical grounds.

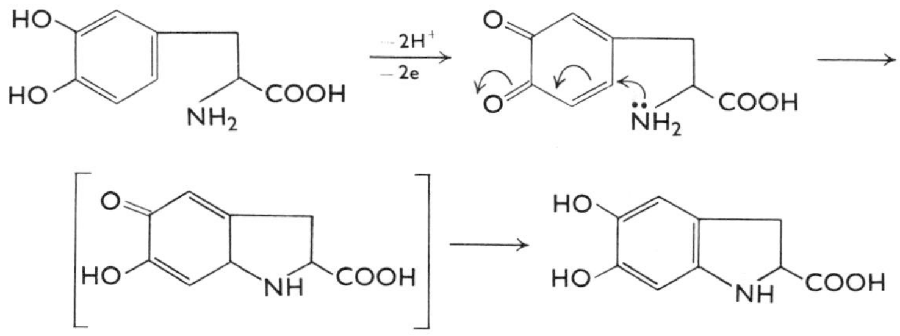

[Eq. 15-25]

The low incorporation of DOPA may be an indication that ring closure of tyrosine occurs before the insertion of the additional hydroxyl group, as indicated in Eq. 15-26. However, this pathway is difficult to account for mechanistically, and the whole question of the biosynthesis of the indolic portion of betanidin must therefore be left open at present.

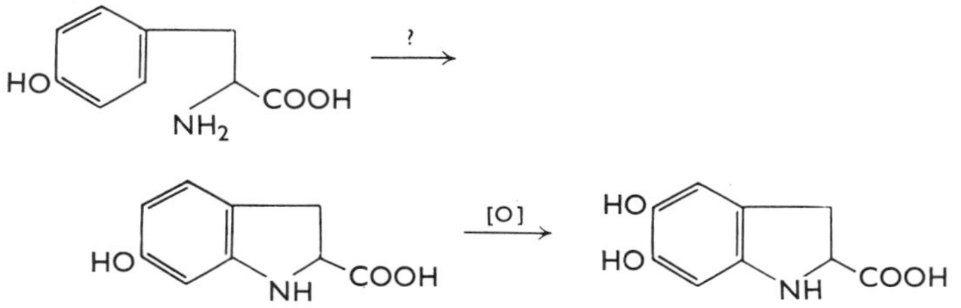

[Eq. 15-26]

15.12 Summary

Although it has not been possible to offer much in the way of experimental proof for certain of the mechanisms discussed in this chapter, the corresponding processes, namely the oxidative modification of N-, C-, and O-methyl groups, and the oxidative fission of aromatic rings, are well established as significant, though minor, pathways of secondary metabolism. Many interesting problems remain to be investigated. The mechanism involved in the formation of the methylenedioxy system is of particular interest in view of the frequent occurrence of this structure in secondary metabolites derived from shikimic acid. This is an area of inquiry in which the study of laboratory models can be expected to do much to increase our understanding of the processes involved.

XVI CHAPTER

∿∿∿∿∿∿∿∿∿∿∿∿∿∿∿∿∿∿∿∿∿∿∿∿∿∿∿∿∿∿∿∿∿∿∿∿∿

REFERENCES FOR FURTHER READING

General information: The reader will find much information relating to the various classes of alkaloid discussed in this chapter in the series *The Alkaloids, Chemistry and Physiology*, R. H. F. Manske, Ed., Academic Press, New York and London. Volume XI of this series (1968) contains a cumulative chapter index to which the reader is referred for specific details of the contents of earlier volumes.

Further references:

1. G. A. Swan, *An Introduction to the Alkalodis*, Blackwell, Oxford, 1967.
2. H-G Boit, *Ergebnisse der Alkaloid-Chemie bis 1960*, Akademie-Verlag, Berlin, 1961.
3. R. Robinson, *The Structural Relations of Natural Products*, Clarendon Press, Oxford, 1955.
4. A. R. Battersby, *Alkaloid Biosynthesis*, Quart. Rev. (Chem. Soc.), *15*, (1961), 259.
5. K. Mothes and H. R. Schütte, *The Biosynthesis of Alkaloids*, Angew. Chem. Intl. Ed., *2*, 341 (Part 1); *2*, 441 (Part 2), (1963).
6. K. Mothes, *Biogenesis of Alkaloids and the Problem of Chemotaxonomy*, Lloydia, *29*, (1966), 156.
7. E. Leete, *Alkaloid Biosynthesis*, Ann. Rev. Plant Physiol., *18*, (1967), 179.
8. E. Leete, *Alkaloid Biogenesis* in Biogenesis of Natural Compounds, P. Bernfeld, Ed., 2nd Edition, Pergamon Press, Oxford, (1967), 953.

General Aspects of Alkaloid Biosynthesis. Alkaloids Derived from Ornithine, Lysine, and Nicotinic Acid

16.1 Introduction

The alkaloids are organic, nitrogenous bases which occur chiefly in plants, but to a lesser extent also in microorganisms and in animals. The marked physiological activity of many alkaloids provided the stimulus for early investigations leading to the isolation and characterization of such well-known representatives as strychnine, morphine, quinine, nicotine, and cocaine. Frequently, the physiological activity of an alkaloid manifests itself in an extreme toxicity; on the other hand, many alkaloids have therapeutically useful pharmacological properties at sublethal dosage and have become established as valuable drugs in general medical practice.

The continued and increasing interest in alkaloids is partly attributable to their importance in medicine, but is also to a large extent a reflection of the fascinating problems which they present to the organic chemist in the elucidation of their structures and, in more recent years, in the investigation of the multifarious biosynthetic pathways by which they are produced in plants and in other organisms.

The problem of extracting alkaloids from plant material is greatly simplified by their basic nature, which permits a ready separation from acidic or neutral components. Partition of the crude plant extract between an organic and aqueous-acidic phase, followed by basification of the acidic solution and re-extraction with an organic solvent, usually serves to furnish the alkaloidal components in a reasonable state of purity.

Certain alkaloids, which occur as quaternary bases, are frequently isolated by precipitation of their reineckate salts; these can be further purified by recrystallization or by partition chromatography. Occasionally an alkaloid may be present in a plant as the N-oxide, a structure which often results in low solubility in organic solvents. In such an event, the free base is usually readily obtained by reduction with zinc and dilute mineral acid or with sulphur dioxide.

Modern spectroscopic methods have played an important part in the elucidation of alkaloid structures. NMR and mass spectrometry have proved to be especially valuable. Many alkaloids give characteristic fragmentation patterns in the mass spectrometer, so that it is often possible to tell, almost at a glance, whether or not a given type of heterocyclic structure is present. NMR spectroscopy has also been widely used, not only as an aid to the elucidation of gross structure, but also in establishing precise stereochemical relationships in alkaloids containing many asymmetric centers.

Classical methods, however, still have their place in structure determination. The Hofmann degradation, in particular, is still widely used as a means of effecting the controlled elimination of the nitrogen function. Although alkaloids rarely occur as glycosides, in contrast to the flavonoids, they are often found as the esters of a wide variety of acids. In these cases, an initial hydrolysis serves to furnish the simpler basic and acidic components. Many other techniques of natural product chemistry, such as oxidative degradation, reduction, etc., also play their part.

16.2 Alkaloids and Amino Acids

By the early twentieth century, the structures of many alkaloids were known with reasonable certainty, and comparisons with the structures of other natural products became possible. Arising out of such comparisons came the idea, developed by Winterstein and Trier in 1910, that the plant alkaloids were related biogenetically to the amino acids. As the structures of more and more alkaloids were elucidated, this relationship became firmly established and was expanded by Robinson, Schöpf, and others into formal schemes for alkaloid biosynthesis which took the common amino acids as their starting point. Many of the theoretical ideas propounded during this period have since been substantiated, largely through the application of radiotracer techniques.

The amino acids currently regarded as most often participating in alkaloid biosynthesis are shown in Fig. 16-1.

The consistency with which amino acids have been shown to be the natural precursors of alkaloids has led to the suggestion that this biogenetic relationship should serve to define a true alkaloid; all other nitrogenous bases are to be regarded as "pseudo alkaloids" or "proto alkaloids". Unfortunately, nature has no regard for our desire to package secondary metabolites under convenient headings, so that this distinction, in any but the biogenetic sense, tends to be rather artificial.

Many alkaloids, for example, are basically terpenoid in nature, and among these the mono-, sesqui-, di-, and triterpenes, as well as the steroids, all have their

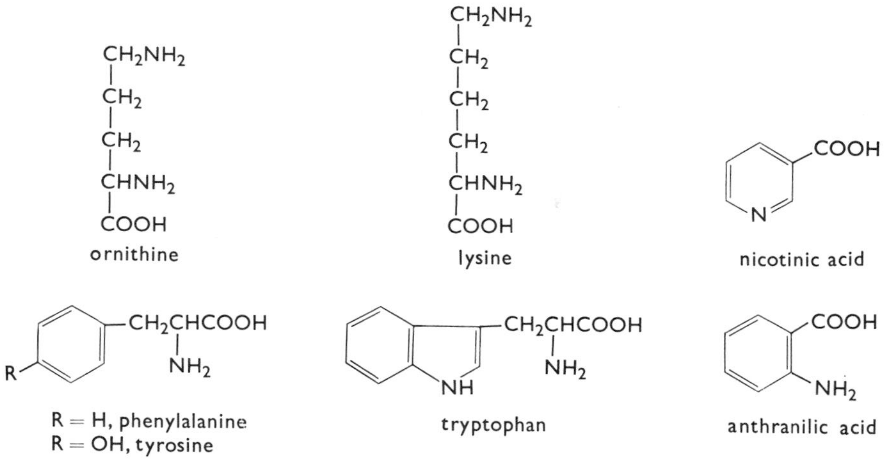

Fig. 16-1. Amino Acids Most Often Participating in Alkaloid Biosynthesis.

representatives. Some typical examples are discussed in Chapter 19. Other alkaloids are formed by the incorporation of nitrogen into a polyketide framework. The hemlock alkaloids, to be discussed in a later section, are the best known representatives of this group.

16.3 Common Reactions Encountered in Alkaloid Biosynthesis

Although an extraordinary diversity of structures is encountered among the various classes of alkaloid, certain reactions, centered on the functionality of the amino group, are consistently observed in their biosynthesis. Consequently, the alkaloids can be regarded as the products of a major biosynthetic production line which ranks in importance with the polyketide, mevalonate, and shikimic acid pathways.

Arising out of the original theoretical proposals of Trier, Robinson, Schöpf, and others, many investigations were undertaken into the reactivity of various hypothetical alkaloid precursors under "physiological" conditions. As a result of these investigations, certain basic types of reaction were postulated to be of major importance in alkaloid biosynthesis. The usefulness of such model studies is evident from the fact that subsequent investigations have done nothing to detract from these early mechanistic proposals.

Basically, three reactions are thought to be involved: firstly, Schiff base formation (Eq. 16-1a), secondly Mannich condensations (Eq. 16-1b) (which also involve

Schiff base formation as a preliminary step), and thirdly, condensations of the aldol type between compounds containing imino (C=N) groups (Eq. 16-1c).

a. $\quad$ >C=O + H$_2$N—R $\quad\xrightarrow{-H_2O}\quad$ >C=N—R

b. $\quad$ —CH + >C=O + H$_2$N—R $\quad\xrightarrow{-H_2O}\quad$ —C—C—NHR

c. $\quad$ —N$^+$=CH—CH$_2$— $\qquad\longrightarrow\qquad$ —NH—CH—CH$_2$—

$\qquad$ —CH$_2$—CH=N— $\qquad\qquad\qquad$ —CH—CH=N—   [Eq. 16-1]

In the Mannich condensation, a C—C—N system is generated by the addition of a carbanion to the Schiff base formed by the condensation of a ketone or aldehyde with an amine (Eq. 16-2a). This reaction is not restricted to primary amines; secondary amines may also participate through the formation of quaternary Schiff base intermediates (Eq. 16-2b). Charged intermediates of this kind facilitate the reaction by increasing the electron deficiency at the carbon atom which is subject to attack by the carbanion species. A similar effect is achieved in non-quaternary Schiff base intermediates by protonation of the nitrogen function, which explains the observation that in the laboratory, Mannich condensations often proceed most rapidly at or around neutral pH. This condition allows for the simultaneous formation of appreciable amounts both of the protonated Schiff base and of the attacking anionic species.*

a. $\quad$ R—NH$_2$ + O=C< $\quad\xrightarrow[H^+]{-H_2O}\quad$ R—N$^+$=C< $\cdots$ C< $\quad\longrightarrow\quad$ R—NH—C—C<

$\qquad\qquad\qquad\qquad\qquad\qquad$ H

b. $\quad$ R$_2$NH + O=C< $\quad\xrightarrow{-OH^-}\quad$ R$_2$N$^+$=C<   [Eq. 16-2]

The Mannich reaction is encountered in a wide variety of guises. The carbanion intermediate, for example, may be generated by delocalization of the negative charge in a phenolate anion, as in the laboratory synthesis of (±)-salsolin, an alkaloid found in various *Salsola* species (fam. Chenopodiaceae)

---

* It must be acknowledged that the view of the Mannich reaction taken here is somewhat arbitrary, since the experimental evidence that might allow a precise description of the mechanism is, unfortunately, not available. It is by no means certain, for example, that carbanion addition is the rate controlling step, as implied in the above discussion. Moreover, it is probable that the mechanism varies according to the nature of the subtrates and to the experimental conditions (pH, solvent etc.). The same reservations apply, to an even greater degree, in the biological situation. These interpretative difficulties, however, in no way detract from the importance of the Mannich condensation as a biosynthetic *process*.

(Eq. 16-3). The formation of the heterocyclic ring in this synthesis is an example of the well-known Pictet-Spengler reaction.

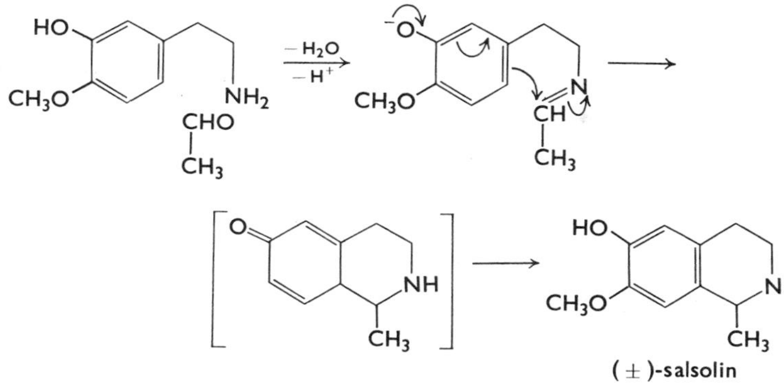

[Eq. 16-3]

(±)-salsolin

The "aldol"-type condensation between two imino structures is illustrated by the process shown in Eq. 16-4, in which this mechanism operates to link two Δ^1-piperideine nuclei together. This precise reaction will be encountered later in an established pathway of alkaloid biosynthesis.

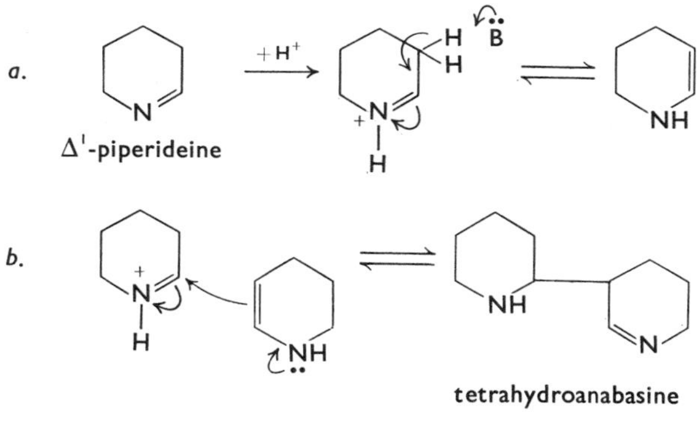

a. Δ^1-piperideine

b.

[Eq. 16-4]

tetrahydroanabasine

In the addition step (Eq. 16-4b), the cationic nature of the α-carbon atom in the "acceptor" molecule is increased by protonation of the nitrogen atom. The double bond isomerization in the "attacking" molecule is also shown as an acid-catalyzed rearrangement. This formulation is consistent with the observation that Δ^1-piperideine and tetrahydroanabasine are in equilibrium at physiological pH (Eq. 16-4b), conditions under which the nitrogen function would be extensively protonated.

Some important secondary reactions which are often implicated in the further elaboration of the initially formed nitrogenous structures are as follows:

a. Hydrogenation of an imino function (Eq. 16-5).

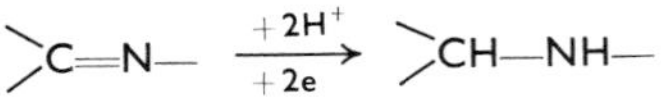

$$\text{>C=N—} \quad \xrightarrow[\text{+ 2e}]{\text{+ 2H}^+} \quad \text{>CH—NH—}$$ [Eq. 16-5]

b. Formation of an imino function by dehydrogenation of a saturated amine (Eq. 16-6).

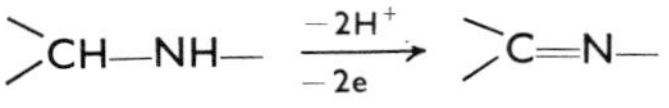

$$\text{>CH—NH—} \quad \xrightarrow[\text{- 2e}]{\text{- 2H}^+} \quad \text{>C=N—}$$ [Eq. 16-6]

A continuation of this process is frequently observed, especially when favored by the ultimate formation of an aromatic system, as in Eq. 16-7.

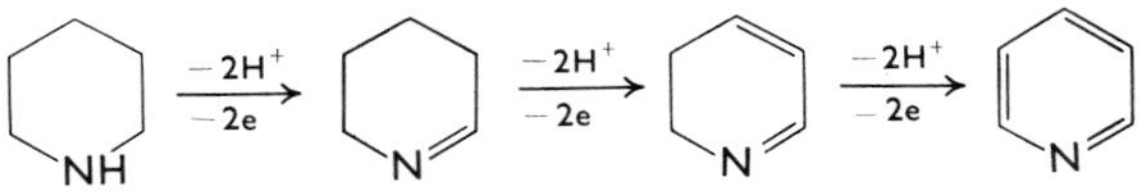

[Eq. 16-7]

c. Isomerization of an imino- to an α,β-unsaturated amino function (Eq. 16-8). (This isomerization is implicated in the mechanism postulated for the conversion of Δ^1-piperideine into tetrahydroanabasine noted in Eq. 16-4a, above.)

$$\text{—N=C—CH—} \quad \rightleftharpoons \quad \text{—NH—C=C—}$$ [Eq. 16-8]

d. Oxidation at the activated position adjacent to a nitrogen function. The products are either carbinolamines or amides (Eq. 16-9).

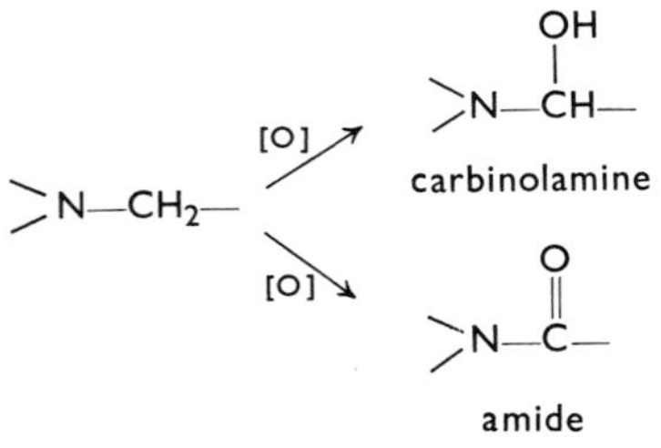

[Eq. 16-9]

Although oxidations of this kind, for which there are numerous laboratory analogies, are readily explicable on mechanistic grounds, it is to be noted that many pathways of alkaloid biosynthesis, and indeed, of secondary metabolism in general, appear to involve oxidations at positions which lack formal activation.

It will be seen in the sections to follow, that the simple processes just described are sufficient to account for the formation of a wide variety of alkaloid structures which range from the very simple to the highly complex.

16.4 Basic Pathways of Amino Acid Metabolism

Before considering any detailed pathways of alkaloid biosynthesis, it is necessary to discuss the various enzymatic reactions by which amino acids are transformed into the intermediates required for the operation of the basic reactions described in the previous section.

A coenzyme of fundamental importance in amino acid metabolism is vitamin B_6. This exists in the two biologically active forms, pyridoxal-5'-phosphate and

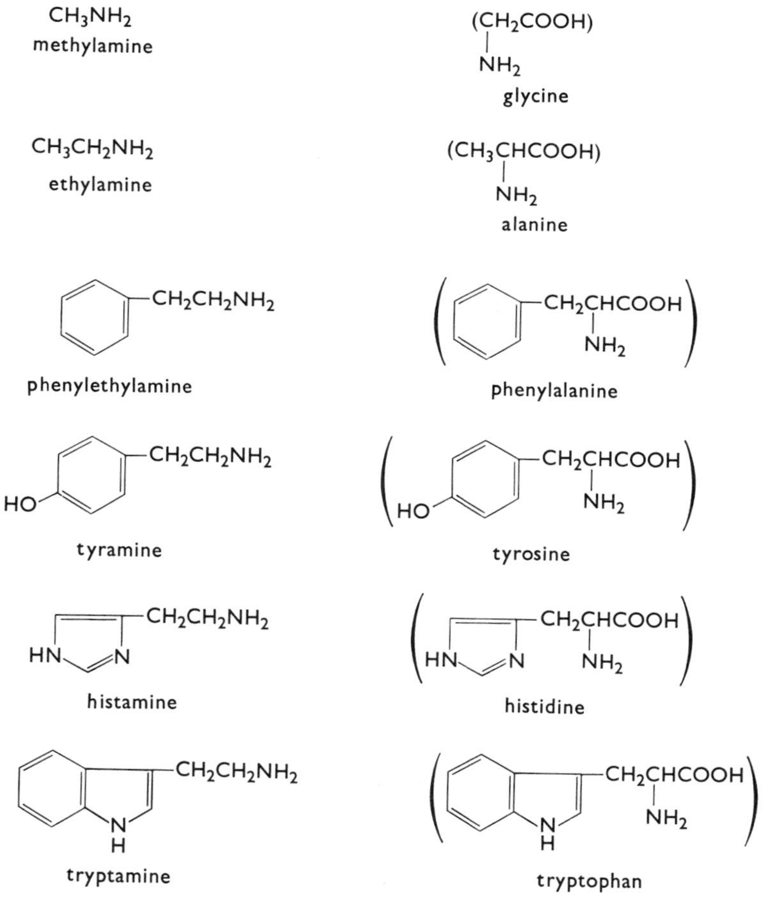

CH_3NH_2
methylamine

(CH_2COOH)
|
NH_2
glycine

$CH_3CH_2NH_2$
ethylamine

$(CH_3CHCOOH)$
|
NH_2
alanine

$-CH_2CH_2NH_2$
phenylethylamine

$\left(-CH_2CHCOOH \atop NH_2 \right)$
phenylalanine

$HO-\!\!-CH_2CH_2NH_2$
tyramine

$\left(HO-\!\!-CH_2CHCOOH \atop NH_2 \right)$
tyrosine

$HN\!\!-\!\!N\!\!-CH_2CH_2NH_2$
histamine

$\left(HN\!\!-\!\!N-CH_2CHCOOH \atop NH_2 \right)$
histidine

$-CH_2CH_2NH_2$ (indole) N–H
tryptamine

$\left(-CH_2CHCOOH \atop NH_2 \right)$ (indole) N–H
tryptophan

(Many simple N-methyl derivatives of the above amines also occur in nature,
e.g. dimethylamine, N-methyltyramine, N-methyltryptamine (dipterine),
N,N-dimethyltryptamine, etc.)

Fig. 16-2. Some Simple Amines from Higher Plants, and their Corresponding Amino Acids.

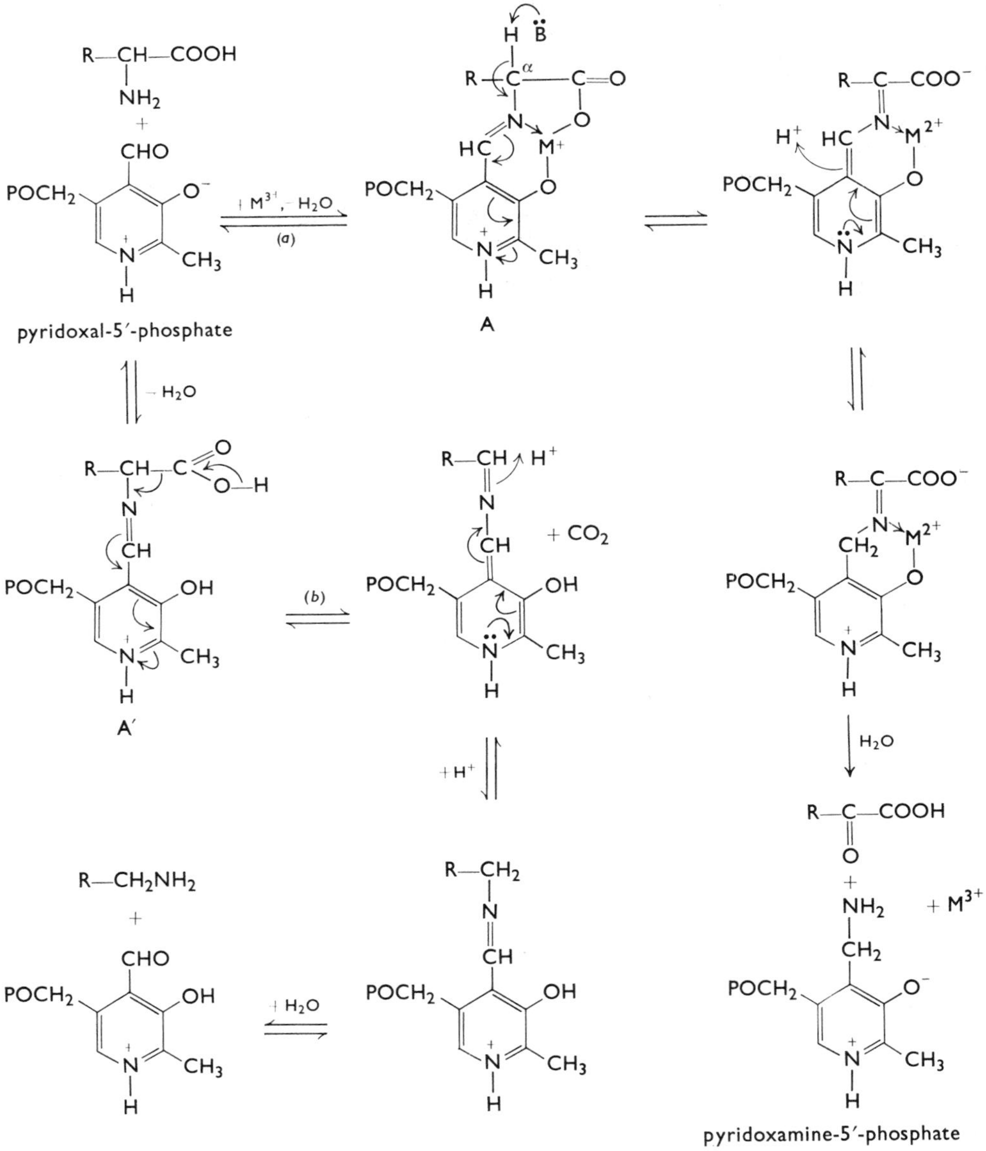

pyridoxal-5′-phosphate

A

$+ M^{3+}, - H_2O$

(a)

$- H_2O$

A′

(b)

$+ CO_2$

$+ H^+$

$R—CH_2NH_2$
$+$
CHO

$+ H_2O$

$R—CH_2$

$+ H_2O$

$R—C—COO^-$

H_2O

$R—C—COOH$
O
$+$
NH_2 $+ M^{3+}$
CH_2

pyridoxamine-5′-phosphate

[Eq. 16-10]

(n.b. Although the amino-acid structure in this and subsequent representations is shown for convenience in the unionized form, it is to be noted that it normally exists either as the zwitterion, $R—CH—COO^-$,

$^+NH_3$

or in the protonated or deprotonated forms, $R—CH—COOH$ and $R—CH—COO^-$, respectively,

$^+NH_3$ NH_2

depending on the pH of the medium and the isoelectric point of the particular amino acid.)

pyridoxamine-5'-phosphate, the mode of action of which may be illustrated by the following mechanism for the conversion of an amino acid into the corresponding α-ketoacid (Eq. 16-10a).

The specific function of the coenzyme is centered on the reactivity of the Schiff base intermediate Eq. 16-10A, in which the substituents attached to the α-carbon atom of the original amino acid are strongly activated by conjugation with the protonated pyridinium nucleus and by coordination with a metal ion as shown. Rearrangement to the isomeric Schiff base followed by hydrolysis leads to the required α-ketoacid.

Reactivation of the coenzyme is effected by a simple reversal of the sequence shown in Eq. 16-10, but with a different α-keto acid (usually α-ketoglutaric acid) acting as the amino group acceptor. The net result of these transformations, as summarized in Eq. 16-11, is that an amino group is transferred from the amino acid to the α-ketoacid "acceptor" in an overall process which is known as "transamination".

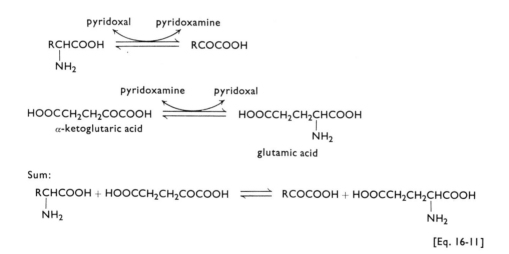

Sum:

$$RCHCOOH + HOOCCH_2CH_2COCOOH \rightleftharpoons RCOCOOH + HOOCCH_2CH_2CHCOOH$$

[Eq. 16-11]

The electronegative character of the pyridinium nucleus in the Schiff base intermediate Eq. 16-10A' facilitates an alternative pathway of decomposition through decarboxylation followed by hydrolysis to the corresponding amine (Eq. 16-10b). Many simple amines, widely distributed among higher plants, evidently arise in this way. Some typical examples are given in Fig. 16-2.

A further oxidative pathway for the conversion of amino acids into α-ketoacids, which has been widely studied in animal tissues and in microorganisms, and which may be of importance in alkaloid biosynthesis, is illustrated in Eq. 16-12. In this transformation, flavin-adenine dinucleotide (FAD), a coenzyme which functions in hydrogenation-dehydrogenation reactions, catalyzes the dehydrogenation of the amino function to an imine. This, on hydrolysis, furnishes the α-ketoacid.

$$\underset{\underset{NH_2}{|}}{RCHCOOH} \xrightarrow[\text{FAD} \quad \text{FAD}-H_2]{} \underset{\underset{NH}{\|}}{RCCOOH} \xrightarrow{H_2O} RCOCOOH + NH_3$$

[Eq. 16-12]

A pathway for the non-oxidative deamination of aromatic amino acids is illustrated in Eq. 16-13. This reaction has already been described in connection with the formation of cinnamic acids from phenylalanine and tyrosine (Chap. 5).

$$R \!-\!\!\left\langle\bigcirc\right\rangle\!\!-\!\underset{\underset{NH_2}{|}}{CH_2CHCOOH} \xrightarrow[\substack{\text{("ammonia-}\\ \text{lyase")}}]{\text{deaminase}} R\!-\!\!\left\langle\bigcirc\right\rangle\!\!-\!CH\!\!=\!\!CHCOOH$$
$$+$$
$$R = H, OH \qquad\qquad\qquad\qquad NH_3$$

[Eq. 16-13]

Oxidation of an amine to the corresponding aldehyde is a further reactio of some consequence in alkaloid biosynthesis, as the aldehydes formed are able to participate in Mannich condensations of the kind discussed in the previous section. The enzymes which catalyze these oxidations are broadly classified into two groups, the monoamine oxidases and the diamine oxidases. Monoamine oxidases act on monoamines (Eq. 16-14a), whereas diamine oxidases act on diamines such as putrescine and cadaverine, the decarboxylation products of ornithine and lysine respectively (Eq. 16-14b).

$$a. \quad RCH_2NH_2 \xrightarrow[\text{oxidase}]{\text{monoamine}} RCHO$$

$$b. \quad \underset{\underset{CH_2NH_2}{|}}{\overset{\overset{CH_2NH_2}{|}}{(CH_2)n}} \xrightarrow[\text{oxidase}]{\text{diamine}} \underset{\underset{CH_2NH_2}{|}}{\overset{\overset{CHO}{|}}{(CH_2)n}}$$

[Eq. 16-14]

$$n = 2, \text{putrescine}$$
$$n = 3, \text{cadaverine}$$

Little is known about the detailed mode of action of these enzymes, although a mechanism involving dehydrogenation followed by hydrolysis of the resulting imine has received some support (cf. oxidative deamination, Eq. 16-12).

In addition to these basic reactions involving the amino group, many further reactions including oxidations, reductions, rearrangements, etc., are also encountered in alkaloid biosynthesis. In the benzylisoquinoline series, for example, oxidative phenol coupling processes are of major importance (Chap. 18), whilst the biosynthesis of a large and important group of indole alkaloids involves the coupling of a tryptophan-derived nucleus with a C_{9-10} fragment of terpenoid origin (Chap. 19).

Discussion of the simpler alkaloids derived from phenylalanine, tyrosine, tryptophan, and anthranilic acid will be deferred until Chapter 17. The remainder of this chapter will be devoted to a discussion of some detailed pathways of alkaloid biosynthesis stemming mainly from ornithine, lysine, and nicotinic acid.

16.5   Simple Pyrrolidine and Piperidine Derivatives

The simple pyrrolidine alkaloids N-methylpyrrolidine, hygrine and cuscohygrine, illustrate in a straightforward manner some of the basic reactions of alkaloid biosynthesis discussed in the foregoing sections. Their probable biosynthesis from ornithine is illustrated in Eq. 16-15.

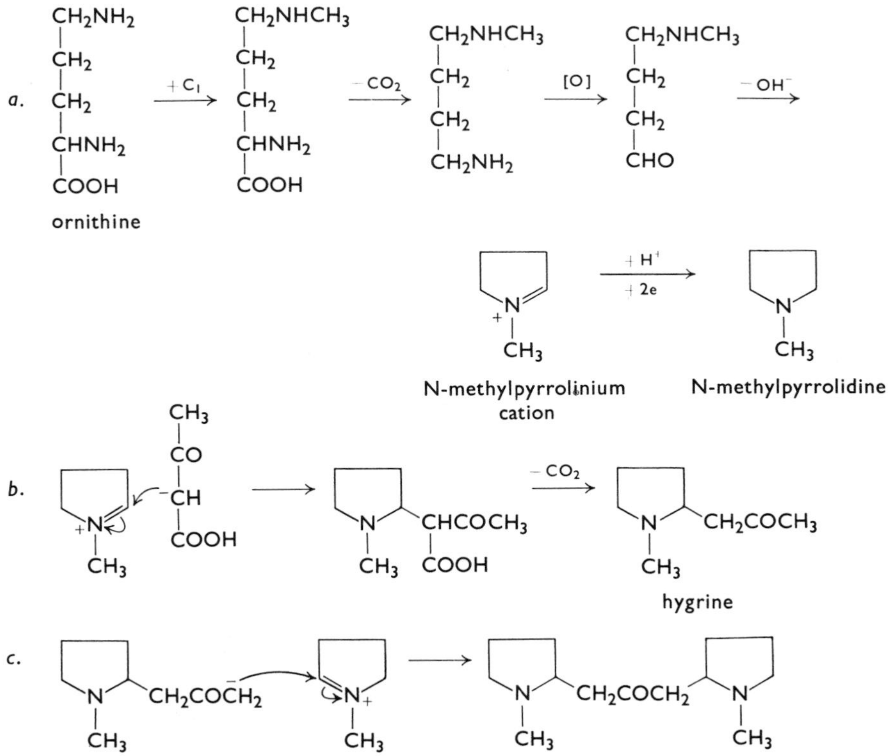

[Eq. 16-15]

(n.b. Acetoacetic acid may participate as the coenzyme A ester.)

It can be seen that the pathway leading to hygrine and cuscohygrine centers on a Mannich-type condensation involving a quaternary Schiff base intermediate, (the N-methyl-Δ^1-pyrrolinium cation), and an anion derived from acetoacetate.

Various investigators have been able to simulate, under "physiological conditions", the biosynthesis of hygrine and cuscohygrine from N-methyl-2-hydroxy-pyrrolidine (a source of the N-methyl-Δ^1-pyrrolinium cation) and acetone dicarboxylic acid, as shown in Eq. 16-16. The use of acetone dicarboxylic acid in the laboratory synthesis, instead of acetoacetate, as in the pathway of Eq. 16-15, is an artifice designed to give a little extra activation for the second addition step. In nature, the nucleophile is almost certainly the anion derived from acetoacetate rather than that from acetone dicarboxylic acid, since the latter has not been found in higher plants.

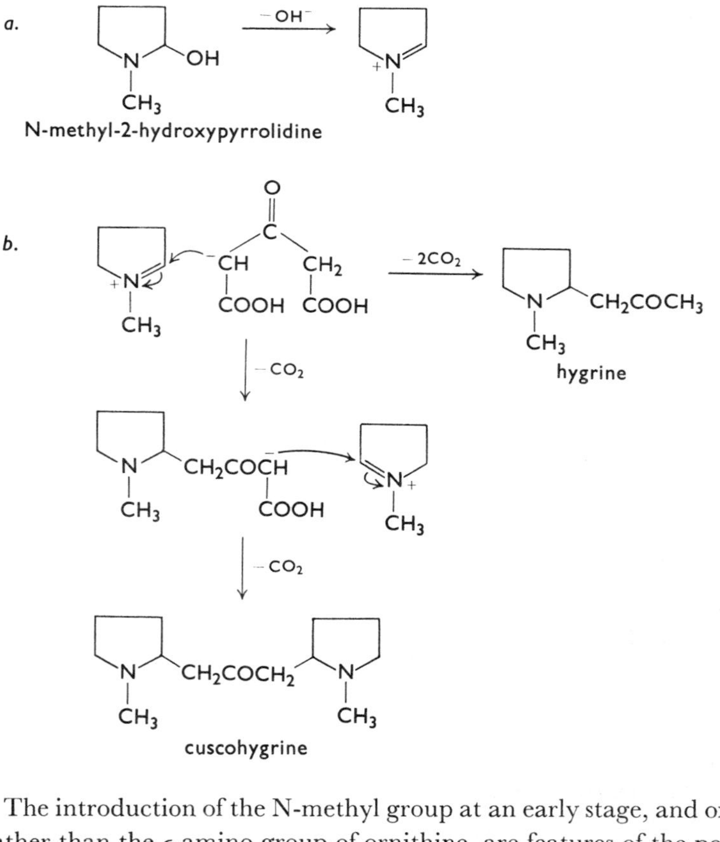

[Eq. 16-16]

The introduction of the N-methyl group at an early stage, and oxidation of the α- rather than the ε-amino group of ornithine, are features of the postulated pathway of hygrine biosynthesis which are not readily predictable on mechanistic considerations alone, but which are rendered likely in the light of the established pathway of biosynthesis of the closely related tropane alkaloids. Thus if hygrine undergoes a secondary dehydrogenation to a Δ^5-pyrroline derivative, the anion produced by removal of a proton from the methyl terminus of the side chain can add to the double bond, rather than to a further Δ^1-pyrroline nucleus as in the pathway of cuscohygrine biosynthesis (Eq. 16-15). By this simple means, the bicyclic nucleus of the tropane alkaloids is generated, as shown in Eq. 16-17. The

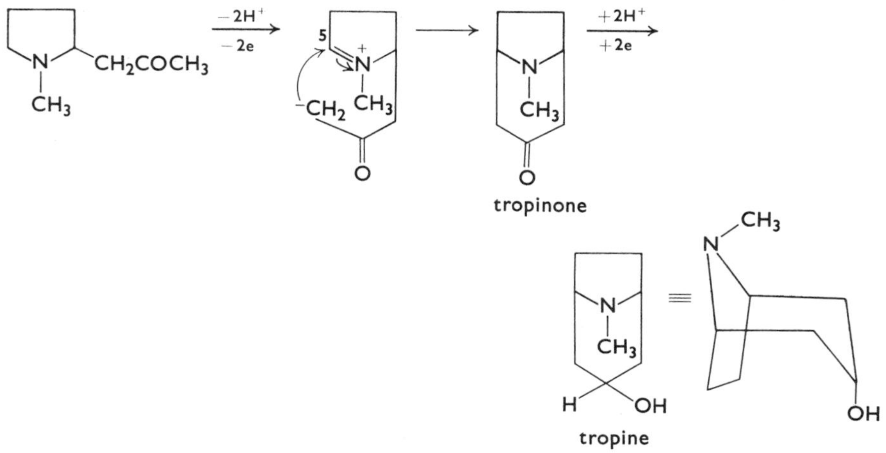

tropinone

tropine

[Eq. 16-17]

immediate product of the cyclization step is the ketone tropinone, which is not known in nature. Simple reduction, however, leads to tropine, from which a number of different alkaloids are derived, both by esterification of the hydroxyl function with a variety of acids, and by modification of the tropane nucleus.

The probable biosynthetic pathway of Eq. 16-17 is readily simulated in the laboratory by allowing succindialdehyde, methylamine, and acetone dicarboxylic acid to react in aqueous solution at neutral pH. The reaction probably follows the mechanistic course illustrated in Eq. 16-18.

Having established the relationship between the tropane alkaloids and alkaloids of the hygrine-cuscohygrine family, it will be appropriate to note the distribution of these compounds in nature. With few exceptions, alkaloids of these structural classes are found only in species of the family Solanaceae, and in particular in species of the genera *Atropa, Datura, Hyoscyamus,* and *Scopolia.* The close biogenetic relationship between the two groups is underlined by the co-occurrence of N-methylpyrrolidine, cuscohygrine (Eq. 16-15), and tropine (Eq. 16-17) together with related alkaloids in the deadly nightshade, *Atropa belladonna* L. Cuscohygrine, in particular, is a frequent companion of tropane alkaloids in species of the family Solanaceae.

$$\text{[structure: cyclic dialdehyde (—CHO, —CHO)]} + H_2NCH_3 \xrightarrow[-H_2O]{pH7} \text{[NCH}_3, \text{—CHO structure]} + \begin{array}{c} COOH \\ | \\ CH \\ | \\ C=O \\ | \\ CH_2 \\ | \\ COOH \end{array} \longrightarrow$$

$$\begin{array}{c} COOH \\ | \\ \text{[NHCH}_3\text{]} \quad =O \\ \text{—CHO} \quad CH_2 \\ | \\ COOH \end{array} \xrightarrow[-OH^-]{-CO_2} \text{[}^+NCH_3 \text{ ring} =O, -CH, COOH\text{]} \xrightarrow{-CO_2} \text{tropinone} \dagger \qquad \text{[Eq. 16-18]}$$

_____

† The symbol "—OH⁻" in this equation (and in others of this chapter) is a formal device. There is no doubt that, with the intervention of a proton donor, it is H_2O that is lost.

_____

The biosynthesis of tropine has been thoroughly studied,* with the gratifying result that the scheme shown in Eq. 16-19 is now supported by a considerable body of experimental evidence. Some of the key results which serve to delineate this pathway are as follows:

$$\begin{array}{c} 5\ CH_2NH_2 \\ | \\ 4\ CH_2 \\ | \\ 3\ CH_2 \\ | \\ 2\ ^*CHNH_2 \\ | \\ 1\ COOH \\ \text{ornithine} \end{array} \xrightarrow{+C_1} \begin{array}{c} CH_2NHCH_3 \\ | \\ CH_2 \\ | \\ CH_2 \\ | \\ ^*CHNH_2 \\ | \\ COOH \end{array} \xrightarrow{-CO_2} \begin{array}{c} CH_2NHCH_3 \\ | \\ CH_2 \\ | \\ CH_2 \\ | \\ ^*CH_2NH_2 \end{array} \xrightarrow{[O]} \begin{array}{c} CH_2NHCH_3 \\ | \\ CH_2 \\ | \\ CH_2 \\ | \\ ^*CHO \end{array} \xrightarrow{-OH^-}$$

$$\text{[}^+NCH_3 \text{ ring, }^*\text{]} \begin{array}{c} COOH \\ | \\ CH \\ | \\ C=O \\ | \\ CH_3 \end{array} \xrightarrow{-CO_2} \text{[NCH}_3 \text{ ring, }^*, =O, CH_3\text{]} \xrightarrow[-2e]{2H^+} \text{hygrine}$$

$$\text{[}^+NCH_3 \text{ ring, }^*, =O, -CH_2\text{]} \longrightarrow \text{[NCH}_3 \text{ ring, }^*, =O\text{]} \xrightarrow[+2e]{+2H^+} \text{[tropine bicyclic, }1^*,2,3H,NCH_3,OH,5,4\text{]}$$

tropine

[Eq. 16-19]

* In most of the investigations, the alkaloid actually studied was hyoscyamine, the ester of tropine with tropic acid (Fig. 16-4).

a. N-methylputrescine, ornithine, δ-N-methylornithine, and hygrine, in labeled form, are all incorporated into tropine.

b. 2-^{14}C-ornithine is incorporated stereospecifically into tropine, the label appearing at C-1 and not at the formally equivalent C-5 position.

c. Labeled acetate is incorporated into tropine, predominantly into positions 2, 3, and 4 of the tropane nucleus.

d. Tropine, obtained from an experiment in which N-methylputrescine, doubly labeled with ^{14}C and ^{15}N in the N-methyl group was fed to *Datura metel*, had nearly the same ^{14}C:^{15}N ratio as the precursor (Eq. 16-20).

$$\begin{array}{l} CH_2{}^{15}NH{}^{14}CH_3 \\ | \\ CH_2 \\ | \\ CH_2 \\ | \\ CH_2NH_2 \end{array} \quad \xrightarrow{\textit{Datura metel}} \quad \boxed{}NCH_3 \begin{array}{l} H \\ OH \end{array}$$

[Eq. 16-20]

$$\frac{^{15}N}{^{14}C} = 100 \qquad\qquad \frac{^{15}N}{^{14}C} = 92.7$$

tropine

The experiment described in (d) is of general significance, as it illuminates an important aspect of alkaloid biosynthesis that has not so far been discussed, that is, the origin of the nitrogen functions. This experiment, when considered together with others of a similar kind, leads to the conclusion that in general, for pathways of alkaloid biosynthesis which stem from amino acids, the nitrogen in the finished alkaloid is that present in the amino acid precursor.

A second point of importance relates to the unsymmetrical incorporation of ornithine into tropine. It will be evident from the pathway of Eq. 16-19, that C-2 and C-5 of ornithine could become equivalent through reversible double bond isomerization in the intermediate N-methyl-Δ^1-pyrrolinium cation, as shown in Eq. 16-21. However, the evidence from the incorporation experiments indicates that

[Eq. 16-21]

such an equilibrium situation does not arise, and this conclusion is supported by the evidence from laboratory studies, in which it has been shown that isomerization of the N-methyl-Δ^1-pyrrolinium cation is not a significant process at physiological pH. Many related pathways of alkaloid biosynthesis in which ornithine and lysine are involved display a similar specificity. On the other hand, pathways in which these amino acids are elaborated through symmetrical intermediates are also known. Both situations will be encountered in the examples to be quoted in the following pages.

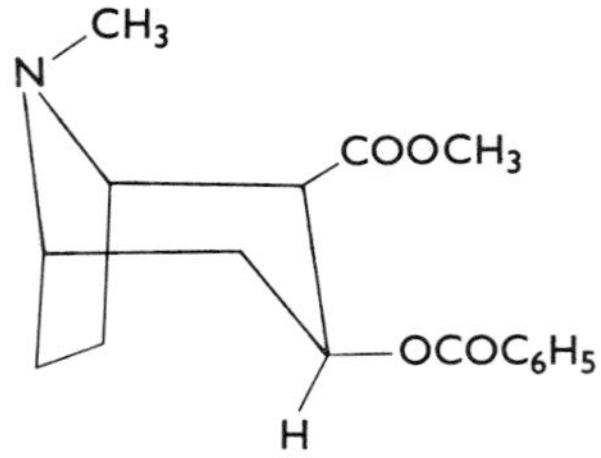

cocaine

Fig. 16-3.

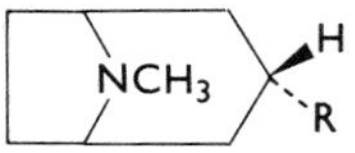

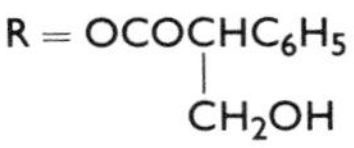

$R = OCOCHC_6H_5$ ((−)-tropic acid): hyoscyamine 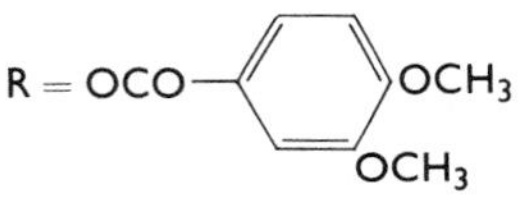
       |
       CH_2OH

$R = OCO$—⟨benzene ring⟩—OCH_3 (veratric acid): convolamine 
                          OCH_3

$R = OCOCH= C$⟨CH_3 / CH_3⟩ (senecioic acid): tropine senecioic ester

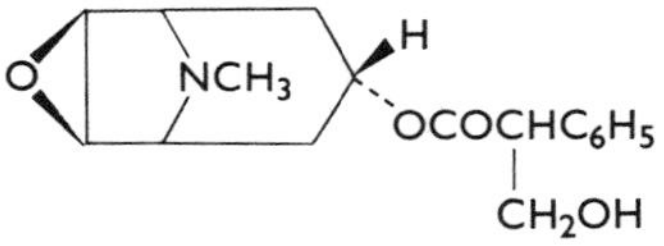

scopolamine
(scopine + tropic acid)

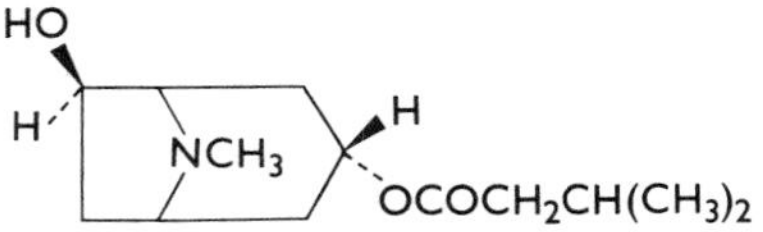

valeroidine
(dihydroxytropane +
isovaleric acid)

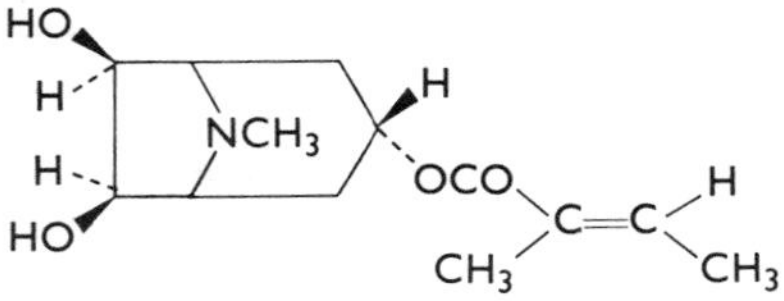

meteloidine
(teloidine + tiglic acid)

Fig. 16-4. Some Representative Tropane Alkaloids.

It will be noted that the acetoacetate-derived moiety undergoes decarboxylation in the pathway of tropine biosynthesis shown in Eq. 16-19. Occasionally this carboxyl group survives the biosynthetic process, as in ecgonine (2-carboxytropine). Ecgonine is the tropane nucleus of cocaine (Fig. 16-3), the familiar narcotic alkaloid found in *Erythroxylum coca* Lam. (fam. Erythroxylaceae).

In nature, the tropane nucleus is elaborated in two ways: by esterification and by oxidative modification.

An example of a tropane ester alkaloid, cocaine, has already been noted. Some further representative ester alkaloids are illustrated in Fig. 16-4. Examples of tropane bases exhibiting various structural features arising through secondary oxidative processes are also shown.

A number of plant species utilize lysine in biosynthetic pathways which lead to piperidine analogues of the pyrrolidine and tropane alkaloids considered above. Thus the alkaloids of *Punica granatum* L. (fam. Punicaceae), N-methylisopelletierine, and pseudopelletierine, evidently arise from lysine as follows (Eq. 16-22):

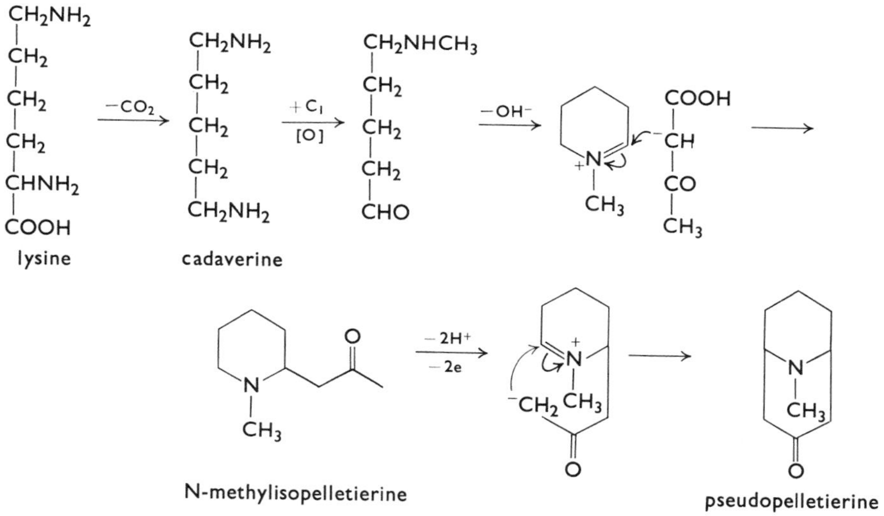

(n.b. Although cadaverine is shown as a precursor, it is not yet known with certainty whether lysine is incorporated *via* a symmetrical or an unsymmetrical intermediate.)

[Eq. 16-22]

Some obvious extensions of these pathways can be seen in the alkaloids of *Withania somnifera* Dunal. (fam. Solanaceae) which comprise, in addition to cuscohygrine, isopelletierine and various tropane alkaloids, the desmethyl analogue of cuscohygrine, anaferine, and the interesting ornithine-lysine hybrid alkaloid anahygrine (Fig. 16-5).

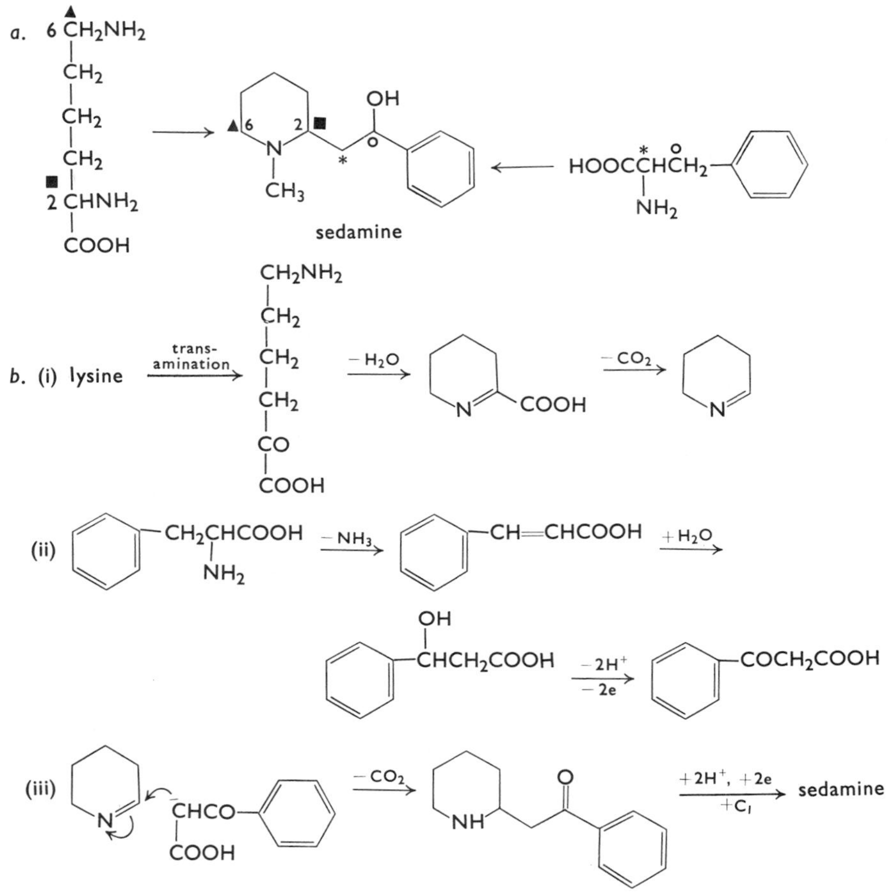

[Eq. 16-23]

The alkaloids so far discussed have all been seen to arise by pathways involving Mannich condensations in which the carbanion species is provided by acetoacetate. Related pathways of alkaloid biosynthesis are known, which involve carbanion species derived from other β-ketoacids. An instructive example is provided by sedamine, the biosynthesis of which has been investigated in *Sedum acre* L. (fam. Crassulaceae) by administering ^{14}C-labeled lysine and phenylalanine, with the results indicated in Eq. 16-23a. It will be noted that lysine is incorporated in an un-symmetrical manner, since C-2 and C-6 in sedamine are derived from C-2 and C-6 of lysine respectively.

The probable pathway of biosynthesis which emerges from these results is illustrated in Eq. 16-23b. (The N-methyl group could be inserted at an earlier stage without altering the essential nature of the pathway.) It will be noted that the

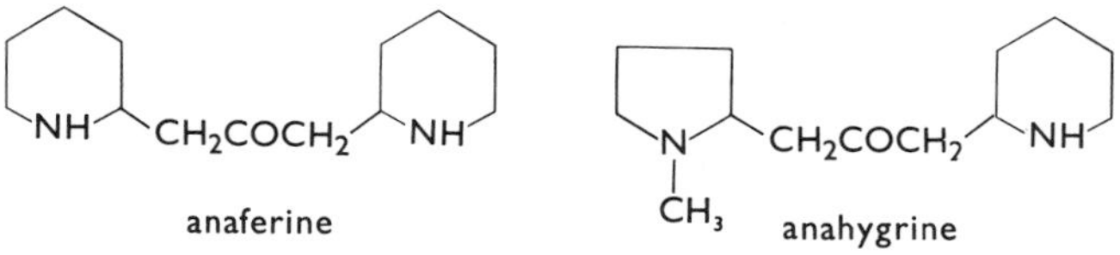

anaferine   anahygrine

Fig. 16-5.

carbanion species for the Mannich condensation is postulated to arise from 3-oxo-3-phenylpropanoic acid, which in turn could readily be derived from phenylalanine by non-oxidative deamination, followed by hydration and oxidation as in the normal pathway of β-oxidation of fatty acids (Chap. 3), as shown.

16.6 α,β′-Bipiperidine Alkaloids

The formation of tetrahydroanabasine from Δ^1-piperideine (Eq. 16-4b) provides a laboratory model for the key step in the probable biosynthetic pathway leading to the α,β′-bipiperidine alkaloids encountered in a number of species of the family Leguminosae. The demonstration that cadaverine can serve as a precursor of the representative base ammodendrine, in *Ammodendron conollyi* Bge., provides evidence to support the pathway of biosynthesis illustrated in Eq. 16-24.

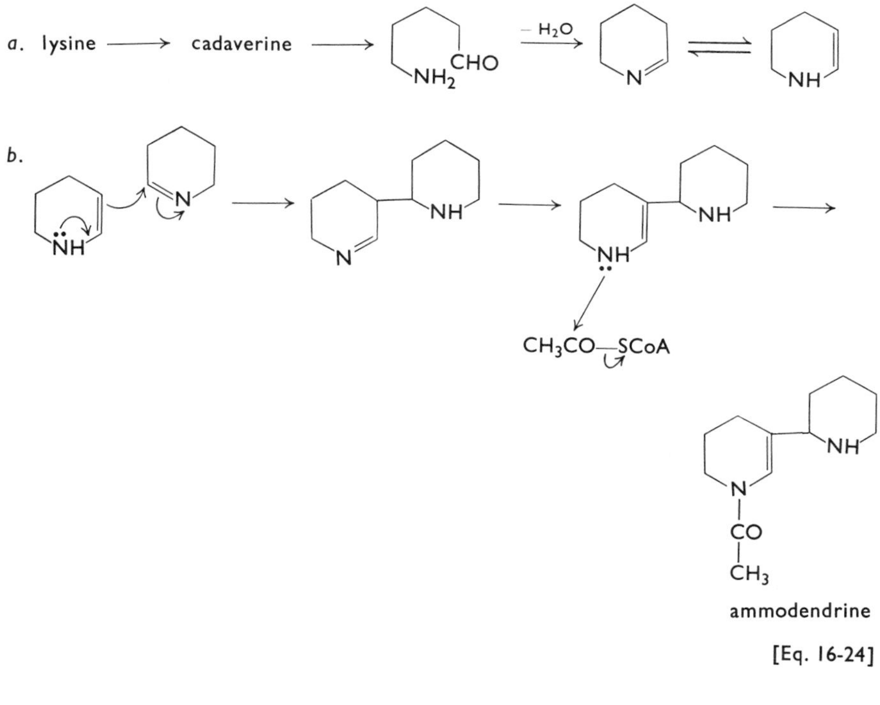

ammodendrine

[Eq. 16-24]

16.7 Pyrrolizidine Alkaloids

Pyrrolizidine alkaloids have a wide distribution, but are particularly characteristic of certain genera of the families Boraginaceae (*Heliotropium, Cynoglossum*), Compositae (*Senecio*), and Leguminosae (*Crotalaria*). The basic heterocyclic framework of the pyrrolizidine alkaloids arises from ornithine, *via* putrescine, by the probable pathway illustrated in Eq. 16-25.

a. ornithine $\xrightarrow{-CO_2}$ putrescine $\xrightarrow{[O]}$ ... $\xrightarrow{-H_2O}$

$\xrightarrow[+2H^+, +2e]{[O]}$

$-OH^-\rightarrow$

a

$\xrightarrow[+2e]{+2H^+}$

trachelanthamidine
(etc.)

[Eq. 16-25]

The evidence from incorporation experiments suggests (a) that at some stage in the pathway C-2 and C-5 of ornithine become equivalent, and (b) that a symmetrical intermediate is probably involved. To accommodate these results, the pathway illustrated, which leads to the simple representative base trachelanthamidine, is postulated to center on a Mannich-type condensation involving the symmetrical dialdehyde intermediate (Eq. 16-25*a*), a process which is readily simulated in the laboratory.

The early steps in this sequence, whereby two molecules of putrescine are linked together, can be reasonably formulated as shown. However, it is to be noted that the available evidence does not permit one to be definitive as to the precise mechanism of this process, and future investigations may require the adoption of an alternative scheme.

Further elaboration of the basic pyrrolizidine structure frequently involves the type of oxidative process noted in relation to the biosynthesis of the pyrrolidine and piperidine alkaloids. Thus retronecine and heliotridine, the two pyrrolizidine bases most often encountered in nature, are unsaturated, hydroxylated compounds, differing only in the configuration at C-7 (Fig. 16-6).

In the related base otonecine (Eq. 16-26), the C-8—N bond of the pyrrolizidine nucleus has been broken in a manner which is repeated sporadically in alkaloids

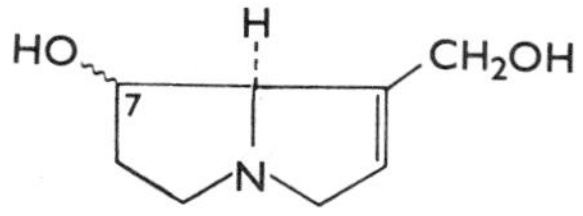

7α OH, heliotridine
7β OH, retronecine

Fig. 16-6.

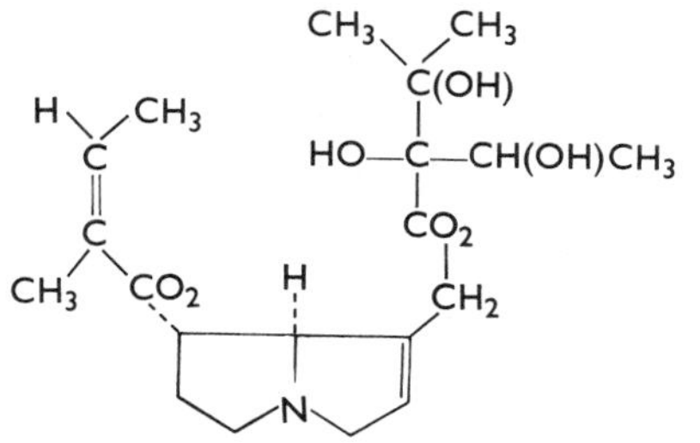

heliosupine
(heliotridine + angelic
and echimidinic acids)
[Boraginaceae]

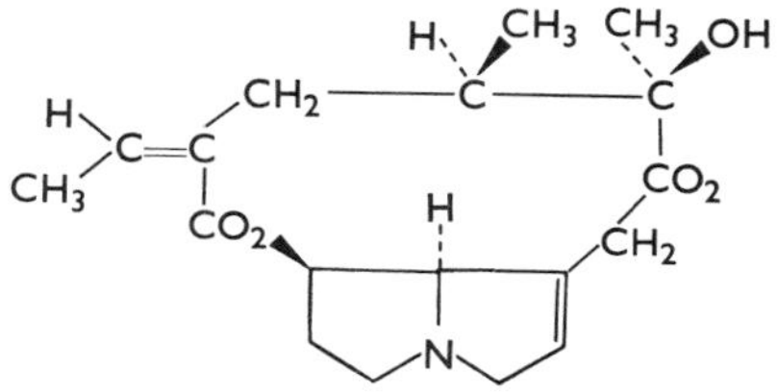

senecionine
(retronecine +
senecic acid
[Compositae]

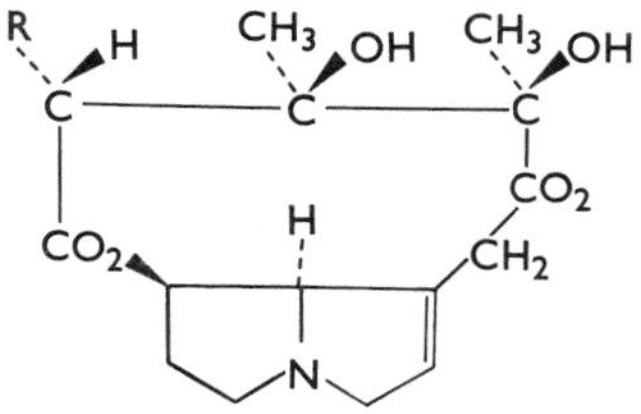

R = CH₃, monocrotaline (retronecine + monocrotalic acid)
R = (CH₃)₂CH, trichodesmine (retronecine + trichodesmic acid)
[Leguminosae]

Fig. 16-7. Some Characteristic Pyrrolizidine Alkaloids.

of a wide variety of structural types. This process is best conceived as proceeding from retronecine by hydroxylation at C-8, followed by methylation of the nitrogen function and ring cleavage, possibly in a concerted manner. The methyl donor in this reaction is undoubtedly S-adenosylmethionine, as shown.

Pyrrolizidine bases occasionally but rarely occur in nature in the free form; more often they are found in ester combination with mono- or dibasic acids, most of which are unique to this series. Various examples of these so-called necic acids

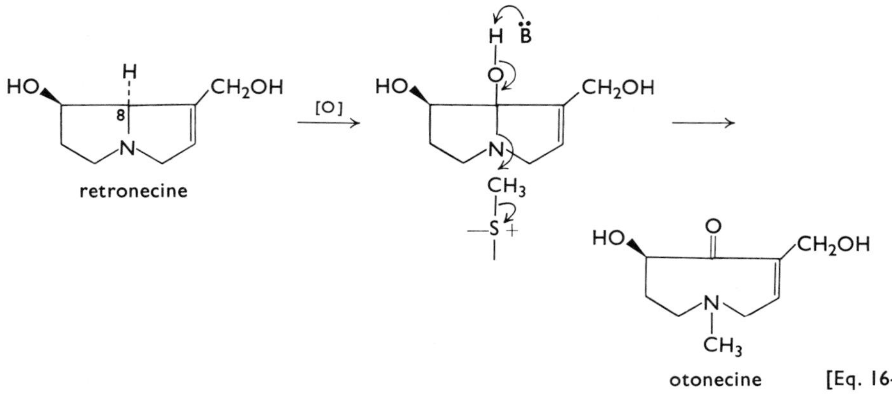

retronecine

otonecine   [Eq. 16-26]

were discussed in Chapter 13. Some representative alkaloids, which illustrate the most characteristic structural types encountered in the families Boraginaceae, Compositae, and Leguminosae are shown in Fig. 16-7.

16.8 Lupin Alkaloids

Certain genera of the Leguminosae are particularly adept in the biosynthetic elaboration of lysine. The compounds resulting from this synthetic activity constitute a group frequently referred to as "lupin alkaloids," from their widespread occurrence in species of *Lupinus*, although it is to be noted that they are by no means confined solely to this genus.

The simplest representative, lupinine, evidently arises from lysine in a manner entirely analogous to the formation of trachelanthamidine from ornithine (Eq. 16-27). As in the pyrrolizidine series, radiotracer experiments have shown that lysine is incorporated *via* a symmetrical intermediate (cf. the dialdehyde Eq. 16-27a) and that C-2 and C-6 become equivalent during the biosynthetic process.

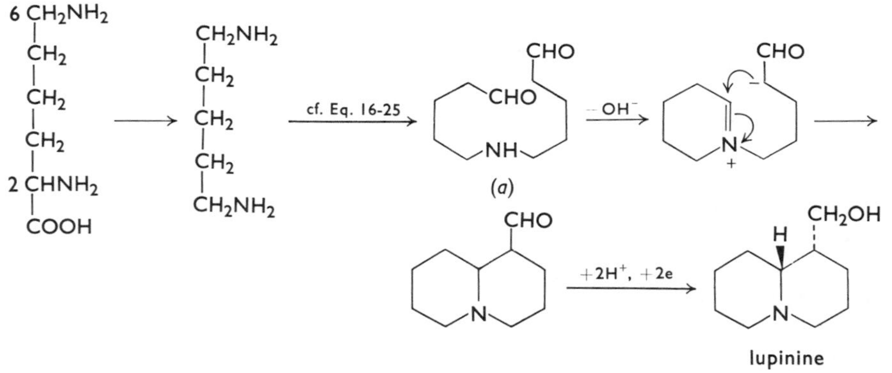

lupinine

[Eq. 16-27]

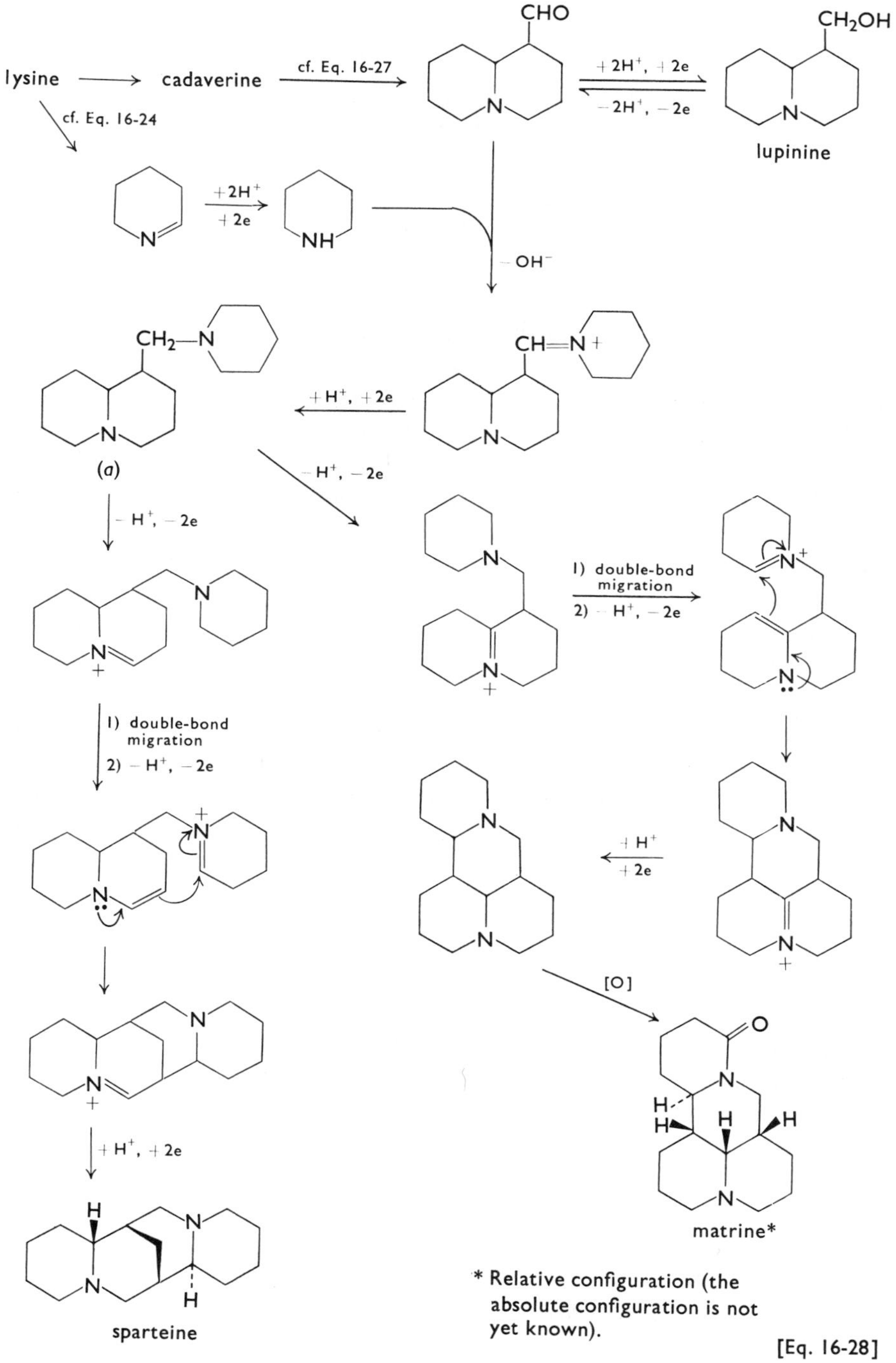

lysine ⟶ cadaverine

cf. Eq. 16-27

cf. Eq. 16-24

+ 2H⁺
+ 2e

+ 2H⁺, + 2e
− 2H⁺, − 2e

lupinine

− OH⁻

+ H⁺, + 2e

− H⁺, − 2e

(a)

− H⁺, − 2e

1) double-bond
migration
2) − H⁺, − 2e

1) double-bond
migration
2) − H⁺, − 2e

+ H⁺
+ 2e

[O]

+ H⁺, + 2e

sparteine

matrine*

* Relative configuration (the
absolute configuration is not
yet known).

[Eq. 16-28]

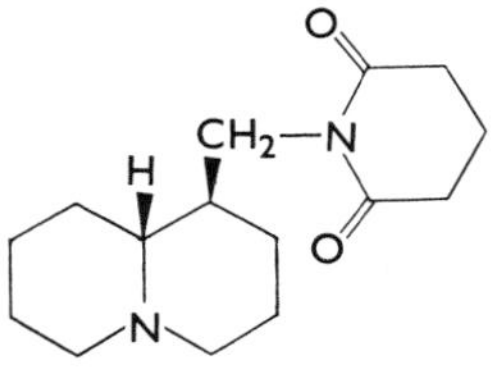

lamprolobine

Fig. 16-8.

The synthetic potential of the simple processes discussed in the previous sections is well exemplified in the probable pathways of biosynthesis leading to sparteine and matrine (Eq. 16-28), which represent two important classes of tetracyclic lupin alkaloid. It will be noted that the ring forming step in each sequence is represented as an aldol-type condensation of the kind previously described.

The mechanistic details of the pathways shown in Eq. 16-28 have yet to be verified experimentally. However, it is well established that lysine and cadaverine are incorporated into sparteine and matrine and that lupinine can serve as a precursor of sparteine in *Lupinus* species. It is also of interest that an alkaloid, lamprolobine (Fig. 16-8), which has the basic structure of the postulated common intermediate Eq. 16-28*a*, has been discovered in the Australian plant *Lamprolobium fruticosum* Benth. (fam. Leguminosae).

Cytisine, which, after sparteine is the most widely distributed lupin alkaloid, has been shown to be derived by the loss of ring D from sparteine in *Lupinus luteus* (Eq. 16-29). (The oxidative modification of ring A in this transformation clearly

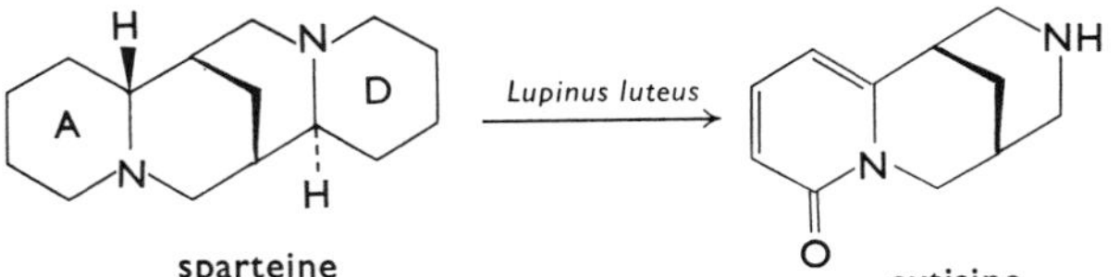

sparteine   cytisine   [Eq. 16-29]

presents no conceptual difficulties.) An intermediate stage in a ring D degradation of this type is seen in the structures of the related alkaloids angustifoline and rhombifoline (Fig. 16-9).

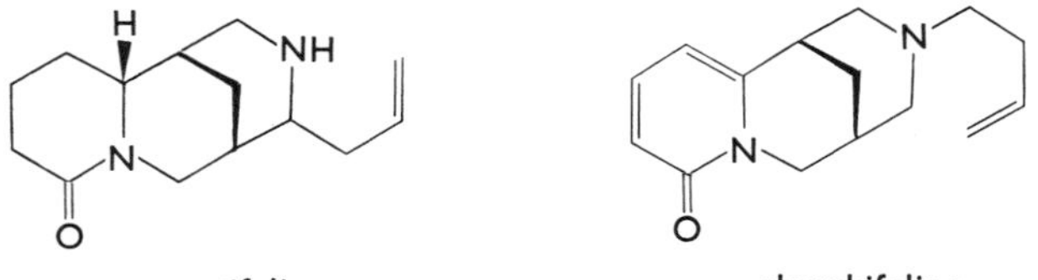

angustifoline   rhombifoline

Fig. 16-9.

16.9 The Ormosia Alkaloids

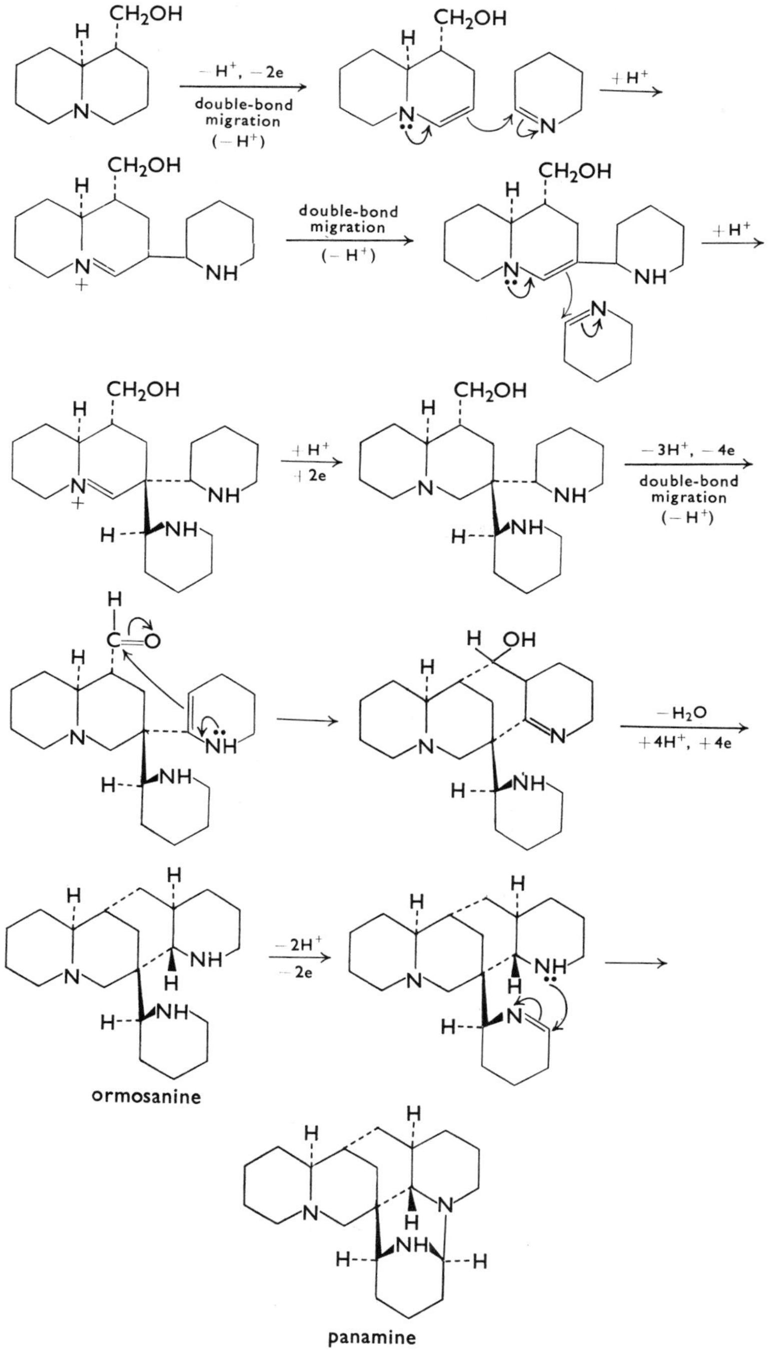

ormosanine

panamine

[Eq. 16-30]

Various species of *Ormosia* (fam. Leguminosae) are able to elaborate intermediates derived from lysine and cadaverine to the construction of penta- and
hexacyclic alkaloids such as ormosanine and panamine (Eq. 16-30). A family relationship with the lupin alkaloids is indicated by the occurrence of (−)-sparteine
(Eq. 16-28) and angustifoline (Fig. 16-9) in certain *Ormosia* species.

The complexity of the *Ormosia* alkaloids made for rather slow progress in the
elucidation of their structures until X-ray crystallographic methods were applied.
By this means, the structures of both panamine and jamine (related to ormosanine)
were elucidated, which led, through established chemical correlations, to the structures of other members of the group.

The biosynthesis of both ormosanine and panamine is readily rationalized
without recourse to processes other than those already considered, as shown in
Eq. 16-30.

It should be emphasized that this pathway of biosynthesis is entirely speculative
since no tracer experiments of any kind have as yet been reported which would
either confirm or invalidate the scheme shown. Its main purpose here is to show
that the biosynthesis of complex structures such as those of panamine and ormosanine, can be entirely explained in terms of the basic reactions used in related
schemes throughout this chapter.

16.10   The Lycopodium Alkaloids

The club mosses (*Lycopodium* spp.) belong to a primitive plant division, the
vascular cryptogams. The commonest alkaloid structure encountered in this genus
is represented by lycopodine. Until radiotracer experiments proved otherwise, the
view was held that this structure probably arose from two polyketide chains, each
consisting of four acetate units, as shown in Eq. 16-31.

lycopodine   [Eq. 16-31]

Although ^{14}C-labeled acetate was incorporated into lycopodine, the labeling
pattern clearly demonstrated that this particular pathway could not be correct. On
the other hand, two molecules of lysine were incorporated in a specific manner.

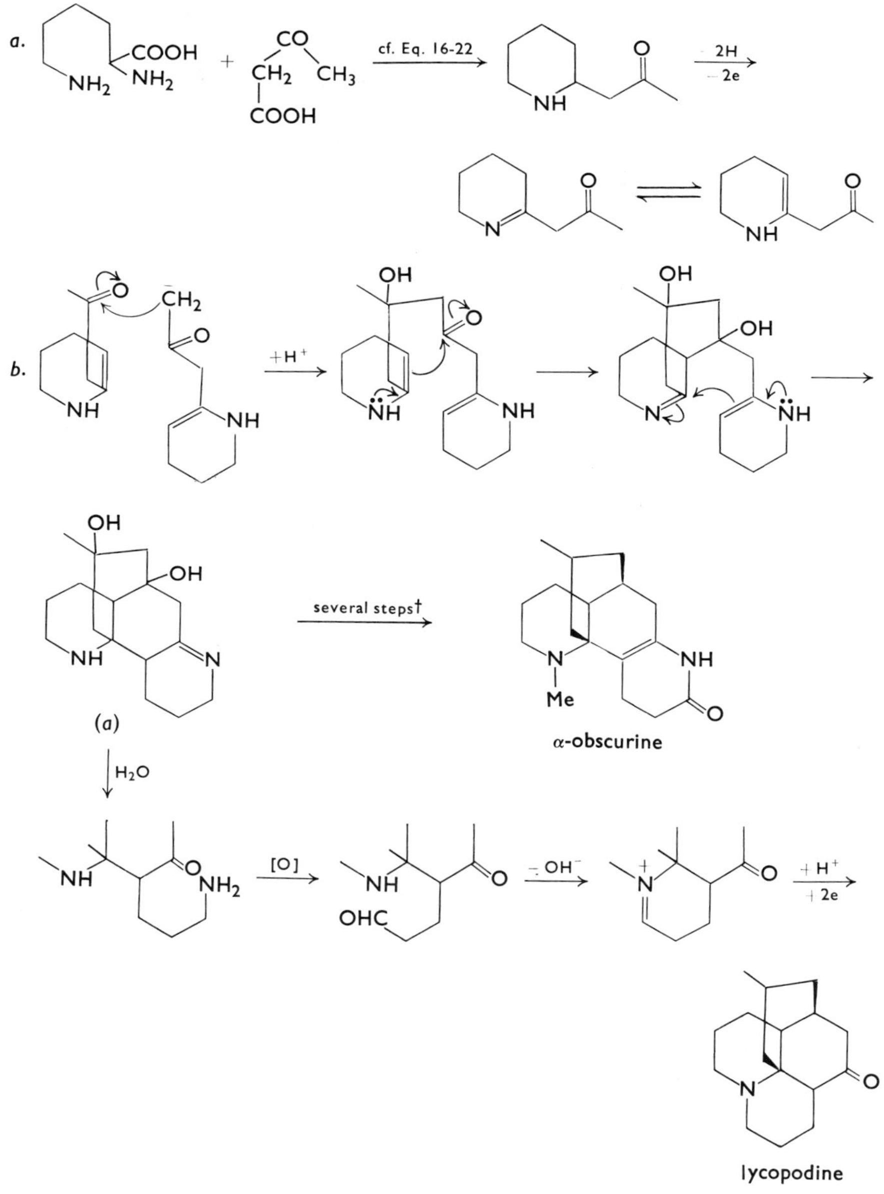

a.

b.

cf. Eq. 16-22

+H⁺

several steps†

(*a*)

H₂O

[O]

α-obscurine

lycopodine

[Eq. 16-32]

<hr />

† These steps can be formulated as oxidation, methylation, double-bond migration, dehydration, and reduction. The latter two steps are also involved in the conversion of intermediate *a* into lycopodine.

On the basis of these results, a scheme for lycopodine biosynthesis is suggested in which isopelletierine plays a central role. This scheme, shown in Eq. 16-32, at the same time satisfactorily accounts for the genesis of related alkaloids such as α-obscurine.

It will be noted that each step in this pathway has ample precedent in biological reactions already discussed.

Again, it must be emphasized that the detailed pathway shown in Eq. 16-32 has yet to be tested by appropriate radiotracer experiments. There is no doubt, however, that the *Lycopodium* alkaloids provide a further illustration of the versatile way in which plants can elaborate simple precursors, such as lysine, to alkaloids of a surprising degree of complexity.

16.11   The Hemlock Alkaloids

At first sight, the structure of coniine (Fig. 16-10), the principal alkaloid of hemlock, *Conium maculatum* L. (fam. Umbelliferae), bears such a strong resemblance

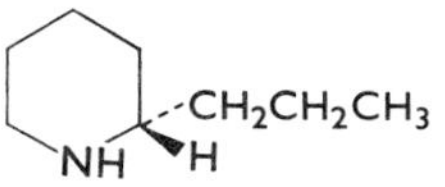

coniine

Fig. 16-10.

to that of N-methylisopelletierine (Eq. 16-22) that an investigation of its biosynthesis might have seemed rather superfluous. Although we can now speak with the benefit of hindsight, a note of caution in accepting this conclusion too readily might have been sounded by the fact that the plant family in which the genus *Conium* is placed, the Umbelliferae, is only distantly related to the families in which N-methylisopelletierine is found (the Punicaceae and Solanaceae).

When tracer experiments were eventually undertaken, it was found, contrary to expectation, that lysine was only a very poor precursor of the piperidine ring. Accordingly, a second hypothesis for the biosynthesis of coniine was considered, in which a polyketide intermediate, derived from four molecules of acetate, was invoked, as illustrated in Eq. 16-33.

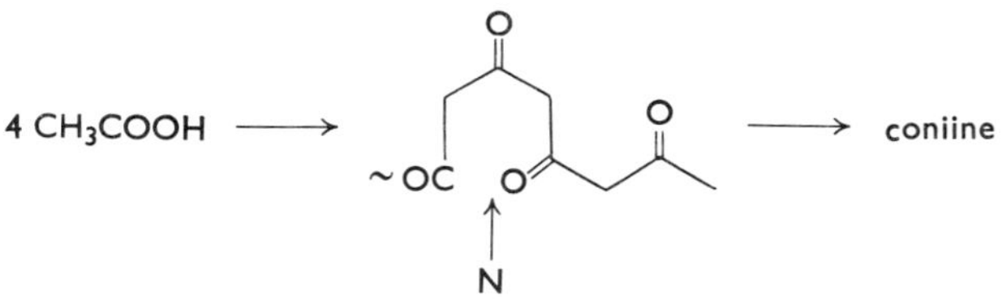

$$4 \; CH_3COOH \longrightarrow \qquad \longrightarrow \text{coniine}$$

[Eq. 16-33]

The results obtained from appropriate feeding experiments, which were carried out to test this hypothesis, are summarized in Eq. 16-34. The labeling pattern which emerged clearly shows the participation of four molecules of acetate in the biosynthesis of coniine. This discovery should perhaps be regarded as a cautionary tale against automatically equating, for two related compounds, a structural similarity with a common biogenesis.

$$CH_3{}^{14}COOH \xrightarrow{\text{Conium maculatum}}$$

% Activity at each position: 3′ 2′ 1′ 2 3 4 5 6
1.6 22 1.3 26 1.6 22 1 24   [Eq. 16-34]

16.12 Pyridine Alkaloids

Few alkaloids have attracted the attention of chemists as much as nicotine, the characteristic base of *Nicotiana* species (fam. Solanaceae). Its well known physiological properties, together with its wide distribution in a number of plant families besides the Solanaceae, account for the numerous investigations which have been carried out into its biosynthesis.

The pathway summarized in Eq. 16-35 is supported by the following evidence, all of which has been obtained from studies with radioactive precursors.

a. Nicotinic acid and ornithine serve as efficient precursors of the pyridine and pyrrolidine rings respectively.

b. Quinolinic acid is as efficient a precursor of the pyridine ring as nicotinic acid.

c. Putrescine, N-methylputrescine, and 4-methylaminobutanal are all efficiently incorporated into the pyrrolidine ring.

d. 2,3,7-^{14}C-nicotinic acid gives nicotine labeled almost exclusively at positions 2 and 3 of the pyridine ring.

e. 2-^{14}C-ornithine gives nicotine labeled equally at positions 2′ and 5′ of the pyrrolidine ring.

f. The carboxyl group of nicotinic acid is not incorporated into nicotine.

Item (e) shows that ornithine is incorporated *via* a symmetrical precursor, which is undoubtedly putrescine, as indicated in (c). Item (d) shows that the pyrrolidine ring becomes attached specifically to C-3 of nicotinic acid. This evidence also shows that nicotinic acid is not incorporated *via* a symmetrical intermediate.

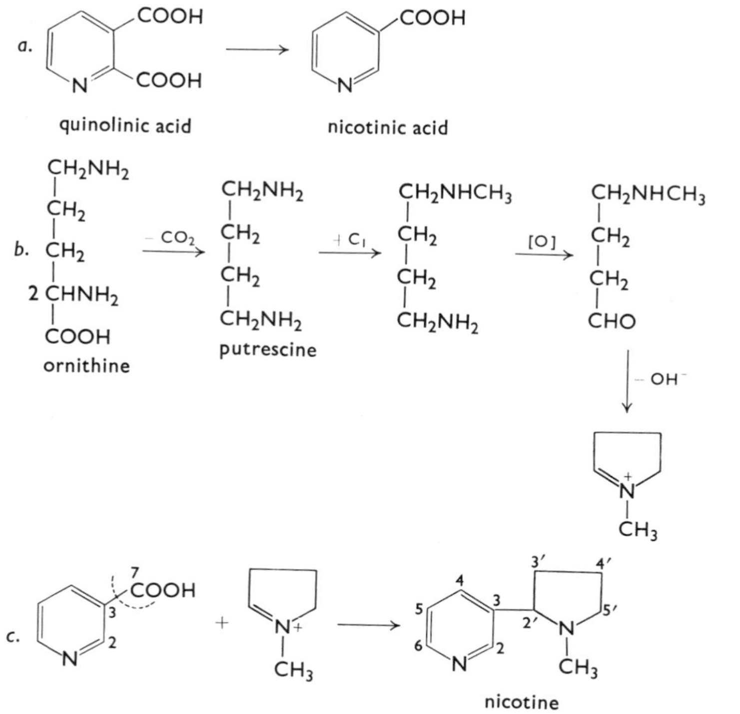

quinolinic acid   nicotinic acid

b.

ornithine   putrescine

c.

nicotine   [Eq. 16-35]

Thus far the evidence discussed is quite clear. A difficulty arises, however, when we come to consider the mechanism by which the pyrrolidine ring becomes attached to the pyridine nucleus. It we are to invoke a mechanism similar to that previously discussed for nucleophilic addition to Δ^1-pyrroline derivatives, we must account somehow for the development of nucleophilic potential at C-3 in nicotinic acid (Eq. 16-35c). Strong evidence that the coupling step does indeed involve nucleophilic addition to the N-methyl-Δ^1-pyrrolinium cation, has been provided by the observation that this compound, labeled with ^{14}C at C-2, is incorporated into nicotine in *Nicotiana tabacum*, with the label appearing exclusively at C-2' (Eq. 16-36).

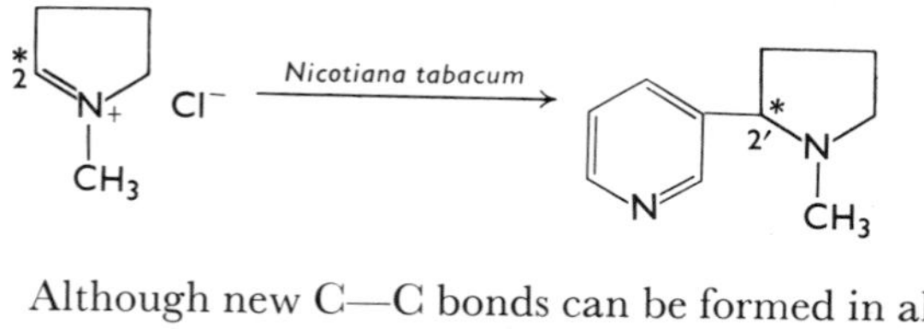

Nicotiana tabacum

[Eq. 16-36]

Although new C—C bonds can be formed in aldol-type reactions, by utilizing the developing negative charge at the α-position in the decarboxylation of picolinic acids, as shown, for example, in Eq. 16-37 (the Hammick reaction), this behavior is not exhibited by nicotinic acid.

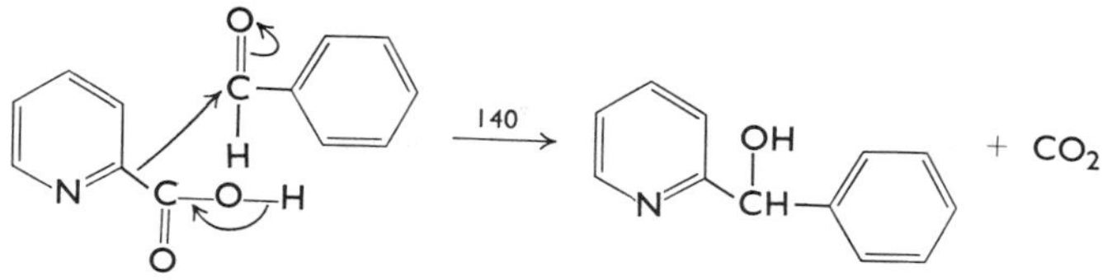

[Eq. 16-37]

A possible mechanism by which the required nucleophilic character could be developed is shown in Eq. 16-38. The reduction step (a) leading to the dihydro derivative is analogous to the reduction of NAD^+ to NADH (page 51).

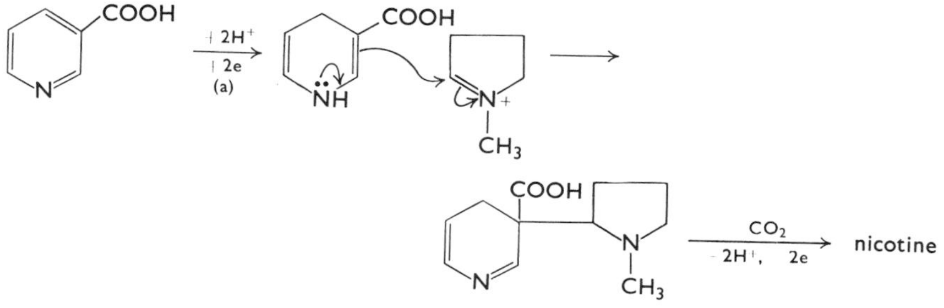

[Eq. 16-38]

In the structures of the tobacco alkaloids anabasine and anatabine we can see an obvious variation of nicotine biosynthesis in which a piperidine ring derived from lysine replaces the pyrrolidine ring in nicotine. The biosynthetic pathway shown in Eq. 16-39 is adequately supported by evidence from radiotracer experiments. It will be noted, however, that in this pathway, as in sedamine biosynthesis

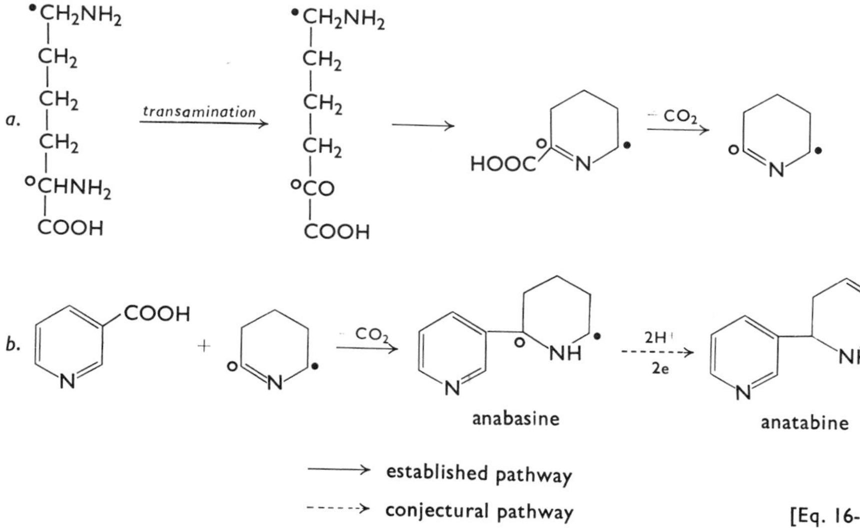

anabasine

anatabine

⟶ established pathway

- - - -→ conjectural pathway

[Eq. 16-39]

(Eq. 16-23), C-2 and C-6 of lysine do not become equivalent. A non-symmetrical intermediate such as 6-amino-2-oxohexanoic acid is therefore indicated as the substrate for the cyclization step, rather than a symmetrical precursor such as cadaverine.

Ricinine, the toxic alkaloid of the castor oil plant,* *Ricinus communis* L. (fam. Euphorbiaceae), is a further example of an alkaloid derived from nicotinic acid (Eq. 16-40). The derivation of ricinine from intermediates of the nicotinic acid group (nicotinic acid, nicotinamide, and quinolinic acid) has been well established by appropriate tracer experiments. The elaboration of the pyridine ring in nicotinic acid to ricinine, by oxidation and methylation, clearly presents no conceptual diffi-

nicotinamide   ricinine

[Eq. 16-40]

culties. The presence of a nitrile group, however, is a novel feature, which arises through dehydration of the amide group in nicotinamide.

16.13 Primary Metabolic Processes Related to Ornithine and Lysine Biosynthesis

Delineation of the pathways of ornithine and lysine biosynthesis will allow us to retrace many of the pathways discussed in this chapter to their sources in processes of primary metabolism.

Although the pathway of biosynthesis of ornithine has been mainly studied in bacteria, a similar pathway is probably involved in higher plants. The pathway in bacteria stems from glutamic acid and proceeds by way of the steps shown in Eq. 16-41.

Two pathways to lysine are known. The one which appears to operate in higher plants uses as its starting materials pyruvic and aspartic acids, as shown in Eq. 16-42 (the α,ϵ-diaminopimelic acid pathway). This scheme is an abbreviated version of the full sequence and shows only the essential chemical transformations.

Nicotinic acid arises in bacteria from tryptophan, by a rather involved process of ring cleavage and recyclization. However, in higher plants, a completely dif-

---

* The extreme toxicity of castor oil seeds is not due primarily to ricinine but to ricin, a polypeptide of undetermined structure.

$$
\begin{array}{c}
\text{COOH} \\ | \\ \text{CH}_2 \\ | \\ \text{CH}_2 \\ | \\ \text{CHNH}_2 \\ | \\ \text{COOH}
\end{array}
\xrightarrow{\text{acetylation}}
\begin{array}{c}
\text{COOH} \\ | \\ \text{CH}_2 \\ | \\ \text{CH}_2 \\ | \\ \text{CHNHCOCH}_3 \\ | \\ \text{COOH}
\end{array}
\xrightarrow[-\text{H}_2\text{O}]{+2\text{H}^+,\, +2\text{e}}
$$

glutamic acid

$$
\begin{array}{c}
\text{CHO} \\ | \\ \text{CH}_2 \\ | \\ \text{CH}_2 \\ | \\ \text{CHNHCOCH}_3 \\ | \\ \text{COOH}
\end{array}
\longrightarrow
\begin{array}{c}
\text{CH}_2\text{NH}_2 \\ | \\ \text{CH}_2 \\ | \\ \text{CH}_2 \\ | \\ \text{CHNHCOCH}_3 \\ | \\ \text{COOH}
\end{array}
\xrightarrow{\text{hydrolysis}}
\begin{array}{c}
\text{CH}_2\text{NH}_2 \\ | \\ \text{CH}_2 \\ | \\ \text{CH}_2 \\ | \\ \text{CHNH}_2 \\ | \\ \text{COOH}
\end{array}
\qquad \text{[Eq. 16-41]}
$$

ornithine

$$
\begin{array}{c}
\text{COOH} \\ | \\ \text{CH}_2 \\ | \\ \text{CHNH}_2 \\ | \\ \text{COOH}
\end{array}
\xrightarrow[-\text{H}_2\text{O}]{+2\text{H}^+,\, +2\text{e}}
\begin{array}{c}
\text{COOH} \\ | \\ \text{CO} \\ | \\ -\text{CH}_2 \\ \text{H}-\text{C}=\text{O} \\ | \\ \text{CH}_2 \\ | \\ \text{CHNH}_2 \\ | \\ \text{COOH}
\end{array}
\xrightarrow{-\text{H}_2\text{O}}
\begin{array}{c}
\text{COOH} \\ | \\ \text{CO} \\ | \\ \text{CH} \\ \| \\ \text{CH} \\ | \\ \text{CH}_2 \\ | \\ \text{CHNH}_2 \\ | \\ \text{COOH}
\end{array}
\xrightarrow[+2\text{e}]{+2\text{H}^+}
$$

aspartic acid

$$
\begin{array}{c}
\text{COOH} \\ | \\ \text{CO} \\ | \\ \text{CH}_2 \\ | \\ \text{CH}_2 \\ | \\ \text{CH}_2 \\ | \\ \text{CHNH}_2 \\ | \\ \text{COOH}
\end{array}
\xrightarrow{\text{transamination}}
\begin{array}{c}
\text{COOH} \\ | \\ \text{CHNH}_2 \\ | \\ \text{CH}_2 \\ | \\ \text{CH}_2 \\ | \\ \text{CH}_2 \\ | \\ \text{CHNH}_2 \\ | \\ \text{COOH}
\end{array}
\xrightarrow{-\text{CO}_2}
\begin{array}{c}
\text{CH}_2\text{NH}_2 \\ | \\ \text{CH}_2 \\ | \\ \text{CH}_2 \\ | \\ \text{CH}_2 \\ | \\ \text{CHNH}_2 \\ | \\ \text{COOH}
\end{array}
\qquad \text{[Eq. 16-42]}
$$

meso-α,ϵ-diamino-   lysine
pimelic acid

ferent pathway is observed. This has been shown to involve glycerol and aspartic acid, which are incorporated into the pyridine ring of nicotine, and therefore presumably into nicotinic acid, in the manner indicated in Eq. 16-43.

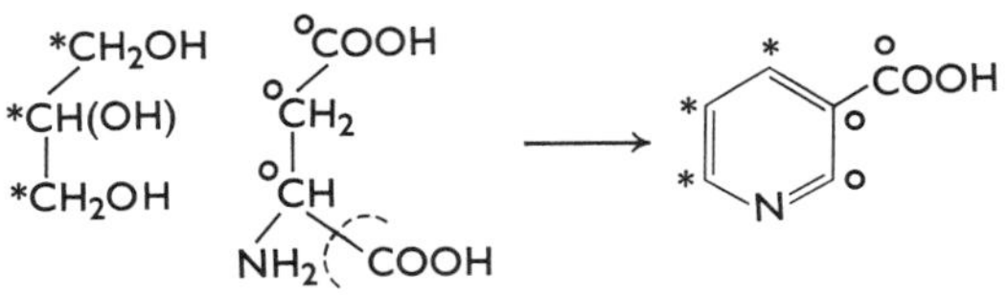

[Eq. 16-43]

A reasonable mechanism to account for this transformation is shown in Eq. 16-44.

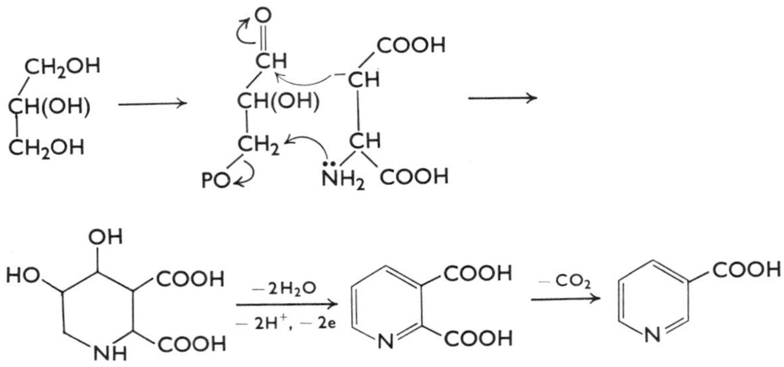

[Eq. 16-44]

Glutamic acid, the precursor of ornithine, arises by way of transamination from 2-oxoglutaric acid, an intermediate of the citric acid cycle (Chap. 2). Aspartic acid likewise arises from oxaloacetate, another citric acid cycle intermediate. The pyruvate available for synthetic operations in plants arises mainly from the catabolism of glucose (Chap. 2). The alkaloids discussed in this chapter therefore have in common a biogenetic origin, predominantly in intermediates of the citric acid cycle, supplemented, in the case of alkaloids derived from lysine and nicotinic acid, by intermediates drawn from the pathway of carbohydrate metabolism.

16.14 Summary

It will be evident from the preceding discussion that many questions relating to the mechanisms involved in the biosynthesis of alkaloids of the ornithine-lysine-nicotinic acid family remain to be answered. However, in surveying the various mechanisms which have been proposed, one is impressed by the way in which a relatively small number of simple reactions can be used to rationalize the biosynthesis of almost all of the very varied alkaloid structures encountered. This internal consistency is in itself a persuasive argument for the validity of the basic reactions formulated. In most cases these have the added support of appropriate laboratory analogies.

Now that the broad outlines of the secondary metabolism of ornithine, lysine, and nicotinic acid have been sketched in, future investigations will undoubtedly be concentrated on defining the precise mechanisms of the individual steps in the various pathways. It is to be hoped that these investigations will be accompanied by parallel research into the various enzyme systems involved, since this will bring to alkaloid biosynthesis the same depth of understanding that we now have of the early stages of terpene and steroid biosynthesis.

XVII CHAPTER

REFERENCES FOR FURTHER READING

The reader is referred to the general references given at the beginning of Chapter 16 for general information on the chemistry and biosynthesis of the alkaloids discussed in this chapter.

1. A. R. Battersby, R. Binks, and R. Huxtable, *Biosynthesis of Cactus Alkaloids,* Tetrahedron Letters, (1967), 563.
2. J. Lundström and S. Agurell, *Biosynthesis of Mescaline and Anhalamine in Peyote. II.,* Tetrahedron Letters, (1968), 4437.
3. S. Agurell and J. Lundström, *Apparent Intermediates in the Biosynthesis of Mescaline and Related Tetrahydroisoquinolines,* Chem. Comm., (1968), 1638.
4. D. G. O'Donovan and H. Horan, *The Biosynthesis of Lophocereine,* J. Chem. Soc. (C), (1968), 2791.
5. S. Agurell and J. L. Nilsson, *Biosynthesis of Psilocybin,* Acta Chem. Scand., 22, (1968), 1210.
6. K. Stolle and D. Gröger, *Investigations into the Biosynthesis of Harmine,* Arch. Pharm., 301, (1968), 561.
7. H. R. Schütte and B. Maier, *On the Biosynthesis of the Calycanthine Alkaloids,* Arch. Pharm., 298, (1965), 459.
8. D. G. O'Donovan and M. F. Keogh, *The Biosynthesis of Folicanthine,* J. Chem. Soc. (C), (1966), 1570.
9. D. Munsche and K. Mothes, *Feeding Experiments on the Biosynthesis of Damascenine in Nigella Damascena L.,* Phytochemistry, 4, (1965), 705.
10. D. R. Liljegren, *The Biosynthesis of Quinazoline Alkaloids of Peganum Harmala L.,* Phytochemistry, 7, (1968), 1299.
11. D. Gröger and S. Johne, *On the Biosynthesis of Some Alkaloids of Glycosmis arborea (Rutaceae),* Z. Naturforsch., 23b, (1968), 1072.
12. J. R. Price, *The Distribution of Alkaloids in the Rutaceae,* in Chemical Plant Taxonomy, T. Swain, Ed., Academic Press, London, (1963), 429.

Simple Alkaloids Derived from the Aromatic Amino Acids Phenylalanine, Tyrosine, Tryptophan, and Anthranilic Acid

17.1 Introduction

As an interlude between the variously complex alkaloids discussed in Chapter 16 and the biosynthetic pyrotechnics of the benzylisoquinoline and indole alkaloids to be considered in Chapters 18 and 19, we shall survey in this chapter some simpler alkaloids derived from the aromatic amino acids. The compounds to be described, although formed by relatively direct pathways, nevertheless present some interesting and instructive aspects of secondary metabolism.

Alkaloids Derived from Phenylalanine and Tyrosine

17.2 The Hordeum Alkaloids

Incorporation studies have shown that the simple amines N-methyltyramine and hordenine are formed in barley (*Hordeum vulgare* L. fam. Gramineae) from tyrosine, as shown in Eq. 17-1.

[Eq. 17-1]

None of the steps in this sequence require comment, as they are all familiar from pathways described in previous chapters. It is of some significance, however, that phenylalanine has also been found to be a precursor of hordenine. This result implies the ability of *Hordeum* to convert phenylalanine into tyrosine by hydroxylation of the aromatic ring. It should be noted that, in general, higher plants do not appear to be able to carry out this transformation, and that the Gramineae (grasses) appear to be unusual in this respect. A clear distinction is therefore usually observed between pathways of alkaloid biosynthesis which stem from phenylalanine and tyrosine, as will be further noted in Chapter 18.

17.3   The Ephedra Alkaloids

Species of the genus *Ephedra* (fam. Gnetaceae) commonly produce the bases ephedrine and the diastereoisomeric pseudoephedrine (Eq. 17-2), together with the corresponding N-methyl and N-demethyl derivatives. The specific conversion of phenylalanine and ω-aminoacetophenone into ephedrine in *Ephedra* is suggestive of the pathway illustrated in Eq. 17-2*a*. The only feature of this scheme which requires comment derives from the observation that formate but not methionine was the donor of the C-methyl group in feeding experiments, a result which suggests the sequence indicated in Eq. 17-2*b* for the introduction of this substituent. (The N-methyl group is derived as expected from methionine.)

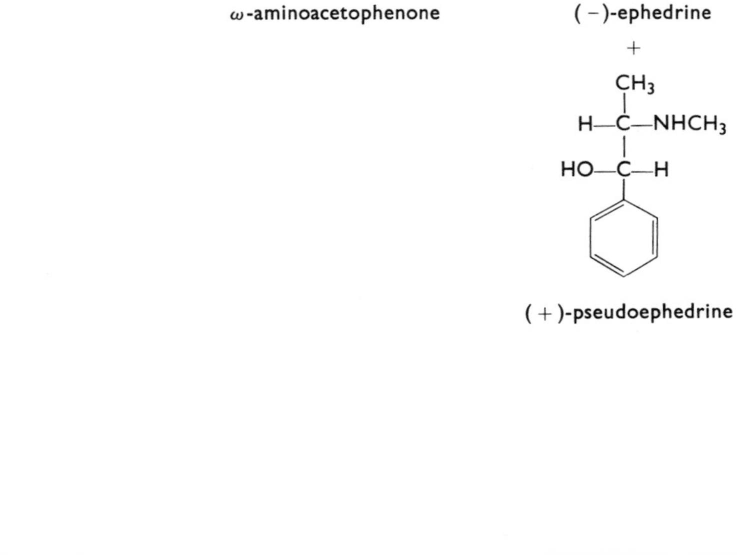

$$HCOOH \xrightarrow[- H_2O]{\substack{+2H^+ \\ +2e}} H-\overset{\displaystyle O}{\underset{\displaystyle |}{C}}-H$$

b.

$$\text{C}_6\text{H}_5\text{COCH}_2\text{NH}_2 \xrightarrow{-H^+} \text{C}_6\text{H}_5\text{COCHNH}_2 \longrightarrow \text{C}_6\text{H}_5\text{COCHNH}_2\ (\text{CH}_2\text{OH}) \xrightarrow{\text{reduction}}$$

$$\text{C}_6\text{H}_5\text{COCHNH}_2\ (\text{CH}_3) \xrightarrow[+2e]{+2H^+} \text{C}_6\text{H}_5\text{CH(OH)CHNH}_2\ (\text{CH}_3) \xrightarrow{+C_1} \text{ephedrine} \qquad [\text{Eq. 17-2}]$$

17.4 The Cactus Alkaloids

Some of the most interesting of the simpler alkaloids derived from tyrosine are found in various cactus species. The well-known hallucinogenic base mescaline (Eq. 17-3) occurs in "peyote" (*Lophophora williamsii* (Lem.) Coult, fam. Cactaceae) and in a number of other species. Since tyrosine and tyramine have been firmly established as precursors of mescaline, it will be evident that the only remaining question concerning its biosynthesis is that of the order in which the subsequent methylation and hydroxylation steps take place. The number of possibilities is reduced by the observation that both dopamine and 3,4,5-trihydroxyphenylethyl-amine are well incorporated into mescaline and that 5-hydroxy-3,4-dimethoxy-phenylethylamine has been detected in "peyote." The pathway shown in Eq. 17-3 is therefore indicated.

$$\text{HO}-\text{C}_6\text{H}_4-\text{CH}_2\text{CH(NH}_2)\text{COOH} \xrightarrow{-CO_2} \text{HO}-\text{C}_6\text{H}_4-\text{CH}_2\overset{\bullet}{\text{C}}\text{H}_2\text{NH}_2 \xrightarrow{[O]}$$
$$\text{tyramine}$$

$$(\text{HO})_2\text{C}_6\text{H}_3-\text{CH}_2\overset{*}{\text{C}}\text{H}_2\text{NH}_2 \xrightarrow{[O]} (\text{HO})_2\text{C}_6\text{H}_2(\text{OH})-\text{CH}_2\overset{o}{\text{C}}\text{H}_2\text{NH}_2 \xrightarrow{\text{methylation}}$$
$$\text{dopamine}$$

$$(\text{CH}_3\text{O})_2\text{C}_6\text{H}_2(\text{OH})-\text{CH}_2\text{CH}_2\text{NH}_2 \xrightarrow{+C_1} (\text{CH}_3\text{O})_2\text{C}_6\text{H}_2(\text{OCH}_3)-\text{CH}_2\overset{\bullet*o}{\text{C}}\text{H}_2\text{NH}_2 \qquad [\text{Eq. 17-3}]$$
$$\text{mescaline}$$

$\bullet * o \ ^{14}$C label. The indicated labeling pattern in mescaline relates to separate feeding experiments with *Lophophora williamsii* in which each of the marked intermediate compounds were used.

However, the discovery of 3-methoxy-4-hydroxy- and 4-hydroxy-3,5-dimethoxyphenylethylamine in *Trichocereus pachanoi* Britton and Rose, another mescaline-producing species, reveals a possible alternative pathway (Eq. 17-4):

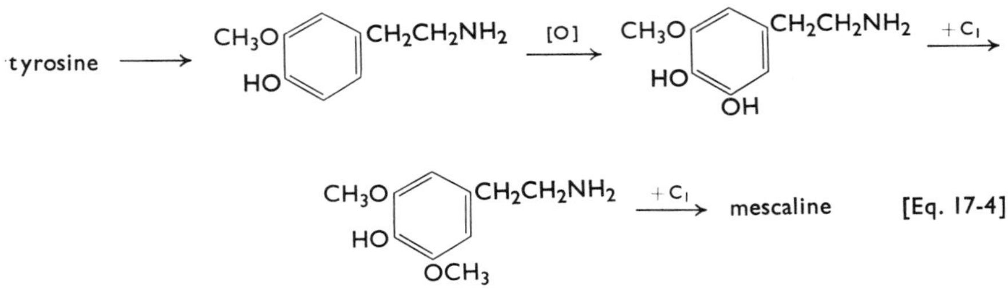

$$\text{tyrosine} \longrightarrow \quad \begin{array}{c}CH_3O\\HO\end{array}\!\!\!\!\text{—}CH_2CH_2NH_2 \quad \xrightarrow{[O]} \quad \begin{array}{c}CH_3O\\HO\\\;\;OH\end{array}\!\!\!\!\text{—}CH_2CH_2NH_2 \quad \xrightarrow{+C_1}$$

$$\begin{array}{c}CH_3O\\HO\\\;\;OCH_3\end{array}\!\!\!\!\text{—}CH_2CH_2NH_2 \quad \xrightarrow{+C_1} \quad \text{mescaline} \qquad \text{[Eq. 17-4]}$$

It would appear that the Cactaceae are rather versatile with respect to the methylation of phenolic substrates and that more than one pathway to mescaline may exist, even within a single species.

The next stage of elaboration in the cactus alkaloids is illustrated by the structures of anhalamine, anhalidine, anhalonidine, and pellotine (Fig. 17-1), in which ring-closure to a tetrahydroisoquinoline system has taken place.

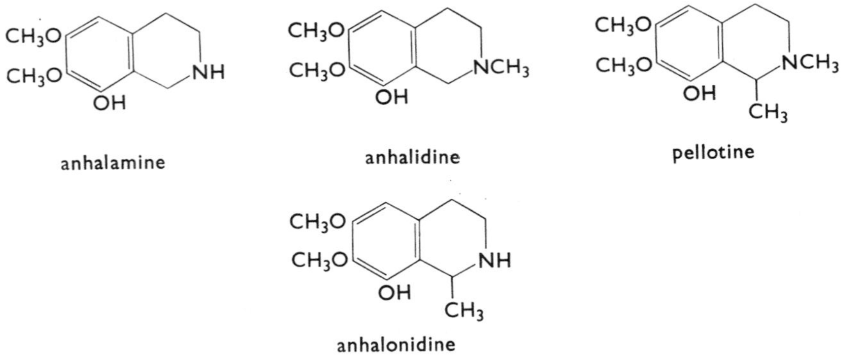

anhalamine

anhalidine

pellotine

anhalonidine

Fig. 17-1.

The manner in which the "berberine bridge" is constructed (Chap. 15), suggests that anhalamine may be formed by a similar oxidative ring closure of an N-methylphenylethylamine precursor, as follows (Eq. 17-5):

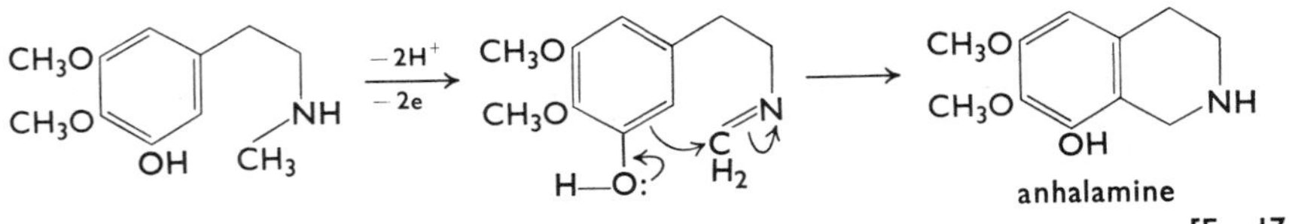

$$\xrightarrow[-2e]{-2H^+} \qquad \longrightarrow \qquad \text{anhalamine}$$

[Eq. 17-5]

An experiment which has been carried out to test this proposal gave the results indicated in Eq. 17-6.

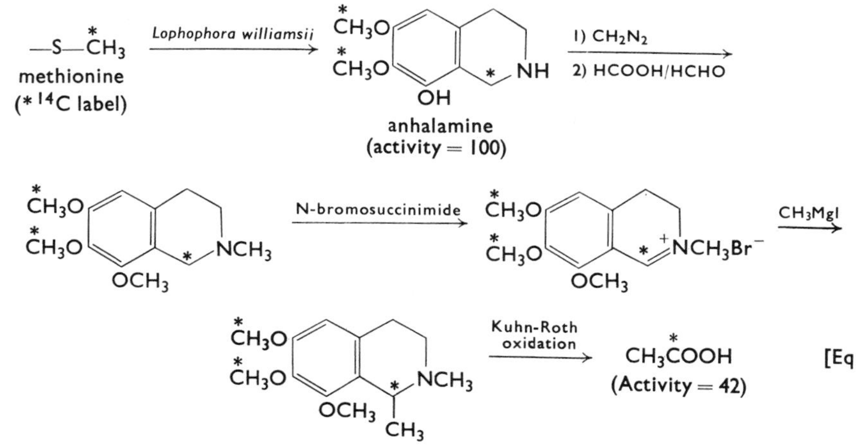

—S—CH3
methionine
(* 14C label)
Lophophora williamsii
CH3O
CH3O
NH
OH
anhalamine
(activity = 100)
1) CH2N2
2) HCOOH/HCHO
NCH3
OCH3
N-bromosuccinimide
NCH3Br−
CH3MgI
CH3
Kuhn-Roth
oxidation
CH3COOH
(Activity = 42)

[Eq. 17-6]

(The methyl groups in anhalamine contained 53 per cent of the total activity in this experiment.)

It will be noted that the methyl group of methionine provided C-1 in anhalamine with an efficiency comparable to that with which the O-methyl groups were furnished. The oxidative cyclization pathway shown in Eq. 17-5 is therefore strongly supported by the experimental results.

The laboratory synthesis of salsolin, described on page 433, has been suggested as a model for the probable biosynthetic pathway leading to the 1-methyltetrahydroisoquinoline alkaloids. As applied to pellotine biosynthesis the following sequence is indicated (Eq. 17-7):

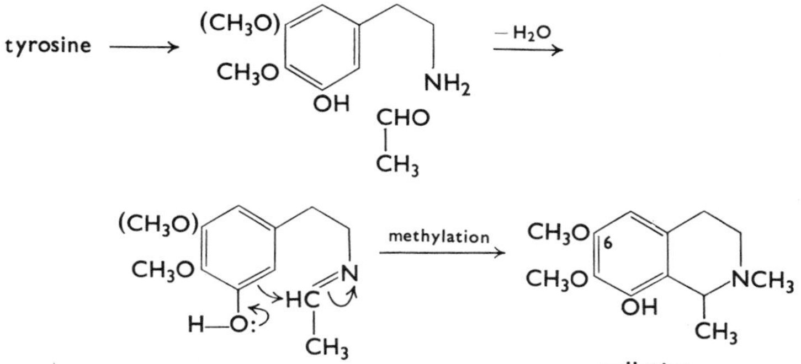

tyrosine
(CH3O)
CH3O
OH
NH2
CHO
CH3
−H2O
N
HC
H—O:
methylation
6
NCH3

pellotine

[Eq. 17-7]

(n.b. In nature, the process shown in this equation and elsewhere as nucleophilic addition to the C=N group, would probably be assisted by protonation of the nitrogen (cf. section 16-3).)

It is to be noted that the precise point at which the C-6-hydroxylation and methylation steps occur is not yet known. It is possible that some of these processes may take place after the formation of the heterocyclic ring.

By analogy with the pathways leading to harmine (see below) and to the benzylisoquinoline alkaloids (Chap. 18), it is probable that in nature, the cyclization step involves pyruvate rather than acetaldehyde, as indicated in Eq. 17-8.

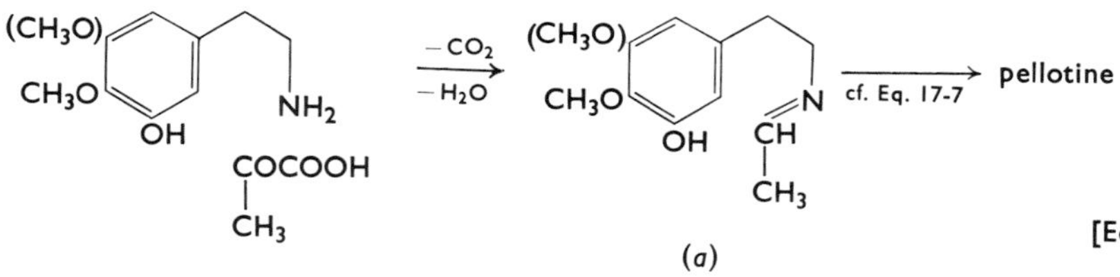

(a)   [Eq. 17-8]

In the light of the foregoing discussion, the main problem associated with the formation of lophocereine (from *Lophocereus schottii* Britton and Rose) will be seen to lie in the origin of the five-carbon unit comprising C-1 and the isobutyl substituent (Eq. 17-10). By analogy with the pathway suggested for pellotine (Eq. 17-8), a probable precursor would be 4-methyl-2-oxopentanoic acid, which could readily arise from leucine by way of transamination (Eq. 17-9).

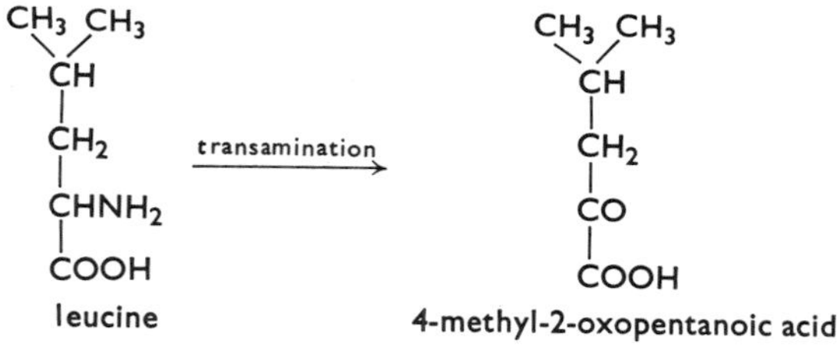

[Eq. 17-9]

On the other hand, structural considerations suggest that mevalonic acid should also be considered as a possible precursor.

When we turn to the information available from incorporation experiments, we find that in fact *both* of these precursors are reported to be incorporated into lophocereine, with comparable efficiencies (Eq. 17-10).

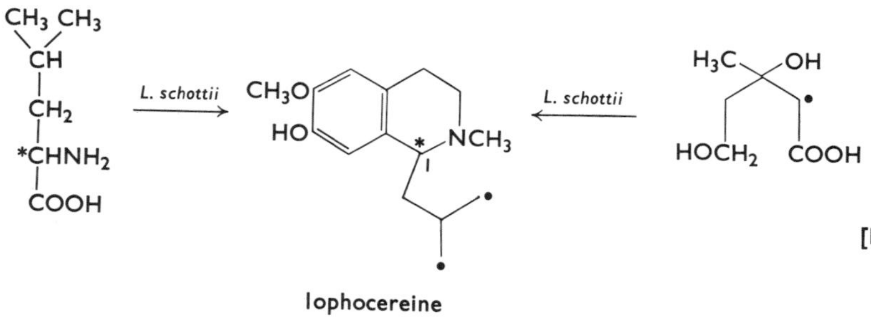

[Eq. 17-10]

lophocereine

These results recall the early investigations into steroid biosynthesis, before the discovery of mevalonic acid. In a search for the "active isoprene" intermediate, a number of compounds were tested as steroid precursors, and it was during these investigations that leucine was found to be incorporated into cholesterol to a small but significant extent. Subsequent investigations showed that leucine undergoes a sequence of transformations culminating in the formation of the coenzyme A ester of β-hydroxy-β-methylglutaric acid (Eq. 17-11), which, it will be recalled, is an intermediate in the biosynthesis of mevalonic acid (Chap. 8). Thus we have a possible explanation for the incorporation of both leucine and mevalonate into lophocereine.

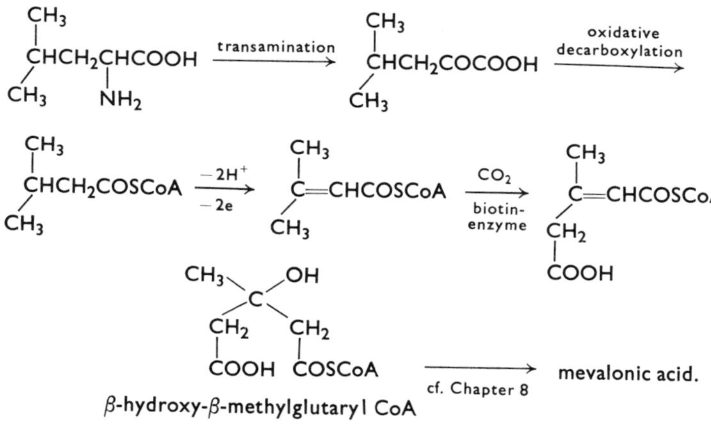

β-hydroxy-β-methylglutaryl CoA   cf. Chapter 8   mevalonic acid.   [Eq. 17-11]

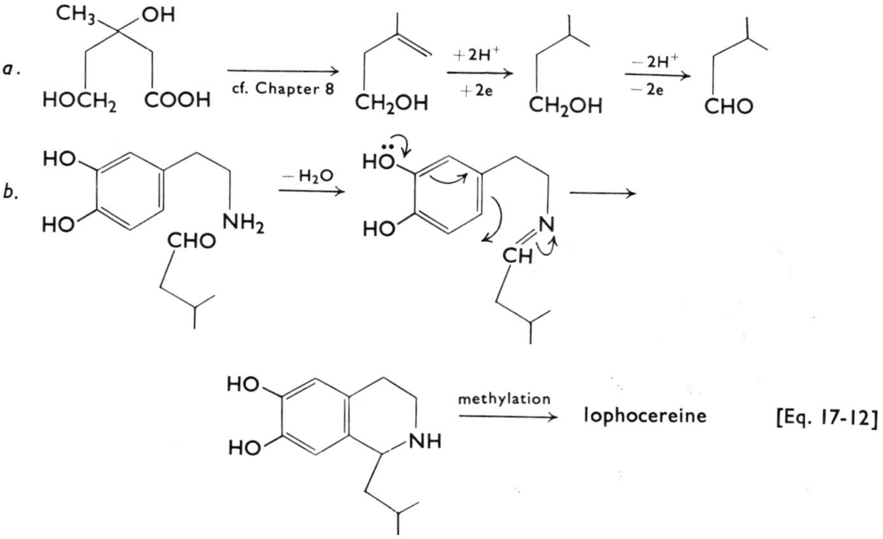

a.

b.

methylation ⟶ lophocereine   [Eq. 17-12]

It is not possible to be definitive about the precise way in which mevalonate participates in lophocereine biosynthesis. An imino-intermediate of the type Eq. 17-8*a* is probable by analogy with similar pathways, but this could arise from mevalonate by various routes other than the single alternative illustrated below (Eq. 17-12).

The formation of the unique trimeric alkaloid pilocereine, a congener of lophocereine, is discussed in Chapter 18.

Alkaloids Derived from Tryptophan

Some simple derivatives of tryptamine, the decarboxylation product of tryptophan, were mentioned in Chapter 14. In nature, a number of related bases are formed by pathways involving hydroxylation at C-5 in the indole nucleus (Fig. 17-2).

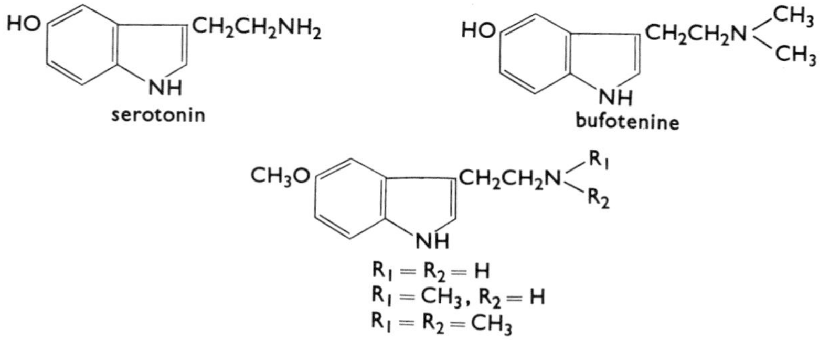

Fig. 17-2. Some Simple Alkaloids formed from Tryptophan by Pathways Involving Hydroxylation at C-5.

Hydroxylation at C-4 is observed in psilocin and psilocybin, which occur in species of the hallucinogenic mushroom *Psilocybe*. Incorporation experiments have established that psilocin is the precursor of psilocybin and that both compounds stem from tryptophan, probably *via* N-dimethyltryptamine (Eq. 17-13).

A further indole derivative, gramine (Fig. 17-3), is found in germinating barley (*Hordeum vulgare*) and in certain species of *Acer* (sycamore, fam. Aceraceae). It evidently arises by the side-chain degradation of tryptophan, but the precise manner in which this occurs is not known.

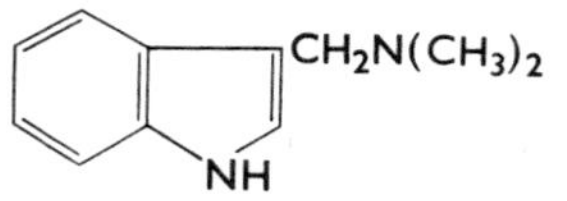

gramine

Fig. 17-3.

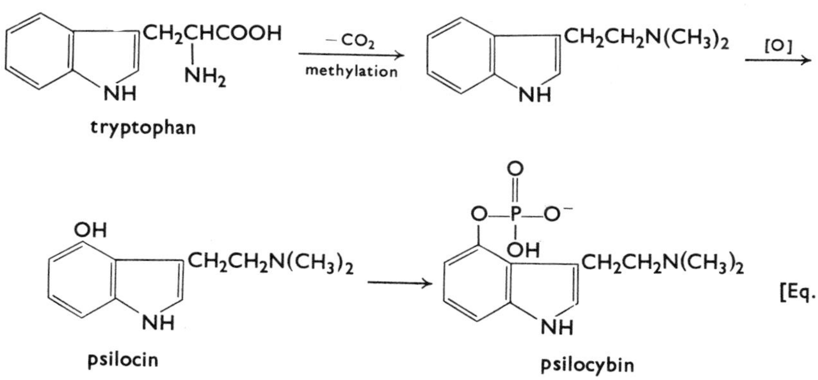

[Eq. 17-13]

17.5 β-Carboline Alkaloids

Alkaloids based on the tetrahydro-β-carboline system, although not common, occur sporadically in a number of plant families. The typical representatives harmine, harmaline, and harmalol co-occur in *Peganum harmala* L. (fam. Zygophyllaceae) (Fig. 17-4).

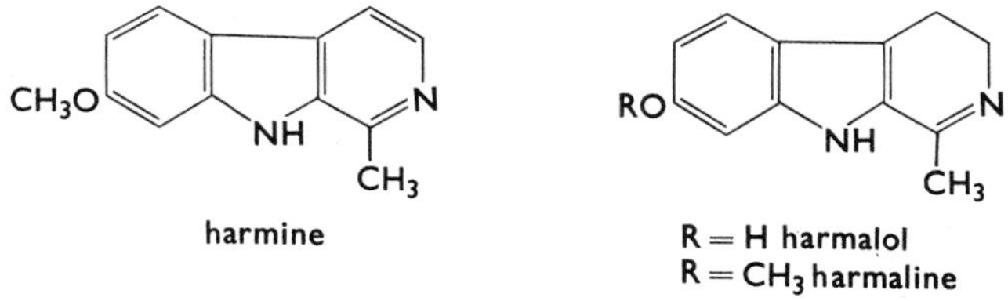

R = H harmalol
R = CH₃ harmaline

Fig. 17-4.

In order to account for the formation of harmine, it is only necessary to recall that positions C-2 and C-3 in indole are possible points of nucleophilic attack in Mannich-type condensations. With this information at hand, the observed specific incorporations of tryptophan, tryptamine, and pyruvate into harmine in *Peganum harmala*, are readily rationalized in terms of the following pathway (Eq. 17-14). It will be noted that the nucleophilic character of the indole ring in this reaction resembles that of the aromatic ring in Eq. 17-7.

It is to be noted that the introduction of the methoxyl function at the end of this sequence is an arbitrary suggestion, since there is no available information as to the precise point at which the requisite hydroxylation and methylation steps take place.

The nucleophilic potential at C-2 and C-3 in the indole nucleus (cf. tryptamine, Eq. 17-14) will be seen to be of prime importance in the biosynthesis of the complex indole alkaloids to be discussed in Chapter 19.

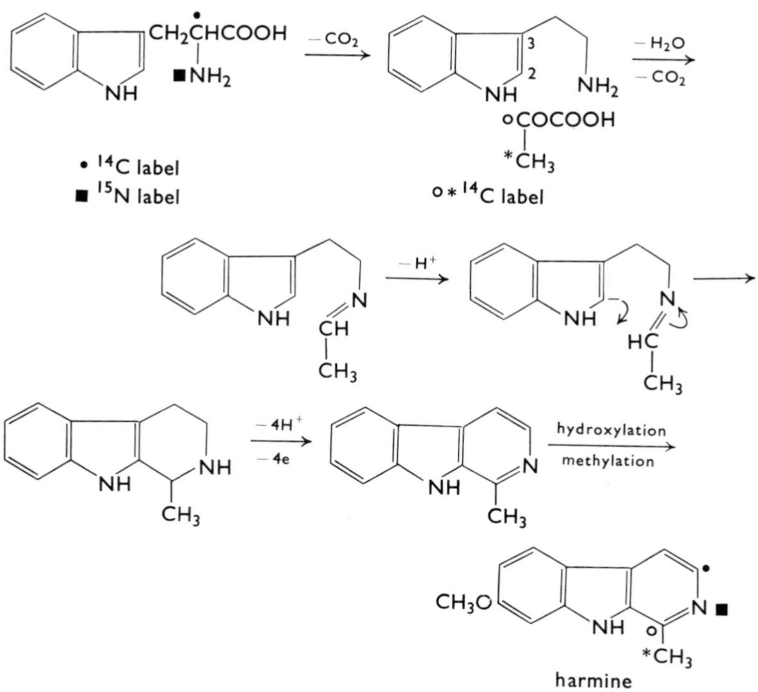

474

CHAPTER 17—

• ^{14}C label
■ ^{15}N label

o * ^{14}C label

[Eq. 17-14]

harmine

(Feeding experiments in *Peganum harmala*, with tryptophan and pyruvic acid, labeled as shown, gave harmine with the labeling pattern indicated.)

17.6 Alkaloids of Physostigma venesosum

The calabar bean (the seed of *Physostigma venesosum* Balf. fam. Leguminosae) is so-called because it was formerly used as an ordeal drug in Old Calabar, on the coast of Eastern Nigeria. The bases found in the calabar bean (Fig. 17-5), contain a novel heterocyclic system encountered only in this group and in certain of the *Calycanthus* alkaloids to be described in the following section.

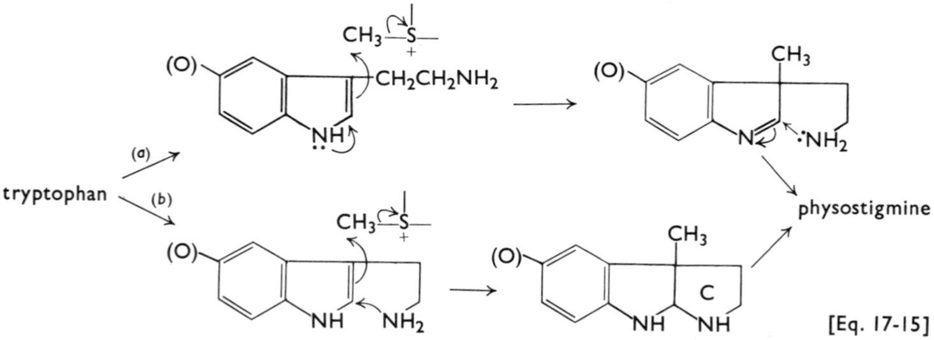

tryptophan

physostigmine

[Eq. 17-15]

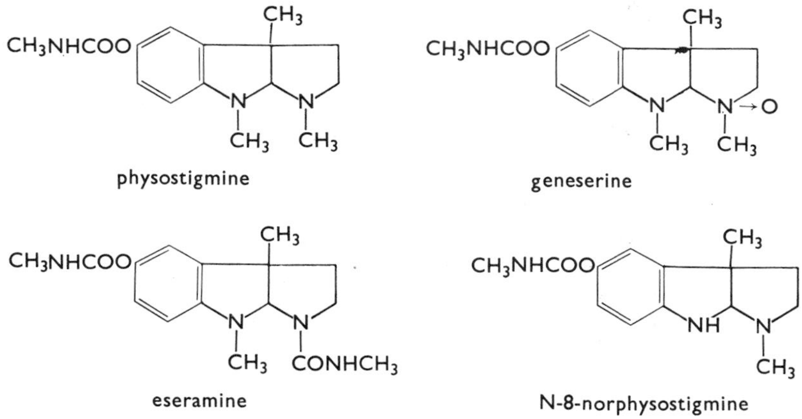

physostigmine

geneserine

eseramine

N-8-norphysostigmine

Fig. 17-5.

Although experimental evidence is lacking, it would appear probable that in the formation of the basic structure of physostigmine, the nucleophilic character at C-3 in tryptamine (or its 5-hydroxy derivative) is utilized in an attack on the methyl function of S-adenosylmethionine. Introduction of the angular methyl group in this way could be followed by (Eq. 17-15a), or concerted with (Eq. 17-15b), closure of ring C as shown.

The origin of the methylcarbamate substituent is not known at present.

17.7   The Calycanthus Alkaloids

The Calycanthaceae, one of the smallest of all plant families, comprise only two genera (*Calycanthus* and *Chimonanthus*) and nine species; they produce several alkaloids of a novel and interesting kind.

The two structural varieties encountered are postulated to arise through the dimerization of a β-indolenine radical, formed by the one-electron oxidation of N-methyltryptamine (Eq. 17-16). The immediate product of the dimerization step undergoes a double cyclization to give chimonanthine and then, by stepwise methylation, calycanthidine and folicanthine. Hydrolysis of the dimerization product (Eq. 17-16a) leads to calycanthine by a Mannich-type ring closure in which the alkylamino function takes the role of the usual carbanion species.

The laboratory synthesis of chimonanthine illustrated in Eq. 17-17 provides a good analogy for the proposed pathway. It should be remarked, however, that this reaction can be formulated equally satisfactorily by postulating a two-electron oxidation of one of the participants in the "dimerization."

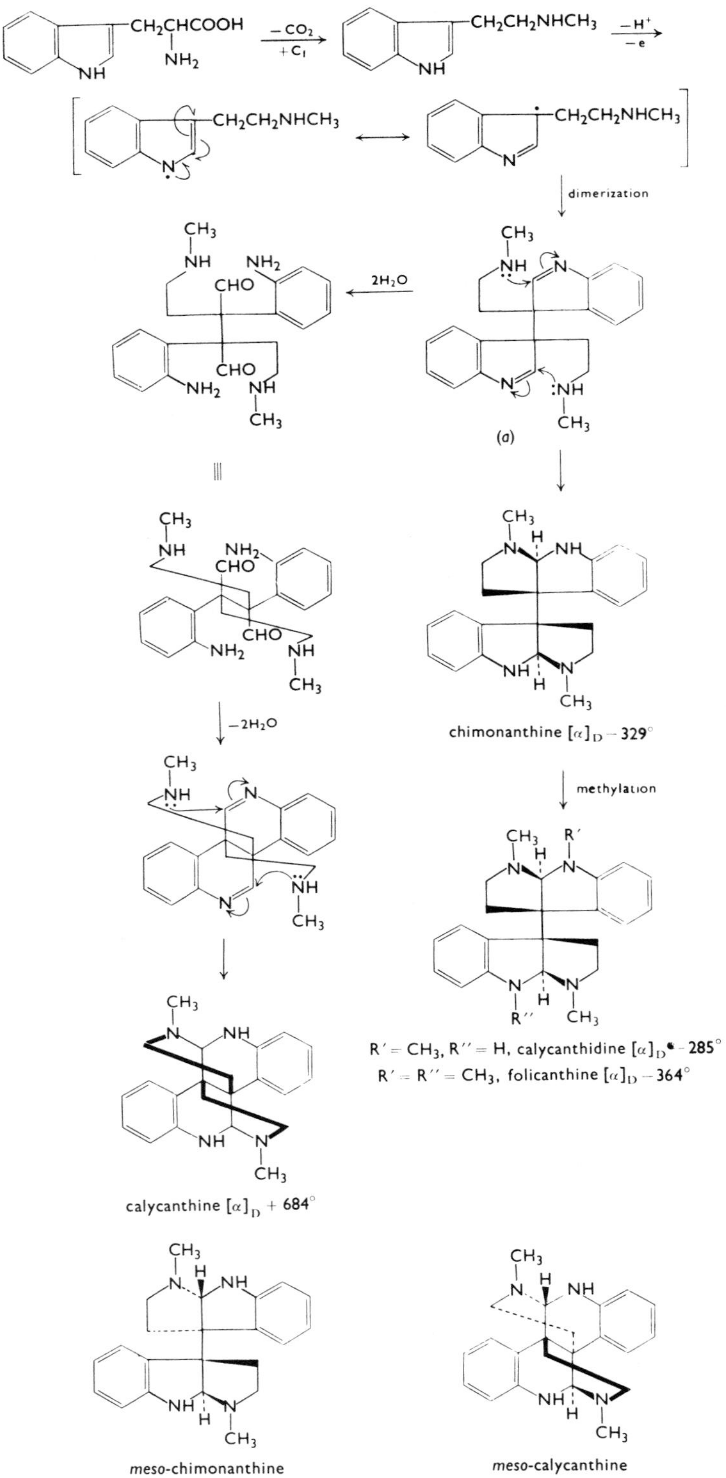
CH2CHCOOH
NH2
NH
− CO2
+ C1
CH2CH2NHCH3
− H+
− e
dimerization
2H2O
CHO
(a)
− 2H2O
methylation
chimonanthine [α]D − 329°
R′ = CH3, R″ = H, calycanthidine [α]D − 285°
R′ = R″ = CH3, folicanthine [α]D − 364°
calycanthine [α]D + 684°
meso-chimonanthine
meso-calycanthine

[Eq. 17-16]

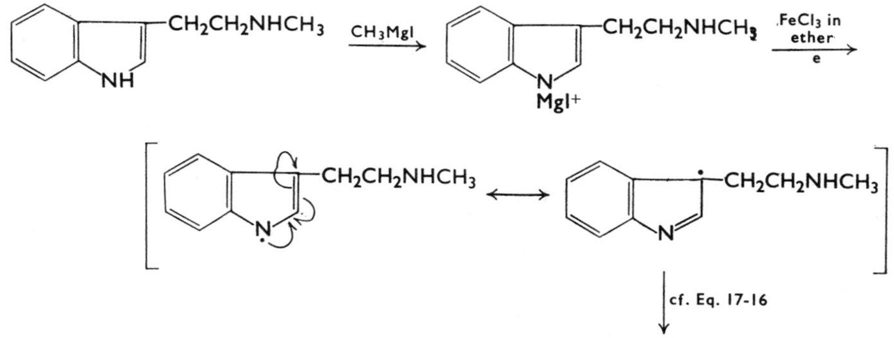

$$(\pm)\text{-chimonanthine}$$

$$+$$

meso-chimonanthine   [Eq. 17-17]
(minor product)

folicanthine

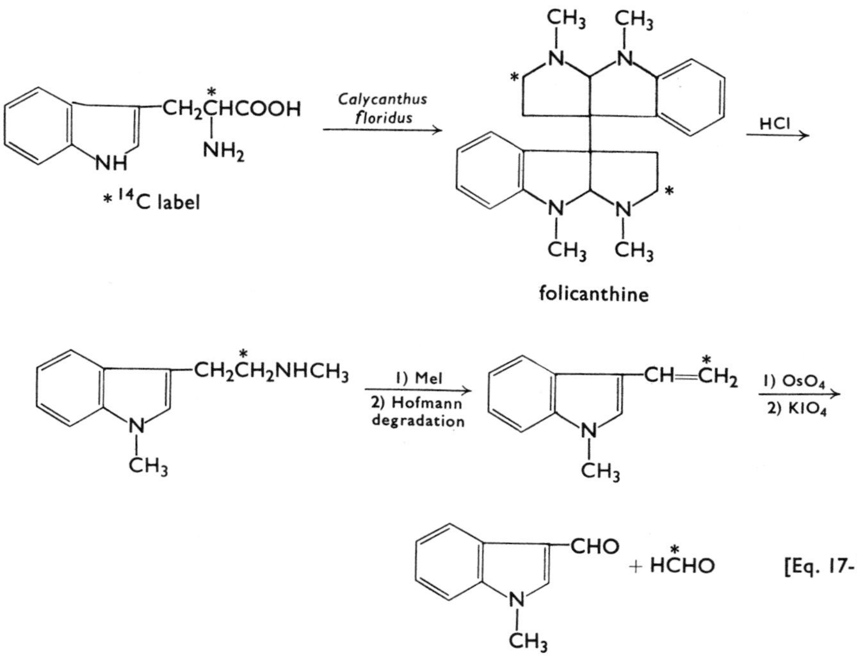

[Eq. 17-18]

It will be noted that these alkaloids are shown with the ($\pm$) rather than the *meso* configuration (Eq. 17-16). (The absolute configurations are not yet known.) The *meso* configuration is ruled out by the marked optical activity of all four bases. Calycanthine is strongly dextrarotatory whereas alkaloids of the chimonanthine group all have strongly negative rotations (Eq. 17-16).

Incorporation experiments have demonstrated the expected specific incorporation of tryptophan into the *Calycanthus* alkaloids. 2-^{14}C-tryptophan, when fed to *Calycanthus floridus* L., for example, gave folicanthine, which was degraded as shown in Eq. 17-18. The activity of the formaldehyde finally obtained showed conclusively that the label in the original folicanthine was located at the expected positions.

Alkaloids Derived from Anthranilic Acid

17.8 Damascenine

Damascenine is the simplest representative of a group of alkaloids derived from anthranilic acid. It is found in *Nigella damascena* L. (fam. Ranunculaceae) and has been shown to arise from glucose *via* shikimic acid and anthranilic acid (cf. Chap. 5). The exact order of the hydroxylation and methylation steps in this pathway is not known with certainty, but the fact that 3-methoxyanthranilic acid is incorporated without prior degradation, suggests the sequence illustrated in Eq. 17-19.

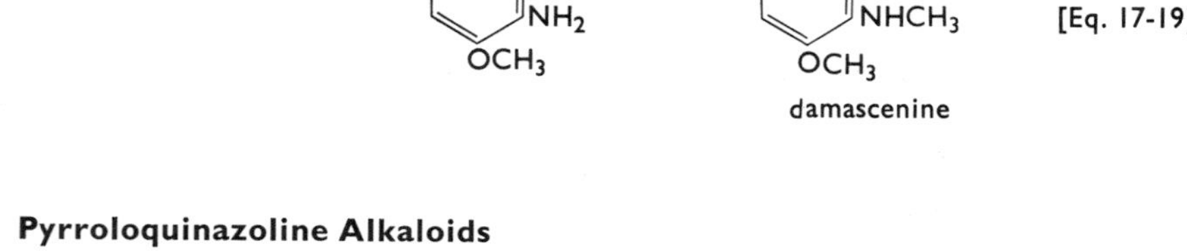

anthranilic acid

[Eq. 17-19]

damascenine

17.9 Pyrroloquinazoline Alkaloids

Quinazoline alkaloids are found in a number of plant families. The pyrroloquinazoline type to be considered here is represented by vasicine, vasicinone, and desoxyvasicinone (Fig. 17-6), which occur together in *Perganum harmala* L. (fam. Zygophyllaceae) together with alkaloids of the harmine group (page 473).

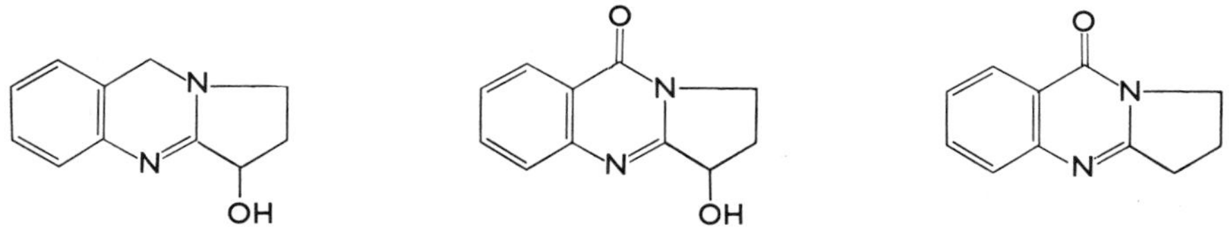

vasicine
(peganine)

vasicinone

desoxyvasicinone

Fig. 17-6.

An early suggestion that vasicine might be formed from anthranilic acid and proline was reinforced by the elegant laboratory synthesis of desoxyvasicine illustrated in Eq. 17-20.

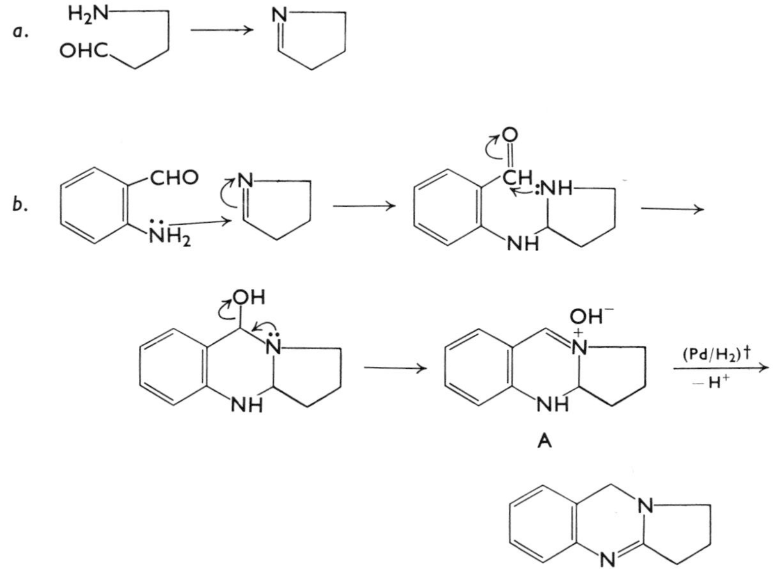

[Eq. 17-20]

desoxyvasicine

(The quaternary hydroxide, A, was obtained by incubating together 4-aminobutanal and 2-aminobenzaldehyde at pH 5.)

† These conditions were used to provide a reducing environment for the rearrangement.

This synthetic pathway can be translated into biological terms as shown in Eq. 17-21.

The overall features of this pathway have been shown to be correct by the demonstration that anthranilic acid, ornithine, and putrescine are precursors of vasicine and its congeners in *Peganum harmala*. Although various pathways from

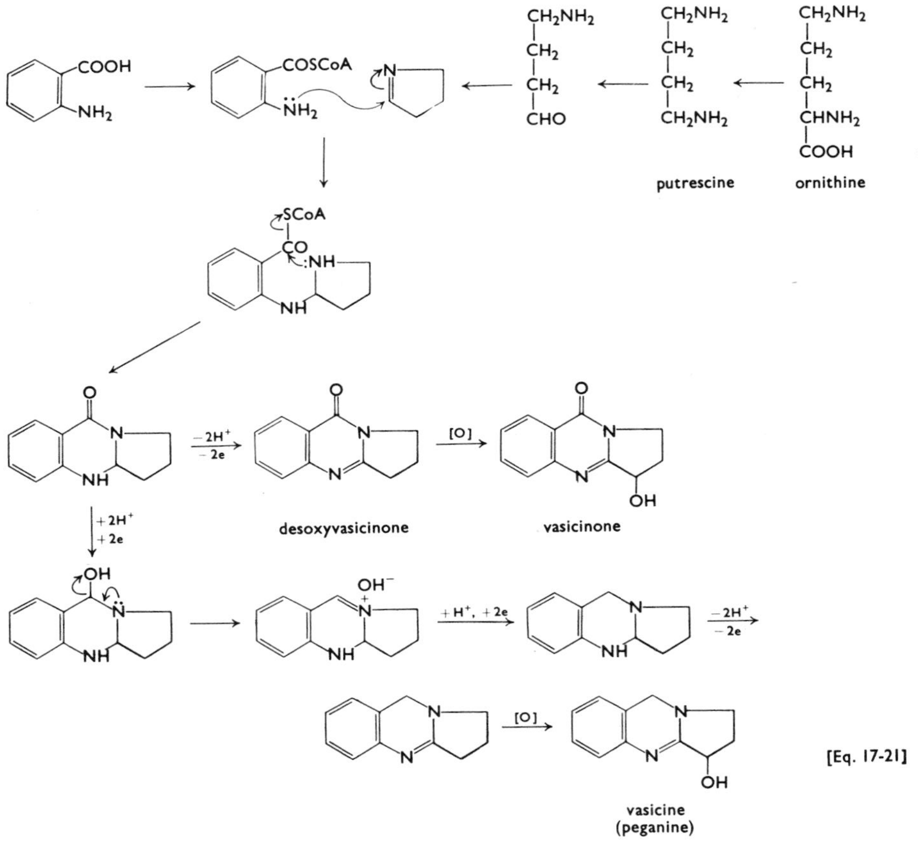

desoxyvasicinone   vasicinone

[Eq. 17-21]

vasicine
(peganine)

these amino acids might be formulated, the sequence suggested in Eq. 17-21 illustrates one way in which the vasicine structure can arise by way of established biological reactions, each of which has ample analogy in pathways previously
discussed.

17.10 Alkaloids of Rutaceae

Alkaloids derived from anthranilic acid undoubtedly occur in the greatest
abundance in plants of the family Rutaceae. The two largest groups encountered
are based respectively on the quinoline and acridine skeletons (Fig. 17-7).

quinoline   acridine

Fig. 17-7.

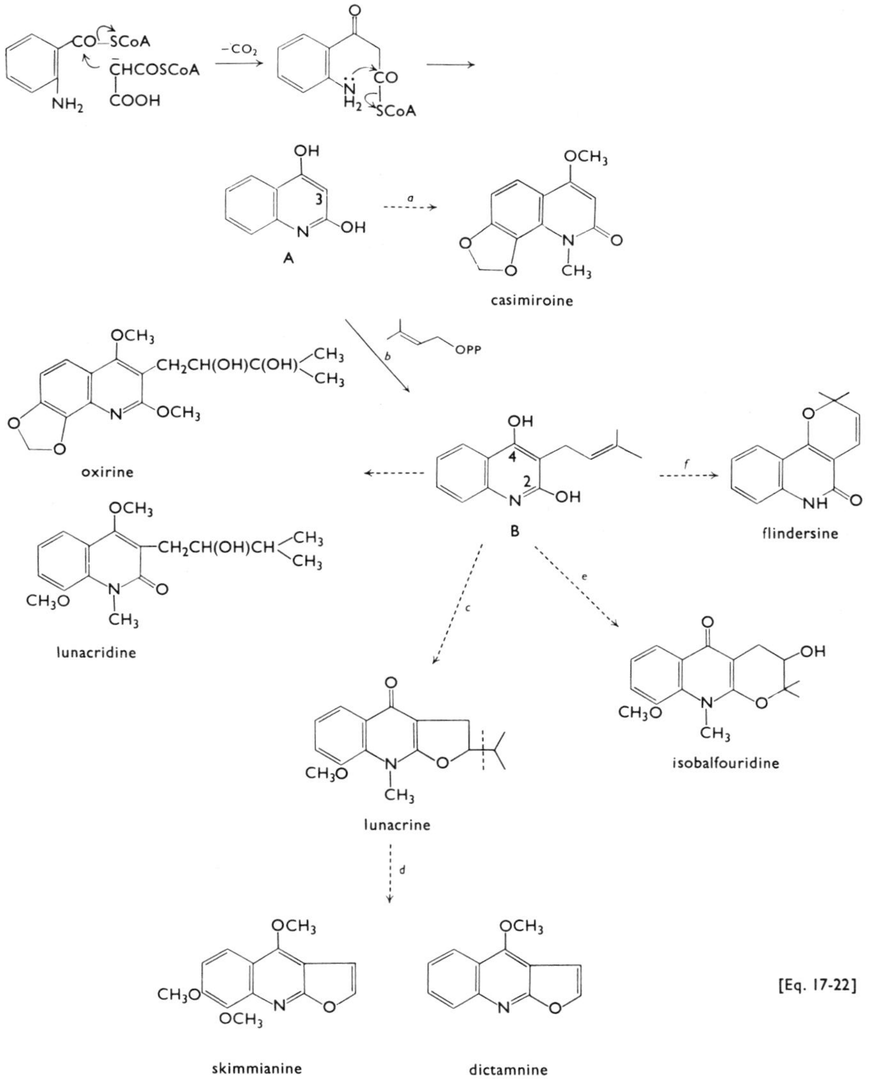

[Eq. 17-22]

skimmianine   dictamnine

(n.b. The dotted arrows indicate the general relationships between the various structures shown and are not intended to represent specific biosynthetic pathways.)

Evidence obtained from a number of incorporation experiments points to a derivation of the heterocyclic framework of the quinoline alkaloids from anthranilic acid and acetic acid. The quinoline system can plausibly be considered to arise by condensation of an anthranilic acid derivative (possibly the coenzyme A ester) with acetyl or malonyl coenzyme A, followed by cyclization (Eq. 17-22). The formation of casimiroine requires only the intervention of the usual processes of hydroxylation, methylation, and methylenedioxy ring closure at appropriate stages in the pathway (Eq. 17-22a).

Position C-3 in the 2,4-dihydroxyquinoline intermediate (Eq. 17-22A) is obviously highly nucleophilic and therefore subject to ready prenylation, as shown in Eq. 17-22b. Alkaloids of the oxirine and lunacridine type evidently arise at this stage of elaboration by hydroxylation of the side chain as shown. Alternatively, ring closure, by addition of the 2-hydroxyl function to the olefinic bond, leads directly to the basic structures of lunacrine and related alkaloids (Eq. 17-22c).

The simple furanoquinolines skimmianine and dictamnine evidently arise by loss of the isopropyl substituent from alkaloids of the lunacrine type (Eq. 17-22d). Although there is at present no experimental evidence to support the postulated cleavage step in these alkaloids, it will be recalled that an exactly corresponding pathway has been demonstrated for the formation of the furan ring in the furanocoumarin series (Chap. 8).

The formation of the pyran ring in isobalfouridine simply requires the addition of the 2-hydroxy substituent in the prenylated intermediate (Eq. 17-22B), to the distal end of the side chain olefinic bond (Eq. 17-22e). The alternative mode of ring closure towards the 4-hydroxy substituent is observed in flindersine (Eq. 17-22f).

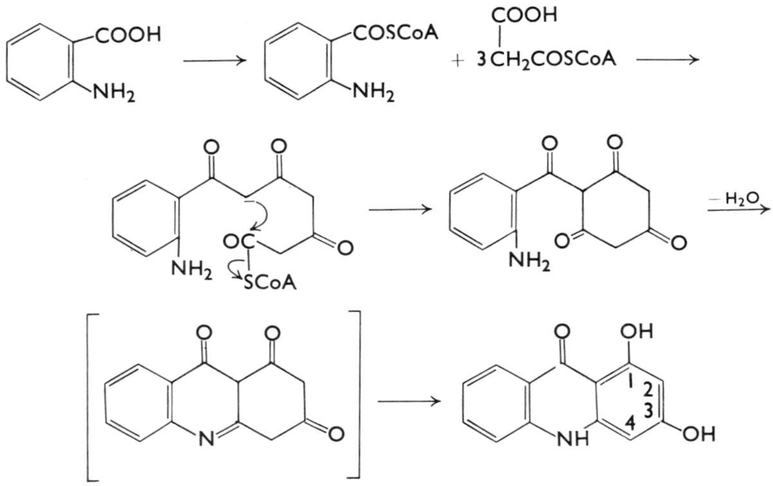

[Eq. 17-23]

Nothing is known about the relative order of the secondary hydroxylation and methylation steps in the formation of the quinoline alkaloids. However, these are simple and familiar processes, which offer no conceptual difficulties.

In order to arrive at the ring structure of the acridine alkaloids, an extension of the carboxyl side chain of anthranilic acid by three acetate units is required (Eq. 17-23). The tricyclic system is then readily obtained by successive ring closure steps, as shown.

Since no experimental results are available to support this pathway, we are forced to rely for our evidence on structural comparisons and biogenetic analogy. One important consequence of the proposed route (Eq. 17-23) is that positions C-1 and C-3 in the acridine nucleus would be expected to carry oxygen substituents with greater frequency than positions C-2 and C-4. Although positions C-1 and C-3 are almost invariably oxygenated, this line of argument is weakened by the observation that most of the known alkaloids also have a substituent at C-2 and nearly half have a substituent at C-4 (Fig. 17-8). The value of a statistical analysis of the substitution pattern is therefore greatly diminished. However, if we look to the

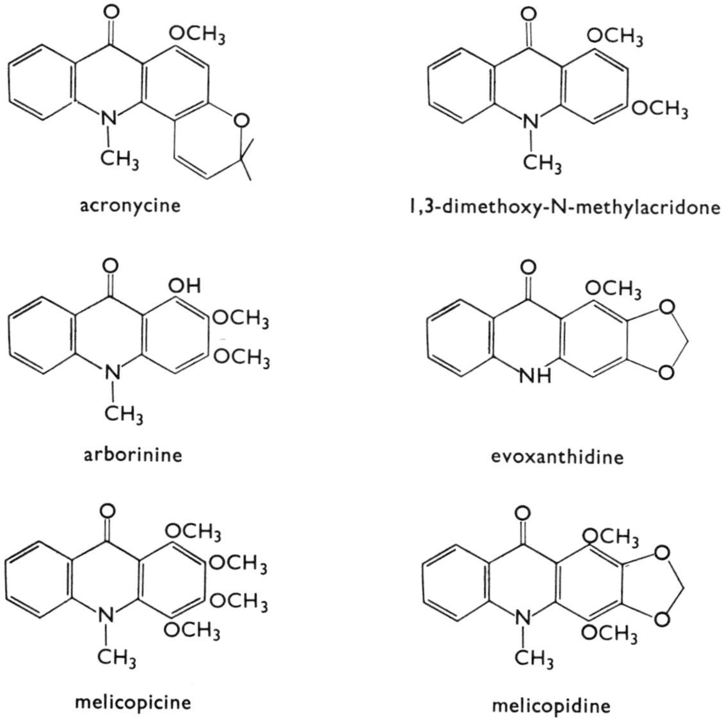

acronycine

1,3-dimethoxy-N-methylacridone

arborinine

evoxanthidine

melicopicine

melicopidine

Fig. 17-8. Some Typical Acridine (Acridone) Alkaloids of the Rutaceae.

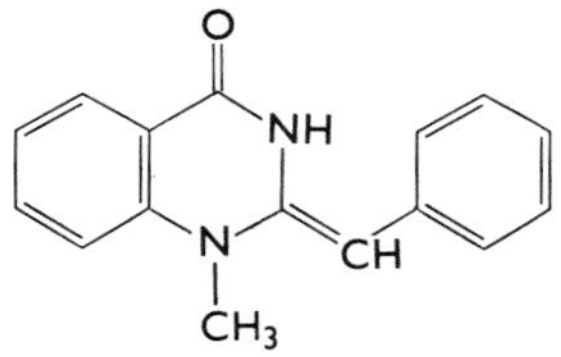

arborine

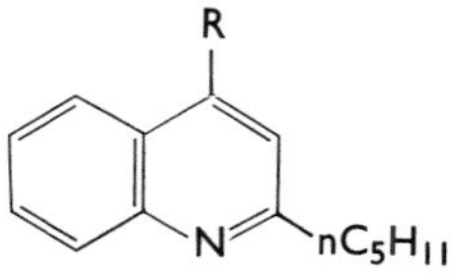

R = H, OCH₃
(From *Galipea officinalis* Hancock)

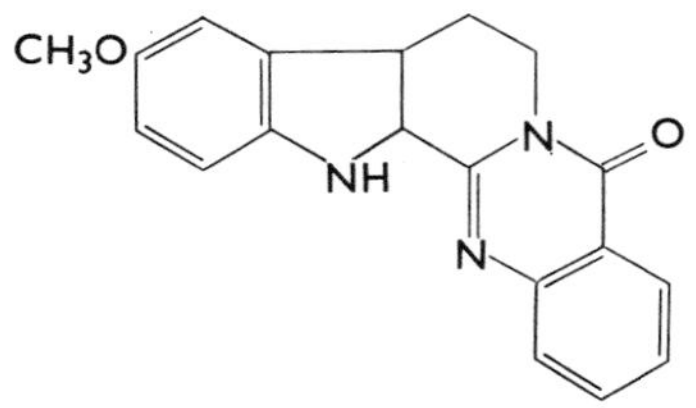

hortiacine

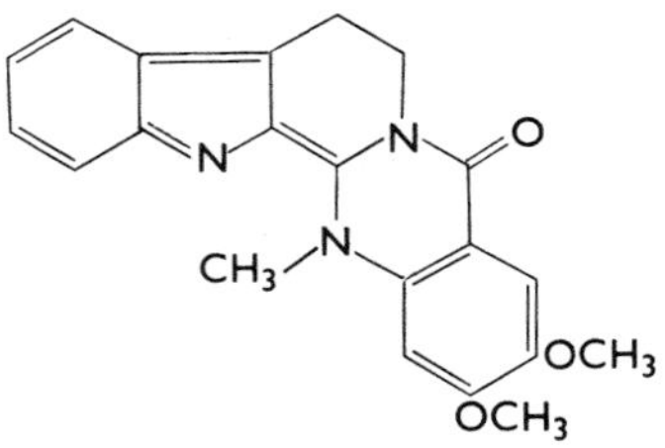

euxylophorine

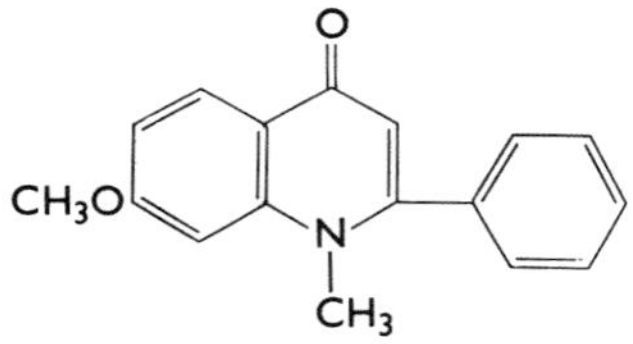

eduleine

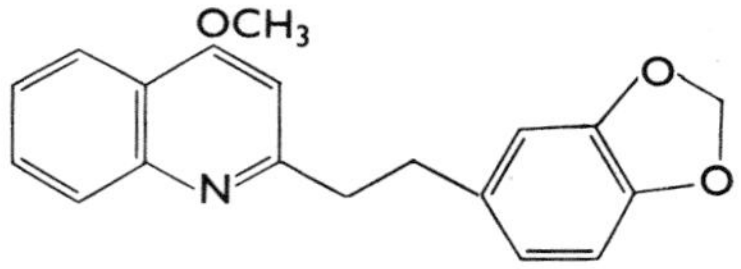

cusparine

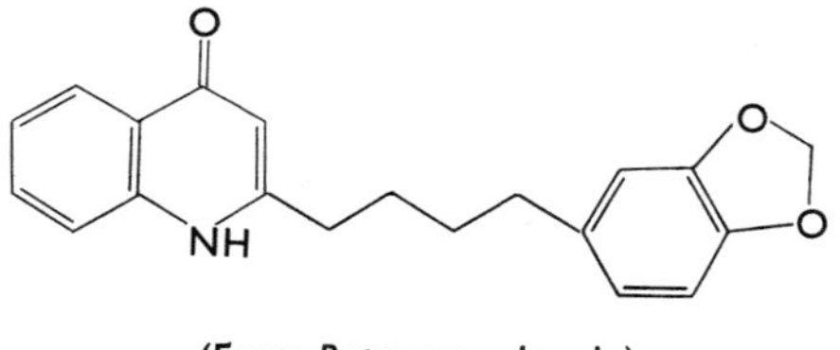

(From *Ruta graveolens* L.)

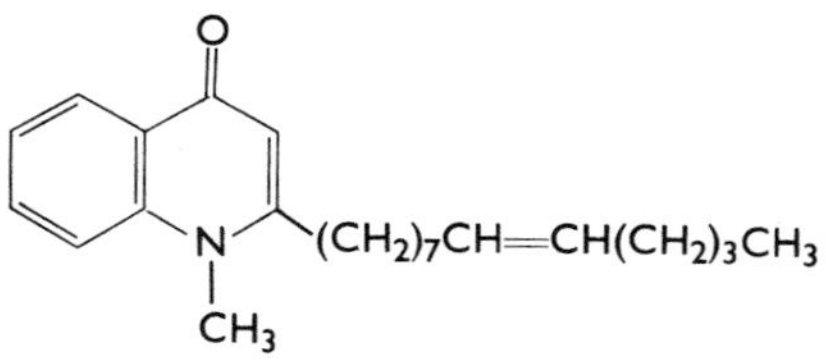

evocarpine

Fig. 17-9. Miscellaneous Alkaloids from the Rutaceae Containing Anthranilic Acid Residues.

simpler representatives, acronycine, and 1,3-dimethoxy-N-methylacridone (Fig. 17-8), whose structures are likely to be more informative under these circumstances, we do indeed observe the expected oxygenation pattern.

An anthranilic acid residue can be seen by inspection to be present in various other alkaloids produced by Rutaceae (Fig. 17-9). Certain of these also contain structural elements derived from other amino acids, such as phenylalanine (arborine), and tryptophan (hortiacine, euxylophorine).

17.11 Biosynthesis of the Aromatic Amino Acids

The alkaloids considered in this chapter are related by a common biogenetic ancestry in the aromatic amino acids. These in turn arise out of the synthetic processes of carbohydrate metabolism, specifically by way of the glucose-shikimic acid pathway. The formation of phenylalanine and anthranilic acid was considered in Chapter 5. Tyrosine arises from prephenic acid by a sequence involving oxidation and decarboxylation (Eq. 17-24). The product, p-hydroxyphenylpyruvic acid, is converted into tyrosine by transamination.

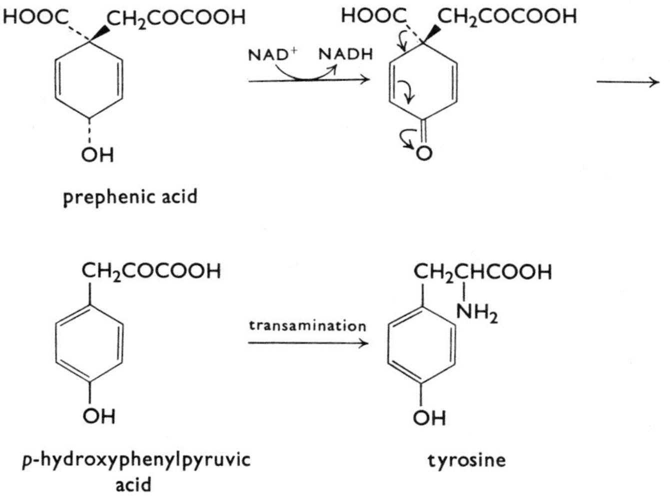

prephenic acid

p-hydroxyphenylpyruvic
acid

tyrosine

[Eq. 17-24]

In bacteria, the biosynthesis of tryptophan follows a rather unexpected course in which anthranilic acid provides the benzene ring of the indole nucleus, ribose the C-2,3 component and serine the alanyl side chain (Eq. 17-25).

The available evidence, although of a rather fragmentary nature, suggests that a similar pathway is followed in higher plants.

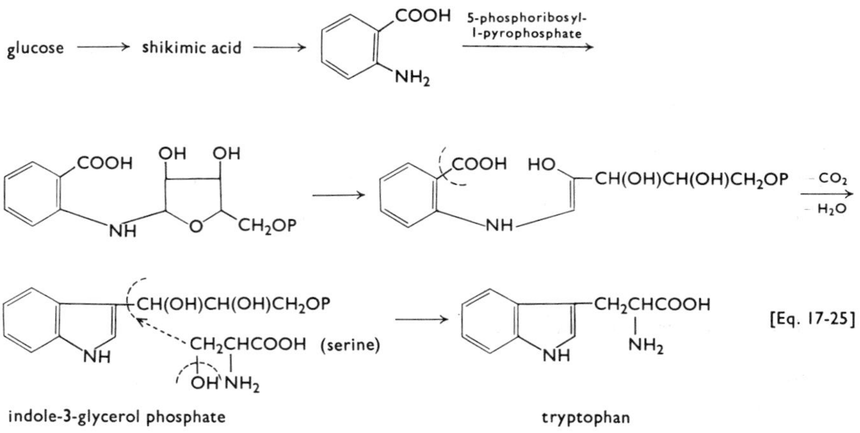
glucose
shikimic acid
COOH
NH2
5-phosphoribosyl-1-pyrophosphate
COOH
OH OH
NH
O
CH2OP
COOH HO
CH(OH)CH(OH)CH2OP
NH
CO2
H2O
CH(OH)CH(OH)CH2OP
NH
CH2CHCOOH (serine)
OH NH2
indole-3-glycerol phosphate
CH2CHCOOH
NH2
NH
tryptophan

[Eq. 17-25]

17.12 Conclusion

Because they do not possess the bifunctional characteristics of the basic amino acids, ornithine and lysine, the aromatic amino acids are relatively circumscribed with respect to biosynthetic processes involving the amino acid side chains. They cannot be elaborated, for example, by condensation reactions of the kind postulated to involve cyclic imines, as in lupin alkaloid biosynthesis (Chap. 16). On the other hand, the potential which exists for the development of phenolic structures provides an alternative avenue of biosynthesis, through the intervention of oxidative coupling processes of the type discussed in Chapter 14. Many plant families take advantage of this synthetic capability and apply it to phenylalanine and tyrosine to produce a variety of complex alkaloid structures, which represent the highest development in the biosynthetic elaboration of these amino acids. The relevant pathways are discussed in detail in the following chapter. Other plant families are able to utilize intermediates of terpenoid origin, together with metabolites derived from tryptophan, in biosynthetic pathways leading to an important group of indole alkaloids. These are described in Chapter 19.

XVIII CHAPTER

REFERENCES FOR FURTHER READING

Much information relating to the chemistry and biosynthesis of the alkaloids discussed in this chapter is contained in the references listed at the beginning of Chapter 16.

1. A. R. Battersby, *Phenol Oxidations in the Alkaloid Field,* in Oxidative Coupling of Phenols, W. I. Taylor, and A. R. Battersby, Eds., Edward Arnold Ltd., London; Marcel Dekker Inc., New York, (1967), 119.
2. K. L. Stuart and M. P. Cava, *The Proaporphine Alkaloids,* Chem. Revs., 6, (1968), 321.
3. D. H. R. Barton, *Some Studies in the Biogenesis of Plant Products,* Pure Appl. Chem., 9, (1964), 35.
4. D. H. R. Barton, R. James, G. W. Kirby, D. W. Turner, and D. A. Widdowson, *Phenol Oxidation and Biosynthesis. Part XVIII. The Structure and Biosynthesis of Erythrina Alkaloids,* J. Chem. Soc. (C), (1968), 1529.
5. E. Leete and Sister John Brendan Murrill, *Biosynthesis of the Alkaloids of Chelidonium Majus-II. The Formation of Chelidonine from Stylopine,* Phytochemistry, 6, (1967), 231.
6. A. R. Battersby, M. Hirst, D. J. McCaldin, R. Southgate, and J. Staunton, *Alkaloid Biosynthesis. Part XII. The Biosynthesis of Narcotine,* J. Chem. Soc. (C), (1968), 2163.
7. A. R. Battersby, *Biosynthesis of the Indole and Colchicum Alkaloids,* Pure Appl. Chem., 14, (1967), 117.

CHAPTER XVIII

Oxidative Phenol Coupling in Alkaloid Biosynthesis

18.1 Introduction

In few areas of biosynthetic enquiry has the organic chemist had such success as in the unraveling of the pathways leading to a large and varied group of alkaloids derived from the simple 1-benzylisoquinoline system (Fig. 18-1). These alkaloids

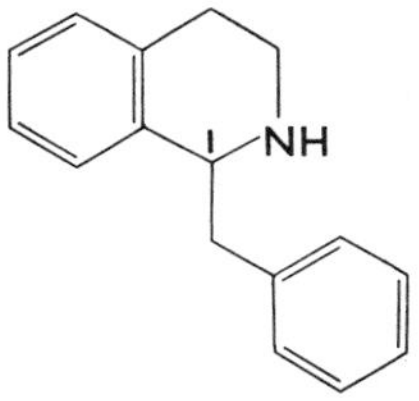

Fig. 18-1.

are related, not only in their biogenetic origins but also by the participation in their formation of oxidative phenol coupling processes of the kind discussed in Chapter 14.

The interlocking evidence from biosynthetic investigations and the laboratory study of model reactions has provided the basis for the elucidation of the inter-relationships of many important alkaloid structures in this series. For certain path-ways the combined evidence is so compelling that investigators have been able to predict with considerable accuracy the existence and properties of postulated intermediates, just as Mendeleef was able to predict the existence and properties of unknown elements from the gaps in his periodic table. These intermediates have sometimes been discovered by chance, but have also come to light on occasion as the result of a deliberate search.

A discussion of the formation of the benzylisoquinoline alkaloids can be conveniently separated into two parts. First, we may consider the biosynthesis of the benzylisoquinoline system itself, and second, we may follow the progress of this basic structure through many secondary changes, the most significant of which involve the oxidative coupling processes mentioned above.

18.2 Biosynthesis of the Simple Benzylisoquinoline Alkaloids

Simple benzylisoquinoline alkaloids* have a very wide distribution; their taxonomic limits can be delineated only in the broad terms that the families in which they appear are confined to the sub-classes Rosidae and Magnoliidae (Table 18-1).

Table 18-1. THE DISTRIBUTION OF BENZYLISOQUINOLINE ALKALOIDS BY FAMILIES

Annonaceae*, Berberidaceae*, Combretaceae*, Hernandiaceae*, Lauraceae*, Magnoliaceae*, Menispermaceae*, Monimiaceae*, Nymphaeaceae*, Papaveraceae, Ranunculaceae*, Rhamnaceae, Rutaceae.

---

  * Families in which bisbenzylisoquinoline alkaloids have also been found (cf. page 521).

The biosynthesis of the simple benzylisoquinoline system is conveniently illustrated by reference to papaverine, one of the chief alkaloidal constituents of the opium poppy, *Papaver somniferum* L. (fam. Papaveraceae). It was one of the most venerable postulates of biogenetic theory as propounded by Winterstein and Trier in 1910, that this structure could arise by condensation of 3,4-dihydroxyphenylethylamine with 3,4-dihydroxyphenylacetaldehyde as shown in Eq. 18-1.

If we disregard for the moment the O-methyl groups and consider the formation of the primary condensation product, norlaudanosoline, we see that this can readily arise from tyrosine by a pathway involving well-established reactions (Eq. 18-2).

Support for this pathway has been found in incorporation experiments in the opium poppy. 2-^{14}C-tyrosine gave labeled papaverine which was degraded by the method shown in Eq. 18-3. The radioactivity was located equally, and almost exclusively, at the predicted positions.

  * It will be noted that most of the alkaloids described in this section are at the oxidation level of tetrahydrobenzylisoquinoline. However, as the oxidation state is of secondary importance to the present discussion, the term "benzylisoquinoline" will be taken to include all members of this group.

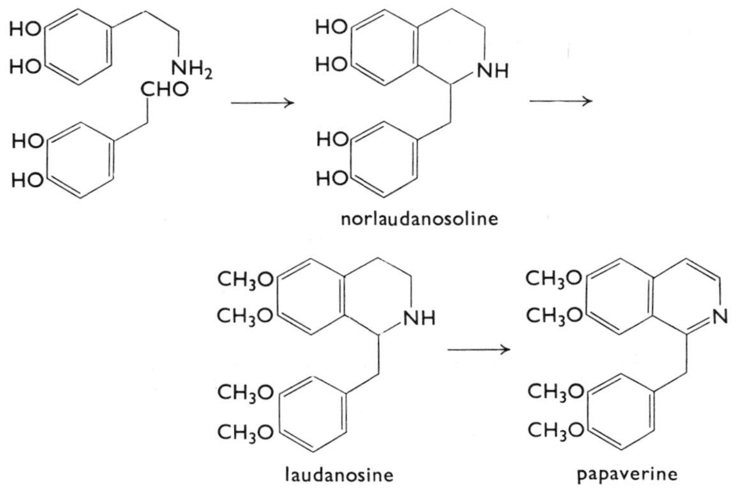
norlaudanosoline
laudanosine
papaverine

[Eq. 18-1]

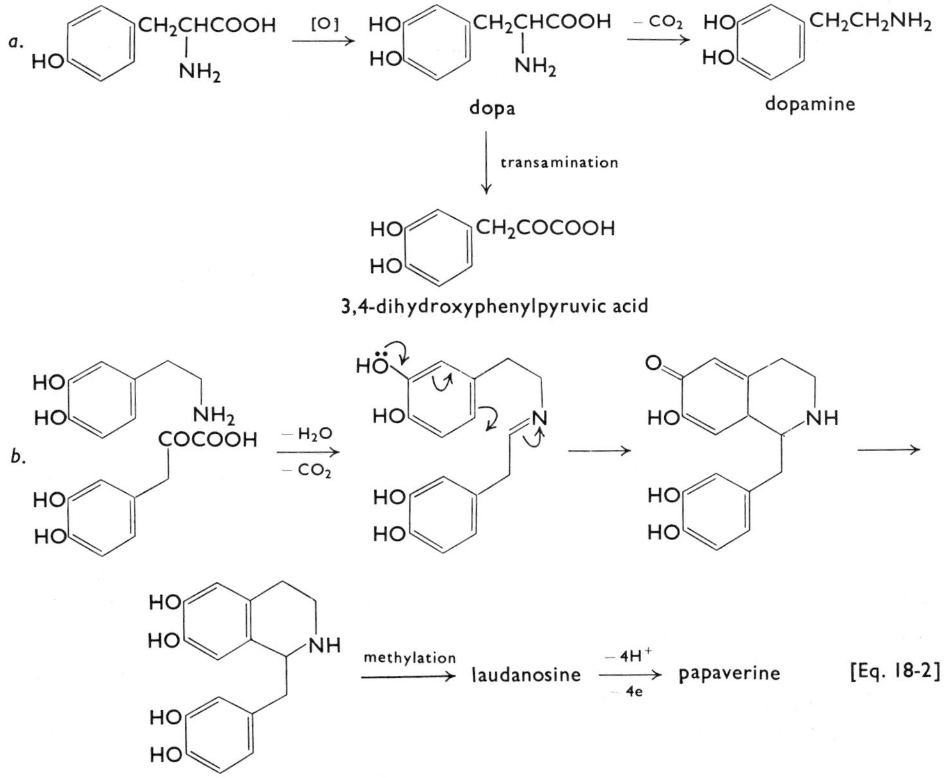
a.
[O]
dopa
$-CO_2$
dopamine
transamination
3,4-dihydroxyphenylpyruvic acid
b.
$-H_2O$
$-CO_2$
methylation
laudanosine
$-4H^+$
$-4e$
papaverine

[Eq. 18-2]

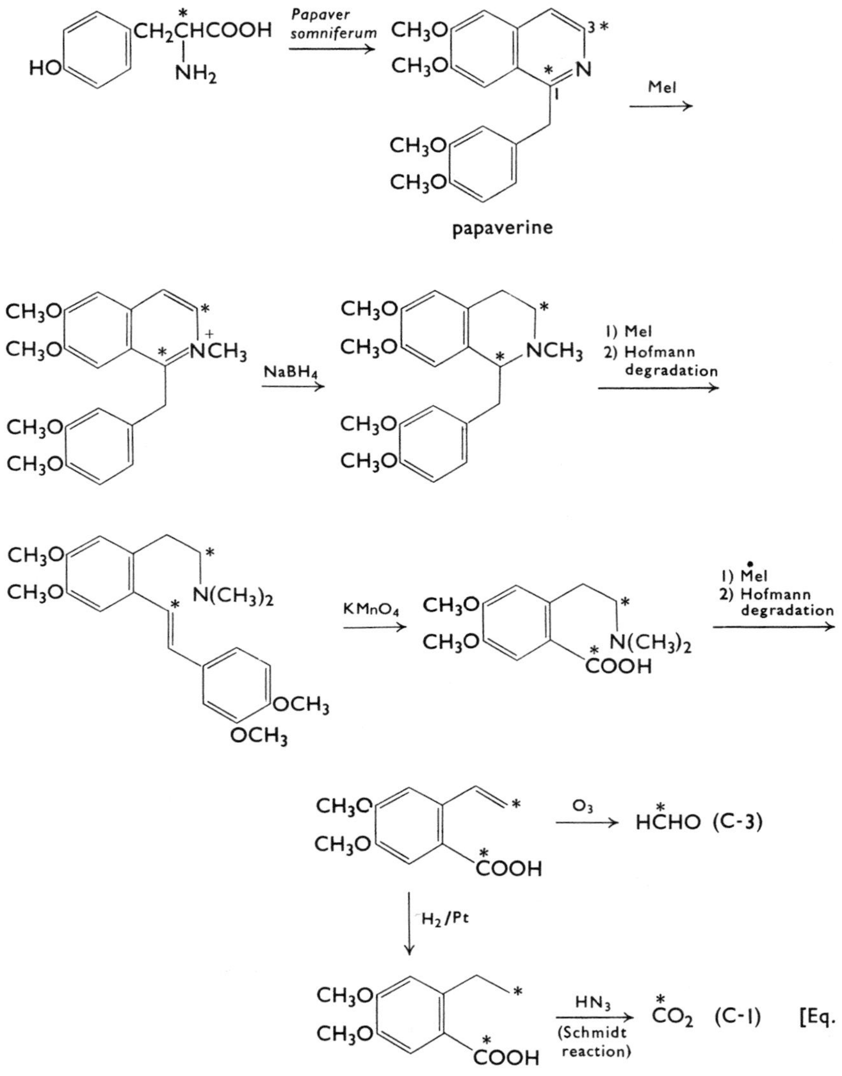

papaverine

Methylation evidently takes place after formation of the tetrahydroiso-
quinoline system, but before dehydrogenation to papaverine, as implied in Eq. 18-2.
Two pieces of evidence suggest this order of events; first, the observation that norlaudanosoline is an efficient precursor of papaverine; and second, the co-occurrence
of laudanosine (Eq. 18-1) with papaverine in the opium poppy.

It will be noted that the initial formation of the isoquinoline system (Eq. 18-2)
is shown as a Mannich-type condensation involving 3,4-dihydroxyphenylpyruvic

acid, rather than the corresponding aldehyde. This suggestion is based on the observation that dopamine (3,4-dihydroxyphenylethylamine) is incorporated only into the isoquinoline moiety of benzylisoquinoline and related alkaloids, a result which is indicative of a branch at an early point in the pathway. Although more than one explanation for this observation can be offered, the suggestion that 3,4-dihydroxyphenylpyruvic acid is an intermediate is the most obvious, since this compound cannot be furnished by dopamine but is readily derived from DOPA by transamination (Eq. 18-4).

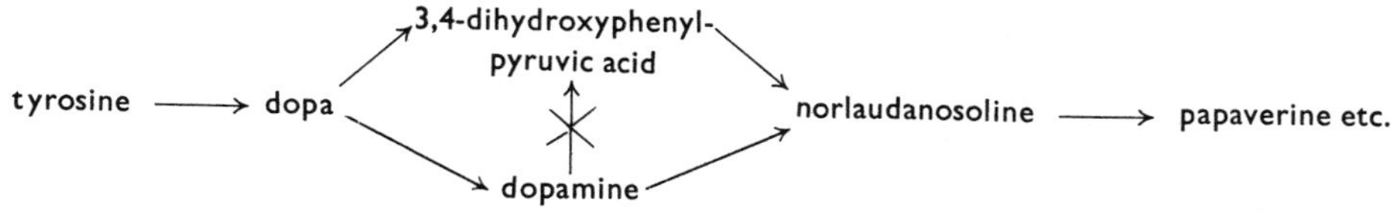

[Eq. 18-4]

The dehydrogenation of laudanosine to papaverine requires no further comment in the light of the discussion given in Chapter 16. The derivation of O-methyl groups by transmethylation from methionine also occurs so frequently in this series that special mention will not be necessary for each specific example in the discussion to follow.

From the biogenetic point of view, the most important benzylisoquinoline alkaloid is undoubtedly reticuline (Fig. 18-2). Reticuline is the precursor of a number of more elaborate compounds (notably the opium alkaloids), a fact which is reflected in its wide distribution. Reticuline has an asymmetric centre at C-1 (Fig. 18-2) and usually occurs in the dextrorotatory form, as for example in *Annona reticulata* Linn. (fam. Annonaceae), *Cinnamomum camphora* (Linn.) Sieb. (fam. Lauraceae), and in *Phylica rogersii* Pillans (fam. Rhamnaceae). In the opium poppy, however, it occurs partly in racemic form, with the (+)-isomer predominating. This observation will be seen to be of considerable significance in the biosynthesis of morphine and its congeners.

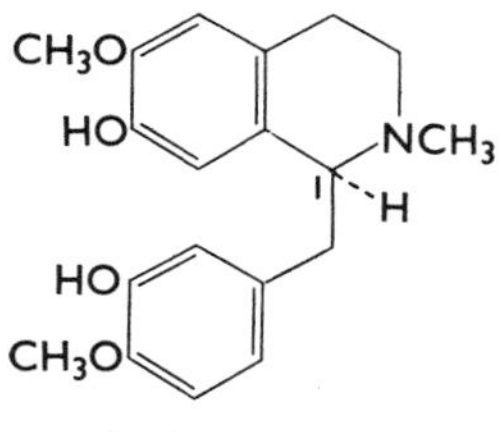

(+)-reticuline

Fig. 18-2.

Papaverine, laudanosine, and reticuline illustrate one of the two common oxygenation patterns in this series; the other is represented by coclaurine (Fig. 18-3) which has been found in species of *Cocculus* (fam. Menispermaceae) and *Machilus* (fam. Lauraceae).

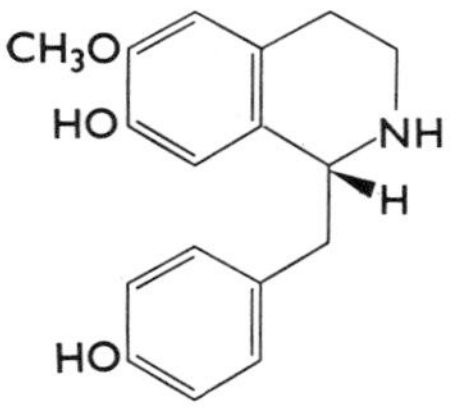

(+)-coclaurine 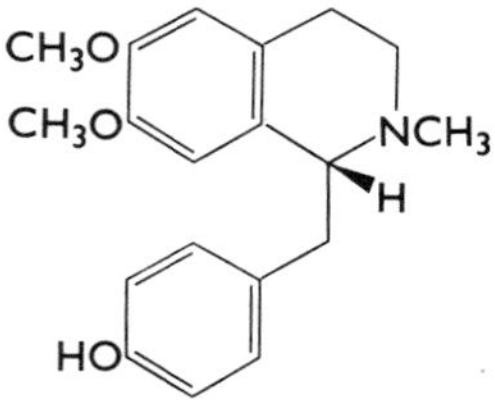   (−)-armepavine

Fig. 18-3.

Armepavine (Fig. 18-3), an alkaloid of various species of *Papaver* (fam. Papaveraceae), is another example of this oxygenation type.

It will be noticed that the heterocyclic ring in these alkaloids exists in the fully reduced form. However, it is encountered at the higher oxidation level represented by papaverine (Eq. 18-1) in a few instances. Quaternary bases are also found, as for example tembetarine (Fig. 18-4), which is N-methyl-(+)-reticuline.

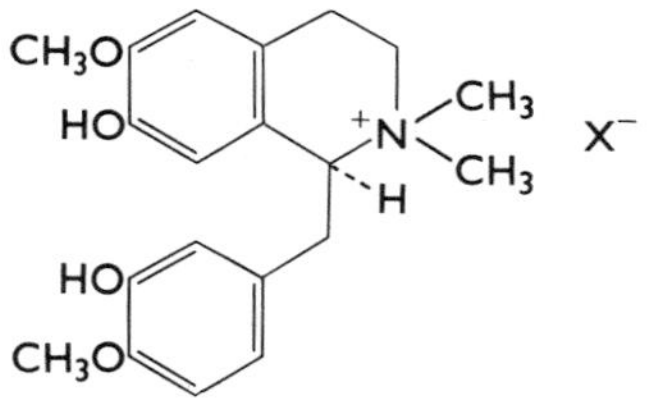

tembetarine

Fig. 18-4.

18.3   The Aporphine Alkaloids

The preceding discussion has sketched in the background against which the formation of an extensive class of alkaloids based on the aporphine skeleton (Fig. 18-5) can now be considered. When it is noted that the aporphine and simple benzylisoquinoline alkaloids have an almost identical distribution, and when the role of oxidative coupling processes in the formation of biaryl structures is recalled (Chap. 14), the derivation of the aporphines by simple oxidative coupling of

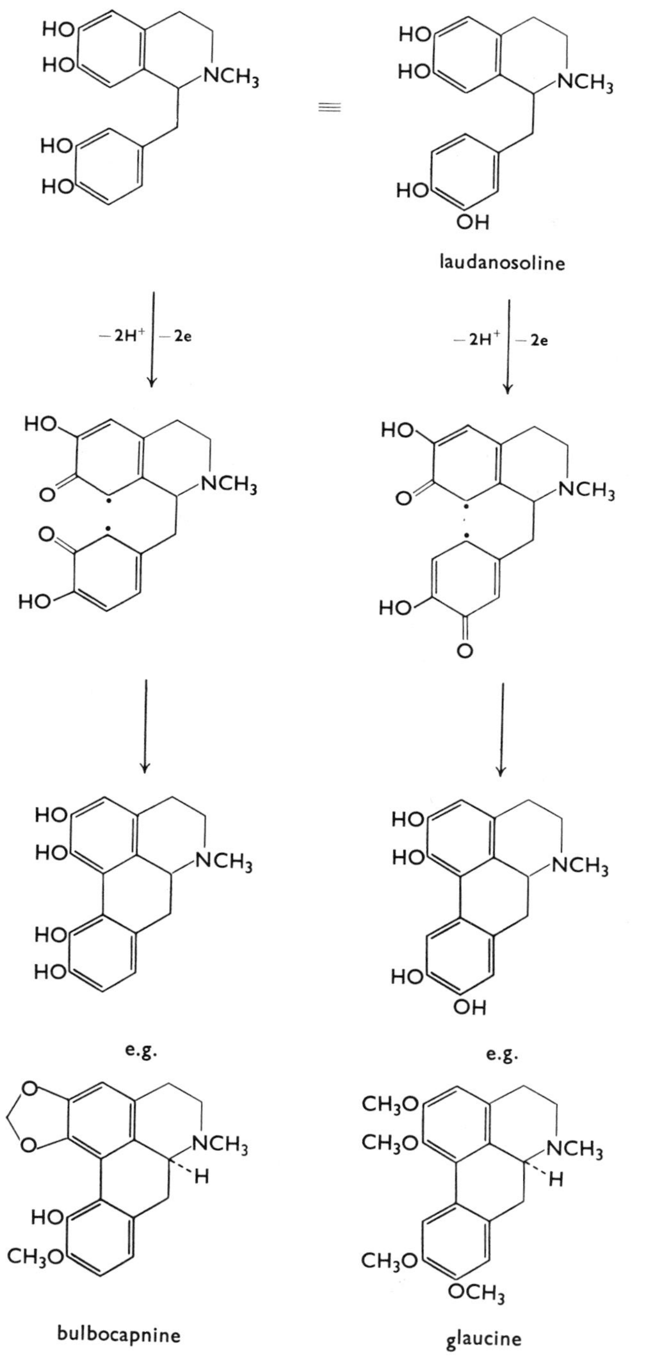

laudanosoline

$-2H^+$ $-2e$

$-2H^+$ $-2e$

e.g.

e.g.

bulbocapnine

glaucine

[Eq. 18-5]

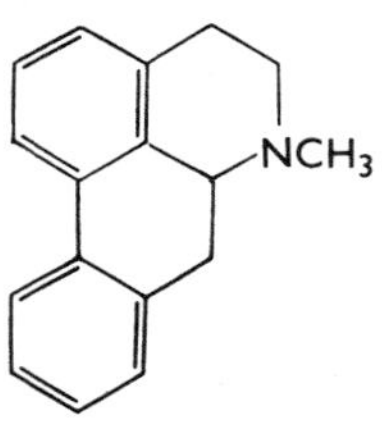

aporphine

Fig. 18-5.

benzylisoquinoline precursors becomes obvious. Thus by *ortho-ortho* or *ortho-para* coupling of laudanosoline, the basic structures of the representative alkaloids bulbocapnine and glaucine can be produced (Eq. 18-5).

A considerable body of evidence has been accumulated in support of this general pathway. Bulbocapnine, for example, has been shown to arise in *Corydalis cava* Schweigg and Kort (fam. Papaveraceae) by the oxidative coupling of reticuline, as shown in Eq. 18-6.

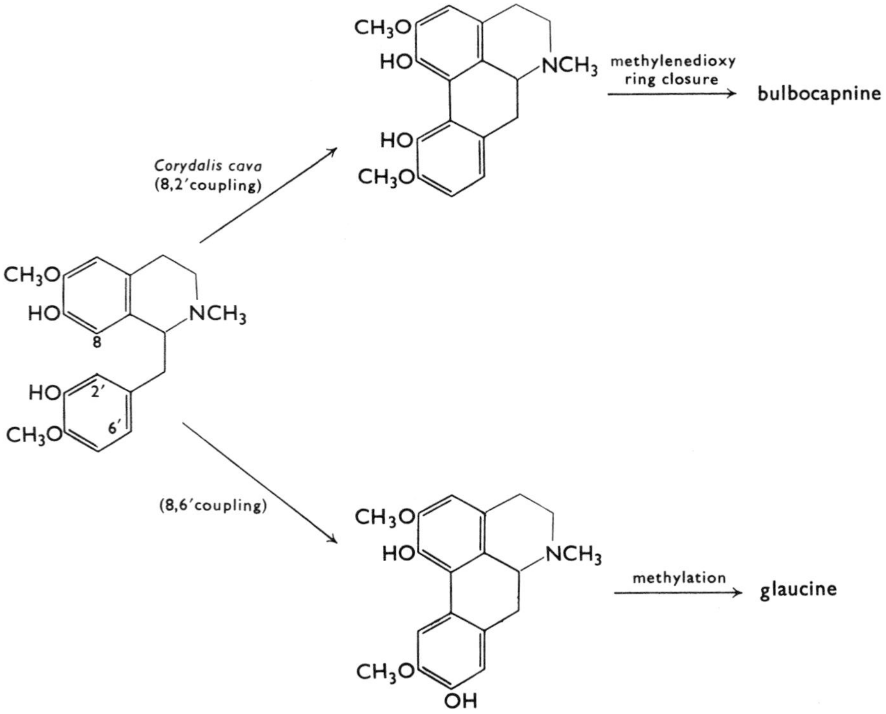

[Eq. 18-6]

Glaucine probably arises through the alternative *ortho-para* mode of coupling, as shown, although experimental proof is lacking for this specific example.

It is to be noted that methylation of two of the phenolic hydroxyl groups in reticuline considerably reduces the number of possible coupling modes, since it is well established that in processes of this kind, coupling only takes place *ortho* or *para* to free phenolic groups (cf. Chap. 14). The use of methylation as a device to block undesirable pathways in oxidative coupling reactions *in vivo* appears to be quite general, as will be seen in the sections to follow.

It will be noted that the proposed biosynthetic pathways leading to bulbocapnine and glaucine (Eq. 18-6) present no conceptual difficulties; each step is readily accounted for in terms of established biological processes. We face a different situation, however, when we come to consider the formation of certain other aporphine alkaloids such as stephanine, laureline, and isothebaine (Fig. 18-6).

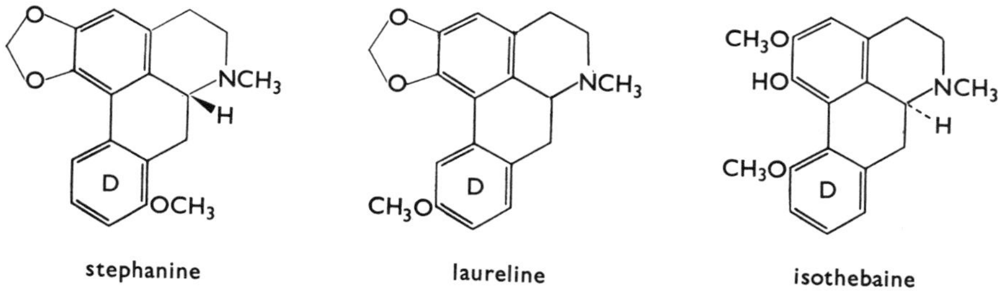

stephanine   laureline   isothebaine

Fig. 18-6.

Thus ring D in stephanine and laureline lacks the *ortho* or *para* oxygen function which would be required for the direct oxidative coupling of a benzylisoquinoline precursor. Isothebaine has an appropriately placed substituent, but this is in the unusual position for an isolated oxygen function, *meta* to the benzylic carbon atom.

In order to account for the formation of these apparently anomalous structures, Barton and Cohen made the important suggestion that the corresponding biosynthetic pathways might involve the rearrangement of intermediates which could be formed by oxidative coupling in the usual way. The participation of two related rearrangements was envisaged. These are the dienone-phenol rearrangement (Eq. 18-7*a*) and the dienol-benzene rearrangement (Eq. 18-7*b*). Both are promoted by acid catalysis; the dienols required for the latter rearrangement are readily derivable by reduction of the corresponding dienones.*

The dienone-phenol rearrangement can be used to rationalize the formation of laureline from N-methylcoclaurine as follows (Eq. 18-8).

---

* Although both rearrangements are now very familiar, it is interesting to note that the proposal concerning the dienol-benzene rearrangement antedated its discovery in the laboratory.

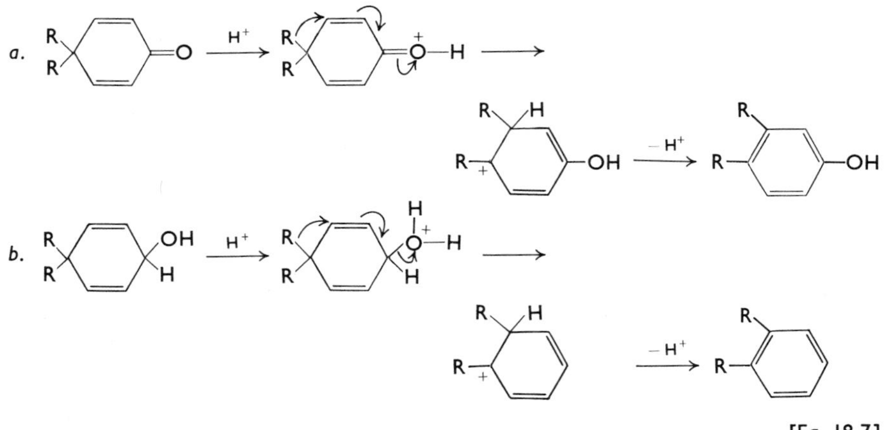

[Eq. 18-7]

N-methylcoclaurine

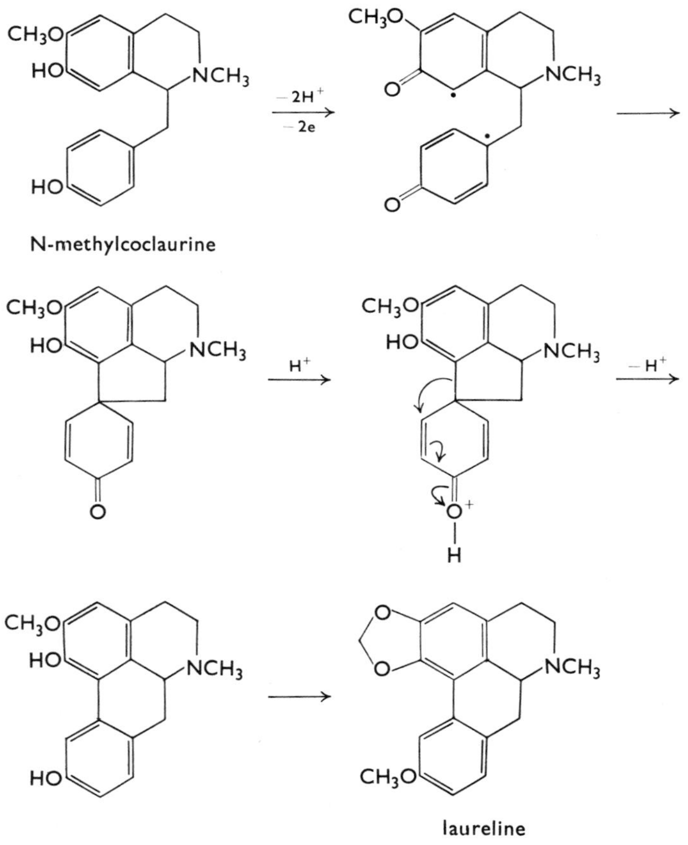

laureline

[Eq. 18-8]

a.

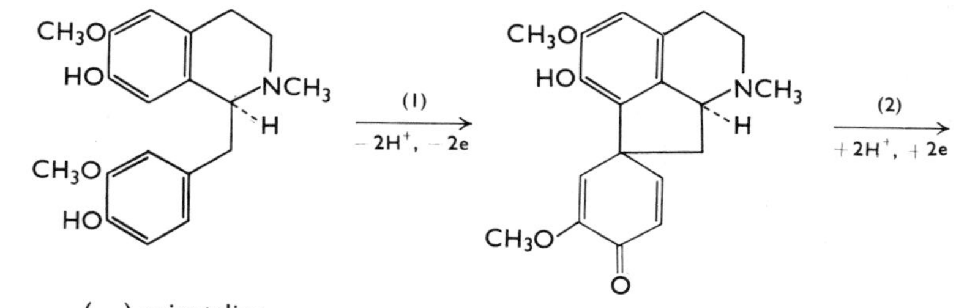

$(-)$-orientaline

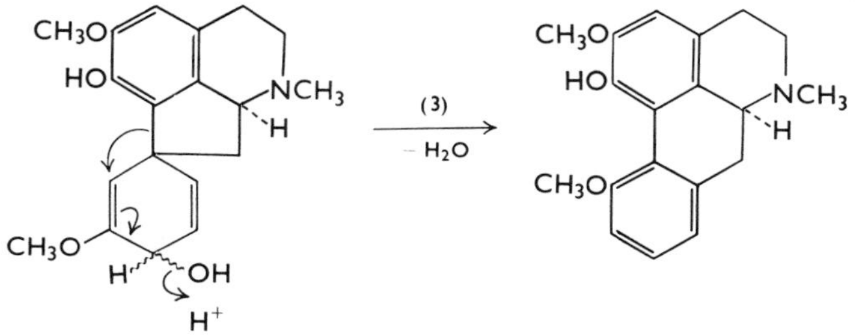

(1) $\quad -2H^+,\ -2e$

(2) $\quad +2H^+,\ +2e$

(3) $\quad -H_2O$

A

$(+)$-isothebaine

(1) $K_3Fe(CN)_6$ (2) NaBH$_4$ (3) H$^+$

b.

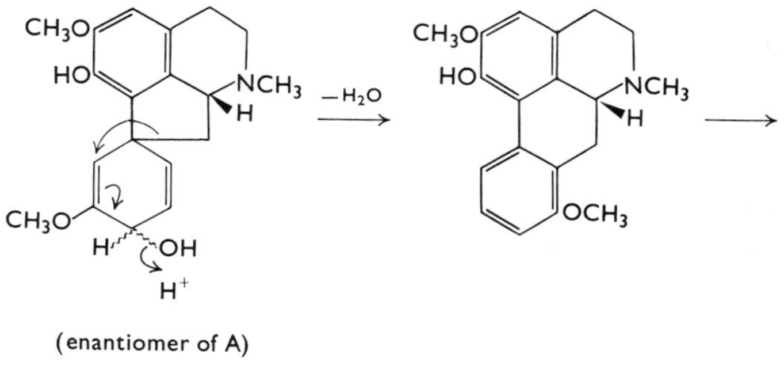

(enantiomer of A)

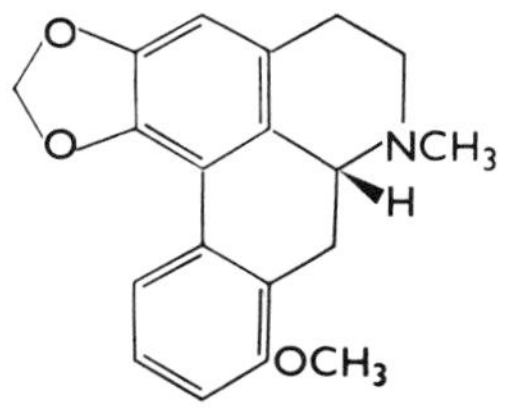

$-H_2O$

stephanine

[Eq. 18-9]

(n.b. This pathway would start from $(+)$-orientaline)

Similarly, the formation of isothebaine from orientaline is readily explained in terms of a dienol-benzene rearrangement (Eq. 18-9a).

Migration of the alkyl rather than the aryl group in an intermediate enantiomeric with the dienone A (Eq. 18-9a) leads to an aporphine from which stephanine is readily derived by oxidative closure of the *o*-methoxyphenol system (Eq. 18-9b).

The preceding pathways are amply supported by appropriate laboratory analogies. Orientaline, for example, on ferricyanide oxidation furnishes orientalinone, which undergoes dienone-phenol rearrangement to give isocorytuberine (Eq. 18-10).

orientaline   orientalinone   isocorytuberine

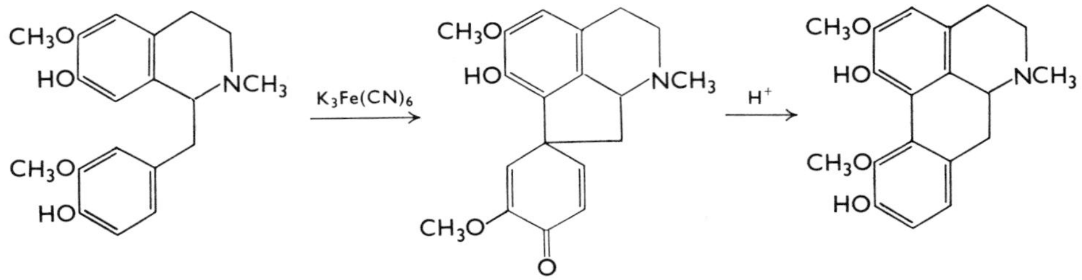

[Eq. 18-10]

An illustration of the dienol-benzene rearrangement is found in the laboratory conversion of orientaline into isothebaine, which followed the precise pathway given in Eq. 18-9a. The reagents used for effecting each step are indicated at the foot of the equation.

The latter pathway has been elegantly confirmed as an *in vivo* process by administering both orientaline and orientalinone, labeled as shown (Eq. 18-11) to *Papaver orientale* plants. Both precursors were efficiently incorporated into isothebaine, with the labels appearing at the predicted positions.

The evidence for the proposed pathway appeared to be so conclusive that a deliberate search for orientalinone in *Papaver orientale* was instigated. Initial proof

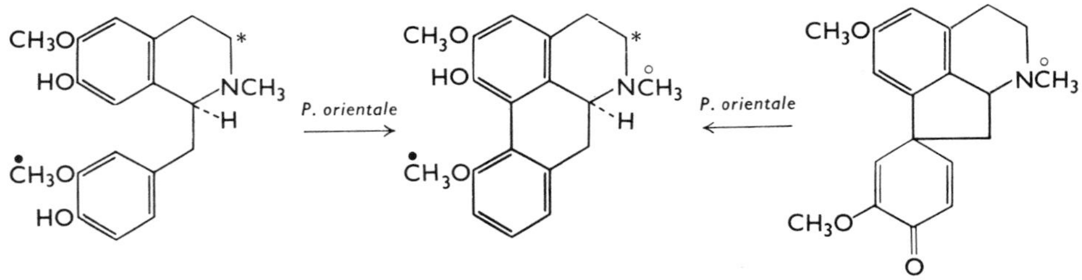

(--)-orientaline   isothebaine   (±)-orientalinone

[Eq. 18-11]

of its existence was obtained by the application of the isotope dilution technique, which has been of great use in similar searches for biosynthetic intermediates. This procedure is based on the assumption that as a result of the conversion of a labeled precursor into a given metabolite, the biological pools of all intervening intermediates will also become labeled. A very minute amount of a suspected intermediate can thus be detected, and its activity measured, by entraining it in a relatively large quantity of added, inactive "carrier" compound, which can then be re-isolated and purified in the usual way. By applying this technique to the alkaloidal residues remaining after the extraction of isothebaine, in the foregoing experiment with doubly labeled orientaline, the presence of orientalinone in *P. orientale* was confirmed. Prompted by this result, a large scale extraction of the alkaloids from *P. orientale* was undertaken. The alkaloid mixture, on separation by countercurrent distribution and chromatography, yielded a small quantity of a base which proved to be identical in all respects with synthetic $(-)$-orientalinone.

Since 1963, many dienone alkaloids of the type represented by orientalinone have been isolated and characterized. In many cases, the acid-catalyzed rearrangement to an aporphine structure has been demonstrated; and this, taken together with the biogenetic relationship to the naturally occurring aporphines, has led to the designation "proaporphines" for this group.

It will be noted that the demonstration of the incorporation of orientaline into orientalinone, above, provides evidence for the participation of a phenol coupling step in the formation of the latter. Comparable results have been obtained in other experiments relating to proaporphine biosynthesis, so that the sequence benzylisoquinoline → proaporphine → aporphine can be regarded as an established pathway for the biosynthesis of aporphines with "abnormal" substitution patterns in ring D.

18.4 The Opium Alkaloids

It is to Robinson and Gulland that we owe the conception of the formation of aporphines by the oxidative coupling of benzylisoquinoline precursors. The same authors were the first to point out that through a different mode of coupling, the basic carbon framework of the opium alkaloids thebaine, codeine, and morphine could arise. This is readily appreciated if we rewrite the structure of reticuline as in Eq. 18-12. It is then evident that by *ortho-para* coupling the basic framework of morphine will be generated. The reason for choosing reticuline to illustrate this relationship will be clear from the methylation pattern, which is such as to block other, undesirable, coupling modes and thereby favor the desired pathway.

It was left to Barton and Cohen to draw together their mechanistic proposals concerning the formation of Pummerer's ketone (Chap. 14) with the biogenetic

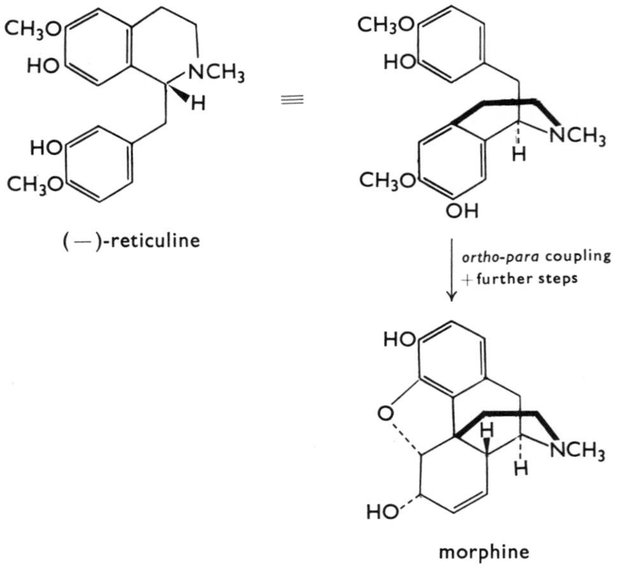

(−)-reticuline

≡

ortho-para coupling
+ further steps

morphine

[Eq. 18-12]

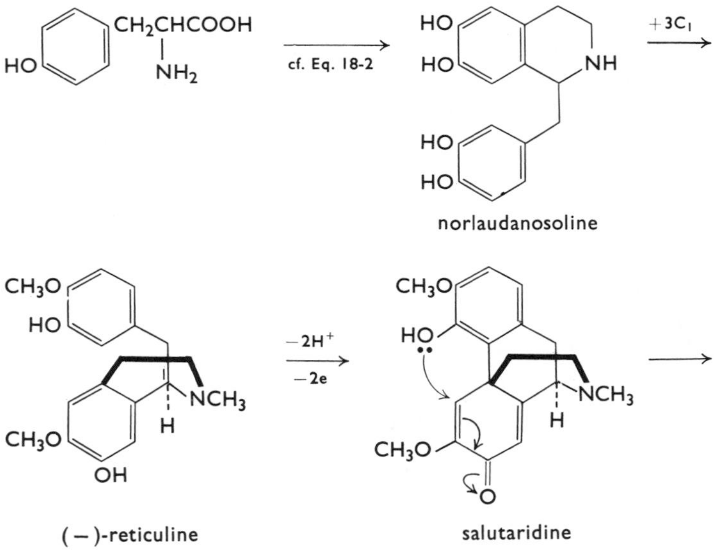

cf. Eq. 18-2

+3C₁

norlaudanosoline

−2H⁺
−2e

(−)-reticuline

salutaridine

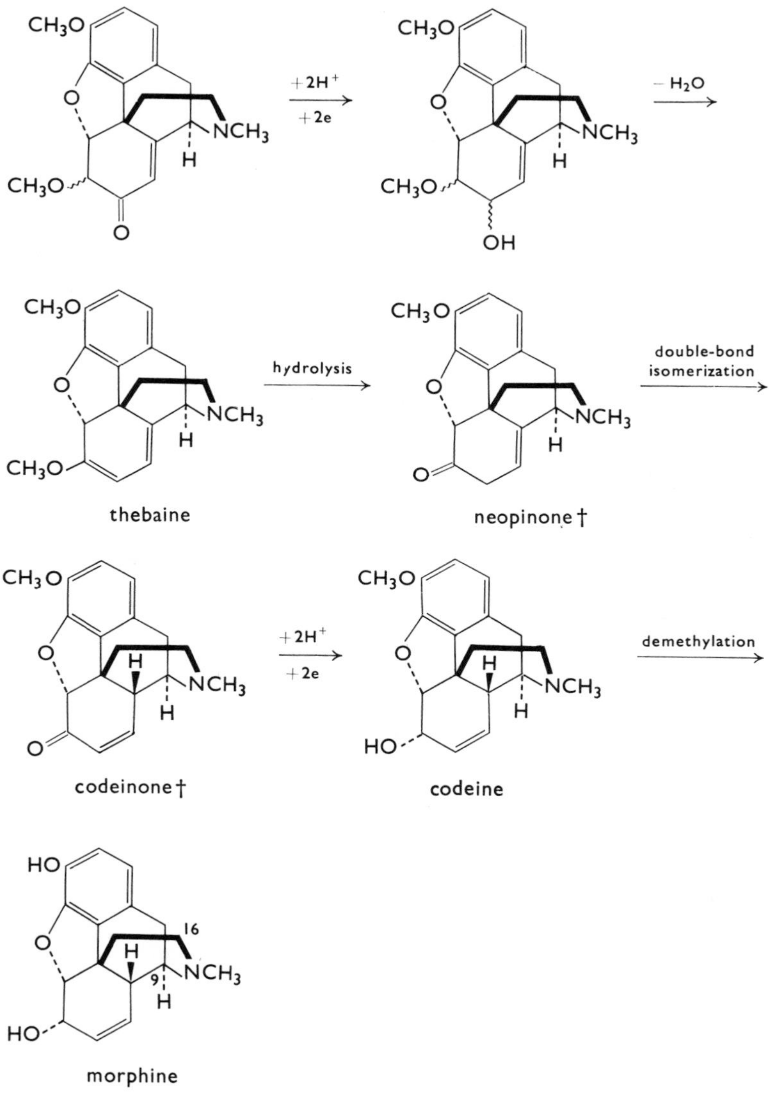

thebaine

neopinone †

codeinone †

codeine

morphine

[Eq. 18-13]

---

† These intermediates have not yet been detected in *Papaver somniferum*.

speculations of Robinson and Gulland and combine them into the rational scheme for morphine biosynthesis given in Eq. 18-13.

The steps involving the hydrolysis of a vinyl methyl ether structure, double bond isomerization, reduction, and demethylation, in the conversion of thebaine into morphine, are readily acceptable on mechanistic grounds. The preceding steps have ample analogy in reactions previously discussed.

As the result of prodigious experimental efforts by many workers, it is now known that with one small but significant modification, the sequence given in Eq. 18-13 represents the true pathway of morphine biosynthesis in the opium poppy, *Papaver somniferum.*

Some key experimental results which serve to define this pathway are as follows:

  a. $2\text{-}^{14}C\text{-}$tyrosine gives morphine labeled exclusively at C-9 and C-16.

  b. $1\text{-}^{14}C\text{-}$dopamine gives morphine labeled exclusively at C-16.

  c. Norlaudanosoline is an efficient precursor of morphine.

  d. Studies of the relative rates of incorporation of radioactivity into the alkaloids in poppy plants growing in an atmosphere of $^{14}CO_2$, clearly demonstrated the sequence thebaine $\to$ codeine $\to$ morphine.

  e. Quadruply labeled reticuline was specifically incorporated into thebaine (Eq. 18-14).

  f. Tritium-labeled salutaridine was also specifically incorporated (see below).

(−)-reticuline	thebaine	[Eq. 18-14]

The predictive power of the suggested pathway has been underlined by the discovery of the key intermediate salutaridine, in a Brazilian plant, *Croton salutaris* Casar (fam. Euphorbiaceae).* Subsequent isotope dilution experiments demonstrated the presence of salutaridine in low concentration in *Papaver somniferum.*

The modification to the pathway of Eq. 18-13 mentioned above, relates to the formation of the oxygen bridge. The proposed variation is illustrated in Eq. 18-15a where it can be seen that the new O—C bond is shown as arising by an S_N2' dis-

---

  * The name salutaridine was of course given to the morphine precursor only after it had been discovered as a natural product in *C. salutaris.*

placement of the hydroxyl function in salutaridinol, the reduction product of salutaridine, rather than by addition to the dienone system of salutaridine itself (Eq. 18-13).

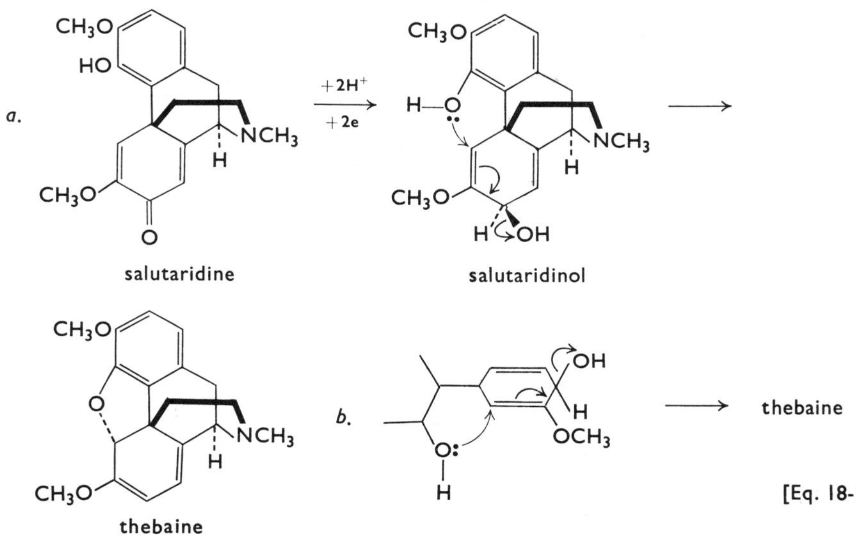

salutaridine

salutaridinol

thebaine

thebaine

[Eq. 18-15]

As the result of detailed incorporation experiments, it is now known that the sequence given in Eq. 18-15, accurately represents the manner in which the oxygen bridge in thebaine is formed. It is also known that of the two isomeric forms of salutaridinol, the true biological intermediate (salutaridinol I) has the β orientation of the secondary hydroxyl function, as shown. It is to be noted, however, that the *trans-cis* stereochemistry of the overall displacement process (cf. Eq. 18-15*b*) is such that a concerted mechanism is less likely than a sequence involving two or more discrete enzymatic steps.

Throughout the foregoing account, the use of labeled precursors has been mentioned. However, in presenting the results of incorporation experiments, we have merely been describing the tip of the iceberg in terms of the total labour involved, since it will be evident from the complexity of the compounds under discussion that their synthesis in labeled form must often represent a major undertaking. In studies of this kind, the preparation of labeled precursors often consumes far

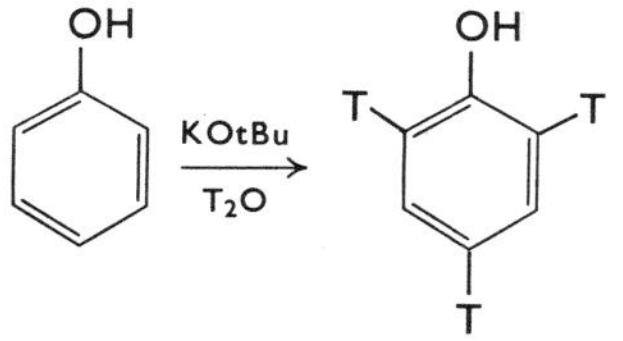

[Eq. 18-16]

more time and effort than the actual incorporation experiments themselves and makes considerable demands on the ingenuity and resourcefulness of the chemist.

In general, two approaches to the synthesis of radioactive precursors can be adopted; (a) standard synthetic routes may be used, suitably modified to allow the inclusion of label at the required positions; (b) the intact precursor may be labeled

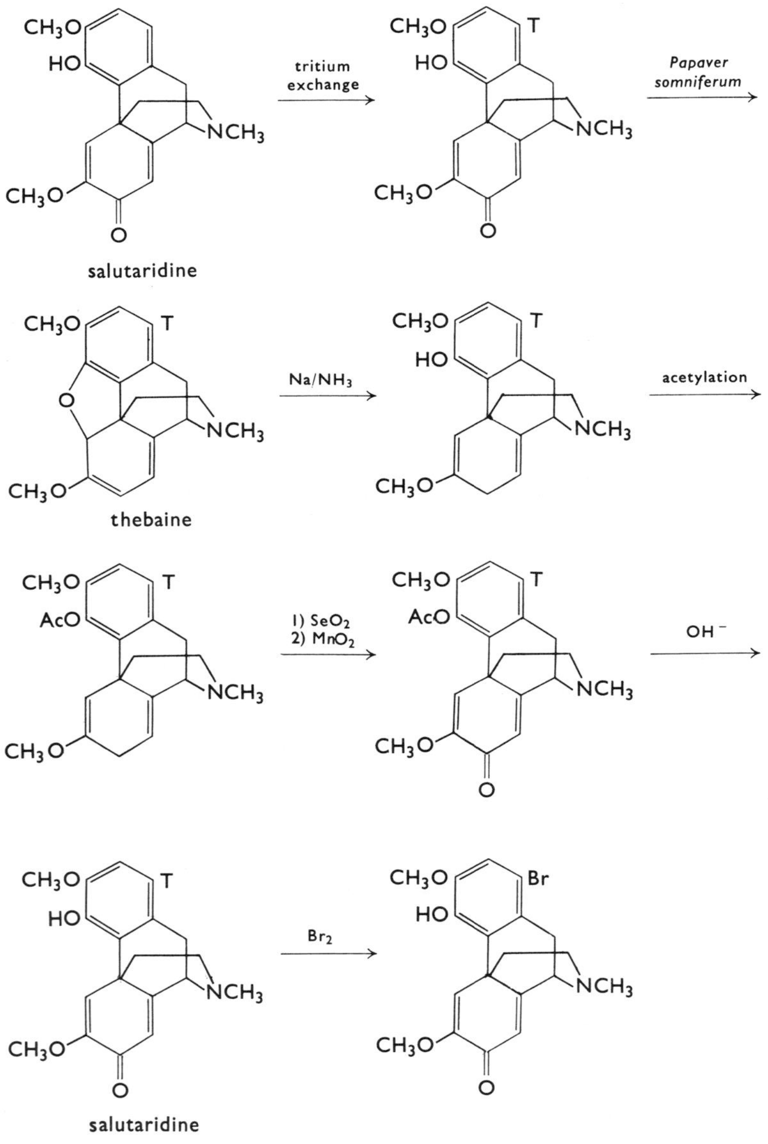

[Eq. 18-17]

by isotope exchange. (This latter method is most frequently used for the introduction of tritium.)

Isotope exchange has been extremely useful in experiments relating to benzyl-isoquinoline alkaloid biosynthesis as it provides a means of obtaining labeled precursors without recourse to total radiochemical synthesis. A method frequently used depends on the observation that aromatic protons *ortho* and *para* to phenolic hydroxyl groups are labile under strongly basic conditions and may be exchanged for tritium in the presence of a tritiated proton donor. A typical system would comprise potassium *tert*-butoxide and tritiated water, as illustrated in Eq. 18-16.

This method has the advantages (a) that it is specific for exchange *ortho* and *para* to free hydroxyl groups and (b) that the position of the label in the product can be demonstrated by equally specific electrophilic displacement.

The isotope exchange technique has been used to investigate the role of salutaridine in opium alkaloid biosynthesis as illustrated in Eq. 18-17. Salutaridine, labeled by base-catalyzed tritium exchange, was converted into thebaine in *P. somniferum*. In order to demonstrate the position of the label in the product, the thebaine was reconverted into salutaridine by the method illustrated. Bromination then gave the mono-bromo derivative which was completely inactive, thereby demonstrating the specific retention of the tritium label in the biological transformation.

18.5 The Laboratory Simulation of Aporphine and Morphine Biosynthesis

Attempts to synthesize the basic structures of the aporphine and opium alkaloids by oxidative coupling date from the publication of the original proposals of Robinson and Gulland. Early attempts at the oxidation of laudanosoline, however, did not give the required type of coupling, but resulted in the formation of a dibenzopyrrocoline structure by the probable mechanism shown in Eq. 18-18.

[Eq. 18-18]

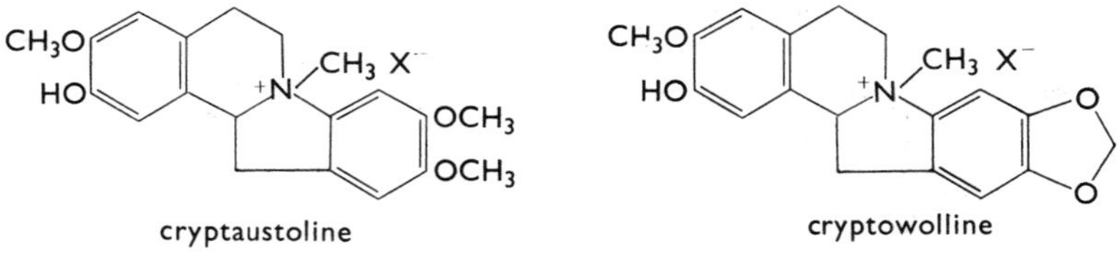

cryptaustoline   cryptowolline

Fig. 18-7.

This observation lay fallow for many years, but acquired biogenetic significance with the discovery of the alkaloids cryptaustoline and cryptowolline in an
Australian plant, *Cryptocarya Bowiei* Druce (fam. Lauraceae) (Fig. 18-7).

Later investigations have shown that the desired mode of coupling leading to
the aporphine structure can be achieved if the nitrogen function is first quaternized.
For example, laudanosoline methiodide can be oxidized to give the corresponding
aporphine salt in 62% yield (Eq. 18-19).

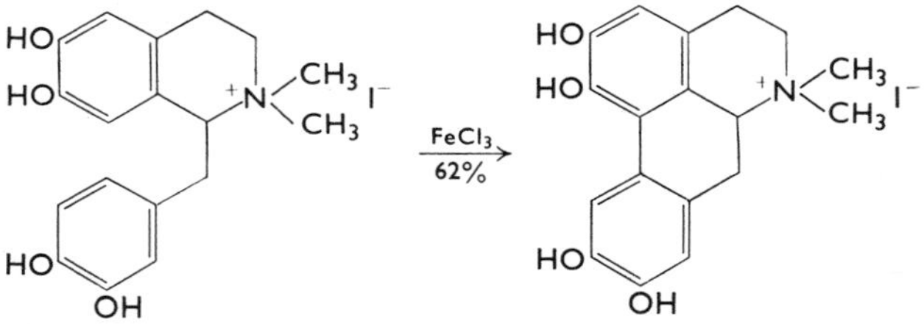

[Eq. 18-19]

It is also found that coupling of tertiary bases can be carried through to an
aporphine structure by using ferric chloride in concentrations sufficiently high to
complex with any catechol units present and prevent the formation of the *o*-
quinone intermediates which lead to the production of dibenzopyrrocolines (cf.
Eq. 18-18).

The coupling of reticuline to give salutaridine (cf. Eq. 18-13) proved to be
rather more difficult to simulate and could only be demonstrated with the aid of
the isotope dilution technique. Manganese dioxide was the oxidant and salutaridine
was obtained from reticuline in 0.01 per cent yield.

18.6   The Argemone Alkaloids

Various species of *Argemone* (fam. Papaveraceae) and the related genus *Eschscholtzia* contain alkaloids with the modified benzylisoquinoline structure represented by (−)-argemonine (Fig. 18-8).

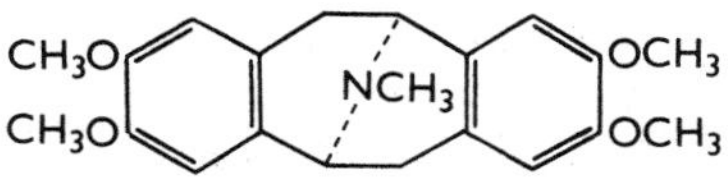

(−)-argemonine

Fig. 18-8.

It is interesting to note that this structure (as the N-demethyl derivative, pavine) was obtained in 1886 by the reduction of papaverine (cf. Eq. 18-1).

The formation of argemonine and related alkaloids is readily rationalized as follows (Eq. 18-20):

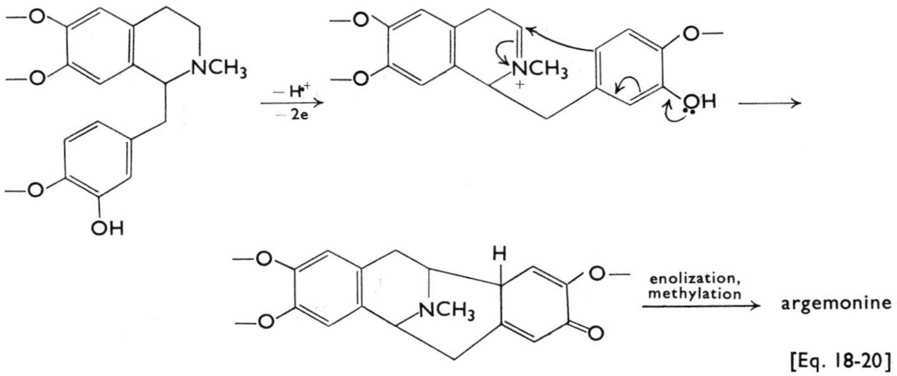

[Eq. 18-20]

It will be noted that this scheme (which is at present hypothetical) employs a mechanism for the cyclization step which is virtually identical with that invoked to explain the formation of the "berberine bridge" (Chap. 15). Reticuline is shown as the precursor for two reasons (a) it has the appropriate substitution pattern and (b) it is known to occur in *Argemone* species.

Related alkaloids differ in the nature of the substituents attached to the hydroxyl functions, as for example in eschscholtzine (Fig. 18-9) from the California Poppy, *Eschscholtzia californica* Cham. (fam. Papaveraceae).

An alternative mode of cyclization, resulting in a different substitution pattern in ring D, is revealed in the structure of (−)-munitagine (Fig. 18-9).

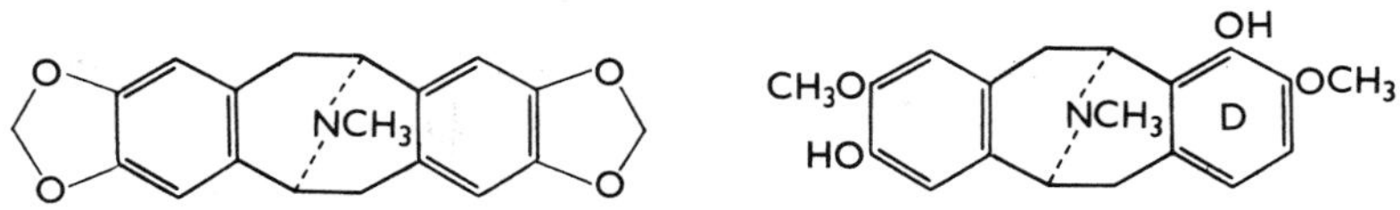

(−)-eschscholtzine   (−)-munitagine

Fig. 18-9.

18.7 Cularine

Hitherto in this chapter, we have been concerned with coupling processes which result in intramolecular C—C bond formation. The corresponding formation of intramolecular O—C linkages is only rarely observed, but is represented in the structures of a small group of alkaloids, typified by cularine (Eq. 18-21), which are found in *Corydalis claviculata* DC. and various *Dicentra* species (both fam. Papaveraceae).

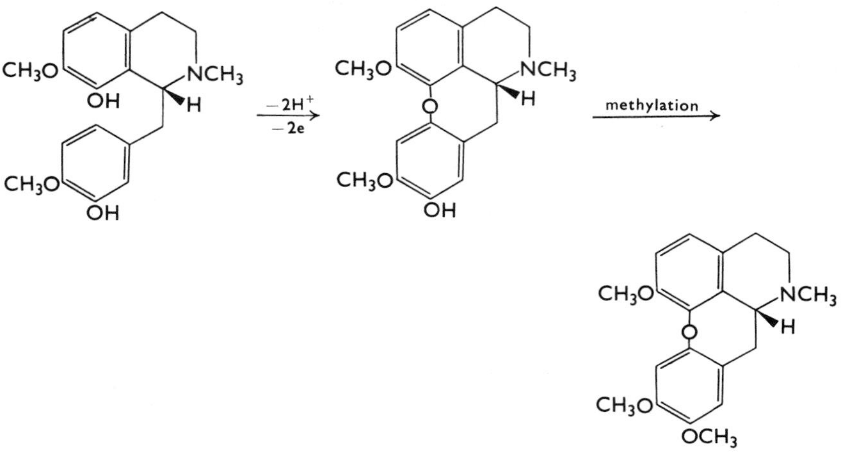

cularine

[Eq. 18-21]

The formation of cularine is most simply rationalized as the direct oxidative coupling of the appropriately substituted benzylisoquinoline precursor, as shown.

18.8 The Erythrina Alkaloids

The genus *Erythrina* (fam. Leguminosae) produces a number of closely related alkaloids with structures based on the "erythrinan" skeleton (Fig. 18-10).

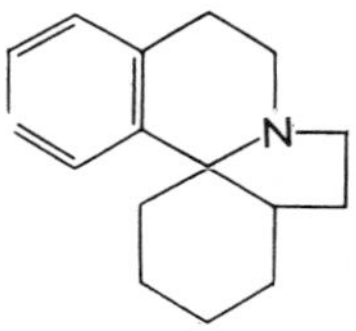

The "erythrinan" skeleton

Fig. 18-10.

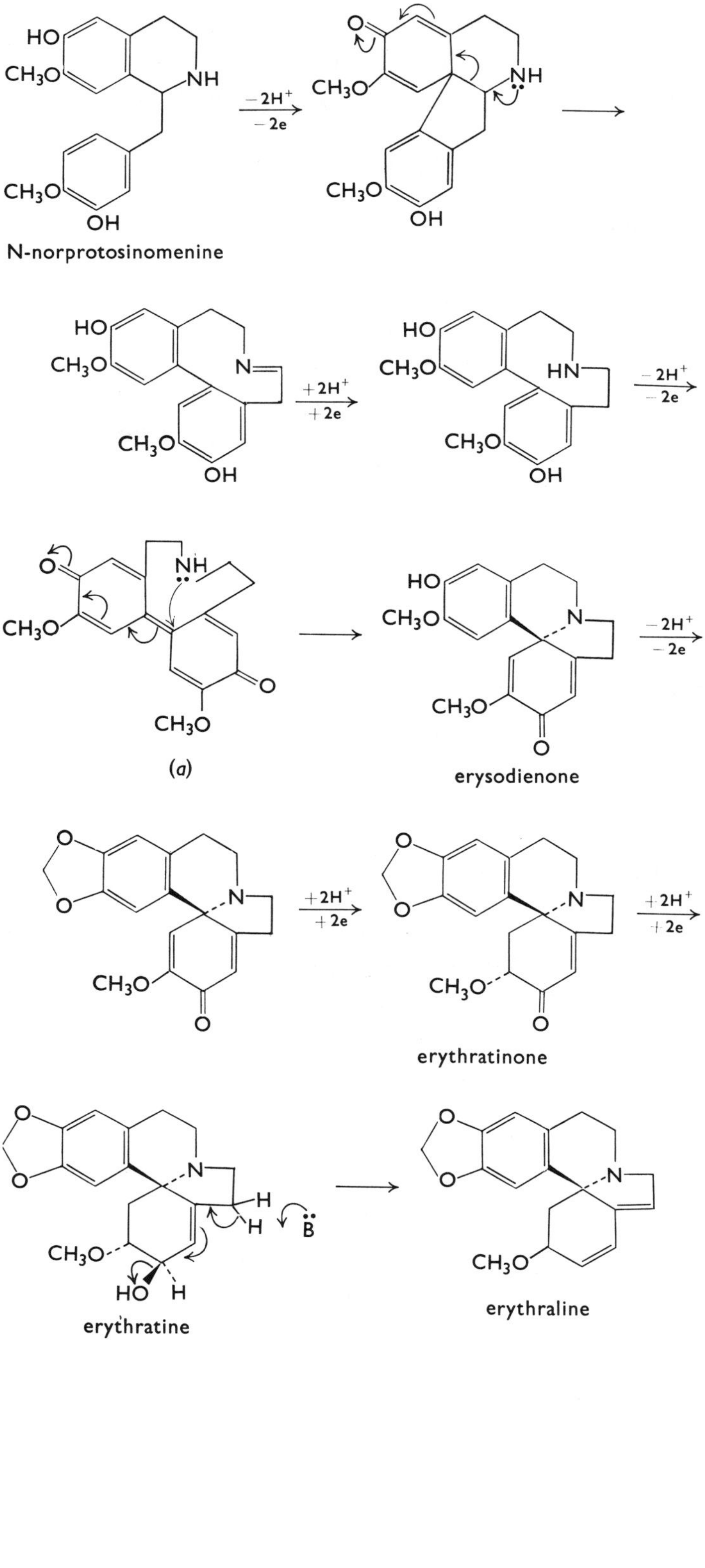

N-norprotosinomenine

(a)   erysodienone

erythratinone

erythratine   erythraline

[Eq. 18-22]

Although conclusive evidence is not yet available, it appears probable that representative bases such as erythratine and erythraline (Eq. 18-22) arise by a pathway involving intramolecular oxidative coupling of the simple benzylisoquinoline precursor N-norprotosinomenine, as shown. Of the succeeding steps, the addition of the nitrogen function to the p,p'-diphenoquinone system of the intermediate Eq. 18-22a will be seen to have an analogy in the biosynthesis of certain of the Amaryllidaceae alkaloids to be discussed in the following section.

The evidence for the proposed pathway rests on the observation that both N-norprotosinomenine and the key intermediate, erysodienone, can serve as precursors of erythratine and erythraline in *Erythrina crista-galli* L., and that erythratinone has been found as a minor component of the alkaloid mixture produced by this species.

At present, therefore, the formation of the erythrinan skeleton, at least in the early stages, would appear to resemble the pathway leading to the simple benzylisoquinoline alkaloids. It is to be noted that the scheme shown in Eq. 18-22 provides yet another example of the use of methylation to block undesirable coupling modes in a biological phenol oxidation.

18.9   The Amaryllidaceae Alkaloids

The unification of the pathways leading to the various types of alkaloid structure encountered in the Amaryllidaceae (daffodil) family, has been one of the most valuable outcomes of the mechanistic proposals of Barton and Cohen. These authors conceived the formation of the three basic skeletons shown in Eq. 18-23, as arising by alternative modes of coupling of precursors related to a single progenitor, norbelladine.

All three pathways are now known to be substantially correct as the result of numerous feeding experiments. We may consider the evidence in two parts, firstly that relating to the formation of the norbelladine system and secondly that relating to the coupling steps and subsequent transformations.

The norbelladine structure arises from tyrosine and phenylalanine, which furnish the C_6—C—C, and the C_6—C components respectively (Eq. 18-24). It will be recalled that tyrosine furnishes both halves of the benzylisoquinoline alkaloids with equal efficiency and that phenylalanine is nowhere implicated. This distinction results from the apparent inability of higher plants* to convert phenylalanine into tyrosine by nuclear hydroxylation. However, at a later stage of elaboration, phenolic compounds may readily arise from phenylalanine by, for example,

---

* With the exception of the Gramineae.

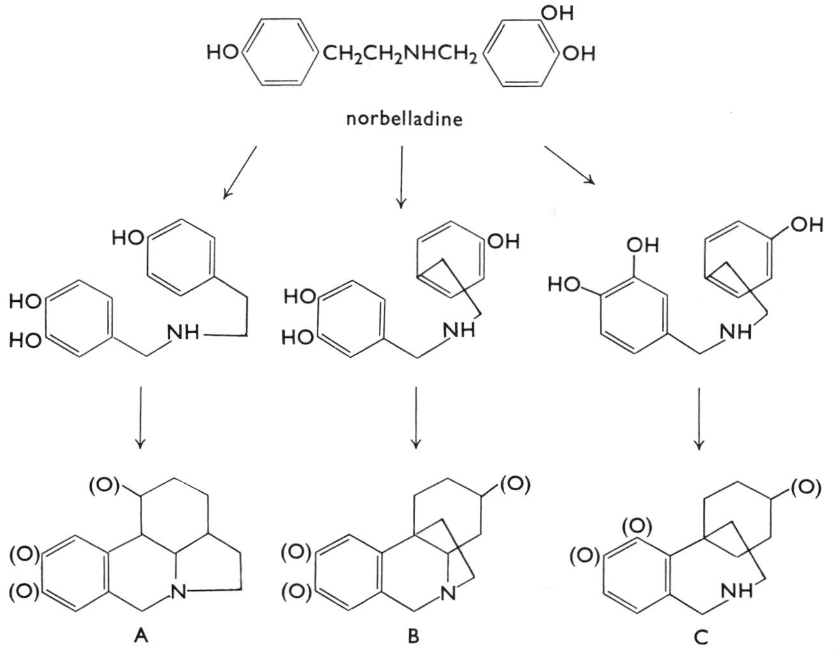

norbelladine

A   B   C

[Eq. 18-23]

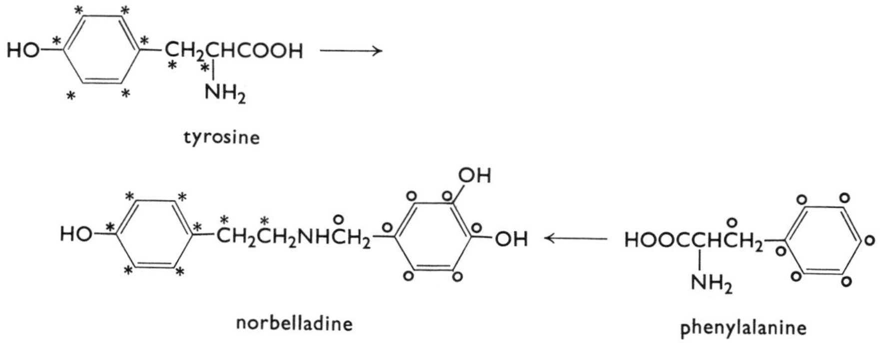

tyrosine

norbelladine   phenylalanine

[Eq. 18-24]

the hydroxylation of derived metabolites such as cinnamic acid. Against this back-ground, the formation of norbelladine by the sequence shown in Eq. 18-25 is readily understood.

Formation of the structural type A (Eq. 18-23) can be illustrated by reference to norpluviine and lycorine, which have been shown to arise from norbelladine and O-methylnorbelladine in various daffodil varieties as shown in Eq. 18-26.

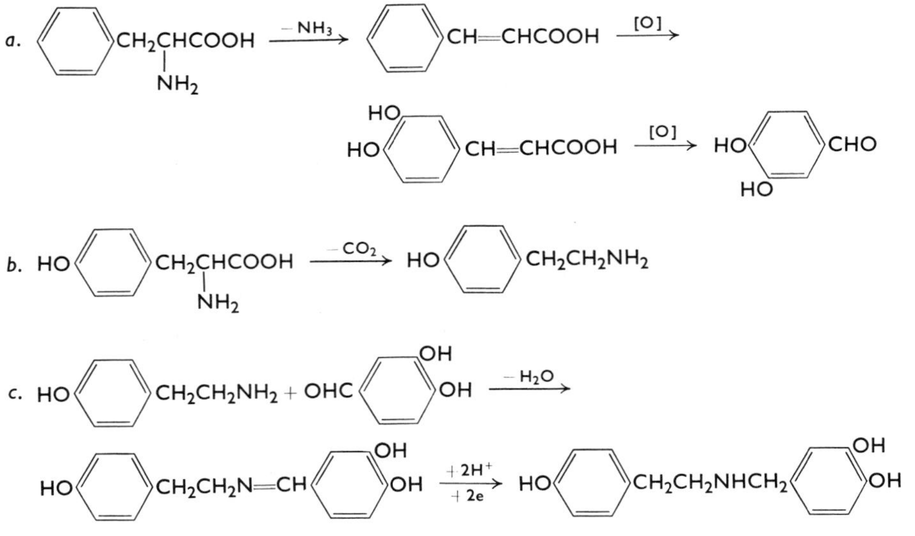

[Eq. 18-25]

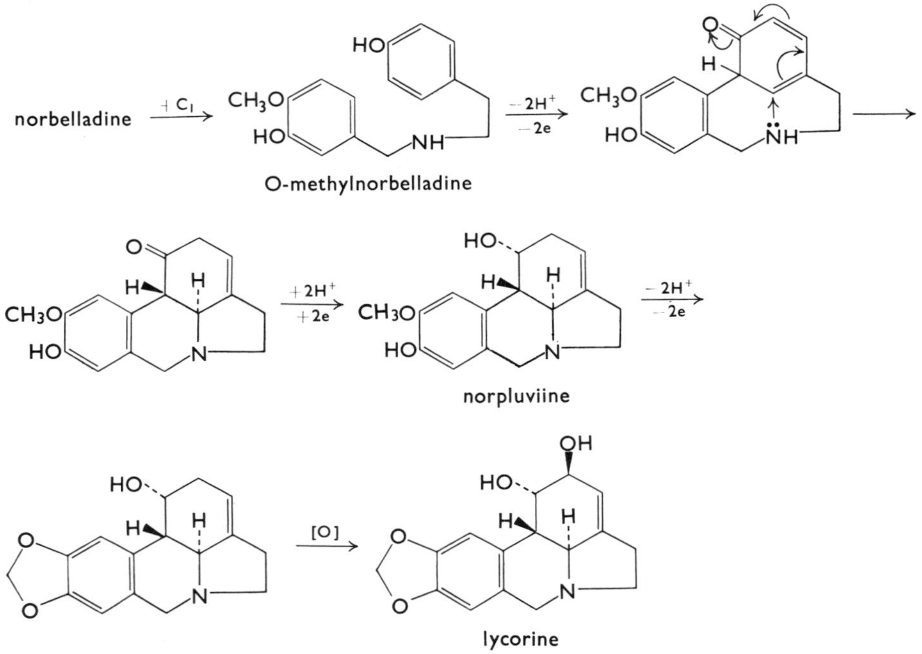

[Eq. 18-26]

It will be noted that this pathway involves the formation of a C—N bond by addition of the nitrogen function to a dienone system, as postulated for erythrinan formation (cf. the preceding section).

O-Methylation of norpluviine, followed by a sequence of hydroxylation, methylation and ring scission, as postulated for otonecine formation (page 448) serves to explain the formation of lycorenine, from which homolycorine can be derived by oxidation, as illustrated in Eq. 18-27.

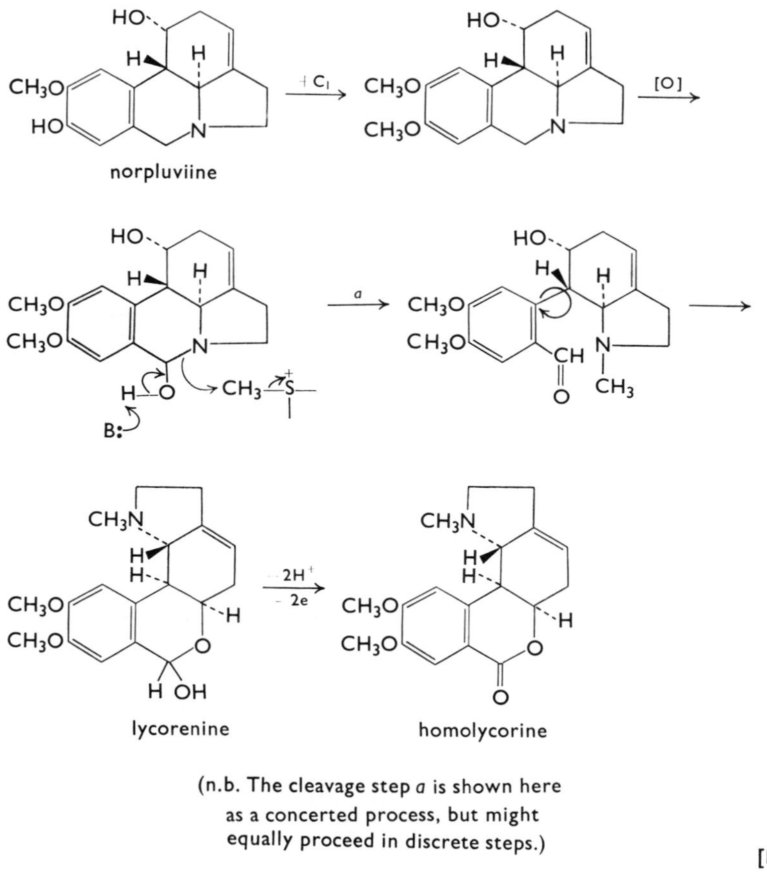

norpluviine

lycorenine   homolycorine

(n.b. The cleavage step a is shown here
as a concerted process, but might
equally proceed in discrete steps.)

[Eq. 18-27]

The genesis of the second structural type, B (Eq. 18-23), is illustrated by the pathway leading to haemanthamine (Eq. 18-28). It is to be noted that O-methylnorbelladine is the precursor as in lycorine formation (cf. Eq. 18-26) with the difference that we here observe a different mode of coupling (*para-para* instead of *ortho-para*). The basic framework is completed by nitrogen addition to the dienone system as before. The

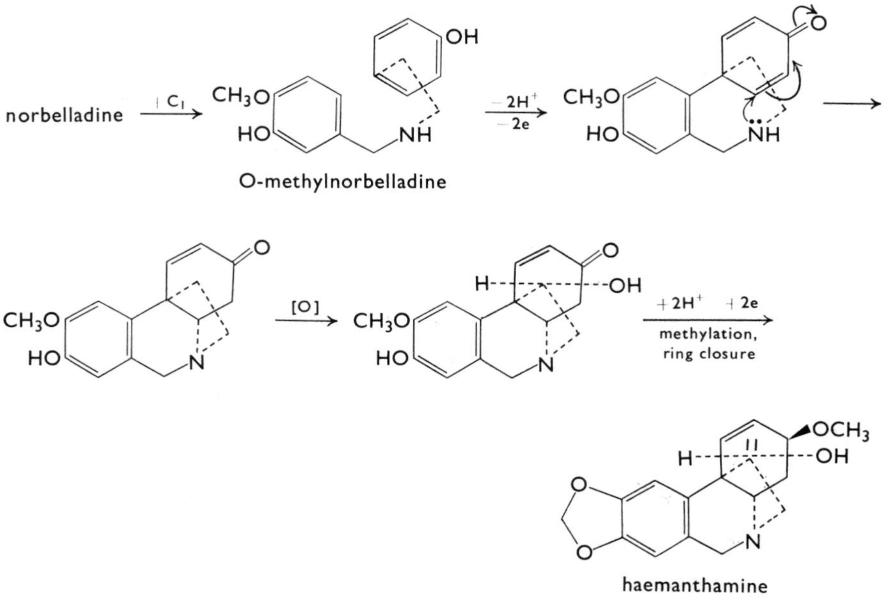
norbelladine
+C1
O-methylnorbelladine
−2H+ −2e
[O]
+2H+ +2e
methylation,
ring closure
haemanthamine

[Eq. 18-28]

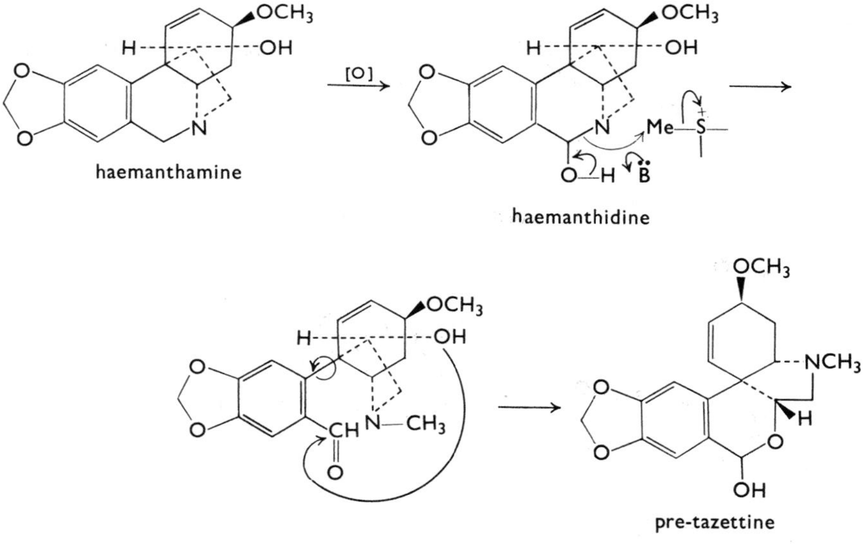
haemanthamine
[O]
haemanthidine
pre-tazettine

[Eq. 18-29]

steps involving the reduction and methylation of the keto group, and the ring-closure of the *o*-methoxyphenol system, have ample precedent in reactions previously discussed. From the mechanical point of view, hydroxylation at C-11 as in this sequence cannot be readily explained, although many other examples are known in secondary metabolism, where hydroxylation occurs at sites lacking formal activation (cf. page 434). The pathway of haemanthamine biosynthesis is well-documented by the appropriate incorporation experiments with *Narcissus* species.

By a process analogous to the conversion of norpluviine into lycorenine, haemanthamine can be converted, *via* the known alkaloid haemanthidine, into pre-tazettine, as shown in Eq. 18-29.

Pre-tazettine undergoes rearrangement under mildly basic conditions to give tazettine (Eq. 18-30). For many years, tazettine was regarded as one of the commonest alkaloids of the Amaryllidaceae, but recent investigations have shown that it is probably an artefact, arising from the true alkaloid, pre-tazettine, under the basic conditions of the normal isolation procedure. When contact with base was carefully avoided, several plant species, previously regarded as rich sources of tazettine, were shown to contain none of this alkaloid, but furnished pre-tazettine in its place. The conversion of pre-tazettine into tazettine can be rationalized as an internal crossed-Cannizzaro reaction, as follows (Eq. 18-30):

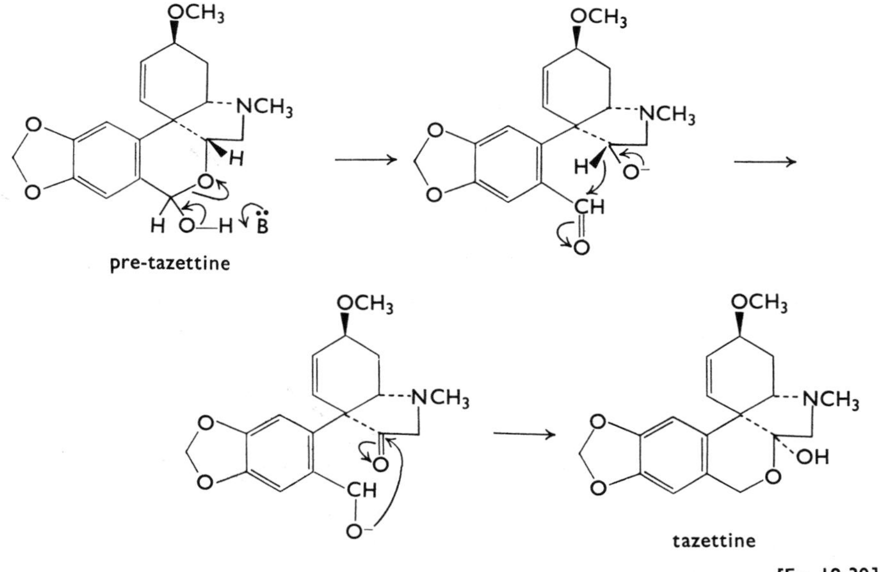

pre-tazettine

tazettine

[Eq. 18-30]

This transformation is accompanied by a considerable relief of ring strain, which accounts for the very mild conditions under which it takes place.

Formation of the skeletal type C (Eq. 18-23) is illustrated by the pathway leading to galanthamine (Eq. 18-31). The coupling step and subsequent formation of the oxygen bridge have obvious parallels in the formation of Pummerer's ketone and in usnic acid biosynthesis (Chap. 14). The proposed pathway has been firmly established by feeding experiments with triply labeled N,O-dimethylnorbelladine, in the King Alfred daffodil, as shown.

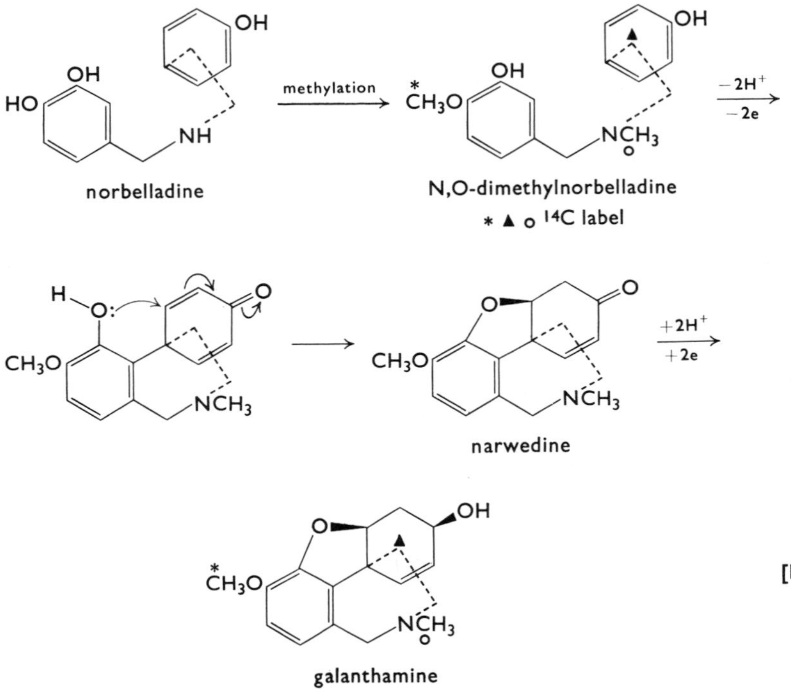

norbelladine

methylation

N,O-dimethylnorbelladine

* ▲ o ¹⁴C label

$-2H^+$
$-2e$

narwedine

$+2H^+$
$+2e$

galanthamine   [Eq. 18-31]

(With the same relative activities at the indicated positions as in the precursor, N,O-dimethylnorbelladine, in feeding experiments with the King Alfred daffodil.)

18.10   Alkaloids Derived by Oxidative Cleavage of Protoberberine Precursors

Formation of the tetrahydroprotoberberine skeleton from a benzylisoquinoline precursor by oxidative ring closure (Eq. 18-32) was discussed in Chapter 15. Various related alkaloids are derived by pathways which involve oxidative fission of the protoberberine structure at one of the positions indicated in Eq. 18-32a.

The simplest transformation is illustrated in the structure of protopine, an alkaloid commonly found in *Corydalis* and *Dicentra* species (both fam. Papaveraceae,

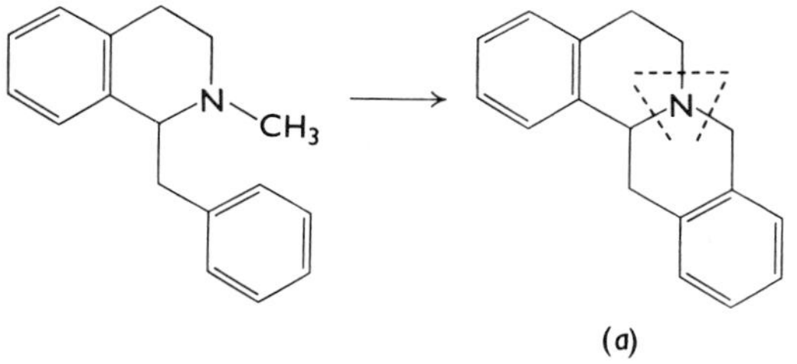

[Eq. 18-32]

(a)

sub-family Fumariaceae). The cleavage reaction leading to protopine (Eq. 18-33) evidently follows the pattern described for the formation of otonecine (page 448) and lycorenine (Eq. 18-27).

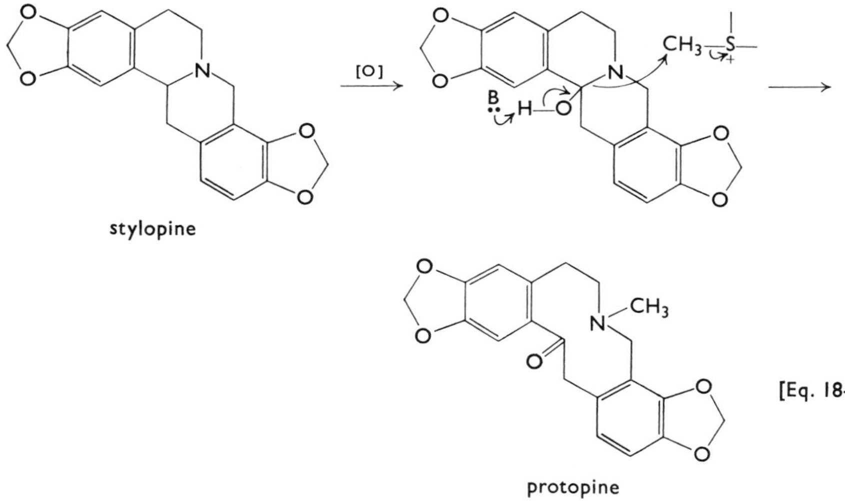

stylopine

[O]

[Eq. 18-33]

protopine

Since the postulated precursor, stylopine, is also frequently found in *Corydalis* and *Dicentra* species, the circumstantial evidence for this pathway is particularly strong.

The benzophenanthridine skeleton encountered in a number of alkaloids of the family Papaveraceae, arises from a protoberberine progenitor, by way of oxidative fission of the C-6—N bond and recyclization. This sequence is illustrated in Eq. 18-34 as it applies to chelidonine biosynthesis in *Chelidonium majus* L. Supporting evidence has come from feeding experiments with multiply labeled reticuline and with labeled stylopine as shown. The results obtained (Eq. 18-34) clearly indicate the specific role of both these alkaloids as precursors of chelidonine. It is to be noted that the tritium label at C-1 in reticuline is lost in this transformation, as is expected for a pathway involving an intermediate of the type Eq. 18-34*a*.

A higher oxidation state is reached in the phthalideisoquinoline alkaloids, a structural type most frequently observed in the Papaveraceae, although occasional representatives are found in the Berberidaceae and Ranunculaceae. The pathway

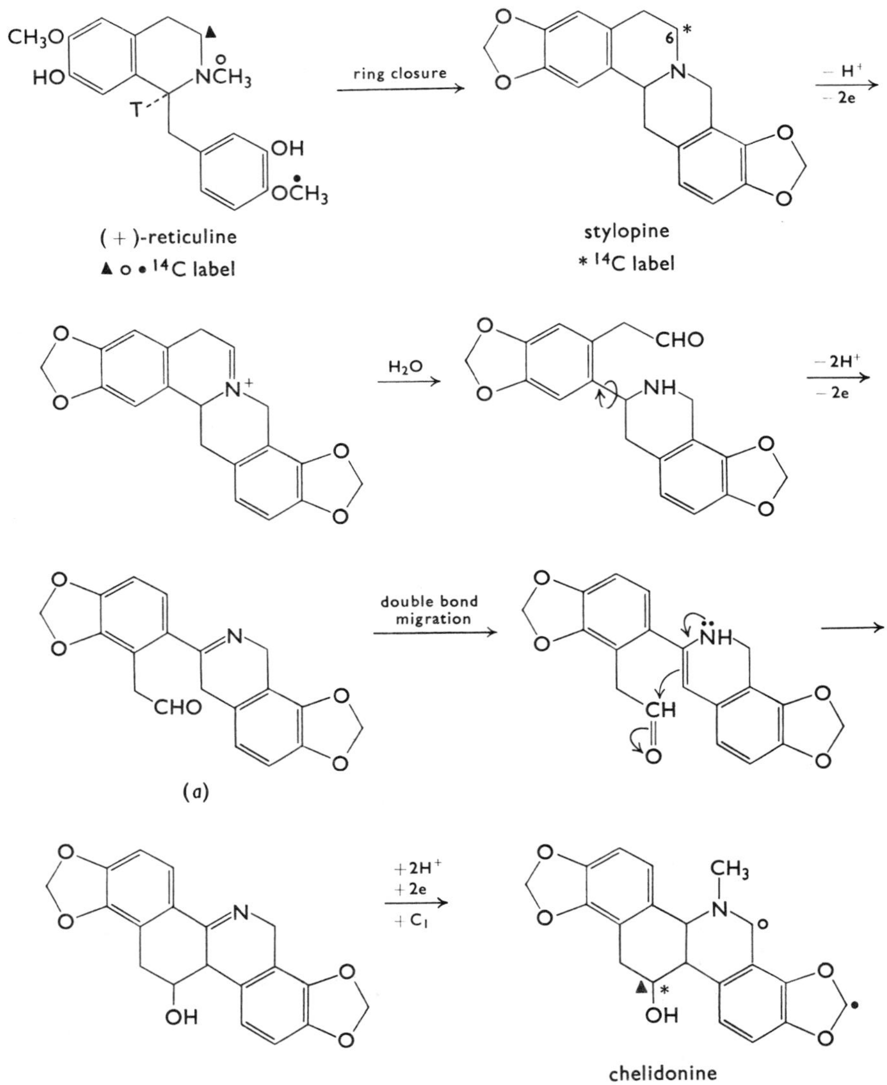

(+)-reticuline
▲ o • ^{14}C label

stylopine
* ^{14}C label

ring closure

$\dfrac{-H^+}{-2e}$

H_2O

$\dfrac{-2H^+}{-2e}$

double bond migration

(a)

$\begin{array}{c} +2H^+ \\ +2e \\ +C_1 \end{array}$

chelidonine

(Activity was found at the indicated positions in chelidonine, when reticuline and stylopine, labeled as shown, were administered to *Chelidonium majus*)

[Eq. 18-34]

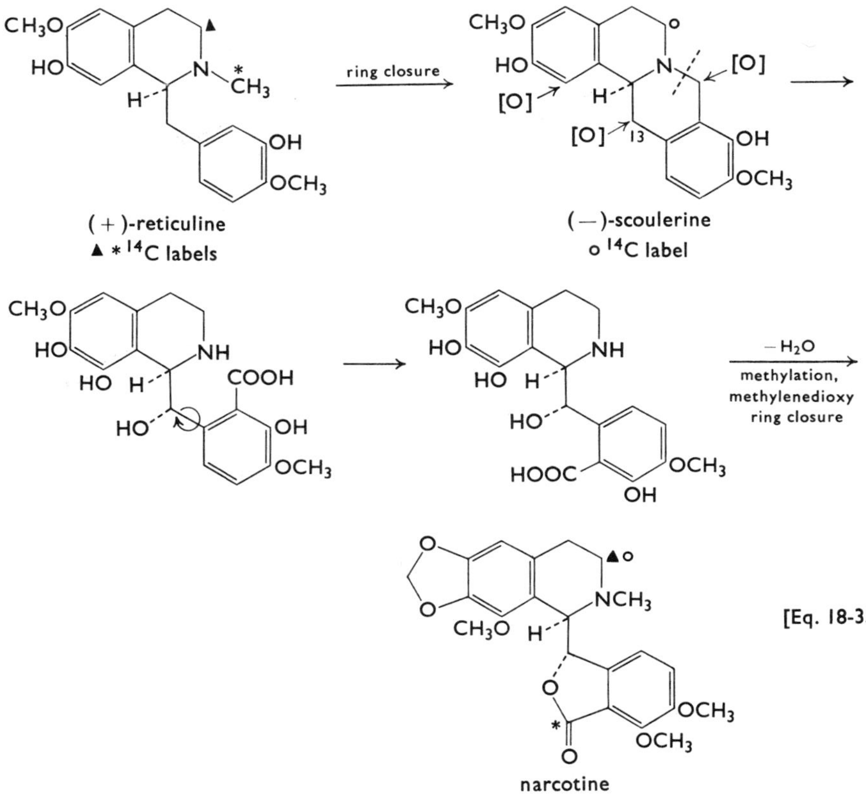

(+)-reticuline
▲ * ^{14}C labels

(−)-scoulerine
o ^{14}C label

narcotine

[Eq. 18-35]

(The location of activity in narcotine at the indicated positions, was observed after administering reticuline and scoulerine, labeled as shown, to *Papaver somniferum*.)

established for narcotine biosynthesis in *Papaver somniferum* involves (+)-reticuline and (−)-scoulerine (Eq. 18-35).

The steps involving hydroxylation, oxidative C—N fission and methylation of the protoberberine precursor can be readily formulated. Hydroxylation at the activated benzylic position, C-13, also presents no conceptual difficulties.

18.11 Bisbenzylisoquinoline Alkaloids

The coupling processes hitherto described have all been of the intramolecular variety. Intermolecular coupling is expressed in an extensive series of bisbenzylisoquinoline alkaloids in which the individual components are usually linked by one or two diphenylether bridges.

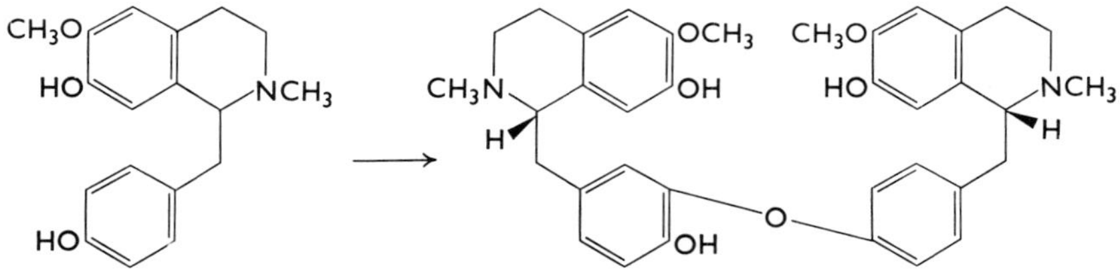

(+) and (−)-N-methylcoclaurine   magnoline   [Eq. 18-36]

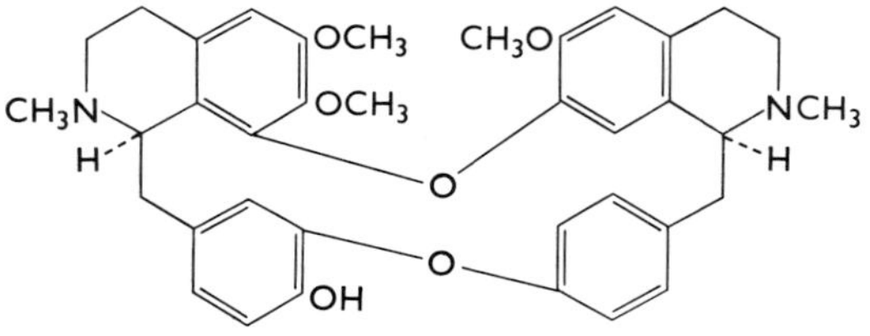

berbamine

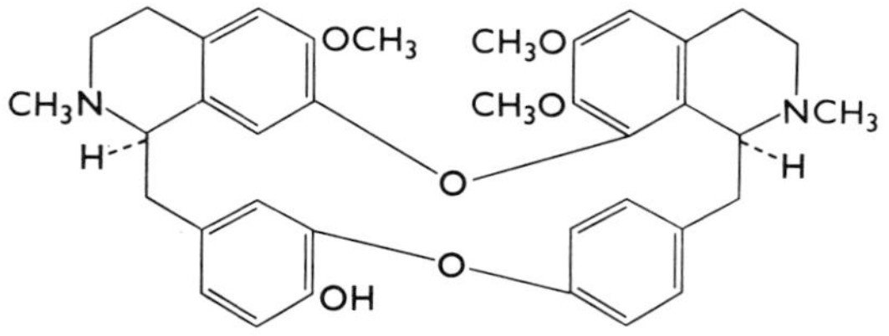

oxyacanthine

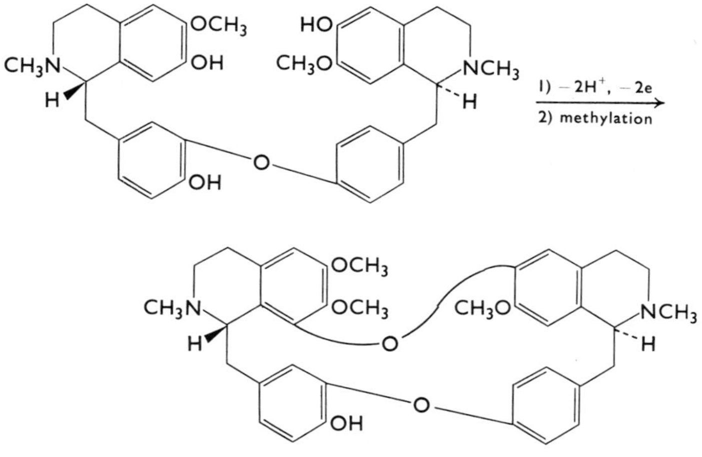

$1) -2H^+, -2e$

$2)$ methylation

[Eq. 18-37]

thalicberine

The majority of bisbenzylisoquinoline alkaloids appear to be derived from norcoclaurine or a suitably methylated derivative. Thus, magnoline can arise directly from N-methylcoclaurine by O—C coupling (Eq. 18-36).

Alkaloids of the magnoline type probably act as precursors of bases containing two ether linkages. Berbamine, oxyacanthine, and thalicberine (Eq. 18-37) illustrate the three common structural varieties in this group. It is to be noted that oxyacanthine and berbamine can be formed from the enantiomer of magnoline by direct O—C coupling followed by methylation. Thalicberine presumably arises from a precursor with an unsymmetrical substitution pattern, as indicated in Eq. 18-37a.

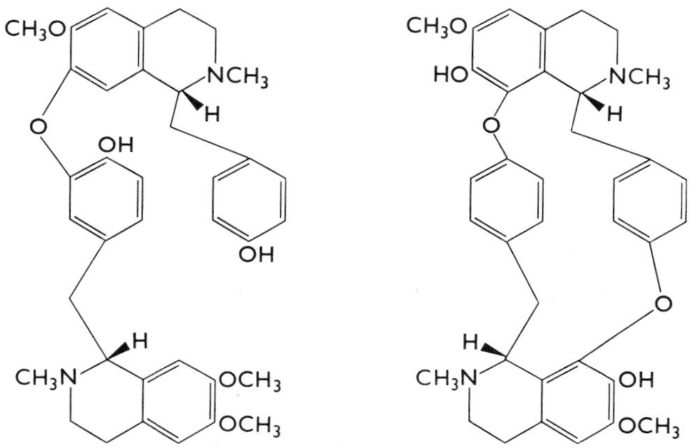

liensinine   isochondrodendrine

Fig. 18-11.

The preceding alkaloids are coupled in what may be described as a "tail-to-tail" manner. The bases liensinine and isochondrodendrine illustrate an alternative "head-to-tail" coupling through the formation of one and two ether linkages respectively (Fig. 18-11).

Tubocurarine, a constituent of South American tube-curare, exhibits a third type of "head-to-tail" coupling (Fig. 18-12).

There are only a few known bases which can be formulated as arising by C—C coupling. A recently discovered example is ocotine, from *Ocotea rodiaei* Mez. (fam. Lauraceae) (Fig. 18-13).

The obvious relationship between the bisbenzyl- and the benzylisoquinoline alkaloids is emphasized by the close coincidence of the plant families in which they appear (cf. table, page 490). Although few incorporation studies have been reported, the available information supports the view that the bisbenzylisoquinoline

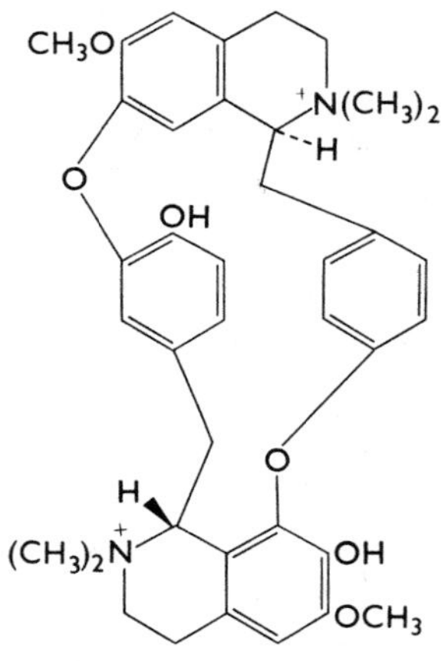

tubocurarine

Fig. 18-12.

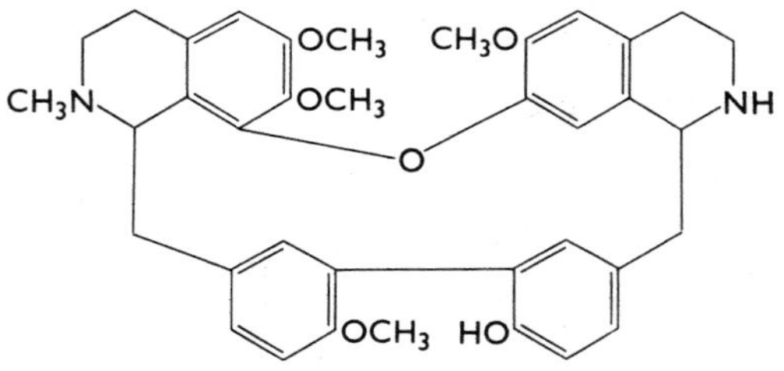

ocotine

Fig. 18-13.

alkaloids are formed as suggested above, i.e. by the direct oxidative coupling of monomers having the appropriate stereochemistry and with a substitution pattern favourable to the desired mode of coupling.

Two further manifestations of intermolecular coupling deserve mention. The first is illustrated by thalicarpine (Fig. 18-14), a base found in various *Thalictrum* species (fam. Ranunculaceae). The aporphine structure in thalicarpine must evidently arise before the *para* hydroxyl function necessary for its formation has been blocked by O—C coupling.

A final structure of quite a different type is exemplified by the unique alkaloid pilocereine, which occurs in species of the genera *Pachycereus*, *Pilocereus*, and *Lophocereus* (fam. Cactaceae) (Fig. 18-14). The genesis of the monomer unit of this alkaloid was discussed in Chapter 17.

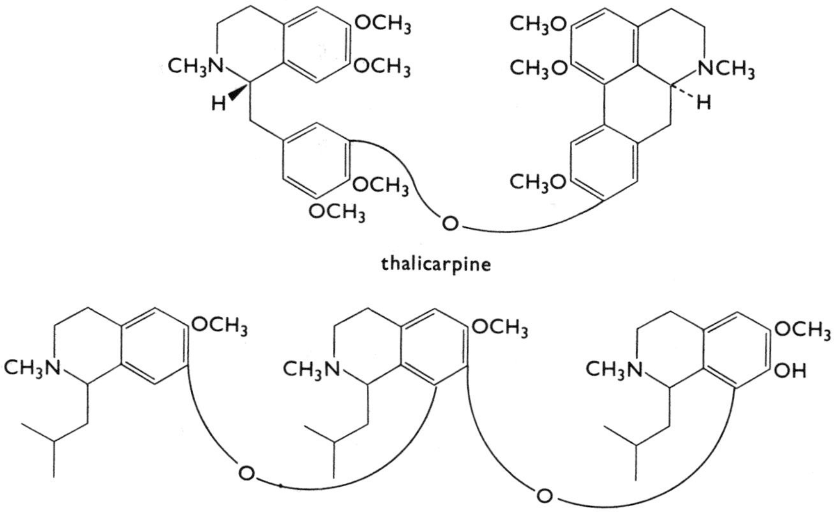

thalicarpine

pilocereine

Fig. 18-14.

18.12 Colchicine

It will be appropriate to conclude this chapter by considering the formation of one of the most intriguing of all alkaloid structures—that of colchicine (Eq. 18-38). This unusual compound is found, together with related bases, in a number of species of the family Liliaceae, notably *Colchicum autumnale* L. (autumn crocus) and *Colchicum byzantium* Ker-Gawl.

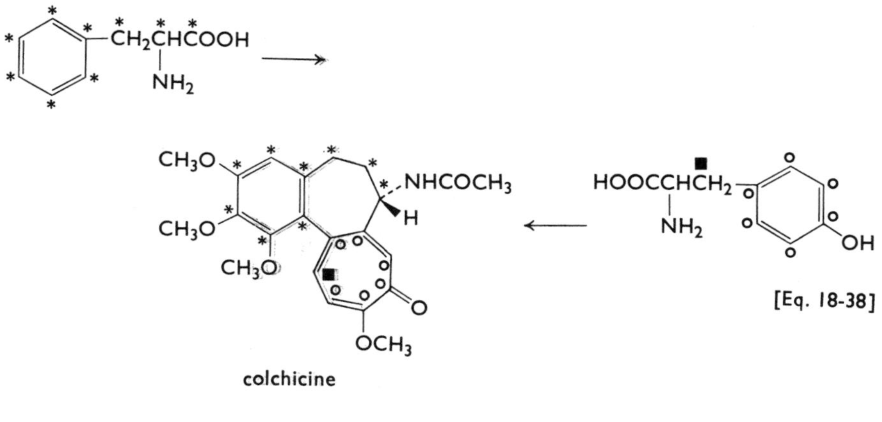

[Eq. 18-38]

colchicine

Incorporation studies provided the following information with respect to the origins of the various rings in colchicine.

  a. Phenylalanine was incorporated *via* cinnamic acid, and furnished the C_6-C_3 component specifically.

  b. C-3 and the aromatic nucleus of tyrosine provided the tropolone ring (Eq. 18-38).

The result noted in (b) was of great importance as it indicated the intervention of a ring expansion step at some stage in the biosynthetic pathway.

As often happens in biosynthetic studies, the way was paved for further progress by the discovery of a possible intermediate in a plant closely related to *Colchicum*. The compound in question, androcymbine, occurs together with colchicine in *Androcymbium melanthoides* Willd. The significance of the structure of androcymbine (Fig. 18-15) lay in its similarity to that of a key intermediate in a provisional pathway of colchicine biosynthesis, which had emerged from preliminary incorporation studies.

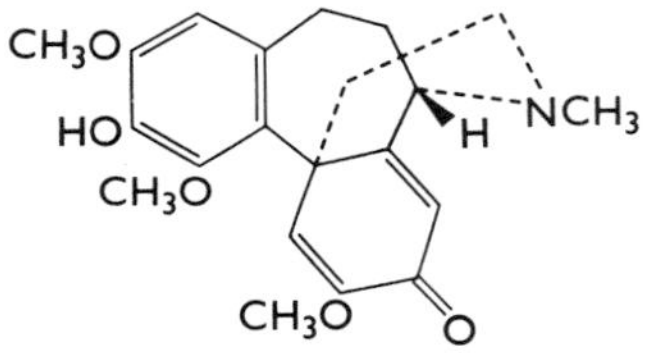

androcymbine

Fig. 18-15.

Although androcymbine itself was eventually considered not to have a place in colchicine biosynthesis, for reasons which will become apparent, a plausible pathway could be developed involving intermediates with closely related structures. This pathway, which is now known to be correct in most details, is given in Eq. 18-39.

It will be noted that according to this scheme, O-methylandrocymbine is postulated as a precursor. Persuasive evidence in support of the proposed pathway was forthcoming with the demonstration that O-methylandrocymbine, labeled as shown (Eq. 18-39), was incorporated into colchicine with very high efficiency.

The pathway was further defined by incorporation experiments involving intermediates *a–d* and demecolcine (Eq. 18-39). (Demecolcine was originally implicated by its co-occurrence with colchicine in *C. autumnale*.) Each of these compounds, in labeled form, was found to be an efficient and specific precursor of colchicine.

The early steps leading to the phenethylisoquinoline *a* (Eq. 18-39), have not yet been elucidated. However, it seems probable that a pathway is involved which is analogous to that leading to the simple benzylisoquinoline alkaloids (cf. Eq. 18-2).

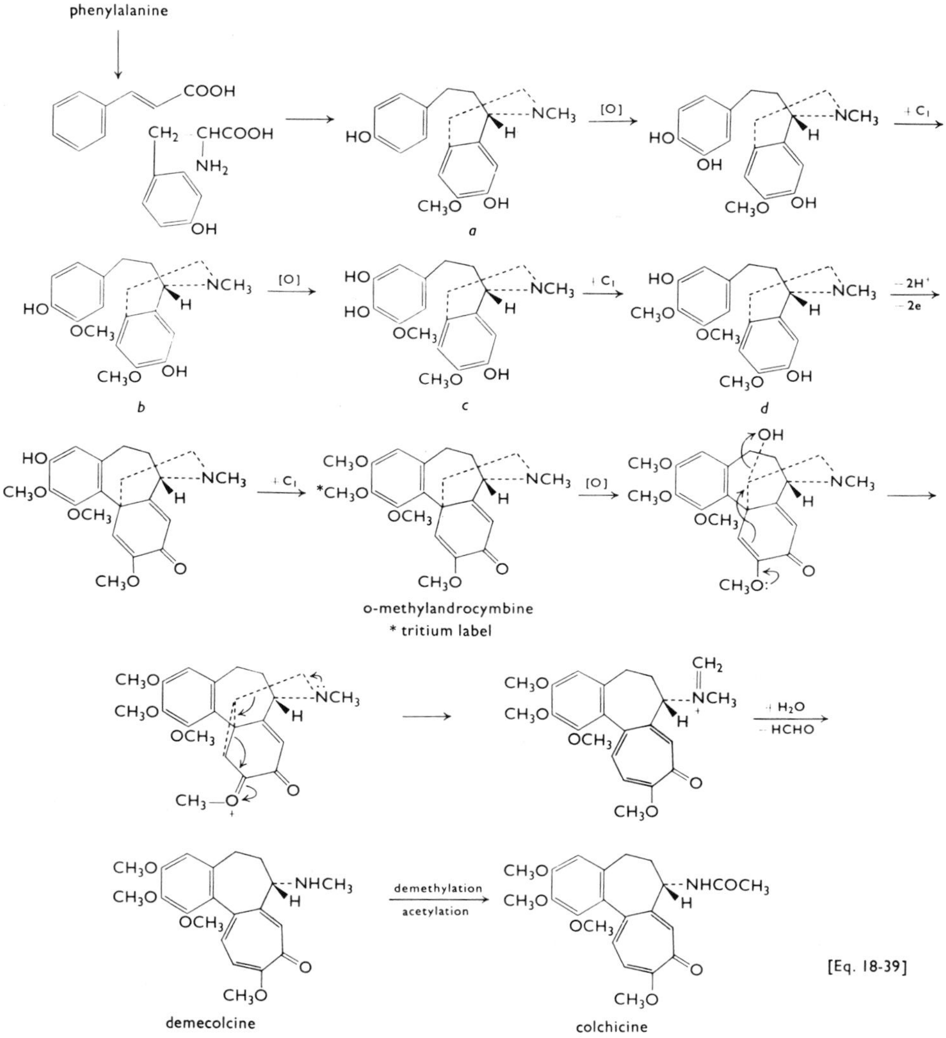

o-methylandrocymbine
* tritium label

[Eq. 18-39]

demecolcine

colchicine

The crucial ring-expansion step in the transformation of O-methylandro-cymbine into colchicine can be formulated as proceeding by way of hydroxylation followed by homoallylic displacement of the hydroxyl function,* a process that in nature would probably be assisted by phosphorylation. The resulting cyclopropane intermediate is postulated to undergo fragmentation followed by hydrolysis, demethylation and acetylation as shown.

* This displacement is analogous to the *iso*-steroid rearrangement. (For a discussion see N. L. Wendler, *Rearrangements in Steroids*, in Molecular Rearrangements, P. de Mayo, Ed., Interscience, New York and London, 1963, Vol. 2, p. 1019.)

The rearrangement has a laboratory analogy in the following reaction (Eq. 18-40):

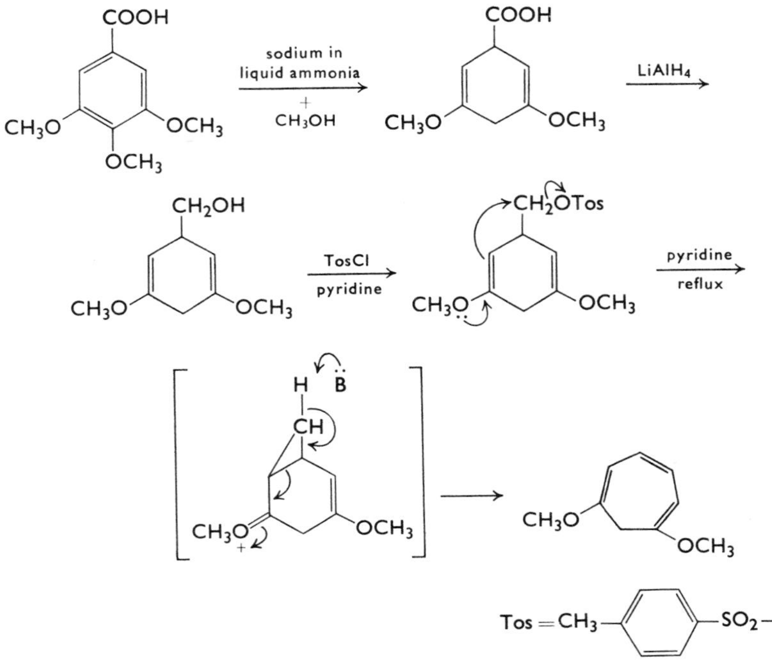

[Eq. 18-40]

$$Tos = CH_3 - \langle \rangle - SO_2 -$$

Although the corresponding sequence in the pathway of Eq. 18-39 has not yet been tested in detail, the following arguments can be presented in its support: (a) it is mechanistically acceptable; (b) it convincingly explains the observed pattern of tyrosine incorporation and (c) it is based on sound laboratory analogies such as the one mentioned.

When the accumulated evidence concerning colchicine biosynthesis is surveyed, it can be seen that what at first sight appears to be a rather extraordinary structure, arises in fact by a straightforward sequence of reactions, most of which have numerous analogies in other pathways of alkaloid biosynthesis. It is particularly noteworthy that in the structure of intermediate *d* (Eq. 18-39) we have yet a further example of the use of methylation to restrict the number of possible orientations in an oxidative coupling process *in vivo*.

18.13   Conclusion

The discussions in this chapter and in Chapter 14 will have illustrated the wide range of biosynthetic pathways in which an oxidative coupling step can be implicated at some point. The original speculations of Robinson and Gulland, Erdtman and Wachmeister, and others, when combined with the mechanistic interpretations due to Barton and Cohen, can be seen to provide one of the most powerful unifying concepts in the chemistry of secondary metabolism. Not the least of the benefits produced by this theory is the stimulus it has provided for the experimental testing of its various proposals. This has resulted in the disclosure of many fascinating biosynthetic pathways which often surpass in elegance and economy the best efforts of the synthetic chemist.

XIX CHAPTER

REFERENCES FOR FURTHER READING

Much additional information on the chemistry and biosynthesis of the indole and terpene alkaloids will be found in the general references given at the beginning of Chapter 16.

1. A. R. Battersby, *Biogenesis of the Indole and Colchicum Alkaloids*, Pure Appl. Chem., *14*, (1967), 117.
2. A. R. Battersby, A. R. Burnett, E. S. Hall, and P. G. Parsons, *The Rearrangement Process in Indole Alkaloid Biosynthesis*, Chem. Comm., (1968), 1582.
3. A. A. Qureshi and A. I. Scott, *Biosynthesis of Indole Alkaloids. Sequential Precursor Formation and Biological Conversion in Vinca rosea*, Chem. Comm., (1968), 948.
4. H. Schmid, *The Chemistry of Calabash Curare*, Bull. Schweiz. Akad. Med. Wiss., *22*, (1967), 415.
5. S. Agurell, *Biosynthetic Studies on Ergot Alkaloids and Related Indoles*, Acta Pharm. Suecica, *3*, (1966), 71.
6. H.-G. Floss, U. Hornemann, N. Schilling, K. Kelley, D. Groeger, and D. Erge, *Biosynthesis of Ergot Alkaloids. Evidence for Two Isomerizations in the Isoprenoid Moiety During the Formation of Tetracyclic Ergolines*, J. Amer. Chem. Soc., *90*, (1968), 6500.
7. R. Tschesche and H. Hulpke, *The Biosynthesis of Conessine from Pregnenolone*, Z. Naturforsch., *23b*, (1968), 283.
8. E. Heftmann, E. R. Lieber, and R. D. Bennett, *Biosynthesis of Tomatidine from Cholesterol in Lycopersicon pimpinellifolium*, Phytochemistry, *6*, (1967), 255.

Alkaloids of Mixed Amino Acid-Mevalonate Origin. Terpenoid Alkaloids

19.1 The Monoterpene-Indole Alkaloids. Introduction and General Biosynthesis

Three plant families, the Apocynaceae, the Loganiaceae, and the Rubiaceae, produce a remarkable series of complex indole alkaloids, which, in the intricacy of their construction, are outstanding among secondary plant metabolites.

As with many other classes of alkaloids, the compounds under discussion first attracted attention because of their pronounced physiological activity. Strychnine, perhaps the most familiar of the complex indole alkaloids, and the related bases of South American calabash curare, are noteworthy for their high toxicity, and the *Cinchona* alkaloid, quinine, is well-known through its widespread use in the prophylaxis and treatment of malaria.*

The isolation, in 1952, of reserpine, from the Indian plant *Rauwolfia serpentina* (L.) Benth. ex Kurz (fam. Apocynaceae), and the discovery of its sedative and antihypertensive properties, initiated a new era in the treatment of nervous disorders, and marked the entry of the tranquilizer into the medical scene. More recently, it has been found that certain indole alkaloids exhibit useful anti-tumor activity. This property was initially observed in the alkaloidal extracts of *Vinca rosea* L. (= *Catharanthus roseus* G. Don) (fam. Apocynaceae), the Madagascar periwinkle. Subsequent investigations led to the isolation and characterization of therapeutically useful compounds such as leurocristine and vincaleukoblastine, which are of value in the treatment of certain forms of leukemia.

The combined stimuli of structural complexity and clinically significant

---

* Although quinine is based structurally on a quinoline nucleus, it will be seen to be biogenetically closely related to the indole alkaloids.

pharmacological activity have inspired enormous efforts in the field of indole alkaloid chemistry, and more than six hundred different bases in this group have now been isolated and characterized. However, this profusion of individual compounds can be reduced to a relatively small number of structural types. Some of the most important of these are illustrated by the following representative bases (Fig. 19-1):

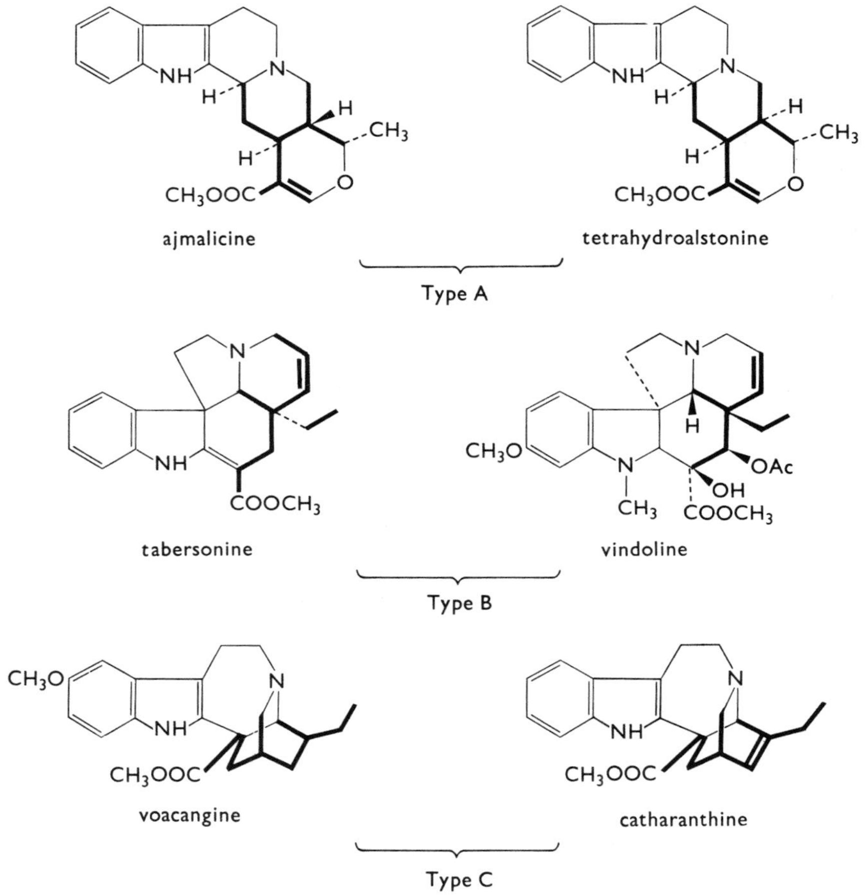

ajmalicine   tetrahydroalstonine

Type A

tabersonine   vindoline

Type B

voacangine   catharanthine

Type C

Fig. 19-1.

Most of the known alkaloids have structures which can be dissected into an indole component, which almost invariably appears as a tryptamine unit (cf. Fig. 19-1), and a further fragment, of variable structure, containing nine or ten carbon atoms.

The observation, based on a number of incorporation experiments, that tryptophan furnishes the tryptamine component in various representative alkaloids, quickly settles the question of the biogenesis of the indole unit. In many alkaloids the indole nucleus bears hydroxyl or methoxyl substituents. Although it is not known at present exactly when these substituents are introduced, the relevant processes of hydroxylation and methylation are so commonly observed in secondary plant metabolism that no special comment will be necessary for each specific example in the discussion to follow.

An examination of the remaining $C_{9,10}$ components, reveals that in the majority of alkaloids, these have one of the three basic carbon skeletons illustrated in Fig. 19-2 (cf. Fig. 19-1).*

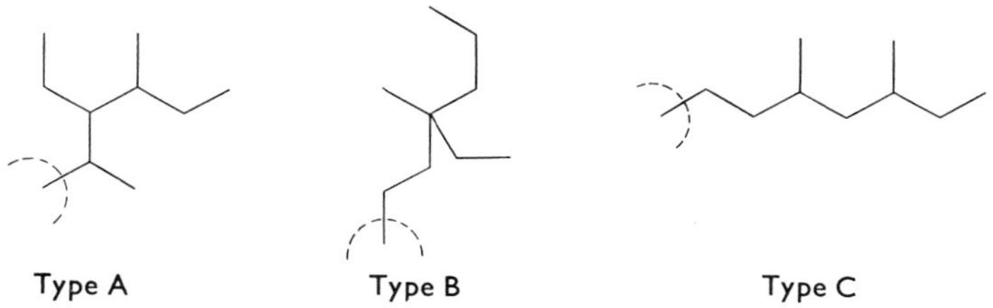

Type A   Type B   Type C

Fig. 19-2.

In alkaloids in which a C_9 component is present, this will be seen to be formally related to one of the C_{10} structures, by bond cleavage at the positions indicated in Fig. 19-2. Examples of typical alkaloids with C_9 components related to the C_{10} structures of Fig. 19-2, are given in Fig. 19-3.

It will be evident that certain basic questions must be answered in order to explain the formation of the complex indole alkaloids. These may be formulated as follows:

  a. What is the biogenetic origin of the various types of $C_{9,10}$ component?
  b. What chemical steps are involved (i) in the elaboration of the $C_{9,10}$ units, (ii) in their attachment to the indole nucleus and (iii) in their subsequent modification?
  c. Are the three principal structural modifications of this unit derived by independent pathways, or are they related as part of a single biosynthetic sequence?

The solution to the problem posed in (a) proved to be remarkably elusive. At various times, it has been proposed that the $C_{9,10}$ units could arise by the polyketide pathway, by ring opening and rearrangement of prephenic acid, by the

* The three principal modifications of the $C_{9,10}$ unit are commonly designated by the names of the genera or species producing their major representatives, viz. Corynanthe type (A) (after the genus *Corynanthe*), *Aspidosperma* type (B) (after the genus *Aspidosperma*), and Iboga type (C) (after *Tabernanthe iboga* Baill.). However, the designations "type A (B, C)" will be used for convenience in the present discussion.

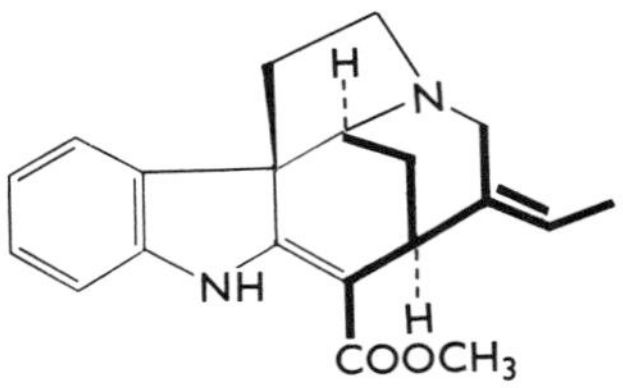

akuammicine
type A, C$_9$

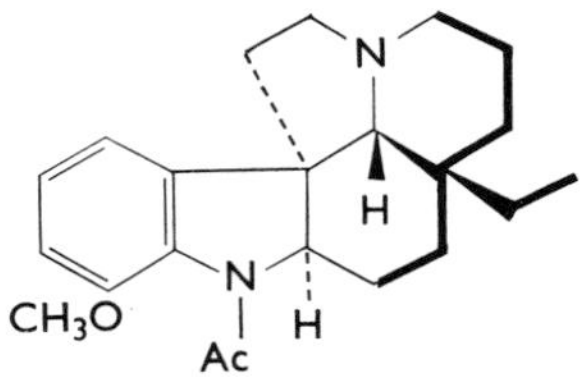

aspidospermine
type B, C$_9$

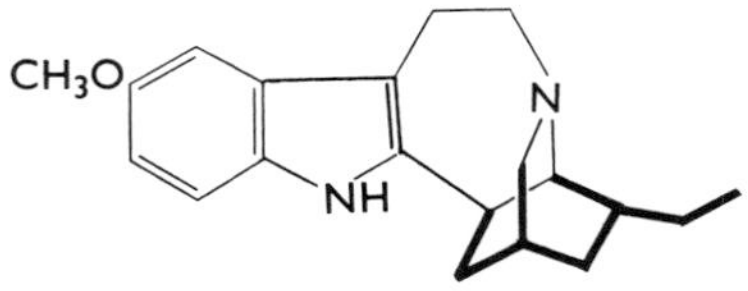

ibogaine
type C, C$_9$

Fig. 19-3.

carboxylation and ring opening of 3,4-dihydroxyphenylacetaldehyde or by the re-arrangement of a monoterpenoid precursor.*

It is now known, as the result of numerous incorporation experiments, that only the last of these hypotheses is tenable, and that the C$_{9,10}$ components of the indole alkaloids are derived by way of the acetate-mevalonate pathway.

Before discussing the relevant experimental results, it is necessary to consider the ways in which the C$_{9,10}$ units could arise from a monoterpenoid precursor.

It will be evident from an examination of the structures shown in Fig. 19-2, that none of these has the "normal" monoterpene skeleton, as exemplified, for example, by geraniol (Fig. 19-4). Structure A, however, has a carbon skeleton identical with that of the secoiridoid compounds described in Chapter 8, of which

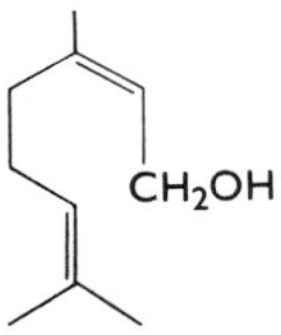

geraniol

Fig. 19-4.

* For a discussion of the many interesting proposals concerning indole alkaloid biogenesis, the reader is referred to the chapter by E. Leete, *Alkaloid Biogenesis*, in Biogenesis of Natural Compounds, P. Bernfeld Ed., Pergamon Press, Oxford, 2nd Edition, 1967, p. 953.

gentiopicroside (Eq. 19-1) may be taken as a typical example. The secoiridoids, it will be recalled, are known to arise by ring cleavage of precursors which belong to the iridoid class of monoterpene, as shown.

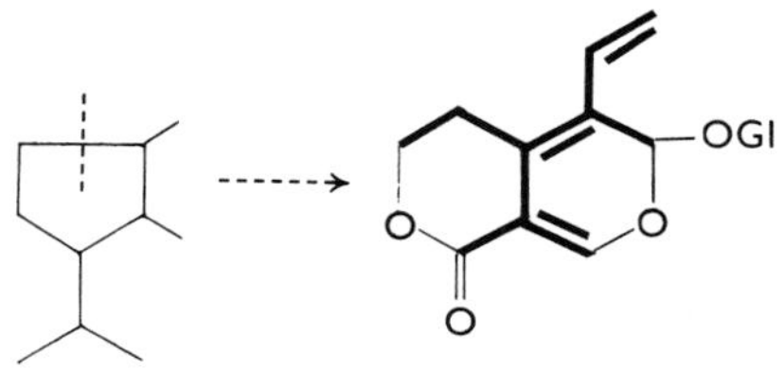

[Eq. 19-1]

iridoid skeleton   gentiopicroside

The sequence outlined in Eq. 19-2a can thus be written, by analogy, to illustrate a possible pathway for the conversion of mevalonate into the type A C_{10} unit of the indole alkaloids.

In addition, the rearrangements shown in Eq. 19-2b, c may be postulated for the formation of the C_{10} units of types B and C.

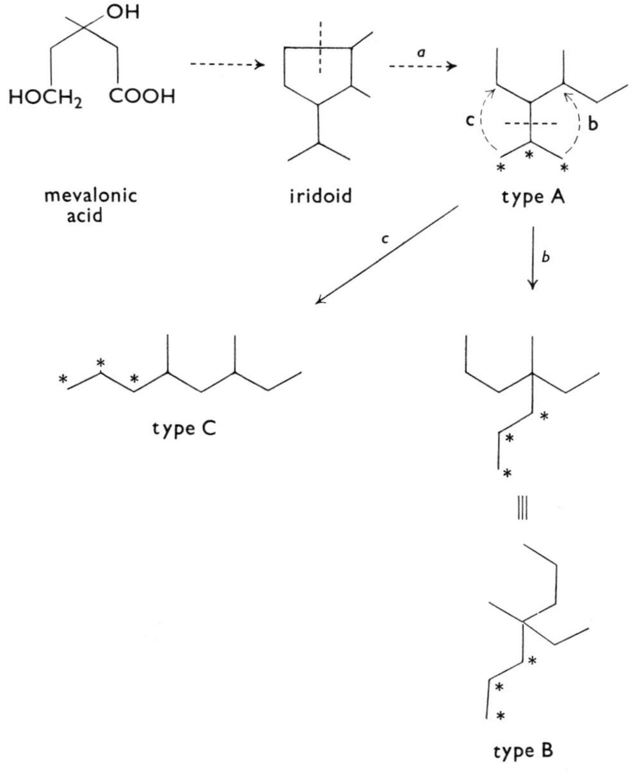

mevalonic   iridoid   type A
acid

type C

[Eq. 19-2]

type B

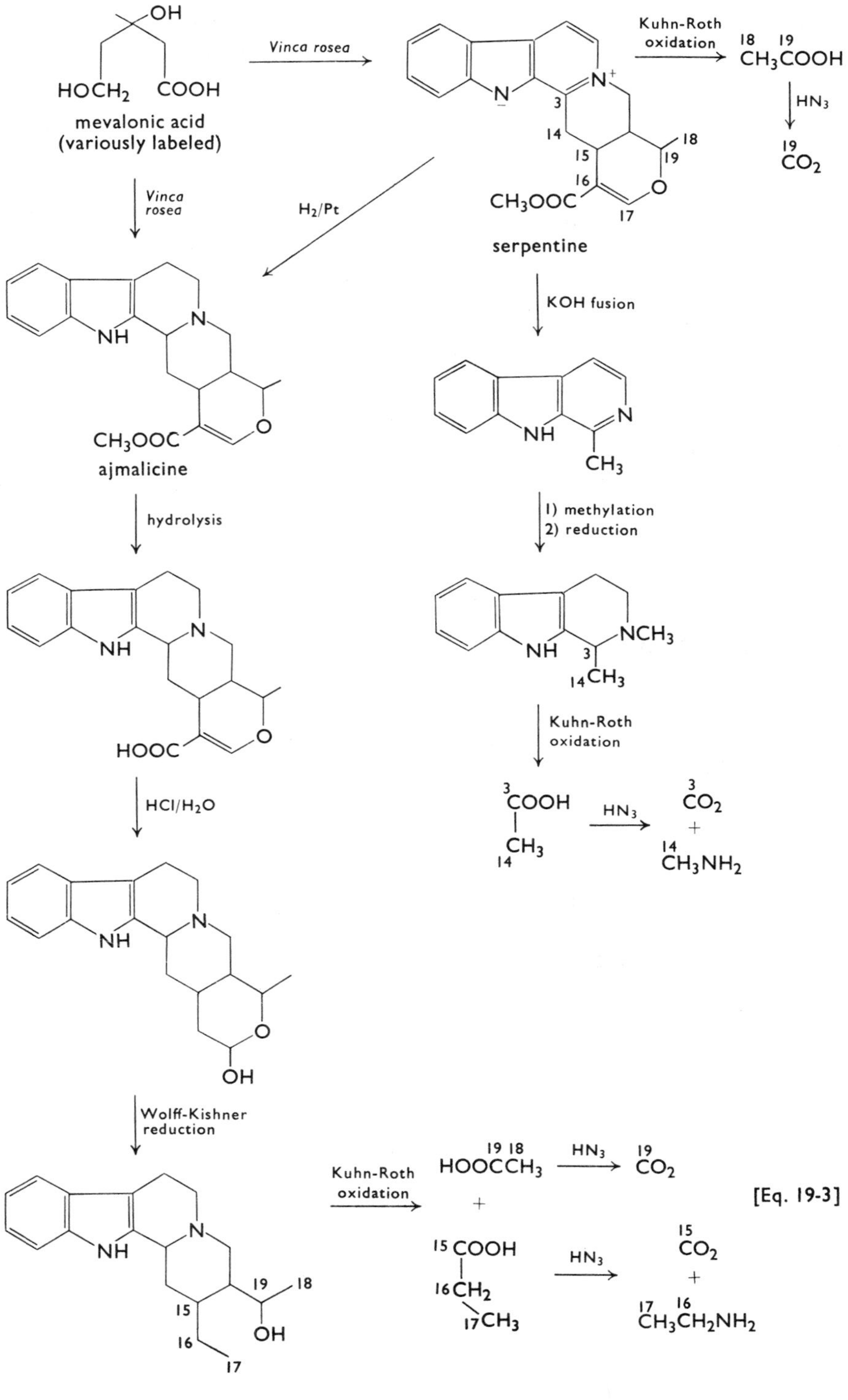

mevalonic acid
(variously labeled)

serpentine

CH_3COOH

CH_3
CO_2

ajmalicine

CH_3OOC

hydrolysis

$HOOC$

HCl/H_2O

OH

Wolff-Kishner
reduction

Kuhn-Roth
oxidation

$HOOCCH_3$ $\xrightarrow{HN_3}$ CO_2

+

$COOH$
CH_2
CH_3 $\xrightarrow{HN_3}$ CO_2
+
$CH_3CH_2NH_2$

[Eq. 19-3]

$COOH$
CH_3 $\xrightarrow{HN_3}$ CO_2
+
CH_3NH_2

Kuhn-Roth
oxidation

1) methylation
2) reduction

NCH_3
CH_3

KOH fusion

CH_3

It is to be noted that at this point we are considering only the *formal* derivation of the C_{10} units and are taking no cognisance of the possible mechanisms of these various rearrangements. However, the relationships suggested in Eq. 19-2 have been used to formulate experiments by means of which the possible role of an iridoid precursor in indole alkaloid biosynthesis could be tested. As an example, we may consider the experiments relating to the biosynthesis of the C_{10} unit of type A (Fig. 19-2) as it appears in two of the alkaloids of *Vinca rosea*, ajmalicine and serpentine. Specifically labeled mevalonic acid was fed to *V. rosea* plants, and the resulting labeled alkaloids were degraded as shown in Eq. 19-3.

The results from these experiments are summarized in Eq. 19-4*a*, and may be compared with the predictions arising from the postulated sequence mevalonate → iridoid → secoiridoid → C_{10} unit, shown in Eq. 19-4*b*.

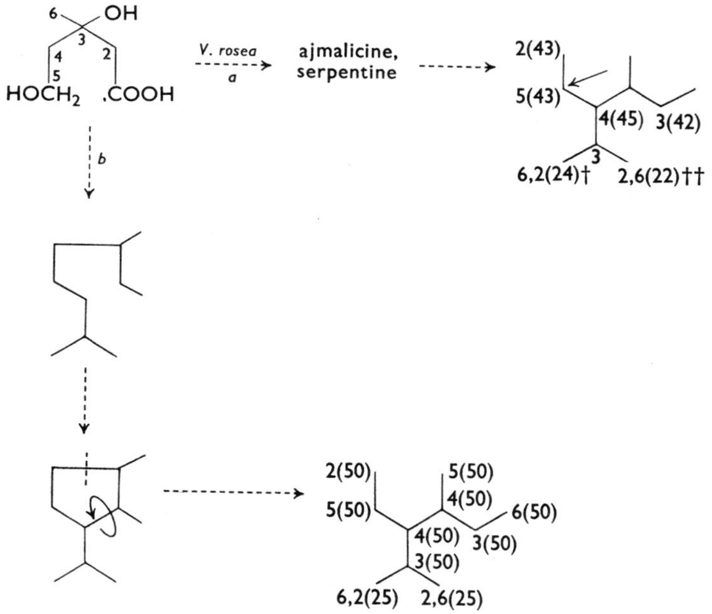

[Eq. 19-4]

† Results from feeding experiments with 2-^{14}C-mevalonate.

†† This figure includes the activity at the adjacent position derived from C-3 of mevalonic acid.

The figures in parentheses in the C_{10} structure of Eq. 19-4*a*, indicate the percentage activity found at the corresponding position in the experiments outlined in Eq. 19-3. For example, the carbon atom indicated by an arrow is predicted to be derived from C-5 of mevalonic acid. The figure in parentheses denotes that 43 per cent of the total activity of the alkaloid was found at this position when meval-onate, specifically labeled at C-5, was used in the feeding experiment.

It will be noted from the incorporation pattern (Eq. 19-4a) that C-2 and C-6 of mevalonic acid become equivalent in one of the isoprene units of the C_{10} structure.* However, when this is taken into account, a very good agreement is observed between the predicted and experimentally determined activities for each of the investigated positions. Similar studies relating to the origins of the remain-ing two types of C_{10} structure have likewise given results which are in close agree-ment with the requirements imposed by the postulated relationships of Eq. 19-2. Taken together, these experiments provide powerful support for the involvement of iridoid and secoiridoid precursors in indole alkaloid biosynthesis.

The conclusions arising out of these experiments with mevalonic acid, have been underscored by further incorporation experiments involving geraniol, which, according to the accepted pathway of monoterpene biosynthesis (Chap. 8), should be an immediate precursor of the postulated iridoid intermediate in indole alkaloid biosynthesis. Without entering into a detailed discussion, it can be stated that feed-ing experiments with specifically labeled geraniol have given results which are in agreement with the proposed pathway.

At this stage, the various strands of evidence emerging from the experiments just described, can be summarized in the following statements:

  a. The indole alkaloids are derived biogenetically from tryptophan (*via* tryptamine) and mevalonic acid.
  b. The evidence relating to the formation of the three basic $C_{9,10}$ components of terpenoid origin is consistent with the sequence mevalonate → geraniol → iridoid → secoiridoid → C_{10} unit.

Further progress evidently required the identification of the iridoid and seco-iridoid intermediates, of which more than a single related pair might be involved. When a number of iridoid compounds were scrutinized as possible precursors of the $C_{9,10}$ units, attention gradually became focused on loganin (Fig. 19-5) as the most

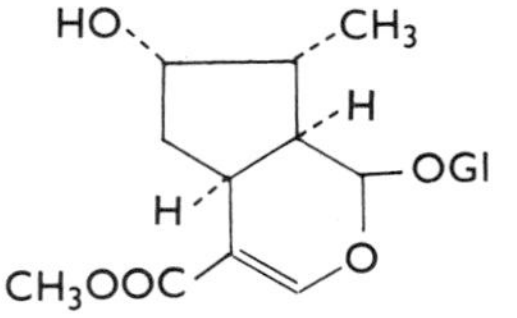

loganin

Fig. 19-5.

* A similar equivalence has been observed in the biosynthesis of the iridoid monoterpene, plumieride.

likely candidate. The reasons for favouring loganin were firstly taxonomic, in that it occurs in a number of species of the family Loganiaceae, and secondly structural, in that it has an arrangement of functional groups strongly reminiscent of similar arrangements in a number of indole alkaloids containing C_{10} components of type A.

An alkaloid noted to bear a particularly strong resemblance to loganin was ipecoside (Eq. 19-5). Ipecoside is representative of a group of alkaloids with structures analogous to the indole alkaloids, but based on an isoquinoline rather than on an indole nucleus. Ipecoside is found in *Cephaelis ipecachuanha* Rich, a plant best known as a source of emetine (see below). Since the genus *Cephaelis* is placed in the family Rubiaceae, biogenetic comparisons between the *Ipecachuanha* and indole alkaloids are placed on a valid taxonomic basis.

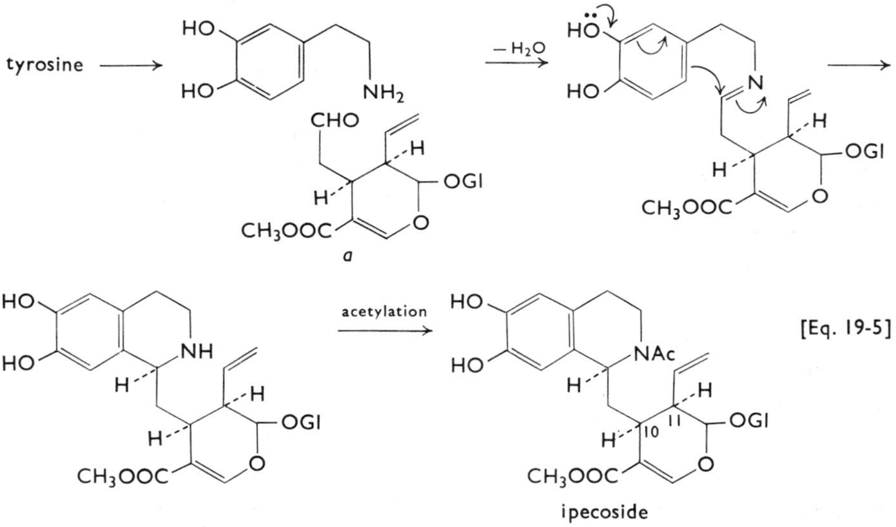

[Eq. 19-5]

ipecoside

The putative connection between loganin and ipecoside can be more readily appreciated if the probable biosynthetic pathway to the latter is considered (Eq. 19-5). Exactly analogous pathways were invoked to explain the formation of the simple 1-alkylisoquinoline alkaloids described in Chapter 17.

The intermediate aldehyde Eq. 19-5a (which is now known as secologanin) can be considered to arise from loganin in a number of ways. The fragmentation mechanism shown in Eq. 19-6, for example, illustrates one possibility.

When the proposals linking loganin with indole alkaloid biosynthesis had reached this stage of development, it was obviously necessary to consider whether the configurations at the asymmetric centers in loganin, corresponded with those in supposedly related alkaloids such as ipecoside. It was subsequently found, by un-ambiguous stereochemical correlation, that positions C-10 and C-11 in ipecoside

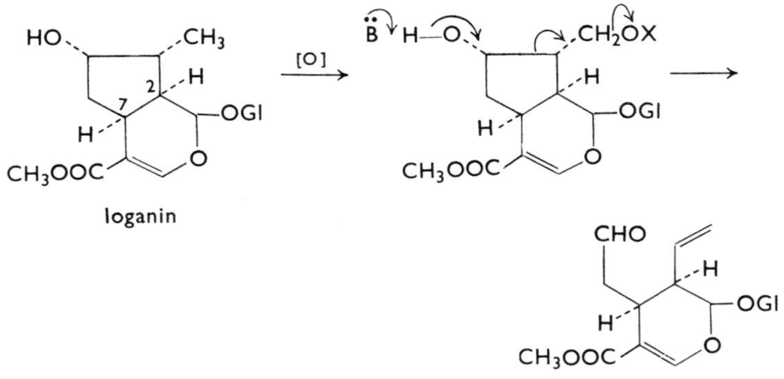

loganin

secologanin

[Eq. 19-6]

(Eq. 19-5) and the corresponding positions C-7 and C-2, respectively, in loganin (Eq. 19-6) had the same absolute configurations. A similar correspondence has been observed, in all but a few alkaloids, for centers corresponding to C-7 in loganin. However, although the absolute configuration at C-2 in loganin persists in ipecoside, many pathways of indole alkaloid biosynthesis apparently involve inversion at this center, by readily explicable mechanisms which will be discussed in the sequel.

To complete the circumstantial evidence regarding the precursor role of loganin, mention should be made of the recent discovery, in *Rhazya stricta* Decaisne (fam. Apocynaceae), of the glucosidic alkaloid strictosidine (Fig. 19-6), which is an indole analogue of ipecoside. Strictosidine has also been shown by isotope dilution analysis to be present in *Vinca rosea*.

It will be evident from the foregoing discussion, that it was necessary for projected incorporation experiments involving loganin to be able to provide answers to two questions: (a) Is loganin biosynthesized in a manner which is consistent with its role as a precursor, in the light of the results obtained from incorporation experiments relating to the biosynthesis of the C_{10} units from mevalonate (cf. Eq. 19-4a)? (b) Can loganin be utilized directly for the biosynthesis of indole alkaloids?

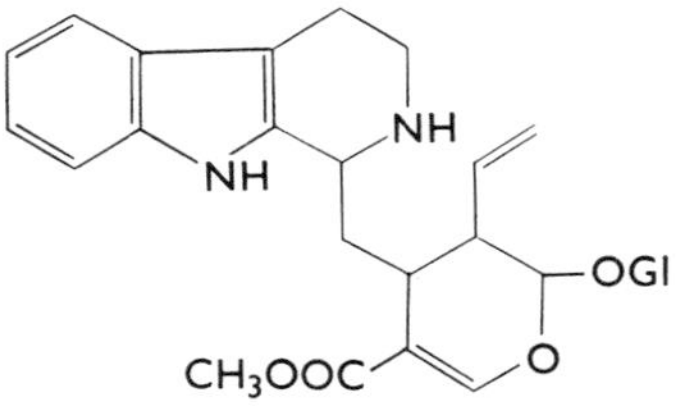

strictosidine

Fig. 19-6.

Experiments relating to loganin biosynthesis have been carried out with *Menyanthes trifoliata* L. This species, although not placed in any of the three major indole-alkaloid producing families, is classified in the family Menyanthaceae, which is closely related both to the Loganiaceae and to the Apocynaceae.

Experiments with labeled mevalonate in *M. trifoliata* were not particularly informative, as negligible incorporations into loganin were observed. However, this result should not be taken to mean that mevalonate is not a precursor; the most probable explanation for the observed result is that the administered compound failed to penetrate to the site of loganin biosynthesis. Similar negative results have often been observed in investigations into terpene biosynthesis in higher plants. However, experiments with the more immediate precursor, geraniol, had a satisfactory outcome. The synthesis of specifically labeled geraniol, and its conversion into loganin, in *M. trifoliata*, are illustrated in Eq. 19-7.*

a. $Br\overset{*}{C}H_2COOCH_3 + (C_6H_5)_3P \longrightarrow (C_6H_5)_3\overset{+}{P}-\overset{*}{C}H_2COOCH_3 \xrightarrow{base} (C_6H_5)_3P=CHCOOCH_3$

Br$^-$

* 14C label

b.

$+ (C_6H_5)_3P=\overset{*}{C}HCOOCH_3 \xrightarrow{\substack{Wittig \\ reaction}} \overset{*}{C}HCOOCH_3 \xrightarrow{LiAlH_4}$

Menyanthes
trifoliata
(0.25%)

14C-geraniol   loganin   [Eq. 19-7]

Proof that the derived loganin was labeled at the expected position, was obtained by an experiment which at the same time economically provided an answer to the question posed in (b) above. Thus the biosynthetically labeled loganin, obtained from the feeding experiment just described, was fed to *Vinca rosea* plants to afford the labeled alkaloids shown in Eq. 19-8. The various degradations illustrated, clearly established the location of activity at the expected positions, in alkaloids representative of the three main types of $C_{9,10}$ unit. (The skeletal type of each alkaloid is indicated in parentheses.) These results also served to confirm the specific conversion of geraniol into loganin (cf. Eq. 19-7).

* Additional evidence regarding loganin biosynthesis was described in Chapter 8.

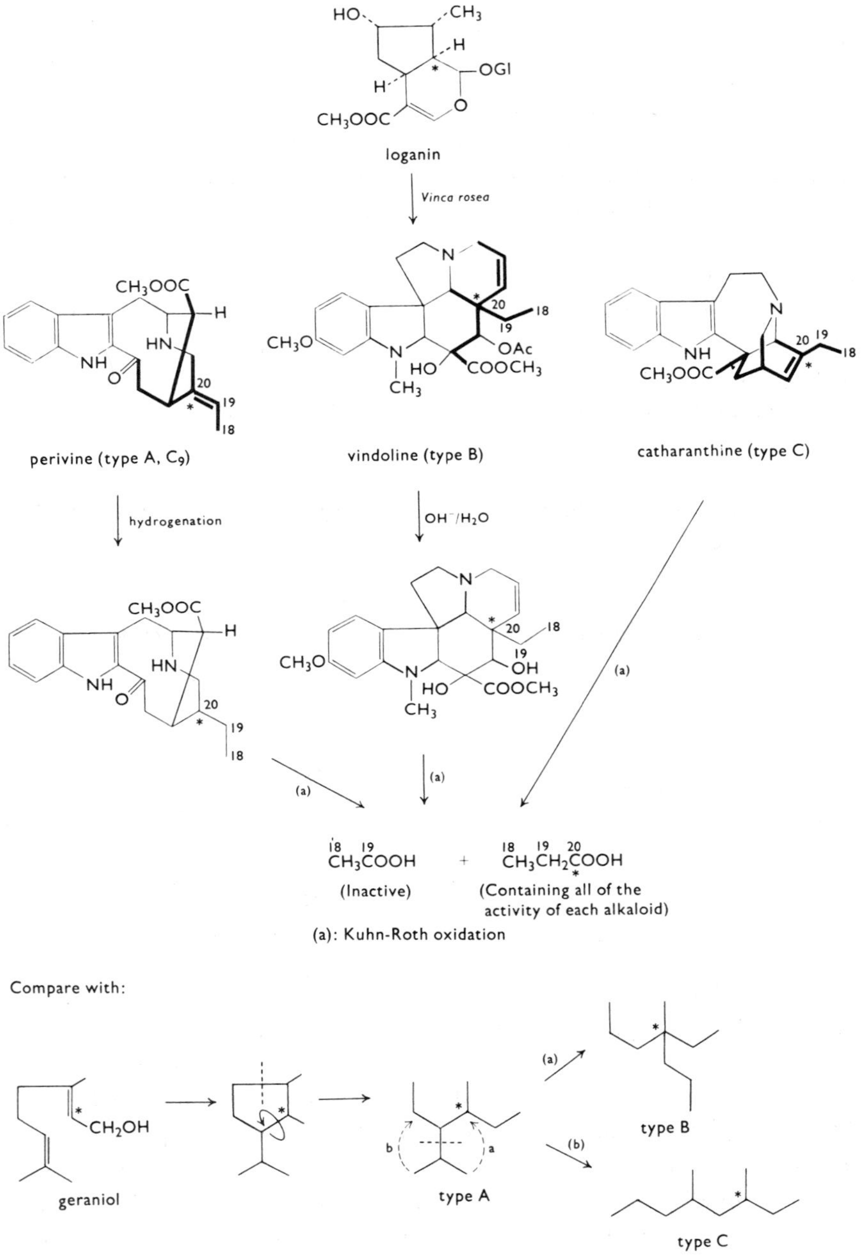

loganin

Vinca rosea

perivine (type A, C₉)

vindoline (type B)

catharanthine (type C)

hydrogenation

OH⁻/H₂O

(a)

(a)

(a)

18 19
CH₃COOH   +   CH₃CH₂COOH
(Inactive)   (Containing all of the
                          activity of each alkaloid)

(a): Kuhn-Roth oxidation

Compare with:

geraniol

type A

type B

type C

[Eq. 19-8]

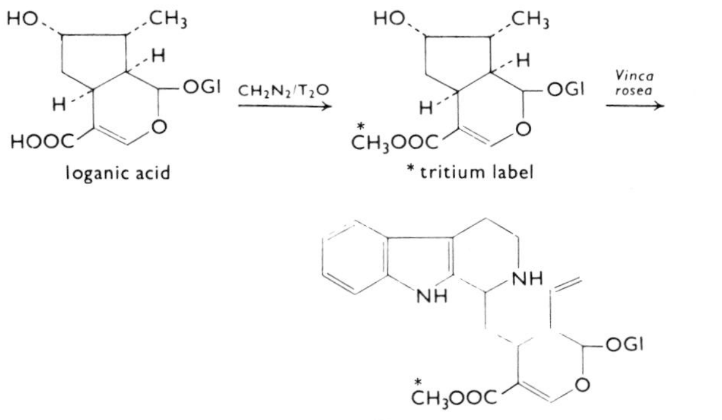

loganic acid   * tritium label

[Eq. 19-9]

strictosidine (5.2% incorporation of radioactivity)

R = ⟋⟍ CH₂OH ⟍COO—   foliamenthin

R = ⟋⟍ CH₂OH ⟍COO—   dihydrofoliamenthin

R = OH ⟍COO—   menthiafolin

a.

secologanin

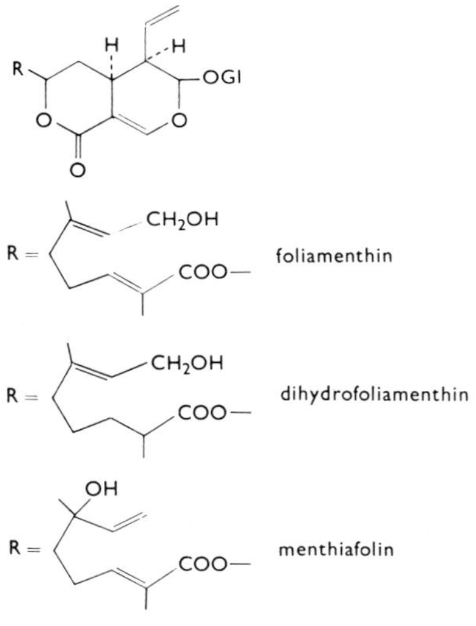

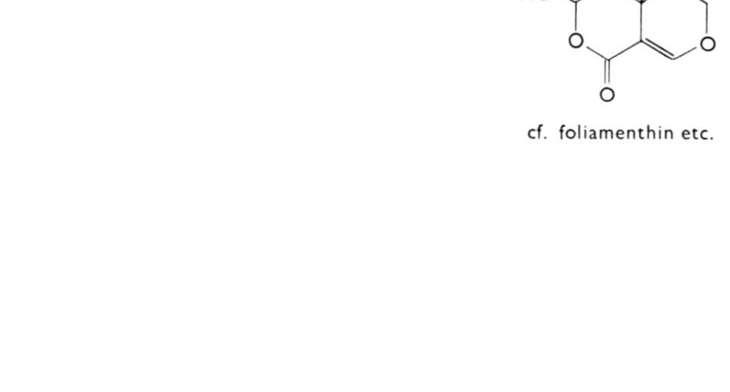

[Eq. 19-10]

cf. foliamenthin etc.

Similar experiments have given confirmatory proof of the conversion of loganin into indole alkaloids. As an example, we may quote the very efficient incorporation of O-methyl labeled loganin into strictosidine, in *Vinca rosea* plants, as shown in Eq. 19-9.

These investigations, together with others not described, served to put the speculations concerning the participation of loganin in indole alkaloid biosynthesis on a firm experimental basis. It is particularly to be noted that they demonstrate the formation from loganin, not only of the C_{10} unit of type A (cf. Eq. 19-2), but also of the rearranged types B and C.

The investigations so far discussed were founded on reasonable biogenetic speculations arising out of an examination of the structural and chemo-taxonomic relationships between various alkaloidal and terpenoid plant metabolites. These led to the designing of experiments by which the monoterpene theory could be tested, and finally to the identification of loganin as a major, if not unique precursor of the $C_{9,10}$ terpenoid components of the indole alkaloids. The pathway emerging from these various theoretical and experimental approaches also required the participation of secologanin as an intermediate. The recent discovery, in *Menyanthes trifoliata*, of compounds closely related to secologanin, serves to confirm the essential validity of the biosynthetic proposals. Three glucosides, foliamenthin, dihydrofoliamenthin, and menthiafolin (Eq. 19-10) have been isolated by careful fractionation of the glycosidic mixture from this species. Each of these glucosides is an acyclic monoterpene ester of the same secoiridoid component, which can be regarded as a lactol form of the acid corresponding to secologanin, as indicated in Eq. 19-10*a*.

The preparation of secologanin from menthiafolin has been carried through according to the following scheme (Eq. 19-11):

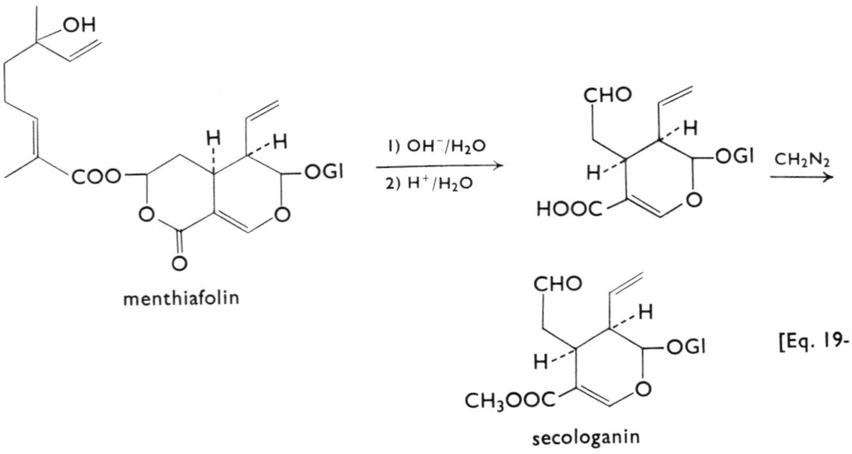

menthiafolin

secologanin

[Eq. 19-11]

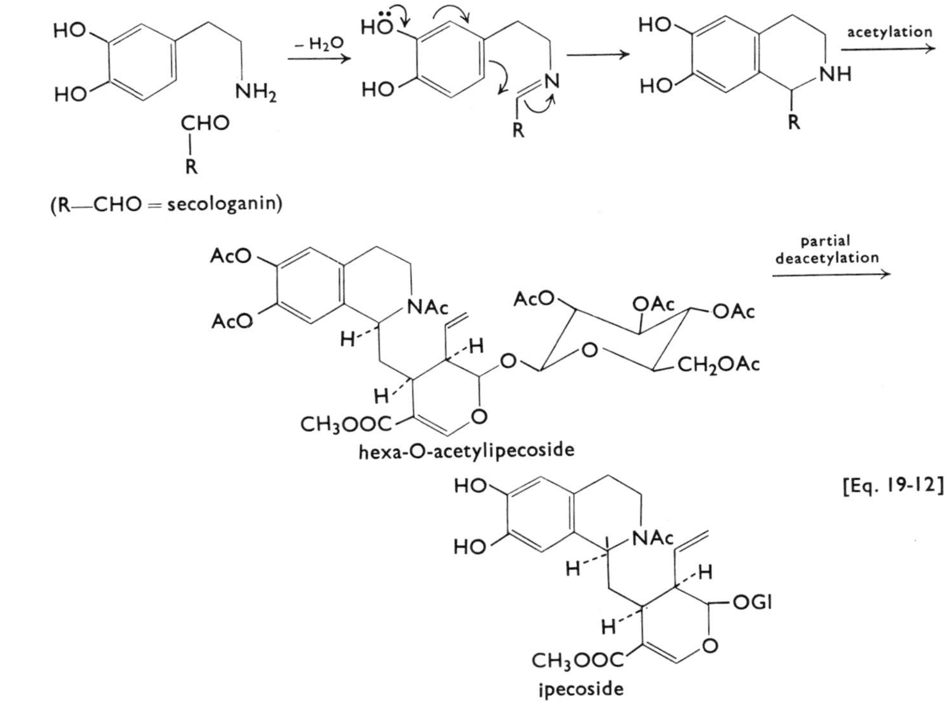

(R—CHO = secologanin)

hexa-O-acetylipecoside

[Eq. 19-12]

ipecoside

Condensation of the secologanin thus obtained, with 3,4-dihydroxyphenyl-ethylamine, gave ipecoside (Eq. 19-12), together with the C-1 epimer as a minor product. The chemical feasibility of the postulated pathway of ipecoside biosynthesis (Eq. 19-5) was thus assured. Similar condensation of secologanin with tryptamine gave a glucosidic product, vincoside, and its C-5 epimer isovincoside,*

a.

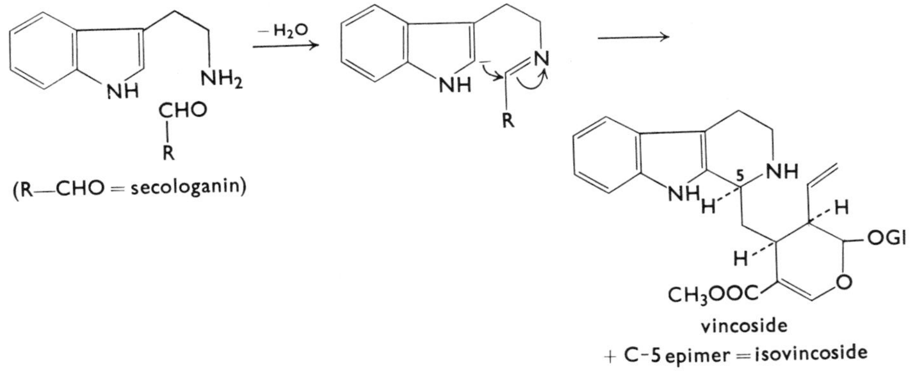

(R—CHO = secologanin)

vincoside
+ C-5 epimer = isovincoside

* One of these isomers is probably identical with strictosidine (Fig. 19-6).

b.

$-H_2O$

A   [Eq. 19-13]

together with a base having the probable structure Eq. 19-13A. This latter compound, which is readily converted into vincoside and its epimer on acid treatment, is evidently formed by a sequence in which the nucleophilic potential at C-3 in the indole nucleus is utilized in a Mannich-type condensation as shown (Eq. 19-13*b*). In the formation of vincoside and isovincoside, the potential anionic character at C-2 in tryptamine is utilized in the now familiar Mannich-type condensation (Eq. 19-13*a*). (cf. harmine, Chap. 17.)

It was evident that vincoside and isovincoside marked the probable confluence of the pathways of amino acid and terpene metabolism in indole alkaloid biosynthesis, and that experiments to test their effectiveness as precursors were therefore of crucial importance. In the event, the administration of a labeled mixture of vincoside and isovincoside to *Vinca rosea* plants resulted in a very efficient and specific conversion into alkaloids representative of all three major structural types. Further, both vincoside and isovincoside were shown by isotope dilution analysis to be present among the alkaloids of *Vinca rosea*. Finally, secologanin has also been shown by isotope dilution analysis to be present in *Vinca rosea*.

If the reader will refer to page 533, he will now find that the questions posed there, relating to the biogenetic origin of the C_{10} components and to their elaboration and mode of incorporation into the indole nucleus, have been satisfactorily answered. In addition, a partial answer has been provided to the question concerning the point at which the pathways leading to the three major structural types diverge, in that a common pathway is evident, at least as far as the stage represented by vincoside and isovincoside.

Passing now to the question of the further elaboration of the terpenoid units, it will be noted that ipecoside (Eq. 19-5) contains two masked aldehyde groups in the form of the enol ether and glucosidic functions which are present in loganin and which survive the various subsequent transformations. These aldehyde groups, if released in free form, are available to participate in further reactions such as Schiff base formation, Mannich condensations etc.

The realization of some of these possibilities may again be illustrated by reference to the alkaloids of *Cephaelis ipecachuanha*. Thus the formation of emetine and cephaeline in this species, can be rationalized according to the following scheme (Eq. 19-14):

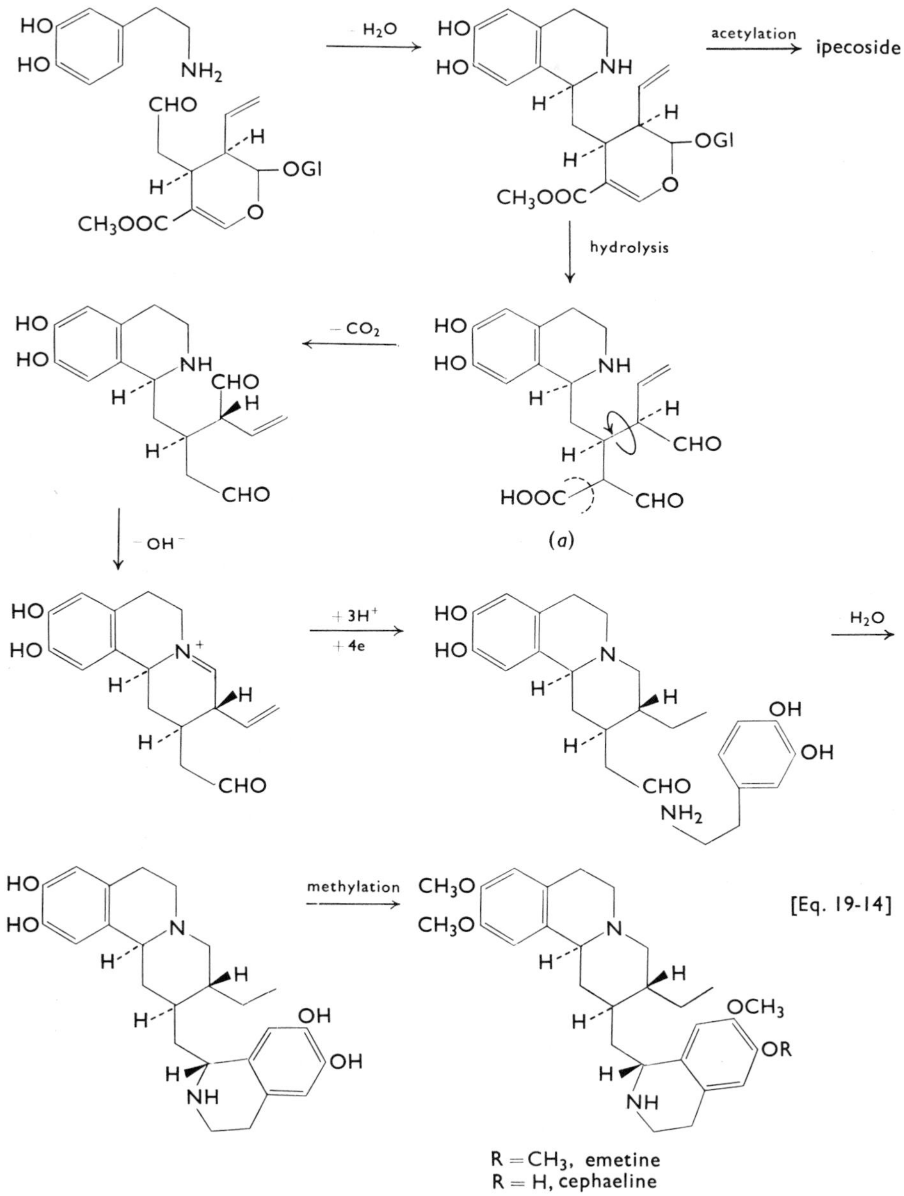

R = CH₃, emetine
R = H, cephaeline

[Eq. 19-14]

Although this sequence is subject to confirmation with regard to the details of the various individual steps, its overall features are supported by the evidence from appropriate incorporation experiments. Thus the non-quinoline component of cephaeline has been shown to be terpenoid in nature by feeding experiments with specifically labeled geraniol. In addition, the efficient incorporation of doubly-labeled loganin provides good evidence for the role of secologanin as a precursor. (Precisely analogous results have been obtained in parallel investigations relating to ipecoside biosynthesis).

It will be noted that ipecoside itself is not an intermediate in this suggested pathway, as ring closure towards the nitrogen function of the tetrahydroiso-quinoline nucleus is prevented by a blocking acetylation. However, with respect to the biosynthesis of the indole alkaloids, it is of some significance that this pathway is also postulated to involve as an intermediate the β-aldehydo-acid Eq. 19-14a. Since this compound has an arrangement of functional groups conducive to ready decarboxylation, an explanation is at hand for the frequently observed loss of a one-carbon unit from the basic C_{10} skeleton of secologanin. It is very likely that the formation of the C_9 units corresponding to the C_{10} units of types B and C, in the indole alkaloid series, is also attributable to a similar decarboxylation, as reference to Eq. 19-2 will show that in each case, the carbon atom lost is that corresponding to C-10 (or less probably, C-9) in loganin (cf. Fig. 19-5).

We are now in a position to formulate a complete sequence leading to indole alkaloids such as ajmalicine and serpentine, which contain C_{10} units of type A, as follows (Eq. 19-15):

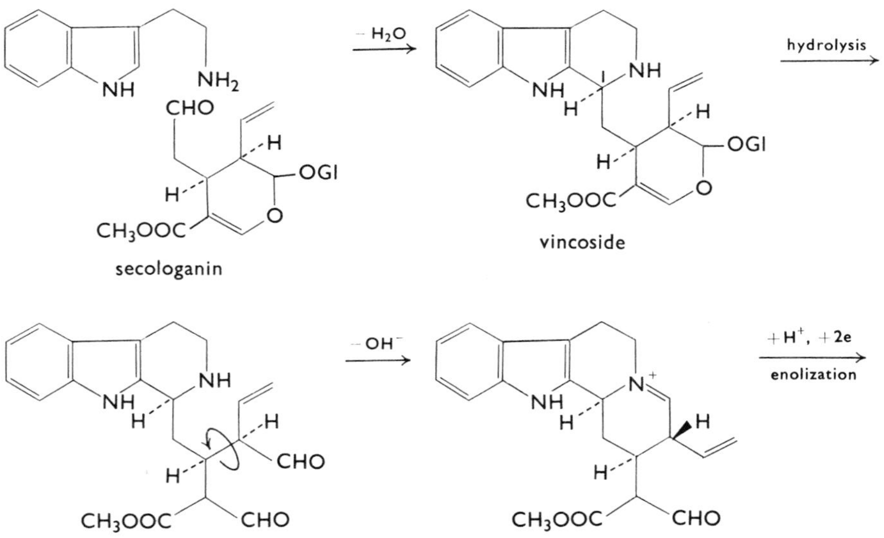

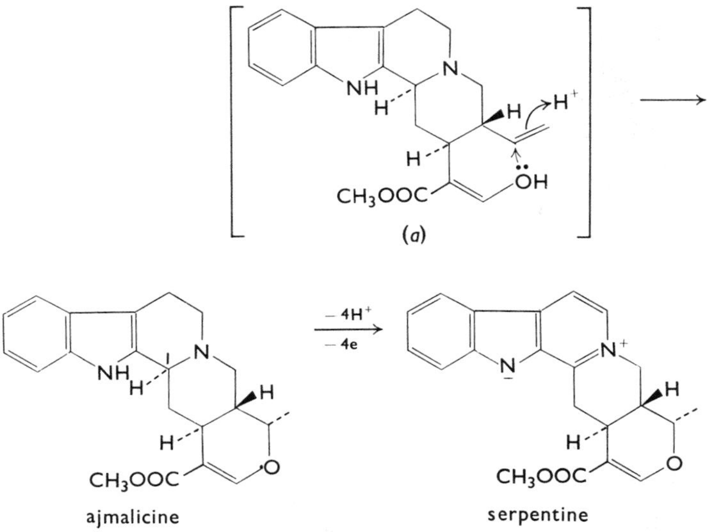

(a)

ajmalicine

$$-4H^+ \atop -4e$$

serpentine

[Eq. 19-15]

The stereospecificity of this pathway is evident from the fact that whereas radio-activity from O-methyl-labeled vincoside was efficiently incorporated into ajmalicine and serpentine in *Vinca rosea*, neither of these bases was significantly labeled in the corresponding experiment with isovincoside. Since isovincoside has the "wrong" configuration at C-1 (cf. ajmalicine, Eq. 19-15), this result is easily understood.

Turning to the relationship between the principal classes of indole alkaloid, two lines of experimental evidence, based on studies made both *in vitro* and *in vivo*, suggest that these are related by interconversions in the sequence type A → type B → type C.

The first indication that such interconversions might be chemically feasible, came from laboratory studies into the effect of mildly acidic conditions on certain selected alkaloids. Thus tabersonine (Eq. 19-16), a representative of structural type B, is partly converted into the type C alkaloid catharanthine when heated under reflux in acetic acid solution. This transformation is most simply explained in terms of reverse and forward Diels-Alder cyclizations, as shown. However it is to be noted that alternative mechanisms, based on reverse Mannich-type reactions, can also be written.

A connection between types B and C and type A, has been established through the reactions of the alkaloid stemmadenine (type A). This base, in refluxing acetic acid, is partly converted into tabersonine (type B) and catharanthine (type C) (Eq. 19-17). Stemmadenine evidently undergoes double bond isomerization and fragmentation to furnish the common intermediate Eq.19-16a. Cyclization in two ways, as shown, leads either to tabersonine or to catharanthine.

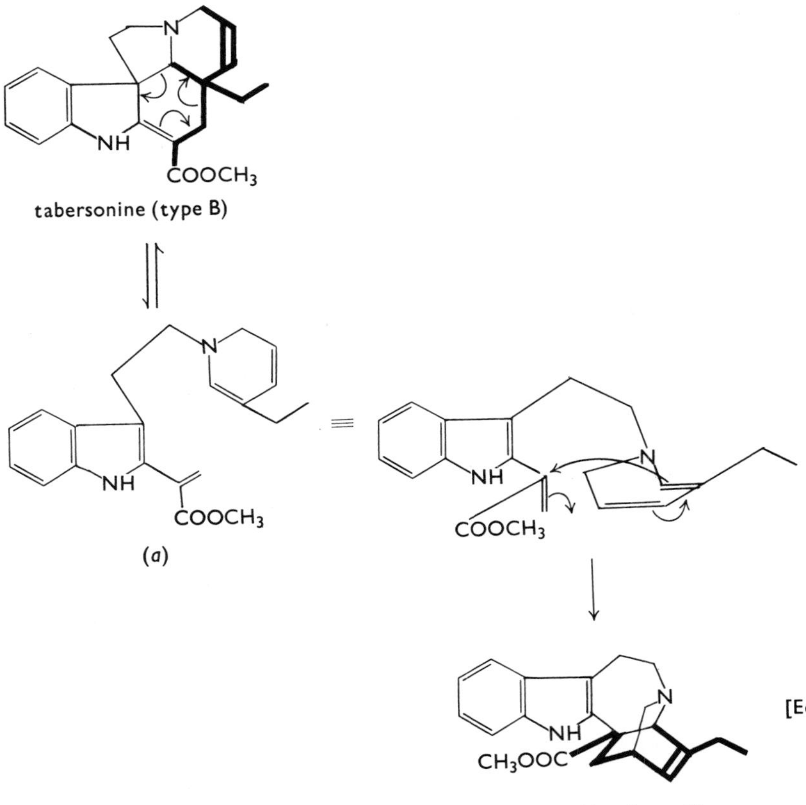

tabersonine (type B)

(a)

[Eq. 19-16]

catharanthine (type C)

The rearrangements illustrated in Eq. 19-17 provide a possible laboratory model for the formal changes postulated in Eq. 19-2. They are also compatible with the results of the feeding experiments with specifically labeled mevalonic acid noted on page 537 and in Eq. 19-4.

It is evident that the formation of stemmadenine from the prototype structure for alkaloids of type A (cf. Eq. 19-15a) requires both rearrangement and reduction to a lower oxidation level. A plausible sequence to account for these changes is shown in Eq. 19-18. It will be seen below, that pentacyclic intermediates of the type Eq. 19-18a, can be invoked to explain the formation of strychnine and related bases.

When the laboratory transformations illustrated in Eq. 19-17 are taken to-gether with the provisional sequences of Eq. 19-15 and Eq. 19-18, a unified scheme for the formation of the three basic classes of indole alkaloid emerges. It will be noted, however, that although the sequence shown in Eq. 19-17 points to a deriva-tion of alkaloids of types B and C from precursors of type A, it does not provide un-

stemmadenine (type A)

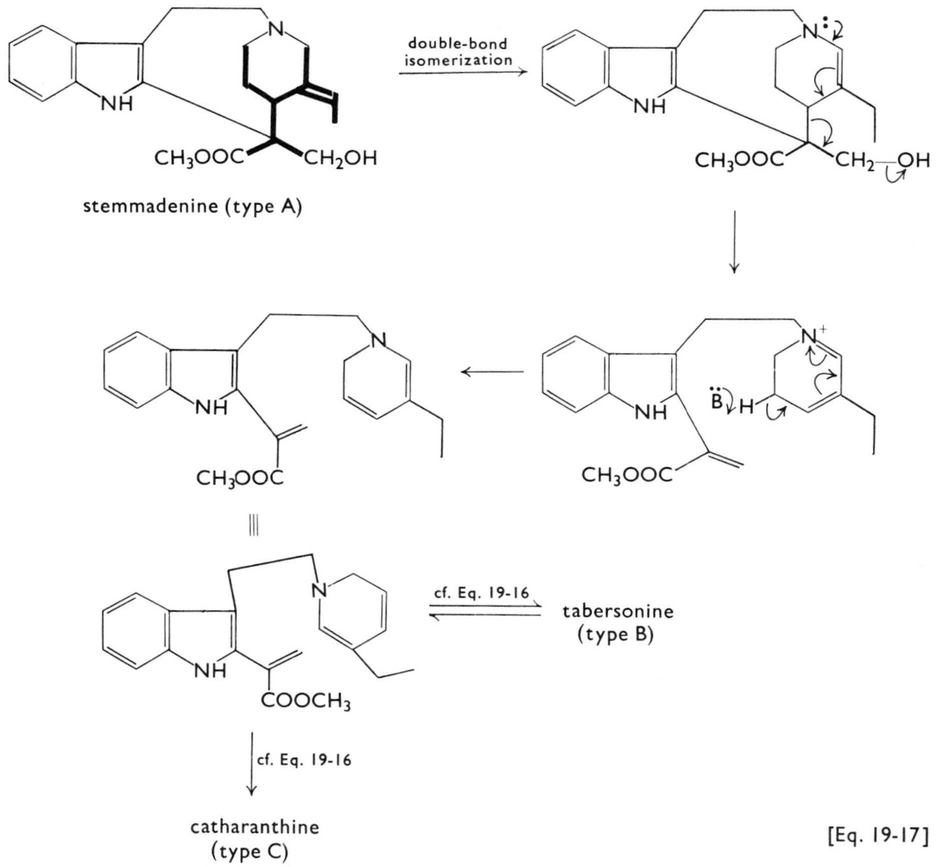

double-bond
isomerization

CH₃OOC   CH₂OH

CH₃OOC   CH₂—OH

CH₃OOC

CH₃OOC

cf. Eq. 19-16   tabersonine
(type B)

COOCH₃

cf. Eq. 19-16

catharanthine
(type C)

[Eq. 19-17]

ambiguous evidence as to the relationship between types B and C. However, information on this latter point is available from feeding experiments. Thus, labeled stemmadenine (type A), when fed to *Vinca rosea* plants, gave labeled tabersonine (type B), vindoline (type B) and catharanthine (type C), whereas labeled tabersonine (type B) gave labeled vindoline (type B) and catharanthine (type C). Labeled catharanthine, on the other hand, was not incorporated into either tabersonine of vindoline. These results, which are summarized in Eq. 19-19, clearly indicate the sequence: type A → type B → type C.

The results relating to vindoline are of further interest, in that they indicate the late stage in the biosynthetic pathway at which the secondary processes of hydroxylation and methylation occur.

The foregoing discussion summarizes those aspects of indole alkaloid biosynthesis for which experimental evidence is at present available. However, it must

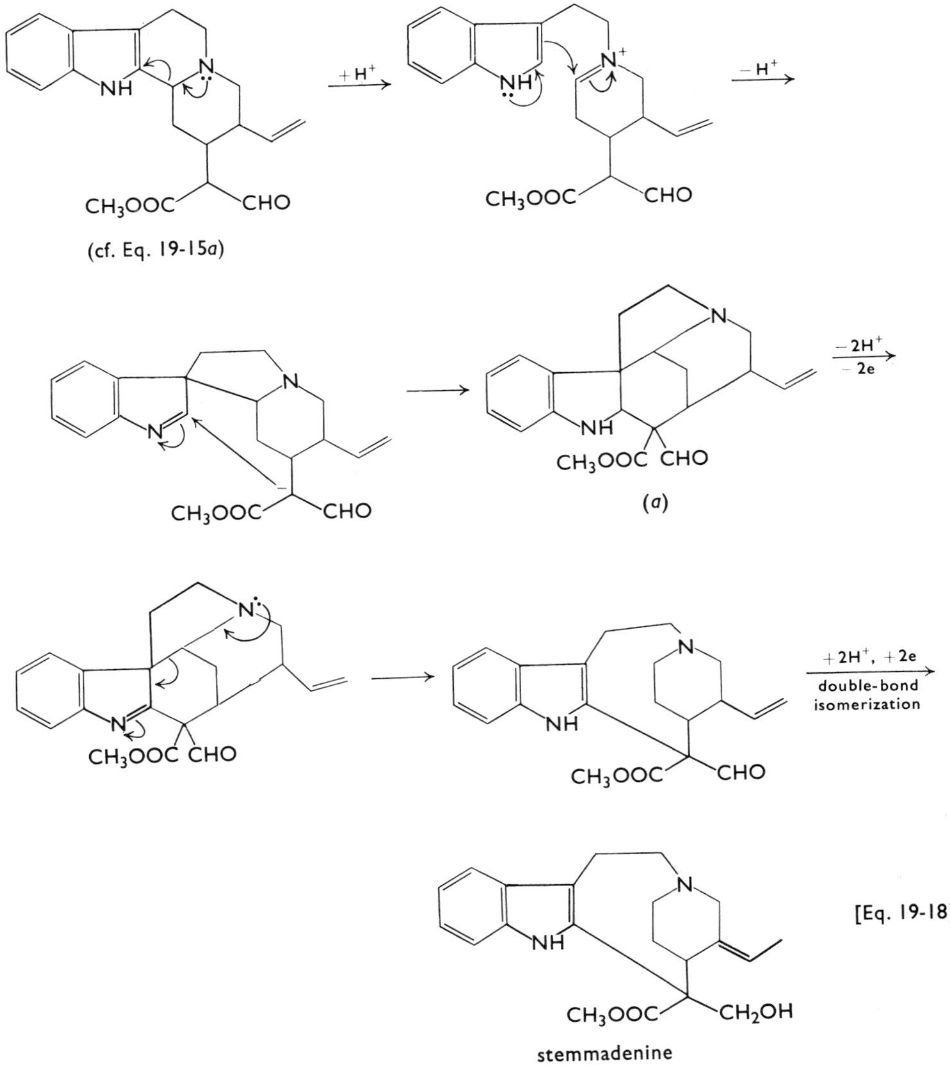

(cf. Eq. 19-15a)

(a)

[Eq. 19-18]

stemmadenine

be pointed out that certain parts of the proposed sequence are more firmly estab-lished than others, and further detailed incorporation experiments will be necessary before they can be regarded as acceptable models for the actual biological processes.

It is to be noted that incorporation studies relating to the precursor roles of loganin and secologanin have been restricted to a few plant species only, and that the possible intermediacy of different iridoid-secoiridoid pairs in the biosynthesis of indole alkaloids in other species cannot be ruled out.

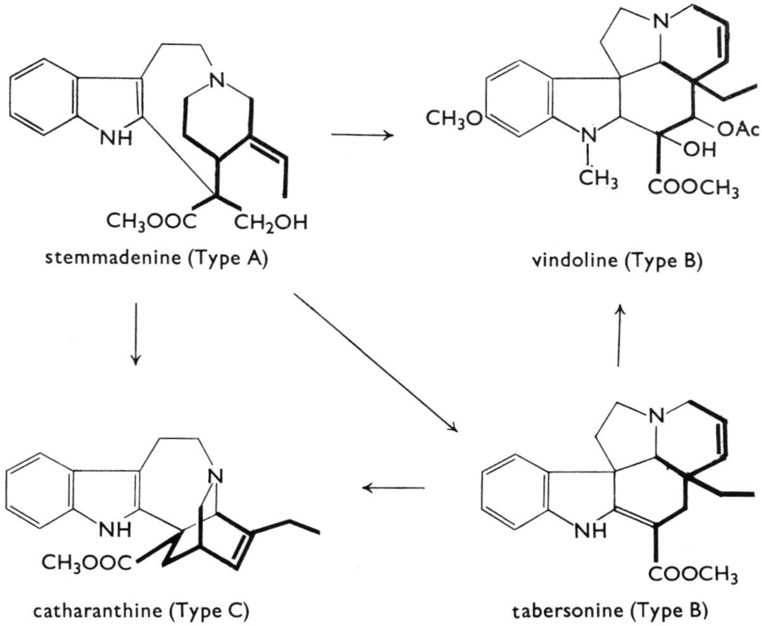

stemmadenine (Type A)

vindoline (Type B)

catharanthine (Type C)

tabersonine (Type B)

[Eq. 19-19]

Nevertheless, bearing these provisions in mind, it can be seen that the biosynthetic studies so far reported bring an astonishing degree of order to a large group of natural products which at first sight are of bewildering complexity and variety.

Many variations of the basic structures just described are encountered in the indole alkaloid series. Although a discussion of each individual type is beyond the scope of this book, three groups of particular interest deserve mention. These are represented by strychnine, reserpine and quinine respectively.

19.2 Strychnine

This alkaloid has been found in many species of *Strychnos* (fam. Loganiaceae), a genus which is believed to be the main source of South American calabash curare. Although the non-tryptamine portion of strychnine (Fig. 19-7) evidently belongs to the type A structural class, it will be noted that it contains eleven, rather than ten carbon atoms. The explanation for this apparent anomaly is readily forthcoming when it is noted that related alkaloids such as spermostrychnine (from *Strychnos psilosperma* F. Muell) (Fig. 19-7) bear an acetyl group on the indolic nitrogen function. This feature suggests that the non-indolic C_{11} moiety of strychnine arises

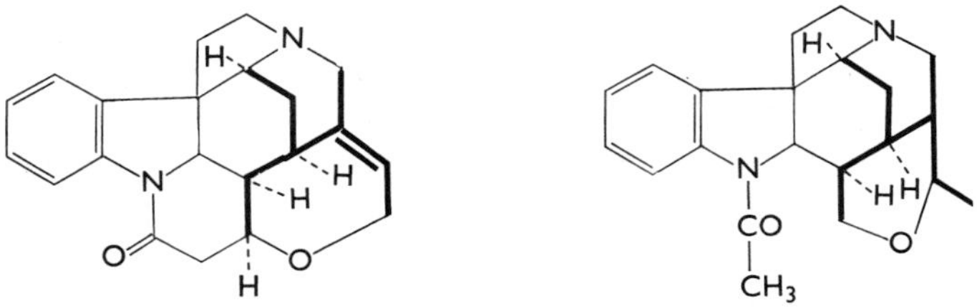

strychnine
(Type A, C₉)

spermostrychnine
(Type A, C₉)

Fig. 19-7.

from a C_9 unit of type A and a C_2 unit derived from acetic acid. A plausible bio-synthetic pathway can thus be suggested, which starts from the pentacyclic inter-mediate Eq. 19-18a, and proceeds by way of the following steps (Eq. 19-20):

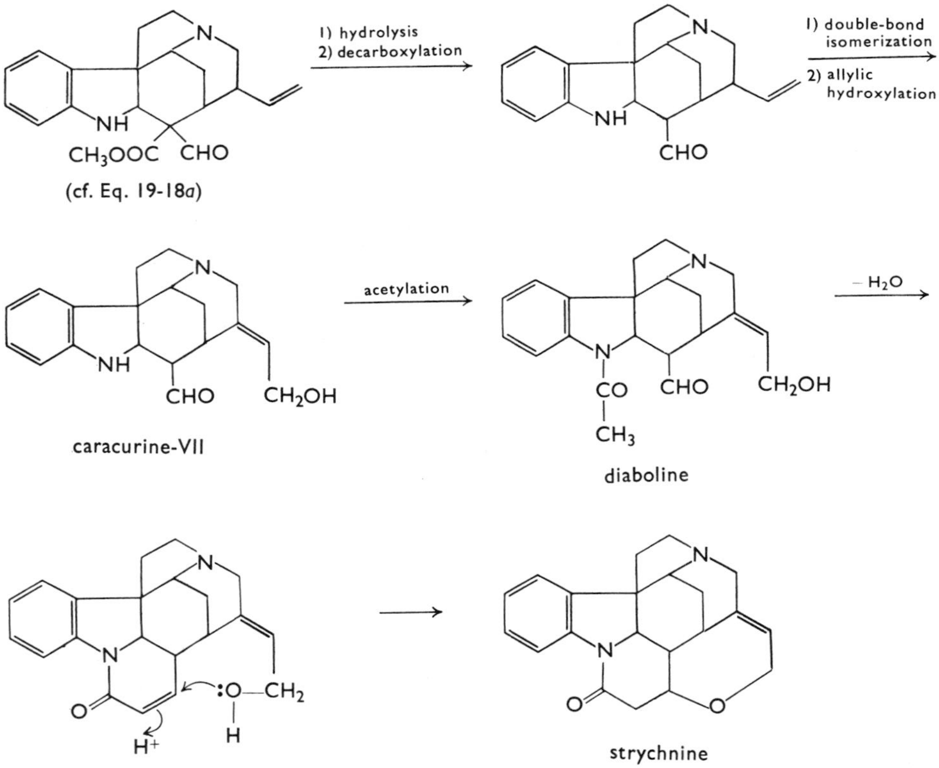

[Eq. 19-20]

It is of particular interest that two of the intermediates in the sequence shown in Eq. 19-20 occur in nature. Thus caracurine VII, long known as a degradation product of strychnine (the Wieland-Gumlich aldehyde), has also been found as one of the components of calabash curare. Similarly, diaboline occurs in *Strychnos diaboli* Sandwith.

19.3 Reserpine

Reserpine (Fig. 19-8), an alkaloid found in many species of *Rauwolfia* (fam. Apocynaceae), is the trimethylgallate ester of a base belonging to the type A structural series. The group which includes reserpine is usually named after the archetypal alkaloid yohimbine (Fig. 19-8).

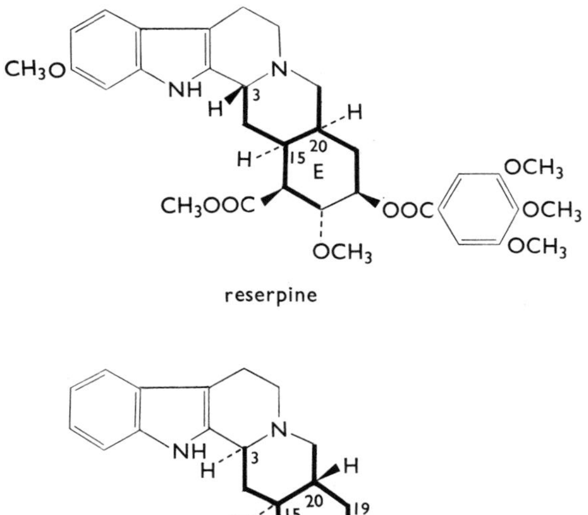

reserpine

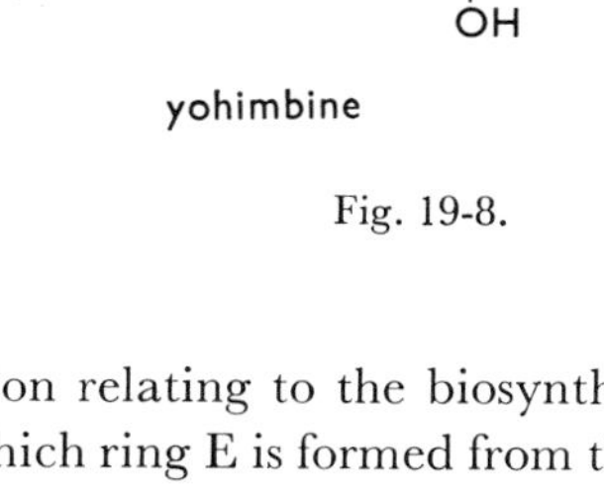

yohimbine

Fig. 19-8.

The major question relating to the biosynthesis of reserpine and yohimbine concerns the way in which ring E is formed from the probable tetracyclic precursor

a.

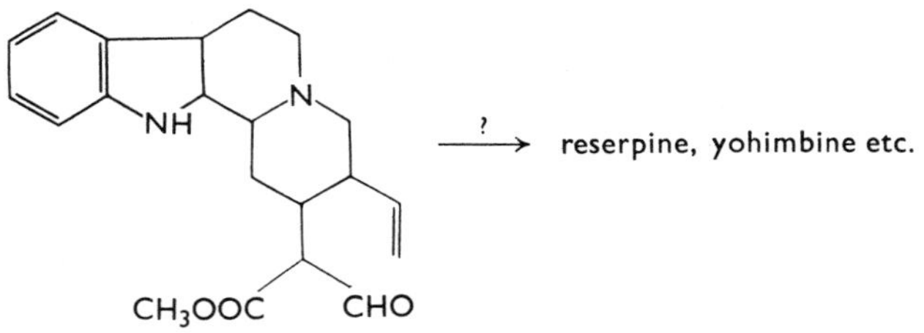

$\xrightarrow{\ ?\ }$ reserpine, yohimbine etc.

cf. Eq. 19-15*a*

b.

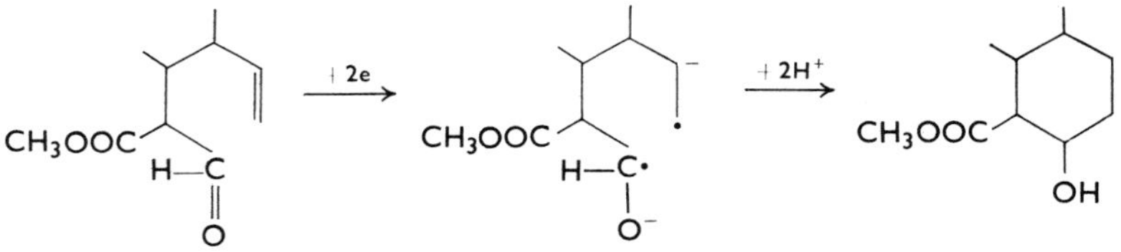

[Eq. 19-21]

vincoside $\xrightarrow[\text{cf. Eq. 19-15}]{\text{hydrolysis}}$

a.

b.

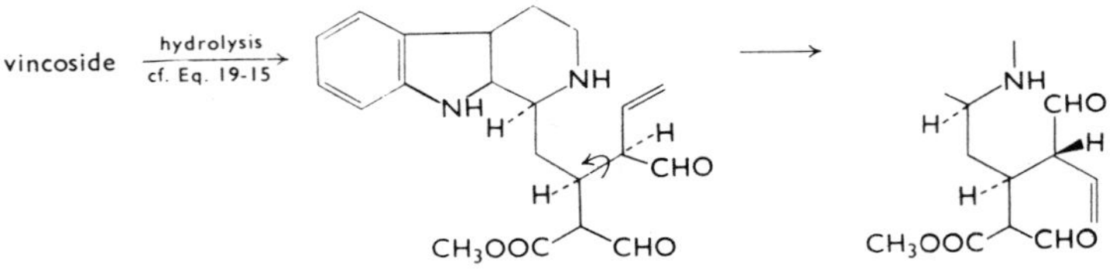

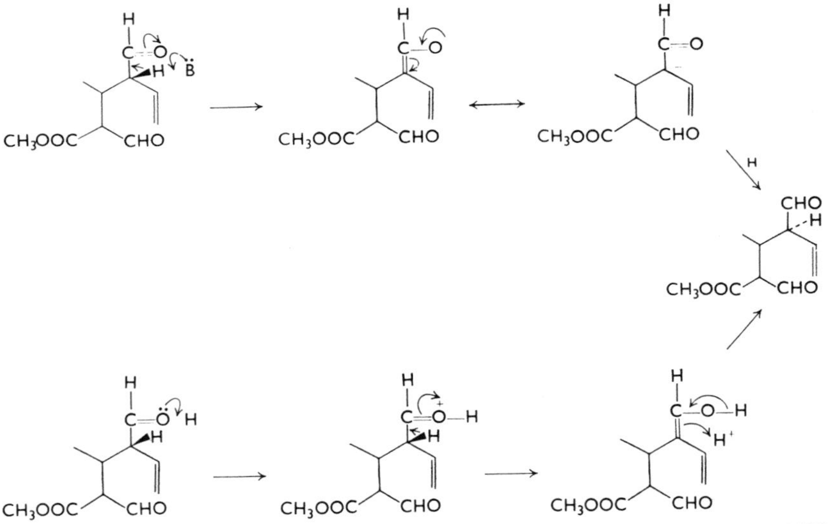

[Eq. 19-22]

shown in Eq. 19-21a (cf. Eq. 19-15). (The stereochemical features of the pathway leading to these alkaloids will be discussed below.) Since the relationship of the yohimbine alkaloids to the bases of the type A series has still to be investigated, proposals concerning the probable mechanism of the ring closure step can only be tentatively formulated. The lack of functionality at positions C-18 and C-19 in yohimbine, suggests that a direct reductive cyclization may be involved, as indicated in Eq. 19-21b. However, although such a mechanism has a number of indirect laboratory analogies, it must be considered to be purely speculative at present.

We may most usefully employ the structures of reserpine and yohimbine to illustrate certain stereochemical aspects of the elaboration of the C_{10} components, particularly as they relate to the configurations at C-3, C-15, and C-20 in these alkaloids (cf. Fig. 19-8).

It will be noted that reserpine and yohimbine have the opposite configurations at C-3. The stereochemistry at this center must be established during the initial Mannich-type condensation between secologanin* and tryptamine. Since products with both configurations are formed with comparable ease *in vitro* (cf. vincoside and isovincoside, Eq. 19-13), control of the absolute stereochemistry under the asymmetric conditions of the enzymatic synthesis clearly presents no conceptual difficulty.

Reserpine and yohimbine, and indeed the vast majority of comparable indole alkaloids, have identical configurations at C-15, as mentioned previously. Position C-15 corresponds to position C-7 in loganin, and since the postulated sequence for the elaboration of loganin into alkaloids of structural type A nowhere involves a reaction affecting this center (cf. Eq. 19-15), the preservation of its absolute configuration can readily be understood.

Finally, it will be noted that reserpine and yohimbine have opposite configurations at C-20, the configuration in reserpine being the same as that of the corresponding centers in loganin and secologanin. It must be concluded from this observation, that epimerization at this position is possible at some stage in the biosynthetic pathway. Again, this can easily be explained if a dialdehyde intermediate of the type arising by the hydrolysis of vincoside or isovincoside is involved (Eq. 19-22, cf. Eq. 19-15). It will be noted that the methine group in this intermediate, corresponding to C-20 in the yohimbine series, has an aldehyde group attached. Such a structure would be subject to ready epimerization by either a base catalyzed (Eq. 19-22a) or an acid catalyzed (Eq. 19-22b) mechanism.

---

* The participation of secologanin in the biosynthesis of alkaloids of the yohimbine series has not been demonstrated, but is assumed here as a basis for discussion.

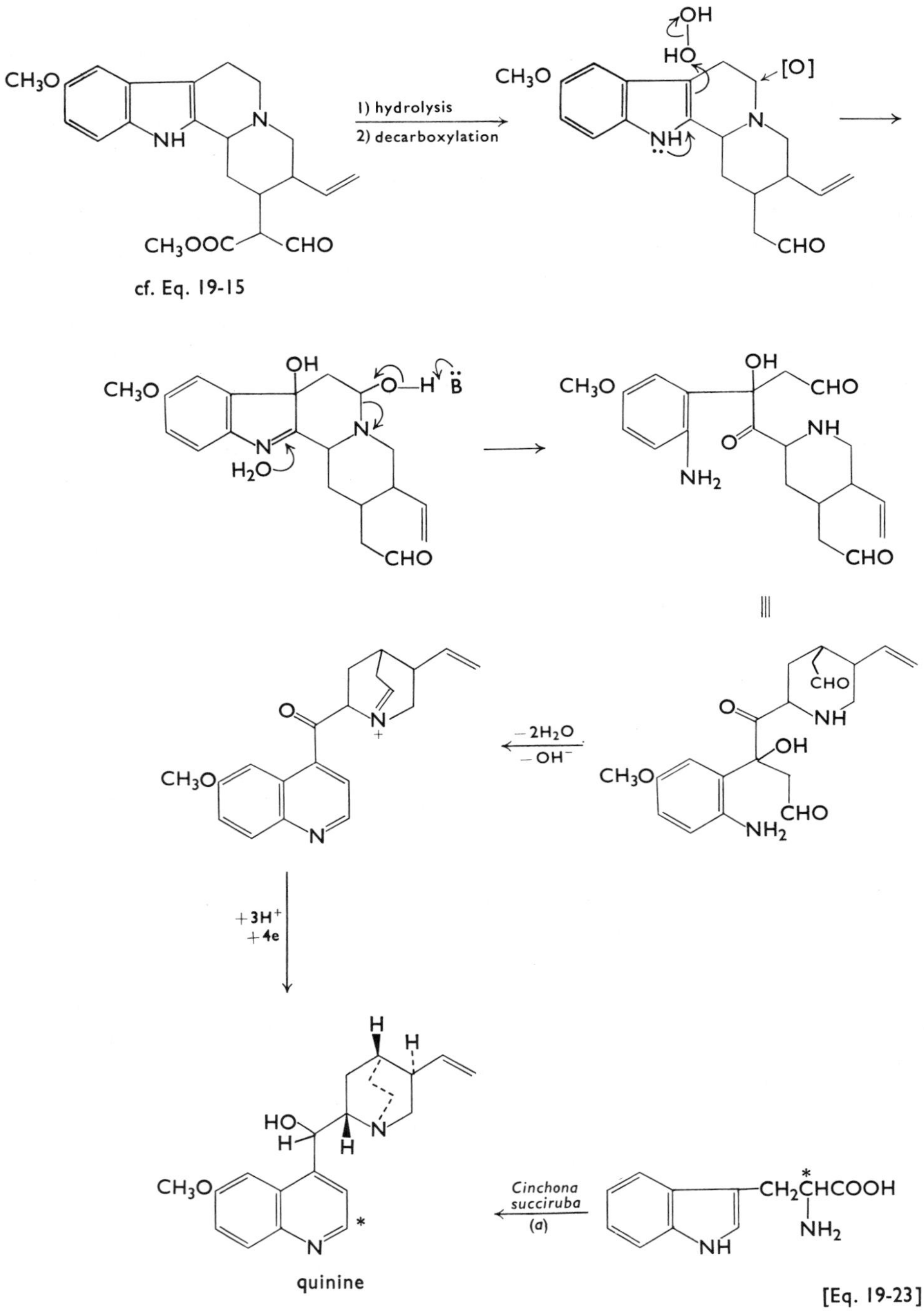

cf. Eq. 19-15

quinine

[Eq. 19-23]

19.4 Quinine

Species of the genera *Cinchona* and *Remija* (both fam. Rubiaceae), produce a series of alkaloids typified by quinine (Eq. 19-23). Although quinine is based structurally on a quinoline nucleus, the close taxonomic relationship between the genera *Cinchona* and *Remija*, and other indole alkaloid producing genera of the Rubiaceae, suggests a biogenetic connection between quinine and the indole alkaloids.

A reasonable pathway to account for the formation of quinine from the standard precursor of the type A indole alkaloids, is illustrated in Eq. 19-23. The initial hydroxylation step is shown as a nucleophilic displacement in which the negative character at C-3 in the indole nucleus is utilized in an attack on hydrogen peroxide. This process is equivalent to electrophilic substitution at C-3 by a species which is often written for convenience as "OH$^+$", in descriptions of biological hydroxylating systems (cf. Chap. 11). Although the precise nature of the hydroxylating species is not known, hydrogen peroxide has the appropriate electrophilic character, and may be taken as a reasonable model for the natural reagent in the present context.

The remaining steps in the sequence will be seen to involve unexceptional processes such as hydroxylation, Schiff base formation, dehydration, etc.

Future investigations may require the modification of this sequence in various respects. However, the basic biogenetic proposals are supported by the evidence from appropriate feeding experiments. Thus labeled geraniol has been shown to be specifically incorporated into the quinuclidine nucleus, and 2-^{14}C-tryptophan has been found to furnish quinine labeled solely at C-2 (Eq. 19-23a).

19.5 Dimeric Indole Alkaloids

Up to the present, more than fifty bases have been isolated from calabash curare. Many of the most potent constituents are found to be dimeric compounds containing forty or more carbon atoms. The structures of many of these highly complex alkaloids have been elucidated, but only through the joint application of practically every spectroscopic technique available to the organic chemist.

Most of the alkaloids examined are structurally related to the Wieland-Gumlich aldehyde (caracurine VII) and evidently arise by double Schiff-base condensations followed by various secondary processes. The typical representative C-toxiferine I, probably arises from the Wieland-Gumlich aldehyde as shown in Eq. 19-24.

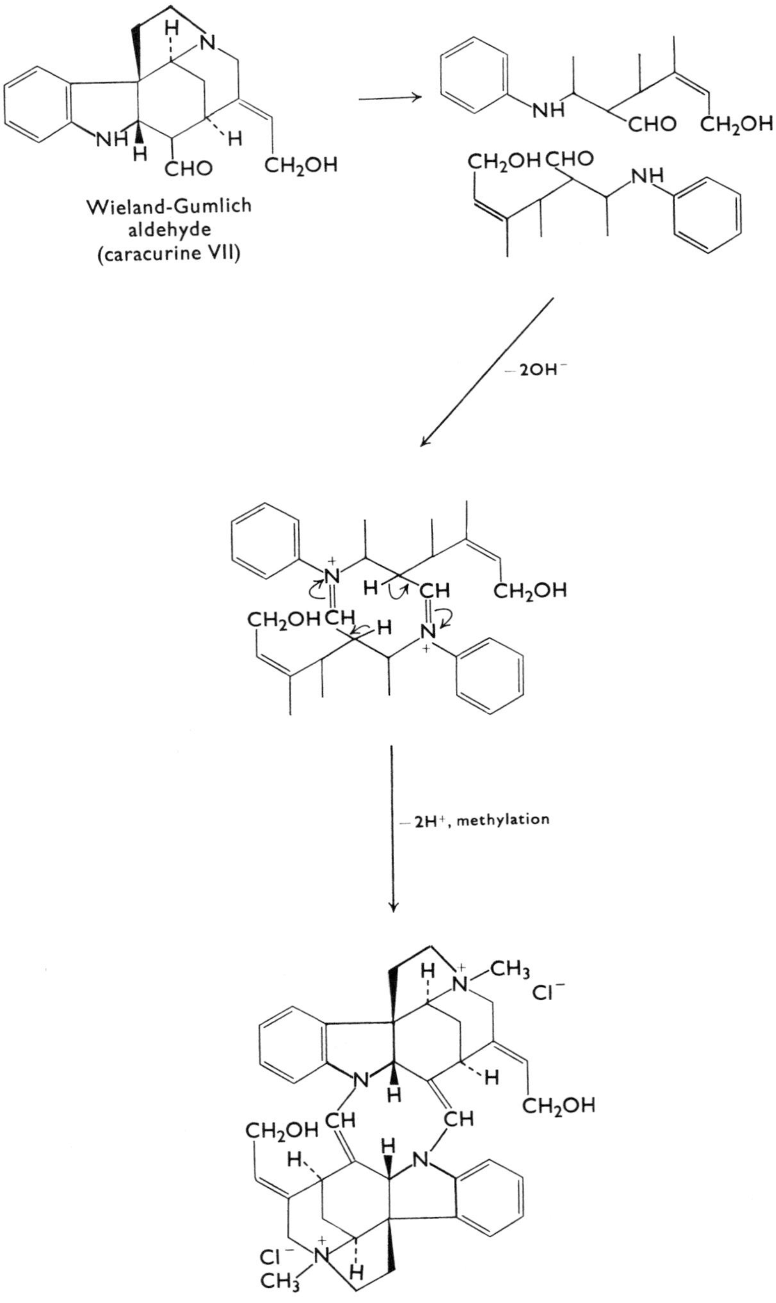

Wieland-Gumlich
aldehyde
(caracurine VII)

$-2OH^-$

$-2H^+$, methylation

C-toxiferine I

[Eq. 19-24]

19.6 Monoterpene-Indole Alkaloids. Summary

In the last few years our understanding of the way in which the monoterpene indole alkaloids are formed in nature has undergone a complete transformation—from a state of almost total ignorance to the present situation, where the broad outlines of the biosynthetic highway are now clear. A multitude of minor by-roads remain to be investigated, but with the information summarized in the preceding pages at hand, the task of elucidating new structures and exploring secondary biosynthetic pathways, is now placed on a sound theoretical basis.

19.7 The Ergot Alkaloids

One of the pestilences of the Middle Ages in Europe was "St Anthony's fire" or "heiliges Feuer", which was caused by the toxic alkaloids present in bread prepared from infected rye. The infectious agent is now known to have been ergot (*Claviceps purpurea* Fr. Tul), the spores of which are carried by wind and insects to the ovaries of the rye, where they develop eventually into the black, sickle-shaped sclerotia, about one centimetre or so in length, which represent the resting state of the fungus.

The symptoms of ergot poisoning are two-fold. On the one hand there may be deep-seated mental disturbances and on the other severe gangrene, brought about by the vasoconstrictory action of the alkaloids. The disease is frequently fatal. *Claviceps purpurea* is a specific parasite of rye, but many other species of *Claviceps* are known, which between them are capable of infecting more than three hundred species of Gramineae (grasses).

In spite of its occasional unwelcome presence in rye, ergot has achieved a position of great importance in medicine, as a number of its constituent alkaloids have valuable pharmacological properties. Thus ergotamine is widely used in obstetrics for promoting contraction of the uterus after childbirth, and is also valuable in the treatment of migraine. The diethylamide of lysergic acid (LSD) is used in certain forms of psychotherapy.

The ergot alkaloids are divided, for convenience, into two groups, comprising on the one hand, lysergic acid and its derivatives (Fig. 19-9), and on the other, the so-called clavine alkaloids. In the latter, the C-17 carboxyl group of the lysergic acid series is replaced by a methyl or hydroxymethyl function. In addition, certain alkaloids are differentiated by having a peptide residue attached to the non-indolic nitrogen function (cf. ergotamine, Fig. 19-9).

An inspection of the structures of the ergot alkaloids will readily reveal the structural elements of a tryptamine unit and an isoprene residue. Accordingly, the

Clavine type:

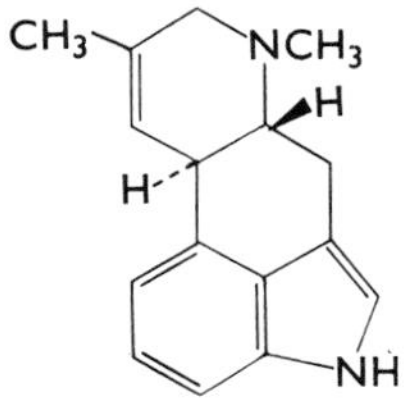

agroclavine

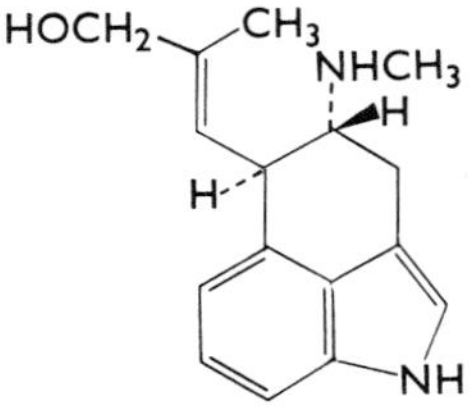

chanoclavine-l

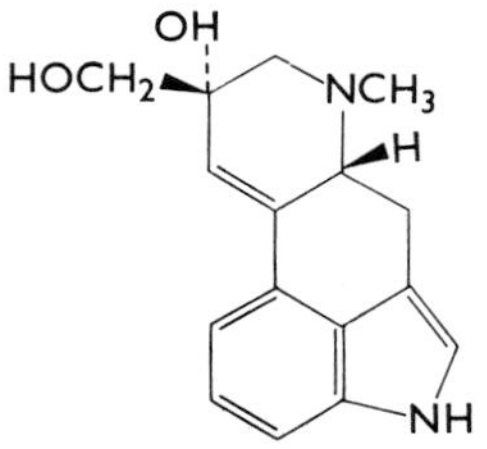

penniclavine

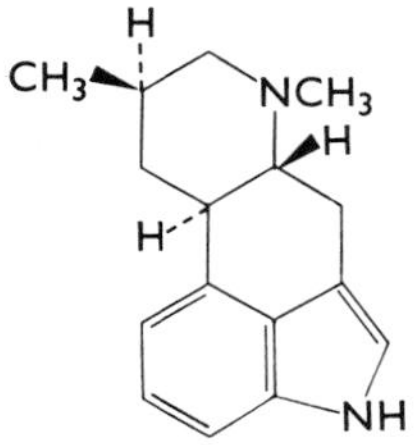

festuclavine

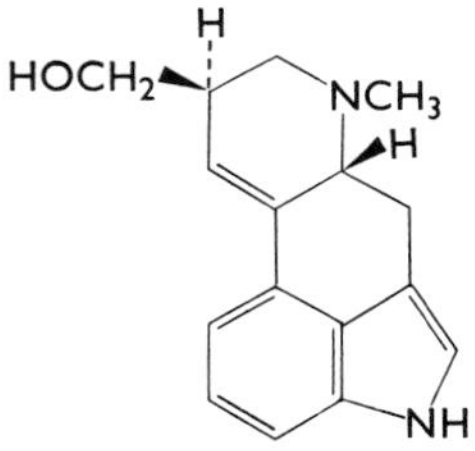

lysergol

Lysergic acid derivatives:

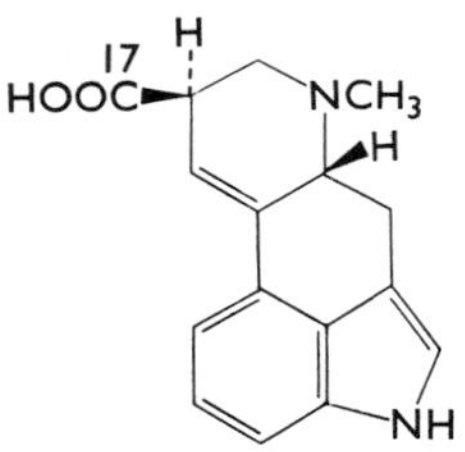

lysergic acid

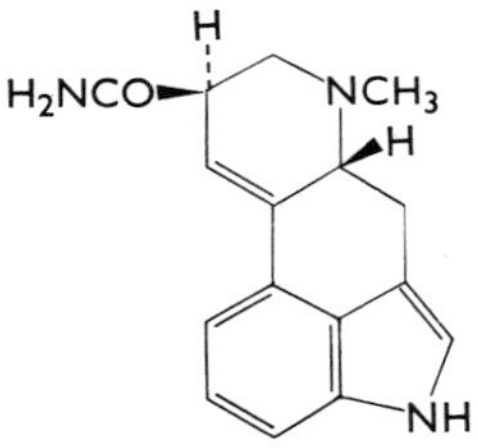

lysergic acid amide

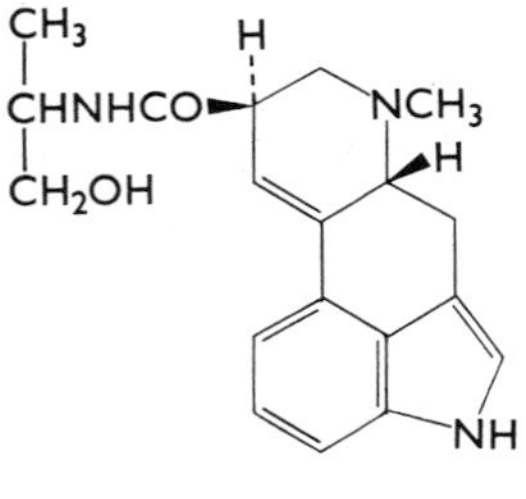

ergometrine

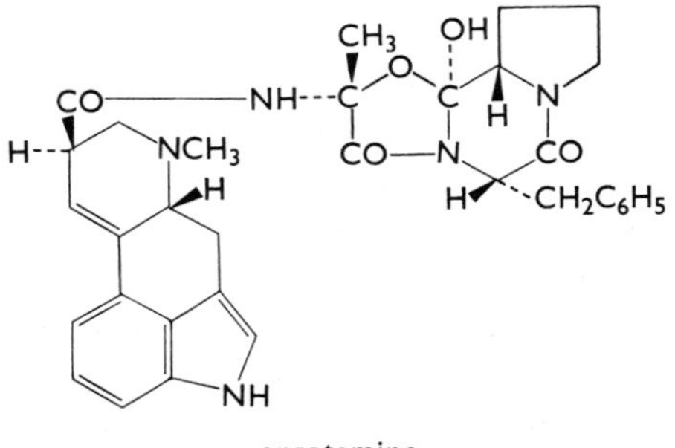

ergotamine

Fig. 19-9. Some Ergot Alkaloids.

pathway of ergot alkaloid biosynthesis has been postulated to stem from 4-dimethylallyltryptophan (a known metabolite of ergot) which could readily arise from dimethylallylpyrophosphate and tryptophan, as shown in Eq. 19-25.

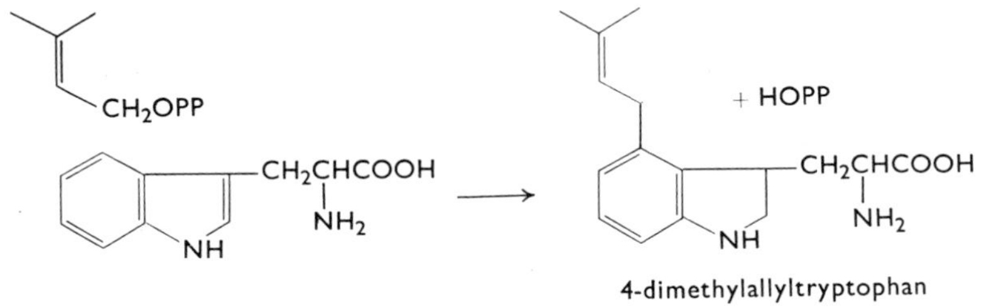

4-dimethylallyltryptophan

[Eq. 19-25]

Numerous incorporation experiments have established the biosynthetic sequence leading to lysergic acid, illustrated in Eq. 19-26. It is to be noted that this pathway also encompasses the biosynthesis of the clavine-type alkaloids.

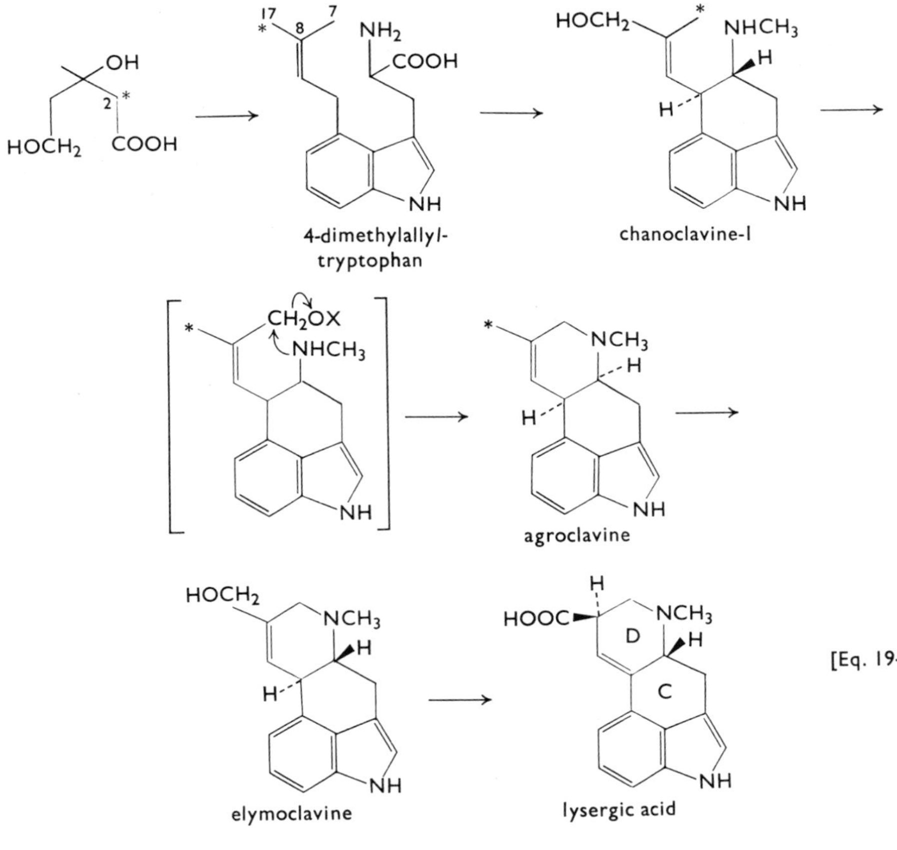

4-dimethylallyl-tryptophan

chanoclavine-I

agroclavine

elymoclavine

lysergic acid

[Eq. 19-26]

At present, the mechanism of the cyclization step leading to closure of ring C is not understood. However, it is probable that formation of the heterocyclic D ring involves a simple nucleophilic displacement with the primary hydroxyl function of the precursor suitably esterified (Eq. 19-26). The allylic nature of such an ester would facilitate the type of substitution indicated.

The most intriguing feature of the pathway shown in Eq. 19-25 lies in the remarkable gyrations performed by the C-7,8,17 component about the Δ^8-double bond. Thus it appears that a *cis-trans* isomerization is involved both in the sequence between 4-dimethylallyltryptophan and chanoclavine-I, and in the conversion of the latter into agroclavine. These changes may be appreciated by noting the changes in the position of the starred carbon atom (Eq. 19-26) which corresponds, for each intermediate, with C-2 of mevalonic acid, as shown.

An experiment which clearly demonstrates the intervention of a *cis-trans* isomerization in the conversion of chanoclavine-I into agroclavine, is illustrated in Eq. 19-27.

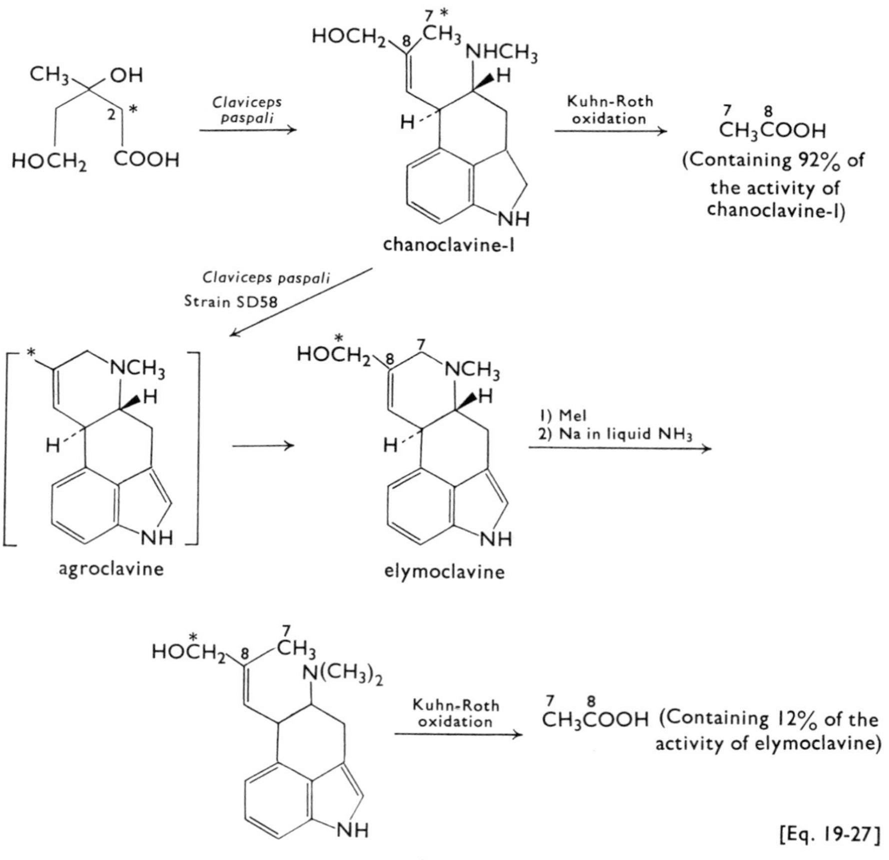

[Eq. 19-27]

The reason for these unusual isomerizations, and the mechanisms by which they are brought about, are not known at present.

In view of the highly specialized structures of the ergot alkaloids, it is remarkable that various representatives have been found in species of *Ipomoea* (morning glory) and *Rivea* (both fam. Convolvulaceae), since these genera are far removed from ergot on the evolutionary scale. A new name, the "ergolines", has therefore been suggested for alkaloids of this group as being more in keeping with their distribution in plant species as well as in fungi.

19.8   Terpene Alkaloids

Many alkaloids appear to be formed by the apparently adventitious incorporation of nitrogen into a molecule of fundamentally terpenoid origin. It is evident that the questions of the biosynthesis of alkaloids in this group are largely those of the biosynthesis of the corresponding classes of terpene, since in most cases, the alkaloid structures encountered are based on recognizable terpenoid frameworks.

The best known examples of monoterpenoid alkaloid have the iridoid or seco-iridoid structure and are sometimes noted to occur together with the corresponding monoterpenes or with a terpene of closely related structure. Examples are matatabi lactone and actinidine (from *Actinidia polygama* Franch and Sav., fam. Actinidiaceae) and gentiopicroside and gentianine, which co-occur in a number of species of *Gentiana* (fam. Gentianaceae) (Fig. 19-10).

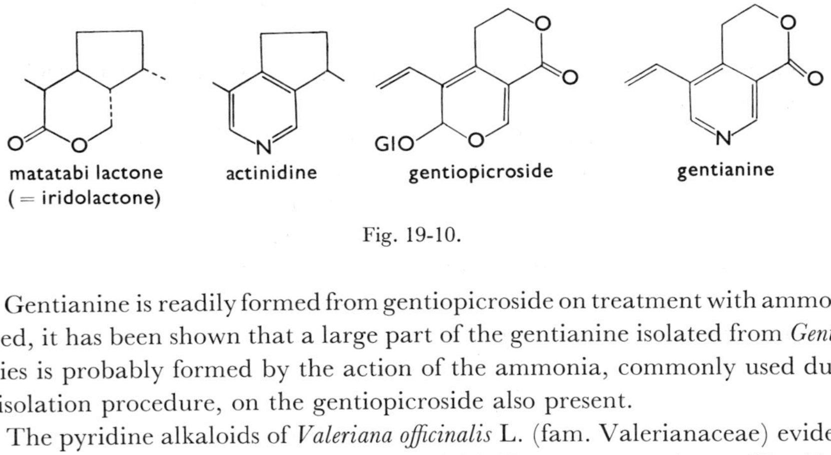

matatabi lactone   actinidine   gentiopicroside   gentianine
(= iridolactone)

Fig. 19-10.

Gentianine is readily formed from gentiopicroside on treatment with ammonia; indeed, it has been shown that a large part of the gentianine isolated from *Gentiana* species is probably formed by the action of the ammonia, commonly used during the isolation procedure, on the gentiopicroside also present.

The pyridine alkaloids of *Valeriana officinalis* L. (fam. Valerianaceae) evidently arise from tyramine and the corresponding iridoid precursor as shown (Eq. 19-28).

A number of sesquiterpene alkaloids are found in various species of water lily, particularly in the genera *Nymphaea* and *Nuphar* (fam. Nymphaeaceae). Two representative bases are shown in Fig. 19-11. It is probable that quinolizidine alkaloids

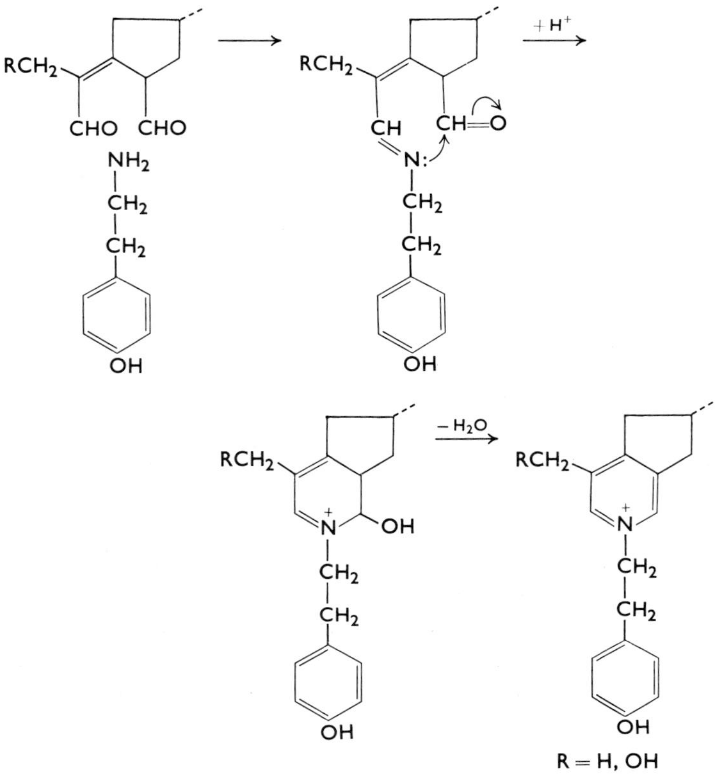

[Eq. 19-28]

R = H, OH

such as deoxynupharidine are formed in nature by the cyclization of piperidino precursors such as nuphamine.

Species of the genera *Aconitum* and *Delphinium* (fam. Apocynaceae) and *Garrya* (fam. Garryaceae), produce diterpene alkaloids which are structurally related to (−)-kaurene. The three structural varieties encountered are represented by atisine, veatchine, and lycoctonine (Fig. 19-12). Of these, veatchine has the carbon framework of (−)-kaurene, but atisine and lycoctonine have structures which possibly arise from a kaurene-like precursor by rearrangement.

The yew tree (*Taxus baccata* L. fam. Taxaceae) produces a number of toxic alkaloids including the unique compounds taxine I and taxine II (Fig. 19-13).

Various species of *Buxus* (box) (fam. Buxaceae) produce triterpene alkaloids which are structurally, and therefore probably biogenetically related to the widely distributed plant triterpene, cycloartenol. This relationship is clearly demonstrated in the structure of cycloprotobuxine-C (Fig. 19-14), which is plausibly derived from cycloartenol by degradation of the C-17 side chain, followed by introduction of the nitrogen substituents at C-3 and C-20.

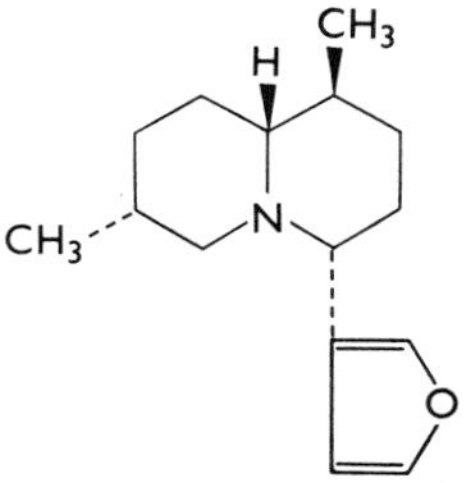

deoxynupharidine

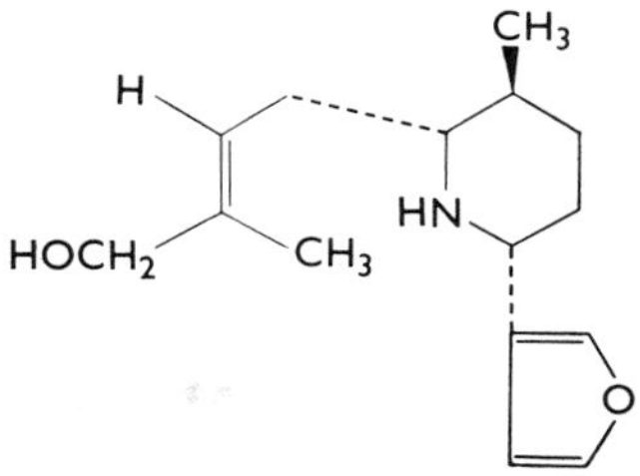

nuphamine

Fig. 19-11.

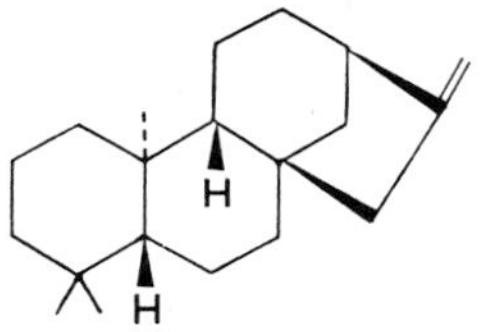

(—)-kaurene

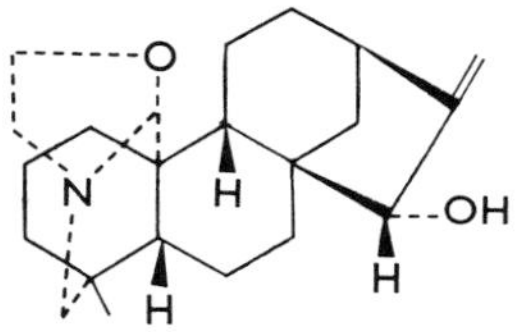

veatchine

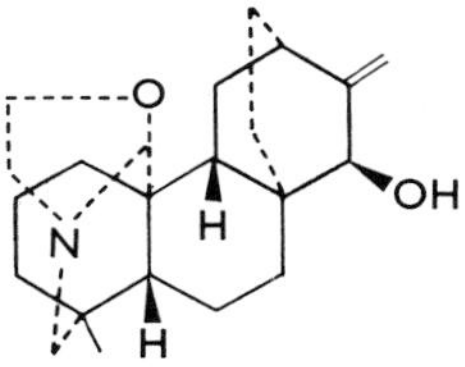

atisine

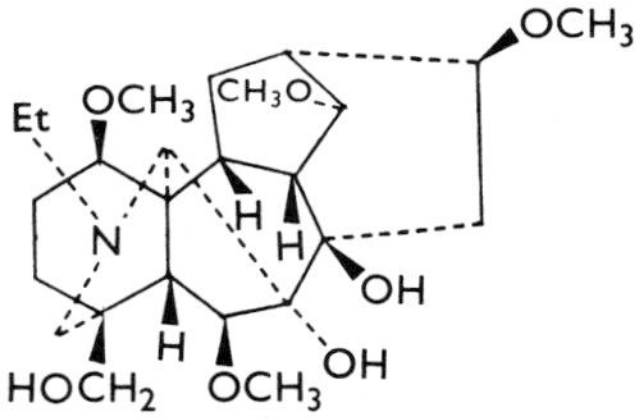

lycoctonine

Fig. 19-12.

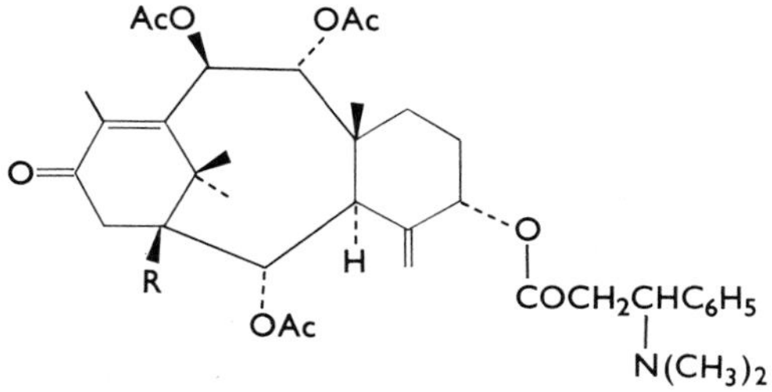

R = OH, taxine-I
R = H, taxine-II

Fig. 19-13.

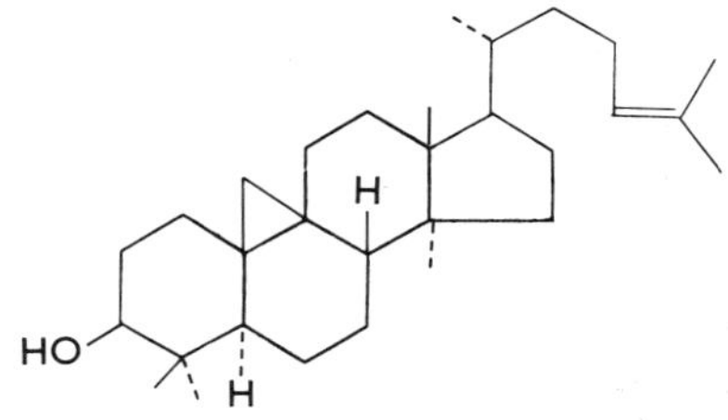

cycloartenol

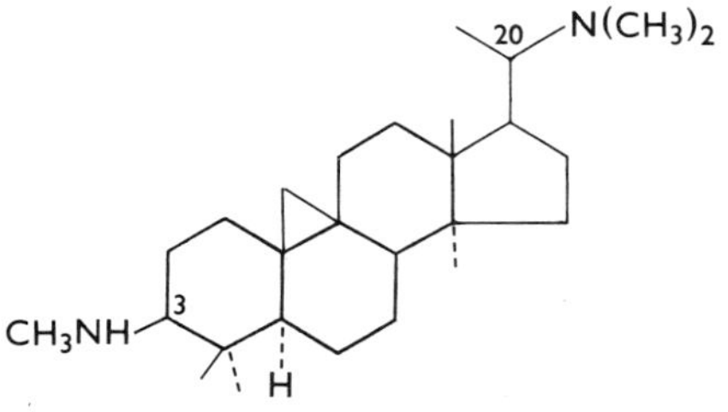

cycloprotobuxine-C

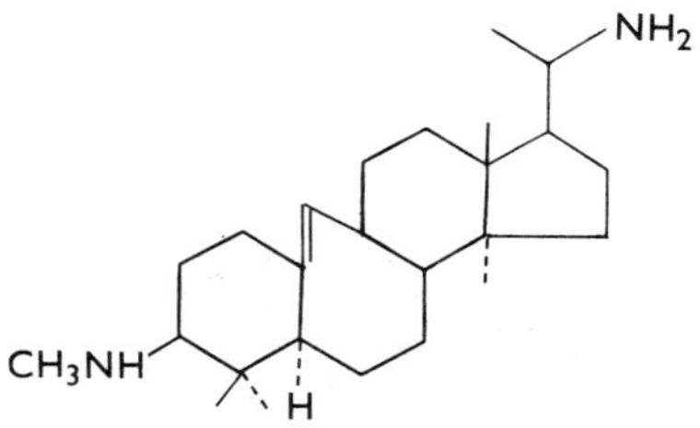

buxamine-G

Fig. 19-14.

In certain of the *Buxus* alkaloids, such as buxamine-G, a seven-membered B-ring is present. This evidently arises by cleavage of the cyclopropane ring in precursors with the cycloartenol skeleton (Fig. 19-14).

19.9 Steroidal Alkaloids

Several plant families produce alkaloids which are evidently formed from steroidal precursors. Certain genera of the Apocynaceae (notably *Holarrhena*, *Funtumia*, and *Malouetia*) and of the Buxaceae (*Sarcococca* and *Pachysandra*), produce alkaloids based on the 5α-pregnane skeleton (Fig. 19-15). The two basic structural

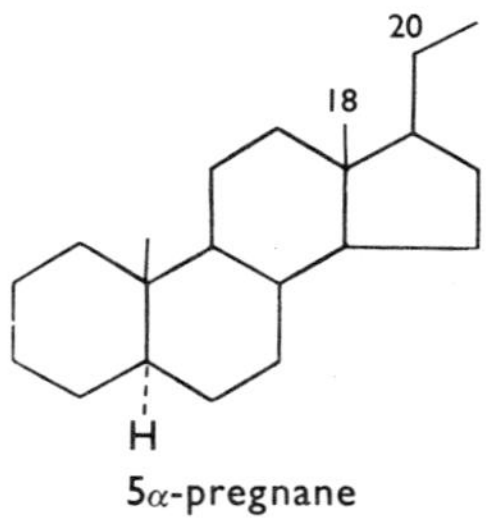

5α-pregnane

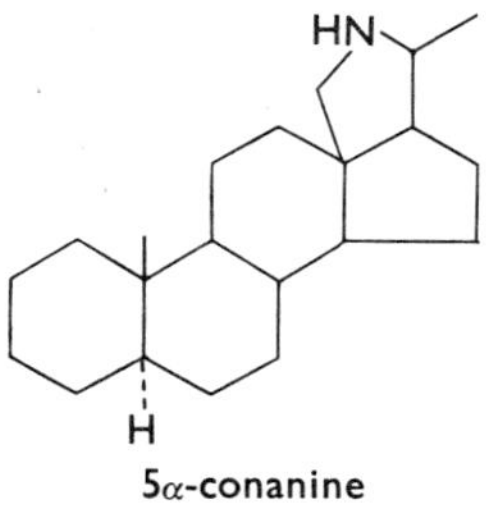

5α-conanine

Fig. 19-15.

varieties encountered, are based either on 5α-pregnane itself or on a heterocyclic derivative, 5α-conanine, in which C-18 and C-20 are joined by a nitrogen bridge (Fig. 19-15).

In recent years, it has become apparent that cholesterol, far from being a metabolite exclusively confined to the animal kingdom, has a wide distribution among higher plants. Accordingly, it has been proposed that the biosynthetic pathways leading to representative alkaloids such as holaphyllamine and conessine involve as an intermediate, pregnenolone, which could arise, as in animal systems, by the degradation of cholesterol. Evidence is available from incorporation experiments to support the roles of both cholesterol and pregnenolone as intermediates in the biosynthesis of holaphyllamine and conessine, as indicated in Eq. 19-29.

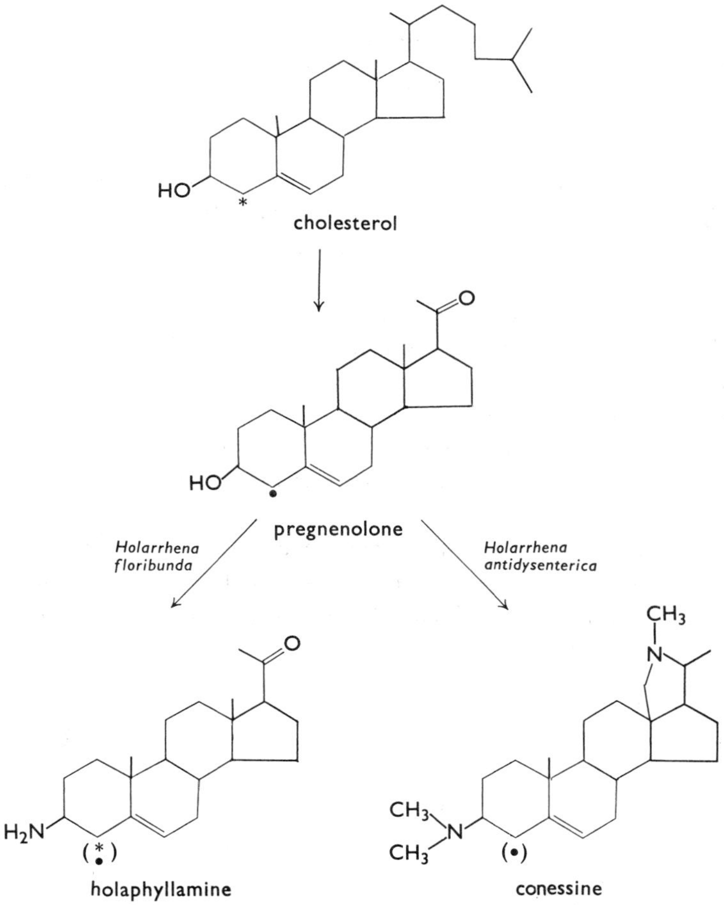

cholesterol

pregnenolone

Holarrhena floribunda

Holarrhena antidysenterica

[Eq. 19-29]

holaphyllamine

conessine

* • ¹⁴C label (n.b. The position of the label in the products was not determined).

It will be noted that the pathway from cholesterol to conessine must involve at some point the oxidative modification of the C-18 methyl group. In this connection, it is interesting to note the co-occurrence with conessine, in *Holarrhena antidysenterica* Wall, of the steroidal derivative holadysone (Fig. 19-16), the formation of which evidently involves just such an oxidative process.

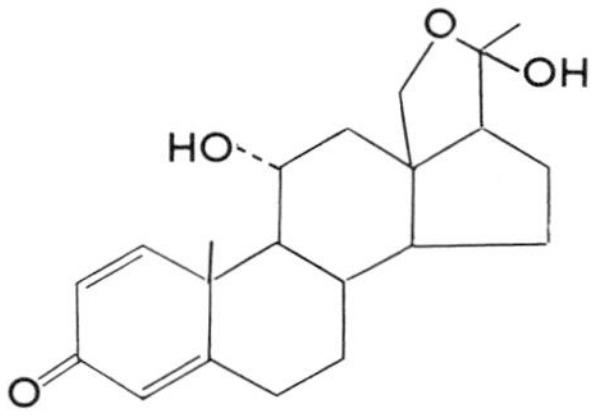

holadysone

Fig. 19-16.

Many species of *Solanum* and *Lycopersicon* (both fam. Solanaceae), produce steroidal alkaloids with structures closely related to the steroidal sapogenins. Tomatidine (Fig. 19-17), first isolated from tomato leaves, but subsequently found in many *Solanum* species, has a structure identical with that of tigogenin, apart from the substitution of a nitrogen atom for oxygen in the spiro-ketal system. Related bases may have an amino function at C-3 and may also differ in the structural modification of the C-17 side chain, as illustrated by solanidine and solanocapsine (Fig. 19-17).

The close relationship between the *Solanum* alkaloids and the steroidal sapogenins, is emphasized by the fact that both classes usually occur in nature as glycosides. Tomatidine, for example, is usually found as the glycoside tomatine (Fig. 19-16).

As with the steroidal alkaloids of the Apocynaceae and Buxaceae, structural considerations indicate a close biogenetic relationship between the *Solanum* alkaloids and cholesterol. Preliminary evidence from incorporation experiments suggests that this proposal is well founded.

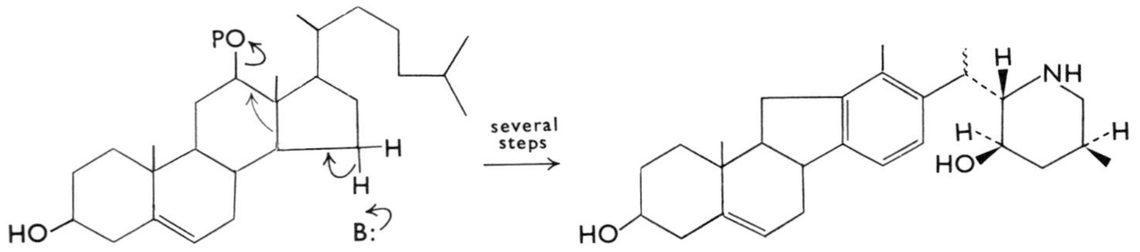

several steps

veratramine

[Eq. 19-30]

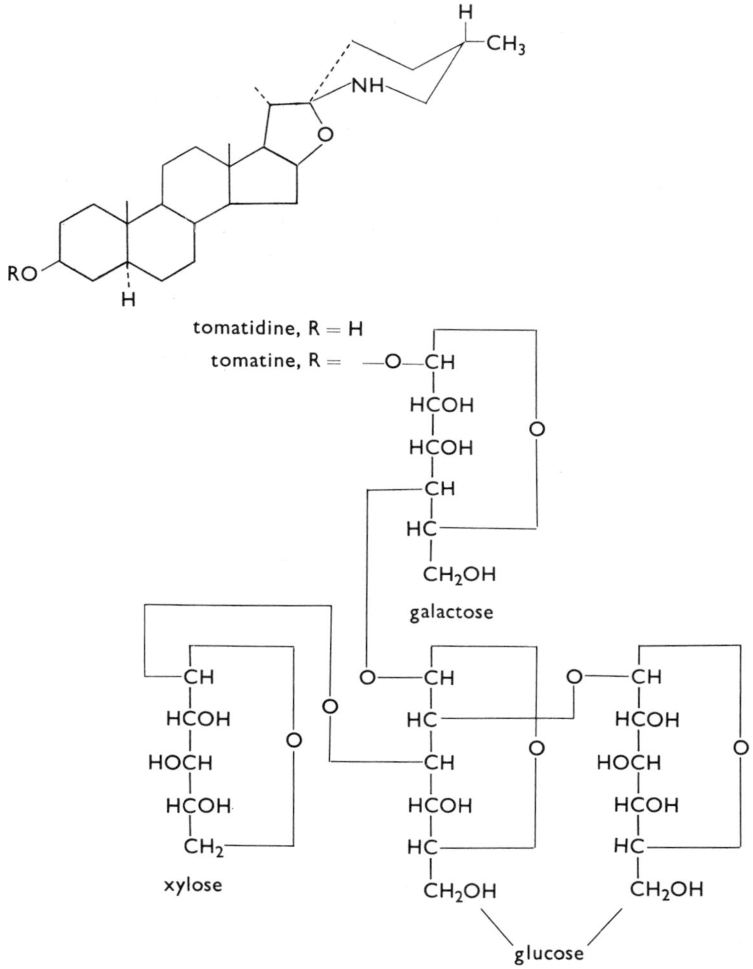

tomatidine, R = H

tomatine, R =

galactose

xylose

glucose

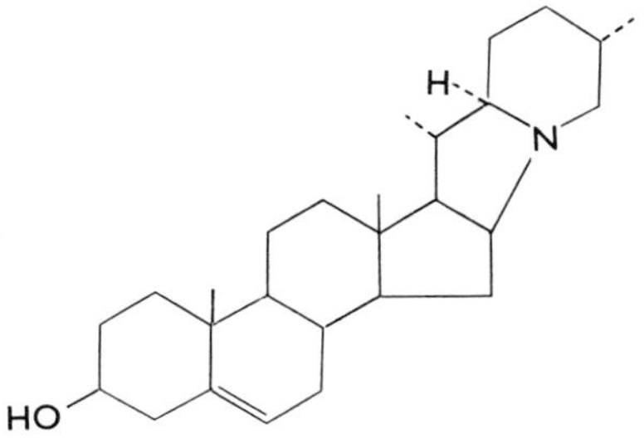

solanidine

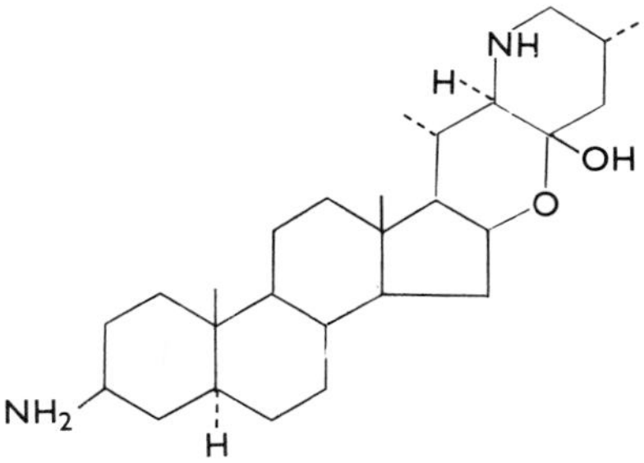

solanocapsine

Fig. 19-17.

Species of the genera *Veratrum* and *Fritillaria* (fam. Liliaceae), produce steroidal alkaloids similar to the solanaceous type described above. However, more often, the alkaloids encountered are based on a modified steroid nucleus in which the C- and D-rings are five and six membered respectively. Veratramine (Eq. 19-30) is typical of the alkaloids in this series.

It has been suggested that the formation of the *Veratrum* and *Fritillaria* alkaloids may involve a ring expansion reaction of the type illustrated in Eq. 19-30.

Index